SNAP and XSight can help you improve your marks!

Your purchase of the third European edition of Malhotra and Birks, *Marketing Research: An Applied Approach*, includes a CD-ROM containing valuable Snap and XSight software demos. Snap and XSight work at the cutting edge of marketing research practice and set industry standards. Using these demos will dramatically enhance your understanding of quantitative and qualitative design and analysis issues in marketing research.

DON'T THROW IT AWAY!

What are Snap and XSight and how will they help you?

Snap is a user-friendly program for marketing research, enabling you to design surveys, create and publish questionnaires, and collect and analyse the replies. This powerful survey software is an industry standard that has been helping researchers and educators in more than 50 countries for 25 years. Snap consists of a core product, Snap Professional, and specialist modules that may be added to extend its capabilities to surveys via the Internet, Personal Digital Assistants (PDAs), tablets, kiosks, scanning and telephone interviewing. You will find direct references to the use of Snap in Chapter 10 (Survey and quantitative observation techniques), Chapter 13 (Questionnaire design), Chapter 17 (Data preparation) and Chapter 18 (Frequency distribution, cross-tabulation and hypothesis testing).

XSight is a user-friendly program for qualitative data analysis software, customised for marketing research.

Conventional qualitative data analysis software was designed for and used mainly by academic researchers. XSight was designed for marketing researchers by marketing researchers who understood the particular problems faced by their profession. Created by QSR International, a qualitative research software company with years of experience in developing solutions to a wide array of research problems, XSight is seen as a breakthrough tool for every qualitative marketing researcher. It will enable you to explore unstructured qualitative data gathered via focus groups, interviews or open ended surveys much more easily. This will allow you much more time to devote to the real art of qualitative research – interpretation. With XSight you will be able to compile, compare and make logical connections in qualitative data almost instantaneously. It can help you identify even the most subtle data patterns. You will find direct references and a case to illustrate the use of XSight in Chapter 9 (Qualitative research: data analysis).

Using SNAP and XSight

With the enclosed free trial version of Snap, simply install it on your personal computer at a time that's convenient. You'll then be able to design a 'mini-survey' of up to 9 questions and up to 25 respondents. You'll also be able to see examples of much larger surveys designed with Snap. **There is no time limit to the use of Snap.**

With XSight, we advise you to work through the tutorials before using your software. First, simply install XSight on your personal computer at a time that's convenient. The tutorials can then be accessed from within the software. You'll need to open XSight and click on the 'Help' menu. From there, click on 'XSight Tutorials'. Once you are familiar with how XSight works, you're ready to get started. The software we've provided you with lets you enjoy **the full suite of XSight features for a period of 90 days**. Once you have experienced the benefits of using Snap and XSight, they will become integral to your work in the design, data collection and analysis of quantitative and qualitative data. Working without them may become inconceivable.

To use the CD:

1. Put the CD in your machine.
2. Select the options to install Snap; or install XSight.
3. Follow the on-screen instructions.
4. XSight only: when prompted, input the password on the CD.

PEARSON
Education

We work with leading authors to develop the strongest educational materials in marketing, bringing cutting-edge thinking and best learning practice to a global market. Under a range of well-known imprints, including Financial Times Prentice Hall, we craft high quality print and electronic publications which help readers to understand and apply their content, whether studying or at work.

To find out more about the complete range of our publishing please visit us on the World Wide Web at: **www.pearsoned.co.uk**

Visit the *Marketing Research: An Applied Approach, Third European edition* Companion Website at **www.pearsoned.co.uk/malhotra_euro** to find valuable **student** learning material including:

- Annotated links to relevant sites on the web
- Online glossary
- Flashcards to test your knowledge of key terms and definitions
- Introduction to the valuable Snap/XSight software on the CD that accompanies this book
- Foreword by the Managing Director of Sports Marketing Surveys, who has provided many of the case studies throughout the book

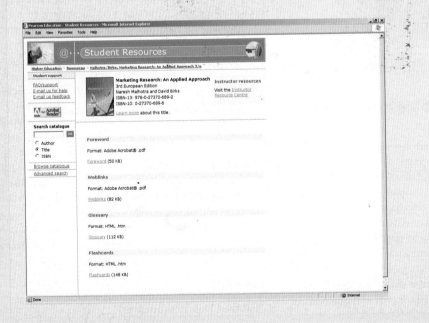

Third Edition

Marketing Research
An Applied Approach

Naresh K. Malhotra

David F. Birks

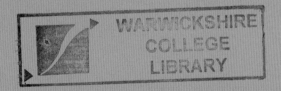

FT Prentice Hall
FINANCIAL TIMES

An imprint of **Pearson Education**

Harlow, England • London • New York • Boston • San Francisco • Toronto • Sydney • Singapore • Hong Kong
Tokyo • Seoul • Taipei • New Delhi • Cape Town • Madrid • Mexico City • Amsterdam • Munich • Paris • Milan

Pearson Education Limited

Edinburgh Gate
Harlow
Essex CM20 2JE
England

and Associated Companies around the world

Visit us on the World Wide Web at:
www.pearsoned.co.uk

Original 3rd entitled *Marketing Research: An Applied Orientation*
published by Prentice Hall, Inc., a Pearson Education company
Copyright © 1999 Prentice Hall Inc.

This edition first published 2006
Third edition published 2007

© Pearson Education Limited 2000, 2003, 2006, 2007

Authorised for sale only in Europe, the Middle East and Africa.

ISBN-13: 978-0-273-70689-2
ISBN-10: 0-273-70689-6

British Library Cataloguing-in-Publication Data
A catalogue record for this book is available from the British Library

Library of Congress Cataloging-in-Publication Data
A catalog record for this book is available from the Library of Congress

10 9 8 7 6 5 4 3 2 1
09 08 07

Typeset in 10/12.5 pt Minion by 30.
Printed and bound by Mateu Cromo, Artes Graficas, Spain.

The publisher's policy is to use paper manufactured from sustainable forests.

Brief contents

Preface   xiii
Publisher's acknowledgements   xvii
Guided tour   xviii
About the authors   xxi

1   Introduction to marketing research   1
2   Defining the marketing research problem and developng a research approach   32
3   Research design   62
4   Secondary data collection and analysis   92
5   Internal secondary data and the use of databases   122
6   Qualitative research: its nature and approaches   148
7   Qualitative research: focus group discussions   179
8   Qualitative research: depth interviewing and projective techniques   205
9   Qualitative research: data analysis   231
10   Survey and quantitative observation techniques   264
11   Causal research design: experimentation   301
12   Measurement and scaling: fundamentals, comparative and non-comparative scaling   334
13   Questionnaire design   369
14   Sampling: design and procedures   403
15   Sampling: final and initial sample size determination   431
16   Survey fieldwork   459
17   Data preparation   474
18   Frequency distribution, cross-tabulation and hypothesis testing   502
19   Analysis of variance and covariance   544
20   Identifying relationships   573
21   Discriminant analysis   617
22   Factor analysis   645
23   Cluster anaylsis   670
24   Multidimensional scaling and conjoint analysis   692
25   Report preparation and presentation   722
26   International marketing research   742
27   Business-to-business (b2b) marketing research   766

Appendix: Statistical tables   795
Glossary   806
Indexes   821

To the memory of Harry Birks

Contents

Preface   xiii
Publisher's acknowledgements   xvii
Guided tour   xviii
About the authors   xxi

1 Introduction to marketing research   1

Objectives   1
Overview   2
What does market research encompass?   2
Definition of marketing research   6
The marketing research process   7
A classification of marketing research   11
The global marketing research industry   13
The limitations of marketing research   17
The future – the growing demand for managerial
    skills in marketing researchers   21
Supporting decision-makers in sports marketing   24
International marketing research   24
Ethics in marketing research   25
Internet and computer applications   27
Summary   28
Questions   29
Exercises   30
Notes   30

2 Defining the marketing research problem and developing a research approach   32

Objectives   32
Overview   33
Importance of defining the problem   34
The marketing research brief   35
The marketing research proposal   38
The process of defining the problem and developing a
    research approach   42
Marketing decision problem and marketing research
    problem   46
Defining the marketing research problem   47
Components of the research approach   49
International marketing research   55
Ethics in marketing research   57
Internet and computer applications   58
Summary   59
Questions   60
Exercises   60
Notes   61

3 Research design   62

Objectives   62
Overview   63
Research design definition   64

Research design from the decision-makers'
    perspective   65
Research design from the respondents' perspective   66
Research design classification   69
Descriptive research   73
Causal research   79
Relationships between exploratory, descriptive and
    causal research   79
Potential sources of error in research designs   83
International marketing research   86
Ethics in marketing research   87
Internet and computer applications   88
Summary   88
Questions   89
Exercises   90
Notes   90

4 Secondary data collection and analysis   92

Objectives   92
Overview   93
Defining primary data, secondary data and marketing
    intelligence   94
Advantages and uses of secondary data   96
Disadvantages of secondary data   96
Criteria for evaluating secondary data   97
Classification of secondary data   100
Published external secondary sources   101
Computerised databases   104
Classification of computerised databases   104
Syndicated sources of secondary data   106
Syndicated data from households   108
Syndicated data from institutions   114
International marketing research   115
Ethics in marketing research   116
Internet and computer applications   117
Summary   118
Questions   119
Exercises   119
Notes   120

5 Internal secondary data and the use of databases   122

Objectives   122
Overview   123
Internal secondary data   124
Scanning devices   126
Relating customer data to scanning systems   126
Geodemographic data   129
Linking different types of data   134
Stages of development in using databases and survey
    data to build portfolios of customers and model
    marketing decisions   135

Contents

The datawarehouse 136
Data mining 138
Databases and marketing research 139
International marketing research 141
Ethics in marketing research 142
Internet and computer applications 143
Summary 144
Questions 145
Exercises 146
Notes 147

6 Qualitative research: its nature and approaches 148

Objectives 148
Overview 149
Primary data: qualitative versus quantitative research 152
Rationale for using qualitative research 153
Philosophy and qualitative research 155
Ethnographic research 161
Grounded theory 166
Action research 169
Ethics in marketing research 172
Internet and computer applications 173
Summary 175
Questions 176
Exercises 177
Notes 177

7 Qualitative research: focus group discussions 179

Objectives 179
Overview 180
Classifying qualitative research techniques 181
Focus group discussions 182
Planning and conducting focus groups 188
The moderator 193
Other variations of focus groups 194
Other types of qualitative group discussions 195
Misconceptions about focus groups 196
International marketing research 198
Ethics in marketing research 200
Internet and computer applications 201
Summary 202
Questions 203
Exercises 203
Notes 204

8 Qualitative research: in-depth interviewing and projective techniques 205

Objectives 205
Overview 206
In-depth interviews 207
Projective techniques 217
Comparison between qualitative techniques 222
International marketing research 223
Ethics in marketing research 224
Internet and computer applications 226

Summary 227
Questions 228
Exercises 229
Notes 229

9 Qualitative research: data analysis 231

Objectives 231
Overview 232
The qualitative researcher 233
The process of qualitative data analysis 236
Grounded theory 248
Content analysis 251
Semiotics 252
Using computers in qualitative research and analysis 254
International marketing research 258
Ethics in marketing research 259
Summary 260
Questions 261
Exercises 261
Notes 262

10 Survey and quantitative observation techniques 264

Objectives 264
Overview 265
Survey techniques 265
Telephone interviews 267
Personal interviews 269
Mail interviews 272
Electronic interviews 273
A comparative evaluation of survey techniques 275
Selection of survey method(s) 283
Observation techniques 283
Observation techniques classified by mode of administration 285
A comparative evaluation of observation techniques 288
Advantages and disadvantages of observation techniques 289
International marketing research 290
Ethics in marketing research 292
Internet and computer applications 294
Summary 296
Questions 297
Exercises 298
Notes 298

11 Causal research design: experimentation 301

Objectives 301
Overview 302
Concept of causality 302
Conditions for causality 303
Definitions and concepts 306
Definition of symbols 307
Validity in experimentation 307
Extraneous variables 308

Controlling extraneous variables   310
A classification of experimental designs   312
Pre-experimental designs   313
True experimental designs   315
Quasi-experimental designs   317
Statistical designs   319
Laboratory versus field experiments   322
Experimental versus non-experimental designs   323
Application: test marketing   324
International marketing research   326
Ethics in marketing research   327
Internet and computer applications   329
Summary   329
Questions   330
Exercises   331
Notes   331

12 Measurement and scaling: fundamentals, comparative and non-comparative scaling   334
Objectives   334
Overview   335
Measurement and scaling   336
Primary scales of measurement   336
A comparison of scaling techniques   341
Comparative scaling techniques   342
Non-comparative scaling techniques   347
Itemised rating scales   348
Itemised rating scale decisions   351
The development and evaluation of scales   355
Choosing a scaling technique   360
Mathematically derived scales   360
International marketing research   361
Ethics in marketing research   362
Internet and computer applications   362
Summary   363
Questions   364
Exercises   365
Notes   365

13 Questionnaire design   369
Objectives   369
Overview   370
Questionnaire definition   371
Questionnaire design process   372
Specify the information needed   374
Specify the type of interviewing method   375
Determine the content of individual questions   377
Overcome the respondent's inability and unwillingness to answer   378
Choose question structure   381
Choose question wording   384
Use unambiguous words   385
Arrange the questions in proper order   387
Identify the form and layout   390
Reproduce the questionnaire   390

Eliminate problems by pilot-testing   391
Summarising the questionnaire design process   392
International marketing research   394
Ethics in marketing research   396
Internet and computer applications   397
Summary   398
Questions   399
Exercises   400
Notes   400

14 Sampling: design and procedures   403
Objectives   403
Overview   404
Sample or census   405
The sampling design process   406
A classification of sampling techniques   410
Non-probability sampling techniques   411
Probability sampling techniques   415
Choosing non-probability versus probability sampling   421
Summary of sampling techniques   422
International marketing research   424
Ethics in marketing research   425
Internet and computer applications   425
Summary   427
Questions   428
Exercises   428
Notes   429

15 Sampling: final and initial sample size determination   431
Objectives   431
Overview   432
Definitions and symbols   433
The sampling distribution   434
Statistical approaches to determining sample size   436
The confidence interval approach   436
Multiple characteristics and parameters   442
Other probability sampling techniques   442
Adjusting the statistically determined sample size   443
Non-response issues in sampling   443
International marketing research   450
Ethics in marketing research   451
Internet and computer applications   452
Summary   452
Questions   453
Exercises   454
Appendix: The normal distribution   455
Notes   457

16 Survey fieldwork   459
Objectives   459
Overview   460
The nature of survey fieldwork   461
Survey fieldwork and the data collection process   461
Selecting survey fieldworkers   461

Training survey fieldworkers 462
Recording the answers 465
Supervising survey fieldworkers 467
Validating survey fieldwork 468
Evaluating survey fieldworkers 468
International marketing research 469
Ethics in marketing research 470
Internet and computer applications 470
Summary 471
Questions 472
Exercises 472
Notes 473

17 Data preparation 474
Objectives 474
Overview 475
The data preparation process 476
Checking the questionnaire 477
Editing 477
Coding 479
Transcribing 485
Cleaning the data 486
Statistically adjusting the data 488
Selecting a data analysis strategy 491
International marketing research 494
Ethics in marketing research 496
Internet and computer applications 497
Summary 499
Questions 499
Exercises 500
Notes 500

18 Frequency distribution, cross-tabulation and hypothesis testing 502
Objectives 502
Overview 503
Frequency distribution 506
Statistics associated with frequency distribution 508
Measures of shape 510
A general procedure for hypothesis testing 511
Cross-tabulations 516
Hypothesis testing related to differences 525
Parametric tests 526
Non-parametric tests 532
Internet and computer applications 537
Summary 539
Questions 539
Exercises 540
Notes 542

19 Analysis of variance and covariance 544
Objectives 544
Overview 545
Relationship among techniques 546
One-way ANOVA 547

Statistics associated with one-way ANOVA 548
Conducting one-way ANOVA 548
N-way ANOVA 555
Analysis of covariance (ANCOVA) 560
Issues in interpretation 561
Repeated measures ANOVA 564
Non-metric ANOVA 565
Multivariate ANOVA 566
Internet and computer applications 566
Summary 567
Questions 568
Exercises 569
Notes 571

20 Identifying relationships 573
Objectives 573
Overview 574
Product moment correlation 575
Partial correlation 578
Non-metric correlation 581
Regression analysis 581
Bivariate regression 582
Statistics associated with bivariate regression analysis 582
Conducting bivariate regression analysis 583
Multiple regression 590
Statistics associated with multiple regression 591
Conducting multiple regression analysis 592
Multicollinearity 601
Relative importance of predictors 601
Cross-validation 602
Regression with dummy variables 603
Analysis of variance and covariance with regression 603
Structural equation modelling 604
Internet and computer applications 609
Summary 611
Questions 612
Exercises 612
Notes 615

21 Discriminant analysis 617
Objectives 617
Overview 618
Basic concept 618
Relationship to regression and ANOVA 619
Discriminant analysis model 620
Statistics associated with discriminant analysis 620
Conducting discriminant analysis 621
Conducting multiple discriminant analysis 631
Stepwise discriminant analysis 638
Internet and computer applications 640
Summary 640
Questions 641
Exercises 641
Appendix: Estimation of discriminant function coefficients 642
Notes 643

22 Factor analysis — 645

Objectives — 645
Overview — 646
Basic concept — 646
Factor analysis model — 647
Statistics associated with factor analysis — 648
Conducting factor analysis — 649
Applications of common factor analysis — 660
Internet and computer applications — 664
Summary — 664
Questions — 665
Exercises — 666
Appendix: Fundamental equations of factor analysis — 667
Notes — 669

23 Cluster analysis — 670

Objectives — 670
Overview — 671
Basic concept — 671
Statistics associated with cluster analysis — 673
Conducting cluster analysis — 674
Applications of non-hierarchical clustering — 684
Clustering variables — 686
Internet and computer applications — 687
Summary — 688
Questions — 689
Exercises — 689
Notes — 690

24 Multidimensional scaling and conjoint analysis — 692

Objectives — 692
Overview — 693
Basic concepts in MDS — 694
Statistics and terms associated with MDS — 695
Conducting MDS — 695
Assumptions and limitations of MDS — 702
Scaling preference data — 702
Correspondence analysis — 703
Relationship between MDS, factor analysis and discriminant analysis — 704
Basic concepts in conjoint analysis — 704
Statistics and terms associated with conjoint analysis — 705
Conducting conjoint analysis — 706
Assumptions and limitations of conjoint analysis — 714
Hybrid conjoint analysis — 714
Internet and computer applications — 716
Summary — 717
Questions — 717
Exercises — 718
Notes — 719

25 Report preparation and presentation — 722

Objectives — 722
Overview — 723
Importance of the report and presentation — 724
Preparation and presentation process — 724
Report preparation — 725
Oral presentation — 733
Research follow-up — 735
International marketing research — 736
Ethics in marketing research — 736
Internet and computer applications — 737
Summary — 738
Questions — 740
Exercises — 740
Notes — 741

26 International marketing research — 742

Objectives — 742
Overview — 743
What is international marketing research? — 744
A framework for international marketing research — 746
Secondary data — 752
Qualitative techniques — 753
Survey methods — 755
Measurement and scaling — 758
Questionnaire translation — 760
Ethics in marketing research — 761
Internet and computer applications — 762
Summary — 763
Questions — 764
Exercises — 764
Notes — 765

27 Business-to-business (b2b) marketing research — 766

Objectives — 766
Overview — 767
What is b2b marketing? — 769
Introducing the distinction between b2b and consumer marketing — 769
Bases for the distinction of b2b marketing research — 771
Implications of the differences between business and consumer purchases for marketing researchers — 773
The growth of competitive intelligence — 785
International marketing research — 787
Ethics in marketing research — 789
Internet and computer applications — 790
Summary — 791
Questions — 792
Exercises — 792
Notes — 793

Appendix: Statistical tables — 795
Glossary — 806
Subject index — 821
Name index — 833
Company index — 834

Supporting resources

Visit **www.pearsoned.co.uk/malhotra_euro** to find valuable online resources

Companion Website for students
- Annotated links to relevant sites on the web
- Online glossary
- Flashcards to test your knowledge of key terms and definitions
- Introduction to the valuable Snap/XSight software on the CD that accompanies the book
- Foreword by the Managing Director of Sports Marketing Surveys, who has provided many of the case studies throughout the book

For instructors
- Customisable, colour PowerPoint slides, including key figures and tables from the book
- Extensive Instructor's Manual, including sample answers for all question material in the book
- Video case studies that are integrated with the book, with sample answers to the questions in the book
- Extra case study material
- MRS and ESOMAR material on specific countries around the world

Also: The Companion Website provides the following features:
- Search tool to help locate specific items of content
- E-mail results and profile tools to send results of quizzes to instructors
- Online help and support to assist with website usage and troubleshooting

For more information please contact your local Pearson Education sales representative or visit **www.pearsoned.co.uk/malhotra_euro**

Preface

Working as a marketing researcher is a very creative task. This creativity is nurtured by an industry and a discipline that is undergoing enormous changes. Decision-makers that use marketing research are demanding greater value for their research spend, a much quicker turnaround of research projects and more insight to, and integration of, any information collected. Industry competition is emerging and growing from suppliers of competitive intelligence, management consultants, customer database analysts and low-cost survey suppliers using new technologies. In addition, respondents are becoming more aware of the value of their knowledge. With many surveys used to generate news items or sales leads, respondents are more sceptical of the motives and value of surveys, creating major challenges for the genuine marketing researcher. These challenges also create enormous opportunities for marketing researchers who use their skills to fully grasp the changes occurring in today's business world.

Marketing researchers must be able to cope with the technical challenges to plan, gather, analyse and interpret information. They must be aware of the challenges faced by the array of decision-makers that trust sound marketing research. They must be able to empathise with the people they aim to question and observe, and to treat them with care and respect. Marketing researchers that rise to the emerging challenges can have a genuine impact on the strategic direction of a company. Their future is very bright, stimulating and rewarding.

Understanding the emerging marketing research challenges, developing creativity, finding the confidence to conduct research and to discover insight in findings may seem difficult with so many options to consider. This is where we believe *Marketing Research: An Applied Approach*, Third European Edition can help. Founded on the enormously successful American editions and the First and Second European editions, this text aims to be comprehensive, authoritative and applied. This edition includes an array of European and international examples, practices and illustrations. It portrays a balance of qualitative and quantitative approaches to conducting research that allows the creative support of decision-makers. It will guide the reader through the challenges faced in conducting marketing research of the highest quality. This is achieved through an appropriate blend of scholarship with a highly applied and managerial orientation.

The book

The book is written for use at both the undergraduate and postgraduate levels. The coverage is comprehensive and the depth and breadth of topics are well suited to both levels. The material is presented in a manner that is easy to read and understand. There are numerous diagrams, tables and examples to help explain and illustrate the basic concepts. If a chapter does not cover a particular topic in sufficient depth, there are numerous references to follow a line of enquiry. The web addresses presented throughout allow for further illustration of ideas and, in many instances, demonstration versions of software. The companion website presents a *Marketing Research Software* section, links to the book's companion Marketing Research agency – Sports Marketing Surveys – more European cases, exercises and web links.

Marketing research is defined as a topic with a clear demonstration of how it may support effective decision-making. This definition is set in the context of the nature and dynamics of the marketing research industry. The limitations of marketing research are recognised, as are other means of information support that decision-makers turn to. The process of conducting marketing research is described in six stages. Each of these stages is fully described and illustrated. Working out an approach and research design is discussed as a foundation to administering techniques. The justification for the use of qualitative and quantitative techniques is made, with a demonstration of how they may mutually support each other. The administration of a broad range of qualitative and quantitative techniques is presented. Sampling issues for both qualitative and quantitative studies are discussed. Issues of ensuring the quality of data and preparing for data analysis are covered. Qualitative data analysis is discussed in detail. Quantitative data analysis from simple descriptive statistics to sophisticated multivariate techniques is worked through in seven chapters. Presenting research findings in both oral and written formats is covered, with an emphasis on ensuring that the interpretation of research findings really supports decision-makers.

Applications of marketing research in an international context are tackled in most chapters; this vital topic also has a distinct chapter in its own right. Applying marketing research in a b2b context is illustrated in many parts of the text but, as a vital topic for the industry with many challenges, it has a distinct chapter in its own right. The ethical practice of marketing research and the dilemmas that researchers face are also tackled in most chapters. Discussion of the impact of the Internet and IT on marketing research is integrated throughout the text but is also dealt with at the end of each chapter.

Being an excellent marketing researcher requires an appreciation of, and continual practice of, all the elements discussed in this text. This book firmly sets you on that path of creativity and excellence.

New for this edition

Revisions to existing chapters We have retained the most desirable features of the first five American editions and the first two European editions. In all chapters that tackle quantitative techniques and analysis, none of the well-regarded material has been lost. Changes have been made to improve the clarity of explanations, with many new examples and updated references. Developments in the use of databases have made substantial changes in how decision-makers are supported. These developments are tackled in the revisions to the chapter that covers 'internal secondary data and the use of databases'. In the chapter devoted to qualitative data analysis, particular emphasis has been placed upon clarifying the nature of grounded theory, content analysis and semiotics. In the chapter devoted to correlation and regression, a new section is devoted to structural equation modelling. All chapters have benefitted from more up-to-date references and, where appropriate, more relevant examples that reflect the European and international focus. At the end of each chapter, a new section is presented with five stimulating Exercises that can be conducted individually or in teams, both in and out of the classroom.

Web links The pace of new technological developments in the marketing research industry is breathtaking. Trying to keep up with them is a thankless task. It can be guaranteed that as soon as any publication hits the shelves, much material on technology can be out of date. Many of the new developments that have a demonstrable impact on the practice of marketing research, especially through the use of the Internet, have been incorporated into each chapter. To maintain the currency of technology, the web addresses of the major research associations, national statistical bodies, and research organisations are presented. The web addresses of major suppliers of qualitative analysis packages, questionnaire design, survey processing and statistical analysis are also presented. Care has been taken to choose those where good case illustrations and demo versions are available, in a variety of formats to suit individual users.

CD demonstration software The CD that accompanies this edition contains demonstration software for quantitative and qualitative researchers.

- Snap8 **www.snapsurveys.com** is powerful user-friendly software that has driven standards in survey design and analysis in the marketing research industry for over 25 years. It is now used in over 50 countries worldwide. With Snap8, questionnaires can be created and published for surveys that use paper, web, email and computer-assisted personal and telephone interviews. It can then offer options to key or scan data or even to collect data automatically. Survey results can be analysed, statistics calculated and tables and charts produced. These features briefly summarise how the software helps to manage a great array of survey designs. By working through the demo, the detail of support in survey design, i.e. the array of functions available, will become apparent. The demo will bring to life the challenges to questionnaire and survey designers and the solutions they use in practice.
- XSight **www.qsrinternational.com** is a new product that offers customised data analysis software for qualitative marketing researchers. The software has been developed by QSR International who are world leaders in qualitative research software as used in a variety of applications. Academic marketing researchers that use qualitative analysis software would be familiar with QSR's NVivo package, which we discuss in Chapter 9. In this chapter, we discuss why for many practitioner qualitative marketing researchers, manual methods or basic computer-based methods have been the norm. XSight has been developed in close consultation with practitioner marketing researchers to bridge the gap between the packages designed for the needs of academics and traditional manual methods. The demo will bring to life the challenges faced by qualitative researchers in the amount and nature of qualitative data they may collect and how they make sense of that data.

Sports Marketing Surveys There is a new 'companion' marketing research agency, whose work forms a running case throughout the text. In most chapters, examples will be presented based upon work conducted by the marketing research agency **Sports Marketing Surveys**. This independent marketing research agency has specialised in the sponsorship and sports industry for the past 20 years. The sports industry and many sponsorship deals are often multi-country in their reach and activity and to meet these challenges Sports Marketing Surveys has the capability of working and reporting on a worldwide basis, in over 200 countries, for events such as the Olympic Games, Wimbledon, the Ryder Cup and the Football World Cup. Work from four projects conducted by Sports Marketing Surveys will be used as running examples throughout this book:

Racetrack 2003 – a syndicated study to measure the attitudes and opinions of, and profile, the Formula One fan across eight countries worldwide.

Nestea – sponsorship evaluation in '*Wind, Water and Waves*' Hungary and Germany, and *Beach Volleyball* in Italy, Germany and Sweden.

Flora London Marathon 2004 – TV media analysis, public awareness tracking and target market research.

Rugby League – understanding and quantifying the core values of Rugby League and new branding concepts for the game.

Elements of these commercially sensitive projects will be chosen to show how Sports Marketing Surveys managed the challenges of conducting actionable marketing research. There will also be a distinct section on the companion website devoted to Sports Marketing Surveys.

Companion website The companion website has been updated to reflect the changes in this edition. There are new European case studies with discussion points and questions to tackle. All the referenced websites on the text are described with notes of key features to look for on a particular site.

There is a new section on the website devoted to *Marketing Research Software*. This section is based upon the work of three contributors:

Peter Wills is the CEO of SNAP Surveys and a Senior Visiting Fellow at the University of Southampton. He has contributed to the first two editions of this text, writing Professional Perspectives on the impact of the Internet on marketing research and how technology changes affect questionnaire and survey design. Peter has helped a huge variety of organisations with marketing research problems. As well as the SNAP software, his business encompasses training, software implementation and bespoke survey and questionnaire design, data entry, analysis and reporting; especially utilising the Internet but also incorporating the latest technological developments to capture data. He has worked directly with research users and research companies.

Tim Macer is the Managing Director of Meaning and a Senior Visiting Fellow at the University of Southampton. He has established a reputation internationally as an authoritative and independent analyst and commentator on software for survey research, data collection and analysis. He is often called on by industry bodies such as the Association of Users of Market Research Agencies (AURA), the Council of American Survey Research Organisations (CASRO), the Marketing Research Association (MRA) and the Market Research Society (MRS) to speak as an impartial commentator at conferences or training events. Tim regularly contributes to two industry-respected magazines – *Research* in the UK and *Quirk's Review* in the USA – on software and technology. He has contributed to the first two editions of this text, allowing access to his published reviews of the huge variety and applications of software that support marketing research activity.

Karen Thomas is the marketing director of QSR International. She is responsible for their Marketing Strategy, Communications, Customer Service and Business Analyst functions. Karen drew experience from working in Australia and the UK, including senior management positions with a global IT firm and consultancy. QSR are the world's leading supplier of qualitative data analysis software. Their products – NVivo, N6 and XSight – are used in over 90 countries throughout the world. More researchers use QSR products than all other qualitative research software. Karen's work on the marketing research impact of XSight illustrates the innovations of a company with over 20 years' experience in data analysis software development and an in-depth understanding of qualitative research.

Instructors manual The instructors manual is very closely tied to the text, but is not prescriptive in how the material should be handled in the classroom. The manual offers teaching suggestions, answers to all end-of-chapter questions, Professional Perspective discussion points, and case study exercises. The manual includes PowerPoint slides, incorporating all the new figures and tables.

Photography Photographs that accompany any management textbook may be perceived as trivial and mere embellishments. I do not take this view. I see textbook photographs as a means to encapsulate the essence of a subject, its joys and its challenges. In putting together the new colour photographs for this edition, I wanted images that portray the competitiveness, dynamism and creativity of marketing research. The work of Sports Marketing Surveys and many of the other text examples exemplify these characteristics, and the images amplify them. The four-colour design of the book portrays the vitality of marketing research. Some of the images in this edition have a serious intent, linking a particular image to concepts and aiding the recall of a concept. Others are there to lighten the sometimes difficult technical passages. In their own right, each image has many technical and artistic merits.

Acknowledgements

Many people have been most generous in helping me to write the three European editions.

In developing the critical approach I take in marketing research practice and writing, I must thank my Consumer Behaviour teacher and PhD supervisor, John Southan of Salford University. My friend and former work colleague, the late Kevin Fogarty, deserves special mention for his humour, creativity and for shaping many of the values I continue to hold dear.

Many thanks must go to Stephen Proctor, Managing Director of Sports Marketing Surveys Ltd. I enjoyed working with the fascinating case material of a truly inspirational marketing research company. Many thanks also to Sandra Greer, John Bushell and Erica George, who supported my work with great patience and care.

In putting together the Marketing Research Software section, the demonstration versions of SNAP and XSight and for support in many aspects of my thinking and writing I would like to thank Tim Macer, Karen Thomas and Peter Wills.

For their critique, insight and excellent feedback, I am most grateful to Dr Johan van Rekom of the Erasmus University Rotterdam, Professor Peter Navde of Manchester Business School and Professor David Ford of the University of Bath.

To David Cox at Pearson Education with whom I started this edition, I'm so glad that you've returned from your trip around the globe to see it through! David has been very patient, kind and helpful through some trying times. His advice has always been incisive and inspiring, and he's managed me with great humour and a superb eye for detail. I could not have had better support and I'm very much in your debt.

At Pearson Education the book has also come together with the help of Georgina Clark-Mazo, Desk Editor; Kelly Meyer, who designed the cover; Colin Reed, who helped with the internal design; and Andrew Harrison, Editorial Assistant.

Last but by no means least, to be able to find the time and space to write, the love, support and understanding of your family is vital. Thank you so much mum for all your love. To my partner Helen, enormous thanks and love for all you have put up with in giving me the space and peace to write and to my beautiful son Jesse, who with Helen brings me so much light and joy.

David F. Birks

Publishers acknowledgements

We are grateful to the following for permission to reproduce copyright material:

pp. 7, 68, 162, 190, 215, 339, 488, 519, 665 and 697 Alamy; pp. 32, 573 and 722 Photodisc/Getty Images/Cadmium; p. 49 Mika/Zefa/CORBIS; pp. 62, 92, 122, 179, 205, 231, 264, 301, 334, 369, 403, 414, 431, 444, 459, 465, 474, 502, 544, 559, 598, 617, 630, 670, 683, 692 and 766 Getty Images; p. 112 George Disario/CORBIS; pp. 128 and 311 Science Photo Library; pp. 148, 645 and 742 EMPICS; p. 240 Bryan Allen/CORBIS; p. 284 Russell Underwood/ CORBIS; p. 389 Patrik Giardino/CORBIS; p. 739 Jim Craigmyle/CORBIS; p. 748 TopFoto/ImageWorks; p. 785 Laureen March/CORBIS

In some instances we have been unable to trace the owners of copyright material and we would appreciate any information that would enable us to do so.

Guided tour

Full colour photography throughout vibrantly illustrates key points and examples

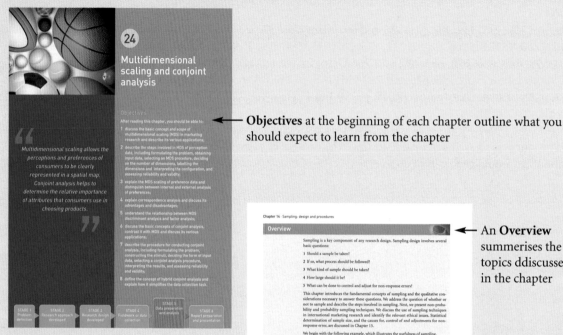

Objectives at the beginning of each chapter outline what you should expect to learn from the chapter

Stage flowcharts show how the chapter fits into the six stages of the marketing research process

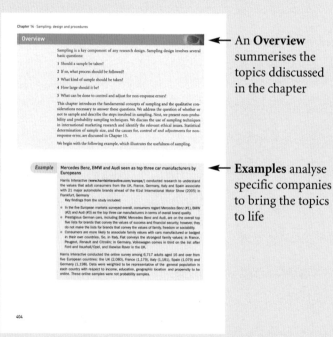

An **Overview** summarises the topics ddiscussed in the chapter

Examples analyse specific companies to bring the topics to life

Marginal definitions highlight the key terms in the text

A **Glossary** of these terms is provided both at the end of the book and on the website at **www.pearsoned.co.uk/malhotra_euro**

Focus on Sports Marketing Surveys is a set of sports marketing case studies that run throughout the text, including material on the Olympics, Formula One racing and Beach Volleyball

Take these case studies further at
www.pearsoned.co.uk/malhotra_euro

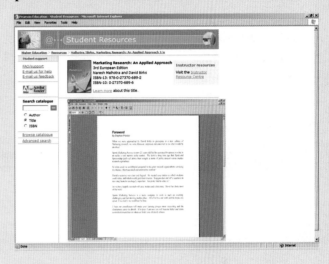

International marketing research shows how different aspects of the marketing research process fit into an international context

Ethics in Marketing Research focus on the ethical practice of marketing research and the dilemmas that researchers face

Internet and computer applications illustrate the impact of technology and the Internet on marketing research

Test yourself at the end of each chapter with a set of **Questions**

Exercises help you to apply what you have learnt, by testing your understanding in a practical context

Test your understanding of the key concepts with **Flash Cards** at the *Marketing Research* website

Notes at the end of each chapter list sources to help you take your reading further

Dr Naresh K. Malhotra is Regents' Professor, DuPree College of Management, Georgia Institute of Technology. He is listed in *Marquis Who's Who in America*, 51st Edition (1997), 52nd Edition (1998), 53rd Edition (1999), and in the *National Registry of Who's Who* (1999).

In an article by Wheatley and Wilson (1987 AMA Educators' Proceedings), Professor Malhotra was ranked number one in the country based on articles published in the *Journal of Marketing Research* from 1980 to 1985. He also holds the all-time record for the most publications in the *Journal of Health Care Marketing*. He is ranked number one based on publications in the *Journal of the Academy of Marketing Science* (JAMS) from its inception through volume 23, 1995. He is also number one based on publications in JAMS from 1986 to 1995. He is listed as one of the best researchers in marketing in John Fraedrich, 'The best researchers in marketing', *Marketing Educator* (Summer 1997), p. 5.

He has published more than 75 papers in major refereed journals including the *Journal of Marketing Research, Journal of Consumer Research, Marketing Science, Journal of Marketing, Journal of Academy of Marketing Science, Journal of Retailing, Journal of Health Care Marketing*, and leading journals in statistics, management science and psychology. In addition, he has also published numerous refereed articles in the proceedings of major national and international conferences. Several articles have received research awards.

He was Chairman, Academy of Marketing Science Foundation, 1996–1998, and was President, Academy of Marketing Science, 1994–1996, and Chairman of the Board of Governors from 1990 to 1992. He is a Distinguished Fellow of the Academy and Fellow of the Decision Sciences Institute. He serves as an Associate Editor of *Decision Sciences Journal* and has served as Section Editor, Health Care Marketing Abstracts, *Journal of Health Care Marketing*. Also, he serves on the Editorial Boards of eight journals.

His book entitled *Marketing Research: An Applied Orientation*, Third Edition, was published by Prentice Hall, Inc. An International Edition and an Australian Edition of his book have also been published, along with a Spanish translation. The book has received widespread adoption at both the graduate and undergraduate levels with more than 100 schools using it in the USA.

Dr Malhotra has consulted for business, non-profit and government organisations in the USA and abroad and has served as an expert witness in legal and regulatory proceedings. He is the winner of numerous awards and honours for research, teaching and service to the profession.

Dr Malhotra is a member and Deacon, First Baptist Church of Atlanta. He lives in the Atlanta area with his wife, Veena, and children, Ruth and Paul.

Dr David Frederick Birks is a Senior Lecturer in Marketing in the School of Management at the University of Southampton, England. He is the Programme Director for their MSc in Marketing Analytics. Marketing Analytics combines the disciplines of marketing research, database and web metrics, competitor intelligence and the information systems used to support strategic marketing decision making. David teaches quantitative and qualitative marketing research and consumer metrics. His industrial experience was gained in the construction and housing industry in England and Germany. Before university lecturing he worked in purchasing, planning, marketing and research. He has Masters degrees in Marketing Management and in Social Statistics and a PhD in Marketing Information Systems.

David has continued to practise marketing research throughout his university career, managing projects in financial institutions, retailers, industrial organisations, local authorities and charities. He has managed projects as part of undergraduate, MSc, MBA and PhD degree programmes. He was the Head of Marketing Research on the GlobalCash Project, a major study of European cash management banking practices that ran from 1994 to 2004. David helped to develop the research design, research instruments and analyses by coordinating the demands of major pan-European and American banks, and the research requirements of 19 business schools throughout Europe. He edited and made a major contribution to the text *Global Cash Management in Europe* that resulted from the combined research efforts of colleagues in Britain, Denmark, Germany, Ireland, Italy, Norway and Sweden. He has published further research from GlobalCash with colleagues from Aarhus, Denmark. In addition to his Cash Management work, David's publications have covered the fields of Housing, Statistics, Marketing and Information Systems.

David lives in the heart of the city of Winchester in Hampshire. From this very English setting, he brings a cosmopolitan background to this European edition, having an English father, German mother, French grandfather and Belgian great-grandparents.

1

Introduction to marketing research

Marketing researchers support decision-makers by collecting, analysing and interpreting information needed to identify and solve marketing problems.

Objectives

After reading this chapter, you should be able to:

1 understand the nature and scope of marketing research and its role in supporting the design and implementation of successful marketing decisions;

2 describe a conceptual framework for conducting marketing research as well as the steps of the marketing research process;

3 distinguish between problem identification and problem-solving marketing research;

4 appreciate the relative importance of marketing research in countries throughout the world;

5 understand the types and roles of research suppliers, including internal and external, full-service and limited-service suppliers;

6 understand why some marketers may be sceptical of the value of marketing research;

7 appreciate the demands for marketing researchers to supplement their technical research skills with managerial skills;

8 appreciate the complexities involved in international marketing research;

9 understand the basis of ethical aspects of marketing research and the responsibilities that marketing research stakeholders have to them-selves, each other and to the research project;

10 appreciate the potential opportunities and threats of the Internet to marketing researchers.

| STAGE 1 Problem definition | STAGE 2 Research approach developed | STAGE 3 Research design developed | STAGE 4 Fieldwork or data collection | STAGE 5 Data preparation and analysis | STAGE 6 Report preparation and presentation |

Overview

Marketing research comprises one of the most important and fascinating facets of marketing. In this chapter, we describe the nature and scope of marketing research, emphasising its role of supporting marketing decision making, and provide several real-life examples to illustrate the basic concepts of marketing research. We give a formal definition of marketing research and show how this links to a six-stage description of the marketing research process. This description is extended to illustrate many of the interconnected activities in the marketing research process. We then subdivide marketing research into two areas: problem identification and problem-solving research. The extent and growth rates of marketing research expenditure throughout the world are then presented followed by an overview of marketing research suppliers and services.

There are many successful marketing decisions that have been founded upon sound marketing research: however marketing research does not replace decision making. The limitations of marketing research are established and these lead on to the growing demands upon the marketing research industry to produce research findings that are actionable and relevant to marketing decision makers. Many individual examples will be presented to illustrate the managerial challenges of making marketing research actionable and relevant, but beyond these individual examples we showcase the exciting work of Sports Marketing Surveys. This independent marketing research agency has specialised in the sponsorship and sports industry over the past 20 years. The sports industry and many sponsorship deals are often multi-country in their reach and activity, and to meet these challenges Sports Marketing Surveys has the capability of working and reporting on a worldwide basis, in over 200 countries for events such as the Olympic Games and the Football World Cup. Work from four projects conducted by Sports Marketing Surveys will be used as running examples throughout this book.

The topic of international marketing research is introduced. International marketing research will be discussed systematically in subsequent chapters and will be tackled in a dedicated chapter.

The ethical aspects of marketing research and the responsibilities that marketing research stakeholders have to themselves, to each other and to the research project are presented and developed in more detail throughout the text.

Finally, a general introduction to the use of the Internet in the marketing research industry is made. Specific issues relating to the impact of the Internet and computers will be developed throughout the text.

What does marketing research encompass?

The term 'marketing research' is broad in meaning. This breadth will be explored and illustrated throughout this chapter. What will become apparent is that it is related to supporting marketing decision making in many ways. The following example illustrates the variety of marketing research techniques used at Royal Ahold and the role of marketing research in supporting decision-makers.

Example | **Listening to the customer – research at Royal Ahold[1]**

Royal Ahold is a world supermarket leader. In the Netherlands Ahold operates six chains with over 1,750 outlets, including the flagship Albert Heijn supermarkets. Worldwide, Ahold serves 20 million customers weekly in 3,400 stores in 17 countries across the USA, Central and Western Europe, Latin America and Asia. Customer orientation is at the top of the fundamental principles of the company. Its credo is that the customer comes first: 'However big we become, however international, it is ultimately the customer who determines our success.'

The following list summarises the ways that Royal Ahold 'listens' to its customers to maintain its customer orientation and continued success:

- Produces economic analyses and forecasts. It does this by gathering secondary data and intelligence that give it an understanding of retail developments, competitive threats and market changes.
- Uses and contributes to audit data from A.C. Nielsen to obtain global data about developments in their markets.
- Sees its stores as a major 'market research laboratory' to study customers. It knows when they come in, how often and what they buy. Fundamental to these observations is the use of scanner systems and loyalty cards.
- Uses focus groups as a major source of information about how customers and non-customers feel. It insists that management teams watch and listen to these discussions.
- Uses observation approaches to watch how customers behave in store, using protocol tapes (where people think aloud about the purchases they are making).
- Selects some researchers to supply raw data, where it performs its own analyses and interpretations, whilst in other projects it uses specialised strategic input from researchers to provide added value.
- Shares its best practices and know-how. It has an electronic market research platform where researchers discuss their projects and any problems they have. For example, if a successful approach has been used in the Netherlands, they can consider using it in the USA.
- Circulates a digest to the Corporate Executive Board and management teams all over the world. *Market Research Findings* is issued twice a year, giving details of important papers, articles and reports on retail research from inside or outside the Ahold company.

Bert L. J. van der Herberg, Vice President Market Research, summarises the role of market researchers at Royal Ahold:

Researchers are backroom consultants. I see the market researcher as a philosopher who can take a critical view of the internal and external world. The researcher can act as 'the serious fool' to the court. The Board takes on our ideas and our language, but the market researcher is not the spokesman for the company. They are listeners and interpreters.[1]

The use of a variety of techniques is vital to support a variety of key marketing decisions. The following two examples from Philips and the Nordea Bank illustrate how integral marketing research can be to sound decision making.

Example | **Research is integral to marketing at Philips[2]**

A few years ago, Philips Consumer Electronics determined that the market for traditional personal audio was diminishing. Its researchers looked into what the key needs and drivers of teenagers were and came up with concepts such as adaptability, choice flexibility, sharing experiences and spontaneity. They selected a few of these as a basis for their designers to start developing products. They also meticulously identified the value proposition they wanted to offer with new products coming out of the designer pipeline. Subsequently, when a product was presented during the trial phase, Philips let the researchers determine, through qualitative research, what the consumer saw as the primary benefits and concerns of the product. Philips wanted to identify exactly why it would make a product, for whom it would make it and how it would be differentiated from other products. After Philips had decided to go to market with these products (a series of very small portable MP3 players/cameras that fit on a key ring), it again turned to its researchers to test the advertising campaign that was developed for the product.

Example   ## Nordea: a new brand in the making[3]

Nordea is a leading bank in the Nordic region with around 1,200 branch offices and some 11 million clients of which 3.9 million are e-customers. It was created around 2000 through a series of mergers between Nordbanken in Sweden, Merita Bank in Finland, Unibank in Denmark and Christiana Bank og Kreditkasse in Norway. Before the merger, each original bank conducted ongoing customer and employee satisfaction surveys, including monitoring its reputation and image. At the time of the merger there was a solid basis to continue these surveys. Since branding of the new name was central to creating Nordea, concurrent with the satisfaction surveys, specific surveys were needed to support the brand building process.

This consisted of five phases:

1 **Establishing common core values**: surveys were instituted to ensure the basis to launch the new brand, for instance a comprehensive laddering survey to form the basis of Nordea's positioning strategy.
2 **Choosing a new name**: the name studies took several months to complete and substantial resources were committed to test associations with potential candidates including 'Nordea'.
3 **Ensuring name awareness**: on launching the Nordea name, a frequent and detailed name awareness tracking was initiated. As awareness grew, the tracking was phased out and eventually focused exclusively on the quality of the awareness.
4 **Positioning the brand**: the initial purpose of the brand positioning survey was to create a common understanding of the original banks' positioning and to identify the position towards which the brand should move based on the company's business strategy. As the survey had to reflect feelings and values in four different languages when employees did not even 'speak the same language', linguistic pitfalls had to be taken into account.
5 **Building reputation**: as a company turn-around process was initiated at the time, the focus shifted towards the bank's corporate reputation. This was measured by Reputation Excellence, a syndicated Nordic survey marketed by Danish MarkedsConsult. Nordea took an active role in designing the survey when launched in 2003. The survey was based on 15,000 CATI interviews in the Nordic countries carried out by Nordic Norstat.

These examples illustrate only a few of the methods used to conduct marketing research, which may range from highly structured surveys with large samples to in-depth interviews with small samples; from the collection and analysis of readily available data to the generation of 'new' data; from direct interaction with consumers to the distant observation of consumers. These examples illustrate a few of the applications of marketing research in supporting decision-makers. This book will introduce you to the full complement of marketing research techniques. These examples also illustrate the crucial role played by marketing research in designing and implementing successful marketing plans.[4] This book will also introduce you to a broad range of marketing applications supported by marketing research.

The role of marketing research can be better understood in light of the basic marketing paradigm depicted in Figure 1.1. The emphasis in marketing, as illustrated in the Royal Ahold example above, is on the identification and satisfaction of customer needs. To

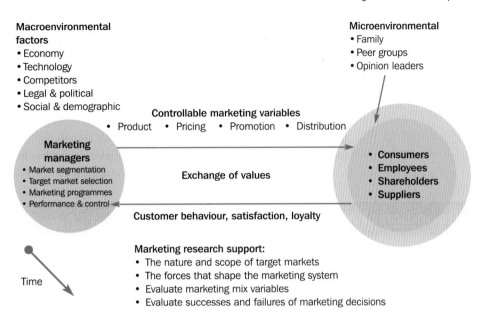

Figure 1.1
The role of marketing research within the marketing system

determine customer needs and to implement marketing strategies and plans aimed at satisfying those needs, marketing managers need information about customers, competitors and other forces in the marketplace. In recent years, many factors have increased the need for more accurate and timely information. As firms have become national and international in scope, the need for information on larger, and more distant, markets has increased. As consumers have become more affluent, discerning and sophisticated, marketing managers need better information on how they will respond to new products and other marketing offerings. As competition has become more intense, managers need information on the effectiveness of their marketing tools. As the environment is changing more rapidly, marketing managers need more timely information to cope with the impact of changes.[5]

Marketers make decisions about what they see as potential opportunities and problems, i.e. a process of identifying issues. They go on to devise the most effective ways to realise these opportunities and overcome problems they have identified. They do this based on a 'vision' of the distinct characteristics of the target markets and customer groups. From this 'vision' they develop, implement and control marketing programmes. This 'vision' of markets and subsequent marketing decisions may be complicated by the interactive effects of an array of environmental forces that shape the nature and scope of target markets. These forces also affect the marketers' ability to satisfy their chosen target markets.

Within this framework of decision making, marketing research helps the marketing manager link the marketing variables with their environment and customer groups. It helps remove some of the uncertainty by providing relevant information about marketing variables, environment and consumers.

The role of the marketing researcher in supporting the marketing decision-maker can therefore be summarised as helping to:

- describe the nature and scope of customer groups;
- understand the nature of forces that shape customer groups;
- understand the nature of forces that shape the marketer's ability to satisfy targeted customer groups;
- test individual and interactive marketing mix variables;
- monitor and reflect upon past successes and failures in marketing decisions.

Traditionally, marketing researchers were responsible for assessing information needs and providing the relevant information, while marketing decisions were made by the managers. These roles are changing, however, and marketing researchers are becoming more involved in decision making; conversely, marketing managers are becoming more involved with research. This trend can be attributed to better training of marketing managers and advances in technology; we will discuss this in more detail towards the end of this chapter. There has also been a shift in the nature and scope of marketing research, where increasingly marketing research is being undertaken on an ongoing basis rather than in response to specific marketing problems or opportunities on an ad hoc basis.[6]

This crucial role of marketing research is recognised in its definition.

Definition of marketing research

The European Society for Opinion and Marketing Research (ESOMAR) defines marketing research as given below. For the purpose of this book, which emphasises the need for information in the support of decision making, marketing research is defined as:

Marketing research
A key element within the total field of marketing information. It links the consumer, customer and public to the marketer through information which is used to identify and define marketing opportunities and problems; to generate, refine and evaluate marketing actions; and to improve understanding of marketing as a process and of the ways in which specific marketing activities can be made more effective.

> **Marketing research** *is a key element within the total field of marketing information. It links the consumer, customer and public to the marketer through information which is used to identify and define marketing opportunities and problems; to generate, refine and evaluate marketing actions; and to improve understanding of marketing as a process and of the ways in which specific marketing activities can be made more effective.*

Several aspects of this definition are noteworthy. First, it reinforces the notion of basing marketing decisions upon a strong understanding of target customers. It stresses the role of 'linking' the marketer to the consumer, customer and public to help improve the whole process of marketing decision making.

ESOMAR further qualifies its definition of marketing research by stating:

> *Marketing research specifies the information required to address these issues* [of linking the consumer, customer and public to the marketer]; *designs the method for collecting information; manages and implements the data collection process; analyses the results; and communicates the findings and their implications.*

Marketing research process
A set of six steps which define the tasks to be accomplished in conducting a marketing research study. These include problem definition, developing an approach to the problem, research design formulation, fieldwork, data preparation and analysis, and report generation and presentation.

The above qualification of the definition of marketing research encapsulates the **marketing research process**. The process is founded upon an understanding of the marketing decision(s) needing support. From this understanding, research aims and objectives are defined. To fulfil defined aims and objectives, an approach to conducting the research is established. Next, relevant information sources are identified and a range of data collection methods are evaluated for their appropriateness, forming a research design. The data are collected using the most appropriate method; they are analysed and interpreted, and inferences are drawn. Finally, the findings, implications and recommendations are provided in a format that allows the information to be used for marketing decision making and to be acted upon directly.

Marketing research should aim to be objective. It attempts to provide accurate information in an impartial manner. Although research is always influenced by the researcher's research philosophy, it should be free from the personal or political biases of the researcher or decision-makers. Research motivated by personal or political gain involves a breach of professional standards. Such research is deliberately biased to result in predetermined findings. The motto of every researcher should be 'Find it and tell it like it is.' Second, it is worth noting the term 'total field of information'. This recognises that marketing decisions are not exclusively supported by marketing research. There are other

Source: © Alamy

means of information support for marketers from management consult-ants, raw data providers such as call centres, direct marketing, database marketing and telebusinesses.[7] These alternative forms of support are now competing with a 'traditional' view of marketing research. The methods of these competitors may not be administered with the same scientific rigour and/or ethical standards applied in the marketing research industry. Nonetheless, many marketing decision-makers are increasingly using these other sources which collectively are changing the nature of skills demanded in marketing researchers. These demands will be discussed in more detail later in this chapter.

The marketing research process

The marketing research process consists of six broad stages. Each of these stages is developed in more detail in subsequent chapters; thus, the discussion here is brief. The process illustrated in Figure 1.2 is of the marketing research seen in simple stages. Figure 1.3 takes the process a stage further to show the many iterations and connections between stages. This section will explain the stages and illustrate the connections between the stages.

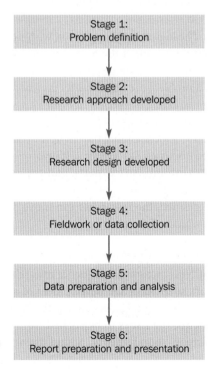

Figure 1.2
Simple description of the marketing research process

Stage 1:
Problem definition

Stage 2:
Research approach developed

Stage 3:
Research design developed

Stage 4:
Fieldwork or data collection

Stage 5:
Data preparation and analysis

Stage 6:
Report preparation and presentation

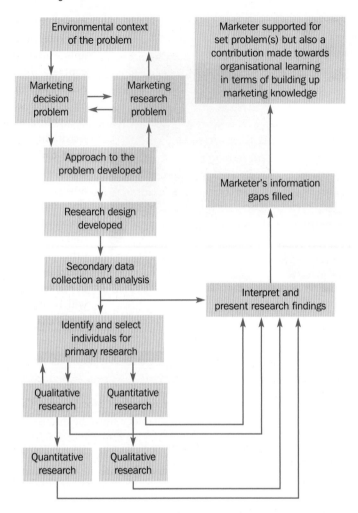

Figure 1.3
The marketing research process, detailing iterations between stages

Step 1: problem definition. The logical starting point in wishing to support the decision-maker is trying to understand the nature of the marketing problem that requires research support. Marketing problems are not simple 'givens', as will be discussed in Chapter 2, and the symptoms and causes of a problem are not as neatly presented as they may be in a case study such as those found in marketing textbooks. In Figure 1.3, the first three stages show the iterations between *environmental context of the problem, marketing decision problem and marketing research problem*. Understanding the environmental context of the problem has distinct stages that will be discussed in Chapter 2. It involves discussion with decision-makers, in-depth interviews with industry experts, and the collection and analysis of readily available published information (from both inside and outside the firm). Once the problem has been precisely defined, the researcher can move on to designing and conducting the research process with confidence.

Step 2: development of an approach to the problem. The development of an approach to the problem involves identifying factors that influence research design. A key element of this step involves the selection, adaptation and development of an appropriate theoretical framework to underpin a research design. Understanding the interrelated characteristics of the nature of target respondents, the issues to be elicited from them and the context in which this will happen rely upon 'sound' theory. 'Sound' theory helps the researcher to decide 'what should be measured or understood' and 'how best to encapsulate and communicate the measurements or understandings'. In deciding what should be either measured or encapsulated, the researcher also develops a broad appreciation of how the data collected will be analysed. The issues involved in developing an approach are tackled in more detail in Chapter 2.

Step 3: research design developed. A research design is a framework or blueprint for conducting a marketing research project. It details the procedures necessary for obtaining the required information. Its purpose is to establish a study design that will either test the hypotheses of interest or determine possible answers to set research questions, and ultimately provide the information needed for decision making. Conducting any exploratory techniques, precisely defining variables to be measured, and designing appropriate scales to measure variables can also be part of the research design. The issue of how the data should be obtained from the respondents (e.g. by conducting a survey or an experiment) must be addressed. These steps are discussed in detail in Chapters 3 to 13.

Step 4: fieldwork or data collection. In Figure 1.2, this stage could be simplified to 'collecting the required data'. In Figure 1.3, a whole array of relationships between stages of data collection is shown, starting at *Secondary data collection and analysis* through to *Quantitative research* or *Qualitative research*. The process starts with a more thorough collection and analysis of secondary data sources. Secondary data are data collected for some other purpose than the problem at hand. They may be held within the organis-ation as databases that detail the nature and frequency of customer purchases, through to surveys that may have been completed some time ago that may be accessed through libraries, CD-ROMs or the Internet. Going through this stage avoids replication of work and gives guidance in sampling plans and in deciding what to measure or encapsulate using quantitative or qualitative techniques. Secondary data collection and analysis may complete the research process, i.e. sufficient information may exist to interpret and report findings to a point whereby the information gaps that the decision-maker has are filled. Secondary data forms a vital foundation and essential focus to primary data collection.

In Figure 1.3, the stage of *Identify and select individuals for primary research* covers sampling issues for both quantitative and qualitative studies. This stage may include the selection of individuals for in-depth qualitative research. In qualitative research, issues of 'representativeness' are less important than the quality of individuals targeted for investigation and the quality of response elicited. However, as can be seen from the line leading up from *Qualitative research* to *Identify and select individuals for primary research*, the qualitative research process may help in the identification and classification of individuals who may be targeted using more formal sampling methods. These sampling methods are covered in detail in Chapters 14 and 15.

Beyond the issues of identifying and selecting individuals, the options available for primary data collection vary considerably. A stage of *Qualitative research* alone may be sufficient to support the decision-maker, as indeed could a stage of *Quantitative research*. The following example illustrates the use of qualitative observation to support marketing decision making. This example mirrors one of the research techniques used by Royal Ahold (presented at the start of this chapter), helping it to build up a 'picture' of its customers. As a technique in its own right, it does not necessarily have to be followed by a survey or quantitative work to confirm the observations. This technique will be developed under the heading 'Ethnographic research' in Chapter 6.

Example   **Supermarket Sweep[8]**

Video camera analysis can be used to gain vital information about the way in which supermarket consumers spend their money. People behave in certain ways within the supermarket environment, according to store design specialist company ID Magasin. Patterns of consumer behaviour can be used to maximise profits. Store managers who work on store design without video footage are sometimes wrong about their conclusions. Consumers, for example, often ignore the products placed on shelves at eye level, despite popular belief to the contrary.

The research problem may require a stage of qualitative and quantitative research to run concurrently, perhaps measuring and encapsulating different characteristics of the problem under investigation.

A stage of qualitative research could be used to precede a stage of quantitative research. For example, a series of focus groups may help to generate a series of statements or expectations that are subsequently tested out in a survey to a representative sample. Conversely, a survey may be conducted and, upon analysis, there may be clear statistically significant differences between two distinct target markets. A series of qualitative in-depth interviews may follow to allow a more full exploration and understanding of the reasons for the differences between the two groups.

Step 5: data preparation and analysis. Data preparation includes the editing, coding, transcription and verification of data. In Figure 1.3, this stage is not drawn out as a distinct stage in its own right, but is seen as integral to the stages of *Secondary data collection and analysis* through to *Quantitative research* or *Qualitative research*. The process of data preparation and analysis is essentially the same for both quantitative and qualitative techniques, for data collected from both secondary and primary sources. Considerations of data analysis do not occur after data have been collected; such considerations are an integral part of the development of an approach, the development of a research design, and the implementation of individual quantitative or qualitative methods. If the data to be collected are qualitative, the analysis process can occur as the data are being collected, well before all observations or interviews have been completed. An integral part of qualitative data preparation and analysis requires researchers to reflect upon their own learning and the ways they may interpret what they see and hear. These issues will be developed in Chapters 6 to 9.

If the data to be analysed are quantitative, each questionnaire or observation form is inspected or edited and, if necessary, corrected. Number or letter codes are assigned to represent each response to each question in the questionnaire. The data from the questionnaires are transcribed or keypunched into a proprietary data analysis package. Verification ensures that the data from the original questionnaires have been accurately transcribed, whereas data analysis gives meaning to the data that have been collected. Univariate techniques are used for analysing data when there is a single measurement of each element or unit in the sample; if there are several measurements of each element, each variable is analysed in isolation (see Chapter 18). On the other hand, multivariate techniques are used for analysing data when there are two or more measurements of each element and the variables are analysed simultaneously (see Chapters 18 to 24).

Step 6: report preparation and presentation. The entire project should be documented in a written report that addresses the specific research questions identified, describes the approach, research design, data collection and data analysis procedures adopted, and presents the results and major findings. Research findings should be presented in a comprehensible format so that they can be readily used in the decision-making process. In addition, an oral presentation to management should be made using tables, figures and graphs to enhance clarity and impact. This process is encapsulated in Figure 1.3 with the reminder that the marketer's information gaps are filled and that the marketer is supported for the set problem, but also a contribution is made towards organisational learning in terms of building up marketing knowledge (see Chapter 25).

A classification of marketing research

The ESOMAR definition encapsulates two key reasons for undertaking marketing research: (1) to identify opportunities and problems, and (2) to generate and refine marketing actions. This distinction serves as a basis for classifying marketing research into problem identification research and problem-solving research, as shown in Figure 1.4. Linking this classification to the basic marketing paradigm in Figure 1.1, problem identification research can be linked to: the description of the nature and scope of customer groups, understanding the nature of forces that shape customer groups, and understanding the nature of forces that shape the marketer's ability to satisfy targeted customer groups. Problem-solving research can be linked to: test individual and interactive marketing mix variables, and to monitor and reflect upon past successes and failures in marketing decisions.

Problem identification research
Research undertaken to help identify problems that are not necessarily apparent on the surface, yet exist or are likely to arise in the future.

Problem identification research is undertaken to help identify problems that are, perhaps, not apparent on the surface and yet exist or are likely to arise in the future. Examples of problem identification research include market potential, market share, brand or company image, market characteristics, sales analysis, short-range forecasting, long-range forecasting and business trends research. Research of this type provides information about the marketing environment and helps diagnose a problem. For example, a declining market potential indicates that the firm is likely to have a problem achieving its growth targets. Similarly, a problem exists if the market potential is increasing but the firm is losing market share. The recognition of economic, social or cultural trends, such as changes in consumer behaviour, may point to underlying problems or opportunities.

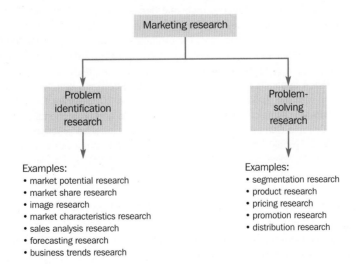

Figure 1.4
A classification of marketing research

11

Example

Beer research shows overspill[9]

The proliferation of new brands in Europe's booming beer market could result in shorter product lifecycles and, ultimately, destroy brand loyalty. The report 'Western European Beer' reveals that the industry is in danger of an overspill of brands, with the number of brands available exceeding demand. As a result, consumers are likely to fall back on 'tried and tested brands', normally owned by large manufacturers, at the expense of lesser known brands, which are likely to fall by the wayside.

The example above presents either a problem or an opportunity for beer manufacturers, depending largely upon whether their brand is 'tried and tested' or not. The research could be classified as 'business trends research' or even 'market potential research'. It could be followed by individual beer manufacturers conducting their own 'image research' to reveal the extent to which their brand(s) are perceived as being 'tried and tested'.

Problem-solving research
Research undertaken to help solve specific marketing problems.

Once a problem or opportunity has been identified, **problem-solving research** may be undertaken to help develop a solution. The findings of problem-solving research are used to support decisions that tackle specific marketing problems. Problem-solving research linked to problem identification research is illustrated by the following example of developing a new cereal at Kellogg's.

Example

Crunchy Nut Red adds colour to Kellogg's sales[10]

In 2001, Kellogg's was faced with the challenge of reviving low cereal sales. Through problem identification research, it was able to identify the problem, and through problem-solving research, to develop several solutions to increase the sales of cereals.

To identify the problem, Kellogg's researchers interviewed decision-makers within the company, interviewed industry experts, conducted analyses of available secondary data, conducted some qualitative research and surveyed consumers about their perceptions and preferences for cereals. Several important problems were identified:

- Current products were being targeted at children.
- Bagels and muffins were becoming more favoured breakfast foods.
- High prices were turning consumers to generic brands.
- Quick breakfast foods that required liitle or no preparation were becoming more popular.

These issues helped Kellogg's to define the problem: Kellogg's was not being creative in introducing new products to meet the needs of adult consumers. Based on this definition, Kellogg's introduced new flavours that were more suited to the adult palette but were not tasteless varieties of the past. For example, it introduced Crunchy Nut Red. This new cereal included cranberry pieces, almonds and yogurt-flavoured flakes. The new cereal was supported by a national television advertising campaign, major in-store promotions, and 2 million specially produced sachets for a nationwide sampling campaign. Kellogg's partnered with the 2002 US Olympic team and the 2002 Winter Olympic Games. The company distributed Olympic themed packages, products and promotional offers as a way to welcome the Olympic Games back to the USA. Through creative problem identification research followed by problem-solving research, Kellogg's has seen not only an increase in sales, but also an increase in consumption of cereal at times other than breakfast.

This example illustrates how the careful crafting of problem identification research can help to develop a clear focus to problem-solving research. The outcome was research that supported marketing decisions in many ways. A problem-solving perspective enabled Kellogg's management to focus on issues of product development and an integrated promotions campaign. Table 1.1 shows the different types of issues that can be addressed using problem-solving research.

Table 1.1 Examples of problem-solving research

Segmentation research	Determine basis of segmentation
	Establish market potential and responsiveness for various segments
	Select target markets and create lifestyle profiles: demography, media, and product image characteristics
Product research	Test concept
	Determine optimal product design
	Package tests
	Product modification
	Brand positioning and repositioning
	Test marketing
Pricing research	Importance of price in brand selection
	Pricing policies
	Product line pricing
	Price elasticity of demand
	Initiating and responding to price changes
Promotions research	Optimal promotional budget
	Optimal promotion mix
	Copy decisions
	Creative advertising testing
	Evaluation of advertising effectiveness
Distribution research	Attitudes of channel members
	Intensity of wholesale and retail coverage
	Channel margins
	Retail and wholesale locations

Problem identification research and problem-solving research go hand in hand as seen in the Kellogg's case, and a given marketing research project may combine both types of research. A marketing research project for a European beer manufacturer that sees its market share diminish may determine through image research that its brand is perceived in a most positive manner. This may indicate that the brand should be extended into other types of beer or even into clothes and fashion accessories. Appropriate target markets may be selected, with detailed profiles of potential customers and an associated media and product image. These decisions can clearly be supported with problem-solving research. Whether the focus is upon problem identification or problem-solving research, it is vital that the process of marketing research is conducted in a systemic and rigorous manner.

The global marketing research industry

With the rising demand for managerial skills in marketing researchers, we turn our attention to the relative rates of demand for marketing research and industry growth rates across the globe. To monitor rates of expenditure and growth, we follow the annual ESOMAR Global Market Research Industry Study (**www.esomar.nl**), with summaries and commentary from the magazine *Research World*.

The figures presented are estimates of all the work conducted within individual countries, by research agencies. Not included in the data is marketing research undertaken by non-profit research institutes, governments, universities or advertising agencies using their own resources. The data also do not include the internal supply of marketing research, i.e. the costs of a marketing research function located within a firm. In addition, not included are costs incurred by the more sophisticated users of marketing research who integrate the data and analyses of their operational databases to understand customers and support marketing decision making. Though these estimates are static, may quickly go out of date and only tell part of the story of supporting marketing decision making, they are a vital means to illustrate developments in the marketing research industry.

The total global expenditure on marketing research in 2004 amounted to €17,415 million. Where this money was spent is illustrated in Table 1.2 which lists the top 20 countries with the highest marketing research spend per capita. Though it is clear to see that the USA as a country spent the most on marketing research, on a per capita basis a different story emerges. Five European countries spent more than the USA, with the UK spending €32.18 on marketing research for every citizen, with Sweden second at €27.96 and France at €24.70. The top 20 is dominated by countries with mature marketing research industries and with relatively high price levels for their research services.

In countries with marketing research industries that are relatively young, though the overall turnover and per capita rates may be low, the potential for growth may be immense. This is not the case in many developed economies: for example, in 2003, of the EU15 countries[12] the UK, Germany, the Netherlands, Sweden, Belgium, Denmark and Ireland had negative growth rates, with the Netherlands and Belgium continuing this decline in 2004. These negative growth rates increased the competitive intensity in marketing research suppliers and exacerbate the demand for managerial skills from marketing researchers. Marketing research in Europe is far from in decline as illustrated by the healthy growth rates of the new EU member states and other non-EU European countries.

Table 1.2 Top 20 countries with highest MR spend per capita, 2004[11]

Country	Turnover (€m)	Population (million)	Spend per capita (€ per capita)
1 UK	1,901	59.07	32.18
2 Sweden	248	8.87	27.96
3 France	1,478	59.84	24.70
4 Switzerland	147	7.17	20.50
5 Germany	1,677	82.41	20.35
6 USA	5,892	291.04	20.24
7 Finland	103	5.20	19.81
8 Denmark	101	5.35	18.88
9 Australia	367	19.54	18.78
10 Norway	78	4.51	17.29
11 New Zealand	65	3.85	16.88
12 Netherlands	271	16.07	16.86
13 Ireland	63	3.91	16.11
14 Canada	430	31.27	13.75
15 Belgium	131	10.30	12.72
16 Austria	87	8.16	10.65
17 Italy	540	57.48	9.39
18 Spain	382	41.16	9.28
19 Singapore	36	4.18	8.61
20 Japan	1,042	127.48	8.17

When set in a global context, Table 1.3 shows that Central and South America have the highest regional growth rates for marketing research expenditure in the world. This table presents the turnover, growth rates and market share for all regions of the world. It also shows that Europe as a whole has the largest share of the global market for marketing research at 44.93%.

Though Table 1.3 presents the relative expenditure, growth rates and shares on a regional basis, it masks the individual countries where marketing research is growing at the greatest rates. Table 1.4 ranks the countries with a real growth rate over 10%. Countries with healthy economic growth show the highest growth levels in marketing research. This table shows the increased demand for and expenditure in the booming Central and Latin America, where several countries like Venezuela, Argentina and Mexico have emerged from recession and are displaying high growth rates for marketing research. Examples of marketing research conducted in these emerging and fast-growing economies will be used throughout the text in the sections of International Marketing Research.

Table 1.3 Turnover, growth rates and market share per region, 2003–2004[13]

Region	Turnover 2003, (€m)	Growth rate (unadjusted for inflation) (%)	Real growth rate (adjusted for inflation) (%)	Share of global market, 2003 (%)
EU15	7,150	5.2	3.0	41.06
New member states	242	10.5	6.0	1.39
Other Europe	433	10.7	6.1	2.48
Total Europe	**7,825**	**5.6**	**3.2**	**44.93**
North America	6,361	9.5	6.7	36.53
Central & South America	672	14.8	8.2	3.86
Asia Pacific	2,319	6.5	5.2	13.32
Middle East & Africa	238	8.6	6.3	1.37
Total World	**17,415**	**7.5**	**5.0**	

Table 1.4 Countries with growth rate expectations over 10% for 2005[14]

Region	Expected growth rate, 2005
Venezuela	30
Argentina	25
Russian Fed.	25
Ukraine	20
Poland	19
Turkey	17
Kenya	15
Lithuania	15
Mexico	15
Singapore	12.5
Brazil	10
Cyprus	10

External suppliers
Outside marketing research companies hired to supply marketing research services.

Full-service suppliers
Companies that offer the full range of marketing research activities.

Syndicated services
Companies that collect and sell common pools of data designed to serve information needs shared by a number of clients.

Standardised services
Companies that use standardised procedures to provide marketing research to various clients.

Customised services
Companies that tailor research procedures to best meet the needs of each client.

Internet services
Companies which specialise in the use of the Internet to collect, analyse and distribute marketing research information.

Limited-service suppliers
Companies that specialise in one or a few phases of a marketing research project.

Field services
Companies whose primary service offering is their expertise in collecting data for research projects.

The bases for the estimates in Tables 1.2 to 1.4 emerge from external marketing research suppliers or agencies. **External suppliers** are outside firms hired to supply marketing research data. These external suppliers collectively comprise the 'marketing research industry'. They range from small (one or a few persons) operations to very large global corporations. We now examine the nature of services that may be supplied by external suppliers. As illustrated in Figure 1.5, external suppliers can be classified as full-service or limited-service suppliers.

Full-service suppliers offer the entire range of marketing research services: for example, defining a problem, developing a research design, conducting focus group interviews, designing questionnaires, sampling, collecting, analysing and interpreting data, and presenting reports. They may also address the marketing implications of the information they present, i.e. have the management skills to interpret and communicate the impact of their research findings at the highest levels. They may also manage customer database analyses, being able to integrate the management and analyses databases with the management and analyses of conventional marketing research techniques.

The services provided by these suppliers can be further broken down into syndicated services, standardised services and customised services (see Figure 1.5).

Syndicated services collect information that they provide to subscribers. Surveys, diary panels, scanners and audits are the main means by which these data are collected.

Standardised services are research studies conducted for different clients but in a standard way. For example, procedures for measuring advertising effectiveness have been standardised so that the results can be compared across studies and evaluative norms can be established.

Customised services offer a variety of marketing research services specifically designed to suit a client's particular needs. Each marketing research project is treated uniquely.

Internet services offer a combination or variety of secondary data and intelligence gathering, survey or qualitative interviewing, and the analysis and publication of research findings, all through the Internet.

Limited-service suppliers specialise in one or a few phases of a marketing research project. Services offered by such suppliers are classified as field services, coding and data entry, analytical services, data analysis and branded products.

Field services collect data through mail, personal interviews or telephone interviews, and firms that specialise in interviewing are called field service organisations. These

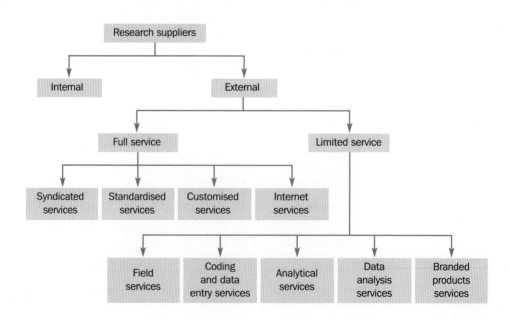

Figure 1.5
Marketing research suppliers

organisations may range from small proprietary organisations that operate locally to large multinationals. Some organisations maintain extensive interviewing facilities across the country for interviewing shoppers. Many offer qualitative data collection services such as focus group interviewing (discussed in detail in Chapter 7).

Coding and data entry services include editing completed questionnaires, developing a coding scheme and transcribing the data for input into a computer.

Analytical services include designing and pretesting questionnaires, determining the best means of collecting data, and designing sampling plans, as well as other aspects of the research design. Some complex marketing research projects require knowledge of sophisticated procedures, including specialised experimental designs (discussed in Chapter 10) and analytical techniques such as conjoint analysis and multidimensional scaling (discussed in Chapter 24). This kind of expertise can be obtained from firms and consultants specialising in analytical services.

Data analysis services are offered by firms, also known as tab houses, that specialise in computer analysis of quantitative data such as those obtained in large surveys. Initially, most data analysis firms supplied only tabulations (frequency counts) and cross-tabulations (frequency counts that describe two or more variables simultaneously). Now, many firms offer sophisticated data analysis using advanced statistical techniques. With the proliferation of microcomputers and software, many firms now have the capability to analyse their own data, but data analysis firms with expert statisticians are still in demand.

Branded marketing research products and services are specialised data collection and analysis procedures developed to address specific types of marketing research problems. These procedures may be patented, given brand names, and marketed like any other branded product. *Microscope* by Retail Marketing (In-Store) Services is an example of a branded product. It is a test marketing package for new product development that supplies cost-effective measurements of new product performance.

Coding and data entry services
Companies whose primary service offering is their expertise in converting completed surveys or interviews into a usable database for conducting statistical analysis.

Analytical services
Companies that provide guidance in the development of research design.

Data analysis services
Firms whose primary service is to conduct statistical analyses of quantitative data.

Branded marketing research products
Specialised data collection and analysis procedures developed to address specific types of marketing research problems.

The limitations of marketing research

It must be recognised that using researchers, even if they follow the marketing research process to the letter, does not guarantee that a marketing decision supported by that research will be successful. The act of decision making and conducting marketing research are distinctive activities and there are examples where the vital link between these activities has resulted in failure. In the following example, the entrepreneur Sahar Hashemi makes the case for marketing research, but not for the use of external suppliers as discussed above. Following her points, we then move on to the arguments and examples of the limitations of marketing research.

Example   The birth of an idea[15]

Sahar Hashemi, co-founder of the coffee chain Coffee Republic, believes marketing research to be tremendously important. 'You shouldn't ever start a business without it. Of course you have to make gut instinct decisions but they should be informed by market research, like educated guesses.' However, Sahar believes in the importance of doing marketing research yourself. 'Why would you give research to an agency to do?' she asks. 'You have to become a real expert in the area you want to work in. You have to get your head around these things.' Sahar believes that a slick research agency might give you a glossy report packed with facts and figures, but if you do the work yourself you'll gain more insight. She also thinks that better ideas can grow out of research – facts and figures mixing with inspired thought to create what she calls 'fertile ground in which to cultivate new ideas'.

If decision-makers have gaps in their knowledge, if they perceive risk and uncertainty in their decision making and cannot find support at hand within their organisation, they can gain support from marketing research. However, many marketers can recount cases where the use of marketing research has resulted in failure or where decisions based upon gut feeling or intuition have proved to be successful. Such cases present a challenge to marketing researchers, especially in light of the competition faced by the industry from alternative information sources. Reflecting upon such cases should remind marketing researchers to maintain a focus of offering real and valuable support to decision-makers. Understanding what real and valuable support means should underpin the whole array of creative data collection and analysis procedures available to the marketing researcher. The following example starts this reflection process with a case that is very close to home!

Example   What's this marketing research then, Dave?

James Birks founded and successfully ran a kiln construction company for over 40 years. He designed, built and maintained kilns for some of the most demanding porcelain and ceramics manufacturers worldwide, including Wedgwood, Royal Doulton and Spode. At retirement age he sold his company as a going concern – a very wealthy man.

James was presented with a copy of the first edition of this text by his nephew, David Birks. He was very pleased with the present but was intrigued by the title and asked 'What's this marketing research then, Dave?' He certainly had a clear idea of what marketing meant to his business and what was involved in being a successful marketer in his industry, but the notion of researching marketing activities was alien to him.

The intriguing aspect of this question is that James Birks had run a successful business on an international basis for over 40 years without the need to be aware of or to use marketing research. Had he used marketing research, could he have been even more successful, or would it have been a wasted investment? Could he have been practising marketing research 'activities' in a very informal manner to support marketing decisions? In his business-to-business marketing situation, he knew his customers and competitors well, and knew what shaped their demands. This knowledge he acquired on a day-to-day basis, nurturing a curiosity about opportunities and how to realise them – without resorting to support from formal ad hoc marketing research. The example of James Birks shows that decision-makers do not rely solely upon marketing research, and in certain circumstances can survive and perform well without it.

Another view to reflect upon is the damning comment from Anita Roddick of The Body Shop, who said that 'market research is like looking in the rear view mirror of a speeding car'.[16] This may be a valid point if one sees the relationship of marketing and marketing research from the perspective illustrated by the respected research practitioner, Wendy Gordon:[17]

> Traditional marketers delegate responsibility to the processes of marketing research. They believe that you can ask people what they want and need in the future and then deliver it to them. It is a fallacy. Marketing research removes people from experiencing reality, where the signs of change bubble up in unexpected places. Sitting in comfort behind a one-way mirror, listening to a debrief from researchers describing the world 'out there' or reading statistical reports on markets and the 'aggregate consumer' is not real, it is sanitised and second-hand.

Given the above criticisms, it is a fair point to acknowledge that there are cases where the use of marketing research has resulted in poor decision making or even failure. Ultimately, this examination should lead to a stronger justification of what ensures strong and valuable marketing research support. It may be a painful path to tread but this journey has to be made!

There are two areas of misconception of the role of marketing research:[18]

1 *Marketing research does not make decisions.* The role of marketing research is not to make decisions. Rather, research replaces hunches, impressions or a total lack of knowledge with pertinent information.
2 *Marketing research does not guarantee success.* Research, at best, can improve the odds of making a correct decision. Anyone who expects to eliminate the possibility of failure by doing research is both unrealistic and likely to be disappointed. The real value of research can be seen over a long period where increasing the percentage of good decisions should be manifested in improved bottom-line performance and in the occasional revelation that arises from research.

The last point shows the long-term benefits of conducting marketing research, i.e. that the results of a study may help decision-makers with an immediate problem, but by building their knowledge they can also have long-term benefits.

A great proportion of marketing research money has been spent on developing and testing new products. Questions have been posed that examine the role marketing research plays in poor success rates of new products across a wide range of industries.[19] Clearly, marketing research cannot be blamed for every failure, and the following two reasons may explain why decision-makers can make poor decisions when sound research has been conducted:

1 *Blind optimism/disbelief in research.* Many patently bad products have been launched because marketing management did not believe research findings.
2 *Political pressures.* Given how many personal reputations may be at stake in the lengthy and costly process of new product development, there may be political pressures to launch a 'borderline' case.

The following example illustrates where research was used in new product development but the designer and entrepreneur chose to ignore the findings, and ultimately achieved immense levels of success.

Example | **Doing a Dyson[20]**

Just 23 months after its launch in the UK, the Dyson bagless vacuum cleaner became the country's best seller, overtaking sales of Hoover, Electrolux, Panasonic, Miele and all other vacuum cleaners. The Dyson clear bin was given a resounding thumbs-down in marketing research. People said they did not like the dirt being visible in the bin in case their neighbours saw how much dirt had been picked up in their homes. Some retailers said they would not want to have dust on display in demonstration machines. Yet, the dust was there because they began using Dyson display machines to clean their shops. Dyson felt compelled to launch its vacuum cleaner with a clear bin, believing that it is important to see when it is full. Moreover, what better way was there to show stockists, sales staff and customers proof of its increased efficiency than to see the dirt being collected?

How would consumers react to a new vacuum cleaner with totally radical styling, revolutionary internal engineering and a price tag almost twice that of the current brand leader? The public's response proved immediately that innovative products do sell, even at a premium price. However, marketing research did not point to this product having the potential to be a success. James Dyson argued that 'marketing research will only tell you what has happened. No research can tell you what is going to happen.'

This is a theme that James Dyson has reiterated over the years. In an interview in 2006, giving tips to would-be inventors and entrepreneurs, he said:

you can't go out and do marketing research to try and solve these problems about what to do next because usually, or very often, you're doing the opposite of what marketing research would tell you. You can't base a new project two years ahead on current market trends and what users are thinking at the moment. That sounds very arrogant. But it isn't arrogance. You can't go and ask your customers to be your inventors. That's your job.

Other researchers offer reasons why decision-makers may reject research findings. These go beyond the confines of developing and testing new products. Examples of these reasons include:

- *Invalidity of research methods.* If the decision-maker suspects the accuracy or appropriateness of the methods for the problem faced, lack of confidence would lead to a rejection of findings.
- *Faulty communication.* This would lead to the findings being difficult to comprehend or utilise, or being unconvincing.
- *Irrelevance.* The decision-maker may see the findings as irrelevant to the perceived marketing problem.

If decision-makers reject research findings, and have been taken to task as a consequence, they can easily support their stance. They could question the time taken to conduct research (and the possible consequences of delays in decision making), and the cost required (not only in paying for marketing research projects but also in managerial effort). They could point to the few reliable methods of evaluating the return on investment in marketing research. They may also question the amount of support that can be given by a researcher who may have little understanding of the context and environment in which the decisions are made.

Collectively, the examples in this section illustrate that out of the array of research and information support approaches, there is no one guaranteed approach, research design or technique that can create the perfect means to support decision-makers. Given the vast array of marketing decisions and styles of marketing decision-maker, the hallmark of marketing decision making is creativity. Creativity in decision making can be supported well by accurate and relevant information. Generating accurate and relevant information is also a creative act. The diagnosis of problems, the measurement of consumers and the interpretation of those measurements are all creative acts, not a set system. The following PlayStation example illustrates the task of researching creative images, using a creative research design. It shows how the marketing researcher 'stepped back' and devised a creative solution to encapsulate the impact of the film being used in the advert.

Example — Marketing research supports PlayStation advertising[21]

Trevor Beattie, Creative Director of the ad agency TBWA (**www.tbwa-europe.com**), describes that the 'The Third Place' campaign for PlayStation2 was about 'the experience'. He wanted to create imagery that would live with people long after the commercial break had finished. Neil Hourston, TBWA London Head of Planning, described the creative intention: 'Our desired response on the creative brief was "excited fear",' he says. 'If we were going to be true to that then in the research we were looking for an idea that made people both excited and a little bit worried.'

London agency Firefish was given the job of researching how to develop what turned out to be an odd bit of 60 seconds. 'The finished ad was an incredibly surreal David Lynch piece of film. It was utterly random and bizarre and quite dark and incredibly original,' recalls Jem Fawcus, Co-founder and Director of Firefish:

We made a conscious decision not to begin trying to research anything like the finished film. We took a huge step back and just researched the idea of The Third Place: what do you think of the idea of The Third Place? What would it be like? Does it strike a chord with people? Is it something that could be used to support PlayStation2's new positioning? If we had gone in and said, 'We got a really weird film by David Lynch, and its got a duck and a man dressed up in bandages in it, and its all in black and white, and its got strange music,' it would have absolutely bombed. No one would have understood what we were talking about.

Whether or not PlayStation2 gamers, or anyone else for that matter, understood what David Lynch was on about does not matter. It got consumers excited about the arrival of the new video game experience. 'We used research for that properly, which was for development,' says Neil. 'We gave Jem some executional elements rather than the whole thing. We asked him to work with the respondents to see whether it had the potential in bits to create the response that we were looking for.'

If decision-makers complain that research is misleading or is only telling them what they already know, the marketing researcher may argue that the fault lies with managers who pose the wrong questions or problem in the first place. If one takes the narrow view that the decision-maker poses the questions and the researcher finds the answers, there may be some validity in such an argument. It does not hold if one considers that the decision-maker and the researcher have a joint commitment to solve problems. In this joint commitment they have quite distinct but complementary creative skills that they can bring together to understand what problem they should be researching, how they conduct the research and how they interpret their findings.

Can marketing researchers survive in an age of increasing competition from other information providers? How can the industry fend off the challenge from the armies of consultants and other information suppliers? To achieve this, the industry has to offer clients insights rather than just data analysis. The marketing researcher's input must be seen to benefit the bottom line. Initiatives that bring clients and researchers closer together are needed – initiatives that educate buyers that marketing research has as much if not more to offer than very expensive consultancy firms.[22]

The future – the growing demand for managerial skills in marketing researchers

Over the past few years, a debate has emerged about the value of marketing research and consultancy in supporting marketing decisions.[23] Many marketing researchers are feeling the pressure to move away from a position of being seen as mere data collectors and data analysts towards becoming providers of strategic marketing intelligence. One of the drivers behind this change is that data collection is seen by many marketers as a 'commodity' with comparatively low added value. An example of this pressure on marketing researchers emerges from Denmark, which is home to a number of high-quality research organisations. In Denmark the industry is faced with concerns about commoditisation. 'Many research buyers now see marketing research as a commodity' explains Erik Liljeberg of the Association of Market Research Institutes in Denmark.[24] 'They think that if you go to one research agency or another it won't make much of a difference. If an agency will not give you a discount, then you try someone else who will.' In Germany, ADM (Arbeitskreis Deutscher Markt), the association of private market and social research agencies, reports a development from straightforward marketing research 'data supply' to information-based consultancy. It describes the growing competition from research providers outside the traditional marketing research industry, with advertising and media agencies, business consultants and academic research institutions entering the arena.[25]

Many marketing research agencies have concluded that in the long term, information will become a commodity, and that it therefore now makes sound business sense to extend their offer beyond the provision of professionally collected data. These agencies are seeking to provide value-added services, around their skills of being able to interpret data, and relate this precisely to business decision-making processes.[26] Professor Frank Wimmer, board member at the German agency GfK, believes that a seat at the decision-maker's table is what most career-driven marketing researchers desire. 'To have a genuine impact on company policy, rather than being restricted to a role as a numbers-supplier.'[27] He contends that marketing research should develop into a more decision-making, management-orientated direction. That way, the researcher will be taken seriously by businesses, and no longer be looked upon as a 'number cruncher'. In the following two examples, we see this development illustrated by the perspectives of the Premier Automotive Group of Ford and Phillip Morris International in their need to work with marketing researchers with managerial skills.

Example ### Luxury cars – a key role for research[28]

Ford is a multi-faceted company, with different divisions facing their own particular challenges. At the Premier Automotive Group – its collection of European luxury brands comprising Jaguar, Volvo, Aston Martin and Land Rover – it's a matter of predicting which of its vehicles will be important in an evermore congested market. The ability of the Premier Automotive Group, as elsewhere in the Ford empire, to get closer to the hearts and minds of its consumers has been enhanced by changes to the marketing research function within the company. Instead of being specialists in one particular methodology or another, they are being transformed into consultants who will have a more holistic view of the business. 'Marketing researchers have always had a tendency to be backroom people', says their Marketing Research Manager, Simon Wilson. 'There is a much greater need nowadays for communication of research and this can only be achieved effectively if you are say, front of house.' This change in attitude has meant a certain amount of retraining, and even recruiting internally and externally, but Wilson is convinced that investment in this area will be well worth it. It should mean that, in time, most of his staff would be capable of looking at the big picture.

Example ### What do clients want from research?[29]

Richard Henchoz, Director Marketing Planning Services with responsibility for marketing research for Africa and the Middle East and Duty Free at Phillip Morris International, expects that clients increasingly want and ask for actionable insights from researchers, the kind of insights that include an answer to the question: 'What would you do if you were in my place?' Henchoz believes researchers must be able to provide this kind of strategic information. Richard, a Swiss national based at Phillip Morris International's headquarters in Lausanne, puts into perspective concerns about the feared loss of relevance of the research function:

I have been in research for about 20 years now and the call for more creativity has been going on for a long time. In the 1980s, when working as a researcher for Proctor & Gamble, I already aspired to move on from just executing research projects to a role in which I could be more creative, by making concrete recommendations to decision-makers. To me, it seemed an almost natural inclination for a researcher. And yes, clients will indeed require far more creativity and business intelligence from providers and international researchers. We are definitely working towards this goal at Phillip Morris.

The emerging generation of marketing researchers will be expected to continue to master the skill of borrowing and adapting tried and tested techniques from the social sciences. The challenges of writing engaging questionnaires, drawing meaningful samples, and making sense of data will still have to be met. Increasingly, marketing decision-makers demand a far more integrated approach to analysing often contradictory and imperfect sources of evidence; there is a mounting need for the capacity to work in an eclectic and holistic way with qualitative and quantitative data. Increasingly, marketing researchers have to analyse multiple and often imperfect datasets. To do this, they need new holistic analytic frameworks to be able to make sense of the data and to present this to decision-makers in a coherent, confident and effective manner.[30]

John Forsyth, Partner of McKinsey and Company and Director of the firm's global Customer Insights Practice, believes that adding new skills to the current set of capabilities of marketing researchers is crucial. Describing some of the lingering shortcomings of research professionals, he points out that marketing researchers in many cases still tend to focus on their own processes instead of client's needs:

> *Senior decision-makers don't want a 15 page explanation of why a specific tool and technique has been used. They want researchers to tell them what they should do. Marketing researchers should provide actionable consumer insights that can be used to improve the decision-making process for key executives. This requires a twist in researchers' approach. Interacting with senior management is different from dealing with management at the mid-level, then you really need to understand the business issue, you need to know how to communicate with them and understand how they make decisions. Marketing researchers should be more comfortable with them and understand how they take decisions.[31]*

The marketing research industry is seeing a broad differentiation between types of marketing research companies and marketing researchers. One type is the marketing researcher who becomes 'techniques focused', driven by the demands of marketers and buyers who view marketing research as a commodity. The alternative is the marketing researcher driven by the demands described by Richard Henchoz of Phillip Morris International in his search for researchers with more creativity and strategic marketing intelligence. Moving towards a business model that is driven by marketing researchers offering strategic marketing intelligence means that researchers and the marketing research industry of the future will be required to:[32]

- **Think conceptually** – by recruiting a new generation of 'conceptual' thinkers, i.e. researchers who feel comfortable working with higher order business concepts and talking the language of senior decision-makers. These individuals must understand the relationship between information and key business concepts. They must go beyond their technical and skill-based knowledge and offer strategic and tactical advice for business advantage based on detailed consumer and market knowledge.
- **Communicate in the way that those who commission research think** – by knowing how to communicate in the way senior people think, i.e. researchers presenting findings as a compelling narrative, not as disparate blocks of information.
- **Interpret findings in terms of the whole picture** – by thinking holistically about 'evidence', i.e. researchers with the skills to work in a 'holistic' way with all available customer evidence, recognising the need to interpret often imperfect marketing information. They must draw knowledge from a host of different sources including qualitative and quantitative techniques, a variety of forms of observation, customer relationship management systems, financial and customer profile information. These individuals will have to draw heavily upon the use of analytical models that represent the way customers think and behave.
- **Integrate findings with others that support marketing decision-makers** – by working in a multi-disciplinary way with related marketing services companies, with researchers working alongside branding and design and other marketing specialisms to gain a wider market understanding. This makes sure that everything is tailored to business solutions and is not just the result of rigid prescriptive research designs. This bottom-up, multi-disciplinary approach provides flexibility and differentiates 'strategic marketing

intelligence' from the 'top-down' approach of full-blown management consultants. This will also mean the cultivating of a more creative environment with a more 'hands-off' management style rather than a prescriptive techniques-driven approach.

Supporting decision-makers in sports marketing

 ### Focus on Sports Marketing Surveys

Sports Marketing Surveys quality research for management action

In most chapters of the text, examples will be presented based upon work conducted by the marketing research agency **Sports Marketing Surveys**. Four of its projects have been selected to illustrate how marketing research is managed in practice. Elements of these commercially sensitive projects will be chosen to show how the Agency managed the challenges of conducting actionable marketing research. The four chosen projects are:

Racetrack 2003 – a syndicated study to measure the attitudes and opinions of and profile the Formula 1 fan across eight countries worldwide.

Nestea – sponsorship evaluation in *Water, Wind and Waves* in Hungary and Germany, and Beach Volleyball in Italy, Germany and Sweden.

Flora London Marathon 2004 – TV media analysis, public awareness tracking and target market research.

Rugby Football League – evaluation of the core values of the sport and a deeper understanding of its target audience.

Sports Marketing Surveys (**www.sportsmarketingsurveys.com**) is a full-service independent marketing research agency that has specialised in the sponsorship and sports industry over the past 20 years. The sports industry and many sponsorships are often multi-country in their reach and activity. Sports Marketing Surveys has responded to this by having the capability of working and reporting on a worldwide basis in over 200 countries for events such as the Olympic Games and the Football World Cup. Its head office is in Surrey in the UK with global offices in: **Europe** – Belgium, France, Greece, Italy, Netherlands, Spain, Turkey: the **Americas** – Brazil, USA; **Australasia** – Australia; **Asia** – Japan, Korea, Singapore.

The sectors in which it specialises include: **sponsorship** (exposure and evaluation, effectiveness and event research), **sports goods** (sports equipment and footwear companies, e.g. golf, tennis and snow sports), **sports leisure and tourism** (supporting sports federations, venues and local governments).

The services they offer include: **media research** (covering TV, press, Internet and radio), **marketing research** (on an ad hoc or syndicated basis), **publications** (reports covering, e.g. European sports fans, profile of the European golfer and motorsport fans), **selection and valuation** (analytical model to select appropriate sponsorship and a tool to value the sponsorship investment) and **consultancy** (combining all the knowledge bases within the company and helping clients to use multiple sources in areas such as matching the understanding of potential markets and the strategic plans to maximise that potential).

 ## International marketing research

With the spread of marketing and research skills has come a noticeable decline in a 'national research culture'. There was a time when each country had a stubbornly distinctive approach to research, making it extremely difficult to get a consistent research design across markets. Most people are aware now that there are different, equally legitimate, ways to approach research problems and that no one school of thought has absolute authority for all types of problem. This greater flexibility has made multi-country coordinated projects much more feasible – not easier, as they represent intellectually, logistically and diplomatically the most demanding of problems.

Conducting international marketing research is much more complex than conducting domestic marketing research. All research of this kind will be discussed and illustrated in individual chapters as individual techniques are developed and in greater detail in Chapter 26. The marketing, government, legal, economic, structural, socio-cultural and informational environments prevailing in target international markets, and the characteristics of target consumers that are being studied, influence the manner in which the marketing research process should be performed. Examples of these environmental factors and their impact on the marketing research process are illustrated in detail in subsequent chapters. The following example illustrates the problems and challenges faced by researchers in the European context.

Example ### Crossing borders[33]

What is this thing called Europe? Despite binding influences like a single currency, Europe's national marketing research markets have distinct cultural, cost and quality characteristics. For example, German marketing research still feels the effects of reunification, while Spanish agencies are trying to leverage Spain's historical links with Latin America to capture a slice of the coordination market there.

For research buyers and users, the diversity of Europe is very real, and the trickiest part of their remit is to get comparable data systems across the different country markets. Andrew Grant, European Research Director at Ford, says: 'From our perspective, actually getting to a single methodology, a single questionnaire, a single data collection method and a single set of attributes that means the same thing across markets is a hugely difficult part of what we do.'

Europe may be moving towards becoming a single market, but from a research cost perspective it is still far from being a level playing field. In the absence of tax and social cost harmonisation across Europe, countries like France and Sweden are two of the region's most expensive places to conduct research. The euro will have an increasingly positive effect, agencies say, for those countries that participate. 'It makes contracting and financing easier,' says Klaus Wübbenhorst, Chief Executive of German-based group GfK. 'The euro won't mean that prices in all European countries will be the same, you have to take into account different levels of productivity and efficiency. But it makes pricing more transparent between countries.'

Against a background of centralisation, standardisation and increasing cooperation, Europe's researchers believe that the region's defining diversity will survive. 'The fact that we're multicultural means that we have great creative potential,' says Meril James of GIA.

Ethics in marketing research

Marketing research often involves contact with the respondents and the wider public, usually by way of data collection, dissemination of the research findings, and marketing activities such as advertising campaigns based on these findings. Thus, there is the potential to abuse or misuse marketing research by taking advantage of these people. If respondents feel that they or their views are being abused or misrepresented, they either will not take part in future studies or may do so without honesty or full engagement in the issues being researched. They may also lobby politicians to protect them from what they see as intrusions into their privacy and liberties. In short, unethical research practices can severely impair the quality of the research process, undermine the validity of research findings and ultimately inflict serious damage upon the body of professional marketing researchers. If respondents cannot distinguish between genuine marketing research and unethical telemarketing or direct marketing where surveys are used to gain access to respondents to deliver a sales pitch or to generate sales, there can be severe repercussions for the marketing research industry through legislation designed to protect the privacy of citizens. The marketing research industry in Europe and the USA has got to a point where it has had to defend the quality of its practices.

The Alliance for Research, based in Brussels, was established in May 2002 as the first representative and lobbying body with a prime objective to improve understanding of the value and distinctive characteristics of marketing research among European parliamentarians and officials at the European Commission. The Alliance was initially funded by ESOMAR and from its inception it has been closely liaising with equivalent organisations in the USA for global alignment on legislative issues. The concern of such bodies was based on their assessment that parliamentarians, in both Europe and the USA (CASRO, Council of American Survey Research Organisations, and CMOR, Council for Marketing and Opinion Research), were very eager to protect citizens' privacy, especially against intrusive actions by telemarketers or direct marketers. Protection against intrusive actions tended to be afforded through legislation that also hurt the freedom to conduct research. In many cases, legislators were not aware of the differences between telemarketing and direct marketing on the one hand and marketing and opinion research on the other. Often they just did not realise that banning unsolicited phone calls across the board would infringe upon the ability to collect through social research some of the information they themselves needed as input for formulating their policies.[34] The Alliance for Research monitors all potentially damaging EU legislation and has been engaged in a dialogue with the EU data protection authorities. The Alliance is stepping up efforts to work in partnership with the authorities and to replace 'self-regulation' by 'co-regulation'. In the USA, the achievements of CASRO and CMOR include a ban by the federal authorities on selling or fundraising under the guise of research.[35]

Beyond support for the Alliance for Research, ESOMAR have been proactive in a review and reform of the entire framework of marketing research codes and guidelines. In the Quo Vadis project, initiated by ESOMAR in 2003, experts from the USA, Japan and Europe met for a workshop in Amsterdam in July 2003 to discuss the latest developments in the industry and their impact upon the quality of marketing research. They recognised the effect of a shift in focus of marketing research from data collection towards organisational decision making and agreed that current codes and guidelines had not kept up with this development. The experts pointed out that a concise list of codes would be a tool for self-regulation and support international convergence: 'A good ethical basis helps minimise legal restrictions.' They agreed and presented eight principles that would encapsulate to the outside world the scientific aim and character of marketing research as well as its special responsibility towards respondents, clients and the public.

The eight principles that have now been incorporated into the ESOMAR code of conduct are:[36]

1 Marketing researchers will conform to all relevant national and international laws.
2 Marketing researchers will behave ethically and will not do anything which might damage the reputation of marketing research.

3 Marketing researchers will take special care when carrying out research among children and other vulnerable groups of the population.

4 Respondents' cooperation is voluntary and must be based on adequate, and not misleading, information about the general purpose and nature of the project when their agreement to participate is being obtained and all such statements must be honoured.

5 The rights of respondents as private individuals will be respected by marketing researchers and they will not be harmed or disadvantaged as the result of cooperating in a marketing research project.

6 Marketing researchers will never allow personal data they collect in a marketing research project to be used for any purpose other than marketing research.

7 Marketing researchers will ensure that projects and activities are designed, carried out, reported and documented accurately, transparently, objectively and to appropriate quality.

8 Marketing researchers will conform to the accepted principles of fair competition.

The basic principles of the ESOMAR code of conduct and the full array of ESOMAR codes of conduct can be viewed at: **www.esomar.nl/codes_and_guidelines.html**.

ESOMAR distinguishes marketing research from other competitive forms of data gathering, primarily through the issue of the anonymity of respondents. It stresses that in marketing research the identity of the provider of information is not disclosed. It makes a clear distinction between marketing research and database marketing where the names and addresses of the people contacted are to be used for individual selling, promotional, fundraising or other non-research purposes. The distinction between marketing research and the database as a research tool is ultimately not so clear. There is a growing amount of support given to marketing decision-makers from database analyses that are not 'respondent specific'. It is possible to perform database analyses with the same level of professional standards as is applied in the marketing research industry.

There are many instances where database analyses can add clarity and focus to marketing research activities. For example, since the start of 1995 the highly respected marketing research agency Taylor Nelson AGB has been building the European Toiletries & Cosmetics Database (ETCD). Some 14,000 usage diaries of personal care products are collected each year, across the UK, France, Germany, Italy and Spain. Given the huge impact that database analyses are having upon marketing decision making, these issues will be developed more fully in Chapter 5. In the meantime, the maxim stated by ESOMAR of preserving the anonymity of respondents is vital for the continuing support of respondents and the ultimate health of the marketing research industry.

Internet and computer applications

As the applications of the Internet in research first became apparent, there was no real consensus within the marketing research industry of just what its impact would be. Many predicted that the Internet would ultimately replace all other methods of data collection, whilst others argued that it would just add another means to measure, understand or observe respondents.[37] In 2004, online research methods accounted for an estimated 11% of global research turnover. This is still some way behind telephone (20%) and face-to-face (31%). However, the actual usage, the amount of projects that use the Internet compared with other techniques, is likely to be much higher because the low-cost nature of the Internet keeps its revenue contributions down. The Internet may not have gained such popularity had it not been for its low-cost characteristics and the ever-increasing cost and time pressures on research agencies. As an example, online access panels are seen as faster and more cost efficient than other methods of research. According to the ESOMAR 2005 Prices Study, for a tracking study they are on average 60% cheaper than face-to-face interviewing.[38]

Many argue that the growth of online research will be driven by new research clients, who see that they can enjoy the benefits of marketing research at a level they could not previously afford. The downside of the low costs of the technique is that the barriers to entry to the marketing research industry have been lowered. Effectively, anyone can establish a business with online survey software, a data analysis package and a basic understanding of research, undertaking surveys, customer satisfaction studies, and so on. This may have profound effects upon the quality and ethical standards of marketing research.

Given the importance of the Internet and developing technologies to the marketing research process and industry, key issues and debates in this subject will be continually addressed. Throughout this book we show how the stages of the marketing research process are facilitated by the Internet and other developing technologies and software. On the Companion Website to this text, demonstration versions of marketing research software will illustrate the use of computing technology in the process of questionnaire design, data entry, data analysis and reporting, and the application of geodemographic information systems.

Summary

Marketing research provides support to marketing decision-makers by helping to describe the nature and scope of customer groups, understand the nature of forces that shape the needs of customer groups and the marketer's ability to satisfy those groups, test individual and interactive controllable marketing variables, and monitor and reflect upon past successes and failures in marketing decisions. The overall purpose of marketing research is to assess information needs and provide the relevant information in a systematic and objective manner to improve marketing decision making. The marketing research process consists of six broad steps that must be followed creatively and systematically. The process involves problem definition, research approach development, research design formulation, fieldwork or data collection, data preparation and analysis, and report preparation and presentation. Within these six broad steps are many iterations and routes that can be taken, reflecting the reality of marketing research in practice. Marketing research may be classified into problem identification research and problem-solving research. In general terms, problem identification uncovers the potential that may be exploited in markets, problem-solving uncovers the means to realize that potential.

The major developed economies, especially in Europe and the USA, are the biggest users of marketing research on a per capita and total expenditure basis. The growth rates for the marketing research industries in these economies are low, the major growth occurring in countries like Chile, China and Bulgaria. Marketing research may be conducted internally (by internal suppliers) or may be purchased from external suppliers. Full-service suppliers provide the entire range of marketing research services, from problem definition to report preparation and presentation. They may also manage customer database analyses, being able to integrate the management and analyses databases with the management and analyses of conventional marketing research techniques. Limited-service suppliers specialise in one or a few phases of the marketing research project. Services offered by these suppliers can be classified as field services, coding and data entry, data analysis, analytical services or branded products.

Marketing research is not a panacea for all marketing problems. There are examples where marketing research has not adequately supported decision-makers. Many of the problems that arise from poor marketing research derive from poor communications between decision-makers and researchers. In order to resolve these problems, there are growing demands upon the marketing research industry to produce research findings that are more actionable and relevant to marketing decision-makers. As well as having the technical skills to conduct research in a professional and ethical manner, marketing researchers are increasingly expected to have the ability to interpret their findings in a manner that is relevant to decision-makers.

International marketing research can be much more complex than domestic research because the researcher must consider the environments prevailing in the international markets being researched. Research is founded upon the willing cooperation, of the public and of business organisations. Ethical marketing research practices nurture that cooperation, allowing a more professional approach and more accurate research information. Marketing research makes extensive use of the great opportunities afforded by the Internet. There are also many competitive threats to the marketing research industry that have been exacerbated by the Internet.

Questions

1. Describe the task of marketing research.

2. What decisions are made by marketing managers? How does marketing research help in supporting these decisions?

3. What do you see as the major challenges for marketing researchers that emerge from the ESOMAR definition of marketing research?

4. What problems are associated with using consumer databases in marketing research?

5. How may the sound practice of problem identification research enhance the sound practice of problem-solving research?

6. What challenges exist in trying to quantify the size and growth of the marketing research industry on a global basis?

7. Explain one way to classify marketing research suppliers and services.

8. Describe the steps in the simple marketing research process.

9. Explain why there may be the need for iterations between stages of the marketing research process.

10. What arguments can be used by sceptics of marketing research?

11. What management skills are increasingly being demanded from marketing researchers?

12. What arguments would you use to defend investment in marketing research?

13. What factors fuel the growth of international marketing research?

14. Discuss the ethical issues in marketing research that relate to (a) the client, (b) the supplier, and (c) the respondent.

15. Summarise the nature of threats and opportunities that the Internet offers the marketing researcher.

Exercises

1   Visit the website of Taylor Nelson Sofres **www.tns-global.com**. Examine the nature of the Research Services and the Business Solutions it offers. How do you see these fitting together and what is the impact of this fit upon the career opportunities the company advertises?

2   Visit the website of the Market Research Society, **www.mrs.org.uk**. Work through the array of publications and support it gives to its members. Specifically examine and register for **www.research-live.com/** and examine the published code of conduct. Compare the MRS code of conduct with that available on the ESOMAR website, **www.esomar.org**. Are there any differences in their respective approaches to maintaining professional standards in the marketing research industry?

3   Visit the website **www.trendwatching.com** and register for trend-watching updates if you wish. Critically evaluate the worth of trend watching for the marketing researcher.

4   From national or international newspapers, track down stories of successful entrepreneurial ventures. Evaluate the extent to which marketing research is attributed to their success and/or an awareness of their market(s).

5   In a small group discuss the following issues: 'What is the ideal educational background for someone seeking a career in marketing research?' and 'Is it possible to enforce ethical standards within the marketing research industry?'

Video Case Exercise: Burke Inc.

Burke describes marketing research as 'an important and dynamic component of modern business'. How are other means of supporting the marketing decision-maker affecting the importance and dynamism of marketing research?

video case

download from
www.pearsoned.co.uk/
malhotra_euro

Notes

1   Vangelder, P., 'Listening to the customer – research at Royal Ahold', *ESOMAR Newsbrief* 4 (April 1999), 14–15.

2   Johansen, T. and Herlin, K., 'Banner advertising – more than clicks', *Admap* (October 2001), 15–17.

3   Jensen, N.M. and Wegloop, P., 'Nordea: a new brand in the making', *Research World*, (January 2005), 34.

4   For the strategic role of marketing research, see Jarratt, D. and Fayed, R., 'The impact of market and organizational challenges on marketing strategy decision making', *Journal of Business Research* 51 (January 2001), 61–72; Higgins, L.F., 'Applying principles of creativity management to marketing research efforts in high-technology markets', *Industrial Marketing Management* 28 (3) (May 1999), 305–317; Zabriskie, N.B. and Huellmantel, A.B., 'Marketing research as a strategic tool', *Long-Range Planning* 27 (February 1994), 107–118.

5   For relationships between information processing, marketing decisions and performance, see Glazer, R. and Weiss, A.M., 'Marketing in turbulent environments: decision process and the time-sensitivity of information', *Journal of Marketing Research* 30 (November 1993), 509–521.

6   Samuels, J., 'Research methodologies', *Research World* (November 2003), 20–21.

7   Savage, M., 'Downstream danger', *Research* (May 2000), 25–27.

8   Anon., 'Supermarket sweep', *The Grocer* (13 July 1996), 28.

9   Anon., 'Beer research shows overspill', *Marketing* (9 October 1997), 6.

10 Anon, 'Kellogg's brings Olympic spirit to America's breakfast table', PR Newswire (6 December 2001); 'Anon, Kellogg's Crunchy Nuts gets ready for adult breakfast', *Grocer* 224 (7524) (October 6 2001), 53.

11 Vonk, T., 'ESOMAR Annual Study on the Market Research Industry 2003', *Research World* (September 2004), 28–33.

12 The 15 EU member countries in 2003.

13 ESOMAR – *Industry study on 2004*, 8.

14 ESOMAR – *Industry study on 2004*, 15.

15 Tarran, B., 'The birth of an idea', *Research* (August 2003), 23.

16 Lury, G., 'Market research cannot cover for the "vision thing"', *Marketing* (9 November 2000), 34.

17 Gordon, W., 'Be creative to innovate', *Research* (January 2000), 23.

18 Lehmann, D.R., *Market Research and Analysis*, 3rd edn (Homewood, IL: Irwin, 1994), 14.

19 Sampson, P. and Standen, P., 'Predicting sales volume and market shares', in *New Product Development Research Contributions to Strategy Formulation, Idea Generation and Screening Product, Product Testing and Final Marketing*, ESOMAR (November 1983).

20 Muranka, T. and Rootes, N., *Doing a Dyson* (Dyson Appliances, 1996), 22; Mesure, S., 'A day in the life of James Dyson', *Independent* (27 May 2006), 55.

21 Escobales, R., 'A little less conversation', *Research*, (January 2004), 18.

22 Chervi, B. and Savage, M., 'Innovate to survive', *Research* (October 1999), 16.

23 Havermans, J., 'A seat at the boardroom table', *Research World* (January 2004), 16.

24 Wilson, V., 'Worldwide: Denmark', *Research* (August 2005), 28.

25 Heeg, R., 'Back on the path of growth', *Research World* (April 2005), 19.

26 Van Hamersveld, M. and Smith, D., 'From data collection to decision support (3)' *Research World* (December 2003), 19.

27 Heeg, R., 'A career in market research is a hard sell', *Research World* (September 2004), 11.

28 Miles, L., 'Luxury cars – a key role for research', *Research World* (January 2004), 14.

29 Havermnans, J., 'What do clients want from research?', *Research World* (March 2005), 10.

30 Van Hamersveld, M. and Smith, D., 'From data collection to decision support (2)', (November 2003), 18.

31 Havermans, J., 'Revive apprenticeship in research', *Research World* (September 2004), 14.

32 Van Hamersveld, M. and Smith, D., 'From data collection to decision support (3)', *Research World* (December 2003), 20.

33 McElhatton, N., 'Crossing borders', *Research, Guide to Europe* (May 2000), 4–5.

34 Havermans, J., 'Look out post for research', *Research World* (November 2004), 30.

35 Havermans, J., 'Market research leaders agree on next steps in industry effort', *Research World* (February 2005), 8.

36 Havermans, J., 'New international MR practice in 8 principles', *Research World* (May 2004), 20–21.

37 Tarran, B., 'Worldwide global', *Research* (November 2005), 27.

38 Ibid.

Visit the *Marketing Research* Companion Website at www.pearsoned.co.uk/malhotra_euro for additional learning resources including annotated weblinks, an online glossary and a suite of downloadable video cases.

2

Defining the marketing research problem and developing a research approach

> *The correct diagnosis of marketing research problems cannot be compromised. Regardless of how well subsequent stages are conducted, the whole process may be worthless if the diagnosis is weak.*

Objectives

After reading this chapter, you should be able to:

1 understand the importance of, and the process used, in defining marketing research problems;

2 describe the tasks involved in problem definition;

3 discuss in detail the nature and various components of a research brief and a research proposal;

4 discuss the environmental factors affecting the definition of the research problem;

5 clarify the distinction between the marketing decision problem and the marketing research problem;

6 explain the structure of a well-defined marketing research problem, including the broad statement and the specific components;

7 understand the role of theory in the development and execution of applied marketing research;

8 acquire an appreciation of the complexity involved in defining the problem and developing a research approach in international marketing research;

9 understand the ethical issues and conflicts that arise in defining the problem and developing a research approach;

10 appreciate the ways in which the Internet can support the process of problem diagnosis and the development of a research design.

STAGE 1	STAGE 2	STAGE 3	STAGE 4	STAGE 5	STAGE 6
Problem definition	Research approach developed	Research design developed	Fieldwork or data collection	Data preparation and analysis	Report preparation and presentation

Overview

This chapter covers the first two of the six steps of the marketing research process described in Chapter 1: defining the marketing research problem and developing a research approach to tackle the problem. Defining the problem is the most important step, since only when a problem has been clearly and accurately identified can a research project be conducted properly. Defining the marketing research problem sets the course of the entire project. Regardless of how well a research plan is designed and subsequent stages are carried out, if the problem is not correctly diagnosed, research findings could be misleading or even dangerous. In this chapter, we allow the reader to appreciate the complexities involved in defining a problem, by identifying the factors to be considered and the tasks involved.

In practical terms, the means to communicate and facilitate the diagnosis of research problems is achieved through the preparation of a research brief and research proposal. The rationale and components of the research brief and research proposal are presented. We provide guidelines for appropriately defining the marketing research problem and avoiding common types of errors. We also discuss in detail the characteristics or factors influencing the research design and components of an approach to the problem: objective/theoretical framework, analytical models, research questions and hypotheses. The special considerations involved in defining the problem and developing a research approach in international marketing research are discussed. Finally, several ethical issues that arise at this stage of the marketing research process are considered.

We introduce our discussion with an example. The ABC Global Kids Study illustrates that, starting from broad research questions, a clear set of research questions can be developed. There are many difficulties in designing a research approach that will allow comparable findings from six countries on three continents and in questioning children. Without a precise diagnosis of marketing and research problems, such a complicated research approach would be doomed to failure.

Example   Is there one global village for our future generation?[1]

The ABC Global Kids Study was conducted in the spring of 1996 among 2,400 children aged 7–12 years and their mothers, in China, Japan, France, the UK, Germany and the USA. The study was sponsored by multinational corporations such as Mars, Kodak and McDonald's. The key topic areas were as follows:

- Child wealth and spending patterns
- Influence on household purchases
- Media habits
- Technology ownership and usage
- Social issues and concerns
- Daily activities
- Food and beverages
- Toys and games
- Cartoon and movie awareness and attitudes
- Recreation.

The study was designed to quantify the size of business opportunities in given product categories and to provide fact-based direction on how to create an exciting child product portfolio and marketing programme.

While uniformity of survey, method and instrument were maintained for cross-country comparison, adaptations were sought locally to capture unique retail and cultural characteristics. A pictorial response scale was used when interviewing children on emotions and preferences. Product usage frequency was asked of mothers, instead of children.

The survey revealed considerable spending power for children aged 7–12, as well as active participation from children in making family purchase decisions in a number of product categories. It was apparent that, worldwide, children basically have many common dreams and aspirations.

Importance of defining the problem

Problem definition
A broad statement of the general problem and identification of the specific components of the marketing research problem.

Although each step in a marketing research project is important, problem definition is the most important step. As mentioned in Chapter 1, for the purpose of marketing research, problems and opportunities are treated interchangeably. **Problem definition** involves stating the general problem and identifying the specific components of the marketing research problem. Only when the marketing research problem has been clearly defined can research be designed and conducted properly:

Of all the tasks in a marketing research project, none is more vital to the ultimate fulfilment of a client's needs than an accurate and adequate definition of the research problem. All the effort, time, and money spent from this point on will be wasted if the problem is misunderstood and ill-defined.[2]

An analogy to this is the medical doctor prescribing treatment after a cursory examination of a patient – the medicine may be even more dangerous than the condition it is supposed to cure!

The importance of clearly identifying and defining the research problem cannot be overstated. The foundation of defining a research problem is the communication that develops between marketing decision-makers and marketing researchers. In some form or another, marketing decision-makers must communicate what they see as being the problems they face and what research support they need. This communication usually comes in the form of a research brief. The marketing researcher responds to the research brief with a research proposal, which encapsulates the researcher's vision of a practical solution to the set research problem. The following example illustrates that a research brief may not always be particularly well thought out. The marketing researcher is expected to develop the brief into a research proposal and in doing so has a vital role to play in the diagnosis of research problems.

| *Example* | ### How to bait the interview hook for those top 1,000 big fish[3] |

The groans from researchers when another brief arrives asking for 100 or 200 interviews with chief executive officers (CEOs) or equivalents within the Times Top 1000 companies typify the attitude generated by business-to-business marketers' constant demand to reach this audience. When the research brief arrives, it is certainly worth examining whether, practically, what is requested can actually be done. The research proposal developed must reflect the practicalities of questioning managers who are constantly bombarded with requests to respond to research questions. The number of interviews, the timescale, the nature of questions and the structure of the sample all need to be taken into account. For example, is it really worth undertaking 200 interviews within any single European country? If we were limited to one per organisation, we would be interviewing to strike rates of between 1 in 2.5 and 1 in 5. If the research targets companies throughout Europe, individual countries such as the UK and France may have few large companies compared with the USA, while Italy has a limited number of very large companies and a great many smaller ones. In actually reaching the target audience, a number of issues need to be taken into account. International business-to-business research with senior business audiences brings with it not only the particular difficulties of reaching them but also the need to understand both country and cultural issues that impact on the research. Telephone interviews (even if possible) are considered inappropriate for these audiences in many Far East and Middle East markets, especially South Korea and Japan, while in Singapore and Hong Kong, provided the interviews are not too long (over 15 minutes), telephone is fine.

The marketing research brief

Research brief
A document produced by the users of research findings or the buyers of a piece of marketing research. The brief is used to communicate the perceived requirements of a marketing research project.

The marketing **research brief** is a document produced by the users of research findings or the buyers of a piece of marketing research. The brief may be used to communicate the perceived requirements of a marketing research project to external agencies or internally within an organisation to marketing research professionals. It should act as the first step for decision-makers to express the nature of a marketing and research problem as they see it. This first step is vital in developing an agreement of an appropriate research approach. As a first step of problem diagnosis and negotiation, *the marketing research brief should not be carved in tablets of stone!*

It has been contended that the greatest form of potential error in marketing research lies in the initial relationship between marketing decision-makers and marketing researchers.[4] In developing a sound initial relationship, the research brief plays a vital role. Without some formal method of communicating the nature of a marketing problem, there is great potential for ambiguities, illogical actions (by both parties), misunderstandings and even forgetfulness.

The purpose of a written marketing research brief may be summarised as:

- It makes the initiator of the brief more certain of how the information to be collected will support decision making.
- It ensures an amount of agreement or cohesion among all parties who may benefit from the research findings.
- It helps both the marketer and the researcher to plan and implement the research design.
- It helps to reduce disputes that can occur when the gaps in marketers' knowledge are not 'filled' as intended.
- It can form the basis for negotiation with a variety of research organisations.

In all, the research brief saves resources in time and money by helping to ensure that the nature of the problem or opportunity under investigation has been thought through.

Components of the marketing research brief

The rationale for a marketing research brief may seem logical, but actually generating a brief from marketing decision-makers can be extremely difficult. These difficulties will be tackled later in this chapter. If a decision-maker has a very clear idea of the nature of decision support needed *and* can define the research objectives that will create such support *and* define the research design that will fulfil the research objectives – the decision-maker could write a research brief that is highly structured. A structured brief created in these conditions would basically be a tender document, allowing a number of research suppliers to pitch for business on a like-for-like basis. Not all marketing decision-makers have such clarity of the marketing research support they need. Even if they do, by sticking to highly structured and prescriptive marketing research briefs, they can underutilise the experience and creativity of marketing researchers. The following format for a research brief helps to make the most of the experience and creativity of both the marketing decision-maker and the researcher and has clear advantages for both parties. First, it does not demand that decision-makers have a great deal of technical knowledge about research. Their focus can remain upon the gaps in their knowledge, the nature of support they need, not the technicalities of how data are to be collected and analysed. Second, it allows the researchers the opportunity to demonstrate their creative abilities and awareness of the latest techniques. Using their experiences from problems faced by other decision-makers, perhaps from a great variety of contexts and industries, researchers have the possibility of examining the marketing and research problem from many different perspectives. They can create, develop and adapt a research design to the research problem that supports the marketing decision-maker within clear time and cost parameters (Figure 2.1):

1 *Background information.* The background serves to put research objectives into context, helping the researcher to understand why certain research objectives are being pursued. Marketers would detail what they see as being the main events that have caused or contributed to the problem under study. Such a background gives a framework for the researcher to investigate other potential events, contributory factors or causes.

2 *Objectives.* The first part of this section would detail which marketing decisions are to be completed once the research has been undertaken. This requires decision-makers to explain what they see as the focus of the decisions they plan to make. They then go on to explain what gap(s) they see in their knowledge. Those gaps create the focus to planned research activities and set the research objectives. The formulation of the marketing objectives can encompass two areas: organisational objectives and personal objectives of the decision-maker. For a research project to be successful, it must serve the objectives of the organisation and of the decision-maker. For the researcher this may not be explicit or obvious to discern. It may take some time working with a decision-maker or a particular organisation to see potential conflicts in organisational and personal objectives. The problem faced by researchers is that decision-makers may not formulate marketing objectives clearly. Rather, it is likely that objectives tend to be

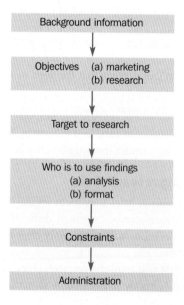

**Figure 2.1
Components of the
marketing research
brief**

stated in terms that have no operational significance, such as 'to improve corporate image'. Ultimately this does not matter, as this 'first-step' brief offers the opportunity for the researcher to draw out and develop a much clearer vision of marketing and research objectives. Drawing out and developing decision-makers' perspectives of objectives, even if they have no operational significance, helps the process of developing a common understanding of what the decision-maker is trying to achieve.

3 *Target to research.* Any marketing research project will measure, understand or observe a target group of individuals. These may be distinct groups of consumers, channel members such as retailers or competitors, or company employees. In this section, details of the characteristics of the target group(s) can help in many research design decisions. These cover areas of identification, gaining access to conduct research, understanding which techniques are appropriate to measure or understand these individuals, and the best environment or context in which to conduct research.

4 *Who is to use the findings.* This section would outline brief details of the decision-makers who will use the research findings. For example, certain decision-makers may be entrepreneurial and introspective, looking for short-term tactical advantages. Presenting research findings that make tactical advantages apparent would be the best way to communicate to such managers. Managers with a background and training in statistics may expect results to be analysed and presented in a particular manner to have any credibility. Other managers may not have such training or may even be distrustful of statistical analyses and seek a more qualitative interpretation. These issues have an impact upon the nature and extent of analysis conducted upon the data collected and the style and format in which research findings will be presented.

5 *Constraints.* The main limitation to marketing researchers carrying out what they may perceive as being the correct way to research a problem is the time and money that a marketer can afford. Proposing a large-scale project that would cost €200,000 when only €50,000 has been budgeted obviously will not meet management approval. In many instances, the scope of the marketing research problem may have to be reduced to accommodate budget constraints. With knowledge of time and cost constraints, the researcher can develop a research design to suit these needs. The researcher may also demonstrate other courses of action that could demand greater amounts of money or time, but could have clear benefits that the marketer may be unaware of. Other constraints, such as those imposed by the client firm's personnel, organisational structure and culture, or decision making styles, should be identified to determine the scope of the research project. Yet, constraints should not be allowed to diminish the value of the research to the decision-maker or to compromise the integrity of the research process. In instances where the resources are too limited to allow a project of sufficient quality, the firm should be advised not to undertake formal marketing research. In the following example, Marketing Researchers Marc Brenner and David Miln warn of the pressures on researchers to reduce their costs and that, ultimately, the good marketing researcher should guide marketers in getting the best value from their research investments.

Example	The big trap[5]

'Either cut your rates or we will move our account to another agency.' 'Sadly times are tough, though the brand is doing well, profitability is down and the agency must help us out here.' 'We all have to reduce costs.' 'I am under great pressure to reduce agency fees, indeed all expenditure and, unless we can sort something out, I may, reluctantly, be forced to go out to competitive tender – you know what the purchasing people are like.' Such stances from clients that buy and use marketing research can understandably create stress in a client–agency relationship. The marketing research agency may feel unappreciated or mistrusted. Such stances are by no means a new phenomenon but are becoming more common. Marketing research agency profit margins are being squeezed by the competitive pressure on client businesses that require them to reduce their own costs. Marketing research agencies generally respond by demonstrating the quality and effectiveness of their work and by pointing out the real and hidden costs of making an agency change, and the risks involved. The more demanding the client, the more likely is the agency to give a real (or apparent) cost reduction, arguing that it is necessary for the good of the relationship and ultimately the retention of business. The big trap for the marketing research agency is to think that, to improve its client relationship, it is necessary to sacrifice what it gets paid. It is a big mistake to appear to support or encourage the idea that there is a legitimate trade-off between the two by treating the matter as if it were a zero sum game. It's not. The reality is that while a good relationship and the financial deal with the client are indeed related, they move together. Better price leads to a better relationship, a better job and a better contribution to the client. It is also a big mistake for an agency to fail to act as a steward of its client's resources.

6 *Administrative considerations.* These would lay out administrative details in completing the research project. Examples could be the expected delivery of interim reports, contacts in an organisation who may be able to help supply further information, or reference to sources of materials and individuals that are needed to complete the research successfully.

With a formal marketing research brief and perhaps preliminary discussions with the organisation that is to commission the research, the marketing researcher has the necessary material to develop a research proposal. In many instances, however, the marketing researcher does not enjoy the luxury of a written research brief. The marketing decision-maker may outline ideas in an oral manner, perhaps on an informal basis. This can happen if the decision-maker is not aware of the personal benefits of producing a written research brief detailed above. Decision-makers may see the brief as a time-consuming process that really is the job of the researcher. If marketing researchers are faced with an oral brief, they can use the proposed brief outline above as a guideline to the issues they should elicit in informal discussions in order to develop an effective proposal.

The marketing research proposal

Research proposal
The official layout of the planned marketing research activity.

In response to a research brief, the marketing researcher will develop a research plan (covered in detail in Chapter 3) and will develop a **research proposal** to communicate this plan. The marketing research proposal contains the essence of the project and, in its final format, serves as a contract between the researcher and management. The research proposal covers all phases of the marketing research process. It allows the researcher to present an interpretation of the problems faced by management and to be creative in developing a research solution that will effectively support decision-makers. Although the format of a research proposal may vary considerably, most proposals address all the steps of the marketing research process and contain the elements shown in Figure 2.2:

1 *Executive summary.* The proposal should begin with a summary of the major points from each of the other sections, presenting an overview of the entire proposal.
2 *Background.* The researcher would be expected to have developed ideas beyond those presented in the brief 'background'. Other potential causes of the problems faced or alternative interpretations of the factors that shape the background in an environmental context should be presented. The extent of developmental work on the background

to a research project will depend mostly upon how much past work marketing researchers have done for the decision-makers. In projects where researchers and marketers are working together for the first time, much exploratory work may be undertaken by the marketing researcher to understand an industry, organisation, decision-makers, planned campaigns, etc. After a number of projects, much of this may be understood and not need restating. The following example from a proposal to Nestea illustrates how Sports Marketing Surveys presents a relatively short but well-focused background. The two companies have worked together before and are building upon their shared knowledge and their shared language.

 Sports Marketing Surveys

Nestea research proposal: background

Nestea has entered into two sponsorships for 2004 that it believes match its target market and key lifestyle attributes:

- *Water, Wind and Waves*. The initial title sponsorship of windsurfing through the Professional Windsurfers Association Racing World Tour and individual races. In Italy, however, sailing has been chosen in preference since local market indications are that windsurfing does not fit the key criteria. The intention would be to widen the field to include other relevant sports in this category.
- *Beach Volleyball*. Sponsorship within the Beach Volleyball European Championship Tour. This is not a title sponsorship of events but major sponsor benefits are expected.

The popularity of iced tea varies across Europe, with Spain having relatively low levels of consumption compared with high levels in Italy. In turn, the penetration of Nestea varies by territory and it has a major competitor – Lipton, who is active in sponsorship and has been involved in some of the sports currently being looked at by Nestea.

Sponsorship is being viewed as a marketing option to increase the Nestea brand share in key countries and to link the sponsored properties'* markets and lifestyle images with activation and leverage† support – the most crucial area to ensure optimisation of sponsorship impact.

* A 'property' in a sponsorship context can mean an event, a league, or an individual sports star.
† Leverage in a sponsorship context means investment in other marketing communications that will integrate with and enhance the sponsorship.

3 *Problem definition.* Again, if necessary, the researcher may go beyond the problem definition presented in the brief. If the researcher sees potential to add value for the marketer through alternative diagnoses of the problem presented in the brief, then these should be shown. If the researcher sees a problem in the brief that is ambiguous or unattainable, again alternative diagnoses should be presented. From this section, the marketer's gaps in knowledge should be apparent.

4 *Research objectives.* These may be presented in the form of clear hypotheses that may be tested. They may also cover broader areas in terms of 'research questions' that are to be explored rather than formally measured in a conclusive manner.

5 *Research design.* The research design to be adopted, in broad terms classified as exploratory, descriptive or causal, should be specified. Beyond such a broad classification should be details of the individual techniques that will be adopted and how they will unfold and connect to each other. This means that the reader will clearly see methods of collecting the desired data, justification for these methods, and a sampling plan to include details of sample size(s). This applies to both quantitative and qualitative approaches. The following example from Sports Marketing Surveys' Nestea project is a

descriptive research design. This summarises the stages but note that each stage is developed in more detail in the actual proposal. Of particular note is the foundation to the study in the form of the proprietary model to evaluate the effectiveness of sponsorship – and how this model is used to interpret the data collected from different sources and to form strategic recommendations.

 Sports Marketing Surveys

Nestea research proposal: research design

1 **Model build.**
2 **Desk and database research.**
3 **Primary research:**
   - **Close market: spectator studies** – we will undertake 10–15 interviews at each event based on a more qualitative 10–15 minute in-depth discussion. These will take place over one day at each event and will be based around a topic guide to be discussed. This topic guide will focus more on the lifestyle values and how these fit with the desired attributes of Nestea.
   - **Distant market: target market** – 150 interviews in each country in the region of the relevant events will be undertaken. However, in terms of timing where two events are being undertaken (Germany), we propose the research to be in two stages immediately after each event:
     - Germany: 75 interviews after each event to give a total of 150 for each country. This will provide post-event data for the first event and pre- and post-information for the second event. It also ensures that there is not a large time difference from event to research if the first event is held much earlier in the summer.
     - Spain, Italy and Hungary: 150 interviews in each country after completion of each event in the region(s).
4 **Model evaluation and strategic analysis.**

6 *Fieldwork/data collection.* The proposal should discuss how the data will be collected and who will collect them. If the fieldwork is to be subcontracted to another supplier, this should be stated. Control mechanisms to ensure the quality of data collected should be described.
7 *Data analysis.* This should describe the kind of data analysis that will be conducted, e.g. content analysis, simple cross-tabulations, univariate analysis or multivariate analysis. If software packages are to be used in these analyses, they should be specified, as they will be indicative of the potential analyses that can be conducted. There should be further description of the extent to which the results will be interpreted in light of the set marketing objectives, beyond the specified analysis techniques.
8 *Reporting.* The proposal should specify the nature of any intermediate reports to be presented, what will be the form of the final report, and whether an oral presentation of the results will be made.
9 *Cost and timetable.* The cost of the project and a time schedule, broken down by phases, should be presented. A critical path method chart might be included. In large projects, a payment schedule is also worked out in advance.
10 Research organisation and key researchers working on the project. When an organisation is working with researchers for the first time, some idea of past research projects and clients should be displayed. This can help the marketer to trust the researcher in problem diagnosis, research design and implementation (e.g. how credible the researchers may be seen by the individuals they are to research and how this may affect respondent openness and honesty), and interpretation of the findings.

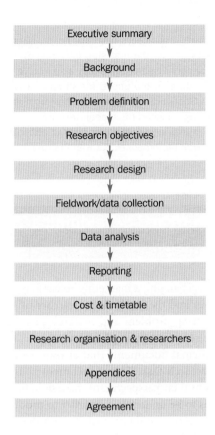

Executive summary

Background

Problem definition

Research objectives

Research design

Fieldwork/data collection

Data analysis

Reporting

Cost & timetable

Research organisation & researchers

Appendices

Agreement

Figure 2.2
Components of the marketing research proposal

11 *Appendices.* Any statistical or other information of interest to only a few people should be contained in appendices.

12 *Agreement.* All parties concerned with fulfilling the research plan should sign and date their agreement to the proposal.

Preparing a research proposal has several advantages. It ensures that the researcher and management agree about the nature of the project, and it helps sell the project to a wider array of decision-makers who may contribute to and benefit from the research findings. As preparation of the proposal entails planning; it helps the researcher conceptualise and execute the marketing research project. The following example illustrates the language problems in writing a pan-European research proposal. In this example, a problem lies with English speakers wanting to negotiate and work with other English speakers and having little experience of the countries in which they will undertake research.

Example | **Some dos and don'ts of pan-European research[6]**

Many European studies are commissioned by English speakers who want to work with English speakers. They want to agree questionnaires in English, and they want reports and tables in English. And so they come to the UK.

In addition, it is simpler for someone commissioning international research to accept an English proposal written by a first-language English speaker. Even the best European – used here in its not-British sense – English speaker finds it hard to write a creative proposal in good idiomatic English. But it is creativity that sells proposals.

A problem in writing proposals for research in Europe is often lack of familiarity with European habits and behaviour. Most British researchers' experience of Europe is derived from holidays backed up (in all too few cases) by limited work experience in one or more countries. Faced by a proposal on TV viewing, on grocery purchasing, on holiday habits or on headache remedies, few British researchers have any notion of how Italians, Spaniards or Germans treat these subjects. Hence the first step in writing an international proposal on an unfamiliar subject is secondary research. This may also involve calling a dozen homes in the relevant country, and chatting on the phone for an hour or two with locals. Soon you start to identify how Italians, Spaniards and Germans differ from the British and what these main differences are. Designing a piece of European research in an unfamiliar area without taking this first simple step is like taking up power boating without learning to swim. It is a route to disaster, not maybe with the proposal, but with the research when commissioned.

The process of defining the problem and developing a research approach

By formally developing and exchanging a marketing research brief and research proposal, the marketing decision-maker and the marketing researcher utilise their distinctive skills. They ensure that the marketing problem and research problems have been correctly defined and an appropriate research approach is developed. The research brief and the research proposal are the formal documents that ensure each party is clear about the nature and scope of the research task. These documents allow decision-makers and researchers formally to present their perspective of the task in hand. The following section details the process that needs to be undertaken in order to produce these documents. The detail of defining the nature of problems and developing an appropriate research approach to the point of creating a research design is shown in Figure 2.3.

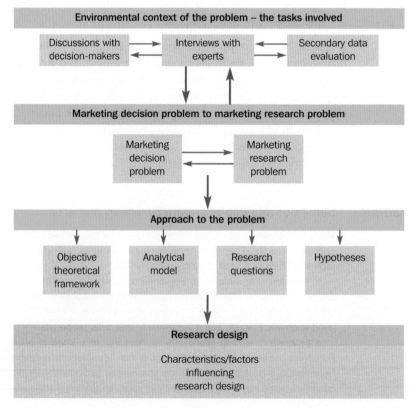

Figure 2.3
The process of defining the problem and developing an approach

The tasks involved in problem definition consist of discussions with decision-makers, qualitative interviews with industry experts and other knowledgeable individuals, and analysis of readily available secondary data. These tasks help the researcher to understand the background of the problem by analysing the environmental context. Certain essential environmental factors bearing on the problem should be evaluated. An understanding of the environmental context facilitates the identification of the marketing decision problem. Then, the marketing decision problem is translated into a marketing research problem. Based on the definition of the marketing research problem, an approach to the problem is established and an appropriate research design is developed. The components of the approach may consist of an objective/theoretical framework, analytical models, research questions and hypotheses. Further explanation of the problem definition process begins with a discussion of the tasks involved.

Environmental context of the problem

The tasks involved in understanding the environmental context of the marketing and research problem can include discussions with decision-makers, qualitative interviews with industry experts, and secondary data analysis. The purposes of these tasks are to develop an understanding of forces that may affect the nature of decision-makers' problems and related research problems.

Discussions with decision-makers

Discussions with the decision-makers beyond the formal presentation of a research brief and research proposal are usually vital. The decision-maker needs to understand the capabilities and limitations of research.[7] Research provides information relevant to management decisions, but it cannot provide solutions, because solutions require managerial creativity and judgement. Conversely, the researcher needs to understand the nature of the decision that managers face – the marketing problem, and what they hope to learn from the research.

To identify the marketing problem, the researcher must possess considerable skill in interacting with the decision-maker. Several factors may complicate this interaction. Access to decision-makers may be difficult, and some organisations have complicated protocols for access to top executives. The organisational status of the researcher or the research department may make it difficult to reach the key decision-maker in the early stages of the project. Finally, there may be more than one key decision-maker, and meeting collectively or individually may be difficult. All of the problems make it difficult to develop a research brief. Despite these problems, though, it is necessary that the researcher interacts directly with the key decision-makers.[8]

Problem audit
A comprehensive examination of a marketing problem to understand its origin and nature.

A **problem audit** provides a useful framework to develop ideas from a brief, allowing the researcher to interact with the decision-maker and identify the underlying causes of the problem. A problem audit, like any other type of audit, is a comprehensive examination of a marketing problem with the purpose of understanding its origin and nature.[9] A problem audit involves discussions with the decision-maker on the following issues:

1 The events that led to the decision that action is needed, or the history of the problem.
2 The corporate culture as it relates to decision making.[10] For example, in some firms, the decision-making process is dominant; in others, the personality of the decision-maker is more important.
3 The alternative courses of action available to the decision-maker. The set of alternatives may be incomplete at this stage, and qualitative research may be needed to identify the more innovative courses of action.
4 The criteria that will be used to evaluate the alternative courses of action. For example, new product offerings might be evaluated based on sales, market share, profitability, or return on investment.

5 What the decision-maker perceives to be gaps in their knowledge.

6 The manner in which the decision-maker will use each item of information in making the decision.

It may be necessary to perform a problem audit, because the decision-maker may have only a vague idea of what the problem is. For example, the decision-maker may know that the firm is losing market share but may not know why; decision-makers may tend to focus on symptoms rather than on causes. An inability to meet sales forecasts, a loss of market share and a decline in profits are all symptoms. The researcher should treat the underlying causes, not merely address the symptoms. For example, loss of market share may be caused by much better advertising campaigns by the competition, inadequate distribution of the company's products, or any number of other factors. Only when the underlying causes are identified can the problem be successfully addressed.

A problem audit, which involves extensive interaction between the decision-maker and the researcher, can greatly facilitate problem definition by determining the underlying causes. The interaction between the researcher and the decision-maker is facilitated when one or more people in the client organisation serve to liaise and form a team with the marketing researcher. To be fruitful, the interaction between the decision-maker and the researcher can be characterised by the following:

1 *Communication.* A free exchange of ideas between the decision-maker and the researcher is essential.

2 *Cooperation.* Marketing research is a team project in which both parties (decision-maker and researcher) must cooperate, from problem diagnosis through to the interpretation and presentation of findings.

3 *Confidence.* Mutual trust of each other's distinct skills and contribution should underlie the interaction between the decision-maker and the researcher.

4 *Candour.* There should not be any hidden agendas, and an attitude of openness should prevail.

5 *Closeness.* An understanding of each other's problems should result in a closeness that should characterise the relationship between the decision-maker and the researcher.

6 *Continuity.* The decision-maker and the researcher must interact continually rather than sporadically.

7 *Creativity.* The interaction between the decision-maker and the researcher should be creative rather than formulaic. Though the research process may be laid out in 'easy-to-follow' steps, in reality great amounts of creativity are needed at every stage.

Interviews with industry experts

In addition to discussions with decision-makers, qualitative interviews with industry experts, individuals knowledgeable about the firm and the industry, can help in diagnosing the nature of the marketing and research problem.[11] These experts may be found both inside and outside the firm. Typically, expert information is obtained by unstructured personal interviews, without a formal questionnaire. It is helpful, however, to prepare a list of topics to be covered during the interview. The order in which these topics are covered and the questions to ask should not be predetermined. Instead, they should be decided as the interview progresses, which allows greater flexibility in capturing the insights of the experts (see Chapter 8 for full details of depth interviewing techniques). The list of topics to cover and the type of expert sought should evolve as the researcher becomes more attuned to the nature of the marketing problem. The purpose of interviewing experts is to explore ideas, make new connections between ideas, and create new perspectives in defining the marketing research problem. If the technique works well, and an amount of trust and rapport is developed, the potential to generate and test ideas can be immense. Experts may have other contacts that the researcher may not be aware of or may not be able to get access to. They may also have secondary data which, again, the researcher may not be aware of or have access to. Unfortunately, two potential difficulties may arise when seeking advice from experts:

1 Some individuals who claim to be knowledgeable and are eager to participate may not really possess expertise.
2 It may be difficult to locate and obtain help from experts who are outside the client organisation, i.e. access to these individuals may be problematic.

For these reasons, interviews with experts are more useful in conducting marketing research for industrial firms and for products of a technical nature, where it is relatively easy to identify and approach the experts. This method is also helpful in situations where little information is available from other sources, as in the case of radically new products. Experts can provide valuable insights in modifying or repositioning existing products, as illustrated in the following example of the development of brand values at Visa.

Example	### Visa to travel[12]

Visa ran a major brand-building campaign spanning Europe. The aim of the campaign was to create the same brand values in different countries. Although the benefits of uniform branding are obvious, many companies have found that targeting a number of countries with the same campaign is fraught with danger. However, with research that revealed perceptions of Visa and cash to be consistent across Europe, that 'plastic is better than cash', the message was simple to translate – simple if one is aware of cultural sensibilities and the relationship between countries, the company and the target audience. With industry expertise emphasising the appeal of locally produced campaigns, Visa has succeeded. As an example, Visa has been running a separate campaign for the Electron debit card in Spain, Portugal and Italy for some time. It has won many awards in Spain where people think it is a Spanish campaign, but then they think the ad is locally produced in Italy and Portugal as well.

Initial secondary data analyses

Secondary data
Data collected for some purpose other than the problem at hand.

Primary data
Data originated by the researcher specifically to address the research problem.

Secondary data collection and analysis will be addressed in detail in Chapters 4 and 5. A brief introduction here will demonstrate the worth of secondary data at the stage of problem diagnosis. Secondary data are data collected for some purpose other than the problem at hand. Primary data, on the other hand, are originated by the researcher for the specific purpose of addressing the research problem. Secondary data include data generated within an organisation, information made available by business and government sources, commercial marketing research firms, and computerised databases. Secondary data are an economical and quick source of background information. Analysis of available secondary data is an essential step in the problem definition process: primary data should not be collected until the available secondary data have been fully analysed. Past information and forecasts of trends with respect to sales, market share, profitability, technology, population, demographics and lifestyle can help the researcher to understand the underlying marketing research problem. Where appropriate, this kind of analysis should be carried out at the industry and firm levels. For example, if a firm's sales have decreased but industry sales have increased, the problems will be very different than if the industry sales have also decreased. In the former case, the problems are likely to be specific to the firm. Past information and forecasts can be valuable in uncovering potential opportunities and problems.

Marketing decision problem and marketing research problem

Marketing decision problem
The problem confronting the marketing decision-maker, which asks what the decision-maker needs to do.

Marketing research problem
A problem that entails determining what information is needed and how it can be obtained in the most feasible way.

The **marketing decision problem** asks what the decision-maker needs to do, whereas the **marketing research problem** asks what information is needed and how it can best be obtained.[13] The marketing decision problem is action oriented. It is concerned with the possible actions the decision-maker can take. How should the loss of market share be arrested? Should the market be segmented differently? Should a new product be introduced? Should the promotional budget be increased?

In contrast, the marketing research problem is information oriented. It involves determining what information is needed and how that information can be obtained effectively and efficiently. Consider, for example, the loss of market share for a particular product line. The decision-maker's problem is how to recover this loss. Alternative courses of action can include modifying existing products, introducing new products, changing other elements in the marketing mix, and segmenting the market. Suppose that the decision-maker and the researcher believe that the problem is caused by inappropriate segmentation of the market and want research to provide information on this issue. The research problem would then become the identification and evaluation of an alternative basis for segmenting the market. Note that this process requires much interaction, in the sense that both parties critically evaluate, develop and defend each other's ideas to clarify the nature of decision and research problems, and to ensure there is a clear and logical connection between them. The following example further illustrates the distinction between the marketing decision problem and the marketing research problem. It also illustrates the interactive nature of identifying the marketing decision problem and the research problem, each one unfolding and informing the understanding of the other.

The following examples further distinguish between the marketing decision problem and the marketing research problem.

Example   Defining the problem

Bank X: We are experiencing a loss of market share in Ireland in corporate banking.

Researcher: Is it just Ireland?

Bank X: No, but as we conduct the majority of our business there, the loss is causing us the greatest amount of concern.

Researcher: Why do you think you are losing market share?

Bank X: We wish we knew!

Researcher: How are your competitors coping?

Bank X: We suspect that other Irish banks are also suffering, but that the multinational banks are capturing market share.

Researcher: How do your customers feel about the quality of services you deliver?

Bank X: We recently attained our ISO 9000 for service quality, which we are proud of!

Researcher: But how does your service delivery compare with your competitors?

After a series of discussions with key decision-makers, analysis of secondary data within the bank and from other sources, the problem was identified as follows:

● *Marketing decision problem*. What should be done to arrest the decline in market share of Bank X?
● *Marketing research problem*. Determine the relative strengths and weaknesses of Bank X, vis-à-vis other major competitors in Ireland. This would be done with respect to factors that influence a company in its choice of a bank to handle its transactions.

Marketing decision problem	Marketing research problem
Should a new product be introduced?	To determine consumer preferences and purchase intentions for the proposed new product
Should the advertising campaign be changed?	To determine the effectiveness of the current advertising campaign
Should the price of the brand be increased?	To determine the price elasticity of demand and the impact on sales and profits of various levels of price changes

Defining the marketing research problem

The general rule to be followed in defining the research problem is that the definition should:

1 allow the researcher to obtain all the information needed to address the marketing decision problem;
2 guide the researcher in maintaining focus and proceeding with the project in a consistent manner.

Researchers make two common errors in problem definition. The first arises when the research problem is defined too broadly. A broad definition does not provide clear guidelines for the subsequent steps involved in the project. Some examples of excessively broad marketing research problem definitions are: developing a marketing strategy for a brand, improving the competitive position of the firm, or improving the company's image. These are not specific enough to suggest an approach to the problem or a research design.

The second type of error is just the opposite: the marketing research problem is defined too narrowly. A narrow focus may preclude consideration of some courses of action, particularly those that are innovative and not obvious. It may also prevent the researcher from addressing important components of the marketing decision problem. For example, in a project conducted for a consumer products firm, the marketing problem was how to respond to a price cut initiated by a competitor. The alternative courses of action initially identified by the firm's research staff were to:

1 decrease the price of the firm's brand to match the competitor's price cut;
2 maintain price but increase advertising heavily; or
3 decrease the price somewhat, without matching the competitor's price, and moderately increase advertising.

None of these alternatives seemed promising. When outside marketing research experts were brought in, the problem was redefined as improving the market share and profitability of the product line. Qualitative research indicated that in blind tests consumers could not differentiate products offered under different brand names. Furthermore, consumers relied on price as an indicator of product quality. These findings led to a creative alternative: increase the price of the existing brand and introduce two new brands – one priced to match the competitor and the other priced to undercut it.

Broad statement of the problem
The initial statement of the marketing research problem that provides an appropriate perspective on the problem.

The likelihood of committing either error of problem definition can be reduced by stating the marketing research problem in broad, general terms and identifying its specific components (see Figure 2.4). The **broad statement of the problem** provides perspective

Figure 2.4
Proper definition of the marketing research problem

Specific components of the problem
The second part of the marketing research problem definition that focuses on the key aspects of the problem and provides clear guidelines on how to proceed further.

and acts as a safeguard against committing the second type of error. The **specific components of the problem** focus on the key aspects and provide clear guidelines on how to proceed further, and act as a safeguard against committing the first type of error. Examples of appropriate marketing research problem definitions are provided in the following two examples.

Example ## Net has yet to prove its value[14]

As the stampede to set up websites continues, those companies without a clear long-term strategy are looking increasingly rudderless as they search for ways to capitalise on their investment. A recent survey by Gallup and the *Wall Street Journal* of 603 board-level executives in the UK, France and Germany has revealed that Europe's businesses continue to embrace the Internet on the somewhat vague grounds that it is in the interests of their 'competitiveness'. Yet, they remain unsure about how, specifically, to use the medium for generating profits in the longer term.

The notable exception has been the financial services sector. Exploratory secondary data gathering and analyses revealed the opportunities that have been grasped by this sector. It also revealed the strategies adopted by financial companies. To develop these ideas into relevant actions, case histories of exemplary financial companies were built, key decision-makers were targeted and questions focused upon technology, design and financial returns were developed.

Specifically the following issues could be addressed (as examples of many) for a company embarking on developing a website:

1 To what extent is the Net used by competitors?
2 What specific information types and services do they offer?
3 How can the Net generate knowledge of customers?
4 How can the Net add to marketing communication strategies?
5 How can the Net help to generate actual sales?
6 What types of existing or potential customers could use our site?

In the following *Tennis* magazine example, the broad statement of the problem focused upon gathering information about subscribers, and specific components identified the particular information about subscribers that was needed.

Example ## Research serves *Tennis* magazine[15]

Tennis magazine wanted to obtain information about its readers, which numbered 1.6 million in 2003, though it had 700,000 subscribers. The management decision problem was: '*What changes should be made in Tennis magazine to make it more appealing to its readers?*'

The broad marketing research problem was defined as: '*to build a profile of subscribers of Tennis magazine*'

Specific components of the problem included the following:

1 **Demographics.** Who are the men and women who subscribe to the magazine?
2 **Psychological characteristics and lifestyle.** How do subscribers spend their money and their free time? Lifestyle indicators to be examined were: fitness, travel, car rental, apparel, consumer electronics, credit cards and financial investments.
3 **Tennis activity.** Where and how often do subscribers play tennis? What are their skill levels?
4 **Relationship to *Tennis* magazine.** How much time do subscribers spend with the issues? How long do they keep them? Do they share the magazine with other tennis players?

Because the questions were so clearly defined, the information provided by this research helped management design their editorial and layout with features on tennis instruction, equipment, famous tennis players and locations to play tennis.

Components of the research approach

Once the marketing decision-maker and researcher have clarified the decision problem and established the research problem they face, it has to be decided how to approach the research problem. The research problem may be very clear in the sense that there are strong established theories of what should be measured and how to conduct the measurements. Conversely, the research problem may lack theoretical foundation, with the researcher trying to cope with a broad set of issues that have not been sufficiently researched beforehand and unable to trust existing theories. How the researcher perceives the research problem affects the **paradigm** he or she will adopt in either an implicit or explicit manner. The researcher's adopted paradigm is built upon a set of assumptions. These assumptions consist of 'agreed-upon' knowledge, criteria of judgement, problem fields and ways to consider them[16] (these factors will be developed further in Chapter 6). What is 'agreed-upon' refers to how strong the theories are in defining and encapsulating the issues that make up a research problem. Bringing together the 'agreed upon' knowledge, criteria of judgement, problem fields and ways to consider them can be undertaken by considering the objective/theoretical framework, analytical models, research questions and hypotheses. Each of these components is discussed in the following sections. Collectively they may be considered to be the 'approach' that a researcher will take.

Paradigm
A set of assumptions consisting of agreed-upon knowledge, criteria of judgement, problem fields and ways to consider them.

Source: © Mike/Zefa/CORBIS

Objective/theoretical framework

Theory
A conceptual scheme based on foundational statements, or axioms, that are assumed to be true.

Objective evidence
Perceived to be unbiased evidence, supported by empirical findings.

In general, researchers should aim to base their investigations upon objective evidence, supported by **theory**. A theory is a conceptual scheme based on foundational statements called axioms that are assumed to be true. **Objective evidence** is gathered by compiling relevant findings from secondary sources. Likewise, an appropriate theory to guide the research might be identified by reviewing academic literature contained in books, journals and monographs. The researchers should rely on theory to help them to measure or understand the variables they are investigating. Academic sources of new developments to measure, understand and analyse consumers should be constantly evaluated; the following two examples illustrates why.

Example   Not afraid of theory[17]

An abundance of innovations have emerged from academics over the past decades to the benefit of marketing research practitioners. Conjoint analyses, for instance, started in the academic world, and really caught on in the 1980s. Choice-based conjoint analysis or CBC is a good example of this, which has been popularised over the past 10 years, after its inception in the academic circles of econometricians and psychologists. Other contributions have been in segmentation, pricing and customer satisfaction research. Latent class models and structural equation models (used in customer satisfaction research) are clear examples of academic developments that have been popularised for use in marketing research practice

---

Example   Innovation or hype?[18]

Many qualitatitive researchers are shifting from the familiar focus group discussions and in-depth interviews to embrace new methods of semiotics, linguistics, bricolage, diaries, observations, workshops and neuroscience. It has been claimed that these new techniques can generate better information and insight. How valid is this viewpoint? David Penn, Managing Director of Conquest Research Ltd, says:

> We need to understand the theory that underpins each new technique so we can make a sound judgement about when and how to use it and also see its limitations. You need to understand the intellectual tradition behind, say, semiotics to be able to assess its value for a particular research project. This means we should place more emphasis on theory in marketing research.

Marketing researchers should also rely on theory to determine which variables should be investigated. Past research on theory development and testing can provide important guidelines on determining dependent variables (variables that depend on the values of other variables) and independent variables (variables whose values affect the values of other variables). Furthermore, theoretical considerations provide information on how the variables should be operationalised and measured, as well as how the research design and sample should be selected. A theory also serves as a foundation on which the researcher can organise and interpret the findings: 'nothing is so practical as a good theory'.[19] Conversely, by neglecting theory, researchers increase the likelihood that they will fail to understand the data obtained or be unable to interpret and integrate the findings of the project with findings obtained by others. The role of theory in the various phases of an applied marketing research project is summarised in Table 2.1.

Applying a theory to a marketing research problem requires creativity on the part of the researcher. A theory may not specify adequately how its abstract constructs (variables) can be embodied in a real-world phenomenon. Marketing researcher must therefore take the best of what they believe to be the most novel theories to represent and encapsulate consumer thinking and behaviour.

Example **Brands are recorded in our brains[20]**

All the human and biological sciences – social, behavioural psychology, cognitive psychology, psychoanalytical psychology, linguistics, and the newer discoveries within the science of the brain – are an attempt to find out why human beings do what they do. That is what research is about. You cannot read a book about linguistics or brain science and expect to know all about these complex and specialised subjects. What you have to do is try to identify relevant principles and integrate these with the pragmatic experience of being an active researcher. Something new, a new way of thinking, is the result. Nearly all of our work consists of several strands. It's not possible to say 'I'm using cognitive psychology here, or now I'm using a bit of linguistics'. They become part of your model of thinking about how human beings interact with brands, communications and organisations. We do practice 'bricolage' very seriously – not for the sake of novelty but for the sake of research rigour.

It is also vital for marketing researchers to recognise that theories are incomplete; they deal with only a subset of variables that exist in the real world. Hence, the researcher must also identify and examine other variables that have yet to be published as theories. This may involve the researcher developing 'grounded theory', which will be explained and developed in Chapter 6.

Table 2.1 The role of theory in applied marketing research

Research task	Role of theory
Conceptualising and identifying key variables	Provides a conceptual foundation and understanding of the basic processes underlying the problem situation. These processes will suggest key dependent and independent variables
Operationalising key variables	Provides guidance for the practical means to measure or encapsulate the concepts or key variables identified
Selecting a research design	Causal or associative relationships suggested by the theory may indicate whether a causal, descriptive or exploratory research design should be adopted (see Chapter 3)
Selecting a sample	Helps in defining the nature of a population, characteristics that may be used to stratify populations or to validate samples (see Chapter 14)
Analysing and interpreting data	The theoretical framework and the models, research questions and hypotheses based on it guide the selection of a data analysis strategy and the interpretation of results (see Chapter 17)
Integrating findings	The findings obtained in the research project can be interpreted in the light of previous research and integrated with the existing body of knowledge

Analytical model
An explicit specification of a set of variables and their interrelationships designed to represent some real system or process in whole or in part.

Verbal models
Analytical models that provide a written representation of the relationships between variables.

Graphical models
Analytical models that provide a visual picture of the relationships between variables.

Analytical model

An **analytical model** is a set of variables and their interrelationships designed to represent, in whole or in part, some real system or process. Models can have many different forms. The most common are verbal, graphical and mathematical structures. In **verbal models**, the variables and their relationships are stated in prose form. Such models may be mere restatements of the main tenets of a theory. **Graphical models** are visual. They are used to isolate variables and to suggest directions of relationships but are not designed to provide numerical results. They are logical, preliminary steps to developing mathematical models.[21] **Mathematical models** explicitly specify the relationships among variables, usually in equation form.[22] These models can be used as guides for formulating the research design and have the advantage of being amenable to manipulation.[23] The different models are illustrated in the context of the proprietary sponsorship model used by Sports Marketing Surveys.

As can be seen from this example, the verbal, graphical and mathematical models depict the same phenomenon or theoretical framework in different ways. The phenomenon of 'sponsorship impact', stated verbally, is represented for clarity through a figure (graphical model) and is put in equation form (mathematical model) for ease of statistical estimation and testing. Graphical models are particularly helpful in clarifying the concept or approach to the problem.

The verbal, graphical and mathematical models complement each other and help the researcher identify relevant research questions and hypotheses.

Mathematical models
Analytical models that explicitly describe the relationships between variables, usually in equation form.

Focus on **Sports Marketing Surveys**

After the initial decision has been taken to use sponsorship as a marketing tool, it is vital to ensure that the most appropriate sponsorship is selected. It is also essential from both the rights holder's and sponsor's point of view to have an independent assessment of the value of a sponsorship. To this end, Sports Marketing Surveys has its own sponsorship selection and valuation model in partnership with IEG (International Events Group, **www.sponsorship.com**).

Model building

Verbal model

A marketing manager wishes to include an investment in sponsorship as part of the portfolio of integrated marketing communications. She wishes to understand the impact of her sponsorship investment. She starts by deciding what key objectives should be fulfilled through a sponsorship relationship. She then selects a sector (sports, arts, culture, environment, broadcast) and the type of property (event, team, performance, individual, programme). Once the sector and property have been selected, she sets specific objectives that can be developed to help to set realistic targets and a set of metrics as a means to measure success.

Graphical model

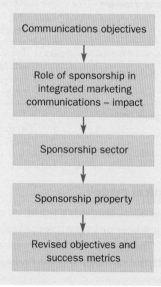

Mathematical model

$$y = a_0 + \sum_{i=1}^{n} a_i x_i$$

where y = sponsorship impact
a_0, a_i = model parameters to be estimated statistically
x_i = sponsorship requirement factors

Research questions

Research questions
Refined statements of the specific components of the problem.

Research questions are refined statements of the components of the problem. Although the components of the problem define the problem in specific terms, further detail may be needed to develop an approach. Each component of the problem may have to be broken down into subcomponents or research questions. Research questions ask what specific information is required with respect to the problem components. If the research questions are answered by the research, then the information obtained should aid the decision-maker. The formulation of the research questions should be guided not only by the problem definition, but also by the theoretical framework and the analytical model adopted. For a given problem component, there are likely to be several research questions.

 Sports Marketing Surveys

Racetrack 2003

Research questions

In 1993 Sports Marketing Surveys completed its first international syndicated study to measure the attitudes and opinions of, and profile of, the Formula One fan. Racetrack 2003 was the fifth study, covering Formula One fans from: Australia, Brazil, France, Germany, Italy, Japan, Spain and the UK.
The key research questions tackled in the study were:

- What is the image of Formula One and its manufacturers at the end of 2003?
- What is the awareness of Formula One sponsors (car sponsors and tyre suppliers)?
- What changes have occurred in sponsor awareness?
- What levels of support exist for teams and drivers?
- What are the attitudes towards sponsorship amongst Formula One fans?
- What is the Internet and merchandise profile of Formula One fans?

These research questions were then further refined by precisely defining the variables and determining how they could be turned into specific questions, i.e. operationalised. To illustrate, in wishing to measure the level of support for teams and drivers, the following two questions were posed:

1 Which *one* Formula One team do you support?
2 Which *one* current Formula One driver do you support?

The biggest response to question 1 was 'Ferrari', the most popular team in 2001, 2002 and 2003. The biggest response to question 2 was 'Michael Schumacher', the most popular driver in 2001, 2002 and 2003.

Hypotheses

Hypothesis
An unproven statement or proposition about a factor or phenomenon that is of interest to a researcher.

A **hypothesis** is an unproven statement or proposition about a factor or phenomenon that is of interest to the researcher. For example, it may be a tentative statement about relationships between two or more variables as stipulated by the theoretical framework or the analytical model. Often, a hypothesis is a possible answer to the research question.[24] Hypotheses go beyond research questions because they are statements of relationships or propositions rather than merely questions to which answers are sought. Research questions are interrogative; hypotheses are declarative and can be tested empirically (see Chapter 18). An important role of a hypothesis is to suggest variables to be included in the research design.[25] The relationship between the marketing research problem, research questions and hypotheses, along with the influence of the objective/theoretical framework and analytical models, is described in Figure 2.5 and illustrated by the following example from Sports Marketing Surveys.[26]

Hypotheses are an important part of the approach to a research problem. When stated in operational terms, as H_1 and H_2 in the Sports Marketing Surveys example, they provide guidelines on what, and how, data are to be collected and analysed. When operational hypotheses are stated using symbolic notation, they are commonly referred to as statistical hypotheses.

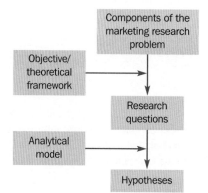

Figure 2.5
Development of research questions and hypotheses

Focus on **Sports Marketing Surveys**

Racetrack 2003

Hypotheses

The following hypotheses were formulated in relation to the research question on team/driver support:

H_1: German Formula One fans show the highest level of support for Michael Schumacher.
H_2: French Formula One fans show the highest level of support for the Renault team.

These hypotheses guide the research by ensuring that variables which affect relationships are included in the research design. The connection between questions that form hypotheses and the appropriate analyses needed are thought out clearly before the research plan and questionnaire are designed.

It is important to note that not all research questions can be developed into hypotheses that may be tested. Certain research questions may be exploratory in nature, with the researcher having no preconceived notions of possible answers to the research questions, nor the ability to produce statements of relationships or propositions. If the researcher is faced with such a situation, it does not mean that the investigation will not be as valid as one where hypotheses are clearly established. It means that the researcher may have to adopt a different approach or paradigm to establish its validity.

International marketing research

The precise definition of the marketing research problem is more difficult in international marketing research than in domestic marketing research. Unfamiliarity with the environmental factors of the country where the research is being conducted can greatly increase the difficulty of understanding the problem's environmental context and uncovering its causes.

Example — Heinz Ketchup couldn't catch up in Brazil[27]

In 2003, Heinz was selling products in over 200 countries and sales were over €10 billion. Despite good records of global sales, the H.J. Heinz Company failed in Brazil, a market that seemed to be South America's biggest and most promising market. Heinz entered a joint venture with Citrosuco Paulista, a giant orange juice exporter, because of the future possibility of buying the profitable company. Yet, the sales of its products, including ketchup, did not take off. Where was the problem? A problem audit revealed that the company lacked a strong local distribution system. Heinz lost control of the distribution because it worked on consignment. Distribution could not reach 25% penetration. The other related problem was that Heinz concentrated on neighbourhood shops because this strategy was successful in Mexico. The problem audit, however, revealed that 75% of the grocery shopping in São Paulo is done in supermarkets and not the smaller shops. Although Mexico and Brazil may appear to have similar cultural and demographic characteristics, consumer behaviour can vary greatly. A closer and intensive look at the Brazilian food distribution system and the behaviour of consumers could have averted this failure.

As the Heinz example illustrates, many international marketing efforts fail not because research was not conducted, but because the relevant environmental factors were not taken into account and fully appreciated. Generally, this leads to a definition of the problem that is too narrow. A major problem for researchers is that their perception of problems may be reflected through their own social and cultural development. Before defining the problem, researchers should reflect upon their unconscious reference to cultural values. The following steps help researchers to reflect upon their own cultural values:[28]

1 Define the marketing research problem in terms of domestic environmental and cultural factors. This involves an identification of relevant European traits, economics, values, needs or habits.
2 Define the marketing research problem in terms of foreign environmental and cultural factors. Make no judgements. This involves an identification of the related traits, economics, values, needs or habits in the proposed market culture. This task requires input from researchers familiar with the foreign environment.

3 Examine the differences between steps 1 and 2. The unconscious reference to cultural values can be seen to account for these differences.

4 Redefine the problem without the social/cultural influence and address it for the foreign market situation. If the differences in step 3 are significant, the impact of the social/cultural influences should be carefully considered.

Whilst the above steps may seem at face value to be straightforward, note the words 'unconscious reference' in step 3. They mean that the researchers need to reflect upon their own values and attitudes, the factors that may bias the way they perceive things and what they observe. As these factors may be 'unconscious', this reflection and introspection may take some time to realise. These issues will be more fully developed in Chapter 9.

While developing theoretical frameworks, models, research questions and hypotheses, remember that differences in the environmental factors, especially the socio-cultural environment, may lead to differences in the formation of perceptions, attitudes, preferences and choice behaviour. For example, orientation towards time varies considerably across cultures. In many parts of Asia, Latin America and the Middle East, people tend not to be as time conscious as Westerners. This influences their perceptions of and preferences for convenience foods such as frozen foods and prepared dinners. In developing an approach to the problem, the researchers should consider the equivalence of consumption and purchase behaviour and the underlying factors that influence them. This is critical to the identification of the correct research questions, hypotheses and characteristics/factors that influence the research design.

The following example reveals how the use of focus groups could have helped to reveal social/cultural characteristics of the Japanese. Focus groups would have allowed the correct identification of research questions, leading to a more successful product launch.

Example | **Surf Superconcentrate faces a super washout in Japan[29]**

Unilever attempted to break into the Japanese detergent market with Surf Superconcentrate. It initially achieved 14.5% of the market share during test marketing but fell down to a shocking 2.8% when the product was introduced nationally. Where did Unilever go wrong? Surf was designed to have a distinctive pre-measured packet as in teabag-like sachets, joined in pairs because convenience was an important attribute to Japanese consumers. It also had a 'fresh smell' appeal. Japanese consumers, however, noticed that the detergent did not dissolve in the wash, partly because of weather conditions and because of the popularity of low-agitation washing machines. Surf was not designed to work in the new washing machines. Unilever also found that the 'fresh smell' positioning of new Surf had little relevance since most consumers hang their washing out in the fresh air. The research approach was certainly not without flaw, as Unilever failed to identify critical attributes that are relevant in the Japanese detergent market. Furthermore, it identified factors such as 'fresh smell' that had no relevance in the Japanese context. Appropriate qualitative research such as focus groups across samples from the target market could have revealed the correct characteristics or factors leading to a suitable research design. Despite having to withdraw from the Japanese market, Surf continued to perform well in several markets including India. With the success and increasing popularity of its other detergent, Omo, in Latin America and China, Unilever is evaluating how the product will fare in Japan.

Ethics in marketing research

Ethical situations arising from the process of problem definition and developing an approach are likely to occur between the marketing researcher and the client. As explained earlier, identifying the correct marketing research problem is crucial to the success of the project. This process can, however, be compromised by the personal agendas of the researcher or the decision-maker. For example, the researcher, after performing the tasks involved in problem definition and analysing the environmental context of the problem, realises that the correct marketing research problem may be defined in a way that makes primary research unnecessary. This would reduce the cost of the project and the research firm's profit margin substantially. Does the researcher define the problem correctly, fabricate a research problem that involves primary data collection, or refuse to proceed with this project in lieu of those more profitable? The researcher is faced with an ethical dilemma, as in the following example.

Example

Taste (profits) or image (ethics)?[30]

A marketing research firm is hired by a soft drinks company to conduct taste tests to determine why its newly introduced soft drink brand has not captured the expected market share. The researcher, after following the process outlined in this chapter, determines that the problem is not one of taste but of image and product positioning. The client, however, has already defined the problem as a taste problem and not as the broader, market-share problem. The researcher must weigh the relatively high profit margin of taste test research against the less lucrative survey research needed to answer questions pertaining to soft drink image. What should the research firm do? Should it simply conduct the research the client wants rather than the research it feels the client needs? The guidelines indicate that:

> the researcher has a professional obligation to indicate to the client that, in his or her judgement, the research expenditure is not warranted. If, after this judgement has been clearly stated, the client still desires the research, the researcher should feel free to conduct the study. The reason for this is that the researcher can never know for certain the risk preferences and strategies that are guiding the client's behaviour.

Such ethical situations would be satisfactorily resolved if the client–researcher relationship developed with both the client and the researcher adhering to the seven Cs discussed earlier: communication, cooperation, confidence, candour, closeness, continuity and creativity. This would provide a relationship of mutual trust that would check any unethical tendencies.

Ethical situations affecting the researcher and the client may also arise in developing an approach to the problem. When researchers conduct studies for different clients in related industries (e.g. banking and financial services) or in similar research areas (e.g. customer satisfaction) they may be tempted to cut corners in theoretical framework and model development. Take an example where a grocery chain client has on its board of directors the chairman of a bank. The bank had recently conducted customer satisfaction research using a client-specific model, and the bank-affiliated board member has access to this research. The researcher feels that a customer satisfaction model for the bank could be easily adapted to work for the grocery chain. The client feels that it would

→

not be a good business decision to have access to this information and not use it. Is it ethical for the client and researcher to obtain and use this model developed for another company by another research firm? There is an underlying trust between the researcher and the client that the research firm is honour bound not to reuse client-specific models or findings for other projects.

The client also has an ethical responsibility not to solicit proposals merely to gain the expertise of the research firms without pay. It is unethical for a client to solicit proposals from a few research firms, then adopt one or a combination of the approaches suggested in them, and conduct the project in-house. The client must respect the rights of a firm by realising that an unpaid proposal belongs to the research firm that generated it. However, if the client firm pays for the development of the proposal, it has a right to use the information contained in it.

Internet and computer applications

There are several ways in which the Internet can support the process of problem diagnosis and research design.

Discussions with the decision-maker

The Internet can help the researcher gain access to a wide variety of marketing decision-makers who may use and benefit from proposed research. Thanks to email, it is possible to reach decision-makers anywhere, at any time.

The Internet can also provide chat rooms so that decision-makers and researchers can exchange and test ideas. The availability of the responses to be seen by whoever enters the chat room has the effect of getting all the relevant decision-makers together at the same time without requiring that they be physically present at the same time.

Interviews with industry experts

The Internet can be used to enhance the researcher's ability to obtain advice from experts. It can be searched to find industry experts outside the organisation that commissions a research project.

Secondary data location and analysis

Search engines can be used to locate secondary data quickly and economically. This can be vital in helping to understand the issues to be examined and the approach to examining those issues. We will discuss the availability, acquisition and quality of secondary data on the Internet in more detail in Chapter 4.

In setting the environmental context of the research problem, client-specific information can be gained from the company home page. Generally, companies provide information about their products and services in their home page, making it the ideal starting point for information about the company. Further, the user can also search for competitor and industry information on the Internet. While these searches may not provide complete answers for the marketing researcher, they may raise issues and identify contacts where further exploration may prove beneficial.

Summary

Defining the marketing research problem is the most important step in a research project. Problem definition is a difficult step, because frequently management have not determined the actual problem or have only a vague notion about it. The marketing researcher's role is to help management identify and isolate the problem.

The formal ways in which decision-makers and researchers communicate their perspectives on a research problem and how to solve it are through the development of a research brief and a research proposal. To develop these documents fully, researchers should be proactive in arranging discussions with key decision-makers, which should include a problem audit whenever possible. They should also conduct, where necessary, interviews with relevant experts, and secondary data collection and analyses. These tasks should lead to an understanding of the environmental context of the problem.

Analysis of the environmental context should assist in the identification of the marketing decision problem, which should then be translated into a marketing research problem. The marketing decision asks what the decision-maker needs to do, whereas the marketing research problem asks what information is needed and how it can be obtained effectively and efficiently. The researcher should avoid defining the marketing research problem either too broadly or too narrowly. An appropriate way of defining the marketing research problem is to make a broad statement of the problem and then identify its specific components.

Developing an approach to the problem is the second step in the marketing research process. The components of an approach may consist of an objective/theoretical framework, analytical models, research questions and hypotheses. It is necessary that the approach developed be based upon objective evidence or empirical evidence and be grounded in theory as far as it is appropriate. The relevant variables and their interrelationships may be neatly summarised in an analytical model. The most common kinds of model structures are verbal, graphical and mathematical. The research questions are refined statements of the specific components of the problem that ask what specific information is required with respect to the problem components. Research questions may be further refined into hypotheses. Finally, given the problem definition, research questions and hypotheses should be used to create a method either to measure or elicit an understanding of target respondents.

When defining the problem in international marketing research, researchers must be aware of the impact of their own cultural values when evaluating the environmental impact upon the nature of a problem. Likewise, when developing an approach, the differences in the environment prevailing in the domestic market and the foreign markets should be carefully considered. Several ethical issues that have an impact on the client and the researcher can arise at this stage but can be resolved by adhering to the seven Cs: communication, cooperation, confidence, candour, closeness, continuity and creativity.

Questions

1 What is the nature of the first step in conducting a marketing research project?

2 Why is it vital to define the marketing research problem correctly?

3 What is the role of the researcher in the problem definition process?

4 What are the components of a marketing research brief?

Questions

5 What are the components of a marketing research proposal?

6 How may a marketing researcher be creative in interpreting a research brief and developing a research proposal?

7 What is the significance of the 'background' section of a research brief and research proposal?

8 Describe some of the reasons why management are often not clear about the 'real' problem they face.

9 What interrelated events occur in the environmental context of a research problem?

10 What are some differences between a marketing decision problem and a marketing research problem?

11 Describe the factors that may affect the approach to a research problem.

12 What is the role of theory in the development of a research approach?

13 What are the most common forms of analytical models?

14 What are the differences between research questions and hypotheses?

15 Is it necessary for every research project to have a set of hypotheses? Why or why not?

Exercises

1 Imagine that you are the Marketing Director of KLM airlines.

   a Make a list of potential marketing objectives whose fulfilment could improve the performance of KLM.

   b Select what you feel would be the most important marketing objective. Develop a set of marketing research objectives that you consider would support the decisions needed to fulfil that marketing objective

2 You are a consultant to the Ford Premier Automotive Group, working on a project for Aston Martin.

   a Use online databases to compile a list of articles related to the Ford Premier Automotive Group, Aston Martin and the global high-performance luxury car market in the past year.

   b Visit the Aston Martin and Ferrari websites and evaluate the extent of competitive information available at each.

   c Based upon the information collected from a and b, write a report on the environmental context surrounding Aston Martin.

3 Visit the websites of competing mobile phone manufacturers and/or their distributors (Motorola, Nokia and Siemens). Determine the factors of choice criteria used by consumers in selecting a mobile phone. Evaluate the extent to which there are different sets of choice criteria used by one company, e.g. Siemens, to target specific consumer segments.

4 Select any 'Premier League' football club in a country of your choice. Using secondary data sources, obtain information on the annual sales of official club merchandise and the 'industry' (your definition of this) sales over the last five years. Use a spreadsheet package to analyse this information and develop a graphical model relating the club's sales to the industry's sales.

5 In a small group discuss the following issues: 'Is it feasible that marketing decision-makers may not conceive of or be able to express the nature of decision support they need? What are the implications of such a possibility in the development of research proposals?' And 'From where may theory emerge to ground applied marketing research and what may be the relative worth of the source of theories used by marketing researchers?'

Video Case Exercise: Burke Inc.

Burke describe how, beyond just collecting marketing research data, they help to diagnose problems.
They describe how they engage with clients to help define the marketing research problem to be studied.
What barriers may prevent them being able to engage with clients in the way they describe the process?

video case

download from
www.pearsoned.co.uk/
malhotra_euro

Notes

1 Carey, G., Zhao, X., Chiaramonte, J. and Eden, D., 'Is there a global village for our future generation? Talking to 7–12-year-olds around the world', *Marketing and Research Today* (February 1997), 12.

2 Sheth, J.N. and Sisodia, R.S., 'Marketing productivity: issues and analysis', *Journal of Business Research* 55, (5) (May 2002), A9; Butler, P., 'Marketing problem: from analysis to decision', *Marketing Intelligence & Planning* 12 (2) (1994), 4–12.

3 Ingledew, S., 'How to bait the interview hook for those Top 1000 big fish', *ResearchPlus* (October 1996), 4.

4 Greenhalgh, C., 'How should we initiate effective research?', The Market Research Society Conference, 1983.

5 Brenner, M. and Miln, D., 'In search of a signature', *Research* (November 2004), 23.

6 Clemens, J., 'Some dos and don'ts of pan-European research', *ResearchPlus* (November 1996), 4.

7 Marshall, G.W., 'Selection decision making by sales managers and human resource managers: decision impact, decision frame and time of valuation', *Journal of Personal Selling and Sales Management* (Winter 2001), 19–28; Wierenga, B. and van Bruggen, G.H., 'The integration of marketing problem solving modes and marketing management support systems', *Journal of Marketing* 61 (3) (July 1997), 21–37.

8 Anon., 'How to decide who should get what data', *HR Focus* (May 2001), 7; Cronin, M.J., 'Using the web to push key data to decision makers', *Fortune* 36 (6) (29 September 1997), 254.

9 Morgan, N.A., 'Marketing productivity, marketing audits, and systems for marketing performance assessment: integrating multiple perspectives', *Journal of Business Research* 55, (5) (May 2002), 363; Merrilyn, A.T., 'Quick marketing audit', *Law Practice Management* 23 (6) (September 1997), 18, 63; Berry, L.L., Conant, J.S. and Parasuraman, A., 'A framework for conducting a services marketing audit', *Journal of the Academy of Marketing Science* 19 (Summer 1991), 255–258; Ackoff, R.L., *Scientific Method* (New York: Wiley, 1961), 71; Ackoff, R.L., *The Art of Problem Solving* (New York: Wiley, 1978).

10 Charan, R., 'Conquering a culture of indecision', *Harvard Business Review* (April 2001), 74; Saviour, L.S., Nwachukwu and Vitell, S.J. Jr, 'The influence of corporate culture on managerial ethical judgments', *Journal of Business Ethics* 16 (8) (June 1997), 757–776.

11 Malo, K., 'Corporate strategy requires market research', *Marketing News* 36 (2) (21 January 2001), 14; Winett, R., 'Guerilla marketing research outsmarts the competition', *Marketing News* 29 (1) (January 1995), 33; Armstrong, J.S., 'Prediction of consumer behaviour by experts and novices', *Journal of Consumer Research* 18 (September 1991), 251–256.

12 Barrett, P., 'Abroad minded', *Marketing* (24 April 1997), 20.

13 Thieme, R.J., 'Artificial neural network decision support systems for the new product development project selection', *Journal of Marketing Research* (November 2000), 499–507; Heyl, S.M., 'Decision matrix points the way to better research ROI', *Marketing News* 21 (19) (15 September 1997), 18, 30.

14 Shannon, J., 'Net has yet to prove its value', *Marketing Week* (26 June 1997), 25.

15 www.tennis.com/external.cfm?articleid=2141 13 January 2002.

16 Potter, G., *The Philosophy of Social Science: New Perspectives* (Harlow: Pearson, 2000), 242.

17 Havermans, J., 'Bridging the gap between science and the timely result', *Research World* (July/August 2004), 18–20.

18 Havermans, J., 'Innovation or hype?' *Research World* (June 2005), 13–15.

19 Lilien, G.L., 'Bridging the marketing theory', *Journal of Business Research* 55 (2) (February 2002), 111; Hunt, S.D., 'For reason and realism in marketing', *Journal of Marketing* 56 (April 1992), 89–102; Hunt; S.D. 'Truth in marketing theory and research', *Journal of Marketing* 54 (July 1990), 1–15.

20 Gordon, W., 'Brands are recorded in our brains', *Research* (September 2004), 12.

21 For an illustration of a graphical model of software piracy, see Figure 1 of Givon, M., Mahajan, V. and Muller, E., 'Software piracy: estimation of lost sales and the impact on software diffusion', *Journal of Marketing* 59 (January 1995), 29–37.

22 For an example of developing a theoretical framework and a mathematical model based on it, see Miller, C.M., McIntyre, S.H. and Mantrala, M.K., 'Toward formalizing fashion theory', *Journal of Marketing Research* 30 (May 1993), 142–157.

23 Malhotra, N.K. and Wu, L., 'Decision models and descriptive models: complementary roles', *Marketing Research* 13 (4) (December 2001), 43–44; Leefang, P.S.H., 'Building models for marketing decisions: past, present and future', *International Journal of Research in Marketing* (September 2000) 105.

24 For an example of hypothesis formulation, see Smith, N.C. and Cooper-Martin, E., 'Ethics and target marketing: the role of product harm and consumer vulnerability', *Journal of Marketing* 61 (July 1997), 1–20.

25 Kerlinger, F.N., *Foundations of Behavioral Research*, 3rd edn (New York: Holt, Rinehart & Winston, 1986). See pp. 17–20 for a detailed discussion of the characteristics and role of hypotheses in research. For an alternative view, see Lawrence, R.J., 'To hypothesize or not to hypothesize? The correct "approach" to survey research', *Journal of the Market Research Society* 24 (October 1982), 335–343. For an example of model development and hypothesis formulation see Bitner, M.J., 'Servicescapes: the impact of physical surroundings on customers and employees', *Journal of Marketing* 56 (April 1992), 57–71.

26 The integrated role of theory, models, research questions and hypotheses in marketing research can be seen in Nygaard, A. and Dahlstrom, R., 'Role stress and effectiveness in horizontal alliances', *Journal of Marketing*, 66 (April 2002), 61–82; Nunes, J.C., 'A cognitive model of people's usage estimations', *Journal of marketing Research*, 37 (4) (November 2000), 397–409.

27 Reyes, S., 'Heinz builds on EZ squirt success with adult skewing kick'rs line', *Brandweek*, 43 (3) (21 January 2002), 4; Judann, D., 'Why Heinz went sour in Brazil', *Advertising Age* (5 December 1988).

28 Westhead, P., 'International market selection strategies selected by "Micro" and "Small" firms', *Omega* 30 (1) (February 2002), 51; Orpen, C., 'Developing international marketing strategies in small companies', *Journal of International Marketing & Marketing Research* 20 (2) (June 1995), 89–96; Douglas, S.P. and Craig, C.S., *International Marketing Research* (Englewood Cliffs, NJ: Prentice Hall, 1983).

29 Singh, S., 'Unilever picks global brand director for Surf', *Marketing Week* (7 March 2002), 7; Kilbum, D., 'Unilever struggles with Surf in Japan', *Advertising Age* (6 May 1991).

30 Brans, J.P., 'Ethics and decisions', *European Journal of Operations Research* 136 (2) (16 January 2002), 340; Laczniak, G.R. and Murphy, P.E., *Ethical Marketing Decisions, the Higher Road* (Boston: Allyn & Bacon, 1993), 64.

Source: © Getty Images

3

Research design

There are a huge array of alternative research designs that can satisfy research objectives. The key is to create a design that enhances the value of the information obtained, whilst reducing the cost of obtaining it.

Objectives

After reading this chapter, you should be able to:

1 define research design, classify various research designs, and explain the differences between exploratory and conclusive research designs;

2 compare and contrast the basic research designs: exploratory, descriptive and causal;

3 understand how respondents or the subjects of research design affect research design choices;

4 describe the major sources of errors in a research design, including random sampling error and the various sources of non-sampling error;

5 explain research design formulation in international marketing research;

6 understand the ethical issues and conflicts that arise in formulating a research design

7 appreciate the ways in which the Internet can support the process of research design.

| STAGE 1 Problem definition | STAGE 2 Research approach developed | STAGE 3 Research design developed | STAGE 4 Fieldwork or data collection | STAGE 5 Data preparation and analysis | STAGE 6 Report preparation and presentation |

Overview

Chapter 2 discussed how to define a marketing research problem and develop a suitable approach. These first two steps are critical to the success of the whole marketing research project. Once they have been completed, attention should be devoted to designing the formal research project by formulating a detailed research design (as a reminder, see Figure 2.3).

This chapter defines and classifies research designs. We examine the nature of research design from the perspectives of decision-makers and respondents. Two major types of research design are then discussed: exploratory and conclusive. We further classify conclusive research designs as descriptive or causal and discuss both types in detail. The differences between the two types of descriptive designs are then considered (cross-sectional and longitudinal) and sources of errors are identified. The special considerations involved in formulating research designs in international marketing research are discussed. Several ethical issues that arise at this stage of the marketing research process are considered. A better appreciation of the concepts presented in this chapter can be gained by first considering the following example, which illustrates the use of a number of interrelated techniques to build a research design.

Example | **Getting to know you[1]**

Building a relationship with consumers is a challenge facing all organisations, but particularly so in the case of 'emergent drinkers', those of legal drinking age up to 25. Allied Domecq Spirits and Wines (ADSW) recognised the danger of being distanced from this crucial group, particularly across geographical markets. ADSW worked with Pegram Walters International (PWi) on a project that went far beyond an exploration of the current usage and attitudes towards spirits. The objectives of the project encompassed an exploration of the target groups' personal values, their feelings about their lives, their universe, their hopes and dreams.

There were three stages to the research design. In the first stage the researchers conducted one-hour depth interviews. There were three clear objectives for this stage: to understand personal viewpoints on marketing and lifestyle issues; to clarify and/or narrow down topics for subsequent exploration; and to recruit appropriate 'information gatherers'. From this stage hypotheses were formulated on issues such as how respondents saw themselves and their future, relationships, self-discovery and opting in or out of the system.

In the second stage, from 20 depth interviews, 10 respondents were retained as 'information gatherers'. 'Leading-edge' bars were rented out and 50 adult emergent drinkers were invited to participate in workshops. Given a task guideline, the information gatherers led discussions. As an additional record, the workshops were video recorded. The participants felt comfortable within their peer group and, in the more natural bar environment, fed back real, relevant and honest information.

The third stage occurred on the night following the workshops. Focus groups were used, made up of the 'information gatherers'. They discussed what happened in the workshops and their interpretation of what it actually meant.

In order to ensure that the information remained topical, useful and easily accessible, it was felt important to create a vehicle for an ongoing communication and dialogue with the target market. To achieve this, a high-impact 'magazine' was created to bring the research to life after the presentation of findings. This was referred to as a magazine and not a research report to reflect the lifestyle of the consumer group in question: it contained images, layouts and fonts typically associated with the generation.

The above example illustrates a very creative and useful exploratory research design. As a research design it worked well in that it achieved a balance of the needs and expectations of marketing decision-makers and respondents. Decision-makers helped to set clear research objectives based upon the gaps in their knowledge of the target market. Respondents related well to the issues posed to them, in a context and environment that was comfortable to them. An understanding of the fundamentals of research design, its components, and the trade-offs between the parties involved in making the design work, enabled the researchers to formulate the most appropriate design for the problem at hand.

Research design definition

Research design
A framework or blueprint for conducting the marketing research project. It specifies the details of the procedures necessary for obtaining the information needed to structure or solve marketing research problems.

A **research design** is a framework or blueprint for conducting a marketing research project. It details the procedures necessary for obtaining the information needed to structure or solve marketing research problems. Although a broad approach to the problem has already been developed, the research design specifies the details – the practical aspects – of implementing that approach. A research design lays the foundation for conducting the project. A good research design will ensure that the marketing research project is conducted effectively and efficiently. Typically, a research design involves the following components or tasks, which will be discussed in detail in various chapters:

1 Define the information needed (Chapter 2).
2 Decide whether the overall design is to be exploratory, descriptive or causal (Chapter 3).
3 Design the sequence of techniques of understanding and/or measurement (Chapters 4 to 12).
4 Construct and pretest an appropriate form for data collection or questionnaire (Chapters 7, 8 and 13).
5 Specify the qualitative and/or quantitative sampling process and sample size (Chapters 6, 14 and 15).
6 Develop a plan of qualitative and/or quantitative data analysis (Chapters 9 and 17).

In formulating a research design, the researcher has to balance the perspectives of marketing decision-makers and target respondents. From their education and experience, marketing decision-makers may have certain techniques that they believe to be the most effective and in which they subsequently have more confidence. There is no problem with this, providing the technique is the best means to measure or understand the issue under investigation, from the perspective of respondents. In the example at the start of this chapter, decision-makers had confidence in the qualitative techniques and the data generated. The techniques worked well with the respondents, drawing out a rich picture of respondent behaviour, lifestyle and aspirations. However, should the decision-makers feel that survey techniques are the most effective, giving them the most confidence to support their decisions, the researchers may face a dilemma. If they use survey techniques they may find that respondents may have a different relationship with interviewers, do not reflect in the same manner and ultimately do not reveal so much. Thus, research design involves the researchers developing an understanding of the type of data decision-makers have confidence in, plus an understanding of how respondents may respond to different techniques. The first part of this balancing act involves understanding research design from the decision-makers' perspective; the second part involves understanding the respondents' perspective.

Research design from the decision-makers' perspective

Marketing decision-makers seek support from marketing researchers that is of practical relevance to the decisions they face. To give practical support, decision-makers expect information that is:

- *Accurate*, i.e. the most valid representation of the phenomena under investigation, that has come from the most reliable or consistent form of measurement or understanding, that is sufficiently sensitive to the important differences in individuals being measured or understood. Combining these three criteria refers to the degree to which information may be deemed as 'accurate'.
- *Current*, i.e. as up to date as possible. This is particularly important where consumer attitudes, lifestyle or behaviour change rapidly, perhaps due to rapid technology changes or new product offerings in a highly competitive market.
- *Sufficient*, i.e. the completeness or clarity of a 'picture' that reflects the characteristics of the marketing problem the decision-makers face.
- *Available*, i.e. that access to the relevant information can be made when a decision is imminent. This is particularly important where competitive activity forces the decision-maker into making a rapid response.
- *Relevant*, i.e. that the support given 'makes sense' to decision-makers. In very general terms, decision-makers may criticise qualitative techniques for being biased and unrepresentative and quantitative techniques for lacking depth and a holistic perspective. Ideally, whichever technique is adopted, decision-makers should be aware of the benefits, limitations and even alternatives. With this awareness they can use the findings with confidence to build upon their existing experiences and knowledge.

Generating information that fulfils all the above characteristics is extremely difficult, if not impossible to achieve in marketing research. The evaluation of sources of error, presented later in this chapter, and the restrictions of budget and timescales mean that this list represents 'ideals'. Realistically, trade-offs must be made among the above characteristics. Within the first characteristic of accuracy there are further trade-offs which are primarily caused by what the marketing researcher is attempting to measure or understand:[2]

1 The subject of investigation is usually human.
2 The process of measuring or observing humans may cause them to change.
3 It is difficult to assess the effect of extraneous variables in marketing experiments and thus their applications are limited.

Given the complexity of the subjects under study, the context or environment in which measurements are taken, and the skills required to perform and interpret measurements, it is difficult (if not impossible) to gain completely objective and accurate measurements. Of all the potential trade-offs, if one were to remove *relevance* then the whole rationale of supporting the marketing decision-maker would be removed. Therefore this characteristic can never be compromised.

Relevance embraces, *inter alia*, the ability to plan and forecast from research findings, to be able to distinguish real differences in consumer traits, and to know that characteristics are representative of groups of individuals. With relevant information such as this, the decision-maker can build up a stronger understanding or awareness of markets and the forces that shape them. In building up this understanding, the decision-maker cannot turn to a single technique or even body of techniques that may be deemed 'ideal' in ensuring that information is relevant. In different types of decision-making scenarios, different techniques will offer the best support for that decision-maker. Establishing the best form of support is the essence of research design.

A fundamental starting point in deciding an appropriate design is viewing the process from the point of view of the potential subject or respondent to a marketing research study.

Research design from the respondents' perspective

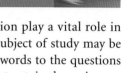

The potential respondents to any marketing research investigation play a vital role in deciding which research design will actually work in practice. A subject of study may be complex and need time for respondents to reflect upon and put words to the questions posed. Certain methods are more likely to build up a rapport and trust, in these circumstances putting the respondents in the right frame of mind, and getting them to respond in a full and honest manner. Figure 3.1 is a framework that serves to remind how respondents may be accessed, and what kinds of response may be generated.[3]

In Figure 3.1 the box under the heading 'Layers of response from respondents' represents how respondents may react to questions posed to them. In the first layer of 'Spontaneous, Reasoned, Conventional' are questions that respondents can express a view about quickly, and that are simple for them to reflect upon, relating to common everyday occurrences that are at the forefront of their minds. In such circumstances, simple struc-

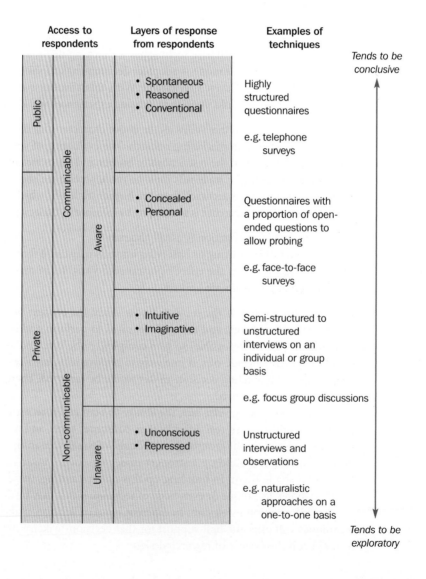

**Figure 3.1
Responses to
interviewing**

tured questioning (or self-reporting) in a standardised manner is possible. Further, the same procedure can be conducted in a consistent manner to a whole array of 'types' of respondent such as age groups, social class and intellectual levels. For example, if questions were posed on which newspapers someone reads, it is a reasonable assumption that respondents are aware of the title(s), the title(s) can be communicated and the topic is not a sensitive issue. In these circumstances, where answers to questions on reading habits are relatively easy to access and respond to, highly structured questionnaires are appropriate. Clearly, in such situations, quantitative techniques are applicable that allow very detailed descriptions or experiments to be made.

Progressing down Figure 3.1, at the second level are questions that are more personal and more sensitive. There are two characteristics that can turn otherwise mundane topics into sensitive ones.[4] The first involves any private, sacred or stressful aspect of a respondent's life. The second is the real or perceived stigma associated with specific thoughts or actions. A great amount of business-to-business research can be added to these in terms of commercially sensitive information. Again, structured questionnaires can measure the relevant issues but an amount of rapport may be needed to induce respondents to trust the interviewer and reveal their 'more personal' attitudes and behaviour. Where the presence of the interviewer causes discomfort or bias, the method of audio-computer-assisted-self-interviewing may be used.[5] This technique combines the higher response rates of personal interviews with the privacy of self-administered questionnaires.

At the third level are questions that require respondents to be creative. For example, if respondents were to be asked about their attitudes and behaviour towards eating yogurt, this could be done in a very structured manner. Questions could be set to determine when it was eaten, favourite flavours and brands, where it was bought, how much was spent, etc. The same can be said of alcohol consumption, though this could well be a sensitive issue for many respondents. Now imagine a new product idea that mixes yogurt and alcohol. What combinations of alcohol and yogurt would work, and what types of consumer would be attracted to them? Would they be a dessert liqueur such as Baileys Irish Cream or frozen yogurt to compete with the Häagen Dazs luxury ice creams? Would champagne, advocaat, whisky or beer be the best alcoholic ingredient? Should any fruits be added? Individually? Forest fruits? Tropical fruits? How would the product be packaged? What name would best suit it? What price level would it sell at? On what occasions would it be consumed?

Answering these questions demands a great amount of creativity and imagination. It demands that respondents reflect upon ideas, can play with ideas and words and dig deep to draw out ideas in a relaxed manner. Structured questionnaires cannot do this; such a scenario would work best with the use of focus groups.

At the fourth level may be questions that respondents may not be able to conceptualise, never mind be willing to express what they feel about a particular issue. Consumers may absorb masses of marketing related stimuli, react to them and 'intend' to behave without really knowing why or even being aware of the true drivers of their intentions or behaviour.[6] An example may be trying to understand the childhood influences of family and friends on an individual's perception and loyalty to brands of washing-up liquid. Another example may be understanding the image consumers have of themselves and an image they wish to portray by spending €20,000 on a Rolex wristwatch. Respondents do not normally have to think through such issues or articulate them, until a marketing researcher comes along!

There is an implicit assumption in research that people carry attitudes around in their head that determine their buying behaviour. Most of the time, we don't give much thought to the burger we've eaten or even the flight we've made. Our natural inclination is to be polite and cooperative. If a researcher asks us to give an opinion we will do our best to formulate one on the spot.[7]

Source: © Alamy

In circumstances where the marketing researcher is digging deep into topics that respondents do not normally think about or articulate, polite responses to questions may be very misleading. The characteristics of the individual respondent may determine what is the best way to probe and elicit appropriate responses. Nothing is standardised or consistent in these circumstances, the researchers having to shape the questions, probes and observations as they see fit in each interview.

As well as understanding how respondents may react to particular issues, researchers should also understand how the context or environment may affect respondents. The following example sets out aspects about the meaning of 'context' when conducting interviews. Sarah Brown, a senior marketing research executive, reveals a variety of methods that help to create an environment that allows respondents to feel and think naturally.

Example **Keeping it real[8]**

One of the most frequent criticisms of focus groups and depth interviews is that they are conducted in artificial environments, placing respondents in synthetic situations and drawing out unnatural responses.

Home turf

To understand specialised subpopulations, e.g. video gamers, horse lovers, or jobseekers, it is vital to reach people in the context of their specialisation. Researchers should visit the places where people live this part of their identity; read their newsletters; visit their chat rooms; and attend their conventions. Talk to those who deal with the subpopulation on a regular basis. To understand students, interview teachers; to understand drivers, talk to traffic police; and so on.

Object poverty

Objects or pictures from daily life are powerful stimulants for emotions and memories and can trigger respondents to recall their behaviour with greater clarity. Sometimes how we think we behave differs from how we really behave, and working with objects helps to keep respondents grounded and personally engaged.

Act natural

On-location groups or depth interviews, whether in a store, respondents' homes, or another 'real' location in which the behaviour of interest takes place, are an effective way to keep respondents relaxed, lively and as natural as possible.

Networking

This is often used to research young people to reflect their highly social character. Respondents work in pairs and act as consultants, interviewing members of their friendship peer group. Researchers thereby understand both the individual and the individual in his or her social context, accessing the views and behaviours of a range of people through a single respondent.

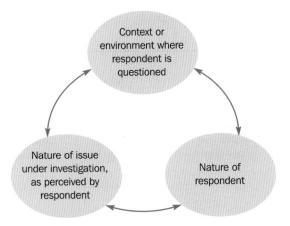

Figure 3.2
Understanding respondents – to help choose optimum research techniques

As a further example, return to the first level of Figure 3.1, where respondents may be more relaxed and feel in control if they can answer the set questions about their newspaper reading habits on the Internet rather than on the street. In the example at the start of this chapter that explored the hopes and dreams of 'emergent drinkers', techniques were used at the third and fourth levels of Figure 3.1. The context of the interviews was in 'leading-edge bars'. This context could have helped the target respondents to relax, to develop a better rapport with interviewers and other respondents, and to think more about the issues and express their feelings more clearly. If the interviews were conducted over the Internet, the same levels of relaxation and rapport would not work. If the interviews were targeted at older respondents, they would have felt very self-conscious in 'leading-edge bars', which may restrict their responses. Researchers therefore must understand characteristics of respondents, how they react to particular issues and how they react in different contexts or environments. These factors are illustrated in Figure 3.2, which acts as a reminder of the understanding of respondents that researchers must develop, in order to choose and apply the best research technique.

Research design classification

Exploratory research
A research design characterised by a flexible and evolving approach to understand marketing phenomena that are inherently difficult to measure.

Conclusive research
A research design characterised by the measurement of clearly defined marketing phenomena.

Research designs may be broadly classified as exploratory or conclusive (see Figure 3.3). The differences between **exploratory research** and **conclusive research** are summarised in Table 3.1.

The primary objective of exploratory research is to provide insights into and an understanding of marketing phenomena.[9] It is used in instances where the subject of the study cannot be measured in a quantitative manner or where the process of measurement cannot realistically represent particular qualities. For example, if a researcher was trying to understand what 'atmosphere' meant in a restaurant, exploratory research may help to establish all the appropriate variables and how they connected together. What role did music play? What type of music? How loud? What types of furniture? What colours and textures? What types of lighting? What architectural features? This list could go on to consider what 'atmosphere' may mean in the context of a restaurant experience for particular types of consumer. 'Atmosphere' may not be measurable from the respondent's perspective. From the perspective of the creative director in an advertising agency, quantitative measurements of the individual components of 'atmosphere' may not create the holistic feel of a restaurant in a manner the creative director can relate to.

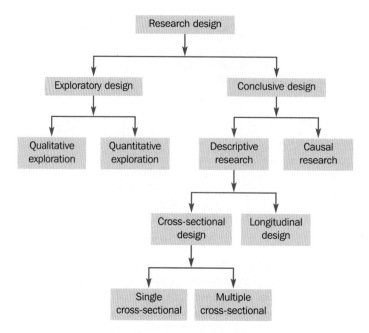

Figure 3.3
A classification of
marketing research
designs

Table 3.1 Differences between exploratory and conclusive research

	Exploratory	Conclusive
Objectives	To provide insights and understanding of the nature of marketing phenomena To understand	To test specific hypotheses and examine relationships To measure
Characteristics	Information needed may be loosely defined Research process is flexible, unstructured and may evolve Samples are small Data analysis can be qualitative or quantitative	Information needed is clearly defined Research process is formal and structured Sample is large and aims to be representative Data analysis is quantitative
Findings/results	Can be used in their own right May feed into conclusive research May illuminate specific conclusive findings	Can be used in their own right May feed into exploratory research May set a context to exploratory findings
Methods	Expert surveys Pilot surveys Secondary data Qualitative interviews Unstructured observations Quantitative exploratory multivariate methods	Surveys Secondary data Databases Panels Structured observations Experiments

Exploratory research may also be used in cases where you must define the problem more precisely, identify relevant courses of action, or gain additional insights before going on to confirm findings using a conclusive design. The following example of researching computer games players illustrates the connection between exploratory and conclusive designs.

Example   Greedy Gamers[10]

Future Publishing, a leading computer games magazine publisher, wanted to identify the role that the specialist games press plays within the gaming community. In particular, it was interested in the extent to which games magazines can both influence the decision-making process for games purchases and generate positive word-of-mouth recommendations. Future asked Continental Research to conduct the research. Qualitative research was initially conducted with active gamers. It quickly became clear that gaming is a very competitive activity for some, and it was therefore important to understand the difference between reported gaming activity and success, and reality. For example, there was talk of dusk-til-dawn gaming sessions; of the 'friend' who could complete four games within one day; and the teenager whose mum had to write him a sick note because his thumbs ached and his vision went blurry after a heavy gaming session! The key role of the qualitative research in all of this was to identify different gaming typologies in terms of not only their gaming activity, but also their communication role in the gaming fraternity.

For example: **Greedy Gamers** *eat and breathe gaming (some of them quite literally, as they would eat while playing a game one-handed). For them, it was a key topic of conversation with everyone that they came into contact with.*

Once different typologies had been identified, Continental was able to hypothesise about the likelihood of communication between different types of gamers. For the quantitative research stage of the project, Continental spoke to a representative sample of active gamers aged between 10 and 35. Continental's Grapevine matrix analysis tool enabled it to use the typologies in its questionnaire. The matrix identified the extent to which readers of the gaming press (whether exposed to adverts, reviews, previews or demo discs) were transmitting knowledge to other gamers.

The research findings gave publishers and editors a greater insight into their readers and core target market. It was also of great use to advertising sales, providing a better understanding of how advertising within Future's magazines works.

In this example, the information needed was loosely defined at an exploratory stage, using research questions rather than specific hypotheses or actual measurements. The research process that was initially adopted can be characterised as flexible, loosely structured and, in some circumstances, evolutionary in nature.

In an example of a flexible, loosely structured and evolutionary approach, consider conducting personal interviews with industry experts. The sample, selected to generate maximum insight, is small and non-representative. However, the emphasis in the sampling procedure is focused upon 'quality' individuals who are willing to open up, use their imagination, be creative and reveal perhaps sensitive thoughts and behaviour. 'Quality' also may emerge from their level of expertise; for example, there may only be a small population of chief executives in airline companies in Europe. If a small sample of, say, six chief executives from the largest and fastest developing airlines allowed access to a marketing researcher and revealed their attitudes and behaviour, insights may be gained that no conclusive study could achieve. By being flexible in the issues to discuss, loosely structured in how probes and additional issues emerge, and evolutionary in the nature of who to talk to and the best context in which to gain their confidence and get them to express what they really feel, an exploratory design can be very beneficial.

There is an exception to exploratory designs being built around qualitative techniques. There are examples of quantitative findings being used for exploratory purposes. For example, within a survey that examines specific research questions and hypotheses lies the opportunity to examine additional connections between questions that had not been initially considered. Simple correlations through to multivariate techniques that explore potential connections between questions may be conducted; this process is known as data mining (examined in more detail in Chapter 5). In essence, data mining searches for significant connections or patterns in a dataset that a researcher or decision-maker may be unaware of.

To summarise, exploratory research is meaningful in any situation where the researcher does not have enough understanding to proceed with the research project. Exploratory research is characterised by flexibility and versatility with respect to the methods, because formal research protocols and procedures are not employed. It rarely involves structured questionnaires, large samples and probability sampling plans. Rather, researchers are alert to new ideas and insights as they proceed. Once a new idea or insight is discovered, they may redirect their exploration in that direction. That new direction is pursued until its possibilities are exhausted or another direction is found. For this reason, the focus of the investigation may shift constantly as new insights are discovered. Thus, the creativity and ingenuity of the researcher play a major role in exploratory research. Exploratory research can be used for any of the purposes listed in Table 3.2.

Table 3.2 A summary of the uses of exploratory research designs

1	To obtain some background information where absolutely nothing is known about the problem area
2	To define problem areas fully and to formulate hypotheses for further investigation and/or quantification
3	To identify and explore concepts in the development of new product or forms of marketing communications
4	During a preliminary screening process such as in new product development, in order to reduce a large number of possible projects to a smaller number of probable ones
5	To identify relevant or salient behaviour patterns, beliefs, opinions, attitudes, motivations, etc., and to develop structures of these constructs
6	To develop an understanding of the structure of beliefs and attitudes in order to aid the interpretation of data structures in multivariate data analyses
7	To explore the reasons that lie behind the statistical differences between groups that may emerge from secondary data or surveys
8	To explore sensitive or personally embarrassing issues from the respondents' and/or the interviewer's perspective
9	To explore issues that respondents may hold deeply, that are difficult for them to rationalise and that they may find difficult to articulate
10	To 'data-mine' or explore quantitative data to reveal hitherto unknown connections between different measured variables

The objective of conclusive research is to describe specific phenomena, to test specific hypotheses and to examine specific relationships. This requires that the information needed is clearly specified.[11] Conclusive research is typically more formal and structured than exploratory research. It is based on large, representative samples, and the data obtained are subjected to quantitative analysis. Conclusive research can be used for any of the purposes listed in Table 3.3.

As shown in Figure 3.3, conclusive research designs may be either descriptive or causal, and descriptive research designs may be either cross-sectional or longitudinal. Each of these classifications is discussed further, beginning with descriptive research.

Table 3.3 A summary of the uses of conclusive research designs

1	To describe the characteristics of relevant groups, such as consumers, salespeople, organisations, or market areas
2	To estimate the percentage in a specified population exhibiting a certain form of behaviour
3	To count the frequency of events, especially in the patterns of consumer behaviour
4	To measure marketing phenomena to represent larger populations or target markets
5	To be able to integrate findings from different sources in a consistent manner, especially in the use of marketing information systems and decision support systems
6	To determine the perceptions of product or service characteristics
7	To compare findings over time that allow changes in the phenomena to be measured
8	To measure marketing phenomena in a consistent and universal manner
9	To determine the degree to which marketing variables are associated
10	To make specific predictions

Descriptive research

Descriptive research
A type of conclusive research that has as its major objective the description of something, usually market characteristics or functions.

As the name implies, the major objective of **descriptive research** is to describe something, usually market characteristics or functions.[12] A major difference between exploratory and descriptive research is that descriptive research is characterised by the prior formulation of specific research questions and hypotheses. Thus, the information needed is clearly defined. As a result, descriptive research is preplanned and structured. It is typically based on large representative samples. The following example illustrates the use of descriptive research in an image study that determines consumer perceptions of Flora and its products.

 Sports Marketing Surveys

Flora London Marathon 2004

Flora has sponsored the London Marathon (**http://www.london-marathon.co.uk/**) for a number of years. Flora wished to evaluate the impact of its sponsorship investment and employed Sports Marketing Surveys to measure the impact of Flora's brand on TV, evaluating the nature of the Marathon TV audience and the exposure of its brand to this audience. In conjunction with this work, Flora wished to measure characteristics of its image. In order to measure this image Sports Marketing Surveys conducted 225 interviews with 18–70 year olds, immediately after the Marathon. These interviews were conducted on a face-to-face basis in the homes of respondents, allowing their interviewers to present visual prompts.

A descriptive research design specifies the methods for selecting the sources of information and for collecting data from those sources.

Examples of descriptive studies in marketing research are as follows:

- Market studies describing the size of the market, buying power of the consumers, availability of distributors, and consumer profiles.
- Market share studies determining the proportion of total sales received by a company and its competitors.
- Sales analysis studies describing sales by geographic region, product line, type of account and size of account.
- Image studies determining consumer perceptions of the firm and its products.

- Product usage studies describing consumption patterns.
- Distribution studies determining traffic flow patterns and the number and location of distributors.
- Pricing studies describing the range and frequency of price changes and probable consumer response to proposed price changes.
- Advertising studies describing media consumption habits and audience profiles for specific TV programmes and magazines.

These examples demonstrate the range and diversity of descriptive research studies. Descriptive research can be further classified into cross-sectional and longitudinal research (Figure 3.3).

Cross-sectional designs

The cross-sectional study is the most frequently used descriptive design in marketing research. **Cross-sectional designs** involve the collection of information from any given sample of population elements only once. They may be either single cross-sectional or multiple cross-sectional (Figure 3.3). In **single cross-sectional designs**, only one sample of respondents is drawn from the target population, and information is obtained from this sample only once. These designs are also called sample survey research designs. In **multiple cross-sectional designs,** there are two or more samples of respondents, and information from each sample is obtained only once. Often, information from different samples is obtained at different times. The following examples illustrate single and multiple cross-sectional designs respectively.

Cross-sectional design
A type of research design involving the collection of information from any given sample of population elements only once.

Single cross-sectional design
A cross-sectional design in which one sample of respondents is drawn from the target population and information is obtained from this sample once.

Multiple cross-sectional design
A cross-sectional design in which there are two or more samples of respondents, and information from each sample is obtained only once.

Example | **Designing coupons from cross-sections[13]**

A cross-sectional study based on a single survey was conducted to determine the effectiveness of sales promotion coupons in stimulating sales, as well as to assess coupon user and non-user profiles. The data were collected from 8,000 households. The results showed that 31% of all coupon-redeeming households accounted for 72% of all redemptions. Demographically, heavy coupon redeemers were large households with children and annual incomes exceeding €30,000, with female heads of household aged 35–54 who worked part-time. Light users of coupons were smaller households with female heads who were younger and worked full-time. Such information was useful to consumer products firms like Procter & Gamble that rely heavily on coupon promotion, as it enabled the company to target its promotions to heavy coupon redeemers.

Example | **Chase and Grabbits multiply like rabbits[14]**

Eating behaviour trends were examined in a marketing research project commissioned by the Pillsbury Company. This project involved data from food diaries collected over three time waves. Each wave had a different sample of 1,000 households for a total sample size of 3,000 in the multiple cross-sectional design. Based on an analysis of eating patterns, the market was divided into five segments: Chase and Grabbits, Functional Feeders, Down Home Stokers, Careful Cooks and Happy Cookers. The changes in composition of these segments were examined over time. For example, the Chase and Grabbits experienced the biggest increase over the 15-year period (+136%). Currently, this group represents 26% of the total sample. The group's desire for more convenience also increased over time. Says one Chase and Grabbit, 'Someday all you'll have to do is take a pill and it'll give you everything you need.' This information enabled the Pillsbury Company to target different products for different segments. For example, the Chase and Grabbit segment represented a prime segment for prepared foods and TV dinners.

The survey of coupon use, a single cross-sectional design, involved only one group of respondents who provided information only once. On the other hand, the Pillsbury study involved three different samples, each measured only once, with the measures obtained five years apart. Hence, the latter study illustrates a multiple cross-sectional design. A type of multiple cross-sectional design of special interest is cohort analysis.

Cohort analysis consists of a series of surveys conducted at appropriate time intervals, where the cohort serves as the basic unit of analysis. A cohort is a group of respondents who experience the same event within the same time interval.[15] For example, a birth (or age) cohort is a group of people who were born during the same time interval, such as 1951–1960. The term 'cohort analysis' refers to any study in which there are measures of some characteristics of one or more cohorts at two or more points in time.

It is unlikely that any of the individuals studied at time 1 will also be in the sample at time 2. For example, the age cohort of people between 8 and 19 years was selected, and their soft drink consumption was examined every 10 years for 30 years. In other words, every 10 years a different sample of respondents was drawn from the population of those who were then between 8 and 19 years old. This sample was drawn independently of any previous sample drawn in this study from the population of 8 to 19 years. Obviously, people who were selected once were unlikely to be included again in the same age cohort (8 to 19 years), as these people would be much older at the time of subsequent sampling. This study showed that this cohort had increased consumption of soft drinks over time. Similar findings were obtained for other age cohorts (20–29, 30–39, 40–49, and 50+). Further, the consumption of each cohort did not decrease as the cohort aged. These results are presented in Table 3.4 in which the consumption of the various age cohorts over time can be determined by reading down the diagonal. These findings contradict the common belief that the consumption of soft drinks will decline with the greying of Western economies. This common but erroneous belief has been based on single cross-sectional studies. Note that if any column of Table 3.4 is viewed in isolation (as a single cross-sectional study) the consumption of soft drinks declines with age, thus fostering the erroneous belief.[16]

Cohort analysis
A multiple cross-sectional design consisting of surveys conducted at appropriate time intervals. The cohort refers to the group of respondents who experience the same event within the same interval.

Table 3.4 Consumption of soft drinks by various age cohorts (*percentage consuming on a typical day*)

Age	1950	1960	1970	1980	
8–19	53	63	73	81	
20–29	45	61	76	76	C8
30–39	34	47	68	71	C7
40–49	23	41	59	68	C6
50+	18	29	50	52	C5
	C1	C2	C3	C4	

C1: cohort born prior to 1900	C4: cohort born 1921–1930	C7: cohort born 1951–1960
C2: cohort born 1901–1910	C5: cohort born 1931–1940	C8: cohort born 1961–1970.
C3: cohort born 1911–1920	C6: cohort born 1941–1950	

Cohort analysis is also used to predict changes in voter opinions during a political campaign. Well-known marketing researchers such as MORI or Gallup, who specialise in political opinion research, periodically question cohorts of voters (people with similar voting patterns during a given interval) about their voting preferences to predict election results. Thus, cohort analysis is an important cross-sectional design. The other type of descriptive design is longitudinal design.

Longitudinal designs

Longitudinal design
A type of research design involving a fixed sample of population elements measured repeatedly. The sample remains the same over time, thus providing a series of pictures that, when viewed together, vividly illustrate the situation and the changes that are taking place.

In **longitudinal designs**, a fixed sample (or samples) of population elements is measured repeatedly as in the following example at Ford motors.

Scores impact on margins at Ford[17]

Apart from ad hoc marketing research projects and new product development studies, Ford also runs a number of big continuous studies which are mainly company performance related. One major study measures the effectiveness of its distribution channels. Ford measures customer satisfaction in every Ford dealership in 19 European markets, in terms of both sales and after-sales performance. This covers over 5,000 dealers. Ford produces a monthly report for every dealer and it is available on a website showing the action plans that have been developed with Ford staff to remedy any problems. There is an added incentive that performance scores are keyed in on a quarterly basis, to dealer margins. It's a popular motivational tool and it works. With the help of this longitudinal study, the strength and performance of Ford's dealer network in Europe provides the company with a significant competitive advantage.

Example

A longitudinal design differs from a cross-sectional design in that the sample or samples remain the same over time. In other words, the same people are studied over time. In contrast to the typical cross-sectional design, which gives a snapshot of the variables of interest at a single point in time, a longitudinal study provides a series of 'pictures'. These 'pictures' give an in-depth view of the situation and the changes that take place over time. For example, the question 'how did the German people rate the performance of Chancellor Helmut Kohl immediately after unification of West and East Germany?' would be addressed using a cross-sectional design. A longitudinal design, however, would be used to address the question 'how did the German people change their view of Kohl's performance during his term of office?'

Panel
A sample of respondents who have agreed to provide information at specified intervals over an extended period.

Often, the term **panel** is used interchangeably with the term 'longitudinal design'. A panel consists of a sample of respondents, generally households, who have agreed to provide general or specific information at set intervals over an extended period. The emphasis of the panel is on measuring facts, e.g. who in the household bought what, where they bought it, when, and other aspects of their behaviour. Panels are really only established when observations or measurements over an extended period are meaningful. The observations are usually gathered through questionnaires such as purchase diaries or electronically, e.g. by scanning purchasing. Panels are maintained by syndicated firms, and panel members are compensated for their participation with gifts, coupons, information or cash.[18]

Access panel
A general 'pool' of individuals or households who have agreed to be available for surveys of widely varying types and topics.

Access panels are made up of a 'pool' of individuals or households who have agreed to be available for surveys of widely varying types and topics.[19] They are used to provide information for ad hoc decisions rather than for longitudinal studies, a typical use being for new product testing. A pre-recruited panel that is willing to participate makes it easier to set up the test and conduct interviews after the test. Access panels are also used to test concepts, advertising and pricing decisions.

Online consumer access panels are becoming increasingly more prevalent in marketing research. Rising rates of non-response or refusal to take part in telephone or personal interviews (to be discussed in Chapters 10 and 13) make it more difficult to recruit for a single survey. This increases the attractiveness of representative and motivated panels of pre-recruited respondents. Using the Internet enables international surveys to be conducted at relatively low cost and short time frames, adding to the attractiveness of the technique.

Data obtained from panels may provide information on market shares that are based on an extended period of time. Such data may also allow the researcher to examine changes in market share over time.[20]

Relative advantages and disadvantages of longitudinal and cross-sectional designs

The relative advantages and disadvantages of longitudinal versus cross-sectional designs are summarised in Table 3.5. A major advantage of longitudinal design over cross-sectional design is the ability to detect change as a result of repeated measurement of the same variables on the same sample.

Table 3.5 Relative advantages and disadvantages of longitudinal and cross-sectional designs

Evaluation criteria	Cross-sectional design	Longitudinal design
Detecting change	−	+
Large amount of data collection	−	+
Accuracy	−	+
Representative sampling	+	−
Response bias	+	−

Note: A + indicates a relative advantage over the other design, whereas a − indicates a relative disadvantage.

Tables 3.6 and 3.7 demonstrate how cross-sectional data can mislead researchers about changes over time. The cross-sectional data reported in Table 3.6 reveal that the purchases of Brands A, B and C remain the same in periods 1 and 2. In each survey, 20% of the respondents purchase Brand A, 30% Brand B and 50% Brand C. The longitudinal data presented in Table 3.7 show that substantial change, in the form of brand switching, occurred in the study period. For example, only 50% (100/200) of the respondents who purchased Brand A in period 1 also purchased it in period 2. The corresponding repeat purchase figures for Brands B and C are, respectively, 33.3% (100/300) and 55% (275/500). Hence, during this interval Brand C experienced the greatest loyalty and Brand B the least. Table 3.7 provides valuable information on brand loyalty and brand switching (such a table is called a turnover table or a brand-switching matrix).[21]

Longitudinal data enable researchers to examine changes in the behaviour of individual units and to link behavioural changes to marketing variables, such as changes in advertising, packaging, pricing and distribution. Since the same units are measured repeatedly, variations caused by changes in the sample are eliminated and even small variations become apparent.[22]

Another advantage of panels is that relatively large amounts of data can be collected. Because panel members are usually compensated for their participation, they are willing to participate in lengthy and demanding interviews. Yet another advantage is that panel data can be more accurate than cross-sectional data.[23] A typical cross-sectional survey

Table 3.6 Cross-sectional data may not show change

Brand purchased	Time period	
	Period 1 survey	Period 2 survey
Total surveyed	1,000	1,000
Brand A	200	200
Brand B	300	300
Brand C	500	500

Table 3.7 Longitudinal data may show substantial change

Brand purchased in period 1	Brand purchased in period 2			
	Brand A	Brand B	Brand C	Total
Total surveyed	200	300	500	1,000
Brand A	100	50	50	200
Brand B	25	100	175	300
Brand C	75	150	275	500

requires the respondent to recall past purchases and behaviour; these data can be inaccurate because of memory lapses. Panel data, which rely on continuous recording of purchases in a diary, place less reliance on the respondent's memory. A comparison of panel and cross-sectional survey estimates of retail sales indicates that panel data give more accurate estimates.[24]

The main disadvantage of panels is that they may not be representative. Non-representativeness may arise because of:

1 *Refusal to cooperate*. Many individuals or households do not wish to be bothered with the panel operation and refuse to participate. Consumer panels requiring members to keep a record of purchases have a cooperation rate of 60% or less.
2 *Mortality*. Panel members who agree to participate may subsequently drop out because they move away or lose interest. Mortality rates can be as high as 20% per year.[25]
3 *Payment*. Payment may cause certain types of people to be attracted, making the group unrepresentative of the population.

Another disadvantage of panels is response bias. New panel members are often biased in their initial responses. They tend to increase the behaviour being measured, such as food purchasing. This bias decreases as the respondent overcomes the novelty of being on the panel, so it can be reduced by initially excluding the data of new members. Seasoned panel members may also give biased responses because they believe they are experts or they want to look good or give the 'right' answer. Bias also results from boredom, fatigue and incomplete diary entries.[26] The following example from the marketing research agency Taylor Nelson Sofres (TNS) illustrates how it copes with potential panel bias.

Example   Rubbish in, rubbish out[27]

Arno Hummerston, Head of Interactive Solutions Worldwide at TNS Interactive (**www. tnsinteractive.com**), notes that companies like TNS spend a lot of money on recruiting respondents to online panels. 'If you start with rubbish you end up with rubbish.' As part of the ESOMAR Project Team on online panels, TNS has been looking at how to define a well-recruited panel. For TNS, a panel is recruited from multiple sources with the panellist's details verified. Arno argues that care must be taken to account for the differences between the type of people who take part in online panels and those who do not, to ensure that the panel is truly representative. TNS deals with this issue by running parallel studies to make sure that online panellists are responding in the same way online as they would offline. If a bias is found, the results are calibrated to account for it. In this respect, he argues, online is no different from any other form of research:

> When we interpret the data, we take all the factors into account, in the same way that any decent research company should take into account the factors and biases they encounter in telephone or face-to-face research. If you only phone people during the day for example, that will have an effect on the type of person you are speaking to. So long as you can identify the bias, you can account for it.

Causal research

Causal research
A type of conclusive research where the major objective is to obtain evidence regarding cause-and-effect (causal) relationships.

Causal research is used to obtain evidence of cause-and-effect (causal) relationships. Marketing managers continually make decisions based on assumed causal relationships. These assumptions may not be justifiable, and the validity of the causal relationships should be examined via formal research.[28] For example, the common assumption that a decrease in price will lead to increased sales and market share does not hold in certain competitive environments. Causal research is appropriate for the following purposes:

1 To understand which variables are the cause (independent variables) and which variables are the effect (dependent variables) of marketing phenomena.
2 To determine the nature of the relationship between the causal variables and the effect to be predicted.
3 To test hypotheses.

Like descriptive research, causal research requires a planned and structured design. Although descriptive research can determine the degree of association between variables, it is not appropriate for examining causal relationships. Such an examination requires a causal design, in which the causal or independent variables are manipulated in a relatively controlled environment. Such an environment is one in which the other variables that may affect the dependent variable are controlled or checked as much as possible. The effect of this manipulation on one or more dependent variables is then measured to infer causality. The main method of causal research is experimentation.[29]

Due to the complexity and importance of this subject, Chapter 11 has been devoted to causal designs and experimental research.

Relationships between exploratory, descriptive and causal research

We have described exploratory, descriptive and causal research as major classifications of research designs, but the distinctions among these classifications are not absolute. A given marketing research project may involve more than one type of research design and thus serve several purposes.[30] Which combination of research designs to employ depends on the nature of the problem. We offer the following general guidelines for choosing research designs.

1 When little is known about the problem situation, it is desirable to begin with exploratory research. Exploratory research is appropriate for the following:
   a When the nature of the topic under study cannot be measured in a structured, quantifiable manner.
   b When the problem needs to be defined more precisely.
   c When alternative courses of action need to be identified.
   d When research questions or hypotheses need to be developed.
   e When key variables need to be isolated and classified as dependent or independent.
2 Exploratory research may be an initial step in a research design. It may be followed by descriptive or causal research. For example, hypotheses developed via exploratory research can be statistically tested using descriptive or causal research.
3 It is not necessary to begin every research design with exploratory research. It depends on the precision with which the problem has been defined and the researcher's degree of certainty about the approach to the problem. A research design could well begin with descriptive or causal research. To illustrate, a consumer satisfaction survey that is conducted annually need not begin with or include an exploratory phase.

4 Although exploratory research is generally the initial step, it need not be. Exploratory research may follow descriptive or causal research. For example, descriptive or causal research results in findings that are hard for managers to interpret. Exploratory research may provide more insights to help understand these findings.

The relationships between exploratory, descriptive and causal research are further illustrated by the following example. The example starts with a description of the environmental context of a marketing problem, shows the related marketing decision problem and the related marketing research problem, and then evaluates potential research designs that could work.

Example | **How would you like your alligator cooked, madam?**

Environmental context

Supermarket X has seen a continual decline in the sales of beef over the past five years. Over this period, a number of factors have emerged which collectively may have eroded consumers' confidence in the product and changed their attitudes and behaviour. The factors may be summarised as follows:

- *Animal health scares* related to diseases in cattle throughout Europe, including BSE and foot-and-mouth disease.
- *Health awareness* in terms of relationship between diet, nutrition and health has become a topic that is more widely debated – especially the role and benefits of red meats.
- The *organic food* movement has significantly grown over this period, raising awareness in consumers of food production and what they deem to be 'quality' food.
- *Animal welfare*, in terms of how animals are treated on farms, on their journey to the abattoir and in the slaughter process, has become a topic that is more widely debated.

Marketing decision problem and related marketing research problem

The marketing decision-makers in Supermarket X could perceive these issues as threats or opportunities and react in a number of ways. The following are two examples of a multitude of directions they could choose. The **marketing decision problem** could be '*should a new product be introduced?*', i.e. beef is in decline, therefore determine which product is felt to be the 'replacement', setting a **marketing research problem** of '*to determine consumer preferences and purchase intentions for the proposed new product*'. The **marketing decision problem** could alternatively be '*should the advertising campaign be changed to allay consumer fears?*', i.e. having a belief that 'ex-consumers' of beef can be tempted back, if only the negative connotations related to the product are addressed, setting a **marketing research problem** of '*to understand the nature of consumer fears and to test the impact of various advertising formats in terms of changing consumer attitudes*'.

Research design

The marketing research problem '*to determine consumer preferences and purchase intentions for the proposed new product*' could be tackled with a descriptive research design, further classified as a cross-sectional design. The second description of a marketing research problem, '*to understand the nature of consumer fears and to test the impact of various advertising formats in terms of changing consumer attitudes*', has two components, so it may have a more complex research design. The first component, to understand the nature of fears and ways of overcoming those fears, could be tackled with an exploratory research design. This could be followed by a causal research design where the impacts of different advertising formats are tested out.

The implication of the above connections between a marketing research problem and a research design may be that there is a simple, single design that will answer all the questions that the decision-maker faces; this is not always the case. There may be a number of research techniques that need to run simultaneously or cannot be effectively applied unless other techniques precede or succeed them. As one learns of the nature of different research techniques and their benefits and limitations, it becomes clear that techniques can connect together. By combining different research techniques, greater power in understanding and measuring consumers may be achieved, ultimately giving greater support to decision-makers.

The following research design illustrates this point by pulling together a number of research techniques to create a research design (Figure 3.4). This design should not be seen as the 'ideal' solution; it is but one of many research designs that could be used to tackle the marketing research problem.

The research design starts with **internally generated secondary data** where, depending upon how data have been collected and stored, a huge array of issues could be examined. For example, sales trends of beef could be analysed to determine whether there are differences in the decline based upon beef cuts, e.g. minced beef vs. steaks, or geography, e.g. sales patterns in different stores. If different sales promotions have been tried out, the correlations with increased sales could be examined. If different alternatives such as ostrich meat, kangaroo meat or even soya-based cuts have been sold, how have they performed?

In conjunction with this stage, the researcher could collect and analyse **externally generated secondary data**. Again, a huge array of issues could be examined. For example, production levels of different alternatives to beef could be examined, looking in detail at the levels of growth or decline in new products and established products and where these products come from. In this stage, statistics that set out the wider forces that shape the market can be quantified.

In conjunction with this stage, the researcher could collect and examine different forms of **intelligence** (covered in detail in Chapter 4). For example, the writings of economists, health experts and even chefs from leading newspapers and magazines all over the world could be evaluated. This source, being far more qualitative, may help in the interpretation of some of the analyses of internal and external secondary data. It may spark off new ideas of data to track down and new connections between data sources. Intelligence may help to locate experts who may have access to secondary data or be willing to talk in more detail.

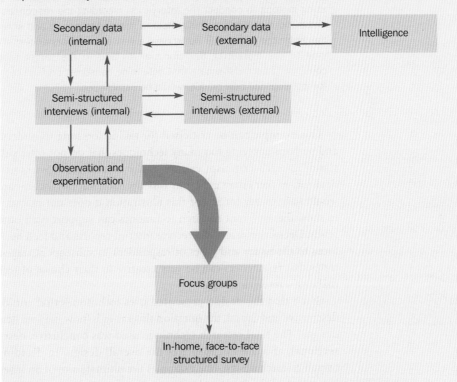

Figure 3.4 Should a new product be introduced to replace beef? – research design

With a very rich descriptive base of secondary data and intelligence, the researcher could conduct exploratory **semi-structured interviews** with managers within Supermarket X. These qualitative interviews could help to interpret many of the secondary data and intelligence analyses. They could help explain, for example, the reasons behind varying levels of success in advertising and sales promotion activities in regenerating beef sales. Why different alternatives were chosen and how they were promoted, positioned in the store and priced could be examined.

Concurrently, semi-structured interviews could be conducted with individuals who work outside Supermarket X and subsequently may be more difficult to gain access to. These interviews could be directed at experts with knowledge of health issues, culinary trends and lifestyle changes. Again, on a qualitative basis, the future of different alternatives to beef could be examined and the comparative benefits and limitations to beef evaluated. Ideas could be generated that could be discussed and developed in interviews with managers in Supermarket X, making the semi-structured interviews concurrent and interrelated in nature.

The exploratory stage of semi-structured interviewing could generate ideas about the nature of alternatives to beef, the types of consumer they should be targeted to and the ways in which these alternatives may be promoted. Having an array of stores, researchers could set up an **experiment** to try to establish what may be influencing purchases of beef and alternatives. If consumers using the supermarket have loyalty or store cards, an **observation** of their patterns of purchase may also be made.

Having established an understanding of the variables that may affect the choice of beef and alternatives, the researcher may seek a more in-depth understanding of the most significant variables. By setting up **focus groups** with representatives from, for example, young single persons, single parents, young families and elderly couples, chosen issues can be explored in a most creative manner. Discussion may ensue, recipes can be tasted, packages and forms of promotions can be commented upon, all resulting in a much stronger understanding of consumer preferences and purchase intentions for the proposed new product.

Finally, the researcher may wish to test out the ideas developed from the focus groups in a conclusive manner. A **face-to-face survey** may be conducted in target respondents' homes, using laptops to conduct the interviews, recording the responses but also showing video and audio recordings that may help to convey the nature and style of beef alternatives. By this stage the researcher would have a very clear understanding of the issues that are relevant to the marketing decision-makers and to the target respondents and ultimate consumers. Conclusive data that determine consumer preferences and purchase intentions for the proposed new product would be established.

This example can be criticised for taking too long to undertake, being too expensive and perhaps applying too many techniques that do not offer sufficient additional understanding. Such criticism cannot really be addressed without knowing the value that decision-makers may get from this decision support, compared with how much they would have to pay for it. For this illustration it does not matter, in that the intention was to show that different research techniques can support each other and can work concurrently. Decision-makers can receive interim reports and feed back their ideas to give more focus to the issues and types of respondent in subsequent stages. The example also illustrates that researchers can be very creative in their choice of techniques that combine to make up a research design.

Given that the design presented uses techniques that could be termed exploratory, descriptive and causal, the question this raises is 'how may we describe the overall research design?' The final research technique used was **conclusive, descriptive and single cross-sectional**, and this encapsulates the overall design. In deciding what encapsulates the overall research design, one examines the ultimate aim of an investigation, and in this case it was to describe in a conclusive manner.

Potential sources of error in research designs

Several potential sources of error can affect a research design. A good research design attempts to control the various sources of error. Although these errors are discussed in detail in subsequent chapters, it is pertinent at this stage to give brief descriptions.

Where the focus of a study is a quantitative measurement, the **total error** is the variation between the true mean value in the population of the variable of interest and the observed mean value obtained in the marketing research project. For example, the annual average income of a target population may be €85,650, as determined from census information via tax returns, but a marketing research project estimates it at €62,580 based upon a sample survey. As shown in Figure 3.5, total error is composed of random sampling error and non-sampling error.

Total error
The variation between the true mean value in the population of the variable of interest and the observed mean value obtained in the marketing research project.

Random sampling error

Random sampling error occurs because the particular sample selected is an imperfect representation of the population of interest. Random sampling error is the variation between the true mean value for the population and the true mean value for the original sample. Random sampling error is discussed further in Chapters 14 and 15.

Random sampling error
The error arising because the particular sample selected is an imperfect representation of the population of interest. It may be defined as the variation between the true mean value for the sample and the true mean value of the population.

Non-sampling error

Non-sampling errors can be attributed to sources other than sampling, and may be random or non-random. They result from a variety of reasons, including errors in problem definition, approach, scales, questionnaire design, interviewing methods, and data preparation and analysis. Non-sampling errors consist of non-response errors and response errors.

Non-sampling error
An error that can be attributed to sources other than sampling and that can be random or non-random.

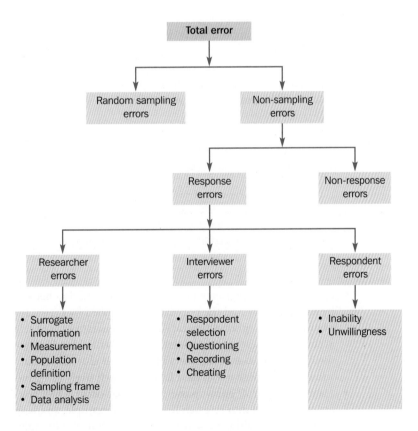

Figure 3.5
Potential sources of error in research designs

Non-response error
A type of non-sampling error that occurs when some of the respondents included in the sample do not respond. This error may be defined as the variation between the true mean value of the variable in the original sample and the true mean value in the net sample.

Response error
A type of non-sampling error arising from respondents who do respond but who give inaccurate answers or whose answers are mis-recorded or mis-analysed. It may be defined as a variation between the true mean value of the variable in the net sample and the observed mean value obtained in the market research project.

A **non-response error** arises when some of the respondents included in the sample do not respond. The primary causes of non-response are refusals and not-at-homes (see Chapter 15). Non-response will cause the net or resulting sample to be different in size or composition from the original sample. Non-response error is defined as the variation between the true mean value of the variable in the original sample and the true mean value in the net sample.

Response error arises when respondents give inaccurate answers or their answers are mis-recorded or mis-analysed. Response error is defined as the variation between the true mean value of the variable in the net sample and the observed mean value obtained in the marketing research project. Response error is determined not only by the non-response percentage but also by the difference between respondents and those who failed to cooperate, for whatever reason, as response errors can be made by researchers, interviewers or respondents.[31] A central question in evaluating response error is whether those who participated in a survey differ from those who did not take part, in characteristics relevant to the content of the survey.[32]

Errors made by the researcher include surrogate information, measurement, population definition, sampling frame and data analysis errors:

- *Surrogate information error* may be defined as the variation between the information needed for the marketing research problem and the information sought by the researcher. For example, instead of obtaining information on consumer choice of a new brand (needed for the marketing research problem), the researcher obtains information on consumer preferences because the choice process cannot be easily observed.
- *Measurement error* may be defined as the variation between the information sought and information generated by the measurement process employed by the researcher. While seeking to measure consumer preferences, the researcher employs a scale that measures perceptions rather than preferences.
- *Population definition error* may be defined as the variation between the actual population relevant to the problem at hand and the population as defined by the researcher. The problem of appropriately defining the population may be far from trivial, as illustrated by the case of affluent households. Their number and characteristics varied depending on the definition, underscoring the need to avoid population definition error. Depending upon the way the population of affluent households was defined, the results of this study would have varied markedly.

Example   How affluent is affluent?

The population of the affluent households was defined in four different ways in a study:

1 Households with income of €80,000 or more.
2 The top 20% of households, as measured by income.
3 Households with net worth over €450,000.
4 Households with discretionary income to spend being 30% higher than that of comparable households.

- *Sampling frame error* may be defined as the variation between the population defined by the researcher and the population as implied by the sampling frame (list) used. For example, the telephone directory used to generate a list of telephone numbers does not accurately represent the population of potential landline consumers due to unlisted, disconnected and new numbers in service. It also misses out the great number of consumers that choose not to have landlines, exclusively using mobile telephones
- *Data analysis error* encompasses errors that occur while raw data from questionnaires are transformed into research findings. For example, an inappropriate statistical procedure is used, resulting in incorrect interpretation and findings.

Response errors made by the interviewer include respondent selection, questioning, recording and cheating errors:

- *Respondent selection error* occurs when interviewers select respondents other than those specified by the sampling design or in a manner inconsistent with the sampling design. For example, in a readership survey, a non-reader is selected for the interview but classified as a reader of *Le Monde* in the 15–19-year-old category in order to meet a difficult quota requirement.
- *Questioning error* denotes errors made in asking questions of the respondents or in not probing, when more information is needed. For example, while asking questions an interviewer does not use the exact wording or prompts as set out in the questionnaire.
- *Recording error* arises due to errors in hearing, interpreting and recording the answers given by the respondents. For example, a respondent indicates a neutral response (undecided) but the interviewer misinterprets that to mean a positive response (would buy the new brand).
- *Cheating error* arises when the interviewer fabricates answers to a part or the whole of the interview. For example, an interviewer does not ask the sensitive questions related to a respondent's debt but later fills in the answers based on personal assessment.

Response errors made by the respondent comprise inability and unwillingness errors:

- *Inability error* results from the respondent's inability to provide accurate answers. Respondents may provide inaccurate answers because of unfamiliarity, fatigue, boredom, faulty recall, question format, question content and other factors. For example, a respondent cannot recall the brand of toothpaste purchased four weeks ago.
- *Unwillingness error* arises from the respondent's unwillingness to provide accurate information. Respondents may intentionally misreport their answers because of a desire to provide socially acceptable answers, to avoid embarrassment, or to please the interviewer.[33] For example, to impress the interviewer, a respondent intentionally says that they read *The Economist* magazine.

These sources of error are discussed in more detail in subsequent chapters; what is important here is that there are many sources of error. In formulating a research design, the researcher should attempt to minimise the total error, not just a particular source. This admonition is warranted by the general tendency among naive researchers to control sampling error with large samples. Increasing the sample size does decrease sampling error, but it may also increase non-sampling error, e.g. by increasing interviewer errors. Non-sampling error is likely to be more problematic than sampling error. Sampling error can be calculated, whereas many forms of non-sampling error defy estimation. Moreover, non-sampling error has been found to be the major contributor to total error, whereas random sampling error is relatively small in magnitude. The point is that total error is important. A particular type of error is important only in that it contributes to total error.

Sometimes, researchers deliberately increase a particular type of error to decrease the total error by reducing other errors. For example, suppose that a mail survey is being conducted to determine consumer preferences in purchasing shoes from a chain of specialist shoe shops. A large sample size has been selected to reduce sampling error. A response rate of 30% may be expected. Given the limited budget for the project, the selection of a large sample size does not allow for follow-up mailings. Past experience, however, indicates that the response rate could be increased to 45% with one follow-up mailing and to 55% with two follow-up mailings. Given the subject of the survey, non-respondents are likely to differ from respondents in many features. Hence, it may be desirable to reduce the sample size to make money available for follow-up mailings. While decreasing the sample size will increase random sampling error, the two follow-up mailings will more than offset this loss by decreasing non-response error.

International marketing research

While conducting international marketing research, it is important to realise that, given environmental differences, the research design appropriate for one country may not be suitable in another. Consider the problem of determining household attitudes towards major appliances in the Netherlands and Saudi Arabia. While conducting exploratory research in the Netherlands, it is appropriate to conduct focus groups jointly with male and female heads of households. It would be inappropriate to conduct such focus groups in Saudi Arabia, however. Given the traditional culture, wives are unlikely to participate freely in the presence of their husbands. It would be more useful to conduct one-on-one in-depth interviews with both male and female heads of households being included in the sample. An understanding of environmental influences can affect the choice and application of individual research techniques. Ultimately, the rules of using different techniques to build up an understanding of consumers remains the same, regardless of geographic boundaries, as illustrated in the following example.

Example

Chinese sport a favourable attitude towards sporting goods[35]

A marketing research study was performed to gain insight and understanding into the behaviour of consumers in China in relation to sports and sporting goods. The research design included both exploratory and conclusive research. Exploratory research was necessary to gain an understanding of the social, cultural, economic and legal environment of China. The researcher also utilised both secondary data and one-to-one depth interviews with retail outlet managers to gather this information.

For the conclusive research, a single cross-sectional design was used. A survey was developed and 4,000 questionnaires were distributed to respondents in 10 Chinese cities. Of these, 54% were completed and returned. A single cross-sectional design was appropriate because the researcher wanted to gain an understanding of the current state of consumers' attitudes, motivations and behaviours in relation to sporting goods.

As well as findings such as the strong brand recognition of Adidas, Nike, Asics and Reebok, specific social, cultural and environmental trends were also identified. For instance, China is becoming more fitness conscious. China is also becoming a more casual society, which is leading to the use of sporting goods for facilitation of the casual lifestyle. Also, the Chinese tend to shop a lot on Sundays and the Chinese wife tends to make family purchasing decisions.

In many countries, particularly developing countries, consumer panels have not been developed, making it difficult to conduct descriptive longitudinal research. Likewise, in many countries the marketing support infrastructure – that is, retailing, wholesaling, advertising and promotional infrastructure – is lacking, making it infeasible to implement a causal design involving a field experiment. In formulating a research design, considerable effort is required to ensure the equivalence and comparability of secondary and primary data obtained from different countries. In the context of collecting primary data, qualitative research, survey methods, scaling techniques, questionnaire design and sampling considerations are particularly important. These topics are discussed in more detail in subsequent chapters.

Ethics in marketing research

During the research design stage, not only are the concerns of the researcher and the client involved, but the rights of the respondents also must be respected. Although normally there is no direct contact between the respondents and the other stakeholders (client and researcher) during the research design phase, this is the stage when decisions with ethical ramifications, such as using hidden video or audio tape recorders, are made.

The basic question of the type of research design which should be adopted (i.e. descriptive or causal, cross-sectional or longitudinal) has ethical overtones. For example, when studying brand switching in toothpaste purchases, a longitudinal design is the only actual way to assess changes in an individual respondent's brand choice. A research firm that has not conducted many longitudinal studies may try to justify the use of a cross-sectional design. Is this ethical?

Researchers must ensure that the research design utilised will provide the information needed to address the marketing research problem that has been identified. The client should have the integrity not to misrepresent the project and should describe the constraints under which the researcher must operate and not make unreasonable demands. Longitudinal research takes time. Descriptive research might require interviewing customers. If time is an issue, or if customer contact has to be restricted, the client should make these constraints known at the start of the project. The client buying services from a marketing research firm should not take undue advantage of it to ask for unreasonable concessions or discounts for a current project by making false promises of future research contracts as illustrated in the following example.

Example   ## Big Brother or Big Bully?[36]

Ethical dilemmas may arise due to the strong desire of marketing research firms to become suppliers to large organisations who invest heavily in marketing research projects. Many companies in financial services, airlines, beverages and automobiles, for example, have enormous marketing budgets and regularly employ external marketing research firms. Large clients can manipulate the price for a current project or demand unreasonable concessions in the research design (e.g. the examination of additional variables, more focus groups, a larger or more targeted sample for the survey, or additional data analyses) by implying that there is the potential for the marketing research firms to become a regular supplier. This may be considered just business, but it becomes unethical when there is no intention to follow up with a larger study or to use the research firm in the future.

Responsibilities to research respondents must not be overlooked. The researcher should design the study so as not to violate the respondents' right to safety, right to privacy, or right to choose. Furthermore, the client must not abuse power to jeopardise the anonymity of the respondents.

As well as its general code of conduct, ESOMAR produces a series of guidelines that are specific to particular research techniques (Internet research), types of respondent (children) and types of industry (pharmaceutical).

To see how ESOMAR guides the ethical practices of the marketing research industry in Europe, and how marketing research associations in individual countries throughout the world guide the ethical practices of domestic marketing research, visit **www.esomar.nl**.

Internet and computer applications

The Internet can facilitate the implementation of different types of research designs.

Exploratory research

If an exploratory research design is to be utilised, discussion groups, chat rooms or newsgroups can be used to discuss a particular topic to great depth. Files can be exchanged that can include moving images and sounds, allowing questions and probes to be built around this material. Formal focus groups may be conducted with experts or individuals representing target groups, all on a global basis if needed. Illustrations of qualitative interviews using the Internet are presented in Chapters 6 to 8.

Listservers could also be used to obtain initial information needed to develop a research design. Listservers make interactive discussion possible for special interest groups, user groups and customer service forums. Messages sent to the listener are forwarded to all subscribers of that listserver. Broad or specific questions could be asked of listserver subscribers. The questions might not constitute a specifically developed survey, and the members of the listservers might not represent the target respondents precisely, but if they are chosen based upon their relationship to the area being researched, they can provide a means of quickly receiving responses that can begin to clarify the research area. Discussion groups or lists allow for ongoing discussions among members, with or without moderation. Every member can write to the group, and, in doing so, everyone will receive a copy of the message. More information on listservers can be obtained at **www.lsoft.com/lists/listref.html**.

Conclusive research

Many descriptive studies utilise secondary data in defining the nature of a problem, as a technique in its own right and as a means to develop sampling plans. The use of the Internet for these purposes is discussed in Chapter 4. In primary data collection, the Internet can be used for surveys (discussed in Chapter 10) and in panels (Chapters 4 and 10). The use of the Internet for causal research designs is discussed in Chapter 11.

In addition to Internet applications, computers can also help to control total error. By using computers, researchers can model and calculate how the various sources of error may affect the results and what levels of errors could be acceptable. It is relatively easy to estimate random sampling error when probability sampling schemes are used. Estimating the impact of various non-sampling errors, however, is much more problematic. Simulation can be conducted to determine how the distributions and levels of various non-sampling errors will affect final results.[37]

Summary

A research design is a framework or blueprint for conducting the marketing research project. It specifies the details of how the project should be conducted in order to fulfil set research objectives. The challenge faced by marketing researchers in developing a research design is that they need to balance an understanding of research design from the decision-makers' perspective with an understanding of potential respondents' reactions to issues researched using different techniques, applied in differing contexts. Research designs may be broadly classified as exploratory or conclusive. The primary purpose of exploratory research is to develop understanding and provide insights.

Conclusive research is conducted to measure and describe phenomena, test specific hypotheses and examine specific relationships. Conclusive research may be either descriptive or causal. The findings from both exploratory and conclusive research can be used as input into marketing decision-making.

The major objective of descriptive research is to describe market characteristics or functions. Descriptive research can be classified into cross-sectional and longitudinal research. Cross-sectional designs involve the collection of information from a sample of population elements at a single point in time. These designs can be further classified as single cross-sectional or multiple cross-sectional designs. In contrast, in longitudinal designs repeated measurements are taken on a fixed sample. Causal research is designed for the primary purpose of obtaining evidence about cause-and-effect (causal) relationships.

Many research designs combine techniques that can be classified as exploratory, descriptive and causal. In cases where there is an array of interrelating techniques, the researcher should examine the ultimate aim of an investigation, and decide what encapsulates the overall research design, i.e. a desire to explore, describe or experiment.

A research design consists of six components. Error can be associated with any of these components. The total error is composed of random sampling error and non-sampling error. Non-sampling error consists of non-response and response errors. Response error encompasses errors made by researchers, interviewers and respondents. In formulating a research design when conducting international marketing research, considerable effort is required to ensure the equivalence and comparability of secondary and primary data obtained from different countries. In terms of ethical issues, the researchers must ensure that the research design used will provide the information sought and that the information sought is the information needed by the client. The client should have the integrity not to misrepresent the project and should describe the situation within which the researcher must operate and must not make unreasonable demands. Every precaution should be taken to ensure the respondents' or subjects' right to safety, right to privacy, or right to choose.

Questions

1 Define research design in your own words.

2 What expectations do marketing decision-makers have of research designs?

3 How does the subject of enquiry as seen by potential research respondents affect research design?

4 How does formulating a research design differ from developing an approach to a problem?

5 Differentiate between exploratory and conclusive research.

6 What are the major purposes for which exploratory research is conducted?

7 Describe how quantitative techniques may be used in exploratory research.

8 What are the major purposes for which descriptive research is conducted?

9 Discuss the advantages and disadvantages of panels.

10 Compare and contrast cross-sectional and longitudinal designs.

11 Describe cohort analysis. Why is it of special interest?

12 What is a causal research design? What is its purpose?

13 What is the relationship between exploratory, descriptive and causal research?

14 What potential sources of error can affect a research design?

15 Why is it important to minimise total error rather than any particular source of error?

Exercises

1 Imagine that you are the marketing researcher appointed by BMW and that you have been hired to conduct a study of its corporate image.

  a Discuss the potential issues that may affect your choice of context in which to interview female executives that buy the 7-series cars.

  b Discuss the potential issues that may affect your choice of context in which to interview teenagers whose parent(s) own a BMW.

2 Visit the website of the Association of Qualitative Research Practitioners, **www.aqrp.co.uk**. Browse through the business directory to get a feel for the nature of industries and marketing issues that may be supported by exploratory studies. Find the agency MORI and examine the work of its specialist qualitative agency **www.mori.com/qualitative**. In what manner(s) does this agency link exploratory designs to conclusive designs?

3 Imagine that you are conducting an image study for the online dating agency **www.match.com**. What elements of the way that it presents its services and how its customers use the site could help you in an exploratory stage of this study?

4 Visit the website of the research organisation JD Power and Associates, **www.jdpower.com**. Work through its corporate site and choose a study that it has conducted to examine. What research design has it used for this study and what potential error issues could emerge given the nature of what it was investigating?

5 In a small group discuss the following issues: 'There are many potential sources of error in a research project. It is impossible to control all of them. Hence, all marketing research contains errors and we cannot be confident of the findings.' And 'If a research budget is limited, small sample sizes through exploratory studies are the best solution.'

Video Case Exercise: Nike

Innovation is a core value of the Nike brand. What factors may demand an innovative research design for challenges such as measuring or understanding the brand values of Nike?

video case

download from www.pearsoned.co.uk/ malhotra_euro

Notes

1 Acreman, S. and Pegram, B., 'Getting to know you', *Research* (November 1999), 36–41.

2 Tait, B., 'How 'marketing science' undermines brands', *Admap* (October)2004, 46–48; Boyd, H.W. Jr, Westfall, R. and Stasch, S.F., *Marketing Research, Text and Cases*, 7th edn (Homewood, IL: Irwin, 1989), 49.

3 Adapted from Cooper, P. and Braithwaite, A., 'Qualitative technology – new perspectives on measurement and meaning through qualitative research', Market Research Society Conference, 2nd pre-conference workshop, 1979.

4 Chambers, K., 'Lies, damn lies and sensitive topics', *Imprints*, July 2004, 5.

5 Ibid., p. 6.

6 Gordon, W. 'Consumer decision making', *Admap*, October 2004, 74.

7 Clegg, A. 'What do you really think?', *Marketing Week* (25 November 2004), 39.

8 Brown, S., 'Keeping it real', *Research* (August 2004), 22.

9 Halman, I.M., 'Evaluating effectiveness of project start-ups: an exploratory study', *International Journal of Project Management*, 20 (January 2002), 81 and Semon, T.T., 'Marketing research need basic research', *Marketing News*, 28 (14 March 1996), 12.

10 Beaumont, J. and Horton, L., 'They got game', *Research* (May 2005), 36–37.

11 Creswell, J.W., *Research Design: Qualitative, quantitative, and mixed method approaches*, 2nd edn (Thousand Oaks, CA: Sage, 2002); Lee, H., Lindquist, J.D. and Acito, F., 'Managers' evaluation of research design and its impact on the use of research: an experimental approach', *Journal of Business Research* 39 (3) (July 1997), 231–240; Wilson, R.D., 'Research design: qualitative and quantitative approaches', *Journal of Marketing Research* 33 (2) (May 1996), 252–255.

12 For examples of descriptive research, see Robinson, W.Y., 'Is the first to market the first to fail?', *Journal of Marketing Research* 39 (1) (February 2002), 120–128; Song, S.M. and Perry, M.E., 'The determinants of Japanese new product success', *Journal of Marketing Research* 34 (February 1997), 64–76.

13 Anon., 'Coupon use low among young, working women', *Marketing News* (10 April 1987), 24.

14 Anon., 'Eating behaviour trends revealed in Pillsbury study', *Quirk's Marketing Research Review* (June–July 1988), 14–15, 39, 44.

15 Creswell, J., *Research Design: Qualitative, quantitative and mixed method approaches*, 2nd edn (Thousand Oaks CA, Sage, 2002); Misra, R. and Panigrahi, B., 'Changes in attitudes toward women: a cohort analysis', *International Journal of Sociology & Social Policy* 15 (6) (1995), 1–20; Glenn, N.D., *Cohort Analysis* (Beverly Hills, CA: Sage, 1981).

16 Rentz, J.O., Reynolds, F.D. and Stout, R.G., 'Analyzing changing consumption patterns with cohort analysis', *Journal of
Marketing Research* 20 (February 1983), 12–20. See also
Rentz, J.O. and Reynolds, F.D., 'Forecasting the effects of an
aging population on product consumption: an age-period-
cohort framework', *Journal of Marketing Research* (August
1991), 355–360.

17 Miles, L., 'Keeping a lid on overcapacity', *Research World*
(January 2004), 12.

18 For example, see Elrod, T. and Keane, M.P., 'A factor-analytic
probit model for representing the market structure in panel
data', *Journal of Marketing Research* 32 (February 1995), 1–16.

19 Michaelsen, F., 'A quick ABC of panels', *Research World*
(February 2005), 27.

20 Lee, J.K.H., Sudhir, K. and Steckel, J.H., A multiple ideal point
model: capturing multiple preference effects from within an
ideal point framework', *Journal of Marketing Research* 39 (1)
(February 2002), 73–86. For a basic treatment see Markus,
G.B., *Analyzing Panel Data* (Beverly Hills, CA: Sage, 1979).

21 Table 3.7 can also be viewed as a transition matrix. It depicts the
brand-buying changes from period to period. Knowing the proportion of consumers who switch allows for early prediction of
the ultimate success of a new product or change in market
strategy. See Sudman, S. and Ferber, R., *Consumer Panels*
(Chicago: American Marketing Association, 1979), 19–27.

22 Johnston, M.W., Parasuraman, A., Futrell, C.M. and Black,
W.C., 'A longitudinal assessment of the impact of selected
organizational influences on salespeople's organizational
commitment during early employment', *Journal of Marketing
Research* (August 1990), 333–344.

23 Sudman, S. and Ferber, R., 'A comparison of alternative procedures for collecting consumer expenditure data for
frequently purchased products', and Wright, R.A., Beisel,
R.H., Oliver, J.D. and Gerzowski, M.C., 'The use of a multiple
entry diary in a panel study on health care', both in Ferber, R.
(ed.), *Readings in Survey Research* (Chicago: American
Marketing Association, 1978), 487–502, 503–512; Wind, Y.
and Lemer, D., 'On the measurement of purchase data: surveys versus purchase diaries', *Journal of Marketing Research* 16
(February 1979), 39–47; McKenzie, J., 'The accuracy of telephone call data by diary methods', *Journal of Marketing
Research* 20 (November 1983), 417–427.

24 Brannas, K., 'A new approach to modelling and forecasting
monthly guest nights in hotels', *International Journal of
Forecasting*, 18, (1) (January–March 2002), 19; Coupe, R.T. and
Onudu, N.M., 'Evaluating the impact of CASE: an empirical
comparison of retrospective and cross-sectional survey
approaches', *European Journal of Information Systems* 6 (1)
(March 1997), 15–24. Sudman, S. and Ferber, R., *Consumer
Panels* (Chicago: American Marketing Association, 1979), 19–27.

25 Taris, T.W., *A primer in longitudinal data analysis* (Thousand
Oaks, CA: Sage, 2001); Van Den Berg, D.G., Lindeboom, M.
and Ridder, G., 'Attribution in longitudinal panel data and the
empirical analysis of dynamic labour market behaviour',
Journal of Applied Econometrics 9 (4) (October–December
1994), 421–435; Winer, R.S., 'Attrition bias in econometric
models estimated with panel data', *Journal of Marketing
Research* 20 (May 1983), 177–186.

26 Lee, J.K.H., Sudir, K. and Steckel, J.H., 'A multiple ideal point
model: capturing multiple preference effects from within an
ideal point framework', *Journal of Marketing Research*, 39 (1)
(February 2002), 73–86; Maytas, L. and Sevestre, P. (eds), *The
Econometrics of Panel Data: A Handbook of the Theory with
Applications* (Norwell, MA: Kluwer Academic, 1996).

27 Murphy, D., 'More efficiency and integration of data', *Research
World* (February 2005), 29.

28 Gould, G.F. and Gould, J.L. *'Chance and Causation: To experimental design and statistics'* (New York: W.H. Freeman, 2001);
Hulland, J., Ho, Y. and Lam, S., 'Use of causal models in marketing research: a review', *International Journal of Research in
Marketing* 13 (2) (April 1996), 181–197. See also Cox, K.K.
and Enis, B.M., *Experimentation for Marketing Decisions*
(Scranton, PA: International Textbook, 1969), 5.

29 Winer, R.S., 'Experimentation in the 21st century: the importance of external validity', *Journal of the Academy of Marketing
Science* (Summer 1999), 349–358.

30 Cooper, P.J., Diamond, I. and High, S., 'Choosing and using
contraceptives: integrating qualitative and quantitative
research methods in family planning', *Journal of the Market
Research Society* 35 (October 1993), 325–340.

31 Lee, E., 'Are consumer survey results distorted? Systematic
impact of behavioural frequency and duration on survey
response errors', *Journal of Marketing Research* (February
2000), 125–133; Dutka, S. and Frankel, L.R., 'Measuring
response error', *Journal of Advertising Research* 37 (1)
(January/February 1997), 33–39.

32 Loosveldt, G., Carton, A. and Billiet, J., 'Assessment of survey
data quality: a pragmatic approach focused on interviewer tasks',
International Journal of Market Research, 46 (1) (2004), 68.

33 Brooks, D.V. 'A hands on approach to response rates', *Imprints*
(October 2003), 24.

34 Sinha, P., 'Determination of reliability of estimations
obtained with survey research: A method of simulation',
International Journal of Market Research 42 (3) (Summer
2000), 311–318; Rollere, M.R., 'Control is elusive in research
design', *Marketing News* 31 (19) (15 September 1997), 17;
Corlett, T. ,'Sampling errors in practice', *Journal of the Market
Research Society* 38 (4) (April 1997), 307–318.

35 Geng, L., 'Sports marketing strategy: a consumer behaviour
case analysis in China', *Multinational Business Review* (Spring
1997), 147–154.

36 Herndon, N.C., Jnr. 'An investigation of moral values and the
ethical content of the corporate culture: Taiwanese versus US
sales people', *Journal of Business Ethics* 30 (1) (March 2001),
73–85.

37 Leu, S.S., 'A generic algorithm-based optimal resource-con-
strained scheduling simulation model', *Construction
management and Economics*, 20 (2) (March 2002), 131–141;
Leung, J.W.K. and Lai, K.K., 'A structured methodology to
build discrete-event simulation models', *Asia Pacific Journal of
Operations Research* 14 (1) (May 1997), 19–37.

Source: © Getty Images

4

Secondary data collection and analysis

The act of sourcing, evaluating and analysing secondary data can realise great insights for decision-makers. It is also vital to successful problem diagnosis, sample planning and collection of primary data.

Objectives

After reading this chapter, you should be able to:

1 define the nature and scope of secondary data and distinguish secondary data from primary data;

2 analyse the advantages and disadvantages of secondary data and their uses in the various steps of the marketing research process;

3 evaluate secondary data using the criteria of specifications, error, currency, objectives, nature and dependability;

4 describe in detail the different sources of secondary data, focusing upon external sources in the form of published materials and syndicated services;

5 discuss in detail the syndicated sources of secondary data, including household and consumer data obtained via surveys, mail diary panels and electronic scanner services, as well as institutional data related to retailers, wholesalers and industrial or service firms;

6 explain the need to use multiple sources of secondary data and describe single-source data;

7 identify and evaluate the sources of secondary data useful in international marketing research;

8 understand the ethical issues involved in the use of secondary data.

| STAGE 1 Problem definition | STAGE 2 Research approach developed | STAGE 3 Research design developed | STAGE 4 Fieldwork or data collection | STAGE 5 Data preparation and analysis | STAGE 6 Report preparation and presentation |

Overview

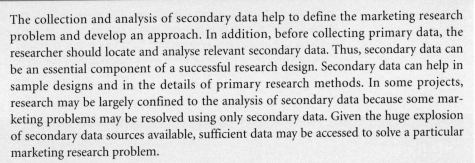

The collection and analysis of secondary data help to define the marketing research problem and develop an approach. In addition, before collecting primary data, the researcher should locate and analyse relevant secondary data. Thus, secondary data can be an essential component of a successful research design. Secondary data can help in sample designs and in the details of primary research methods. In some projects, research may be largely confined to the analysis of secondary data because some marketing problems may be resolved using only secondary data. Given the huge explosion of secondary data sources available, sufficient data may be accessed to solve a particular marketing research problem.

This chapter discusses the distinction between primary data, secondary data and marketing intelligence. The advantages and disadvantages of secondary data are considered, and criteria for evaluating secondary data are presented, along with a classification of secondary data. Internal secondary data are described and major sources of external secondary data, such as published materials, online and offline databases, and syndicated services, are also discussed. Useful sources of secondary data in international marketing research are discussed. Several ethical issues that arise in the use of secondary data are also identified.

To begin with, we present an example that illustrates the nature of secondary data, how it may be evaluated, and its relationship to primary data collection.

Example   Flying high on secondary data[1]

Money magazine published the results of a study conducted to uncover the airline characteristics that consumers consider most important. In order of importance, these characteristics were safety, price, baggage handling, on-time performance, customer service, ease of reservations and ticketing, comfort, frequent flyer schemes and food.

If Air France was considering conducting a marketing research study to identify characteristics of its service that should be improved, this article might be a useful source of secondary data. Before using the data, Air France should evaluate them according to several criteria.

First, the research design used to collect the data should be examined. This *Money* magazine article includes a section that details the research design used in the study. *Money* used a face-to-face survey of 1,017 'frequent flyers'. The results of the survey had a margin of error of 3%. Air France would have to decide whether 'frequent flyers' in the USA could be generalised to the population it wishes to understand, whether 1,017 was a sufficient sample size for its purposes and whether a margin of error of 3% was acceptable. In addition, Air France should evaluate what type of response or non-response errors may have occurred in the data collection or analysis process.

The currency of the data and objective of the study would be important to Air France in deciding whether to utilise this article as a source of secondary data. Air France would also need to look at the nature and dependability of the data. For example, it would need to examine how the nine choice criteria were defined. If the criterion price was measured in terms of fare per kilometre, is this a meaningful and acceptable definition to decision-makers at Air France? With regard to dependability, Air France would need to evaluate the reputation of *Money* magazine and of ICR, the research company hired by *Money* to undertake the survey. It would also need to recognise the fact that *Money* used secondary data in its study; how dependable are the sources it used?

The *Money* magazine article might be useful as a starting place for a marketing research project for Air France. It could be helpful in formulating the nature of decision-making problems and associated research objectives. There may be limitations in regard to reliability, dependability or even how generalisable it may be to Air France's target consumers. Many lessons and ideas may be generated from this article that may lead to other secondary data sources and in the design of a well-focused primary data collection.

Defining primary data, secondary data and marketing intelligence

Primary data
Data originated by the researcher specifically to address the research problem.

Primary data are data originated by a researcher for the specific purpose of addressing the problem at hand. They are individually tailored for the decision-makers of organisations that pay for well-focused and exclusive support. Compared with readily available data from a variety of sources, this exclusivity can mean higher costs and a longer time frame in collecting and analysing the data.

Secondary data
Data collected for some purpose other than the problem at hand.

Secondary data are data that have already been collected for purposes other than the problem at hand. At face value this definition seems straightforward, especially when contrasted to the definition of primary data. However, many researchers confuse the term, or quite rightly see some overlap with marketing intelligence.

Marketing intelligence
Qualified observations of events and developments in the marketing environment.

Marketing intelligence can be defined as 'qualified observations of events and developments in the marketing environment'. The use of the word 'observations' is presented in a wide sense to include a variety of types of data, broadly concerned with 'environmental scanning'.[2] In essence, though, marketing intelligence is based upon data that in many instances have been collected for purposes other than the problem at hand. To clarify this overlap in definitions, Table 4.1 compares secondary data with marketing intelligence through a variety of characteristics.

Table 4.1 A comparison of secondary data and marketing intelligence[3]

Characteristic	Secondary data	Marketing intelligence
Structure	Specifications and research design tend to be apparent	Can be poorly structured; no universal conventions of reporting
Availability	Tend to have regular updates	Irregular availability
Sources	Generated in-house and from organisations with research prowess	Generated in-house and from unofficial sources
Data type	Tend to be quantitative; many issues need qualitative interpretation	Tends to be qualitative; many issues difficult to quantify
Source credibility	Tend to be from reputable and trustworthy research sources of credibility	Questionable credibility; can be generated from a broad spectrum
Terms of reference	Tend to have clear definitions of what is being measured	Ambiguous definitions; difficult to compare over different studies
Analysis	Mostly conventional quantitative techniques	Opinion based, interpretative
Ethics	In-company data gathering may be covered by Data Protection Acts; externally generated data may be covered by research codes of conduct, e.g. ESOMAR	Some techniques may be seen as industrial espionage – though there is an ethical code produced by the Society of Competitive Intelligence Professionals

Note in these comparisons the repeated use of the word 'tend'. The boundaries between the two are not absolutely rigid. Consider the example at the start of this chapter, an article published in *Money* magazine. The journalist may have collected, analysed and presented quantitative data to support the qualitative interpretation of the future developments of a market. The data used and presented may come from credible sources and be correctly analysed, but what about the choice of data to support the journalist's argument? Other sources of data that may contradict this view may be ignored. The data presented can be seen as a secondary data source and interpreted in its own right by a researcher. The interpretation and argument of the journalist can be seen as intelligence and have some credibility. In its entirety, such an article has elements of both secondary data and marketing intelligence, and it may be impossible to pull them apart as mutually exclusive components.

As will become apparent in this chapter, there are clear criteria for evaluating the accuracy of secondary data, which tend to be of a quantitative nature. Marketing intelligence is more difficult to evaluate but this does not mean that it has less value to decision-makers or researchers. Certain marketing phenomena cannot be formally measured: researchers may not be able to gain access to conduct research, or the rapid unfolding of events means that it is impracticable to conduct research. The following example illustrates the importance of intelligence to many companies.

Example **Behind enemy lines[4]**

Robin Kirkby, Director of European Consulting for intelligence specialist Fuld & Company, says there are three principal factors driving investment in intelligence:

The Internet, globalisation and higher expectations from customers are all putting companies under more pressure to differentiate themselves from the competition. It's frustrating that intelligence gets associated with spying; it's actually a highly ethical activity, focused on underlying competitive dynamics and planning future change.

According to research by The Futures Group (TFG), 60% of companies have an organised system for collecting competitive intelligence, while 82% of companies with revenues over €10 billion make systematic use of it. TFG ranked the leading eight users of competitor intelligence as:

1   Microsoft
2   Motorola
3   IBM
4   Procter & Gamble
5= General Electric
5= Hewlett-Packard
7= Coca-Cola
7= Intel

Shadow team
A small cross-functional boundary-spanning group that learns everything about a competitive unit.

Many major organisations invest huge amounts in the hardware and software needed for a systematic approach to gathering intelligence, some even engaging in the use of 'shadow teams'. A **shadow team** is a small cross-functional boundary-spanning group that learns everything about a competitive unit. A competitive unit can be a competitor, product line, supply chain or prospective partner in a strategic alliance. The objective of a shadow team is to learn everything possible about its target through published data, personnel and network connection, and organisation knowledge or hearsay. It brings together knowledge from across an organisation, so that it can think, reason and react like the competitive unit.[5] Competitive intelligence will be discussed in more detail in the context of business-to-business marketing research in Chapter 27.

Such widespread use of intelligence in major organisations means it has a role to play in supporting decision-makers, but it has many limitations, which are apparent in Table 4.1. In the development of better founded information support, credible support can come from the creative collection and evaluation of secondary data. This requires researchers to connect and validate different data sources, ultimately leading to decision-maker support in its own right and support of more focused primary data collection. As this chapter and Chapter 5 unfold, examples of different types of secondary data will emerge and the applications of secondary data will become apparent.

Advantages and uses of secondary data

Secondary data offer several advantages over primary data. Secondary data are easily accessible, relatively inexpensive and quickly obtained. Some secondary data, such as those provided by the National Censuses, are available on topics where it would not be feasible for a firm to collect primary data. Although it is rare for secondary data to provide all the answers to a non-routine research problem, such data can be useful in a variety of ways.[6] Secondary data can help you to:

1 Diagnose the research problem.
2 Develop an approach to the problem.
3 Develop a sampling plan.
4 Formulate an appropriate research design (e.g., by identifying the key variables to measure or understand).
5 Answer certain research questions and test some hypotheses.
6 Interpret primary data with more insight.
7 Validate qualitative research findings.

Given these advantages and uses of secondary data, we state the following general rule:

Examination of available secondary data is a prerequisite to the collection of primary data. Start with secondary data. Proceed to primary data only when the secondary data sources have been exhausted or yield marginal returns.

The rich dividends obtained by following this rule are illustrated in the example at the start of this chapter. It shows that the collection and analysis of even one relevant secondary data source can provide valuable insights. The decision-maker and researcher can use the ideas generated in secondary data as a very strong foundation to primary data design and collection. However, the researcher should be cautious in using secondary data, because they have some limitations and disadvantages.

Disadvantages of secondary data

Because secondary data have been collected for purposes other than the problem at hand, their usefulness to the current problem may be limited in several important ways, including relevance and accuracy. The objectives, nature and methods used to collect the secondary data may not be appropriate to the present situation. Also, secondary data may be lacking in accuracy or may not be completely current or dependable. Before using secondary data, it is important to evaluate them according to a series of factors.[7] These factors are discussed in more detail in the following section.

Criteria for evaluating secondary data

The quality of secondary data should be routinely evaluated, using the criteria presented in Table 4.2 and the discussion in the following sections.[8]

Specifications and research design

The specifications or the research design used to collect the data should be critically examined to identify possible sources of bias. Such design considerations include size and nature of the sample, response rate and quality, questionnaire design and administration, procedures used for fieldwork, and data analysis and reporting procedures. These checks provide information on the reliability and validity (these concepts will be further developed in Chapter 13) of the data and help determine whether they can be generalised to the problem at hand. The reliability and validity can be further ascertained by an examination of the error, currency, objectives, nature and dependability associated with the secondary data.

Error and accuracy

The researcher must determine whether the data are accurate enough for the purposes of the present study. Secondary data can have a number of sources of error or inaccuracy, including errors in the approach, research design, sampling, data collection, analysis, and

Table 4.2 Criteria for evaluating secondary data

Criteria	Issues	Remarks
Specifications and research design	• Data collection method • Response rate • Population definition • Sampling method • Sample size • Questionnaire design • Fieldwork • Data analysis	Data should be reliable, valid and generalisable to the problem at hand
Error and accuracy	Examine errors in: • Approach • Research design • Sampling • Data collection • Data analysis • Reporting	Assess accuracy by comparing data from different sources
Currency	Time lag between collection and publication. Frequency of updates	Census data are periodically updated by syndicated firms
Objective	Why the data were collected	The objective will determine the relevance of data
Nature	• Definition of key variables • Units of measurement • Categories used • Relationships examined	Reconfigure the data to increase their usefulness, if possible
Dependability	Source: • Expertise • Credibility • Reputation • Trustworthiness	Preference should be afforded to an original rather than an acquired source

reporting stages of the project. Moreover, it is difficult to evaluate the accuracy of secondary data because the researcher did not participate in the research. One approach is to find multiple sources of data if possible, and compare them using standard statistical procedures.

Example | **Number crunch[9]**

In December 1997, the Audit Bureau of Circulations (ABC) met UK newspaper publishers and major media buyers from the Institute of Practitioners in Advertising. The meeting aimed to thrash out a formula that could restore ABC's credibility in measuring newspaper readship which forms the basis of negotiation for advertising rates.

Most observers agreed that ABC's troubles were a direct result of squabbling between media owners. As newspaper circulations continued to slide, they fought to hold on to market share through price cuts, promotions and enhanced editorial packages. This has introduced an unprecedented volatility into their sales figures. Not content with trumpeting their own gains, some newspapers have sought to show up the deficiencies in their rivals' sales figures.

Figures under fire

The argument is best understood through an example of what was at stake. The October 1997 ABC figure for *The Times* was 814,899. This was a monthly circulation average which, prior to the dispute, would have been the only official benchmark that agencies used as a negotiating point between newspapers and advertisers (though they turn to data from the National Readership Survey and the Target Group Index to argue their case). At the heart of the dispute was what that monthly figure comprised. For example, were all the issues sold at the full price or were some given away cheaply as part of a subscription or promotional offer? Were any sold or given in bulk to an airliner or retailer, and if so how many? What about papers sold to Ireland or Spain? Were they included in the total, and if so how could that be justified as a piece of credible advertising data?

Another hot issue was the reliability of the monthly figure. Advertisers were dissatisfied with a number that they believe fails to reflect the reality of what they were buying. Director of Press Buying at The Media Centre, Tim Armes, says:

we'd like to know what each paper sells daily and we'd like to know week to week fluctuations. The papers all boast about Saturday but keep quiet about Tuesday and Thursday. If one day is dramatically higher than the average, you don't have to be a brain surgeon to realise the others are lower.

As this example indicates, the accuracy of secondary data can vary: What is being measured? What rules apply to those measurements? What happens if there are rapid changes in what is being measured? With different researchers potentially measuring the 'same' phenomena, data obtained from different sources may not agree. In these cases, the researcher should verify the accuracy of secondary data by conducting pilot studies or by other exploratory work that verifies the analytical framework used to arrive at certain figures. Often, by judicious questioning of those involved in compiling the figures, this can be done without much expense or effort.

Currency: when the data were collected

Secondary data may not be current and the time lag between data collection and publication may be long, as is the case with much census data which may take up to two years from collection to publication. Moreover, the data may not be updated frequently enough for the purpose of the problem at hand. Decision-makers require current data; therefore, the value of secondary data is diminished as they become dated. For instance, although the Census of Population data are comprehensive, they may not be applicable to major cities in which the population has changed rapidly during the last two years.

Objective: the purpose for which the data were collected

Data are invariably collected with some objective in mind, and a fundamental question to ask is why the data were collected in the first place. The objective for collecting data will ultimately determine the purpose for which that information is relevant and useful. Data collected with a specific objective in mind may not be appropriate in another situation. In the example at the start of this chapter, the sample surveyed by *Money* magazine was made up of 'frequent flyers'. The objective of the study was 'to uncover the airline characteristics consumers consider most important'. Air France, however, may wish to target 'business class' flyers and 'to uncover perceptions related to trade-offs made in customer service–price–safety'. Even though there may be identical questions used in both studies, the target respondents may be different, the rationale for the study presented to respondents will be different, and ultimately the 'state of mind' respondents may be in when they come to comparable questions will be different. The *Money* survey was conducted for entirely different objectives from those Air France has for its study. The findings from the *Money* survey may not directly support decision making at Air France, though they may help to define who Air France should talk to and what questions it should put to them.

Nature: the content of the data

The nature, or content, of the data should be examined with special attention to the definition of key variables, the units of measurement, the categories used and the relationships examined. If the key variables have not been defined or are defined in a manner inconsistent with the researcher's definition, then the usefulness of the data is limited. Consider, for example, secondary data on consumer preferences for TV programmes. To use this information, it is important to know how preference for programmes was defined. Was it defined in terms of the programme watched most often, the one considered most needed, most enjoyable, most informative, or the programme of greatest service to the community?

Likewise, secondary data may be measured in units that may not be appropriate for the current problem. For example, income may be measured by individual, family, household or spending unit and could be gross or net after taxes and deductions. Income may be classified into categories that are different from research needs. If the researcher is interested in high-income consumers with gross annual household incomes of over €120,000, secondary data with income categories of less than €20,000, €20,001–€50,000, €50,001–€75,000 and more than €75,000 will not be of use. Determining the measurement of variables such as income may be a complex task, requiring the wording of the definition of income to be precise. Finally, the relationships examined should be taken into account in evaluating the nature of data. If, for example, actual behaviour is of interest, then data inferring behaviour from self-reported attitudinal information may have limited usefulness. Sometimes it is possible to reconfigure the available data – for example, to convert the units of measurement – so that the resulting data are more useful to the problem at hand.

Dependability: how dependable are the data?

An overall indication of the dependability of data may be obtained by examining the expertise, credibility, reputation and trustworthiness of the source. This information can be obtained by checking with others who have used the information provided by the source. Data published to promote sales, to advance specific interests, or to carry on propaganda should be viewed with suspicion. The same may be said of data published anonymously or in a form that attempts to hide the details of the data collection research design and process. It is also pertinent to examine whether the secondary data came from an original source, one that generated the data, or an acquired source, one that procured the data from an original source and published it in a different context. Generally, secondary data should be secured from an original rather than an acquired source. There are at least two reasons for this rule: first, an original source is the one that specifies the details of the data collection research design; and, second, an original source is likely to be more accurate and complete than a surrogate source.

Classification of secondary data

Internal data
Data available within the organisation for whom the research is being conducted.

Figure 4.1 presents a classification of secondary data. Secondary data may be classified as either internal or external. **Internal data** are those generated within the organisation for which the research is being conducted. An example of this source of data for any marketing decision-maker and marketing researcher is the corporate sales ledger at individual transaction level. Analyses of who is buying and the different ways that these customers may be classified or segmented, what they bought, how frequently and the monetary value of their purchases, can give a basic level of understanding customer buying behaviour. With a number of years of transaction data, the lifestages of customer segments can be better understood and how customers have reacted to an array of marketing activities. One of the main problems that marketing researchers face with accessing and analysing transaction data is 'corporate territorialism', i.e. the attitude that each department should only be concerned with the operational data it needs for the business to run on a day-to-day basis. Given that the marketing department in many companies is still not expected to need access to data beyond that needed to execute direct mail campaigns, analysing transactional data may well be a major internal political challenge.[10] Given the importance of this element of marketing decision support, secondary data generated from internal sources will be examined in more detail in Chapter 5.

External data
Data that originate outside the organisation.

External data, on the other hand, are those generated by sources outside the organisation. These data may exist in the form of published material, online databases, or information made available by syndicated services. Externally generated secondary data may be more difficult to access, more expensive and more difficult to evaluate for accuracy, in comparison with internal secondary data. These factors mean that, before collecting external secondary data, it is vital to gather, analyse and interpret any readily available internal secondary data and intelligence.

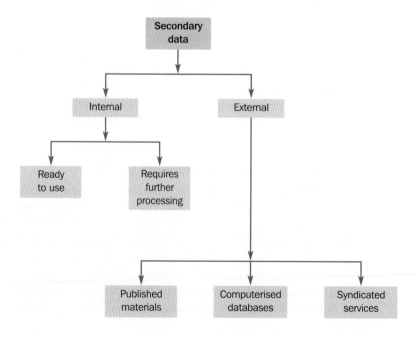

Figure 4.1
A classification of secondary data

Published external secondary sources

Sources of published external secondary data include local authorities, regional and national governments, the EU, non-profit organisations (e.g. Chambers of Commerce), trade associations and professional organisations, commercial publishers, investment brokerage firms and professional marketing research firms.[11] In fact, such a quantity of data is available that the researcher can be overwhelmed. Therefore, it is important to classify published sources (see Figure 4.2). Published external sources may be broadly classified as general business data or government data. General business sources comprise guides, directories, indexes and statistical data. Government sources may be broadly categorised as census data and other publications. These data types are discussed further with specific sources used as examples.

General business sources

Businesses publish a lot of information in the form of books, periodicals, journals, newspapers, magazines, reports and trade literature. This information can be located by using guides, directories and indexes. Sources are also available to identify statistical data.

Guides. Guides are an excellent source of standard or recurring information. A guide may help identify other important sources of directories, trade associations and trade publications. Guides are one of the first sources a researcher should consult. The following example illustrates the Global Industry Guide for Orthopaedics (**www.bioportfolio.com**).

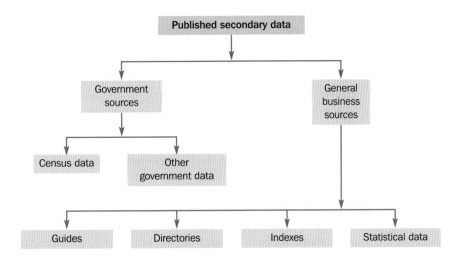

Figure 4.2
A classification of published secondary sources

Example	**Orthopaedics: Global Industry Guide**

Datamonitor's Orthopaedics Global Industry Guide is an essential resource for top-level data and analysis covering the orthopaedics industry. It includes detailed data on market size and segmentation, textual analysis of the key trends and competitive landscape, and profiles of the leading companies. This incisive report provides expert analysis on a global, regional and country basis.

Scope of the report

It contains an executive summary and data on value, volume and segmentation. It provides textual analysis of the industry's prospects, competitive landscape and leading companies; covers global, European, Asia–Pacific and 11 individual country markets; and includes a five-year forecast of the industry.

Highlights

Detailed information is included on market size, measured by both value and volume. Market shares are covered by manufacturer and by brand, including private label. Distribution channels are also analysed. Published December 2004, 162 pages, PDF. Price: $995.00 (€780).

Directories. Directories are helpful for identifying individuals or organisations that collect specific data. An example of a directory that you can examine on the Internet is the Central and Eastern European Business Directory. This interactive site provides current information on businesses and organisations in 24 Central and Eastern European countries (**www.ceebd.co.uk**). Another example is Europages, a reference business directory in Europe that classifies 500,000 companies in 30 European countries. Again, this can be accessed through the Internet and is available in English, French, German, Italian and Spanish versions (**www.europages.com**). Other directories worth exploring include **www.bizeurope.com**.

Indexes. It is possible to locate information on a particular topic in several different publications by using an index and abstracts. Indexes and abstracts, therefore, can increase the efficiency of the search process. Several indexes and abstracts are available for both academic and business sources. Examples of newspaper indexes include the *Financial Times Index* (**www.ft.com**), *Le Monde Index* (**www.le-monde.fr**) and the Japanese Business News online, *The Nikkei Weekly* (**www.nikkei.co.jp**). These indexes allow researchers to identify sources of particular topics, industries and individuals.

An example of a marketing index is the *Marketing Surveys Index* published by Euromonitor (**www.euromonitor.com**). This is a most comprehensive and up-to-date directory of business research on European and world markets. The index contains details of published research reports, a brief summary of its contents, a keyword index to the markets and products covered, and bibliographic details of the report.

A most valuable directory for marketing researchers is the *Directory of Research Organisations* published by ESOMAR (**www.esomar.com**). Finally, a particularly useful abstract source for marketing researchers is the *Market Research Abstracts* published by the Market Research Society in the UK (**www.warc.com**). Major European and American journals that relate to marketing research are reviewed and an abstract of each article is presented. The abstract is published twice a year. It is divided into sections that cover survey techniques; statistics, models and forecasting; attitude and behaviour research; psychographics, personality and social psychology; advertising and media research; applications of research; industrial market research; market research and general applications; and new product development. Such an abstract allows the researcher to identify and evaluate quickly the worth of journal papers that are relevant to the particular study.

Non-government statistical data. Published statistical data are of great interest to researchers. Graphic and statistical analyses can be performed on these data to draw important insights. Examples of non-governmental statistical data include trade associations such as the Swedish Tourism Trade Association (**www.sverigeturism.se**). The Swedish Information 'Smorgasbord' is a large single source of information in English on Sweden, Swedish provinces, nature, culture, lifestyle, society and industry. Another example is Euromonitor (**www.euromonitor.com**), which publishes monthly market research journals covering subjects under the headings of Market Research Europe, Market Research GB, Market Research International and Retail Monitor International.

The United Nations provides an example of an organisation with a Statistics Division that provides a wide range of statistical outputs on a global basis (**www.unstats. un.org/unsd**). The

Statistics Division produces printed publications of statistics and statistical methods in the fields of international merchandise trade, national accounts, demography and population, social indicators, gender, industry, energy, environment, human settlements and disability. The Statistics Division also produces general statistical compendiums including the *Statistical Yearbook* and *World Statistics Pocketbook*. Many of its databases in these fields are available as electronic publications in the form of CD-ROM and on the Internet.

Government sources

European governments and the EU also produce large amounts of secondary data. Each European country has its own statistical office which produces lists of the publications available (and the costs involved). Examples of national statistical offices include the Centraal Bureau voor de Statistiek Nederlands (**www.cbs.nl**), Danmarks Statistik (**www.dst.dk**), the Federal Statistical Office of Germany (**www.destatis.de**), the French Institut National de la Statistique et des Études Economiques (**www.insee.fr**) and the British Office for National Statistics (**www.statistics.gov.uk**). All of these offices have Internet links that allow you to examine quickly the array of publications that they produce. Their publications may be divided into census data and other publications.

Census data. Most European countries produce either catalogues or newsletters that describe the array of census publications available and the plans for any forthcoming census. In the UK, for example, *Census News* (**www.statistics.gov.uk/census**) is a newsletter that contains the latest information about the 2007 and 2011 Censuses and previous censuses and is available four to six times a year. Census Marketing in Britain can supply unpublished data from the 1961, 1971, 1981, 1991, 2001 Censuses in the form of Small Area Statistics (SAS). SAS are available for standard census areas within England and Wales, such as counties, local government districts, London boroughs, wards, civil parishes and enumeration districts. Maps can also be purchased to complement the data.

Census data can be kept in electronic format, allowing them to be analysed and presented in a variety of formats at a detailed geographical level. Given the long periods between the national Censuses and the amount of change that can occur in these periods, other data sources are used to maintain an up-to-date picture of specific regions.

As well as general population censuses, national statistical offices produce an array of industrial censuses. These may include industrial production, housing, construction, agriculture, restaurants and hotels, and financial services, e.g. **www.statistics.gov.uk/statbase/ mainmenu.asp**.

Other government publications. In addition to the census, national statistical offices collect and publish a great deal of statistical data. Examining the Department of Statistics and Research in Cyprus as an example (**www.mof.gov.cy**), major industrial categories such as agriculture, construction, retailing and tourism are classified, with a whole array of available statistics. More generally, demographic, health, household income and expenditure, and labour statistical reports are also available.

Examples of reports from the British Office for National Statistics include *Social Trends*. *Social Trends* draws together social and economic data from a wide range of government departments and other organisations to provide a comprehensive guide to British society today, and how it has been changing. In 2005 *Social Trends* celebrated 35 years of social reporting. The 2005 edition featured an overview chapter that highlights some of the major changes in society since *Social Trends* was first published. The UK has an ageing population, and growth in the minority ethnic population has resulted in a more diverse society. Household income has risen over the past 35 years, although income inequality has widened. Life expectancy has also increased but so have the number of years that the population can expect to live in poor health or with a disability. Technology has transformed many lives and dependence on the car is greater than ever.

In the EU, statistics are collected and published by the Statistical Office of the European Community (SOEC) in a series called Eurostat (**www.europa.eu**) (**www.epp.eurostat. cec.eu.int**). Tables normally contain figures for individual member states of the EU plus totals for all countries. Eurostat divides its publications into themes, which are:

- *Theme 1* – General and regional statistics
- *Theme 2* – Economy and finance
- *Theme 3* – Population and social conditions
- *Theme 4* – Industry trade and services
- *Theme 5* – Agriculture and fisheries
- *Theme 6* – External trade
- *Theme 7* – Transport
- *Theme 8* – Environment and energy
- *Theme 9* – Science and technology.

It also produces general titles which include *Eurostat Yearbook* (annual), *Basic Statistics* (annual), *Europe in Figures* (annual), *Key Figures* (monthly) and *Eurostatistics* (monthly).

To examine any of the national statistics offices in Europe and Global Regions, visit the excellent Central Statistics Office Ireland website **www.cso.ie/links/** and follow the country links. There are also links to many other important organisations with relevant statistics such as the European Central Bank and the International Monetary Fund.

Computerised databases

Most published information is also available in the form of computerised databases. Computerised databases contain information that has been made available in computer-readable form for electronic distribution. From the 1980s to today, the number of databases, as well as the vendors providing these services, has grown enormously.[12] Computerised databases offer a number of advantages over printed data, including:[13]

1 The data are current and up to date, as publishers and data compilers are now using computers as the primary production technology.
2 The search process is more comprehensive, quicker and simpler. Online vendors provide ready access to hundreds of databases. Moreover, this information can be accessed instantaneously, and the search process is simplified as the vendors provide uniform search protocols and commands for accessing the database.
3 The cost of accessing these is relatively low, because of the accuracy of searching for the right data, and the speed of location and transfer of data.
4 It is convenient to access these data using a personal computer fitted with an appropriate communication device, such as a modem or a communication network.

While computerised database information can be helpful, it is vast and can be confusing. Thus a classification of computerised databases is helpful.

Classification of computerised databases

Computerised databases may be classified as online, Internet or offline as shown in Figure 4.3. Online databases consist of a central data bank that is accessed with a computer (or dumb terminal) via a telecommunications network. Internet databases can be accessed, searched and analysed on the Internet. It is also possible to download data from the Internet and store it in the computer or on an auxiliary storage device.[14] Offline databases

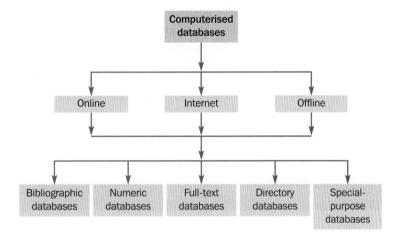

**Figure 4.3
A classification of
computerised
databases**

make the information available on CD-ROM. Thus, offline databases can be accessed at the user's location without the use of an external telecommunications network.[15]

Online, Internet and **offline databases** may be further classified as bibliographic, numeric, full text, directory or special-purpose databases. **Bibliographic databases** are composed of citations to articles in journals, magazines, newspapers, marketing research studies, technical reports, government documents and the like.[16] They often provide summaries or abstracts of the material cited. The earlier example of *Market Research Abstracts* (**www.imriresearch.com**) is an example of a bibliographic database. Another example is the *Aslib Index to Theses* (**www.theses.com**); this bibliographic database lists theses at masters and doctoral level and research degrees, including abstracts from the UK and Ireland.

Numeric databases contain numerical and statistical information. For example, some numeric databases provide time series data about the economy and specific industries. The earlier examples of census-based numeric databases using data over a series of censuses provide an example of a numeric database.

Full-text databases contain the complete text of the sources of the database. Examples include *World Advertising Research Center WARC* (**www.warc.com**), *FT Intelligence* (**www.ft.chadwyck.co.uk**) and *Infotrac Searchbank* (accessed through academic library links). WARC is a supplier of intelligence to the global marketing, advertising, media and research communities. *Searchbank* has over 100 full-text journals on subjects including business, economics, current affairs and new technologies. It includes a spectrum of journals from professional trade publications through to refereed academic journals. *FT Intelligence*, which includes *Europe Intelligence Wire*, was developed to offer access to a range of key sources of accurate and unbiased financial, economic and political news. It is possible to search on specific countries, sectors and publications based upon over 150 daily and weekly newspapers and business magazines from the UK and Europe.

Directory databases provide information on individuals, organisations and services. *European Interactive Directories* (**www.euroyellowpages.com**) is an example of a directory that has channels based upon EU community activities, country channels and thematic channels such as suppliers, wholesalers and shopping centres. Another example worth examining is the *ESOMAR directory* (**www.esomar.nl**) which provides details of member organisations throughout the world as well as many other publications of value to marketing researchers based in Europe.

Finally, there are **special-purpose databases**. For example, the *Non-Governmental Organisation NGO directory* (**www.rec.org/REC/Databases/databases.html**) helps to track down information about environmental organisations working in Central and Eastern Europe. It has contact information for over 2,700 organisations from over 15 Central and Eastern European countries.

Online databases
Databases, stored in computers, that require a telecommunications network to access.

Internet databases
Databases that can be accessed, searched and analysed on the Internet. It is also possible to download data from the Internet and store it on the computer or an auxiliary device.

Offline databases
Databases that are available on CD-ROM.

Bibliographic databases
Databases composed of citations to articles in journals, magazines, newspapers, marketing research studies, technical reports, government documents, and the like. They often provide summaries or abstracts of the material cited.

Numeric databases
Databases containing numerical and statistical information that may be important sources of secondary data.

Full-text databases
Databases that contain the complete text of secondary source documents comprising the database.

Directory databases
Databases that provide information on individuals, organisations and services.

Special-purpose databases
Databases that contain information of a specific nature, e.g. data on a specialised industry.

In addition, virtually all libraries of major universities maintain special-purpose databases of research activities that reflect the distinct specialisms of that university. Beyond the internally generated, special-purpose databases, university libraries and reference libraries maintain computerised databases with instructions relating to what may be accessed and how it may be accessed. Another library source worth examining for computerised sources is the European Commission's 'Libraries' site (**www.europa.eu.int**). The site, which is multilingual, is distributed by the EUROPA server. EUROPA is the portal site of the EU. It provides up-to-date coverage of European affairs and essential information on European integration. Users can access websites of each of the EU institutions.

Syndicated sources of secondary data

Syndicated sources (services)
Information services offered by marketing research organisations that provide information from a common database to different firms that subscribe to their services.

In addition to published data or data available in the form of computerised databases, syndicated sources constitute the other major source of external secondary data. **Syndicated sources**, also referred to as **syndicated services**, are companies that collect and sell common pools of data designed to serve information needs shared by a number of clients. These data are not collected with a focus on a specific marketing problem, but the data and reports supplied to client companies can be personalised to fit specific needs. For example, reports could be organised based on the clients' sales territories or product lines. Using syndicated services is frequently less expensive than commissioning tailored primary data collection. Figure 4.4 presents a classification of syndicated sources. Syndicated sources can be classified based on the unit of measurement (house-

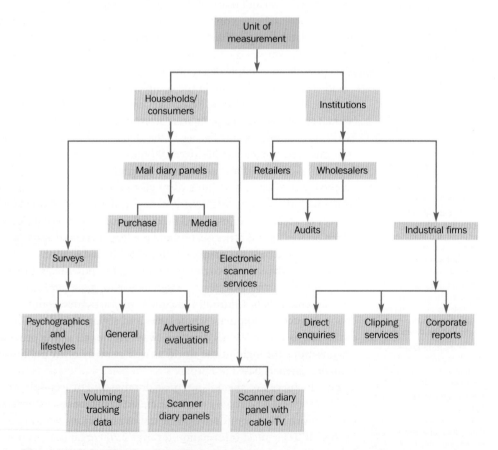

Figure 4.4 A classification of syndicated services

holds and consumers or institutions). Household and consumer data may be obtained from surveys, diary panels or electronic scanner services. Information obtained through surveys consists of values and lifestyles, advertising evaluation, or general information related to preferences, purchase, consumption and other aspects of behaviour. Diary panels emphasise information on purchases or media consumption. Electronic scanner services might provide scanner data only, scanner data linked to diary panels, or scanner data linked to diary panels and (cable) TV. When institutions are the unit of measurement, the data may be obtained from retailers, wholesalers or industrial firms. An overview of the various syndicated sources is given in Table 4.3. Each of these sources will be discussed.

Table 4.3 Overview of syndicated services

Type	Characteristics	Advantages	Disadvantages	Uses
Surveys	Surveys conducted at regular intervals	Most flexible way of obtaining data; information on underlying motives	Interviewer errors; respondent errors	Market segmentation, advertising theme selection and advertising advertising effectiveness
Mail diary panels	Households provide specific information regularly over an extended period of time; respondents asked to record specific behaviour as it occurs	Recorded purchase behaviour can be linked to the demographic/ psychographic characteristics	Lack of representativeness; response bias; maturation	Forecasting sales, market share and trends; establishing consumer profiles, brand loyalty and switching; evaluating test markets, advertising and distribution
Diary media panels	Electronic devices automatically recording behaviour, supplemented by a diary	Same as mail diary panel	Same as mail diary panel	Establishing advertising selecting media programme or air time; establishing viewer profiles
Scanner volume tracking data	Household purchases recorded through electronic scanners in supermarkets	Data reflect actual purchases; timely data, less expensive	Data may not be respresentative; errors in recording purchases; difficult to link purchases to elements of marketing mix other than price	Price tracking, modelling effectiveness of in-store modelling
Scanner diary panels with cable TV	Scanner panels of households that subscribe to cable TV	Data reflect actual purchases; sample control; ability to link panel data to household characteristics	Data may not be representative; quality of data limited	Promotional mix analyses, copy testing, new product testing, positioning
Audit services	Verification of product movement by examining physical records or performing inventory analysis	Relatively precise information at retail and wholesale levels	Coverage may be be incomplete; matching of data on competitive activity may be difficult	Measurement of consumer sales and market share; competitive activity; analysing distribution patterns; tracking of new products
Industrial firms	Data banks on industrial establishments created through direct enquiries of companies, clipping services and corporate reports	Important source of information in industrial firms; particularly useful in initial phases of the projects	Data are lacking in terms of content, quantity and quality	Determining market potential by geographic area, defining sales territories, allocating advertising budget

Syndicated data from households

Surveys

Surveys
Interviews with a large number of people using a questionnaire.

Various syndicated services regularly conduct **surveys** and **omnibus surveys**. In general, these surveys involve interviews with a large number of respondents using a pre-designed questionnaire. The distinction of the omnibus survey is that it targets particular types of respondents such as those in certain geographic locations, e.g. Luxembourg residents, or consumers of particular types of products, e.g. business air travellers. The following example illustrates just one of many omnibus surveys conducted by Taylor Nelson Sofres Omnibus Services (**www.tns-global.com**) and the nature of interpretation that can emerge from an omnibus survey.

Example **Children are savvy consumers who increasingly understand the role of marketing[17]**

Anita Emery, Group Director of TNS Omnibus Services, argues that children also have a strong influence on the buying decisions of their peers or family members. Despite children showing high recognition and awareness of advertising campaigns, TNS's children's omnibus research with youngsters aged 10–19 shows that only 8% say 'you can trust everything you read or hear in an ad'. Even among 10 year olds, just 16% agreed with this statement, a relatively cynical attitude normally associated with much older consumers. Marketers cannot underestimate the influence children have on consumer decisions and the impact that advertising campaigns have on children's appeal and appreciation of brands and products.

Omnibus survey
A distinctive form of survey that serves the needs of a syndicate group. The omnibus survey targets particular types of respondents such as those in specific locations, e.g. Luxembourg residents, or customers of particular types of product, e.g. business air travellers. With that target group of respondents, a core set of questions can be asked with other questions added as syndicate members wish.

With a defined target group of respondents, a core set of questions can be asked with other questions added as syndicate members wish. Other syndicate members can 'jump on the omnibus' and buy the answers to all the questionnaire responses or to specific questions of their choice. Surveys and omnibus surveys may be broadly classified based on their content as psychographics and lifestyles, advertising evaluation, or general surveys.

Psychographics and lifestyles. **Psychographics** refer to the psychological profiles of individuals and to psychologically based measures of lifestyle. **Lifestyles** refer to the distinctive modes of living of a society or some of its segments. Together, these measures are generally referred to as activities, interests and opinions. A good example of a marketing research agency that works upon the measurement and marketing applications of psychographics and lifestyles can be found at **www.espconsultancy.co.uk**.

Psychographics
Quantified profiles of individuals based upon lifestyle characteristics.

Lifestyles
Distinctive patterns of living described by the activities people engage in, the interests they have, and the opinions they hold of themselves and the world around them.

Advertising evaluation. The purpose of advertising evaluation surveys is to assess the effectiveness of advertising using print and broadcast media. TV commercials are evaluated using either the recruited audience method or the in-home viewing method. In the former method, respondents are recruited and brought to a central viewing facility, such as a theatre or mobile viewing laboratory. The respondents view the commercials and provide data regarding knowledge, attitudes and preferences related to the product being advertised and the commercial itself. In the in-home viewing method, consumers evaluate commercials at home in their normal viewing environment. New commercials can be pretested at the network level or in local markets. A survey of viewers is then conducted to assess the effectiveness of the commercials. The following example illustrates the importance of advertising evaluation, how qualitative research helps in the development of advertisements and quantitative research measures their performance.

Example **Gut or numbers? Pretesting ads[18]**

Larry Friedman, Global Director of Brand and Advertising Research at TNS, confirms that testing advertising has grown faster than other forms of research over the past few years. 'Everyone is trying to build a connection between their brands and consumers and trying to understand how advertising contributes to that,' he explains. Research to pretest advert can be qualitative (focus groups and one-to-one interviews; the moderator elicits general discussion about the advert) or quantitative (interviewees answer specific questions that aim to measure their responses to the advert). Qualitative research tends to be used in early stages of an advert's production, with groups of consumers discussing concepts before anything is created. Then an animatic, a moving storyboard, is often drawn up, and this is researched quantitatively. Millward Brown is the market leader in ad testing (**www.imsl.ie**). Millward Brown's quantitative 'Link' tests are used across the industry. Link measures three areas of ad performance: communication, branded memorability and consumer response. Branded memorability is measured as an AI (Awareness Indicator) number, which is made up of scores for branding, enjoyment and engagement. Link now incorporates a facility for measuring the following emotional responses: surprised, excited, attracted, proud, inspired, confident, contented, affectionate, hatred, repelled, annoyed, inadequate, disappointed, guilty, unimpressed, sad.

The following example illustrates one element of the media research work that is conducted by Sports Marketing Surveys. It describes the techniques for media exposure analysis. Visit the agency's website at **www.sportsmarketingsurveys.com** to see the nature of, and how it manages, media evaluation, media coverage and compliance monitoring.

Focus on **Sports Marketing Surveys**

Media exposure analysis

TV exposure

The majority of sports sponsorships are focused on the opportunity of exposure through TV. Media exposure is recorded if the sighting is at least 1 second in duration and the brand/logo is clearly readable. This is monitored using Sports Marketing Surveys' leading-edge TV monitoring systems: FREDI (Freeze Frame Enhanced Digital Imaging) and Magellan (automated image recognition).

Press exposure

In the UK, national newspapers, mostly with a large sports section, are read by four out of five adults every week and sponsor mentions and logos can return notable media values. In other markets there are one or more daily papers devoted to sport. Sports Marketing Surveys undertakes press analysis in a number of countries on a regular basis. Sports Marketing Surveys has access to national, regional and specialist publications through specialist press agencies, which are monitored for brand exposure. Brand exposure is recorded if all letters of a sponsor' s name appear in full and the brand/logo is clearly readable, with a method comparable with TV.

Radio exposure

Sports coverage is considerable on national and regional radio stations and commentators and presenters alike offer verbal mentions for event and team sponsors. Sports Marketing Surveys monitors sponsor mentions on national, regional and specialist sports stations. Since verbal mentions carry more impact than visual exposure, each mention is offered the equivalent of 10 seconds of exposure.

Internet exposure

The Internet is now proving to be a major source of information to sports fans and a value can be placed on the exposure of sponsor logos. Sports Marketing Surveys can monitor brand exposure across the Web using specialist web-search agencies or in-house searches for selected sites.

General surveys. Surveys are also conducted for a variety of other purposes, including examination of purchase and consumption behaviour. Because a variety of data can be obtained, survey data have numerous uses. They can be used for market segmentation, as with psychographic and lifestyle data, and for establishing consumer profiles. Surveys are also useful for determining product image, measurement and positioning, and conducting price perception analysis. Other notable uses include advertising theme selection and evaluation of advertising effectiveness.

Purchase and media panels

About a quarter of all research budgets is spent on panels in their various formats, the largest investors in this format in Europe being Switzerland at 41%, Germany 35% and the Netherlands 31%.[19] Panels were discussed in Chapter 3 in the context of longitudinal research designs. Panels are samples of respondents who provide specified information at regular intervals over an extended period of time. These respondents may be organisations, households or individuals, although household diary panels are most common. The distinguishing feature of panels is that the respondents record specific behaviours as they occur. Previously, behaviour was recorded in a diary, and the diary returned to the research organisation every one to four weeks. Panel diaries have been gradually replaced by electronic diaries. Now, most of the panels are online and the behaviour is recorded electronically, either entered online by the respondents or recorded automatically by electronic devices as illustrated by the following example.

Example   **The battle for media measurement[20]**

Audience measurement for radio has traditionally used weekly diaries, where respondents record their own listening habits. However, this method is completely reliant on the memory of respondents, and has often led to excessive claims for stations or programmes they listen to regularly and to reduced claims for those they listen to less frequently. Passive measurement of radio usage is being developed through the following methods.

The Personal People Meter (PPM)

A small pager-type device is worn by respondents throughout the day. This inserts an inaudible code into a broadcast transmission at the radio station. The codes are then downloaded to a central computer. PPM is used in Belgium, Canada, Norway and Singapore.

The Media Monitor

This samples sounds to which respondents are exposed using an audio matching pager-type device. It can collect other information such as the location of respondents and active or passive listening. The technology is still being tested. There are plans to start a multimedia survey in Italy in 2006.

The Media Watch

The unit is built into a wristwatch and is designed to record exposure to radio, TV, cinema, posters as well as readership. It is currently used in Switzerland, Liechtenstein and the UK with testing in Denmark, France, Germany, the Netherlands, Sweden and Tokyo. Recent formal tests were less than satisfactory as the watch identified fewer listening occasions compared with other methods.

The Mobile Phone

This works on an encoded signal basis using mobile phone technology to capture and transmit the encoded signal for analysis. This is being tested in the UK. Interest is strongest in South America and the larger markets in Europe, and Commercial Radio Australia is working with the manufacturer.

Media panels
A data gathering technique composed of samples of respondents whose TV viewing behaviour is automatically recorded by electronic devices, supplementing the purchase information recorded in a diary.

In diary media panels, electronic devices automatically record viewing behaviour, thus supplementing a diary. Diary **media panels** yield information helpful for establishing advertising rates by radio and TV networks, selecting appropriate programming, and profiling viewer or listener subgroups. Advertisers, media planners and buyers find panel information particularly useful. Another media vehicle that competes heavily for advertising budgets is the Internet. The following example illustrates how A.C. Nielsen use media panels to understand Internet usage.

Example   ## The Nielsen way[21]

The Nielsen/NetRatings (**www.netratings.com**) approach to monitoring consumer behaviour online is to employ panels of randomly selected consumers to form a representative subset of the total online population. The panel's behaviour is used to provide estimates of behaviour in the population as a whole. Panellists install unobtrusive tracking software on their PCs that records everything they do, providing continual information on their behaviour. This allows comparison of all the sites that appear in the research and provides data that can be tested against 13 different panels established in other countries. People are the focus of this research: who they are, how they behave online, and how their behaviour changes over time, by country and demographic profile. This ability to link visits to sites to an individual and hence to track usage behaviour within a session and across many sessions is unique to panel-based research. It provides a complete picture of the Internet landscape, allowing key players to understand not only their performance, but also that of their competitors.

Purchase panels
A data gathering technique in which respondents record their purchases in a diary.

Purchase panels provide information useful for forecasting sales, estimating market shares, assessing brand loyalty and brand-switching behaviour, establishing profiles of specific user groups, measuring promotional effectiveness, and conducting controlled store tests.

Compared with sample surveys (see Chapter 10), diary panels offer certain distinct advantages.[22] Panels can provide longitudinal data (data can be obtained from the same respondents repeatedly). People who are willing to serve on panels may provide more and higher quality data than sample respondents. In diary purchase panels, information is recorded at the time of purchase, eliminating recall errors.[23] Information recorded by electronic devices is accurate because it eliminates recall errors.

Source: © George Disano/CORBIS

The disadvantages of diary panels include lack of representativeness, maturation and response biases. They may under-represent certain groups such as minorities and those with low education levels. This problem is further compounded by refusal to respond and attrition of panel members. Over time, maturation sets in, and the panel members must be replaced. Response biases may occur, since simply being on the panel may alter behaviour. Because purchase or media data are entered by hand, recording errors are also possible (see Chapter 3).

Electronic scanner services

The following example illustrates the nature and scope of electronic scanner services as undertaken by A.C. Nielsen, which conducts consumer panel services in 18 countries around the world.

Example | **A.C. Nielsen – the business economist at work[24]**

Most of A.C. Nielsen's revenue comes from selling information on *fast-moving consumer goods* (FMCG). This information is compiled either from scanner data obtained from thousands of supermarkets, pharmacists and department stores, or from a 40,000-household panel who electronically record every aspect of every goods purchase they made using that item's bar code.

Panel members go beyond their standard forms of analysing and presenting existing data to more creative interpretations that attempt to tell the marketer something he or she does not know. Often, creativity is valued more than sophisticated econometric techniques, as illustrated in the following two examples.

Inventory and sales data are available on food store retail sales, so an inventory–sales ratio can be calculated. This ratio had been increasing for several years up to 1992 when it began to shrink. Yet it is generally accepted that the size of the average new store is increasing, implying the need for additional inventories relative to sales. Coincidentally, more sophisticated inventory management techniques have become especially prevalent in food stores in recent years. Apparently, the ratio is being driven more by improved inventory management than by the opening of new, larger stores. A discrete cause and effect cannot be proven, but a linkage between the ratio and better inventory control mechanisms is highly probable.

Consumer spending patterns in Asia are very difficult to analyse, given the paucity of data available and the lack of data comparability across countries or spending components. By calculating consumer spending on food as a share of total consumer spending, and then ordering the results by per capita GDP, a relationship becomes obvious. Poorer countries spend proportionately more of their resources on food, around 50%. For middle-income countries, this ratio slides from around 40% to 20%, and then holds steady near 20% for the developed economies. The implication is that, as a country obtains a middle-income status, because of this declining ratio, food sales will not grow as fast as other categories of consumer spending.

Although information provided by surveys and diary panels is useful, electronic scanner services are becoming increasingly popular. The role of scanned data as a foundation to developing sophisticated consumer databases is developed in Chapter 5. In this chapter we examine scanned data as a distinct source of syndicated data. **Scanner data** reflect some of the latest technological developments in the marketing research industry. They are collected by passing merchandise over a laser scanner that optically reads the bar-coded description (Universal Product Code, or UPC) printed on the merchandise. This code is then linked to the current price held in the computer memory and used to prepare a sales slip. Information printed on the sales slip includes descriptions as well as prices of all items purchased. Checkout scanners, now used in many retail stores, are revolutionising packaged goods marketing research.

Three types of scanner data are available: **volume tracking data, scanner diary panels** and **scanner diary panels with cable TV**. Volume tracking data provide information on purchases by brand, size, price and flavour or formulation, based on sales data collected from the checkout scanner. This information is collected nationally from a sample of supermarkets with electronic scanners. In scanner diary panels, each household member is given an ID card that looks like a credit card. Panel members present the ID card at the checkout counter each time they shop. The checker keys in the ID numbers and each item of that customer's order. The information is stored by day of week and time of day.[25]

Scanner diary panels with cable TV combine diary panels with new technologies growing out of the cable TV industry. Households on these panels subscribe to one of the cable or TV systems in their market. By means of a cable TV 'split', the researcher targets different commercials into the homes of the panel members. For example, half the households may see test commercial A during the 6 p.m. newscast while the other half see test commercial B. These panels allow researchers to conduct fairly controlled experiments in a relatively natural environment.[26]

Scanner data are useful for a variety of purposes.[27] National volume tracking data can be used for tracking sales, prices and distribution, for modelling, and for analysing early warning signals. Scanner diary panels with cable TV can be used for testing new products, repositioning products, analysing promotional mixes, and making advertising decisions, including budget, copy and media, and pricing. These panels provide marketing researchers with a unique controlled environment for the manipulation of marketing variables. The following example gives a basic description of GfK's BEHAVIORSCAN.

Scanner data
Data obtained by passing merchandise over a laser scanner that reads the UPC from the packages.

Volume tracking data
Scanner data that provide information on purchases by brand, size, price and flavour or formulation.

Scanner diary panels
Scanner data where panel members are identified by an ID card, allowing information about each panel member's purchases to be stored with respect to the individual shopper.

Scanner diary panels with cable TV
The combination of a scanner diary panel with manipulations of the advertising that is being broadcast by cable TV companies.

Example

GfK BEHAVIORSCAN: Europe's first experimental test market using targetable TV

GfK's household panel is demographically, nationally representative. It helps to answer important questions such as: How successful will a new product be? Who are the purchasers of a new product? How well does TV advertising drive sales? Which level of media spending is optimal? Which TV ad copy is more successful at increasing sales? GfK cooperates with all relevant outlets and all test stores utilise scanners. GfK personnel handle all elements associated with the test, and execute promotions, price changes, handle product stocking and check the test stores daily to ensure 100% distribution and no out-of-stocks. Their three European test markets are:

1 **Hassloch, Germany**: *3,000 households* with GfK ID card, 2,000 households with targetable TV and 1,000 control households, *TV Broadcasters*: ARD, ZDF, Kabel 1, Pro7, Sat.1, RTL, RTL2, VOX, Super RTL, *Print*: Hörzu (with split-panel), daily newspapers, supplements.

2 **Angers, France**: *4,000 households* with GfK ID card, *11 partner stores, TV broadcasters*: 14 channels; TF1, France 2, France 3, Canal+, France 5, M6, Paris Première, Série Club,

LCI, Eurosport, TMC Monte Carlo, MCM, Canal J, RTL9, *Print*: Femme Actuelle or Télé Loisirs (with split-panel), *Radio*: 10 channels: Alouette, Chérie FM, Europe 1, Europe 2, MFM, Nostagie, RFM, NRJ, RTL, RTL2, *Postering, Cinema, Internet.*

3 **Le Mans, France**: *4,000 households* with GfK ID card, *9 partner stores, TV broadcasters*: 14 channels; TF1, France 2, France 3, Canal+, France 5, M6, Paris Première, Série Club, LCI, Eurosport, TMC Monte Carlo, MCM, Canal J, RTL9, *Postering, Cinema, Internet.*

Scanner data have an obvious advantage over surveys and diary panels: they reflect purchasing behaviour that is not subject to interviewing, recording, memory or expert biases. The record of purchases obtained by scanners is complete and unbiased by price sensitivity, because the panellist is not required to be particularly conscious of price levels and changes. Another advantage is that in-store variables such as pricing, promotions and displays are part of the dataset. The data are also likely to be current and can be obtained quickly. Finally, scanner panels with cable TV provide a highly controlled testing environment.

The quality of scanner data may be limited by several factors. Not all products may be scanned. For example, to avoid lifting a heavy item, a sales assistant may use the register to ring it up. If an item does not scan on the first try, the assistant may key in the price and ignore the bar code. Sometimes a consumer purchases many flavours of the same item, but the assistant scans only one package and then rings in the number of purchases. Thus, the transaction is inaccurately recorded. Although scanner data provide behavioural and sales information, they do not provide information on underlying attitudes and preferences and the reasons for specific choices.

Syndicated data from institutions

Retailer and wholesaler audits

As Figure 4.4 shows, syndicated data are available from retailers and wholesalers as well as industrial firms (see the example of the work of German marketing research company GfK at **www.gfkms.com** which conducts retail and wholesale audits in the following sectors: automotive aftermarket, consumer electronics/brown goods, do-it-yourself, entertainment, furniture, gardening, imaging photo, information technology, lighting products, luggage, major domestic appliances/white goods, office equipment, optics, small domestic appliances, stationery, telecommunication, wristwatches).

Audit
A data collection process derived from physical records or performing inventory analysis. Data are collected personally by the researcher, or by representatives of the researcher, and are based on counts usually of physical objects rather than people.

The most popular means of obtaining data from retailers and wholesalers is an audit. An **audit** is a formal examination and verification of product movement carried out by examining physical records or analysing inventory. Retailers and wholesalers who participate in the audit receive basic reports and cash payments from the audit service. Audit data focus on the products or services sold through the outlets or the characteristics of the outlets themselves.

Example   ### Retail auditing for retailing information[28]

In the USA in 1933, A.C. Nielsen pioneered food and drug indices to measure and understand the performance and dynamics of product sales. The Retail Measurement Service of A.C. Nielsen uses store audit data on product movement, market share, distribution, price and other market-sensitive information in over 80 countries across six continents. Using in-store scanning of product codes and store visits by auditors, sample and census information is gathered across the food, household, health and beauty, durables, confectionery and beverage industries.

Retail audit data can be useful to consumer product firms. For example, if Colgate-Palmolive is contemplating the introduction of a new toothpaste brand, a retail audit can help determine the size of the total market and distribution of sales by type of outlet and by different regions.

Wholesale audit services, the counterpart of retail audits, monitor warehouse withdrawals. Participating operators, which include supermarket chains, wholesalers and frozen-food warehouses, typically account for over 80% of the volume in the area.

The uses of retail and wholesale audit data include:

- determining the size of the total market and the distribution of sales by type of outlet, region or city;
- assessing brand shares and competitive activity;
- identifying shelf space allocation and inventory problems;
- analysing distribution problems;
- developing sales potentials and forecasts;
- developing and monitoring promotional allocations based on sales volume.

Audits provide relatively accurate information on the movement of many different products at the wholesale and retail levels. Furthermore, this information can be broken down by a number of important variables, such as brand, type of outlet and size of market. Audits have limited coverage, however; not all markets or operators are included. In addition, audit information may not be timely or current, particularly compared with scanner data. Typically, there is a two-month gap between the completion of the audit cycle and the publication of reports. Another disadvantage is that, unlike scanner data, audit data cannot be linked to consumer characteristics. In fact, there may even be a problem in relating audit data to advertising expenditures and other marketing efforts. Some of these limitations are overcome in computerised audit panels.

Industrial firms

These provide syndicated data about industrial firms, businesses and other institutions. Syndicated data are collected by making direct enquiries to organisations, from clipping services (see an example at **www.romeike.com**) to the analysis of corporate reports (see example of corporate analysis of the telecoms market at www.insight-corp.com). Dunn & Bradstreet's International Business Locator (**www.dnb.com**) provides access to over 28 million public/private companies in over 200 countries. After finding a business, the Locator will provide key business data including full address information, line of business details, business size (sales, net worth, employees), names of key principals, and identification of this location's headquarters, domestic parent company and/or global parent company.

Industrial firm information is useful for sales management decisions, including identifying prospects, defining territories, setting quotas, and measuring market potential by geographic areas. It can also aid in advertising decisions such as targeting prospects, allocating advertising budgets, selecting media, and measuring advertising effectiveness. This kind of information is useful for segmenting the market and for designing custom products and services for important segments.

International marketing research

A wide variety of secondary data are available for international marketing research.[29] The problem is not a lack of data but the potential overabundance of information. The international marketing researcher has to work through an array of potential sources to find accurate, up-to-date and relevant information. Evaluation of secondary data is even more critical for international than for domestic projects. Different sources report different values for a given statistic, such as the GDP, because of differences in the way the unit is defined. Measurement units may not be equivalent across countries. In France, for example, some workers are still paid a 13-monthly salary each year as an automatic bonus, resulting in a measurement construct that is different from those in other countries.[30] The accuracy of secondary data may also vary from country to country. Data from highly industrialised countries in Europe are likely to be more accurate than those from developing nations. Business and income statistics are affected by the taxation structure and the extent of tax evasion. Population censuses may vary in frequency and year in which the data are collected. In the UK, for example, the census is conducted every 10 years, whereas in the People's Republic of China there was a 29-year gap between the censuses of 1953 and 1982. This situation, however, is changing quickly. Several syndicated firms are developing huge sources of international secondary data, as illustrated in the following example.

Example

Los Medios y Mercados de Latinoamerica (LMML)[31]

Started in 1994 by Roper Audits & Surveys Worldwide (**www.roperasw.com**), *Los Medios y Mercados de Latinoamerica* (The Markets and Media of Latin America) is the largest multinational survey of media and consumer habits that is conducted in Latin America to provide managers with important information for their marketing strategies. The study, which is repeated every year, aims at tracking the development of media and consumer habits in Latin America.

A recent multinational survey was conducted in 18 Latin American countries, including Argentina, Brazil, Colombia, Mexico and Venezuela. It sampled 6,634 respondents between the ages of 12 and 64. Its probability sample, representing urban as well as rural Latin America, can be projected to 280 million people or 79 million households.

The research design for this survey involved two steps. First, the personal interview technique was used to measure the variety of media, including newspapers, multinational and local magazines, TV and radio. Then a 25-page self-administered booklet was passed to the respondents to measure their product consumption and usage in over 100 categories and 800 brands. Demographic data gathered about the respondents included country/region, age, sex, employment status, occupation, education, household size, annual household income, car ownership, household goods owned and services taken. Subscribing companies can easily use these data, as the survey results are provided in a set of 14 printed volumes, and also in computer database formats including an SPSS format.

Ethics in marketing research

Possible ethical dilemmas exist when using internal or external secondary data. Some ethical issues that are pertinent include:

- The unnecessary and expensive collection of primary data when the problem can be addressed based on secondary data alone.
- Cutting corners through the use of only secondary data when primary data are needed.
- The use of secondary data that are not applicable.

- The use of secondary data that have been gathered through morally questionable means.
- Compromising the anonymity of customer details held on databases.

As was discussed in Chapter 2, the unnecessary collection of expensive primary data when the research problem can be addressed using only secondary data is unethical. In this case, the researcher is using a more expensive method that is less appropriate. Similarly, the exclusive reliance on secondary data when the research problem requires primary data collection could raise ethical concerns. This is particularly true if the researcher is charging a fixed fee for the project and the research design was not specified in advance. Here again, the researcher's profit goes up, but at the expense of the client.

The researcher is ethically obliged to ensure the relevance and usefulness of secondary data to the problem at hand. The secondary data should be evaluated by the criteria discussed earlier in this chapter. Only data judged to be appropriate should be used.

Internet and computer applications

The World Wide Web as an online source of secondary data

The World Wide Web is a vital source of secondary data and intelligence for the marketing researcher. Given the global nature of the technology, the Internet is a vital tool for the international marketing researcher. One can go directly to the websites of traditional suppliers of secondary data from government or business sources. Many of those sites also have inside search engines that sort data from the supplier's internal database. Information on the Web is of great value as generally it is current, though care must be taken to note when web pages have been updated. It should be noted that not all secondary data on the Web is free. The Web may reveal the existence of data on a particular subject or industry, but remember the costs involved in conducting quality research. Hence the Web may be used to give an awareness and a 'taste' of secondary data but it does not necessarily mean 'free' data.

Internal secondary data

Large organisations have intranets, which greatly facilitate the search for access to secondary data. The Coca-Cola Company (**www.cocacola.com**), for example, has developed powerful intranet applications that enable Coca-Cola managers worldwide to search for past and present research studies and a wide variety of marketing-related information on the basis of keywords. Once located, the information can be accessed online. Even sensitive and restricted information can be accessed by obtaining permission electronically. Visit **www.intranets.com** for a fuller description of intranet technology, evaluations of software and an interactive tour.

External secondary data

As we have illustrated throughout this chapter, information can be obtained by visiting various business-related sites that provide sales leads and mailing lists, business profiles and credit ratings. Various newspapers, magazines and journals can be accessed on the Web with excellent indexing facilities to locate particular subjects, companies and individuals. Government data for the European Community and for individual countries through to regional and city councils can be accessed via the Web, though the quality and quantity of data available through government sources can vary enormously.

Online and syndicated sources of information

A substantial amount of face-to-face and telephone research in Europe has been replaced by the cheaper option of online panel research in recent years through many Western European countries.[32] With European data protection laws, other EU rules such as the Distance Selling Directive and falling response rates, many commentators predict more growth for online panels. It is worth examining the approaches used and case histories of online panel research at **www.him.uk.com**, **www.greenfieldonline.com**, **www.lightspeedresearch.com** and **www.intelliquest.com**.

For syndicated sources of information one can visit the home pages of the various marketing research companies and providers of syndicated information. The A.C. Nielsen home page at **www.acnielsen.com** is a good example. This site provides links to various manufacturers and to various countries such as the UK, Canada and Spain. Other good sources of syndicated data include Mintel, which can be reached at **www.mintel.co.uk**, Euromonitor at **www.euromonitor.com** and Taylor Nelson Sofres at **www.tnsofres.com** (it is worth working through the great array of marketing research products they offer).

International secondary data

The Internet has emerged as the most extensive source of secondary information. The utility of the Internet for the marketing researcher is further enhanced by the easy accessibility and retrieval of information and the ability to cross-validate information from a variety of sources. Most of the Internet links highlighted in this chapter allow for secondary data to be gathered from countries all over the world. Whilst necessarily we have a focus on European matters, it is well worth visiting **www.quirks.com**. This website is a most thorough source for information on marketing research, including case studies of successful research projects and a comprehensive list of directories.

Summary

In contrast to primary data, which originate with the researcher for the specific purpose of the problem at hand, secondary data and intelligence are data originally collected for other purposes. Secondary data can be obtained quickly and are relatively inexpensive. They have limitations, and should be carefully evaluated to determine their appropriateness for the problem at hand. The evaluation criteria consist of specifications, error, currency, objectivity, nature and dependability.

A wealth of information exists in the organisation for which the research is being conducted. This information constitutes internal secondary data. External data are generated by sources outside the organisation. These data exist in the form of published (printed) material, online and offline databases, or information made available by syndicated services. Published external sources may be broadly classified as general business data or government data. General business sources comprise guides, directories, indexes and statistical data. Government sources may be broadly categorised as census data and other data. Computerised databases may be online or offline. Both online and offline databases may be further classified as bibliographic, numeric, full-text, directory or specialised databases.

Syndicated sources are companies that collect and sell common pools of data designed to serve a number of clients. Syndicated sources can be classified based on the unit of measurement (households and consumers or institutions). Household and consumer data may be obtained via surveys, diary purchase or media panels, or electronic scanner services. When institutions are the unit of measurement, the data may be obtained from retailers, wholesalers or industrial units. It is desirable to combine information obtained from different secondary sources.

Several specialised sources of secondary data are useful for conducting international marketing research. The evaluation of secondary data becomes even more critical, however, because the usefulness and accuracy of these data can vary widely. Ethical dilemmas that can arise include the unnecessary collection of primary data, the use of only secondary data when primary data are needed, the use of secondary data that are not applicable, and the use of secondary data that have been gathered through morally questionable means.

Questions

1 What are the differences between primary data, secondary data and marketing intelligence?

2 What are the relative advantages and disadvantages of secondary data?

3 At what stages of the marketing research process can secondary data be used?

4 Why is it important to locate and analyse secondary data before progressing to primary data?

5 How may secondary data be used to validate qualitative research findings?

6 What is the difference between internal and external secondary data?

7 How can intranet technology help in the location and dissemination of secondary data?

8 By what criteria may secondary data be evaluated?

9 What criteria would you look for when examining the design and specifications of secondary data? Why is it important to examine these criteria?

10 To what extent should you use a secondary data source if you cannot see any explicit objectives attached to that research?

11 If you had two sources of secondary data for a project, the first being dependable but out of date, the second not dependable but up to date, which would you prefer?

12 Evaluate the desirability of using multiple sources of secondary data and intelligence.

13 List and describe the main types of syndicated sources of secondary data.

14 Explain what an online panel is, giving examples of different types of panel. What are the advantages and disadvantages of online panels?

15 What is an audit? Describe the uses, advantages and disadvantages of audits.

Exercises

1 Select an industry of your choice. Using secondary sources, obtain industry sales and the sales of the major firms in that industry for the past year. Estimate the market shares of each major firm. From another source where this work may have already been completed, e.g. Mintel, compare and contrast the estimates:
   a To what extent do they agree?
   b If there are differences in the estimates, what may account for these differences?

→

2 Select an industry of your choice. Write a report on the potential growth in that industry and the factors that are driving that growth. Use both secondary data and intelligence sources to build your case.

3 You are a brand manager for Proctor & Gamble, in charge of a shampoo brand. How would you use the information available from a store audit? Ask another student to play the role of marketing director. What case would you make to the marketing director about the value of investing in store audit information related to shampoos?

4 Visit the Central Statistics Office Ireland website (**www.cso.ie/links/**) and follow a link to the national

statistics office in a country of your choice. Write a report about the secondary data available from this office that would be useful to a national housing developer for the purpose of formulating its marketing strategy

5 In a small group discuss the following issues: 'What is the significance and limitations of government census data for marketing researchers?' and 'Given the growing array of alternative data sources that describe characteristics of individuals and households in a country, would it be a disaster for marketing researchers if formal government censuses were scrapped?'

Notes

1 Keating, P., 'The best airlines to fly today', *Money* (November 1997), 118–128.

2 Rothberg, H.N. and Erickson, G.S., *From knowledge to intelligence: creating competitive advantage in the next economy*, (Burlington MA: Butterworth-Heinemann, 2005); Aguilar, F.J., *Scanning the Business Environment* (London: Macmillan, 1967).

3 Adapted from Brownlie, D., 'Environmental scanning', in Baker, M.J., *The Marketing Book*, 3rd edn (Oxford: Butterworth–Heinemann), 158.

4 Curtis, J., 'Behind enemy lines', *Marketing* (24 May 2001), 28–29.

5 Rothberg, H.N. and Erickson, G.S., *From knowledge to intelligence: creating competitive advantage in the next economy* (Burlington MA: Butterworth-Heinemann, 2005), 21.

6 For applications of secondary data, see Kotabe, M., 'Using Euromonitor database in international marketing research', *Journal of the Academy of Marketing Science* 30 (2) (Spring 2002), 172; Bottomley, P.A. and Holden, S.J.S., 'Do we really know how consumers evaluate brand extensions? Empirical generalizations based on secondary analysis of eight studies', *Journal of Marketing Research* 38 (4) (November 2001) 494–500.

7 Jacob, H., *Using Published Data: Errors and Remedies* (Beverly Hills, CA: Sage, 1984).

8 Stewart, D.W., *Secondary Research: Information Sources and Methods* (Beverly Hills, CA: Sage, 1984), 23–33.

9 Fry, A., 'Number crunch', *Marketing* (4 December 1997), 29.

10 Lawson, J., 'Buying behaviour', *Database Marketing* (October 2004), 35–38.

11 Fries, J.R., 'Library support for industrial marketing research', *Industrial Marketing Management* 11 (February 1982), 47–51.

12 Schwartz, E., 'Dawn of a new database', *InfoWorld* 24 (11) (18 March, 2002), 32.

13 Post, C., 'Marketing data marts help companies stay ahead of the curve and in front of the competition', *Direct Marketing* 59 (April 1997), 37–40.

14 Tucker, D.M., 'Technology: online database set to debut this summer', *Business Press* (18 March 2002), 8; Notess, G.R., 'Searching the hidden Internet', *Database* 20 (June/July 1997), 37–40.

15 Quint, B., 'Assume the position, take the consequences', *Information Today* 13 (June 1996), 11–13.

16 Tenopir, C., 'Links and bibliographic databases', *Library Journal* 126 (4) (1 March 2001), 34–35; Notess, G.R., 'The Internet as an on-line service: bibliographic databases on the net', *Database* 19 (August/September 1996), 92–95.

17 Kilby, N., 'Trends insight', *Marketing Week* (21 July 2005), 33.

18 Murphy, C., 'Gut or numbers?', *Marketing* (15th June 2005), 31.

19 ESOMAR, 'Industry Study on 2004', Esomar World Research Report (2005), 27.

20 Mareck, M., 'The battle for media measurement', *Research World* (July/August 2005), 24–25.

21 Green, L., 'We know what you're looking at', *Research* (November 2004), 16.

22 Eunkyu, L., Hu, M.Y. and Toh, R.S., 'Are consumer survey results distorted? Systematic impact of behavioural frequency and duration on survey response errors', *Journal of Marketing Research* 37 (1) (February 2000), 125–133; Parfitt, J.H. and Collins, B.J.K., 'Use of consumer panels for brand share predictions', *Journal of the Market Research Society* 38 (4) (October 1996), 341–367; Ramaswamy, V. and Desarbo, W.S., 'SCULPTURE: a new methodology for deriving and analyzing hierarchical product-market structures from panel data', *Journal of Marketing Research* 27 (November 1990), 418–427

23 Clancy, K.J., 'Brand confusion', *Harvard Business Review* 80 (3) (March 2002), 22; Sudman, S., *On the Accuracy of Recording of Consumer Panels II*, Learning Manual (New York: Neal-Schumen, 1981).

24 Handler, D., 'The business economist at work: linking economics to market research: A.C. Nielsen', *Business Economics* 31 (October 1996), 51.

25 Andrew, R.L. and Srinivasan, T.C., 'Studying consideration effects in empirical choice models using scanner panel data', *Journal of Marketing Research* 32 (February 1995), 30–41; Bucklin, R.E., Gupta, S. and Han, S., 'A brand's eye view of response segmentation in consumer brand choice behaviour', *Journal of Marketing Research* 32 (February 1995), 66–74.

26 It is possible to combine store-level scanner data with scanner panel data to do an integrated analysis. See, for example, Russell, G.J. and Kamakura, W.A., 'Understanding brand competition using micro and macro scanner data', *Journal of Marketing Research* 31 (May 1994), 289–303.

27 Examples of scanner data applications include Lemon, K.W. and Nowlis, S.M., 'Developing synergies between promotions and brands in different price-quality tiers', *Journal of Marketing Research* 39 (2) (May 2002), 171–185; Chintagunta, P.K., 'Investigating category pricing behaviour at a retail chain', *Journal of Marketing Research* 39 (2) (May 2002), 141–154.

28 Based on information obtained from the suppliers.

29 For an example of international marketing research based on secondary data see Luk, S.T.K., 'The use of secondary infor-mation published by the PRC Government', *Journal of the Market Research Society* 41 (3) (3rd Quarter 1999), 355–365.

30 Chisnall, P.M., 'Marketing research: state of the art perspec-tives', *Journal of the Market Research Society* 44 (1) (1st Quarter 2002), 122–125.

31 Rydholm, J., 'A united effort', *Quirk's Marketing Research Review* (October 1996).

32 ESOMAR, 'Industry study on 2004', Esomar World Research Report (2005), 6.

Visit the *Marketing Research* Companion Website at www.pearsoned.co.uk/malhotra_euro for additional learning resources including annotated weblinks, an online glossary and a suite of downloadable video cases.

Source: © Photodisc/Getty Images/Cadmium

5

Internal secondary data and the use of databases

> *If all you do is stick to research in an organisation like this, then you're dead really.*[1]

Objectives

After reading this chapter, you should be able to:

1 describe the nature and purpose of internal sources of secondary data;

2 describe how different technological developments have increased the array of internally generated secondary data;

3 understand how databases are developing into powerful means to understand consumer behaviour through 'electronic observation';

4 understand how databases support traditional forms of marketing research to build up behavioural and attitudinal 'pictures' of target markets;

5 understand how geodemographic information systems can help in integrating data sources and in the graphical display of findings in a non-statistical manner;

6 describe how the link-up of different databases and survey data can be developed through the use of datawarehouses and be analysed through data mining techniques;

7 understand international data capture issues;

8 understand the ethical problems of having individual consumer data held on databases.

STAGE 1
Problem definition

STAGE 2
Research approach developed

STAGE 3
Research design developed

STAGE 4
Fieldwork or data collection

STAGE 5
Data preparation and analysis

STAGE 6
Report preparation and presentation

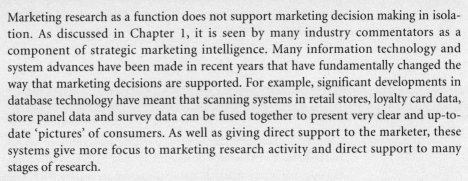

Overview

Marketing research as a function does not support marketing decision making in isolation. As discussed in Chapter 1, it is seen by many industry commentators as a component of strategic marketing intelligence. Many information technology and system advances have been made in recent years that have fundamentally changed the way that marketing decisions are supported. For example, significant developments in database technology have meant that scanning systems in retail stores, loyalty card data, store panel data and survey data can be fused together to present very clear and up-to-date 'pictures' of consumers. As well as giving direct support to the marketer, these systems give more focus to marketing research activity and direct support to many stages of research.

This chapter describes how internal secondary data and databases have developed to make major impacts upon how decision-makers are supported. The data collected and analysed through database marketing can be seen as secondary data sources. As with all good secondary data sources, they have a major impact upon the conduct and direction of primary data collection, analyses and interpretation. There are also many ethical issues related to utilising internally generated customer data and the use of databases.

We introduce our discussion with an example of the use of databases. Databases generated within companies or bought in from specialist sources are primarily viewed as a tool to generate direct sales and target promotion activities. However, internally generated customer databases are a secondary data source of value to marketing researchers. Technological developments in the collection, analysis and presentation of data present great opportunities to researchers. There are also potential conflicts with the core premise of anonymity in marketing research. The following example illustrates how a customer database can reveal behavioural characteristics of customers, valuable information to decision-makers in its own right. From an understanding of who Homebase's customers were and how they were behaving, marketing research could be designed to understand the underlying motives for this behaviour. The database analysis acted as an excellent foundation of a research design in deciding who to research and what issues to focus upon.

<table>
<tr><td>Example</td><td>Database mining meets marketing research[2]</td></tr>
</table>

The Save and Spend loyalty card of DIY retailer Homebase helped to create a database of more than 4 million active customers and their sales transactions. Homebase could see there were many different types of purchase patterns emerging and asked its marketing research agency for help to understand them. The database told it where people lived and what they were spending, but not things like what sort of house they lived in or their attitudes towards DIY. If Homebase could understand what lay behind patterns of DIY purchasing behaviour for customer types, it could use this information to target its advertising and promotions. Data from store exit surveys were overlaid onto purchasing behaviour from the database. Factors such as the frequency of store visits dominated a base level of segmentation. Statistical modelling then revealed the importance of factors such as distance to store, lifestage and attitudes. This resulted in a clear and actionable segmentation approach. For example, from taking one segment of people looking to decorate their homes in a period style, and overlaying that on the level of disposible income, strong differences were found between men and women. Advertising and promotions could then be tailored to three core types of cardholder: those who dislike DIY and just want value for money; those doing DIY for recreation; and those who want to distinguish their property and hence want the latest gadgets. Homebase calculated that the project enabled it to generate £10 return for every £1 marketing spend.

Internal secondary data

Chapter 4 described the nature, purpose and value of secondary data to marketing researchers. A vital source of secondary data comes from within organisations that commission marketing research, namely internal secondary data. These data are generally seen as being 'operational data', i.e. data that represent the daily activities and transactions of a business. Daily transactions may be held in different departments such as sales, accounts or human resources and stored in different manners. The use of operational data has presented opportunities to researchers for as long as businesses have been recording their daily transactions. Even in the days of transactions being recorded manually, it has been a task for marketing researchers to track down different sources of data and analyse them. Locating and analysing internal sources of secondary data should be the starting point in any marketing research project. The main reasons are that, as these data have already been collected, there are no additional data collection costs, there should be no access problems (though individual managers may make access difficult for personal or political reasons) and the quality of the data should be easier to establish (in comparison with externally generated data).

Most organisations have a wealth of in-house information even if they are not marketing or customer focused, so some data may be readily available. For example, imagine a timber merchant that sells wood to builders and cabinetmakers. It creates invoices for all its sales. Its accounts department handles this process and maintains the data that it generates. Yet, there exists much consumer behaviour data in these invoices. They could be analysed by:

- What products customers buy.
- Which customers buy the most products.
- Which customers repeat purchases.
- Which customers appear only when there are special offers.
- Where these customers are located.
- How these customers pay – by cash or credit.
- Which customers are the most profitable.
- Seasonal patterns of purchasing behaviour by product types and customer types.

There may also be data that relate to promotional activities such as spending on advertising, trade fairs, sponsorship deals or personal selling. The researcher could look for details of spending in these areas and seek correlations with any of the analyses of customer behaviour. The task facing the marketing researcher is to search for such data, conduct analyses and present these to decision-makers to interpret. Such a process may focus the thoughts of decision-makers, by realising the potential that lies in these data. With this focus, other types of **operational data** and their value may be realised, managers in other parts of the organisation may release data that they guarded, and connections to sources of intelligence may be generated. Here lies the basis of generating clearly focused primary data collection, and effective marketing research.

Operational data
Data generated about an organisation's customers, through day-to-day transactions.

More marketing decision-makers have realised the benefits of analysing customer data. This realisation and technological developments in collecting, analysing and presenting customer data have given birth to a concept known as customer relationship management (CRM). The growth of CRM has emerged from the use and subsequent integration of various direct marketing channels (direct mail, telemarketing) and the rise of e-business, e-communication and the increasing use of the Internet as a conduit for customer care and sales.[3] The main challenge of implementing CRM is to integrate customer data from the post, telephone, personal visits and the Internet into a central database so that it holds all transactions and contacts with each customer allied with the ability to update the data constantly and to access it immediately whenever necessary.[4] An illustration of the use and effect of CRM is presented in the following example.

Example   **Getting to know clients lifts profits[5]**

The principles of CRM are simple. Businesses gather accurate information about customers and prospects. Having identified the customers or segments that account for the highest profits, they devise marketing strategies that differentiate between different groups. Greater resources are focused on higher value customers. Every opportunity is used to amass additional information about each client to personalise sales messages and build a closer relationship.

When Mercury Asset Management began to experiment with CRM, it was able to demonstrate that 59% of its profits came from 1% of its customers. Over six months it moved from having a standard type of literature for all its customers and prospects to no fewer than 7,700 types of literature. Digital printing made this personalisation relatively simple. The first stage of this personalisation process was the compilation of comprehensive information about customers.

Customer database
A database that details characteristics of customers and prospects that can include names and addresses, geographic, demographic and buying behaviour data.

Many companies see the benefits of compiling comprehensive information about their customers and invest great amounts in developing and maintaining a **customer database**. The customer database for many companies is used to drive all marketing strategies. Customer data can be created by companies from past records, promotional devices such as competitions or direct response advertising. The database is used to stimulate marketing activities, and the response from these activities is fed back to improve and update it. Database marketing is a circular activity where every iteration improves the total value of the database. So, when consumers 'hook up' to an online company, through their PC, their TV or even their mobile phone, they help to develop the customer database.[6] They supply personal details, their choice of products or services and their means of payment. From the knowledge gained from these transactions, new targeted offerings can be formulated, and the nature of the customers' response can be recorded. As the decision-maker learns more about the customers from transaction data, the awareness of gaps in knowledge becomes more focused. Where those gaps cannot be filled with transaction data, the marketing researcher plays a vital role in the generation and interpretation of bespoke primary data. In the development of good research design, the customer database can be seen as a resource to the marketing researcher when conducting internal secondary data searches.

There is a whole array of different means to capture electronically customer transaction behaviour and even potential customers through their search for information to buy services and products. It is beyond the scope of this text to describe the array of CRM technologies, Internet trading and online business. We therefore will just concentrate on a concept introduced in the last chapter, concerning scanned data. From a basis of scanned data we illustrate how other data sources, including primary data from marketing research studies, can be integrated. This serves as a link to examine how decision-makers and researchers make sense of the masses of customer data that may be collected.

Scanning devices

Scanning device
Technology that reads the UPC from merchandise by passing it over a laser scanner.

One of the most fundamental technological breakthroughs that has allowed the monitoring of product sales has been the bar code. With **scanning devices** to read bar codes we now have the ability to count and analyse sales quickly. If a new product is launched, scanning data can monitor sales on a daily basis, breaking down the sales by advertising region and the type of outlet. The scanning device is an electronic means of observation. Consumers do not answer any questions, do not identify themselves; they merely enjoy the benefits of supermarket queues moving far more quickly compared with the days of checkout assistants manually entering the prices for individual goods.

What product bar codes and scanning devices do not do is classify consumers. Classification is fundamental to marketing research, marketing segmentation techniques and ultimately a vast array of marketing decisions. Is the new brand of yogurt more popular with younger age groups compared with older groups? Have more Calvin Klein shirts been sold to male or female buyers? The following example of the Tesco loyalty card illustrates perhaps one of the most sophisticated means of understanding the characteristics of consumers and of linking their characteristics to their purchasing behaviour. When consumers sign up for a loyalty card, they supply Tesco with personal details that enables them to be classified in a number of manners. Using their loyalty card when making a purchase allows Tesco to make the link between what has been bought with who made the purchase. The example shows what impact this means of electronic observation had upon the performance of Tesco.

Relating customer data to scanning systems

Example **Tesco Clubcard[7]**

On 13 February 1995, the face of retailing in the UK started to change, with the national rollout of Tesco's loyalty scheme, the Clubcard. It began as an attempt to maintain market share by sustaining and developing the value of Tesco's customer base against the then market leader Sainsbury's and fending off threats lower down the grocery food chain, from price cutters such as Asda. The Clubcard enables it to track £4 out of every £5 spent in its stores and helped to transform its entire retail strategy, helping it to leapfrog over Sainsbury's to be the market leader. The Clubcard has 10 million active members and generates more than £100 million in incremental sales every year. The primary reason for its success is the rich seam of data it provides for the chain. This, says a Tesco spokesman, 'helps us to understand what customers want and develop products and services that are relevant'. The transactional data generated by Clubcard gives Tesco almost unparalleled customer insight. This, combined with the intelligence generated from the past use of the data, makes it one of the most successful schemes of its sort. The card is helping Tesco stay well ahead of its rivals and has been instrumental in winning £1 out of every £8 spent nationally and helping it break the £2 billion profit barrier.

The essence of the Tesco example is that the scanned data of products sold in Tesco's stores is linked to known customers: the system links customer identification to product usage. Any promotional offers, competitive activity, new product offerings, discounts, where to locate a new store, to name but a few marketing activities, can be analysed and related to classifications of customer. Many businesses have seen the transformation in the fortunes of Tesco and have tried to replicate the performance through the introduction of their own loyalty card schemes.

Loyalty card
At face value, a sales promotion device used by supermarkets, pharmacists, department stores, petrol stations and even whole shopping centres and towns to encourage repeat purchases. For the marketing researcher, the loyalty card is a device that can link customer characteristics to actual product purchases.

The **loyalty card** is the device that supermarkets, pharmacists, department stores, petrol stations and even whole shopping centres and towns have developed in order to link customer characteristics to actual product purchases.

The loyalty card may be offered to customers as they make a purchase in a store. They normally complete an application form which may include their name and address, demographic details, household details, media usage and even some lifestyle characteristics. Once the customers use their loyalty cards, the products they have purchased are scanned and a link can be made through the 'swiped' card to their characteristics that can then be related to the scanned data of their product purchases. In return, the customers earn 'points' for their total spend and may earn additional points for buying particular products. The points gained may be redeemed for cash, additional purchases or even goods and services in other retailers or restaurants.

From the marketing decision-makers' perspective, many benefits accrue from a loyalty card and product scanning system. The following list summarises the benefits to the marketer:

1 *Profiles of customers can be built up.* The types of individual that are being attracted to a store can be monitored. The returns and contributions made by particular types of customer can be measured. Profiles of the 'ideal' customer type can be built up, and plans developed to attract that type of customer.

2 *Products used and not used.* The types of product that are being bought or not bought can be monitored. From the customer profile, other types of product can be added to the range offered. Cross-selling of related products can be undertaken. Linked to the customer profile, actual customer behaviour can be understood more fully.

3 *Communications that have worked and not worked.* Merchandising displays, money-off coupons, three for the price of two, or a clip-out coupon from a local newspaper, for example, can be linked to individuals and products. The effectiveness of particular types of communication for particular types of consumer can be developed. Reassurance that the customer has made the right decision can be given where the size of purchase warrants it.

4 *Distribution methods can be tailored.* Certain customer types may prefer the convenience of a small store that they visit more than once a week for small purchases of 'staple' goods. Other customer types may shop once a month for the total household. Retailers can have different shop formats for different customers, may develop home delivery programmes or even develop Internet shopping systems.

The above four factors interact to allow marketing decision-makers to redefine their market(s) and the offerings they make to those markets. The iteration of target market definition and marketing mix tailored to those markets is at the heart of strategic marketing.

From the marketing researchers' perspective, many benefits also accrue from a loyalty card and product scanning system. The following list summarises the benefits to the marketing researcher:

1 *One big laboratory.* Experimental methods will be described in Chapter 11, but, in essence, the monitoring of customers, markets and interrelated marketing mix activities allows for many causal inferences to be established. For example, what is the effect, and upon whom, of raising the price of Häagen Dazs ice cream by 10%? What is the effect of inserting a cut-out coupon to give a discount on after-sun lotion, placed in *Cosmopolitan* magazine?

2 *Refining the marketing process.* With time series of responses to planned marketing activities, statistical models of consumer response can be built with associated probabilities of a particular outcome. Likewise, models of the consumers over their lifetimes can be built. Again, statistical models can be built with associated probabilities of particular types of product being bought at different stages of a consumer's life.

3 *Developing a clear understanding of 'gaps' in the knowledge of consumers.* The scanner and loyalty card electronically observe behaviour but do not encapsulate attitudinal data. The nature and levels of satisfaction, what is perceived as good-quality service, or what brand image is associated with a particular brand of vodka are examples of attitudinal data. The use of the database helps to identify target populations to measure and the attitudinal data that need to be collected. In all there can be a much greater clarity in the nature of primary marketing research that tackles attitudinal issues.

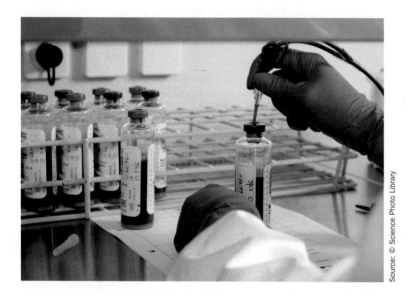

Source: © Science Photo Library

4 *Linking behavioural and attitudinal data.* If attitudinal data are elicited from consumers, the data gathered can be analysed in their own right. It is possible, however, to link the gathered data back to the behavioural data in the database. The term 'fusing' the data from different sources is used. The key to fusing lies in identifying individual respondents so that one large dataset is built up. The notion of fusing together databases and survey data from different sources is at the heart of building a strong understanding of consumers. The analytical power that emerges from linking behavioural and attitudinal data has been realised by SPSS as illustrated in the following example.

Example   The art of SPSS[8]

The days of pure data processing are over at SPSS. The company has embarked on a strategy to combine the art of working with massive amounts of transactional data, which provide insight into the behaviour of consumers, with the art of working with attitudinal insights, which are typically derived from marketing research. The combination of database analytics and marketing research results in what SPSS calls predictive analytics. The software company decided to take this route when it realised that, for decades, the craft of analysing transactional data was wrongly separated from the marketing research profession. In many companies' headquarters, the departments dealing with data mining and CRM were strictly separated from the other field of providing business intelligence: marketing research. SPSS sees huge opportunities in this convergence both for its clients and for itself. It has started to develop software products that embody this convergence between transactional data analysis and marketing research. SPSS has several products that embody the convergence of database analytics and marketing research, such as Predictive Text Analytics. This application enables companies automatically to process large volumes of answers to open-ended questions, collected through surveys, and combine these with transactional data as well as analyses of a company's own call centre transcripts.

The benefits listed above show why many marketers and marketing researchers welcome the power of building an iterative customer database, through scanned product purchases and knowledge of customers who make those purchases. There are drawbacks, however, that focus on the nature of the 'loyalty card'. Loyalty card schemes may be viewed more as a sales promotion technique in much the same manner as giving trading stamps, a dividend or coupons to be redeemed after a period of saving rather than as a means to capture customer data. Many loyalty schemes fail because they have been founded upon short-term goals and do not capitalise on the consumer insight generated through analysis of the data. Loyalty cards should not be seen as a short-term means to boost sales, because, compared with other sales promotion techniques, they incur huge operating costs. Proficient companies that use loyalty cards do so to identify profitable consumers and their needs and tailor the entire shopping experience to them, rather than merely deliver discounts to bargain-hungry fickle consumers.[9]

There are few questions about the huge costs involved in developing and administering loyalty card schemes. For many retailers, however, the investment allows many marketing and marketing research benefits to be realised. It is only when viewed in the light of offering strategic decision-making power and a complement to an integrated marketing information system that such an investment makes sense. One means of integrating scanned data with knowledge of customers, and of presenting the relationships and analyses in a spatial manner, is through the use of geodemographic information systems.

Geodemographic data

Geodemographic information system (GIS)
At a base level, a GIS matches geographic information with demographic information. This match allows subsequent data analyses to be presented on maps.

Thematic maps
Maps that solve marketing problems. They combine geography with demographic information and a company's sales data or other proprietary information.

One of the main elements of database power illustrated in the preceding section is the linking of different data sources from both scanner data and customer databases. The ability to create those links and to display analyses graphically has been achieved with the development of **geodemographic information systems** (GISs). At a base level, a GIS matches geographic information with demographic information, allowing analyses to be presented on **thematic maps**. This base can be built upon with data from customer databases, databases from other sources and surveys. The combined data again can be presented on maps and in conventional statistical tables.

The geographic dimension is vital as a base to the system. Growing up and living in different geographical locations has an effect upon what we buy and the nature of our lifestyle. Look at the huge diversity of consumers around Europe! It is easy to see differences in consumers and their spending habits, between countries and regions within countries, between cities and towns and areas within a town, and even between different sides of a street. These differences emerge from a variety of factors. The following list summarises the main factors, using extreme examples in places. With closer analysis, more subtle differences can be seen which will be illustrated later in this chapter.

1 *Physical geography and climate.* Consumers living in hot Mediterranean climates in villages close to the sea may have many different needs and wants compared with consumers in Scandinavian inner cities.
2 *Economic history, working opportunities.* Consumers who are primarily semi-skilled, working in a declining manufacturing sector, may have many different needs, wants and spending priorities compared with those in a region that attracts recent graduates to work in a burgeoning financial services sector.
3 *Political and legal differences.* Locations with a history of political and legal domination can affect the types of property and subsequently the types of people who live there. The differences may be national, e.g. with policies that encourage state ownership of property, or tax breaks and discounts so that a rented property may be bought by its tenant. The differences may be regional, e.g. a local council may have structural plans to allow the building of new housing estates for families on greenfield sites on the outskirts of cities.

4 *Demographic make-up.* Regions made up of consumers living in predominantly retirement areas, such as seaside towns, will have many different requirements from regions that are heavily populated with single young people.

5 *Infrastructure links.* Infrastructure can include the means of travelling around an area as well as the nature and quality of leisure, sports and shopping facilities. Areas with different levels and quality of infrastructure attract different types of consumer. Families with two cars who can comfortably drive to facilities have different needs and wants when compared with individuals living alone who own a bicycle but not a car.

6 *Property types.* In different locations particular styles of property may dominate: flats rather than houses, multi-storey rather than low-rise, detached rather than terraced, bungalow rather than house. The type, size, quality and costs of property within an area attract different types of consumer.

Thus, differences can be seen between geographic locations that affect the lifestyle of residents, the array of products and services they buy, their ability to buy different types of products and services, and their hopes, fears and aspirations. The founding premise of a GIS is that the type of property a consumer lives in says much about the consumer's lifestyle and consumption patterns. Property type also encapsulates the other five factors that discriminate between consumers living in different geographic regions. For example, consumers living in small one-bedroom flats over shops in a city centre will tend to have very different lifestyles and consumption patterns from those living in large detached rural properties. Consumers in different property types have different propensities or probabilities of buying particular goods and services and of undertaking activities that make up their lifestyle. They also have different propensities to use and be exposed to different types of media.

From a marketing decision-making perspective, geography also plays a vital role. Knowing where one's consumers are located affects the means and costs of distribution. For example, should a retail outlet be built to gain the most returns? Which customers will have to pass our competitors in order to get to us? What features and facilities should the outlet have? The location of consumers also affects the means to communicate with them. Are consumers dispersed over a wide area or tightly clustered together? Do they read the same type of newspaper or magazine? Do they watch the same TV programmes or films at the cinema? The following example of Fred Olsen Cruise Lines illustrates how the firm used geodemographic analyses; it also reveals the links from the firm's customer database to its survey work.

Example **Crusing for customers[10]**

Founded in 1848, Fred Olsen Cruise Lines (**www.fredolsencruises.com**) has built a reputation for luxurious voyages in ships that are smaller and more intimate than the norm. With some extremely loyal customers, until recently it required little in the way of marketing to fill the relatively small number of cabins available during the cruising season. This all changed with the launch of *Braemar* in 2001 and increased competition from P&O, Cunard and Carnival. The company has invested in means to create greater customer insight through its customer database, website and marketing research practices. Geographic analysis has helped to pinpoint locations to target for prospective customers. The company has selected catchments around travel agents to target by direct mail. If it runs a 'cruise evening' then it does targeted mailing to publicise it. Depending upon where customers are located, possible attendees of exhibitions are also selected by location and other segmentation criteria and mailed or emailed with free ticket offers. The company's website works directly with the customer database so that segmentation codes and other preference data can be used to target returning customers with cookie-based personalised offers on the home page. In the future, customers will be able to update their own preferences, including preferred contact channel, online. Though the company already keys in data from post-cruise questionnaires, another goal of the site is to gather extra personal attributes each time a customer visits and also to perform short surveys. Overall, the site helps to give a much deeper understanding of why customers respond to the Fred Olsen offerings.

A map therefore forms the foundation of a GIS – a map that can identify all properties in a country, all roads, shopping centres and major facilities in towns and cities. On top of a base map can be laid a range of statistical measures. They typically originate from a number of sources and have the common feature of being able to relate to a specific postcode or zip code. An example of such a system is one produced by Experian (**www.experian.com.**) It has developed systems specifically tailored for a number of countries throughout the world. The sources and details of data available in each of the above countries differ, as does the legislation that determines what can be stored and analysed on databases. Typically for each country, statistics can be gathered and used to develop individual GISs based upon census data, postal address files, electoral registers, consumer credit data, directories of company directors, mail order purchase records, car registrations and data on access to retail outlets.

From the data collected, the purpose is to classify consumers on a geodemographic basis. Experian defines a **geodemographic classification** as follows:

Geodemographic classification groups consumers together based on the types of neighbourhood in which they live. If a set of neighbourhoods are similar across a wide range of demographic measures, they will also offer similar potential across most products, brands, services and media.

Geodemographic classification
This groups consumers together based on the types of neighbourhood in which they live. If a set of neighbourhoods are similar across a wide range of demographic measures, they may also offer similar potential across most products, brands, services and media.

With the variables chosen for a particular country, i.e. the types of data that are available to build a GIS, cluster analyses are performed (Chapter 23 details the nature and purpose of cluster analysis). These analyses help to create consumer classifications, based upon the types of property the consumers live in and the propensity of consumers to have certain lifestyles and behave in particular manners. The analyses ensure that each of the descriptions used is reasonably homogeneous in terms of demographic measurements and consumer behaviour. As well as being able to discriminate and describe distinctive groups of consumers, the analyses have to produce 'pictures' of consumers that are meaningful to marketing decision-makers.

Experian has also produced 'Mosaic Global' as a consistent segmentation system that covers over 284 million of the world's households. It is based on the proposition that the world's cities share common patterns of residential segregation. Each country has its ghettos of Metropolitan Strugglers, suburbs of Career and Family, and communities of Sophisticated Singles. In terms of their values and lifestyles, each type of neighbourhood displays strong similarities in whichever country it is found. Using local data from 16 countries and statistical methods, Experian has identified 10 distinct types of residential neighbourhood, each with a distinctive set of values, motivations and consumer preferences, which can be found in each of the countries. Mosaic Global uses the data from the national Mosaic classification systems for the following countries: Australia, China (Beijing, Guangzhou, Shanghai), Denmark, Finland, France, Germany, Greece, Hong Kong, Ireland, the Netherlands, New Zealand, Norway, Spain, Sweden, the UK and the USA.

The resulting analyses have produced a classification of 10 main consumer types. Table 5.1 lists these types and the percentages of each type in the populations of Australia and Sweden. The following example describes characteristics of the Mosaic Global group labelled as *Sophisticated Singles*.

Table 5.1 Mosaic Global classification of the global, Australian and Swedish populations

Classification descriptor	% of global population*	% in Australian population	% in Swedish population
Sophisticated Singles	7.90	10.40	4.34
Bourgeois Prosperity	9.20	22.40	18.61
Career and Family	8.60	3.50	7.13
Comfortable Retirement	2.90	2.00	2.54
Routine Service Workers	9.30	3.80	11.40
Hard Working Blue Collar	10.90	18.90	5.59
Metropolitan Strugglers	18.50	5.00	26.02
Low Income Elders	6.20	4.20	10.25
Post Industrial Survivors	12.20	16.80	2.89
Rural Inheritance	14.60	13.30	11.22

* The countries where Experian is able to access data and build its groups.

Example   Sophisticated Singles

Sophisticated Singles contains young people, mostly single and well educated, who positively enjoy the variety and stimulation afforded by life in large cities. Typically international in their outlook and with a rich network of personal contacts, they are quick to explore and adopt new social and political attitudes and are important agents of innovation, in terms of both lifestyles and the adoption of consumer products. Most are at the stage of their lives when the development of 'human' capital, i.e. skills, contacts, knowledge, continues to take precedence over the maximization of their incomes or indeed the accumulation of financial assets and much of their income is spent on 'experiences', such as entertainment, eating out, travel, books and magazines, rather than on equipment. They exhibit a variety of household arrangements and typically marry and have children late in their lives. Such people gravitate towards the smarter downtown areas of major cities where they spend short periods of time living in small, rented apartments.

With a GIS, it is possible to pinpoint where the *Sophisticated Singles* are in any of the countries analysed, whether they are clustered in particular regions or cities, or whether they are dispersed. From Table 5.1 differences between the countries in the distribution of groups are clearly seen. If one were to dig deeper within each country there would be clear differences in the proportions of these groups between cities and regions. From these classifications and the data that can be added from other databases, models of consumer behaviour can be developed. Customers can be mapped out to see how far they live from a retail outlet or to see whether they pass a competitor's store to reach a retail outlet. The profile of customers that a company has can be compared with national, regional or city profiles. Data that are captured on customer databases can be mapped out. For example, the ABN AMRO bank can map out which customers have responded to an offer to take out a personal loan at a discounted rate, as well as building up a profile of those who respond. The following example illustrates how Experian's data and systems are merged with customer databases.

Building long-lasting partnerships for Parfümerie Douglas

Parfümerie Douglas is the largest subsidiary of the Douglas Lifestyle Group in Germany. It is the market leader in retail perfumery in Europe, with more than 430 stores in Germany and a further 300 in the Netherlands, Italy, Austria, France, Switzerland, Spain and Portugal. Retail perfumery is a highly competitive market with little customer brand loyalty. The challenge facing Parfümerie Douglas was to maintain its market leadership and achieve its growth ambitions by encouraging greater customer loyalty and increasing average customer spend. Parfümerie Douglas launched its loyalty card in 1995 and by 2001 had issued 1.4 million cards. Since the card's inception, Experian has partnered with Parfümerie Douglas, merging the data generated from the card with its data and systems to provide a full-service account processing function. The Douglas card has met the company's objectives with regard to customer loyalty, sales per customer, payment security and bad debt management. Douglas had its account processing system already in place when German regulations regarding discounts were liberalised in 2001. This gave it an advantage over its competitors by having the ability to test market special offers and discounts through the card's existing database.

In addition to customer behaviour being added to the GIS, survey data can also be added. The key that would link the survey to the customer database may be either a named customer or a postcode. The following example illustrates a major survey that utilises the power of Experian's Mosaic to enable more detailed analyses of target markets. Table 5.2 illustrates and provides links to a number of established and well-respected surveys that connect to and use geodemographic classifications to generate more insightful analyses of target markets.

Table 5.2 Example of marketing research surveys that are linked to geodemographic classifications

Marketing research survey tions	Markets covered	Linked geodemographic classifica-
FRS – NOP's Financial Research Survey (**www.gfknop.co.uk**)	Financial	Acorn (**www.acorn.caci.co.uk**)
MFS – MORI's Financial Survey (**www.mori.com**)	Financial	Mosaic (**www.experian.co.uk**), CAMEO (**www.eurodirect.co.uk**)
TNS – Taylor Nelson Sofres' Superpanel	Fast-moving consumer goods	Acorn (**www.acorn.caci.co.uk**)

The MORI MFS Continuous Tracking Survey

The MFS (**www.mori.com**) Continuous Tracking Survey is widely syndicated to many of the UK's leading banks, building societies, insurance companies and other organisations operating in the personal finance sector. All major markets are measured and the questionnaire is constantly updated to reflect developments in this rapidly changing sector; 2000 different adults are interviewed each fortnight in-home, face to face, by MORI's fieldforce. Quotas are set to reflect the British population by age, sex, class and region. This large annual sample size of 48,000 enables detailed analyses to be run. The types of questions asked by the MFS Omnibus cover the following topics: credit cards, personal loans, life & pensions, technology tracker, current accounts, general insurance (home & motor, pet, travel & medical), future buyer behaviour, savings & investments, loyalty/store cards. All MFS respondents are postcoded and therefore geodemographic analyses can be run against any group of respondents. This can then be compared with clients' own marketing database for any industry classification.

In this example, an insurance company can map out who bought a new policy from it. It may be able to profile and map out the types of individual who bought different types of financial services beyond insurance. The company may be interested about the levels of satisfaction related to the different financial service companies used by the respondents. The results of the survey can be analysed by the different Mosaic classifications, and levels of customer satisfaction can be mapped out. Additional purchases of insurance related to satisfaction or customer loyalty can be captured. It can be seen from the above that through the use of a GIS, profiles of target markets, measures of the success of marketing decisions and the means to model consumer behaviour can all be achieved. Graphical representations can be made of customers' behaviour, their attitudes and their levels of satisfaction. Using these data, the insurance company additionally has the potential to measure the propensity of potential customers in new locations to buy particular types of insurance policy and other financial services. Using the Mosaic Global classification, the propensity of potential customers could lead to new locations throughout the world.

Linking different types of data

The previous example illustrated how different types of data can be merged and mapped out to represent customer characteristics. One of the main applications of collecting customer data from different sources and linking the data together would be to perform segmentation analyses. Examining the means by which target markets can be segmented, it is clear to see that the five methods as illustrated in Figure 5.1 can be individually utilised or combined to build clearer 'pictures' or profiles of target consumers.

Figure 5.1 gives examples of where data may be obtained from, to help build up profiles of customers and markets. In the example of 'psychographics' or lifestyle measurements, data may be generated from electronic point of sale (EPOS) systems or surveys. In the case of the EPOS collection, the purchasing of particular types of products can indicate characteristics of a lifestyle. In a more direct manner, questions in a survey can help to build a profile of lifestyle behaviour. In its own right, 'lifestyle' can be a valid means of segmenting a market, perhaps positioning products and services to consumers who aspire to a particular lifestyle. However, being able to combine demographic measurements, broader behavioural characteristics and a knowledge of where these consumers live helps to build a 'picture' of consumers that facilitates strong marketing decision-making support.

Figure 5.1 indicates that as one moves from the demographic through to psychological characteristics the measurement process becomes more difficult. Putting aside the differences in techniques to capture 'demography', 'behaviour' or 'psychology', what is being captured becomes more difficult as one moves towards psychological variables. If one

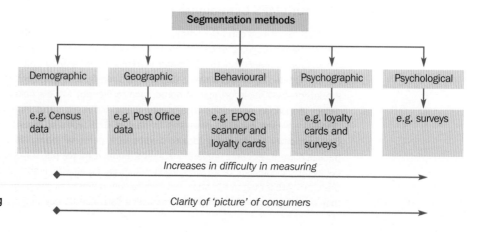

**Figure 5.1
Methods of segmenting markets**

considers psychological variables that are vital to marketing which could be captured, examples such as satisfaction, loyalty, trust and quality are not as easy to capture as questions such as gender, age or where one lives. Chapter 12 will explore the concept of measurement in more depth, but at this stage consider what 'satisfaction' actually means, and then the problems of measuring that concept in a valid and consistent manner.

Conversely, as the measurements become more difficult to conduct, they add more to the 'picture' of consumer and market profiles. To say that a market is primarily female, aged between 25 and 40 and lives in a detached property with a mortgage starts to build a 'picture' of target consumers. To add details of their media behaviour, the array of products and services they buy, characteristics of their lifestyle and their expectations helps to build up a rich and, for decision-makers, very useful 'picture' of target consumers.

Examining the variety of data sources that can be used in the interrelated variables that build market profiles, it is clear to see a role for traditional survey work, scanned data, customer data, externally generated secondary data and the use of loyalty cards. There is a clear interdependence among the different data sources with the increased sophistication of decision support systems that allow 'fusing' of the data to be conducted.[11]

Stages of development in using databases and survey data to build profiles of consumers and model marketing decisions

The last section discussed how different data could be combined to build strong 'pictures' of consumers. Reflecting upon the role of the marketing researcher in supporting the marketing decision-maker as detailed in Chapter 1, it is clear that the combination of survey data and databases plays a major role in fulfilling the following, helping to:

- describe the nature and scope of customer groups;
- understand the nature of forces that shape the needs of customer groups and the marketer's ability to satisfy those groups;
- test individual and interactive controllable marketing variables;
- monitor and reflect upon past successes and failures in marketing decisions.

The actual implementation of the decision support systems that allow the combination of data sources to be used in supporting decision-makers can take a great deal of time, expense and organisational learning. It is not the intention here to go through the planning, training and organisational issues in making the systems work, but broadly to summarise the stages that an organisation may go through in combining survey and database data. Figure 5.2 summarises the stages of integration. The following descriptions develop the summarised stages in more detail:

1 *Analyse existing consumer database.* These data could include the daily operational transactions or enquiries made to a company. As an internal secondary data source these are the cheapest and most readily available data – providing the organisation culture allows access and analysis to marketing researchers.

2 *Use supplied geodemographic profiles.* There are a growing number of GIS vendors, some of which have been in operation for over 25 years.[12] In this time they have been able to refine the data they collect and the analyses they produce to build consumer profiles. Companies can buy a base system 'off the shelf' from systems vendors, and add a variety of different databases.

3 *Combine existing consumer data with geodemographic profiles.* Using the mapping functions of the GIS, existing customer data can be analysed using the profiles supplied with the system. Maps can be used to illustrate the catchment and types of customer and then to evaluate potential in new locations.

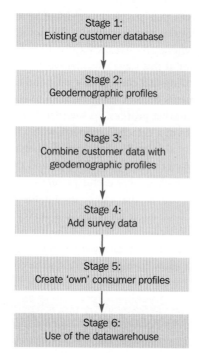

Figure 5.2
Stages of development in using databases and survey data to build profiles of consumers and model marketing decisions

4 *Use other surveys (either own or from external sources) that build on geodemographic sources and customer database.* Surveys conducted by a company where either a customer identification or postcode is recorded can be added. Survey data can be analysed using the geographic profiles and analyses represented using maps.

5 *Use combined data sources to create own profiles of customers.* Companies gain experience from using the geodemographic profiles and adding their own data. Over a period of time they may see that the generalised definitions of consumers from the GIS do not accurately represent their existing and target customers. With the benefit and use of their own data, they may take the raw data from the geodemographics vendor and produce their own classifications.

6 *Datawarehouse analytics.* Essentially, this is using many database sources to build one huge database that may be accessed, allowing data to be fused and analysed. The more sophisticated developments of datawarehousing would include the capture and integration of qualitative data that can emerge from intelligence and primary data sources. The analyses that emerge from datawarehouse analytics would be done to suit particular reporting requirements or specific queries from either marketing research or marketing managers. With the growth and significance of this development in decision support, the next section describes the datawarehouse in more detail.

The datawarehouse

Datawarehouse
This may be seen as a 'super-database', but more specifically it may be defined as a process of gathering disparate data from database and survey sources, and converting the data into a consistent format that can aid business decision making.

One of the most prolific users and innovators in **datawarehouses** is the banking industry. The following example illustrates the problems and opportunities for the banking industry of having many different departments with quite distinctive databases.

Example ## You say 'warehouse', I say 'database'...[13]

Three major changes are sweeping through bank marketing: banks are becoming even more customer driven, they are becoming increasingly information rich, and they are now dependent on constantly evolving computer technologies.

Being more customer driven results in a breaking down of the previously hermetically sealed functional areas of banking. Synergistic marketing and sales is now the name of the game. But as these invisible walls come tumbling down, banks are confronting the unintended result of departments with unique informational needs and personal computers: databases of highly valuable information that have no connection with each other. It is as if the tide has gone out, leaving tidal pools teeming with rich data separate from one another along a beach. In this case, the whole of the data really is greater than the sum of its parts. These pools of customer data are not just valuable in and of themselves. The greatest value is in the across-the-board juxtaposition of all the data pools with one another. That's where the confusing conceptual model of a datawarehouse comes in. 'Datawarehousing', then, is simply about the creation of a super-database.

The datawarehouse may be seen as a super-database, but more specifically it may be defined thus:[14]

A datawarehouse is as much a process of gathering disparate data, converting it into a consistent format that can aid business decision making, as it is a configuration of software and hardware. Datawarehouses empower users by providing them with access to a whole array of information in an organisation, making it available for use in other applications.

From this definition, the datawarehouse can be described as having the following three qualities:

1 It is a collection of integrated databases designed to support managerial decision making and problem solving.
2 It essentially becomes a giant database that can include survey data held in a database format.
3 It physically separates an organisation's operational data systems from its decision support systems.

At its most fundamental level, the datawarehouse has three components.

1 *Acquisition.* This includes all the programs, applications and various interfaces that extract data from existing databases. It continues with preparing the data and exporting them to the datawarehouse.
2 *Storage.* This is synonymous with any database. It simply involves a storage area to hold a vast amount of data from a variety of sources. The storage area is organised to make it easy to find and use the data. It will be updated from a variety of sources which could be through scanner and loyalty card data on customers, or through the use of intranet data as described in Chapter 4 when examining the compilation of competitor data.
3 *Access.* This encompasses both set reporting of predetermined events and the means of performing individual analyses, querying 'what-if' scenarios. The process of exploring the databases uses **data mining** techniques. As marketing researchers and decision-makers learn about markets and their effects upon those markets, the development of predictive models is facilitated. Predictive models are built and tested using historical customer and transactional data, and then used to predict how customers might respond in any number of future situations. As well as the classic marketing application of who may respond to a particular offer, they help to evaluate how likely different individuals or groups are to end their relationship with a company, default on a loan or

Data mining
The process of discovering meaningful correlations, patterns and trends by sifting through large amounts of data stored in repositories, using pattern recognition as well as statistical and mathematical techniques.

buy an extra product. The use of predictive modelling started out in credit risk: who is most likely to pay up rather than moving out and disappearing? Analysts found that by appropriately weighting different variables such as income they could predict with some accuracy the degree of risk that customers presented. Awareness of the power of modelling outside credit and direct marketing rose dramatically with the use of techniques like collaborative filtering by online vendors such as Amazon. If you buy certain books, they you may well be interested in other books bought by customers with a similar history to yours.[15]

Data mining

Data mining is a process of discovering meaningful correlations, patterns and trends by sifting through large amounts of data stored in repositories. The process uses pattern recognition as well as statistical and mathematical techniques.[16] Data mining should not be confused with datawarehousing. The datawarehouse could be termed a 'repository' or a place where large amounts of sometimes disparate sources of data are stored; data mining is a process that depends upon access to the data held in that repository.

Examples of what data mining aims to do are as follows:

- Classify customers into specific categories that are meaningful to decision-makers.
- Identify potential target markets that possess the characteristics that decision-makers seek.
- Forecast sales or the use of services.
- Discover which types of products or services are purchased together.
- Discover patterns and trends over time, such as 'after graduation, students take a holiday', and be able to show the probabilities associated with them buying different types of holiday.

Data mining is a way of exploiting the data held by organisations to help discover and develop specific information or knowledge. As well as using proprietary software to perform pattern recognition, statistical and mathematical techniques, data mining can also be seen as a mental process undertaken by decision-makers. The decision-makers who interact with large datasets using data mining are generally not specialists in statistics, data analysis, datawarehousing and other data tools; they are information users, seeking support for their decision-making processes. With the aid of data mining software, the decision-maker is encouraged to think in new ways and ask new questions. The decision-maker discovers more from the data and explores in new areas, integrating other sources of data, going through iterative processes to dig deeper. The exploration process involves the discovery of non-trivial relationships of dependence or associations, non-trivial clusters, factors or trends and an understanding of the managerial significance of these discoveries. A data mining process must be 'user oriented' and that user is typically the decision-maker. The following example illustrate the processes described above by showing how data mining has been used to explore the customer database of one of Europe's leading banks.

| **Example** | **Credit Suisse** |

As one of the world's leading financial services companies, Credit Suisse Group provides banking and insurance solutions for private clients, companies and institutions. Based in Zurich, Switzerland, Credit Suisse employs 80,000 people worldwide. Competition in the financial services industry is intense, and obtaining new customers is expensive. In order to maximise profitability, Credit Suisse focused on three areas. First, identifying profitable current customers. Second, managing customer relationships to ensure longevity. Third, retaining profitable customer accounts. In 1997, Credit Suisse started the 'Loyalty Based Management' programme, with the primary goal of retaining profitable customers. It invested in a six-member 'data mining team' that used the Clementine tool (**www.spss.com/ clementine**) to analyse a data warehouse of its 2.5 million customers, each with more than 400 attributes. The analysis was used to identify potential leads among Credit Suisse's customers and intelligently market to them based on their individual preferences and histories. With the help of SPSS, Credit Suisse's data mining activities, analysis and modelling have been fully integrated into its business processes and have proven their value in many different applications. As a result of the success of the Loyalty Based Management project, Credit Suisse consultants began to see data mining's benefits and started to use it to sell specific customers targeted services. Credit Suisse can now identify customers, typically the top 1%, who are extremely likely to buy a service, thus increasing the opportunities for cross-selling and retaining customers. Detailed segmentation of its vast customer base allows Credit Suisse to develop targeted solutions for its customers. This segmentation is executed inductively using the cluster algorithm and the dimensions are tailored directly to the customer requirements. Each cluster serves as a starting point for individual marketing campaigns. This hierarchical system is advantageous because the customer database is continually researched and monitored. As a result, changes in the cluster structure are quickly identified and appropriate responses are triggered.

Databases and marketing research

There has been a phenomenal growth in the use of databases to support marketing decision making. In larger organisations with many divisions or where mergers and acquisitions have taken place, the datawarehouse has facilitated 'fusing' of data from many sources. Such developments are seen as a threat by many in the marketing research industry. However, many marketing research companies and marketing research departments within companies are embracing database techniques, utilising the synergistic benefits of matching database analyses with traditional survey data through data mining. To illustrate this point, consider the following quote from Greg Ward, Development Director for Taylor Nelson (**www.tns-global.com**), the largest marketing research company in the UK:

The marketing research industry needs to acknowledge that databases are serious products and that both types of information have benefits. If you take the best of both – what we call information based marketing – you get something that is significantly more powerful. The 'them and us' situation does nobody any favours and the idea that the two disciplines bear no resemblance to each other is wrong.

As marketing decision-makers become more willing and able to interrogate databases and to generate creatively their own decision support, this does not mean the end of 'traditional' marketing research. As illustrated earlier when examining types of data that are used to build consumer and market profiles, psychological data play a vital role that is fulfilled by qualitative and quantitative marketing research. The marketing researcher needs to develop a greater awareness of both how data captured through traditional methods can be integrated with data held on databases *and* how the combined data creatively support decision-makers.

Databases, the development of datawarehouses and the use of data mining techniques are allowing a wider and shared use of data. The graphical formats of presenting data, especially using maps, break down many barriers in decision-makers who resist formal statistical analyses. They encourage managers to tailor output to meet their individual needs. The creativity that is the hallmark of marketing decision making is supported by the creative collection and connections between data. Where there are gaps in decision-makers' knowledge, they can be more focused and precise in determining what marketing research support they need. Many marketing researchers are rising to meet this challenge.[17]

The next example illustrates how data mining can provide in-depth analyses of survey data at great speed or it can help combine research data with other types of data to provide a much richer source of insight. It illustrates how companies can integrate databases and traditional marketing research, seeing the disciplines as complementary, not competitive.

Example **TrustMark CFI**

TrustMark CFI, part of the worldwide CFI Group, is a market research and management consulting business in Zollikon, Switzerland. In a project for a banking customer, TrustMark CFI consultants used Clementine (**www.spss.com/clementine**) to analyse customer satisfaction data with operational data, and then build models that would forecast future consumer activity. By combining the two data sources, the models produced by Clementine were more accurate – and comparing the predictions from the Clementine model with reality proved this. When using operational data only, Clementine correctly identified 65.4% of the customers who had increased their asset volume significantly, and 56.9% of those who had greatly reduced it. However, using the two data sources together, the model was correct in 67.9% and 60.7% of cases respectively. According to Leonie van de Vijfeijken, a research analyst at TrustMark CFI:

> the results would have been even better if there hadn't been a large time lag between gathering the operational and survey data. Although the difference in the figures does not sound remarkable, it is significant to the bank's business and helps reduce its marketing costs.

Using these models on current data allows the bank to predict whether an account is likely to be profitable, at risk, or inactive. This information enables it to target marketing resources more effectively and, in the final analysis, improve financial performance. Interestingly, had the bank not used predictive models and simply run standard analyses on the survey research data, a very different picture would have emerged. When past research data was compared with reality, it was shown that only 21% of the respondents who said they were going to increase their asset volume actually did so.

There is a blurring of the lines between traditional marketing research and other corporate intelligence activities, including data mining. Whilst some research departments are reinforcing the line that separates the marketing research department from other functions, many are embracing the change. The reason that this integration matters is that it should be the case that the marketing research department is in the best position to drive the understanding of the 'why' of behaviour, rather than just describing the behaviour.[18] Given the different but complementary roles that marketing research and database analytics perform, put together there can be a great synergistic effect. If a company has a customer transactional database, it is very unlikely that it can tell the company why its customers use the products they do and what media they consume. What marketing research can do is overlay those attitudes, identify segments and make the whole database actionable.[19]

International marketing research

Linking databases and survey data is transforming international marketing research. Within individual companies, customers may be analysed from operational data within a country, showing different patterns of behaviour between different regions or cities and relating that behaviour to their marketing activities. When a company operates across borders, country differences become just another geographical variable.

In deciding to operate or develop in a particular country, companies may buy a geodemographic information system (should one be developed for that country). A GIS may be used as a foundation to add to their operational data. From this point they may go through the stages of database development as laid out in Figure 5.2. However, international marketers face a dilemma in choosing between 'consistency' and 'richness of detail'.

It is possible to create systems GISs to individual countries across the globe based upon the data sources available within that country, its data protection laws and how current and accurate those data sources are. Such systems work extremely well if one's marketing activities are based within that country. The problem arises when, as an international marketer, one wishes to have consumer classifications that are consistent across borders. Mosaic Global is one of many solutions to this problem. However, in resolving the problem of consistency across countries, an amount of the richness of individual country detail may be lost. To illustrate this dilemma, examine the following summaries of Mosaic Global, UK and London. See how, as the system becomes more focused geographically, there is a greater richness of detail but a loss of consistency in the measurements and classification across borders

---

Example   **Mosaic classifications in London, the UK and across the globe**

Mosaic Global is a consistent segmentation system that covers over 400 million of the world's households. Using local data from 25 countries, Experian has identified 10 types of residential neighbourhood that can be found in each of the countries, each with a distinctive set of values, motivations and consumer preferences. Mosaic Global is based on a simple proposition that the world's cities share common patterns of residential segregation. In terms of their values and lifestyles, each type of neighbourhood displays strong similarities in whichever country it is found.

Mosaic UK is the latest version of the market-leading consumer segmentation product. It classifies all 24 million British households into 11 groups, 61 types and 243 segments, and is updated each year. A development team of over 30 staff took over two years to build Mosaic UK. The result is a classification that paints a rich picture of British consumers in terms of their socio-demographics, lifestyles, culture and behaviour, providing the most accurate and comprehensive view of British society at the start of the twenty-first century.

Mosaic London is a geodemographic classification of London. The classification covers 5.9 million households (25% of the UK) in approximately 380,000 postcodes. Mosaic London describes Londoners in depth: each postcode has been allocated to one of 41 types and 12 groups that are specific to London. Groups of people are identified that are important to the London community but may not occur elsewhere in the country.

Performing analyses within countries can be most fruitful, provided a base GIS has been established. Problems start where there is no base GIS. In many countries there are great problems in tracking down and combining data sources that can be relied upon. Further, even if reliable data can be located, legislation may make the use of certain data types illegal. In many developing countries, the data needed to build a GIS are sparse. With the data that are available, much experimentation is needed to enable valid classifications that reflect consumer types which are useful to marketers and marketing researchers.

Ethics in marketing research

Marketing researchers are confronted by problems posed by the wording of ESOMAR and individual country marketing research associations' codes of conduct.[20] The codes specify that the compilation of lists, registers or databanks of names and addresses for any non-research purpose shall in no way be associated directly or indirectly with marketing research. The view is that whilst marketing research and marketing database analytics are complementary, because the two activities are subject to different legislative requirements and in the interests of transparency for respondents, the ICC/ESOMAR International Code states:

> *When acting in their capacity as researchers, the latter must not undertake any non-research activities, for example database marketing involving data about individuals which will be used for direct marketing and promotional activities. Any such non-research activities must always, in the way they are organized and carried out, be clearly differentiated from marketing research activities.*
>
> *For more details see www.esomar.org/codesandguidelines.*

However, the examples detailed in this chapter show that supporting marketing decision-makers through databases and marketing research can be seen as part of a total information industry. Evidence of the many leading marketing research agencies involved in data collection and analyses through databases illustrates that databases need not be unethical. With due care it is possible to combine marketing research ethics and databases generated through database marketing. There are a growing number of companies that have used marketing research for many years that now combine the traditional role of marketing research manager with a wider role including database management. An essential part of this combined role lies in the management of customer databases, adding survey details to respondents' individual details, at either an individual or an aggregated level.

Given the phenomenal growth of databases in marketing and the support they offer to marketing decision makers, they are here to stay. With well-planned 'traditional' marketing research integrated into database analyses, the strategic power of consumer and market analyses is phenomenal. If marketers abuse their knowledge of consumers, they stand to do great harm to their brands and corporate image. For example, in bank databases there are many opportunities for the cross-selling of products. Rather than welcoming the approach from another division of a bank trying to sell insurance to an investment client, there can be a reaction against the approach, affecting the original business. Consumers are now more aware of how valuable knowledge of their behaviour is and how it is used by marketers. They are willing to trade this knowledge for the kind of rewards that are gained from the use of their loyalty cards. Marketers are aware of the dangers of abusing the knowledge that their customers impart to them. However, there are issues of civil liberties that cannot be ignored. These are touched upon in the following example.

Example **Loyalty for sale[21]**

Provided that shoppers like the benefits and do not object to a system which records every bar of chocolate and bottle of gin purchased, no great harm will be done. However, there is a danger that, despite the safeguards of Data Protection Acts, this mass of information on consumers' habits could leak across the networks into unscrupulous hands. Issues of civil liberty would be raised if, for example, insurance companies could use the data to identify people whose purchases indicated an unhealthy lifestyle; or if the police could draw up a list of suspects by monitoring the purchase of specific items or unusual consumption patterns.

One of the benefits of the use of GISs is that in many cases the individual does not have to be identified; the postcode is a sufficient key to make a link between databases. This maintains the marketing research industry's maxim of respondent confidentiality.

Internet and computer applications

At the start of the 1990s, this chapter would not have existed in a marketing research text. The idea of conducting internal secondary data searches and analyses would have merited a paragraph or two as part of the process of developing primary data collection. Since then, the massive technological changes that have made the global use of the Internet commonplace, the increased storage space, speed and analysis capabilities of computers, and the increased sophistication of software collectively have made fundamental changes to the environment in which marketing researchers operate. The collection and analysis of customer data held within businesses have developed enormously and marketing researchers cannot ignore these developments.

In Chapter 1 we discussed how, for many years, marketing researchers have recognised the competition they face from an array of management consultants, but more recently competition has emerged from raw data providers such as call centres, direct marketing, database marketing and telebusinesses.[22] Much of the new competition has emerged from organisations that have utilised and developed Internet and computer applications and have been able to offer support to decision-makers, in faster, cheaper and more user-friendly formats, though not necessarily more rigorously or ethically. Leading marketing researchers have developed means of integrating many of the new formats for supporting decision-makers with traditional marketing research methods and have maintained their customary rigour and ethical behaviour. In order to get a feel of how decision-makers may be supported by some of the means discussed in this chapter, we recommend that you explore the following websites. These websites contain case studies of the applications of decision support. When working through these cases, consider what 'gaps' may still exist in the knowledge of decision-makers that may be filled only by the use of traditional marketing research techniques. The following example illustrates such a case. It shows how SPSS is using the integration of different data sources to build consumer behaviour models and predict behaviour. The SPSS concept of predictive analytics was presented earlier in the chapter; this example illustrates its application in combining data mining and marketing research (**www.spss.com**).

Example   **Top Dutch insurer Interpolis selects SPSS software for lead generation**

Interpolis (www.interpolis.com) is the largest single-brand consumer property and casualty insurance company in the Netherlands. The company is also active in Luxembourg and Ireland. It has about 6,000 employees, and realised a turnover of €5 billion in 2004. Interpolis has purchased SPSS's predictive analytics software to grow its business further through lead generation. Harnessing SPSS's PredictiveMarketing, Interpolis wants to predict which customers are most likely to buy its insurance products. With SPSS, Interpolis aims to increase sales to its existing customers and broaden its customer base, which can amount to millions of euros in additional revenue. Interpolis generates 85% of its revenues from Rabobank's branch network. The insurer selected SPSS's analytics software better to understand and predict customer needs and feed this information to branch staff, providing a clear indication of opportunities to sell its insurance products. Interpolis's marketing department will also utilise SPSS software to identify which customers are most likely to defect once an insurance contract has ended, the reasons for defection and the best actions to minimise it. 'Interpolis is a great example of a predictive enterprise – leveraging and acting upon customer knowledge across multiple channels: at its marketing campaigns, in branch offices, and in the call center,' added Marcel Holsheimer, Vice President of Marketing for SPSS's Platform and Applications, and, 'Deploying predictive analytics gives it the ability to improve across several business processes and considerably enhance bottom line performance.'

Two major suppliers of software that help with customer relationship management mentioned at the start of this chapter are SAP (www.netsuite.com) and AIT (www.ait.co.uk). They also show how operational data generated in organisations may be integrated. The main GISs to examine individual countries and across boundaries were listed earlier in the chapter, but as a reminder, they were: Acorn (www.acorn.caci.co.uk), Mosaic (www.experian.com) and CAMEO (www.eurodirect.co.uk). Numerous data mining software programs are now available. Kdnuggets (www.Kdnuggets.com) is an online resource for data miners which has identified the most popular data mining software packages. The most popular vendors and their datamining software programs include the following:

SPSS (www.spss.com/clementine),
SAS (www.sas.com/technologies/analytics)
IBM (www-306.ibm.com/software/data/db2bi)
Angoss (www.angoss.com)
Megaputer (www.megaputer.com).

Each of these programs can run on client–server platforms and includes a wide range of analysis tools and techniques, including neural networks and decision trees.[23] A French datawarehouse supplier with a case based on the Renault Company can be found at www.decisionnel.fr. Finally, visit www.crisp-dm.org to see an organisation devoted to the development of data mining methodology.

Summary

The overall tone of this chapter has been to demonstrate that internally generated secondary data offer great opportunities not only for decision-makers but also for researchers. As with all good secondary data sources, they have a major impact upon the conduct and direction of primary data collection, analyses and interpretation.

Databases, including customer operational data, geodemographic data and survey data, are radically changing how marketing decision making is being supported. There is much debate as to whether the use of databases is compatible with traditional techniques of marketing research. With the junk mail connotations of databases and compromises of respondent anonymity, many marketing researchers may seek to keep the marketing database at arm's length. However, handled with the professional acumen that marketing researchers have displayed for many years, the database presents great opportunities for the marketing researcher. In Europe, many of the leading marketing research agencies and research functions within companies have embraced the marketing database as an essential component of their desire to create 'customer insight'.

For the marketer, databases help to build profiles of consumers, linked to the products, communications and distribution methods those consumers favour. For the marketing researcher, databases can present the opportunity to experiment in 'one big laboratory', build models of consumer behaviour, develop an understanding of the gaps in knowledge of consumers and make links between behavioural and attitudinal data.

Much of the data that offer these benefits have been gained using data that capture customer buying behaviour. The use of the 'loyalty card' is one example. Different types of data, including scanner data, loyalty card data and survey data, may be combined using geodemographic information systems (GISs). Using base geographic and demographic data, existing customers can be analysed and mapped out.

Disparate database sources are pulled together through the use of datawarehouses. The datawarehouse integrates databases and survey data, allowing creative connections between data to be explored. Integrated databases and survey data can be explored using data mining techniques. These processes involve the use of proprietary software and inquisitive, creative decision-makers who search for trends and patterns in customer behaviour and attitudes. The development of datawarehouse and data mining expertise especially helps to cope with the problems of disparate databases and survey data from different countries.

The ethics of using databases provokes much debate in the marketing research industry. As many research practitioners grow more accustomed to using databases, marketing research guidelines and codes of practice are being developed to reflect the good practices that exist in many companies.

Questions

1 How may 'operational data' held in organisations help to build up an understanding of customer behaviour?

2 What is a customer database? Why may a marketing researcher wish to analyse the data held in a customer database?

3 What kinds of data can be gathered through electronic scanner devices?

4 What other sources beyond electronic scanner devices electronically observe customer behaviour?

5 Describe the benefits to the *marketing decision-maker* of being able to capture data that identify characteristics of consumers and their shopping behaviour in a store.

6 Describe the benefits to the *marketing researcher* of being able to capture data that identify characteristics of consumers and their shopping behaviour in a store.

7 Why may the characteristics of consumers differ, based upon where they live?

8   What is a geodemographic classification of consumers?

9   How can the graphical representation of consumer characteristics using maps help marketing decision making?

10 What benefits may be gained from fusing together customer characteristics held as internal secondary data, with a proprietary geodemographic information system held as external secondary data?

11 How does the compilation of different types of data help to build a strong 'picture' of consumer characteristics?

12 Describe the stages of development in using databases and survey data to build profiles of consumers and model marketing decisions.

13 What is a datawarehouse?

14 What is the difference between a datawarehouse and data mining?

15 Why may there be a difference between a individual country geodemographic classification and a European or global classification of that same country?

Exercises

1   Visit the websites of Acorn (**www.acorn.caci.co.uk**), Mosaic (**www.experian.com**) and CAMEO (**www.eurodirect.co.uk**). Imagine that you have been commissioned to select a geodemographic system to help a newspaper publisher in a major European city.

a   For such a business, how may a geodemographic system be used for marketing decision making?
b   For such a business, how may a geodemographic system aid marketing research design?
c   Present the case of which of the above systems would best suit such a business.

2   Call in at a supermarket or store that operates a reward or loyalty card scheme that requires you to apply for membership. Pick up an application form and examine the nature of questions you are expected to answer.

a   What marketing research use can be made of the data collected from this application form?
b   Evaluate the design of this form and make recommendations on how the nature of questions could be improved.

3   You are a marketing manager for Carlsberg beer. One of your major customers is a supermarket that uses a loyalty card scheme to electronically observe its customers.

a   What would this supermarket know about beer buying behaviour through its scheme?
b   If it would not share this with you, evaluate any marketing research techniques that you think could generate the same knowledge.

4   Visit the SPSS website **www.spss.com** and follow a link to its 'predictive analytics' products. Write a report on how marketing research may feed into and/or feed from predictive analytics in either a bank or major retailer.

5   In a small group discuss the following issues: 'What ethical problems exist with the use of marketing databases for marketing researchers?' and 'If, on ethical grounds, marketing researchers refused to utilise the benefits of marketing databases, what inherent weaknesses may exist in their research designs?'

Video Case Exercise: Subaru

How could Subaru's survey analyses and internal and external secondary data collection help them to profile and target female drivers?

video case

download from
www.pearsoned.co.uk/
malhotra_euro

Notes

1 McElhatton, N., 'Customer insight in stereo', *Research World* (December 2004), 21.

2 Ibid., p. 20.

3 Evans, M., Nancarrow, C., Tapp, A. and Stone, M., 'Future marketers: future curriculum; future shock?', *Journal of Marketing Management* 18 (5–6), (2002), 579–596.

4 Dawe, A., 'Integration is the thing', *The Times – Special Edition e–CRM* (11 April 2001), 2–3.

5 Sumner–Smith, D., 'Getting to know clients lifts profits', *The Sunday Times* (26 September 1999), 17.

6 Fletcher, K., 'The evolution and use of information technology in marketing', in Baker, M.J. (ed.), *The Marketing Book*, 3rd edn (Oxford: Butterworth–Heinemann, 1994), 352.

7 Mistry, B., 'A question of loyalty', *Marketing* (2 March 2005), 42.

8 Havermans, J., 'Do-it-yourself surveys offer opportunity for MR', *Research World* (June 2004), 20–21.

9 Kilby, N. and Bedwell, R., 'Women stand by their stores', *Marketing Week* (2 June 2005), 32–33.

10 Lawson, J., 'Cruising for customers', *Database Marketing* (December 2003), 29–30.

11 An example of fusing research data with databases is presented in Leventhal, B., 'An approach to fusing market research with database marketing', *Journal of the Market Research Society* 39 (4) (October 1997), 545–561.

12 Sleight, P., 'Newest neighbourhoods', *Database Marketing* (June 2005), 31–34.

13 Man, D., 'You say "warehouse", I say "database" …', *Bank Marketing* 29 (4) (April 1997), 37.

14 Man, D., 'The faqs on datawarehousing', *Bank Marketing* 29 (4) (April 1997), 38.

15 Lawson, J., 'No rocket scientists required', *Database Marketing* (June 2003), 30.

16 Jambu, M., 'Data mining for better knowledge: a case study for the telecommunications industry', ESOMAR, Power of Knowledge Conference, Berlin (September 1998).

17 McElhatton, N., 'Raiding the data bank', *Research* (September 1999), 28–30. See also the arguments in Brand, C. and Jarvis, S., 'Mind games – the new psychology of research', Market Research Society Conference, 2000.

18 Pinnell, J., 'Customer relationships – manage, measure or just understand?' ESOMAR (January 2003), **www.warc.com/print/78475p.asp**.

19 McElhatton, N., 'Customer insight in stereo', *Research World* (December 2004), 21.

20 Hodgson, P., 'Databases: the time for decisions is nigh', *Research* (October 1993), 19.

21 'Loyalty for sale', *Financial Times* (18 September 1998).

22 Smith, D.V.L. 'Bridging the gap between data and decision', *Research World*, (November 2004), 20–21; Savage, M., 'Downstream danger', *Research* (May 2000), 25–27.

23 For illustrations of neural networks and decision trees in marketing, see Garver, M.S., 'Using data mining for customer satisfaction research', *Marketing Research* (Spring 2002), 8–12.

Visit the *Marketing Research* Companion Website at www.pearsoned.co.uk/malhotra_euro for additional learning resources including annotated weblinks, an online glossary and a suite of downloadable video cases.

Source: © EMPICS

6

Qualitative research: its nature and approaches

Qualitative research helps the marketer to understand the richness, depth and complexity of consumers.

Objectives

After reading this chapter, you should be able to:

1 explain the difference between qualitative and quantitative research in terms of the objectives, sampling, data collection and analysis, and outcomes;

2 describe why qualitative research is used in marketing research;

3 understand the basic philosophical stances that underpin qualitative research;

4 understand the nature and application of ethnographic approaches;

5 understand how qualitative researchers develop theory through a grounded theory approach;

6 explain the potential of action research to qualitative marketing researchers;

7 discuss the considerations involved in collecting and analysing qualitative data collected from international markets;

8 understand the ethical issues involved in collecting and analysing qualitative data.

STAGE 1
Problem
definition

STAGE 2
Research approach
developed

STAGE 3
Research design
developed

STAGE 4
Fieldwork or data
collection

STAGE 5
Data preparation
and analysis

STAGE 6
Report preparation
and presentation

Qualitative research forms a major role in supporting marketing decision making, primarily as an exploratory design but also as a descriptive design. Researchers may undertake qualitative research to help define a research problem, to support quantitative, descriptive or causal research designs or as a design in its own right. Qualitative research is often used to generate hypotheses and identify variables that should be included in quantitative approaches. It may be used after or in conjunction with quantitative approaches where illumination of statistical findings is needed. In some cases qualitative research designs are adopted in isolation, after secondary data sources have been thoroughly evaluated or even in an iterative process with secondary data sources.

In this chapter, we discuss the differences between qualitative and quantitative research and the role of each in marketing research. We present reasons for adopting a qualitative approach to marketing research (Stage 2 of the marketing research process). These reasons are developed by examining the basic philosophical stances that underpin qualitative research. The concept of ethnographic techniques is presented, with illustrations of how such techniques support marketing decision-makers. The concept of grounded theory is presented, illustrating its roots, the steps involved and the dilemmas for researchers in attempting to be objective and sensitive to the expressions of participants. Action research is an approach to conducting research that has been adopted in a wide variety of social and management research settings. Action research is developing in marketing research and offers great potential for consumers, decision-makers and researchers alike. The roots of action research are presented, together with the iterative stages involved and the concept of action research teams. The considerations involved in conducting qualitative research when researching international markets are discussed, especially in contrasting approaches between the USA and Europe. Several ethical issues that arise in qualitative research are identified.

Before the chapter moves on to the substantive issues, one key point to note in the application of qualitative research is the name applied to the individuals who take part in interviews and observations. Note the emphasis in the following example.

Example 'Research is War'[1]

Dutch agency MARE is calling for respondents to be promoted to the status of participants in research. The method that it has been developing puts the respondent in the position of participant rather than a passive reactive pawn in research. We take two participants, show them an image or commercial, and then invite one participant to ask the other what he or she just saw. This results in a conversation that is not directed by researchers, which is an important aspect. Our intervention is mostly focused on finding a good match between two participants who can communicate with one another. The method reveals how a consumer absorbs information and reports about it to fellow consumers, and it shows the client which elements of a commercial message work and which elements do not. Clients were reluctant to use this approach when it was first used in 1995. MARE senses there is a market for it now, so with an amount of refining, adjusting and testing, it ran from September 2005. A multinational in the Netherlands which has young marketers will apply it in research among young consumers.

This example illustrates the creative thinking necessary to get the most from qualitative research and the respect that should be given to individuals who may be asked to engage in a process that sometimes goes way beyond simple questioning. Embracing this attitude, the term 'participant' rather than 'respondent' or 'informant' is used throughout Chapters 6 to 9, i.e. the core qualitative research chapters of the text.

We now move on to the nature of qualitative research with three examples. Given the nature of its products and competitive environment, the first example illustrates why L'Oréal feels that qualitative research is of importance to it. The second example illustrates how Philips uses qualitative techniques to support its trend forecasting and product design. Note in this example the use of an analytical framework to help researchers and decision-makers gain insight from the data they collect. In the third example, Sports Marketing Surveys uses qualitative brainstorming techniques and focus groups as part of a research design to support the development of rugby league. These examples illustrate the rich insights into the underlying behaviour of consumers that can be obtained by using qualitative techniques.

Example A research commitment more than skin deep[2]

L'Oréal is the largest supplier of toiletries and cosmetics in the world. The group tucks under its umbrella some of the best known brands and companies in the beauty business: cosmetics houses Lancôme, Vichy and Helena Rubenstein, and fragrance houses Guy Laroche, Cacharel and Ralph Lauren. Given the French penchant for qualitative research, and given the nature of the cosmetics industry, Anne Murray, Head of Research, was asked which type of research she favoured.

We're not particularly pro-quantitative or qualitative. Nevertheless, I do think qualitative in our area is very important. There are many sensitive issues to cover – environmental concerns, animal testing, intimate personal products. And increasingly, we have given to us very technical propositions from the labs, and what is a technical breakthrough to a man in a white coat is not necessarily so to a consumer. So the research department has to be that interface between the technical side and the consumer.

Example Trend forecasting at Philips[3]

Marco Bevolo is in the future business. At Philips Design, the design department of the electronics multinational, he is responsible for identifying short-term trends in popular culture and aesthetics design. Marco believes his job has a lot in common with marketing research. Trend forecasting at Philips is carried out through a model developed by Marco and his team called CultureScan. The theoretical background of their approach comes from the Birmingham school of popular culture analysis as well as from the kind of cultural analysis performed by scholars who study phenomena such as 'punks' in Western cities as if they were a tribe in New Guinea. Rather than hinting at tangible design solutions – colour, 'touch and feel' or shape – of TVs, MP3 players or other specific products, CultureScan is supposed to provide an insight into the broader, longer term undercurrents in popular culture and aesthetics design all over the world. These broad trends are then customised by Philips decision teams. CultureScan uses both an internal and external network of experts to collect information on a wide variety of trends. These insights are then filtered by objective tools in order to validate the outcomes and make them actionable. The predictive horizon of CultureScan is 18 to 36 months with the trends refined every two or three years.

Sports Marketing Surveys

Rugby league study

Sports Marketing Surveys was commissioned by the Rugby Football League (the governing body of rugby league in the UK) to:

- gain an understanding of the target audience for rugby league;
- investigate the core values of rugby league;
- verify the core values and quantify the new branding concepts.

The figure below sets out the research design adopted for the project, setting out the research objectives, the qualitative and quantitative techniques used, and how each stage feeds the development of subsequent stages.

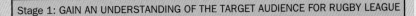

Rugby league study – research design

Stage 1: GAIN AN UNDERSTANDING OF THE TARGET AUDIENCE FOR RUGBY LEAGUE

Sporting insights: Online specialist sports fan research tool using a pool of rugby league fans and links to Rugby Football League websites

BRAINSTORM/WORKSHOP 1
Construct initial draft definition statements and unique sales propositions for the sport, use as a basis for Stage 2 discussion guide and stimulus materials

Stage 2: INVESTIGATE THE CORE VALUES OF RUGBY LEAGUE

Focus/discussion groups: Gain insight into views, attitudes and aspirations for the sport, evaluate and validate values/definition statement, identify representative images of the sport. Stimulus constructed from Stage 1 results

BRAINSTORM/WORKSHOP 2
The basis for a final definition statement for the sport. Develop the unique sales propositions for the sport, identify/validate the brand hierarchy and understanding barriers for entry. Develop creative brief to complete brand image changes.

Stage 3: QUANTIFY THE CORE VALUES AND NEW BRANDING CONCEPTS

Face-to-face interviews – Test reactions amongst a wider quantitative audience, representing the rugby league target market
Sporting insights – Test on 1,000 general sports fans and 500 rugby leagues fans through online survey

In qualitative research, research agencies and companies are continually looking to find better ways to understand consumers' thought processes and motivations. This has led to a wealth of research approaches, including techniques borrowed from anthropology, ethnography, sociology and psychology. For example, Intel has a specialist team of researchers, including ethnographers, anthropologists and psychologists, whose principal form of research is in the home. 'People don't tell you things because they don't think you'll be interested. By going into their homes you can see where and how they use their computers,' says Wendy March, Intel's interaction designer of Intel Architecture.[4]

Primary data: qualitative versus quantitative research

Qualitative research
An unstructured, primarily exploratory design based on small samples, intended to provide insight and understanding.

Quantitative research
Research techniques that seek to quantify data and, typically, apply some form of statistical analysis.

As explained in Chapter 4, primary data are originated by the researcher for the specific purpose of addressing the problem at hand. Primary data may be qualitative or quantitative in nature, as shown in Figure 6.1.

Dogmatic positions are often taken in favour of either **qualitative research** or **quantitative research** by marketing researchers and decision-makers alike. The positions are founded upon which approach is perceived to give the most accurate understanding of consumers. The extreme stances on this issue mirror each other. Many quantitative researchers are apt to dismiss qualitative studies completely as giving no valid findings – indeed as being little better than journalistic accounts. They assert that qualitative researchers ignore representative sampling, with their findings based on a single case or only a few cases. Equally adamant are some qualitative researchers who firmly reject statistical and other quantitative methods as yielding shallow or completely misleading information. They believe that to understand cultural values and consumer behaviour requires interviewing or intensive field observation. Qualitative techniques they see as being the only methods of data collection sensitive enough to capture the nuances of consumer attitudes, motives and behaviour.[5]

There are great differences between the quantitative and qualitative approaches to studying and understanding consumers. The arguments between qualitative and quantitative marketing researchers about their relative strengths and weaknesses are of real practical value. The nature of marketing decision making encompasses a vast array of problems and types of decision-maker. This means that seeking a singular and uniform approach to supporting decision-makers by focusing on one approach is futile. Defending qualitative approaches for a particular marketing research problem through the positive benefits it bestows and explaining the negative alternatives of a quantitative approach is healthy – and vice versa. Business and marketing decision-makers use both approaches and will continue to need both.[6]

The distinction between qualitative and quantitative research can be in the context of research designs as discussed in Chapter 3. There is a close parallel in the distinctions between 'exploratory and conclusive research' and 'qualitative and quantitative research'. There is a parallel, but the terms are not identical. There are circumstances where qualitative research can be used to present detailed descriptions that cannot be measured in a quantifiable manner: for example, in describing characteristics and styles of music that may be used in an advertising campaign or in describing the interplay of how families go through the process of choosing, planning and buying a holiday.

Conversely, there may be circumstances where quantitative measurements are used conclusively to answer specific hypotheses or research questions using descriptive or experimental techniques. Beyond answering specific hypotheses or research questions, there may

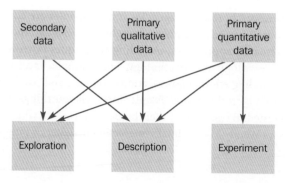

Figure 6.1
A classification of marketing research data

be sufficient data to allow data mining or an exploration of relationships between individual measurements to take place. The concept of data mining illustrated in Chapter 5 allows decision-makers to be supported through exploratory quantitative research.

The nature of qualitative research

Qualitative research encompasses a variety of methods that can be applied in a flexible manner, to enable participants to reflect upon and express their views or to observe their behaviour. It seeks to encapsulate the behaviour, experiences and feelings of participants in their own terms and context; for example, when conducting research on children, an informality and child-friendly atmosphere is vital, considering features such as the decoration of the room with appropriately themed posters.[7]

Qualitative research is based on at least two intellectual traditions.[8] The first and perhaps most important is the set of ideas and associated methods from the broad area of depth psychology.[9] This movement was concerned with the less conscious aspects of the human psyche. It led to a development of methods to gain access to individuals' subconscious and/or unconscious levels. So, while individuals may present a superficial explanation of events to themselves or to others, these methods sought to dig deeper and penetrate the superficial.

The second tradition is the set of ideas and associated methods from sociology, social psychology and social anthropology, and the disciplines of ethnography, linguistics and semiology. The emphases here are upon holistic understanding of the world-view of people. The researcher is expected to 'enter' the hearts and minds of those they are researching, to develop an empathy with their experiences and feelings.

Both traditions have a concern with developing means of communication between the researcher and those being researched. There can be much interaction between the two broad traditions, which in pragmatic terms allows a wide and rich array of techniques and interpretations of collected data.

Qualitative research is a significant contributor to the marketing research industry, accounting for substantial expenditure (around 16% of all spending on marketing research methods),[10] and is growing. In commercial terms, it is a billion-euro-plus global industry. However, it is not just a matter of business value. Qualitative thinking has had a profound effect upon marketing and the marketing research industry as a whole.

Rationale for using qualitative research

It is not always possible, or desirable, to use structured quantitative techniques to obtain information from participants or to observe them. Thus, there are several reasons to use qualitative techniques. These reasons, either individually or in any combination, explain why certain marketing researchers adopt a particular approach (Stage 2 of the marketing research process) to how they conduct research, analyse data and interpret their findings.

1 *Preferences and/or experience of the researcher.* Some researchers are more oriented and temperamentally suited to do this type of work. Just as some researchers enjoy the challenge of using statistical techniques, there are researchers who enjoy the challenges of qualitative techniques and the interpretation of diverse types of data. Such researchers have been trained in particular disciplines (e.g. anthropology) and philosophies (e.g. hermeneutics) that traditionally make use of qualitative research designs and techniques.

2 *Preferences and/or experience of the research user.* Some decision-makers are more oriented to receiving support in a qualitative manner. This orientation could come from their training but it could also be due to the type of marketing decisions they have to

take. Decision-makers working in a creative environment of advertising copy or the development of brand 'personalities', for example, may have a greater preference for data that will feed such 'artistic' decisions. In the following example, consider how decision-makers would get to understand and represent the language used by teenagers. Consider also the implications for a brand if marketers do not fully understand the language and values of their target markets.

Example   ## First get the language right, then tell them a story[11]

Teenagers immediately recognise a communication in their language and are very quick to judge whether advertisers have got it right. They see ads and like them, reject them, ignore them or, in many cases, discuss them. Teenagers are so fluent in 'marketing speak' because marketing and advertising are perceived by them to be the kind of work which can be creative, interesting and acceptable. They discuss with one another the advertising which they perceive to be targeting them.

Pelgram Walters International conducted a study called Global Village. The main contention of the study was that teenagers around the world have a common language, which speaks to them in the filmed advertising medium. Part of the study consisted of focus group discussions of 12–18 year olds. Pepsi's Next Generation advertisement was criticised by more media-literate teenage markets (the UK, Germany and the USA) for stereotyping teens and misunderstanding who they are. The ad was a montage of very hip skateboarding teens, male teens wearing make-up, perhaps implying that Pepsi is for the next generation which looks thus. The main complaint was 'we don't look like that', the teens saying that they were not all the same as one another. By aligning the brand image with these extreme images, the commercial was less appealing to mainstream teen consumers.

---

3   *Sensitive information.* Participants may be unwilling to answer or to give truthful answers to certain questions that invade their privacy, embarrass them, or have a negative impact on their ego or status. Questions that relate to sanitary products and contraception are examples of personally sensitive issues. In industrial marketing research, questions that relate to corporate performance and plans are examples of commercially sensitive issues. Techniques that build up an amount of rapport and trust, that allow gentle probing in a manner that suits individual participants, can help researchers get close to participants, and may allow sensitive data to be elicited.

4   *Subconscious feelings.* Participants may be unable to provide accurate answers to questions that tap their subconscious. The values, emotional drives and motivations residing at the subconscious level are disguised from the outer world by rationalisation and other ego defences. For example, a person may have purchased an expensive sports car to overcome feelings of inferiority. But if asked 'Why did you purchase this sports car?' that person may say 'I got a great deal', 'My old car was falling apart', or 'I need to impress my customers and clients.' The participants do not have to put words to their deeper emotional drives until researchers approach them! In tapping into those deeper emotional drives, qualitative research can take a path that evolves and is right for the participant.

5   *Complex phenomena.* The nature of what participants are expected to describe may be difficult to capture with structured questions. For example, participants may know what brands of wine they enjoy, what types of music they prefer or what images they regard as being prestigious. They may not be able to clearly explain why they have these feelings or where these feelings are coming from.

6   *The holistic dimension.* The object of taking a holistic outlook in qualitative research is to gain a comprehensive and complete picture of the whole context in which the phenomena of interest occur. It is an attempt to describe and understand as much as possible

about the whole situation of interest. Each scene exists within a multi-layered and inter-related context and it may require multiple methods to ensure the researcher covers all angles. This orientation helps the researcher discover the interrelationships among the various components of the phenomenon under study. In evaluating different forms of consumer behaviour, the researcher seeks to understand the relationship of different contextual environments upon that behaviour. Setting behaviour into context involves placing observations, experiences and interpretations into a larger perspective.[12] An example of this may be of measuring satisfaction with a meal in a restaurant. A questionnaire can break down components of the experience in the restaurant and quantify the extent of satisfaction with these. But what effect did the 'atmosphere' have upon the experience? What role did the type of music, the colour and style of furniture, aromas coming from the kitchen, other people in the restaurant, the mood when entering the restaurant, feelings of relaxation or tension as the meal went on, contribute to the feeling of atmosphere? Building up an understanding of the interrelationship of the context of consumption allows the qualitative researcher to build up this holistic view. This can be done through qualitative observation and interviewing.

7 *Developing new theory.* This is perhaps the most contentious reason for conducting qualitative research. Chapter 11 details how causal research design through experiments helps to generate theory. Qualitative researchers may argue that there are severe limitations in conducting experiments upon consumers and that quantitative approaches are limited to elaborating or extending existing theory. The development of 'new' theory through a qualitative approach is called 'grounded theory', which will be addressed later.

8 *Interpretation.*[13] Qualitative techniques often constitute an important final step in research designs. Large-scale surveys and audits often fail to clarify the underlying reasons for a set of findings. Using qualitative techniques can help to elaborate and explain underlying reasons in quantitative findings.

Philosophy[14] and qualitative research

Positivist perspectives

Theory
A conceptual scheme based on foundational statements, or axioms, that are assumed to be true.

Operationalised
The derivation of measurable characteristics to encapsulate marketing phenomena, e.g. the concept of 'customer loyalty' can be operationalised through measurements such as the frequency of repeat purchases or the number of years that a business relationship has existed.

Empiricism
A theory of knowledge. A broad category of the philosophy of science that locates the source of all knowledge in experience.

Positivism
A philosophy of language and logic consistent with an empiricist philosophy of science.

In Chapter 2 we discussed the vital role that **theory** plays in marketing research. Researchers rely on theory to determine which variables should be investigated, how variables should be **operationalised** and measured, and how the research design and sample should be selected. Theory also serves as a foundation on which the researcher can organise and interpret findings. Good marketing research is founded upon theory and contributes to the development of theory to improve the powers of explanation, prediction and understanding in marketing decision-makers.[15]

The dominant perspective of developing new theory in marketing research has been one of **empiricism** and more specifically **positivism**. The central belief of a positivist position is a view that the study of consumers and marketing phenomena should be 'scientific' in the manner of the natural sciences. Marketing researchers of this persuasion adopt a framework for investigation akin to the natural scientist. For many, this is considered to be both desirable and possible. A fundamental belief shared by positivists is the view that the social and natural worlds 'conform to certain fixed and unalterable laws in an endless chain of causation'.[16] The main purpose of a scientific approach to marketing research is to establish causal laws that enable the prediction and explanation of marketing phenomena. To establish these laws, a scientific approach must have, as a minimum, reliable information or 'facts'. The emphasis on facts leads to a focus upon objectivity, rigour and measurement.

Paradigm
A set of assumptions consisting of agreed-upon knowledge, criteria of judgement, problem fields, and ways to consider them.

As an overall research approach (using the description of a **paradigm** or research approach as developed in Chapter 2) qualitative research does not rely upon measurement or the establishment of 'facts' and so does not fit with a positivist perspective. However, if qualitative research is just seen as a series of techniques, they can be used to develop an understanding of the nature of a research problem, and to develop and pilot questionnaires. In other words, the positivist perspective of qualitative research is to see it as a set of techniques, applied as preliminary stages to more rigorous techniques that measure, i.e. surveys and questionnaires. This use of qualitative techniques is fine but may be limiting. To conduct in-depth interviews, focus groups or projective techniques, to understand the language and logic of target questionnaire participants makes good sense. However, using qualitative techniques just to develop quantitative techniques can affect how those techniques are used. As an illustration, we will examine how focus groups may be conducted.

The term 'focus group discussion' is commonly used across all continents, yet it subsumes different ways of applying the technique. There are two main schools of thought, which may be termed 'cognitive' and 'conative'.

1 *Cognitive.* American researchers generally follow this tradition, which largely follows a format and interviewing style as used in quantitative studies. 'American-style groups' is shorthand in Europe for large groups (10 participants on average), a structured procedure and a strong element of external validation. Within the cognitive approach, the analysis or articulation has been worked on before, and so the interviews are largely meant to confirm or expand on known issues.
2 *Conative.* European researchers generally follow this tradition. This style assumes a different starting point, one that emphasises exploration, with analysis taking place during and after the group. There is less structure to the questions, with group members being encouraged to take their own paths of discussion, make their own connections and let the whole process evolve.

Table 6.1 summarises the differences between the American (cognitive) and European (conative) approaches to conducting focus groups. Note the longer duration of the European approach to allow the exploration to develop. To maintain the interest and motivation of participants for this time period, the interview experience must be stimulating and enjoyable.

International marketers have always been aware that qualitative research as it developed in the USA and Europe involves quite different practices, stemming from different premises and yielding different results. American-style qualitative research started from the same evaluative premise as quantitative research but on a smaller scale. This made it cheaper, quicker and useful for checking out the less critical decisions. European-style qualitative research started from the opposite premise to quantitative research: it was developmental, exploratory and creative rather than evaluative. It was used as a tool of understanding, to get underneath consumer motivation.[17]

The American style uses a detailed discussion guide which follows a logical sequence and is usually strictly adhered to. The interviewing technique involves closed questions and straight answers. This type of research is used primarily to inform about behaviour and to confirm hypotheses already derived from other sources. For this reason, clients who have attended groups often feel they do not need any further analysis; the group interaction supplies the answers. Transcripts are rarely necessary and reports are often summarised or even done away with altogether.

The European style is used primarily to gain new insight; it also works from a discussion guide, but in a less structured way. The interviewing technique is opportunistic and probing. Projective techniques are introduced to help researchers understand underlying motivations and attitudes. Because the purpose is 'understanding', which requires a creative synthesis of (sometimes unconscious) consumer needs and brand benefits, analysis is time consuming and usually involves full transcripts.

Table 6.1 The two schools of thought about 'focus group discussions'[18]

Characteristics	Cognitive	Conative
Purpose	Demonstration	Exploration
Sample size	10–12	6–8
Duration	1.5 hours	1.5 to 6 hours
Interviewing	Logical sequence	Opportunistic
Questions	Closed	Open
Techniques	Straight question, questionnaires, hand shows, counting	Probing, facilitation, projectives, describing
Response required	Give answers	Debate issues
Interviewer	Moderator	Researcher
Observer's role	To get proof	To understand
Transcripts	Rarely necessary	Usually full
Analysis	On the spot	Time-consuming
Focus of time	Preplanning	Post-fieldwork
Accusations against other style	'Formless'	'Over-controlling'
Suited for	Testing or proving ideas	Meaning or understanding
Output	To be confirmed in quantitative studies	Can be used in its own right to support decision-makers

In the above descriptions of American and European traditions of applying qualitative techniques, it is clear to see that the American perspective is positivist, i.e. aims to deliver a 'factual' impression of consumers. The facts may be established, but they may not be enough – they may not provide the richness or depth of understanding that certain marketing decision-makers demand. So, although a positivist perspective has a role to play in developing explanations, predictions and understanding of consumers and marketing phenomena, it has its limitations and critics. The following quote from the eminent qualitative practitioner Peter Cooper cautions us of what we really mean by the term 'qualitative':

> There is much qualitative research that still hangs on the positivist model or is little more than investigative journalism. Competition also comes from the media with increasing phone-ins and debates described as 'research'. We need to be careful about the abuse of what goes under the title 'qualitative'.[19]

The dominance of positivist philosophy in marketing research has been and is being challenged by other philosophical perspectives, taken and adapted from disciplines such as anthropology and sociology. These perspectives have helped marketing researchers to develop richer explanations and predictions and especially an understanding and a meaning as seen through the eyes of consumers.

Interpretivist perspectives

In general there are considered to be two main research paradigms that are used by marketing researchers.[20] These are the positivist paradigm and the interpretivist paradigm (though these are by no means the only research paradigms that may be adopted by marketing researchers).[21] Table 6.2 presents alternative names that may be used to describe these paradigms.

Table 6.2 Alternative paradigm names[22]

Positivist	Interpretivist
Quantitative	Qualitative
Objectivist	Subjectivist
Scientific	Humanistic
Experimentalist	Phenomenological
Traditionalist	Revolutionist

Whilst it may be easier to think of these as quite clear, distinct and mutually exclusive perspectives of developing valid and useful marketing knowledge, the reality is somewhat different. There is a huge array of versions of these paradigms, presented by philosophers, researchers and users of research findings. These versions change depending upon the assumptions of researchers and the context and subjects of their study, i.e. the ultimate nature of the research problem. It has long been argued[23] that both positivist and interpretivist paradigms are valid in conducting marketing research and help to shape the nature of techniques that researchers apply.

In order to develop an understanding of what an interpretivist paradigm means, Table 6.3 presents characteristic features of the two paradigms.

Table 6.3 Paradigm features[24]

Issue	Positivist	Interpretivist
Reality	Objective and singular	Subjective and multiple
Researcher–participant	Independent of each other	Interacting with each other
Values	Value free = unbiased	Value laden = biased
Researcher language	Formal and impersonal	Informal and personal
Theory and research design	Simple determinist Cause and effect Static research design Context free Laboratory Prediction and control Reliability and validity Representative surveys Experimental design Deductive	Freedom of will Multiple influences Evolving design Context bound Field/ethnography Understanding and insight Perceptive decision making Theoretical sampling Case studies Inductive

Comparison of positivist and interpretivist perspectives

The paradigms can be compared through a series of issues. The descriptions of these issues do not imply that any particular paradigm is stronger than the other. In each issue there are relative advantages and disadvantages specific to any research question under investigation. The issues are dealt with in the following subsections.

Reality. The positivist supposes that reality is 'out there' to be captured. It thus becomes a matter of finding the most effective and objective means possible to draw together information about this reality. The interpretivist stresses the dynamic, participant-constructed and evolving nature of reality, recognising that there may be a wide array of interpretations of realities or social acts.

Researcher–participant. The positivist sees the participant as an 'object' to be measured in a consistent manner. The interpretivist may see participants as 'peers' or even 'companions', seeking the right context and means of observing and questioning to suit individual participants. Such a view of participants requires the development of rapport, an amount of interaction and evolution of method as the researcher learns of the best means to elicit information.

Values. The positivist seeks to set aside his or her own personal values. The positivist's measurements of participants are being guided by established theoretical propositions. The task for the positivist is to remove any potential bias. The interpretivist recognises that his or her own values affect how he or she questions, probes and interprets. The task for interpretivists is to realise the nature of their values and how these affect how they question and interpret.

Researcher language. In seeking a consistent and unbiased means to measure, the positivist uses a language in questioning that is uniformly recognised. This uniformity may emerge from existing theory (to allow comparability of findings) or from the positivist's vision of what may be relevant to the target group of participants. Ultimately, the positivist imposes a language and logic upon target participants in a consistent manner. The interpretivist seeks to draw out the language and logic of target participants. The language used may differ between participants and develop in different ways as the interpretivist learns more about a topic and the nature of participants.

Theory and research design. In the development of theory, the positivist seeks to establish **causality** (discussed in detail in Chapter 11) through experimental methods. Seeking causality helps the positivist to explain phenomena and hopefully predict the recurrence of what has been observed in other contexts. There are many **extraneous variables** that may confound the outcome of experiments, hence the positivist will seek to control these variables and the environment in which an experiment takes place. The ultimate control in an experiment takes place in a laboratory situation. In establishing causality through experiments, questions of causality usually go hand in hand with questions of **determinism**, i.e. if everything that happens has a cause, then we live in a determinist universe.

The positivist will go to great pains to diagnose the nature of a research problem and establish an explicit and set research design to investigate the problem. A fundamental element of the positivist's research design is the desire to generalise findings to a **target population**. Most targeted populations are so large that measurements of them can only be managed through representative sample surveys. The positivists use theory to develop the consistent and unbiased measurements they seek. They have established rules and tests of the **reliability** and **validity** of their measurements and continually seek to develop more reliable and valid measurements.

In the development of theory, the interpretivist seeks to understand the nature of multiple influences of marketing phenomena through **case studies**. The search for multiple influences means focusing upon the intrinsic details of individual cases and the differences between different classes of case. This helps the interpretivist to describe phenomena and hopefully gain new and creative insights to understand ultimately the nature of consumer behaviour in its fullest sense. The consumers that interpretivists focus

---

Causality
Causality applies when the occurrence of X increases the probability of the occurrence of Y.

Extraneous variables
Variables other than dependent and independent variables which may influence the results of an experiment.

Determinism
A doctrine espousing that everything that happens is determined by a necessary chain of causation.

Target population
The collection of elements or objects that possess the information sought by the researcher and about which inferences are made.

Reliability
The extent to which a measurement reproduces consistent results if the process of measurement were to be repeated.

Validity
The extent to which a measurement represents characteristics that exist in the phenomenon under investigation.

Case study
A detailed study based upon the observation of the intrinsic details of individuals, groups of individuals and organisations.

upon, live, consume and relate to products and services in a huge array of contexts, hence the interpretivist will seek to understand the nature and effect of these contexts on the chosen cases. The contexts in which consumers live and consume constitute the field in which interpretivists immerse themselves to conduct their investigations. In understanding the nature and effect of context upon consumers, the interpretivist does not consider that *everything* that happens has a cause and that we live in a determinist universe. There is a recognition and respect for the notion of free will.

The interpretivist will go to great pains to learn from each step of the research process and adapt the research design as his or her learning develops. The interpretivist seeks to diagnose the nature of a research problem but recognises that a set research design may be restrictive and so usually adopts an **evolving research design**. A fundamental element of the interpretivist's research design is the desire to generalise findings to different contexts, such as other types of consumer. However, rather than seeking to study large samples to generalise to target populations, the interpretivist uses **theoretical sampling**. This means that the data gathering process for interpretivists is driven by concepts derived from evolving theory, based on the notion of seeking out different situations and learning from the comparisons that can be made. The purpose is to go to places, people or events that will maximise opportunities to discover variations among concepts. Interpretivists use theory initially to help guide which cases they should focus upon, the issues they should observe and the context of their investigation. As their research design evolves they seek to develop new theory and do not wish to be 'blinkered' or too focused on existing ideas. They seek multiple explanations of the phenomena they observe and create what they see as the most valid relationship of concepts and, ultimately, theory. Interpretivists seek to evaluate the strength of the theory they develop. The strongest means of evaluating the strength of interpretivist theory lies in the results of decision making that is based on the theory. Interpretivists continually seek to evaluate the worth of the theories they develop. A principal output of research generated by an interpretivist perspective should therefore be findings that are accessible and intended for use. If they are found to be meaningful by decision-makers and employed successfully by them, this may constitute further evidence of the theory's validity. If employed and found lacking, questions will have to be asked of the theory, about its comprehensibility and comprehensiveness and about its interpretation. If it is not used, the theory may be loaded with validity but have little value.

Evolving research design
A research design where particular research techniques are chosen as the researcher develops an understanding of the issues and participants.

Theoretical sampling
Data gathering driven by concepts derived from evolving theory and based on the concept of 'making comparisons'.

Summarising the broad perspectives of positivism and interpretivism

The positivist seeks to establish the legitimacy of his or her approach through **deduction**. In a deductive approach, the following process unfolds:

Deduction
A form of reasoning in which a conclusion is validly inferred from some premises, and must be true if those premises are true.

- An area of enquiry is identified, set in the context of well-developed theory, which is seen as vital to guide researchers, ensuring that they are not naive in their approach and do not 'reinvent the wheel'.
- The issues to focus an enquiry upon emerge from the established theoretical framework.
- Specific variables are identified that the researchers deem should be measured, i.e. hypotheses are set.
- An 'instrument' to measure specific variables is developed.
- Participants give answers to set and specific questions with a consistent language and logic.
- The responses to the set questions are analysed in terms of a prior established theoretical framework.
- The researchers test theory according to whether their hypotheses are accepted or rejected. From testing theory in a new context, they seek to develop existing theory incrementally.

Such a process means that positivists reach conclusions based upon agreed and measurable 'facts'. The building and establishment of 'facts' forms the premises of deductive arguments. Deductive reasoning starts from general principles from which the deduction is to be made, and proceeds to a conclusion by way of some statement linking the particular case in question.

A deductive approach has a well-established role for existing theory: it informs the development of hypotheses, the choice of variables and the resultant measures.[25] Whereas the deductive approach starts with theory expressed in the form of hypotheses, which are then tested, an inductive approach avoids this, arguing that it may prematurely close off possible areas of enquiry.[26]

The interpretivist seeks to establish the legitimacy of his or her approach through **induction**. In an inductive approach, the following process unfolds:

Induction
A form of reasoning that usually involves the inference that an instance or repeated combination of events may be universally generalised.

- An area of enquiry is identified, but with little or no theoretical framework. Theoretical frameworks are seen as restrictive, narrowing the researcher's perspective, and an inhibitor to creativity.
- The issues to focus an enquiry upon are either observed or elicited from participants in particular contexts.
- Participants are aided to explain the nature of issues in a particular context.
- Broad themes are identified for discussion, with observation, probing and in-depth questioning to elaborate the nature of these themes.
- The researchers develop their theory by searching for the occurrence and interconnection of phenomena. They seek to develop a model based upon their observed combination of events. Such a process means that interpretivists reach conclusions without 'complete evidence'.

With the intense scrutiny of individuals in specific contexts that typify an interpretivist approach, tackling large 'representative' samples is generally impossible. Thus, the validity of the interpretivist approach is based upon 'fair samples'. Interpretivists should not seek only to reinforce their own prejudice or bias, seizing upon issues that are agreeable to them and ignoring those that are inconvenient. If they are to argue reasonably they should counteract this tendency by searching for conflicting evidence.[27] Their resultant theory should be subject to constant review and revision.

Ethnographic research

It is clear that an interpretive approach does not set out to test hypotheses but to explore the nature and interrelationships of marketing phenomena. The focus of investigation is a detailed examination of a small number of cases rather than a large sample. The data collected are analysed through an explicit interpretation of the meanings and functions of consumer actions. The product of these analyses takes the form of verbal descriptions and explanations, with quantification and statistical analysis playing a subordinate role. These characteristics are the hallmark of a research approach that has developed and been applied to marketing problems over many years in European marketing research. This research approach is one of ethnographic research.

Ethnography as a general term includes observation and interviewing and is sometimes referred to as participant observation. It is, however, used in the more specific case of a method which requires a researcher to spend a large amount of time observing a particular group of people, by sharing their way of life.[28] Ethnography is the art and science of describing a group or culture. The description may be of a small tribal group in an exotic land or a classroom in middle-class suburbia. The task is much like the one taken on by the investigative reporter, who interviews relevant people, reviews records, weighs

Ethnography
A research approach based upon the observation of the customs, habits and differences between people in everyday situations.

the credibility of one person's opinions against another's, looks for ties to special interests and organisations and writes the story for a concerned public and for professional colleagues. A key difference between the investigative reporter and the ethnographer, however, is that whereas the journalist seeks out the unusual, the murder, the plane crash, or the bank robbery, the ethnographer writes about the routine daily lives of people. The more predictable patterns of human thought and behaviour are the focus of enquiry.[29]

The origins of ethnography are in the work of nineteenth-century anthropologists who travelled to observe different pre-industrial cultures. An example in a more contemporary context could be the study of death rituals in Borneo, conducted over two years by the anthropologist Peter Metcalf.[30] Today, 'ethnography' encompasses a much broader range of work, from studies of groups in one's own culture, through experimental writing, to political interventions. Moreover, ethnographers today do not always 'observe', at least not directly. They may work with cultural artefacts such as written texts, or study recordings of interactions they did not observe at first hand,[31] or even, as in the following example, the observations of a refrigerator.

Example **The Electrolux 'screen fridge'**

Electrolux and Ericsson joined forces to test new products using ethnographic methods. They provided a group of Swedish consumers with 'screen fridges' which download recipes from the Internet, store shopping lists and have a built-in video camera to record messages. By putting the fridges in people's homes Electrolux could see how the technology was actually used and find out whether participants would be prepared to pay for it. This type of research is relatively expensive, but it gives in-depth information that could not be generated from a focus group or one-to-one interview.

Before developing an understanding of the ethnography in marketing research, it is worth summarising the aims of ethnographic research:

- *Seeing through the eyes of others.* Viewing events, actions, norms and values from the perspective of the people being studied.
- *Description.* Attending to mundane detail to help understand what is going on in a particular context and to provide clues and pointers to other layers of reality.
- *Contextualism.* The basic message that ethnographers convey is that whatever the sphere in which the data are being collected, we can understand events only when they are situated in the wider social and historical context.
- *Process.* Viewing social life as involving an interlocking series of events.
- *Avoiding early use of theories and concepts.* Rejecting premature attempts to impose theories and concepts which may exhibit a poor fit with participants' perspectives.[32] This will be developed further in this chapter when we examine grounded theory.
- *Flexible research designs.* Ethnographers' adherence to viewing social phenom-

Source: © Alamy

ena through the eyes of their subjects has led to a wariness regarding the imposition of prior and possibly inappropriate frames of reference on the people they study. This leads to a preference for an open and unstructured research design which increases the possibility of coming across unexpected issues.

This final point is illustrated in the following example. This example can be explored in more depth by actually viewing the reviewed film.

Example   Kitchen Stories[33]

Kitchen Stories was an unlikey contender for one of the best movies of 2004. Kitchen Stories (Salmer Fra Kjokkenet), a Norwegian/Swedish co-production, is about an ethnographic study of the 1950s into the kitchen routines of single Norwegian men. Beneath the light humour, the film seeks to make a more serious point about whether the rules governing research stand in the way of reaching a true understanding of people. The film is based upon the real-life story of a team of Swedish researchers who set out to design the perfect kitchen. The researcher, Folke, finds himself partnered with the participant from hell: the doddering, grumpy recluse, Isak. Assuming his position on a shaky high chair stuck in the corner of the kitchen, it quickly dawns on Folke that Isak is determined to make his stay as difficult as possible. Both men are under strict instructions not to communicate and in these circumstances, much humour is wrought from Isak's petty behaviour such as leaving a tap dripping in an attempt to infuriate the well-mannered researcher. Folke's flouting of the rules marks him out as a less than perfect researcher. The film does not judge Folke but the method he has to work with. The objective nature of the research translates on screen as cold, dispassionate voyeurism. Ethnography in *Kitchen Stories* is not the science of observing but a clumsy foolish exercise that imposes rules on both men. It is only when Folke climbs down from his 'pedestal' that he truly begins to understand Isak. Both the formal impartiality adopted by Folke and Isak's bizarre behaviour cease, and the two are no longer 'researcher' and 'participant' – simply friends.

The use of ethnographic approaches has rapidly developed in marketing research. Decision-makers are finding great support from the process and findings, as the following example illustrates.

Example   Demonstrating the value of air time[34]

Capital Radio has been looking at the way the radio affects people's lives. It wanted to show advertisers how listeners relate to the brand and to demonstrate the value of air time. It teamed up with the Henley Centre for a project called Modal Targeting, which highlighted different modes that listeners go through during the day. The intention was to establish when they were most susceptible to certain advertisements. On six occasions it sent researchers to observe listeners for three days at a time. They do not stay overnight, and they do not tell the people what they are looking for because that might affect the way they behave. The skill is that they blend into the background and almost become part of the fixtures and fittings. The study showed that there can be a greater difference between how one consumer feels at the start of the day and the end of the day than how two consumers feel at the same time of the day. Advertisers will now be able to be more effective as they know what 'mode' listeners are in. They should not be aiming to sell financial products when people are rushing for a train in the morning.

Ethnography cannot reasonably be classified as just another single method or technique.[35] In essence, it is a research discipline based upon culture as an organising concept and a mix of both observational and interviewing tactics to record behavioural dynamics. Above all, ethnography relies upon entering participants' natural life worlds – at home, while shopping, at leisure and in the workplace. The researcher essentially becomes a naive visitor in that world by engaging participants during realistic product usage situations in the course of daily life.

Whether called on-site, observational, naturalistic or contextual research, ethnographic methods allow marketers to delve into actual situations in which products are used, services are received and benefits are conferred. Ethnography takes place not in laboratories but in the real world. Consequently, clients and practitioners benefit from a more holistic and better nuanced view of consumer satisfactions, frustrations and limitations than in any other research method.[36]

A growing trend is for marketers to apply ethnographic methods in natural retail or other commercial environments. There are several objectives that lie behind these studies, one of which is orientated towards a detailed ecological analysis of sales behaviour. In other words, all of the elements that comprise retail store environments – lighting, smells, signage, display of goods, the location, size and orientation of shelving – have an impact upon the consumers' experience and their ultimate buying behaviour. The ethnographer's role is to decode the meaning and impact of these ecological elements. Often, these studies utilise time-lapse photography as a tool for behavioural observation and data collection over extensive periods of time and avoid actual interaction with consumers, as illustrated in the following example.[37]

Example | **Top of the Pops**[38]

The point of purchase (POP) is a manufacturer's last opportunity to have an effect on the customers' decisions. Awareness of the crucial role of in-store influences is growing, and several POP companies have started offering detailed research on how customers react at the point of sale. To achieve this awareness, Electronic Surveillance of Behaviour (ESOB) gives a detailed understanding of how consumers behave in a shop. Kevin Price, Managing Director of Coutts Design, has formed a partnership with The In-Store Audit to utilise ESOB.

Says Kevin:

with ESOB, shoppers are tracked remotely on video around the store and their movements and actions are followed. Because this technique is fairly unobtrusive, we are able to capture natural shopper behaviour as people are not being followed around by a researcher.

He goes on to explain the complexity of the computer software:

The cameras are specially modified and they record a large sample size. They can measure consumer behaviour from entry to exit, following customers around the store and noting the items they touch and the visual cues that they give and get. The cameras may operate for between 10 and 14 days. The information is then analysed and the key clips from the video are used to reinforce the key points that have emerged from the analysis.

One of the key elements of the above example is the context in which the consumer is behaving. The researcher observes shoppers, taking in and reacting to their retail experience, behaving naturally in the set context. The context of shoppers does not just mean the retail outlet they visit. The processes of choosing and buying products, of using products or giving them as gifts, of reflecting upon and planning subsequent purchases, are all affected by contextual factors. Context operates on several levels, including the immediate physical and situational surroundings of consumers, as well as language, character, culture and history. Each of these levels can provide a basis for the meaning and significance attached to the roles and behaviour of consumption.

'Can we divorce the ways we buy, use and talk about products from the cultural and linguistic context within which economic transitions occur? The answer is an emphatic *no*.'[39]

The ethnographer may observe the consumer acting and reacting in the context of consumption. The ethnographer may see a shopper spending time reading the labels on cat food, showing different brands to his or her partner, engaged in deep conversation, pondering, getting frustrated and putting tins back on the shelf. The ethonographer may see the same shopper more purposefully putting an expensive bottle of cognac into a shopping trolley without any discussion and seemingly with no emotional attachment to the product. The ethnographer may want to know what is going on. How may the consumer explain his or her attitudes and motivations behind this behaviour? This is where the interplay of observation and interviewing helps to build such a rich picture of consumers. In questioning the shopper in the above example, responses of 'we think that Rémy Martin is the best' or 'we always argue about which are the prettiest cat food labels' would not be enough. The stories and contexts of how these assertions came to be would be explored. The ethnographer does not tend to take simple explanations for activities that in many circumstances may be habitual to consumers. Ethnographic practice takes a highly critical attitude towards expressed language. It challenges our accepted words and utterances at face value, searching instead for the meanings and values that lie beneath the surface. In interviewing situations, typically this involves looking for gaps between expressed and non-verbal communication elements. For example, if actual practices and facial and physical gestures are inconsistent with a subject's expressed attitudes towards the expensive cognac, we are challenged to discover both the reality behind the given answer and the reasons for the 'deception'.

Ethnographic research is also effective as a tool for learning situationally and culturally grounded language, the appropriate words for everyday things as spoken by various age or ethnic groups. Copywriters and strategic thinkers are always pressed to talk about products and brands in evocative and original ways. Ethnography helps act as both a discovery and an evaluation tool.[40] To summarise, ethnographic approaches are useful when the marketing research objectives call for:[41]

1 *High-intensity situations.* To study high-intensity situations, such as a sales encounter, meal preparation and service, or communication between persons holding different levels of authority.
2 *Behavioural processes.* To conduct precise analyses of behavioural processes, e.g. radio listening behaviour, home computer purchasing decisions or home cleaning behaviour.
3 *Memory inadequate.* To address situations where the participant's memory or reflection would not be adequate. Observational methods can stand alone or can complement interviewing as a memory jog.
4 *Shame or reluctance.* To work with participants who are likely to be ashamed or reluctant to reveal actual practices to a group of peers. If they were diabetic, for example, participants may be reluctant to reveal that they have a refrigerator full of sweet snacks, something that an ethnographic observer would be able to see without confronting the subject.

In these applications, the ethnographer is expected to analyse critically the situations observed. The critique or analysis can be guided by theory but in essence the researcher develops a curiosity, thinks in an abstract manner and at times steps back to reflect and see how emerging ideas connect. By reacting to the events and participants as they face them, to draw out what they see as important, ethnographers have the ability to create new explanations and understandings of consumers. This ability to develop a new vision, to a large extent unrestricted by existing theory, is the essence of a grounded theory approach, which is explained and illustrated in the next section.

Grounded theory

Grounded theory
Theory derived from data, systematically gathered and analysed.

The tradition of **grounded theory** was developed by Glaser and Strauss in the late 1950s and published in their seminal work in 1967.[42] At that time, qualitative research was viewed more as impressionistic or anecdotal, little more than 'soft science' or journalism.[43] It was generally believed that the objective of sociology should be to produce scientific theory, and to test this meant using quantitative methods.[44] Qualitative research was seen to have a place, but only to the extent to which it developed questions which could then be verified using quantitative techniques. Glaser and Strauss accepted that the study of people should be scientific, in the way understood by quantitative researchers. This meant that it should seek to produce theoretical propositions that were testable and verifiable, produced by a clear set of replicable procedures. Glaser and Strauss defined theory as follows:

theory in sociology is a strategy for handling data in research, providing modes of conceptualization for describing and explaining. The theory should provide clear enough categories and hypotheses so that crucial ones can be verified in present and future research; they must be clear enough to be readily operationalized in quantitative studies when these are appropriate.[45]

The focus upon developing theory was made explicit in response to criticisms of ethnographic studies that present lengthy extracts from interviews or field observations. Strauss sought to reinforce his view of the importance of theory, illustrated by the following quote:

much that passes for analysis is relatively low level description. Many quite esteemed and excellent monographs use a great deal of data, quotes or field note selections. The procedure is very useful when the behavior being studied is relatively foreign to the experiences of most readers or when the factual assertions being made would be under considerable contest by skeptical and otherwise relatively well-informed readers. Most of these monographs are descriptively dense, but alas theoretically thin. If you look at their indexes, there are almost no new concepts listed, ones that have emerged in the course of research.[46]

In contrast to the perhaps casual manner in which some ethnographers may be criticised for attempts at developing theory, the grounded theorist follows a set of systematic procedures for collecting and analysing data. This systematic procedure is used to encourage researchers to use their intellectual imagination and creativity to develop new theories, to suggest methods for doing so, to offer criteria to evaluate the worth of discovered theory, and to propose an alternative rhetoric of justification.[47] The most distinctive feature of grounded theory is its commitment to 'discovery' through direct contact with the social phenomena under study, coupled with a rejection of a priori theorising. This feature does not mean that researchers should embark on their studies without any general guidance provided by some sort of theoretical understanding. It would be nigh on impossible for a researcher to shut out the ideas in the literature surrounding a particular subject. However, Glaser and Strauss argued that preconceived theories should be rejected as they obstruct the development of new theories by coming between researchers and the subjects of their study. In other words, the strict adherence to developing new theory built upon an analytical framework of existing theory can result in 'narrow-minded' researchers who do not explore a much wider range of explanations and possibilities. With the rejection of *a priori* theorising and a commitment to imaginative and creative discovery comes a conception of knowledge as emergent. This knowledge is created by researchers in the context of investigative practices that afford them intimate contact with the subjects and phenomena under study.[48]

The following example illustrates the use of grounded theory in the development of theory related to the marketing of health visitors. The example is then followed by a description of the process involved in developing theory through a grounded theory process.[49]

Example | **Grounded theory and the marketing of health visitors[50]**

Grounded theory was used to conduct a study into the effectiveness of marketing related to health visiting. The collection and analysis of data were conducted simultaneously as the study worked through interviews and observations, all guided through theoretical sampling. There was a line-by-line analysis of interview transcripts with concepts drawn from these to describe events. Categories based on attitudes, behaviour and the characteristics of informants were built through constantly comparing the data in the transcripts and the emerging concepts. The theory that emerged from this process was further guided by a contextual knowledge of the *conditions* under which any interactions took place, the nature of the interactions between the informants and health visitors, and the *consequences* of the actions and *interactions* undertaken by the informants. In addition, memos gathered throughout the process played a crucial part in developing the theory.

The findings and emergent theory centred around the attitudes of the health visitors' clients. The theory identified tactics which could enhance 'selling' in health visiting, strategies for gaining new clientele and methods for influencing behaviour in order to encourage the prevention of illness. The study addressed the nature of the 'process' of health visiting, and the need to promote the service through personal presentations and advertising. Further practical implications emerged from the study by identifying tactics for raising awareness by getting clients to recognise problems early.[51]

Attempting to gain an objective viewpoint

For the grounded theorist, data collection and analysis occur in alternating sequences. Analysis begins with the first interview and observation, which leads to the next interview or observation, followed by more analysis, more interviews or fieldwork, and so on. It is the analysis that drives the data collection. Therefore there is a constant interplay between the researcher and the research act. Because this interplay requires immersion in the data, by the end of the enquiry the researcher is shaped by the data, just as the data are shaped by the researcher. The problem that arises during this mutual shaping process is how one can become immersed in the data and still maintain a balance between objectivity and sensitivity. Objectivity is necessary to arrive at an impartial and accurate interpretation of events. Sensitivity is required to perceive the subtle nuances and meanings of data and to recognise the connections between concepts. Both objectivity and sensitivity are necessary for making discoveries. Objectivity enables the researcher to have confidence that the findings are a reasonable, impartial representation of a problem under investigation, whereas sensitivity enables creativity and the discovery of new theory from data.[52]

During the analytic process, grounded researchers attempt to set aside their knowledge and experience to form new interpretations about phenomena. Yet, in their everyday lives, they rely on knowledge and experience to provide the means for helping them to understand the world in which they live and to find solutions to problems encountered. Most researchers have learned that a state of complete objectivity is impossible and that in every piece of research, quantitative or qualitative, there is an element of subjectivity. What is important is to recognise that subjectivity is an issue and that researchers should take appropriate measures to minimise its intrusion into their investigations and analyses.

In qualitative research, objectivity does not mean controlling the variables. Rather it means an openness, a willingness to listen and to 'give voice' to participants, be they individuals or organisations. Though this may seem odd, listening is not necessarily a quality that some researchers possess. The following example illustrates the challenges of 'listening'.

> **Example** Listening is not the same as researching[53]
>
> According to the Coca-Cola Retail Research Group study, the German discount supermarket Aldi is now the strongest retail brand in Europe. Dieter Brandes was an architect of Aldi's success, and contends that in reaching this position, Aldi never had a 'grand' strategy. 'We just groped our way forward. It was a dynamic process driven by intuition, incremental adjustments and decisions, whose consequences were not always foreseeable.' This approach is one of being endlessly curious and being confident to take an experimental approach with much thinking and reflection. The essence of this curiosity is listening. Listening is not the same as researching. Research pursues a pre-identified agenda, that of the researcher. Listening gives other people's agendas top priority. Because it can pick up looming dangers and new opportunities, listening lies at the heart of effective innovation. But it is very hard to do.

Thus, good qualitative research means hearing what others have to say, seeing what others do and representing these as accurately as possible. It means developing an understanding of those they are researching, whilst recognising that researchers' understandings are often based on the values, culture, training and experiences that they bring from all aspects of their lives; these can be quite different from those of their participants.[54] As well as being open to participants, qualitative researchers reflect upon what makes them, as observers, 'see' and 'listen' in particular ways. This usually means that, while working on a particular project, the researcher keeps a diary or journal. This diary is used to make notes about the conditions of interviews and observations, of what worked well and what did not, of what questions the researcher would have liked to ask but did not think of at the time. As the researcher reads through the diary in the analysis process, the entries become part of the narrative explored, and reveal to the researcher and to others the way the researcher has developed their 'seeing' and 'listening'. Research diaries will be covered in more detail in examining qualitative data analysis in Chapter 9.

Developing a sensitivity to the meanings in data

Having sensitivity means having insight into, and being able to give meaning to, the events and happenings in data. It means being able to see beneath the obvious to discover the new. This quality of the researcher occurs as they work with data, making comparisons, asking questions, and going out and collecting more data. Through these alternating processes of data collection and analysis, meanings that are often elusive at first later become clearer. Immersion in the data leads to those sudden insights.[55] Insights do not just occur haphazardly; rather, they happen to prepared minds during interplay with the data. Whether we want to admit it or not, we cannot completely divorce ourselves from who we are and what we know. The theories that we carry around in our heads inform our research in multiple ways, even if we use them quite unselfconsciously.[56]

Ultimately, a grounded theory approach is expected to generate findings that are meaningful to decision-makers, and appropriate to the tasks they face. As with other interpretivist forms of research, if it is found meaningful by decision-makers and employed successfully by them, there is further evidence of the theory's validity. Another qualitative approach that is absolutely meaningful to decision-makers in that its primary focus is to deliver actionable results is called action research.

Action research

Background

The social psychologist Kurt Lewin had a main interest in social change and specifically in questions of how to conceptualise and promote social change. Lewin is generally thought to be the person who coined the term **action research** and gave it meanings that are applicable today.[57] In action research, Lewin envisaged a process whereby one could construct a social experiment with the aim of achieving a certain goal.[58] For example, in the early days of the Second World War, Lewin conducted a study, commissioned by the US authorities, on the use of tripe as part of the regular daily diet of American families. The research question was: 'To what extent could American housewives be encouraged to use tripe rather than beef for family dinners?' Beef was scarce and was destined primarily for the troops.

Lewin's approach to this research was to conduct a study in which he trained a limited number of housewives in the art of cooking tripe for dinner. He then surveyed how this training had an effect on their daily cooking habits in their own families. In this case, action research was synonymous with a 'natural experiment', meaning that the researchers in a real-life context invited participants into an experimental activity. This research approach was very much within the bounds of conventional applied social science with its patterns of authoritarian control, but it was aimed at producing a specific, desired social outcome.

The above example can be clearly seen from a marketing perspective. It is easy to see a sample survey measuring attitudes to beef, to tripe, to feeding the family and to feelings of patriotism. From a survey, one can imagine advertisements extolling the virtues of tripe, how tasty and versatile it is. But would the campaign work? Lewin's approach was not just to understand the housewives' attitudes but to engage them in the investigation and the solution – to *change* attitudes and behaviour.

Lewin is credited with coining a couple of important slogans within action research that hold resonance with the many action researchers that practise today. The first is 'nothing is as practical as a good theory' and the second is 'the best way to try to understand something is to change it'. In action research it is believed that the way to 'prove' a theory is to show how it provides an in-depth and thorough understanding of social structures, understanding gained through planned attempts to invoke change in particular directions. The appropriate changes are in the proof.

Lewin's work was a fundamental building block to what today is called action research. He set the stage for knowledge production based on solving real-life problems. From the outset, he created a new role for researchers and redefined criteria for judging the quality of the enquiry process. Lewin shifted the researcher's role from being a distant observer to involvement in concrete problem solving. The quality criteria he developed for judging a theory to be good focused on its ability to support practical problem solving in real-life situations.[59]

From Lewin's work has developed a rich and thriving group of researchers who have developed and applied his ideas throughout the world. In management research, the study of organisational change with the understanding and empowerment of different managers and workers has utilised action research to great effect. There has been little application of action research in marketing research, though that is changing. Marketing researchers and marketing decision-makers alike are learning of the nature of action research, the means of implementing it and the benefits it can bestow.

Approach

The term 'action research' includes a whole range of approaches and practices, each grounded in different traditions, in different philosophical and psychological assumptions, sometimes pursuing different political commitments. Sometimes it is used to describe a positivist approach in a 'field' context, or where there is a trade-off between the theoretical interests of researchers and the practical interests of organisation members. Sometimes it is used to describe relatively uncritical consultancy based on information gathering and feedback.[60] It is beyond the scope of this text to develop these different traditions, so the following describes an approach that is grounded in the Lewin foundations of the approach, and, like his work, is applicable to marketing.

Action research is a team research process, facilitated by one or more professional researchers linking with decision-makers and other stakeholders who together wish to change or improve particular situations. Together, the researcher and decision-makers or stakeholders define the problems to be examined, generate relevant knowledge about the problems, learn and execute research techniques, take actions, and interpret the results of actions based on what they have learned.[61] There are many iterations of problem definition, generating knowledge, taking action and learning from those actions. The whole process of iteration evolves in a direction that is agreed by the team.

Action researchers accept no a priori limits on the kinds of research techniques they use. Surveys, statistical analyses, interviews, focus groups, ethnographies and life histories are all acceptable, if the reason for deploying them has been agreed by the action research collaborators and if they are used in a way that does not oppress the participants.

Action research is composed of a balance of three elements. If any one of the three is absent, then the process is not action research.

1 *Research*. Research based on any quantitative or qualitative techniques, or combination of them, generates data and, in the analyses and interpretation of the data there is shared knowledge.

2 *Participation*. Action research involves trained researchers who serve as facilitators and 'teachers' to team members. As these individuals set their action research agenda, they generate the knowledge necessary to transform the situation and put the results to work. Action research is a participatory process in which everyone involved takes some responsibility.

3 *Action*. Action research aims to alter the initial situation of the organisation in the direction of a more self-managed and more rewarding state for all parties.

An example of an action research team in marketing terms could include:

- *Marketing researchers*: trained in a variety of qualitative and quantitative research techniques, and with experience of diagnosing marketing and research problems.
- *Strategic marketing managers*: decision-makers who work at a strategic level in the organisation and have worked with researchers, as well as those who have no experience of negotiating with researchers.
- *Operational marketing managers*: decision-makers who have to implement marketing activities. These may be the individuals who meet customers on a day-to-day basis and who really feel the impact and success of marketing ideas.
- *Advertising agency representatives*: agents who have worked with strategic decision-makers. They may have been involved in the development of communications campaigns to generate responses from target groups of consumers.
- *Customers*: existing customers who may be loyal and have had many years of experience of the company (initiating and funding the action research) its products and perhaps even its personnel.
- *Target customers*: potential customers who may be brand switchers or even loyal customers to competitive companies.

Figure 6.2[62] illustrates how action research may be applied. This model of action research is taken from the subject area of the management of change, which is relevant to many of the problems faced by marketing decision-makers. The process aims to create a learning community in a team such as that above. The team develops an understanding of issues to the extent that it makes sound judgements and takes effective action to implement the changes it wishes to make.

The process in Figure 6.2 can be described as follows.

- *Diagnosis.* The present state of affairs would be set out, including the perceived barriers to change and an initial broad statement of desired direction for the organisation. Diagnosis would include documenting the change process and all data gathering activities such as secondary data gathering, surveys, interviews or observations.
- *Analysis.* An initial interpretation of data gathered would be made. From this the issues to be tackled would be identified. Summary findings and the development of a framework, with set tasks for team members in subsequent data gathering, would be drawn up.
- *Feedback.* Data analyses would be fed back for examination and discussion in the team. 'Ownership' of the diagnosis would be developed to formulate a commitment to action.
- *Action.* Individual courses of action and the development of broader strategies would be formulated.
- *Evaluation.* There would be an ongoing review of methods and outcomes. The effectiveness of any action would be evaluated against agreed criteria and critical success factors.

All of these stages are interrelated, so there is no definitive path that the team would take. In subsequent iterations of activities, the team could move around the stages in any order that suits its needs.

The process is illustrated in the following example where action research was used to evaluate a youth Drop-In Centre. The detail of the case is limited, but there is sufficient to see action research being successfully practised in an area that could be considered as a marketing research challenge. It also presents the challenge of what other research designs could have worked in these circumstances?

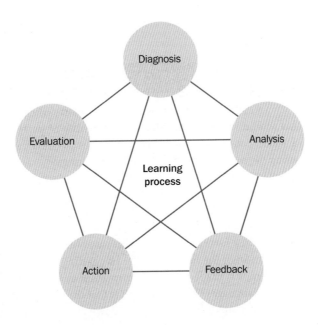

Figure 6.2
The action research approach

Example   Creating 'The Kit'[63]

A Drop-In Centre for street-involved youth, in a Canadian city, had been running for four years and it was time to evaluate its services. The Centre's mission and clientele were controversial. Some people felt that a safe place to 'hang out' met the initial needs of street-involved youth and allowed staff to reach out informally, build trust, and intervene effectively in crises. Others wanted more structured activities and stricter rules, whilst others thought the Centre attracted 'high-risk' youth to the area and wanted it shut down completely. The evaluation, identified four objectives:

1 To involve youth in designing and implementing an evaluation to measure the impact of Drop-In services.
2 To improve service delivery to youth.
3 To collaborate with community members on long-term solutions to help integrate street youth into the community.
4 To make the evaluation instrument available to other youth centres.

A team was built of six youth, two staff members and one outside professional researcher. The group met two afternoons per week at the Drop-In. The evaluation began with the team considering three questions: 'What do we want to know?', 'How will we find out?' and 'Who do we need to talk to?' The team worked together and in small groups to develop the initial questionnaire. Framing questions that would get the information it wanted was a lengthy process, with many drafts and redrafts. The team moved on to try alternative methods with the youth working together to develop tools that would fit the Centre milieu and engage other street-involved youth. When the tools were ready, each session was advertised in the Drop-In, with pizza as an incentive for participation. An iterative process was established for data analysis, 'walking through' responses to open-ended questions to learn the principles and techniques of analysis. The youth worked in pairs to describe and summarise the data. The team produced a formal report, a 'Kit' and participated in community and academic presentations about its work. The formal written report was produced by everyone brainstorming the contents, the professional researcher drafting each section, submitting it for feedback to the team and redrafting. The result was a thorough, well-crafted document. The youth took the main role in community and academic presentations. Sharing their expertise publicly helped them gain confidence and pride in their hard work and impressive results. Perhaps the most interesting reporting mechanism was 'The Kit', a colourful guide for other youth evaluators. 'The Kit' was designed and produced entirely by the youth team members.

Ethics in marketing research

The researcher and the client must respect participants when conducting qualitative research. This should include protecting the anonymity of participants, not misleading or deceiving them, conducting research in a way not to embarrass or harm the participants, and using the research results in an ethical manner.[64]

The above advice from the Market Research Society contrasts sharply with a controversial approach to retail research that sometimes goes by the name of 'guerrilla ethnography' or 'street research'. This involves observing and talking with consumers in their natural habitats. Researchers in this case commonly do not identify their role as a researcher, nor do they formally state the objectives behind their interaction with consumers. Instead, through the normal course of chatting with fellow customers or sales personnel, an attempt is made to glean information about customer preferences, sales cues and customer language. The benefit here is that the social distance and formal barriers between researcher and subject are broken down and interaction is more 'natural' and less subject to contrivance. The main objection expressed by critics is the potential invasion of privacy and somewhat manipulative structure of interaction, and the confusion that may be caused by not being absolutely open to those being observed or questioned.[65]

In 1994, addressing the ESOMAE Annual Conference, Karl Vorsteen, chairman of Heineken exhorted the virtues of observing consumers. He positively encouraged his managers to visit bars to see consumers enjoying their products in their natural context. This he saw as part of a natural curiosity that decision-makers should have of their customers. Decision-makers naturally meet many of their customers on a day-to-day basis, especially sales personnel, and much is to be learned from these encounters. As long as these encounters respect the anonymity of participants, do not mislead or deceive them, and in no way embarrass or harm them, these encounters are a healthy part of conducting business.

It is up to the researcher to be aware of the harm that participants may suffer and the damage such harm will inflict on all parties involved in an investigation. A reminder of why researchers must be aware of the potential for harm is presented in the following example.

Example **The need to pay greater attention to issues of the balance of power, to ensure public cooperation[66]**

There are two primary reasons why researchers must be aware of the potential harm to participants and the need to foster a continual willingness to cooperate in research:

1 Qualitative research is doubly dependent on public cooperation. Not only do we rely on participants' cooperation in taking part, but the non-directive and open-ended nature of qualitative questioning techniques means that we also rely on their being positively engaged by the process, willing and eager to apply their minds, and happy to reveal their thoughts.
2 The nature of qualitative interviews and groups means that moderators will always try to encourage participants to reveal more. This brings with it a responsibility to ensure that safeguards are in place, to deter coercion and avoid the potential danger of abuse of power and control over participants in qualitative research.

Internet and computer applications

The Internet presents huge opportunities for the qualitative researcher. Computer-mediated communication (CMC) can be used to run online versions of semi-structured or in-depth interviews, 'observation' of virtual communities, the collection of personal documents, and focus groups. Applying these techniques using the Internet rather than face to face presents a whole array of advantages and challenges.[67] These may be summarised as follows.

Advantages

- *Extending access to participants.* Provided that potential participants have access to the technology, researchers can cross time and space barriers. They can reach a much wider geographical span of participants, and also populations that are normally hard to reach, such as people with disabilities.

- *Sensitive subjects.* For some participants the sensitivity of the subject being studied may mean that they would not discuss it in a face-to-face manner. The anonymity and distance can help to draw out views from such participants.
- *Interest groups.* A variety of online formats, such as chat rooms, mailing lists and conferences, focus on specific topics, drawing together geographically dispersed participants who may share interests, experiences or expertise.
- *Cost and time savings.* Issues such as the time and travelling expenses of researchers, the hire of venues and the costs of producing transcripts can make face-to-face interviewing an expensive option for many researchers, especially if they are using qualitative approaches for the first time. The Internet dramatically reduces or eliminates many of these costs and thus makes qualitative approaches more accessible to a wider array of companies and decision-makers.
- *Handling transcripts.* As interviews or observations are built up through dialogue on the Internet, many of the potential biases or mistakes that occur through audio recordings can be eliminated.

Challenges

- *Computer literacy for the researcher.* Applying qualitative research on the Internet means that some degree of technical expertise is required of the researcher. The extent of expertise depends upon which techniques are being used. For example, moderators of focus groups online will have to learn about the capabilities of the chosen software for running a focus group. They will also have to learn about the specific skills in making the group experience work well online, perhaps by participating in online research conferences or gaining exposure to alternative discussion practices online.
- *Making contact and recruitment.* Establishing contact online requires a mutual exchange of email addresses. There is an array of techniques that can encourage potential participants to reveal their address (which will be developed in Chapters 7 and 8) but in essence the researcher has to develop rapport and trust to draw the most out of participants.
- *Interactive skills online.* Even if the researcher develops his or her skills online, it must be remembered that participants use their computing equipment with varying degrees of expertise.
- *Losing access.* A key challenge for online studies is to sustain electronic connection with participants for the whole period of the qualitative research process. This is a reminder that, unlike a survey which may be a short, one-off contact with a participant, qualitative techniques may unfold and evolve over time and involve returning to participants as issues develop and theory emerges.

The issues above lay out the broad advantages and challenges of the Internet for the qualitative researcher. As we develop more detailed descriptions and evaluations of qualitative techniques in Chapters 7 to 9, we will examine these points in more detail as there are many rapid innovations occurring to support qualitative researchers.

The impact of the Internet has had a profound effect upon how qualitative research is conducted, especially the geographic extent, the nature of data that can be gathered and the sharing and communicating of its analysis. The following example is an illustration of this impact. It is just one of the means that the Internet and mobile phone technology can significantly improve qualitative data gathering and analysis.

Example   **Red Bull re-energising its customer feedback teams**[68]

Red Bull was facing an 'administrative nightmare'. Its energy teams – roving groups of employees who meet directly with consumers to discuss the product and collect customer feedback – were having to fax details of their meetings with consumers through to head office. They were getting stacks of paper through that took a lot of time to compile into anything worthwhile. What they wanted was a system that gave them 'real-time' results. Blue Trail (**www.bluetrail.co.uk**), a mobile technology specialist, was chosen to implement a new system. Each of Red Bull's 30 energy teams (consisting of 4 people each) was given an IPAQ pocket PC which was used to store customer responses. Information was then uploaded via Orange mobile phones to a Red Bull web page, hosted by Blue Trail. The programme drives a workforce that can be used for multiple tasks, including trade audits and customer research. Most recently, the IPAQs were equipped with Nexicam digital camera attachments. The energy teams have always been asked to produce photographic diaries, but the use of the Nexicam enables the images to be used for a fraction of the cost of conventional photography.

Summary

Qualitative and quantitative research should be viewed as complementary. Unfortunately, many researchers and decision-makers do not see this, taking dogmatic positions in favour of either qualitative or quantitative research. The defence of qualitative approaches for a particular marketing research problem, through the positive benefits it bestows and through explaining the negative alternatives of a quantitative approach, should be seen as healthy, as should the defence of quantitative approaches. Business and marketing decision-makers use both approaches and will continue to need both.

Qualitative and quantitative approaches to marketing research are underpinned by two broad philosophical schools, namely positivism and interpretivism. The central belief of a positivist position is a view that the study of consumers and marketing phenomena should be 'scientific' in the manner of the natural sciences. Marketing researchers of this persuasion adopt a framework for investigation akin to that of the natural scientist. The interpretivist researcher does not set out to test hypotheses but to explore the nature and interrelationships of marketing phenomena. The focus of investigation is a detailed examination of a small number of cases rather than a large sample. The data collected are analysed through an explicit interpretation of the meanings and functions of consumer actions. The product of these analyses takes the form of verbal descriptions and explanations, with quantification and statistical analysis playing a subordinate role.

In examining qualitative approaches, ethnography as a general term includes observation and interviewing and is sometimes referred to as participant observation. It is, however, used in the more specific case of a method which requires a researcher to spend a large amount of time observing a particular group of people, by sharing their way of life. The ethnographer is expected to analyse critically the situations observed. The critique and the analysis can be guided by theory but in essence the researcher develops a curiosity, thinks in an abstract manner and at times steps back to reflect and see how emerging ideas connect. By reacting to the events and participants as they face them, to draw out what they see as important, ethnographers have the ability to create new explanations and understandings of consumers.

$\rightarrow$

Some ethnographers may be criticised in their attempts at developing theory. In response, the grounded theorist follows a set of systematic procedures for collecting and analysing data. A distinctive feature of a grounded theory approach is that the collection of data and its analysis take place simultaneously, with the aim of developing general concepts, to organise data and integrate these into a more general, formal set of categories.

Ethnographic techniques and a grounded theory approach can be applied in an action research framework. Action research is a team research process, facilitated by one or more professional researchers, linking with decision-makers and other stakeholders who together wish to improve particular situations. Together, the researcher and decision-makers or stakeholders define the problems to be examined, generate relevant knowledge about the problems, learn and execute research techniques, take actions, and interpret the results of actions based on what they have learned. There are many iterations of problem definition, generating knowledge, taking action and learning from those actions. The whole process of iteration evolves in a direction that is agreed by the team.

The Internet presents huge opportunities for the qualitative researcher. Computer-mediated communication (CMC) can be used to run online versions of semi-structured or in-depth interviews, 'observation' of virtual communities, the collection of personal documents, and focus groups. Being able to conduct such techniques online offers great opportunities to the qualitative marketing researcher and also many challenges.

When conducting qualitative research, the researcher and the client must respect participants. This should include protecting the anonymity of participants, honouring all statements and promises used to ensure participation, and conducting research in a way not to embarrass or harm the participants.

Questions

1 What criticisms do qualitative marketing researchers make of the approaches adopted by quantitative marketing researchers, and vice versa?

2 Why is it not always possible or desirable to use quantitative marketing research techniques?

3 Evaluate the differences between a European and an American approach to qualitative research.

4 Describe the characteristics of positivist and interpretivist marketing researchers.

5 In what ways may the positivist and the interpretivist view potential research participants?

6 What role does theory play in the approaches adopted by positivist and interpretivist marketing researchers?

7 What does ethnographic research aim to achieve in the study of consumers?

8 Why may marketing decision-makers wish to understand the context of consumption?

9 Describe and illustrate two research techniques that may be utilised in ethnographic research.

10 What stages are involved in the application of a grounded theory approach?

11 Is it possible for marketing researchers to be objective?

12 Why may the Kurt Lewin case of action research be deemed an application of marketing research?

13 Describe the key elements to be balanced in the application of action research.

14 Describe the five interrelated phases of an action research approach.

15 What do you see as the key advantages and challenges of conducting qualitative research using the Internet?

Exercises

1 An advertising agency has selected three pieces of music that it could use in a new advertising campaign. It has come to you as a marketing researcher to help in making the case for selecting the right piece of music for the campaign. What would be the case for using qualitative techniques for this task?

2 Would a 12-year-old schoolchild who has not been exposed to any academic theories about 'service delivery quality' be more creative and open-minded, and thus better suited to conduct a grounded theory approach, compared with a 22-year-old business studies graduate? Would your view change in any way if the study were about a game or toy that was specifically targeted at 12 year olds?

3 You are a brand manager for Lynx deodorant. You wish to invest in an ethnographic study of young men. Ask another student to play the role of marketing director. What case would you make to the marketing director about the value of investing in an ethnographic study?

4 In the above case of an ethnographic study of young men for Lynx deodorant, what would you feel to be appropriate contexts or circumstances to conduct this work?

5 In a small group discuss the following issues: 'Quantitative research is more important than qualitative research because it generates conclusive findings' and 'Qualitative research should always be followed by quantitative research to confirm the qualitative findings'.

Video Case Exercise: Wild Planet

What does ethnographic research mean for Wild Planet? How do they conduct ethnographic techniques? What challenges do they face in conducting these techniques?

video case

download from www.pearsoned.co.uk/ malhotra_euro

Notes

1 Havermans, J., 'Research is war', *Research World* (June 2005), 20–21.
2 McElhatton, N., 'A research commitment more than skin deep', *Research* (May 1994), 10.
3 Havermans, J. 'Trend forecasting applied to fashion and consumption', *Research World* (February 2005), 22–24.
4 Clarke, A., 'Research takes an inventive approach', *Marketing* (13 September 2001), 25.
5 Strauss, A. and Corbin, J.M., *Basics of Qualitative Research: Techniques and Procedures for Developing Grounded Theory*, 2nd edn (Thousand Oaks, CA: Sage, 1998), 27–34.
6 Cooper, P., 'Consumer understanding, change and qualitative research', *Journal of the Market Research Society* 41 (1) (January 1999), 3.
7 Kenway, J., 'Keep on moving', Research, (November 2005), 36.
8 Sykes, W., 'Validity and reliability in qualitative market research: a review of the literature', *Journal of the Market Research Society* 32 (3) (1990), 289.
9 De Groot, G., 'Qualitative research: deeply dangerous or just plain dotty?', *European Research* 14 (3) (1986), 136–141.
10 ESOMAR, 'Industry study on 2004', Esomar World Research Report (2005), 21.
11 Flaster, C., 'First get the language right, then tell them a story', *ResearchPlus* (November 1997), 11.
12 Gilmore, A. and Carson, D., '"Integrative" qualitative methods in a service context', *Marketing Intelligence and Planning* 14 (6) (June 1996), 21.
13 Mariampolski, H., *Qualitative marketing Research: A comprehensive guide*, (Thousand Oaks, CA: Sage, 2001), 24.
14 It is recognised that this topic is treated in a superficial manner and is really a basic introduction to the key ideas. Students who are interested in developing these ideas further should see Hunt, S.D., *Modern Marketing Theory* (Cincinnati, OH: South Western Publishing, 1991); Potter, G., *The Philosophy of Social Science: New Perspectives* (Harlow: Prentice Hall, 2000); Silverman, D., *Interpreting Qualitative Data: Methods for Analysing Talk, Text and Interaction* (London: Sage, 2001).
15 Hunt, S., *Marketing Theory: The Philosophy of Marketing Science* (Homewood, IL: Irwin, 1983), 2.
16 Hughes, J.A., *Sociological Analysis: Methods of Discovery* (London: Nelson, 1976), 19.
17 Broadbent, K., 'When East meets West, quite what does "qualitative" mean?', *ResearchPlus* (March 1997), 14.
18 Goodyear, M., 'Divided by a common language: diversity and deception in the world of global marketing', *Journal of the Market Research Society* 38 (2) (April 1996), 105.
19 Cooper, P., 'Consumer understanding, change and qualitative research', *Journal of the Market Research Society* 41 (1) (January 1999), 3.
20 Hussey, J. and Hussey, R., *Business Research* (Basingstoke: Macmillan Business, 1997).
21 See Healy, M. and Perry, C., 'Comprehensive criteria to judge validity and reliability of qualitative research within the realism paradigm', *Qualitative Market Research: An International Journal* 3 (3) (2000), 118–126.
22 Hussey, J. and Hussey, R., *Business Research* (Basingstoke: Macmillan Business, 1997).

23 Channon C., 'What do we know about how research works?', *Journal of the Market Research Society* 24 (4) (1982), 305–315.

24 Creswell, J.W., *Research Design: Qualitative and Quantitative Approaches* (Thousand Oaks, CA: Sage, 1994).

25 Ali, H. and Birley, S., 'Integrating deductive and inductive approaches in a study of new ventures and customer perceived risk', *Qualitatitive Market Research: An International Journal* 2 (2) (1999), 103–110.

26 Bryman, A., *Quantity and Quality in Social Research* (London: Unwin Hyman, 1988).

27 St Aubyn, G., *The Art of Argument* (London: Christophers, 1956), 61–75.

28 Travers, M., *Qualitative Research through Case Studies* (London: Sage, 2001), 4.

29 Fetterman, D.M., *Ethnography: Step by step* (Thousand Oaks, CA: Sage, 1998), 1.

30 Metcalf, P., *A Borneo Journey into Death: Berawan Eschatology from its Rituals* (Kuala Lumpur: Abdul Majeed, 1991).

31 Silverman, D., *Interpreting Qualitative Data: Methods for Analysing Talk, Text and Interaction*, 2nd edn (London: Sage, 2001), 45.

32 Ibid., p. 46.

33 Tarran, B., 'Northern exposure', *Research* (February 2004), 7.

34 Steiner, R., 'Homing in on consumers', *The Sunday Times* (25 August 2002), 3.8.

35 Stewart, A., *The Ethnographer's Method* (Thousand Oaks, CA: Sage, 1998), 5.

36 Mariampolski, H., 'The power of ethnography', *Journal of the Market Research Society* 41 (1) (January 1999), 79.

37 Ibid., p. 84.

38 Witthaus, M., 'Top of the Pops', *Marketing Week* (21 September 2001), 75–78.

39 Mariampolski, H., 'The power of ethnography', *Journal of the Market Research Society* 41 (1) (January 1999), 82.

40 Ibid., p. 81.

41 Mariampolski, H., *Qualitative Marketing Research: A comprehensive guide* (Thousand Oaks, CA: Sage, 2001), 52.

42 Glaser, B. and Strauss, A., *The Discovery of Grounded Theory* (Chicago: Aldine, 1967).

43 Blumer, H., 'Sociological analysis and the variable', in Blumer, H., *Symbolic Interactionism: Perspective and Method* (Berkeley, CA: University of California Press, 1969), 127–139.

44 Travers, M., *Qualitative Research through Case Studies* (London: Sage, 2001).

45 Glaser, B. and Strauss, A., *The Discovery of Grounded Theory* (Chicago: Aldine, 1967), 3.

46 Strauss, A., Fagerhaugh, S., Suczek, B. and Wiener, C., *The Social Organisation of Medical Work* (Chicago: University of Chicago Press, 1985).

47 Locke, K., *Grounded theory in management research* (London: Sage, 2001), 33.

48 Ibid., p. 34.

49 This outline summarises a quite detailed procedure. For a definitive practical guideline to performing grounded theory see Goulding, C., *Grounded Theory: A practical guide for management, business and market researchers* (London: Sage, 2002); Strauss, A. and Corbin, J.M., *Basics of Qualitative Research: Techniques and Procedures for Developing Grounded Theory*, 2nd edn (London: Sage, 1998).

50 De La Cuesta, C., 'Marketing: a process in health visiting', *Journal of Advanced Nursing* 19 (2) (2001), 347–353.

51 Goulding, C., *Grounded Theory: A practical guide for management, business and market researchers* (London: Sage, 2002), 86–87.

52 Strauss, A. and Corbin, J.M., *Basics of Qualitative Research: Techniques and Procedures for Developing Grounded Theory*, 2nd edn (London: Sage, 1998), 53.

53 Mitchell, A., 'The path to success is simple – why do so few stay the course', *Marketing Week* (19 May 2005), 20–21.

54 Bresler, L., 'Ethical issues in qualitative research methodology', *Bulletin of the Council for Research in Music Education* 126 (1995), 29–41; Cheek, J., 'Taking a view: qualitative research as representation', *Qualitative Health Research* 6 (1996), 492–505.

55 Strauss, A. and Corbin, J.M., *Basics of Qualitative Research: Techniques and Procedures for Developing Grounded Theory*, 2nd edn (London: Sage, 1998), 46–47.

56 Sandelowski, M., 'Theory unmasked: the uses and guises of theory in qualitative research', *Research in Nursing and Health* 16 (1993), 213–218.

57 Greenwood, D.J. and Levin, M., *Introduction to Action Research: Social Research for Social Change* (Thousand Oaks, CA: Sage, 1998), 17.

58 Lewin, K., 'Forces behind food habits and methods of change', *Bulletin of the National Research Council* 108 (1943), 35–65.

59 Greenwood, D.J. and Levin, M., *Introduction to Action Research: Social Research for Social Change* (Thousand Oaks, CA: Sage, 1998), 19.

60 Reason, P. and Bradbury, H., *Handbook of Action Research* (London: Sage, 2002), xxiv.

61 Greenwood, D.J. and Levin, M., *Introduction to Action Research: Social Research for Social Change* (Thousand Oaks, CA: Sage, 1998), 4.

62 Bate, S.P., 'Changing the culture of a hospital: from hierarchy to network', *Public Administration* 78 (3) (2000), 487.

63 Witmore, E. and McKee, C., 'Six street youths who could…', in Reason, P. and Bradbury, H. (eds), *Handbook of Action Research*, (London: Sage, 2002), 396–402.

64 *MRS Code of Conduct* (The Market Research Society, London).

65 Mariampolski, H., 'The power of ethnography', *Journal of the Market Research Society* 41 (1) (January 1999), 84.

66 Murphy, D., 'Fishing by the Net', *Marketing* (22 August 1996), 25.

67 Mann, C. and Stewart, F., *Internet Communication and Qualitative Research: A Handbook for Researching Online* (London: Sage, 2000), 17–38.

68 Case studies, *Research in Business* (March 2004), 14.

Source: © Getty Images

7

Qualitative research: focus group discussions

The best moderators of focus groups are those that create a spirit of spontaneity and a passion for the issues under discussion.

Objectives

After reading this chapter, you should be able to:

1 understand why the focus group is defined as a direct qualitative research technique;

2 describe focus groups in detail, with an emphasis on planning and conducting focus groups;

3 evaluate the advantages, disadvantages and applications of focus groups;

4 describe alternative ways of conducting qualitative research in groups;

5 discuss the considerations involved in conducting qualitative research in an international setting, extending the contrast between European and American traditions of running focus groups;

6 understand the ethical issues involved in conducting focus groups;

7 describe the difference between real-time and non-real-time online focus groups.

STAGE 1
Problem definition

STAGE 2
Research approach developed

STAGE 3
Research design developed

STAGE 4
Fieldwork or data collection

STAGE 5
Data preparation and analysis

STAGE 6
Report preparation and presentation

Overview

In this chapter, we start by presenting a means of classifying qualitative research techniques and we examine the implications of such classification. The characteristics of the focus group are presented along with their advantages and disadvantages. The manner in which focus groups should be planned and conducted is then presented. Running successful focus groups depends upon the skills of a moderator, i.e. the person who manages the group, and the ensuing discussion. We present the qualities needed in moderators to get the most out of focus group discussions. There are variations on the main theme of running a focus group; these are described as well as other qualitative group activities. Some of the misconceptions of focus groups are examined, with a reminder of the qualities that make group techniques work well. Running focus groups using the Internet is a rapidly developing technique; we describe how focus groups can be run in 'real time' and 'non-real time'. In Chapter 6 we contrasted the purpose and different ways of running focus groups in the USA and in Europe; this contrast is developed and illustrated further in examining international marketing research issues. Several ethical issues that arise in running focus groups are identified.

The following example illustrates how using focus groups helps researchers and decision-makers to understand the issues faced by consumers and, in this case, advertisement viewers. The issues are expressed in consumers' own words and sometimes in ways that words cannot convey. The example also illustrates that researchers and decision-makers may think that they know of all the issues they should be questioning, but once the exploration starts, participants can reveal new issues that they perceive to be of more importance, and these issues can drive very innovative marketing decisions.

Example   Save the Children's emotive appeal[1]

Save the Children's work is focused on helping the world's most vulnerable children. A new direct response TV advertisement in September 2004 formed part of a wider communications plan which included press inserts, online advertising and door-drops. In order to achieve an acceptable return on investment, TV channels chosen to screen the advertisements were predominantly cable/satellite with low active viewing, such as MTV and Paramount Comedy. Low activity enables the viewers to walk away from what they have been watching and telephone the donation line, rather than remaining to view the rest of the programme. The advertisement began with a startling call to attention, a 'gunshot', to grab the viewer. Save the Children could draw upon a broad archive of relevant, harrowing footage, so focus groups were convened to assess the acceptable bounds of the imagery that could be used that would encourage an instant response. One of the key focus group findings was that, in addition to presenting 'the problem', the advertisement must also offer hope, reassurance that a donation could actually make a difference. For these individuals, a very emotive appeal was required to stir them into action.

Classifying qualitative research techniques

A classification of qualitative research techniques is presented in Figure 7.1.

These techniques are classified as either direct or indirect, based on whether the true purpose of the project is known to the participants. A **direct approach** is not disguised. The purpose of the project is disclosed to the participants or is otherwise obvious to them from the questions asked. Focus groups and in-depth interviews are the major direct techniques. Even though the purpose of the project is disclosed, the extent to which the purpose of the research is revealed at the start of a focus group or in-depth group may vary. Suppose that the researcher wanted to understand how participants felt about the Prada brand, what their views were of Prada advertising campaigns, the style and quality of Prada clothes, how 'cool' the brand was, the importance of its being an Italian company – to name but a few issues that could be tackled. Rather than stating these objectives or even that the study was for Prada right at the start, the researcher may initially hide these issues. If revealed at the start, participants may focus straight on to these issues and not the surrounding contextual issues that may reveal the 'relative' impact of the Prada brand. Thus the researcher may initially reveal that the discussion is going to be about 'what clothes mean to you'. The researcher may explore what participants feel to be good and poor examples of clothing advertisements and why – what types of clothing and accessories do participants see as stylish, how important is it to wear stylish clothes, how important is it to wear 'cool' clothes? – drawing out examples of brands to illustrate these views. Italy as a country could be explored in terms of characteristics of Italians or Italian design and style. If participants bring up Prada in the discussion, the researcher can then focus upon specific questions about the brand, contrast it with other brands and clearly see which subjects generated positive or negative views of Prada. Participants may deduce that the study is being conducted for Prada as the discussion proceeds, which may be apparent by the end of the discussion, or the researcher may clarify this point and explain why it was not revealed at the beginning.

In using focus groups or in-depth interviews, the researcher employs a direct approach but has control over how much 'directness' to reveal at the start of the discussion. The researcher must consider what 'frame of mind' participants should be in at the start of the discussion, as a too narrow or set focus at the start can impede the thought processes and creativity of the participants and the success of the discussion.

In contrast, research that takes an **indirect approach** totally disguises the purpose of the project. In an indirect approach, the researcher wants participants to behave as naturally as possible without any impediment of research purposes. In observation or ethnographic techniques, consumers may be seen shopping, choosing products, using

Direct approach
A type of qualitative research in which the purposes of the project are disclosed to the participant or are obvious given the nature of the interview.

Indirect approach
A type of qualitative research in which the purposes of the project are disguised from the participants.

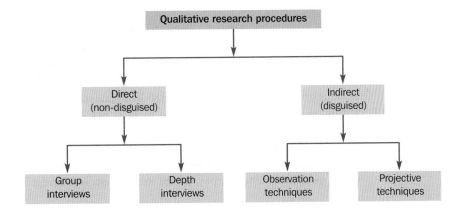

Figure 7.1
A classification of qualitative research techniques

products, interacting with other people and objects, hopefully in a natural environment and a natural manner. The 'participants' may not know that they are being observed, or if they do and have agreed to be observed, may not really know why. The purpose of using projective techniques (presented in Chapter 8) is to discover underlying motivations, beliefs, attitudes or feelings regarding consumer behaviour. The techniques allow indirect questioning to allow participants to discover novel ways to think about and express their feelings, where direct questioning would fail.

Figure 7.1 presents a useful way to remember which qualitative techniques tend towards directness and indirectness. Another way of thinking about these issues would be to visualise a continuum with 'totally direct' at one extreme and 'totally indirect' at the other. Qualitative techniques may then be positioned on this continuum and the implications of that position addressed. The implications for the researcher are as follows:

- *Ethical.* What are the ethical issues concerning revealing what a study is about? Would participants get involved in the study if they knew what it was really about? Will participants feel cheated or abused by not being told the purpose or finding it out as they go along?
- *Data richness.* If participants know what a study is about, to what extent does this 'close' their minds or destroy their creativity? Qualitative techniques aim to draw out deeply held views, issues that may be difficult to conceive or express. Researchers need to be able to get participants in the right frame of mind to be able to elicit these rich data. To what extent does revealing the purpose of a study impede this process?

Researchers cannot resolve this issue by stating, for example, that 'they will only use direct techniques' to resolve the ethical issues. Successful focus groups and in-depth interviews can utilise certain observation techniques. As an example, consider recording a simple answer of 'no' to a question. This 'no' may be interpreted in different ways, depending upon facial expressions ('was the participant smiling?'), the tone of the participant's voice ('was it sharp and direct?'), the participant's posture and body language ('were they hunched and hiding their faces?'), or their positioning and reactions to others around them ('were they seeking support from others of the same view, by gestures directed towards those participants?'). The researcher can use and manipulate scenarios to observe participants as a means of interpreting the answers they give to questions. The same can be said of projective techniques, all of which can be used to great effect in focus groups and in-depth interviews.

The researcher ultimately has to work out the extent of directness or indirectness of the chosen qualitative techniques and address the ethical and data richness issues before setting out the detail of how to administer the qualitative techniques. These issues may be unique in each investigation, depending upon the nature of participants being studied and the questions they face. In practice, the qualitative researcher may resolve the best means to administer a technique by experimenting and adapting; these issues are tackled later in this chapter.

Focus group discussions

Focus group
A discussion conducted by a trained moderator among a small group of participants in an unstructured and natural manner.

A **focus group** is a discussion conducted by a trained moderator in a non-structured and natural manner with a small group of participants. A **moderator** leads and develops the discussion. The main purpose of focus groups is to gain insights by creating a forum where participants feel sufficiently relaxed to reflect and to portray their feelings and behaviour, at their pace and using their language and logic. It has been argued that the single most compelling purpose of the focus group is to bridge social and cultural differ-

Moderator
An individual who conducts a focus group interview, by setting the purpose of the interview, questioning, probing and handling the process of discussion.

ences between researchers and their target participants.[2] The value of the technique and its role in bridging social and cultural differences lies in discovering unexpected findings, often obtained from a free-flowing discussion that is respectful and not condescending to participants.[3] Focus groups are the most important qualitative marketing research procedure accounting for 11% of all global marketing research expenditure in 2004.[4] They are used extensively in new product development, advertising development and image studies. They are so popular that many marketing research practitioners consider this technique synonymous with qualitative research.[5] Given their importance and popularity, we describe the salient characteristics of focus groups in detail.[6]

Characteristics

The major characteristics of a focus group are summarised in Table 7.1.

Table 7.1 Characteristics of focus groups

Key benefit	Group members 'feed' off each other and creatively reveal ideas that the researcher may not have thought of or dared to tackle
Key drawback	Group members may feel intimidated or shy and may not reveal anything
Group size	6–10
Group composition	Homogeneous, participants pre-screened
Physical setting	Relaxed, informal atmosphere
Stimulating discussion	Use of storyboards, mood boards, products, brochures
Time duration	1.5 to 6 hours
Recording	Use of audiocassettes, videotapes and notes from observations
Moderator	Observational, interpersonal and communication skills

One of the main characteristics and key benefits lies in the amount of creative discussion and other activities that may be generated. Group members have the time to reflect upon the discussion and range of stimuli that may be presented to them. The stimuli may come from other group members or from the moderator. Using their intuition and imagination, group members can explain how they feel or behave, in words they are comfortable with and using logic that is meaningful to them. The key drawback lies in how intimidating the group scenario may be to certain individuals. Many individuals may be self-conscious in expressing their ideas, feeling they may be ridiculed by others, or they may be shy and unable to express themselves freely in a group. A focus group is generally made up of 6–10 members. Groups of fewer than six are unlikely to generate the momentum and group dynamics necessary for a successful session. Likewise, groups of more than 10 may be too crowded and may not be conducive to a cohesive and natural discussion.[7] Large groups have a tendency to splinter into subgroups as group members compete to get their views across.

A focus group generally should be homogeneous in terms of demographic and socio-economic characteristics. Commonality among group members avoids interactions and conflicts among group members on side issues.[8] An amount of conflict may draw out issues or get participants to rationalise and defend their views in a number of ways; it can also mean that the discussion does not get stale with everybody agreeing with each other and setting a scenario where genuine disagreement gets stifled. However, major conflicts should and can be avoided by the careful selection of participants. Thus, for many topics, a women's group should not combine married homemakers with small children, young unmarried working women and elderly divorced or widowed women, because their lifestyles are substantially different. Participants should be carefully screened to meet stated criteria. These criteria are set by the researcher to ensure that participants have had adequate experience with the object or issue being discussed. The most fundamental basis screening of participants is through demographic classification. Common demographic characteristics for determining group composition are: gender, race or ethnicity, age, household location, education level, occupation, income and marital status or family composition. Selecting participants using these characteristics can help increase compatibility but does not guarantee it; their background should be carefully balanced with their experiences.[9] Participants who have already taken part in numerous focus groups should not be included. These so-called professional participants are atypical, and their participation leads to serious validity problems.[10]

The physical setting for the focus group is also important. A relaxed, informal atmosphere helps group members to forget they are being questioned and observed. What is meant by a relaxed, informal atmosphere may change depending upon the type of participant and the subject being tackled. Examples of what 'relaxed and informal' means can include the home of a friend within a particular community, a works canteen, a village hall, a room in a leisure centre, a meeting room in a hotel or a purpose-built discussion group room. The poor acoustics and hard seats of a works canteen may not seem relaxed and informal. To group participants, however, it may be the place where they are happy to talk and willing to open up to a moderator. An example of this could be using part of a furniture store to discuss issues around house decoration, furnishings and cleaning or maintaining the home. Such a setting may set a very strong frame of reference to start the focus group and provide lots of stimuli. This example does not mean that all research needs to be conducted *in situ*, but that the technique can be designed to allow the findings from the real and the research environments to inform the overall recommendations.[11] Light refreshments should be served before the session and made available throughout; these become part of the context of relaxation. The nature of these refreshments largely depends upon how long the discussion lasts, the nature of tasks faced by the participants and the ethical viewpoint of the researcher.

Although a focus group may last from one to six hours, a duration of one and a half to two hours is typical. When a focus group lasts up to six hours, participants may be performing a series of projective techniques such as building 'mood boards' or 'role playing'.

The following example shows how mood boards were used in the Sports Marketing Surveys project on rugby league. The photographs represent one of four mood boards that were used to great effect in eliciting the core values of rugby league. Imagine how the discussion may flow around these images as participants reflect upon the images and the connotations they see. In a relaxed, engaging and fun context, respondents could take their time to focus on the passions, feelings and stereotypes associated with the sport and the match-day experience.

Sports Marketing Surveys

Rugby league study

In the focus groups four mood boards were presented to participants. The themes presented on the mood boards encapsulated '*impact*', '*athletic*', '*north*' and '*entertainment*'. These were built following the findings that emerged from an Internet survey and a brainstorming workshop. The aim of the mood boards was to ascertain:

● Was there an overall theme?
● What were the pictures about?

- What relevance did they have to rugby league?
- What did they say about rugby league?
- What word or phrase would sum up the board?

Avid male fans described these images as:

- *Demolition*, power, damage, aggression, impact.
- *Wildlife programme*, locking horns like a scrum.
- *Car crash*, implies permanent damage.

They did not want to see the sport portrayed like this – not what it's all about, it's not representing the game, aggressive in a negative manner. Whilst it was not the main theme of the game, the image had contextual applications. The hardness and contact of the sport is an important variable, but not the core factor of the sport.

Avid female fans described these images as:

- *Negative aggression*, injury, violence, pain.
- *Distasteful face*, not appealing to children, dummy suggests fatality.
- *More like football*, does not say anything about rugby league

They saw rugby league as far more colourful than these images. They recognised that appropriate pictures must capture the toughness and determined aggression of the sport. It is combative and compelling, but not violent and threatening.

Participants can also be given additional stimuli to discuss such as advertising storyboards and products (new, existing, competitors) to handle and examine. A focus group that lasts for up to six hours will invariably require a break for a meal, but in all circumstances a flow of drinks and snacks should be made available, noting special dietary requirements, e.g. vegan food and drinks. The opportunities and problems that occur by serving alcoholic drinks in focus groups will be discussed in the 'Ethics in marketing research' section later in this chapter.

The lengthy period of discussion in a focus group is needed to establish rapport with the participants, to get them to relax and be in the right frame of mind, and to explore in depth their beliefs, feelings, ideas, attitudes and insights regarding the topics of concern. Focus group discussions are invariably recorded, mostly using audiotape but often on videotape, for subsequent replay, transcription and analysis. Videotaping has the advantage of recording facial expressions and body movements, but it can increase the costs significantly. Frequently, where focus groups are conducted in purpose-built studios, decision-makers as 'clients' observe the session from an adjacent room using a two-way mirror or through video transmission as described in the following example.

Example | How wrong can you be?[12]

Many management boards of blue-chip companies now watch consumer qualitative research as a regular part of their board activities. EVO Research and Consulting has managed this approach on many occasions. In one instance, a European board agreed that the business as a whole needed to get closer to its customers and they must lead by example. EVO organised a one-off research event in which the board would view a cross-section of their customer base taking part in a series of group discussions. To make it more interesting, the board members who were watching via a two-way mirror were each asked to make some assumptions about the types of people they were expecting to see; the lives they imagined these people led; and, importantly, the types of relationships thay felt the participants had with various brands within their portfolio. The most outstanding aspect of this exercise was the level of surprise at how 'wrong' board perceptions of customers could be, especially when they prided themselves by how 'in touch' they were with their customers.

The approach taken in the above example could work even if board members could not physically attend the group discussion. Video transmission technology also enables the clients to observe focus group sessions live from a remote location (see **www.focusvision. co.uk** for an example). Care must be taken with both audio and video recording in terms of how comfortable participants are with being recorded and what effects recorders have on how much they relax and honestly portray how they feel, especially when projective techniques are used (these techniques will be detailed in Chapter 8) , which some participants may find embarrassing. Many moderators can give rich examples of how the most interesting points to emerge from a focus group occur when recorders are switched off at the end of the discussion. This happens when a group of participants have really become involved in the subject of discussion and have enjoyed talking to their fellow participants. Even when the moderator has finished the discussion, some participants carry on discussing the issues between themselves as they put their coats on, leave the room and even perhaps as they walk to their cars. Moderators can hear issues discussed in this informal manner that they wish had been tackled with the full group.

The moderator plays a vital role in the success of a focus group. The moderator must establish rapport with the participants and keep the discussion flowing, including the **probing** of participants to elicit insights. Typically, probing differs from questioning in that the probes and the nature of probing are more spontaneous, and involve comments such as:[13]

Probing
A motivational technique used when asking questions to induce the participants to enlarge on, clarify or explain their answers.

- Would you explain further?
- Can you give me an example of what you mean?
- Would you say more?
- Is there anything else?
- Please describe what you mean.

- I don't understand.
- Tell me more about that.
- How does that work?

Sometimes the moderator may put a probe question to the whole group such as:

- Who else has something?
- What about the rest of you?
- I see people nodding their heads; tell me about it.
- We want to hear all the different points of view. Who else has something that might be a bit different?

It is seen as good practice to probe early in the discussion in order to communicate the importance of precision or a developed explanation, and to use probes sparingly in later discussion.

In addition, the moderator may have a central role in the analysis and interpretation of the data. Therefore, the moderator should possess skill, experience, knowledge of the discussion topic, and an understanding of the nature of group dynamics.

Advantages and disadvantages of focus groups

Focus groups offer several advantages over other data collection techniques. These may be summarised by the nine S's:[14]

1 *Synergy.* Putting a group of people together will produce a wider range of information, insight and ideas than will individual responses secured privately.
2 *Snowballing.* A bandwagon effect often operates in a group discussion in that one person's comment triggers a chain reaction from the other participants. This process facilitates a very creative process where new ideas can be developed, justified and critically examined.
3 *Stimulation.* Usually after a brief introductory period, the participants want to express their ideas and expose their feelings as the general level of excitement over the topic increases in the group.
4 *Security.* Because the participants' feelings may be similar to those of other group members, they feel comfortable and are therefore willing to 'open up' and reveal thoughts where they may have been reluctant if they were on their own.
5 *Spontaneity.* Because participants are not required to answer specific questions, their responses can be spontaneous and unconventional and should therefore provide an accurate idea of their views.
6 *Serendipity.* Ideas are more likely to arise unexpectedly in a group than in an individual interview. There may be issues that the moderator had not thought of. The dynamics of the group can allow these issues to develop and be discussed. Group members, to great effect, may clearly and forcibly ask questions that the moderator may be reluctant to ask.
7 *Specialisation.* Because a number of participants are involved simultaneously, the use of a highly trained, but expensive, interviewer is justified.
8 *Scientific scrutiny.* The group discussion allows close scrutiny of the data collection process in that observers can witness the session and it can be recorded for later analysis. Many individuals can be involved in the validation and interpretation of the collected data.
9 *Structure.* The group discussion allows for flexibility in the topics covered and the depth with which they are treated. The structure can match the logical structure of issues from the participants' perspective as well as the language and expressions they are comfortable with.

Disadvantages of focus groups may be summarised by the five Ms:

1 *Misjudgement.* Focus group results can be more easily misjudged than the results of other data collection techniques. As discussed in Chapter 6, as a qualitative technique, focus groups can evolve through a line of questioning and probing. The specific direction of questioning and the ultimate interpretation of findings can be susceptible to the bias of the moderator and other researchers working on a project.

2 *Moderation.* As well as being great fun to moderate, focus groups can be difficult to moderate. Much depends upon the 'chemistry' of the group in terms of how group members get on with each other and draw ideas and explanations from each other. Even moderators with many years of experience may not connect with particular groups of respondents or topics and can get into difficulty with group members who disrupt the discussion. The quality of the results depends upon how well the discussion is managed and ultimately on the skills of the moderator.

3 *Messiness.* The unstructured nature of the responses makes coding, analysis and interpretation difficult in comparison with the structure of quantitative techniques. Focus group data tend to be messy and need either strong theoretical support or the discipline of a grounded theory approach to ensure that decision-makers can rely upon the analyses and interpretations.

4 *Misrepresentation.* Focus group results concentrate on distinct target groups, describing them and contrasting them to other groups or types of participant. Trying to generalise to much wider groups, in the same manner as with a quantitative survey based on a representative sample, can be very misleading.

5 *Meeting.* There are many problems in getting potential participants to agree to take part in a focus group discussion. Even when they have agreed to participate, there are problems in getting focus group participants together at the same time. Running focus groups on the Internet has helped to resolve these problems to some extent, but for some target groups even this does not offer a solution. An example is in conducting business research with managers as participants. Given the amount of travel and tight schedules that many managers have, getting them together at the same time is very difficult. With many managers reluctant to reveal their company's behaviour and plans in front of other managers, one can see that the focus group may be very difficult to administer in getting managers to meet up and discuss issues.

Planning and conducting focus groups

The procedure for planning and conducting focus groups is described in Figure 7.2.

Planning begins with an examination of the marketing research problem(s) and objectives. In most instances, the problem has been defined by this stage, but it is vital to ensure that the whole process is founded upon a clear awareness of the gaps in the knowledge of marketing decision-makers. Given the problem definition, the objectives of using focus groups should be clarified. There should be a clear understanding of what information can be elicited and what the limitations of the technique are.

Topic guide
A list of topics, questions and probes that are used by a moderator to help manage a focus group discussion.

The next step is to develop a list of issues, or **topic guide**, that are to be tackled in the focus groups. This list may be a series of specific questions but is more likely to be a set of broad issues that can be developed into questions or probes as the focus group actually takes place. Specific questions may be of help to the moderator who feels that a consistent set of points needs to be presented to different groups in order to allow clear comparisons to be made. Specific questions also act as a 'prop' when the discussion is failing; indeed some group participants may initially feel that their role is to react to specific questions. However, treating the whole discussion as a means to present set questions may stifle the

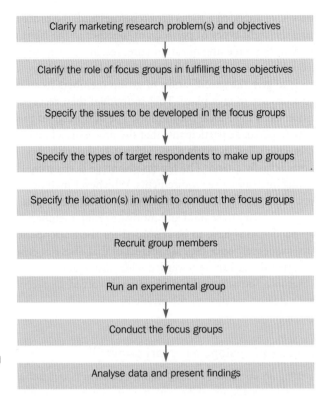

Figure 7.2
Procedure for planning and conducting focus groups

Clarify marketing research problem(s) and objectives

Clarify the role of focus groups in fulfilling those objectives

Specify the issues to be developed in the focus groups

Specify the types of target respondents to make up groups

Specify the location(s) in which to conduct the focus groups

Recruit group members

Run an experimental group

Conduct the focus groups

Analyse data and present findings

creativity and spontaneity that are the hallmarks of successful focus groups. The moderator should open the discussion with a general *introductory question* to make participants comfortable with the subject and the purpose of the research. This question should encourage conversation and interaction amongst the participants. It should not be threatening, it may even question in the third person, i.e. not asking participants what they do or think, and as such it may not be critical to the analysis, though there can be much revealed at this point. The discussion moves onto one or two *transition questions*, which move the discussion towards the key questions and issues. Transition questions help participants to envision the topic in a broader scope. Through these questions, participants become more aware of their fellow participants. Transition questions can ask participants to go into more depth about their experiences and uses of a product, making the connection between the participant and the topic under investigation.[15] The moderator can then move on to the *key questions* developing specific questions, issues and probes that can advance as the moderator tunes into the dynamics of the group. There may be additional, new issues that develop and, indeed, issues that group members do not see as being appropriate, and these can be discussed. The emphasis should be upon an evolution and learning process rather than administering a consistent set of questions.

The types of group members to take part in the discussions are then specified. From this specification, a questionnaire to screen potential participants is prepared. Typical information obtained from the questionnaire includes product familiarity and knowledge, usage behaviour, attitudes towards and participation in focus groups, and standard demographic characteristics. With the types of participants specified, consideration must be taken of what would make them relaxed and comfortable, balanced in both a physical and psychological sense.

Having decided on the location of the focus groups, the actual recruitment of group members progresses. This is one of the most difficult tasks, as potential group members may be sceptical of what may happen at the group, sometimes fearing that they are exposing themselves to a hard-sell campaign of time-share holidays or home improvements! If individuals have attended a focus group beforehand, the process of recruitment is easier, but getting the right types of participant together at the right place and time can prove difficult. With the screening questionnaire, recruitment may take place on a face-to-face basis through street interviews or through database details by telephone. One traditional approach is to give the specification of group members to an individual in whose home the discussions are to take place. That individual then recruits participants who fit that specification from their local community. The advantage of this approach is the individual's ability to persuade participants that the process is a bona fide research process and is going to be rewarding in many ways; ultimately the individual makes sure that potential participants actually attend. The big disadvantage is ensuring that those recruited match the screening questionnaire requirements. Whichever method of recruiting participants is used, even when individuals have said that they will participate in the group, a telephone follow-up is necessary to remind and motivate group members.

Group participants have to be rewarded for their attendance. Usually they enjoy the experience immensely once they are there, but that does not ensure that they attend in the first place. Attendance can be rewarded with cash, a donation to charity or a gift. The following example illustrates the difficulties involved in recruitment and a marketing researcher's creative solution to the problem.

Example — So how do you upstage a Ferrari owner?[16]

Researching an upmarket, socially active audience is difficult at the best of times. The target is opinionated, demanding, often resistant to research and almost impossible to reach. So, when we got the brief to conduct focus groups among Ferrari, Porsche, top Mercedes and other exotic sports car owners, we were tempted to panic. We knew we could find them, but how could we persuade them to participate?

Source: © Alamy

We realised the one thing that would link our target, who were also defined as keen drivers, not just poseurs, was their love of cars and desire to know the latest news about new models (and to try them out if possible).

That's why we decided to offer the carrot of a drive around a race and proving track and the opportunity to meet the design and management team at our famous sports car maker. If anything might motivate people who clearly already had sufficient money to indulge a very expensive taste, it should be this package. It worked like a dream, and we had great success getting the right people to come and, more importantly, to participate.

Experimental group
An initial focus group run to test the setting of the interview, the opening question, the topic guide and the mix of participants that make up the group.

The first focus group to be run should be seen as an **experimental group**. All aspects of running the group should be evaluated. Were the group members relaxed and comfortable in the chosen location, i.e. did the context work as intended? How did they react to the tape recorder, video or two-way mirror, i.e. at what point did they seem to relax and forget that they were being recorded? What types of member interacted well or not, and what issues helped or hindered interaction? How did the introductory and transition questions work in opening up and developing the discussion? How did the topic guide work; were there issues missing or issues that individuals would not tackle? How comfortable was the moderator handling the topics; did he or she have to interject to liven the discussion? How much did the moderator have to know about the subject to have credibility with the participants? With reflection on these issues, any necessary alterations can be made to the way that the remaining focus groups are administered. There may be very useful information that emerges from the experimental group that can be included in the main analysis. However, if the group does not work well, the information gleaned may be of little use, but the lessons learnt are invaluable in running the remaining groups.

Finally, the focus groups can be actually run. The question arises here of how many groups should be run. Beyond the first experimental group, the number of groups needed can vary. The extent to which comparisons are sought in analyses can determine how many groups are needed. Seeking comparisons means recruiting participants with different backgrounds or experiences. If there are a great variety of types of individual that make up a target market, then many homogeneous groups may be needed to reflect the variety of types, e.g. a group of 18–25-year-old single-male car owners compared with groups of women or groups of older males, married men or non-car owners. The definition of these distinct target groups to question is entirely bound by the nature of the research problem.

A confounding factor in the definition of these groups is the extent to which different types of participant will mix together in a single group. In an experimental focus group that explored attitudes and behaviour related to sports activities in the English city of Bath, distinct target groups of participants did not work well together. Older participants who participated in more 'gentle' sports activities did not particularly appreciate, listen to or respect the views of younger participants. In addition, there was a gender split in that male participants showed very little respect for the views of female participants. The older male participants were particularly patronising to younger females. As a result it was decided to run groups that separated younger and older participants and males and females. This meant an increase in the total number of focus groups conducted but also meant that the remaining focus groups worked well and that the views of distinct target groups were clearly presented

If target participants are geographically widespread, then many groups may be needed to represent this diversity. The following example of an A.C. Nielsen hypermarket study illustrates the comparisons made in focus group analyses. The important markets they concentrated upon were Russia, Hungary, Poland and the Czech Republic and so focus groups would be needed to represent each country. Further analyses of two distinct target groups were also needed. Thus, a minimum of two groups per country, i.e. eight groups plus an experimental group, would be needed, which would be doubled if it were subsequently felt to be important to run exclusively male and female groups.

Example   **Hypermarkets in Eastern Europe and Russia[17]**

International retailers have pounced upon the opportunity to dominate grocery retailing in Central Eastern Europe and Russia. Given the inefficiencies of many local networks, this has created enormous changes in the way that people shop. Never before have they had such choice in store numbers, formats and product assortment. To better understand these changes, A.C. Nielsen conducted eight focus group discussions with housewives aged 25-40 years in Moscow, Warsaw, Prague and Budapest. Participants who were active shoppers, visiting at least three retail formats every month, provided further insights through self-completion questionnaires.

Hungarians were the most enthusiastic about hypermarkets, which they might visit up to twice a week, compared with the fortnightly trip for Czechs. Russians are more budget minded and perfer no-frills discounters. Shoppers in Poland were the most satisfied with hypermarkets although this could be because they were a relatively new phenomenon.

Another factor to be considered in determining the number of focus groups to conduct relates to whether the researcher is using focus groups as part of a grounded theory approach. With such an approach (as described in Chapter 6) theoretical sampling is adopted whereby further examples or instances are sought that may contradict the nature of the emerging grounded theory. The complexity of the developing grounded theory and the extent to which the qualitative researcher makes sense of the issues being explored will ultimately determine the number of discussions needed. This can be contrasted to focus groups conducted from a positivist perspective, focusing upon generating an understanding of issues to be confirmed in a subsequent survey. In the latter scenario, the researcher may not need to continue to search for more contradictory perspectives. Whichever paradigm underpins the application of focus groups, resources permitting, one should conduct additional discussion groups until the moderator can anticipate what will be said. The last sentence is a reminder of the final factor determining the number of discussions – the time and money afforded by the client.

In summary, the number of focus groups that should be conducted on a single subject depends on the following factors:

- The extent to which comparisons between types of participants are sought.
- The different types of participant to be targeted and how well they mix together.
- The geographic spread of participants.
- The paradigm that underpins the focus group.
- The time and budget available.

Another dimension of running the groups, beyond the actual number of groups, is the nature of stimuli that the moderator chooses to input. At certain times, examples of particular products or brands may be introduced for participants to examine, or even taste or sample if the nature of the product permits. Advertising material such as brochures, posters or even video recordings of TV or cinema adverts can be shown and a response generated. One of the most frequently used forms of stimuli is the **mood board**.

The 'mood board' is really the creation of a collage. Focus group participants are given a pile of magazines and asked to snip words and pictures from them. The direction they are given is to select images and words that they think represent characteristics of a brand, a consumer type or lifestyle or whatever issue the researcher wishes to be illustrated in this manner. The resultant collage can then be used to stimulate discussion and to help draw together ideas and connect them. Creative marketing decision-makers in copywriting or advertisement development may develop many ideas directly from the collages or mood boards. The mood board has two main functions:

1 *Reference point.* The moderator can use the mood board to reflect upon the discussion, in which case issues can emerge that were not so apparent in the heat of a discussion.
2 *Enabling device.* The mood board gets participants to loosen up and talk more freely. The focus group is not to get participants to talk rationally but to display what 'feels

Mood board
A collage created in a focus group setting. Focus group participants are asked to snip words and pictures from magazines that they see as representing the values a particular brand is perceived to have. In some circumstances, collages can also be made up from audio- and videotapes.

right' to them. The collage can help to express feelings they may not be able to put into words, or enable those words to have more clarity. This can happen by questioning what is included in a mood board as well as what is omitted.[18]

The following example illustrates that the mood board can develop beyond two-dimensional images.

Example | **Art of the matter[19]**

Paul Walton, Chairman of new product development consultancy The Value Engineers, explains:

In the early stages of a new product or brand reassessment project, words might be appropriate. Beyond the words come picture collages and as you learn more and you start to give the brand a clearer identity, you introduce mock-ups of packaging and other props to 'three-dimensionalise' the world.

Alex Authers, Research Director at branding consultancy New Solutions, argues the case for stimuli beyond the mood board:

We've moved on from static visuals, to using videos. It's often useful to show a series of fast-edited clips set to some sort of soundtrack. People are now much more video literate. So, instead of having a mood board, we have a mood video. Video collages are particularly good for exploring the emotional resonances of brands.

Other props used in qualitative research include swatches of material and even fragrances. Authers says smells and colours can 'help to create a mood and evoke a positioning'.

The final stage in planning and conducting focus groups involves the analysis of data. Chapter 9 discusses qualitative data analysis in more detail. However, at this point there are two essential points to note:

1 *Evolving analysis.* Focus groups can change and develop in terms of the issues discussed and the stimuli used to draw out views from participants. The changes are made as the moderator generates and develops new ideas as each focus group progresses. The moderator makes observations and notes to help as the discussion progresses and also for when it is over. These observations and notes are part of the total analysis in that they decide which issues to probe, which issues to drop and the form of summarising issues that may be presented to groups at certain stages of the discussion.

2 *Not just the narrative.* If the discussion is recorded then transcripts can be produced which can be analysed with proprietary software. These transcripts form a major part of the analysis procedure but the accumulation and reflection upon observations and notes forms a key part of the analysis.

The moderator

Throughout this chapter we have referred to the moderator as an individual who conducts a focus group discussion, by setting the purpose of the discussion, questioning, probing and handling the process of discussion. This individual may be the researcher handling the project. More likely it will be someone who specialises in the technique, or, given the number of groups to run and the time allowed to complete them, a number of specialist moderators will be employed. Whoever is to undertake the task of 'moderating' will require the following qualities:[20]

1 *Kindness with firmness.* The moderator must quickly develop an empathy with group members. From this the moderator should show kindness to make participants feel welcome, combined with a firmness to stop particular individuals taking over the discussion.

2 *Permissiveness.* The moderator must be permissive, allowing the flow of discussion to develop as the group sees fit. However, the moderator must be alert to signs that the group's cordiality or purpose is disintegrating.

3 *Involvement.* The moderator must encourage and stimulate intense personal involvement. In certain circumstances, this may mean becoming involved in the actual discussion itself. This can happen if a tendency for 'group speak' emerges. 'Group speak' happens when little debate or creativity in ideas develops, as particular individuals may not wish to be seen as going against a perceived group norm.

4 *Incomplete understanding.* The moderator must encourage participants to be more specific about generalised comments by exhibiting a feigned naivety or incomplete understanding.

5 *Encouragement.* The moderator must encourage unresponsive members to participate.

6 *Flexibility.* The moderator must be able to improvise and alter the planned outline amid the distractions of the group process.

7 *Sensitivity.* The moderator must be sensitive enough to guide the group discussion at an intellectual as well as emotional level. The moderator must also be attuned to mood changes and issues that fire up enthusiastic responses or conversely cause the discussion to dry up.

8 *Observation.* As the group progresses, notes must be made of ideas or questions to come back to, interpretations of particular silences or bouts of laughter, and how group members are interacting with each other. These observations help the group discussion to progress well and the interpretation of the discussion to have greater meaning.

Other variations of focus groups

Focus groups can use several variations of the standard procedure. These include:

- *Two-way focus group.* This allows one target group to listen to and learn from a related group. In one application, physicians viewed a focus group of arthritis patients discussing the treatment they desired. A focus group of these physicians was then held to determine their reactions.[21]

- *Dual-moderator group.* This is a focus group discussion conducted by two moderators. One moderator is responsible for the smooth flow of the session, and the other ensures that specific issues are discussed.

- *Duelling-moderator group.* Here also there are two moderators, but they deliberately take opposite positions on the issues to be discussed. This allows the researcher to explore both sides of controversial issues. It also encourages participants who may support a particular perspective to express their views without fear that they will be 'attacked' by the rest of the group.

- *Participant-moderator group.* In this type of focus group, the moderator asks selected participants to play the role of moderator temporarily to improve group dynamics.

- *Client-participant group.* Client personnel are identified and made part of the discussion group. Their primary role is to offer clarifications that will make the group process more effective.

- *Mini group.* These groups consist of a moderator and only four or five participants. They are used when the issues of interest require more extensive probing than is possible in the standard group of 6–10.

- *Telephone focus groups.* These are conducted using a telephone conferencing system with the same number of participants as conventional focus groups, but typically within a narrower time frame, no more than an hour. These can work well in gaining access to widely dispersed experts in a range of professions or specialists. They would not be cost effective with 'average' consumers, except perhaps in cases where follow-up from survey respondents is desired.[22]

Other types of qualitative group discussions

Brainstorming

Traditional brainstorming[23] has been used for several decades, especially in the context of management or marketing issues. Whether formal or informal, the process is the same: think of as many ideas as you can and say them out loud; leave the evaluation until later; build on and combine others' ideas; be as imaginative as possible, the wilder the ideas the better. The group moderator seeks to nurture an atmosphere of creativity, tapping into the intuition of participants, generating novel ideas and connections between ideas.

When it works well, ideas flow freely from an interplay that may never have occurred if the group had not brainstormed together.

Two problems plague traditional brainstorming: namely, production blocking and evaluation apprehension:

- *Production blocking* occurs when a group member has an idea, but someone else is talking. When it's their turn, they have forgotten the idea, or think their idea is redundant or not that good. If the group is large or dominated by talkative people, they lose interest and do not say what they think.
- *Evaluation apprehension* occurs when participants become anxious about what others think of their thoughts. Ideas may be censored, as there is a fear of being labelled as odd. When participants feel this apprehension, they do not produce as many new and potentially useful ideas but keep them to themselves and therefore defeat the purpose of brainstorming.

Industrial group discussions

As noted earlier, the focus group has limited use in industrial or business research. Getting managers together at the same time and place is a big operational problem. Getting them to be open about their companies in a group scenario is also very difficult to achieve. The following example illustrates how this problem was overcome, essentially by not using the term 'focus group'.

Example **Is a 'workshop' a focus group?**

In a major pan-European business-to-business survey, group discussions were seen as important in order to explore and develop issues that could not be measured in a questionnaire. What was measured in the questionnaire produced many statistics whose analyses necessitated further exploration and elaboration. Developing an elaboration of the statistical findings could be tackled in a group discussion. To overcome the above issues of getting managers to sit down together, part of the incentive to complete the questionnaire was an invitation to take part in a 'closed forum for questionnaire participants'. This meant that a date was set to present findings from the survey exclusively to questionnaire participants. The date and meeting place of The Management Centre in Brussels were established well in advance to allow managers the chance to put the date in their diaries. The day started with an initial session of presenting statistical findings to the whole group of managers who had responded to the questionnaire. As questions were fielded in this forum, particular topics of interest were identified and focus groups named as 'workshops' were built around these topics. By mid-morning, groups of around 10 managers were together tackling a theme of importance to them. With a loose set of topics to develop into questions and probes, the format for a focus group was achieved. In the afternoon, the same format continued with a presentation of questionnaire findings and further group discussions. By splitting the day in this manner, managers could attend and contribute to two subject areas of interest to them. Finally, individual managers could be identified who could be interviewed in depth on their own at a later date.

Misconceptions about focus groups

There has been much debate about the use and value of focus group discussions. Much of the debate has been misinformed through the development of myths and misconceptions built around the technique. Misconceptions about focus groups have emerged from assumptions made by researchers or the users of focus group findings or even journalists. Their assumptions may have been useful at one time, in a particular context, or when tackling a certain subject. The assumptions may well apply to specific contexts but may not be applicable to focus groups in general. Working through the misconceptions can help marketing researchers make decisions about when and how to use focus groups, and even if they should be using them at all.[24] The misconceptions about focus groups can be summarised by the five Es:

1 *Economical – they are low cost and quick.* The idea that focus groups are low cost and quick has emerged through comparison with other research methods. In comparison with survey research, focus groups may be conducted with a smaller budget and more quickly. This is not a fair comparison given the sample sizes the techniques work with and the type of data they generate. In comparison with other qualitative methods, focus groups are often more expensive than observation and individual interviewing, primarily due to more expensive recruiting methods. The biggest resource involved in the technique, however, is that of the researcher in the careful planning, execution and analysis of focus groups. The analysis of the data generated can be 'cheap and quick' if it is a case of decision-makers taking away their own conclusions from focus groups they have observed. Analysis can be far more expensive and time consuming if the careful planning and execution is followed up by the assembly of data, reflective diaries and memos and the full immersion into that data of the researcher as detailed in Chapter 9.

2 *Experts – they require professional moderators.* The qualities of a good moderator were detailed above. A professional moderator with experience of tackling different subjects, questioning and probing different types of participant and working in a variety of contexts undoubtedly has much to offer any project. However, in many instances it is not the amount of experience that matters most in moderating. Sometimes a less experienced moderator who has more contact with the issues under question, more contact with the participants, and is perhaps more comfortable in the interview location, can elicit better data. This is especially true when working with distinctive ethnic, linguistic or cultural groups. For example, an undergraduate student working on a project for a leading deodorant brand was about to enter the room to conduct a focus group. Looking at the 18–20 year olds before he entered the room, he realised that he was wearing the 'wrong' logo. With a quick change of sweatshirt, he continued with the dis-

cussion to great effect. Upon reflection, he revealed that the logo he was wearing and indeed the colour of his sweatshirt would have said things about him to the group that would have affected his credibility. He felt that he would not have been able to engage with the group and get them to reveal so much in his original clothing. His acute sensitivity to this cultural nuance made this focus group particularly effective; an older and more experienced moderator may not have picked this up. The best moderators are not necessarily those with the most experience. It is the individual that can best engage with, listen to and draw out the best of target participants.

3 *Easily upset – they do not work for sensitive topics.* Focus groups are regularly used in projects related to sexual behaviour, substance abuse and stressful life events, which have marketing or other social implications. This misconception is based upon what may be deemed as socially acceptable in conversations, perhaps around the dinner table. However, focus groups present an atypical setting for discussion. The moderator is encouraging everyone in the group to share values and experiences that they all have an interest in. There may be little consequence to what they say, especially if they are meeting with strangers that they may never meet again. Handled with caution, the moderator can encourage participants to reveal things they would normally keep to themselves. Researchers and moderators working with sensitive issues must make plans to encourage appropriate self-disclosures, and to cope with disclosures that go beyond the boundaries of the project. These plans go beyond the wording of the questions and probes, into the atmosphere they wish to create at the discussion, the nature of the location being particularly important here.

4 *Endorsement – they must be validated by other research methods.* This is part of the general misconception that all qualitative techniques play a preliminary role that prepares the way for a conclusive technique. Focus groups can serve a useful role as the first stage of developing questionnaires or experiments, but that is not their sole purpose. Focus groups can illuminate and indeed help to validate many of the statistical findings that emerge from surveys, e.g. helping to understand and describe findings from factor and cluster analyses. They can be used in isolation to produce the kind of in-depth understanding of an issue that no other technique can provide: for example, if the use of a particular celebrity in an advertisement can generate a series of emotional responses that could impact upon the brand values – and those values are compounded by the particular use of music and who is playing that music. To uncover what is happening to the viewers and how their values may have changed, the focus group may well be the most efficient and effective technique, of all qualitative or quantitative options.

5 *Exposure – they reveal how consumers will behave.* Focus groups, depth interviews and surveys all depend upon verbal reporting. They depend upon a belief in what participants say about how they intend to behave. In many circumstances, even when it comes down to it, the most sincere participants can change their minds. In focus groups, participants may talk about their likely behaviour in many hypothetical scenarios, moderators can watch other participants nod their heads in agreement and the evidence is compelling. It must be recognised that the data generated are attitudinal, and trying to predict behaviour from attitudes is most problematic. The rise in customer databases and ethnographic methods has helped marketing researchers to predict consumer behaviour and validate the findings of focus groups and surveys.

The focus group, like every research technique, is never foolproof or perfect. To get the most from focus groups, the following thinking should be encouraged.[25] First, the quality of moderating is crucial to the success of the discussion. The quality of the findings is directly related to the talents, preparation and attentiveness of the moderator. Second, teamwork is vital. As well as star moderators, there must be quality recruiters, notetakers, analysts and reporters. Third, this team has always something to learn from the participants. For a short period of time, the participants open their lives (and sometimes souls) and share their experiences, preferences and beliefs. The most destructive thing a researcher can do in a focus group is to display arrogance, condescension or superiority. It is much better to sit back and let participants tell you everything you wanted to know, and more! Finally, there are many ways to conduct successful focus groups. Given the nature of the topic under investigation and the nature of the target participants, there are many options to choose for the best context and approach to draw out the best from participants. Focus groups vary enormously in how they are planned, administered and analysed, from the very structured interview in a studio bristling with technology, through to a passionate dialogue conducted globally over the Internet, to a riotous exchange on a tropical beach. Experimentation with new ways of conducting focus groups should be positively encouraged rather than being bound by the thought that there is one ideal way to conduct them.

International marketing research

The term 'focus group' is commonly used across all continents, yet it subsumes approaches that are different. For many European marketing researchers, one of the biggest headaches associated with focus groups is its name. The technique has been disparaged by a popular media impression that implies that focus groups are a means to get answers to set questions. Many see this as the American approach to conducting focus groups and thus see the name as an unwanted Americanism that has displaced what they see as the favoured term, 'group discussion'.

> The best people at moderating focus groups are ones who can create that spirit of spontaneity. You can't do it with a crowded agenda. You can't do it if you're focused, which is why focus is wrong.[26]

The above quotation implies a criticism of an American approach that can be highly structured rather than an approach that is truly spontaneous and exploratory in its fullest sense. It is not advocated at this stage that the word 'focus' be removed, but it is a reminder that there are different research approaches that can affect how the technique is administered. American and European approaches were presented in Chapter 6 to illustrate how different philosophies that underpin research techniques can affect how the technique is applied.[27] In examining the use of focus groups, two main schools of thought were presented: the *cognitive* approach, which largely follows a format and interviewing style as used in quantitative studies and is generally used by American researchers; and the *conative* approach, which has less structure to the questions, with group members being encouraged to take their own paths of discussion, make their own connections and let the whole process evolve, and is generally used by European researchers. It is not advocated that one particular approach is better than the other. Each approach has its own distinctive strengths and weaknesses depending upon why the technique is being used, the nature of the participants and the nature of researchers and decision-makers who are to use the data.

Viewing laboratory
A room where a focus group may be conducted and simultaneously observed, usually by using a two-way mirror.

For example, in the USA, observing focus groups through the use of purpose-built focus group rooms or a **viewing laboratory** with a two-way mirror is a *policy*. Typically there will be five to eight observers, sometimes more, with agency and marketing company matching level for level to maintain a balance of power. American researchers and clients defend the value of observers. People with different perspectives can listen in a way that a moderator cannot, since the moderator is often 'dipping in for the moment' on one specific issue while the clients 'have the brand in their bones'. Probably the most deeply felt reason for being there is just being there; there is no substitute for the touchy–feely benefit of experiencing the consumer first-hand. More than ever, marketing people are isolated in their small worlds (probably in atypical New York or Chicago), making assumptions about their users. Seeing them is a reality check. Hearing tonality, watching body language, observing the consumer interact with the product, enrich the learning process. Sometimes brand people will get rejuvenated and creatives will get inspired.[28]

Example　**A client's view of observing the focus group through the two-way mirror[29]**

It's a strange experience, sitting on the other side of a two-way mirror watching your product being analysed in a focus group. It's like being locked out of your house and peering through the windows as burglars rifle through your drawers and take the piss out of your record collection.

You want to bang on the glass and plead with them to stop, but then they say something nice about your product and you want to grab the person next to you and shout 'I thought of that!'

You tell yourself not to take the criticism too personally, to be professional, but it's hard when you've had sleepless nights agonising over minute details only to see them ignored or ripped apart in the space of half an hour.

It's great to get raw feedback like this, but remember just how raw it is. One group can say completely different things to another and some may just like the sport of making the suits behind the mirror suffer.

At face value, the above description of the use of viewing labs seems to show a feature of American practice that has many benefits, but consider the following problems:

- *Incomplete data.* Clients may not have seen all the groups, leaving gaps in the total picture. Observers admit that they focus on the most lively and self-serving points; that they identify positively and negatively with certain responses and filter accordingly; that they are attentive to ideas that affirm their positions and dismissive of contrary viewpoints.
- *Instant analysis.* Rather than waiting for a moderator's report or even the conclusions of the group, observers often jump to conclusions on little evidence or, worse still, stop listening once they have an 'impression' of the results.
- *Moderator reflection.* Often the moderator gets trapped into debriefing immediately after the group and taking positions that are hard to retreat from but which might be very different after a thoughtful review.
- *Effect on participants.* There is little research on the effect of the two-way mirrors on participants. The setting is not exactly conducive to natural expression and participants may alter their responses for effect, stay silent or be self-conscious.

Supporters of the European approach to focus groups may console themselves that they can overcome these drawbacks. They may argue that the context in which they run groups is more conducive to relaxed participants, that moderators are not under such pressure to produce 'instant analysis' and that they can take more time to reflect upon and interpret the data generated. But in Europe, and especially in the UK (which has had the biggest tradition of running focus groups in people's homes), marketing researchers are embracing the use of the viewing lab. Marketing researchers should not take a dogmatic position, believing that their approach is the most 'correct'. The marketing researcher should be open-minded to learn from focus group practices in different countries and be able to evaluate critically why they have been administered in that way.

Ethics in marketing research

A number of ethical issues related to running focus groups have emerged in this chapter. The focus group can be a direct qualitative research technique where the purpose of the discussion is made clear to participants before it starts. However, the focus group can incorporate observational and projective techniques that introduce elements of indirectness, i.e. elements or all of the purpose of the discussion being hidden from participants. This is where marketing researchers face a real ethical dilemma. If they fully reveal the purpose of their study, would this put off potential participants whose views are important to the success of the study? Even if they do manage to recruit potential participants, the researchers have to consider how they may feel when the real purpose of the study becomes apparent through the nature of the discussion or by the moderator revealing all at the end. The nature of the dilemma faced by marketing researchers is that by revealing too much at the start of the study they may compromise the quality of their discussion. A full revelation may not be conducive to participants reflecting, making new connections and expressing themselves about issues that may be deeply held, difficult to conceive and express.

Researchers should take all reasonable precautions to ensure that participants are in no way adversely affected or embarrassed as a result of the focus group. What is meant by an adverse effect and embarrassment will largely depend upon the issues being explored and how they are perceived by target participants. Some participants may find personal hygiene issues very embarrassing to talk about in a group scenario, but not financial issues. Other individuals may be very frank about their sexual behaviour, while others would be shocked at the notion of talking about sex with a group of strangers. The researchers must get to know how the issues they wish to explore are perceived by their target participants by examining the literature, secondary data and the use of experimental focus groups.

Another major ethical problem that is research issue and participant specific is the use of alcoholic drinks during focus groups. For certain groups of participants, relaxing and socialising in a comfortable context, drinking wine or beer is very natural. Researchers with experience of running many focus groups would argue that serving alcoholic drinks can help to reduce tension in certain participants and give them the confidence to express their particular viewpoint. Other researchers would argue that this is unethical practice, that in effect the researcher is 'drugging' the participants. Whatever the researcher decides is right for the type of participants, the issues he or she is questioning them about and the context in which the discussion takes place, there are practical problems involved with serving alcohol. Controlling the flow of alcohol and how much is given to certain participants may take attention away from the discussion. If control is not exerted, particular participants may get out of hand and disrupt or even destroy the discussion. Researchers could be accused of not taking reasonable precautions to ensure that participants are in no way adversely affected or embarrassed as a result of the focus group, should the use of alcohol be abused by certain participants.

Finally, in no circumstances should researchers use audio or video recording or two-way mirrors in focus groups without gaining the consent of participants. It must be made clear to participants that recording or observation equipment is to be used and why it needs to be used. Participants must then be free to decline any offer to take part in a discussion.

Internet and computer applications

The development of the Internet, the increasing numbers of individuals with access and who are comfortable using the Internet have presented many opportunities to run focus groups online. For online focus groups, virtual facilities can be used, providing the same facilities as real-life facilities including 'rooms' such as a reception room, discussion room and client backroom. Online focus groups can be conducted in two ways: 'real time' or 'non-real time':[30]

- *Real time*. In this method, all participants are online at the same time. The transmission of messages is immediate or as close to immediate as can be. As one participant types in a message, it is transmitted to the group as a whole. Other participants can read the message and can reply as soon as they receive it. Real-time focus groups can be highly interactive with a fast 'passionate' exchange of views. This is the big advantage of real-time groups, that the passion for a subject and the nature of rapid exchange can develop a very creative atmosphere. Participants do not have to wait for others to comment in order to send further messages, so as they have been stimulated to think in particular ways, their thoughts and ideas can flow straight out on to the screen. The drawback is that the participant with the most proficiency at typing has the power to dominate the discussion. Compared with face-to-face focus groups where the moderator and audio and video recordings can track participant statements and the responses stimulated, this cannot be done online in real time. The distinction of replying and sending becomes a blur as participants do not take their turn as they would face to face. This means that much of the structure of conversation is lost.
- *Non-real time*. In this method there is no requirement for participants to be online at the same time. This method is analogous to the use of email. Unlike email, though, this form of focus group is conducted using a 'conference site' as opposed to individual email addresses. Participants can send their views about a particular issue to a conference folder. Messages can be read in real time but this does not usually happen. The reality is that all responses are archived in the folder and can be opened and responded to by other participants. This method of running focus groups can overcome difficulties in running focus groups in different time zones and therefore is an excellent tool in conducting international research. Participants with weak typing skills do not lose their voice or feel intimidated. The major benefit of this approach is that, akin to face-to-face focus groups, participants can 'sit back' and reflect upon how they really feel about an issue. Even better than in face-to-face scenarios, they can take time to express how they really feel about an issue.

Online focus groups have a number of logistical requirements. Depending upon how the online focus group is to be conducted, participants may have to gain access to proprietary conferencing software. Real-time and non-real-time focus groups can operate from particular websites, requiring potential participants to have a web browser and to know the web address from which the group will be run.

In summary, the key benefits of running focus groups online include the following:[31]

- More potential participants can be recruited through the growing use of the Internet, and the growing ease of conducting discussions online.
- Participants can be made to feel that they have the ability to contribute; their confidence can be quickly built up.

→

- Conflicts in face-to-face focus groups that may stem from participants taking a dislike to other participants from their physical appearance can be avoided.
- A great breadth of information may be collected, through the types of participant that can be recruited and the geographic spread of participants.
- The practical difficulties of getting individuals together at the same time in the same location can be overcome.
- The nature of a discussion location that is 'comfortable' to the participant is largely overcome by each participant setting the conditions that they feel comfortable in.

Summary

In direct qualitative methods, participants are able to discern the true purpose of the research, whereas indirect methods disguise the purpose of the research to some extent. Focus groups can be a completely direct qualitative method, though by the use of observational and projective techniques elements of indirectness can be introduced. In deciding how 'direct' a focus group should be, researchers have to face ethical issues and questions related to the richness of data that they can draw from participants. Focus group discussions are the most widely used qualitative research technique.

Focus groups are conducted by a moderator in a relaxed and informal manner with a small group of participants. The moderator leads and develops the discussion. In a focus group, participants can portray their feelings and behaviour, using their own language and logic. The value of the technique lies in the unexpected findings that emerge when participants are allowed to say what they really feel. An experimental focus group should always be run at the start of any series of discussions. The researcher needs to understand how comfortable target participants feel in the chosen location for discussion, how the opening question works, the topic guide, the probes, the mix of participants and the refreshments, including any alcoholic drinks. In a nutshell, one could argue that one should continue running focus groups until nothing new is learned from target participants. This perspective oversimplifies how diverse and spread out different participants may be and how well they mix together in a group situation. The time and budget available will also mean that a cut-off point has to be drawn and the strongest analysis and interpretation has to be made at that point. Developments in the use of the Internet means that group discussions can take place away from the traditional 'viewing' or meeting room. The maxim of participants being relaxed and comfortable with the context and means of communicating still applies.

There are a variety of different styles of running focus groups. The variations and adaptations are used to draw the best out of particular types of participant, tackling particular types of issue. The most significant development in the variation of technique has been afforded by developments in Internet technology and take-up. Participants can be targeted from all over the world, discussing issues online in 'real time' or 'non-real time'. Another factor that affects the style of running focus groups lies in the underlying philosophy for conducting research. American and European styles can be broadly encapsulated as being respectively 'highly structured' or 'highly spontaneous'. There is no one absolute correct method to administer a focus group; the researchers should understand the factors that will make the technique work for their particular research problem and the type of participants they have to work with. A key element of ensuring that the focus group works well lies in the ethical issues of how much is revealed to participants before they get involved and during the discussion. Getting participants to relax and be open may involve the use of alcoholic drinks which for many researchers creates no problems but for some creates ethical and practical problems.

Questions

1. Why may marketing researchers not wish to reveal fully the purpose of a focus group discussion with participants before it starts?

2. What are the key benefits and drawbacks of conducting focus group discussions?

3. What are the difficulties in conducting focus groups with managers or professionals?

4. What determines the questions, issues and probes used in a focus group?

5. Evaluate the purpose of running an experimental focus group discussion.

6. What does a 'comfortable setting' mean in the context of running a focus group?

7. To what extent can a moderator achieve an 'objective detachment' from a focus group discussion?

8. Why is the focus group moderator so important to the success of a focus group discussion?

9. What are the relative advantages and disadvantages of being able to observe covertly a focus group discussion?

10. What can the researcher do to make potential participants want to take part in a focus group?

11. What determines the number of focus groups that should be undertaken in any research project?

12. Describe the purpose and benefits of using stimulus material in a focus group.

13. What is the difference between a dual-moderator and a duelling-moderator group?

14. Describe the opportunities and difficulties that may occur if alcoholic drinks are served during focus group discussions.

15. Evaluate the benefits and limitations of conducting focus group discussions on the Internet.

Exercises

1. Following the methods outlined in this chapter, develop a plan for conducting a focus group study to determine consumers' attitudes towards organic foods. Specify the objectives for the groups, write a screening questionnaire, list potential props or physical stimuli that you could use in the discussion and develop a moderator's outline.

2. Your campus sports centre is trying to recruit more members from the local non-student community. In achieving this aim, evaluate the marketing decisions that could be supported by focus groups, either as a technique in its own right or validated with other techniques.

3. You are a brand manager for Johnny Walker whiskies. You wish to invest in an Internet focus group study of whisky buyers and drinkers. Explain how you would

identify and recruit such respondents from across the globe. What incentive(s) would you offer potential participants?

4. Visit the website of the Association of Qualitative Research Practitioners (**www.aqrp.co.uk**). Examine the reports and views of contributing practitioners and write a report on what you feel are the latest developments and/or exciting opportunities in the use of focus groups.

5. In a small group discuss the following issues: 'The dress, appearance and speech of the moderator create biases in group discussions that cannot be evaluated' and 'Mood boards created in focus groups are more useful to marketing decision-makers compared to a formal written analysis of the discussions'.

Video Case Exercise: Nike

For Nike, how could focus groups have helped in the development of the 'Presto' new product line?

video case

download from www.pearsoned.co.uk/ malhotra_euro

Notes

1 Murphy, D., 'What can be more real than a result?' *Research World* (December 2004), 19.

2 Morgan, D.L. 'Focus group interviewing', in Gulbrium, J.F. and Holstein, J.A. (eds), *Handbook of Interview Research: Context and Method* (Thousand Oaks, CA: Sage, 2002), 141–159.

3 Morgan, D.L. and Krueger, R.A. 'When to use focus groups and why', in Morgan, D.L. (ed.), *Successful focus groups: Advancing the state of the art,* (Newbury Park, CA: Sage, 1993), 3–19.

4 ESOMAR, 'Industry study on 2004', *Esomar World Research Report* (2005), 26.

5 Bloor, M., Frankland, J., Thomas, M. and Robson, K., *Focus groups in Social Research* (Thousand Oaks, CA: Sage, 2001).

6 Kreuger, R.A., and Casey, M.A., *Focus Groups: A practical guide for applied research*, 3rd edn (Thousand Oaks, CA: Sage, 2000); Drayton, J. and Tynan, C., 'Conducting focus groups – a guide for first-time users', *Marketing Intelligence and Planning* 6 (1) (1988), 5–9.

7 For more discussion, see Morgan, D.L., *Planning focus groups* (Thousand Oaks, CA: Sage, 1998), 71–76; Dachler, H.P., 'Qualitative methods in organization research', *Organizational Studies* 18 (4) (1997), 709–724.

8 Forrest, C., 'Research with a laugh track', *Marketing News* 36 (5) (4 March 2002), 48; Mazella, G.F., 'Show-and-tell focus groups reveal core bloomer values', *Marketing News* 31 (12) (9 June 1997), H8.

9 Morgan, D.L. *Planning focus groups* (Thousand Oaks, CA: Sage, 1998), 71–76.

10 MacDougall, C., 'Planning and recruiting the sample for focus groups and in-depth interviews', *Qualitative Health Research* 11 (1) (January 2001), 117–126; Kahn, H., 'A professional opinion', *American Demographics* (Tools Supplement) (October 1996), 14–19.

11 Gordon, W., 'New life for group discussions', *ResearchPlus* (July 1993), 1.

12 O'Donoghue, D., 'Taking the plunge', *Research* (December 2005) 46–47.

13 Krueger, R.A., *Moderating focus groups* (Thousand Oaks, CA: Sage, 1998), 30.

14 Goldsmith, R.E., 'The Focus Group Research Handbook', *The Services Industries Journal* 20 (3) (July 2000), 214–215;

Greenbaum, T.L., *The Handbook for Focus Group Research* (Newbury Park, CA: Sage, 1997).

15 Krueger, R.A., *Developing questions for focus groups* (Thousand Oaks, CA: Sage, 1998), 25.

16 Ellis, R., 'So how do you upstage a Ferrari owner?', *ResearchPlus* (November 1994), 10.

17 Ghosh, S., 'Hypermarkets lead to new shopping habits', *Research World* (November 2004), 32–33.

18 Croft, M., 'Art of the matter', *Marketing Week* (9 October 1997), 71.

19 Ibid.

20 Katcher, B.L., 'Getting answers from the focus group', *Folio: The Magazine for Magazine Management* (Special Sourcebook Issue for 1997 Supplement) 25 (18) (1997), 222; and an adaptation from Chase, D.A., 'The intensive group interviewing in marketing', *MRA Viewpoints* (1973).

21 Silverstein, M., 'Two-way focus groups can provide startling information', *Marketing News* (4 January 1988), 31.

22 Mariampolski, H., *Qualitative marketing Research: A comprehensive guide,* (Thousand Oaks, CA: Sage, 2001), 47.

23 Gallupe, R.B. and Cooper, W.H., 'Brainstorming electronically', *Sloan Management Review* 35 (1) (Fall 1993), 27.

24 Morgan, D.L. *The focus group guidebook* (Thousand Oaks, CA: Sage, 1998), 45–52.

25 Ibid., pp. 52–54.

26 Savage, M., 'Soft focus', *Research* (September 1999), 32–33.

27 Note that the expression 'American' or 'European focus group' does not mean that such methods are exclusively used in these continents. The term is used to show that there is a greater propensity for a particular approach to running a focus group in a particular manner in each of these continents.

28 Sonet, T., 'See the USA, through the looking glass', *ResearchPlus* (June 1994), 6.

29 Dwek, R., 'Through the looking glass', *Marketing* (11 September 1997), 37.

30 Mann, C. and Stewart, F., *Internet Communication and Qualitative Research: A Handbook for Researching Online* (London: Sage, 2000), 101–102.

31 Sweeney, J.C., Soutar, G.N., Hausknecht, D.R., Dallin, R.F. and Johnson, L.W., 'Collection of information from groups: a comparison of two methods', *Journal of the Market Research Society* 39 (2) (April 1997), 397.

Source: © Getty Images

8

Qualitative research: in-depth interviewing and projective techniques

Objectives

After reading this chapter, you should be able to:

1 understand why the in-depth interview is defined as a direct qualitative research technique and observation and projective techniques are defined as indirect techniques;

2 describe in-depth interview techniques in detail, citing their advantages, disadvantages and applications;

3 explain how theory may be used to create structure to questioning and analysis in in-depth interviewing by reference to the laddering technique and the repertory grid technique;

4 describe projective techniques in detail and compare association, completion, construction and expressive techniques;

5 understand the language problems that should be considered by international qualitative researchers;

6 understand the ethical dilemmas faced by qualitative research practitioners.

| STAGE 1 Problem definition | STAGE 2 Research approach developed | STAGE 3 Research design developed | STAGE 4 Fieldwork or data collection | STAGE 5 Data preparation and analysis | STAGE 6 Report preparation and presentation |

Overview

Having discussed qualitative research in terms of its nature and approach, and evaluated focus groups as the main marketing research technique, we now move on to describe and evaluate other qualitative techniques.

We start by describing and evaluating what is meant by an in-depth interview and the procedure of in-depth interviewing. The role of the in-depth interviewer is described and the advantages and disadvantages of the technique are summarised. In the process of conducting in-depth interviews, the techniques of 'laddering' and 'repertory grid' can be applied to help to structure the elicitation and analysis process. Laddering and repertory grid techniques will be described and illustrated. The indirect qualitative association, completion, construction and expressive projective techniques are described and illustrated. The applications of these techniques are detailed, followed by an evaluation of their advantages and disadvantages. This is developed into an overall summary of the relative strengths and weaknesses of qualitative techniques under the headings of 'focus groups', 'in-depth interviews', 'projective techniques' and 'ethnographic techniques'.

The following example illustrates a subject that for some individuals is difficult to discuss in a group: personal hygiene issues and even their fantasies when bathing. The subject requires a qualitative technique to generate data of a kind that will support creative advertising decisions. The subject matter, however, is ideal for the application of in-depth interviews and projective techniques where time can be spent building trust and rapport between the interviewer and participant. In-depth interviews allow participants talking about bathing the time and space to express ideas about everyday events that normally they just get on with and do not have to explain or rationalise to anyone!

| Example | Soaps look for a fresh way to work consumers into a lather[1] |

In studies of bath soaps, participants invariably say that a good soap makes them feel 'clean and fresh'. However, they often have difficulty explaining what 'clean and fresh' means. Copywriters trying to find a new way to talk about freshness in their advertising do not find such results supportive or relevant to the decisions they have to take. Hence, participants have been probed on a one-to-one basis through in-depth interviews about all the things 'clean and fresh' meant to them: the times they felt this way, their mental pictures, the moods and feelings connected with it, what music and colours come to mind, and even what fantasies it evoked.

Escape from ordinary life was one of the main themes that emerged from the in-depth interviews – getting away from the cramped rushed city to the free, relaxed, unhindered life, surrounded by nature, in the countryside. The words and images sparked by this theme offered new ideas for creative advertising ideas.

In-depth interviews

The meaning of 'in-depth'

An **in-depth interview** is an unstructured, direct, personal interview in which a single participant is probed by an experienced interviewer to uncover underlying motivations, beliefs, attitudes and feelings on a topic.[2] It is a qualitative interview and as such is based upon conversation, with the emphasis on researchers asking questions and listening, and participants answering.[3] The purpose of most qualitative interviews is to derive meaning through interpretations, not necessarily 'facts' from participant talk. The emphasis should be upon a full interaction to understand the meaning of the participant's experiences and life worlds.[4] In order to tap into these experiences and life worlds, in-depth interviewing involves a certain style of social and interpersonal interaction. In order to be effective and useful, in-depth interviews develop and build upon intimacy; in this respect, they resemble the forms of talking one finds among close friends. They can resemble friendship, and may even lead to long-term friendship. They are also very different from the nature of talking one finds between friends, mainly because the interviewer seeks to use the information obtained in the interaction for some other purpose.[5] As the name implies, in-depth interviewing seeks 'deep' information and understanding. The word 'deep' has four meanings in this context.[6] These meanings will be illustrated with a scenario of a researcher trying to understand the Ebay (**www.ebay.com**) shopping experience:

1 **Everyday events.** Deep understandings are held by the participants in some everyday activity, event or place. The interviewer seeks to achieve the same deep level of knowledge or understanding as the participants. For example, if the interviewer has never used Ebay to buy or sell goods and this experience is what is being investigated, in-depth interviewing can be used as a way to learn the meanings of participants' actions. In this respect, the participant acts as a kind of teacher and the interviewer a student, one interested in learning the ropes.

2 **Context.** Deep understandings go beyond common-sense explanations of some cultural form, activity, event, place or artefact. In-depth interviewing aims to explore contextual boundaries to uncover what is usually hidden from ordinary view and to penetrate the more reflexive understandings about the nature of that experience. In an Ebay investigation, the interviewer can explore the meanings of different shopping experiences, the thrill of 'winning' a deal, and the 'joy' of owning a particular artefact, to name but a few contextual boundaries.

3 **Multi-faceted.** Deep understandings allow multiple views and perspectives on and meanings of some activity, event, place or cultural object. The researcher may wish to explore the many perspectives of Ebay buyers and sellers, family members who 'enjoy' or 'suffer' Ebay transactions in their household, executives who manage Ebay, Ebay competitors, high-street retailers, again to name but a few facets of the total experience.

4 **Interviewer reflection.** Deep understandings can help to reveal the interviewer's common-sense assumptions, practices, ways of talking and self-interests. This issue will be developed in Chapter 9. In this example, however, if the interviewer traditionally buys goods from the high street, wanting to examine the goods before buying, or has not conducted an Internet transaction, what will he or she 'see' or 'hear' in a particular in-depth interview? This situation mirrors children–parent relationships. Children do not learn what their parents tell them, but what they are prepared and ready to hear. The same holds for in-depth interviewers: researchers do not necessarily 'hear' what their informants tell them, but only what their own intellectual, social, cultural and ethical development has prepared them to hear.

Going deep into the minds of consumers is a learning process. Researchers make mistakes; they sometimes say the wrong things or upset participants in some way. They learn that their race, age, gender, social class, appearance or voice makes one kind of difference with some participants and another kind of difference with other informants.[7] The lesson from this is that there is no 'ideal' means to conduct the in-depth interview. Researchers learn from their experiences, discovering strengths and playing to them, realising weaknesses and understanding how to compensate for them. In this spirit of experimentation and learning we present a procedure that encapsulates how a marketing researcher may approach the in-depth interview.

Procedure

To illustrate the technique, a scenario is set whereby the researcher is interviewing the marketing director of a soap manufacturer that has successfully sponsored a major athletics event. The sponsorship has resulted in many industry awards, increased sales and better employee–employer relations. The researcher wishes to understand why the soap manufacturer became involved in the sponsorship and how it achieved such success.

The in-depth interview with this busy executive may take from 30 minutes to well over an hour. It may occur on a one-off basis or it may unfold over a number of meetings as more understanding is developed. Once the interviewer has gained access to the marketing director (which can be very problematic, why should he or she give up valuable time and share commercial knowledge?), the interviewer should begin by explaining the purpose of the interview, showing what both will get out of taking part in the interview and explaining what the process will be like. Beyond the introduction the interviewer may ask the marketing director a general introductory question such as 'what impacts have the industry awards had upon your business?' The interviewer would be expected to have done their homework to know what the awards were, what they were awarded for and who the manufacturer was competing against. This is a very positive feature of the sponsorship experience, and it would be hoped to boost the ego of the marketing director and encourage them to talk freely about the different impacts of the awards. The impact of sponsorship could be upon existing and potential new customers, employees and suppliers. The discussion could then flow into any of these areas. After asking the initial question, the interviewer uses an unstructured format, guided by a topic guide as a reminder of important subject areas to cover. The subsequent direction of the interview is determined by the participant's initial reply, the interviewer's probes for elaboration and the participant's answers.

As with the focus group topic guide and the moderator managing that guide, spontaneity ensures that the process is creative and meaningful to the participant. Suppose that the participant replies to the initial question by saying

> The award for the 'best use of sponsorship' in the launch of a new product gave us the most satisfaction. It has made us review how we execute all of our new product launches and integrate our different marketing agencies, our employees and supply chains.

The interviewer might then pose a question such as 'was it the award that initiated the review or would you have done that anyway?' If the answer is not very revealing, e.g. 'we may have', the interviewer may ask a probing question, such as 'what did the award tell you about how you worked as a team?' This question could open up a whole series of issues such as 'trust', 'relationship development' or 'technical support', to name a few. Such an exchange of questions and answers could emerge from a heading of '*Integrating sponsorship with other marketing communications*' on the topic guide. The interviewer will keep an eye on the topic guide to ensure that all the important issues are tackled, but the specific wording of the questions and the order in which they are asked is influenced by the participant's replies.

Probing is of critical importance in obtaining meaningful responses and uncovering hidden issues. Probing can be done by asking general questions such as 'why do you say that?', 'that's interesting, can you tell me more?' or 'would you like to add anything else?'[8] Probing can search for general issues but also be more specific, an example in the above scenario being 'what does good teamwork mean to you?' One of the main success factors of specific probing is that the researcher understands something about the nature of the subject being researched. This means the researcher appreciates the significance of particular revelations, understands the language (even technical language and jargon in certain areas, like the soap industry) and has a credibility with the participant that encourages him or her to open up to the interviewer.

The interviewer must be alert to the issues to go through but also the issues that the participant is willing to talk about, and must listen carefully to and observe which issues fire enthusiasm in the participant. The questions and probes the interviewer puts to participants should follow the interest and logic of the participants, making them feel motivated to respond in a manner that suits them. As with a focus group discussion, the participants should feel comfortable and relaxed, which could mean holding the interview in their office, their home, a bar, a sports club – any context in which they will feel comfortable and more willing to be reflective, honest and open. Answering in a manner that suits the participant helps to make the interview more comfortable and relaxed. For a great amount of business research, the in-depth interview is the best way to gain access and to talk to managers. Much of the interviewing takes place in their office at a time that is convenient to them. Researchers can also observe characteristics of the manager in his or her office environment that can be of help in their analyses. Examples of this could be levels of formality in the workplace, reports and books that the manager has for reference, the manager's use of IT equipment, or the tidiness of the workplace. In the example above, it could be how awards are displayed, photographs from advertisements, displays of new products. These observations would be entirely based upon the purpose of the study, but the context of the office can be of help to the manager and the researcher. In order to make the above process work, the interviewer should:

1 Do his or her utmost to develop an empathy with the participant.
2 Make sure the participant is relaxed and comfortable.
3 Be personable to encourage and motivate participants.
4 Note issues that interest the participant and develop questions around these issues.
5 Not be happy to accept brief 'yes' or 'no' answers.
6 Note where participants have not explained clearly enough issues that need probing.

In marketing research that focuses upon managers or professionals as illustrated above, the context of the in-depth interview helps to set the frame of mind of the participant. The context should also help the participant and interviewer to relax, engendering an atmosphere to explore and develop issues that they feel to be relevant. The following arguments help to focus on the issues faced by the interviewer coping with managers and professionals, trying to find the right context to allow these participants to express how they really feel.[9] The in-depth interview helps to overcome:

1 *Hectic schedules.* The best participants tend also to be the busiest and most successful people. They can make time for an interview, but are rarely able to spare the much greater time needed for them to come to a group discussion at some location away from their office. So groups exclude the best participants.
2 *Heterogeneity.* Whereas mothers evaluating nappy ads, or beer drinkers the latest lager, have only their personal preferences to consider, it is very different for executives evaluating copiers, airline advertisements or computer software. This is because their reactions are complicated by the type of job they do and who they work for. The group discussion

is dependent on the group's composition being fairly homogeneous; the job backgrounds of business people make them too varied to be entirely comfortable in a group.

3 *Live context.* A lot of information comes from seeing the participant at his or her desk, which is missed in a group discussion. Work schedules pinned to the wall, the working atmosphere, the freebies from suppliers on the desk, the way coffee is served, all help to fill out the picture.

4 *Interviewer reflection.* Groups do not allow the researcher enough thinking time. Two groups, each taking an hour and a half over successive evenings, do not even begin to compare with two or three full days of non-stop interviewing. Individual interviews give much more scope for experimentation. If one way does not work, it is only one participant, not a whole group, that is affected.

Another major application of in-depth interviews where the context of the interview plays a major part, is in the interviewing of children. Researchers into children and teenagers spend considerable time working out the best research approach. Debates proliferate on the most appropriate research designs and interviewing techniques: in-depth interviews versus group, mini groups versus standard groups, friendship pairs versus stranger groups, association projective techniques versus expressive, and so on. These debates make researchers focus on the implications of how research is conducted and which technique provides the best results. One vital element is often overlooked, and that is the issue of context: in other words, the need to ensure that the situation in which children are interviewed is relevant to the research needs.

Like adults, children have multi-faceted personalities. The same teenager can be sullen at home, obstructive in the classroom, but the life and soul of the peer group. The essential difference between children and adults, however, is the extent to which different aspects of the persona can be accessed on one occasion and in one situation, the research setting. Adults have insight into the different roles and behaviour, which they adopt in different contexts, and can project other aspects of themselves which they bring into the research situation. Children and young teenagers, on the other hand, react to the moment and thus project only one aspect of themselves. They lack the maturity, experience and self-knowledge to draw on other parts of themselves and therefore find it almost impossible to know, let alone admit or explore, how they might behave in another circumstance.[10]

The above evaluation of the importance of context also shows that question formulation, the very heart of marketing research, can be more important in interviewing children than when dealing with adults. A straightforward 'what do you think about X?' may throw children into confusion. A formulation such as 'if you were to call your friends about this, what would you tell them?' would be more likely to produce illuminating responses. An innovative approach to interviewing children is illustrated in the following example.

Example   Quantifying the emotional aspects of advertising[11]

In order to understand how to 'talk' to children we need to find ways to connect to them, and hence explore what it is like to be a 10 year old. The way Quæstor (**www.quaestor.co.uk**) goes about researching children taps into the very areas where they are not adults. It is about how we as adults adapt to who they are, finding a way to engage with every child, and building a bridge to help us reach their world. A good starting point is often an awareness of the skills they have developed in school, using these as the building blocks for the technique. So, rather than asking a child a direct question, which more often than not will result in a long blank look, we can ask children to draw a picture, or select a photograph, or even write a story that simply relates to the question we are trying to ask. Children react well to this approach and find the prop easy to talk around, often giving the researchers more than they hoped for.

On a project for Cartoon Network, a child depicted in a picture one of the pressures of the fierce consumer society we live. The picture was about exclusion and showed a group of boys; outside the group, another boy was crying. On closer inspection it was not the boy crying that told the story, but why he was doing so. A Nike tick was distinctly missing from his trainers.

Friendship pair
A technique used to interview children as two friends or classmates together.

An effective technique when working with children is the use of **friendship pairs** – interviewing two friends or classmates together. This helps to cut out lying because children are not alone with strangers and because if one tells a lie, the other tells on them. The ingrained honesty of children arguably makes them easier to research than adults, who of course are far more accomplished exponents of deception.

Advantages and challenges of in-depth interviews

In-depth interviews have the following advantages. They can:

- Uncover a greater depth of insights than focus groups. This can happen through concentrating and developing an issue with the individual. In the group scenario, interesting and knowledgeable individuals cannot be solely concentrated upon.
- Attribute the responses directly to the participant, unlike focus groups where it is often difficult to determine which participant made a particular response.
- Result in a free exchange of information that may not be possible in focus groups because there is no social pressure to conform to group response. This makes them ideally suited to sensitive issues, especially commercially sensitive issues.
- Be easier to arrange than the focus group as there are not so many individuals to co-ordinate and the interviewer can travel to the participant.

The following are not necessarily disadvantages, but really the challenges that researchers face when using this very valuable technique:

1 The lack of structure makes the results susceptible to the interviewer's influence, and the quality and completeness of the results depend heavily on the interviewer's skills. As with all qualitative techniques, the interviewer needs to develop an awareness of the factors that make him or her 'see' in a particular way.

2 The length of the interview, combined with high costs, means that the number of in-depth interviews in a project tends to be few. If few in-depth interviews can be managed, the researcher should focus upon the quality of the whole research experience. 'Quality' in this context means the qualities that the participant possesses in terms of richness of experience and how relevant the experiences are to the study; the quality of drawing out and getting participants to express themselves clearly and honestly; and the quality of analysis in terms of interpretation of individual participants and individual issues evaluated across all the interviews conducted.

3 The data obtained can be difficult to analyse and interpret. Many responses may not be taken at face value; there can be many hidden messages and interpretations in how participants express themselves. The researcher needs a strong theoretical awareness to make sense of the data or the technical means to develop theory if using a grounded theory approach. As well as the transcripts of the interview, additional observations add to the richness and multi-faceted analyses and potential interpretations.

The following technique illustrates how a theoretical awareness can help to develop structure, elicit or draw more out of participants and help to make sense of the data they generate. It is an illustration of how the three challenges outlined above can be overcome.

The laddering technique

The in-depth interview can be driven by a topic guide, made up of just a few topics covering a very broad range of issues. From these few topics, the nature of questions, the order of questions and the nature of probes can be driven by the interviewer's perception of what will draw the best out of participants. Alternatively, an in-depth interview can be semi-structured where parts of the interview use consistent and highly structured questions, with set response categories, interspersed with open-ended questions involving probes that again suit the nature of the participant. There are other variations on the technique that can help the interviewer and participant to apply useful structure to issues that can be very 'messy' and unstructured. One of the most popular techniques to apply structure is called **laddering**. Laddering requires interviewers to be trained in specific probing techniques in order to develop a meaningful 'mental map' of the consumer's view towards a particular product. The ultimate goal is to combine mental maps of consumers who are similar, which lead to the reasons why people purchase particular products.

Laddering
A technique for conducting in-depth interviews in which a line of questioning proceeds from product characteristics to user characteristics.

The laddering technique is made up of a linking or ladder of elements that represent the link between products and the consumer's perception process. It enables an understanding of how consumers translate product attributes, through personal meanings associated with them.[12] Theories of consumer behaviour act as a foundation to this approach, based on the contention that consumption acts produce consequences for the consumer. Consumers learn to associate these consequences to specific product attributes. These associations are reinforced through consumers' buying behaviour and, as a result, they learn to choose products that have certain attributes in order to obtain the consequences they desire. There are two features of this theory that the researcher using laddering technique will focus upon:

1 *Motivation.* The laddering technique focuses upon generating insight to the motives behind the consumption of certain products. It represents a more contemporary approach to classical motivation research.[13] The technique aims to stimulate participants to reflect upon their buying behaviour in a way unconnected from their usual behaviour.
2 *Cognitive structure.* This feature is also a development of theory, in this case means–end–chain (MEC), developed by Guttman.[14] MEC starts from a point of consumer motivation. It contends that motivation leading towards a form of behaviour is derived from the connection between tangible product attributes and more abstract cognitive structures that involve the physical and emotional consequences derived from these attributes. At a more abstract level, the consequences lead to values held by the consumer.

The laddering technique is therefore designed to identify and follow the chain of

$$\text{attributes} \rightarrow \text{consequences} \rightarrow \text{values (A–C–V)}$$

The in-depth interview using the laddering technique is based on comparisons of the consumer's choice alternatives. These can include, for example, different products used for the same purpose, such as an electric toothbrush and a conventional toothbrush, and/or varieties in a product line such as full-fat and skimmed milk, and/or product brands such as Heineken and Amstel beer, and/or kinds of packaging such as wine in bottles and in cartons. Other elements that can affect consumer choices can be added to the above list. In making the comparisons, the interviewer poses a question that hopes to encourage the participants to put aside their established rationale and reflect upon their consumption behaviour, in ways that they would not normally do. In other words, questions are posed that make participants think about consumption from other points of view to try to release participants from fixed attitudes, perceptions and values. The interviewer's role is to build up a rapport with participants and get them to relax and feel comfortable to respond with whatever comes to mind. The interview revolves around three basic questions based on the A–C–V chain. The questions posed would be:

1 *Values*. How important is this for you? (e.g. health)
2 *Consequences*. What does this difference mean? (e.g. not fattening)
3 *Attributes*. What is different about these alternatives? (e.g. low calories)

From the attribute of 'low calories' in comparing different product varieties in a product line such as full-fat and skimmed milk, a further and negative consequence of 'watery taste' could be elicited, followed by the values of 'unnatural'. The interviewer aims to build a great repertoire of chains through these levels spontaneously, choosing the right comparisons to draw out the next link in the chain. The resulting responses are analysed to establish possible categories of attributes, consequences and values. The categories are then organised according to the qualitative comments made between the relationship of an attribute, its consequence and value. The result is an association matrix that graphically displays the categories and the connections that have emerged.

Laddering requires an interviewer with experience of in-depth interviewing, with a realisation of what will relax participants and get them in a frame of mind to 'play' with the associations sought. The interviewer needs to appreciate the theoretical foundations of the technique,[15] not only to help determine what should be elicited from participants, but also to help generate sound and meaningful analyses. The following example illustrates the consumer insights and marketing implications that emerged through the use of laddering.

Example **Climbing the ladder to PlayStation2 success[16]**

The laddering technique was used to determine consumer attitudes and purchasing motivations towards the Sony PlayStation2 (**www.scea.com**). The key laddering insights for this product included:

- My friends come over and we spend an evening working together through a game or playing against each other.
- Challenging games require more critical thinking and decision making. It feels more like a puzzle than a game.
- Some games are suited to adults only, so I don't feel like I'm playing a 'kids' game, but taking part in a high-quality gaming experience.

The marketing implications that emerged from these insights include:

- Set up kiosks in large cities to attract adults.
- Advertise through programmes such as *Friends* with Joey and Chandler playing games on a PlayStation2.
- Target magazines such as *Wired* and *Sports Illustrated* with more mature advertisements.

The insights generated helped to develop further research at Sony and helped with creative marketing decisions in all aspects of designing products, distribution, pricing and promotions.

The repertory grid technique

Another widely used technique that applies structure to qualitative in-depth interviewing is the repertory grid technique (RGT). This technique was originally developed by George Kelly in 1955[17] to explore the meanings that people attach to the world around them, which they find particularly hard to articulate. As with the laddering technique, there is a theoretical underpinning, personal construct psychology.[18] Given the debate around this theory, there are a number of variations of the technique and arguments about whether it should be implemented and analysed in a positivist or interpretivist manner,[19] but in essence the stages involved in the repertory grid technique are:

1 Element selection
2 Construct elicitation
3 Element comparisons
4 Data analysis.

Element selection. The elements selected will depend upon the nature of consumer behaviour that the interviewer wishes to examine. In a study that wished to understand *broad-based patterns of consumer behaviour*[20] the elements chosen included 30 generic products and services such as newspapers, holidays, chocolate bars, eggs, alcoholic drinks, shoes, toothpaste, savings accounts, restaurant meals and shampoo. In another study that wished to understand *the process of effective new product development*[21] the elements chosen included 30 successful new products and services such as Slim Fast, Pull Ups, Loed Tea, Ultraglide, Baby Jogger, Gourmet Coffee, Zantac, Paragliders, MTV and Carmen Soft. These elements should be chosen by the participants, not just chosen and presented by the interviewer. There should be some homogeneity in the elements in the sense that the participant sees the elements relating to and representative of the behaviour being studied.

Construct elicitation. Having selected elements that the participant believes to encapsulate the behaviour being studied, the interviewer now seeks to understand what connects them together. The first stage of this involves the interviewer selecting three of the chosen elements at random and then presenting to the participant small cards with a summary of these elements. The participant is then asked to describe how he or she sees two of the three to be alike and how the third may be different. The researcher selects different 'triads' to the point where all the elements have been contrasted or the participant cannot describe further 'similarities' or 'differences'. Construct elicitation therefore draws out the participant's perspective of the important features that encapsulate a particular form of consumer behaviour.

Element comparisons. The constructs elicited from participants are now turned into bipolar descriptions in a manner similar to the semantic differential scale described and illustrated in Chapter 12. For example, suppose that in a study of *the process of effective new product development*, three elements were compared: MTV, Gourmet Coffee and Paragliders. The participant may say that MTV and Gourmet Coffee are alike in that there are many similar competitive products that they can be compared with, whereas Paragliders is different in that there are few competitive 'personal' means to fly long distances. Whether this is factually correct or whether the interviewer agrees with this is immaterial; it is how the participant sees it that is important. Such a belief could be turned into a bipolar scale as illustrated below:

| No other products like this in the market | — — — — — — — (1) (2) (3) (4) (5) (6) (7) | Lots of competitive products |

Other scales would be constructed to cover the ways that participants compared the chosen elements, i.e. the constructs elicited would be turned into a series of bipolar scales. Participants would then be expected to evaluate all the original elements using these scales. If they felt that Gourmet Coffee has many competitors they could tick a line at the (6) or (7) point. So, if there were 30 elements that encapsulate the behaviour under study and 20 constructs elicited to evaluate these elements, a total of 30 × 20 or 600 ratings would need to be performed.

Data analysis. A grid can be assembled for each participant to represent in the above example the 30 × 20 ratings. Again, an illustration of this comes from a small extract of *the process of effective new product development* study. The following represents an extract of the total response from one participant:

Construct	MTV	Gourmet Coffee	Paragliders
Market newness	6	6	2
Company newness	3	7	1
Technology newness	2	4	6

With a number of these completed grids, factor analysis (Chapter 22) can be performed to discover the important underlying factors or dimensions that encapsulate a particular form of behaviour.[22] The analysis can continue by performing cluster analysis (Chapter 23) to explore patterns of similarity or dissimilarity in different types of participant, i.e. to discover and describe groups of participants who may view particular forms of behaviour in similar ways.

The above process can take a great deal of time to select the elements, to elicit the means to compare the elements and to evaluate them. It requires an amount of rapport between the interviewer and the participant and patience in working through the stages. All of the stages may not be completed in one interview. It may require the interviewer to return to the participant to develop the next stage, especially in transferring the elicited elements to bipolar descriptions to allow all the elements to be evaluated.

The Zaltman metaphor elicitation technique

Another technique that creates a 'mental map' of the consumer's view towards a particular product is the Zaltman metaphor elicitation technique (ZMET). It is a qualitative in-depth technique that is used by companies such as Procter & Gamble, AT&T, Kodak, Ford and General Motors. It was developed at the Harvard Business School by Professor Jerry Zaltman and is patented in the USA. The technique uses images and metaphors to reveal how consumers think and feel about brands, issues or other research topics. It does not ask consumers 'what they think about the things researchers think about'. Instead, it lets respondents' own frames of reference shape the in-depth interview, without losing sight of the research aims. The technique and its application are illustrated in the following example.

Source: © Alamy

Example Diving for pearls[23]

ZMET allows the participant to define the frame of reference for an interview. The use of metaphor is extremely effective in revealing submerged thoughts and feelings and specifically in allowing access to the emotional domain. Respondents are given a question a few days before their actual interview, and asked to source (non-literal) images reflecting their feelings. For example, in a study of looking at how people choose which financial products to buy and which suppliers to use, one respondent brought in a picture of two dogs, a fully grown Saint Bernard towering over a tiny Chihuahua, to express his feeling of being intimidated by large companies. This period of reflection brings tacit knowledge to the surface. At an in-depth interview, participants explain the significance of each image and how it relates to the question. Probing for clarification, cause and consequence reveals the meaning behind each idea and the connections between ideas. The results reveal the consumers' mindset: the issues most salient to them and the thoughts and feelings they attach to each issue. In ZMET, the main ideas are coded and mapped by Metaphoria, proprietary software that shows the links between them. The result is a consensus map of 'the mind of the market'. Although product performance remains central to this map, the process also allows highly emotional outcomes, such as confidence, joy, fear and alienation to emerge.

ZMET aims to understand the images and associations that underpin both spoken and tacit thoughts and feelings through the elicitation of both rational and emotional thinking. The process especially allows the emotional aspects of products and their use to shine through. The resultant analysis creates a graphical visualisation of the 'mind of the market'. This visualisation creates a link between consumer perceptions and those involved in creative activities of product design and marketing communications. Such an approach accelerates the creative process and helps design and advertising agencies to add more emotional value to their work.

Applications of in-depth interviews

Applying in-depth interviews, with high or low levels of structure, with a strong theoretical foundation such as laddering, the repertory grid technique or ZMET, or with the desire to generate grounded theory, presents challenges but also many rewards. There are many marketing decisions that can be made with support from marketing researchers using the broad array of techniques under the heading of 'in-depth interviews'. The following summarises the applications:[24]

1. Interviews with professional people (e.g. finance directors using banking services).
2. Interviews with children (e.g. attitudes towards a theme park).
3. Interviews with elite individuals (e.g. wealthy individuals involved in large philanthropic ventures).
4. Detailed probing of the participant (e.g. new product development for cars).
5. Discussion of confidential, sensitive or embarrassing topics (e.g. personal hygiene issues).
6. Situations where strong social norms exist and where the participant may be easily swayed by group response (e.g. attitudes of university students towards sports).
7. Detailed understanding of habitual or tacit behaviour (e.g. the route a consumer may take around a supermarket).
8. Detailed understanding of complicated behaviour (e.g. the purchase of fashion or 'high-status' goods).
9. Interviews with competitors who are unlikely to reveal the information in a group setting (e.g. travel agents' perceptions of airline travel packages).
10. Situations where the product consumption experience is sensory in nature, affecting mood states and emotions (e.g. perfumes, bath soap).

In the application of in-depth interviews, the researcher can use other techniques to help maintain the interest of participants, to make the experience more enjoyable for the participants and the researcher alike, and ultimately to draw out the true feelings of participants. A set of techniques that help to achieve all this, that have been applied with great success over many years, is the body of indirect techniques called 'projective techniques'.

Projective techniques

Projective technique
An unstructured and indirect form of questioning that encourages participants to project their underlying motivations, beliefs, attitudes or feelings regarding the issues of concern.

Projective techniques are a category of exercises designed to provoke imagination and creativity that can be used in in-depth interviews. A projective technique is an unstructured, indirect form of questioning that encourages participants to project their underlying motivations, beliefs, attitudes or feelings regarding the issues of concern.[25] They are useful techniques for drawing out emotional values, exploring issues in a non-linear manner or for bypassing participants' rational controls. They also help participants to verbalise unframed, subconscious, low-salience or low-involvement attitudes.[26] In projective techniques, participants are asked to interpret the behaviour of others rather than to describe their own behaviour. In interpreting the behaviour of others, it is contended that participants indirectly project their own motivations, beliefs, attitudes or feelings into the situation. Thus, the participants' attitudes are uncovered by analysing their responses to scenarios that are deliberately unstructured, vague and ambiguous. The more ambiguous the situation, the more participants project their emotions, needs, motives, attitudes and values, as demonstrated by work in clinical psychology on which projective techniques are based.[27] As in psychology, these techniques are classified as association, completion, construction and expressive. Each of these classifications is discussed below.[28]

Association techniques

Association technique
A type of projective technique in which participants are presented with a stimulus and are asked to respond with the first thing that comes to mind.

Word association
A projective technique in which participants are presented with a list of words, one at a time. After each word, they are asked to give the first word that comes to mind.

In **association techniques**, an individual is presented with a stimulus and asked to respond with the first thing that comes to mind. Word association is the best known of these techniques. In **word association**, participants are presented with a list of words, one at a time, and encouraged to respond without deliberation to each with the first word that comes to mind. The words of interest, called test words, are interspersed throughout the list, which also contains some neutral, or filler, words to disguise the purpose of the study. For example, in the Sports Marketing Surveys – Racetrack Project, individual Formula One teams may be examined with test words such as competitive, dangerous, inspirational, elitist, sexy. The subject's response to each word is recorded verbatim and responses are timed so that participants who hesitate or reason out (defined as taking longer than 3 seconds to reply) can be identified. The interviewer, not the participant, records the responses.

The underlying assumption of this technique is that association allows participants to reveal their inner feelings about the topic of interest. Responses are analysed by calculating:

1 The frequency with which any word is given as a response.
2 The amount of time that elapses before a response is given.
3 The number of participants who do not respond at all to a test word within a reasonable period.

Those who do not respond at all are judged to have an emotional involvement so high that it blocks a response. It is often possible to classify the associations as favourable, unfavourable or neutral. An individual's pattern of responses and the details of the response are used to determine the person's underlying attitudes or feelings on the topic of interest, as shown in the following example.

| Example | Dealing with dirt |

Word association was used to study women's attitudes towards detergents. Below is a list of stimulus words used and the responses of two women of similar age and household status. The sets of responses are quite different, suggesting that the women differ in personality and in their attitudes towards housekeeping. Ms M's associations suggest that she is resigned to dirt. She sees dirt as inevitable and does not do much about it. She does not do hard cleaning, nor does she get much pleasure from her family. Ms C sees dirt too, but is energetic, factual minded and less emotional. She is actively ready to combat dirt, and she uses soap and water as her weapons.[29]

Stimulus	Ms M	Ms C
Washday	Everyday	Ironing
Fresh	And sweet	Clean
Pure	Air	Soiled
Scrub	Does not; husband does	Clean
Filth	This neighbourhood	Dirt
Bubbles	Bath	Soap and water
Family	Squabbles	Children
Towels	Dirty	Wash

These findings suggest that the market for detergents could be segmented based on attitudes. Firms (such as Procter & Gamble) that market several different brands of washing powders and detergents could benefit from positioning different brands for different attitudinal segments.

There are several variations to the standard word association procedure illustrated here. Participants may be asked to give the first two, three or four words that come to mind rather than only the first word. This technique can also be used in controlled tests, as contrasted with free association. In controlled tests, participants might be asked 'what Formula one teams come to mind first when I mention "boring"?' More detailed information can be obtained from completion techniques, which are a natural extension of association techniques.

Completion techniques

Completion technique
A projective technique that requires participants to complete an incomplete stimulus situation.

In **completion techniques**, participants are asked to complete an incomplete stimulus situation. Common completion techniques in marketing research are sentence completion and story completion.

Sentence completion is similar to word association. Participants are given incomplete sentences and are asked to complete them. Generally, they are asked to use the first word or phrase that comes to mind, as illustrated in the context of the Sports Marketing Surveys – Racetrack Project*.

Sentence completion
A projective technique in which participants are presented with a number of incomplete sentences and are asked to complete them.

This example illustrates one advantage of sentence completion over word association: participants can be provided with a more directed stimulus. Sentence completion may provide more information about the subjects' feelings than word association. Sentence completion is not as disguised as word association, however, and many participants may be able to guess the purpose of the study. A variation of sentence completion is paragraph completion, in which the participant completes a paragraph beginning with the stimulus phrase. A further expanded version of sentence completion and paragraph completion is story completion.

Story completion
A projective technique in which participants are provided with part of a story and are required to give the conclusion in their own words.

In **story completion**, participants are given part of a story, enough to direct attention to a particular topic but not to hint at the ending. They are required to give the conclusion in their own words, as in the following example.

* The Racetrack Project did not use Projective Techniques. The examples presented illustrate how this could have been applied.

Focus on · Sports Marketing Surveys – Racetrack Project

Sentence completion

A Formula One fan that supports a team rather than a driver is _____
_____

A sponsor who selects drivers based on how competitive they are is _____
_____

The Ferrari team is most preferred by _____
_____

When I think of watching Formula One on television, I _____
_____

Focus on · Sports Marketing Surveys – Racetrack Project

Story completion

The marketing director of a bank had championed the sponsorship of a Formula One team for 10 years. A new chief executive has been appointed and he believes that the sponsorship is just an excuse for senior executives to party at the bank's expense. He wants to see a measurable impact in terms of sales for any sponsorship activity. The marketing director has tried to defend the Formula One sponsorship in terms of corporate image development in being associated with the sport. She has also pointed out the impact of hospitality events upon major clients and other stakeholders that are important to the bank. She has tried to get the next chief executive to attend the Monaco Grand Prix, but is having great difficulty.

What should the Marketing Director do? _____

Why? _____

The participants' completion of this story could reveal characteristics of successful sponsorship that may not be measurable. It could examine why, after such a lengthy relationship, the bank should explore other sponsorship activities. The relationship between the marketing director and the chief executive could be explored as could many directions and facets of the sponsor relationship.

Construction techniques

Construction technique
A projective technique in which participants are required to construct a response in the form of a story, dialogue or description.

Picture response technique
A projective technique in which participants are shown a picture and are asked to tell a story describing it.

Construction techniques are closely related to completion techniques. Construction techniques require the participants to construct a response in the form of a story, dialogue or description. In a construction technique, the researcher provides less initial structure to the participants than in a completion technique. The two main construction techniques are picture response techniques and cartoon tests.

The roots of **picture response techniques** can be traced to the thematic apperception test (TAT), which consists of a series of pictures of ordinary as well as unusual events. In some of these pictures, the persons or objects are clearly depicted, while in others they are relatively vague. The participant is asked to tell stories about these pictures. The participant's interpretation of the pictures gives indications of that individual's personality. For example, an individual may be characterised as impulsive, creative, unimaginative, and so on. The term 'thematic apperception test' is used because themes are elicited based on the subject's perceptual interpretation (apperception) of pictures.

In **cartoon tests**, cartoon characters are shown in a specific situation related to the problem. Participants are asked to indicate what one cartoon character might say in response to the comments of another character. The responses indicate the participants' feelings, beliefs and attitudes towards the situation. Cartoon tests are simpler to administer and analyse than picture response techniques.

Expressive techniques

In **expressive techniques**, participants are presented with a verbal or visual situation and asked to relate the feelings and attitudes of other people to the situation. The participants express not their own feelings or attitudes, but those of others. The main expressive techniques are role playing, the third-person technique and personification.

In **role playing**, participants are asked to play the role or to assume the behaviour of someone else. Participants are asked to speak as though they were someone else, such as another household member with whom they would share a decision or an authority figure. For example, 'Bernard, you are a 15-year-old boy; Eva, you play Bernard's mother; George, you play Bernard's father. Imagine you are at home deciding which summer holiday you would like this year as a family'. The discussion that emerges is likely to reveal unspoken objections as well as those of overcoming resistance to features of the holiday, locations, and ways of travelling there that may be favoured by Bernard but not his parents, or even his mother and not by the two males. The researcher assumes that the participants will project their own feelings into the role.[30]

In the **third-person technique**, participants are presented with a verbal or visual situation and are asked to relate the beliefs and attitudes of a third person rather than directly expressing personal beliefs and attitudes. This third person may be a friend, a neighbour, a colleague, or any person that the researcher chooses. Again, the researcher assumes that the participants will reveal personal beliefs and attitudes while describing the reactions of a third party. Asking an individual to respond in the third person reduces the social pressure to give an acceptable answer.

In the **personification technique**, participants imagine that the brand is a person and then describe characteristics of that person, e.g. their lifestyle, status, demographics, home(s). They can build up layers of this description using words and images from a variety of sources. These descriptions help to uncover and develop the perceived nature of a brand's personality. The following example shows why the brand personality is of importance to the marketer and how an understanding of personality may be used in advertising.

Cartoon tests
Cartoon characters are shown in a specific situation related to the problem. Participants are asked to indicate the dialogue that one cartoon character might make in response to the comment(s) of another character.

Expressive technique
A projective technique in which participants are presented with a verbal or visual situation and are asked to relate the feelings and attitudes of other people to the situation.

Role playing
Participants are asked to assume the behaviour of someone else or a specific object.

Third-person technique
A projective technique in which participants are presented with a verbal or visual situation and are asked to relate the beliefs and attitudes of a third person in that situation.

Personification technique
Participants are asked to imagine that the brand is a person and then describe characteristics of that person.

Example

It's a bit of an animal[31]

Brand personality

A brand has a human-made personality and it can survive only if those responsible for it think long term, safeguard its consistency, and ensure its adherence to and compatibility with the needs and attitudes of those for whom it caters. The brand's personality is sacrosanct. Its owners need to guard against squatters, parallel traders, plagiarists and the threat of the brand becoming generic. Above all, they must guard against inconsistency.[32]

The oddball snack product Peperami, strongly flavoured and meat based, in a world where sweet confectionery snacks are the norm, has been an enormous success. Advertising for the product could not be developed without first obtaining real insights into how consumers related to Peperami. Research revealed that there was a widespread view of the brand's personality. Children and adults alike referred to it as bizarre, mischievous, anarchic, impulsive, rebellious and manic. More than 50 rough advertising concepts were then tested to establish how the brand personality could be expressed, from mere eccentricity to naked aggression. What emerged was a swaggering character with a mischievous desire to shock. All the ingredients were there for the advertising solution – the manic, animated Peperami, and the pay-off line, 'It's a bit of an animal.'

Brand personality can also be uncovered using role playing. In a group discussion scenario, participants may be asked to play out the personality of a brand. In the Peperami example, the setting could be a cocktail bar after work on a Friday evening, with individuals acting out a Peperami brand, Pringles, a Snickers Bar and a Lidl (store) branded packet of salted peanuts. What the individuals as a brand do, what they say, how they interact with each other in the cocktail scenario, all allow an expression of personality that straight questioning may not reveal. Video recording of the event, played back to the group, acts as a means to discuss and elicit further meaning of a brand's personality, highlighting any positive and negative associations of the brand.

Advantages and disadvantages of projective techniques

The major advantage of projective techniques is that they may elicit responses that subjects would be unwilling or unable to give if they knew the purpose of the study. At times, in direct questioning, the participant may intentionally or unintentionally misunderstand, misinterpret or mislead the researcher. In these cases, projective techniques can increase the validity of responses by disguising the purpose. This is particularly true when the issues to be addressed are personal, sensitive or subject to strong social norms. Projective techniques are also helpful when underlying motivations, beliefs and attitudes are operating at a subconscious level.[33]

Projective techniques suffer from many of the disadvantages of unstructured direct techniques, but to a greater extent. These techniques generally require personal interviews with individuals who are experienced interviewers and interpreters, hence they tend to be expensive. Furthermore, as in all qualitative techniques, there is the risk of interpretation bias. With the exception of word association, all are open-ended techniques, making the analysis and interpretation more problematic.

Some projective techniques such as role playing require participants to engage in what may seem to be unusual behaviour. Certain participants may not have the self-confidence or the ability to express themselves fully with these techniques. In role playing, for example, the skills of acting may make some participants more articulate at expressing their feelings compared with others. The same may be said of techniques where pictures and cartoons are put together and interpreted, in that distinctive skills may make certain participants more adept and comfortable in expressing themselves. To counter this, one could argue that there is a great amount of skill required in expressing oneself in an open-ended in-depth interview. One could point to fiction writers or poets who are able to encapsulate particular feelings most clearly and succinctly, which again is enormously skilful.

With such skill requirements, the disadvantage of the technique lies in the nature of the participants who agree to participate, and how characteristic they are of distinct target markets.

Applications of projective techniques

Projective techniques are used less frequently than unstructured direct methods (focus groups and in-depth interviews). A possible exception may be word association, which is commonly used to test brand names and occasionally to measure attitudes about particular products, brands, packages or advertisements. As the examples have shown, projective techniques can be used in a variety of situations.[34] The usefulness of these techniques is enhanced when the following guidelines are observed. Projective techniques should be used:

1 Because the required information cannot be accurately obtained by direct questioning.
2 In an exploratory manner to elicit issues that participants find difficult to conceive and express.
3 To engage participants in the subject, by having fun in expressing themselves in interesting and novel ways.

Comparison between qualitative techniques

To summarise comparisons between qualitative techniques, Table 8.1 gives a relative comparison of focus groups, in-depth interviews, projective techniques and ethnographic approaches (qualitative observation).

The nature of qualitative research is such that, within the broad categories above, there are numerous variations of the techniques with distinct strengths and weaknesses in eliciting and representing consumer feelings. Really, it is not possible to say that one technique is better or worse than the other. Faced with a given problem, it would seem to be the case of deciding which technique is the most appropriate to represent or understand consumers.[35] What may affect this choice is the confidence that marketing decision-makers may have in particular techniques. Thus, for example, any number of arguments may be made for the use of a projective technique as being the best way to tackle indirectly a sensitive issue. If the marketer who has to use the research findings does not believe it to be a trustworthy technique, then other, perhaps less appropriate, techniques may have to be used.

Table 8.1 A comparison of focus groups, in-depth interviews, projective techniques and ethnographic techniques

Criteria	Focus groups	In-depth interviews	Projective techniques	Ethnographic techniques
Degree of structure	Can vary from highly to loosely structured	Can vary from highly to loosely structured	Tends to be loosely structured	Loosely structured, though can have a framework to guide observation
Probing of individual participants	Low	High	Medium	None when used in isolation and in a covert manner
Moderator bias	Medium	Relatively high	Low to high	None when used in isolation and in a covert manner
Uncovering subconscious information	Low	Medium to high	High	High
Discovering innovative information	High	Medium	Low	Medium
Obtaining sensitive information	Low	Medium	High	High
Involving unusual behaviour or questioning	No	To a limited extent	Yes	Perhaps on the part of the observer

International marketing research

One of the major contributors to the success of in-depth interviews and projective techniques is getting the context of questioning right. The context of questioning can have two key components.

The first component is the actual location, such as an office, hotel room or even a bar. Given the issues that are to be tackled and the characteristics of the target participants, the location plays a significant role in helping the participant to relax and feel comfortable about responding in a manner that the interviewer is looking for. For some participants, e.g. a young graduate manager, being questioned about issues relating to 'night life and entertainment', talking in a noisy, smoky bar may be far more natural than talking in a 'business suite' at a hotel. The same participants being questioned about cleaning their homes may be far more comfortable in a quiet 'home' environment, though perhaps not their own home. The interviewer has to work out what location will work best for the target participants and the issues that will be discussed. The interviewer has to appreciate that this location may change between different participants and may also change as he or she discovers what effect location has on getting the most out of participants.

The second component of the context of questioning is the protocol of conducting the interview. The protocol can include the clothes the interviewer wears, the manner in which the inteviewer greets participants, introduces the interview, conducts the interview and terminates it. This means that, even if an interviewer is technically adept at questioning, the interviewer may still not get the most out of participants. For example, an interviewer who dresses formally when the participants see themselves 'off duty' may result in an interview that is tense and lacking in spontaneity.

There are no firm rules about the balance of participant characteristics, related to issues to be questioned and the context of questioning. The interviewer has to be aware of the balance, and make adjustments as he or she learns of what works well in drawing out a quality response. Much of what works in a particular context is culturally bound. There can be striking differences between countries in how comfortable participants may feel talking about issues in their home, for example. There can be striking differences in the protocol of clothing, greeting people, questioning in a direct manner and giving 'gifts' as a reward for taking part in an interview. The problem of 'context' was paramount in the following example. This example illustrates a case in which in-depth interviews helped to probe in detail the views of professionals, which given the detail of banking relationships could be deemed as highly complex and sensitive.

| *Example* | **Why are you going to make more use of electronic banking?** |

A syndicated study of banking in Europe was conducted by a consortium of banks from Finland, France, Germany, Ireland, Norway, Spain, the UK and the USA. These banks formed a steering committee that helped shape the research design, which was primarily a postal survey followed by in-depth interviews. Each bank had different information requirements to support their marketing strategies, which meant that there was a big demand for a wide array of questions to be asked. There was much debate about which questions should be tackled and, given the detail of information sought, whether these would be best achieved through a structured questionnaire or with in-depth interviews. For example, the questionnaire asked companies what future changes they planned. An example of a response to this question was 'to make greater use of electronic banking'. Statistical analyses could reveal the the types of respondent (e.g. utility companies) who were to make greater use of electronic banking. However, the questionnaire could not

Example

question *why* they were going to make more use of electronic banking. When around 50% of the responses to the postal survey were received, an interim report was presented to the steering committee. The issues that they deemed the most important to probe formed a topic guide for in-depth interviews. With the completed questionnaires, profiles of the participants could be analysed and those with behaviour relevant to the issues that needed to be explored in depth could be contacted. For example, 'sophisticated' users of cash management services could be profiled. These 'sophisticated' users were then contacted and invited to take part in an in-depth interview. Around 60 in-depth interviews were conducted, with a minimum of 2 interviews in any one country.

In the above example, each interview had the same interviewer who ensured a degree of consistency in the approach. This required the interviewer to visit 20 countries in order to conduct the 60 interviews. This interviewer had to have a strong awareness of the technical issues of cash management banking in order to be seen as credible by the participants, to be able to question and probe, and to appreciate the relevance of the responses elicited. He had to be aware of the context of interviewing in each of the target countries in order to get the most out of participants. The first component of context, the actual location for the interviews, was consistent throughout each country. The interviews were held in the offices of the finance directors of Europe's largest companies, who made up the participants. This was an environment where the participants are naturally used to thinking and talking about the issues under question. It was also an environment where they could talk uninterrupted; the participant was in control of the interview space and could relax. The second component of context, i.e. the protocol of the interview, was where the interviewer needed local support. Most of the technical language and terms used in cash management banking are 'American'. Many finance directors speak English, but some did not, and even if they did, at times they needed to express a view in their native tongue. To understand the protocol and language issues, the interviewer was supported by another interviewer in each country, drawn from local business schools. This interviewer helped to explain the protocol of individual countries, the peculiarities of greeting participants, posing questions in particular ways and closing an interview. These interviewers could help with the translation of questions and responses and ultimately in interpreting the findings. Using one main interviewer allowed a full understanding of the interplay between the participant, the issues and the context of interview. Using a fellow interviewer in individual countries allowed for the subtle characteristics of protocol and language to be incorporated into the whole process.

Understanding the interplay of participant, issue and context is vital to the success of in-depth interviewing and projective techniques. Working in alien cultures in international markets makes this understanding more difficult. Investing in the time and means to develop this understanding ensures that the interviewer generates quality information, getting to reflect really what international participants feel.

Ethics in marketing research

The essence of qualitative research is that consumers are examined in great depth. They may be questioned and probed in depth about subjects they hardly reflect upon on a day-to-day basis, never mind talk to strangers about. Great care must be taken not to upset or disturb participants through such intensive questioning. In survey work, reassuring participants that their responses will be confidential can work if there is a demonstrable link between their responses to questions and a means of aggregating all of the findings – making the individual response 'hidden'. In qualitative research, the process is far more intimate and the link between the response and the participant is far more difficult to break. This is illustrated in the following example.

Example Just how 'anonymous' is a quali participant?[36]

From both a practical and a methodological perspective, 'confidentiality' in qualitative research is a different concept from confidentiality as applied to survey work. In survey work the emphasis is upon anonymity, i.e. the identity of individual participants should not be revealed. This creates two problems for qualitative research:

1 Anonymity cannot be promised in qualitative research, especially in the light of current practices where it is increasingly common for clients and others to come to groups, or hear audiotapes, see videotapes and other primary data. This issue further demands consideration of the question: 'where does the identity reside?' In a name, a face, the voice, perhaps even a turn of phrase? It is of course also pertinent to ask: 'do participants actually care if their identity is revealed?'

2 In quantitative research, participant identity is generally unimportant. The very essence of sampling theory is that a sufficiently large and randomly chosen sample will represent the views, behaviour or attitudes of any known population as a whole. As such, the identity of any one individual is irrelevant to quantitative findings. In sharp contrast, in qualitative research the relationship between the specific individuals and their views is at the heart of analysis and interpretation. You cannot reach qualitative findings without having 'revealed' the individual as part of the research process. Therefore, confidentiality through anonymity is a methodologically untenable concept wherever anyone other than the interviewer is privy to any part of the research process. Yet at the same time, more clients attend groups and more groups take place in viewing facilities.

At the end of the second point above comes the reason why the marketing research industry is so concerned about how qualitative research participants are handled. More consumers are being questioned in both domestic and business scenarios. If they are to 'open up' and reveal deeply held feelings, perhaps in front of a group of strangers, or if they are to take part in projective techniques that they may see as being unorthodox, they have to be reassured of how the data captured will be used. As well as the ethical questions of potentially damaging participants come the problems of participants either not willing to take part or, if they do, being very guarded with their responses.

Ethical questions also arise when videotaping sessions with the participants. Some of the pertinent questions are how much to tell participants and when the clients should be allowed access. When videotaping participants, regardless of whether or not they were aware of the camera during the meeting, at the end of the meeting they should be asked to sign a written declaration conveying their permission to use the recording. This declaration should disclose the full purpose of the video, including who will be able to view it. If any participant refuses, the tape should be either destroyed or edited to omit that participant's identity and comments completely. The researcher should be sensitive to the comfort level of the participants, and respect for the participants should warrant restraint. When a participant feels uncomfortable and does not wish to go on, the researcher should not aggressively probe or confront any further. It has also been suggested that participants should be allowed to reflect on all they have said at the end of the interview and should be given the opportunity to ask questions. This may help return the participants to their pre-interview emotional state.

Internet and computer applications

The following example illustrates the use of a computer application in interviewing participants using projective techniques. It presents one solution to the problem of participants feeling self-conscious when undertaking what they may see as strange and unorthodox research techniques.

Example ### Quantifying the emotional aspects of advertising[37]

Much research demonstrates that people are typically on 'autopilot' in their everyday lives, and that reactions to advertising are intuitive rather than rational, and subliminal rather than conscious. News International felt that it was clear how qualitative research could help it, but it wished to quantify the emotions, feelings and intuition generated by the very nature of advertising. News International chose QualiQuant International (**www.qiqinternational.com**) because of its creative approach to this problem. Its approach involved novel applications of projective methods, applied in PC/web-based interviewing.

Surf is a well-known British washing powder brand, and the *Sun* is the UK's best selling tabloid newspaper. The objectives were to assess whether a particular advertisement was communicating Surf's brand values amongst *Sun* readers. The interviewees (n = 351) were regular readers of the *Sun* or other tabloid newspapers, recruited on the street for central location interviewing. Once in location, the respondents were shown to a PC. They were then asked to perform various free association tasks on Surf and the *Sun*, including playful exercises such as dragging and dropping selected visual images and words onto relevant brand or subject areas. They were then encouraged to pour their hearts out in projective techniques designed to elicit moods and feelings.

An important feature of the process was that the interviewer was 'virtual', whereby respondents go through the computer questionnaire themselves, the vast majority finding it easy and fun to complete the tasks on screen. This gives freedom and encourages spontaneity, whereas the presence of an interviewer can force respondents into a more rational justifying mode.

The Internet has opened up many possibilities to marketing researchers who wish to use in-depth interviews and projective techniques. Through the use of email, interviewers can reach and question participants from all over the world. To be able to track down and talk to individuals with the desired qualities for a particular study, without the time and cost implications of travelling, presents a significant benefit of the Internet.

Being able to track down and talk to participants, i.e. gaining access to qualitative participants, is vital, but the quality of the discussion with these participants should be considered.[38] In the case of in-depth interviews, a full dialogue can develop between an interviewer and participant, either in real time or in non-real time, i.e. a series of emails over a period of time. The discussion, questions and probes can be tailored to specific participants, allowing them time to reflect upon the issues and express their views in their own manner. The interviewer can present stimuli in terms of images or audio recordings that may help to elicit more from the participants. It is possible to use webcams to observe participants and for participants to view interviewers, provided of course that both parties have this technology.

However, even with the use of webcams, much of the non-verbal communication that makes in-depth interviews work is lost. Subtle changes in facial expression and body language may be missed. These non-verbal forms of communication are important in developing a rapport between interviewer and participant and are vital in the development of dialogue and the analysis of data. The limitation of visual interaction can make projective techniques difficult to implement. For certain projective techniques such as the array of completion and construction techniques, the anonymity afforded by the distance between interviewer and participant can be a positive feature. Some participants may find the presence of an interviewer inhibiting when they are trying to think of and present a story completion. Where participants feel inhibited, working through a response in their own space and time may be the ideal context in which to tackle particular issues.

In evaluating the worth of the Internet in in-depth interviewing and projective techniques we can return to the example in the 'International marketing research' section. Meeting participants face to face allowed a great richness of dialogue and understanding to be built up. There was no question about how successful the interviews were in understanding *why* participants behaved in particular ways. However, consider the travel and other costs involved. Consider the time involved in conducting the interviews and just typing up the transcripts of the interviews. Compare the cost and timing requirements of meeting face to face in an international setting with a dialogue by email. The process could have been conducted by email much more quickly and cheaply. The dilemma faced is whether the participants would have allowed such a dialogue in the first place and how much they would open up and develop a dialogue.

Summary

The qualitative technique of in-depth interviewing allows researchers to focus upon individuals with the qualities they deem to be important to their research objectives. With a 'quality individual' the researcher can question and probe to great depth and elicit a quality understanding of that individual's behaviour or feelings. The technique is well suited to tackling commercially and personally sensitive issues. It is also well suited to interviewing children. There are many types of interview that can be applied under the term 'in-depth interview'. They can range from the very open and unstructured to semi-structured exchanges. The application of structure in an in-depth interview can be founded on a theoretical underpinning of how individuals should be questioned and probed. Three relevant and widely used examples of interviews using a theoretical underpinning are laddering, repertory grid techniques and the Zaltman metaphor elicitation technique (ZMET). Laddering seeks to reveal chains of attributes, consequences and values that participants associate with products. The repertory grid seeks to elicit the underlying elements and the connection of those elements, related to a particular form of consumer behaviour. ZMET seeks to understand the images and associations that underpin both spoken and tacit thoughts and feelings through the elicitation of both rational and emotional thinking.

Indirect projective techniques aim to project the participant's motivations, beliefs, attitudes and feelings onto ambiguous situations. Projective techniques may be classified as association (word association), completion (sentence completion, story completion), construction (picture response, cartoon tests) and expressive (role playing, third-person, personification) techniques. Projective techniques are particularly useful when participants are unwilling or unable to provide the required information by direct methods.

The qualitative researcher needs to develop an understanding of the interplay between characteristics of the target participants, the issues they will be questioned about and the context in which they will be questioned. The context can be broken down into the physical location of the interview and the protocol of starting, running and terminating the interview. Building up this understanding is vital to the success of conducting in-depth interviews and projective techniques in international markets.

The marketing research industry is concerned about how qualitative research participants are handled in interviews and observations. More consumers are being questioned in both domestic and business scenarios. If they are to 'open up' and reveal deeply held feelings, perhaps in front of a group of strangers, or if they are to take part in projective techniques that they may see as being unorthodox, they have to be reassured of how the data captured will be used.

The Internet has opened up many possibilities to conduct in-depth interviews and use projective techniques on a global basis. A rich dialogue between an interviewer and a participant can be developed and recorded with much lower cost and time demands when compared with meeting face to face. The loss of subtle eye contact and body language can be a price to pay for the savings afforded by using the Internet.

Questions

1 What is an in-depth interview? Summarise the process of administering an in-depth interview.

2 What are the major advantages of in-depth interviews?

3 What are the requirements of the researcher undertaking in-depth interviews? Why are these requirements particularly important when conducting interviews with managers?

4 Why may a structure be applied to the in-depth interview in the form of laddering or the repertory grid technique?

5 Describe the process of administering the repertory grid technique.

6 Evaluate the context and timing requirements that you think would be needed to make the repertory grid technique work.

7 Choose any particular application of an in-depth interview and present a case for why you think the technique may work much better than a focus group.

8 What are projective techniques? Under what circumstances should projective techniques be used?

9 Describe the word association technique. Give an example of a situation in which this technique is especially useful.

10 Describe the story completion technique. Give an example of the type of participant and the context in which such a technique would work.

11 Describe the criteria by which marketing researchers may evaluate the relative worth of qualitative techniques.

12 Why is the context of questioning particularly important when conducting in-depth interviews in international marketing research?

13 Why may in-depth interviews or projective techniques upset or disturb participants?

14 Describe a projective technique that you feel would work particularly well by email – without the use of webcams.

15 What limitations are there to conducting in-depth interviews by email, compared with meeting participants face to face?

Exercises

1 Could an in-depth interview about the phenomenon of Internet casinos be conducted via the Internet? Present a case for how you would conduct such interviews and set out what you see as the advantages and disadvantages of this approach.

2 Baileys Irish Cream wishes to understand something of the nuances of serving and enjoying its drink. Develop a cartoon test for this purpose.

3 A cosmetics firm would like to increase its penetration of the student market through a new range of organic and 'ethical' products. Conduct two experimental in-depth interviews with a male and female student. Write a report setting out plans for any subsequent form of in-depth interviews and associated

techniques, showing how the experimental interviews have impacted upon these plans.

4 Jeffery West shoes (**www.jeffery-west.co.uk**) wishes to develop an understanding of its brand personality. Design a role-playing scenario that will help to achieve this aim. Who would you invite to the sessions? Where would you run the sessions? What roles would you ask the participants to play?

5 In a small group discuss the following issues: 'Are there any dangers (for researchers and participants) in conducting in-depth studies on issues that participants hardly reflect upon on a day-to-day basis?' and 'Projective techniques cannot work well with shy and introverted participants.'

Notes

1 De Chernatony, L. and Dall Olmo Riley, F., 'Brand consultants' perspectives on the concept of the brand', *Marketing and Research Today* 25 (1) (February 1997), 45–52.

2 Harris, L.M., 'Expanding horizons', *Marketing Research: A Magazine of Management and Application* 8 (2) (Summer 1996), 12.

3 Kvale, S., *Interviews: An introduction to qualitative research interviewing* (Thousand Oaks, CA: Sage, 1996); Rubin, H.J. and Rubin, I.S., *Qualitative Interviewing: The art of hearing data* (Thousand Oaks, CA: Sage, 1995).

4 Warren, C.A.B., 'Qualitative interviewing', in Gubrium, J.F. and Holstein, J.A. (eds), *Handbook of interview research: Context and method* (Thousand Oaks, CA: Sage, 2002), 83–101.

5 Johnson, J.M., 'In-depth Interviewing', in Gubrium, J.F. and Holstein, J.A. (eds), *Handbook of interview research: Context and method* (Thousand Oaks, CA: Sage, 2002), 104.

6 Ibid., pp. 106–107.

7 Schwalbe, M.L. and Wolkomir, M., 'Interviewing men', in Gubrium, J.F. and Holstein, J.A. (eds), *Handbook of interview research: Context and method* (Thousand Oaks, CA: Sage, 2002), 203–220.

8 'Looking for a deeper meaning', *Marketing* (Market Research Top 75 Supplement) (17 July 1997), 16–17.

9 Bloom, N., 'In-depth research? A bit controversial!', *ResearchPlus* (June 1993), 12.

10 Parke, A., 'When not to rely on the young imagination', *ResearchPlus* (March 1997), 14.

11 Milling, A., 'Don't supersize me', *Research* (November 2005), 38–39.

12 De Andrade Marseilles Reis, A.H.M., 'Laddering: an efficient tool for the formation of product positioning strategies and ways of communication', *The Dynamics of Change in Latin America*, ESOMAR Conference in Rio de Janeiro (1997).

13 Dichter, E., *The Strategy of Desire* (New York: Doubleday, 1960).

14 Guttman, J., 'Laddering: extending the repertory grid methodology to construct attribute-consequence-value hierarchies', in Heath, D.C (ed.), *Personal Values and Consumer Psychology* (Lanham, MD: Lexington Books, 1984).

15 For example, Grunert, G.K. and Grunert, S.C., 'Measuring subjective meaning structures by the laddering method: theoretical considerations and methodological problems', *International Journal of Research in Marketing* 12 (1995) 209–225.

16 Guth, R.A., 'PlayStation2 helps Sony beat forecasts', *Wall Street Journal* (28 January 2002), A12; Wasink, B., 'New techniques to generate key marketing insights', *Marketing Research* (Summer 2000), 28–36.

17 Kelly, G.A., *The Psychology of Personal Constructs* (New York: Norton, 1955).

18 Kelly, G.A., *A Theory of Personality: The Psychology of Personality* (New York: Norton, 1969).

19 Marsden, D. and Littler, D., 'Exploring consumer product construct systems with the repertory grid technique', *Qualitative Market Research: An International Journal* 3 (3) (2000), 127–144.

20 Van Raaij, W.F. and Verhallen, T.M.M., 'Domain specific market segmentation', *European Journal of Marketing* 28 (10) (1994), 49–66.

21 Jin, Z.Q., Birks, D.F. and Targett, D., 'The context and process of effective NPD: a typology', *International Journal of Innovation Management* 1 (3) (September 1997), 275–298.

22 Fransella, F. and Bannister, D., *Manual for Repertory Grid Technique* (London: Academic Press, 1977).

23 Wornell, T., 'Diving for pearls', *Research*, (April 2005), 39.

24 Sokolow, H., 'In-depth interviews increasing in importance', *Marketing News* (13 September 1985), 26.

25 Chandler, J. and Owen, M., *Developing brands with qualitative market research*, (Thousand Oaks, CA: Sage, 2002, 86–100; Best, K., 'Something old is something new in qualitative research', *Marketing News* 29 (18) (28 August 1995), 14.

26 Mariampolski, H., *Qualitative Marketing Research: A comprehensive guide* (Thousand Oaks, Sage, 2001), 206.

27 Zaichowsky, J.L., 'The why of consumption: contemporary perspectives and consumer motives, goals, and desires', *Academy of Marketing Science* 30 (2) (Spring 2002), 179; Levy, S.J., 'Interpreting consumer mythology: structural approach to consumer behaviour focuses on story telling', *Marketing Management* 2 (4) (1994), 4–9.

28 Catterall, M., 'Using projective techniques in education research', *British Educational Research Journal* 26 (2) (April 2000), 245–256; Kennedy, M.M., 'So how'm I doing?', Across the Board 34 (6) (June 1997), 53–54; Lindzey, G., 'On the classification of projective techniques', *Psychological Bulletin* (1959), 158–168.

29 Walsh, K., 'Soaps and detergents', *Chemical Week* 164 (3) (23 January 2002), 24–26; 'Interpretation is the essence of projective research techniques', *Marketing News* (28 September 1984), 20.

30 For issues involved in role playing, see Suprenant, C., Churchill, G.A. and Kinnear, T.C. (eds) 'Can role playing be substituted for actual consumption?', *Advances in Consumer Research* (Provo, UT: Association for Consumer Research, 1984), 122–126.

31 *Campaign* (28 October 1994), S13.

32 Van Mesdag, M., 'Brand strategy needs turning back to front', *Marketing Intelligence and Planning* 15(2–3) (February–March 1997), 157.

33 Gill, J., and Johnson, P., *Research Methods for Managers*, 3rd edn (Thousand Oaks, CA: Sage, 2002); Varki, S., Cooil, B. and Rust, R.T., 'Modeling fuzzy data in qualitative marketing research', *Journal of Marketing Research* 37 (4) (November 2000), 480–489.

34 For more on projective techniques, see Valentine, V. and Evans, M., 'The dark side of the onion: rethinking the meaning of "rational" and "emotional" responses', *Journal of the Market Research Society* 35 (April 1993), 125–144.

35 Colwell, J., 'Qualitative market research: a conceptual analysis and review of practitioner criteria', *Journal of the Market Research Society* 32 (1) (1990), 33.

36 Imms, M., 'Just how "anonymous" is a quali participant?', *Research* (April 1997), 20.

37 Sharman, N., Pawle, J. and Cooper, P., 'Quantifying the emotional aspects of advertising', *Research World* (September 2003), 32–36.

38 Pincott, G. and Branthwaite, A., 'Nothing new under the sun?', *International Journal of Market Research* 42 (2) (2000), 137–155.

Visit the *Marketing Research* Companion Website at www.pearsoned.co.uk/malhotra_euro for additional learning resources including annotated weblinks, an online glossary and a suite of downloadable video cases.

Source: © Getty Images

9

Qualitative research: data analysis

> *Qualitative analysis involves the process of making sense of data that are not expressed in numbers.*

Objectives

After reading this chapter, you should be able to:

1 understand the importance of qualitative researchers being able to reflect upon and understand the social and cultural values that shape the way they gather and interpret qualitative data;

2 describe the stages involved in analysing qualitative data;

3 describe the array of data types that qualify as qualitative data;

4 explain the nature and role of coding in the stage of reducing qualitative data;

5 appreciate the benefits of being able to display the meaning and structure that qualitative researchers see in their data;

6 understand why qualitative data analysis pervades the whole process of data gathering and why the stages of analysis are iterative;

7 appreciate the nature and roles of grounded theory, content analysis and semiotics in qualitative data analysis;

8 appreciate the strengths and weaknesses of analysing data using qualitative analysis software and have the means to experiment with demonstration software;

9 understand the ethical implications of the ways that qualitative researchers interpret data.

STAGE 1
Problem definition

STAGE 2
Research approach developed

STAGE 3
Research design developed

STAGE 4
Fieldwork or data collection

STAGE 5
Data preparation and analysis

STAGE 6
Report preparation and presentation

Overview

The application of qualitative techniques can see researchers changing direction as they learn what and who they should focus their attention on. The techniques, the nature of participants and the issues explored can change and evolve as a project develops. This chapter starts by examining how researchers reflect upon what happens to the way they perceive and observe as these changes occur. It discusses how these reflections form a key source of qualitative data to complement the narrative generated from interviews and observations.

The stages involved in a generic process of analysing qualitative data are outlined and described. The first stage of the process involves assembling qualitative data in their rich and varying formats. The second stage progresses on to reducing the data, i.e. selecting, classifying and connecting data that researchers believe to be of the greatest significance. A key element of this stage is the concept of coding. The third stage involves display data, i.e. using graphical means to display the meaning and structure that researchers see in the data they have collected. Manual and electronic means of displaying data are discussed. The final stage involves verifying the data. Marketing researchers aim to generate the most valid interpretation of the data they collect, which may be supported by existing theories or through the concept of theoretical sampling. Though these stages seem quite distinct, the reality is that they are iterative and totally interdependent upon each other; the stages unfold in 'waves' to produce an ultimate interpretation of great value to decision-makers. Three alternative perspectives of analysing qualitative data are presented. First, the purpose and concept of grounded theory are discussed, with the stages involved in building theory. Second, content analysis is presented, a much simpler approach to analysing qualitative data, which is sometimes viewed as a quantitative technique. Third, the purpose and concept of semiotics are presented. This approach adopts the view that consumers should be viewed as products of culture, constructed and largely determined by the popular culture within which they live. It allows for the integrated analysis of cues that emerge from text, pictures and sounds.

The use of computers in the stages of qualitative data collection and analyses is described. There are many distinct advantages to the use of qualitative data analysis software, but many researchers contend that it should be a 'hands-on' process that cannot be mechanised. The arguments from both of these perspectives are presented. To be able to cope with the great amount of data generated from qualitative techniques, a great variety of software packages are available. Examples of analysis software are briefly described followed by Internet addresses that allow demonstration versions of the software to be downloaded and explored. XSight, the qualitative data analysis package specifically designed for marketing researchers, is presented. This is the software package that is available with this text as a full-working version, for use over 90 days.

The social and cultural values of qualitative researchers affect how qualitative researchers gather and analyse data. Understanding the social and cultural norms of participants in international environments is discussed. The chapter concludes by examining how the social and cultural values of researchers affect their interpretation of qualitative data and the ethical implications of not reflecting upon these values.

The qualitative researcher

Self-reflection of social and cultural values

In Chapter 2, when discussing the diagnosis of research problems on page 55, we stated:

A major problem for researchers is that their perception of problems may be reflected through their own social and cultural development. Before defining the problem, researchers should reflect upon their unconscious reference to cultural values . . . The unconscious reference to cultural values can be seen to account for these differences.

This implies that marketing researchers need to reflect upon their own values and attitudes, the factors that may bias the way they perceive and what they observe. This reflection is just as important in the analysis of qualitative data as it is in the diagnosis of research problems. To illustrate why researchers need to reflect upon what may bias the way they perceive and what they observe, we start this chapter with an example from the world of literature and the treatment of narrative. The example is a precis of an English translation of a Japanese novel; the example could be taken from any novel.

Example **South of the Border, West of the Sun**[1]

This novel tells the story of an only child, Hajime, growing up in the suburbs of postwar Japan. His childhood sweetheart and sole companion in childhood was Shimamoto, also an only child. As children they spent long afternoons listening to her father's record collection. When Hajime's family moved away, the childhood sweethearts lost touch. The story moves to Hajime in his thirties. After a decade of drifting he has found happiness with his loving wife and two daughters, and success in running a jazz bar. Then Shimamoto reappears. She is beautiful, intense, enveloped in mystery. Hajime is catapulted into the past, putting at risk all he has at the present.

Imagine that you had been asked to read this novel, but before you read it you were expected to prepare by reading a description of conditions in postwar Japan. From that you may appreciate the significance of a record collection of 15 albums, and how privileged a family may be to own a record player and to have this collection. Imagine someone else being asked to prepare by reading a biography of the author. From that you may appreciate the social and economic conditions of his upbringing, the literature, music and education that he enjoyed. Preparing to read the novel in these two ways may mean that a reader sees very different things in the story. The reader may interpret passages differently, have a different emotional attachment with the conditions and behaviour of the characters, and appreciate the effect of quite subtle events upon the characters.

Put aside any prior reading and imagine a female reader enjoying the book. She may empathise with the main female character Shimamoto and understand her attitudes, values and behaviour in the way that male readers may not be able to comprehend. In the story, Shimamoto suffered from polio as a child, which made her drag her left leg. Imagine a reader who has had to cope with a disability and who may appreciate how as a child one copes with the teasing of young children. The two main characters were 'only children'; imagine the reader who was an only child and who can recall how they would view large families and appreciate the emotions of the only child. The list could go on of the different perspectives of the story that may be seen. The reader, with his or her inherent values and attitudes, may perceive many different things happening in the story. The reader does not normally reflect upon his or her unconscious values and attitudes, but just enjoys the story. In talking to others about the story, the reader may be surprised about how others see it. In watching the film version of the book, the reader may be shocked at the different images the film director presents, images that are very different from the one that resides in his or her head. Now consider whether there is one ultimate interpretation of the novel, one ultimate 'truth'. It is very difficult to conceive that there is one ultimate interpretation. One may question why anyone would want to achieve such a thing; surely the enjoyment of literature is the ability to have multiple interpretations and 'truths' of a novel.[2]

Narrative for the qualitative researcher

What is the link from the interpretation of a novel to qualitative data analysis in marketing research? Quite simply, the qualitative marketing researcher builds up a narrative and creates a story of the consumers whom decision-makers wish to understand. Imagine yourself as a qualitative marketing researcher, supporting decision-makers who wish to develop advertisements for an expensive ride-on lawnmower. The key target market they wish to understand is 'wealthy men, over the age of 60, who own a home(s) with at least 1 hectare of garden'. The decisions they face may include the understanding of:

1 What gardening and cutting grass mean to target consumers.
2 How they feel about the process of using a lawnmower.
3 What relative values (tangible and intangible) are inherent in different brands of lawnmower.
4 What satisfaction they get from the completed job of mowing a large lawn.
5 The nature and qualities of celebrities they admire (who may be used to endorse and use the product in an advertisement).

These questions may be tackled through the use of focus groups. Imagine yourself running these groups. What could you bring to the groups if you have personally gone through the experience of buying an expensive ride-on lawnmower and have gardening and lawnmowing experiences? You may have an empathy with the participants in the same manner as the 'only child' reading of the experiences and emotions of an only child in a story. From this empathy, you may be able to question, probe and interpret the participants' answers really well, drawing an enormous amount from them. Without those experiences you may have to devise ways to 'step into the shoes' of the participants. You may look to the attitudes, values and behaviour of your parents, grandparents or friends for a start, looking for reference points that you are comfortable with, that make sense to you. As you go through a pilot or experimental focus group, you may be surprised by certain participants talking about their lawnmowers as 'friends', giving them pet names and devoting lavish care and attention upon them. Getting an insight into this may mean looking at cases from past research projects or literature from analogous situations such as descriptions of men forming a 'bond' with their cars.

The direction that qualitative marketing researchers take in building up their understanding and ultimately their narrative is shaped by two factors. The first factor is the *theoretical understanding* of the researchers as they collect and analyse the data. This theoretical understanding can be viewed from two perspectives. The first is the use of theory published in secondary data, intelligence and literature. The use of theory from these sources may help the researchers to understand what they should focus their attention upon, in their questioning, probing, observations and interpretations. The second is the use of theory from a grounded theory perspective. The researchers may see limitations in existing theory that do not match the observations they are making. These limitations help the researchers to form the focus of their questioning, probing, observations and interpretations.

The second factor that shapes the direction that the researchers take is a *marketing understanding*. In the case of understanding the wealthy male lawnmower owner, the researchers need to understand what marketing decision-makers are going to do with the story they create. The researchers need to appreciate the decisions faced in creating an advertisement, building a communications campaign or perhaps changing features of the product. Reference to theoretical and marketing understanding in the researchers helps them to present the most valid interpretation of their story to decision-makers. Unlike writing a novel, where the author is happy for the readers to take their own 'truth', marketing researchers are seeking an ultimate interpretation and validity in their story. Achieving a valid interpretation enables the researchers to convey to decision-makers a vision or picture of a target market that they can quickly 'step into'. Marketing decision-makers, for example, may wish to include a passage of music in an advertisement that the target market has an emotional attachment to, which they find positive and uplifting. With a rich picture or vision of this target market they may be able to choose the right piece of music. The decision-makers' cultural and social development may mean that the piece of music is meaningless to them, but you as a researcher have given them the confidence and enabled them to step into the world of the target market. The following example represents the views of an advertising practitioner praising the support gained from qualitative researchers through their understanding of the issues faced by decision-makers.

Example   **Cinderella's getting ready for the ball[3]**

I think a lot of researchers have worked hard at understanding advertising and the advertising process and are now regarded as quite critical contributors. What has allowed them to become 'wise' advisers rather than providers of fuel for literal and obedient fools? I think the following:

1   *There has been more crossover between planners and qualitative researchers.* Qualitative researchers understand their role in the process of developing advertisements and building brands. They want to know what the creative brief is and what responses or feelings an advert is meant to elicit. For example, when developing a current and famous premium package lager, we purposely discussed what levels of initial bewilderment or mild alienation were acceptable. The campaign had to challenge consumers – hopefully the brightest ones would let their mates in on the secret jokes down the pub!

2   *Good researchers work to more 'holistic' views of how ads work and thus avoid mechanistic and simplistic diagnoses.* We may therefore use projective techniques to help consumers express feelings. Whatever it is, good researchers try and look at advertisements in totality, not as a disaggregated series of frames.

3   *Good qualitative researchers, planners and clients are much more conscious about stimuli in advertising research.* People put more effort into defining stimuli, e.g. using film clips to get across production values or special effects, mood boards to give texture alongside traditional animatics, narratives or key frames. We have showed *Terminator 2* to help consumers imagine products 'metamorphosing' from one thing to another, and music snippets to conjure up different feelings of sensuality and sexuality.

4   *Interpretation has improved.* Good qualitative researchers know that consumers in group discussions are likely to be evaluative/judgemental, cynical and literal. It is the researcher's job to get them to 'imagine' beyond that and to interpret responses using one's cumulative knowledge of advertising chemistry.

The researcher's learning as qualitative data

Qualitative marketing researchers have to reflect upon their own social and cultural development, their own attitudes and values to see how these have shaped the narrative and how they shape their interpretation of the narrative. The researchers should recognise their own limitations and the need to develop and learn; in the case above, this means learning about wealthy men and their relationship with lawnmowers. Ultimately they wish to present the most valid story that they see, to have examined the story from many perspectives, to have immersed themselves in the world of their target markets.

If you are reading a novel, you may not be inclined to make notes as your reading progresses. You may not make notes of other books to read that may help you to understand the condition of particular characters, or to understand the environment in which they behave. You may not wish to write down the way that you change and learn as you read through the story. A reflection of your unconscious social and cultural values as revealed through your interpretation of the novel may be the last thing you want to do.

As a qualitative researcher you need to do all the above as you build and interpret your story of target consumers. A notebook or diary should be on hand to note new question areas or probes you wish to tackle, and to reflect upon how they have worked. As interviews unfold and you feel your own development and understanding progress, a note of these feelings should be made. As you seek out specific secondary data, intelligence or theory to develop your understanding, you should note why. If you see limitations in existing theories or ideas, you should note why. As an understanding of how decision-makers can use the observations that are being made, these should be recorded. Included in these notes should be feelings of failure to ask the right question or probe, emotional states should be noted, of feeling up or down, sad or angry, or nervous.[4] Ultimately the story that emerges in your own notebook should be a revelation of your own social and cultural values. There should be an explicit desire to develop this self-awareness and understand how it has shaped the direction of an investigation and the ultimate story that emerges.

The creation and development of the researcher's notebook is a major part of the narrative that is vital to the successful interpretation of questions and observations of consumers. The key lesson that emerges from the creation and development of the researcher's notebook is that qualitative data analysis is an ongoing process through all stages of data collection, not just when the data have been collected.

> *Analysis is a pervasive activity throughout the life of a research project. Analysis is not simply one of the later stages of research, to be followed by an equally separate phase of 'writing up results'.*[5]

The evolution of questions and probes, deciding who should be targeted for questions and observations and even deciding the context for questioning or observing, means that analysis takes place as data are being gathered.

The process of qualitative data analysis

We go through four perspectives of analysing qualitative data starting with a generic process. Many of the terms used here differ from those linked to specific types of software or to researchers that follow a particular theoretical approach derived from a specific discipline. The generic process outlined is designed to give an understanding of what is involved in qualitative data analysis and how the stages link and interact. The four stages of the generic process are outlined in Figure 9.1. The concept of coding is introduced in this section, a vital concept to understand in all approaches to analysing qualitative data. The second perspective presented is the concept of grounded theory. The third perspective is the process of content analysis. The fourth is the discipline of semiotics.

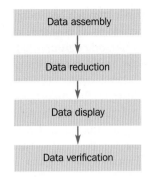

Figure 9.1
Stages of qualitative data analysis

Data assembly

Data assembly
The gathering of data from a variety of disparate sources.

Data assembly means the gathering of data from a variety of sources. These would include:

1 Notes taken during or after interviewing or observations.
2 Reflections of researchers, moderators or observers involved in the data collection process.
3 Theoretical support – from secondary data, intelligence or literature sources.
4 Documents produced by or sourced from participants.
5 Photographs, drawings, diagrams, i.e. still visual images.
6 Audiotape recordings and transcripts of those recordings.
7 Videotape recordings.
8 Records made by participants such as mood boards or collages.

Field notes
A log or diary of observations, events and reflections made by a researcher as a study is planned, implemented and analysed.

As discussed in the previous section, the researcher should get into the habit of maintaining a notebook, diary or **field notes**. As a qualitative investigation evolves in terms of the issues to explore and the participants to target, the researcher goes through a learning process. This learning process means that the researcher may see things differently as interviews or observations progress. Keeping field notes aids the researcher's memory when it comes to the formal process of data analysis and helps enormously in categorising and interpreting collected data. It ultimately helps to generate a 'deeper and more general sense of what is happening'.

In order to make 'deeper and more general sense of what is happening', it is suggested[6] that researchers keep four separate sets of notes in order to systematise the process and thus improve their reliability:

1 Short notes made at the time of observation or interview.
2 Expanded notes made as soon as possible after each session of interviews or observations.
3 A fieldwork journal to record problems and ideas that arise during each stage of fieldwork.
4 A provisional running record of analysis and interpretation.

Data assembly also includes deciding lines of enquiry which should be developed and those that should be dropped. Given that qualitative research is primarily exploratory in nature, questions and probes are not fixed. As an interview or observation takes place, the researcher learns more about an issue and can develop a new question or probe and decide that a question, initially thought to be vital, is no longer relevant. There may be issues that can be compared over a series of interviews or observations, but the whole data collection and data assembly can evolve. Keeping notes is vital as memory alone is fallible, unreliable and potentially biased. Being able to recall, for example, the hesitation in replying to a question displayed by a focus group participant may upon reflection be seen as someone evading the issue. After all the group discussions have been completed and the same question has been posed to others, the interpretation may change to the individual being embarrassed about an issue, primarily through becoming aware of his or her own ignorance. The researchers' notes help them to recall how they were feeling at the point of setting the question, and recall the situation in other groups that gives meaning to a pause that shows up as a quiet spot in an audio or video recording. They may also help the researcher appreciate what is happening when laughter occurs by participants in qualitative techniques. The following example illustrates the importance of humour in devising a strategy to develop a brand. It shows the dilemma facing the researcher in interpreting the meaning of laughter. In this example, the marketing researcher Chris Forrest suggests that the humour in an advert can be sensed through the 'relative energy in the room'. If this is the case, group dynamics, the pitch and intensity of laughter, or even the sly smile that masks a feeling that something is incredibly funny, would need to be recorded in the researcher's notes, to set a vital context to the narrative of any discussion.

Example	### Funny business, serious money[7]

Humour is something that can communicate a strategy very powerfully, but is not a solution in its own right. There are pitfalls in understanding humour in the research process, with the focus group seen as a poor place to find out if an advertisement is funny. In groups people laugh to show they fit in, to please the moderator or other participants, or simply because laughter can be contagious. In short, laughter (or its absence) is an unreliable piece of evidence. However, Chris Forrest from the research agency The Nursery argues that the focus group can detect what is funny and what is not:

> *A really strong script will have a group in stitches, participants will even insist it is an ad that has to be made. Naturally one cannot always hope to be researching a knock-out script, and in these cases its useful to have more than one script.*

Then, Chris says, 'It is possible to benchmark a group's reaction. Even when a group isn't laughing a lot, you can tell from the relative energy in the room which one they respond to the best.'

Unfortunately, the recording and use of field notes or a diary is limited in many qualitative marketing research projects. This may be due to the contents of such notes which could include photographs and other non-verbal data sources. These are unavoidably 'subjective', being what the researcher has chosen to notice. They are developmental, representing the learning and self-reflection that the researcher goes through. The subjective choices are reasoned choices, where issues are deliberately included or excluded. Understanding the reasons for those choices, recognising the learning and self-development that can emerge from these notes, can add so much more depth and greater insight into qualitative data. By developing self-awareness, qualitative marketing researchers can take a more balanced view of the data they collect as they realise many of their own biases and hidden agendas.

Beyond taking notes or keeping a diary, many qualitative techniques make extensive use of material of a semi- or non-verbal nature, generated through participant tasks such as the use of projective techniques. These materials can include drawings, lists, stories, clay models or structures, and collages of photographs, video footage and music. The commonly held view is that it is not these materials that should be analysed but the meanings attached to them by the participants who produced them.[8] These meanings as narrative will have been captured as part of the discussion on tape or are in the notes of the researcher.[9] The materials themselves would normally be available during analysis, enabling the possibility to notice useful features such as consistencies and differences between participants. They can also be useful in communicating and illustrating findings. Other qualitative researchers go further, taking the view that it is legitimate to 'read' these materials in the absence of the participants who produced them. They would argue that significant and valid meaning can be extracted from them provided they have a strong theoretical basis to drawing their conclusions and meanings.

This relationship between participants' discourse and non-verbal materials mirrors the debate in using photography in ethnographic studies (a common occurrence in qualitative marketing research where participants are given disposable or digital cameras to capture stills or moving images of their experiences). Many significant anthropological ethnographies dating from the mid-1920s onward include photographs relating to the fieldwork. The question that faces anthropologists relates to why photographs may be used in analysis and the relationship, if any, between the photograph and the written text. It is difficult to generalise, but it seems to be the case that photographs have been included in ethnographic reports more for evidential than analytic purposes. The photographs serve essentially presentational and illustrative purposes rather than providing a focus for a more sustained analysis of the visual dimensions of culture.[10]

There is however, a class of anthropological works (that includes marketing phenomena) in which the phenomenon investigated is itself clearly a visual one that benefits from visual representation:[11] the cross-cultural study of the visual arts, plastic and graphic, costume, self-decoration, masks, architecture, religious iconography, and other aspects of material culture. The following example describes a seminal anthropological study where photographs were seen as a valid form of data

Example **Gender advertisements**

A study that exemplifies the use of photographs as data is Goffman's *Gender Advertisements*.[12] Goffman presents more than 500 photographs, drawn mainly from illustrated newspaper and magazine advertisements. The aim was to analyse 'gender displays': the culturally conventional expressions of sex–class membership that are ordinarily available to us 'at a glance'. Goffman examines the various senses in which pictures can and cannot be regarded as depictions of some 'real' state of affairs. He is well aware that advertisements present a distorted view of the world, one that is prettier and more affluent than the everyday reality. However, using pictorial materials has the considerable advantage of allowing subtle features of gender displays to be exhibited where words alone would stand deficient.[13]

They key feature of the above example is to note the subtlety of features that may be displayed where words alone would be deficient. This feature has an impact for qualitative marketing researchers for two reasons. The first can be seen from the perspective of qualitative technique participants. Certain participants may not be able to express what they feel about a product, service, advertisement, brand, etc., using words. They may, however, be able to use visual cues from sources like photographs to represent their feelings. The second can be seen from the perspective of decision-makers who use qualitative research findings. Certain marketing decision-makers working in visually creative fields such as advertising, product and package design, and branding work better with visual data compared with words or statistics. They may understand the impact of how consumers feel and will react to their designs through very subtle interpretations of visual data. Given the importance of visual data to this type of marketing decision-maker, we explore the concept of semiotics later in this chapter.

Data reduction

Data reduction
The organising and structuring of qualitative data.

Data reduction involves handling the data. This process involves organising and structuring the data. It means having to throw some data away! Imagine a series of 10 focus group discussions and the amount of data that can be collected. There are the memories and notes of the moderator and any other observers who took part, there are the transcripts of what was actually said in interviews, and there may be contributions from participants in the form of mood boards. The **transcripts** are a vital and for most studies the primary data source in qualitative data analysis and much care should be taken in typing them up. Transferring the dialogue from tape is tortuous as tape recordings are notoriously 'unclear'. Imagine a focus group in full swing: not every participant takes their turn to speak without talking over other participants, and then they may not speak clearly and loudly enough. As a result it can take a great deal of time to work out what participants actually said and how the questions, responses and ideas connect together. In producing transcripts, it is much better for the researchers to work through the tape recordings and piece together the components using their notes and memory of events. This is very time consuming, so many researchers use typists to transcribe their tape recordings of interviews, arguing that their time is better spent reading through and editing transcripts produced in this manner. The use of the Internet in in-depth interviews and focus groups means that this time-consuming task is eliminated as the transcript is built up as the interview progresses.

The researchers with their transcripts, notes and other supporting material have to decide what is relevant in all these data. Reducing the data involves a process of **coding data**, which means breaking down the data into discrete chunks and attaching a reference to those chunks of data. Coding is a vital part of coping with qualitative data analysis and, given this importance, the process is discussed in some detail.

Coding data. Researchers need to be able to organise, manage and retrieve the most meaningful bits of qualitative data that they collect. This is normally done by assigning 'labels' or codes to the data, based upon what the researcher sees as a meaningful categorisation. What happens is that the researcher condenses the great mass of data from a qualitative study into analysable units by creating categories from the data.[14] This process is termed the coding of data. Coding is the process of bringing together participants' responses into categories that bring together similar ideas, concepts, themes, or steps or stages in process. Coding can also enable the categorisation of names, evidence or time sequences. Any hesitations, emotional states or levels of humour can be coded. Indeed, anything that is felt to be revealing in the data can be coded. Data such as a simple response to a question can be coded in many different ways, or placed into many different categories; there is no expectation of mutual exclusivity and data can be recoded as often as is thought necessary.[15]

Source: © Bryan Allen/CORBIS

An illustration of coding is presented using the data presented in the Table 9.1. This table presents the verbatim responses from an open-ended question in a self-completion survey targeted at 12–14 year olds. The question asked participants what facilities they would like in a planned new community centre. Though the technique used was quantitative, the survey generated qualitative data and in its much shortened format demonstrates the process that qualitative researchers must go through.

In categorising the responses, the researcher could create codes of '**swimming pool**' or '**disco**' and count the times that these were literally expressed. Alternatively, the researcher

Transcripts
'Hard copies' of the questions and probes and the corresponding answers and responses in focus group or in-depth interviews.

Coding data
Breaking down qualitative data into discrete chunks and attaching a reference to those chunks of data.

Table 9.1 Teenager requests for facilities at a planned community centre

Requested feature of new community centre	Gender
Skate park, death slide, basketball courts, swimming pool	Male
Computer room	Male
Stuff for all ages	Male
Swimming pool	Male
Computers, snooker room	Male
A space for computers, tuck shop	Male
Music, television, up-to-date magazines, pool tables	Female
Music, discos	Female
Swimming pool	Female
Music, pool/snooker, discos	Female
What people will enjoy	Female
All the things people enjoy	Female

could code on the basis of '**sports activities**' or '**recreational activities**' and group together activities such as 'swimming, basketball and snooker' for sports and 'computers, television, discos and tuck shop' for recreational activities. The researcher could code '**indoor activities**' and '**outdoor activities**', or activities that would need supervision and those that would need no supervision. There are many ways that the researcher can categorise the data, it is his or her choice. Consider how the researcher may cope with the requests for a 'computer room' and 'computers'. Could these be combined under one heading of '**computing**' or would this lose the meaning of having a devoted space, away from other activities that could be noisy and distracting? Consider also how the researcher would cope with the requests for 'stuff for all ages', 'what people will enjoy' and 'all the things people enjoy'. It may seem obvious that a new leisure centre needs to develop facilities that people enjoy and that these may be discarded, but there may be a hint in the first statement of 'stuff for all ages' that may link to the word 'people' used in the two other statements. If the researcher interprets the statements in this way, a category of '**activities to draw in all ages**' could be created; these responses may be seen as tapping into a notion of a leisure centre that is welcoming and not exclusive.

Table 9.2 presents a small selection of the verbatim responses from the same open-ended question in a self-completion survey, this time targeted at adults.

Table 9.2 Adult requests for facilities at a planned community centre

Requested feature of new community centre	Gender
Regards for residents living nearby, special car parking area to avoid streets nearby being jammed	Male
New centre would soon bring the wrong sort of people; it could form a centre for thugs and crime	Male
Strict rules so as to inconvenience local people living close by as little as possible, e.g. noise	Male
Run and organised well to run functions at affordable prices with dress rules for the lounge and bar	Male
Membership should be given on signature of applicants to a strict set of rules	Male
Emphasis on youth on the estate and run in a way to encourage rather than regiment them	Male
Supervised youth activities, daytime crèche, dance floor, serve coffee/soft drinks for youths	Female
Should be very welcoming and developed for all kinds of people	Female
Active participation by those using the facilities which should give opportunities for the young	Female
To make a safe place for all people of all ages to enjoy	Female
Exterior should be modern. Inside decorated tastefully with nice seats and tables, plenty of hall space	Female
Youth club with a youth leader. Luncheon club for older groups and gentle keep-fit for the elderly	Female

The interesting feature in comparing the statements from the adults with those from the teenagers is how they express themselves in more detail and how they thought beyond specific facilities that make up the leisure centre. These statements were unprompted, so one can imagine how much richer the explanations and justifications would be with an in-depth interview or a focus group. Again, there are many ways that the researcher can categorise the data, perhaps even more than with the teenagers. Categorising these adult statements is not as straightforward as for the teenagers. The researcher could draw out the words '**youth**' or '**rules**' and set these as categories. The researcher could pull out named '**facilities**' such as '**dance floor**' and '**nice seats and tables**' or '**activities**' such as '**youth club**' and '**luncheon club**'. What becomes apparent in reading through the statements (especially with the full set of responses) are implied problems related to issues of parking, the types of people that are attracted or could be attracted, and how 'regimented' or not the centre should be. These are categories or patterns that may be apparent to a reader, though not explicitly expressed. There may be words expressed that make up the categories, but the words broken down and taken in isolation may lose their impact, if they are just counted.

Table 9.2 illustrates that categorisation into the component words may mean that the contextual material that gives these words meaning can be lost. From the above example, coding can be thought of as a means to:

1 *Retrieve data*, i.e. from the whole mass of data, particular words or statements can be searched for and retrieved to examine the 'fit' with other words or statements.
2 *Organise the data*, i.e. words or statements can be reordered, put alongside each other and similarities and differences evaluated.
3 *Interpret data*, i.e. as words or statements are retrieved and organised in different ways, different interpretations of the similarities and differences can be made.

Coding is a process that enables the researcher to identify what he or she sees as meaningful and to set the stage to draw conclusions and interpret the meaning. Codes are essentially labels to assign meaning to the data compiled during a study.

In broad terms the coding process involves the following stages:

1 *Set up a broad group of coding categories.* These would emerge from an initial reading of the gathered data and the intended purpose of the study. For example, these may be the themes that structured a number of focus group interviews or in-depth interviews.
2 *Work through the data to uncover 'chunks' of data that may be put into brackets or underlined or highlighted.* Codes are usually attached to 'chunks' of varying size, i.e. words, phrases, sentences, paragraphs, an extended story, an image, indeed any component of the collected data, connected or unconnected to a specific context.[16] Sometimes a single sentence or paragraph might be coded into several categories. For example, one paragraph where participants are overtly discussing parking problems at a community centre may also be discussing issues of 'mobility' or 'independence'. Once the start and end of a chunk to be coded is established, a name or number is assigned to it.
3 *Review the descriptions given to the codes.* Working through the data, it may be clear that important themes emerging from the data do not fit into the preset categories or that one theme blurs into two or more separate concepts. At this point new categories have to be set to fit the data. With new categories, the data must then be reviewed and recoded where appropriate. This stage therefore is one of immersion in the data and refining the nature of categories as more meaning is uncovered in the data.
4 *Examine differences between types of participant.* This could be simple demographic comparisons, e.g. to see if there are differences between men and women in how they view independence. The comparisons could be between types of respondent that emerge from other codes, e.g. lifestyle aspirations may emerge from the data with

groups emerging that may be labelled 'sophisticated minimalists' and 'spiritual warriors'. Comparisons of the behaviour between these emerging groups can be made. Through these comparisons, new insights may emerge about the assigned codes and the descriptors applied to them. New insights may also emerge about the way that participants are described and categorised, combining knowledge of their demographic, geographic, behavioural, psychographic and psychological characteristics. The following Sports Marketing Survey example on rugby league illustrates how it classified focus group participants to perform the analyses.

 Sports Marketing Surveys

Rugby league study

In the rugby league study, Sports Marketing Surveys analysed its focus group findings based upon gender, behavioural and attitudinal characteristics. The analysis focused upon four distinctive groups that it labelled and described as:

Male Avid Rugby League Fans – whose interest in the game ranged from 7–65 years, following and experience, averaging over 30 years. Most of them were brought up with the game encapsulated by *'first match inside mother's stomach!'* *'since I was a student'*, *'Grandad used to play, I used to play'*. They all attended matches with their family: *'go with my daughter'*, *'the wife, she's madder about it than me!'*, *'the whole family – my aunts, uncles, cousins ... everyone!'*

Female Family Rugby League Fans – whose interest in the game ranged from half to 'all' of their lives, initiated by *'dad made us watch it when we were small'*, *'thought it would be good for my son, and social for me'*, *'kids got tickets from school'*. They all attended matches with their family from a single parent with her son, through to attending with a husband after all the children had grown up and moved on.

Male Occasional Rugby League Fans – whose interest in the game was part of an overall 'sports interest'. Around half also played other sports but 'armchair involvement' was popular: *'mad about all sports!'*, *'sports freak all my life'*, *'play golf, badminton, swim, go to football with friends, rugby league finals sometimes'*. They were all family men with children ranging from toddler age to young adults, but more likely to attend games with friends and colleagues (albeit usually football).

Male General Sports Fans – whose interest in the game was part of an overall 'sports interest', were 'non-rejectors' of rugby league but were predominantly avid football supporters: *'watch anything with a ball!'*, *'like all sports'*, *'watch all sports, but selectively!'* They were all family men with two or three children, who were most likely to watch live football games outside their family unit or *'prefer to watch in the pub where there are no distractions'*.

5 *Develop models of interconnectivity amongst the coded categories.* This involves basic graphical modelling to explain a sequence of events or a process that the data describe. It could show how categories relate to each other, how participants may be alike or differ and how different contexts impact upon the categories and participants. Again, new insights may emerge about the meaning seen in the data, and the coding process may be further refined.

6 *Iterate between the code descriptions and the developing model.* This stage is again one of immersion in the data, with continual refining of the nature of categories and the structural relationship of those categories. These iterations continue until the researchers have what they believe to be the most valid meaning that they see in the data.

The approach described above can be completed manually or proprietary software can be used. The relative advantages and disadvantages of manual or electronic approaches to analysing qualitative data, and especially the iterative process of coding and modelling, are presented later in the chapter. The point to consider at this stage is that the immersion in the data to draw out meaning is not formulaic. Reducing qualitative data to the essence of meaning as seen by the researchers is a highly creative and subjective process. Given the time that may be allocated to this process, coding can be observed from two perspectives. First, if there is relative little time for the researchers to immerse themselves in the data, it can be thought of as a means to simplify or reduce the mass of data. If an initial broad group of coding categories is kept and their number is relatively small, then the data can be 'stripped down' to a simple general form. This coding approach can be compared directly with simple forms of content analysis.[17] Second, if more time can be afforded, it can be thought of as a means to expand, transform and reconceptualise data, opening up more diverse ideas and analytical possibilities. The general analytical approach is to open up the categories in order to interrogate them further, to try to identify and speculate about further features. Coding here is about going beyond the data, thinking creatively with the data, asking the data questions, and generating theories and frameworks.[18]

Coding is a major process involved in data reduction. The process forces the researchers to focus upon what they believe to be the most valid meaning held in the data. In order to develop that meaning further, the researchers need to communicate their vision to others, to evaluate their interpretations of the data and to reflect upon their own vision. The stage of data display is the means by which researchers communicate their vision of meaning in the data.

Data display

Data display
Involves summarising and presenting the structure that is seen in collected qualitative data.

Data display is an organised, compressed assembly of information that permits conclusion drawing and action.[19] The most frequent form of display for qualitative data in the past has been *extended text*. Such an approach is cumbersome, dispersed and sequential, poorly structured and extremely bulky. The qualitative researcher can resolve these problems with the use of matrices, graphs, charts and networks. All are designed to assemble information into an immediately accessible, compact form so that the analyst can see what is happening and either draw justified conclusions or move on to the next step of analysis the displays suggests may be useful. The creation and use of displays is not an end output of analysis, it is an integral part of the analytic process. For example, designing a matrix as a display involves decisions on what should be displayed in the rows and columns, and deciding what qualitative data, in which form, should be entered in the cells.

Data display also allows a 'public' view of how the researcher has made connections between the different 'data chunks'. Even if others may not have made the same connections and interpret the data in exactly the same manner, the logic of connections should be clear. The display may be in a graphical format, with boxes summarising issues that have emerged and connecting arrows showing the interconnection between issues. Verbatim quotes can be used to illustrate the issues or the interconnections. Pictures, drawings, music or advertisements can also be used to illustrate issues or interconnections. The overall structure allows the marketing decision-maker who is to use the analysis to see the general meaning in the collected data. The illustration of issues or interconnections brings that meaning to life.

One of the simplest means to display data is through the use of a spreadsheet. This can be built up and displayed in a manual or electronic format. Table 9.3 presents an example of how a spreadsheet may be set out. This spreadsheet is a sample of all the interviews that may be conducted and the number of issues that may be tackled. The example relates to a bus and tram operator who wishes to understand the attitudes and behaviour of 18–25 year olds related to using public transport. In the columns, details of each interview are presented, and in the final column, notes are made of observations between interviews with a focus on each issue. In the rows, the issues that were discussed in the interviews are presented. These issues may be generated from the topic guide used and/or from the notes of the researcher related to what he or she sees as the emerging issues. The final row details notes of the dynamics of the group, explaining why particular exchanges may be interpreted in a particular way. The analyst cuts and pastes extracts from the transcripts into the relevant cells. With the spreadsheet built up of the reordered transcripts (each focus group may tackle the issues in a different order and with different emphases), comparisons can be made across the columns on particular issues, looking for similarities and differences. Connections between issues can be mapped out with the use of arrows to show the flow of dialogue. The responses from types of participants such as 'city-dwellers' or 'suburb-dwellers' can be colour coded to examine differences. Different notes, images or any other supplementary material can be pasted onto the spreadsheet to help in the interpretation; all the assembled data can be displayed, or more probably a reduced and coded set of data can be displayed.

Table 9.3 Spreadsheet data display of focus group discourse

Interviews? Issues, e.g.?	Group 1 – 18–25-year-old male car drivers	Group 2 – 18–25-year-old female car drivers	Group 3 – 18–25-year-old male bus and tram users	Group 4 – 18–25-year-old female bus and tram users	Notes on the similarities and differences between groups on issues?
Evening travel	Verbatim discourse taken from the interview that relates to this issue				
Commuting					
Freedom					
Friends					
Notes on the dynamics of individual groups?					

Such a spreadsheet can be built up manually using large sheets of paper from, for example, flip charts, divided into a grid, and the evidence such as chunks of the transcript physically pasted in. The big advantage of this approach is being able to visualise the whole body of data and to move around the data to 'play' with ideas and connections. This works particularly well when there is more than one person working on the analysis and they are drawing ideas and questions out of each other as they relate to the data. The disadvantage is that editing, moving data around and recategorising data can become very cumbersome and messy. This is where electronic means of displaying the data work well. With electronic means, images and notes can be scanned in and added to the transcripts. Changes can be made very easily and quickly in moving data around, recategorising and incorporating new material. Different versions can be easily stored to allow an evaluation of how the thought processes of the researcher have developed. The disadvantage of the approach is that, when attempting to view the data in their entirety, the entire dataset is there but in effect is viewed through a 'window' with a limited field of vision. The 'window' can be readily moved about but the overall perspective is limited.

Another simple means to display data is through the use of a qualitative cross-tabulation. Table 9.4 presents an example of how a cross-tabulation may be set out. Again, the example relates to a bus and tram operator who wishes to understand the attitudes and behaviour of 18–25 year olds related to using public transport. The table shows a sample of categories that have been built around issue of 'evening travel'. As the analyst works through the transcripts and codes distinct chunks of data, and with knowledge of who expressed a particular view that is embodied in that chunk, that relationship can be displayed. The table shows that the analyst has established codes to represent views of 'expense', 'personal attacks' 'spontaneity' and 'style'. With a simple classification of participants, in this case by gender, the analyst can display differences in the number of incidences that a specific code emerges. The large differences between males and females in how they brought up the issues 'expense' and 'personal attacks' can help the analyst to explore the data further, or indeed collect more data to understand what is creating such divergent attitudes and behaviour. Again, different notes, images or any other supplementary material can be pasted onto the cross-tabulation to help in the interpretation.

Table 9.4 Cross-tabulation of emerging categories related to evening travel by gender

Evening travel	Gender	
	Male	Female
Expense	16	2
Personal attacks	8	24
Spontaneity	5	5
Style	3	5

The other major means of displaying data is to use flow charts. Figure 9.2 displays a very basic structure of the issues or major categories and subcategories related to how 18–25 year olds view the use of public transport after an evening out.

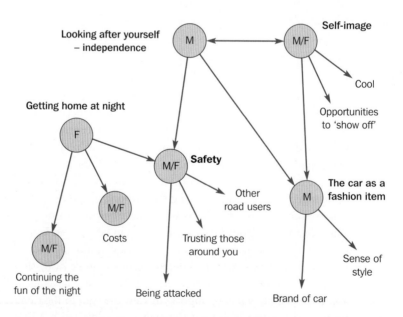

Figure 9.2
Flow chart depicting how 18–25-year-olds view public transport

Visualising the data in this matter can allow the researchers to dip back into the transcripts and their notes to seek alternative ways of connecting evidence and justifying connections. This means that this form of graphic can play a vital role in data reduction and coding, i.e. in making sense of the data, as well as in portraying a final interpretation of the data. Most proprietary qualitative analysis software packages allow data structures to be displayed as in Figure 9.2 but with far more sophisticated features to display structure, differences and supporting evidence. A simple illustration of this in Figure 9.2 is the 'M/F' label attached to categories, used to display behavioural tendencies of male or female participants. With an analysis package, quite distinctive structures for participant types may be mapped, with the ability to tap into supporting evidence in actual categories or in the links between categories.[20]

Once the researchers have displayed what they see as the meaning in the data, they need to demonstrate the credibility of their vision. This involves data verification.

Data verification

Data verification
Involves seeking alternative explanations of the interpretations of qualitative data, through other data sources.

Data verification involves seeking alternative explanations through other data sources and theories. From the start of data collection, qualitative researchers are beginning to decide the meaning of their observations, and noticing regularities, patterns, explanations, possible configurations, causal flows and propositions. The researcher should form these meanings 'lightly' maintaining openness and scepticism, developing conclusions that are embryonic and vague at first, then increasingly explicit and grounded. Final conclusions may not appear until data collection is over, depending upon the volume of data collected in all their forms, the coding, storage and retrieval methods used, and the resource constraints placed upon the researchers. When final conclusions have been drawn, researchers need to demonstrate that they have presented a valid meaning of the data that they have collected. They need to show that the structure or meaning they see is not just a reflection of their own views. This is where the concept of theoretical understanding as discussed at the start of this chapter can help. It is also where the use of the researchers' field notes proves to be invaluable. The use of theory from secondary data, intelligence and the literature can help to guide what may be reasonably expected as a meaning. Other means to verify the data can be through seeking 'similar' research findings and explanations taken from different contexts, different time frames and different researchers.[21] Though the findings from these different scenarios will not be the same, there can be categories that give qualitative researchers the confidence that they are representing a valid view of their participants.

Two forms of validation have been suggested as particularly appropriate to the logic of qualitative research.[22] The first is termed 'triangulation', a term derived from navigation, where different bearings give the correct position of an object. In research terms, comparing different kinds of data (e.g. dialogue and photographs, quantitative and qualitative) and different methods (e.g. observations and interviews) allows reflection upon the extent of corroboration, and what may be the causes of any differences.[23] The second is termed 'participant validation'. This involves taking one's findings back to the participants under study. Where the feedback from participants on emergent conclusions is verified by them, there can be more confidence in the validity of the findings.

The concept of validity will be examined in more detail in Chapter 12.[24] At this stage it is worth noting that the qualitative researchers should not just present an interpretation and then seek validation or verification of that perspective. The search for verification is a quest that permeates the whole research process. At face value, data assembly, reduction, display and verification appear to be quite distinct and consecutive stages of data analysis. The reality is that they are iterative and totally interdependent upon each other. As the researchers assemble new data, they should be thinking of means to validate their views, asking questions of different individuals in different ways and recording these thoughts in their field notes. As data are being reduced and coded, the researchers seek different possible explanations and evidence to support categorising, naming and connecting views in a particular manner. The researchers will question their interpretations of words and gestures and their own ways of seeing. This questioning process adds to the verification. The use of data display is a means to communicate to others the meaning and structure that researchers 'see' in qualitative data. The display allows others to understand that vision, to question and evaluate it. The exposure and critique of the vision by other researchers and decision-makers further verify the data. Ultimately, such critique can direct the researchers to further data assembly, reduction and display; the stages may unfold in 'waves' to produce an ultimate interpretation of great value to decision-makers.

Grounded theory

Grounded theory
A qualitative approach to generating theory through the systematic and simultaneous process of data collection and analysis.

In 1967 Glaser and Strauss published the seminal work *The discovery of grounded theory.*[25] It was their formal description of the approach to handling and interpreting qualitative data that they had developed in the 1960s in a participant observation study of hospital staff's care and management of dying patients.[26] The method they developed was labelled **grounded theory** to reflect the source of the developed theory which is ultimately grounded in the behaviour, words and action of those under study.[27] The essence of their beliefs was:[28]

- The need to get out into the field if one wants to understand what is going on.
- The importance of theory grounded in reality.
- The nature of experience in the field for the subjects and researcher as continually evolving.
- The active role of persons in shaping the worlds they live in through the process of symbolic interaction.
- An emphasis on change and process and the variability and complexity of life.
- The interrelationship between meaning in the perception of subjects and their action.

Grounded theory methods consist of guidelines that aid the researcher to:[29]

1 Study social and social psychological processes (the essence of consumption experiences).
2 Direct data collection.
3 Manage data analysis.
4 Develop an abstract theoretical framework that explains the studied process.

Grounded theory researchers collect data and analyse them simultaneously from the initial phases of research. They would argue that they cannot know exactly what the most significant social and social psychological processes are in particular settings. They could be guided by existing theories which may predict the processes, but they would argue that such guidance may constrain their observations, forcing them to observe a particular setting from a narrow perspective. So they start with broad areas of interest and form preliminary interviewing questions to open up those areas. They explore and examine participants' views and then further develop questions around those views, seeking out participants whose experiences address the emerging issues. This sequence is repeated several times during a research project, which means that researchers are kept 'close' to their data. Grounded theory gives researchers tools to analyse data that are concurrent with obtaining additional focused data that inform, extend and refine emerging analytical themes. This means that interviews become more focused with a tight fit between the collected data and the data analysis. With grounded theory, the researcher works in the actual environments in which the actions take place, in natural situations in order analytically to relate participant's perspectives to the environments through which they emerge (such as ethnographers sharing the homes of families to observe how they use and listen to the radio).[30] The style of grounded theory adapts well to capturing the contextual complexities in which action unfolds, enabling researchers to understand better the interrelationships of context and action.

Essentially the approach is most commonly used to:

1 Generate new theory where little is already known,
2 Provide a fresh perspective on existing knowledge, i.e. to supplement existing theories.
3 Challenge existing theories. Researchers may challenge or disagree with existing theories for two reasons. The first is based upon the substantive representation of what the theory expounds, e.g. of how toddlers respond to certain forms of advertising. The second may be based upon how the theory was created, i.e. the research approach, techniques or forms of analysis.

The grounded theory approach to analysing data

Grounded theory provides researchers with guidelines for analysing data at several points in the research process, not simply at an end point or 'analysis stage'. It involves the following four stages:[31]

Coding data in grounded theory
A form of shorthand that distils events and meanings without losing their essential properties.

1 **Coding data.** Grounded theory coding is at least a two-step process. It starts with an initial or open coding process, which forces the researchers to begin making broad analytical decisions about the data they are collecting. It moves on to more selective or focused coding in which the researchers use the most frequently appearing initial codes to synthesise and conceptualise large amounts of data. In essence, coding is a form of shorthand that distils events and meanings without losing their essential properties. During the coding process, the researchers work through their collected data on a line-by-line basis, use 'active' terms or descriptors to define what is happening in the data, and ultimately follow leads in the initial coding through further data gathering. Throughout the process of coding in grounded theory, the researchers should regularly address the data, as they are built up and in their entirety, with the following list of questions. Attempting to answer these facilitates the questioning of how codes are defined, connected and subsumed into broader categories:[32]
   a *What?* What is it about here? Which phenomenon is mentioned?
   b *Who?* Which persons are involved? What roles do they play? How do they interact?
   c *How?* Which aspects of the phenomenon are mentioned (or not mentioned)?
   d *When? How long? Where?* Time, course, location?
   e *How much? How strong?* Aspects of intensity.
   f *Why?* Which reasons are given or can be reconstructed?
   g *What for?* With what intention, to what purpose?
   h *By which?* Means, tactics and strategies for reaching that goal.

Memo writing
Loosely written notes through to fully formed analytical arguments which are added to the original data and interpretations.

2 **Memo writing.** Memo writing links coding to the writing of the first draft of the analysis. This stage helps researchers to: define the properties of the categories that they have created, specify conditions under which each category has developed, note the impact of each category and the interrelationships with other categories. Memos can be loosely written notes to fully formed analytical arguments which are added to the original data and interpretations. The process of memo writing helps the researcher to achieve the following:[33]
   a Stop and think about what is emerging from the data.
   b Generate ideas to explore through other means of collecting data.
   c Reflect upon gaps and missed opportunities in earlier interviews and observations.

    d Reflect upon the meanings and impact of personal field notes.

    e Treat coded data as distinct categories to analyse.

    f Clarify categories, through their definitions, properties, distinctive elements, consequences and interconnectivity with other categories.

    g Make explicit comparisons of data with data, category with category, concept with concept.

Theoretical sampling
Data gathering driven by concepts derived from evolving theory and based on the concept of 'making comparisons'.

3 **Theoretical sampling.** This concept was introduced in Chapter 6 in our discussion of the differences between a positivist and interpretivist approach to research. This type of sampling is not designed to represent a chosen population, but to develop theory by seeking out new data. The process of gathering more data is driven by the challenges in building categories and concepts that are derived from evolving theory. It is based on the notion of seeking out different situations and learning from the comparisons that can be made. The purpose is to go to places, people or events that will maximise opportunities to discover variations amongst concepts. By generating more focused data to fill in any gaps in emerging categories and concepts, the whole process of theory building becomes more precise, explanatory and predictive. The process of theoretical sampling helps the researcher to achieve the following:[34]

    a Define gaps within and between categories.

    b Discover variation within categories.

    c Seek out and gather more focused and rich data.

    d Develop the strength of categories and their interconnections.

Integrating analysis
Creating an order and connectivity that is seen to be emerging from memos.

4 **Integrating analysis.** Producing more focused and well-developed memos as the analysis proceeds should enable the researchers to produce theory that is clear and well validated. The researchers should aim to integrate the memos they have crafted in order to reflect the theoretical direction of their analysis or stages of a process. They have to create the order (how do the ideas fit together?) and the connectivity (what order makes the most sense?) that they see emerging from their memos. The process of integrating the analysis helps the researchers to achieve the following:

    a Sort the memos, usually done by the titles of categories.

    b Map out a number of ways to order the memos.

    c Choose an order that works for the analysis and the target audience.

    d Create clear links between categories.

When ordering memos the researchers should consider whether a particular order reflects or challenges the logic of the experiences of participants and their target audiences of marketing decision-makers. A balance needs to be made between both parties, which may mean collapsing categories for clarity and ease of reading.

Limitations of grounded theory

Grounded theory has been criticised for its failure to acknowledge implicit theories which guide qualitative researchers in the early stages of their work. Grounded theorists argue that such guidance may constrain their observations, forcing them to question and observe a particular setting from a narrow perspective. The downside of claiming to have such an approach is that it may be extremely difficult to ignore theories that may be embedded into their way of thinking. It may also be counterproductive to ignore relevant theories (used with a healthy dose of scepticism) that could be useful in creating focus in gathering and interpreting data. Another major criticism of grounded theory is that the process can degenerate into a fairly empty building of categories, especially when aided by data analysis software.[35]

Content analysis

Content analysis
The objective, systematic and quantitative description of the manifest content of a communication.

In qualitative research, **content analysis** is one of the classical procedures for analysing textual material or communication rather than behaviour or physical objects. The text being analysed may come from the narrative held in brochures or advertising copy, to dialogues held in interview data. Primarily the objective of content analysis is to 'reduce' the data, to simplify by summarising and structuring the data according to rules derived from existing theory. In effect, even though a researcher may be working with qualitative data, content analysis should be classified as a quantitative technique based upon classifying and 'counting'. Content analysis is seen by many as an 'objective', systematic and quantitative description of the manifest content of a communication.[36] The term 'content analysis' is set to include observation as well as analytic activity. The unit of analysis may be words (different words or types of words in the message), characters (individuals or objects), themes (propositions), space and time measures (length or duration of the message) or topics (subject of the message). Analytical categories for classifying the units are developed, and the communication is broken down according to prescribed rules. Marketing research applications involve observing and analysing the content or message of advertisements, newspaper articles, TV and radio programmes and the like. For example, the frequency of appearance of ethnic minorities and women in advertising has been studied using content analysis.

Content analysis has several virtues.[37] First of all, it is a standardised technique that permits the processing of large amounts of data covering long time spans. It is an unobtrusive research method, avoiding the problems of researcher effects on the data that are inherent in interpretative research methods such as in-depth interviewing.

Limitations of content analysis

Content analysis has its shortcomings; the most serious involve the issues of manifest content, data fragmentation and quantification. For qualitative researchers, these set limits on the usefulness of the method for the analysis of visual representations:

1 *Manifest content.* A crucial requirement to the success of content analysis is that the established categories of analysis are sufficiently precise to enable different coders to arrive at the same results when the same body of material (e.g. advertising copy) is examined. Thus, manifest content refers to what may be seen to be manifestly apparent in the established categories of any communication. This means that in coding the meanings in any communication a clearly defined category system must plainly state the characteristics of content, there can be no implicit or hidden meanings from the coding operation. For some analysts,[38] the insistence upon coding only manifest content is too restrictive. The essence of their argument is that excessive emphasis on a standardised approach can result in reliability being attained at the expense of validity. The significance of the message may lie more in its context than in its manifest content.

2 *Data fragmentation.* By virtue of the constraint of focusing upon manifest content, the tendency is to break up communications into their elements, and it is solely the presence, absence or frequency of these elements that is deemed relevant to the investigation. This categorisation isolates those elements of the communication determined by the researcher's analytical framework or theory. This process decontextualises the message in a communication, a process described as losing the phenomenon, or failing to respect the original right of the data.[39]

3 *Quantification.* Berelson[40] argued that content analysis is essentially a quantitative research technique. He would be suspicious of any attempt to bring qualitative considerations into the technique – to do so would risk its objectivity and systematicness. He

argued that its strength lies in allowing the selection and rational organisation of categories to condense the substantive meanings of a communication, with an aim to testing assumptions or hypotheses. If the aim of a study were to count frequencies in order to test hypotheses about communications, then the technique would have much to offer. In this case it could be argued that the requirements of objectivity and systematicness should be the prime aim of the content analyst, and that the issue of manifest content be treated on a case-by-case basis. When examining individual cases and contexts, the presence or absence of a 'theme' may be measured, but not the frequency with which it occurs in the communication. What the essence is of that 'theme' takes the method into the realms of qualitative research.

Semiotics

Semiotics
The study of signs in the context of consumer experience.

We have described a range of different qualitative techniques and approaches that primarily focus on the participants or the consumers; questioning and observing them in a direct or indirect manner. **Semiotics** takes a different approach in that consumers are not viewed as independent, self-determining agents, making their own choices. Rather, consumers are viewed as products of culture, constructed and largely determined by the popular culture within which they live. Consumer needs and aspirations are seen as not being the result of freely made choices of the individual, but a reflection of the surrounding cultural discourses. Semiotics therefore moves the marketing researcher's focus towards the cultural context of the consumer, including both popular culture and the marketing context.[41] Semiotics combines knowledge and research techniques from across a spectrum of disciplines, including linguistics, psychology, anthropology, cultural studies and the visual arts. It analyses data such as paintings and photography that some other qualitative research methods do not tackle so well.[42] It is based on a detailed analysis of language and images which untangle how meaning is conveyed as well as what that meaning is. The difference between a semiotic approach and other qualitative approaches can be illustrated using the following examples.

Example   Just a sign of the times?[43]

Semiotics contributed to the cult status achieved by Pot Noodle by depicting the brand as food pornography. Semiotics consultant Greg Rowland drew the unlikely comparison between dried noodles and pornography:

> We looked at the relationship between instant snacks and real food and saw parallels in the relationship of porn to love. Neither claim to be the real thing or to be good for you. It's instant gratification and overly intense hits of pleasure.

The idea was taken up and developed into the notorious 'Slag of all snacks' campaign, which portayed Pot Noodle as a shameful, but irresistible pleasure that has consumers irredeemably hooked.

Example   Fish out of water[44]

Pulse (**www.pulse.com**) explored the world of electronic music communication (linguistic and visual) to understand the cues that define the genre, and those that do not. Pulse also looked beyond the music sector, to related markets such as alcohol and fashion, to understand better the cultural interplay and genre references. Pulse sees the study of communications, cultural signs, cues and signifiers as really adding value, providing extra evidence to back up the researcher's intuitive thoughts or inherent knowledge of the sector. This approach was taken in a project using semiotics to evaluate album covers for a dance music label.

A conventional qualitative researcher might ask, 'Why does Frank buy Pot Noodle?' The semioticians would be more likely to ask, 'How does consumer culture give meaning to Pot Noodle, and what are these meanings?' They might argue that if we can answer these questions, we will be able to make a good guess not just at why Frank buys it, but also why anyone buys it. This is because its meanings are constructed within popular culture, and consumers are influenced and constrained by this cultural context. An understanding of the broader cultural context is something that semiotic analysis is uniquely well placed to provide, because it focuses on the culture and not just on the consumer.[45]

Examples of how semiotics can help marketing decision-makers are:[46]

- Mapping out a new market or a whole field of cultural activity.
- Seeing the opportunities to position new brands.
- Analysing how different aspects of marketing communications work together, and the means to create synergies across different media.
- Evaluating in-store developments and harmonising the different aspects of marketing communications.
- Diagnosing problems with brand or marketing communications.
- Providing models and guidelines for successful brand communications, indicating the key signifiers within the relevant context.
- Understanding the process of encoding and decoding more precisely, to minimise the potential for misunderstanding between the marketer and the consumer.

As can be seen from the above list, semiotics can play a major role in the development of a wide array of marketing communications. In terms of conducting a qualitative analysis of marketing communications, the approach goes into far more depth in comparison with content analysis. Semioticians investigate the subtext of communication. They begin with the brand, combing through the cultural connotations of advertising imagery and language, the colour, shape and forms of corporate identity, where the brand is distributed and how it is displayed. Then they look outwards to the consumer's world, hunting for shifts in cultural meaning – how concepts such as masculinity, heroism or indulgence have changed over time and how they might be reinterpreted.[47] To illustrate this point, the following questions may be set by a researcher examining the advertising of a particular brand, looking at the past, the potential and the competition. The questions would be directed at the text, sounds and images of the advertisements, the wide breadth of qualitative data:[48]

- What are the major signifiers (i.e. the material signs – what it is)?
- What signifieds (i.e. the conceptual sign – what it means) might they be creating and to whom?
- How do the advertisements work on a symbolic/metaphorical and on a product/metonymical (literal) level?
- How do the form and content of the advertisement work together?
- What codes (i.e. bundles of signs) do the advertisements use?
- How does the advertisement measure up to the brand's historical codes and those of its competitors?
- How do the advertisements work in relation to the brand's history and its futures?

- Is the advertisement using a dominant (everyday, mainstream), emergent (leading edge, culturally dynamic) or residual (old fashioned, lacking in energy) set of codes or are residual codes being applied in an emergent way?
- What kinds of discourse or discourses are apparent, e.g. postmodernism, feminism, spirituality?

This set of questions and processes will illuminate the advertising for the researcher. They will help the researcher to understand more completely the material that viewers will be evaluating. However, this may not be readily achievable using a single researcher. To maximise the potential of semiotics, an action research approach (described in Chapter 6) may offer the best results. This would involve taking a more facilitative and involving approach; sharing the actual techniques and questions of semiotic analysis with researchers and decision-makers working together towards the co-creation of knowledge. This would be more open and interactive. Semiotics specialists would be vital to the process, but as facilitators and mentors in a workshop style of joint working, helping clients identify and understand the way forward themselves. A more involving approach also provides the tools to recode, enabling the client to move from insight to the successful implementation of new strategy in any of the applications above.[49]

Limitations of semiotics

Although semiotics is able to analyse a great breadth of interrelated qualitative data, there are four core criticisms of semiotics:

1 *Reliability.* The main criticism of semiotics lies in how reliable or replicable it is.[50] Although an individual analyst's interpretation may be very insightful and could be a valid representation of cultural influences upon the consumer, there is little guaranteeing that another analyst would come to the same conclusion about the relevant codes or structures.

2 *Qualitative dataset.* In practice it can be hard to assemble the relevant data to analyse, given that there is usually no discourse or discussion as may be assembled with a series of focus groups or in-depth interviews.

3 *Logic of interpretation.* It is not usually clear how the analyst has arrived at an interpretation. It must be accepted that there is no unique way to interpret text or other types of qualitative data. On this score, Derrida[51] makes the point that no single interpretation can ever claim to be the final one.[52] In the case of semiotics, in many instances an interpretation seems to rely upon a shared knowledge of a cultural background and intuition, which may be valid but extremely difficult to validate. This is where an action research approach can help, where the team of researchers and marketing decision-makers share and 'own' the interpretation.

4 *Consumer theory.* The position of the consumer can be unclear in semiotic analysis. In principle, the consumer is seen as passive, determined by culture and unable to break out of his or her contextual frame.[53] Many consumer theorists would disagree with this view, giving the consumer a more active role in interpreting, accepting or resisting the brand's semiotically encoded meanings.

Using computers in qualitative research and analysis

A major problem for the qualitative researcher is the sheer volume of data that may be collected. In an attempt to 'step into the shoes' of target consumers, a whole array of questions, probes, observations, answers and personal notes have to be analysed. As with quantitative data analyses, it is possible to complete analyses without the aid of a computer. Using the computer should provide speed, memory, ease of data access and the ability to transform and manipulate data in many ways. Overall it allows a much more efficient and ultimately effective process, as the researcher's effort may be focused upon generating the most effective support for decision-makers as quickly as possible rather than upon laborious administrative tasks. The following list summarises qualitative research activities that may be supported by the use of computers:

1 *Field notes*. Making notes before, during and after interviews and observations. Writing and editing these notes if needed as part of a data display to justify a particular interpretation.
2 *Transcripts*. Building up transcripts to represent the discourse in interviews.
3 *Coding*. Attaching keywords to chunks of data or text.
4 *Storage, search and retrieval*. Keeping data in an organised manner, so that relevant segments of data or text can be located, pulled out and evaluated.
5 *Connection*. Linking relevant data segments with each other.
6 *Memoing*. Writing up reflective comments that can be 'pasted' onto relevant codes and connections.
7 *Data display*. Placing selected or reduced data in a condensed and organised format using a spreadsheet matrix or network. The display can be part of the development of the analysis or in the final vision produced by the researcher.
8 *Drawing conclusions and verification*. Aiding the researcher to interpret the data display and to test or confirm findings.
9 *Theory building*. Developing systematic and conceptually coherent explanations of findings that are meaningful to marketing decision-makers.
10 *Reporting*. Presenting interim and final reports of the findings in a written and oral manner.

Many of these tasks can be performed with readily available word-processing, spreadsheet and presentation packages. Many researchers may be very comfortable using such packages to gather and record data and to present findings. What may be new to many researchers is the use of proprietary software to help with the technical integration of data assembly, reduction, display and verification. Improvements in the functions and power of software that copes with this technical integration occur at a rapid pace. To see an array of different qualitative data analysis packages, download demos and evaluate how applicable they may be to a particular qualitative technique, visit the following websites:

Qualitative data analysis software	Website
NVivo and XSight	www.qsrinternational.com
Atlas ti	www.atlasti.com
Ethnograph	www.qualisearch.com
C-I-SAID	www.code-a-text.co.uk

The demo disc attached to this book is the QSR International product XSight. Conventional qualitative data analysis software was designed for and used mainly by academic researchers in the social sciences. XSight was designed for marketing researchers by marketing researchers who understood the challenges faced by the profession. The following example summarises a review of the software and shows how it has changed the data analysis practices of the leading marketing research agency MORI. We recommend that you visit the QSR website to review descriptions of applications and cases. You can then choose when you wish to start working with the XSight demo disc. Remember that this demo has the full suite of XSight features and that, once it is installed, you will be able to use it for a period of 90 days.

| *Example* | XSight reviewed[54] |

Sara Butler, an associate director at MORI's Qualitative Hothouse (**www.mori.com/ qualitative/**) used QSR's XSight qualitative software to handle a six-month 'mega-project' of some 80 focus groups throughout the UK. Not only did XSight impose a discipline and rigour on the process, but also it reduced the burden of management, made it easier for her to monitor the job in progress and the consistency of work from different moderators, and brought her extra thinking time. The tool is now in regular use at MORI. Sara rates XSight highly for overall design, ease of use and 'the way it pulls everything together, like a virtual whiteboard'. She estimates it saved her about two hours of work on each group, while through the project tracking capabilities, she achieved much higher levels of consistency across all groups because she could get her hands on the data much sooner. Sara observes: 'People are taking on larger and larger qualitative projects, which opens up a whole new world of project management. One of its key strengths is that it provides a project management tool too.'

XSight is a computer-assisted qualitative data analysis (or CAQDAS) tool from QSR, an Australian software developer (**www.qsrinternational.com**). QSR started by developing NUD*IST and NVIVO, both widely used in academic and social research but rarely applied in the world of marketing research where there is still much scepticism about the use of software to analyse qualitative data.

The core of XSight is based upon three components:

1 Transcripts.
2 The analysis framework, which can equate to the interview guide.
3 Interviewer observations, selected verbatim quotes and other notes.

The framework is a tree structure of headings and subheadings which can be broken down to many levels. So if 'packaging' for a product was a high-level topic, 'colour', 'images' and 'wording' might be the next level down, and within, say, 'colour', could be listed 'pink', 'blue', 'white', then down to 'like', 'dislike', and so on. With a framework set up from the start, this could be used to supplement or even replace the interview guide. The screen is divided into three main areas: transcript, analysis framework and a space for comments and observations. When coding the transcript, the relevant level is chosen from the analysis hierarchy. Comments are now focused only on that single analysis heading, and they can be amended or new ones added, which can be paraphrases, notes, hunches or actual, selected verbatim, which are simply dragged from the transcript and dropped into place. This usefully creates a hyperlink back to the text which means that, several hundred comments later, they can always be seen in the full context of any verbatim quote, simply by clicking on the link. The real power comes once all of the coding has been completed. Bringing everything together is done through the 'query' window, where all the responses can be sifted and any classification or any level of the analysis framework enables all of the responses to be pulled out for all the groups, or filtered by demographics. This is where the real thinking goes on, and at the bottom of the window, a document can be opened up which can gradually be developed into a report. Reports can be destined for either Microsoft Word or PowerPoint.

Qualitative data analysis packages do not automate the analysis process, nor is that their purpose. The process of coding, as described in the data verification section, depends upon the interpretations made by the researcher. The overall description, model or theory that emerges from the analysis also depends upon interpretations made by the researcher. No analysis package can perform such interpretations.

Qualitative data analysis is not formulaic; it requires an approach that gives quick feedback to the researcher on the results of emergent questions. This involves an iterative cycle of reflection and innovation, which means total interaction between the researcher and the computer. So, rather than seeing analysis as an automated process, the purpose of software is to aid the researcher to analyse data in a systematic and thorough manner. The researcher seeks patterns, meanings and interconnections in the qualitative data. This can be conducted manually, but by using software the researcher can manipulate the data far more efficiently to help see patterns, meanings and interconnections and ultimately to develop theory. In summary, software packages offer the qualitative researcher the following advantages.

Advantages of computer-assisted qualitative data analysis

1 *Speed*. The speed at which programs can carry out sorting procedures on large volumes of data is remarkable, and continues to get faster. This gives the data analyst more time to think about the meaning of data, enabling rapid feedback of the results of particular analytic ideas so that new ones can be formulated. Analysis becomes more devoted to creative and intellectual tasks, less immersed in routine.

2 *Rigour*. Rigour adds to the trust placed in research findings. In this context it means counting the number of times things occur as well as demonstrating that negative incidences have been located rather than selecting anecdotes that support a particular interpretation.

3 *Team*. In collaborative research projects where researchers need to agree on the meaning of codes, a check can easily be made of whether team members are interpreting segments in the same way. This is particularly useful as coding moves from the more descriptive and mundane codes to ones that reflect broader theoretical concerns. Researchers can pass coded interviews between them, and compare the results.

4 *Sampling*. It is easy to keep track of who *has* been interviewed, compared with the intentions of who *should* be interviewed. Beyond the sampling of individuals is the concept of theoretical sampling, i.e. the inclusion of events that corroborate or contradict developing theory. As researchers have more time to spend on creative and intellectual tasks, they can develop stronger descriptions and theories and strengthen the validity of their views by ensuring they have sampled sufficient incidences.[55]

It must be reinforced, however, that software packages cannot interpret and find meaning in qualitative data. The programs do facilitate, and in some cases automate, the identification and coding of text. But there is sometimes a false assumption that identification and coding are simple and unproblematic, and critical evaluation and scrutiny of coded segments and code counts are not needed. By facilitating quick analyses which focus on quantitative category relationships, the software may discourage more time-consuming, in-depth interpretations. Thus while the programs are intended as a means of allowing the researcher to stay close to the data, their misuse can have the unintended result of distancing the researcher from the data. As discussed earlier, many decision-makers who use qualitative marketing research do not question how analysis is completed, or indeed why it should be completed. The following arguments illustrate the nature of their concerns.[56]

Disadvantages of computer-assisted qualitative data analysis

1 *Mechanistic data analysis*. The computer cannot replace the creative process expected of the qualitative researcher. The researcher can evaluate the interrelated play on particular words, the tone of voice or the gestures of a particular participant. The sensitivity towards these relationships and connections can be lost in a mechanistic search for statements.

2 *Loss of the overview*. The researcher may be seduced into concentrating on the detail of individual chunks of data and assigning codes to the data. This focus may detract from the overall context that is so vital to identify and name chunks of data. Making sense of codes can be greatly facilitated by an ability to visualise the data in their entirety.

3 *Obsession with volume.* Given the ability to manipulate large amounts of data, there may be a push to increase the number of interviews. This may be counterproductive in that the emphasis should be on the interrelated *qualities* of:
- individual participants
- the interview process.

4 *Exclusion of non-text data.* As noted earlier, qualitative 'text' can include notes, observations, pictures and music that make up the total 'picture' or representation of individuals. Many programs can only cope with the narrative of questions and answers recorded in transcripts (though rapid developments are being made to overcome this shortcoming).

Many software developers recognise these limitations and have gone to great pains to overcome them. One of the trade-offs faced by software developers in overcoming these limitations is the user-friendliness of their programs compared with the sophistication of being able to manipulate and represent the structure that may lie in multifarious data. As qualitative researchers use and learn how to generate the most from the software, user-friendliness may take a lesser though not ignored role. Experienced qualitative researchers can demand more sophistication to match the realities of coping with qualitative data. For the novice qualitative researcher the packages may seem daunting, but this problem is analogous to an initial exposure to sophisticated survey design packages such as SNAP or statistical packages such as SPSS. In all cases researchers need to appreciate how the software may serve them and work through the examples and cases, to experiment and to build up their knowledge and confidence.

International marketing research

If one were to take the very naive view of qualitative data analysis being to feed data into an analysis package, and to wait for processed data to emerge, then international analysis would focus purely upon issues of language and translation. Such a perspective of qualitative analysis would ignore the context and process of collecting data and the role that context and process play in interpreting the meaning that emerges from interviews and observations. As discussed at the start of this chapter, qualitative marketing researchers need an acute self-awareness of how they 'see' – which affects the way they pose questions and interpret answers.

Consumers in any country use their social and cultural frames of reference to interpret questions posed to them by qualitative researchers and to present a response. Likewise, qualitative researchers use their social and cultural frames to present questions and interpret answers. If the researcher and the participant share the same or similar social and cultural frames of reference, the analysis and interpretation of the data can be relatively straightforward. If the qualitative researcher goes into an international market, there is the potential for big differences in social and cultural frames between the researcher and the researched. The qualitative researcher needs to develop an understanding of the social and cultural frames of the types of participant in an international market. At the same time, they must have a strong awareness of their own social and cultural frames. Only when qualitative researchers have examined both perspectives can they start to interpret consumer responses.

The process is summarised by leading qualitative researchers Virginia Valentine and Malcolm Evans as:[57]

Consumers give a 'coded' version of the social and cultural relationship with products and brands that drive their 'feelings'. Because language (and language systems) are the medium of culture, the rules of language become the rules of the code. Qualitative research then becomes a matter of working with the code through understanding the rules of language.

Thus, simple literal translations of transcripts of interviews from international markets entered into a qualitative data analysis package are doomed to failure. Understanding the rules of language and understanding oneself are vital for the qualitative researcher to interpret interviews and observations. As the rules of language, with the social and cultural forces that shape those rules, become more alien to the researcher in international markets, the task of analysis and meaningful interpretation becomes more difficult.

Ethics in marketing research

It is interesting to note that within the ESOMAR code of conduct, little reference is made to what is deemed the ethical practice of data analysis, be that quantitative or qualitative. This is understandable, as the chief concern for the marketing research industry is how participants are handled, i.e. the process of eliciting data from them. Care must be taken to ensure that the precious resource of participants is not misled or manipulated.

With quantitative data, as will be seen in Chapters 18–24, there are many established and consistent procedures of analysis. With qualitative data, even though there exists a broad framework to manage analysis procedures, there does not exist a body of consistent and established procedures of analysis. The difficulty in establishing consistent procedures lies primarily in the great diversity of data that can be included in the analysis procedure. Go back to the 'Data assembly' subsection to see the list of types of qualitative data and it is easy to see why this is so. Combining the researcher's notes, transcripts of interviews, pictures, audio and video recordings and mood boards does not lead to a structured process. It is a messy process that owes much to individual patience, creativity and vision.

In searching for support of ethical practice to cope with such a 'messy process', there is one area of support that comes from the code of conduct of the Market Research Society in the UK. In its section 'Mutual Rights and Responsibilities of Researchers and Clients', Rule B26 states:

When reporting on the results of a marketing research project the Researcher must make a clear distinction between the findings as such, the Researcher's interpretation of these and any recommendations based on them.

The key element of this rule is that the researcher should be explicit about his or her interpretation of the data collected. This takes us back to the start when we discussed the self-reflection of the social and cultural values of researchers. If qualitative researchers fail or cannot be bothered to reflect upon their own values and cultural norms, their interpretation of qualitative data may be extremely biased. It therefore follows that, for the most valid as well as the most ethical interpretation of qualitative data, researchers must continually reflect and test the extent and effect of their social and cultural values.

Summary

Qualitative marketing researchers should reflect upon how their social and cultural values affect the way they perceive and observe target participants. These reflections should be built up as field notes as the whole process of data gathering develops and evolves. These notes form a key source of qualitative data to complement the broad array of qualitative data generated from interviews and observations. To successfully draw together a valid interpretation, qualitative data analysis must be set in the context of a theoretical understanding of the issue being researched, and an understanding of the marketing decision-makers' use of the findings.

The first stage of the process of analysing qualitative data involves assembling data in their rich and varying formats. The second stage involves reducing the data, i.e. selecting, classifying and connecting data that are believed to be of the greatest significance. A key element of this stage is the concept of coding. The third stage involves displaying data, i.e. using graphical means to display the meaning and structure that a researcher sees in the data collected. The final stage involves verifying the data. The marketing researcher aims to generate the most valid interpretation of these data, which may be supported by existing theories or through the concept of theoretical sampling. The stages of analysis seem quite distinct but in reality they are totally dependent upon each other.

Three of the most commonly used approaches to analysing qualitative marketing research lie in grounded theory, content analysis and semiotics. Grounded theory is an approach that develops theory which is ultimately grounded in the behaviour, words and action of those under study. Content analysis is used to 'reduce' qualitative data, to simplify them by summarising and structuring the data according to rules derived from existing theory. Semiotics combines research techniques from across a spectrum of disciplines, including linguistics, psychology, anthropology, cultural studies and the visual arts. It helps to analyse visual data that some other qualitative research methods do not tackle so well.

To be able to cope with the great amount of data generated from qualitative techniques, a great variety of software packages are available. Used correctly, they can facilitate a speedy and rigorous exploration of qualitative data, allowing teams of researchers to perform creative and incisive analyses and interpretations. The main concern with the use of qualitative data analysis packages lies in the potential for them to be mechanistic and to encourage yet more interviews to be completed, sacrificing the quality of data capture. The qualitative researcher needs to develop an understanding of the social and cultural frames of target participants in international markets. At the same time, qualitative researchers must have a strong awareness of their own social and cultural frames. Only when they have examined both perspectives can they effectively interpret consumer responses. There are ethical implications of the extent to which researchers seek the valid interpretations they can make of the qualitative data they have gathered.

Questions

1 How may the social and cultural background of researchers affect the way they:
   - gather qualitative data?
   - interpret the whole array of qualitative data they have gathered?

2 What is the significance of a qualitative researcher having a theoretical and marketing understanding of the subject he or she is researching?

3 Why should a qualitative researcher maintain a field notebook?

4 What should be recorded in a field notebook?

5 What may be classified as 'data' when assembling data as part of the data analysis process?

6 What does the word 'coding' mean in the context of qualitative data analysis? What problems do you see associated with the process of coding?

7 What are the advantages and disadvantages of handing over audiotapes of qualitative interviews to a typist who has taken no part in the interviews?

8 Evaluate the purpose of displaying qualitative data.

9 What advantages and disadvantages do you see in displaying qualitative data in a spreadsheet format?

10 Evaluate 'when' the stage of data verification should occur.

11 How may theoretical sampling aid the process of verification?

12 How may computers help in the whole process of qualitative data gathering and analysis?

13 Evaluate the main concerns that exist with the use of computers in qualitative data analysis.

14 Why is the researcher's understanding of his or her social and cultural values particularly important in international marketing research?

15 Why does the interpretation of qualitative findings have ethical implications?

Exercises

1 You have been given the task of conducting a series of in-depth interviews about luxury cruises targeted at women of 50 years of age and over. What preparatory work could you do to understand characteristics of this subject, the target group and how the target group relate to the subject?

2 You have just started to work for a major qualitative marketing research agency. The CEO notes that her researchers use a great variety of methods to keep field notes, ranging from scrappy notes taken at interviews to detailed diaries. You have been given the task of designing a format of field notes that will incorporate 'short notes made at the time of observation or interview', 'expanded notes made as soon as possible after each session of interviews or observations', 'a fieldwork journal to record problems and ideas that arise during each stage of fieldwork', and 'a provisional running record of analysis and interpretation'. Present the design and the case you would make to other researchers to use your format.

3 You have conducted a series of focus groups with 18–21 year olds about travelling home from evening events. As you complete each group, you give each participant a disposable camera to record significant events of their journeys home for the forthcoming weekend. What would you do with the images that they send to you?

4 An ethnographic study is planned of young men using Lynx deodorant. You have been asked to compare the relative merits of the qualitative data analysis packages Ethnograph (www.qualisearch.com) and XSight (www.qsrinternational.com) in terms of coping with the types of data that will be generated and the interpretations that will be performed.

5 In a small group discuss the following issues: 'Quantitative techniques of analysis and data display have no role to play in qualitative data analysis?' and 'Theoretical sampling could never work in commercial marketing research given that it creates an open-ended agenda of issues to explore and participants to pursue.'

Video Case Exercise: Wild Planet

To what extent do you feel the gender of qualitative researcher has an impact upon how they interpret the differences between boys and girls playing with Wild Planet toys?

video case

download from
www.pearsoned.co.uk/
malhotra_euro

Notes

1 Murakami, H., *South of the Border, West of the Sun* (London: Harvill, 1999).

2 Interpreting narrative, i.e. the nature and scope of analysing literature is a major subject area in its own right. For a simple introduction into the field see Culler, J., *Literary Theory: A very short introduction* (Oxford: Oxford University Press, 1997).

3 Payne, G., 'Cinderella's getting ready for the ball', *Research Plus* (February 1993), 7.

4 Rubin, H.J. and Rubin, I.S., *Qualitative Interviewing: The art of hearing data* (Thousand Oaks, CA: Sage, 1995), 120.

5 Coffey, A. and Atkinson, P., *Making Sense of Qualitative Data Complementary Research Strategies* (Thousand Oaks, CA: Sage, 1996), 10–11.

6 Spradley, J.P., *The Ethnographic Interview* (New York: Holt, Rinehart & Winston, 1979).

7 Southgate, N., 'Funny business, serious money', *Research*, (March 2004) 28–30.

8 Ereaut, G., *Analysis and Interpretation in Qualitative Market Research* (London: Sage, 2002), 63.

9 Gordon, W. and Langmaid, R., *Qualitative Market Research: A practitioner's and buyer's guide* (Aldershot: Gower, 1988).

10 Ball, M.S. and Smith, G.W.H., *Analyzing visual data* (Newbury Park, CA: Sage, 1992), 9.

11 Ibid., p. 11.

12 Goffman, E., *Gender Advertisements*, (London: Macmillan 1979).

13 Ball, M.S. and Smith, G.W.H., *Analyzing visual data* (Newbury Park, CA: Sage, 1992), 15.

14 Coffey, A. and Atkinson, P., *Making Sense of Qualitative Data* (Thousand Oaks, CA: Sage, 1996), 26.

15 Rubin, H.J. and Rubin, I.S., *Qualitative Interviewing: The art of hearing data* (Thousand Oaks, CA: Sage, 1995), 238.

16 Hubermann, A.M. and Miles, M.B., 'Data management and analysis methods', in Denzin, N.K. and Lincoln, Y.S. (eds), *Handbook of Qualitative Research* (Thousand Oaks, CA: Sage, 1994), 428–444.

17 Krippendorf, K., *Content Analysis: An Introduction to its Methodology* (Beverly Hills, CA: Sage, 1980).

18 Coffey, A. and Atkinson, P., *Making Sense of Qualitative Data: Complementary Research Strategies* (Thousand Oaks, CA: Sage, 1996), 29–30.

19 Miles, M.B. and Huberman, A.M., *Qualitative data analysis: An expanded sourcebook*, 2nd edn. (Thousand Oaks, CA: Sage, 1994), 11.

20 This is a very basic overview of the different means to display qualitative data. For a fuller discussion, the following five chapters devoted to data display are recommended: Miles, M.B. and Huberman, A.M., *Qualitative data analysis: An expanded sourcebook*, 2nd edn. (Thousand Oaks, CA: Sage, 1994), 90–244.

21 This process is known as triangulation. For a fuller description of this topic, set in the context of researcher bias, see Griseri, P., *Management Knowledge: A Critical View* (Basingstoke: Palgrave, 2002), 60–78.

22 Silverman, D., *Interpreting qualitative data: Methods for analysing text, talk and interaction*, 2nd edn (London: Sage, 2001), 233.

23 Patton, M., *Qualitative evaluation and research methods*, 2nd edn (Newbury Park, CA: Sage), 1990.

24 For a fuller explanation of validity in qualitative research, see Kirk, J. and Miller, M.L., *Reliability and Validity in Qualitative Research* (Newbury Park, CA: Sage, 1986).

25 Glaser, B.G. and Strauss, A.L., *The discovery of grounded theory* (Chicago: Aldine, 1967).

26 Locke, K., *Grounded theory in management research* (London: Sage, 2001), 1.

27 Goulding, C., *Grounded theory: A practical guide for management, business and market researchers* (London: Sage, 2002), 40.

28 Glaser, B.G., *Basics of grounded theory analysis: Emergence v Forcing* (Mill Valley, CA: Sociology Press, 1992), 16.

29 Charmaz, K., 'Qualitative interviewing and grounded theory analysis', in Gubrium, J.F. and Holstein, J.A., *Handbook of Interview Research* (Thousand Oaks, CA: Sage, 2002), 675–694.

30 Baszanger, I., 'The work sites of an American interactionist: Anselm L. Strauss, 1917–1996', *Symbolic Interaction* 21 (4) (1998), 353–378.

31 Charmaz, K., 'Qualitative interviewing and grounded theory analysis', in Gubrium, J.F. and Holstein, J.A., *Handbook of Interview Research* (Thousand Oaks, CA: Sage, 2002), 683–690.

32 Böhm, A., Legewie, H. and Muhr, T., *Kursus Textinterpretation: Grounded Theory* (Berlin: Technische Universität, Bericht aus dem IfP Atlas), 92–93, MS.

33 Adapted from Charmaz, K., 'Qualitative interviewing and grounded theory analysis', in Gubrium, J.F. and Holstein, J.A., *Handbook of Interview Research* (Thousand Oaks, CA: Sage, 2002), 687.

34 Ibid., p. 689.

35 Silverman, D., *Interpreting qualitative data: Methods for analysing text, talk and interaction*, 2nd edn (London: Sage, 2001), 71.

36 Neundorf, A.N., *The Content Analysis Guidebook* (Thousand Oaks, CA: Sage, 2002); Wang, C.L., 'A content analysis of connectedness vs separateness themes used in US and PRC print advertisements', *International Marketing Review* 18 (2) (2001), 145.

37 Ball, M.S. and Smith, G.W.H., *Analyzing visual data*, (Thousand Oaks, CA: Sage, 1992), 15

38 Glassner, B., and Corzine, J., 'Library research as fieldwork: a strategy for qualitative content analysis', *Sociology and Social Research* 66 (1982), 305–319.

39 Waksler, F., 'Studying children: phenomenological insights', *Human Studies* 9 (1986), 71–82.

40 Berelson, B., *Content analysis in communication research* (New York: Free Press, 1952).

41 Desai, P., *Methods beyond interviewing in qualitative market research* (London: Sage, 2002), 84.

42 Lawes, R., 'The research gallery', *Research* (October 2003), 23.

43 Clegg, A., 'Just a sign of the times?', *Marketing Week* (19 August 2004), 36.

44 Braier, S., 'Fish out of water', *Research* (December 2003), 40.

45 Desai, P., *Methods beyond interviewing in qualitative market research* (London: Sage, 2002), 85.

46 Adapted from the Semiotics Solutions website **www. semioticsolutions.com**, in Desai, P., *Methods beyond interviewing in qualitative market research* (London: Sage, 2002), 85.

47 Clegg, A., 'Just a sign of the times?', *Marketing Week* (19 August 2004), 36.

48 Wardle, J., *Developing advertising with qualitative research* (London: Sage, 2002), 53.

49 Clatworthy, T. and Flanagan, C., 'White light white heat', *Research* (December 2003), 41.

50 Slater, D., 'Analysing cultural objects: content analysis and semiotics', in Seale, C. (ed.), *Researching society and culture* (London: Sage, 2002), 233–244.

51 Derrida, J., *Positions*, A. Bass (trans.) (Chicago: Chicago University Press, 1981).

52 O'Shaughnessy, J. and Holbrook, M.B., 'The linguistic turn in marketing research', *Journal of the Market Research Society* 30 (3) (April 1988), 210.

53 Desai, P., *Methods beyond interviewing in qualitative market research* (London: Sage, 2002), 97.

54 The full text of this review, written by Tim Macer, can be accessed at **www.meaning.co.uk**. Review 108: 06/05 *XSight 1.1* Qualitative data analysis tool from QSR International.

55 Seale, C., in Silverman, D., *Doing Qualitative Research: A Practical Handbook* (London: Sage, 2000), 161.

56 Wolfe, R.A., Gephart, R.P. and Johnson, T.E., 'Computer-facilitated qualitative data analysis: potential contributions to management research', *Journal of Management* 19 (3) (Fall 1993), 637; Dembrowski, S. and Hanmer-Lloyd, S., 'Computer applications – a new road to qualitative data analysis?', *European Journal of Marketing* 29 (11) (November 1995), 50.

57 Valentine, V. and Evans, M., 'The dark side of the onion: rethinking the meanings of "rational" and "emotional" responses', *Journal of the Market Research Society* 35 (2) (April 1993), 127.

Visit the *Marketing Research* Companion Website at www.pearsoned.co.uk/malhotra_euro for additional learning resources including annotated weblinks, an online glossary and a suite of downloadable video cases.

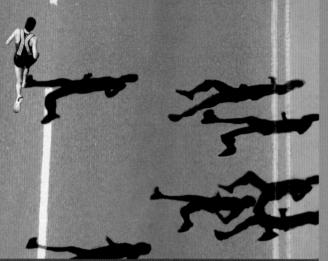

Source: © Getty Images

10

Survey and quantitative observation techniques

> *Know exactly what you want to measure – and then select a survey or observation technique that creates cooperative respondents, willing to think and be honest.*

Objectives

After reading this chapter, you should be able to:

1. discuss and classify survey techniques available to marketing researchers, and describe various survey techniques;

2. identify the criteria for evaluating survey techniques, compare the different techniques and evaluate which is the best for a particular research project;

3. explain and classify the different quantitative observation techniques;

4. identify the criteria for evaluating observation techniques, compare the different techniques, and evaluate which are suited for a particular research project;

5. describe the relative advantages and disadvantages of observation techniques and compare them with survey techniques;

6. discuss the considerations involved in implementing surveys and observation techniques in an international setting;

7. understand the ethical issues involved in conducting survey and observational research.

STAGE 1
Problem definition

STAGE 2
Research approach developed

STAGE 3
Research design developed

STAGE 4
Fieldwork or data collection

STAGE 5
Data preparation and analysis

STAGE 6
Report preparation and presentation

Overview

In this chapter, we focus on the major techniques employed in descriptive research designs: surveys and quantitative observation. As explained in Chapter 3, descriptive research has as its prime objective the description of something, usually consumer or market characteristics. Survey and quantitative observation techniques are vital techniques in descriptive research designs. Survey techniques may be classified by mode of administration as traditional telephone interviews, computer-assisted telephone interviews, personal in-home or office interviews, street interviews, computer-assisted personal interviews, postal surveys, mail panels, email and Internet surveys. We describe each of these techniques and present a comparative evaluation of all the survey techniques. Then we consider the major observational techniques: personal observation including mystery shopping research, electronic observation, audit, and trace analysis. The relative advantages and disadvantages of observation over survey techniques and the considerations involved in conducting survey and observation research when researching international markets are also discussed. Several ethical issues that arise in survey research and observation techniques are identified.

To begin our discussion, we present an example of how technological advances are enabling different survey approaches to be conducted in a single study. Such advances are helping in the challenges to overcome respondent reluctance to participate in surveys.

Example   ### Different strokes[1]

Mixed-mode research, where one research survey may embrace several different fieldwork methods side by side, is a relatively recent development. It may be achieved by conducting some interviews in for example CATIs and others on the Web. It could even take this idea a stage further and allow respondents to switch modes part way through an interview. Those who dare to mix modes find it does improve response rates quite dramatically if respondents get to choose the mode for themselves. John Allison and Chris O'Konis, researchers at the US financial firm Fidelity, found that a staggering 88% of their customers contacted in a computer-assisted telephone interview (CATI) agreed to participate in the web survey. Whilst this figure included a number of covert 'soft refusals', 54% did complete the web survey and a small proportion also completed the survey on the telephone.

Completion rate is not the only issue that mixed-mode can tackle. A more subtle problem is the effect of differential response rates within a sample, meaning that certain groups may be under- or over-represented. A mixed-mode approach inevitably exposes the in-built tendencies of some modes to favour certain types of respondent. CATI, especially in consumer surveys, has been observed to favour female respondents, the less well educated and those outside urban areas. Web surveys tend to favour males, the young and the better educated. Mixing modes allows these in-built biases to be tackled.

Survey techniques

Survey techniques
Techniques based upon the use of structured questionnaires given to a sample of a population.

Survey techniques are based upon the use of structured questionnaires given to a sample of a population. Respondents may be asked a variety of questions regarding their behaviour, intentions, attitudes, awareness, motivations, and demographic and lifestyle characteristics. These questions may be asked verbally, in writing or via a computer, and

Structured data collection
Use of a formal questionnaire that presents questions in a prearranged order.

the responses may be obtained in any of these forms. 'Structured' here refers to the degree of standardisation imposed on the data collection process. In **structured data collection**, a formal questionnaire is prepared and the questions are asked in a prearranged order; thus, the process is also direct. Whether research is classified as direct or indirect is based on whether the true purpose is known to the respondents. As explained in Chapter 7, a direct approach is undisguised in that the purpose of the project is disclosed to the respondents or is otherwise obvious to them from the questions asked.

In a typical questionnaire, most questions are fixed-response alternative questions that require the respondent to select from a predetermined set of responses. Consider, for example, the following question, designed to measure a dimension of students' attitudes towards the way they are assessed in marketing research classes:

	Strongly agree	*Agree*	*Neutral disagree*	*Disagree*	*Strongly agree*
I prefer written examinations compared with continual assessment	☐	☐	☐	☐	☐

The survey method has several advantages. First, the questionnaire is simple to administer. Second, the data obtained are consistent because the responses are limited to the alternatives stated. The use of fixed-response questions reduces the variability in the results that may be caused by differences in interviewers. Finally, coding, analysis and interpretation of data are relatively simple.[2]

Fixed-response alternative questions
Questions that require respondents to choose from a set of predetermined answers.

The disadvantages are that respondents may be unable or unwilling to provide the desired information. For example, consider questions about motivational factors. Respondents may not be consciously aware of their motives for choosing specific brands or shopping at particular stores. Therefore, they may be unable to provide accurate answers to questions about their motives. Respondents may be unwilling to respond if the information requested is sensitive or personal. In addition, structured questions and **fixed-response alternative questions** may result in loss of validity for certain types of data such as beliefs and feelings. Finally, wording questions properly is not easy (see Chapter 13 on questionnaire design). In other words, the survey imposes the language and logic of the researcher on the questionnaire respondents. Given this core characteristic of survey techniques, great care must be taken to ensure that the language and logic used in questionnaires are meaningful and valid to potential respondents. Despite the above disadvantages, the survey approach is by far the most common method of primary data collection in marketing research, representing around 69% of all marketing research spending.[3] The following example demonstrates how one company has realised the benefits of the survey by the creative integration of an online survey with its customer relationship management system.

Example   **Survey supports customer support[4]**

Ariba (**www.ariba.com**), a b2b (business-to-business) software provider, uses both the Internet and other computer applications to collect survey data. Ariba has integrated its Vantive Enterprise Customer Relationship Management platform (a proprietary software system) with the Web Survey System from CustomerSat.com. With this setup, Ariba has the ability to gain real-time feedback, track trends, and obtain immediate notification about unsatisfied customers. The system works by administering an online survey to each customer (respondent) who asks for customer support. This survey gathers not only specifics about the problem customers are experiencing but also data that can be used to make executive decisions down the road (e.g. current product needs, likes/dislikes). The system then analyses the responses and routes the respondent to an appropriate specialist. Customers can rate and comment on their customer support experience within 24 hours of the case being closed.

Survey questionnaires may be administered in four major modes: (1) telephone interviews, (2) personal interviews, (3) mail interviews and (4) electronic interviews (see Figure 10.1). Telephone interviews may be further classified as traditional telephone interviews and computer-assisted telephone interviews (CATIs). Personal interviews may be conducted in the home or office, as street interviews, or as computer-assisted personal interviews (CAPIs). The third major method, mail interviews, takes the form of traditional mail surveys, or surveys conducted using mail panels. Finally, electronic interviews can be conducted via email or administered on the Internet. We now describe each method.

Telephone interviews

As stated earlier, telephone interviews may be categorised as traditional or computer-assisted. They constitute around 20% of the worldwide total spend on research methods. Examples of countries with low and high spending on this technique range from Japan at 4% to Denmark at 41%.[5]

Traditional telephone interviews

Traditional telephone interviews involve phoning a sample of respondents and asking them a series of questions. The interviewer uses a paper questionnaire and records the responses with a pencil. From a central location, a wide geographical area can be covered, including international markets. Given that telephone interviewers cannot give respondents any visual prompts, they have to write down answers to any open-ended questions and may have to flick through the questionnaire to find appropriate questions for a particular respondent (filtering). These interviews tend to be short in duration and have questions with few options as answers. Today, this approach is rarely used in commercial marketing research, the common approach being CATI.

Computer-assisted telephone interviews (CATI)

CATI uses a computerised questionnaire administered to respondents over the telephone. A computerised questionnaire may be administered using a networked computer or a PC. The interviewer sits in front of a terminal and wears a small headset. The terminal replaces a paper and pencil questionnaire, and the headset substitutes for a telephone.

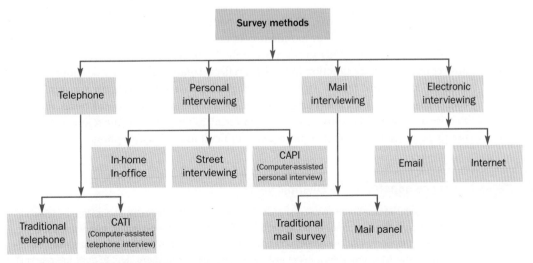

Figure 10.1 A classification of survey techniques

Upon command, the computer dials the telephone number to be called. When contact is made, the interviewer reads questions posed on the screen and records the respondent's answers directly into the computer memory, ready for immediate analysis. The following example illustrates how the technique has developed over the years. The main benefit of the technique illustrated here is the speed of collecting data and analyses. Speed is of the essence in subjects where respondent attitudes and behaviour can change quickly, an example being the 'latest' toys that parents may wish to buy for their children. One of the most widespread uses of CATI is for political opinion polls.

With CATI, the computer systematically guides the interviewer. Only one question at a time appears on the screen. The computer checks the responses for appropriateness and consistency. It uses the responses as they are obtained to personalise the questionnaire. Data collection flows naturally and smoothly. Interviewing time is reduced, data quality is enhanced, and the laborious steps in the data collection process, coding questionnaires and entering data into the computer are eliminated. Because the responses are entered directly into the computer, interim and update reports on data collection or results can be provided almost instantaneously. The following example shows how CATI is being used in a major study throughout Europe.

Example **They're free and young people love them[6]**

Free newspapers, such as *Metro* or *20 Minutes*, now available in many metropolitan areas around the world, have seen their readerships soar, according to the 2004 Metro Global Readership Study. The study is based on a sample of 24,000 in two waves using CATI. The study has been conducted every year since 2000 by TNS Gallup in Denmark on behalf of Metro International. Unlike most other pan-European surveys, which tend to focus on a selective business or affluent consumer audience, this survey represents a universe of all 114.2 million people aged 13 or more who live in the 51 'Metro-Cities' in 16 countries.

With 14.5 million readers worldwide (up from 3.7 million in 2000) *Metro* now claims to be the third largest newspaper, behind Japan's *Yomiuri Shimbun* and *Asahi Shimbun*, but ahead of Germany's *Bild Zeitung*. Its daily reach in 11 European countries is 10.2 million or 15% of the survey universe. The main strength of *Metro*'s various editions is its young readership: 41% are between 18 and 34 years of age, a group that accounts for only 31% of the population in all Metro-Cities. At the other end of the spectrum, those aged 55 or more are considerably less likely to be attracted by *Metro*'s offering and tend to stick with their traditional newspapers.

The biggest drawback of CATI lies in respondents' willingness to be interviewed by telephone. In a 2003 study respondent cooperation by the Council for Marketing and Opinion Research (CMOR) in the USA, only 7% of respondents called were willing to answer questions. The situation in the USA reflects conditions in other developed markets such as Europe and Japan. Although average response rates in Japan are significantly higher than in the USA and Europe, they show a continuous downward trend, mainly by the rise of refusals.[7] This situation is not universal, as illustrated by the following example, but there are many factors that make it very difficult to conduct telephone interviews.

Example Greece hopeful in the Olympic year

At Research International (**www.research-int.com**) whose main Greek clients are in telecommunications, food, alcohol and cigarettes, CEO Dimitris Manoussakis has witnessed the growth of the worldwide phenomenon known as the non-response ratio. 'This has risen significantly in the past few years, especially in the Athens area, where door-to-door interviewing can no longer ensure a representative sample.' As an alternative to face-to-face interviews, telephone surveys are already seen by Manoussakis as growing rapidly, offering the advantage of more representative results. Telephone surveys will be the best approach to tackle the non-response problem for the foreseeable future, as Greece has not started to go online on a large scale (Internet penetration in 2004 was less than 20%). However, it has grown significantly over the past few years, especially among the younger, urban population.

At times the technique may be confused in the minds of respondents with cold-call selling techniques. To overcome this problem requires interviewers who are trained to reassure respondents and to make the interviewing experience worthwhile. In most businesses, phone calls are screened; how else could managers avoid calls from companies and individuals they do not want to talk to? Many businesses have set up formal procedures to minimise unnecessary calls to management. This is a hurdle well-trained interviewers are taught to circumvent. Experienced interviewers can 'run the gauntlet' of three or four screenings and still secure an interview without in any way upsetting the interviewee.

The usual blocking responses of '(s)he's busy', '(s)he wouldn't be interested', '(s)he doesn't deal in that area', or '(s)he's in a meeting', have been joined by 'we don't allow marketing research interviews – it's company policy'. Even this will not deter telephone interviewers from seeking interviews but it is a continuing and worrying trend.[9]

So why do companies which commission marketing research themselves restrict their own employees from participating? The reasons given are:

- The confidentiality of information divulged to interviewers.
- The length of interviews.
- The frequent apparent or real irrelevance of questions.
- The number of requests.
- *Taking part is seen as providing no direct benefit to the company.*

The last point is set in italics as a reminder to all researchers to place themselves in the shoes of potential respondents. Marketing researchers, and the decision-makers they support, may have distinct information requirements, but why should respondents supply this information? What benefits do they gain from giving this information? This issue will be dealt with in examining questionnaire design in Chapter 13, but here we have a reminder of the impact of ignoring the benefits that respondents gain from participating in a survey.

Personal interviews

Personal interviewing techniques may be categorised as in-home, in-office, street or computer-assisted. They constitute around 31% of the worldwide total spend on research methods. Examples of countries with low and high spending on this technique range from Sweden at 6% to Russia at 65%.[10]

Personal in-home and in-office interviews

In personal in-home interviews, respondents are interviewed face to face in their homes or in their workplace. The interviewer's task is to contact the respondents, ask the questions and record the responses. In recent years, the use of personal in-home interviews has declined due to their high cost. There are many situations where they are used because of the reassurances of quality of the interview process and the nature of the questions that are being administered. The following Sports Marketing Surveys example illustrates such a case where it was paramount to use a personal in-home survey.

Sports Marketing Surveys

Flora London Marathon 2004

In the study to evaluate the impact of Flora's sponsorship of the London Marathon the following factors were considered vital to measure:

- The connection between the London Marathon and Flora.
- The image of the London Marathon.
- The impact of a number of new Flora/London Marathon promotions.
- The impact of new Flora branding.

Omnibus survey
A distinctive form of survey that serves the needs of a syndicated group. The omnibus survey targets particular types of respondents such as those in specific geographic locations, e.g. Luxembourg residents, or consumers of particular types of products, e.g. business air travellers. With that target group of respondents, a core set of questions can be asked, with other questions added as syndicate members wish.

The 225 interviews, targeted at 18–70 year olds, occurred immediately after the London Marathon. These interviews were conducted on a face-to-face basis in the homes of respondents. Given the focus on image-based issues in this study, a face-to-face survey method gave interviewers the ability to present and build questions around a number of visual prompts, in the comfort of respondents' homes. The survey revealed that 85% of respondents were aware of the connection between Flora and the London Marathon with this figure increasing year on year.

As well as using face-to-face interviews for individual surveys, they are also widely used by syndicated firms, as illustrated in the following example. The use of **omnibus surveys** for marketing decision-makers is shown with examples of the types of marketing research projects that are supported by this technique.

Example **Omnibus – the flexible research tool for many jobs[11]**

The tracking aspect of an omnibus is important for a number of clients, not least because it enables the following:

- A continuous assessment of awareness and effectiveness of marketing/advertising activity.
- A monitor of opinion/behaviour in constantly changing competitive markets, which in addition may be highly fragmented.
- The accumulation of ongoing data to provide robust bases and thus build, for example, profiles of customers that would otherwise be inaccessible for small brands.
- Access to competitors' performance, without introducing overt bias among respondents' answers.
- Detection of early signs of change in a defined marketplace.
- Opportunities for syndication (with additional benefits, such as shared costs).

Omnimas offers omnibus facilities, each week interviewing 2,000 adults face to face in their homes. A number of continuous tracking projects are conducted that range over the following:

- Advertising awareness tracking (which, depending on the client and subject matter, is conducted on a weekly, monthly or less frequent basis), monitoring whether the advertisement has been seen or heard and how it is communicated or interpreted.
- Regular (weekly) behavioural monitors (the Eating Out Of Home Monitor examines consumers' eating habits outside their own homes in restaurants and similar outlets).
- Ongoing tracking of people's awareness, usage and participation in loyalty schemes across a number of retail sectors.
- Using ongoing information about consumers' intentions to buy video titles to predict volume sales (data are supplied for Buena Vista Entertainment, the Disney Video Company).

In-office research is used extensively in business-to-business research to research subjects who cannot be effectively interviewed by telephone or mail. Managers being interviewed have the comfort and security of their office and can control the timing and pace of the interview. For the researcher, the big benefit of meeting managers in their office is the ability to build up a rapport, probe and gain the full attention of the manager.

Street interviews

In street interviews, respondents are intercepted while they are shopping in town centres or shopping centres. They may be questioned there and then in the street or taken to a specific test facility. In the testing of new product formulations, test facilities are ideal to allow respondents the time and context to sample and evaluate products. The technique can also be used to test merchandising ideas, advertisements and other forms of marketing communications. The big advantage of the street interview is that it is more efficient for the respondent to come to the interviewer than for the interviewer to go to the respondent.[12]

Computer-assisted personal interviews (CAPI)

In CAPI, the third form of personal interviewing, the respondent sits in front of a computer terminal and answers a questionnaire on the screen by using the keyboard or a mouse. There are several user-friendly electronic packages that design relatively simple questions for the respondent to understand. Help screens and courteous error messages are also provided. The colourful screens and on- and off-screen stimuli can all contribute to making the interview process interesting and stimulating. This method has been classified as a personal interview technique because an interviewer is usually present to serve as a host or hostess and to guide the respondent as needed.

CAPI has been used to collect data at test facilities from street interviews, product clinics, conferences and trade shows. It may also be used for in-home or in-office interviews. You may wonder, however, how CAPI compares with the traditional method of conducting personal interviews, using paper and pencil questionnaires. The following example illustrates an application of CAPI where many visual aspects of football sponsorship could be displayed for questioning.

Example **Brands fall short of their goal[13]**

Major consumer brands use a plethora of sports sponsorship platforms, from players to stadiums, to communicate with a global consumer market and gain international exposure and recognition. Sporting events are an effective vehicle to gain access to a swathe of potential customers yet, according to the CAPI study conducted by TNS Sport, young people and children have a greater awareness than adults of those brands that sponsor leading football clubs. Its research among people who watch football on TV revealed that spontaneous recall of brands by adults (aged 16 plus) across a range of sponsors was generally less than that of children (aged 10–19).

A major development for marketers, especially in financial services, has been the use of customer satisfaction surveys to guide strategic and operational decisions. With traditional interview techniques, the interviewer may have to carry a huge questionnaire to cope with questions that measure attitudes to a range of banks and a range of services taken from those banks. With CAPI, when a particular bank is chosen, particular questions may be filtered out, and choosing a particular service from that bank can filter out further questions. Questions specific to the respondent may then be asked, in all making the interview process far more efficient.

Mail interviews

Mail interviews, the third major form of survey administration, can be conducted via traditional mail, or the mail panel. They constitute around 7% of the worldwide total spend on research methods. Examples of countries with low and high spending on this technique range from Portugal at 1% to Japan at 14%.[14]

Traditional mail surveys

In the traditional mail survey, questionnaires are mailed to preselected potential respondents. A typical mail survey package consists of the outgoing envelope, cover letter, questionnaire, return envelope and possibly an incentive.[15] The respondents complete and return the questionnaires. There is no verbal interaction between the researcher and the respondent in the survey process.[16] There may be an initial contact with potential respondents, to establish who is the correct person to send the questionnaire to, and to motivate them before they receive the survey.

Before data collection can begin, however, the respondents need to be at least broadly identified. Therefore, an initial task is to obtain a valid mailing list. Mailing lists can be compiled from telephone directories, customer databases or association membership databases, or can be purchased from publication subscription lists or commercial mailing list companies.[17] Regardless of its source, a mailing list should be current and closely related to the population of interest. (Chapters 13 and 14 will detail the full questionnaire design and sampling implications of this approach.) With an understanding of characteristics of target respondents and what will motivate them to respond honestly, as fully and as quickly as possible, the researcher must also make decisions about the various elements of the mail interview package (see Table 10.1).

Table 10.1 Some decisions related to the mail survey package

Outgoing envelope	Method of addressing	Envelope size, colour	Postage	
Covering letter	Personalisation	Sponsorship	Type of appeal	Signature
Questionnaire	Size, length and content	Colour and layout	Format and reproduction	Respondent anonymity
Instructions	As part of covering letter	A separate sheet	Alongside individual questions	
Return envelope	Whether to include one	Type of envelope	Postage	
Incentives	Feedback of findings	Monetary vs. non-monetary	Prepaid vs. promised amount	

Mail panels

Mail panel
A large and nationally representative sample of households that have agreed to participate in periodic mail questionnaires and product tests.

Mail panels were introduced in Chapters 3 and 4. A **mail panel** consists of a large, nationally representative sample of households that have agreed to participate in periodic mail questionnaires and product tests.[18] A pre-recruited panel that is willing to participate makes it easier to set up a product test and conduct interviews after the test. Panels are made up of a 'pool' of individuals or households who have agreed to be available for surveys of widely varying types and topics. The households are compensated with various incentives. Mail panels can be used to obtain information from the same respondents repeatedly. Thus, they can be used to implement a longitudinal design. Online consumer access panels are becoming increasingly more prevalent in marketing research. With the growth in electronic survey methods, email and Internet panels are rapidly becoming more prevalent than the traditional mail formats.

Electronic surveys

Electronic surveys can be conducted via email, or administered on the Internet. They constitute around 11% of the worldwide total spend on research methods. Examples of countries with low and high spending on this technique range from Italy at 1% to Australia at 20%.[19]

Email surveys

Text-based email surveys can be convenient for respondents because they require no facilities or expertise beyond those that they use in their day-to-day email communications. To conduct an email survey, a list of email addresses is obtained. The survey is written within the body of the email message which is then sent out over the Internet. Email surveys use pure text (ASCII) to represent questionnaires and can be received and responded to by anyone with an email address, whether or not they have access to the Web. Respondents type the answers to either closed-ended or open-ended questions at designated places, and click on 'reply'. Responses are then data entered and tabulated in the manner of a traditional mail survey. Alternatively, a program can be written that interprets the emailed responses and reads the answers directly into a format compatible with the requirements of an analysis package.

Email surveys have several limitations, chief of which is that they can appear dry and uninteresting.[20] Given the technical limitations of most email systems, questionnaires cannot utilise programmed skip patterns, logic checks or randomisation. The limited intelligence of ASCII text cannot keep a respondent from, say, choosing both 'yes' and 'no' to a question where only one response is meaningful. Skipping instructions (e.g. 'If the answer to Question 5 is yes, go to Question 9') must appear explicitly, just as on paper. These factors can reduce the quality of data from an email survey and can require much post-survey data cleaning.[21] There are also problems in locating accurate and current email address lists and even if these can be located, given spam protection software, there is no guarantee that an email will reach intended respondents.

Internet surveys

**Hypertext marku
p language (HTML)**
The language of the Web.

In contrast to email surveys, Internet or web surveys use **hypertext markup language** (HTML), the language of the Web, and are posted on a website. Respondents may be recruited online from potential respondent databases maintained by the marketing research firm or they can be recruited by conventional techniques (mail, telephone). Respondents are asked to go to a particular web location to complete the survey. Frequently, respondents are not recruited, but those who happen to be visiting the website on which the survey is posted (or other popular websites) are invited to participate in the survey. Either all or every *i*th Web visitor is allowed to participate. Web surveys offer several advantages over email surveys. It is possible in HTML, but not in ASCII text, to construct buttons, checkboxes and data entry fields that prevent respondents from selecting more than one response where only one is intended, or from otherwise typing where no response is required. Skip patterns can be programmed and performed automatically as in CATI or CAPI. It is possible to validate responses as they are entered. Finally, additional survey stimuli such as graphs, images, animations and links to other web pages may be integrated into or around the survey. The responses are collected in an adjoining database. The data require some processing before they can be tabulated or used in a statistical package. All these factors contribute to a higher quality experience and elicitation process. With the growth of the use of email and the Internet as a means of communication, electronic mail is rapidly becoming the most feasible and popular means of conducting surveys. Most survey analysis packages that include the function of questionnaire design have the ability to formulate the questionnaire into email and Internet formats. Big sampling problems exist with electronic mail, which will be tackled in Chapter 14. The speed of administering the survey, collecting and analysing the data, linked with very low costs, make electronic mail very attractive as illustrated in the following example.

Example   **How Canon used the Internet to pick the right respondents**[22]

Canon's European research arm wanted to study the printer usage and attitudes of 400 different print owners in five separate countries. Marketing Co-ordinator Stuart McGown says, 'ten years ago, carrying out a survey of this scope and complexity would have been a major operation, whose fieldwork might have taken a number of months'. Canon began conducting studies online in 2002:

> *"Using the internet means that data can be collected from countries in just a matter of days. This means that we can adapt much faster to the changing needs of the market. Our marketing and communications strategy is far more responsive than ever before. The cost of online methods has been advantageous. I would say it has allowed us to run more projects, more frequently; we get more for our Euros."*

The following lists summarise the advantages and disadvantages of Internet surveys:[23]

Advantages

- *Speed.* Compared with a postal survey, especially on an international basis, the time taken can be reduced to a matter of days rather than weeks. Even if one includes the time taken to contact respondents by email, to establish their willingness to take part in a survey, for them to reply, for the survey to be sent, for it to be completed and then emailed back (the procedure adopted to reduce the perception of 'junk' email), such a survey can be completed far more quickly than a postal procedure. There can be a 'seamless' international coordination that using traditional mail would be very time consuming to organise.
- *Cost.* Once the electronic questionnaire is set up, it is almost as easy to mail it to 10,000 people as to 10, since there are no printing, stationery and postage costs.
- *Quality of response.* Quality can be measured by the number and clarity of responses to open-ended questions. Graphics can be displayed to maintain the interest of respondents but also to put them in a frame of mind that elicits more from them.
- *Interviewer bias removed.* The method maintains the key advantage of mail surveys in being able to present a consistent form of measurement.
- *Data quality.* Logic and validity checks can be built in, and in areas where open-ended or 'other – please state' responses are required, the respondent types in answers ready for analysis.
- *Contacting certain target groups.* Such groups are mostly those who are regular users of the Internet and certain business target markets.

Disadvantages

- *Sampling frames.* There are a growing number of directories that provide email addresses but there are still major questions surrounding their currency, accuracy and means of classifying different types of target respondent. Another sampling issue is that the questions are self-completion based and the researcher does not know whether those who choose to take part are really representative of a target population. Being able to generalise findings to a particular population becomes difficult with a self-selecting sample.
- *Access to the Web.* At present the penetration of households and businesses is highly variable within countries and across countries. The adoption of the Internet is growing rapidly worldwide and in businesses the Web is rapidly being adopted as the medium of communication. However, there are many types of respondent that cannot be accessed via the Web.
- *Technical problems.* Depending upon the hardware and software that respondents use, the questionnaire may 'work' or not as was intended by the designer.

A comparative evaluation of survey techniques

Not all survey techniques are appropriate in a given situation. Therefore, the researcher should conduct a comparative evaluation to determine which techniques are appropriate. Table 10.2 compares the different survey techniques through a range of criteria. For any particular research project, the relative importance attached to these criteria will vary. The criteria consist of flexibility of data collection, diversity of questions, use of physical stimuli, sample control, control of the data collection environment, control of field force, quantity of data, response rate, perceived respondent anonymity, social desirability, obtaining sensitive information, potential for interviewer bias, potential to probe respondents, potential to build rapport, speed and cost.

Flexibility of data collection

The flexibility of data collection is determined primarily by the extent to which the respondent can interact with the interviewer and the survey questionnaire. The personal interview, whether conducted as an in-home, in-office or street interview, allows the highest flexibility of data collection. Because the respondent and the interviewer meet face to face, the interviewer can administer complex questionnaires, explain and clarify difficult questions, and even use unstructured techniques.

By contrast, the traditional telephone interview allows only moderate flexibility because it is more difficult to use unstructured techniques, ask complex questions, or obtain in-depth answers to open-ended questions over the telephone. CATI and CAPI and Internet surveys allow somewhat greater flexibility because the researcher can use various question formats, can personalise the questionnaire, and can handle complex skip or filter patterns (directions for skipping questions in the questionnaire based on the subject's responses). Because the electronic and mail questionnaire allows for no interaction between the interviewer and the respondent, mail surveys, mail panels and email surveys have low flexibility.

An often-overlooked benefit of Internet survey research is the ease with which an Internet survey can be quickly modified. For example, early data returns may suggest additional questions that should be asked. Changing or adding questions as the need becomes apparent would be almost impossible with a traditional mail survey, possible but difficult with personal or telephone questionnaires, but achievable in a matter of minutes with some Internet survey systems.

Table 10.2 A comparative evaluation of survey techniques

	Telephone CATI	In-home, in-office interviews	Street interviews	CAPI	Traditional mail surveys	Mail panels	Email	Internet
Flexibility of data collection	Moderate to high	High	High	Moderate to high	Low	Low	Low	Moderate to high
Diversity of questions	Low	High	High	High	Moderate	Moderate	Moderate	Moderate to high
Use of physical stimuli	Low	Moderate to high	High	High	Moderate	Moderate	Low	Moderate
Sample control	Moderate to high	Potentially high	Moderate to high	Moderate	Low	Moderate	Low	Low to moderate
Control of data collection environment	Moderate	Moderate to high	High	High	Low	Low	Low	Low
Control of field force	Moderate	Low	Moderate	Moderate	High	High	High	High
Quantity of data	Low	High	Moderate	Moderate	Moderate	High	Moderate	Moderate
Response rate	Moderate	High	High	High	Low	Moderate	Low	Low
Perceived respondent anonymity	Moderate	Low	Low	Low	High	High	Moderate	High
Social desirability	Moderate	Low to moderate	Low	Low to high	High	High	High	High
Obtaining sensitive information	Low	High	Low	Moderate	Moderate	Moderate	Moderate	Moderate
Potential for interviewer bias	Moderate	High	High	Low	None	None	None	None
Potential to probe respondents	Low	High	Moderate	Moderate	Low	Low	Low	Low
Potential to build rapport	Moderate	High	Moderate to high	Moderate to high	Low	Low	Low	Low
Speed	High	Moderate to high	Moderate	Moderate to high	Low	Low to high	High	High
Cost	Moderate	High	Moderate to high	Moderate to high	Low	Low to moderate	Low	Low

Diversity of questions

The diversity of questions that can be asked in a survey depends on the degree of interaction the respondent has with the interviewer and the questionnaire, as well as the respondent's ability actually to see the questions. A variety of questions can be asked in a personal interview because the respondent can see the questionnaire and the interviewer is present to clarify ambiguities. Thus in-home and in-office interviews, street interviews and CAPI allow for diversity. In Internet surveys, multimedia capabilities can be utilised and so the ability to ask a diversity of questions is moderate to high, despite the absence of an interviewer. In mail surveys, mail panels and email surveys, less diversity is possible. In traditional telephone interviews and CATI, the respondent cannot see the questions while answering, and this limits the diversity of questions. For example, in a telephone interview or CATI, it would be very difficult to ask respondents to rank 15 TV programmes in terms of preference.

Use of physical stimuli

Often it is helpful or necessary to use physical stimuli such as products, product prototypes, commercials or promotional displays during an interview. For the most basic example, a taste test involves tasting the product and evaluating the taste. In other cases, photographs, maps or other audio-visual cues are helpful. In these cases, personal interviews conducted at central locations (guided through street interviews and CAPI) are more preferable to in-home interviews. In the central location, many intricate visual stimuli can be set up prior to the actual interview. Mail surveys and mail panels are moderate on this dimension, because sometimes it is possible to mail the facilitating aids or even product samples. Internet surveys are also moderately suitable. Because they are web based, the questionnaires can include multimedia elements such as prototype web pages and advertisements. The use of physical stimuli is limited in traditional telephone interviews and CATI, as well as in email surveys (depending upon the respondent's ability to open attachments).

Sample control

Sample control
The ability of the survey mode to reach the units specified in the sample effectively and efficiently.

Sample control is the ability of the survey mode to reach the units specified in the sample effectively and efficiently.[24] At least in principle, in-home and in-office personal interviews offer the best sample control. It is possible to control which sampling units are interviewed, who is interviewed, the degree of participation of other members of the household, and many other aspects of data collection. In practice, to achieve a high degree of control, the researcher has to overcome several problems. It is difficult to find respondents at home during the day because many people work outside the home. Also, for safety reasons, interviewers are reluctant to venture into certain neighbourhoods and people have become cautious of responding to strangers at their door. Street interviews allow only a moderate degree of sample control. Although the interviewer has control over which respondents to intercept, the choice is limited to individuals who are walking down a street or through a shopping centre, and frequent shoppers have a greater probability of being included. Also, potential respondents can intentionally avoid or initiate contact with the interviewer. Compared with street interviews, CAPI offers slightly better control, as sampling quotas can be set and respondents randomised automatically.

Sampling frame
A representation of the elements of the target population that consists of a list or set of directions for identifying the target population.

Moderate to high sampling control can be achieved with traditional telephone interviews and CATI. Telephones offer access to geographically dispersed respondents and hard-to-reach areas. These procedures depend upon a **sampling frame**, a list of population units with their telephone numbers.[25] The sampling frames normally used are telephone directories, but telephone directories are limited in that:

1 Not everyone has a phone or even a 'conventional' phone, while some individuals have several phone numbers partly due to the growing use of mobile phones with rapidly changing numbers.[26]

2 The growth in number portability which allows people to transfer their landline telephone number to a cell phone and to move to any geographical area of the country.[27]

3 Some individuals have unlisted phones or are ex-directory.

4 Directories do not reflect new phones in service or recently disconnected phones.

Internet, email and traditional mail surveys require a list of addresses of individuals or households eligible for inclusion in the sample. Mail surveys can reach geographically dispersed respondents and hard-to-reach areas. However, mailing lists are sometimes unavailable, outdated or incomplete, especially for electronic addresses. Another factor outside the researcher's control is whether the questionnaire is answered and who answers it. Some subjects refuse to respond because of lack of interest or motivation; others cannot respond because they are illiterate.[28] Given these reasons, the degree of sample control in electronic and mail surveys is low.[29]

Mail panels, on the other hand, provide moderate to high control over the sample. They can provide samples matched to national census statistics on key demographic variables. It is also possible to identify specific user groups within a panel and to direct the survey to households with specific characteristics. Specific members of households in the panel can be questioned. Finally, low-incidence groups, groups that occur infrequently in the population, can be reached with panels, but there is a question of the extent to which a panel can be considered representative of the entire population.

Not all populations are candidates for Internet survey research. Although respondents can be screened to meet qualifying criteria and quotas imposed, the ability to meet quotas is limited by the number and characteristics of respondents who visit the website. However, there are some exceptions to this broad statement. For example, computer products purchasers and users of Internet services are ideal populations. Business and professional users of Internet services are also an excellent population to reach with Internet surveys. Sample control is low to moderate for Internet surveys, whilst email surveys suffer from many of the limitations of mail surveys and thus offer low sample control.

Control of the data collection environment

The context in which a questionnaire is completed can affect the way that a respondent answers questions. An example of this would be the amount of distraction from other people around, noise and temperature. The degree of control a researcher has over the context or environment in which the respondent answers the questionnaire differentiates the various survey modes. Personal interviews conducted at central locations (from street interviews and CAPI) offer the greatest degree of environmental control. For example, the researcher can set up a special facility for demonstrating a product upon which a survey is based. In-home and in-office personal interviews offer moderate to high control because the interviewer is present. Traditional telephone interviews and CATI offer moderate control. The interviewer cannot see the environment in which the interview is being conducted, but he or she can sense the background conditions and encourage the respondent to be attentive and involved. In mail surveys, panels, email and Internet surveys, the researcher has little or no control over the environment.

Control of field force

Field force
Both the actual interviewers and the supervisors involved in data collection.

The **field force** consists of interviewers and supervisors involved in data collection. Because they require no such personnel, mail surveys, mail panels, email and Internet surveys eliminate field force problems. Traditional telephone interviews, CATI, street interviews and CAPI all offer moderate degrees of control because the interviews are conducted at a central location, making supervision relatively simple. In-home and in-office personal interviews are problematic in this respect. Because many interviewers work in many different locations, continual supervision is impractical.[30]

Quantity of data

In-home and in-office personal interviews allow the researcher to collect large amounts of data. The social relationship between the interviewer and the respondent, as well as the home or office environment, motivates the respondent to spend more time in the interview. Less effort is required of the respondent in a personal interview than in a telephone or mail interview. The interviewer records answers to open-ended questions and provides visual aids to help with lengthy and complex scales. Some personal interviews last for as long as 75 minutes. In contrast to in-home and in-office interviews, street interviews and CAPI provide only moderate amounts of data. Because these interviews are conducted in shopping centres and other central locations, a respondent's time is more limited. Typically, the interview time is 20 minutes or less.

Mail surveys also yield moderate amounts of data. Fairly long questionnaires can be used because short questionnaires do not necessarily generate higher response rates than long ones. The same is true for email and Internet surveys, although the Internet is a better medium in this respect. Mail panels, on the other hand, can generate large amounts of data because of the special relationship between the panel members and the sponsoring organisation.

Traditional telephone interviews and CATI result in the most limited quantities of data. They tend to be shorter than other surveys because respondents can easily terminate the telephone conversation at their own discretion. These interviews commonly last about 15 minutes, although longer interviews may be conducted when the subject matter is of interest to the respondents.[31]

Response rate

Response rate
The percentage of the total attempted interviews that are completed.

Survey **response rate** is broadly defined as the percentage of the total attempted interviews that are completed. Personal, in-home and in-office, street and CAPI interviews yield the highest response rates, though this is not generalisable to all countries as illustrated in the next example.

Example   **Where respondents are particularly reluctant to give their opinions[32]**

Non-response is a common problem in most countries, but Germany has a particularly bad reputation when it comes to closed doors. A manager, responsible for supplier management at a domestic products giant, works with most global agencies in Germany for quantitative research. For products in for instance the baby care line, it proved very cumbersome to find out German opinion: 'Door to door is virtually impossible, due also to the fact that there are a lot of apartment blocks here. Telephone research is very difficult too, Germans are very careful before answering.' John Attfield of RMM Marketing Research International worked in England before his 11-year stint in Germany. The differences in response he observes are dramatic. He takes extra special care in designing questionnaires, for instance: 'One cannot approach Germans with the same introductory texts as in, for instance, the US. In the US the assumption is made that the respondent is going to enjoy the survey. But in Germany people think it is a pain.'

Telephone interviews, traditional and CATI, also suffer from not-at-homes or no-answers. In a study involving qualitative interviews and a census of all Australian telephone market research providers it was reported that about half of all placed telephone calls go unanswered; and refusals can outnumber interviews by up to six to one. Three call-backs per survey were built into the research design in most companies but surprisingly, in some cases, there were none, despite research that shows that call-backs can increase response rates by up to 76%.[33]

Mail surveys have the poorest response rate. In a mail survey of randomly selected respondents, without any pre- or postmailing contact, response rates can be less than 15%. Such low response rates can lead to serious bias (**non-response bias**). This is because whether a person responds to a mail survey is related to how well the benefits of taking part in the survey are meaningful to the person and are clearly communicated to them. The magnitude of non-response bias increases as the response rate decreases. Response

Non-response bias
Bias caused when actual respondents differ from those who refuse to participate.

rates in mail panels are much higher than in traditional mail techniques because of assured respondent cooperation.

Internet surveys can have very poor response rates, much depending upon how comprehensive and current the sampling frame is. With a well-constructed sampling frame that is relevant to the survey topic, response rates on the Internet can be relatively high.

A comprehensive review of the literature covering 497 response rates in 93 journal articles found weighted average response rates of 81.7%, 72.3% and 47.3% for, respectively, personal, telephone and mail surveys.[34] The same review also found that response rates increase with the following:

- Either prepaid or promised monetary incentives.
- An increase in the amount of monetary incentive.
- Non-monetary premiums and rewards (pens, pencils, books).
- Preliminary notification.
- Foot-in-the door techniques. These are multiple request strategies. The first request is relatively small, and all or most people agree to comply. The small request is followed by a larger request, called the **critical request**, which is actually the target behaviour being researched.
- Personalisation (sending letters addressed to specific individuals).
- Follow-up letters.

A further discussion of improving response rates is given in Chapter 15.

Perceived respondent anonymity

Perceived respondent anonymity refers to the respondents' perceptions that their identities will not be discerned by the interviewer or the researcher. Perceived anonymity of the respondent is high in mail surveys, mail panels and Internet surveys because there is no contact with an interviewer while responding. It is low in personal interviews (in-home, street and CAPI) due to face-to-face contact with the interviewer. Traditional telephone interviews and CATI fall in the middle. It is also moderate with email; while there is no contact with the interviewer, respondents know that their names can be located on the return email.

Social desirability

Social desirability is the tendency of respondents to give answers that they feel to be acceptable in front of others, including interviewers. When respondents are questioned face to face by an interviewer, they may give an answer that they feel to be 'acceptable' rather than how they really feel or behave. An example of this phenomenon occurred during the opinion polls that led up to the British General Election of 1992. The opinion polls placed the Labour Party a clear 8% ahead of the Conservative Party. In the actual election, the Conservative Party won, confounding all of the opinion poll predictions. This outcome resulted in an investigation by the Royal Statistical Society and the Market Research Society into why all the opinion polls had consistently predicted that the Labour Party would win. The investigation revealed that many respondents (who primarily had been interviewed face to face and by telephone) said they would vote Labour, as this was seen to be the socially acceptable thing to do. In the privacy of the polling booth, they voted Conservative.

The best techniques to avoid respondents distorting their views are those where face-to-face contact is avoided; this is the case with all mail methods. Traditional telephone interviews and CATI are moderately good at handling socially desirable responses, as there is an amount of anonymity afforded by not meeting face to face. The weakest techniques are face-to-face interviews, though in the case of in-home and in-office interviews, the chance to build up a rapport with respondents may nurture them to reveal how they really feel.[35]

Critical request
The target behaviour being researched.

Perceived respondent anonymity
The respondents' perceptions that their identities will not be discerned by the interviewer or researcher.

Social desirability
The tendency of respondents to give answers that may not be accurate but may be desirable from a social standpoint.

Obtaining sensitive information

Sensitive information may mean an issue that is personally sensitive, such as the way in which a respondent may be classified or the use of hygiene products. What may be deemed 'sensitive' varies enormously between different types of respondent. For some respondents, asking questions about the type and amount of household cleaning products may be seen as revealing characteristics of their personal cleanliness; they see it as a sensitive issue and would need a lot of reassurance before revealing the truth. Many classification questions in a survey, such as the respondent's age, gender, educational or income level, can also be seen as highly sensitive. In business research, characteristics of an organisation's activities may be seen as commercially sensitive.

In some situations, the interviewer plays a very important role in explaining to respondents why they are being asked such a question and that their views will be handled in a confidential and proper manner. In-home and in-office interviews allow the time and context to build up such explanations and reassure respondents. Interviews conducted in this way may be seen as the best means to handle certain sensitive topics. For some issues, respondents may not wish to face any interviewer and would like to complete the survey alone. CAPI can be set up so that the interviewer introduces the respondent to a terminal and then leaves the respondent to get on with the on-screen interview.[36] All mail surveys can be seen as moderately successful in handling sensitive questions. Their success depends upon how well the purpose of sensitive questions is introduced. Handled correctly, respondents can take their time to answer questions without any embarrassing contact. For telephone and street interviews, the interviewer can reassure the respondent about the questions being asked, but may not have the time and context really to relax respondents and overcome any embarrassment.

Potential for interviewer bias

An interviewer can bias the results of a survey by the manner in which he or she:

1 selects respondents (e.g. interviewing a male aged 34 when required to interview a male aged between 36 and 45);
2 asks research questions (omitting questions);
3 poses questions in another way when respondents do not understand the question as presented on the questionnaire;
4 probes (e.g. by offering examples to encourage respondents);
5 records answers (recording an answer incorrectly or incompletely).

The extent of the interviewer's role determines the potential for bias.[37] In-home, in-office and street personal interviews are highly susceptible to interviewer bias. Traditional telephone interviews and CATI are less susceptible, although the potential is still there. For example, with inflection and tone of voice, interviewers can convey their own attitudes and thereby suggest answers. CAPI has a low potential for bias. Mail surveys, mail panels, email and Internet surveys are free of it.

Potential to probe respondents

Although the interviewer has the potential to create bias in the responses elicited from respondents, it is balanced somewhat by the amount of probing that can be done. For example, a survey may ask respondents which brands of beer they have seen advertised on TV over the past month. A list of brands could be presented to respondents and they could simply look at the list and call out the names. What may be important in the survey is what brands they could remember. There may be a first response, of a brand that could be remembered unaided. A simple probe such as 'any others?' or 'any involving sports personalities?' could be recorded as a second response.

Much deeper prompts and probes can be conducted, within limits. The intention is not to turn the interview into a qualitative interview but, for example, some of the reasons why a respondent has chosen a brand may be revealed. In-home, in-office and street personal interviews have great potential for probing respondents. Traditional telephone interviews and CATI can also probe but not to the same extent as being face to face. CAPI has limited potential to probe, though particular routines can be built into a survey to ask for further details. Mail surveys, mail panels, email and Internet surveys have very limited means to probe respondents.

Potential to build rapport

Another counter to the bias in the responses elicited from respondents by personal interviews is the amount of rapport that can be built up with respondents. Rapport may be vital to communicate why the survey is being conducted, with a corresponding rationale for the respondent to spend time answering the questions. Beyond motivating respondents to take part in a survey is the need for the respondent to answer truthfully, to reflect upon the questions properly and not to rush through the questionnaire. Building up a good rapport with respondents can be vital to gain a full and honest response to a survey.

In-home, in-office and street personal interviews have great potential to build up rapport with respondents. Traditional telephone interviews and CATI can also develop rapport but not to the same extent as being face to face. CAPI has limited potential to build up rapport through particular graphics and messages that can be built into a survey. When recruiting respondents to mail panels, an amount of rapport can be built up. Mail surveys, email and Internet surveys have very limited means to build up a rapport with respondents.

Speed

First, there is the speed with which a questionnaire can be created, distributed to respondents, and the data returned. Because printing, mailing and data keying delays are eliminated, data can be in hand within hours of writing an Internet or telephone questionnaire. Data are obtained in electronic form, so statistical analysis software can be programmed to process standard questionnaires and return statistical summaries and charts automatically. Thus, the Internet can be an extremely fast method of obtaining data from a large number of respondents. The email survey is also fast, although slower than the Internet, since more time is needed to compile an email list and data entry is also required.

Traditional telephone interviews and CATI are also fast means of obtaining information. When a central telephone facility is used, several hundred telephone interviews can be done per day. Data for even large national surveys can be collected in a matter of days or even within a day. Next in speed are street and CAPI interviews that reach potential respondents in central locations. In-home personal interviews are slower because there is dead time between interviews while the interviewer travels to the next respondent. To expedite data collection, interviews can be conducted in different markets or regions simultaneously. Mail surveys are typically the slowest. It usually takes several weeks to receive completed questionnaires; follow-up mailings to boost response rates take even longer. Mail panels are faster than mail surveys because little follow-up is required.[38]

Cost

For large samples, the cost of Internet surveys is the lowest. Printing, mailing, keying and interviewer costs are eliminated, and the incremental costs per respondent are typically low, so studies with large numbers of respondents can be done at substantial savings compared with mail, telephone or personal surveys. Personal interviews tend to be the most expensive mode of data collection per completed response, whereas mail surveys tend to be the least expensive. In general, Internet, email, mail surveys, mail panel, traditional telephone, CATI, CAPI, street and personal in-home interviews require progressively larger field staff and greater supervision and control. Hence, the cost increases in this order. Relative costs, however, depend on the subject of enquiry and the procedures adopted.[39]

Selection of survey method(s)

As is evident from Table 10.2 and the preceding discussion, no survey method is superior in all situations. Depending on such factors as information requirements, budgetary constraints (time and money) and respondent characteristics, no, one, two or even all techniques may be appropriate.[40] Remember that the various data collection modes are not mutually exclusive. Rather, they can be employed in a complementary fashion to build on each other's strengths and compensate for each other's weaknesses. The researcher can employ these techniques in combination and develop creative twists within each technique. Mixed-mode research offers one of the most serious ways to tackle falling response rates. The key features of making mixed-mode research work are:[41]

- Common questions across all modes.
- Different templates applied to different modes to ensure that each looks right.
- Mode-specific text alternatives in addition to support for foreign language translations.
- A single database for all survey data, updated in real time.
- The ability to determine the mode of initial contact from the sample.
- Easy switching of any interview from one mode to another.
- Automatic concealment of any interviewer-recorded data when switching a self-completion mode.
- Management tools that allow progress to be viewed across all modes and identify separate modes.
- Support for mode-specific questions or question types.

Observation techniques

Quantitative observation
The recording and counting of behavioural patterns of people, objects and events in a systematic manner to obtain information about the phenomenon of interest.

Quantitative observation techniques are extensively used in descriptive research. Observation involves recording the behavioural patterns of people, objects and events in a systematic manner to obtain information about the phenomenon of interest. The observer does not question or communicate with the people being observed unless he or she takes the role of a **mystery shopper**. Information may be recorded as the events occur or from records of past events. Observational techniques may be structured or unstructured, disguised or undisguised. Furthermore, observation may be conducted in a natural or a contrived environment.[42]

Mystery shopper
An observer visiting providers of goods and services as if he or she was really a customer, and recording characteristics of the service delivery.

Structured versus unstructured observation

Structured observation
Observation where the researcher clearly defines the behaviours to be observed and the techniques by which they will be measured.

For **structured observation**, the researcher specifies in detail what is to be observed and how the measurements are to be recorded, such as when an auditor performs a stock or inventory analysis in a store. This reduces the potential for observer bias and enhances the reliability of the data. Structured observation is appropriate when the phenomena under study can be clearly defined and counted. For example, suppose that the researcher wished to measure the ratio of visitors to buyers in a store. The reason for such observations could be to understand the amount of browsing that occurs in a store. The researcher could observe and count the number of individuals who enter the store and the number who make a purchase. Counting people who enter a shop could be a manual observation, and could have a rule that the store visitors are counted 'if they actually look at any of the products on display'. Counting the number of transactions through the till may be a simpler electronic observation. With these two counts the researcher could simply calculate the required ratio. Structured observation is suitable for use in conclusive research.

Unstructured observation
Observation that involves a researcher monitoring all relevant phenomena, without specifying the details in advance.

Ethnography
A research approach based upon the observation of the customs, habits and differences between people in everyday situations.

In **unstructured observation** the observer monitors all aspects of the phenomenon that seem relevant to the problem at hand, such as observing children playing with new toys and trying to understand what activities they enjoy the most. This form of observation can be used when a research problem has yet to be formulated precisely and when flexibility is needed in observation to identify essential components of the problem and to develop hypotheses. Unstructured observation is most appropriate for exploratory research and as such was discussed in detail in Chapter 6 under the heading of **ethnography**. Ethnographic techniques require a researcher to spend a large amount of time observing a particular group of people, by sharing their way of life.[43]

Disguised versus undisguised observation

In disguised observation, the respondents are unaware that they are being observed. Disguise enables respondents to behave naturally because people tend to behave differently when they know they are being observed. Disguise may be accomplished by using two-way mirrors, hidden cameras or inconspicuous electronic devices. Observers may be disguised as

Source: © Russell Underwood/CORBIS

shoppers, sales assistants or other appropriate roles. One of the most widespread techniques of observation is through the use of mystery shoppers. Typically a mystery shopper would go into, for example, a bank, note practical things such as the number of counter positions open, the number of people queuing, or the availability of specific leaflets, and then ask a number of specific questions. The mystery shopper takes the role of the ordinary 'man or woman in the street', behaves just as a normal customer would, asks the same sorts of questions a customer would, leaves, and fills in a questionnaire detailing the various components observed in the visit. Mystery shopping differs from conventional survey research in that it aims to collect facts rather than perceptions. Conventional customer service research is all about customer perceptions. Mystery shopping, on the other hand, aims to be as objective as possible and to record as accurately as possible what actually happened in encounters such as the following:[44]

Personal visits
- How long were you in the queue?
- How many tills were open?
- Did the counter clerk apologise if you were kept waiting?
- What form of greeting or farewell was given?

Telephone calls
- How many rings were there before the phone was answered?
- Did the person who answered the phone go on to answer all your questions?
- Were you asked a password?
- How many times during the conversation was your name used?

| **Example** | **The mystery behind mystery shopping[45]** |

The Bose Corporation (www.bose.com) is one of the world's leading audio brands, selling a variety of audio products. As of 2003, Bose relied on an array of sales channels, such as retail stores, direct mail operations and online sales to drive about €1.5 billion in annual sales. One strategy that Bose uses effectively is selling directly to consumers through its own retail shops around the country with its own employees who know the products and can explain them to customers. Bose uses mystery shopping to ensure that its customers get the best customer service available. This method combines the use of personal observation with questioning to evaluate different features of the retail shops. Shoppers are recruited and trained in the observation and questioning process.

The mystery shopping process begins with a telephone call to the retail shop. Shoppers ask questions about products and record how helpful the employee was in answering questions. Customers also rate the employee's friendliness and other factors on an excellent–satisfactory–unsatisfactory scale. Next, there is the in-person visit where the shopper, pretending to be a buyer, gets a more in-depth look at the employee's people skills and knowledge of the product. The process is more involved during the in-person visit. The employees are graded on their language, the store environment and their demonstrations of the products. Shoppers are instructed to complete the observation form immediately after the experience, while everything is still fresh in their minds. The feedback is used to make changes in the personal selling and marketing strategy. When mystery shopping revealed that some salespeople were not very knowledgeable about the products, Bose strengthened its basic training programme and made it mandatory for all its salespeople.

In undisguised observation, respondents are aware that they are under observation. Respondents may be aware of the situation either by being told that an observer is in their presence or by its being obvious that someone is recording their behaviour. Researchers disagree on how much effect the presence of an observer has on behaviour. One viewpoint is that the observer effect is minor and short-lived.[46] The other position is that the observer can seriously bias the behaviour patterns.[47] There are ethical considerations to disguised versus undisguised observations that will be tackled at the end of this chapter.

Natural versus contrived observation

Natural observation
Observing behaviour as it takes place in the environment.

Contrived observation
Observing behaviour in an artificial environment.

Natural observation involves observing behaviour as it takes place in the environment. For example, one could observe the behaviour of respondents eating a new menu option in Burger King. In **contrived observation**, respondents' behaviour is observed in an artificial environment, such as a test kitchen.

The advantage of natural observation is that the observed phenomenon will more accurately reflect the true phenomenon, as the behaviour occurs in a context that feels natural to the respondent. The disadvantages are the cost of waiting for the phenomenon to occur and the difficulty of measuring the phenomenon in a natural setting.

Observation techniques classified by mode of administration

As shown in Figure 10.2, observation techniques may be classified by mode of administration as personal observation, electronic observation, audit, and trace analysis.

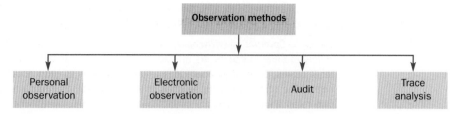

**Figure 10.2
A classification of
observation techniques**

Personal observation

Personal observation
An observational research
strategy in which human
observers record the
phenomenon being observed
as it occurs.

In **personal observation**, a researcher observes actual behaviour as it occurs. The observer does not attempt to control or manipulate the phenomenon being observed but merely records what takes place. For example, a researcher might record the time, day and number of shoppers who enter a shop and observe where those shoppers 'flow' once they are in the shop. This information could aid in designing a store's layout and determining the location of individual departments, shelf locations and merchandise displays.

Electronic observation

Electronic observation
An observational research
strategy in which electronic
devices, rather than human
observers, record the
phenomenon being
observed.

In **electronic observation**, electronic devices rather than human observers record the phenomenon being observed. The devices may or may not require the respondents' direct participation. They are used for continuously recording ongoing behaviour for later analysis.

Of the electronic devices that do not require respondents' direct participation, the A.C. Nielsen audimeter is best known. The audimeter is attached to a TV set to record continually the channel to which a set is tuned. Another way to monitor viewers is through the people meter. People meters attempt to measure not only the channels to which a set is tuned but also who is watching.[48] Other common examples include turnstiles that record the number of people entering or leaving a building and traffic counters placed across streets to count the number of vehicles passing certain locations.

The most significant electronic observation form as detailed in Chapter 5 is through the use of the bar code on products. As goods are sold, optical scanners can determine which products have been sold. With a link to a 'loyalty card', electronic observation links the whole array of purchases made by a consumer to the actual identity of that consumer. In this example, electronic observation does not require direct involvement of the participants.

In contrast, there are many electronic observation devices that do require participant involvement. These electronic devices may be classified into five groups: (1) eye tracking monitors, (2) pupilometers, (3) psycho-galvanometers, (4) voice pitch analysers and (5) devices measuring response latency. **Eye tracking equipment** – such as oculometers, eye cameras or eye view minuters – records the gaze movements of the eye. These devices can be used to determine how a respondent reads an advertisement or views a TV commercial and for how long the respondent looks at various parts of the stimulus. Such information is directly relevant to assessing advertising effectiveness. The **pupilometer** measures changes in the diameter of the pupils of the respondent's eyes. The respondent is asked to look at a screen on which an advertisement or other stimulus is projected. Image brightness and distance from the respondent's eyes are held constant. Changes in pupil size are interpreted as changes in cognitive (thinking) activity resulting from exposure to the stimulus. The underlying assumption is that increased pupil size reflects interest and positive attitudes towards the stimulus.[49]

The **psycho-galvanometer** measures **galvanic skin response** (GSR) or changes in the electrical resistance of the skin.[50] The respondent is fitted with small electrodes that monitor electrical resistance and is shown stimuli such as advertisements, packages and slogans. The theory behind this device is that physiological changes such as increased perspiration accompany emotional reactions. Excitement leads to increased perspiration, which

Eye tracking equipment
Instruments that record the
gaze movements of the eye.

Pupilometer
An instrument that measures
changes in the eye pupil
diameter.

Psycho-galvanometer
An instrument that measures
a respondent's galvanic skin
response.

Galvanic skin response
Changes in the electrical
resistance of the skin that
relate to a respondent's
affective state.

increases the electrical resistance of the skin. From the strength of the response, the researcher infers the respondent's interest level and attitudes towards the stimuli.

Voice pitch analysis measures emotional reactions through changes in the respondent's voice. Changes in the relative vibration frequency of the human voice that accompany emotional reaction are measured with audio-adapted computer equipment.[51]

Response latency is the time a respondent takes before answering a question. It is used as a measure of the relative preference for various alternatives.[52] Response time is thought to be directly related to uncertainty. Therefore, the longer a respondent takes to choose between two alternatives, the closer the alternatives are in terms of preference. On the other hand, if the respondent makes a quick decision, one alternative is clearly preferred. With the increased popularity of computer-assisted data collection, response latency can be recorded accurately and without the respondent's awareness. Use of eye tracking monitors, pupilometers, psycho-galvanometers and voice pitch analysers assumes that physiological reactions are associated with specific cognitive and affective responses. This has yet to be clearly demonstrated. Furthermore, calibration of these devices to measure physiological arousal is difficult, and they are expensive to use. Another limitation is that respondents are placed in an artificial environment and know that they are being observed.

An interesting development in electronic observation lies in the emergent field of **neuromarketing**. An example of this technique is presented in the following.

Voice pitch analysis
Measurement of emotional reactions through changes in the respondent's voice.

Response latency
The amount of time it takes to respond to a question.

Neuromarketing
The application of neuroscience in marketing, primarily to measure emotions through brain imaging.

Example | ### Dissecting emotions through neuromarketing[53]

The work of Professor Steve Quartz focuses upon the living brain. He gently slides respondents into fMRI (functional Magnetic Resonance Imaging) scanners in order to measure whether they like or dislike commercials, identify with brands, or appreciate a new product or packaging. The scanner measures where the blood flows to the brain and reveals which functional areas are triggered. Steve claims that neuromarketing could fill the traditional gap between qualitative and quantitative research:

Assessing emotions has traditionally been a task for qualitative research. But fMRI is showing how we can break down the distinction between qual and quant, as it allows us to develop quantitative matrices for emotion. Marketers want to know whether or not consumers develop an emotional connection to their product. We know which part of the brain is the connective area and we can measure and scale brain activity. The data also provides insight into the kind of connection and whether or not a product connection is emotional or rational.

Audit

In an audit, the researcher collects data by examining physical records or performing inventory analysis. Audits have two distinguishing features. First, data are collected personally by the researcher. Second, the data are based upon counts, usually of physical objects. Retail and wholesale audits conducted by marketing research suppliers were discussed in the context of secondary data (see Chapter 4). Here we focus on the role of audits in collecting primary data. In this respect, an important audit conducted at the consumer level, generally in conjunction with one of the survey techniques, is the **pantry audit**. In a pantry audit, the researcher takes an inventory of brands, quantities and package sizes in a consumer's home, perhaps in the course of a personal interview. Pantry audits greatly reduce the problem of untruthfulness or other forms of response bias. Obtaining permission to examine consumers' pantries can be difficult, however, and the fieldwork is expensive. Furthermore, the brands in the pantry may not reflect the most preferred brands or the brands purchased most often. Moreover, similar data can be obtained from scanned data more efficiently. For these reasons, pantry audits are no longer commonly used; audits are more common at the retail and wholesale level.

Pantry audit
A type of audit where the researcher inventories the brands, quantities and package sizes of products in a consumer's home.

Trace analysis

Trace analysis
An approach in which data collection is based on physical traces, or evidence, of past behaviour.

An observation method that can be inexpensive if used creatively is **trace analysis**. In trace analysis, data collection is based on physical traces, or evidence, of past behaviour. These traces may be left by the respondents intentionally or unintentionally. Several innovative applications of trace analysis have been made in marketing research:

- The selective erosion of tiles in a museum indexed by the replacement rate was used to determine the relative popularity of exhibits.
- The number of different fingerprints on a page was used to gauge the readership of various advertisements in a magazine.
- The position of the radio dials in cars brought in for service was used to estimate share of listening audience of various radio stations. Advertisers used the estimates to decide on which stations to advertise.
- The age and condition of cars in a car park were used to assess the affluence of customers.
- The magazines people donated to charity were used to determine people's favourite magazines.
- Internet visitors leave traces that can be analysed to examine browsing and usage behaviour through **cookie technology**.

Cookie technology
A group of letters and numbers stored in a web surfer's browser that identify the browser's computer.

Example Have a cookie[54]

The cookie is a group of letters and numbers stored in the web surfer's browser that identifies the user. Companies and individuals that host websites use cookies to observe behavioural characteristics of visitors. Cookies follow the traveller through the website and record the pages accessed by the visitor and the number of minutes spent on each page. The name, address, phone number and access site can be collected by the cookie and saved into a database if the visitor enters any information. During a follow-up visit, the cookie accesses this information and has the ability to repeat it to the visitor. In essence, the cookie collects data on the user during every visit to the site.

Hotwired's Packet (**www.hotwired.com**) uses cookies to collect information about site traffic. The information helps marketing personnel at the electronic and print magazine to collect demographics on the reader. Also, the company can monitor 'hits' on particular topics and gain valuable feedback on user interest. Data collection is based upon visitor behaviour. This disguised technique enables Hotwired to monitor use patterns and to eliminate socially acceptable response bias. Information collected in this manner has been used to modify editorial content and format to make the magazine more appealing.

A comparative evaluation of observation techniques

A comparative evaluation of the observation techniques is given in Table 10.3. The different observation techniques are evaluated in terms of the degree of structure, degree of disguise, ability to observe in a natural setting, observation bias, measurement and analysis bias, and additional general factors.

Structure relates to the specification of what is to be observed and how the measurements are to be recorded. As can be seen from Table 10.3, personal observation is low, trace analysis is medium, and audit is high on the degree of structure. Electronic observation can vary widely from low to high, depending on the techniques used. Techniques such as optical scanners are very structured in that the characteristics to be measured – for example, characteristics of items purchased and scanned in supermarket checkouts – are

Table 10.3 A comparative evaluation of observation techniques

Criteria	Personal observation	Electronic observation	Audit	Trace analysis
Degree of structure	Low	Low to high	High	Medium
Degree of disguise	Medium	Low to high	Low	High
Natural setting	High	Low to high	High	Low
Observation bias	High	Low	Low	Medium
Analysis bias	High	Low to medium	Low	Medium
General remarks	Most flexible	Can be intrusive	Expensive	Limited traces available

precisely defined. In contrast, electronic techniques, such as the use of hidden cameras to observe children at play with toys, tend to be unstructured.

The degree of disguise is low in the case of audits as it is difficult to conceal the identity of auditors. Personal observation offers a medium degree of disguise because there are limitations on the extent to which the observer can be disguised as a shopper, sales assistant, employee and so forth. Trace analysis offers a high degree of disguise because the data are collected 'after the fact': that is, after the phenomenon to be observed has taken place. Some electronic observations such as hidden cameras offer excellent disguise, whereas others, such as the use of psycho-galvanometers, are very difficult to disguise.

The ability to observe in a natural setting is low in trace analysis because the observation takes place after the behaviour has occurred. Personal observation and audits are excellent on this score because human observers can observe people or objects in a variety of natural settings. Electronic observation techniques vary from low (e.g. use of psycho-galvanometers) to high (e.g. use of turnstiles).

Observation bias is low in the case of electronic observation because a human observer is not involved. It is also low for audits. Although the auditors are humans, the observation usually takes place on objects and the characteristics to be observed are well defined, leading to low observation bias. Observation bias is medium for trace analysis. In this technique, human observers are involved and the characteristics to be observed are not very well defined. The observers typically do not interact with human respondents during the observation process, thus lessening the degree of bias. It is high for personal observation due to the use of human observers who interact with the phenomenon being observed.

Data analysis bias is low for audits because the variables are precisely defined, the data are quantitative and statistical analysis can be conducted. Trace analysis has a medium degree of bias as the definition of variables is not very precise. Electronic observation techniques can have a low (e.g. scanner data) to medium (e.g. hidden camera) degree of analysis bias. Unlike personal observation, the bias in electronic observation is limited to the medium level due to improved measurement and classification, because the phenomenon to be observed can be recorded continuously using electronic devices.

In addition, personal observation is the most flexible, because human observers can observe a wide variety of phenomena in a wide variety of settings. Some electronic observation techniques, such as the use of psycho-galvanometers, can be very intrusive, leading to artificiality and bias. Audits using human auditors tend to be expensive. As mentioned earlier, trace analysis is a method that is limited to where consumers actually leave 'traces'. This occurs infrequently and very creative approaches are needed to capture these traces.

Evaluating the criteria presented in Table 10.3 helps to identify the most appropriate observation technique, given the phenomena to be observed, the nature of respondents being observed and the context in which the observation occurs. To strengthen the choice of a particular observation technique, it is also helpful to compare the relative advantages and disadvantages of observation versus survey techniques.

Advantages and disadvantages of observation techniques

Other than the use of scanner data, few marketing research projects rely solely on observational techniques to obtain primary data.[55] This implies that observational techniques have some major disadvantages compared with survey techniques. Yet these techniques offer some advantages that make their use in conjunction with survey techniques quite fruitful.

Relative advantages of observation techniques

The greatest advantage of observational techniques is that they permit measurement of actual behaviour rather than reports of intended or preferred behaviour. There is no reporting bias, and potential bias caused by the interviewer and the interviewing process is eliminated or reduced. Certain types of data can be collected only by observation. These include behaviour patterns which the respondent is unaware of or unable to communicate. For example, information on babies' and toddlers toy preferences is best obtained by observing babies at play, because they are unable to express themselves adequately. Moreover, if the observed phenomenon occurs frequently or is of short duration, observational techniques may cost less and be faster than survey techniques.

Relative disadvantages of observation techniques

The biggest disadvantage of observation is that the reasons for the observed behaviour may be difficult to determine because little is known about the underlying motives, beliefs, attitudes and preferences. For example, people observed buying a brand of cereal may or may not like it themselves; they may be purchasing that brand for someone else in the household. Another limitation of observation is the extent to which researchers are prepared to evaluate the extent of their own bias, and how this can affect what they observe. In addition, observational data can be time consuming and expensive to collect. It is also difficult to observe certain forms of behaviour such as personal activities that occur in the privacy of the consumer's home. Finally, in some cases such as in the use of hidden cameras, the use of observational techniques may border on being or may actually be unethical. It can be argued that individuals being observed should be made aware of the situation, but this may cause them to behave in a contrived manner.

International marketing research

The selection of appropriate interviewing techniques is much more difficult in foreign countries because of the challenges of conducting research there. Given the differences in the economic, structural, informational, technological and socio-cultural environment, the feasibility and popularity of the different interviewing techniques vary widely. In the USA and Canada, for example, the telephone has achieved almost total penetration of households. Consequently, telephone interviewing is a dominant mode of questionnaire administration. The same situation exists in some European countries, such as Sweden. In many other European countries, however, the telephone interview gets confused with telephone sales. This results in high refusal rates and scepticism of what the purpose of a survey is. In developing countries, the problem with the telephone is the low number of households that have telephones as illustrated in the following example:

Example | **Mexico bridges two Americas[56]**

In some layers of the 100 million plus Mexican population (where 61.9% are considered to be of low income) even telephone connections are too scarce for a representative survey. Mexican marketing research therefore depends on face-to-face interviews for 70–80% of all survey work. Western researchers look upon their response rates with some envy as Mexicans are still open and hospitable to personal questioning. The growing higher and middle incomes, who live predominantly in the three large cities – Mexico City, Guadalajara and Monterrey – show an increasing reluctance to personal interviews, but this is largely due to the growing crime rates. The Mexican upper classes surround themselves more and more with security systems and high fences. Behind this screen, they can only be reached by phone and the Internet.

Because of the low cost, mail interviews continue to be used in most developed countries where literacy is high and the postal system is well developed, e.g. in the UK, Canada, Denmark, Finland, Iceland, the Netherlands, Norway, Sweden and the USA. In many parts of Africa, Asia and South America, however, the use of mail surveys and mail panels is low because of illiteracy and the large proportion of the population living in rural areas.

The following example illustrates how CAPI technology has developed to allow consistent approaches to survey techniques across Europe. It shows that, by developing an appreciation of the cultural differences between countries, a research design can be built that allows accurate and comparable surveys to be conducted.

Example | **CAPIBUS Europe[57]**

The concept of the international omnibus is not new; many research groups offer an international service. In reality, however, these have been little more than brokering services, bolting together whatever omnibus is available in each country, with little real standardisation.

Research Services Limited and the IPSOS Group have tackled this problem by calling on the benefits of CAPI technology to introduce CAPIBUS Europe, a weekly omnibus survey covering the six major markets of Europe (the UK, France, Germany, Italy, the Netherlands and Spain).

The use of computer technology means that questionnaires can be scripted in one location and transmitted electronically to other countries. While the need to ensure accurate translation remains, the problems involved in having different questionnaire formats, classification systems and data maps are minimised. At the end of a project, data are again transmitted electronically, to be aggregated by the lead agency in a standardised format for all markets. This can then be weighted to provide information on the European market as well as for each local market.

$\rightarrow$

Selection of survey techniques

No questionnaire administration method is superior in all situations. Table 10.4 presents a comparative evaluation of the major modes of collecting quantitative data in the context of international marketing research. In this table, the survey techniques are discussed only under the broad headings of telephone, personal, mail and electronic interviews. The use of CATI, CAPI, electronic survey and mail panels depends heavily on the state of technological development in the country. Likewise, the use of street interviewing is contingent upon the dominance of shopping centres in the retailing environment.

Table 10.4 A comparative evaluation of survey techniques for international marketing research

Criteria	Telephone	Personal	Mail	Electronic
High sample control	+	+	−	−
Difficulty in locating respondents at home	+	−	+	+
Inaccessibility of homes	+	−	+	+
Unavailability of a large pool of trained interviewers	+	−	+	+
Large population in rural areas	−	+	−	−
Unavailability of maps	+	−	+	+
Unavailability of current telephone directory	−	+	−	+
Unavailability of mailing lists	+	+	−	+
Low penetration of telephones	−	+	+	−
Lack of an efficient postal system	+	+	−	+
Low level of literacy	−	+	−	−
Face-to-face communication culture	−	+	−	−
Poor access to computers and Internet	+	+	+	−

Note: A plus denotes an advantage, and a minus denotes a disadvantage.

Ethics in marketing research

Respondent anonymity was discussed in the context of qualitative research in Chapter 8. It was argued then that large samples could 'hide' the specific answers of individual respondents. This is true to some extent but respondents may still be identifiable. It is up to the marketing researcher to protect a respondent's identity and not disclose it to anyone outside the research organisation, including the client. The client is not entitled to see the names and contact details of respondents. The only instance where respondents' identity can be revealed to the client is when respondents are notified in advance and their consent is obtained prior to administering the survey. Even in such situations, the researcher should have the assurance that the respondents' trust will be kept by the client and their identities will not be used in a sales effort or misused in other ways.

Special care must be taken to ensure that any record which contains a reference to the identity of an informant is securely and confidentially stored during any period before such reference is separated from that record and/or destroyed.[58] Ethical lapses in this respect by unscrupulous researchers and marketers have resulted in a serious backlash for marketing research. The result has been a consistent fall in the levels of response rate, to all forms of survey method. This reinforces the message that considering the needs of survey respondents makes sound research sense as well as being ethically sound. Dubious practices may generate a response for a single survey but may create long-term damage to the marketing research industry.

Another issue facing the marketing research industry is image, as the public may not distinguish between telephone research and telemarketing. This identity crisis is exacerbated by the action of some firms to commit '**sugging** and **frugging**', industry terms for selling or fundraising under the guise of a survey. The damage done to the marketing research industry by the unethical use of survey research as a guise for targeting sales effort was discussed in Chapter 1. The overall effect of these activities has given a poor image in particular to telephone research, raising the cost and making it difficult for researchers to obtain full and representative samples.

Although concerns for the respondents' psychological well-being are mild in survey data collection when compared with either qualitative or experimental research, researchers should not place respondents in stressful situations. Disclaimers such as 'there are no correct responses; we are only interested in your opinion' can relieve much of the stress inherent in a survey. In many face-to-face interview situations, respondents are given a 'thank you booklet' at the end of the interview. As well as saying a genuine thank you for taking part in a survey, the booklet briefly sets out the purpose and benefits of bona fide marketing research. The use of the 'thank you booklet' helps to educate the public to distinguish between genuine, professionally conducted marketing research and 'research' conducted as a front for generating sales leads.

Observation of people's behaviour without their consent is often done because informing the respondents may alter their behaviour.[59] But this can compromise the privacy of the respondents. One guideline is that people should not be observed for research in situations where they would not expect to be observed by the public. Therefore, public places like a shopping centre or a grocery aisle are fair game. These are places where people observe other people routinely. However, notices should be posted in these areas stating that they are under observation by marketing researchers.

With the growth of mystery shopping, where the essence of the technique is that service deliverers cannot spot the observer, the debate over what is ethical practice has intensified. The following example taken from a seminar on mystery shopping illustrates some of the issues that the marketing research industry considers vital to debate for the future 'health' of the technique.

Sugging
The use of marketing research to deliberately disguise a sales effort.

Frugging
The use of marketing research to deliberately disguise fundraising activities.

Example   ### The ethical puzzle of mystery shopping[60]

'For us to believe we can do this without some form of public outrage would make us very naive indeed.' This was the statement of Professor Roger Jowell to delegates attending the Joint Social Research Association/Market Research Society Seminar on Mystery Shopping.

Mystery shopping has been going on for years in one form or another but was formally originated in the USA in the early 1970s. The definition of mystery consumer research used at the seminar states: 'The use of individuals trained to observe ... by acting as a prospective customer.' Whether the individuals should be trained or not brought heated discussion, some suggesting that training would not encourage the shopper to act 'naturally' while others felt training was necessary in some form or another.

$\rightarrow$

The contentious issue of competitive videoing was debated. One agency director said 'this is fly on the wall journalism' and clients should go to a production company rather than a marketing research agency. One agency had been asked by a client to mystery-shop competitors only and, on turning to its code of conduct, found that there was nothing to stop it going ahead with this course of action.

Professor Jowell likened competitive shopping to industrial espionage, at which point Shirley Featherstone, Field Director of ACE Fieldwork, suggested that unlike industrial espionage, mystery shopping is information that is in the public domain.

Colin Brown, an independent consultant, explained that traditionally mystery shopping has been used:

- to campaign on public issues with which sponsoring companies have been able to make changes;
- as a monitor within companies to assess staff performance.

He then pointed to the latest tradition, that of enforcement, which results in people losing their jobs.

The final point in the above example graphically illustrates how important ethical issues are in conducting marketing research. If potential respondents perceive marketing research as a means to generate sales and 'snoop' on service delivery practices, then the goodwill needed to generate full and honest responses will wither. ESOMAR has specific guidelines to help with issues in mystery shopping, which can be seen at **www.esomar.com**.

Internet and computer applications

We begin this section with a description of a technological development that may have profound effects upon how CAPI is undertaken. We then move on to broader Internet and computer issues. A major technological development that has affected the conduct of CAPI has been personal digital assistants (PDAs). PDA is the generic title for a range of devices, from the ubiquitous PalmPilot from 3Com to the Pocket PCs from manufacturers such as Hewlett-Packard/Compaq. Essentially they are computers with a small touch-screen that fit in your hand.

Recent developments have included colour screens, and increasingly telecommunications are being added to new models being released; also the functions of mobile phone and mobile computer are merging together. This will extend their take-up even further, and might see the end of the mobile phone as we know it today.

Marketing research applications for PDAs started to appear in 2001, with Techneos (**www.techneos.com**) producing a specific product for the PalmPilot. Other software developers have opted for the Pocket PCs using variations of Windows CE from Microsoft. These have included SNAP, (**www.snapsurveys.com**). The logic of basing mobile interviewing on Windows-based products has been that software authors are less dependent on the fortunes of a single vendor of hardware.

The main benefits of using PDAs over the more traditional CAPI laptop or even the traditional paper and pencil clipboard solution are:

- Low cost
- Portability
- The fact that they are seen as a technology-based solution and in certain market sectors this is important.

Moving to broader issues, two factors dominate the computer-related aspects of the survey process:

1 It is now likely that 99% of all quantitative surveys today include an element of IT at some stage in their lifecycle. This may be simply for the questionnaire design stage or for the presentation of results. However, the computer is increasingly involved in many stages of the survey process – questionnaire design and printing, preparation of CATI scripts, publication of online surveys, collecting of email responses, scanning of paper questionnaires, keying of replies, data validation, cleaning and verification, data analysis and presentation, electronic distribution of survey results, and integration of results into office products, to name but a few.

2 Surveys increasingly involve more than one method of data collection. A survey might be designed for the Web, but respondents may be emailed a paper version to view the questions, and asked to complete offline if access to the Web is not possible. Surveys are increasingly being designed to incorporate alternative scenarios, perhaps using interviewers with PDAs alongside mailed questionnaires for self-completion.

The result is that researchers are becoming more sophisticated in their IT requirements. They are now less likely to outsource the entire process to the data processing department or an outside agency, and will need to be more heavily involved in the IT process than they were perhaps 10 years ago. This is certainly a beneficial development, as the researchers will acquire a far better understanding of the principles of survey design and analysis.

The increased use of multimode data collection methods may, however, present a further dilemma. On the one hand, an array of different software packages can be used. This approach is likely to generate surveys that are rich in their list of features, but possibly a nightmare to integrate. On the other hand, a single software package may be used that is capable of handling the range of options being requested. This approach may generate a solution that is easier to manage and operate, but possibly less rich in its presentation.

Internet surveys are gaining in popularity and have great potential for the marketing research industry. One reason is that the cost in most cases is less than that of personal, telephone or mail surveys. The cost of designing online surveys (with graphics, colour, buttons, routing, etc.) is likely to be higher than for a standard paper questionnaire, but the cost of data collection and preparation will be greatly reduced. Also, an Internet survey is not as intrusive as a phone call in the middle of dinner or at other inconvenient times. The online survey can be completed in one's own time, place and pace. Quick response time is another advantage cited by those producing online surveys. It is not true, however, that response rates are increased by using online surveys. Indeed, they have been shown to be no more successful than any other method if no follow-up reminders are included.[61]

Internet surveys can be used to target specific populations or potential target markets. There is a growth of specialist directories that include email and Internet addresses, but these are likely to be even less reliable than telephone directories, as online users frequently change their email addresses. Unlike telephone numbers, which do at least result in somebody answering, routing to a voicemail or simply responding as 'unobtainable', invalid email addresses simply bounce back. There is no indication as to whether the address has been misspelt, whether that person still exists at that email address, or whether the email address itself any longer exists. With no way to speak to a human at the end of an email address, the researcher is faced with a lost opportunity.

It has been argued that the use of the Internet to conduct marketing research is more revolutionary than other technological developments such as CATI or CAPI. Practitioners argue that the Internet has fundamentally changed the way that marketing researchers design questionnaires, collect data and analyse them.[62] The Internet is a visual medium: it allows respondents to see images, long text messages, long lists of response options and, as bandwidth grows, video images. It captures the unedited view of the respondent, eliciting responses to open-ended questions that are long, rich and revealing. It may be more effective in addressing sensitive issues; adults may be more willing to reveal information about their experiences of sensitive medical conditions, for example.

The downside of the Internet is its representativeness of broader populations. It is extremely difficult to conduct probability sampling, and the respondent population depends mostly on 'volunteer' or convenience sampling (see Chapter 14 for a full discussion of the sampling implications). Another limitation is the verification of who is actually responding to the survey. The absence of a human facilitator to motivate participants, security and privacy are also areas of concern.

There are also ethical considerations in conducting surveys on the Internet that primarily concern the fact that it is so inexpensive to use and difficult to regulate. This means that it can be open to misuse by less experienced or less scrupulous organisations, often based outside the research industry. Any Internet surveys which fall seriously below the high standards promoted by ESOMAR and other leading professional bodies make it more difficult to use the medium for research and could seriously damage the credibility of such research, as well as being an abuse of the goodwill of Internet users generally. ESOMAR has specific guidelines that address the use of the Internet to protect the interests both of Internet respondents and of the users of Internet research findings. These can be accessed at **www.esomar.nl/guidelines/internet_guidelines.htm**.

Visit **www.snapsurveys.com** to review the SNAP9 survey software, **www.camsp.com** to see Keypoint5, **www.sawtooth.com** (especially the CATI options), **www.voxco.com** for web, CATI and CAPI software in English and French formats, and **www.lesphinx-developpement.fr** for SphinxSurvey and **www.askia.com** for the Askia survey software. On all these sites you will be able to see an array of applications of survey software and to download demo versions.

Summary

The two basic means of obtaining primary quantitative data in descriptive research are through survey and observation techniques. Survey involves the direct questioning of respondents, while observation entails recording respondent behaviour or the behaviour of service deliverers.

Surveys involve the administration of a questionnaire and may be classified, based on the method or mode of administration, as (1) traditional telephone interviews, (2) computer-assisted telephone interviews (CATIs), (3) in-home or in-office personal interviews, (4) street interviews, (5) computer-assisted personal interviews (CAPIs), (6) traditional mail surveys, (7) mail panels, (8) email surveys, and (9) Internet surveys. Of these techniques, CATI, CAPI and Internet surveys have grown enormously in their use in developed Western economies. Each method has some general advantages and disadvantages, however. Although these data collection techniques are usually thought of as distinct and 'competitive', they should not be considered to be mutually exclusive in much the same manner as using quantitative and qualitative techniques should not be considered to be mutually exclusive. It is possible to employ them productively in combination.

Quantitative observational techniques may be classified as structured or unstructured, disguised or undisguised, and natural or contrived. The major techniques are personal observation (including mystery shopping), electronic observation, audit, and trace analysis. Compared with surveys, the relative advantages of observational techniques are that they permit measurement of actual behaviour, there is no reporting bias, and there is less potential for interviewer bias. Also, certain types of data can best, or only, be obtained by observation. The relative disadvantages of observation are that very little can be inferred about motives, beliefs, attitudes and preferences, there is a potential for observer bias, most techniques are time consuming and expensive, it is difficult to observe some forms of behaviour, and questions of ethical techniques of observation are far more contentious. Observation is rarely used as the sole method of obtaining primary data, but it can be usefully employed in conjunction with other marketing research techniques.

In collecting data from different countries, it is desirable to use survey techniques with equivalent levels of reliability rather than to use the same method. Respondents' anonymity should be protected, and their names should not be turned over to clients. People should not be observed without consent for research in situations where they would not expect to be observed by the public. Practitioners argue that the Internet has fundamentally changed the way that marketing researchers design questionnaires, collect survey data and analyse them.

Questions

1 Within a context of survey researchers imposing their language and logic upon potential respondents, what do you see as being the advantages and disadvantages of conducting surveys?

2 Discuss the dilemma faced by the survey designer who wishes to develop a survey that is not prone to interviewer bias but also sees that interviewer rapport with respondents is vital to the success of the survey.

3 Evaluate the reasons why response rates to surveys are declining.

4 Why do interviewers need to probe respondents in surveys? What distinguishes survey probing from probing conducted in qualitative interviews?

5 What are the relevant factors for evaluating which survey method is best suited to a particular research project?

6 What are the distinct advantages of conducting a survey using CAPI technology compared with traditional paper questionnaires?

7 What are the key advantages of conducting interviews on the Internet? Evaluate the potential that this technique holds for the future.

8 How would you classify mystery shopping as an observation technique? Why would you classify it in this way?

9   How may electronic observation techniques be used in supermarkets?

10   Explain, using examples, where trace analysis may be used.

11   Describe the criteria by which you would evaluate the relative benefits of different observation techniques.

12   What is the difference between qualitative and quantitative observation?

13   Describe the relative advantages and disadvantages of observation.

14   Describe a marketing research problem in which both survey and observation techniques could be used for obtaining the information needed.

15   What do you see as being the main ethical problems of mystery shopping?

Exercises

1   The manager of your college/university school/ department has been asked to review which survey method would be the most effective for a study of undergraduate experiences and attitudes at the end of each academic year. She has come to you to help her make the case. Which method would be best and why would it be the best?

2   Visit the Gallup organisation's website at **www.gallup.com**. Which survey methods have been used by Gallup in some of the recent surveys posted at this site? Why were these survey methods selected?

3   Locate an Internet survey, print off the pages and examine the content carefully. What are the relative advantages of administering the same survey via street interviewing? What would a street interviewer need to make this survey effective in a street situation?

4   You have been hired by the campus bookstore to covertly observe students making purchasing decisions while shopping. Spend 30 minutes making these observations and write a report that covers:
     a   How you feel students make their purchasing decisions for books and any other goods available in the shop.
     b   What you feel to be the benefits, limitations and challenges of this approach.

5   In a small group discuss the following issues: 'Telling consumers that they are being observed destroys what you are trying to observe. It is much better to see consumers behaving naturally, even if this requires the use of hidden cameras.' And 'Given the decline in response and cooperation rates to surveys, it would be much better for marketers to invest in quantitative observation techniques and forget conducting surveys.'

Video Case Exercise: Subaru

What technique(s) would you recommend to conduct surveys with Subaru buyers? Why?

video case

download from
www.pearsoned.co.uk/
malhotra_euro

Notes

1   Macer, T., 'Different strokes', *Research in Business* (March 2004), 19–20.

2   Surveys are commonly used in marketing research. See, for example, Malhotra, N. and McCort, D., 'A cross-cultural comparison of behavioural intention models: theoretical consideration and an empirical investigation', *International Marketing Review* 18 (3) (2001), 235–269.

3   ESOMAR – *Industry study on 2004*, 26.

4   Nakwah, R., 'Getting good feedback,' *Quirks Marketing Research Review* (November 2000).

5   ESOMAR – *Industry study on 2004*, 26.

6   Mareck, M., 'They're free and young people love them', *Research World* (November 2004), 25.

7   Havermans, J., 'Strict rules for telemarketers may help research', *Research World* (June 2004), 14–19.

8   Heeg, R., 'MR will be a fundamental tool in our country', *Research World* (May 2004), 6–7.

9   Burrows, S., 'Verbatim', *Research* (September 1995), 20.

10   ESOMAR – *Industry study on 2004*, 26.

11   Luker, J., 'Omnibus – the flexible research tool for many jobs', *ResearchPlus* (February 1996), 12.

12 'Auto-mania at the mall', *American Demographics* (Marketing Tools Supplement) (June 1997), 6; Bush, A.J. and Hair, J.E. Jr, 'An assessment of the mall-intercept as a data collection method', *Journal of Marketing Research* (May 1985), 158–167.

13 Rines, S., 'Brands fall short of their goal', *Marketing Week* (16 June 16 2005), 32–33.

14 ESOMAR – *Industry study on 2004*, 26.

15 Mail surveys are common in institutional and b2b marketing research. See, for example, Brossard, H.L., 'Information sources used by an organisation during a complex decision process: an exploratory study', *Industrial Marketing Management* 27 (1) (January 1998), 41–50.

16 Ganesan, S., 'Determinants of long-term orientation in buyer seller relationships', *Journal of Marketing* 58 (April 1994), 1–19.

17 Schmid, J., 'Assigning value to your customer list', *Catalog Age* 18 (5) (April 2001), 69; Yoegel, R., 'List marketers head to cyberspace', *Target Marketing* 20 (8) (August 1997), 54–55.

18 Michaelsen, R., 'A quick ABC of panels', *Research World* (February 2005), 27.

19 ESOMAR – *Industry study on 2004*, p. 26.

20 Mann, C. and Stewart, F., *Internet Communication and Qualitative Research: A Handbook for Researching Online* (London: Sage, 2000), 67.

21 Schwartz, M., 'Postal and email "Combos" gain favor with marketers', *B to B* 87 (2) (11 February 2002), 25; Stevens, J. and Chisholm, J., 'An integrated approach: technology firm conducts worldwide satisfaction research survey via email, Internet', *Quirk's Marketing Research Review* 11 (8) (October 1997), 12–13, 64–65.

22 Anon., 'How Canon used the internet to pick the right respondents', *Research in Business* (March 2004), 16.

23 Gorman, J.W., 'An opposing view of online surveying', *Marketing News* (24 April 2000); Johnston, A., 'Welcome to the wired world', *Research* (November 1999), 22–25; Comley, P., 'Will working the web provide a net gain?', *Research* (December 1996), 16.

24 Thompson, S.K., *Sampling* (New York: Wiley, 2002); Childers, T.L. and Skinner, S.J., 'Theoretical and empirical issues in the identification of survey respondents', *Journal of the Market Research Society* 27 (January 1985), 39–53.

25 Murphy, G.B., 'The effects of organizational sampling frame selection', *Journal of Business Venturing* 17 (3) (May 2002), 237; Smith, W., Mitchell, P., Attebo, K. and Leeder, S., 'Selection bias from sampling frames: telephone directory and electoral rolls compared to door-to-door population census: results from the Blue Mountain eye study', *Australian & New Zealand Journal of Public Health* 21 (2) (April 1997), 127–133.

26 Heeg, R., 'Every study in Belgium is an international study', *Research World* (February 2004), 8–9.

27 Tarran, B., 'Worldwide USA', *Research* (July 2005), 26–27.

28 Printz, J. and Maltby, D., 'Beyond personalisation: when handwriting makes a difference', *Fund Raising Management* 28 (3) (May 1997), 16–19; Conant, J.S., Smart, D.T. and Walker, B.J., 'Mail survey facilitation techniques: an assessment and proposal regarding reporting practices', *Journal of the Market Research Society* 32 (October 1990), 569–580.

29 Erdogan, B.Z., 'Increasing mail survey response rates from an industrial population: a cost effectiveness analysis of four follow-up techniques', *Industrial Marketing management* 31 (1) (January 2002), 65; Edmonston, J., 'Why response rates are declining', *Advertising Age's Business Marketing* 82 (8) (September 1997), 12; Hubbard, R. and Little, E.L., 'Promised contributions to charity and mail survey responses: replications with extension', *Public Opinion Quarterly* 52 (Summer 1988), 223–230; Erdos, P.L. and Ferber, R. (eds), 'Data collection methods: mail surveys', *Handbook of Marketing Research* (New York: McGraw-Hill, 1974), 102.

30 Fowler, F.J. Jr., *Survey Research Methods* 3rd edn (Thousand Oaks, CA: Sage, 2001); Guengel, P.C., Berchman, T.R. and Cannell, C.E., *General Interviewing Techniques: A Self Instructional Workbook for Telephone and Personal Interviewer Training* (Ann Arbor, MI: Survey Research Center, University of Michigan, 1983).

31 Fletcher, K., 'Jump on the omnibus', *Marketing* (15 June 1995), 25–28.

32 Heeg, R., 'Rigid data-protection and closed doors', *Research World* (April 2004), 6–7.

33 Bednall, D., 'CATI: what researchers, interviewers and clients can do to improve response rates', *Research News* (December 2004), 10.

34 Smith, J., 'How to boost DM response rates quickly', *Marketing News* 35 (9) (23 April 2001), 5; Columbo, R., 'A model for diagnosing and reducing non-response bias', *Journal of Advertising Research* (January/April 2000), 85–93; Nicholls II, W.L., 'Highest response', *Marketing Research: A Magazine of Management and Applications* 8 (1) (Spring 1996), 5–7; Yu, J. and Cooper, H., 'A quantitative review of research design effects on response rates to questionnaires', *Journal of Marketing Research* 20 (February 1983), 36–44. See also James, J.M. and Bolstein, R., 'The effect of monetary incentives and follow-up mailings on the response rate and response quality in mail surveys', *Public Opinion Quarterly* 54 (Fall 1990), 346–361.

35 Ones, D., Reiss, A.D. and Viswesvaran, C., 'Role of social desirability in personality testing for personnel selection: the red herring', *Journal of Applied Psychology* 81 (6) (December 1996), 660–679.

36 Anon. 'Random sampling: homework – yeah right', *Marketing News* 36 (6) (18 March 18 2002), 4; Vinten, G., 'The threat in the question', *Credit Control*, 18 (1) (1997), 25–31; Raghubir, P. and Menon, G., 'Asking sensitive questions: the effects of type of referent and frequency wording in counterbiasing method', *Psychology & Marketing* 13 (7) (October 1996), 633–652.

37 Graeff, T.R., 'Uninformed response bias in telephone surveys', *Journal of Business Research* 55 (3) (March 2002), 251; Singer, E., 'Experiments with incentives in telephone surveys', *Public Opinion Quarterly* 64 (2) (Summer 2000) 171–188; Cannell, C.E., Miller, P.U., Oksenberg, L. and Leinhardt, S. (eds), 'Research on interviewing techniques', in *Sociological Methodology* (San Francisco, CA: Jossey-Bass, 1981); Miller, P.U. and Cannell, C.E., 'A study of experimental techniques for telephone interviewing', *Public Opinion Quarterly* 46 (Summer 1982), 250–269.

38 Bachmann, D.P, Elfrink, J. and Vazzana, G., 'E-mail and snail mail face off in rematch', *Marketing Research*, 11 (Winter 1999/Spring 2000), 10–15.

39 McMaster, M., 'E-Marketing poll vault', *Sales and Marketing Management* 153 (8) (August 2001), 25; Fink, A., *A Survey Handbook* (Thousand Oaks, CA: Sage, 1995).

40 Denstadli, J.M., 'Analyzing air travel: a comparison of different survey methods and data collection procedures', *Journal of Travel Research* 39 (1) (August 2000) 4–10.

41 Macer, T., 'Different strokes', *Research in Business* (March 2004), 20.

42 Milat, A.J., 'Measuring physical activity in public open space – an electronic device versus direct observation', *Australian & New Zealand Journal of Public Health*, 26 (1) (February 2002), 1;

Wilcox, S.B., 'Trust, but verify', *Appliance Manufacturer* 46 (1) (January 1998), 8, 87; Rust, L., 'How to reach children in stores: marketing tactics grounded in observational research', *Journal of Advertising Research* 33 (November–December 1993), 67–72.

43 Travers, M., *Qualitative Research through Case Studies* (London: Sage, 2001), 4.

44 McNeil, R., 'The mystery squad's tougher challenge', *ResearchPlus* (April 1994), 13.

45 Rydholm, J., 'Extending excellence' (January 1998), **www.quirks.com**, Article 0297.

46 Scott, C., Klein, D.M. and Bryant, J., 'Consumer response to humour in advertising: a series of field studies using behavioural observation', *Journal of Consumer Research* 16 (March 1990), 498–501; Kerlinger, F.N., *Foundations of Behavioural Research*, 3rd edn (New York: Holt, Rinehart & Winston, 1986), 538.

47 Kurcina, B., 'Use videos to obtain crucial POP info', *Marketing News* 34 (24) (20 November 2000), 16; Seaton, A.V., 'Unobtrusive observational measures as a qualitative extension of visitor surveys at festivals and events: mass observation revisited', *Journal of Travel Research* 35 (4) (Spring 1997), 25–30; Kerlinger, F.N., *Foundations of Behavioural Research* 3rd edn (New York: Holt, Rinehart & Winston, 1986), 25–30.

48 Ephron, E., 'Nielsen's secret passive meter', *Mediaweek* 10 (36) (18 September 2000); Gold, L.N., 'Technology in television research: the meter', *Marketing Research: A Magazine of Management and Applications* 6 (1) (Winter 1994), 57–58.

49 Pieters, R., Rosbergen, E. and Wedel, M., 'Visual attention to repeated print advertising: a test of Scanpath theory', *Journal of Marketing Research* 36 (4) (November 1999), 424–438; Russo, J.E. and Leclerc, F., 'An eye-fixation analysis of choice processes for consumer non-durables', *Journal of Consumer Research* 21 (September 1994), 274–290.

50 For examples of an application of GSR, see Anthes, G.H., 'Smile, you're on Candid Computer', *Computerworld* 35 (49) (3 December 2001), 50; LaBarbera, P.A. and Tucciarone, J.D., 'GSR reconsidered: a behaviour based approach to evaluating and improving the sales potency of advertising', *Journal of Advertising Research* 35 (5) (September/October 1995), 33–53; Abeele, P.V. and Maclachlan, D.L., 'Process tracing of emotional responses to TV ads: revisiting the warmth monitor', *Journal of Consumer Research* 20 (March 1994), 586–600

51 Croal, N'G., 'Moviefone learns to listen,' *Newsweek* 135 (19) (8 May 2000), 84; Gregory, S., Webster, S. and Huang. G., 'Voice pitch and amplitude convergence as a metric of quality in dyadic interviews', *Language and Communication* 13 (3) (July 1993), 195–217; Buckman, G.A., 'Uses of voice-pitch analysis', *Journal of Advertising Research* 20 (April 1980), 69–73.

52 Haaijer, R., 'Response latencies in the analysis of conjoint choice experiments', *Journal of Marketing Research* (August 2000), 376–382; N. Vasilopoulos, 'The influence of job familiarity and impression management on self-report measure scale scores and response latencies', *Journal of Applied Psychology* 85 (1) (February 2000), 50; Bassili, J.N. and Scott, B.S., 'Response latency as a signal to question problems in survey research', *Public Opinion Quarterly* 60 (3) (Fall 1996), 390–399; Aaker, D.A., Bagozzi, R.P., Carman, J.M. and MacLachlan, J.M., 'On using response latency to measure preference', *Journal of Marketing Research* 17 (May 1980), 237–244.

53 Havermans, J., 'Dissecting emotions', *Research World* (June 2005), 24–26.

54 Verton, D., 'SafeWeb users vulnerable,' *Computerworld* 36 (8) (18 February 2002), 6; Bayan, R., 'Privacy means knowing your cookies,' *Link-Up* 18 (1) (January/February 2001), 22–23.

55 Berstell, G. and Nitterhouse, D., 'Looking outside the box', *Marketing Research: A Magazine of Management and Applications* 9 (2) (Summer 1997), 4–13.

56 Heeg, R., 'Growing business, evolving industry', *Research World* (October 2004), 8.

57 Denny, M., 'How the omnibus hit the fast track – and now, hold very tight', *ResearchPlus* (February 1996), 4.

58 Worcester, R.M. and Downham, J. (eds), 'ICC/ESOMAR International Code of Marketing and Social Research Practice', *Consumer Market Research Handbook* (Amsterdam: North-Holland, 1986), 813–826.

59 Stafford, M.R. and Stafford, T.E., 'Participant observation and the pursuit of truth: methodological and ethical considerations', *Journal of the Market Research Society* 35 (January 1993), 63–76.

60 Social Research Association and Market Research Society Joint Seminar, 11 September 1997.

61 Chan, H., Lee, R., Dillon, T. and Chang, E., *Electronic Commerce: Fundamentals and Applications* (New York: Wiley, 2001).

62 Taylor, H., 'Does Internet research work?', *International Journal of Market Research* 42 (1) (2000), 51–63.

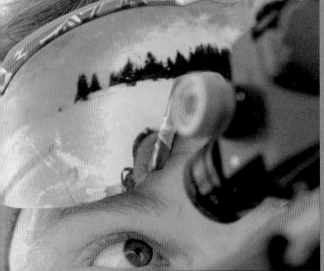

Source: © Getty Images

11

Causal research design: experimentation

> *Causality can never be proved; in other words, it can never be demonstrated decisively. Inferences of cause-and-effect relationships are the best that can be achieved.*

Objectives

After reading this chapter, you should be able to:

1 explain the concept of causality as defined in marketing research and distinguish between the ordinary meaning and the scientific meaning of causality;

2 define and differentiate two types of validity: internal validity and external validity;

3 discuss the various extraneous variables that can affect the validity of results obtained through experimentation and explain how the researcher can control extraneous variables;

4 describe and evaluate experimental designs and the differences among pre-experimental, true experimental, quasi-experimental and statistical designs;

5 compare and contrast the use of laboratory versus field experimentation and experimental versus non-experimental designs in marketing research;

6 describe test marketing and its various forms: standard test market, controlled test market and simulated test market;

7 understand the problems of internal and external validity of field experiments when conducted in international markets;

8 describe the ethical issues involved in conducting causal research and the role of debriefing in addressing some of these issues.

STAGE 1
Problem definition

STAGE 2
Research approach developed

STAGE 3
Research design developed

STAGE 4
Fieldwork or data collection

STAGE 5
Data preparation and analysis

STAGE 6
Report preparation and presentation

Overview

We introduced causal designs in Chapter 3, where we discussed their relationship to exploratory and descriptive designs and defined experimentation as the primary method employed in causal designs. This chapter explores the concept of causality further. We identify the necessary conditions for causality, examine the role of validity in experimentation, and consider the extraneous variables and procedures for controlling them. We present a classification of experimental designs and consider specific designs, along with the relative merits of laboratory and field experiments. An application in the area of test marketing is discussed in detail. The considerations involved in conducting experimental research when researching international markets are discussed. Several ethical issues, which arise in experimentation, are identified. We begin with an example that encapsulates the application and process of experimentation.

Example   ## POP buys[1]

The Eckerd Drug Company (**www.eckerd**) conducted an experiment to examine the effectiveness of in-store radio advertisements to induce point-of-purchase (POP) buys. Twenty statistically compatible stores were selected based on store size, geographic location, traffic flow count and age. Half of these were randomly selected as test stores, and the other half served as control stores. The test stores aired the radio advertisements, whereas the control stores' POP radio systems were removed. Tracking data in the form of unit sales and turnover were obtained for the following three periods: seven days before the experiment, during the course of the four-week experiment, and seven days after the experiment. The products monitored varied from inexpensive items to small kitchen appliances. Results indicated that sales of the advertised products in the test stores at least doubled. Based on this evidence, Eckerd concluded that in-store radio advertising was highly effective in inducing POP buys, and decided to continue it.

In 2001, Point of Purchasing International (**www.popai.com**) conducted a study to determine the growth effects of in-store advertising in the soft drink beverage category in grocery stores. Results revealed that sales increased at an estimated 11% when soft drinks were displayed with free-standing promotional items, and more than 20% when standing promotional items were tied to a themed display. Anheuser-Busch, Pepsi/Frito Lay, Pfizer, Procter & Gamble and Ralston-Purina sponsored this study, with the data gathered by Information Resources from 250 stores.

Concept of causality

Causality
Causality applies when the occurrence of X increases the probability of the occurrence of Y.

Experimentation is commonly used to infer causal relationships. The concept of **causality** requires some explanation. The scientific concept of causality is complex. 'Causality' means something very different to the average person on the street than to a scientist.[2] A statement such as 'X causes Y' will have the following meaning to an ordinary person and to a scientist:

Ordinary meaning	Scientific meaning
X is the only cause of Y	X is only one of a number of possible causes of Y
X must always lead to Y	The occurrence of X makes the occurrence of Y more probable (X is a probabilistic cause of Y)
It is possible to prove that X is a cause of Y	We can never prove that X is a cause of Y. At best, we can infer that X is a cause of Y

The scientific meaning of causality is more appropriate to marketing research than is the everyday meaning.[3] Marketing effects are caused by multiple variables and the relationship between cause and effect tends to be probabilistic. Moreover, we can never prove causality (i.e. demonstrate it conclusively); we can only infer a cause-and-effect relationship. In other words, it is possible that the true causal relation, if one exists, will not have been identified. We further clarify the concept of causality by discussing the conditions for causality.

Conditions for causality

Before making causal inferences, or assuming causality, three conditions must be satisfied: (1) concomitant variation, (2) time order of occurrence of variables, and (3) elimination of other possible causal factors. These conditions are necessary but not sufficient to demonstrate causality. No one of these three conditions, nor all three conditions combined, can demonstrate decisively that a causal relationship exists.[4] These conditions are explained in more detail in the following sections.

Concomitant variation

Concomitant variation
A condition for inferring causality that requires that the extent to which a cause, X, and an effect, Y, occur together or vary together is predicted by the hypothesis under consideration.

Concomitant variation is the extent to which a cause, X, and an effect, Y, occur together or vary together in the way predicted by the hypothesis under consideration. Evidence pertaining to concomitant variation can be obtained in a qualitative or quantitative manner.

For example, in the qualitative case, the management of a travel company may believe that the retention of customers is highly dependent on the quality of its service. This hypothesis could be examined by assessing concomitant variation. Here, the causal factor X is service level and the effect factor Y is retention level. A concomitant variation supporting the hypothesis would imply that travel companies with satisfactory levels of service would also have a satisfactory retention of customers. Likewise, travel companies with unsatisfactory service would exhibit unsatisfactory retention of customers. If, on the other hand, the opposite pattern was found, we would conclude that the hypothesis was untenable.

For a quantitative example, consider a random survey of 1,000 respondents questioned on the purchase of a skiing holiday. This survey yields the data in Table 11.1. The respondents have been classified into high- and low-education groups based on a median or even split. This table suggests that the purchase of a skiing holiday is influenced by education level. Respondents with high education are more likely to purchase a skiing holiday: 73% of the respondents with high education have a high purchase level, whereas only 64% of those with low education have a high purchase level. Furthermore, this is based on a relatively large sample of 1,000 respondents.

Table 11.1 Evidence of concomitant variation between purchase of a skiing holiday and education

		Purchase of a skiing holiday from a travel company, Y		
		High	Low	Total
Education, X	High	363 (73%)	137 (27%)	500 (100%)
	Low	322 (64%)	178 (36%)	500 (100%)

Based on this evidence, can we conclude that high education causes a high purchasing level of skiing holidays? Certainly not! All that can be said is that association makes the hypothesis more tenable; it does not prove it. What about the effect of other possible causal factors such as income? Skiing holidays can be expensive, so people with higher incomes may be more able to afford them. Table 11.2 shows the relationship between the purchase of a skiing holiday and education for different income segments. This is equivalent to holding the effect of income constant. Here again, the sample has been split at the median to produce high- and low-income groups of equal size. Table 11.2 shows that the difference in purchasing levels of a skiing holiday between high- and low-education respondents has been reduced considerably. This suggests that the association indicated by Table 11.1 may be spurious.

Table 11.2 Purchase of skiing holiday by income and education

		Low-income purchase		
		High	Low	Total
Education	High	122 (61%)	78 (39%)	200 (100%)
	Low	171 (57%)	129 (43%)	300 (100%)
		High-income purchase		
		High	Low	Total
Education	High	241 (80%)	59 (20%)	300 (100%)
	Low	151 (76%)	49 (24%)	200 (100%)

We could give similar examples to show why the absence of initial evidence of concomitant variation does not imply that there is no causation. It is possible that considering a third variable will crystallise an association that was originally obscure. The time order of the occurrence of variables provides additional insights into causality.

Time order of occurrence of variables

The time order of occurrence condition states that the causing event must occur either before or simultaneously with the effect; it cannot occur afterwards. By definition, an effect cannot be produced by an event that occurs after the effect has taken place. It is possible, however, for each event in a relationship to be both a cause and an effect of the other event. In other words, a variable can be both a cause and an effect in the same causal relationship. To illustrate, customers who shop frequently in a particular supermarket are more likely to have a loyalty card for that supermarket. In addition, customers who have a loyalty card for a supermarket are likely to shop there frequently.

Consider travel companies and the challenge of retaining their customers. If the quality of their service offering is the cause of retention, then improvements in service must be made before, or at least simultaneously with, an increase in retention. These improvements might consist of training or hiring more staff in their branches. Then, in subsequent months, the retention of customers should increase. Alternatively, retention may increase simultaneously with the training or hiring of additional branch staff. On the other hand, suppose that a travel company experienced an appreciable increase in the level of retaining customers and then decided to use some of that money generated to retrain its branch staff, leading to an improvement in service. In this case, the improved service quality cannot be a cause of increased retention; rather, just the opposite hypothesis might be plausible.

Elimination of other possible causal factors

The absence of other possible causal factors means that the factor or variable being investigated should be the only possible causal explanation. Travel company service quality may be a cause of retention if we can be sure that changes in all other factors affecting retention – pricing, advertising, promotional offers, product characteristics, competition and so forth – were held constant or were otherwise controlled.

In an after-the-fact examination of a situation, we can never confidently rule out all other causal factors. In contrast, with experimental designs it is possible to control some of the other causal factors. It is also possible to balance the effects of some of the uncontrolled variables so that only random variations resulting from these uncontrolled variables will be measured. These aspects are discussed in more detail later in this chapter.

The difficulty of establishing a causal relationship is illustrated by the following example.

Example   ### Which comes first?[5]

There are studies that contend that consumers increasingly make buying decisions in the store while they are shopping. Some studies indicate that as much as 80% of buying decisions are made at point-of-purchase (POP). POP buying decisions have increased concurrently with increased advertising efforts in the stores. These include radio advertisements, advertisements on shopping trolleys and grocery bags, ceiling signs and shelf displays. It is estimated that brand and retail owners spent roughly €1 billion in 2005 trying to influence the consumer at the POP. It is difficult to ascertain from these data whether the increased POP decision making is the result of increased advertising efforts in the store or whether the increase in store advertising results from attempts to capture changing consumer attitudes towards purchasing and to capture sales from the increase in POP decision making. It is also possible that both variables may be both causes and effects in this relationship.

If, as this example indicates, it is difficult to establish cause-and-effect relationships, what is the role of evidence obtained in experimentation?

Evidence of concomitant variation, time order of occurrence of variables, and elimination of other possible causal factors, even if combined, still do not demonstrate conclusively that a causal relationship exists. If all the evidence is strong and consistent, however, it may be reasonable to conclude that there is a causal relationship. Accumulated evidence from several investigations increases our confidence that a causal relationship exists. Confidence is further enhanced if the evidence is interpreted in light of intimate conceptual knowledge of the problem situation. Controlled experiments can provide strong evidence on all three conditions.

Definitions and concepts

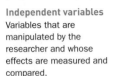

Independent variables
Variables that are manipulated by the researcher and whose effects are measured and compared.

Test units
Individuals, organisations or other entities whose responses to independent variables or treatments are being studied.

Dependent variables
Variables that measure the effect of the independent variables on the test units.

Extraneous variables
Variables, other than dependent and independent variables, which may influence the results of the experiment.

Experiment
The process of manipulating one or more independent variables and measuring their effect on one or more dependent variables, while controlling for the extraneous variables.

Experimental design
The set of experimental procedures specifying (1) the test units and sampling procedures, (2) the independent variables, (3) the dependent variables, and (4) how to control the extraneous variables.

In this section, we define some basic concepts and illustrate them using examples:

- **Independent variables.** Independent variables are variables or alternatives that are manipulated (i.e. the levels of these variables are changed by the researcher) and whose effects are measured and compared. These variables, also known as treatments, may include price levels, package designs and advertising themes. In the Eckerd Drug Company example at the beginning of this chapter, the independent variable was 'in-store radio advertising' (present versus absent).

- **Test units.** Test units are individuals, organisations or other entities whose response to the independent variables or treatments is being examined. Test units may include consumers, stores or geographical areas. The test units were stores in the Eckerd example.

- **Dependent variables.** Dependent variables are the variables that measure the effect of the independent variables on the test units. These variables may include sales, profits and market shares. In the Eckerd example, the dependent variable was the sales level of advertised POP products.

- **Extraneous variables.** Extraneous variables are all variables other than the independent variables that affect the response of the test units. These variables can confound the dependent variable measures in a way that weakens or invalidates the results of the experiment. In the Eckerd example, store size, geographic location, traffic flow count and age of the stores were extraneous variables that had to be controlled.

- **Experiment.** An experiment is formed when the researcher manipulates one or more independent variables and measures their effect on one or more dependent variables, while controlling for the effect of extraneous variables.[6] The Eckerd research project qualifies as an experiment based on this definition.

- **Experimental design.** An experimental design is a set of procedures specifying: (1) the test units and how these units are to be divided into homogeneous subsamples, (2) what independent variables or treatments are to be manipulated, (3) what dependent variables are to be measured, and (4) how the extraneous variables are to be controlled.[7]

As a further illustration of these definitions, consider the following example.

Example — Taking coupons at face value[8]

An experiment was conducted to test the effects of the face value of sales promotion coupons (i.e. the amount saved when a consumer next buys the product) on the likelihood of consumers redeeming those coupons, controlling for the frequency of brand usage. Personal interviews were conducted with 280 shoppers who were entering or leaving a supermarket. Subjects were randomly assigned to two treatment groups. One group was offered a small discount and the other higher value coupons for four products: Tide detergent, Kellogg's Cornflakes, Aim toothpaste and Joy liquid detergent. During the interviews, the respondents answered questions about which brands they used and how likely they were to cash the coupons of the given face value the next time they shopped. An interesting finding was that higher face-value coupons produced a greater likelihood of redemption among infrequent or non-buyers of the promoted brand but had little effect on regular buyers.

In the preceding experiment, the independent variable that was manipulated was the value of the coupon. The dependent variable was the likelihood of cashing the coupon. The extraneous variable that was controlled was brand usage. The test units were individual shoppers. The experimental design required the random assignment of test units (shoppers) to treatment groups (low- or high-value coupon).

Definition of symbols

To facilitate our discussion of extraneous variables and specific experimental designs, we define a set of symbols now commonly used in marketing research:[9]

X = the exposure of a group to an independent variable, treatment or event, the effects of which are to be determined

O = the process of observation or measurement of the dependent variable on the test units or group of units

R = the random assignment of test units or groups to separate treatments

In addition, the following conventions are adopted:

- Movement from left to right indicates movement through time.
- Horizontal alignment of symbols implies that all those symbols refer to a specific treatment group.
- Vertical alignment of symbols implies that those symbols refer to activities or events that occur simultaneously.

For example, the symbolic arrangement

$$X \ O_1 \ O_2$$

means that a given group of test units was exposed to the treatment variable (X) and the response was measured at two different points in time O_1 and O_2.

Likewise, the symbolic arrangement

$$R \ X_1 \ O_1$$
$$R \ X_2 \ O_2$$

means that two groups of test units were randomly assigned to two different treatment groups at the same time, and the dependent variable was measured in the two groups simultaneously.

Validity in experimentation

When conducting an experiment, a researcher has two goals: (1) to draw valid conclusions about the effects of independent variables on the study group, and (2) to make valid generalisations to a larger population of interest. The first goal concerns internal validity, the second external validity. [10]

Internal validity

Internal validity
A measure of accuracy of an experiment. It measures whether the manipulation of the independent variables, or treatments, actually caused the effects on the dependent variable(s).

Internal validity refers to whether the manipulation of the independent variables or treatments actually caused the observed effects on the dependent variables. Thus, internal validity refers to whether the observed effects on the test units could have been caused by variables other than the treatment. If the observed effects are influenced or confounded by extraneous variables, it is difficult to draw valid inferences about the causal relationship between the independent and dependent variables. Internal validity is the basic minimum that must be present in an experiment before any conclusion about treatment effects can be made. Without internal validity, the experimental results are confounded. Control of extraneous variables is a necessary condition for establishing internal validity.

External validity

External validity
A determination of whether the cause-and-effect relationships found in the experiment can be generalised.

External validity refers to whether the cause-and-effect relationships found in the experiment can be generalised. In other words, can the results be generalised beyond the experimental situation, and if so, to what populations, settings, times, independent variables and dependent variables can the results be projected?[11] Threats to external validity arise when the specific set of experimental conditions does not realistically take into account the interactions of other relevant variables in the real world.

It is desirable to have an experimental design that has both internal and external validity, but in applied marketing research we often have to trade one type of validity for another.[12] To control for extraneous variables, a researcher may conduct an experiment in an artificial environment. This enhances internal validity, but it may limit the generalisability of the results, thereby reducing external validity. For example, fast-food chains test customers' preferences for new formulations of menu items in test kitchens. Can the effects measured in this environment be generalised to fast-food outlets that may operate in a variety of other environments? (Further discussion on the influence of artificiality on external validity may be found in the section of this chapter on laboratory versus field experimentation.) Regardless of the deterrents to external validity, if an experiment lacks internal validity, it may not be meaningful to generalise the results. Factors that threaten internal validity may also threaten external validity, the most serious of these being extraneous variables.

Extraneous variables

The need to control extraneous variables to establish internal and external validity has already been discussed. In this section, we classify extraneous variables in the following categories: history, maturation, testing effects, instrumentation, statistical regression, selection bias and mortality.

History

History
Specific events that are external to the experiment but that occur at the same time as the experiment.

Contrary to what the name implies, **history** (H) does not refer to the occurrence of events before the experiment. Rather, history refers to specific events that are external to the experiment but that occur at the same time as the experiment. These events may affect the dependent variable. Consider the following experiment:

$$O_1 \quad X_1 \quad O_2$$

where O_1 and O_2 are measures of ticket sales to a weekend break built around visiting the Christmas market in Nuremberg, Germany, and X_1 represents a new promotional campaign. The difference $(O_2 - O_1)$ is the treatment effect. Suppose that the experiment revealed that there was no difference between O_2 and O_1. Can we then conclude that the promotional campaign was ineffective? Certainly not! The promotional campaign X_1 is not the only possible explanation of the difference between O_2 and O_1. The campaign might well have been effective. What if general economic conditions declined during the experiment and the local area was particularly hard hit by redundancies through several employers closing down their operations (history)? Conversely, even if there was some difference between O_2 and O_1, it may be incorrect to conclude that the campaign was effective if history was not controlled, because the experimental effects might have been confounded by history. The longer the time interval between observations, the greater the possibility that history will confound an experiment of this type.[13]

Maturation

Maturation (MA) is similar to history except that it refers to changes in the test units themselves. These changes are not caused by the impact of independent variables or treatments but occur with the passage of time. In an experiment involving people, maturation takes place as people become older, more experienced, tired, bored or uninterested. Tracking and market studies that span several months are vulnerable to maturation, since it is difficult to know how respondents are changing over time.

Maturation effects also extend to test units other than people. For example, consider the case in which the test units are travel companies. Travel companies change over time in terms of personnel, physical layout, decoration, and the range of holidays and services they have to offer.

Testing effects

Testing effects are caused by the process of experimentation. Typically, these are the effects on the experiment of taking a measure on the dependent variable before and after the presentation of the treatment. There are two kinds of testing effects: (1) main testing effect (MT), and (2) interactive testing effect (IT).

The **main testing effect** (MT) occurs when a prior observation affects a later observation. Consider an experiment to measure the effect of advertising on attitudes towards taking a holiday in Egypt. The respondents are given a pre-treatment questionnaire measuring background information and attitude towards holidaying in Egypt. They are then exposed to the test commercial embedded in a TV programme. After viewing the commercial, the respondents again answer a questionnaire measuring, among other things, attitude towards holidaying in Egypt.

Suppose that there is no difference between the pre- and post-treatment attitudes. Can we conclude that the commercial was ineffective? An alternative explanation might be that the respondents tried to maintain consistency between their pre- and post-treatment attitudes. As a result of the main testing effect, post-treatment attitudes were influenced more by pre-treatment attitudes than by the treatment itself. The main testing effect may also be reactive, causing the respondents to change their attitudes simply because these attitudes have been measured. The main testing effect compromises the internal validity of the experiment.

In the interactive testing effect (IT), a prior measurement affects the test unit's response to the independent variable. Continuing with our advertising experiment, when people are asked to indicate their attitudes towards taking a holiday in Egypt, they become more aware of Egyptian holidays: they are sensitised to Egyptian holidays and become more likely to pay attention to the test commercial than are people who were not included in the experiment. The measured effects are then not generalisable to the population; therefore, the interactive testing effects influence the experiment's external validity.

Instrumentation

Instrumentation (I) refers to changes in the measuring instrument, in the observers or in the scores themselves. Sometimes measuring instruments are modified during the course of an experiment. In the Egyptian holiday experiment, using a newly designed questionnaire to measure the post-treatment attitudes could lead to variations in the responses obtained. Consider an experiment in which sales at a shoe shop are measured before and after exposure to a promotional offer of a discounted music festival ticket (treatment). If there is a non-experimental price change between O_1 and O_2, this could result in a change in instrumentation, because European sales may be measured using different unit prices. In this case, the treatment effect ($O_2 - O_1$) could be attributed to a change in instrumentation.

As shown above, instrumentation effects are likely when interviewers make pre- and post-treatment measurements. The effectiveness of interviewers can be different at different times.

Statistical regression

Statistical regression
An extraneous variable that occurs when test units with extreme scores move closer to the average score during the course of the experiment.

Statistical regression (SR) effects occur when test units with extreme scores move closer to the average score during the course of the experiment. In the Egyptian holiday advertising experiment, suppose that in a pretest measurement some respondents had either very favourable or very unfavourable attitudes towards the country of Egypt. On post-treatment measurement, their attitudes might have moved towards the average. Consumer attitudes change continuously for a wide variety of reasons. Consumers with extreme attitudes have more room for change, so variation may be more likely. This has a confounding effect on the experimental results, because the observed effect (change in attitude) may be attributable to statistical regression rather than to the treatment (test commercial).

Selection bias

Selection bias
An extraneous variable attributable to the improper assignment of test units to treatment conditions.

Selection bias (SB) refers to the improper assignment of test units to treatment conditions. This bias occurs when selection or assignment of test units results in treatment groups that differ on the dependent variable before the exposure to the treatment condition. If test units self-select their own groups or are assigned to groups on the basis of the researchers' judgement, selection bias is possible. For example, consider an experiment in which two different merchandising displays (old *static display* and new *audio-visual display*) are assigned to different branches of a travel company. The branches in the two groups may not be equivalent to begin with. They may vary with respect to a key characteristic, such as branch size. Branch size is likely to affect the sales of holidays, regardless of which merchandising display was assigned to a branch.

Mortality

Mortality
An extraneous variable attributable to the loss of test units while the experiment is in progress.

Mortality (MO) refers to the loss of test units while the experiment is in progress. This happens for many reasons, such as test units refusing to continue in the experiment. Mortality confounds results because it is difficult to determine whether the lost test units would respond in the same manner to the treatments as those that remain. Consider again the merchandising display experiment. Suppose that during the course of the experiment, three branches in the new *audio-visual display* drop out because they feel the noise is not conducive to negotiations with certain types of client (e.g. the type of customer that would spend €10,000 on a luxury cruise). The researcher could not determine whether the average sales of holidays for the new display would have been higher or lower if these three branches had continued in the experiment.

The various categories of extraneous variables are not mutually exclusive; they can occur jointly and also interact with each other. To illustrate, testing–maturation–mortality refers to a situation in which, because of pre-treatment measurement, the respondents' beliefs and attitudes change over time and there is a differential loss of respondents from the various treatment groups.

Controlling extraneous variables

Confounding variables
Variables used to illustrate that extraneous variables can confound the results by influencing the dependent variable; synonymous with extraneous variables.

Extraneous variables represent alternative explanations of experimental results. They pose a serious threat to the internal and external validity of an experiment. Unless they are controlled, they affect the dependent variable and thus confound the results. For this reason, they are also called **confounding variables**. There are four ways of controlling extraneous variables: randomisation, matching, statistical control and design control.

Source: © Science Photo Library

Randomisation

Randomisation refers to the random assignment of test units to experimental groups by using random numbers. Treatment conditions are also randomly assigned to experimental groups. For example, respondents are randomly assigned to one of three experimental groups. One of the three versions of a test commercial, selected at random, is administered to each group. As a result of random assignment, extraneous factors can be represented equally in each treatment condition. Randomisation is the preferred procedure for ensuring the prior equality of experimental groups,[14] but it may not be effective when the sample size is small because it merely produces groups that are equal on average. It is possible, though, to check whether randomisation has been effective by measuring the possible extraneous variables and comparing them across the experimental groups.

Matching

Matching involves comparing test units on a set of key background variables before assigning them to the treatment conditions. In the display experiment, travel company branches could be matched on the basis of turnover, size, proportion of retail to corporate clients, or location. Then one branch from each matched pair would be assigned to each experimental group.

Matching has two drawbacks. First, test units can be matched on only a few characteristics, so the test units may be similar on the variables selected but unequal on others. Second, if the matched characteristics are irrelevant to the dependent variable, then the matching effort has been futile.[15]

Statistical control

Statistical control involves measuring the extraneous variables and adjusting for their effects through statistical analysis. This was illustrated in Table 11.2, which examined the relationship (association) between purchase of skiing holidays and education, controlling for the effect of income. More advanced statistical procedures, such as analysis of covariance (ANCOVA), are also available. In ANCOVA, the effects of the extraneous variable on the dependent variable are removed by an adjustment of the dependent variable's mean value within each treatment condition. ANCOVA is discussed in more detail in Chapter 19.

Design control

Design control involves the use of experiments designed to control specific extraneous variables. The types of controls possible by suitably designing the experiment are illustrated with the following example.

Randomisation
A method of controlling extraneous variables that involves randomly assigning test units to experimental groups by using random numbers. Treatment conditions are also randomly assigned to experimental groups.

Matching
A method of controlling extraneous variables that involves matching test units on a set of key background variables before assigning them to the treatment conditions.

Statistical control
A method of controlling extraneous variables by measuring the extraneous variables and adjusting for their effects through statistical methods.

Design control
A method of controlling extraneous variables that involves using specific experimental designs.

| *Example* | ### Experimenting with new products[16] |

Controlled-distribution electronic test markets are used increasingly to conduct experimental research on new products. This method makes it possible to create a design that controls for several extraneous factors. The control can allow for the manipulation of variables that can affect the success of new products. In manipulating variables, it is possible to ensure that a new product:

- obtains the right level of supermarket acceptance and all commodity volume distribution;
- is positioned in the correct aisle in each supermarket;
- receives the right number of facings on the shelf;
- has the correct everyday price;
- never has out-of-stock problems;
- obtains the planned level of trade promotion, display and price features on the desired time schedule.

By being able to control these variables, a high degree of internal validity can be obtained.

This example shows that controlled-distribution electronic test markets can be effective in controlling for specific extraneous variables. Extraneous variables can also be controlled by adopting specific experimental designs, as described in the next section.

A classification of experimental designs

Pre-experimental designs
Designs that do not control for extraneous factors by randomisation.

True experimental designs
Experimental designs distinguished by the fact that the researcher can randomly assign test units to experimental groups and also randomly assign treatments to experimental groups.

Quasi-experimental designs
Designs that apply part of the procedures of true experimentation yet lack full experimental control.

Statistical designs
Designs that allow for the statistical control and analysis of external variables.

Experimental designs may be classified as **pre-experimental**, **true experimental**, **quasi-experimental** and **statistical designs**: see Figure 11.1.

Pre-experimental designs do not employ randomisation procedures to control for extraneous factors. Examples of these designs include the one-shot case study, the one-group pretest–post test design and the static group. In true experimental designs, the researcher can randomly assign test units to experimental groups and treatments to experimental groups. Included in this category are the pretest–posttest control group design, the posttest-only control group design and the Solomon four-group design. Quasi-experimental designs result when the researcher is unable to achieve full manipulation of scheduling or allocation of treatments to test units but can still apply part of the apparatus of the experimentation. Two such designs are time series and multiple time series designs. A statistical design is a series of basic experiments that allows for statistical control and analysis of external variables. Statistical designs are classified based on their characteristics and use. The important statistical designs include randomised block design, Latin square design and factorial designs.[17] These designs are illustrated in the

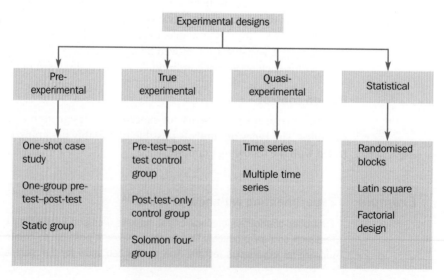

Figure 11.1
A classification of experimental designs

context of a possible extension of Sports Marketing Surveys Racetrack study. It measures the effectiveness of a test advertisement for the Renault Laguna Sport Tourer. The test advertisement could be evaluated in preparation to run in TV coverage of Formula one races (**www.renaultf1.com**). [17a]

We begin our discussion with the first type of experimental design: pre-experimental.

Pre-experimental designs

These designs are characterised by an absence of randomisation. Three specific designs are described: the one-shot case study, the one-group pretest–posttest design and the static group design.

One-shot case study

One-shot case study
A pre-experimental design in which a single group of test units is exposed to a treatment X, and then a single measurement of the dependent variable is taken.

Also known as the after-only design, the one-shot case study may be symbolically represented as

$$X_1 \; O_1$$

A single group of test units is exposed to a treatment X, and then a single measurement on the dependent variable is taken (O_1). There is no random assignment of test units. Note that the symbol R is not used, because the test units are self-selected or selected arbitrarily by the researcher.

The danger of drawing valid conclusions from experiments of this type can be easily seen. They do not provide a basis of comparing the level of O_1 with what would happen if X were absent. In addition, the level of O_1 might be affected by many extraneous variables, including history, maturation, selection and mortality. Lack of control for these extraneous variables undermines the internal validity. For these reasons, the one-shot case study is more appropriate for exploratory than for conclusive research.

Focus on Sports Marketing Surveys

One-shot case study

A one-shot case study to measure the effectiveness of test advertisements for a Renault Lauguna would be implemented as follows. Telephone interviews are conducted with a national sample of respondents who report watching a particular TV programme the previous night, e.g. The Shanghai Grand Prix. The programme selected is one that contains the selected test advertisement, e.g. a Renault Laguna advertisement (X). The dependent variables (O_s) are unaided and aided recall. First, unaided recall is measured by asking the respondents whether they recall seeing a car advertisement, e.g. 'do you recall seeing a car advertisement last night?' If they recall the test advertisement, details about the advertisement content and execution are solicited. Respondents who do not recall the test advertisement are asked about it specifically, e.g. 'do you recall seeing a Renault Laguna advertisement last night?' (aided recall). The results of aided and unaided recall are compared to norm scores to develop an index for interpreting the scores.

One-group pretest–posttest design

One-group pretest–posttest design
A pre-experimental design in which a group of test units is measured twice.

The **one-group pretest–posttest design** may be symbolised as

$$O_1 \; X \; O_2$$

In this design, a group of test units is measured twice. There is no control group. First a pre-treatment measure is taken (O_1), then the group is exposed to the treatment (X).

Finally, a posttreatment measure is taken (O_2). The treatment effect is computed as ($O_2 - O_1$) but the validity of this conclusion is questionable since extraneous variables are largely uncontrolled. History, maturation, testing (both main and interactive testing effects), instrumentation, selection, mortality and regression could possibly be present. The following example shows how this design is used.

Sports Marketing Surveys

One-group pretest-posttest design

A one-group pretest–posttest design to measure the effectiveness of test commercials for Renault cars would be implemented as follows. Respondents are recruited to central cinema locations in different test cities. At the central location, respondents are first administered a personal interview to measure, among other things, attitudes towards the Renault Laguna (O_1). Then they watch a TV programme containing the test commercial (X). After viewing the TV programme, the respondents are again administered a personal interview to measure attitudes towards the Renault Laguna (O_2). The effectiveness of the test commercial is measured as ($O_2 - O_1$).

Static group design

Static group
A pre-experimental design in which there are two groups: the experimental group (EG), which is exposed to the treatment, and the control group (CG). Measurements on both groups are made only after the treatment, and test units are not assigned at random.

The **static group** is a two-group experimental design. One group, called the experimental group (EG), is exposed to the treatment, and the other, called the control group (CG), is not. Measurements on both groups are made only after the treatment, and test units are not assigned at random. This design may be symbolically described as

$$\text{EG: } X\ O_1$$
$$\text{CG: } \quad O_2$$

The treatment effect would be measured as ($O_1 - O_2$). Notice that this difference could also be attributed to at least two extraneous variables (selection and mortality). Because test units are not randomly assigned, the two groups (EG and CG) may differ before the treatment, and selection bias may be present. There may also be mortality effects, as more test units may withdraw from the experimental group than from the control group. This would be particularly likely to happen if the treatment were unpleasant.

In practice, a control group is sometimes defined as the group that receives the current level of marketing activity, rather than a group that receives no treatment at all. The control group is defined in this way because it is difficult to reduce current marketing activities such as advertising and personal selling to zero.

Sports Marketing Surveys

Static group

A static group comparison to measure the effectiveness of a test advertisement for the Renault Laguna would be conducted as follows. Two groups of respondents would be recruited on the basis of convenience. Only the experimental group would be exposed to the TV programme containing the advertisement. Then, attitudes towards the Renault Laguna of both the experimental and control group respondents would be measured. The effectiveness of the test advertisement would be measured as ($O_1 - O_2$).

True experimental designs

The distinguishing feature of true experimental designs, compared with pre-experimental designs, is randomisation. In true experimental designs, the researcher randomly assigns test units to experimental groups and treatments to experimental groups. True experimental designs include the pretest–posttest control group design, the posttest-only control group design and the Solomon four-group design.

Pretest–posttest control group design

Pretest–posttest control group design
An experimental design in which the experimental group is exposed to the treatment but the control group is not. Pretest and posttest measures are taken on both groups.

In the **pretest–posttest control group design**, test units are randomly assigned to either the experimental or the control group and a pre-treatment measure is taken on each group. Then the treatment is applied to the experimental group, and a post-treatment measure is taken from both groups. This design is symbolised as

$$\text{EG: } R\ O_1\ X\ O_2$$
$$\text{CG: } R\ O_3\quad O_4$$

The treatment effect (TE) is measured as

$$(O_2 - O_1) - (O_4 - O_3)$$

This design controls for most extraneous variables. Selection bias is eliminated by randomisation. The other extraneous effects are controlled as follows:

$$O_2 - O_1 = TE + H + MA + MT + IT + I + SR + MO$$
$$O_4 - O_3 = H + MA + MT + I + SR + MO$$
$$= EV \text{ (extraneous variables)}$$

where the symbols for the extraneous variables are as defined previously. The experimental result is obtained by

$$(O_2 - O_1) - (O_4 - O_3) = TE + IT$$

The interactive testing effect is not controlled, because of the effect of the pretest measurement on the reaction of units in the experimental group to the treatment.

Focus on **Sports Marketing Surveys**

Pretest-posttest control group

In the context of measuring the effectiveness of a test advertisement for the Renault Laguna, a pretest–posttest control group design would be implemented as follows. A sample of respondents would be selected at random. Half of these would be randomly assigned to the experimental group, and the other half would form the control group. Respondents in both groups would be administered a questionnaire to obtain a pretest measurement on attitudes towards the Renault Laguna. Only the respondents in the experimental group would be exposed to the TV programme featuring the test advertisement. Then, a questionnaire would be administered to respondents in both groups to obtain posttest measures on attitudes towards the Renault Laguna.

As this example shows, the pretest–posttest control group design involves two groups and two measurements on each group. A simpler design is the posttest-only control group design.

Posttest-only control group design

Posttest-only control group design
Experimental design in which the experimental group is exposed to the treatment but the control group is not and no pretest measure is taken.

The **posttest-only control group design** does not involve any pre-measurement. It may be symbolised as

$$\text{EG: } \mathbf{R}\ \mathbf{X}\ \mathbf{O_1}$$
$$\text{CG: } \mathbf{R}\qquad \mathbf{O_2}$$

The treatment effect is obtained by

$$\mathbf{O_2 - O_1 = TE}$$

This design is fairly simple to implement. Because there is no pre-measurement, the testing effects are eliminated, but this design is sensitive to selection bias and mortality. It is assumed that the two groups are similar in terms of pre-treatment measures on the dependent variable because of the random assignment of test units to groups. Because there is no pre-treatment measurement, this assumption cannot be checked. This design is also sensitive to mortality. It is difficult to determine whether those in the experimental group who discontinue the experiment are similar to their counterparts in the control group. Yet another limitation is that this design does not allow the researcher to examine changes in individual test units.

It is possible to control for selection bias and mortality through carefully designed experimental procedures. Examination of individual cases is often not of interest. On the other hand, this design possesses significant advantages in terms of time, cost and sample size requirements. It involves only two groups and only one measurement per group. Because of its simplicity, the posttest-only control group design is probably the most popular design in marketing research. Note that, except for pre-measurement, the implementation of this design is very similar to that of the pretest–posttest control group design.

 Focus on | **Sports Marketing Surveys**

Posttest-only control group

In the context of measuring the effectiveness of a test advertisement for the Renault Laguna, a posttest-only control group design would be implemented as follows. A sample of respondents would be selected at random. The sample would be randomly split, with half the subjects forming the experimental group and the other half constituting the control group. Only the respondents in the experimental group would be exposed to the TV programme containing the test Renault Laguna advertisement. Then, a questionnaire would be administered to both groups to obtain posttest measures on attitudes towards the Renault Laguna. The differences in the attitudes of the experimental group and the control group would be used as a measure of the effectiveness of the test commercial.

Solomon four-group design
An experimental design that explicitly controls for interactive testing effects, in addition to controlling for all the other extraneous variables.

In this example, the researcher is not concerned with examining the changes in the attitudes of individual respondents. When this information is desired, the **Solomon four-group design** should be considered. The Solomon four-group design overcomes the limitations of the pretest–posttest control group and posttest-only control group designs in that it explicitly controls for the interactive testing effect, in addition to controlling for all the other extraneous variables. However, this design has practical limitations: it is expensive and time consuming to implement. Hence, it is not considered further.[18]

In all true experimental designs, the researcher exercises a high degree of control. In particular, the researcher can control when the measurements are taken, on whom they are taken and the scheduling of the treatments. Moreover, the researcher can randomly select the test units and randomly expose test units to the treatments. In some instances, the researcher cannot exercise this kind of control; then quasi-experimental designs should be considered.

Quasi-experimental designs

A quasi-experimental design results under the following conditions. First, the researcher can control when measurements are taken and on whom they are taken. Second, the researcher lacks control over the scheduling of the treatments and also is unable to expose test units to the treatments randomly.[19] Quasi-experimental designs are useful because they can be used in cases when true experimentation cannot be used, and because they are quicker and less expensive. Because full experimental control is lacking, the researcher must consider the specific variables that are not controlled. Popular forms of quasi-experimental designs are time series and multiple time series designs.

Time series design

Time series design
A quasi-experimental design that involves periodic measurements of the dependent variable for a group of test units. Then the treatment is administered by the researcher or occurs naturally. After the treatment, periodic measurements are continued to determine the treatment effect.

The **time series design** involves a series of periodic measurements on the dependent variable for a group of test units. The treatment is then administered by the researcher or occurs naturally. After the treatment, periodic measurements are continued to determine the treatment effect. A time series experiment may be symbolised as

$$O_1 \, O_2 \, O_3 \, O_4 \, O_5 \, O_6 \, O_7 \, O_8 \, O_9 \, O_{10}$$

This is a quasi-experiment, because there is no randomisation of test units to treatments, and the timing of treatment presentation, as well as which test units are exposed to the treatment, may not be within the researcher's control (hence no specific X symbolised above).

Taking a series of measurements before and after the treatment provides at least partial control for several extraneous variables. Maturation is at least partially controlled, because it would not affect O_5 and O_6 alone but would also influence other observations. By similar reasoning, the main testing effect and statistical regression are controlled as well. If the test units are selected randomly or by matching, selection bias can be reduced. Mortality may pose a problem, but it can be largely controlled by paying a premium or offering other incentives to respondents.

The major weakness of the time series design is the failure to control history. Another limitation is that the experiment may be affected by the interactive testing effect because multiple measurements are being made on the test units. Nevertheless, time series designs are useful, as illustrated by this case. The effectiveness of a test commercial (X) may be examined by broadcasting the commercial a predetermined number of times and examining the data from a pre-existing test panel. Although the marketer can control the scheduling of the test commercial, it is uncertain when or whether the panel members are exposed to it. The panel members' purchases before, during and after the campaign are examined to determine whether the test commercial has a short-term effect, a long-term effect or no effect.

Multiple time series design

Multiple time series design
A time series design that includes another group of test units to serve as a control group.

The **multiple time series design** is similar to the time series design except that another group of test units is added to serve as a control group. Symbolically, this design may be described as

$$\begin{array}{l} \text{EG:} \ O_1 \ \ O_2 \ \ O_3 \ \ O_4 \ \ O_5 \quad\quad X \quad\quad O_6 \ \ O_7 \ \ O_8 \ \ O_9 \ \ O_{10} \\ \text{CG:} \ O_{11} O_{12} O_{13} O_{14} O_{15} \quad\quad\quad\quad\quad O_{16} O_{17} O_{18} O_{19} O_{20} \end{array}$$

If the control group is carefully selected, this design can be an improvement over the simple time series experiment. The improvement lies in the ability to test the treatment effect twice: against the pre-treatment measurements in the experimental group and against the control group. To use the multiple time series design to assess the effectiveness of a commercial, the test panel example would be modified as follows. The test commercial would be shown in only a few of the test cities. Panel members in these cities would make up the experimental group. Panel members in cities where the commercial was not shown would constitute the control group.

Another application of multiple time series design is illustrated in the example opposite.

In concluding our discussion of pre-experimental, true experimental and quasi-experimental designs, we summarise in Table 11.3 the potential sources of invalidity that may affect each of these designs. In this table, a minus sign indicates a definite weakness, a plus sign indicates that the factor is controlled, a question mark denotes a possible source of concern, and a blank means that the factor is not relevant. It should be remembered that potential sources of invalidity are not the same as actual errors.

Table 11.3 Potential sources of invalidity of experimental designs

Source of invalidity								
	Internal variables							External variables
Design	History	Maturation	Testing	Instrumentation	Regression	Selection	Mortality	Interaction of testing and X
Pre-experimental designs								
One-shot case study **X O**	−	−				−	−	
One-group pretest–posttest design **O X O**	−	−	−	−	?			−
Static group comparison **X O** **O**	+	?	+	+	+	−	−	
True experimental designs								
Pretest–posttest control group **R O X O** **R O O**	+	+	+	+	+	+	+	−
Posttest-only control group design **R X O** **R O**	+	+	+	+	+	+	+	+
Quasi-experimental designs								
Time series **O O O X O O O**	−	+	+	?	+	+	+	−
Multiple time series **O O O X O O O** **O O O O O O**	+	+	+	+	+	+	+	

Note: A minus sign indicates a definite weakness, a plus sign indicates that the factor is controlled, a question mark denotes a possible source of concern, and a blank means that the factor is not relevant.

Splitting commercials shows their strength[20]

A multiple time series design was used to examine the build-up effect of increased advertising. The data were obtained from BASES' (**www.bases.com**) split-cable TV advertising field experiment. In the split-cable system, one group of households was assigned to the experimental panel and an equivalent group was assigned to the control panel. The two groups were matched on demographic variables. Data were collected for 76 weeks. Both panels received the same level of advertising for the first 52 weeks for the brand in question. For the next 24 weeks, the experimental panel was exposed to twice as much advertising as the control panel. The results indicated that the build-up effect of advertising was immediate with a duration of the order of the purchase cycle. Information of this type can be useful in selecting advertising timing patterns (allocating a set of advertising exposures over a specified period to obtain maximum impact).

An experimental study, conducted in 2000, showed a new approach to relating advertising exposures of TV media schedules to sales-related market performance. These measures included cumulative sales volume, number of purchases, penetration and repeat purchase patterns. The approach was derived from a match split-cable experimental design. Companies such as BASES can provide the data needed to implement such an approach. In the future, it is expected that companies like BASES will be at the forefront of using technological advances to measure consumer advertising exposure and purchase behaviour simultaneously.

Statistical designs

Statistical designs consist of a series of basic experiments that allow for statistical control and analysis of external variables. In other words, several basic experiments are conducted simultaneously. Thus, statistical designs are influenced by the same sources of invalidity that affect the basic designs being used. Statistical designs offer the following advantages:

1 The effects of more than one independent variable can be measured.
2 Specific extraneous variables can be statistically controlled.
3 Economical designs can be formulated when each test unit is measured more than once.

The most common statistical designs are the randomised block design, the Latin square design and the factorial design.

Randomised block design

Randomised block design
A statistical design in which the test units are blocked on the basis of an external variable to ensure that the various experimental and control groups are matched closely on that variable.

A **randomised block design** is useful when there is only one major external variable – such as sales, store size or income of the respondent – that might influence the dependent variable. The test units are blocked or grouped on the basis of the external variable. The researcher must be able to identify and measure the blocking variable. By blocking, the researcher ensures that the various experimental and control groups are matched closely on the external variable.

As the following example illustrates, in most marketing research situations, external variables such as sales, store size, store type, location, income, occupation and social class of the respondent can influence the dependent variable. Therefore, generally speaking, randomised block designs are more useful than completely random designs. Their main limitation is that the researcher can control for only one external variable. When more than one variable must be controlled, the researcher must use Latin square or factorial designs.

Sports Marketing Surveys

Randomised block design

In the context of measuring the effectiveness of a test advertisement for the Renault Laguna, we extend the example to measure the impact of humour on the effectiveness of advertising.[21] Three test advertisements, A, B and C, have respectively no humour, some humour and high levels of humour. Which of these would be the most effective? Management feel that the respondents' evaluation of the advertisements will be influenced by the extent to which they have driven Renault cars in the past (work vehicle, owning, hire/rental). So, Renault driving experience is identified as the blocking variable, and the randomly selected respondents are classified into four blocks (heavy, medium, light or never driven a Renault car). Respondents from each block are randomly assigned to the treatment groups (test commercials A, B and C). The results reveal that the 'some humour' advertisement B was the most effective (Table 11.4).

Table 11.4 An example of a randomised block design

Block number	Renault usage	Treatment groups		
		Advertisement A	*Advertisement B*	*Advertisement C*
1	*High*	A	B	C
2	*Medium*	A	B	C
3	*Light*	A	B	C
4	*None*	A	B	C

Latin square design

Latin square design
A statistical design that allows for the statistical control of two non-interacting external variables in addition to the manipulation of the independent variable.

A **Latin square design** allows the researcher to control statistically two non-interacting external variables as well as to manipulate the independent variable. Each external or blocking variable is divided into an equal number of blocks or levels. The independent variable is also divided into the same number of levels. A Latin square is conceptualised as a table (see Table 11.5), with the rows and columns representing the blocks in the two external variables. The levels of the independent variable are then assigned to the cells in the table. The assignment rule is that each level of the independent variable should appear only once in each row and each column, as shown in Table 11.5.

Table 11.5 An example of a Latin square design

Renault usage	Interest in watching Formula One races		
	High	*Medium*	*Low*
High	B	A	C
Medium	C	B	A
Light and none	A	C	B

Note: A, B and C denote the three test commercials, which have respectively no humour, some humour and high humour.

Focus on **Sports Marketing Surveys**

Latin square design

To illustrate the Latin square design, suppose that in the previous example, in addition to controlling for Renault usage, the researcher also wanted to control for interest in watching Formula One races (defined as high, medium or low). To implement a Latin square design, Renault usage would also have to be blocked at three rather than four levels (e.g. by combining the low and non-users into a single block). Assignments of the three test advertisements could then be made as shown in Table 11.5. Note that each advertisement – A, B or C – appears once, and only once, in each row and each column.

Although Latin square designs are popular in marketing research, they are not without limitations. They require an equal number of rows, columns and treatment levels, which is sometimes problematic. Note that, in the above example, the low users and non-patrons had to be combined to satisfy this requirement. In addition, only two external variables can be controlled simultaneously. Latin squares do not allow the researcher to examine interactions of the external variables with each other or with the independent variable. To examine interactions, factorial designs should be used.

Factorial design

Factorial design
A statistical experimental design used to measure the effects of two or more independent variables at various levels and to allow for interactions between variables.

A **factorial design** is used to measure the effects of two or more independent variables at various levels. Unlike the randomised block design and the Latin square, factorial designs allow for interactions between variables.[22] An interaction is said to take place when the simultaneous effect of two or more variables is different from the sum of their separate effects. For example, an individual's favourite drink might be coffee and favourite temperature level might be cold, but this individual might not prefer cold coffee, leading to an interaction.

A factorial design may also be conceptualised as a table. In a two-factor design, each level of one variable represents a row and each level of another variable represents a column. Multidimensional tables can be used for three or more factors. Factorial designs involve a cell for every possible combination of treatment variables. Suppose that in the previous example, in addition to examining the effect of humour, the researcher was also interested in simultaneously examining the effect of the amount of information about the performance of the Renault Laguna that came over in the advertisement. Further, the amount of information was also varied at three levels (high, medium and low). As shown in Table 11.6, this would require $3 \times 3 = 9$ cells. The respondents would be randomly selected and randomly assigned to the nine cells. Respondents in each cell would receive a specific treatment combination. For example, respondents in the upper left corner cell would view an advertisement that had no humour and low information about the performance of the Renault Laguna. The results revealed a significant interaction between the two factors or variables. Respondents with a low amount of Renault information preferred the high-humour advertisement (C). Those with a high amount of Renault information, however, preferred the no humour film clip (G). Notice that, although Table 11.6 may appear somewhat similar to Table 11.4, the random assignment of respondents and data analysis are very different for the randomised block design and the factorial design.[23]

Table 11.6 **An example of a factorial design**

Amount of Renault Laguna information	Amount of humour		
	No humour	Some humour	High humour
Low	A	B	C
Medium	D	E	F
High	G	H	I

The main disadvantage of a factorial design is that the number of treatment combinations increases multiplicatively with an increase in the number of variables or levels. In our example of Table 11.6, if the amount of humour and Renault Information had five levels each instead of three, the number of cells would jump from 9 to 25. All the treatment combinations are required if all the main effects and interactions are to be measured. If the researcher is interested in only a few of the interactions or main effects, fractional factorial designs may be used. As their name implies, these designs consist of only a fraction or portion of the corresponding full factorial design.

Laboratory versus field experiments

Field environment
An experimental location set in actual market conditions.

Laboratory environment
An artificial setting for experimentation in which the researcher constructs the desired conditions.

Experiments may be conducted in a laboratory or field environment. A laboratory environment is an artificial one that the researcher constructs with the desired conditions specific to the experiment. The term **field environment** is synonymous with actual market conditions. Our experiment to measure the effectiveness of a test advertisement could be conducted in a **laboratory environment** by showing the advert embedded in a TV programme in a test cinema. The same experiment could also be conducted in a field environment by running the test advertisement on actual TV stations. The differences between the two environments are summarised in Table 11.7.

Table 11.7 **Laboratory versus field experiments**

Factor	Laboratory	Field
Environment	Artificial	Realistic
Control	High	Low
Reactive error	High	Low
Demand artefacts	High	Low
Internal validity	High	Low
External validity	Low	High
Time	Short	Long
Number of units	Small	Large
Ease of implementation	High	Low
Cost	Low	High

Laboratory experiments have the following advantages over field experiments:

- The laboratory environment offers a high degree of control because it isolates the experiment in a carefully monitored environment. Therefore, the effects of history can be minimised.

- A laboratory experiment also tends to produce the same results if repeated with similar subjects, leading to high internal validity.
- Laboratory experiments tend to use a small number of test units, last for a shorter time, be more restricted geographically, and are easier to conduct than field experiments. Hence, they are generally less expensive as well.

Compared with field experiments, laboratory experiments suffer from some main disadvantages:

- The artificiality of the environment may cause reactive error in that the respondents react to the situation itself rather than to the independent variable.[24]
- The environment may cause **demand artefacts**, a phenomenon in which the respondents attempt to guess the purpose of the experiment and respond accordingly. For example, while viewing a film clip, the respondents may recall pre-treatment questions about the brand and guess that the commercial is trying to change their attitudes towards the brand.[25]
- Finally, laboratory experiments are likely to have lower external validity than field experiments. Because a laboratory experiment is conducted in an artificial environment, the ability to generalise the results to the real world may be diminished.

Demand artefacts
Responses given because the respondents attempt to guess the purpose of the experiment and respond accordingly.

It has been argued that artificiality or lack of realism in a laboratory experiment need not lead to lower external validity. One must be aware of the aspects of the laboratory experiment that differ from the situation to which generalisations are to be made. External validity will be reduced only if these aspects interface with the independent variables explicitly manipulated in the experiment, as is often the case in applied marketing research. Another consideration, however, is that laboratory experiments allow for more complex designs than field experiments. Hence, the researcher can control for more factors or variables in the laboratory setting, which increases external validity.[26]

The researcher must consider all these factors when deciding whether to conduct laboratory or field experiments. Field experiments are less common in marketing research than laboratory experiments, although laboratory and field experiments play complementary roles.[27]

Experimental versus non-experimental designs

In Chapter 3, we discussed three types of research designs: exploratory, descriptive and causal. Of these, it may be argued that causal designs are the most appropriate for inferring and measuring cause-and-effect relationships (though not the only way – as may be argued by the adherents to grounded research approaches, introduced in Chapter 6). Although descriptive survey data are often used to provide evidence of 'causal' relationships, these studies do not meet all the conditions required for causality. For example, it is difficult in descriptive studies to establish the prior equivalence of the respondent groups with respect to both the independent and dependent variables. On the other hand, an experiment can establish this equivalence by random assignment of test units to groups. In descriptive research, it is also difficult to establish time order of occurrence of variables. In an experiment, however, the researcher controls the timing of the measurements and the introduction of the treatment. Finally, descriptive research offers little control over other possible causal factors.

We do not wish to undermine the importance of descriptive research designs in marketing research. As mentioned in Chapter 3, descriptive research constitutes the most popular research design in marketing research, and we do not want to imply that it should never be used to examine causal relationships. Indeed, some authors have suggested procedures for drawing causal inferences from descriptive (non-experimental) data.[28] Rather, our intent is to alert the reader to the limitations of descriptive research for examining causal relationships. Likewise, we also want to make the reader aware of the limitations of experimentation. [29]

Experimentation is an important research design that gives the ability to infer causal relationships. However, it has limitations of time, cost and administration of an experiment, with these limitations meaning that experimental techniques have a relatively low penetration into marketing research practice.[30]

Time

Experiments can be time consuming, particularly if the researcher is interested in measuring the long-term effects of the treatment, such as the effectiveness of an advertising campaign. Experiments should last long enough so that the post-treatment measurements include most or all of the effects of the independent variables.

Cost

Experiments are often expensive. The requirements of experimental group, control group and multiple measurements significantly add to the cost of research.

Administration

Experiments can be difficult to administer. It may be impossible in measuring human activity to control for the effects of the extraneous variables, particularly in a field environment. Field experiments often interfere with a company's ongoing operations, and obtaining cooperation from the retailers, wholesalers and others involved may be difficult. Finally, competitors may deliberately contaminate the results of a field experiment. These limitations have given rise to the use of grounded theory approaches, especially in developing an understanding of consumer behaviour that is impossible to encapsulate through experiments.

Application: test marketing

Test marketing
An application of a controlled experiment done in limited, but carefully selected, test markets. It involves a replication of the planned national marketing programme for a product in test markets.

Test market
A carefully selected part of the marketplace particularly suitable for test marketing.

Test marketing, also called market testing, is an application of a controlled experiment conducted in limited but carefully selected parts of the marketplace called **test markets**. In Europe, Switzerland has been used as a test market for European-wide product launches as illustrated in the following example. Usually, however, the test market is more focused on particular cities or regions.

Switzerland – an excellent test market?[31]

Switzerland has the reputation of being the ideal test market for Europe, boasting a well-educated, highly critical population with several cultures and languages within its borders. The population of 7.3 million is divided into four languages: German, French, Italian and Rhaeto-Roman. However, Peter Spichiger-Carlsson of GfS-Forschunginstitut (**www.gfs.ch**) argues that the test-market role of Switzerland is on the wane. 'This is partly caused by the high price-levels in this upper-segment market. For example, the cheapest car in the Netherlands is simply not available in Switzerland.' This is not a concensus view as Knut Hackbarth, Media Research Director at Switzerland's largest marketing research company IHA-GfK (**www.ihagfk.ch**), argues. He still believes firmly in Switzerland's continuing role as an excellent test market. 'With the mix here of southern and northern Europe, you can say that if you test a product and it works in Switzerland, chances are it will work in Germany, France and Italy as well.'

Example

Test marketing involves a replication of a planned national marketing programme in the selected test markets. Often, the marketing mix variables (independent variables) are varied in test marketing and the sales (dependent variable) are monitored so that an appropriate national marketing strategy can be identified. The two major objectives of test marketing are (1) to determine market acceptance of the product, and (2) to test alternative levels of marketing mix variables. Test-marketing procedures may be classified as standard test markets, controlled and mini-market tests, and simulated test marketing.

Standard test market

Standard test market
A test market in which the product is sold through regular distribution channels. For example, no special considerations are given to products simply because they are being test marketed.

In a **standard test market**, test markets are selected and the product is sold through regular distribution channels. Typically, the company's own sales force is responsible for distributing the product. Sales personnel stock the shelves, restock and take inventory at regular intervals. One or more combinations of marketing mix variables (product, price, distribution and promotional levels) are employed.

Designing a standard test market involves deciding what criteria are to be used for selecting test markets, how many test markets to use and the duration of the test. Test markets must be carefully selected. In general, the more test markets that can be used, the better. If resources are limited, at least two test markets should be used for each programme variation to be tested. Where external validity is important, however, at least four test markets should be used. The criteria for selection of test markets may be summarised as:[32]

1 Large enough to produce meaningful projections. They should contain at least 2% of the potential target population.
2 Representative demographically.
3 Representative with respect to product consumption behaviour.
4 Representative with respect to media usage.
5 Representative with respect to competition.
6 Relatively isolated in terms of media and physical distribution.
7 Having normal historical development in the product class.
8 Having marketing research and auditing services available.
9 Not overtested.

The duration of the test depends on the repurchase cycle for the product, the probability of competitive response, cost considerations, the initial consumer response and company philosophy. The test should last long enough for repurchase activity to be observed. This indicates the long-term impact of the product. If competitive reaction to the test is anticipated, the duration should be short. The cost of the test is also an important factor. The longer a test is, the more it costs, and at some point the value of additional information is outweighed by its costs. Recent evidence suggests that tests of new brands whose product lifecycle is projected in 'years' should run for at least 10 months. An empirical analysis found that the final test-market share was reached in 10 months 85% of the time and in 12 months 95% of the time.[33] Test marketing is not without risks, but it can be very beneficial to a product's successful introduction, as the following example demonstrates.

Example | **Bass joins exclusive Czech beer club[34]**

Bass has acquired 34% of Staropramen, a Prague brewer. It launched the Czech beer in six-month test markets in Manchester and Liverpool in bottles, and on draft and in bottles in London. The introduction was backed with a comprehensive promotional package designed to encourage consumer trial and future purchase. This included sampling nights, point-of-sale material and glassware. This standard test market constitutes a one-shot case study.

In addition to the problems associated with this design, test marketing faces two unique problems. First, competitors often take actions such as increasing their promotional efforts to contaminate the test-marketing programme. When Procter & Gamble test marketed a hand-and-body lotion, the market leader, Cheeseborough Ponds, started a competitive buy-one-get-one-free promotion for its flagship brand, Vaseline Intensive Care lotion. This encouraged consumers to stock up on Vaseline Intensive Care lotion and, as a result, the Procter & Gamble product did poorly in the test market. Procter & Gamble still launched the line nationally. Ponds again countered with the same promotional strategy. Vaseline Intensive Care settled with a market share of 22% while Procter & Gamble achieved just 4%.[35] Another problem is that, while a firm's test marketing is in progress, competitors have an opportunity to beat it to the national market.[36]

Sometimes it is not feasible to implement a standard test market using the company's personnel. Instead, the company must seek help from an outside supplier, in which case the controlled test market may be an attractive option.

Controlled test market

Controlled test market
A test-marketing programme conducted by an outside research company in field experimentation. The research company guarantees distribution of the product in retail outlets that represent a predetermined percentage of the market.

In a **controlled test market**, the entire test-marketing programme is conducted by an outside research company. The research company guarantees distribution of the product in retail outlets that represent a predetermined percentage of the market. It handles warehousing and field sales operations, such as stocking shelves, selling and stock control. The controlled test market includes both mini-market (or forced distribution) tests and the smaller controlled store panels. This service is provided by a number of research firms, including GfK (**www.gfk.com**) and BASES (**www.bases.com**).

Simulated test market

Simulated test market
A quasi-test market in which respondents are preselected; they are then interviewed and observed on their purchases and attitudes towards the product.

Also called a laboratory test or test-market simulation, a **simulated test market** yields mathematical estimates of market share based on initial reaction of consumers to a new product. The procedure works as follows. Typically, respondents are intercepted in busy locations, such as shopping centres, and pre-screened for product usage. The selected individuals are exposed to the proposed new product concept and given an opportunity to buy the new product in a real-life or laboratory environment. Those who purchase the new product are interviewed about their evaluation of the product and repeat purchase intentions. The trial and repeat purchase estimates so generated are combined with data on proposed promotion and distribution levels to project a share of the market.[37]

Simulated test markets can be conducted in 16 weeks or fewer. The information they generate is confidential and the competition cannot obtain it. They are also relatively inexpensive. Simulated test markets can cost around 10% of a standard test market.

International marketing research

If field experiments are difficult to conduct in developed Western economies, the challenge they pose is greatly increased in the international arena. In many countries, the marketing, economic, structural, information and technological environment is not developed to the extent that it is in Europe and the USA. For example, in many countries, TV stations are owned and operated by a government that may place severe restrictions on TV advertising. This makes field experiments that manipulate advertising levels extremely difficult. Consider, for example, M & M/Mars, which has set up massive manufacturing facilities in Russia and advertises its sweets on TV. Yet, the sales potential has not been realised. Is Mars advertising too much, too little or just enough? Although the answer could be determined by conducting a field experiment that manipulated the level of advertising, such causal research is not feasible given the tight control by the Russian government on TV stations. Likewise, the lack of major supermarkets in the Baltic states makes it difficult for Procter & Gamble to conduct field experiments to determine the effect of in-store promotions on the sales of its detergents.

In some countries in Asia, Africa and South America, a majority of the population live in small towns and villages. Yet basic infrastructure such as roads, transportation and warehouse facilities are lacking, making it difficult to achieve desired levels of distribution. Even when experiments are designed in such countries, it is difficult to control for the time order of occurrence of variables and the absence of other possible causal factors, two of the necessary conditions for causality. Because the researcher has little control over the environment, control of extraneous variables is particularly problematic. Furthermore, it may not be possible to address this problem by adopting the most appropriate experimental design, as environmental constraints may make that design infeasible.

Thus, the internal and external validity of field experiments conducted overseas is generally lower than in Europe and the USA. Although pointing to the difficulties of conducting field experiments in other countries, we do not wish to imply that such causal research cannot or should not be conducted. On the contrary, as the following example indicates, creatively designed field experiments can work across the globe in quite diverse environments.

Example

Flawless quality and exclusivity at €90,000 a piece[38]

German watchmaker Lange Uhren (**www.langeuhren.com**) conducted simulated test marketing in the USA, Japan and France to determine an effective positioning and pricing strategy for its watches. In each country, the price and positioning strategy were varied and consumer responses were assessed. The results, which were similar across countries, indicted that a prestige positioning with a premium price would be most effective. Lange Uhren used a well-trained workforce and the new positioning strategy exploited the flawless quality of the watches produced by this workforce. The watches are sold by only 22 retailers worldwide for as much as €90,000 each. The strategy has been successful. In 2002, about 4,000 of these exclusive watches were sold.

Ethics in marketing research

As was explained in Chapter 10, it is often believed that, if respondents are aware of the purpose of a research project, they may give biased responses. In these situations, a deliberate attempt is made by the researcher to disguise the purpose of the research. This is often necessary with experimentation, where disguise is needed to produce valid results. Take, for example, a project conducted to determine the effectiveness of TV commercials for a breakfast cereal. The respondents are recruited and brought to a central facility. They are told that they will be watching a TV programme on nutrition and then will be asked some questions. Interspersed in the programme is a test commercial for the breakfast cereal as well as commercials for some other products (filler commercials). After viewing the programme and the commercials, the respondents are given a questionnaire to complete. The questionnaire obtains evaluations on the programme content, the test commercial and some of the filler commercials. Note that the evaluations of the programme content and the filler commercials are not of interest but are obtained to reinforce the nature of the disguise. If the respondents knew that the true purpose was to determine the effectiveness of the test commercial, their responses might be biased. Disguising the purpose of the research, however, should not lead to deception.

Although this seems like a paradox, one solution is to disclose the possible existence of deception before the start of the experiment and allow the participants the right to redress at the conclusion of the experiment. The following four items should be conveyed: (1) inform respondents that in an experiment of this nature a disguise of the purpose is often required for valid results; (2) inform them of the general nature of the experiment and what they will be asked to do; (3) make sure they know that they can leave the experiment at any time; and (4) inform them that the study will be fully explained after the data have been gathered and at that time they may request that their information be withdrawn.

Debriefing
After a disguised experiment, informing test subjects what the experiment was about and how the experimental manipulations were performed.

The procedure outlined in item (4) is called **debriefing**. It could be argued that disclosure in this way would also bias results. There is evidence, however, indicating that data collected from subjects informed of the possibility of deception and those not informed are similar.[39] Debriefing can alleviate the stress caused by the experiment and make the experiment a learning experience for the respondents. However, if not handled carefully, debriefing itself can be unsettling to subjects. In the breakfast cereal example above, respondents may find it disheartening that they spent their time evaluating a cereal commercial. The researcher should anticipate and address this issue in the debriefing session.

One further ethical concern in experimentation involves using the appropriate experimental design to control errors caused by extraneous variables. It is the responsibility of the researcher to use the most applicable experimental design for the problem. As the following example illustrates, determining the most appropriate experimental design for the problem requires not only an initial evaluation but also continuous monitoring.

Example

Correcting errors early: a stitch in time saves nine[40]

A marketing research firm specialising in advertising research examined the effectiveness of a TV commercial for Nike (**www.Nike.com**) athletic shoes. A one-group pretest–posttest design was used. Attitudes held by the respondents towards Nike athletic shoes were obtained prior to being exposed to a sports programme on TV and several commercials, including the one for Nike. Attitudes were again measured after viewing the programme and the commercials. Initial evaluation based on a small sample found the one-group pretest–posttest design adopted in this study to be susceptible to demand artefacts: respondents attempt to guess the purpose of the experiment and respond accordingly. Because time and financial constraints make redesigning the study difficult at best, the research continued with correction. Continuing a research project after knowing errors were made in the early stages is not ethical behaviour. Experimental design problems should be disclosed immediately to the client. Decisions on whether to redesign or accept the flaws should be made jointly.

Internet and computer applications

The Internet can be a useful vehicle for conducting causal research. Different experimental treatments can be displayed on different websites. Respondents can then be recruited to visit these sites and respond to a questionnaire that obtains information on the dependent and extraneous variables. Thus, the Internet can provide a mechanism for controlled experimentation, although in a laboratory type of environment.

An example of testing the effectiveness of advertisements can be used to illustrate the use of the Internet in causal research. Different advertisements can be posted on different websites. Matched or randomly selected respondents can be recruited to visit these sites, with one group visiting only one site. If any pre-treatment measures have to be obtained, respondents can answer a questionnaire posted on the site. Then they are exposed to a particular advertisement on that site. After viewing the advertisement, the respondents answer additional questions providing post-treatment measures. Control groups can also be implemented in a similar way. Thus, all types of experimental designs that we have considered can be implemented in this manner.

To complement the Internet, proprietary software can be used in the design and analysis of experiments. For example, the statistical analysis package Minitab can be used to design experiments – see **www.minitab.com** for details and to download a demo. Minitab is similar in use to SPSS (**www.spss.com**) or SAS (**www.sas.com**). Minitab includes functions and documentation specifically for industrial-quality control work in which factorial designs are encountered. For example, researchers investigating restaurant atmosphere might want to examine some of the interactions of independent variables. The dependent variable in this experiment could be the respondents' rating of the restaurant as a setting for a romantic meal. Three factors would be included in this $2 \times 2 \times 2$ study. Assuming two lighting levels (i.e. low or medium), two sound types (piped music or live music), and two olfactory stimuli (i.e. spicy smells or sweet/confectionery smells), the best combinations of restaurant atmospherics can be examined.

The marketing research company GfK and BASES are major proponents of test-marketing designs. Visit their websites at **www.gfk.com** (search for BEHAVIORSCAN) and **www.bases.com**, and search for their techniques for evaluating new product initiatives in fast-moving consumer goods and pharmaceutical products.

Summary

The scientific notion of causality implies that we can never prove that X causes Y. At best, we can only infer that X is one of the causes of Y in that it makes the occurrence of Y probable. Three conditions must be satisfied before causal inferences can be made: (1) concomitant variation, which implies that X and Y must vary together in a hypothesised way; (2) time order of occurrence of variables, which implies that X must precede Y; and (3) elimination of other possible causal factors, which implies that competing explanations must be ruled out. Experiments provide the most convincing evidence of all three conditions. An experiment is formed when one or more independent variables are manipulated or controlled by the researcher and their effect on one or more dependent variables is measured.

In designing an experiment, it is important to consider internal and external validity. Internal validity refers to whether the manipulation of the independent variables actually caused the effects on the dependent variables. External validity refers to the generalisability of experimental results. For the experiment to be valid, the researcher must control the threats imposed by extraneous variables, such as history, maturation, testing (main and interactive testing effects), instrumentation, statistical regression, selection bias and mortality. There are four ways of controlling extraneous variables: randomisation, matching, statistical control and design control.

Experimental designs may be classified as pre-experimental, true experimental, quasi-experimental and statistical designs. An experiment may be conducted in a laboratory environment or under actual market conditions in a real-life setting. Only causal designs encompassing experimentation are appropriate for inferring cause-and-effect relationships.

Although experiments have limitations in terms of time, cost and administration, they are becoming increasingly popular in marketing. Test marketing is an important application of experimental design.

The internal and external validity of field experiments conducted in developing nations is generally lower than in the developed Western economies. The level of development in many countries is lower and the researcher lacks control over many of the marketing variables. The ethical issues involved in conducting causal research include disguising the purpose of the experiment. Debriefing can be used to address some of these issues.

Questions

1 What are the requirements for inferring a causal relationship between two variables?

2 Differentiate between internal and external validity.

3 List any five extraneous variables and give an example to show how each can reduce internal validity.

4 Describe the various methods for controlling extraneous sources of variation.

5 What is the key characteristic that distinguishes true experimental designs from pre-experimental designs?

6 List the steps involved in implementing the posttest-only control group design. Describe the design symbolically.

7 What is a time series experiment? When is it used?

8 How is a multiple time series design different from a basic time series design?

9 What advantages do statistical designs have over basic designs?

10 What are the limitations of the Latin square design?

11 Compare the characteristics of laboratory and field experimentation.

12 Should descriptive research be used for investigating causal relationships? Why or why not?

13 What is test marketing? What are the three types of test marketing?

14 What is the main difference between a standard test market and a controlled test market?

15 Describe how simulated test marketing works.

Exercises

1   You are the marketing research manager for Louis Vuitton (**www.vuitton.com**). The company would like to determine whether it should increase, decrease or maintain the current spend level of advertising. Design a field experiment to address this issue.

2   What potential difficulties do you see in conducting the experiment above? To what extent could the Louis Vuitton management help you overcome these difficulties?

3   Select two different perfume advertisements for any brand of perfume. Design and conduct an experiment to determine which advertisement is the most effective. Use a student sample with 10 students being exposed to each advertisement (treatment condition). Develop your own measures of advertising effectiveness in this context.

4   Red Bull (**www.redbull.com**) has developed three alternative package designs to replace its current can design. Design an Internet-based experiment to determine which, if any, of these new package designs is superior to the current one.

5   In a small group discuss the following issues: 'Is it possible to prove causality in any aspects of consumer behaviour?' and 'The potential to electronically observe consumer buying behaviour using the Internet has created great growth potential for the application of experimental techniques.'

Notes

1   Anon., 'In-store promo drives soda sales, study says', *Drug Store News* 23 (18) (17 December 2001), 81; Dwek, R., 'Prediction of success', *Marketing* (POP and Field Marketing Supplement) (17 April 1997), XII–XIII; 'POP radio test airs the ads in-store', *Marketing News* (24 October 1986), 16.

2   Sobel, M., 'Causal inference in the social sciences', *Journal of the American Statistical Association* 95 (450) (June 2000), 647–651; Bausall, R.B., *Conducting Meaningful Experiments* (Thousand Oaks, CA: Sage, 1994).

3   For several references on the use of experiments in marketing, see Gardner, D.M. and Belk, R.W., *A Basic Bibliography on Experimental Design in Marketing* (Chicago: American Marketing Association, 1980).

4   Gould, G.F. and Gould, J.L., *Chance and Causation: To Experimental Design and Statistica* (New York: W.H. Freeman, 2001); Boruch, R.F., *Randomized Experiments for Planning and Evaluation* (Thousand Oaks, CA: Sage, 1994).

5   Lee, T., 'Experts say point-of-purchase advertising can influence shoppers choices', *Knight Rider Tribune Business News* (19 January 2002), 1; Witthaus, M., 'POP stars', *Marketing Week* 20 (16) (17 July 1997), 37–41.

6   Leichty, J., Ramaswamy, V. and Cohen, S.H., 'Choice menus for mass customization: an experimental approach for analyzing customer demand with an application to a web-based information service', *Journal of Marketing Research* 38 (2) (May 2001), 183–196; Wyner, G.A., 'Experimental design', *Marketing Research: A Magazine of Management and Applications* 9 (3) (Fall 1997), 39–41; Brown, S.R. and Melamed, L.E., *Experimental Design and Analysis* (Newbury Park, CA: Sage, 1990).

7   Farris, P.W., 'Overcontrol in advertising experiments', *Journal of Advertising Research* (November/December 2000), 73–78.

8   Ben-Zion, U., 'The optimal face value of a discount coupon', *Journal of Economics and Business* 51 (2) (March/April 1999), 159–164; Love, A.A., 'Companies want to cut coupons, but consumers demand bargains', *Marketing News* 31 (10) (12 May 1997), 15; Shoemaker, R.W. and Tibrewala, V., 'Relating coupon redemption rates to past purchasing of the brand', *Journal of Advertising Research* 25 (October–November 1985), 40–47.

9   Banks, S., *Experimentation in Marketing* (New York: McGraw-Hill, 1965), 168–179.

10   In addition to internal and external validity, there also exist construct and statistical conclusion validity. Construct validity addresses the question of what construct, or characteristic, is in fact being measured and is discussed in Chapter 12 on measurement and scaling. Statistical conclusion validity addresses the extent and statistical significance of the covariation that exists in the data and is discussed in the chapters on data analysis. See also Klink, R.R. and Smith, D.C., 'Threats to the external validity of brand extension research', *Journal of Marketing Research* 38 (3) (August 2001), 326–335; Cook, T.D. and Campbell, D.T., *Quasi-Experimentation* (Chicago: Rand McNally, 1979), 52–53; Campbell, D.T. and Stanley, J.C., *Experimental and Quasi Experimental Designs for Research* (Chicago: Rand McNally, 1966).

11   Laurent, G., 'Improving the external validity of marketing models: a plea for more qualitative input', *International Journal of Research in Marketing* 17 (2) (September 2000), 177; Bordia, P., 'Face-to-face computer-mediated communication: a synthesis of the experimental literature', *Journal of Business Communication* 34 (1) (January 1997), 99–120; Bowen, D.M., 'Work group research: past strategies and future opportunities', *IEEE Transactions on Engineering Management* 42 (1) (February 1995), 30–38; Lynch, J.G. Jr, 'On the external validity of experiments in consumer research', *Journal of Consumer Research* 9 (December 1982), 225–244.

12   Winer, R., 'Experimentation in the 21st century: the importance of external validity', *Academy of Marketing Science* 27 (3) (Summer 1999), 349–358; Argyris, C., 'Actionable knowledge: design causality in the service of consequential theory', *Journal of Applied Behavioural Science* 32 (4) (December 1966), 390–406; Lynch, J.G. Jr, 'The role of external validity in theoretical research', Calder, B.J., Phillips, L.W. and Tybout, A., 'Beyond external validity', and McGrath, J.E and Brinberg, D., 'External validity and the research process', *Journal of Consumer Research* (June 1983), 109–111, 112–114 and 115–124, respectively.

13 Berger, P. and Maurer, R., *Experimental Design with Applications in Management, Engineering and the Sciences* (Boston, MA: Boston University Press, 2002); Hirsch, A.R., 'Effects of ambient odors on slot machine usage in a Las Vegas casino', *Psychology and Marketing* 12 (7) (October 1995), 585–594.

14 Rosenbaum, P.R., 'Attributing effects to treatment in matched observational studies', *Journal of the American Statistical Association* 97 (457) (March 2002), 183–192; Durier, C., Monod, H. and Bruetschy, A., 'Design and analysis of factorial sensory experiments with carry-over effects', *Food Quality and Preference* 8 (2) (March 1997), 141–149; Nelson, L.S., 'Notes on the use of randomization in experimentation', *Journal of Quality Technology* 28 (1) (January 1996), 123–126.

15 Rosenbaum, P.R., 'Attributing effects to treatment in matched observational studies', *Journal of the American Statistical Association*, 97 (457) (March 2002), 183–192; Selart, M., 'Structure compatibility and restructuring in judgement and choice', *Organisation Behaviour and Human Decision Processes* 65(2) (February 1996), 106–116; Barker Bausell, R., Conducting Meaningful Experiments (Thousand Oaks, CA: Sage, 1994).

16 Kim, B., 'Virtual field experiments for a digital economy: a new research methodology for exploring an information economy', *Decision Support Systems* 32 (3) (January 2002), 215; Chamis, E., 'Auto dealers test online sales in 90 day experiment', *Washington Business Journal* 19 (11 May 2001), 15; Spethmann, B., 'Choosing a test market', Brandweek 36 (19) (8 May 1995), 42–43; Tarshis, A.M., 'Natural sell-in avoids pitfalls of controlled tests', *Marketing News* (24 October 1986), 14.

17 Other experimental designs are also available. See Borror, C.M., 'Evaluation of statistical designs for experiments involving noise variables', *Journal of Quality Technology* 34 (1) (January 2002), 54–70; Campbell, D.T. and Russo, M.J., *Social Experimentation* (Thousand Oaks, CA: Sage, 1999); Gunter, B., 'Fundamental issues in experimental design', *Quality Progress* 29 (6) (June 1996), 105–113.

17a The Racetrack Project did not use experimental techniques. The example illustrates how they could have been applied.

18 For an application of the Solomon four-group design, see Ayres, J., 'Are reductions in CA an experimental artifact? A Solomon four group answer', *Communications Quarterly* 48 (1) (Winter 2000), 19–26.

19 Simester, D., 'Implementing quality improvement programs designed to enhance customer satisfaction: quasi experiments in the United States and Spain', *Journal of Marketing Research* 37 (1) (February 2000), 102–112; Moorman, C., 'A quasi-experiment to assess the consumer and informational determinants of nutrition information-processing activities – the case of the Nutrition Labeling and Education Act', *Journal of Public Policy and Marketing* 15 (1) (Spring 1996), 28–44.

20 Zufryden, F.S., 'Predicting trial, repeat and sales response from alternative media plans', *Journal of Advertising Research* 40 (6) (November/December 2000), 65–72; Lodish, L.M., Abraham, M.M., Livelsberger, J. and Lubetkin, B., 'A summary of fifty-five in-market experimental estimates of the long-term effects of TV advertising', *Marketing Science* (Summer 1995), G133–G140; Krishnamurthi, L., Narayan, J. and Raj, S.P., 'Intervention analysis of a field experiment to assess the build-up effect of advertising', *Journal of Marketing Research* 23 (November 1986), 337–345.

21 See, for example, Vagnoni, A., 'Fear of funny abating', *Advertising Age* 73 (10) (11 March 2002), 8–9; Weinberger, M.G., Spotts, H., Campbell, L. and Parsons, A.L., 'The use and effect of humor in different advertising media', *Journal of Advertising Research* 35 (3) (May/June 1995), 44–56.

22 For applications of factorial designs, see Sengupta, J. and Gorn, G.J., 'Absence makes the mind grow sharper: effects of element omission on subsequent recall', *Journal of marketing Research* 39 (2) (May 2002), 186–201; Bryce, W.J., Day, R. and Olney, T.J., 'Commitment approach to motivating community recycling: New Zealand curbside trial', *Journal of Consumer Affairs* 31 (1) (Summer 1997), 27–52.

23 Roehm, M.L., Pullins, E.B. and Roehm, H.A., Jr. 'Designing loyalty building programs for packaged goods brands', *Journal of Marketing Research* 39 (2) (May 2002), 202–213; Jones, G.E. and Kavanagh, M.J., 'An experimental examination of the effects of individual and situational factors on unethical behavioural intentions in the workplace', *Journal of Business Ethics* 15 (5) (May 1996), 511–523.

24 Dawar, N., 'Impact of product harm crises on brand equity: the moderating role of consumer expectations', *Journal of Marketing Research* 37 (2) (May 2000), 215–226; Bone, P.F., 'Word-of-mouth effects on short-term and long-term product judgments', *Journal of Business Research* 32 (3) (March 1995), 213–223.

25 Lane, V.R., 'The impact of ad repetition and ad content on consumer perceptions of incongruent extensions', *Journal of Marketing* (April 2000), 80–91; Perrien, J., 'Repositioning demand artifacts in consumer research', *Advances in Consumer Research* 24 (1997), 267–271; Shrimp, T.A., Hyatt, E.M. and Snyder, D.J., 'A critical appraisal of demand artifacts in consumer research', *Journal of Consumer Research* 18 (3) (December 1991), 272–283.

26 Ofir, C. and Simonson, I., 'In search of negative customer feedback: the effect of expecting to evaluate on satisfaction evaluations', *Journal of Marketing Research* 38 (2) (May 2001), 170–182; Laurent, G., 'Improving the external validity of marketing models: a plea for more qualitative input', *International Journal of Research in Marketing* 17 (2, 3) (September 2000), 177.

27 Blumenschein, K., 'Hypothetical versus real willingness to pay in the health care sector: results from a field experiment', *Journal of Health Economics* 20 (3) (May 2001), 441; Alston, R.M. and Nowell, C., 'Implementing the voluntary contribution game: a field experiment', *Journal of Economic Behaviour and Organisation* 31 (3) (December 1996), 357–368.

28 Gould, G.F. and Gould, J.L., *Chance and Causation: To Experimental Design and Statistica* (New York: W.H. Freeman, 2001); Spanos, A., 'On theory testing in econometrics: modeling with nonexperimental data', *Journal of Econometrics* 67 (1) (May 1995), 189–226; Blalock, H.M. Jr, *Causal Inferences in Non-experimental Research* (Chapel Hill, NC: University of North Carolina Press, 1964).

29 In some situations, surveys and experiments can complement each other and may both be used. For example, the results obtained in laboratory experiments may be further examined in a field survey. See Johnston, W.J. and Kim, K., 'Performance, attribution, and expectancy linkages in personal selling', *Journal of Marketing* 58 (October 1994), 68–81.

30 Ryals, L. and Wilson, H., 'Experimental methods in market research: from information to insight', *International Journal of Market Research* 47 (4) (2005), 347–366.

31 Heeg, R., 'Switzerland – an excellent test market', *Research World* (March 2004), 8.

32 Vinarsky, C., 'Test market for smokeless tobacco', *Knight Ridder Tribune Business News* (11 March 2002), 1; Romeo, P., 'Testing, testing', *Restaurant Business* 97 (2) (15 January 1998), 12.

33 Lawrence, K., 'Owensboro, Kentucky could be next test market for new McDonald's eatery concept', *Knight Ridder Tribune Business News* (7 February 2002), 1; Thompson, S., 'Tetley test high value pitches', *Brandweek* 38 (47) (15 December 1997), 8; Rubenstein, E., '7-Eleven tests internet kiosks in Seattle Market', *Nation's Restaurant News* 31 (42) (20 October 1997), 24.

34 'Bass joins exclusive Czech beer club', *Grocer* 216 (7174) (22 October 1994), 34.

35 Anon., 'Vaseline to back Dermacare with Llm Ads activity', *Marketing* (10 January 2002), 4; Mehegan, S., 'Vaseline ups ante via anti-bacterial', *Brandweek* 38 (21) (26 May 1997), 1, 6.

36 Anon., 'Why new products are bypassing the market test', *Management Today* (October 1995), 12.

37 Hayes, D.J., Shogren, J.F., Fox, J.A. and Kliebenstein, B., 'Test marketing new food products using a multitrial nonhypothetical experimental auction', *Psychology and Marketing* 13 (4) (July 1996), 365–379; Anon., 'Simulated test marketing', *Sloan Management Review* 36 (2) (Winter 1995), 112.

38 Costanza, F.S., 'Exports boost German jewelry industry', *National Jeweler* 45 (8) (April 16, 2001), 57; Woodruff, D. and Nickel, K., 'When you think deluxe, think East Germany', *Business Week* (26 May 1997), 124E2.

39 Anon., 'The disclosure dilemma', *Workspan* 45 (1) (January 2002), 72; Schmitt, B.H., 'Contextual priming of visual information in advertisements', *Psychology and Marketing* 11 (1) (January/February 1994), 1–14.

40 Peterson, B., 'Ethics revisited', *Marketing Research: A Magazine of Management and Applications* 8 (4) (Winter 1996), 47–48.

Visit the *Marketing Research* Companion Website at www.pearsoned.co.uk/malhotra_euro for additional learning resources including annotated weblinks, an online glossary and a suite of downloadable video cases.

Source: © Getty Images

12

Measurement and scaling: fundamentals, comparative and non-comparative scaling

> *When you can measure what you are speaking about and express it in numbers, you know something about it.*
>
> Lord Kelvin

Objectives

After reading this chapter, you should be able to:

1 introduce the concepts of measurement and scaling and show how scaling may be considered an extension of measurement;

2 discuss the primary scales of measurement and differentiate nominal, ordinal, interval and ratio scales;

3 classify and discuss scaling techniques as comparative and non-comparative and describe the comparative techniques of paired comparison, rank order, constant sum and Q-sort scaling;

4 explain the concept of verbal protocols and discuss how they could be employed to measure consumer response to advertising;

5 describe the non-comparative scaling techniques, distinguish between continuous and itemised rating scales, and explain Likert, semantic differential and Stapel scales;

6 discuss the decisions involved in constructing itemised rating scales;

7 discuss the criteria used for scale evaluation and explain how to assess reliability, validity and generalisability;

8 discuss the considerations involved in implementing the primary scales of measurement in an international setting;

9 understand the ethical issues involved in selecting scales of measurement.

STAGE 1
Problem definition

STAGE 2
Research approach developed

STAGE 3
Research design developed

STAGE 4
Fieldwork or data collection

STAGE 5
Data preparation and analysis

STAGE 6
Report preparation and presentation

Once marketing researchers have a clear understanding of what they wish to understand in their target respondents, they should consider the concepts of scaling and measurement. These concepts are vital in developing questionnaires or 'instruments of measurement' that will fulfil their research objectives in the most accurate manner. In this chapter we describes the concepts of scaling and measurement and discusses four primary scales of measurement: nominal, ordinal, interval and ratio. We describe and illustrate both comparative and non-comparative scaling techniques in detail. The comparative techniques, consisting of paired comparison, rank order, constant sum and Q-sort scaling, are discussed and illustrated with examples. The non-comparative techniques are composed of continuous and itemised rating scales. We discuss and illustrate the popular itemised rating scales – the Likert, semantic differential and Stapel scales – as well as the construction of multi-item rating scales. We show how scaling techniques should be evaluated in terms of reliability and validity and consider how the researcher selects a particular scaling technique. Mathematically derived scales are also presented. The considerations involved in implementing scaling techniques when researching international markets are discussed. The chapter concludes with a discussion of several ethical issues that arise in scale construction. We begin with an example of how the use of different types of scale can give quite different powers of analysis and interpretation.

Example

Numbers, rankings and ratings: Brazil is on top

According to the international football federation (FIFA) (**www.fifa.com**) post-2006 world cup rankings, the 2002 world champions Brazil maintained their supremacy at the top of the rankings with 1,630 points and the champions Italy took second spot with 1,550 points. The top 10 countries were as follows:

Number	Country	July 2006 ranking	Points
1	Argentina	3	1,472
2	Brazil	1	1.630
3	Czech Republic	10	1,223
4	England	5	1,434
5	France	4	1,462
6	Germany	9	1,229
7	Italy	2	1,550
8	Netherlands	6	1,332
9	Portugal	8	1,301
10	Spain	7	1,309

Note that the countries have been placed in alphabetical order and that at first glance this gives the impression that South American countries have performed better than European countries. An alphabetical order is used to illustrate the first column 'Number'. The 'number' assigned to denote countries is not in any way related to their football-playing capabilities but simply serves the purpose of identification, e.g. drawing numbered balls to decide which teams may play each other in a competition. This identification number constitutes a nominal scale, which says nothing about the respective performances of the countries. So whilst Germany is numbered 6 and the Netherlands is numbered 8, this does not reflect the superior performance of the Netherlands.

A much clearer way to present the list would be to place the countries in the order of their ranking, with Brazil at the top and the Czech Republic at the bottom of the table. The ranking would represent an ordinal scale, where it would be clear to see that the lower the number, the better the performance. But what is still missing from the ranking is the magnitude of differences between the countries.

The only way to really understand how much one country is better than another is to examine the points awarded to each country. The points awarded represent an interval scale. Based on the points awarded, note that only ten points separates the closely ranked Argentina (1,472) and France (1,462), or eight points between Spain (1,309) and Portugal (1,301), but that the difference between Brazil (1,630) ranked at number 1 and Italy (1,550) ranked at number 2 is 80 points.

Measurement and scaling

Measurement
The assignment of numbers or other symbols to characteristics of objects according to certain pre-specified rules.

Measurement means assigning numbers or other symbols to characteristics of objects according to certain pre-specified rules.[1] We measure not the object but some characteristic of it. Thus, we do not measure consumers, only their perceptions, attitudes, preferences or other relevant characteristics. In marketing research, numbers are usually assigned for one of two reasons. First, numbers permit statistical analysis of the resulting data. Second, numbers facilitate universal communication of measurement rules and results.

The most important aspect of measurement is the specification of rules for assigning numbers to the characteristics. The assignment process must be isomorphic, i.e. there must be one-to-one correspondence between the numbers and the characteristics being measured. For example, the same euro (€) figures can be assigned to households with identical annual incomes. Only then can the numbers be associated with specific characteristics of the measured object, and vice versa. In addition, the rules for assigning numbers should be standardised and applied uniformly. They must not change over objects or time.

Scaling
The generation of a continuum upon which measured objects are located.

Scaling may be considered an extension of measurement. Scaling involves creating a continuum upon which measured objects are located. To illustrate, consider a scale for locating consumers according to the characteristic 'attitude towards Formula One racing'. Each respondent is assigned a number indicating an unfavourable attitude (measured as 1), a neutral attitude (measured as 2) or a favourable attitude (measured as 3). Measurement is the actual assignment of 1, 2 or 3 to each respondent. Scaling is the process of placing the respondents on a continuum with respect to their attitude towards Formula One. In our example, scaling is the process by which respondents would be classified as having an unfavourable, neutral or positive attitude.

Primary scales of measurement

There are four primary scales of measurement: nominal, ordinal, interval and ratio.[2] These scales are illustrated in Figure 12.1, and their properties are summarised in Table 12.1 and discussed in the following sections.

Nominal scale
A scale whose numbers serve only as labels or tags for identifying and classifying objects with a strict one-to-one correspondence between the numbers and the objects.

Nominal scale

A **nominal scale** is a figurative labelling scheme in which the numbers serve only as labels or tags for identifying and classifying objects. For example, the numbers assigned to the respondents in a study constitute a nominal scale; thus a female respondent may be

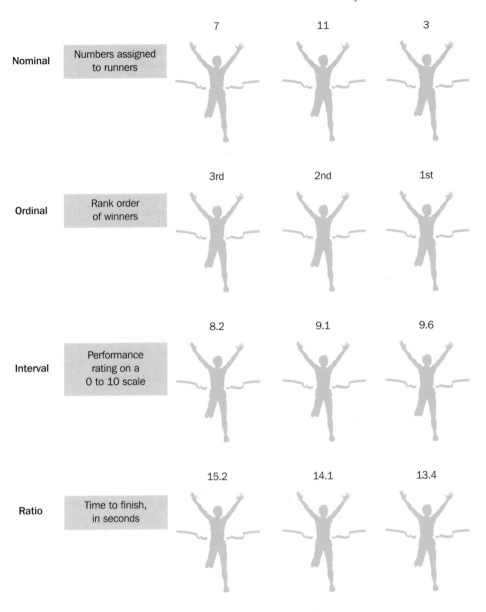

Figure 12.1
An illustration of primary scales of measurement

assigned a number 1 and a male respondent 2. When a nominal scale is used for the purpose of identification, there is a strict one-to-one correspondence between the numbers and the objects. Each number is assigned to only one object, and each object has only one number assigned to it.

Common examples include student registration numbers at their college or university and numbers assigned to football players or jockeys in a horse race. In marketing research, nominal scales are used for identifying respondents, brands, attributes, banks and other objects.

When used for classification purposes, the nominally scaled numbers serve as labels for classes or categories. For example, you might classify the control group as group 1 and the experimental group as group 2. The classes are mutually exclusive and collectively exhaustive. The objects in each class are viewed as equivalent with respect to the characteristic represented by the nominal number. All objects in the same class have the same number, and no two classes have the same number.

The numbers in a nominal scale do not reflect the amount of the characteristic possessed by the objects. For example, a high number on a football player's shirt does not

Table 12.1 Primary scales of measurement

Scale	Basic characteristics	Common examples	Marketing example	Descriptive	Inferential
				Permissible statistics	
Nominal	Numbers identify and classify objects	Student registration numbers, numbers on football players' shirts	Gender classification, bank types	Percentages, mode	Chi-square, binomial test
Ordinal	Numbers indicate the relative positions of the objects but not the magnitude of differences between them	Rankings of the top four teams in the football World Cup	Ranking of service quality delivered by a number of banks. Rank order of favourite TV programmes	Percentile, median	Rank-order correlation, Friedman ANOVA
Interval	Differences between objects can be compared; zero point is arbitrary	Temperature (Fahrenheit, Celsius)	Attitudes, opinions, index numbers	Range, mean, standard deviation	Product moment correlations, t tests, ANOVA, regression, factor analysis
Ratio	Zero point is fixed; ratios of scale values can be computed	Length, weight	Age, income, costs, sales, market shares	Geometric mean, harmonic mean	Coefficient of variation

imply that the footballer is a better player than one with a low number or vice versa. The same applies to numbers assigned to classes. The only permissible operation on the numbers in a nominal scale is counting. Only a limited number of statistics, all of which are based on frequency counts, are permissible. These include percentages, mode, chi-square and binomial tests (see Chapter 18). It is not meaningful to compute an average student registration number, the average gender of respondents in a survey, or the number assigned to an average Formula One team, as in the example opposite.

Ordinal scale

Ordinal scale
A ranking scale in which numbers are assigned to objects to indicate the relative extent to which some characteristic is possessed. Thus, it is possible to determine whether an object has more or less of a characteristic than some other object.

An ordinal scale is a ranking scale in which numbers are assigned to objects to indicate the relative extent to which the objects possess some characteristic. An ordinal scale allows you to determine whether an object has more or less of a characteristic than some other object, but not how much more or less. Thus, an ordinal scale indicates relative position, not the magnitude of the differences between the objects. The object ranked first has more of the characteristic as compared with the object ranked second, but whether the object ranked second is a close second or a poor second is not known. Common examples of ordinal scales include quality rankings, rankings of teams in a tournament and occupational status. In marketing research, ordinal scales are used to measure relative attitudes, opinions, perceptions and preferences. Measurements of this type include 'greater than' or 'less than' judgements from respondents.

In an ordinal scale, as in a nominal scale, equivalent objects receive the same rank. Any series of numbers can be assigned that preserves the ordered relationships between the objects. Ordinal scales can be transformed in any way as long as the basic ordering of the objects is maintained.[3] In other words, any monotonic positive (order-preserving) transformation of the scale is permissible, since the differences in numbers are void of any meaning other than order (see the example opposite). For these reasons, in addition

Focus on

Sports Marketing Surveys

Nominal scale

In the Racetrack study of the Formula One, the numbers 1 through to 10 were assigned to the racing teams (see extracts from the list in Table 12.2). Thus, team 2 referred to Jaguar. It did not imply that Jaguar was in any way superior or inferior to Williams, which was assigned the number 10. Any reassignment of the numbers, such as transposing the numbers assigned to Jaguar and Williams, would have no effect on the numbering system, because the numerals did not reflect any characteristics of the teams. It is meaningful to make statements such as '40% of French respondents named Ferrari as their favourite team'. Although the average of the assigned numbers is 5.5, it is not meaningful to state that the number of the average Formula One team is 5.5.

Table 12.2 Illustration of primary scales of measurement

No.	Nominal scale	Ordinal scale		Interval scale		Ratio scale
	Sponsor	Preference rankings		Preference ratings		Amount (€) spent on merchandise on this team in the past three months
				1–7	11–17	
1	BAR	5	53	5	15	35
2	Ferrari	1	10	7	17	200
3	Jaguar	6	61	5	15	100
4	Jordan	8	82	4	14	0
5	McLaren	2	25	7	17	200
6	Minardi	9	95	4	14	0
7	Renault	3	30	6	16	100
8	Sauber	10	115	2	12	10
9	Toyota	7	79	5	15	0
10	Williams	4	45	6	16	0

 Focus on

Sports Marketing Surveys

Ordinal scale

Table 12.2 gives a particular respondent's preference rankings. Respondents ranked the teams in order of who they preferred, by assigning a rank 1 to the first, rank 2 to the second, and so on. Note that Ferrari (ranked 1) is preferred to McLaren (ranked 2), but how much it is preferred we do not know. Also, it is not necessary that we assign numbers from 1 to 10 to obtain a preference ranking. The second ordinal scale, which assigns a number 10 to Ferrari, 25 to McLaren and 30 to Renault, is an equivalent scale, as it was obtained by a monotonic positive transformation of the first scale. The two scales result in the same ordering of the teams according to preference.

Source: © Alamy

to the counting operation allowable for nominal scale data, ordinal scales permit the use of statistics based on centiles. It is meaningful to calculate percentile, quartile, median (Chapter 18), rank order correlation (Chapter 20) or other summary statistics from ordinal data.

Interval scale

Interval scale
A scale in which the numbers are used to rank objects such that numerically equal distances on the scale represent equal distances in the characteristic being measured.

In an **interval scale**, numerically equal distances on the scale represent equal values in the characteristic being measured. An interval scale contains all the information of an ordinal scale, but it also allows you to compare the differences between objects. The difference between any two scale values is identical to the difference between any other two adjacent values of an interval scale. There is a constant or equal interval between scale values. The difference between 1 and 2 is the same as the difference between 2 and 3, which is the same as the difference between 5 and 6. A common example in everyday life is a temperature scale. In marketing research, attitudinal data obtained from rating scales are often treated as interval data.[4]

In an interval scale, the location of the zero point is not fixed. Both the zero point and the units of measurement are arbitrary. Hence, any positive linear transformation of the form $y = a + bx$ will preserve the properties of the scale. Here, x is the original scale value, y is the transformed scale value, b is a positive constant, and a is any constant. Therefore, two interval scales that rate objects A, B, C and D as 1, 2, 3 and 4 or as 22, 24, 26 and 28 are equivalent. Note that the latter scale can be derived from the former by using $a = 20$ and $b = 2$ in the transforming equation.

Because the zero point is not fixed, it is not meaningful to take ratios of scale values. As can be seen, the ratio of D to B values changes from 2:1 to 7:6 when the scale is transformed. Yet, ratios of differences between scale values are permissible. In this process, the constants a and b in the transforming equation drop out in the computations. The ratio of the difference between D and B values to the difference between C and B values is 2:1 in both the scales.

Statistical techniques that may be used on interval scale data include all those that can be applied to nominal and ordinal data in addition to the arithmetic mean, standard deviation (Chapter 18), product moment correlations (Chapter 20), and other statistics commonly used in marketing research. Certain specialised statistics such as geometric mean, harmonic mean and coefficient of variation, however, are not meaningful on interval scale data. The Sports Marketing Surveys example gives a further illustration of an interval scale.

Focus on | **Sports Marketing Surveys**

Interval scale

In Table 12.2, a respondent's preferences for the 10 teams are expressed on a seven-point rating scale (where a higher number represents a greater preference for a team). We can see that although Williams received a preference rating of 6 and Sauber a rating of 2, this does not mean that Williams is preferred three times as much as Sauber. When the ratings are transformed to an equivalent 11-to-17 scale (next column), the ratings for those teams become 16 and 12, and the ratio is no longer 3 to 1. In contrast, the ratios of preference differences are identical on the two scales. The ratio of preference difference between Ferrari and Sauber to the preference difference between BAR and Sauber is 5 to 3 on both the scales.

Ratio scale

Ratio scale
The highest scale. This scale allows the researcher to identify or classify objects, rank order the objects, and compare intervals or differences. It is also meaningful to compute ratios of scale values.

A **ratio scale** possesses all the properties of the nominal, ordinal and interval scales, and, in addition, an absolute zero point. Thus, in ratio scales we can identify or classify objects, rank the objects, and compare intervals or differences. It is also meaningful to compute ratios of scale values. Not only is the difference between 2 and 5 the same as the difference between 14 and 17, but also 14 is seven times as large as 2 in an absolute sense. Common examples of ratio scales include height, weight, age and money. In marketing, sales, costs, market share and number of customers are variables measured on a ratio scale.

Ratio scales allow only proportionate transformations of the form $y = bx$, where b is a positive constant. One cannot add an arbitrary constant, as in the case of an interval scale. An example of this transformation is provided by the conversion of metres to yards ($b = 1.094$). The comparisons between the objects are identical whether made in metres or yards.

All statistical techniques can be applied to ratio data. These include specialised statistics such as geometric mean, harmonic mean and coefficient of variation. The ratio scale is further illustrated in the context of a Sports Marketing Surveys example.

Focus on | **Sports Marketing Surveys**

Ratio scale

In the ratio scale illustrated in Table 12.2, a respondent is asked to indicate how much had been spent on team merchandise in the last three months. Note that this respondent spent €200 on Ferrari merchandise and only €10 on Sauber. The respondent spent 20 times more euros on Ferrari compared with Sauber. Also, the zero point is fixed because 0 means that the respondent did not spend any money on teams such as Jordan and Minardi. Multiplying these numbers by 100 to convert euros to cents results in an equivalent scale.

The four primary scales discussed above do not exhaust the measurement-level categories. It is possible to construct a nominal scale that provides partial information on order (the partially ordered scale). Likewise, an ordinal scale can convey partial information on distance, as in the case of an ordered **metric scale**. A discussion of these scales is beyond the scope of this text.[5]

Metric scale
A scale that is either interval or ratio in nature.

A comparison of scaling techniques

The scaling techniques commonly employed in marketing research can be classified into comparative and non-comparative scales (see Figure 12.2).

Comparative scales
One of two types of scaling techniques in which there is direct comparison of stimulus objects with one another.

Non-metric scale
A scale that is either nominal or ordinal in nature.

Carryover effects
Where the evaluation of a particular scaled item significantly affects the respondent's judgement of subsequent scaled items.

Comparative scales involve the direct comparison of stimulus objects. For example, respondents may be asked whether they prefer Coke or Pepsi. Comparative scale data must be interpreted in relative terms and have only ordinal or rank order properties. For this reason, comparative scaling is also referred to as **non-metric scaling**. As shown in Figure 12.2, comparative scales include paired comparisons, rank order, constant sum scales, Q-sort and other procedures.

The major benefit of comparative scaling is that small differences between stimulus objects can be detected. As they compare the stimulus objects, respondents are forced to choose between them. In addition, respondents approach the rating task from the same known reference points. Consequently, comparative scales are easily understood and can be applied easily. Other advantages of these scales are that they involve fewer theoretical assumptions, and they also tend to reduce halo or **carryover effects** from one judgement to

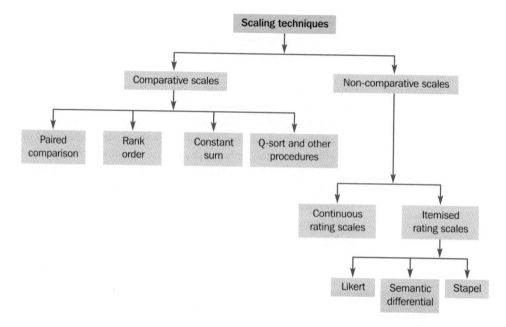

**Figure 12.2
A classification of
scaling techniques**

another.[6] The major disadvantages of comparative scales include the ordinal nature of the data and the inability to generalise beyond the stimulus objects scaled. For instance, to compare Virgin Cola with Coke and Pepsi the researcher would have to do a new study. These disadvantages are substantially overcome by the non-comparative scaling techniques.

In **non-comparative scales**, also referred to as monadic or metric scales, each object is scaled independently of the others in the stimulus set. The resulting data are generally assumed to be interval or ratio scaled.[7] For example, respondents may be asked to evaluate Coke on a 1 to 6 preference scale (1 = not at all preferred, 6 = greatly preferred). Similar evaluations would be obtained for Pepsi and Virgin Cola. As can be seen in Figure 12.2, non-comparative scales can be continuous rating or itemised rating scales. The itemised rating scales can be further classified as Likert, semantic differential or Stapel scales. Non-comparative scaling is the most widely used scaling technique in marketing research.

Non-comparative scale
One of two types of scaling techniques in which each stimulus object is scaled independently of the other objects in the stimulus set. Also called monadic scale.

Comparative scaling techniques

Paired comparison scaling

Paired comparison scaling
A comparative scaling technique in which a respondent is presented with two objects at a time and asked to select one object in the pair according to some criterion. The data obtained are ordinal in nature.

As its name implies, in **paired comparison scaling** a respondent is presented with two objects and asked to select one according to some criterion.[8] The data obtained are ordinal in nature. A respondent may state that he or she prefers Belgian chocolate to Swiss, likes Kellogg's cereals better than supermarket home brands, or likes Adidas more than Nike. Paired comparison scales are frequently used when the stimulus objects are physical products. Coca-Cola is reported to have conducted more than 190,000 paired comparisons before introducing New Coke.[9] Paired comparison scaling is the most widely used comparative scaling technique.

Figure 12.3 shows paired comparison data obtained to assess a respondent's bottled beer preferences. As can be seen, this respondent made 10 comparisons to evaluate five brands. In general, with n brands, $[n(n-1)/2]$ paired comparisons include all possible pairings of objects.[10]

Paired comparison data can be analysed in several ways.[11] The researcher can calculate the percentage of respondents who prefer one stimulus over another by summing the

Instructions
We are going to present you with ten pairs of bottled beer brands. For each pair, please indicate which of the two brands of beer in the pair you prefer.

Recording form

	Holsten	Stella Artois	Grolsch	Carlsberg	Budvar
Holsten		0	0	1	0
Stella Artois	1[a]		0	1	0
Grolsch	1	1		1	1
Carlsberg	0	0	0		0
Budvar	1	1	0	1	
Number of times preferred[b]	3	2	0	4	1

[a] 1 in a particular box means that the brand in that column was preferred over the brand in the corresponding row. 0 means that the row brand was preferred over the column brand.

[b] The number of times a brand was preferred is obtained by summing the 1s in each column.

Figure 12.3
Obtaining bottled beer preferences using paired comparisons

matrices of Figure 12.3 for all the respondents, dividing the sum by the number of respondents, and multiplying by 100. Simultaneous evaluation of all the stimulus objects is also possible. Under the assumption of transitivity, it is possible to convert paired comparison data to a rank order.

Transitivity of preference
An assumption made to convert paired comparison data to rank order data. It implies that if Brand A is preferred to Brand B, and Brand B is preferred to Brand C, then Brand A is preferred to Brand C.

Transitivity of preference implies that if Brand A is preferred to B, and Brand B is preferred to C, then Brand A is preferred to C. To arrive at a rank order, the researcher determines the number of times each brand is preferred by summing the column entries in Figure 12.3. Therefore, this respondent's order of preference, from most to least preferred, is Carlsberg, Holsten, Stella Artois, Budvar and Grolsch. It is also possible to derive an interval scale from paired comparison data using the Thurstone case V procedure. Refer to the appropriate literature for a discussion of this procedure.[12]

Several modifications of the paired comparison technique have been suggested. One involves the inclusion of a neutral/no difference/no opinion response. Another extension is graded paired comparisons. In this method, respondents are asked which brand in the pair is preferred and how much it is preferred. The degree of preference may be expressed by how much more the respondent is willing to pay for the preferred brand. The resulting scale is a euro metric scale. Another modification of paired comparison scaling is widely used in obtaining similarity judgements in multidimensional scaling (see Chapter 24).

Paired comparison scaling is useful when the number of brands is limited, since it requires direct comparison and overt choice. With a large number of brands, however, the number of comparisons becomes unwieldy. Other disadvantages are that violations of the assumption of transitivity may occur, and the order in which the objects are presented may bias the results.[13] Paired comparisons bear little resemblance to the marketplace situation, which involves selection from multiple alternatives. Also respondents may prefer one object over certain others, but they may not like it in an absolute sense.

Example

Paired comparison scaling[14]

The most common method of taste testing is paired comparison. Respondents are asked to taste two different products and say which one they prefer. The test is done in private, either in respondents' homes or some other location such as a hotel suite near to a shopping centre. In these tests a minimum of 1,000 responses is considered an adequate sample.

Ocean Spray (**www.oceanspray.com**), the producer of bottled and canned juices/juice drinks, makes extensive use of taste tests in developing new products. Respondents are asked to sample its new drinks which are presented in pairs. They are evaluated on taste and aspects of flavour and then respondents choose the one they like more than the other. Taste tests showed that a segment of consumers preferred white cranberries to the strong tart taste of red cranberries. Therefore in early 2002, Ocean Spray added White Cranberry drinks, made with natural white cranberries harvested a few weeks earlier than the red variety, and Juice Spritzers, lightly carbonated juice drinks, to its product line.

Rank order scaling

Rank order scaling
A comparative scaling technique in which respondents are presented with several objects simultaneously and asked to order or rank them according to some criterion.

After paired comparisons, the most popular comparative scaling technique is **rank order scaling**. In rank order scaling respondents are presented with several objects simultaneously and asked to order or rank them according to some criterion. For example, respondents may be asked to rank according to overall preference. As shown in Figure 12.4, these rankings are typically obtained by asking the respondents to assign a rank of 1 to the most preferred Fomula One teams, 2 to the second most preferred, and so on, until a rank of n is assigned to the least preferred team. Like paired comparison, this approach is also comparative in nature, and it is possible that the respondents may dislike the team ranked 1 in an absolute sense. Furthermore, rank order scaling also results in ordinal data. See Table 12.2, which uses rank order scaling to derive an ordinal scale.

Rank order scaling is commonly used to measure attributes of products and services as well as preferences for brands. Rank order data are frequently obtained from respondents in conjoint analysis (see Chapter 24), since rank order scaling forces the respondents to discriminate among the stimulus objects. Moreover, compared with paired comparisons, this type of scaling process more closely resembles the shopping environment. It also takes less time and eliminates intransitive responses. If there are n stimulus objects, only $(n - 1)$ scaling decisions need be made in rank order scaling. However, in paired comparison scaling, $[n(n - 1)/2]$ decisions would be required. Another advantage is that most respondents

Instructions
Rank the listed Formula One teams in order of preference. Begin by picking out the team that you like most and assign it a number 1. Then find the second most preferred team and assign it a number 2. Continue this procedure until you have ranked all the teams in order of preference. The least preferred team should be assigned a rank of 10.

No two teams should receive the same rank number.

The criterion of preference is entirely up to you. There is no right or wrong answer. Just try to be consistent.

	Brand	Rank order
1	BAR	
2	Ferrari	
3	Jaguar	
4	Jordan	
5	McLaren	
6	Minardi	
7	Renault	
8	Sauber	
9	Toyota	
10	Williams	

Figure 12.4
Preference for Formula One using rank order scaling

easily understand the instructions for ranking. The major disadvantage is that this technique produces only ordinal data.

Finally, under the assumption of transitivity, rank order data can be converted to equivalent paired comparison data, and vice versa. This point was illustrated by examining the 'Number of times preferred' in Figure 12.3. Hence, it is possible to derive an interval scale from rankings using the Thurstone case V procedure. Other approaches for deriving interval scales from rankings have also been suggested.[15]

Constant sum scaling

Constant sum scaling
A comparative scaling technique in which respondents are required to allocate a constant sum of units such as points, euros, chits, stickers or chips among a set of stimulus objects with respect to some criterion.

In **constant sum scaling**, respondents allocate a constant sum of units, such as points or euros, among a set of stimulus objects with respect to some criterion. As shown in Figure 12.5, respondents may be asked to allocate 100 points to attributes of bottled beers in a way that reflects the importance they attach to each attribute. If an attribute is unimportant, the respondent assigns it zero points. If an attribute is twice as important as some other attribute, it receives twice as many points. The sum of all the points is 100; hence the name of the scale.

The attributes are scaled by counting the points assigned to each one by all the respondents and dividing by the number of respondents. These results are presented for three groups, or segments, of respondents in Figure 12.5. Segment I attaches overwhelming importance to price. Segment II considers a high alcoholic level to be of prime importance. Segment III values bitterness, hop flavours, fragrance and the aftertaste. Such information cannot be obtained from rank order data unless they are transformed into interval data. Note that the constant sum also has an absolute zero; 10 points are twice as many as 5 points, and the difference between 5 and 2 points is the same as the difference between 57 and 54 points. For this reason, constant sum scale data are sometimes treated as metric. Although this may be appropriate in the limited context of the stimuli scaled, these results are not generalisable to other stimuli not included in the

Instructions
Below are eight attributes of bottled beers. Please allocate 100 points among the attributes so that your allocation reflects the relative importance you attach to each attribute. The more points an attribute receives, the more important an attribute is. If an attribute is not at all important, assign it no points. If an attribute is twice as important as some other attribute, it should receive twice as many points.

Note: the figures below represent the mean points allocated to bottled beers by three segments of a target market.

Form

		MEAN POINTS ALLOCATED		
	Attribute	Segment I	Segment II	Segment III
1	Bitterness	8	2	17
2	Hop flavours	2	4	20
3	Fragrance	3	9	19
4	Country where brewed	9	17	4
5	Price	53	5	7
6	High alcohol level	7	60	9
7	Aftertaste	5	0	15
8	Package design	13	3	9
	Sum	100	100	100

Figure 12.5
Importance of bottled beer attributes using a constant sum scale

study. Hence, strictly speaking, the constant sum should be considered an ordinal scale because of its comparative nature and the resulting lack of generalisability. It can be seen that the allocation of points in Figure 12.5 is influenced by the specific attributes included in the evaluation task.

The main advantage of the constant sum scale is that it allows for fine discrimination among stimulus objects without requiring too much time. It has two primary disadvantages, however. Respondents may allocate more or fewer units than those specified. For example, a respondent may allocate 108 or 94 points. The researcher must modify such data in some way or eliminate this respondent from analysis. Another potential problem is rounding error if too few units are used. On the other hand, the use of a large number of units may be too taxing on the respondent and cause confusion and fatigue.

Q-sort and other procedures

Q-sort scaling
A comparative scaling technique that uses a rank order procedure to sort objects based on similarity with respect to some criterion.

Q-sort scaling was developed to discriminate among a relatively large number of objects quickly. This technique uses a rank order procedure in which objects are sorted into piles based on similarity with respect to some criterion. For example, respondents are given 100 attitude statements on individual cards and asked to place them into 11 piles, ranging from 'most highly agreed with' to 'least highly agreed with'. The number of objects to be sorted should not be less than 60 nor more than 140; a reasonable range is 60 to 90 objects.[16] The number of objects to be placed in each pile is pre-specified, often to result in a roughly normal distribution of objects over the whole set.

Another comparative scaling technique is magnitude estimation.[17] In this technique, numbers are assigned to objects such that ratios between the assigned numbers reflect ratios on the specified criterion. For example, respondents may be asked to indicate whether they agree or disagree with each of a series of statements measuring attitude towards different sports. Then they assign a number between 0 and to 100 to each statement to indicate the intensity of their agreement or disagreement. Providing this type of number imposes a cognitive burden on the respondents.

Verbal protocol
A technique used to understand respondents' cognitive responses or thought processes by having them think aloud while completing a task or making a decision.

Another particularly useful procedure (that could be viewed as a very structured combination of observation and depth interviewing) for measuring cognitive responses or thought processes consists of **verbal protocols**. Respondents are asked to 'think out loud' and verbalise anything going through their heads while making a decision or performing a task.[18] The researcher says, 'If you think anything, say it aloud, no matter how trivial the thought may be.' Even with such an explicit instruction, the respondents may be silent. At these times, the researcher will say, 'Remember to say aloud everything you are thinking.' Everything that the respondents say is tape recorded. This record of the respondents' verbalised thought processeses is referred to as a protocol.[19]

Protocols have been used to measure consumers' cognitive responses in actual shopping trips as well as in simulated shopping environments. An interviewer accompanies the respondent and holds a microphone into which the respondent talks. Protocols, thus collected, have been used to determine the attributes and cues used in making purchase decisions, product usage behaviour and the impact of the shopping environment on consumer decisions. Protocol analysis has also been employed to measure consumer response to advertising. Immediately after seeing an ad, the respondent is asked to list all the thoughts that came to mind while watching the ad. The respondent is given a limited amount of time to list the thoughts so as to minimise the probability of collecting thoughts generated after, rather than during, the message. After the protocol has been collected, the individual's thoughts or cognitive responses can be coded into three categories as illustrated in Table 12.3.[20]

Table 12.3 Coded verbal protocols

Category	Definition	Example
Support argument	Support the claim made by the message	'Diet Coke tastes great'
Counter-argument	Refute the claim made by the message	'Diet Coke has an aftertaste'
Source derogation	Negative opinion about the source of the message	'Coca-Cola is not an honest company'

Protocols are, typically, incomplete. The respondent has many thoughts that he or she cannot or will not verbalise. The researcher must take the incomplete record and infer from it a measure of the underlying cognitive response.

Non-comparative scaling techniques

Respondents using a non-comparative scale employ whatever rating standard seems appropriate to them. They do not compare the object being rated either with another object or with some specified standard, such as 'your ideal brand'. They evaluate only one object at a time; thus, non-comparative scales are often referred to as monadic scales. Non-comparative techniques consist of continuous and itemised rating scales, which are described in Table 12.4 and discussed in the following sections.

Table 12.4 Basic non-comparative scales

Scale	Basic characteristics	Examples	Advantages	Disadvantages
Continuous rating scale	Place a mark on a continuous line	Reaction to TV commercials	Easy to construct	Scoring can be cumbersome unless computerised
Itemised rating scales				
Likert scale	Degree of agreement on a 1 (strongly disagree) to 5 (strongly agree) scale	Measurement of attitudes	Easy to construct, administer and understand	More time consuming
Semantic differential scale	Seven-point scale with bipolar labels	Brand product and company images	Versatile	Controversy as to whether the data are interval
Stapel scale	Unipolar 10-point scale, −5 to +5, without a neutral point (zero)	Measurement of attitudes and images	Easy to construct, administered over phone	Confusing and difficult to apply

Continuous rating scale

Continuous rating scale
A measurement scale that has respondents rate the objects by placing a mark at the appropriate position on a line that runs from one extreme of the criterion variable to the other. The form may vary considerably. Also called graphic rating scale.

In a **continuous rating scale**, also referred to as a graphic rating scale, respondents rate the objects by placing a mark at the appropriate position on a line that runs from one extreme of the criterion variable to the other. Thus, the respondents are not restricted to selecting from marks previously set by the researcher. The form of the continuous scale may vary considerably. For example, the line may be vertical or horizontal: scale points, in the form of numbers or brief descriptions, may be provided; and if provided, the scale points may be few or many. Three versions of a continuous rating scale are illustrated in Figure 12.6.

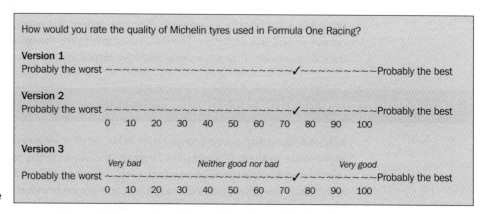

Figure 12.6
Continuous rating scale

Once the respondent has provided the ratings, the researcher divides the line into as many categories as desired and assigns scores based on the categories into which the ratings fall. In Figure 12.6, the respondent exhibits a favourable attitude towards Michelin tyres. These scores are typically treated as interval data. The advantage of continuous scales is that they are easy to construct; however, scoring is cumbersome and unreliable.[21] Moreover, continuous scales provide little new information. Hence, their use in marketing research has been limited. Recently, however, with the increased popularity of computer-assisted personal interviewing and other technologies, their use has become more frequent.

Itemised rating scales

Itemised rating scale
A measurement scale having numbers or brief descriptions associated with each category. The categories are ordered in terms of scale position.

In an **itemised rating scale**, respondents are provided with a scale that has a number or brief description associated with each category. The categories are ordered in terms of scale position, and the respondents are required to select the specified category that best describes the object being rated. Itemised rating scales are widely used in marketing research and form the basic components of more complex scales, such as multi-item rating scales. We first describe the commonly used itemised rating scales – the Likert, semantic differential and Stapel scales – and then examine the major issues surrounding the use of itemised rating scales.

Likert scale
A measurement scale with five response categories ranging from 'strongly disagree' to 'strongly agree' that requires respondents to indicate a degree of agreement or disagreement with each of a series of statements related to the stimulus objects.

Likert scale

Named after its developer, Rensis Likert, the **Likert scale** is a widely used rating scale that requires the respondents to indicate a degree of agreement or disagreement with each of a series of statements about the stimulus objects.[22] Typically, each scale item has five response categories, ranging from 'strongly disagree' to 'strongly agree'. We illustrate with a Likert scale for evaluating attitudes towards Renault cars.

To conduct the analysis, each statement is assigned a numerical score, ranging either from −2 to +2 or from 1 to 5. The analysis can be conducted on an item-by-item basis (profile analysis), or a total (summated) score can be calculated for each respondent by summing across items. Suppose that the Likert scale in Figure 12.7 was used to measure attitudes towards Renault as well as Ford. Profile analysis would involve comparing the two car manufacturers in terms of the average respondent ratings for each item. The summated approach is most frequently used, and, as a result, the Likert scale is also referred to as a summated scale.[23] When using this approach to determine the total score for each respondent on each car manufacturer, it is important to use a consistent scoring procedure so that a high (or low) score consistently reflects a favourable response. This requires that the categories assigned to the negative statements by the respondents be scored by reversing the scale. Note that for a negative statement, an agreement reflects an unfavourable response, whereas for a positive statement, agreement represents a favourable response. Accordingly, a 'strongly agree' response to a favourable statement and a 'strongly disagree' response to an unfavourable statement would both receive scores of 5.[24] In the example in Figure 12.7, if a higher score is to denote a more favourable attitude, the scoring of items 2, 4, 5 and 7 will be reversed. The respondent to this set of statements has an attitude score of 26. Each respondent's total score for each car manufacturer is calculated. A respondent will have the most favourable attitude towards a car manufacturer with the highest score. The procedure for developing summated Likert scales is described later in the section on the development and evaluation of scales.

The Likert scale has several advantages. It is easy to construct and administer, and respondents readily understand how to use the scale, making it suitable for Internet

Instructions

Listed below are different beliefs about Renault cars. Please indicate how strongly you agree or disagree with each by putting a tick next to your choice on the following scale:

1 = Strongly disagree, 2 = Disagree, 3 = Neither agree nor disagree, 4 = Agree, 5 = Strongly agree

	Strongly disagree	Disagree	Neither agree nor disagree	Agree	Strongly agree
1 Renault produces high-quality cars	1	2✓	3	4	5
2 Renault has poor after-sales service	1	2✓	3	4	5
3 I like to visit Renault dealerships	1	2	3✓	4	5
4 Renault does not offer a good range of optional extras for its cars	1	2	3	4✓	5
5 The credit terms at Renault dealerships are terrible	1	2	3	4✓	5
6 Renault is the embodiment of European excellence in car manufacturing	1✓	2	3	4	5
7 I do not like Renault advertising	1	2	3	4✓	5
8 Renault has an excellent selection of car types	1	2	3	4✓	5
9 The price of Renault cars is fair	1	2✓	3	4	5

Figure 12.7
The Likert scale

surveys, mail, telephone or personal interviews. The major disadvantage of the Likert scale is that it takes longer to complete than other itemised rating scales because respondents have to read and fully reflect upon each statement.

Semantic differential scale

Semantic differential
A seven-point rating scale with end points associated with bipolar labels.

The **semantic differential** is a seven-point rating scale with end points associated with bipolar labels that have semantic meaning. In a typical application, respondents rate objects on a number of itemised, seven-point rating scales bounded at each end by one of two bipolar adjectives, such as 'boring' and 'exciting'.[25] We illustrate this scale in Figure 12.8 by presenting a respondent's evaluation of Formula One racing on five attributes.

The respondents mark the blank that best indicates how he or she would describe the object being rated.[26] Thus, in our example, Formula One is evaluated as exciting, innovative, safe, dynamic, though uninspiring. The negative adjective or phrase sometimes appears at the left side of the scale and sometimes at the right. This controls the tendency of some respondents, particularly those with very positive or very negative attitudes, to mark the right- or left-hand sides without reading the labels.

Individual items on a semantic differential scale may be scored either on a –3 to +3 or on a 1 to 7 scale. The resulting data are commonly analysed through profile analysis. In profile analysis, means or median values on each rating scale are calculated and compared by plotting or statistical analysis. This helps determine the overall differences and similarities among the objects. To assess differences across segments of respondents, the researcher can compare mean responses of different segments. Although the mean is most often used as a summary statistic, there is some controversy as to whether the data obtained should be treated as an interval scale.[27] On the other hand, in cases when the researcher requires an overall comparison of objects, such as to determine car manufacturer preference, the individual item scores are summed to arrive at a total score.

Its versatility makes the semantic differential a popular rating scale in marketing research. It has been widely used in comparing brand, product and company images. It has also been used to develop advertising and promotion strategies and in new product development studies.[28]

Stapel scale

Stapel scale
A scale for measuring attitudes that consists of a single adjective in the middle of an even-numbered range of values.

The **Stapel scale**, named after its developer, Jan Stapel, is a unipolar rating scale with 10 categories numbered from –5 to +5, without a neutral point (zero).[29] This scale is usually presented vertically. Respondents are asked to indicate, by selecting an appropriate numerical response category, how accurately or inaccurately each term describes the object. The higher the number, the more accurately the term describes the object, as shown in Figure 12.9. In this example, Formula One is perceived as being prestigious but not elitist.

Instructions
What does Formula One racing mean to you? The following descriptive scales, bounded at each end by bipolar adjectives, summarise characteristics of the sport. Please mark ✗ the blank that best indicates what Formula One means to you.

Form
Formula One is:

Boring	:_::_::_::_::_::✗::_:	Exciting
Conservative	:_::_::_::_::_::✗::_:	Innovative
Dangerous	:_::_::_::_::_::_::✗:	Safe
Staid	:_::_::_::_::_::✗::_:	Dynamic
Uninspiring	:_::✗::_::_::_::_::_:	Inspirational

Figure 12.8
Semantic differential scale

Instructions
Please evaluate how accurately each word or phrase describes Formula One racing. Select a positive number for the phrases you think describe the sport accurately. The more accurately you think the phrase describes the sport, the larger the plus number you should choose. You should select a minus number for the phrases you think do not describe the sport accurately. The less accurately you think the phrase describes the sport, the larger the negative number you should choose. You can select any number from +5 for phrases you think are very accurate, to –5 for phrases you think are very inaccurate.

Form

	Formula One	
	+5	+5
	+4**X**	+4
	+3	+3
	+2	+2
	+1	+1
	Prestigious	*Elitist*
	–1	–1
	–2	–2**X**
	–3	–3
	–4	–4
	–5	–5

**Figure 12.9
The Stapel scale**

The data obtained by using a Stapel scale can be analysed in the same way as semantic differential data. The Stapel scale produces results similar to the semantic differential.[30] The Stapel scale's advantages are that it does not require a pretest of the adjectives or phrases to ensure true bipolarity and that it can be administered over the telephone. Some researchers, however, believe the Stapel scale is confusing and difficult to apply. Of the three itemised rating scales considered, the Stapel scale is used least.[31] Nonetheless, this scale merits more attention than it has received.

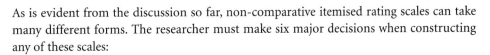

Itemised rating scale decisions

As is evident from the discussion so far, non-comparative itemised rating scales can take many different forms. The researcher must make six major decisions when constructing any of these scales:

1 The number of scale categories to use
2 Balanced versus unbalanced scale
3 Odd or even number of categories
4 Forced versus non-forced choice
5 The nature and degree of the verbal description
6 The physical form of the scale.

Number of scale categories

Two conflicting considerations are involved in deciding the number of scale categories or response options. The greater the number of scale categories, the finer the discrimination among stimulus objects that is possible. On the other hand, most respondents cannot handle more than a few categories. Traditional guidelines suggest that the appropriate number of categories should be between five and nine.[32] Yet there is no single optimal number of categories. Several factors should be taken into account in deciding on the number of categories.

If the respondents are interested in the scaling task and are knowledgeable about the objects, many categories may be employed. On the other hand, if the respondents are not very knowledgeable or involved with the task, fewer categories should be used. Likewise, the nature of the objects is also relevant. Some objects do not lend themselves to fine discrimination, so a small number of categories are sufficient. Another important factor is the mode of data collection. If telephone interviews are involved, many categories may confuse the respondents. Likewise, space limitations may restrict the number of categories in mail questionnaires.

How the data are to be analysed and used should also influence the number of categories. In situations where several scale items are added together to produce a single score for each respondent, five categories are sufficient. The same is true if the researcher wishes to make broad generalisations or group comparisons. If, however, individual responses are of interest or if the data will be analysed by sophisticated statistical techniques, seven or more categories may be required. The size of the correlation coefficient, a common measure of relationship between variables (Chapter 20), is influenced by the number of scale categories. The correlation coefficient decreases with a reduction in the number of categories. This, in turn, has an impact on all statistical analysis based on the correlation coefficient.[33]

Balanced versus unbalanced scale

Balanced scale
A scale with an equal number of favourable and unfavourable categories.

In a balanced scale, the number of favourable and unfavourable categories is equal; in an unbalanced scale, the categories are unequal.[34] Examples of balanced and unbalanced scales are given in Figure 12.10.

In general, in order to obtain objective data, the scale should be balanced. If the distribution of responses is likely to be skewed, however, either positively or negatively, an unbalanced scale with more categories in the direction of skewness may be appropriate. If an unbalanced scale is used, the nature and degree of imbalance in the scale should be taken into account in data analysis.

Odd or even number of categories

With an odd number of categories, the middle scale position is generally designated as neutral or impartial. The presence, position and labelling of a neutral category can have a significant influence on the response. The Likert scale is a balanced rating scale with an odd number of categories and a neutral point.[35]

The decision to use an odd or even number of categories depends on whether some of the respondents may be neutral on the response being measured. If a neutral or indifferent response is possible from at least some of the respondents, an odd number of categories should be used. If, on the other hand, the researcher wants to force a response or believes that no neutral or indifferent response exists, a rating scale with an even number of categories should be used. A related issue is whether the choice should be forced or non-forced.

Balanced scale	
Clinique moisturiser for men is:	
Extremely good	
Very good	✓
Good	
Bad	
Very bad	
Extremely bad	

Unbalanced scale	
Clinique moisturiser for men is:	
Extremely good	
Very good	✓
Good	
Somewhat good	
Bad	
Very bad	

**Figure 12.10
Balanced and unbalanced scales**

Forced versus non-forced choice

Forced rating scale
A rating scale that forces respondents to express an opinion because a 'no opinion' or 'no knowledge' option is not provided.

On **forced rating scales** the respondents are forced to express an opinion because a 'no opinion' option is not provided. In such a case, respondents without an opinion may mark the middle scale position. If a sufficient proportion of the respondents do not have opinions on the topic, marking the middle position will distort measures of central tendency and variance. In situations where the respondents are expected to have no opinion, as opposed to simply being reluctant to disclose it, the accuracy of data may be improved by a non-forced scale that includes a 'no opinion' category.[36]

Nature and degree of verbal description

The nature and degree of verbal description associated with scale categories varies considerably and can have an effect on the responses. Scale categories may have verbal, numerical or even pictorial descriptions. Furthermore, the researcher must decide whether to label every scale category, label only some scale categories, or label only extreme scale categories. Surprisingly, providing a verbal description for each category may not improve the accuracy or reliability of the data. Yet, an argument can be made for labelling all or many scale categories to reduce scale ambiguity. The category descriptions should be located as close to the response categories as possible.

The strength of the adjectives used to anchor the scale may influence the distribution of the responses. With strong anchors (1 = completely disagree, 7 = completely agree), respondents are less likely to use the extreme scale categories. This results in less variable and more peaked response distributions. Weak anchors (1 = generally disagree, 7 = generally agree), in contrast, produce uniform or flat distributions. Procedures have been developed to assign values to category descriptors to result in balanced or equal interval scales.[37]

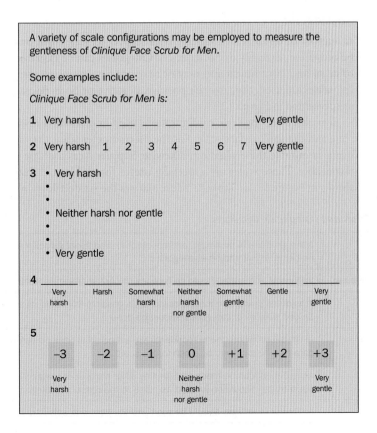

Figure 12.11 Rating scale configurations

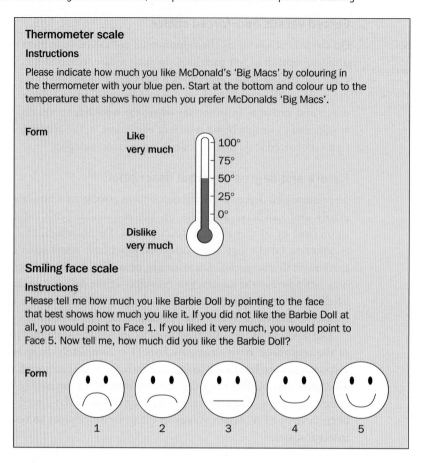

Thermometer scale

Instructions

Please indicate how much you like McDonald's 'Big Macs' by colouring in the thermometer with your blue pen. Start at the bottom and colour up to the temperature that shows how much you prefer McDonalds 'Big Macs'.

Form

Like very much — 100°
75°
50°
25°
0°
Dislike very much

Smiling face scale

Instructions

Please tell me how much you like Barbie Doll by pointing to the face that best shows how much you like it. If you did not like the Barbie Doll at all, you would point to Face 1. If you liked it very much, you would point to Face 5. Now tell me, how much did you like the Barbie Doll?

Form

1 2 3 4 5

Figure 12.12
Some unique rating scale configurations

Physical form of the scale

A number of options are available with respect to scale form or configuration. Scales can be presented vertically or horizontally. Categories can be expressed by boxes, discrete lines or units on a continuum and may or may not have numbers assigned to them. If numerical values are used, they may be positive, negative or both. Several possible configurations are presented in Figure 12.11.

Two unique rating scale configurations used in marketing research are the thermometer scale and the smiling face scale. For the thermometer scale, the higher the temperature, the more favourable the evaluation. Likewise, happier faces indicate evaluations that are more favourable. These scales are especially useful for children.[38] Examples of these scales are shown in Figure 12.12. Table 12.5 summarises the six decisions in designing rating scales.

Table 12.5 Summary of itemised rating scale decisions

1	Number of categories	Although there is no single, optimal number, traditional guidelines suggest that there should be between five and nine categories
2	Balanced versus unbalanced	In general, the scale should be balanced to obtain objective data
3	Odd or even number of categories	If a neutral or indifferent scale response is possible from at least some of the respondents, an odd number of categories should be used
4	Forced versus unforced	In situations where the respondents are expected to have no opinion, the accuracy of the data may be improved by a non-forced scale
5	Verbal description	An argument can be made for labelling all or many scale categories. The category descriptions should be located as close to the response categories as possible
6	Physical form	A number of options should be tried and the best one selected

The development and evaluation of scales

The development of multi-item rating scales requires considerable technical expertise.[39] Figure 12.13 presents a sequence of operations needed to construct multi-item scales.

The characteristic to be measured is frequently called a construct. Scale development begins with an underlying theory of the construct being measured. Theory is necessary not only for constructing the scale but also for interpreting the resulting scores. The next step is to generate an initial pool of scale items. Typically, this is based on theory, analysis of secondary data and qualitative research. From this pool, a reduced set of potential scale items is generated by the judgement of the researcher and other knowledgeable individuals. Some qualitative criterion is adopted to aid their judgement. The reduced set of items may still be too large to constitute a scale. Thus, further reduction is achieved in a quantitative manner.

Data are collected on the reduced set of potential scale items from a large pretest sample of respondents. The data are analysed using techniques such as correlations, factor analysis, cluster analysis, discriminant analysis and statistical tests discussed later in this book. As a result of these statistical analyses, several more items are eliminated, resulting in a purified scale. The purified scale is evaluated for reliability and validity by collecting more data from a different sample (these concepts will be explained on pages 357–359). On the basis of these assessments, a final set of scale items is selected. As can be seen from Figure 12.13, the scale development process is an iterative one with several feedback loops.[40]

A multi-item scale should be evaluated for accuracy and applicability.[41] As shown in Figure 12.14, this involves an assessment of reliability, validity and generalisability of the scale. Approaches to assessing reliability include test–retest reliability, alternative-forms

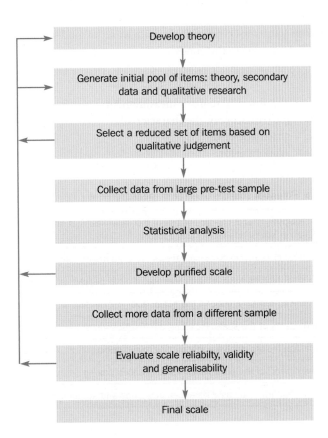

Figure 12.13
Development of a multi-item scale

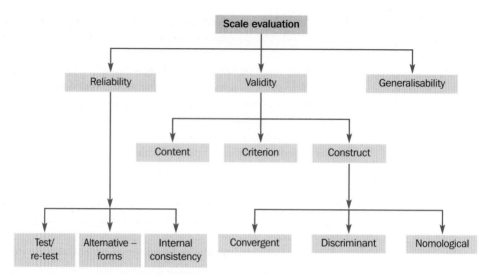

Figure 12.14
Scale evaluation

reliability and internal consistency reliability. Validity can be assessed by examining content validity, criterion validity and construct validity.

Before we can examine reliability and validity we need an understanding of measurement accuracy; it is fundamental to scale evaluation.

Measurement accuracy

A measurement is a number that reflects some characteristic of an object. A measurement is not the true value of the characteristic of interest but rather an observation of it. A variety of factors can cause **measurement error**, which results in the measurement or observed score being different from the true score of the characteristic being measured (see Table 12.6).

Measurement error
The variation in the information sought by the researcher and the information generated by the measurement process employed.

The **true score model** provides a framework for understanding the accuracy of measurement.[42] According to this model,

$$X_O = X_T + X_S + X_R$$

True score model
A mathematical model that provides a framework for understanding the accuracy of measurement.

where X_O = the observed score or measurement
X_T = the true score of the characteristic
X_S = systematic error
X_R = random error

Table 12.6 Potential sources of error in measurement

1	Other relatively stable characteristics of the individual that influence the test score, such as intelligence, social desirability and education
2	Short-term or transient personal factors, such as health, emotions and fatigue
3	Situational factors, such as the presence of other people, noise and distractions
4	Sampling of items included in the scale: addition, deletion or changes in the scale items
5	Lack of clarity of the scale, including the instructions or the items themselves
6	Mechanical factors, such as poor printing, overcrowding items in the questionnaire and poor design
7	Administration of the scale, such as differences among interviewers
8	Analysis factors, such as differences in scoring and statistical analysis

Note that the total measurement error includes the systematic error, X_S, and the random error, X_R. **Systematic error** affects the measurement in a constant way. It represents stable factors that affect the observed score in the same way each time the measurement is made, such as mechanical factors (see Table 12.6). **Random error**, on the other hand, is not constant. It represents transient factors that affect the observed score in different ways each time the measurement is made, such as short-term transient personal factors or situational factors (see Table 12.6). The distinction between systematic and random error is crucial to our understanding of reliability and validity.

Reliability

Reliability refers to the extent to which a scale produces consistent results if repeated measurements are made.[43] Systematic sources of error do not have an adverse impact on reliability, because they affect the measurement in a constant way and do not lead to inconsistency. In contrast, random error produces inconsistency, leading to lower reliability. Reliability can be defined as the extent to which measures are free from random error, X_R. If $X_R = 0$, the measure is perfectly reliable.

Reliability is assessed by determining the proportion of systematic variation in a scale. This is done by determining the association between scores obtained from different administrations of the scale. If the association is high, the scale yields consistent results and is therefore reliable. Approaches for assessing reliability include the test–retest, alternative-forms and internal consistency methods.

In **test–retest reliability**, respondents are administered identical sets of scale items at two different times, under as nearly equivalent conditions as possible. The time interval between tests or administrations is typically two to four weeks. The degree of similarity between the two measurements is determined by computing a correlation coefficient (see Chapter 20). The higher the correlation coefficient, the greater the reliability.

Several problems are associated with the test–retest approach to determining reliability. First, it is sensitive to the time interval between testing. Other things being equal, the longer the time interval, the lower the reliability. Second, the initial measurement may alter the characteristic being measured. For example, measuring respondents' attitude towards low-alcohol beer may cause them to become more health conscious and to develop a more positive attitude towards low-alcohol beer. Third, it may be impossible to make repeated measurements (e.g. the research topic may be the respondent's initial reaction to a new product). Fourth, the first measurement may have a carryover effect to the second or subsequent measurements. Respondents may attempt to remember answers they gave the first time. Fifth, the characteristic being measured may change between measurements. For example, favourable information about an object between measurements may make a respondent's attitude more positive. Finally, the test–retest reliability coefficient can be inflated by the correlation of each item with itself. These correlations tend to be higher than correlations between different scale items across administrations. Hence, it is possible to have high test–retest correlations because of the high correlations between the same scale items measured at different times even though the correlations between different scale items are quite low. Because of these problems, a test–retest approach is best applied in conjunction with other approaches, such as alternative-forms reliability.[44]

In **alternative-forms reliability**, two equivalent forms of the scale are constructed. The same respondents are measured at two different times, usually two to four weeks apart (e.g. by initially using Likert scaled items and then using Stapel scaled items). The scores from the administrations of the alternative scale forms are correlated to assess reliability.[45]

The two forms should be equivalent with respect to content, i.e. each scale item should attempt to measure the same items. The main problems with this approach are that it is difficult, time consuming and expensive to construct an equivalent form of the scale. In a

---

Systematic error
An error that affects the measurement in a constant way and represents stable factors that affect the observed score in the same way each time the measurement is made.

Random error
An error that arises from random changes or differences in respondents or measurement situations.

Reliability
The extent to which a scale produces consistent results if repeated measurements are made on the characteristic.

Test–retest reliability
An approach for assessing reliability, in which respondents are administered identical sets of scale items at two different times, under as nearly equivalent conditions as possible.

Alternative-forms reliability
An approach for assessing reliability that requires two equivalent forms of the scale to be constructed and then the same respondents to be measured at two different times.

strict sense, it is required that the alternative sets of scale items should have the same means, variances and intercorrelations. Even if these conditions are satisfied, the two forms may not be equivalent in content. Thus, a low correlation may reflect either an unreliable scale or non-equivalent forms.

Internal consistency reliability

An approach for assessing the internal consistency of a set of items, where several items are summated in order to form a total score for the scale.

Split-half reliability

A form of internal consistency reliability in which the items constituting the scale are divided into two halves and the resulting half scores are correlated.

Coefficient alpha

A measure of internal consistency reliability that is the average of all possible split-half coefficients resulting from different splittings of the scale items.

Internal consistency reliability is used to assess the reliability of a summated scale where several items are summed to form a total score. In a scale of this type, each item measures some aspect of the construct measured by the entire scale, and the items should be consistent in what they indicate about the construct. This measure of reliability focuses on the internal consistency of the set of items forming the scale.

The simplest measure of internal consistency is **split-half reliability**. The items on the scale are divided into two halves and the resulting half scores are correlated. High correlations between the halves indicate high internal consistency. The scale items can be split into halves based on odd- and even-numbered items or randomly. The problem is that the results will depend on how the scale items are split. A popular approach to overcoming this problem is to use the coefficient alpha.

The **coefficient alpha**, or Cronbach's alpha, is the average of all possible split-half coefficients resulting from different ways of splitting the scale items.[46] This coefficient varies from 0 to 1, and a value of 0.6 or less generally indicates unsatisfactory internal consistency reliability. An important property of coefficient alpha is that its value tends to increase with an increase in the number of scale items.[47] Therefore, coefficient alpha may be artificially, and inappropriately, inflated by including several redundant scale items. Another coefficient that can be employed in conjunction with coefficient alpha is coefficient beta. Coefficient beta assists in determining whether the averaging process used in calculating coefficient alpha is masking any inconsistent items.

Some multi-item scales include several sets of items designed to measure different aspects of a multidimensional construct. For example, car manufacturer image is a multidimensional construct that includes country of origin, range of cars, quality of cars, car performance, service of car dealers, credit terms, dealer location and physical layout of dealerships. Hence, a scale designed to measure car manufacturer image could contain items measuring each of these dimensions. Because these dimensions are somewhat independent, a measure of internal consistency computed across dimensions would be inappropriate. If several items are used to measure each dimension, however, internal consistency reliability can be computed for each dimension.

Validity

Validity

The extent to which a measurement represents characteristics that exist in the phenomenon under investigation.

The **validity** of a scale may be considered as the extent to which differences in observed scale scores reflect true differences among objects on the characteristic being measured, rather than systematic or random error. Perfect validity requires that there be no measurement error ($X_O = X_T$, $X_R = 0$, $X_S = 0$). Researchers may assess content validity, criterion validity or construct validity.[48]

Content validity

A type of validity, sometimes called face validity, that consists of a subjective but systematic evaluation of the representativeness of the content of a scale for the measuring task at hand.

Content validity, sometimes called face validity, is a subjective but systematic evaluation of how well the content of a scale represents the measurement task at hand. The researcher or someone else examines whether the scale items adequately cover the entire domain of the construct being measured. Thus, a scale designed to measure car manufacturer image would be considered inadequate if it omitted any of the major dimensions (country of origin, range of cars, quality of cars, car performance, etc.). Given its subjective nature, content validity alone is not a sufficient measure of the validity of a scale, yet it aids in a common-sense interpretation of the scale scores. A more formal evaluation can be obtained by examining criterion validity.

Criterion validity

A type of validity that examines whether the measurement scale performs as expected in relation to other selected variables as meaningful criteria.

Criterion validity reflects whether a scale performs as expected in relation to other selected variables (criterion variables) as meaningful criteria. If, for example, a scale is designed to measure loyalty in customers, criterion validity might be determined by comparing the results generated by this scale with results generated by observing the extent of repeat purchasing. Based on the time period involved, criterion validity can take two forms, concurrent validity and predictive validity.

Concurrent validity is assessed when the data on the scale being evaluated (e.g. loyalty scale) and the criterion variables (e.g. repeat purchasing) are collected at the same time. The scale being developed and the alternative means of encapsulating the criterion variables would be administered simultaneously and the results compared.

Predictive validity is concerned with how well a scale can forecast a future criterion. To assess predictive validity, the researcher collects data on the scale at one point in time and data on the criterion variables at a future time. For example, attitudes towards how loyal customers feel to a particular brand could be used to predict future repeat purchases of that brand. The predicted and actual purchases are compared to assess the predictive validity of the attitudinal scale.

Construct validity addresses the question of what construct or characteristic the scale is, in fact, measuring. When assessing construct validity, the researcher attempts to answer theoretical questions about why the scale works and what deductions can be made concerning the underlying theory. Thus, construct validity requires a sound theory of the nature of the construct being measured and how it relates to other constructs. Construct validity is the most sophisticated and difficult type of validity to establish. As Figure 12.14 shows, construct validity includes convergent, discriminant and nomological validity.

Convergent validity is the extent to which the scale correlates positively with other measurements of the same construct. It is not necessary that all these measurements be obtained by using conventional scaling techniques. **Discriminant validity** is the extent to which a measure does not correlate with other constructs from which it is supposed to differ. It involves demonstrating a lack of correlation among differing constructs. **Nomological validity** is the extent to which the scale correlates in theoretically predicted ways with measures of different but related constructs. A theoretical model is formulated that leads to further deductions, tests and inferences.

An instance of construct validity can be evaluated in the following example. A researcher seeks to provide evidence of construct validity in a multi-item scale, designed to measure the concept of 'self-image'. These findings would be sought:[49]

- High correlations with other scales designed to measure self-concepts and with reported classifications by friends (convergent validity).
- Low correlations with unrelated constructs of brand loyalty and variety seeking (discriminant validity).
- Brands that are congruent with the individual's self-concept are more preferred, as postulated by the theory (nomological validity).
- A high level of reliability.

Note that a high level of reliability was included as evidence of construct validity in this example. This illustrates the relationship between reliability and validity.

Relationship between reliability and validity

The relationship between reliability and validity can be understood in terms of the true score model. If a measure is perfectly valid, it is also perfectly reliable. In this case, $X_O = X_T$, $X_R = 0$ and $X_S = 0$. Thus, perfect validity implies perfect reliability. If a measure is unreliable, it cannot be perfectly valid, since at a minimum $X_O = X_T + X_R$. Furthermore, systematic error may also be present, i.e., $X_S \neq 0$. Thus, unreliability implies invalidity. If a measure is perfectly reliable, it may or may not be perfectly valid, because systematic error may still be present ($X_O = X_T + X_S$). In other words, a reliable scale can be constructed to measure 'customer loyalty' but it may not necessarily be a valid measurement of 'customer loyalty'. Conversely, a valid measurement of 'customer loyalty' has to be reliable. Reliability is a necessary, but not sufficient, condition for validity.

Concurrent validity
A type of validity that is assessed when the data on the scale being evaluated and on the criterion variables are collected at the same time.

Predictive validity
A type of validity that is concerned with how well a scale can forecast a future criterion.

Construct validity
A type of validity that addresses the question of what construct or characteristic the scale is measuring. An attempt is made to answer theoretical questions of why a scale works and what deductions can be made concerning the theory underlying the scale.

Convergent validity
A measure of construct validity that measures the extent to which the scale correlates positively with other measures of the same construct.

Discriminant validity
A type of construct validity that assesses the extent to which a measure does not correlate with other constructs from which it is supposed to differ.

Nomological validity
A type of validity that assesses the relationship between theoretical constructs. It seeks to confirm significant correlations between the constructs as predicted by a theory.

Generalisability

Generalisability refers to the extent to which one can generalise from the observations at hand to a universe of generalisations. The set of all conditions of measurement over which the investigator wishes to generalise is the universe of generalisation. These conditions may include items, interviewers and situations of observation. A researcher may wish to generalise a scale developed for use in personal interviews to other modes of data collection, such as mail and telephone interviews. Likewise, one may wish to generalise from a sample of items to the universe of items, from a sample of times of measurement to the universe of times of measurement, from a sample of observers to a universe of observers, and so on.[50]

Generalisability
The degree to which a study based on a sample applies to the population as a whole.

In generalisability studies, measurement procedures are designed to investigate each universe of interest by sampling conditions of measurement from each of them. For each universe of interest, an aspect of measurement called a facet is included in the study. Traditional reliability methods can be viewed as single-facet generalisability studies. A test–retest correlation is concerned with whether scores obtained from a measurement scale are generalisable to the universe scores across all times of possible measurement. Even if the test–retest correlation is high, nothing can be said about the generalisability of the scale to other universes. To generalise to other universes, generalisability theory procedures must be employed.

Choosing a scaling technique

In addition to theoretical considerations and evaluation of reliability and validity, certain practical factors should be considered in selecting scaling techniques for a particular marketing research problem.[51] Selecting an appropriate rating scale is a necessary first step in developing a good measurement instrument; establishing statistical reliability and validity through a multi-step testing and retesting process should be accorded the highest priority in selecting a scale. A good rating scale should have the following characteristics:[52]

- Minimal response bias
- Respondent interpretation and understanding
- Discriminating power
- Ease of administration
- Ease of use by respondents
- Credibility and usefulness of results.

As a general rule, using the scaling technique that will yield the highest level of information feasible in a given situation will permit using the greatest variety of statistical analyses. Also, regardless of the type of scale used, whenever feasible, several scale items should measure the characteristic of interest. This provides more accurate measurement than a single-item scale. In many situations, it is desirable to use more than one scaling technique or to obtain additional measures using mathematically derived scales.

Mathematically derived scales

All the scaling techniques discussed in this chapter require the respondents to evaluate directly the constructs that the researcher believes to comprise the object of study, e.g. the cognitive state of customer satisfaction. In contrast, mathematical scaling techniques allow researchers to infer respondents' evaluations of the constructs of the object of study. These evaluations are inferred from the respondents' overall judgements. Two popular mathematically derived scaling techniques are multidimensional scaling and conjoint analysis, which are discussed in detail in Chapter 24.

International marketing research

In designing the scale or response format, respondents' educational or literacy levels should be taken into account.[53] One approach is to develop scales that are pan-cultural, or free of cultural biases. Of the scaling techniques we have considered, the semantic differential scale may be said to be pan-cultural. It has been tested in a number of countries and has consistently produced similar results. The consistency of results occurred in the following example where Xerox successfully used a Russian translation of an equivalent English semantic differential scale.

Example Copying the name Xerox[54]

Xerox was a name well received in the former Soviet Union since the late 1960s. In fact, the act of copying documents was called Xeroxing, a term coined after the name of the company. It was a brand name people equated with quality. With the disintegration of the Soviet Union into the Commonwealth of Independent States, however, Xerox's sales started to fall. The management initially considered this problem to be the intense competition with strong competitors such as Canon, Ricoh, Mitsubishi and Minolta. First attempts to make the product more competitive did not help. Subsequently, marketing research was undertaken to measure the image of Xerox and its competitors in Russia. Semantic differential scales were used, as examples of this type of scale translated well in other countries and were thus considered pan-cultural. The bipolar labels used were carefully tested to ensure that they had the intended semantic meaning in the Russian context.

The results of the study revealed that the real problem was a growing negative perception of Russian customers toward Xerox products. What could have gone wrong? The problem was not with Xerox, but with several independent producers of copying machines that had illegally infringed Xerox's trademark rights. With the disintegration of the Soviet Union, the protection of these trademarks was unclear and trademark infringement kept growing. As a result, customers developed a misconception that Xerox was selling low-quality products.

Although the semantic differential worked well in the Russian context, an alternative approach is to develop scales that use a self-defined cultural norm as a base referent. For example, respondents may be required to indicate their own anchor point and position relative to a culture-specific stimulus set. This approach is useful for measuring attitudes that are defined relative to cultural norms (e.g. attitude towards marital roles). In developing response formats, verbal rating scales appear to be the most suitable. Even less educated respondents can readily understand and respond to verbal scales. Special attention should be devoted to determining equivalent verbal descriptors in different languages and cultures. The end points of the scale are particularly prone to different interpretations. In some cultures, 1 may be interpreted as best, whereas in others it may be interpreted as worst, regardless of how it is scaled. It is important that the scale end points and the verbal descriptors be employed in a manner consistent with the culture.

Finally, in international marketing research, it is critical to establish the equivalence of scales and measures used to obtain data from different countries. This topic is complex and is discussed in some detail in Chapter 26.

Ethics in marketing research

Researchers should not bias scales so as to slant the findings in any particular direction. This is easy to do by biasing the wording of statements (Likert-type scales), the scale descriptors or other aspects of the scales. Consider, for example, the use of scale descriptors. The descriptors used to frame a scale can be manipulated to bias results in any direction. They can be manipulated to generate a positive view of the client's brand or a negative view of a competitor's brand. A researcher who wants to project the client's brand favourably can ask respondents to indicate their opinion of the brand on several attributes using seven-point scales framed by the descriptors 'extremely poor' to 'good'. Using a strongly negative descriptor with only a mildly positive one has an interesting effect. As long as the product is not the worst, respondents will be reluctant to rate the product extremely poorly. In fact, respondents who believe the product to be only mediocre will end up responding favourably. Try this yourself. How would you rate BMW cars on the following attributes?

Reliability	Horrible	1	2	3	4	5	6	7	Good
Performance	Very poor	1	2	3	4	5	6	7	Good
Quality	One of the worst	1	2	3	4	5	6	7	Good
Prestige	Very low	1	2	3	4	5	6	7	Good

Did you find yourself rating BMW cars positively? Using this same technique, a researcher can negatively bias evaluations of competitors' products by providing a mildly negative descriptor (somewhat poor) against a strong positive descriptor (extremely good).

Thus we see how important it is to use balanced scales with comparable positive and negative descriptors. When this guide is not practised, responses are biased and should be interpreted accordingly. This concern also underscores the need to establish adequately the reliability, validity and generalisability of scales before using them in a research project. Scales that are invalid, unreliable or not generalisable to the target market provide the client with flawed results and misleading findings, thus raising serious ethical issues. The researcher has a responsibility to both the client and respondents to ensure the applicability and usefulness of the scale.

Internet and computer applications

All the primary scales of measurement that we have considered can be implemented on the Internet. The same is true for the commonly used comparative scales. Paired comparisons involving verbal, visual or auditory comparisons can be implemented with ease. However, taste, smell and touch comparisons are difficult to implement. It may also be difficult to implement specialised scales such as the Q-sort. The process of implementing comparative scales may be facilitated by searching the Internet for similar scales that have been implemented by other researchers.

Continuous rating scales may be easily implemented on the Internet. The cursor can be moved on the screen in a continuous fashion to select the exact position on the scale that best describes the respondent's evaluation. Moreover, the scale values can be automatically scored by the computer, thus increasing the speed and accuracy of processing the data.

Similarly, it is also easy to implement all of the three itemised rating scales on the Internet. Again, you can use the Internet to search for and locate cases and examples where scales have been used by other researchers. It is also possible that other researchers have reported reliability and validity assessments for multi-item scales. Before generating new scales, a researcher should first examine similar scales used by other researchers and consider using them if they meet the measurement objectives. The following example illustrates how Domino's Pizza uses the Internet to conduct customer surveys and uses the full range of scale types.

Example
Primary scales help Domino's to become a primary competitor[55]

Domino's Pizza builds websites to communicate its image and give information on its products. It also sees its website as a medium to collect information on customers and therefore conduct marketing research. Although no pizza is sold online, the company has a main website (**www.dominos.com**) in addition to websites for its local subsidiaries. For local subsidiaries, the customer is asked to fill in a comment form on the website. This survey helps the local team better to understand its customers' needs and better service them. Different scales are utilised to obtain the following information:

- Name, phone number, email address (nominal scale).
- Preference for pizza restaurants in the local area (ordinal scale).
- Impressions on the service offered by Domino's Pizza as a whole (interval scale).
- Assessments on the products and price (interval scale).
- Customer satisfaction (interval scale).
- Amount spent on pizza and fast foods (ratio scale).

This enables the company to measure customer satisfaction and to use that information for a variety of purposes, including linking it to employee salaries.

Summary

Measurement is the assignment of numbers or other symbols to characteristics of objects according to set rules. Scaling involves the generation of a continuum upon which measured objects are located. The four primary scales of measurement are nominal, ordinal, interval and ratio. Of these, the nominal scale is the most basic in that the numbers are used only for identifying or classifying objects. In the ordinal scale, the numbers indicate the relative position of the objects but not the magnitude of difference between them. The interval scale permits a comparison of the differences between the objects. Because it has an arbitrary zero point, however, it is not meaningful to calculate ratios of scale values on an interval scale. The highest level of measurement is represented by the ratio scale in which the zero point is fixed. The researcher can compute ratios of scale values using this scale. The ratio scale incorporates all the properties of the lower level scales.

Scaling techniques can be classified as comparative or non-comparative. Comparative scaling involves a direct comparison of stimulus objects. Comparative scales include paired comparisons, rank order, constant sum and the Q-sort. The data obtained by these procedures have only ordinal properties. Verbal protocols, where the respondent is instructed to think out loud, can be used for measuring cognitive responses.

In non-comparative scaling, each object is scaled independently of the other objects in the stimulus set. The resulting data are generally assumed to be interval or ratio scaled. Non-comparative rating scales can be either continuous or itemised. The itemised rating scales are further classified as Likert, semantic differential or Stapel scales. When using non-comparative itemised rating scales, the researcher must decide on the number of scale categories, balanced versus unbalanced scales, an odd or even number of categories, forced versus non-forced choices, the nature and degree of verbal description, and the physical form or configuration.

Multi-item scales consist of a number of rating scale items. These scales should be evaluated in terms of reliability and validity. Reliability refers to the extent to which a scale produces consistent results if repeated measurements are made. Approaches to assessing reliability include test–retest, alternative forms and internal consistency. The validity of a measurement may be assessed by evaluating content validity, criterion validity and construct validity.

The choice of particular scaling techniques in a given situation should be based on theoretical and practical considerations. Generally, the scaling technique used should be the one that will yield the highest level of information feasible. Also, multiple measures should be obtained.

In international marketing research, special attention should be devoted to determining equivalent verbal descriptors in different languages and cultures. The misuse of scale descriptors also raises serious ethical concerns. The researcher has a responsibility to both the client and respondents to ensure the applicability and usefulness of scales.

Questions

1 What is measurement?

2 Highlight any marketing phenomena that you feel may be problematic in terms of assigning numbers to characteristics of those phenomena.

3 Describe and illustrate, with examples, the differences between a nominal and an ordinal scale.

4 What are the advantages of a ratio scale over an interval scale? Are these advantages significant?

5 What is a comparative rating scale?

6 What is a paired comparison? What are the advantages and disadvantages of paired comparison scaling?

7 Describe the constant sum scale. How is it different from the other comparative rating scales?

8 Identify the type of scale (nominal, ordinal, interval or ratio) used in each of the following. Give reasons for your choice.

a I like to listen to the radio when I am revising for exams

Disagree   Agree
 1   2   3   4   5

b How old are you? _____

c Rank the following activities in terms of your preference by assigning a rank from 1 to 5 (1 = most preferred, 2 = second most preferred, etc.):
(i) Reading magazines.
(ii) Watching television.
(iii) Going to the cinema.
(iv) Shopping for clothes.
(v) Eating out.

d What is your university/college registration number? _____

e   In an average weekday, how much time do you spend doing class assignments?
  (i)   Less than 15 minutes
  (ii) 15 to 30 minutes
  (iii) 31 to 60 minutes
  (iv) 61 to 120 minutes
  (v)   More than 120 minutes.

f   How much money did you spend last week in the Student Union Bar? _____

9   Describe the semantic differential scale and the Likert scale. For what purposes are these scales used?

10 What are the major decisions involved in constructing an itemised rating scale? How many scale categories should be used in an itemised rating scale? Why?

11 Should an odd or even number of categories be used in an itemised rating scale?

12 How does the nature and degree of verbal description affect the response to itemised rating scales?

13 What is reliability? What are the differences between test–retest and alternative-forms reliability?

14 What is validity? What is criterion validity? How is it assessed?

15 How would you select a particular scaling technique?

Exercises

1   You work in the marketing research department of a firm specialising in decision support systems for the health care industry. Your firm would like to measure the attitudes of hospital administrators towards decision support systems produced by your firm and its main competitors. The attitudes would be measured using a telephone survey. You have been asked to develop an appropriate scale for this purpose. You have also been asked to explain and justify your reasoning in constructing this scale.

2   Develop three comparative (paired comparison, rank order and constant sum) scales to measure attitude towards five popular brands of beer (e.g. Heineken, Guinness, Carlsberg, Stella and Holsten). Administer each scale to five students. No student should be administered more than one scale. Note the time it takes each student to respond. Which scale was the easiest to administer? Which scale took the shortest time?

3   Develop a constant sum scale to determine preferences for restaurants. Administer this scale to a pilot sample of 20 students to determine their preferences for some of the popular restaurants in your town or city. Based on your pilot, evaluate the efficacy of the scale items you chose, and design new scale items that could be used for a full survey.

4   Design Likert scales to measure the usefulness of Renault's website. Visit the site at (**www.renault.com**) and rate it on the scales that you have developed. After your site visit, were there any aspects of usefulness that you had not considered in devising your scales, what were they and why were they not apparent before you made your site visit?

5   In a small group discuss the following issues: 'A brand could receive the highest median rank on a rank order scale of all the brands considered and still have poor sales' and 'It really does not matter which scaling technique you use. As long as your measure is reliable, you will get the right results.'

Notes

1   Newell, S. J., 'The development of a scale to measure perceived corporate credibility', *Journal of Business Research* (June 2001), 235; Gofton, K., 'If it moves measure it', *Marketing* (Marketing Technique Supplement) (4 September 1997), 17; Nunnally, J.C., *Psychometric Theory*, 2nd edn (New York: McGraw-Hill, 1978), 3.

2   Subabrata, B.B., 'Corporate environmentalism: the construct and its measurement', *Journal of Business Research* 55 (3) (March 2002), 177; Stevens, S., 'Mathematics, measurement and psychophysics', in Stevens, S. (ed.), *Handbook of Experimental Psychology* (New York: Wiley, 1951).

3   Moshkovich, H.M., 'Ordinal judgments in multiattribute decision analysis,' *European Journal of Operational Research* 137 (3) (16 March 2002), 625; Cook, W.D., Kress, M. and Seiford, L.M., 'On the use of ordinal data in data envelopment analysis', *Journal of the Operational Research Society* 44 (2) (February 1993), 133–140; Barnard, N.R. and Ehrenberg, A.S.C., 'Robust measures of consumer brand beliefs', *Journal of*

Marketing Research 27 (November 1990), 477–484; Perreault, W.D. Jr. and Young, F.W., 'Alternating least squares optimal scaling: analysis of nonmetric data in marketing research', *Journal of Marketing Research* 17 (February 1980), 1–13.

4　Halme, M., 'Dealing with interval scale data in data envelopment analysis', *European Journal of Operational Research* 137 (1) (February 16, 2002), 22; Lynn, M. and Harriss, J., 'The desire for unique consumer products: a new individual difference scale', *Psychology and Marketing* 14 (6) (September 1997), 601–616.

5　For a discussion of these scales, refer to Miller, D.C., and Salkind, N.J., *Handbook of Research Design and Social Measurement*, 6th edn (Thousand Oaks, CA: Sage, 2002); Taiwo, A., 'Overall evaluation rating scales: an assessment', *International Journal of Market Research* (Summer 2000), 301–311; Coombs, C.H., 'Theory and methods of social measurement', in Festinger, L. and Katz, D. (eds), *Research Methods in the Behavioral Sciences* (New York: Holt, Rinehart & Winston, 1953).

6　Bastell, R.R. and Wind, Y., 'Product development: current methods and needed developments', *Journal of the Market Research Society* 8 (1980), 122–126.

7　There is, however, some controversy regarding this issue. See Campbell, D. T. and Russo, M.J., *Social Measurement* (Thousand Oaks, CA: Sage, 2001); Amoo, T., 'Do the numeric values influence subjects' responses to rating scales?', *Journal of International Marketing and Marketing Research* (February 2001), 41; Kang, M. and Stam, A., 'PAHAP: a pairwise aggregated hierarchical analysis of ratio-scale preferences', *Decision Sciences* 25 (4) (July/August 1994), 607–624.

8　Kellogg, D.L. and Chase, R.B., 'Constructing an empirically derived measure for customer contact', *Management Science* 41 (11) (November 1995), 1734–1749; Corfman, K.P., 'Comparability and comparison levels used in choices among consumer products', Journal of Marketing Research 28 (August 1991), 368–374.

9　Anon., 'Competition between Coca-Cola and Pepsi to start,' *Asiainfo Daily China News* (19 March 2002), 1; Rickard, L., 'Remembering New Coke', *Advertising Age* 66 (16) (17 April 1995), 6; 'Coke's flip-flop underscores risks of consumer taste tests', *Wall Street Journal* (18 July 1985), 25.

10　It is not necessary to evaluate all possible pairs of objects, however. Procedures such as cyclic designs can significantly reduce the number of pairs evaluated. A treatment of such procedures may be found in Bemmaor, A.C. and Wagner, U., 'A multiple-item model of paired comparisons: separating chance from latent performance', *Journal of Marketing Research* 37 (4) (November 2000), 514–524; Malhotra, N.K., Jain, A.K. and Pinson, C., 'The robustness of MDS configurations in the case of incomplete data', *Journal of Marketing Research* 25 (February 1988), 95–102.

11　For an advanced application involving paired comparison data, see Bemmaor, A.C. and Wagner, U., 'A multiple-item model of paired comparisons: separating chance from latent performance', *Journal of Marketing Research* 37 (4) (November 2000), 514–524; Genest, C. and Zhang, S.S., 'A graphical analysis of ratio-scaled paired comparison data', *Management Science* 42 (3) (March 1996), 335–349.

12　Campbell, D. T. and Russo, M.J., *Social Measurement* (Thousand Oaks, CA: Sage, 2001); Likert, R., Roslow, S. and Murphy, G., 'A simple and reliable method of scoring the Thurstone Attitude Scales', *Personnel Psychology* 46 (3) (Autumn 1993), 689–690; Thurstone, L.L., *The Measurement of Values* (Chicago: University of Chicago Press, 1959). For an

application of the case V procedure, see Malhotra, N.K., 'Marketing linen services to hospitals: a conceptual framework and an empirical investigation using Thurstone's case V analysis', *Journal of Health Care Marketing* 6 (March 1986), 43–50.

13　Daniles, E. and Lawford, J., 'The effect of order in the presentation of samples in paired comparison tests', *Journal of the Market Research Society* 16 (April 1974), 127–133.

14　Anon., 'Cranberry juice in a can', *Grocer* 225 (7538) (26 January 2002), 64; The Beverage Network, **www.bevnet.com**.

15　Bottomley, P.A., 'Testing the reliability of weight elicitation methods: direct rating versus point allocation,' *Journal of Marketing Research* 37 (4) (November 2000), 508–513; Herman, M.W. and Koczkodaj, W.W., 'A Monte Carlo study of pairwise comparison', *Information Processing Letters* 57 (1) (15 January 1996), 25–29.

16　Kerlinger, F., *Foundations of Behavioral Research*, 3rd edn (New York: Holt, Rinehart & Winston, 1973), 583–592.

17　Siciliano, T., 'Magnitude estimation', *Quirk's Marketing Research Review* (November 1999); Noel, N.M. and Nessim, H., 'Benchmarking consumer perceptions of product quality with price: an exploration', *Psychology & Marketing* 13 (6) (September 1996), 591–604; Steenkamp, J.-B. and Wittink, D.R., 'The metric quality of full–profile judgments and the number of attribute levels effect in conjoint analysis', *International Journal of Research in Marketing* 11 (3) (June 1994), 275–286.

18　Hayes, J.R., 'Issues in protocol analysis', in Ungson, G.R. and Braunste, D.N. (eds), *Decision Making: An Interdisciplinary Inquiry* (Boston, MA: Kent, 1982), 61–77.

19　For an application of verbal protocols, see Harrison, D.A., McLaughlin, M.E. and Coalter, T.M., 'Context, cognition and common method variance: psychometric properties and verbal protocol evidence', *Organizational Behavior and Human Decision Process*es 68 (3) (December 1996), 246–261; Gardial, S.F., Clemons, D.S., Woodruff, R.B., Schumann, D.W. and Bums, M.J., 'Comparing consumers' recall of prepurchase and postpurchase product evaluation experiences', *Journal of Consumer Research* 20 (March 1994), 548–560.

20　Mick, D.G., 'Levels of subjective comprehension in advertising processing and their relations to ad perceptions, attitudes, and memory', *Journal of Consumer Research* 18 (March 1992), 411–424; Wright, P.L., 'Cognitive processes mediating acceptance of advertising', *Journal of Marketing Research* 10 (February 1973), 53–62; Wright, P.L., 'Cognitive responses to mass media advocacy and cognitive choice processes', in Petty, R., Ostrum, T. and Brock, T. (eds), *Cognitive Responses to Persuasion* (New York: McGraw-Hill, 1978).

21　Murphy, I.P., 'RAMS helps Best Western tout worldwide positioning', *Marketing News* 31 (1) (6 January 1996), 25.

22　Amoo, T. and Friedman, H.H., 'Overall evaluation rating scales: an assessment,' *International Journal of market Research* 42 (3). (Summer 2000), 301–310; Albaum, G., 'The Likert scale revisited – an alternative version', *Journal of the Market Research Society* 39 (2) (April 1997), 331–348; Brody, C.J. and Dietz, J., 'On the dimensionality of 2-question format Likert attitude scales', *Social Science Research* 26 (2) (June 1997), 197–204; Likert, R., 'A technique for the measurement of attitudes', *Archives of Psychology* 140 (1932).

23　However, when the scale is multidimensional, each dimension should be summed separately. See Stanton, J.M., 'Issues and strategies for reducing the length of self-report scales,' *Personnel Psychology* 55 (1) (Spring 2002), 167–194; Aaker, J.L., 'Dimensions of brand personality', *Journal of Marketing Research* 34 (August 1997), 347–356.

24 Herche, J. and Engelland, B., 'Reversed-polarity items and scale unidimensionality', *Journal of the Academy of Marketing Science* 24 (4) (Fall 1996), 366–374.

25 Sethi, R., Smith, D.C. and Whan Park, C., 'Cross-functional product development teams, creativity and the innovativeness of new consumer products', *Journal of Marketing Research* 38 (1) (February 2001) 73–85; Chandler, T.A. and Spies, C.J., 'Semantic differential comparisons of attributions and dimensions among respondents from 7 nations', *Psychological Reports* 79 (3 pt 1) (December 1996), 747–758.

26 Miller, D.C. and Salkind, N.J., *Handbook of research design and social measurement*, 6th edn. (Thousand Oaks, CA: Sage, 2002); Bearden, W.O. and Netemeyer, R.G., *Handbook of Marketing Scales: Multi-Item measures for marketing and consumer behaviour research* (Thousand Oaks, CA: Sage, 1999), 456–464; Millar, R. and Brotherton, C., 'Measuring the effects of career interviews on young people – a preliminary study', *Psychological Reports* 79 (3 pt 2) (December 1996), 1207–1215.

27 There is little difference in the results based on whether the data are ordinal or interval; however, see Nishisato, S., *Measurement and multivariate analysis* (New York: Springer-Verlag, New York, 2002); Gaiton, J., 'Measurement scales and statistics: resurgence of an old misconception', *Psychological Bulletin* 87 (1980), 567.

28 Ofir, C., 'In search of negative customer feedback: the effect of expecting to evaluate on satisfaction evaluations', *Journal of Marketing Research* (May 2001), 170–182; Reisenwitz, T.H. and Wimbush, G.J., Jr. 'Over-the-counter pharmaceuticals: exploratory research of consumer preferences toward solid oral dosage forms', *Health Marketing Quarterly* 13 (4) (1996), 47–61; Malhotra, S., Van Auken, S. and Lonial, S.C., 'Adjective profiles in television copy testing', *Journal of Advertising Research* (August 1981), 21–25.

29 Brady, M.K., 'Performance only measurement of service quality: a replication and extension', *Journal of Business Research* 55 (1) (January 2002), 17; Stapel, J., 'About 35 years of market research in the Netherlands', *Markonderzock Kwartaalschrift* 2 (1969), 3–7.

30 Hawkins, D.I., Albaum, G. and Best, R., 'Stapel scale or semantic differential in marketing research?', *Journal of Marketing Research* 11 (August 1974), 318–322; Menezes, D. and Elbert, N.E., 'Alternative semantic scaling formats for measuring store image: an evaluation', *Journal of Marketing Research* 16 (February 1979), 80–87.

31 Devellis, R.F., *Scale Development: Theories and Applications* (Thousand Oaks, CA: Sage, 1991); Etzel, M.J., Williams, T.G., Rogers, J.C. and Lincoln, D.J., 'The comparability of three Stapel scale forms in a marketing setting', in Bush, R.F. and Hunt, S.D. (eds) *Marketing Theory: Philosophy of Science Perspectives* (Chicago: American Marketing Association, 1982), 303–306.

32 Anderson, E.W., 'Foundations of the American customer satisfaction index', *Total Quality Management* 11 (7) (September 2000), 5869–5882; Coleman, A.M., Norris, C.E. and Peterson, C.C., 'Comparing rating scales of different lengths – equivalence of scores from 5-point and 7-point scales', *Psychological Reports* 80 (2) (April 1997), 355–362; Viswanathan, M., Bergen, M. and Childers, T., 'Does a single response category in a scale completely capture a response?', *Psychology and Marketing* 13 (5) (August 1996), 457–479; Cox, E.P., III, 'The optimal number of response alternatives for a scale: a review', *Journal of Marketing Research* 17 (November 1980), 407–422.

33 Dodge, Y., 'On asymmetric properties of the correlation coefficient in the regression setting', *The American Statistician* 55

(1) (February 2001), 51–54; Alwin, D.F., 'Feeling thermometers versus 7-point scales – which are better?', *Sociological Methods and Research* 25 (3) (February 1997), 318–340; Givon, M.M. and Shapira, Z., 'Response to rating scales: a theoretical model and its application to the number of categories problem', *Journal of Marketing Research* 21 (November 1984), 410–419; Stem D.E. Jr. and Noazin, S., 'The effects of number of objects and scale positions on graphic position scale reliability', in Lusch, R.E. *et al.*, *1985 AMA Educators' Proceedings* (Chicago, IL: American Marketing Association, 1985), 370–372.

34 Jones, B.S., 'Modeling direction and intensity in semantically balanced ordinal scales: an assessment of Congressional incumbent approval', *American Journal of Political Science* 44 (1) (January 2000), 174; Watson, D., 'Correcting for acquiescent response bias in the absence of a balanced scale – an application to class-consciousness', *Sociological Methods and Research* 21 (1) (August 1992), 52–88; Schuman, H. and Presser, S., *Questions and Answers in Attitude Surveys* (New York: Academic Press, 1981), 179–201.

35 Morrel-Samuels, P., 'Getting the truth into workplace surveys', *Harvard Business Review* 80 (2) (February 2002) 111; and Spagna, G.J., 'Questionnaires: which approach do you use?', *Journal of Advertising Research* (February–March 1984), 67–70.

36 McColl-Kennedy, J., 'Measuring customer satisfaction: why, what and how', *Total Quality Management* 11 (7) (September 2000), 5883–5896; Hasnich, K.A., 'The job descriptive index revisited: questions about the question mark', *Journal of Applied Psychology* 77 (3) (June 1992), 377–382; Schneider, K.C., 'Uninformed response rate in survey research', *Journal of Business Research* (April 1985), 153–162.

37 Amoo, T., 'Do numeric values influence subjects' responses to rating scales?', *Journal of International Marketing and Market Research* (February 2001), 41; Gannon, K.M. and Ostrom, T.M., 'How meaning is given to rating scales – the effects of response language on category activation', *Journal of Experimental Social Psychology* 32 (4) (July 1996), 337–360; Friedman, H.H. and Leefer, J.R., 'Label versus position in rating scales', *Journal of the Academy of Marketing Science* (Spring 1981), 88–92.

38 Alwin, D.F., 'Feeling thermometers versus 7-point scales – which are better?' *Sociological Methods and Research* 25 (3) (February 1997), 318–340.

39 For an example of a multi-item scale, see Brown, T., 'The customer orientation of service workers: personality trait effects on self and supervisor-performance ratings', *Journal of Marketing Research* 39 (1) (February 2002), 110–119; Mathwick, C., Malhotra, N.K. and Ridgon, E., 'Experiential value: conceptualization, measurement and application in the catalog and internet shopping environment,' *Journal of Retailing* 77 (2001), 39–56; Aaker, J.L., 'Dimensions of brand personality', *Journal of Marketing Research* 34 (August 1997), 347–356.

40 For example, see Flynn, L. R. and Pearcy, D., 'Four subtle sins in scale development: some suggestions for strengthening the current paradigm', *International Journal of Market Research* 43 (4) (Fourth Quarter 2001), 409–423; King, M.F., 'Social desirability bias: a neglected aspect of validity testing', *Psychology and Marketing* 17 (2) (February 2000), 79; Singhapakdi, A., Vitell, S.J., Rallapalli, K.C. and Kraft, K.L., 'The perceived role of ethics and social responsibility: a scale development', *Journal of Business Ethics* 15 (11) (November 1996), 1131–1140.

41 Borman, W.C., 'An examination of the comparative reliability, validity and accuracy and performance ratings made using computerised adaptive rating scales', *Journal of Applied*

Psychology 86 (5) (October 2001), 965; Kim, K. and Frazier, G.L., 'Measurement of distributor commitment in industrial channels of distribution', *Journal of Business Research* 40 (2) (October 1997), 139–154; Greenleaf, E.A., 'Improving rating scale measures by detecting and correcting bias components in some response styles', *Journal of Marketing Research* 29 (May 1992), 176–188.

42 The true score model is not the only theory of measurement. See Lord, E.M. and Novick, M.A., *Statistical Theories of Mental Test-Scores* (Reading, MA: Addison-Wesley, 1968).

43 Thompson, B., *Score reliability: Contemporary thinking on reliability issues* (Thousand Oaks, CA: Sage, 2002); Sinha, P., 'Determination of reliability of estimations obtained with survey research: a method of simulation', *International Journal of Market Research* 42 (3) (Summer 2000), 311–317; Wilson, E.J., 'Research design effects on the reliability of rating scales in marketing – an update on Churchill and Peter', *Advances in Consumer Research* 22 (1995), 360–365; Perreault, W.D. Jr and Leigh, L.E., 'Reliability of nominal data based on qualitative judgements', *Journal of Marketing Research* 25 (May 1989), 135–148; Peter, J.P., 'Reliability: a review of psychometric basics and recent marketing practices', *Journal of Marketing Research* 16 (February 1979), 6–17.

44 Campbell, D. T. and Russo, M.J., *Social Measurement* (Thousand Oaks, CA: Sage, 2001); Lam, S.S.K. and Woo, K.S., 'Measuring service quality: a test–re-test reliability investigation of SERVQUAL', *Journal of the Market Research Society* 39 (2) (April 1997), 381–396.

45 Hunt, D., Measurement and scaling in statistics, (London: Edward Arnold, 2001); Armstrong, D., Gosling, A., Weinman, J. and Marteau, T., 'The place of inter-rater reliability in qualitative research: an empirical study', *Sociology: The Journal of the British Sociological Association* 31 (3) (August 1997), 597–606; Segal, M.N., 'Alternate form conjoint reliability', *Journal of Advertising Research* 4 (1984), 31–38.

46 Cronbach, L.J., 'Coefficient alpha and the internal structure of tests', *Psychometrika* 16 (1951), 297–334.

47 Brown, T.J., Mowen, J.C., Donavan, D.T. and Licata, J.W., 'The customer orientation of service workers: personality trait effects on self – and supervisor performance ratings', *Journal of Marketing Research* 39 (1) (February 2002), 110–119; Peterson, R.A., 'A meta-analysis of Cronbach's coefficient alpha', *Journal of Consumer Research* 21 (September 1994), 381–391.

48 Chen, G., 'Validation of a new general self-efficacy scale', *Organizational Research Methods* 4 (1) (January 2001), 62–83; McTavish, D.G., 'Scale validity – a computer content analysis approach', *Social Science Computer Review* 15 (4) (Winter 1997), 379–393; Peter, J.P., 'Construct validity: a review of basic issues and marketing practices', *Journal of Marketing Research* 18 (May 1981), 133–145.

49 For further details on validity, see B. Keillor, 'A cross-cultural/cross national study of influencing factors and socially desirable response biases', *International Journal of Market Research* (1st Quarter 2001), 63–84; Sirgy, M.J., Grewal, D., Mangleburg, T.F., Park, J. *et al.*, 'Assessing the predictive ability of two methods of measuring self-image congruence', *Journal of the Academy of Marketing Science* 25(3) (Summer 1997), 229–241; Spiro, R.L. and Weitz, B.A., 'Adaptive selling: conceptualization, measurement, and nomological validity', *Journal of Marketing Research* 27 (February 1990), 61–69.

50 For a discussion of the generalisability theory and its applications in marketing research, see Middleton, K.L., 'Socially desirable response sets: the impact of country culture,' *Psychology and Marketing* (February 2000), 149; Abe, S., Bagozzi, R.P. and Sadarangani, P., 'An investigation of construct validity and generalizability in the self concept: self consciousness in Japan and the United States', *Journal of International Consumer Marketing* 8 (3,4) (1996), 97–123; Rentz, J.O., 'Generalisability theory: a comprehensive method for assessing and improving the dependability of marketing measures', *Journal of Marketing Research* 24 (February 1987), 19–28.

51 Myers, M., 'Academic insights: an application of multiple-group causal models in assessing cross-cultural measurement equivalence,' *Journal of International Marketing* 8 (4) (2000), 108–121; Hinkin, T.R., 'A review of scale development practices in the study of organisations', *Journal of Management* 21 (5) (1995), 967–988.

52 Devlin, S.J., Dong, H.K. and Brown, M., 'Selecting a scale for measuring quality', *Marketing Research* (Fall 2003), 13–16.

53 Page Fisk, A., 'Using individualism and collectivism to compare cultures – a critique of the validity and measurement of the constructs: Comment on Oyserman', *Psychological Bulletin* 128 (1) (January 2002), 78; Mullen, M.R., Milne, G.R. and Didow, N.M., 'Determining cross-cultural metric equivalence in survey research: a new statistical test', *Advances in International Marketing* 8 (1996), 145–157; Gencturk, E., Childers, T.L. and Ruekert, R.W., 'International marketing involvement – the construct, dimensionality, and measurement', *Journal of International Marketing* 3 (4) (1995), 11–37.

54 Unikel, A.L., 'Imitation might be flattering, but beware of trademark infringement,' *Marketing News* 21 (19) (11 September 1997), 200–221; Mckay, B., 'Xerox fights trademark battle', *Advertising Age International* (27 April 1992), 1–39.

55 Zuber, A., 'Pizza chains top customer satisfaction poll', *Nation's Restaurant News* 36 (9) (4 March 2002), 4–5 and **www.dominos.com**.

Visit the *Marketing Research* Companion Website at www.pearsoned.co.uk/malhotra_euro for additional learning resources including annotated weblinks, an online glossary and a suite of downloadable video cases.

13

Questionnaire design

> *The questionnaire must motivate the respondent to cooperate, become involved, and provide complete, honest and accurate answers.*

Objectives

After reading this chapter, you should be able to:

1 explain the purpose of a questionnaire and its objectives of asking questions that respondents can and will answer, encouraging respondents, and minimising response error;

2 understand the array of trade-offs that have to be made in the total process of questionnaire design;

3 describe the process of designing a questionnaire, the steps involved, and guidelines that must be followed at each step;

4 discuss the considerations involved in designing questionnaires for international marketing research;

5 understand the ethical issues involved in questionnaire design.

STAGE 1
Problem definition

STAGE 2
Research approach developed

STAGE 3
Research design developed

STAGE 4
Fieldwork or data collection

STAGE 5
Data preparation and analysis

STAGE 6
Report preparation and presentation

Overview

This chapter discusses the importance of questionnaires and how marketing researchers must put themselves 'in the shoes' of target respondents in order to design an effective questionnaire. There are no scientific principles that can guarantee an optimal questionnaire; it is more of a craft that is honed through experience. Through experience, questionnaire designers will see that, given the information needs of the decision-makers they support and characteristics of target respondents, they must make a series of trade-offs. These trade-offs are described and illustrated. Next, we describe the objectives of a questionnaire and the steps involved in designing questionnaires. We provide several guidelines for developing sound questionnaires. The considerations involved in designing questionnaires when conducting international marketing research are discussed. The chapter concludes with a discussion of several ethical issues that arise in questionnaire design.

We begin with an example that establishes the main principles of good questionnaire design, i.e. to engage respondents and stimulate their interest. These are vital to providing complete and accurate answers. The second example illustrates how the characteristics of target respondents affect the design and implementation of a questionnaire.

Example

Sugging
The use of marketing research to deliberately disguise a sales effort.

The field-good factor[1]

The lifeblood of the marketing research industry is busy people who are bombarded with database marketing, **sugging** and catalogue distributors. They find it difficult to distinguish them from genuine research interviewers. David Jenkins, Chief Executive of Kantor, says:

The problem is partly self induced in terms of sending out long, boring questionnaires and not respecting the value of people's time. There is a big onus on clients to resist the temptation to squeeze every piece of information they can from one interview. The clients signing off questionnaires do not then subject themselves to the fieldwork reality. We've been good at training our interviewers to get bad questionnaires completed. Once it comes back as data, cleaned up and sanitised, the reality of what has happened in the field and therefore what affects the data quality, never surfaces. The vast bulk of what we try and do in marketing research is ambush people to try and get their opinions for free. This ought to be a transaction. It may not be money but consumers need to get something back for their time. A charitable donation, information, increasingly as we do Internet research you could trade something electronic of value – access to data and the like.

Example

Finding the elusive young through cooperative parents[2]

ACCESS to Youth is a specialist survey that comprises around 1,100 in-home interviews targeted at 7–19 year olds. In surveying this age group it was noted that children become fatigued more quickly than adults, and this could affect data quality. In this project strict controls were placed on the interview length – it did not exceed 10 minutes. Wording was kept simple; complicated questions were avoided. The research showed that the ease with which children were able to answer questions correlated with age. The older they were, the easier they found the question; and the more times they were asked the question, the easier they found it. It was also found that children found it more difficult to understand the traditional four- or five-point agree/disagree scale and so a simplified three-point scale was used. Interviewers should be correctly briefed on how to conduct interviews with children. They need to be patient and must treat the child as an equal – impatience or a condescending manner affects the child's ease and hence influences the answers he or she gives.

Questionnaire definition

As discussed in Chapter 10, survey and observation are the two sets of techniques for obtaining quantitative primary data in descriptive research. Both methods require some procedure for standardising the data collection process so that the data obtained are internally consistent and can be analysed in a uniform and coherent manner. If 40 different interviewers conduct personal interviews or make observations in different parts of the country, the data they collect will not be comparable unless they follow specific guidelines and ask questions and record answers in a standard way. A standardised questionnaire or form will ensure comparability of the data, increase speed and accuracy of recording, and facilitate data processing.

A **questionnaire**, whether it is called a schedule, interview form or measuring instrument, is a formalised set of questions for obtaining information from respondents. Typically, a questionnaire is only one element of a data collection package that might also include (1) fieldwork procedures, such as instructions for selecting, approaching and questioning respondents (see Chapter 16); (2) some reward, gift or payment offered to respondents; and (3) communication aids, such as maps, pictures, advertisements and products (as in personal interviews) and return envelopes (in mail surveys).

Any questionnaire has three specific objectives. First, it must translate the information needed into a set of specific questions that the respondents can and will answer. Developing questions that respondents can and will answer and that will yield the desired information is difficult. Two apparently similar ways of posing a question may yield different information. Hence, this objective is most challenging.

Second, a questionnaire must uplift, motivate and encourage the respondent to become involved, to cooperate, and to complete the task. Figure 13.1 uses a basic marketing model of exchange of values between two parties to illustrate this point. Before designing any questionnaire or indeed any research technique, the researcher must evaluate 'what is the respondent going to get out of this?' In other words, the marketing researcher must have an empathy with target respondents and appreciate what they think when approached and questioned. Such an appreciation of what respondents go through affects the design of how they are approached, the stated purpose of the research, the rewards for taking part and the whole process of questioning and question design.

Questionnaire
A structured technique for data collection consisting of a series of questions, written or verbal, that a respondent answers.

What the respondent may want from the researcher:

- Tangible reward
- Confidentiality
- Interesting subject and experience
- Personal benefits from seeing the research completed
- Social benefits from seeing the research completed
- Being 'chosen' as a respondent with expertise on the subject
- Research organisation known for excellence in research
- Rapport and trust

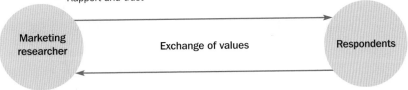

What the researcher wants from respondents:

- Honesty
- Takes in the reason for the study
- Follows the instructions in completing the study
- Thinks through the issues before forming an answer
- Says good things about the rationale for marketing research
- Says good things about the research process

Figure 13.1
Exchange of values between marketing researchers and respondents

371

Not all respondents are the same in what they seek from a questionnaire or interview process. In Figure 13.1, some respondents may want to see some personal benefit, perhaps a tangible reward, while others may be happy to see the social benefits. Taking care in appreciating what respondents expect from the questioning process can nurture responses that have been well thought through, are stated in honesty, and are accurate.

Third, a questionnaire should minimise response error. The potential sources of error in research designs were discussed in Chapter 3, where response error was defined as the error that arises when respondents give inaccurate answers or when their answers are mis-recorded or mis-analysed. A questionnaire can be a major source of response error. Minimising this error is an important objective of questionnaire design.

Questionnaire design process

The great weakness of questionnaire design is a lack of theory. Because there are no scientific principles that guarantee an optimal or ideal questionnaire, questionnaire design is a skill acquired through experience. Similarly, the correct grammatical use of language does not guarantee the optimal questionnaire. There may be certain respondents who do not communicate in a 'correct' grammatical manner; such questionnaires may be confusing and meaningless. Therefore, this section presents guidelines and rules to help develop the craft of questionnaire design. Although these guidelines and rules can help you avoid major mistakes, the fine-tuning of a questionnaire comes from the creativity of a skilled researcher.[3] Developing the craft of questionnaire design requires the creative 'trade-off' of many factors. Figure 13.2 helps to illustrate some of the trade-offs that the questionnaire designer faces and that collectively make the design process problematic.

The design process is founded upon generating information that will effectively support marketing decision-makers. Establishing the nature of marketing problems and corresponding marketing research problems, i.e. defining the nature of effective support, was discussed in Chapter 2. Different techniques and sources of information were outlined to help in the diagnosis process, which feed directly into the stages set out below:

1 The 'source of idea' represents the culmination of marketing decision-maker and marketing researchers' diagnoses and the information they have available at the time of commissioning a marketing research project.

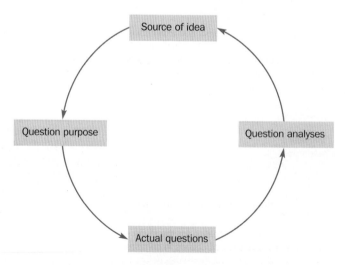

Figure 13.2
Trade-offs faced by the questionnaire designer

2 From the diagnoses, and the statement of marketing and research problems, emerge specific research questions. Based upon the diagnoses, the purpose of each potential question should be established, i.e. 'question purposes'. Some research problems may be tackled through actual measurements in questionnaires. Other research problems may not be tackled by questionnaires.

Example   Establishing question priorities

In a study of pan-European banking practices in Europe, banks wished to know which criteria companies used to choose a bank. Tackling this issue was a straightforward task of establishing criteria and applying scales of importance to these criteria. Banks further wished to know what forces were shaping these criteria and how these forces interacted. The latter issues were qualitative in nature and were captured in follow-up in-depth interviews. In establishing question purposes, priorities had to be set, focusing upon what could be measured using a questionnaire, and out of the array of issues that could be measured, what were seen as the most, down to the least, important.

3 With clear question purposes, the process of establishing 'actual questions' can begin. At this point, the researchers have to put themselves 'in the shoes' of the potential respondent. It is fine to say that certain questions need to be answered, but this has to be balanced with an appreciation of whether respondents are able or indeed willing to answer particular questions, as illustrated in the following example.

Example   Stepping into the shoes of the decision-maker and the respondent

In the study of pan-European banking practices in Europe, a key question focused upon which banks individual companies use in every European country. The purpose of such a question was to establish which banks were gaining market share and to see whether companies were concentrating their business with fewer banks. This seems a straightforward question until one realises the enormity of the task. There were over 20 European countries to concentrate on and in some of them the norm was to conduct business with a large number of banks. In Italy, for example, one company conducted business with 70 banks. Thus, the task of remembering all the banks and writing them down placed an enormous burden on the respondent. Making the question closed by listing all the banks would not help; in Germany, for example, there were over 400 banks that could be listed. The trade-off or final compromise was to ask respondents who their 'lead bank' was, i.e. with whom they did most business. Asking them to name just one bank ensured that the task was not too onerous for them, enabling a more complete and accurate response. The trade-off was that it did not completely satisfy the set question purpose.

4 Deciding how the data collected are to be analysed does not happen when questionnaires have been returned from respondents. 'Question analyses' must be thought through from an early stage. The connections between questions and the appropriate statistical tests that fulfil the question purposes should be established as the questionnaire is designed. Again, trade-offs have to be considered. In Chapter 12, different scale types were linked to different statistical tests. As one progresses from nominal through ordinal to interval and then ratio scales, more sophisticated statistical analyses can be performed. However, as one progresses through these scale types, the task for respondents becomes more onerous. This trade-off can be illustrated again in the following example.

Example   Trading off the respondent task with statistical power

In the study of pan-European banking practices in Europe, companies were asked who they thought were the top four banks in their country (ordinal scale). Respondents were then asked why they thought the top two banks were perceived to be best and second best. This could be completed in a number of ways. A list of characteristics could be given and respondents asked to tick those that they thought matched the bank. This would be easy for respondents to undertake and produce nominal data. The same set of characteristics could be listed with respondents asked to rank-order them. This task requires more thought and effort, though now produces the more powerful ordinal data. The same list could have been presented and respondents asked to allocate 100 points using a constant sum scale. This would have been an even more onerous task but would have produced the more powerful interval scale. The questionnaire designer has to consider how onerous the task is for respondents, especially when set in the context of all the other questions the respondent is being asked, and trade this off against the understanding the designer gets from the data.

5   The understanding that is taken from the data comes back to the 'source of idea'. By now the researcher or questionnaire designers may have collected other data, interpreted existing data differently, or been exposed to new forces in the marketplace. They may even now see what questions they should have been asking!

There can be no theory to encapsulate the trade-offs illustrated in Figure 13.2. Each research project will have different demands and emphases. With the experience of designing a number of questionnaires, the 'craft' of questionnaire design is developed and the balance understood to meet different demands and emphases.

In order to develop a further understanding of questionnaire design, the process will be presented as a series of steps, as shown in Figure 13.3, and we present guidelines for each step. The process outlined in Figure 13.2 shows that in practice the steps are interrelated and the development of a questionnaire involves much iteration and interconnection between stages.[4]

Specify the information needed

The first step in questionnaire design is to specify the information needed. This is also the first step in the research design process. Note that, as the research project progresses, the information needed becomes more and more clearly defined. It is helpful to review the components of the problem and the approach, particularly the research questions, hypotheses and characteristics that influence the research design. To ensure further that the information obtained fully addresses all the components of the problem, the researcher should prepare a set of dummy tables. A dummy table is a blank table used to catalogue data. It portrays how the analysis will be structured once the data have been collected.

It is also vital to have a clear idea of the target respondents. The characteristics of the respondent group have a great influence on questionnaire design. The wording and style of questions that may be appropriate for finance directors being surveyed about their IT needs may not be appropriate for retired persons being surveyed about their holiday needs. The more diversified the respondent group, the more difficult it is to design a single questionnaire appropriate for the entire group.

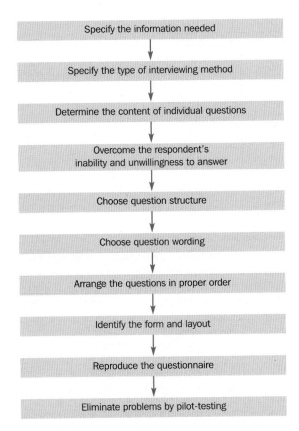

**Figure 13.3
Questionnaire design
process**

Specify the information needed

↓

Specify the type of interviewing method

↓

Determine the content of individual questions

↓

Overcome the respondent's
inability and unwillingness to answer

↓

Choose question structure

↓

Choose question wording

↓

Arrange the questions in proper order

↓

Identify the form and layout

↓

Reproduce the questionnaire

↓

Eliminate problems by pilot-testing

Specify the type of interviewing method

An appreciation of how the type of interviewing method influences questionnaire design can be obtained by considering how the questionnaire is administered under each method (see Chapter 10). In personal interviews, respondents see the questionnaire and interact face to face with the interviewer. Thus, lengthy, complex and varied questions can be asked. In telephone interviews the respondents interact with the interviewer, but they do not see the questionnaire. This limits the type of questions that can be asked to short and simple ones. Mail and electronic questionnaires are self-administered, so the questions must be simple, and detailed instructions must be provided. In Internet surveys and computer-assisted interviewing (CAPI and CATI), complex skip patterns and randomisation of questions to eliminate order bias can be easily accommodated. Questionnaires designed for personal and telephone interviews should be written in a conversational style.[5]

 Sports Marketing Surveys

Effect of interviewing method on questionnaire design

Mail, email and internet questionnaire

Please rank order the following Formula One race teams in order of your preference. Begin by picking out the one team that you like the most and assign it a number 1. Then find the second most preferred team and assign it a number 2. Continue until you have ranked all teams in order of preference. Your least preferred team should be assigned a rank of 10. No two teams should receive the same rank number. The criteria you use to establish your preference are entirely up to you. There are no right or wrong answers. Just try to be consistent.

→

	Team	Rank order
1	BAR	_____
2	Ferrari	_____
3	Jaguar	_____
4	Jordan	_____
5	McLaren	_____
6	Minardi	_____
7	Renault	_____
8	Sauber	_____
9	Toyota	_____
10	Williams	_____

Telephone questionnaire

I will read you the names of Formula One teams. Please rate them in terms of your prefer-ence on a scale of 1 to 10: 10 represents 'greatly preferred' and 1 represents 'not so preferred'. The higher the number, the greater the degree of preference for that team. Now, please tell me your preference for these teams… (READ ONE TEAM AT A TIME.)

	Team	Not so preferred									Greatly preferred
1	BAR	1	2	3	4	5	6	7	8	9	10
2	Ferrari	1	2	3	4	5	6	7	8	9	10
3	Jaguar	1	2	3	4	5	6	7	8	9	10
4	Jordan	1	2	3	4	5	6	7	8	9	10
5	McLaren	1	2	3	4	5	6	7	8	9	10
6	Minardi	1	2	3	4	5	6	7	8	9	10
7	Renault	1	2	3	4	5	6	7	8	9	10
8	Sauber	1	2	3	4	5	6	7	8	9	10
9	Toyota	1	2	3	4	5	6	7	8	9	10
10	Williams	1	2	3	4	5	6	7	8	9	10

Personal questionnaire

(HAND TEAM NAME CARDS TO THE RESPONDENT.) Here is a set of Formula One team names, each written on a separate card. Please examine these cards carefully. (GIVE RESPONDENT TIME.) Now, give me the card with the name of the team that your prefer the most. (RECORD THE TEAM NAME AND TAKE THE CARD FROM THE RESPONDENT.) Would you carry on through the cards and hand over, in order, your second, third, fourth, etc.? (REPEAT THIS PROCESS SEQUENTIALLY UNTIL THE RESPONDENT HAS ONLY ONE CARD LEFT.)

	Team rank	Team name
1	___1___	_____
2	___2___	_____
3	___3___	_____
4	___4___	_____
5	___5___	_____
6	___6___	_____
7	___7___	_____
8	___8___	_____
9	___9___	_____
10	___10___	_____

In the Formula One Racetrack project example, ranking 10 teams is too complex a task to be administered over the telephone. Instead, the simpler ranking task, where the teams are rated one at a time, is selected to measure preferences. Note the use of cards to facilitate the ranking task in the personal interview. Interviewer instructions (typed in capital letters) are much more extensive in the personal interview. Another difference is that whereas the respondent records the ranks in mail and electronic surveys, the interviewer records the team names in the personal interview. The type of interviewing method also influences the content of individual questions.

Determine the content of individual questions

Once the information needed is specified and the type of interviewing method decided, the next step is to determine individual question content: what to include in individual questions.

Is the question necessary?

Every question in a questionnaire should contribute to the information needed or serve some specific purpose. If there is no satisfactory use for the data resulting from a question, that question should be eliminated.

In certain situations, however, questions may be asked that are not directly related to the needed information. It is useful to ask some neutral questions at the beginning of the questionnaire to establish involvement and rapport, particularly when the topic of the questionnaire is sensitive or controversial. Sometimes filter questions are asked to disguise the purpose or sponsorship of the project. For example, rather than limiting the questions to the brand of interest, questions about competing brands may be included to disguise the sponsorship. Questions unrelated to the immediate problem may sometimes be included to generate client support for the project. At times, certain questions may be duplicated for the purpose of assessing reliability or validity.[6]

Are several questions needed instead of one?

Once we have ascertained that a question is necessary, we must make sure that it is sufficient to get the desired information. Sometimes several questions are needed to obtain the required information in an unambiguous manner. Consider the question 'Do you think Coca-Cola is a tasty and refreshing soft drink?' A yes answer will presumably be clear, but what if the answer is no? Does this mean that the respondent thinks that Coca-Cola is not tasty, that it is not refreshing, or that it is neither tasty nor refreshing? Such a question is called a **double-barrelled question**, because two or more questions are combined into one. To obtain the required information, two distinct questions should be asked: 'Do you think Coca-Cola is a tasty soft drink?' and 'Do you think Coca-Cola is a refreshing soft drink?'

Double-barrelled question
A single question that attempts to cover two issues. Such questions can be confusing to respondents and result in ambiguous responses.

Another example of multiple questions embedded in a single question is the 'why' question. In the context of the Formula One Racetrack study, consider the question 'Why did you buy a Renault car?' The possible answers may include: 'it was recommended by my friend', 'the dealer is conveniently located for servicing' and 'it has the best safety record'. Each answer relates to a different question embedded in the 'why' question. The first tells how the respondent learnt about Renault, the second reveals what the respondent likes about Renault compared with other car manufacturers, and the third reveals what features of the car performance the respondent favours. The three answers are not comparable and any one answer may not be sufficient. Complete information may be obtained by asking two separate questions: 'What do you like about Renault compared with other car manufacturers?' and 'How did you first happen to choose a Renault?' Most 'why' questions about the use of a product or choice alternative involve two aspects: (1) attributes of the product and (2) influences leading to knowledge of it.[7]

Overcoming the respondent's inability and unwillingness to answer

Researchers should not assume that respondents can provide accurate or reasonable answers to all questions (assuming that they are willing to!). The researcher should attempt to overcome the respondents' inability to answer. Certain factors limit the respondents' ability to provide the desired information. The respondents may not be informed, may not remember, or may be unable to articulate certain types of responses.

Is the respondent informed?

Respondents are often asked about topics on which they are not informed. Parents may not be informed about their child's daily purchasing or vice versa (especially when one considers that sons and daughters can have an age range from 0 to around 80!).

Filter question
An initial question in a questionnaire that screens potential respondents to ensure they meet the requirements of the sample.

In situations where not all respondents are likely to be informed about the topic of interest, **filter questions** that measure familiarity, product use and past experience should be asked before questions about the topics themselves.[8] Filter questions enable the researcher to filter out respondents who are not adequately informed. The use of CATI, CAPI and Internet surveys allows extensive filtering to produce a variety of questionnaire formats that can be tailored to the familiarity, product use and past experiences of respondents.

The Formula One Racetrack questionnaire included questions related to the sponsors of the sport. In different countries there may be no awareness of certain sponsors, so information on familiarity was obtained for each sponsor. This allowed for separate analysis of data on sponsors about which the respondents were not informed. A 'don't know' option appears to reduce uninformed responses without reducing the overall response rate or the response rate for questions about which the respondents have information. Hence this option should be provided when the researcher expects that respondents may not be adequately informed about the subject of the question.[9]

Can the respondent remember?

Many things that we might expect everyone to know are remembered by only a few. Test this on yourself. Can you remember the brand name of the socks you are wearing (presuming you are wearing socks), what you had for lunch a week ago, or what you were doing a month ago at noon? Further, do you know how many litres of soft drinks you consumed during the last four weeks? Evidence indicates that consumers are particularly poor at remembering quantities of products consumed. In situations where factual data were available for comparison, it was found that consumer reports of product usage exceeded actual usage by 100% or more.[10]

Telescoping
A psychological phenomenon that takes place when an individual telescopes or compresses time by remembering an event as occurring more recently than it actually occurred.

The inability to remember leads to errors of omission, telescoping and creation. Omission is the inability to recall an event that actually took place. **Telescoping** takes place when an individual telescopes or compresses time by remembering an event as occurring more recently than it actually occurred.[11] For example, a respondent reports three trips to the supermarket in the last two weeks when, in fact, one of these trips was made 18 days ago. Creation error takes place when a respondent 'remembers' an event that did not actually occur.

The ability to remember an event is influenced by (1) the event itself, (2) the time elapsed since the event, and (3) the presence or absence of things that would aid memory.

We tend to remember events that are important or unusual or that occur frequently. People remember their wedding anniversary and birthday. Likewise, more recent events are remembered better. A grocery shopper is more likely to remember what he purchased on his last shopping trip than what he bought three shopping trips ago.

Research indicates that questions that do not provide the respondent with cues to the event, and that rely on unaided recall, can underestimate the actual occurrence of an event. For example, testing whether respondents were exposed to a beer commercial at the cinema could be measured in an unaided manner by questions like 'What brands of beer do you remember being advertised last night at the cinema?' (having established that the respondent was at a cinema last night). Naming a brand shows that the respondent saw the advert, took in the brand name and could recall it – three different stages. An aided recall approach attempts to stimulate the respondent's memory by providing cues related to the event of interest. Thus, the important features to measure may be that the respondent saw the advert and took in the brand name – the fact that the respondent cannot say the brand name may not affect his or her purchasing intentions. The aided recall approach would list a number of beer brands and then ask 'Which of these brands were advertised last night at the cinema?' In presenting cues, the researcher must guard against biasing the responses by testing out several successive levels of stimulation. The influence of stimulation on responses can then be analysed to select an appropriate level of stimulation.

Is the respondent able to articulate?

Respondents may be unable to articulate certain types of responses. For example, if asked to describe the 'atmosphere' of a restaurant they would prefer to frequent, most respondents may be unable to phrase their answers. On the other hand, if the respondents are provided with alternative descriptions of restaurant atmosphere, they will be able to indicate the one they like the best. If the respondents are unable to articulate their responses to a question, they are likely to ignore that question and refuse to respond to the rest of the questionnaire. Thus, respondents should be given aids such as pictures, maps and descriptions to help them articulate their responses.

Even if respondents are able to answer a particular question, they may be unwilling to do so, because too much effort is required, the situation or context may not seem appropriate for disclosure, no legitimate purpose or need for the information requested is apparent, or the information requested is sensitive.

Effort required of the respondents

Most respondents are unwilling to devote much effort to providing information. Hence, the researcher should minimise the effort required of the respondents. Suppose that the researcher is interested in determining from which shops a respondent bought goods on the most recent shopping trip. This information can be obtained in at least two ways. The researcher could ask the respondent to list all the items purchased on the most recent shopping trip, or the researcher could provide a list of shops and ask the respondent to indicate the applicable ones. The second option is preferable, because it requires less effort from respondents.

Context

Some questions may seem appropriate in certain contexts but not in others. For example, questions about personal hygiene habits may be appropriate when asked in a survey sponsored by a health organisation but not in one sponsored by a breakfast cereal manufacturer. Respondents are unwilling to respond to questions they consider being inappropriate for the given context. Sometimes, the researcher can manipulate the context in which the questions are asked so that the questions seem appropriate. For example, before asking for information on personal hygiene in a survey for a fast-food restaurant, the context could be manipulated by making the following statement: 'As a fast-food restaurant, we are very concerned about providing a clean and hygienic environment for our customers. Therefore, we would like to ask you some questions related to personal hygiene.'

Legitimate purpose

Respondents are also unwilling to divulge information that they do not see as serving a legitimate purpose. Why should a firm marketing breakfast cereals want to know their age, income and occupation? Explaining why the data are needed can make the request for the information seem legitimate and may increase the respondents' willingness to answer. A statement such as 'To determine how the preferences for cereal brands vary among people of different ages, we need information on …' can make the request for information seem more legitimate.

Sensitive information

Respondents may be unwilling to disclose, at least accurately, sensitive information because this may cause embarrassment or threaten the respondents' prestige or self-image, or be seen as too personal and an invasion of privacy. If pressed for the answer, respondents may give biased responses, especially during personal interviews[12] (see Table 10.2). Sensitive topics include money, personal hygiene, family life, political and religious beliefs, and involvement in accidents or crimes. In industrial surveys, sensitive questions may encompass much of what a company does, especially if it reveals strategic activities and plans. The techniques described in the following subsection can be adopted to increase the likelihood of obtaining information that respondents are unwilling to give.

Increasing the willingness of respondents

Respondents may be encouraged to provide information which they are unwilling to give by the following techniques:[13]

1 Place sensitive topics at the end of the questionnaire. By then, initial mistrust has been overcome, rapport has been created, legitimacy of the project has been established, and respondents are more willing to give information. In this context, consider how sensitive classification questions such as gender, age and income may be perceived.

2 Preface the question with a statement that the behaviour of interest is common. For example, before requesting information on credit card debt, say 'Recent studies show that most European consumers are in debt.' This technique describes the use of counter-biasing statements.

3 Ask the question using the third-person technique (see Chapter 7): phrase the question as if it referred to other people.

4 Hide the question in a group of other questions that respondents are willing to answer. The entire list of questions can then be asked quickly.

5 Provide response categories rather than asking for specific figures.[14] Do not ask 'What is your household's annual income?' Instead, ask the respondent to indicate an appropriate income category. In personal interviews, give the respondents cards that list the numbered choices. The respondents then indicate their responses by number.

6 Use randomised techniques. In these techniques, respondents are presented with two questions, one sensitive and the other a neutral question with a known probability of yes responses (e.g. 'Is your birthday in March?'). They are asked to select one question randomly by flipping a coin, for example. They then answer the selected question yes or no, without telling the researcher which question is being answered.[15] Given the overall probability of a yes response, the probability of selecting the sensitive question, and the

probability of a yes response to the neutral question, the researcher can determine the probability of a yes response to the sensitive question using the law of probability. The researcher cannot, however, determine which respondents have answered yes to the sensitive question.[16]

Choose question structure

A question may be unstructured or structured. We define unstructured questions and discuss their relative advantages and disadvantages and then consider the major types of structured questions: multiple choice, dichotomous and scales.[17]

Unstructured questions

Unstructured questions
Open-ended questions that respondents answer in their own words.

Unstructured questions are open-ended questions that respondents answer in their own words. They are also referred to as free-response or free-answer questions. The following are some examples:

- What is your occupation?
- What do you think of people who patronise secondhand clothes shops?
- Who is your favourite film personality?

Open-ended questions can be good first questions on a topic. They enable the respondents to express general attitudes and opinions that can help the researcher interpret their responses to structured questions. They can also be useful as a final question in a questionnaire. After respondents have thought through and given all their answers in a questionnaire, there may be other issues that are important to them and that may not have been covered. Having an open-ended question at the end allows respondents to express these issues. As well as providing material to help the researcher interpret other responses, the respondents have the chance to express what they feel to be important. Unstructured questions have a much less biasing influence on response than structured questions. Respondents are free to express any views. Their comments and explanations can provide the researcher with rich insights.

A principal disadvantage is that potential for interviewer bias is high. Whether the interviewers record the answers verbatim or write down only the main points, the data depend on the skills of the interviewers. Recorders should be used if verbatim reporting is important.

Another major disadvantage of unstructured questions is that the coding of responses is costly and time consuming, as illustrated in Chapter 9.[18] The coding procedures required to summarise responses in a format useful for data analysis and interpretation can be extensive. Implicitly, unstructured or open-ended questions give extra weight to respondents who are more articulate. Also, unstructured questions are not very suitable for self-administered questionnaires (mail and CAPI), because respondents tend to be briefer in writing than in speaking.

Pre-coding can overcome some of the disadvantages of unstructured questions. Expected responses are recorded in multiple-choice format, although the question is presented to the respondents as an open-ended question. Based on the respondent's reply, the interviewer selects the appropriate response category. Because the response alternatives are limited, this approach may be satisfactory when the respondent can easily formulate the response and when it is easy to develop pre-coded categories. In general, open-ended questions are useful in exploratory research and as opening or closing questions. They should be chosen with great care as their disadvantages can outweigh their advantages in a large survey.[19]

Structured questions

Structured questions specify the set of response alternatives and the response format. A structured question may be multiple choice, dichotomous or a scale.

Multiple-choice questions. In multiple-choice questions, the researcher provides a choice of answers and respondents are asked to select one or more of the alternatives given. Consider the following question:

Do you intend to buy a new car within the next six months?

_____ Definitely will not buy

_____ Probably will not buy

_____ Undecided

_____ Probably will buy

_____ Definitely will buy

_____ Other (please specify)

Of concern in designing multiple-choice questions are the number of alternatives that should be included and the order of potential responses, known as position bias. The response alternatives should include the set of all possible choices. The general guideline is to list all alternatives that may be of importance and to include an alternative labelled 'other (please specify)', as shown above. The response alternatives should be mutually exclusive. Respondents should also be able to identify one, and only one, alternative, unless the researcher specifically allows two or more choices (e.g. 'Please indicate all the brands of soft drinks that you have consumed in the past week'). If the response alternatives are numerous, consider using more than one question to reduce the information processing demands on the respondents.

Order bias or **position bias** is the respondents' tendency to tick an alternative merely because it occupies a certain position or is listed in a certain order. Respondents tend to tick the first or the last statement in a list, particularly the first.[20] For a list of numbers (quantities or prices), there is a bias towards the central value on the list. To control for order bias, several forms of the questionnaire should be prepared with the order in which the alternatives are listed varied from form to form, this is a relatively simple task using electronic questionnaire formats. Each alternative should appear once in each of the extreme positions, once in the middle and once somewhere in between.[21]

Multiple-choice questions overcome many of the disadvantages of open-ended questions because interviewer bias is reduced and these questions are administered quickly. Also, coding and processing of data are much less costly and time consuming. In self-administered questionnaires, respondent cooperation is improved if the majority of the questions are structured.

Multiple-choice questions are not without disadvantages. Considerable effort is required to design effective multiple-choice questions. Qualitative techniques may be required to determine the appropriate response alternatives. It is difficult to obtain information on alternatives not listed. Even if an 'other (please specify)' category is included, respondents tend to choose among the listed alternatives. In addition, showing respondents the list of possible answers produces biased responses.[22] There is also the potential for order bias.

Dichotomous questions. A **dichotomous question** has only two response alternatives, such as yes or no, or agree or disagree. Often, the two alternatives of interest are supplemented by a neutral alternative, such as 'no opinion', 'don't know', 'both' or 'none', as in this example.[23]

The question asked before about intentions to buy a new car as a multiple-choice question can also be asked as a dichotomous question.

Do you intend to buy a new car within the next six months?

✓

Yes

No

Don't know

Note that this question could also be framed as a multiple-choice question using response alternatives 'Definitely will buy', 'Probably will buy', 'Probably will not buy', and so forth. The decision to use a dichotomous question should be guided by whether the respondents approach the issue as a yes-or-no issue. Although decisions are often characterised as series of binary or dichotomous choices, the underlying decision-making process may reflect uncertainty that can best be captured by multiple-choice responses. For example, two individuals may be equally likely to buy a new car within the next six months if the economic conditions remain favourable. One individual, who is being optimistic about the economy, will answer 'yes', while the other, feeling pessimistic, will answer 'no'.

Another issue in the design of dichotomous questions is whether to include a neutral response alternative. If it is not included, respondents are forced to choose between yes and no even if they feel indifferent. On the other hand, if a neutral alternative is included, respondents can avoid taking a position on the issue, thereby biasing the results. We offer the following guidelines. If a substantial proportion of the respondents can be expected to be neutral, include a neutral alternative. If the proportion of neutral respondents is expected to be small, avoid the neutral alternative.[24]

The general advantages and disadvantages of dichotomous questions are very similar to those of multiple-choice questions. Dichotomous questions are the easiest types of questions to code and analyse, but they have one acute problem. The response can be influenced by the wording of the question. To illustrate, the statement 'Individuals are more to blame than social conditions for crime and lawlessness in this country' produced agreement from 59.6% of the respondents. On a matched sample that responded to the opposite statement, 'Social conditions are more to blame than individuals for crime and lawlessness in this country', however, 43.2% (as opposed to 40.4%) agreed.[25] To overcome this problem, the question should be framed in one way on one-half of the questionnaires and in the opposite way on the other half. This is referred to as the split-ballot technique.

Scales. Scales were discussed in detail in Chapter 12. To illustrate the difference between scales and other kinds of structural questions, consider the question about intentions to buy a new laptop computer. One way of framing this using a scale is as follows:

Do you intend to buy a new car within the next six months?

Definitely will not buy	Probably will not buy	Undecided	Probably will buy	Definitely will buy
1	2	3	4	5

This is only one of several scales that could be used to ask this question (see Chapter 12 for more examples).

Choose question wording

Question wording is the translation of the desired question content and structure into words that respondents can clearly and easily understand. Deciding on question wording is perhaps the most critical and difficult task in developing a questionnaire. If a question is worded poorly, respondents may refuse to answer it or answer it incorrectly. The first condition, known as item non-response, can increase the complexity of data analysis.[26] The second condition leads to response error, discussed earlier. Unless the respondents and the researcher assign exactly the same meaning to the question, the results will be seriously biased.[27]

To avoid these problems, we offer the following guidelines: (1) define the issue, (2) use ordinary words, (3) use unambiguous words, (4) avoid leading or biasing questions, (5) avoid implicit alternatives, (6) avoid implicit assumptions, (7) avoid generalisations and estimates, and (8) use positive and negative statements.

Define the issue

A question should clearly define the issue being addressed. Trainee journalists are cautioned to define issues in terms of who, what, when, where, why and way (the six Ws). Consider the following question:

> Which brand of shampoo do you use?

On the surface, this may seem to be a well-defined question, but we may reach a different conclusion when we examine it in terms of 'who', 'what', 'when' and 'where'. 'Who' in this question refers to the respondent. It is not clear, though, whether the researcher is referring to the brand the respondent uses personally or the brand used by the household. 'What' is the brand of shampoo. But what if more than one brand of shampoo is being used? Should the respondent mention the most preferred brand, the brand used most often, the brand used most recently, or the brand that comes to mind first? 'When' is not clear; does the researcher mean last time, last week, last month, last year, or ever? As for 'where', it is implied that the shampoo is used at home, but this is not stated clearly. A better wording for this question would be:

> Which brand or brands of shampoo have you personally used at home during the last month? In the case of more than one brand, please list all the brands that apply.

Use ordinary words

Ordinary words should be used in a questionnaire, and they should match the vocabulary level of the respondents.[29] In other words, even though we may speak the same language as our potential respondents, there may be particular colloquialisms and ways of using words and terms they use which we should acquaint ourselves with. When choosing words, bear in mind the intellectual level of the target group of respondents, and how comfortable they are with technical terms related to any products or services we are measuring. Most respondents do not understand technical marketing words. For example, instead of asking 'Do you think the distribution of soft drinks is adequate?' ask 'Do you think soft drinks are readily available when you want to buy them?' Never forget that you are imposing your language upon respondents in the form of a questionnaire. Your language communicates and puts respondents in a particular frame of mind as they answer the questions you pose. Unless that language is meaningful to respondents, they will be put in a frame of mind that you may not intend, and be answering different questions from those you set.

Use unambiguous words

The words used in a questionnaire should have a single meaning that is known to the respondents.[30] A number of words that appear to be unambiguous have different meanings for different people.[31] These include 'usually', 'normally', 'frequently', 'often', 'regularly', 'occasionally' and 'sometimes'. Consider the following question:

In a typical month, how often do you visit a bank?

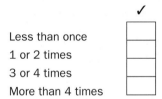

Never
Occasionally
Sometimes
Often
Regularly

The answers to this question are fraught with response bias, because the words used to describe category labels have different meanings for different respondents. Three respondents who visit a bank once a month may tick three different categories: occasionally, sometimes and often. A much better wording for this question would be the following:

In a typical month, how often do you visit a bank?

✓

Less than once
1 or 2 times
3 or 4 times
More than 4 times

Note that this question provides a consistent frame of reference for all respondents. Response categories have been objectively defined, and respondents are no longer free to interpret them in their own way.

In deciding on the choice of words, researchers should consult a dictionary and thesaurus and ask the following questions:

1 Does the word mean what we intend?
2 Does the word mean the same to our target respondents?
3 Does the word have any other meanings?
4 If so, does the context make the intended meaning clear?
5 Does the word have more than one pronunciation or similar pronunciations that may be confusing?
6 Is a simpler word or phrase suggested that may be more meaningful to our target respondents?

Avoid leading or biasing questions

Leading question
A question that gives the respondent a clue as to what the answer should be.

A **leading question** is one that clues the respondent to what the answer should be, as in the following:

Do you think that patriotic French people should buy imported cars when that would put French workers out of employment?

        ✓

Yes

No

Don't know

This question would lead respondents to a 'No' answer. After all, how could patriotic French people put French people out of work? Therefore, this question would not help determine the preferences of French people for imported versus domestic cars.

Bias may also arise when respondents are given clues about the sponsor of the project. Respondents tend to respond favourably towards the sponsor. The question 'Is Colgate your favourite toothpaste?' is likely to bias the responses in favour of Colgate. A more unbiased way of obtaining this information would be to ask 'What is your favourite toothpaste brand?' Likewise, the mention of a prestigious or non-prestigious name can bias the response, as in 'Do you agree with the British Dental Association that Colgate is effective in preventing cavities?' An unbiased question would be to ask 'Is Colgate effective in preventing cavities?'[32]

Avoid implicit alternatives

Implicit alternative
An alternative that is not explicitly expressed.

An alternative that is not explicitly expressed in the options is an **implicit alternative**. Making an implied alternative explicit may increase the percentage of people selecting that alternative, as in the following two questions:

1 Do you like to fly when travelling short distances?
2 Do you like to fly when travelling short distances, or would you rather drive?

In the first question, the alternative of driving is only implicit, but in the second question it is explicit. The first question is likely to yield a greater preference for flying than the second question.

Questions with implicit alternatives should be avoided unless there are specific reasons for including them. When the alternatives are close in preference or large in number, the alternatives at the end of the list have a greater chance of being selected. To overcome this bias, the split-ballot technique should be used to rotate the order in which the alternatives appear.

Avoid implicit assumptions

Implicit assumptions
An assumption that is not explicitly stated in a question.

Questions should not be worded so that the answer is dependent on implicit assumptions about what will happen as a consequence. **Implicit assumptions** are assumptions that are not explicitly stated in the question, as in the following example:[34]

1 Are you in favour of a balanced national budget?
2 Are you in favour of a balanced national budget if it would result in an increase in personal income tax?

Implicit in question 1 are the consequences that will arise as a result of a balanced national budget. There might be a cut in defence expenditure, an increase in personal income tax, a cut in health spending, and so on. Question 2 is a better way to word this question. Question 1's failure to make its assumptions explicit would result in overestimating the respondents' support for a balanced national budget.

Avoid generalisations and estimates

Questions should be specific, not general. Moreover, questions should be worded so that the respondent does not have to make generalisations or compute estimates. Suppose that we were interested in households' annual per capita expenditure on groceries. If we asked respondents the question

> What is the annual per capita expenditure on groceries in your household?

they would first have to determine the annual expenditure on groceries by multiplying the monthly expenditure on groceries by 12 or the weekly expenditure by 52. Then they would have to divide the annual amount by the number of persons in the household. Most respondents would be unwilling or unable to perform these calculations. A better way of obtaining the required information would be to ask the respondents two simple questions:

> What is the monthly (or weekly) expenditure on groceries in your household?

and

> How many members are there in your household?

The researcher can then perform the necessary calculations.

Use positive and negative statements

Many questions, particularly those measuring attitudes and lifestyles, are presented as statements to which respondents indicate their degree of agreement or disagreement. Evidence indicates that the response obtained is influenced by the directionality of the statements: whether they are stated positively or negatively. In these cases, it is better to use dual statements, some of which are positive and others negative. Two different questionnaires could be prepared. One questionnaire would contain half-negative and half-positive statements in an interspersed way. The direction of these statements would be reversed in the other questionnaire. An example of dual statements was provided in the summated Likert scale in Chapter 12 designed to measure attitudes towards Renault cars.

Arrange the questions in proper order

The order of questions is of equal importance to the wording used in the questions. As noted in the last section, questions communicate and set respondents in a particular frame of mind. This frame of mind is set at the start of the questioning process and can change as each question is posed and responded to. It affects how respondents perceive individual questions and respond to those questions. As well as understanding the characteristics of language in target respondents, questionnaire designers must be aware of the logical connections between questions – as perceived by target respondents. The following issues help to determine the order of questions.

Opening questions

The opening questions can be crucial in gaining the confidence and cooperation of respondents. These questions should be interesting, simple and non-threatening. Questions that ask respondents for their opinions can be good opening questions, because most people like to express their opinions. Sometimes such questions are asked although they are unrelated to the research problem and their responses are not analysed.[35] Though classification questions seem simple to start a questionnaire, issues like age, gender and income can be seen as sensitive issues. Opening a questionnaire with these questions tends to make respondents concerned about the purpose of these questions and indeed the whole survey. However, in some instances it is necessary to qualify respondents to determine whether they are eligible to participate in the interview. In this case the qualifying questions serve as the opening questions, and they may have to be classification questions such as the age of the respondent.

Type of information

Classification information
Socio-economic and demographic characteristics used to classify respondents.

Identification information
A type of information obtained in a questionnaire that includes name, address and phone number.

The type of information obtained in a questionnaire may be classified as (1) basic information, (2) **classification information** and (3) **identification information**. Basic information relates directly to the research problem. Classification information, consisting of socio-economic and demographic characteristics, is used to classify the respondents, understand the results, and validate the sample (see Chapter 14). Identification information includes name, address and telephone number. Identification information may be obtained for a variety of purposes, including verifying that the respondents listed were actually interviewed and to send promised incentives or prizes. As a general guideline, basic information should be obtained first, followed by classification and finally identification information. The basic information is of greatest importance to the research project and should be obtained first, before risking alienation of the respondents by asking a series of personal questions.

Difficult questions

Difficult questions or questions that are sensitive, embarrassing, complex or dull should be placed late in the sequence. After rapport has been established and the respondents become involved, they are less likely to object to these questions. Thus, in the Formula One Racetrack Project, information about the nature of Formula One merchandise that has been purchased was asked at the end of the section on basic information. Had respondents perceived (incorrectly) that the survey was being used as a means to sell them merchandise, their trust in the survey and the nature of their subsequent responses could have been impaired. Likewise, income should be the last question in the classification section (if it is to be used at all).

Effect on subsequent questions

Questions asked early in a sequence can influence the responses to subsequent questions. As a rule of thumb, general questions should precede specific questions. This prevents specific questions from biasing responses to the general questions. Consider the following sequence of questions:

Q1: *What considerations are important to you in selecting a bank?*

Q2: *In selecting a bank, how important is convenience of its location?*

Note that the first question is general whereas the second is specific. If these questions were asked in the reverse order, respondents would be clued about convenience of location and would be more likely to give this response to the general question.

Going from general to specific is called the **funnel approach**. The funnel approach is particularly useful when information has to be obtained about respondents' general choice behaviour and their evaluations of specific products.[36] Sometimes the inverted funnel approach may be useful. In this approach, questioning starts with specific questions and concludes with the general questions. The respondents are compelled to provide specific information before making general evaluations. This approach is useful when respondents have no strong feelings or have not formulated a point of view.

Funnel approach
A strategy for ordering questions in a questionnaire in which the sequence starts with the general questions, which are followed by progressively specific questions, to prevent specific questions from biasing general questions.

Logical order

Questions should be asked in a logical order. This may seem a simple rule, but as the researcher takes time to understand respondents and how they use language, the researcher should also take time to understand their logic, i.e. what 'logical order' means to target respondents. All questions that deal with a particular topic should be asked before beginning a new topic. When switching topics, brief transitional phrases should be used to help respondents switch their train of thought.

Branching questions should be designed carefully.[37] Branching questions direct respondents to different places in the questionnaire based on how they respond to the question at hand. These questions ensure that all possible contingencies are covered. They also help reduce interviewer and respondent error and encourage complete responses. Skip patterns based on the branching questions can become quite complex. A simple way to account for all contingencies is to prepare a flow chart of the logical possibilities and then develop branching questions and instructions based on it. A flow chart used to assess the use of electronic payments in clothes purchases via the Internet is shown in Figure 13.4.

Branching question
A question used to guide an interviewer (or respondent) through a survey by directing the interviewer (or respondent) to different spots on the questionnaire depending on the answers given.

Source: © Patrick Giardino/CORBIS

Placement of branching questions is important and the following guidelines should be followed: (1) the question being branched (the one to which the respondents are being directed) should be placed as close as possible to the question causing the branching, and (2) the branching questions should be ordered so that the respondents cannot anticipate what additional information will be required. Otherwise, the respondents may discover that they can avoid detailed questions by giving certain answers to branching questions. For example, the respondents should first be asked if they have seen any of the listed commercials before they are asked to evaluate commercials. Otherwise, the respondents will quickly discover that stating that they have seen a commercial leads to detailed questions about that commercial and that they can avoid detailed questions by stating that they have not seen the commercial.

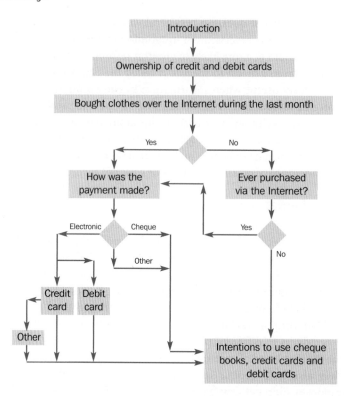

Figure 13.4
Flow chart for
questionnaire design

Identify the form and layout

The format, spacing and positioning of questions can have a significant effect on the results, particularly in self-administered questionnaires. It is good practice to divide a questionnaire into several parts. Several parts may be needed for questions pertaining to the basic information.

The questions in each part should be numbered, particularly when branching questions are used. Numbering of questions also makes the coding of responses easier. In addition, the questionnaires should preferably be pre-coded. In **pre-coding**, the codes to enter in the computer can be printed on the questionnaire. Coding of questionnaires is explained in more detail in Chapter 17 on data preparation.

Pre-coding
In questionnaire design, assigning a code to every conceivable response before data collection.

The questionnaires themselves should be numbered serially. This facilitates the control of questionnaires in the field as well as the coding and analysis. Numbering makes it easy to account for the questionnaires and to determine whether any have been lost. A possible exception to this rule is mail questionnaires. If these are numbered, respondents assume that a given number identifies a particular respondent. Some respondents may refuse to participate or may answer differently under these conditions. However, recent research suggests that this loss of anonymity has little influence on the results.[38]

Reproduce the questionnaire

How a questionnaire is reproduced for administration can influence the results. For example, if the questionnaire is reproduced on poor-quality paper or is otherwise shabby in appearance, the respondents will think that the project is unimportant and the quality of response will be adversely affected. Therefore, the questionnaire should be reproduced on good-quality paper and have a professional appearance.

When a printed questionnaire runs to several pages, it should take the form of a booklet rather than a number of sheets of paper clipped or stapled together. Booklets are easier for the interviewer and the respondents to handle and do not easily come apart with use. They allow the use of a double-page format for questions and look more professional.

Each question should be reproduced on a single page (or double-page spread). A researcher should avoid splitting a question, including its response categories. Split questions can mislead the interviewer or the respondent into thinking that the question has ended at the end of a page. This will result in answers based on incomplete questions.

Vertical response columns should be used for individual questions. It is easier for interviewers and respondents to read down a single column rather than reading sideways across several columns. Sideways formatting and splitting, done frequently to conserve space, should be avoided.

The tendency to crowd questions together to make the questionnaire look shorter should be avoided. Overcrowded questions with little blank space between them can lead to errors in data collection and yield shorter and less informative replies. Moreover, it gives the impression that the questionnaire is complex and can result in lower cooperation and completion rates. Although shorter questionnaires are more desirable than longer ones, the reduction in size should not be obtained at the expense of crowding.[39]

Directions or instructions for individual questions should be placed as close to the questions as possible. Instructions relating to how the question should be administered or answered by the respondent should be placed just before the question. Instructions concerning how the answer should be recorded or how the probing should be done should be placed after the question (for more information on probing and other interviewing procedures, see Chapter 16). It is common practice to distinguish instructions from questions by using different typefaces (such as capital or boldfaced letters).

Although colour does not influence response rates to questionnaires, it can be employed advantageously in some respects. Colour coding is useful for branching questions. The next question to which the respondent is directed is printed in a colour that matches the space in which the answer to the branching question was recorded. Surveys directed at different respondent groups can be reproduced on paper of a different colour.

The questionnaire should be reproduced in such a way that it is easy to read and answer. The type should be large and clear. Reading the questionnaire should not impose a strain.

Eliminate problems by pilot-testing

Pilot-testing
Testing the questionnaire on a small sample of respondents for the purpose of improving the questionnaire by identifying and eliminating potential problems.

Pilot-testing refers to testing the questionnaire on a small sample of respondents to identify and eliminate potential problems.[40] Even the best questionnaire can be improved by pilot-testing. As a general rule, a questionnaire should not be used in the field survey without adequate pilot-testing.[41] A pilot-test should be extensive. All aspects of the questionnaire should be tested, including question content, wording, sequence, form and layout, question difficulty, and instructions. The respondents in the pilot-test should be similar to those who will be included in the actual survey in terms of background characteristics, familiarity with the topic, and attitudes and behaviours of interest.[42] In other words, respondents for the pilot-test and for the actual survey should be drawn from the same population.

Pilot-tests are best done by personal interviews, even if the actual survey is to be conducted by Internet, mail or telephone, because interviewers can observe respondents' reactions and attitudes. After the necessary changes have been made, another pilot-test could be conducted by Internet, mail or telephone if those methods are to be used in the actual survey. The latter pilot-tests should reveal problems peculiar to the interviewing method.

A variety of interviewers should be used for pilot-tests. The project director, the researcher who developed the questionnaire and other key members of the research team should conduct some pilot-test interviews. This will give them a good feel for potential problems and the nature of the expected data. If the survey involves face to face interviews, pilot-tests should be conducted by regular interviewers. It is good practice to employ both experienced and new interviewers. Experienced interviewers can easily perceive uneasiness, confusion and resistance in the respondents, and new interviewers can help the researcher identify interviewer-related problems. Ordinarily the pilot-test sample size is small, varying from 15 to 30 respondents for the initial testing, depending on the heterogeneity (e.g. a wide array of education levels) of the target population. The sample size can increase substantially if the pilot-testing involves several stages.

Protocol analysis and debriefing are two commonly used procedures in pilot-testing. In protocol analysis, the respondent is asked to 'think aloud' while answering the questionnaire, as explained in Chapter 12. Typically, the respondent's remarks are tape recorded and analysed to determine the reactions invoked by different parts of the questionnaire. Debriefing occurs after the questionnaire has been completed. Respondents are told that the questionnaire they just completed was a pilot-test and the objectives of pilot-testing are described to them. They are then asked to describe the meaning of each question, to explain their answers, and to state any problems they encountered while answering the questionnaire.

Editing involves correcting the questionnaire for the problems identified during pilot-testing. After each significant revision of the questionnaire, another pilot-test should be conducted, using a different sample of respondents. Sound pilot-testing involves several stages. One pilot-test is a bare minimum. Pilot-testing should be continued until no further changes are needed.

Finally, the responses obtained from the pilot-test should be coded and analysed. The analysis of pilot-test responses can serve as a check on the adequacy of the problem definition and the data and analysis required to obtain the necessary information. The dummy tables prepared before developing the questionnaire will point to the need for the various sets of data. If the response to a question cannot be related to one of the preplanned dummy tables, either those data are superfluous or some relevant analysis has not been foreseen. If part of a dummy table remains empty, a necessary question may have been omitted. Analysis of pilot-test data helps to ensure that all data collected will be utilised and that the questionnaire will obtain all the necessary data.[43]

Summarising the questionnaire design process

Table 13.1 summarises the questionnaire design process in the form of a checklist.

Table 13.1 Questionnaire design checklist

Step 1: Specify the Information Needed
1 Ensure that the information obtained fully addresses all the components of the problem. Review components of the problem and the approach, particularly the research questions, hypotheses and characteristics that influence the research design.
2 Prepare a set of dummy tables.
3 Have a clear idea of characteristics and motivations of the target population.

Step 2: Specify the Type of Interviewing Method
1 Review the type of interviewing method determined based on considerations discussed in Chapter 10.

Step 3: Determine the Content of Individual Questions
1 Is the question necessary?
2 Are several questions needed instead of one to obtain the required information in an unambiguous manner?
3 Do not use double-barrelled questions.

Step 4: Overcome the Respondent's Inability and Unwillingness to Answer
1 Is the respondent informed?
2 If the respondent is not likely to be informed, filter questions that measure familiarity, product use and past experience should be asked before questions about the topics themselves.
3 Can the respondent remember?
4 Avoid errors of omission, telescoping and creation.
5 Questions that do not provide the respondent with cues can underestimate the actual occurrence of an event.
6 Can the respondent articulate?
7 Minimise the effort required of the respondent.
8 Is the context in which the questions are asked appropriate?
9 Make the request for information seem legitimate.
10 If the information is sensitive:
(a) Place sensitive topics at the end of the questionnaire.
(b) Preface the question with a statement that the behaviour of interest is common.
(c) Ask the question using the third-person technique.
(d) Hide the question in a group of other questions that respondents are willing to answer.
(e) Provide response categories rather than asking for specific figures.
(f) Use randomised techniques, if appropriate.

Step 5: Choose Question Structure
1 Open-ended questions are useful in exploratory research and as closing questions.
2 Use structured questions whenever possible.
3 In multiple-choice questions, the response alternatives should include the set of all possible choices and should be mutually exclusive.
4 In a dichotomous question, if a substantial proportion of the respondents can be expected to be neutral, include a neutral alternative.
5 Consider the use of the split ballot technique to reduce order bias in dichotomous and multiple-choice questions.
6 If the response alternatives are numerous, consider using more than one question to reduce the information processing demands on the respondents.

Step 6: Choose Question Wording
1 Define the issue in terms of 'who', 'what', 'when' and 'where'.
2 Use ordinary words. Words should match the vocabulary level of the respondents.
3 Avoid ambiguous words: usually, normally, frequently, often, regularly, occasionally, sometimes, etc.
4 Avoid leading or biasing questions that cue the respondent to what the answer should be.
5 Avoid implicit alternatives that are not explicitly expressed in the options.
6 Avoid implicit assumptions.
7 Respondent should not have to make generalisations or compute estimates.
8 Use positive and negative statements.

Step 7: Arrange the Questions in Proper Order

1 The opening questions should be interesting, simple and non-threatening.

2 Qualifying questions should serve as the opening questions.

3 Basic information should be obtained first, followed by classification and finally identification information.

4 Difficult, sensitive or complex questions should be placed late in the sequence.

5 General questions should precede specific questions.

6 Questions should be asked in a logical order.

7 Branching questions should be designed carefully to cover all possible contingencies.

8 The question being branched should be placed as close as possible to the question causing the branching, and the branching questions should be ordered so that the respondents cannot anticipate what additional information will be required.

Step 8: Identify the Form and Layout

1 Divide a questionnaire into several parts.

2 Questions in each part should be numbered.

3 The questionnaire should be pre-coded.

4 The questionnaires themselves should be numbered serially.

Step 9: Reproduce the Questionnaire

1 The questionnaire should have a professional appearance.

2 A booklet format should be used for long questionnaires.

3 Each question should be reproduced on a single page (or double-page spread).

4 Vertical response columns should be used.

5 Grids are useful when there are a number of related questions that use the same set of response categories.

6 The tendency to crowd questions to make the questionnaire look shorter should be avoided.

7 Directions or instructions for individual questions should be placed as close to the questions as possible.

Step 10: Eliminate Problems by Pilot-testing

1 Pilot-testing should always be done.

2 All aspects of the questionnaire should be tested, including question content, wording, sequence, form and layout, question difficulty, instructions and rewards for taking part in the survey.

3 The respondents in the pilot-test should be similar to those who will be included in the actual survey.

4 Begin the pilot-test by using personal interviews.

5 The pilot-test should also be conducted by mail or telephone if those methods are to be used in the actual survey.

6 A variety of interviewers should be used for pilot-tests.

7 The pilot-test sample size should be small, varying from 15 to 30 respondents for the initial testing.

8 Use protocol analysis and debriefing to identify problems.

9 After each significant revision of the questionnaire, another pilot-test should be conducted, using a different sample of respondents.

10 The responses obtained from the pilot-test should be coded and analysed.

International marketing research

The questionnaire or research instrument should be adapted to the specific cultural environment and should not be biased in terms of any one culture. This requires careful attention to each step of the questionnaire design process. The information needed should be clearly specified. It is important to take into account any differences in underlying consumer behaviour, decision-making processes, psychographics, lifestyles and demographic variables. In the context of demographic characteristics, information on marital status, education, household size, occupation, income and dwelling unit may have to be specified differently for different countries, as these variables may not be directly comparable across countries. For example, household definition and size varies greatly, given the extended family structure in some countries and the practice of two or even three families living under the same roof.

Although personal interviewing may dominate as a survey method in many Western countries, different survey methods may be favoured in different countries. Hence, the questionnaire may have to be suitable for administration by more than one method. For ease of comprehension and translation, it is desirable to have two or more simple questions rather than a single complex question. In overcoming the inability to answer, the variability in the extent to which respondents in different cultures are informed about the subject matter of the survey should be taken into account. Respondents in some parts of the world may not be as well informed on many issues as people in Europe (and vice versa of course!).

The use of unstructured or open-ended questions may be desirable if the researcher lacks knowledge about the determinants of response in other countries. Because they do not impose any response alternatives, unstructured questions also reduce cultural bias, but they are more affected by differences in educational levels than structured questions. They should be used with caution in countries with low literacy levels.

The questionnaire may have to be translated for administration in different cultures. The researcher must ensure that the questionnaires in different languages are equivalent. The special procedures designed for this purpose are discussed in Chapter 26. the following example illustrates the problems of translation.

Example	**If you board the Asian bus, better mind your language[44]**

On the surface it would appear that the omnibus service could be made very standardised in Asia, even more so than in Europe where one must deal with a different language in almost every country. One might conclude that a questionnaire in Chinese could be used with little or no modification in a number of countries such as China, Hong Kong, Taiwan and Malaysia, thus avoiding the problems of timing, cost and inaccuracies generally associated with translations. However, due to vast differences in the region in terms of language, culture and geography, the 'standard' omnibus survey becomes less standard than would first meet the eye. While the omnibus is a very cost-effective and efficient way of conducting research in Asia, great care must be taken in order to make best use of this service, particularly by companies thinking of entering these markets. Countries such as Japan, Korea and Thailand are typical of South East Asia in that they each possess a single culture and a single language. But, in both Singapore and Malaysia, for example, omnibus questionnaires are always printed in three languages: English, Mandarin and Malay. In Malaysia, in addition to Mandarin, which is spoken by all 'Chinese-literate' consumers, there are three other commonly spoken dialects which have to be dealt with at the respondent level: Cantonese, Hokkien and Hakka. In Singapore the commonly spoken dialects are Cantonese, Hokkien and Teochew.

Pilot-testing the questionnaire is complicated in international research because linguistic equivalence must be pilot-tested. Two sets of pilot-tests are recommended. The translated questionnaire should be pilot-tested on monolingual subjects in their native language, and the original and translated versions should also be administered to bilingual subjects. The pilot-test data from administration of the questionnaire in different countries or cultures should be analysed and the pattern of responses compared to detect any cultural biases.

Ethics in marketing research

Several ethical issues related to the researcher–respondent relationship and the researcher–client relationship may have to be addressed in questionnaire design. Of particular concern are the use of overly long questionnaires, asking sensitive questions, combining questions of more than one client in the same questionnaire or survey (piggybacking) and deliberately biasing the questionnaire.

Respondents are volunteering their time and should not be overburdened by soliciting too much information. The researcher should avoid overly long questionnaires. An overly long questionnaire may vary in length or completion time depending upon variables such as the topic of the survey, the effort required, the number of open-ended questions, the frequency of use of complex scales and the method of administration. According to the guidelines of the Professional Marketing Research Society of Canada (**www.pmrs-aprm.com**), with the exception of in-home personal interviews, questionnaires that take more than 30 minutes to complete are generally considered 'overly long'. Personal in-home interviews can take up to 60 minutes without overloading the respondents. Overly long questionnaires are burdensome on the respondents and adversely affect the quality of responses. Similarly, questions that are confusing, exceed the respondents' ability, are difficult, or are otherwise improperly worded should be avoided.

Sensitive questions deserve special attention. A real ethical dilemma exists for researchers investigating social problems such as poverty, drug use and sexually transmitted diseases like AIDS, or conducting studies of highly personal products like feminine hygiene products or financial products.[45] Candid and truthful responses are needed to generate meaningful results. But how do researchers obtain such data without asking sensitive questions that invade respondents' privacy? When asking sensitive questions, researchers should attempt to minimise the discomfort of the respondents. It should be made clear at the beginning of the questionnaire that respondents are not obligated to answer any question that makes them uncomfortable.[46]

An important researcher–client issue is piggybacking, which occurs when a questionnaire contains questions pertaining to more than one client. This is often done in omnibus surveys (see Chapter 4) that different clients can use to field their questions. One sponsor's questions may take up a part of the questionnaire, while a second sponsor's study takes up the rest. Although there is some risk that one study will contaminate the other or that the questionnaire may not be very coherent, piggybacking can substantially reduce the cost. Thus, it can be a good way for clients with limited research budgets to collect primary data they would not be able to afford otherwise. In these cases all clients must be aware of and consent to the arrangement. Unfortunately, piggybacking is sometimes used without disclosure to the clients for the sole purpose of increasing the researcher's profit. This is unethical.

Finally, the researcher has the ethical responsibility of designing the questionnaire so as to obtain the required information in an unbiased manner. Deliberately biasing the questionnaire in a desired direction, e.g. by asking leading questions, cannot be condoned. In deciding the question structure, the most appropriate rather than the most convenient option should be adopted, as illustrated in the next example. Also, the questionnaire should be thoroughly pilot-tested before fieldwork begins, or an ethical breach has occurred.

Questioning international marketing ethics[47]

In designing a questionnaire, open-ended questions may be most appropriate if the response categories are not known. In a study designed to identify ethical problems in international marketing, a series of open-ended questions was used. The objective of the survey was to elicit the three most frequently encountered ethical problems, in order of priority, to Australian firms that engage in international marketing activities. After reviewing the results, the researcher tabulated and categorised them into 10 categories that occurred most often: traditional small-scale bribery; large-scale bribery; gifts, favours, entertainment; pricing; inappropriate products or technology; tax evasion practices; illegal or immoral practices; questionable commissions to channel members; cultural differences; and involvement in political affairs. The sheer number of categories indicates that international marketing ethics should probably be questioned more closely. The use of structured questions in this case, although more convenient, would have been inappropriate, raising ethical concerns

Internet and computer applications

Word-processing packages/software, such as Microsoft Word, are widely used for designing questionnaires, particularly if they are paper based. Researchers are familiar with their operation as they typically use this type of software to write project briefs and reports. However, although the finished result may be sufficiently presentable, the underlying structures associated with a survey are missing. These include elements such as single or multiple response on any tick box question, data validation and routing.

Even though word-processing software is becoming increasingly more sophisticated, desktop publishing packages, such as QuarkXpress, provide added graphical functionality and are widely used within the design and print industry. Consequently, some researchers are advised to use this type of software. However, the learning curve is fairly steep and researchers rarely undertake design tasks more complex than can be achieved in a standard word-processing package.

One word of caution, though – the print industry is very often Apple Mac based and the marketing research industry is very often PC based. Although software such as QuarkXpress is available for both platforms, and questionnaires can be designed on a PC and then transferred to a Mac for typesetting and printing, the results are not always identical. Do be extremely careful in the proof-checking process. If questionnaires are to be scanned, where the positioning of boxes is even more critical, then the process of proof checking will be even more important and consequently time consuming.

Software such as SNAP enables questionnaires to be designed and printed for all survey formats (paper, the Web, CATI, CAPI, PDA) and can be likened to a word processor with an intelligent template. The processes of selecting boxes, single or multiple responses, routing, etc., are automated, and entire libraries (see the example of surveypaks on **www.snapsurveys.com**) exist to select individual questions or entire questionnaires. These include topics such as customer satisfaction, human resources, travel and tourism, health care and best value. Questions can be selected, pasted in a survey and amendments made where necessary to remove or add new codes. The formatted questionnaire is then ready for the next stages of data collection and data analysis.

→

Internet questionnaires share many of the features of CAPI questionnaires. The questionnaire can be designed using a wide variety of stimuli such as graphics, pictures, advertisements, animations, sound clips and full-motion video. Moreover, the researcher can control the amount of time for which the stimuli are available to the respondents, and the number of times a respondent can access each stimulus. This greatly increases the range and complexity of questionnaires that can be administered over the Internet. As in the case of CATI and CAPI, complicated skip patterns can be programmed into the questionnaire. The questions can be personalised and answers to previous questions can be inserted into subsequent questions. The various types of scales, such as ordinal ranking scales, Likert scales, semantic differential scales and Stapel scales, can be utilised. Open-ended questions can also be posed using the Internet. The data collected may need coding after the survey process, as with all open-ended questions.

As the Internet becomes a more accepted method of administering surveys, the nature and expectations of the sponsors of marketing research increases. Their expectations can include the need to do the following:

- Allow respondents to take a break part way through completing a questionnaire and then return to it later.
- Include a password to control access to a survey.
- Include a user ID to restrict access and avoid multiple completions by the same respondent as well as accessing demographic data of participants on a panel.
- Log information on the time spent by each respondent on each individual question (known as paradata).

Summary

A questionnaire has three objectives. It must translate the information needed into a set of specific questions that the respondents can and will answer. It must motivate respondents to complete the interview. It must also minimise response error.

Designing a questionnaire is more of a craft than a science. This is primarily caused by the interrelationship of stages and the trade-offs that questionnaire designers make in balancing the source of ideas, question purposes, actual questions and question analyses. The steps involved in the questionnaire design process involve:

1 Specifying the information needed. Understanding what information decision-makers need.

2 Specifying the type of interviewing method. Understanding which means of eliciting the information will work best, given the research design constraints that the researcher has to work with.

3 Determining the content of individual questions. Understanding the purpose of each question and working out how a posed question may fulfil that purpose.

4 Overcoming the respondents' inability and unwillingness to answer questions. Understanding the process of approaching and questioning respondents – from their perspective. Knowing what benefits they get from taking part in the survey process.

5 Choosing the question structure. Understanding how individual questions help to elicit information from respondents and help them to express their feelings.

6 Choosing the question wording. Understanding the meaning of words from the perspective of the respondent.

7 Arranging the questions in a proper order. Understanding what 'proper' means from the perspective of the respondent. Recognising that, as each question is posed to a respondent and he or she thinks about the response, the respondent changes. Information is not only drawn out of respondents, it is communicated to them as each question is tackled.

8 Identifying the form and layout of the questionnaire. Understanding how in a self-completion scenario the form and layout motivate and help the respondent to answer the questions properly and honestly. Understanding how the form and layout help the interviewer to conduct and record the interview.

9 Reproducing the questionnaire. Understanding how the professional appearance of a questionnaire affects the perceived credibility and professional ability of researchers.

10 Eliminating problems by pilot-testing. Understanding that no matter how much experience the researcher has in designing questionnaires – the issues, respondent characteristics and context of questioning make each survey unique – pilot-testing is vital.

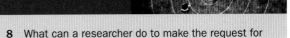

Questions

1 What is the purpose of a questionnaire?

2 What expectations does the marketing researcher have of potential questionnaire respondents – in terms of how they will react to the experience of completing a questionnaire?

3 What does the marketing researcher have to offer potential questionnaire respondents? Why should this question be considered?

4 How would you determine whether a specific question should be included in a questionnaire?

5 What are the reasons why respondents may be (a) unable to answer and (b) unwilling to answer the question asked?

6 Explain the errors of omission, telescoping and creation. What can be done to reduce such errors?

7 Explain the concepts of aided and unaided recall.

8 What can a researcher do to make the request for information seem legitimate?

9 What are the advantages and disadvantages of unstructured questions?

10 What are the issues involved in designing multiple-choice questions?

11 What are the guidelines available for deciding on question wording?

12 What is a leading question? Give an example.

13 What is the proper order for questions intended to obtain basic, classification and identification information?

14 What guidelines are available for deciding on the form and layout of a questionnaire?

15 Describe the issues involved in pilot-testing a questionnaire.

Exercises

1   Visit the website of one of the online marketing research firms, e.g. **www.hostedsurvey.com**. Choose one of the sample surveys and critically analyse the questionnaire using the principles discussed in this chapter.

2   Heineken beer would like to conduct a survey of 18–25-year-old Europeans to determine characteristics of its corporate image. Develop a full questionnaire and use the SNAP software package that accompanies this text (you are able to design nine questions of your survey and administer these to up to 25 respondents). Design nine questions of your questionnaire on SNAP and administer these to 25 fellow students. Write a short report based upon your experience of using the software and the findings you have generated.

3   Develop a questionnaire for determining household preferences for popular brands of cold breakfast cereals. Administer the questionnaire to five adult females, five adult males and five children. How would you modify the questionnaire if it was to be administered by telephone? What changes would be necessary if it was to be administered by the Internet? Are there distinctive characteristics of your different respondent types that could affect your questionnaire design?

4   You have been hired as a management trainee by a firm that manufactures major household appliances. Your boss has asked you to develop a questionnaire to determine how households plan, purchase and use major appliances. This questionnaire is to be used in five European countries. However, you feel that you do not have the expertise or the experience to construct such a complex questionnaire. Present your case to your boss.

5   In a small group discuss the following issues: 'Because questionnaire design is a craft, it is useless to follow a rigid set of guidelines. Rather the process should be left entirely to the creativity and ingenuity of the researcher'. And 'Asking classification questions at the start of a questionnaire only upsets the sensibilities of older respondents; young respondents are not concerned about where these questions are asked'.

Notes

1   Dowding, P., 'The field good factor', *Research*, (Fieldwork Supplement) (July 2000), 4.

2   Abel, S., 'Finding the elusive young through co-operative parents', *ResearchPlus* (February 1996).

3   The founding reference to this subject is Payne, S.L., *The Art of Asking Questions* (Princeton, NJ: Princeton University Press, 1951). See also Schrage, M., 'Survey says', *Adweek Magazines' Technology Marketing*, 22 (1) (January 2002) 11; Gillham, B., *Developing a questionnaire* (New York: Continuum International Publishing Group, 2000).

4   These guidelines are drawn from several books on questionnaire design: Vriens, M., 'Split questionnaire designs: a new tool in survey design and panel management', *Marketing Research* 13 (2) (Summer 2001), 14–19; Jenkins, S., 'Automating questionnaire design and construction', *Journal of the Market Research Society* (Winter 1999–2000), 79–95; Gillham, B., *Developing a questionnaire* (New York: Continuum International, 2000); Peterson, R.A., *Constructing Effective Questionnaires* (Thousand Oaks, CA: Sage, 2000); Schuman, H. and Presser, S., *Questions and Answers in Attitude Surveys* (Thousand Oaks, CA: Sage, 1996); Fink, A., *How to Ask Survey Questions* (Thousand Oaks, CA: Sage, 1995); Sudman, S. and Bradburn, N.M., *Asking Questions* (San Francisco: Jossey-Bass, 1983); Erdos, P.L., *Professional Mail Surveys* (Malabar, FL: Robert E. Krieger, 1983); Fowler, F.J., Jr Backstrom, C.H. and Hursh-Csar, G., Survey Research (Cambridge, MA: Wiley, 1981); Labau, P., *Advanced Questionnaire Design* (Orlando, FL: Abt Books, 1981).

5   Bourque, L.B. and Fielder, E.P., *How to Conduct Self-Administered and Mail Surveys* (Thousand Oaks, CA: Sage, 1995); Frey, J.H. and Oishi, S.M., *How to Conduct Interviews by Telephone and in Person* (Thousand Oaks, CA: Sage, 1995).

6   Bordeaux, D.B., 'Interviewing – part II: Getting the most out of interview questions', *Motor Age*, 121 (2) (February 2002), 38–40; Semon, T.T., 'Asking "how important" is not enough', *Marketing News* 31 (16) (4 August 1997), 19; Hague, P., 'Good and bad in questionnaire design', *Industrial Marketing Digest*, 12 (Third Quarter 1987), 161–170.

7   Hess, J., 'The effects of person-level versus household-level questionnaire design on survey estimates and data quality', *Public Opinion Quarterly* 65 (4) (Winter 2001), 574–584.

8   Knauper, B., 'Filter questions and question interpretation: presuppositions at work', *Public Opinion Quarterly* 62 (1) (Spring 1998), 70–78; Stapel, J., 'Observations: a brief observation about likeability and interestingness of advertising', *Journal of Advertising Research* 34 (2) (March/April 1994), 79–80; Bishop, G.E., Oldendick, R.W. and Tuchfarber, A.J., 'Effects of filter questions in public opinion surveys', *Public Opinion Quarterly* 46 (Spring 1982), 66–85.

9   Graeff, T.R., 'Uninformed response bias in telephone surveys', *Journal of Business Research* 55 (3) (March 2002), 251.

10 Lee, E., Hu, M.Y. and Toh, R.S., 'Are consumer survey results distorted? Systematic impact of behavioural frequency and duration on survey response errors', *Journal of Marketing Research* 37 (1) (February 2000), 125–133; Dutka, S. and Frankel, L.R., 'Measuring response error', *Journal of Advertising*

Research 37 (1) (January/February 1997), 33–39; Haller, T., *Danger: Marketing Researcher at Work* (Westport, CT: Quorum Books, 1983), 149.

11 Gaskell, G.D., 'Telescoping of landmark events: implications for survey research', *Public Opinion Quarterly* 64 (1) (Spring 2000), 77–89; Menon, G., Raghubir, P. and Schwarz, N., 'Behavioural frequency judgments: an accessibility-diagnosticity framework', *Journal of Consumer Research* 22 (2) (September 1995), 212–228; Cook, W.A., 'Telescoping and memory's other tricks', *Journal of Advertising Research* (February–March 1987), 5–8; Sudman, S., Finn, A. and Lannom, L., 'The use of bounded recall procedures in single interviews', *Public Opinion Quarterly* (Summer 1984), 520–524.

12 France, M., 'Why privacy notices are a sham', *Business Week* (18 June 2001), 82; Hill, R.P., 'Researching sensitive topics in marketing – the special case of vulnerable populations', *Journal of Public Policy and Marketing* 1 (1) (Spring 1995), 143–148.

13 Hanrahan, P., 'Mine your own business', *Target Marketing* (February 2000), 32; Tourangeau, R. and Smith, T.W., 'Asking sensitive questions: the impact of data collection mode, question format, and question context', *Public Opinion Quarterly* 60 (20) (Summer 1996), 275–304; Marquis, K.H., Marquis, M.S. and Polich, M.J., 'Response bias and reliability in sensitive topic surveys', *Journal of the American Statistical Association* (June 1986), 381–389.

14 Peterson, R.A., 'Asking the age question: a research note', *Public Opinion Quarterly* (Spring 1984), 379–383; Sheth, J.N., LeClaire, A. Jr and Wachspress, D., 'Impact of asking race information in mail surveys', *Journal of Marketing* (Winter 1980), 67–70.

15 Burton, B.K. and Near, J.P., 'Estimating the incidence of wrongdoing and whistle-blowing: results of a study using randomized response technique', *Journal of Business Ethics* 14 (January 1995), 17–30.

16 Larkins, E.R., Hume, E.C. and Garcha, B.S., 'The validity of the randomized response method in tax ethics research', *Journal of Applied Business Research* 13 (3) (Summer 1997), 25–32; Mukhopadhyay, P., 'A note on UMVU-estimation under randomized-response model', *Communications in Statistics – Theory and Methods* 26 (10) (1997), 2415–2420; Stem, D.E. Jr and Steinhorst, R.K., 'Telephone interview and mail questionnaire applications of the randomized response model', *Journal of the American Statistical Association* (September 1984), 555–564.

17 Patten, M.L., *Questionnaire research: A practical guide* (Los Angeles: Pyrczak, 2001); Newman, L.M., 'That's a good question', *American Demographics* (Marketing Tools) (June 1995), 10–13.

18 Popping, R., *Computer-assisted text analysis* (Thousand Oaks, CA: Sage, 2000); Luyens, S., 'Coding verbatims by computers', *Marketing Research: A Magazine of Management and Applications* 7 (2) (Spring 1995), 20–25.

19 Pothas, A.-M., 'Customer satisfaction: keeping tabs on the issues that matter', *Total Quality Management* 12 (1) (January 2001), 83; Mossholder, K.W., Settoon, R.P., Harris, S.G. and Armenakis, A.A., 'Measuring emotion in open-ended survey responses: an application of textual data analysis', *Journal of Management* 21 (2) (1995), 335–355.

20 Fowler, F.J., Jr *Improving Survey Questions* (Thousand Oaks, CA: Sage, 1995); Krosnick, J.A. and Alwin, D.E., 'An evaluation of a cognitive theory of response-order effects in survey measurement', *Public Opinion Quarterly* (Summer 1987), 201–209.

21 Javeline, D., 'Response effects in polite cultures', *Public Opinion Quarterly*, 63 (1) (Spring 1999), 1–27; Krosnick, J.A. and Alwin, D.F., 'An evaluation of a cognitive theory of response order effects in survey measurement', *Public Opinion Quarterly* (Summer 1987), 201–219; Blunch, N.J., 'Position bias in multiple-choice questions', *Journal of Marketing Research* 21 (May 1984), 216–220, has argued that position bias in multiple-choice questions cannot be eliminated by rotating the order of the alternatives. This viewpoint is contrary to the common practice.

22 Singer, E., 'Experiments with incentives in telephone surveys', *Public Opinion Quarterly* 64 (2) (Summer 2000), 171–188; Schuman, H. and Presser, S., *Questions and Answers in Attitude Surveys* (Thousand Oaks, CA: Sage, 1996).

23 Blumenschein, K., 'Hypothetical versus real willingness to pay in the health care sector: results from a field experiment', *Journal of Health Economics* 20 (3) (May 2001), 441; Herriges, J.A. and Shogren, J.F., 'Starting point bias in dichotomous choice valuation with follow-up questioning', *Journal of Environmental Economics and Management* 30 (1) (January 1996), 112–131; Mizerski, R.W., Freiden, J.B. and Green, R.C., Jr 'The effect of the "don't know" option on TV ad claim recognition tests', *Advances in Consumer Research* 10 (Orlando, FL: Association for Consumer Research, 1983), 283–287.

24 Kalton, G. and Schuman, H., 'The effect of the question on survey responses: a review', *Journal of the Royal Statistical Society Series A* 145, Part 1 (1982), 44–45.

25 Conrad, F.G., 'Clarifying question meaning in a household telephone survey', *Public Opinion Quarterly* 64 (1) (Spring 2000), 1–27; McBurnett, M., 'Wording of questions affects responses to gun control issue', *Marketing News* 31 (1) (6 January 1997), 12; Wanke, M., Schwarz, N. and Noelle-Neumann, E., 'Asking comparative questions: the impact of the direction of comparison', *Public Opinion Quarterly* 59 (3) (Fall 1995), 347–372.

26 Colombo, R., 'A model for diagnosing and reducing nonresponse bias', *Journal of Advertising Research* 40 (1/2) (January/April 2000), 85–93; Etter, J.F. and Perneger, T.V., 'Analysis of nonresponse bias in a mailed health survey', *Journal of Clinical Epidemiology* 50 (10) (25 October 1997), 1123–1128; Omura, G.S., 'Correlates of item non-response', *Journal of the Market Research Society* (October 1983), 321–330; Presser, S., 'Is inaccuracy on factual survey items item-specific or respondent-specific?', *Public Opinion Quarterly* (Spring 1984), 344–355.

27 Bollinger, C.R., 'Estimation with response error and nonresponse: food-stamp participation in the SIPP', *Journal of Business and Economic Statistics* 19 (2) (April 2001), 129–141; Stout, N.J., 'Questionnaire design workshop helps market researchers build better surveys', *Health Care Strategic Management* 12 (7) (July 1994), 10–11.

28 Gillham, B., *Developing a questionnaire* (New York: Continuum International, 2000); Saltz, L.C., 'How to get your news release published', *Journal of Accountancy* 182 (5) (November 1996), 89–91.

29 Couper, M.P., 'Web surveys: a review of issues and approaches,' *Public Opinion Quarterly* 64 (4) (Winter 2000), 464–494; Edmondson, B., 'How to spot a bogus poll', *American Demographics* 8 (10) (October 1996), 10–15; O'Brien, J., 'How do market researchers ask questions?', *Journal of the Market Research Society* 26 (April 1984), 93–107.

30 Semon, T.T., 'Ask simple questions to improve analysis of value perception', *Marketing News* 29 (5) (27 February 1995), 32.

31 Chisnall, P.M., 'Marketing research: state of the art perspectives', *International Journal of Marketing Research* 44 (1) (First Quarter 2002), 122–125; Abramson, P.R. and Ostrom, C.W., 'Question wording and partisanship', *Public Opinion Quarterly* 58 (1) (Spring 1994), 21–48.

32 Becker, B., 'Take direct route when data gathering', *Marketing News*, 33 (20) (27 September 1999, 29–30); and Anon., 'Don't lead: you may skew poll results', *Marketing News* 30 (12) (3 June 1996), H37.

33 Gillham, B., *Developing a questionnaire* (New York: Continuum International, 2000); Adamek, R.J., 'Public opinion and Roe v. Wade: measurement difficulties', *Public Opinion Quarterly* 58 (3) (Fall 1994), 409–418; Neumann, E.N. and Worcester, B., 'International opinion research', *European Research* (July 1984), 124–131.

34 Ouyand, M, 'Estimating marketing persistence on sales of consumer durables in China', *Journal of Business Research* 55 (4) (April 2002), 337; Jacoby, J. and Szybillo, G.J., 'Consumer research in FTC versus Kraft (1991): a case of heads we win, tails you lose?', *Journal of Public Policy and Marketing* 14 (1) (Spring 1995), 1–14; Jaffe, E.D. and Nebenzahl, I.D., 'Alternative questionnaire formats for country image studies', *Journal of Marketing Research* 21 (November 1984), 463–471.

35 Schuman, H. and Presser, S., *Questions and Answers in Attitude Surveys* (Thousand Oaks, CA: Sage, 1996); Krosnick, J.A. and Alwin, D.E., 'An evaluation of a cognitive theory of response-order effects in survey measurement', *Public Opinion Quarterly* (Summer 1987), 201–219.

36 Rating a brand on specific attributes early in a survey may affect responses to a later overall brand evaluation. For example, see Bartels, L.M., 'Question order and declining faith in elections', *Public Opinion Quarterly* 66 (1) (Spring 2002), 67–79; Bickart, B.A., 'Carryover and backfire effects in marketing research', *Journal of Marketing Research* 30 (February 1993), 52–62. See also McAllister, I. and Wattenberg, M.P., 'Measuring levels of party identification: does question order matter?', *Public Opinion Quarterly* 59 (2) (Summer 1995), 259–268.

37 Watson, P.D., 'Adolescents' perceptions of a health survey using multimedia computer-assisted self administered interview', *Australian & New Zealand Journal of Public Health* 25 (6) (December 2001), 520; Willits, F.K. and Ke, B., 'Part-whole question order effects: views of rurality', *Public Opinion Quarterly* 59 (3) (Fall 1995), 392–403; Messmer, D.J. and Seymour, D.J., 'The effects of branching on item non-response', *Public Opinion Quarterly* 46 (Summer 1982), 270–277.

38 Zatz, D., 'Create effective email surveys,' *HRMagazine* 45 (1) (January 2000), 97–103; Milne, G.R., 'Consumer participation in mailing lists: a field experiment', *Journal of Public Policy and Marketing* 16 (2) (Fall 1997), 298–309.

39 Dickinson, S.R. and Kirzner, E., 'Questionnaire item omission as a function of within-group question position', *Journal of Business Research* 38 (February 1985), 71–75; Herzog, A.R. and Bachman, J.G., 'Effects of questionnaire length on response quality', *Public Opinion Quarterly* 45 (Winter 1981), 549–559.

40 Martin, E. and Polivka, A.E., 'Diagnostics for redesigning survey questionnaires – measuring work in the current population survey', *Public Opinion Quarterly* 59 (4) (Winter 1995), 547–567.

41 Mohrle, M.G., 'Empirical testing of a computer-based dialog questionnaire – 11 design rules for successful usage', *Wirtschaftsinformatik* 39 (5) (October 1997), 461.

42 Conrad, F. G., 'Clarifying questions meaning in a household telephone survey', *Public Opinion Quarterly* 64 (1) (Spring 2000), 1–27; Diamantopoulos, A., Schlegelmilch, B.B. and Reynolds, N., 'Pre-testing in questionnaire design: the impact of respondent characteristics on error detection', *Journal of the Market Research Society* 36 (October 1994), 295–314.

43 Gillham, B., *Developing a questionnaire* (New York: Continuum International, 2000); Reynolds, N., Diamantopoulos, A. and Schlegelmilch, B.B., 'Pre-testing in questionnaire design: a review of the literature and suggestions for further research', *Journal of the Market Research Society* 35 (April 1993), 171–182.

44 Hutton, G., 'If you board the Asian bus, better mind your language', *Research Plus* (February 1996), 7.

45 Laczniak, G.R. and Murphy, P.E., *Ethical Marketing Decisions: the Higher Road* (Needham Heights, MA: Allyn and Bacon, 1993).

46 Morris, M.H., Marks, A.S., Allen, J.A. and Peery, N.S., 'Modeling ethical attitudes and behaviours under conditions of environmental turbulence – case of South Africa', *Journal of Business Ethics* 15 (10) (October 1996), 1119–1130.

47 David, M.A., 'Measuring ethical ideology in business ethics: a critical analysis of the ethics position questionnaire', *Journal of Business Ethics* 32 (1) (July 2001), 35–53; Armstrong, R.W., 'An empirical investigation of international marketing ethics: problems encountered by Australian firms', *Journal of Business Ethics* 11 (1992), 161–171.

Source: © Getty Images

14

Sampling: design and procedures

> " *There is no hope of making scientific statements about a population based on the knowledge obtained from a sample, unless we are circumspect in choosing a sampling method.* "

Objectives

After reading this chapter, you should be able to:

1 differentiate a sample from a census and identify the conditions that favour the use of a sample versus a census;

2 discuss the sampling design process: definition of the target population, determination of the sampling frame, selection of sampling technique(s), determination of sample size, execution of the sampling process and validating the sample;

3 classify sampling techniques as non-probability and probability sampling techniques;

4 describe the non-probability sampling techniques of convenience, judgemental, quota and snowball sampling;

5 describe the probability sampling techniques of simple random, systematic, stratified and cluster sampling;

6 identify the conditions that favour the use of non-probability sampling versus probability sampling;

7 understand the sampling design process and the use of sampling techniques in international marketing research;

8 identify the ethical issues related to the sampling design process and the use of appropriate sampling techniques.

STAGE 1
Problem definition

STAGE 2
Research approach developed

STAGE 3
Research design developed

STAGE 4
Fieldwork or data collection

STAGE 5
Data preparation and analysis

STAGE 6
Report preparation and presentation

Overview

Sampling is a key component of any research design. Sampling design involves several basic questions:

1 Should a sample be taken?

2 If so, what process should be followed?

3 What kind of sample should be taken?

4 How large should it be?

5 What can be done to control and adjust for non-response errors?

This chapter introduces the fundamental concepts of sampling and the qualitative considerations necessary to answer these questions. We address the question of whether or not to sample and describe the steps involved in sampling. Next, we present non-probability and probability sampling techniques. We discuss the use of sampling techniques in international marketing research and identify the relevant ethical issues. Statistical determination of sample size, and the causes for, control of and adjustments for non-response error, are discussed in Chapter 15.

We begin with the following example, which illustrates the usefulness of sampling.

Example

Mercedes Benz, BMW and Audi seen as top three car manufacturers by Europeans

Harris Interactive (**www.harrisinteractive.com/europe/**) conducted research to understand the values that adult consumers from the UK, France, Germany, Italy and Spain associate with 21 major automobile brands ahead of the 61st International Motor Show (2005) in Frankfurt, Germany

Key findings from the study included:

● In the five European markets surveyed overall, consumers regard Mercedes Benz (#1), BMW (#2) and Audi (#3) as the top three car manufacturers in terms of overall brand quality.

● Prestigious German cars, including BMW, Mercedes Benz and Audi, are on the overall top five lists for brands that convey the values of success and financial security; however, they do not make the lists for brands that convey the values of family, freedom or sociability.

● Consumers are more likely to associate family values with cars manufactured or badged in their own countries. So, in Italy, Fiat conveys the strongest family values; in France, Peugeot, Renault and Citroën; in Germany, Volkswagen comes in third on the list after Ford and Vauxhall/Opel, and likewise Rover in the UK.

Harris Interactive conducted the online survey among 6,717 adults aged 16 and over from five European countries: the UK (2,080), France (1,179), Italy (1,181), Spain (1,079) and Germany (1,198). Data were weighted to be representative of the general population in each country with respect to income, education, geographic location and propensity to be online. These online samples were not probability samples.

This example illustrates some of the challenges faced by marketing researchers in constructing a 'representative' sample. However, imagine if the researchers in the above example had attempted to question every adult over the age of 16 in the five countries surveyed. The cost involved and the time needed to complete the task would have been astronomical. Even if the sponsors could afford to undertake a census, would it give them a more accurate measurement of people's views?

Sample or census

Population
The aggregate of all the elements, sharing some common set of characteristics, that comprise the universe for the purpose of the marketing research problem.

Census
A complete enumeration of the elements of a population or study objects.

Sample
A subgroup of the elements of the population selected for participation in the study.

The objective of most marketing research projects is to obtain information about the characteristics or parameters of a **population**. A population is the aggregate of all the elements that share some common set of characteristics and that comprise the universe for the purpose of the marketing research problem. The population parameters are typically numbers, such as the proportion of consumers who are loyal to a particular brand of toothpaste. Information about population parameters may be obtained by taking a **census** or a **sample**. A census involves a complete enumeration of the elements of a population. The population parameters can be calculated directly in a straightforward way after the census is enumerated. A sample, on the other hand, is a subgroup of the population selected for participation in the study. Sample characteristics, called statistics, are then used to make inferences about the population parameters. The inferences that link sample characteristics and population parameters are estimation procedures and tests of hypotheses. These inference procedures are considered in Chapters 18 to 24.

Table 14.1 summarises the conditions favouring the use of a sample versus a census. Budget and time limits are obvious constraints favouring the use of a sample. A census is both costly and time consuming to conduct. A census is unrealistic if the population is large, as it is for most consumer products. In the case of many industrial products, however, the population is small, making a census feasible as well as desirable. For example, in investigating the use of certain machine tools by Italian car manufacturers, a census would be preferred to a sample. Another reason for preferring a census in this case is that variance in the characteristic of interest is large. For example, machine tool usage of Fiat may vary greatly from the usage of Ferrari. Small population sizes as well as high variance in the characteristic to be measured favour a census.

If the cost of sampling errors is high (e.g. if the sample omitted a major manufacturer like Ford, the results could be misleading) a census, which eliminates such errors, is desirable. If the cost of non-sampling errors is high (e.g. interviewers incorrectly questioning target respondents) a sample, where fewer resources would have been spent, would be favoured.

Table 14.1 Sample versus census

Factors	Conditions favouring the use of	
	Sample	Census
1 Budget	Small	Large
2 Time available	Short	Long
3 Population size	Large	Small
4 Variance in the characteristic	Small	Large
5 Cost of sampling errors	Low	High
6 Cost of non-sampling errors	High	Low
7 Nature of measurement	Destructive	Non-destructive
8 Attention to individual cases	Yes	No

A census can greatly increase non-sampling error to the point that these errors exceed the sampling errors of a sample. Non-sampling errors are found to be the major contributor to total error, whereas random sampling errors have been relatively small in magnitude.[1] Hence, in most cases, accuracy considerations would favour a sample over a census.

A sample may be preferred if the measurement process results in the destruction or contamination of the elements sampled. For example, product usage tests result in the consumption of the product. Therefore, taking a census in a study that requires households to use a new brand of toothpaste would not be feasible. Sampling may also be necessary to focus attention on individual cases, as in the case of in-depth interviews. Finally, other pragmatic considerations, such as the need to keep the study secret, may favour a sample over a census.

The sampling design process

The sampling design process includes six steps, which are shown sequentially in Figure 14.1. These steps are closely interrelated and relevant to all aspects of the marketing research project, from problem definition to the presentation of the results. Therefore, sample design decisions should be integrated with all other decisions in a research project.[2]

Define the target population

Target population
The collection of elements or objects that possess the information sought by the researcher and about which inferences are to be made.

Element
An object that possesses the information sought by the researcher and about which inferences are to be made.

Sampling unit
An element, or a unit containing the element, that is available for selection at some stage of the sampling process.

Sampling design begins by specifying the **target population**. This is the collection of elements or objects that possess the information sought by the researcher and about which inferences are to be made. The target population must be defined precisely. Imprecise definition of the target population will result in research that is ineffective at best and misleading at worst. Defining the target population involves translating the problem definition into a precise statement of who should and should not be included in the sample.

The target population should be defined in terms of elements, sampling units, extent and time. An **element** is the object about which or from which the information is desired. In survey research, the element is usually the respondent. A **sampling unit** is an element, or a unit containing the element, that is available for selection at some stage of the sampling process. Suppose that Clinique wanted to assess consumer response to a new line of lipsticks and wanted to sample females over 25 years of age. It may be possible to sample females over 25 directly, in which case a sampling unit would be the same as an element. Alternatively, the sampling unit might be households. In the latter case,

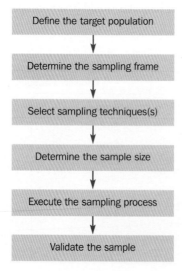

Figure 14.1
The sampling design process

households would be sampled and all females over 25 in each selected household would be interviewed. Here, the sampling unit and the population element are different. Extent refers to the geographical boundaries of the research, and the time refers to the period under consideration. We use the Formula One Racetrack Project to illustrate.

 Focus on | **Sports Marketing Surveys**

Target population

The target population for the Formula One Racetrack Project was defined as follows:

Elements:	male or female aged 18–55
Sampling units:	households
Extent:	Australia, Brazil, France, Germany, the UK, Italy, Japan, Spain
Time:	2005

Defining the target population may not be as easy as it was in this example. Consider a marketing research project assessing consumer response to a new brand of men's moisturiser. Who should be included in the target population? All men? Men who have used a moisturiser during the last month? Men of 17 years of age or older? Should females be included, because some women buy moisturiser for men whom they know? These and similar questions must be resolved before the target population can be appropriately defined.[3]

Determine the sampling frame

Sampling frame
A representation of the elements of the target population that consists of a list or set of directions for identifying the target population.

A **sampling frame** is a representation of the elements of the target population. It consists of a list or set of directions for identifying the target population. Examples of a sampling frame include the telephone book, an association directory listing the firms in an industry, a customer database, a mailing list on a database purchased from a commercial organisation, a city directory, or a map.[4] If a list cannot be compiled, then at least some directions for identifying the target population should be specified, such as random-digit dialling procedures in telephone surveys.

Often it is possible to compile or obtain a list of population elements, but the list may omit some elements of the population or may include other elements that do not belong. Therefore, the use of a list will lead to sampling frame error, which was discussed in Chapter 3.[5]

In some instances, the discrepancy between the population and the sampling frame is small enough to ignore. In most cases, however, the researcher should recognise and attempt to treat the sampling frame error. One approach is to redefine the population in terms of the sampling frame. For example, if a telephone directory is used as a sampling frame, the population of households could be redefined as those with a correct listing in a given area. Although this approach is simplistic, it does prevent the researcher from being misled about the actual population being investigated.[6] Ultimately, the major drawback of redefining the population based upon available sampling frames is that the nature of the research problem may be compromised. Who is being measured and ultimately to whom the research findings may be generalised may not match the target group of individuals identified in a research problem definition. Evaluating the accuracy of sampling frames matches the issues of evaluating the quality of secondary data (see Chapter 4).

Another way is to account for sampling frame error by screening the respondents in the data collection phase. The respondents could be screened with respect to demographic characteristics, familiarity, product usage and other characteristics to ensure that they satisfy the criteria for the target population. Screening can eliminate inappropriate elements contained in the sampling frame, but it cannot account for elements that have been omitted.

Yet another approach is to adjust the data collected by a weighted scheme to counterbalance the sampling frame error. This is discussed in Chapters 15 and 17. Regardless of which approach is used, it is important to recognise any sampling frame error that exists, so that inappropriate inferences can be avoided.

Select a sampling technique

Selecting a sampling technique involves several decisions of a broader nature. The researcher must decide whether to use a Bayesian or traditional sampling approach, to sample with or without replacement, and to use non-probability or probability sampling.

In the **Bayesian approach**, the elements are selected sequentially. After each element is added to the sample, the data are collected, sample statistics computed and sampling costs determined. The Bayesian approach explicitly incorporates prior information about population parameters as well as the costs and probabilities associated with making wrong decisions. This approach is theoretically appealing. Yet it is not used widely in marketing research because much of the required information on costs and probabilities is not available. In the traditional sampling approach, the entire sample is selected before data collection begins. Because the traditional approach is the most common approach used, it is assumed in the following sections.

In **sampling with replacement**, an element is selected from the sampling frame and appropriate data are obtained. Then the element is placed back in the sampling frame. As a result, it is possible for an element to be included in the sample more than once. In **sampling without replacement**, once an element is selected for inclusion in the sample, it is removed from the sampling frame and therefore cannot be selected again. The calculation of statistics is done somewhat differently for the two approaches, but statistical inference is not very different if the sampling frame is large relative to the ultimate sample size. Thus, the distinction is important only when the sampling frame is small compared with the sample size.

The most important decision about the choice of sampling technique is whether to use non-probability or probability sampling. Non-probability sampling relies on the judgement of the researcher, while probability sampling relies on chance. Given its importance, the issues involved in this decision are discussed in detail below, in the section headed 'A classification of sampling techniques'.

If the sampling unit is different from the element, it is necessary to specify precisely how the elements within the sampling unit should be selected. With in-home personal interviews and telephone interviews, merely specifying the address or the telephone number may not be sufficient. For example, should the person answering the doorbell or the telephone be interviewed, or someone else in the household? Often, more than one person in a household may qualify. For example, both the male and female head of household, or even their children, may be eligible to participate in a study examining family leisure-time activities. When a probability sampling technique is being employed, a random selection must be made from all the eligible persons in each household. A simple procedure for random selection is the 'next birthday' method. The interviewer asks which of the eligible persons in the household has the next birthday and includes that person in the sample.

Determine the sample size

Sample size refers to the number of elements to be included in the study. Determining the sample size involves several qualitative and quantitative considerations. The qualitative factors are discussed in this section, and the quantitative factors are considered in Chapter 15. Important qualitative factors to be considered in determining the sample size include

---

Bayesian approach
A selection method where the elements are selected sequentially. The Bayesian approach explicitly incorporates prior information about population parameters as well as the costs and probabilities associated with making wrong decisions.

Sampling with replacement
A sampling technique in which an element *can* be included in the sample more than once.

Sampling without replacement
A sampling technique in which an element *cannot* be included in the sample more than once.

Sample size
The number of elements to be included in a study.

(1) the importance of the decision, (2) the nature of the research, (3) the number of variables, (4) the nature of the analysis, (5) sample sizes used in similar studies, (6) incidence rates, (7) completion rates, and (8) resource constraints.

In general, for more important decisions, more information is necessary, and that information should be obtained very precisely. This calls for larger samples, but as the sample size increases, each unit of information is obtained at greater cost. The degree of precision may be measured in terms of the standard deviation of the mean, which is inversely proportional to the square root of the sample size. The larger the sample, the smaller the gain in precision by increasing the sample size by one unit.

The nature of the research also has an impact on the sample size. For exploratory research designs, such as those using qualitative research, the sample size is typically small. For conclusive research, such as descriptive surveys, larger samples are required. Likewise, if data are being collected on a large number of variables, i.e. many questions are asked in a survey, larger samples are required. The cumulative effects of sampling error across variables are reduced in a large sample.

If sophisticated analysis of the data using multivariate techniques is required, the sample size should be large. The same applies if the data are to be analysed in great detail. Thus, a larger sample would be required if the data are being analysed at the subgroup or segment level than if the analysis is limited to the aggregate or total sample.

Sample size is influenced by the average size of samples in similar studies. Table 14.2 gives an idea of sample sizes used in different marketing research studies. These sample sizes have been determined based on experience and can serve as rough guidelines, particularly when non-probability sampling techniques are used.

The sample size required should be adjusted for the incidence of eligible respondents and the completion rate. Finally, the sample size decision should be guided by a consideration of the resource constraints. In any marketing research project, money and time are limited. The decisions involved in determining the sample size are covered in detail in the next chapter.

Execute the sampling process

Execution of the sampling process requires a detailed specification of how the sampling design decisions with respect to the population, sampling unit, sampling frame, sampling technique and sample size are to be implemented. Whilst individual researchers may know how they are going to execute their sampling process, once more than one individual is involved, a specification for execution is needed to ensure that the process is conducted in a consistent manner. For example, if households are the sampling unit, an operational definition of a household is needed. Procedures should be specified for empty housing units and for call-backs in case no one is at home.

Table 14.2 Usual sample sizes used in marketing research studies

Type of study	Minimum size	Typical range
Problem identification research (e.g. market potential)	500	1,000–2,500
Problem-solving research (e.g. pricing)	200	300–500
Product tests	200	300–500
Test marketing studies	200	300–500
TV, radio or print advertising (per commercial/ad tested)	150	200–300
Test market audits	10 stores	10–20 stores
Focus groups	6 groups	6–12 groups

Validate the sample

Sample validation aims to account for sampling frame error by screening the respondents in the data collection phase. Respondents can be screened with respect to demographic characteristics, familiarity, product usage and other characteristics to ensure that they satisfy the criteria for the target population. Screening can eliminate inappropriate elements contained in the sampling frame, but it cannot account for elements that have been omitted. The success of the validation process depends upon the accuracy of base statistics that describe the structure of a target population.

Once data are collected from a sample, comparisons between the structure of the sample and the target population should be made. Once data have been collected and it is found that the structure of a sample does not match the target population, a weighting scheme can be used (this is discussed in Chapter 17).

The steps involved in the sampling design process are illustrated in the following example based upon a continuous tracking survey.

Example | **Taking the people's temperature – right across Europe[7]**

Since the earliest days of the European Economic Community, the Commission's information, communication, culture and audio-visual directorate, Directorate General X, has conducted regular polls across Europe. In 1996 the need for speed and flexibility in EU surveys led to the introduction of the Continuous Tracking Survey or CTS. The origin of the CTS was a policy initiative on information and communication, established in 1993 as a result of the decline in support for the EU in the period leading up to the Single Market and the ratification of the Maastricht Treaty.

The sample design for this study involved:

1 *Target population*: adults aged 18 years and over (element) in a household with a working telephone number (sampling unit) in individual EU countries (extent) during the survey period (time).
2 *Sampling frame*: computer program for generating random-digit dialling (except in Germany where the code of practice forbids this approach).
3 *Sampling unit*: working telephone numbers.
4 *Sampling technique*: random sampling.
5 *Sample size*: 800 in each of 16 sampling areas making a total of 12,800 interviews in each four-week wave of interviewing – a total of 140,000 interviews each year.
6 *Execution*: CATI, random-digit dialling followed by the random selection of individuals in households; 19 variants of the questionnaire to include people living in countries where more than one national language is common.
7 *Validation*: sample characteristics compared with census statistics in each country.

A classification of sampling techniques

Sampling techniques may be broadly classified as non-probability and probability (see Figure 14.2).

Non-probability sampling
Sampling techniques that do not use chance selection procedures but rather rely on the personal judgement of the researcher.

Non-probability sampling relies on the personal judgement of the researcher rather than on chance to select sample elements. The researcher can arbitrarily or consciously decide what elements to include in the sample. Non-probability samples may yield good estimates of the population characteristics, but they do not allow for objective evaluation of the precision of the sample results. Because there is no way of determining the probability of selecting any particular element for inclusion in the sample, the estimates obtained are not statistically projectable to the population. Commonly used

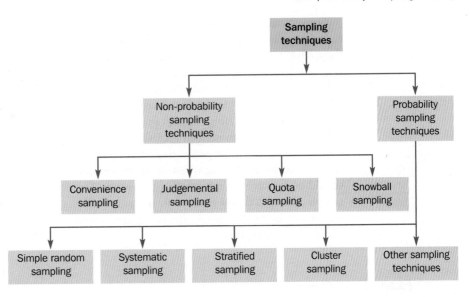

**Figure 14.2
A classification of
sampling techniques**

non-probability sampling techniques include convenience sampling, judgemental sampling, quota sampling and snowball sampling.

Probability sampling
A sampling procedure in which each element of the population has a fixed probabilistic chance of being selected for the sample.

In **probability sampling**, sampling units are selected by chance. It is possible to pre-specify every potential sample of a given size that could be drawn from the population, as well as the probability of selecting each sample. Every potential sample need not have the same probability of selection, but it is possible to specify the probability of selecting any particular sample of a given size. This requires not only a precise definition of the target population but also a general specification of the sampling frame. Because sample elements are selected by chance, it is possible to determine the precision of the sample estimates of the characteristics of interest. **Confidence intervals**, which contain the true population value with a given level of certainty, can be calculated. This permits the researcher to make inferences or projections about the target population from which the sample was drawn. Classification of probability sampling techniques is based on:

Confidence intervals
The range into which the true population parameter will fall, assuming a given level of confidence.

- element versus cluster sampling
- equal unit probability versus unequal unit probability
- unstratified versus stratified selection
- random versus systematic selection
- one-stage versus multistage techniques.

All possible combinations of these five aspects result in 32 different probability sampling techniques. Of these techniques, we consider simple random sampling, systematic sampling, stratified sampling and cluster sampling in depth and briefly touch on some others. First, however, we discuss non-probability sampling techniques.

Non-probability sampling techniques

Convenience sampling

Convenience sampling
A non-probability sampling technique that attempts to obtain a sample of convenient elements. The selection of sampling units is left primarily to the interviewer.

Convenience sampling attempts to obtain a sample of convenient elements. The selection of sampling units is left primarily to the interviewer. Often, respondents are selected because they happen to be in the right place at the right time. Examples of convenience sampling include: (1) use of students, church groups and members of social organisations, (2) street interviews without qualifying the respondents, (3) some forms of email and Internet survey, (4) tear-out questionnaires included in a newspaper or magazine, and (5) journalists interviewing 'people on the street'.[8]

Convenience sampling is the least expensive and least time consuming of all sampling techniques. The sampling units are accessible, easy to measure and cooperative. Despite these advantages, this form of sampling has serious limitations. Many potential sources of selection bias are present, including respondent self-selection. Convenience samples are not representative of any definable population. Hence, it is not theoretically meaningful to generalise to any population from a convenience sample, and convenience samples are not appropriate for marketing research projects involving population inferences. Convenience samples are not recommended for descriptive or causal research, but they can be used in exploratory research for generating ideas, insights or hypotheses. Convenience samples can be used for pretesting questionnaires, or pilot studies. Even in these cases, caution should be exercised in interpreting the results. For example, in the following example, a sample size of 200 was selected to represent visitors to the Sydney Olympics. With no means to validate this sample, how confident would you be in using these findings to represent all of the visitors?

Example **Olympic convenience[9]**

The International Olympic Committee (IOC, **www.olympic.org**) used surveys at the 2000 Olympic Games in Sydney to find out what visitors thought about the level of commercialism in Sydney. One survey was given to a convenience sample of 200 visitors to the games and they were asked about the level of commercialism they find appropriate, whether they thought the event was too commercial, and whether company sponsorship of the games was perceived to be positive. The survey, conducted by Performance Research (**www.performanceresearch.com**), revealed that 77% of the visitors found the presence of large corporations such as Coca-Cola and McDonald's to be appropriate. Furthermore, 88% of the visitors thought the sponsors contributed to the Olympics positively. About 33% said that they thought a company's involvement in Sydney made them feel more positive about that company in general.

Judgemental sampling

Judgemental sampling
A form of convenience sampling in which the population elements are purposely selected based on the judgement of the researcher.

Judgemental sampling is a form of convenience sampling in which the population elements are selected based on the judgement of the researcher. The researcher, exercising judgement or expertise, chooses the elements to be included in the sample because he or she believes that they are representative of the population of interest or are otherwise appropriate. Common examples of judgemental sampling include: (1) test markets selected to determine the potential of a new product, (2) purchase engineers selected in industrial marketing research because they are considered to be representative of the company, (3) product testing with individuals who may be particularly fussy or who hold extremely high expectations, (4) expert witnesses used in court, and (5) supermarkets selected to test a new merchandising display system.

Judgemental sampling is inexpensive, convenient and quick, yet it does not allow direct generalisations to a specific population, usually because the population is not defined explicitly. Judgemental sampling is subjective and its value depends entirely on the researcher's judgement, expertise and creativity. It can be useful if broad population inferences are not required. Judgement samples are frequently used in business-to-business marketing research projects, given that in many projects the target population is relatively small (see Chapter 27).

Quota sampling

Quota sampling
A non-probability sampling technique that is a two-stage restricted judgemental sampling. The first stage consists of developing control categories or quotas of population elements. In the second stage, sample elements are selected based on convenience or judgement.

Quota sampling may be viewed as two-stage restricted judgemental sampling that is used extensively in street interviewing. The first stage consists of developing control characteristics, or quotas, of population elements such as age or gender. To develop these quotas, the researcher lists relevant control characteristics and determines the distribution of these characteristics in the target population, such as Males 49%, Females 51% (resulting in 490 men and 510 women being selected in a sample of 1,000 respondents). Often, the quotas are assigned so that the proportion of the sample elements possessing the control characteristics is the same as the proportion of population elements with these characteristics. In other words, the quotas ensure that the composition of the sample is the same as the composition of the population with respect to the characteristics of interest.

In the second stage, sample elements are selected based on convenience or judgement. Once the quotas have been assigned, there is considerable freedom in selecting the elements to be included in the sample. The only requirement is that the elements selected fit the control characteristics.[10] This technique is illustrated with the following example.

Example   ## How is epilepsy perceived?

A study was undertaken by the Scottish Epilepsy Association to determine the perceptions of the condition of epilepsy by the adult population in the city of Glasgow. A quota sample of 500 adults was selected. The control characteristics were gender, age and propensity to donate to a charity. Based on the composition of the adult population of the city, the quotas assigned were as follows:

Propensity to donate		Male 48%		Female 52%		Totals
		Have a flag	No flag	Have a flag	No flag	
Age		50%	50%	50%	50%	
18 to 30	25%	30	30	33	32	**125**
31 to 45	40%	48	48	52	52	**200**
46 to 60	15%	18	18	19	20	**75**
Over 60	20%	24	24	26	26	**100**
Totals		**120**	**120**	**130**	**130**	
Totals		**240**		**260**		**500**

Note that the percentages of gender and age within the target population can be taken from local census statistics. The percentages of 'propensity to donate' could not be gleaned from secondary data sources and so were split on a 50/50 basis. The interviews were conducted on a Saturday when it was customary to see charity 'flag sellers' operating. One of the hypotheses to be tested in the study was the extent to which those who donated to charities on flag days were more aware of the condition of epilepsy and how to treat epileptic sufferers. Thus the instruction to interviewers was to split interviews between those who wore the 'flag' that they had bought from a street collector and those who had not bought a flag. It was recognised that this was a crude measure of propensity to donate to a charity but was the only tangible clue that could be consistently observed.

In this example, quotas were assigned such that the composition of the sample mirrored the population. In certain situations, however, it is desirable either to under- or over-sample elements with certain characteristics. To illustrate, it may be desirable to over-sample heavy users of a product so that their behaviour can be examined in detail. Although this type of sample is not representative, it may nevertheless be very relevant to allow a particular group of individuals to be broken down into subcategories and analysed in depth.

Even if the sample composition mirrors that of the population with respect to the control characteristics, there is no assurance that the sample is representative. If a characteristic that is relevant to the problem is overlooked, the quota sample will not be representative. Relevant control characteristics are often omitted because there are practical difficulties associated with including certain control characteristics. For example, suppose a sample was sought that was representative of the different strata of socio-economic classes in a population. Imagine street interviewers approaching potential respondents who they believe would fit into the quota they have been set. Could an interviewer 'guess' which potential respondents fit into different classes in the same way that they may guess the gender and age of respondents? The initial questions of a street interview could establish characteristics of potential respondents to see whether they fit a set quota. But given the levels of non-response and ineligibility levels found by such an approach, this is not an ideal solution.

Because the elements within each quota are selected based on convenience or judgement, many sources of selection bias are potentially present. The interviewers may go to selected areas where eligible respondents are more likely to be found. Likewise, they may avoid people who look unfriendly or are not well dressed or those who live in undesirable locations. Quota sampling does not permit assessment of sampling error.[11]

Quota sampling attempts to obtain representative samples at a relatively low cost. Its advantages are the lower costs and greater convenience to the interviewers in selecting elements for each quota. Under certain conditions, quota sampling obtains results close to those for conventional probability sampling.[12]

Snowball sampling

Snowball sampling
A non-probability sampling technique in which an initial group of respondents is selected randomly. Subsequent respondents are selected based on the referrals or information provided by the initial respondents. By obtaining referrals from referrals, this process may be carried out in waves.

In **snowball sampling**, an initial group of respondents is selected, sometimes on a random basis, but more typically targeted at a few individuals who are known to possess the desired characteristics of the target population. After being interviewed, these respondents are asked to identify others who also belong to the target population of interest. Subsequent respondents are selected based on the referrals. By obtaining referrals from referrals, this process may be carried out in waves, thus leading to a snowballing effect. Even though probability sampling can be used to select the initial respondents, the final sample is a non-probability sample. The referrals will have demographic and psychographic characteristics more similar to the persons referring them than would occur by chance.[13]

Source: © Getty Images

The main objective of snowball sampling is to estimate characteristics that are rare in the wider population. Examples include users of particular government or social services, such as parents who use nurseries or child minders, whose names cannot be revealed; special census groups, such as widowed males under 35; and members of a scattered minority ethnic group. Another example is research in industrial buyer–seller relationships, using initial contacts to identify buyer–seller pairs and then subsequent 'snowballed' pairs. The major advantage of snowball sampling is that it substantially increases the likelihood of locating the desired characteristic in the population. It also results in relatively low sampling variance and costs.[14] Snowball sampling is illustrated by the following example.

Sampling horse owners

Dalgety Animal Feeds wished to question horse owners about the care and feeding of their horses. The firm could not locate any sampling frame that listed all horse owners, with the exception of registers of major racing stables. However, the firm wished to contact owners who had one or two horses as it believed this group was not well understood and held great marketing potential. The initial approach involved locating interviewers at horse feed outlets. The interviewers ascertained basic characteristics of horse owners but more importantly they invited them along to focus groups. When the focus groups were conducted, issues of horse care and feeding were developed in greater detail to allow the construction of a meaningful postal questionnaire. As a rapport and trust was built up with those that attended the focus groups, names as referrals were given that allowed a sampling frame for the first wave of respondents to the subsequent postal survey. The process of referrals continued, allowing a total of four waves and a response of 800 questionnaires.

In this example, note the non-random selection of the initial group of respondents through focus group invitations. This procedure was more efficient than random selection, which given the absence of an appropriate sampling frame would be very cumbersome. In other cases where an appropriate sampling frame exists (appropriate in terms of identifying the desired characteristics in a number of respondents, not in terms of being exhaustive – if it were exhaustive, a snowball sample would not be needed), random selection of respondents through probability sampling techniques may be more appropriate.

Probability sampling techniques

Probability sampling techniques vary in terms of sampling efficiency. Sampling efficiency is a concept that reflects a trade-off between sampling cost and precision. Precision refers to the level of uncertainty about the characteristic being measured. Precision is inversely related to sampling errors but positively related to cost. The greater the precision, the greater the cost, and most studies require a trade-off. The researcher should strive for the most efficient sampling design, subject to the budget allocated. The efficiency of a probability sampling technique may be assessed by comparing it with that of simple random sampling.

Simple random sampling

Simple random sampling (SRS)
A probability sampling technique in which each element has a known and equal probability of selection. Every element is selected independently of every other element, and the sample is drawn by a random procedure from a sampling frame.

In **simple random sampling** (SRS), each element in the population has a known and equal probability of selection. Furthermore, each possible sample of a given size (n) has a known and equal probability of being the sample actually selected. This implies that every element is selected independently of every other element. The sample is drawn by a random procedure from a sampling frame. This method is equivalent to a lottery system in which names are placed in a container, the container is shaken and the names of the winners are then drawn out in an unbiased manner.

To draw a simple random sample, the researcher first compiles a sampling frame in which each element is assigned a unique identification number. Then random numbers are generated to determine which elements to include in the sample. The random numbers may be generated with a computer routine or a table (see Table 1 in the Appendix of statistical tables). Suppose that a sample of size 10 is to be selected from a sampling frame containing 800 elements. This could be done by starting with row 1 and column 1 of Table 1, considering the three rightmost digits, and going down the column until 10 numbers between 1 and 800 have been selected. Numbers outside this range are ignored. The elements corresponding to the random numbers generated constitute the sample.

Thus, in our example, elements 480, 368, 130, 167, 570, 562, 301, 579, 475 and 553 would be selected. Note that the last three digits of row 6 (921) and row 11 (918) were ignored, because they were out of range. Using these tables is fine for small samples, but can be very tedious. A more pragmatic solution is to turn to random-number generators in most data analysis packages. For example, in Excel, the Random Number Generation Analysis Tool allows you to set a number of characteristics of your target population, including the nature of distribution of the data, and to create a table of random numbers on a separate worksheet.

SRS has many desirable features. It is easily understood and the sample results may be projected to the target population. Most approaches to statistical inference assume that the data have been collected by SRS. However, SRS suffers from at least four significant limitations. First, it is often difficult to construct a sampling frame that will permit a simple random sample to be drawn. Second, SRS can result in samples that are very large or spread over large geographical areas, thus increasing the time and cost of data collection. Third, SRS often results in lower precision with larger standard errors than other probability sampling techniques. Fourth, SRS may or may not result in a representative sample. Although samples drawn will represent the population well on average, a given simple random sample may grossly misrepresent the target population. This is more likely if the size of the sample is small. For these reasons, SRS is not widely used in marketing research. Procedures such as systematic sampling are more popular.

Systematic sampling

Systematic sampling
A probability sampling technique in which the sample is chosen by selecting a random starting point and then picking every *i*th element in succession from the sampling frame.

In **systematic sampling**, the sample is chosen by selecting a random starting point and then picking every *i*th element in succession from the sampling frame. The sampling interval, *i*, is determined by dividing the population size *N* by the sample size *n* and rounding to the nearest whole number. For example, there are 100,000 elements in the population and a sample of 1,000 is desired. In this case, the sampling interval, *i*, is 100. A random number between 1 and 100 is selected. If, for example, this number is 23, the sample consists of elements 23, 123, 223, 323, 423, 523, and so on.[15]

Systematic sampling is similar to SRS in that each population element has a known and equal probability of selection. It is different from SRS, however, in that only the permissible samples of size *n* that can be drawn have a known and equal probability of selection. The remaining samples of size *n* have a zero probability of being selected.

For systematic sampling, the researcher assumes that the population elements are ordered in some respect. In some cases, the ordering (e.g. alphabetical listing in a telephone book) is unrelated to the characteristic of interest. In other instances, the ordering is directly related to the characteristic under investigation. For example, credit card customers may be listed in order of outstanding balance, or firms in a given industry may be ordered according to annual sales. If the population elements are arranged in a manner unrelated to the characteristic of interest, systematic sampling will yield results quite similar to SRS.

On the other hand, when the ordering of the elements is related to the characteristic of interest, systematic sampling increases the representativeness of the sample. If firms in an industry are arranged in increasing order of annual sales, a systematic sample will include some small and some large firms. A simple random sample may be unrepresentative because it may contain, for example, only small firms or a disproportionate number of small firms. If the ordering of the elements produces a cyclical pattern, systematic sampling may decrease the representativeness of the sample. To illustrate, consider the use of systematic sampling to generate a sample of monthly department store sales from a sampling frame containing monthly sales for the last 60 years. If a sampling interval of 12 is chosen, the resulting sample would not reflect the month-to-month variation in sales.[16]

Systematic sampling is less costly and easier than SRS because random selection is done only once to establish a starting point. Moreover, random numbers do not have to be matched with individual elements as in SRS. Because some lists contain millions of elements, considerable time can be saved, which reduces the costs of sampling. If information related to the characteristic of interest is available for the population, systematic sampling can be used to obtain a more representative and reliable (lower sampling error) sample than SRS. Another relative advantage is that systematic sampling can even be used without knowledge of the elements of the sampling frame. For example, every *i*th person leaving a shop or passing a point in the street can be intercepted (provided very strict control of the flow of potential respondents is exercised). For these reasons, systematic sampling is often employed in consumer mail, telephone and street interviews, as illustrated by the following example.

Example | *Tennis*'s systematic sampling returns a smash[17]

Tennis magazine (**www.tennis.com**) conducted a postal survey of its subscribers to gain a better understanding of its market. Systematic sampling was employed to select a sample of 1,472 subscribers from the publication's domestic circulation list. If we assume that the subscriber list had 1,472,000 names, the sampling interval would be 1,000 (1,472,000/1,472). A number from 1 to 1,000 was drawn at random. Beginning with that number, every subsequent 1,000th was selected.

An 'alert' postcard was mailed one week before the survey. A second, follow-up, questionnaire was sent to the whole sample 10 days after the initial questionnaire. There were 76 post office returns, so the net effective mailing was 1,396. Six weeks after the first mailing, 778 completed questionnaires were returned, yielding a response rate of 56%.

Stratified sampling

Stratified sampling
A probability sampling technique that uses a two-step process to partition the population into subsequent subpopulations, or strata. Elements are selected from each stratum by a random procedure.

Stratified sampling is a two-step process in which the population is partitioned into subpopulations, or strata. The strata should be mutually exclusive and collectively exhaustive in that every population element should be assigned to one and only one stratum and no population elements should be omitted. Next, elements are selected from each stratum by a random procedure, usually SRS. Technically, only SRS should be employed in selecting the elements from each stratum. In practice, sometimes systematic sampling and other probability sampling procedures are employed. Stratified sampling differs from quota sampling in that the sample elements are selected probabilistically rather than based on convenience or judgement. A major objective of stratified sampling is to increase precision without increasing cost.[18]

The variables used to partition the population into strata are referred to as stratification variables. The criteria for the selection of these variables consist of homogeneity, heterogeneity, relatedness and cost. The elements within a stratum should be as homogeneous as possible, but the elements in different strata should be as heterogeneous as possible. The stratification variables should also be closely related to the characteristic of interest. The more closely these criteria are met, the greater the effectiveness in controlling extraneous sampling variation. Finally, the variables should decrease the cost of the stratification process by being easy to measure and apply. Variables commonly used for stratification include demographic characteristics (as illustrated in the example for quota sampling), type of customer (e.g. credit card versus non-credit card), size of firm, or type of industry. It is possible to use more than one variable for stratification, although more than two are seldom used because of pragmatic and cost considerations. Although the number of strata to use is a matter of judgement, experience suggests the use of no more than six. Beyond six strata, any gain in precision is more than offset by the increased cost of stratification and sampling.

Another important decision involves the use of proportionate or disproportionate sampling. In proportionate stratified sampling, the size of the sample drawn from each stratum is proportionate to the relative size of that stratum in the total population. In disproportionate stratified sampling, the size of the sample from each stratum is proportionate to the relative size of that stratum and to the standard deviation of the distribution of the characteristic of interest among all the elements in that stratum. The logic behind disproportionate sampling is simple. First, strata with larger relative sizes are more influential in determining the population mean, and these strata should also exert a greater influence in deriving the sample estimates. Consequently, more elements should be drawn from strata of larger relative size. Second, to increase precision, more elements should be drawn from strata with larger standard deviations and fewer elements should be drawn from strata with smaller standard deviations. (If all the elements in a stratum are identical, a sample size of one will result in perfect information.) Note that the two methods are identical if the characteristic of interest has the same standard deviation within each stratum.

Disproportionate sampling requires that some estimate of the relative variation, or standard deviation of the distribution of the characteristic of interest, within strata be known. As this information is not always available, the researcher may have to rely on intuition and logic to determine sample sizes for each stratum. For example, large retail stores might be expected to have greater variation in the sales of some products as compared with small stores. Hence, the number of large stores in a sample may be disproportionately large. When the researcher is primarily interested in examining differences between strata, a common sampling strategy is to select the same sample size from each stratum.

Stratified sampling can ensure that all the important subpopulations are represented in the sample. This is particularly important if the distribution of the characteristic of interest in the population is skewed. For example, very few households have annual incomes that allow them to own a second home overseas. If a simple random sample is taken, households that have a second home overseas may not be adequately represented. Stratified sampling would guarantee that the sample contains a certain number of these households. Stratified sampling combines the simplicity of SRS with potential gains in precision. Therefore, it is a popular sampling technique and is illustrated in the following example.

Example	### Online retirement plans are on[19]

CIGNA Retirement and Investment Services (**www.cigna.com**) conducted a survey using a stratified sample. The aim of the survey was to learn more about online users' demands for additional Internet retirement services. A telephone survey was conducted of 659 full-time employees over the age of 18 with a quota of 80% to be participants in a retirement plan such as a pension. The sample was stratified by income and age because of differences in the use of the Internet and possible varying concerns about retirement services.

Cluster sampling
A two-step probability sampling technique where the target population is first divided into mutually exclusive and collectively exhaustive subpopulations called clusters, and then a random sample of clusters is selected based on a probability sampling technique such as SRS. For each selected cluster, either all the elements are included in the sample, or a sample of elements is drawn probabilistically.

Cluster sampling

In cluster sampling, the target population is first divided into mutually exclusive and collectively exhaustive subpopulations. These subpopulations or clusters are assumed to contain the diversity of respondents held in the target population. A random sample of clusters is selected, based on a probability sampling technique such as SRS. For each selected cluster, either all the elements are included in the sample or a sample of elements is drawn probabilistically. If all the elements in each selected cluster are included in the sample, the procedure is called one-stage cluster sampling. If a sample of elements is drawn probabilistically from each selected cluster, the procedure is two-stage cluster sampling. As shown in Figure 14.3, two-stage cluster sampling can be either simple two-stage cluster sampling involving SRS or probability proportionate to size sampling. Furthermore, a cluster sample can have multiple (more than two) stages, as in multistage cluster sampling.

The key distinction between cluster sampling and stratified sampling is that in cluster sampling only a sample of subpopulations (clusters) is chosen, whereas in stratified sampling all the subpopulations (strata) are selected for further sampling. The objectives of the two methods are also different. The objective of cluster sampling is to increase sampling efficiency by decreasing costs, but the objective of stratified sampling is to increase precision. With respect to homogeneity and heterogeneity, the criteria for forming clusters are just the opposite of those for strata. Elements within a cluster should be as heterogeneous as possible, but clusters themselves should be as homogeneous as possible. Ideally, each cluster should be a small-scale representation of the population. In cluster sampling, a sampling frame is needed only for those clusters selected for the sample.

Area sampling
A common form of cluster sampling in which the clusters consist of geographical areas such as counties, housing tracts, blocks or other area descriptions.

A common form of cluster sampling is **area sampling**, in which the clusters consist of geographical areas, such as counties, housing districts or residential blocks. If only one level of sampling takes place in selecting the basic elements (e.g. if the researcher samples blocks and then all the households within the selected blocks are included in the sample), the design is called one-stage area sampling. If two or more levels of sampling take place before the basic elements are selected (if the researcher samples blocks and then samples households within the sampled blocks), the design is called two-stage (or multistage) area sampling. The distinguishing feature of one-stage area sampling is that all the households in the selected blocks (or geographical areas) are included in the sample.

There are two types of two-stage cluster sampling designs, as shown in Figure 14.3. Simple two-stage cluster sampling involves SRS at the first stage (e.g. sampling blocks) as well as the second stage (e.g. sampling households within blocks). In this design the number of elements (e.g. households) selected at the second stage is the same for each sample cluster (e.g. selected blocks). This design is appropriate when the clusters are equal in size; that is, when the clusters contain approximately the same number of sampling units. If they differ greatly in size, however, simple two-stage cluster sampling can lead to biased estimates. Sometimes the clusters can be made of equal size by combining clusters. When this option is not feasible, probability proportionate to size (PPS) sampling can be used.

Probability proportionate to size (PPS)
A selection method where the probability of selecting a sampling unit in a selected cluster varies inversely with the size of the cluster. Therefore, the size of all the resulting clusters is approximately equal.

In **probability proportionate to size (PPS)** sampling, the clusters are sampled with probability proportional to size. The size of a cluster is defined in terms of the number of sampling units within that cluster. Thus, in the first stage, large clusters are more likely to be included than small clusters. In the second stage, the probability of selecting a sampling unit in a selected cluster varies inversely with the size of the cluster. Thus, the probability

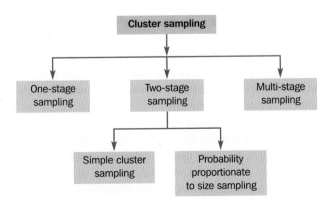

Figure 14.3
Types of cluster sampling

that any particular sampling unit will be included in the sample is equal for all units, because the unequal first-stage probabilities are balanced by the unequal second-stage probabilities. The numbers of sampling units included from the selected clusters are approximately equal.

Cluster sampling has two major advantages: feasibility and low cost. These advantages are illustrated in the following example where alternative means of drawing a sample were severely restricted without incurring great costs.

Example   **Sport and leisure demands in schools**

The Sports Council has supported marketing research in the south west of England that has facilitated new facilities and sports development in a range of cities. The methodology involved using a postal survey which was sent to individuals in households. The Electoral Register acted as the sampling frame and a systematic sampling method was used. A major problem lay in sampling younger members of the community who were not named on the Electoral Register and had no known sampling frame that marketing researchers could access.

The solution lay in the use of a simple two-stage cluster sampling design. All schools and colleges within a target district could be identified; a complete and current sampling frame of schools and colleges was available. A simple random sample of all the schools and colleges constituted the first stage. Then a random sample of classes within the schools and colleges was taken (between the ages of 12 and 18). In this design, the number of elements (classes) selected at the second stage was the same for each sample cluster (school or college).

With the selected classes, permission was gained to administer the questionnaire to the whole class. This resulted in a very cost-effective means of data collection. As all the class completed the task together, a consistent means to motivate respondents and instructions could be given.

In many situations the only sampling frames readily available for the target population are clusters, not population elements. In the above example, the schools and their classes are known but not the pupils. It is often impossible to compile a list of all consumers in a population, given the resources and constraints. Lists of geographical areas, telephone exchanges and other clusters of consumers, however, can be constructed relatively easily. Cluster sampling is the most cost-effective probability sampling technique. This advantage must be weighed against several limitations. Cluster sampling results in relatively imprecise samples, and it is difficult to form clusters in which the elements are heterogeneous, because, for example, households in a block tend to be similar rather than dissimilar.[20] It can be difficult to compute and interpret statistics based on clusters.

Other probability sampling techniques

In addition to the four basic probability sampling techniques, there are a variety of other sampling techniques. Most of these may be viewed as extensions of the basic techniques and were developed to address complex sampling problems. Two techniques with some relevance to marketing research are sequential sampling and double sampling.

In **sequential sampling**, the population elements are sampled sequentially, data collection and analysis are done at each stage, and a decision is made as to whether additional population elements should be sampled. The sample size is not known in advance, but a decision rule is stated before sampling begins. At each stage, this rule indicates whether sampling should be continued or whether enough information has been obtained. Sequential sampling has been used to determine preferences for two competing alternatives. In one study, respondents were asked which of two alternatives they preferred, and sampling was terminated when sufficient evidence was accumulated to validate a prefer-

Sequential sampling
A probability sampling technique in which the population elements are sampled sequentially, data collection and analysis are done at each stage, and a decision is made as to whether additional population elements should be sampled.

ence. It has also been used to establish the price differential between a standard model and a deluxe model of a consumer durable.[21]

Double sampling
A sampling technique in which certain population elements are sampled twice.

In **double sampling**, also called two-phase sampling, certain population elements are sampled twice. In the first phase, a sample is selected and some information is collected from all the elements in the sample. In the second phase, a subsample is drawn from the original sample and additional information is obtained from the elements in the subsample. The process may be extended to three or more phases, and the different phases may take place simultaneously or at different times. Double sampling can be useful when no sampling frame is readily available for selecting final sampling units but when the elements of the frame are known to be contained within a broader sampling frame. For example, a researcher wants to select households in a given city that consume apple juice. The households of interest are contained within the set of all households, but the researcher does not know which ones they are. In applying double sampling, the researcher would obtain a sampling frame of all households in the first phase. This would be constructed from the city directory or purchased. Then a sample of households would be drawn, using systematic random sampling to determine the amount of apple juice consumed. In the second phase, households that consume apple juice would be selected and stratified according to the amount of apple juice consumed. Then a stratified random sample would be drawn and detailed questions regarding apple juice consumption asked.[22]

Choosing non-probability versus probability sampling

The choice between non-probability and probability samples should be based on considerations such as the nature of the research, relative magnitude of non-sampling versus sampling errors, and variability in the population, as well as statistical and operational considerations (see Table 14.3).

Table 14.3 Choosing non-probability vs. probability sampling

Factors	Conditions favouring the use of:	
	Non-probability sampling	*Probability sampling*
Nature of research	Exploratory	Conclusive
Relative magnitude of sampling and non-sampling errors	Non-sampling errors are larger	Sampling errors are larger
Variability in the population	Homogeneous (low)	Heterogeneous (high)
Statistical considerations	Unfavourable	Favourable
Operational considerations	Favourable	Unfavourable

For example, in exploratory research, the judgement of the researcher in selecting respondents with particular qualities may be far more effective than any form of probability sampling. On the other hand, in conclusive research where the researcher wishes to use the results to estimate overall market shares or the size of the total market, probability sampling is favoured. Probability samples allow statistical projection of the results to a target population.

For some research problems, highly accurate estimates of population characteristics are required. In these situations, the elimination of selection bias and the ability to calculate sampling error make probability sampling desirable. Probability sampling will not always result in more accurate results, however. If non-sampling errors are likely to be an important factor, then non-probability sampling may be preferable because the use of judgement may allow greater control over the sampling process.

Another consideration is the homogeneity of the population with respect to the variables of interest. A heterogeneous population would favour probability sampling because it would be more important to secure a representative sample. Probability sampling is preferable from a statistical viewpoint, as it is the basis of most common statistical techniques.

Probability sampling generally requires statistically trained researchers, generally costs more and takes longer than non-probability sampling, especially in the establishment of accurate sampling frames. In many marketing research projects, it is difficult to justify the additional time and expense. Therefore, in practice, the objectives of the study dictate which sampling method will be used.

Non-probability sampling is used in concept tests, package tests, name tests and copy tests where projections to the populations are usually not needed. In such studies, interest centres on the proportion of the sample that gives various responses or expresses various attitudes. Samples for these studies can be drawn using methods such as street interviewing and quota sampling. On the other hand, probability sampling is used when there is a need for highly accurate estimates of market share or sales volume for the entire market. National market tracking studies, which provide information on product category and brand usage rates as well as psychographic and demographic profiles of users, use probability sampling. Studies that use probability sampling generally employ telephone interviews. Stratified and systematic sampling are combined with some form of random-digit dialling to select the respondents.

Summary of sampling techniques

The strengths and weaknesses of cluster sampling and the other basic sampling techniques are summarised in Table 14.4. Table 14.5 describes the procedures for drawing probability samples.

Table 14.4 Strengths and weaknesses of sampling techniques

Technique	Strengths	Weaknesses
Non-probability sampling		
Convenience sampling	Least expensive, least time consuming, most convenient	Selection bias, sample not representative, not recommended for descriptive or causal research
Judgemental sampling	Low cost, convenient, not time consuming. Ideal for exploratory research designs	Does not allow generalisation, subjective
Quota sampling	Sample can be controlled for certain characteristics	Selection bias, no assurance of representativeness
Snowball sampling	Can estimate rare characteristics	Time consuming
Probability sampling		
Simple random sampling (SRS)	Easily understood, results projectable	Difficult to construct sampling frame, expensive, lower precision, no assurance of representativeness
Systematic sampling	Can increase representativeness, easier to implement than SRS, sampling frame not always necessary	Can decrease representativeness depending upon 'order' in the sampling frame
Stratified sampling	Includes all important subpopulations, precision	Difficult to select relevant stratification variables, not feasible to stratify on many variables, expensive
Cluster sampling	Easy to implement, cost effective	Imprecise, difficult to compute and interpret results

Table 14.5 Procedures for drawing probability samples

Simple random sampling

1 Select a suitable sampling frame.

2 Each element is assigned a number from 1 to N (population size).

3 Generate n (sample size) different random numbers between 1 and N using a software package or a table of simple random numbers (Table 1 in the Appendix of statistical tables). To use Table 1, select the appropriate number of digits (e.g. if $N = 900$, select three digits). Arbitrarily select a beginning number. Then proceed up or down until n different numbers between 1 and N have been selected. Discard 0, duplicate numbers and numbers greater than N.

4 The numbers generated denote the elements that should be included in the sample.

Systematic sampling

1 Select a suitable sampling frame.

2 Each element is assigned a number from 1 to N (population size).

3 Determine the sampling interval i, where $i = N/n$. If i is a fraction, round to the nearest whole number.

4 Select a random number, r, between 1 and i, as explained in SRS.

5 The elements with the following numbers will comprise the systematic random sample:

$$r, r + i, r + 2i, r + 3i, r + 4i \ldots r + (n–1)i$$

Stratified sampling

1 Select a suitable sampling frame.

2 Select the stratification variable(s) and the number of strata, H.

3 Divide the entire population into H strata. Based on the classification variable, each element of the population is assigned to one of the H strata.

4 In each stratum, number the elements from 1 to N_h (the population size of stratum h).

5 Determine the sample size of each stratum, n_h, based on proportionate or disproportionate stratified sampling, where

$$\sum_{h=1}^{H} n_h = n$$

6 In each stratum, select a simple random sample of size n_h.

Cluster sampling

We describe the procedure for selecting a simple two-stage sample, because this represents the most commonly used general case.

1 Assign a number from 1 to N to each element in the population.

2 Divide the population into C clusters of which c will be included in the sample.

3 Calculate the sampling interval i, where $i = N/c$. If i is a fraction, round to the nearest whole number.

4 Select a random number, r, between 1 and i, as explained in SRS.

5 Identify elements with the following numbers: $r, r + i, r + 2i, r + 3i, \ldots, r + (c – 1)i$

6 Select the clusters that contain the identified elements.

7 Select sampling units within each selected cluster based on SRS or systematic sampling. The number of sampling units selected from each sample cluster is approximately the same and equal to n/c.

8 If the population of the cluster exceeds the sampling interval i, that cluster is selected with certainty. That cluster is removed from further consideration. Calculate the new proportion size, N^*, the number of clusters to be selected, $c^* (= c – 1)$, and the new sampling interval i^*. Repeat this process until each of the remaining clusters has a population less than the relevant sampling interval. If b clusters have been selected with certainty, select the remaining $c – b$ clusters according to steps 1 to 7. The fraction of units to be sampled from each cluster selected with certainty is the overall sampling fraction n/N. Thus, for clusters selected with certainty, we would select n_s $(n/N)(N_1 + N_2 + \ldots + N_b)$ units. The units selected from clusters selected under two-stage sampling will therefore be $n^* = n – n_s$.

International marketing research

Implementing the sampling design process in international marketing research is seldom easy. Several factors should be considered in defining the target population. The relevant element (respondent) may differ from country to country. In Europe, children play an important role in the purchase of children's cereals and may be seen as target respondents. In countries with authoritarian child-rearing practices, however, the mother or father may be the relevant target respondents. Accessibility also varies across countries. In Mexico, 'upper class' houses cannot be entered by strangers because of boundary walls and servants. Additionally, dwelling units may be unnumbered and streets unidentified, making it difficult to locate designated households.[23]

Developing an appropriate sampling frame is a difficult task. In many countries, particularly developing countries, reliable information about the target population may not be available from secondary sources. Government data may be unavailable or highly biased. Population lists may not be available commercially. The time and money required to compile these lists may be prohibitive. For example, in Saudi Arabia, there is no officially recognised census of population, no elections and hence no voter registration records, and no accurate maps of population centres. In this situation, the interviewers could be instructed to begin at specified starting points and to sample every nth dwelling until the specified number of units has been sampled.

Given the lack of suitable sampling frames, the inaccessibility of certain respondents, such as women in some cultures, and the dominance of personal interviewing, probability sampling techniques are uncommon in international marketing research. Imagine the problems involved in conducting probability sampling in the following example.

Example	### India's vast diversity[24]

Counting 20 official languages (other than English) a truly comprehensive marketing research study in India would need to be executed in at least 8 languages. Language is far from the only variable: there are diverse social, religious and culinary customs. The vast diversity of the Indian population does not limit itself to regions but runs across social strata. Most interesting for advertisers and consumer brands are the upper income inhabitants of cities like the capital New Delhi, Mumbai and Chennai, who most closely resemble Western consumers. Together with the 100 million strong Indian middle class, they form the prime target of most multinational companies. These groups form a stark contrast with the 30% plus of Indians who live in rural areas with minimal facilities – contrasts that make sampling in India a most complex affair.

Quota sampling has been used widely in the developed and developing countries in both consumer and industrial surveys. Quota sampling has a long history of working well in the UK, France and Germany, but is a sampling method that is seen as 'unthinkable' for many US marketing researchers.[25] Snowball sampling is also appealing when the characteristic of interest is rare in the target population or when respondents are hard to reach. For example, it has been suggested that in Saudi Arabia graduate students be employed to hand-deliver questionnaires to relatives and friends.[26] These initial respondents can be asked for referrals to other potential respondents and so on. This approach would result in a large sample size and a high response rate.

Sampling techniques and procedures vary in accuracy, reliability and cost from country to country. If the same sampling procedures are used in each country, the results may not be comparable.[27] To achieve comparability in sample composition and representativeness, it may be desirable to use different sampling techniques in different countries.

Ethics in marketing research

The researcher has several ethical responsibilities to both the client and the respondents pertaining to sampling. With regard to the client, the researcher must develop a sampling design that best fits the project in an effort to minimise the sampling and non-sampling errors (see Chapter 3). When probability sampling can be used it should be.

When non-probability design such as convenience sampling is used, the limitations of the design should be explicit in any findings that are presented. It is unethical and misleading to treat non-probability samples as probability samples and to project the results to a target population. Appropriate definition of the population and the sampling frame, and application of the correct sampling techniques, are essential if the research is to be conducted and the findings used ethically.

Researchers must be extremely sensitive to preserving the anonymity of the respondents when conducting business-to-business research with small populations, particularly when reporting the findings to the client. When the population size is small, it is easier to discern the identities of the respondents than when the samples are drawn from a large population. Special care must be taken when sample details are too revealing and when using verbatim quotations in reports to the client. This problem is acute in areas such as employee research. Here a breach of a respondent's anonymity can cost the respondent a pay rise, a promotion, or their employment. In such situations, special effort should be made to protect the identities of the respondents. In such situations, the researcher has the ethical obligation to protect the identities of respondents, even if it means limiting the level of sampling detail that is reported to the client and other parties.

Internet and computer applications

Sampling potential respondents who are surfing the Internet is meaningful if the sample generated is representative of the target population. More and more industries are meeting this criterion. In software, computers, networking, technical publishing, semiconductors and graduate education, it is now feasible to use the Internet for sampling respondents for quantitative research, such as surveys. For internal customer surveys, where the client's employees share a corporate email system, an intranet survey is practical, even if workers have no access to the external Internet

To avoid sampling errors, the researcher must be able to control the pool from which the respondents are selected. Also, it must be ensured that the respondents do not respond more than once. These requirements are met by email surveys, in which the researcher selects specific respondents. Furthermore, the surveys can be encoded to match the returned surveys with their corresponding outbound emailings. This can also be accomplished with web surveys by emailing invitations to selected respondents and asking them to visit the website on which the survey is posted. In this case, the survey is posted in a hidden location on the Web, which is protected by a password. Hence, non-invited web surfers are unable to access it.

Non-probability as well as probability sampling techniques can be implemented on the Internet. Moreover, the respondents can be pre-recruited or tapped online, as when discussing access panels in Chapter 3. Tapping visitors to a website is an example of convenience sampling. Based on the researcher's judgement, certain qualifying criteria can be introduced to pre-screen the respondents. Even quotas can be imposed. However, the extent to which quotas will be met is limited by the number as well as the characteristics of visitors to the site.

Likewise, SRS is commonly used. To prevent gathering information from the same professional respondents (professional in this context meaning respondents who take part in many surveys for their own enjoyment), some companies use a 'click-stream intercept', which randomly samples online users and gives them the opportunity to participate or decline.

Microcomputers and mainframes can make the sampling design process more effective and efficient. Random-number generators are available in most data analysis packages. For example, in Excel, the Random Number Generation Analysis Tool allows you to set a number of characteristics of your target population, including the nature of distribution of the data, and to create a table of random numbers on a separate worksheet. Computers can also be used in the specification of the sampling frame. In Chapter 5 a number of geodemographic information system providers were described. Their database packages can also be used to store and manipulate sampling frames, especially when the sampling frame is built up from multiple sources and duplicates need to be identified and eliminated. Once the sampling frame has been determined, simulations can be used to generate random numbers and select the sample directly from the database. Another example of sources of national sampling frames (and the costs involved), for households and businesses, can be seen at **www.deutschepost.de** and **www.royalmail.com**.

Finally, in the following example George Terhanian of Harris Interactive Europe (**www.harrisinteractive.com/europe**) offers practical advice on managing a research project online. Here we focus upon key sampling issues

---

Example ### Managing a project online[28]

1 *How do you select respondents for a survey?*
   At times, agencies use a client listing of email addresses. At other times, they administer pop-up surveys. Large Internet panels are particularly useful when the interest lies in interviewing tiny proportions of the population. The panel approach will also allow the agency to include validity checks within surveys. If a woman becomes a man since completing her (or his) previous survey, then something is probably amiss. No matter how the agency selects respondents, it should recognise that older respondents will participate at higher rates than younger ones, and younger women at higher rates than younger men.

2 *How do you ensure that biases due to panel learning do not influence the results?*
   Agencies can reduce or eliminate learning by limiting the number of surveys to which they invite panelists, varying the topics of these surveys, masking screening questions, and measuring and correcting learning biases (through the conduct of validity studies)

3 *How do you weight survey data to ensure that the socio-demographic, attitudinal and behavioural characteristics of the sample reflect those of the target population?*
   No agency should assert that demograhic weighting alone will guarantee representativeness. Panelists are likely to differ from target populations in non-demographic ways as well. Agencies can best understand self-selection (onto the Internet, into the panel) biases by mounting parallel studies whereby they compare panel members (taking into account panel growth, attrition and possible learning) to nationally representative samples interviewed through other modes. The agency can then use the information from the non-Internet study as a check and as a means for potentially adjusting the online data.

Summary

Information about the characteristics of a population may be obtained by carrying out either a sample or a census. Budget and time limits, large population size and small variance in the characteristic of interest favour the use of a sample. Sampling is also preferred when the cost of sampling error is low, the cost of non-sampling error is high, the nature of measurement is destructive, and attention must be focused on individual cases. The opposite set of conditions favours the use of a census.

Sampling design begins by defining the target population in terms of elements, sampling units, extent and time. Then the sampling frame should be determined. A sampling frame is a representation of the elements of the target population. It consists of a list of directions for identifying the target population. At this stage, it is important to recognise any sampling frame errors that may exist. The next step involves selecting a sampling technique and determining the sample size. In addition to quantitative analysis, several qualitative considerations should be taken into account in determining the sample size. Execution of the sampling process requires detailed specifications for each step in the sampling process. Finally, the selected sample should be validated by comparing characteristics of the sample with known characteristics of the target population.

Sampling techniques may be classified as non-probability and probability techniques. Non-probability sampling techniques rely on the researcher's judgement. Consequently, they do not permit an objective evaluation of the precision of the sample results, and the estimates obtained are not statistically projectable to the population. The commonly used non-probability sampling techniques include convenience sampling, judgemental sampling, quota sampling and snowball sampling.

In probability sampling techniques, sampling units are selected by chance. Each sampling unit has a non-zero chance of being selected, and the researcher can pre-specify every potential sample of a given size that could be drawn from the population as well as the probability of selecting each sample. It is also possible to determine the precision of the sample estimates and inferences and make projections to the target population. Probability sampling techniques include simple random sampling, systematic sampling, stratified sampling, cluster sampling, sequential sampling and double sampling. The choice between probability and non-probability sampling should be based on the nature of the research, degree of error tolerance, relative magnitude of sampling and non-sampling errors, variability in the population, and statistical and operational considerations.

When conducting international marketing research, it is desirable to achieve comparability in sample composition and representativeness even though this may require the use of different sampling techniques in different countries. It is unethical and misleading to treat non-probability samples as probability samples and to project the results to a target population.

Questions

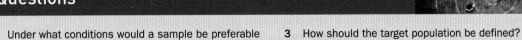

1 Under what conditions would a sample be preferable to a census? A census preferable to a sample?

2 Describe the sampling design process.

3 How should the target population be defined? How does this definition link with the definition of a marketing research problem?

4   What is a sampling unit? How is it different from the population element?

5   To what extent may the availability of sampling frames determine the definition of a population?

6   What qualitative factors should be considered in determining the sample size?

7   How do probability sampling techniques differ from non-probability sampling techniques? What factors should be considered in choosing between probability and non-probability sampling?

8   What is the least expensive and least time consuming of all sampling techniques? What are the major limitations of this technique?

9   What is the major difference between judgemental and convenience sampling? Give examples of where each of these techniques may be successfully applied.

10 Describe snowball sampling. How may the technique be supported by qualitative research techniques?

11 What are the distinguishing features of simple random sampling?

12 Describe the procedure for selecting a systematic random sample.

13 Describe stratified sampling. What are the criteria for the selection of stratification variables?

14 What are the differences between proportionate and disproportionate stratified sampling?

15 Describe the cluster sampling procedure. What is the key distinction between cluster sampling and stratified sampling?

Exercises

1   A company is planning a service that gives respite and support to carers that look after ill or disabled friends or family. It wishes to undertake a face-to-face survey of the carers. What sampling technique would you recommend for this task? Detail the stages involved in making this technique work. What would be the limitations and nearest alternative to the approach that you have recommended?

2   Hewlett-Packard would like to conduct a survey of business attitudes to the use of colour printers. Visit either **www.deutschepost.de** or **www.royalmail.com** and write a report on what support these sites will give you in terms of establishing an up-to-date and accurate sampling frame, and the sampling techniques you could use.

3   The Alumni Office of your University would like to conduct a survey of on-campus students who are in their final year of study. The office wishes to determine attitudes to joining alumni associations as students progress through further study and their careers. As a consultant you must develop a quota sample. What quota variables would you use? Design

a quota matrix. Base this matrix upon your chosen variables and the proportions of these variables within your University.

4   You work as the Marketing Research Manager for ABN AMRO in Amsterdam. Managers would like to know if the attitudes towards saving differ between ethnic groups. They wonder whether, given the varied population of the Netherlands, it is meaningful to segment the market according to ethnic background. A survey is planned. You have been asked to design a sampling plan for this task. Present you plan to a group of students representing the board of ABN AMRO.

5   In a small group discuss the following issues: 'Given that many governments use sampling to check the accuracy of various censuses and that non-response rates to censuses are growing, national decennial censuses should be abolished in favour of the use of existing databases and sample surveys' and 'Because non-sampling errors are greater in magnitude than sampling errors, it really does not matter which sampling method is used.'

Video Case Exercise: Wild Planet

What sampling challenges do Wild Planet face in conducting surveys with children and parents? Evaluate the use of online access panels in resolving these challenges.

video
case

download from
www.pearsoned.co.uk/
malhotra_euro

Notes

1 Anon., 'Random sampling', *Marketing News* (16 July 2001), 10; Wilcox, S., 'Sampling and controlling a TV audience measurement panel', *International Journal of Market Research* 42 (4) (Winter 2000), 413–430; Verma, V. and Le, T., 'An analysis of sampling errors for the demographic and health surveys', *International Statistical Review* 64 (3) (December 1966), 265–294; Assael, H. and Keon, J., 'Non-sampling vs. sampling errors in sampling research', *Journal of Marketing* (Spring 1982), 114–123.

2 Anon., 'Random sampling: bruised, battered, bowed,' *Marketing News* 36 (5) (4 March 2002), 12; Fink, A., *How to Sample in Surveys* (Thousand Oaks, CA: Sage, 1995); Frankel, M.R., 'Sampling theory', in Rossi, P.H., Wright, J.D. and Anderson, A.B. (eds), *Handbook of Survey Research* (Orlando, FL: Academic Press, 1983), 21–67; Jaeger, R.M., *Sampling in Education and the Social Sciences* (New York: Longman, 1984), 28–29; Kalron, G., *Introduction to Survey Sampling* (Beverly Hills, CA: Sage, 1982).

3 Reiter, J.P., 'Topics in survey sampling/finite population sampling and inference: a prediction approach,' *Journal of the American Statistical Association* 97 (457) (March 2002), 357–358; Henry, G.T., *Practical Sampling* (Thousand Oaks, CA: Sage, 1995); Sudman, S., 'Applied sampling', in Rossi, P.H., Wright, J.D. and Anderson, A.B. (eds), *Handbook of Survey Research* (Orlando, FL: Academic Press, 1983), 145–194.

4 Cage, R., 'New methodology for selecting CPI outlet samples', *Monthly Labor Review* 119 (12) (December 1996), 49–83.

5 Couper, M.P., 'Web surveys: A review of issues and approaches,' *Public Opinion Quarterly* 64 (4) (Winter 2000), 464–494; Smith, W., Mitchell, P., Attebo, K. and Leeder, S., 'Selection bias from sampling frames: telephone directory and electoral roll compared with door-to-door population census: results from the Blue Mountain eye study', *Australian & New Zealand Journal of Public Health* 21 (2) (April 1997), 127–133.

6 For the effect of sample frame error on research results, see Murphy, G.B., 'The effects of organizational sampling frame selection', *Journal of Business Venturing* 17 (3) (May 2002) 237; Fish, K.E., Barnes, J.H. and Banahan, B.F., III 'Convenience or calamity', *Journal of Health Care Marketing* 14 (Spring 1994), 45–49.

7 Phillips, A. 'Taking the people's temperature – right across Europe', *ResearchPlus* (November 1996), 6.

8 For an application of convenience sampling, see Ritchie, L., 'Empowerment and Australian community health nurses work with aboriginal clients: the sociopolitical context', *Qualitative Health Research* 11 (2) (March 2001), 190–205; Ho, F., Ong, B.S. and Seonsu, A., 'A multicultural comparison of shopping patterns among Asian consumers', *Journal of Marketing Theory and Practice* 5 (1) (Winter 1997), 42–51.

9 Maddox, K., 'XIX Winter Olympics: marketing hot spot', *B to B* 87 (2) (11 February 2002), 1–2.

10 Thompson, S.K., *Sampling* (New York: Wiley, 2002); Sudman, S., 'Sampling in the twenty-first century', *Academy of Marketing Science Journal* 27 (2) (Spring 1999), 269–277; Kish, L., *Survey Sampling* (New York: John Wiley, 1965), 552.

11 Curtice, J. and Sparrow, N. 'How accurate are traditional quota opinion polls?', *Journal of the Market Research Society* 39 (3) (July 1997), 433–448.

12 Getz, P.M., 'Implementing the new sample design for the current employment statistics survey,' *Business Economics* 35 (4) (October 2000), 47–50; Anon., 'Public opinion: polls apart', *The Economist* 336 (7927) (12 August 1995), 48; Kalton, G., *Introduction to Survey Sampling* (Beverly Hills, CA: Sage, 1982); Sudman, S., 'Improving the quality of shopping center sampling', *Journal of Marketing Research* 17 (November 1980), 423–431.

13 For an application of snowball sampling, see Maher, L., 'Risk behaviours of young Indo-Chinese injecting drug users in Sydney and Melbourne', *Australian & New Zealand Journal of Public Health* (February 2001), 50–54; Frankwick, G.L., Ward, J.C., Hutt, M.D. and Reingen, P.H., 'Evolving patterns of organisational beliefs in the formation of strategy', *Journal of Marketing* 58 (April 1994), 96–110.

14 If certain procedures for listing members of the rare population are followed strictly, the snowball sample can be treated as a probability sample. See Sampath, S., *Sampling Theory and Methods* (Boca Raton, FL: CRC Press, 2000); Henry, G.T., *Practical Sampling* (Thousand Oaks, CA: Sage, 1995); Kalton, G. and Anderson, D.W., 'Sampling rare populations', *Journal of the Royal Statistical Association* (1986), 65–82; Biemacki, P. and Waldorf, D., 'Snowball sampling: problems and techniques of chain referred sampling', *Sociological Methods and Research* 10 (November 1981), 141–163.

15 When the sampling interval, i, is not a whole number, the easiest solution is to use as the interval the nearest whole number below or above i. If rounding has too great an effect on the sample size, add or delete the extra cases.

16 For an application of systematic random sampling, see MacFarlane, P., 'Structuring and measuring the size of business markets', *International Journal of Market Research* 44 (1) (First Quarter 2002), 7–30; Qu, H. and Li, I., 'The characteristics and satisfaction of mainland Chinese visitors to Hong Kong', *Journal of Travel Research* 35 (4) (Spring 1997), 37–41; Chakraborty, G., Ettenson, R. and Gaeth, G., 'How consumers choose health insurance', *Journal of Health Care Marketing* 14 (Spring 1994), 21–33.

17 Adams, M., 'Court Marshall', *Mediaweek* 6 (12) (18 March 1996), 22; 'Readership survey serves *Tennis* magazine's marketing needs', *Quirk's Marketing Research Review* (May 1988), 75–76.

18 For applications of stratified random sampling, see Kjell, G., 'The level-based stratified sampling plan,' *Journal of the American Statistical Association* 95 (452) (December 2000), 1185–1191; Weerahandi, S. and Moitra, S., 'Using survey data to predict adoption and switching for services', *Journal of Marketing Research* 32 (February 1995), 85–96.

19 Anon., 'Charge, losses stifle growth', *Business Insurance* 36 (6) (11 February 2002), 2; Gallucci, J., 'Employees with home Internet access want online retirement plans CIGNA retirement & investment services study reveals', *PR Newswire* (27 June 2000).

20 Geographic clustering of rare populations, however, can be an advantage. See Rao, P.S., *Sampling methodologies with applications* (Boca Raton, FL: CRC Press, 2001); Carlin, J.B., 'Design of cross-sectional surveys using cluster sampling: an overview with Australian case studies', *Australian & New Zealand Journal of Public Health* 23 (5) (October 1999), 546–551; Raymondo, J.C., 'Confessions of a Nielsen Housechild', *American Demographics* 19 (3) (March 1997), 24–27; Sudman,

S., 'Efficient screening methods for the sampling of geographically clustered special populations', *Journal of Marketing Research* 22 (February 1985), 20–29.

21 Walker, J., 'A sequential discovery sampling procedure', *Journal of the Operational Research Society* 53 (1) (January 2002), 119; Park, J.S., Peters, M. and Tang, K., 'Optimal inspection policy in sequential screening', *Management Science* 37 (8) (August 1991), 1058–1061; Anderson, E.J., Gorton, K. and Tudor, R., 'The application of sequential analysis in market research', *Journal of Marketing Research* 17 (February 1980), 97–105.

22 For more discussion of double sampling, see Brewer, K., *Design and Estimation in Survey Sampling* (London: Edward Arnold, 2001); Shade, J., 'Sampling inspection tables: single and double sampling,' *Journal of Applied Statistics* 26 (8) (December 1999), 1020; Baillie, D.H., 'Double sampling plans for inspection by variables when the process standard deviation is unknown', *International Journal of Quality & Reliability Management* 9(5) (1992), 59–70; Frankel, M.R. and Frankel, L.R., 'Probability sampling', in Ferber, R. (ed.), *Handbook of Marketing Research* (New York: McGraw-Hill, 1974), 2-230–2-246.

23 For the use of different non-probability sampling techniques in cross-cultural research, see Malhotra, N.K. and Peterson, M., 'Marketing research in the new millennium: emerging issues and trends', *Market Intelligence and Planning* 19 (4) (2001), 216–235; Malhotra, N.K., Agarwal, J. and Peterson, M., 'Cross-cultural marketing research: methodological issues and guidelines,' *International Marketing Review* 13 (5) (1996), 7–43; Saeed, S. and Jeong, I., 'Cross-cultural research in advertising: an assessment of methodologies', *Journal of the Academy of Marketing Science* 22 (Summer 1994), 205–215.

24 Heeg, R., 'India's vast diversity', *Research World* (December 2004), 14.

25 Taylor, H. 'Horses for courses: how survey firms in different countries measure public opinion with very different methods', *Journal of the Market Research Society* 37 (3) (July 1995), 218.

26 Tuncalp, S., 'The marketing research scene in Saudi Arabia', *European Journal of Marketing* 22 (5) (1988), 15–22.

27 Grosh, M.E. and Glewwe, P., 'Household survey data from developing countries: progress and prospects', *American Economic Review* 86 (2) (May 1996), 15–19.

28 Terhanian, G., 'Managing a project online', *Research in Business* (March 2004), 22–23.

Visit the *Marketing Research* Companion Website at www.pearsoned.co.uk/malhotra_euro for additional learning resources including annotated weblinks, an online glossary and a suite of downloadable video cases.

Source: © Getty Images

15

Sampling: final and initial sample size determination

Making a sample too big wastes resources, making it too small diminishes the value of findings – a dilemma resolved only with the judicious use of sampling theory.

Objectives

1 define key concepts and symbols pertinent to sampling;

2 understand the concepts of the sampling distribution, statistical inference and standard error;

3 discuss the statistical approach to determining sample size based on simple random sampling and the construction of confidence intervals;

4 derive the formulae to determine statistically the sample size for estimating means and proportions;

5 discuss the non-response issues in sampling and the procedures for improving response rates and adjusting for non-response;

6 understand the difficulty of statistically determining the sample size in international marketing research;

7 identify the ethical issues related to sample size determination, particularly the estimation of population variance.

STAGE 1
Problem definition

STAGE 2
Research approach developed

STAGE 3
Research design developed

STAGE 4
Fieldwork or data collection

STAGE 5
Data preparation and analysis

STAGE 6
Report preparation and presentation

Overview

This chapter focuses on the determination of sample size in simple random sampling. We define various concepts and symbols and discuss the properties of the sampling distribution. Additionally, we describe statistical approaches to sample size determination based on confidence intervals. We present the formulae for calculating the sample size with these approaches and illustrate their use. We briefly discuss the extension to determining sample size in other probability sampling designs. The sample size determined statistically is the final or net sample size; that is, it represents the completed number of interviews or observations. To obtain this final sample size, however, a much larger number of potential respondents have to be initially contacted. We describe the adjustments that need to be made to the statistically determined sample size to account for incidence and completion rates and calculate the initial sample size. We also cover the non-response issues in sampling, with a focus on improving response rates and adjusting for non-response. We discuss the difficulty of statistically determining the sample size in international marketing research and identify the relevant ethical issues.

Statistical determination of sample size requires knowledge of the normal distribution and the use of normal probability tables. The normal distribution is bell shaped and symmetrical. Its mean, median and mode are identical (see Chapter 18). Information on the normal distribution and the use of normal probability tables is presented in the appendix to this chapter. The following example illustrates the statistical aspects of sampling.

Example Has there been a shift in opinion?

The sample size used in opinion polls commissioned and published by most national newspapers is influenced by statistical considerations. The allowance for sampling error may be limited to around three percentage points.

The table that follows can be used to determine the allowances that should be made for sampling error. These intervals indicate the range (plus or minus the figure shown) within which the results of repeated samplings in the same time period could be expected to vary, 95% of the time, assuming that the sample procedure, survey execution and questionnaire used were the same.

Recommended allowance for sampling error of a percentage

In percentage points (at 95% confidence level for a sample size of 385)	
Percentage near 10	3
Percentage near 20	4
Percentage near 30	4
Percentage near 40	5
Percentage near 50	5
Percentage near 60	5
Percentage near 70	4
Percentage near 80	4
Percentage near 90	3

The table should be used as follows. If a reported percentage is 43 (e.g. 43% of Norwegian chief executives believe their company will suffer from staff shortages in the next 12 months), look at the row labelled 'percentages near 40'. The number in this row is 5, so the 43% obtained in the sample is subject to a sampling error of 5 percentage points. Another way of saying this is that very probably (95 times out of 100) the average of repeated samplings would be somewhere between 38% and 48%. The reader can be 95% confident that in the total population of Norwegian chief executives between 38% and 48% believe their company will suffer from staff shortages in the next 12 months, with the most likely figure being 43%.

The fortunes of political parties measured through opinion polls are regularly reported in newspapers throughout Europe. The next time that you read a report of a political opinion poll, examine the sample size used, the confidence level assumed and the stated margin of error. When comparing the results of a poll with a previous poll, consider whether a particular political party or politician has *really* grown or slumped in popularity. If there is a news item that the popularity of Party X has grown or the approval of President Y has diminished, is there really anything to report? Can the reported change be accounted for within the set margin of error as summarised in this example?

Definitions and symbols

Confidence intervals and other statistical concepts that play a central role in sample size determination are defined in the following list:

- *Parameter.* A parameter is a summary description of a fixed characteristic or measure of the target population. A parameter denotes the true value that would be obtained if a census rather than a sample was undertaken.
- *Statistic.* A statistic is a summary description of a characteristic or measure of the sample. The sample statistic is used as an estimate of the population parameter.
- *Finite population correction.* The finite population correction (fpc) is a correction for overestimation of the variance of a population parameter – for example, a mean or proportion – when the sample size is 10% or more of the population size.
- *Precision level.* When estimating a population parameter by using a sample statistic, the precision level is the desired size of the estimating interval. This is the maximum permissible difference between the sample statistic and the population parameter.

Table 15.1 **Symbols for population and sample variables**

Variable	Population	Sample
Mean	μ	$\bar{X}$
Proportion	π	p
Variance	σ^2	s^2
Standard deviation	σ	s
Size	N	n
Standard error of the mean	$\sigma\bar{x}$	$S\bar{x}$
Standard error of the proportion	σ_p	S_p
Standardised variate (z)	$\dfrac{X - \mu}{\sigma}$	$\dfrac{X - \bar{X}}{S}$
Coefficient of variation (C)	$\dfrac{\sigma}{\mu}$	$\dfrac{S}{\bar{X}}$

- *Confidence interval.* The confidence interval is the range into which the true population parameter will fall, assuming a given level of confidence.
- *Confidence level.* The confidence level is the probability that a confidence interval will include the population parameter.

The symbols used in statistical notation for describing population and sample characteristics are summarised in Table 15.1.

The sampling distribution

Sampling distribution
The distribution of the values of a sample statistic computed for each possible sample that could be drawn from the target population under a specified sampling plan.

The **sampling distribution** is the distribution of the values of a sample statistic computed for each possible sample that could be drawn from the target population under a specified sampling plan.[1] Suppose that a simple random sample of five sponsors is to be drawn from a population of 20 Formula One sponsors. There are $(20 \times 19 \times 18 \times 17 \times 16)/(1 \times 2 \times 3 \times 4 \times 5)$, or 15,504 different samples of size 5 that can be drawn. The relative frequency distribution of the values of the mean of these 15,504 different samples would specify the sampling distribution of the mean.

Statistical inference
The process of generalising the sample results to a target population.

An important task in marketing research is to calculate statistics, such as the sample mean and sample proportion, and use them to estimate the corresponding true population values. This process of generalising the sample results to a target population is referred to as **statistical inference**. In practice, a single sample of predetermined size is selected, and the sample statistics (such as mean and proportion) are computed. Theoretically, to estimate the population parameter from the sample statistic, every possible sample that could have been drawn should be examined. If all possible samples were actually to be drawn, the distribution of the statistic would be the sampling distribution. Although in practice only one sample is actually drawn, the concept of a sampling distribution is still relevant. It enables us to use probability theory to make inferences about the population values.

The important properties of the sampling distribution of the mean, and the corresponding properties for the proportion, for large samples (30 or more) are as follows:

1 The sampling distribution of the mean is a normal distribution (see the appendix at the end of the chapter). Strictly speaking, the sampling distribution of a proportion is a binomial. For large samples ($n = 30$ or more), however, it can be approximated by the normal distribution.

2 The mean of the sampling distribution of the mean

$$\bar{X} = \left(\sum_{i=1}^{n} X_i / n \right)$$

or of the proportion (p) equals the corresponding population parameter value, μ or π, respectively.

Standard error
The standard deviation of the sampling distribution of the mean or proportion.

3 The standard deviation is called the **standard error** of the mean or the proportion to indicate that it refers to a sampling distribution of the mean or the proportion and not to a sample or a population. The formulae are

Mean	Proportion
$\sigma_{\bar{x}} = \dfrac{\sigma}{\sqrt{n}}$	$\sigma_p = \sqrt{\dfrac{\pi(1 - \pi)}{n}}$

4 Often the population standard deviation, σ, is not known. In these cases, it can be estimated from the sample by using the following formula:

$$s = \sqrt{\frac{\sum_{i=1}^{n}(X_i - \bar{X})^2}{n-1}}$$

or

$$s = \sqrt{\frac{\sum_{i=1}^{n} X_i^2 - \frac{\left(\sum_{i=1}^{n} X_i\right)^2}{n}}{n-1}}$$

In cases where σ is estimated by s, the standard error of the mean becomes

$$\text{est. } \sigma\bar{x} = \frac{s}{\sqrt{n}}$$

where 'est.' denotes that s has been used as an estimate of σ.

Assuming no measurement error, the reliability of an estimate of a population parameter can be assessed in terms of its standard error.

5 Likewise, the standard error of the proportion can be estimated by using the sample proportion p as an estimator of the population proportion, π, as

$$\text{est. } S_p = \sqrt{\frac{p(1-p)}{n}}$$

z value
The number of standard errors a point is away from the mean.

6 The area under the sampling distribution between any two points can be calculated in terms of z **value**. The z value for a point is the number of standard errors a point is away from the mean. The z values may be computed as follows:

$$z = \frac{\bar{X} - \mu}{\sigma\bar{X}}$$

For example, the areas under one side of the curve between the mean and points that have z values of 1.0, 2.0 and 3.0 are, respectively, 0.3413, 0.4772 and 0.4986. (See Table 2 in the Appendix of statistical tables.) In the case of proportion, the computation of z values is similar.

7 When the sample size is 10% or more of the population size, the standard error formulae will overestimate the standard deviation of the population mean or proportion. Hence, these should be adjusted by a finite population correction factor defined by

$$\sqrt{\frac{N-n}{N-1}}$$

In this case,

$$\sigma_{\bar{X}} = \frac{\sigma}{\sqrt{n}}\sqrt{\frac{N-n}{N-1}}$$

Statistical approaches to determining sample size

Several qualitative factors should also be taken into consideration when determining the sample size (see Chapter 14). These include the importance of the decision, the nature of the research, the number of variables, the nature of the analysis, sample sizes used in similar studies, incidence rates (the occurrence of behaviour or characteristics in a population), completion rates and resource constraints. The statistically determined sample size is the net or final sample size: the sample remaining after eliminating potential respondents who do not qualify or who do not complete the interview. Depending on incidence and completion rates, the size of the initial sample may have to be much larger. In commercial marketing research, limits on time, money and expert resources can exert an overriding influence on sample size determination. In the Formula One Racetrack Project, the sample size was determined based on these considerations.

The statistical approach to determining sample size that we consider is based on traditional statistical inference.[2] In this approach the precision level is specified in advance. This approach is based on the construction of confidence levels around sample means or proportions.

The confidence interval approach

The confidence interval approach to sample size determination is based on the construction of confidence intervals around the sample means or proportions using the standard error formula. As an example, suppose that a researcher has taken a simple random sample of 300 households to estimate the monthly amount invested in savings schemes and found that the mean household monthly investment for the sample is €182. Past studies indicate that the population standard deviation σ can be assumed to be €55.

We want to find an interval within which a fixed proportion of the sample means would fall. Suppose that we want to determine an interval around the population mean that will include 95% of the sample means, based on samples of 300 households. The 95% could be divided into two equal parts, half below and half above the mean, as shown in Figure 15.1.

Calculation of the confidence interval involves determining a distance below ($\bar{X}_L$) and above ($\bar{X}_U$) the population mean ($\bar{X}$), which contains a specified area of the normal curve.

The z values corresponding to $\bar{X}_L$ and $\bar{X}_U$ may be calculated as

$$z_L = \frac{\bar{X}_L - \mu}{\sigma_{\bar{X}}}$$

$$z_U = \frac{\bar{X}_U - \mu}{\sigma_{\bar{X}}}$$

where $z_L = -z$ and $z_U = +z$. Therefore, the lower value of is $\bar{X}$ is

$$\bar{X}_L = \mu - z\sigma_{\bar{X}}$$

and the upper value of $\bar{X}$ is

$$\bar{X}_U = \mu + z\sigma_{\bar{X}}$$

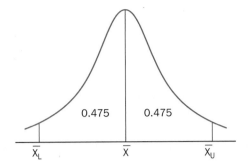

Figure 15.1
The 95% confidence interval

Note that μ is estimated by $\overline{X}$. The confidence interval is given by

$$\overline{X} \pm z\sigma_{\overline{X}}$$

We can now set a 95% confidence interval around the sample mean of €182. As a first step, we compute the standard error of the mean:

$$\sigma_{\overline{X}} = \frac{\sigma}{\sqrt{n}} = \frac{55}{\sqrt{300}} = 3.18$$

From Table 2 in the Appendix of statistical tables, it can be seen that the central 95% of the normal distribution lies within ±1.96 z values. The 95% confidence interval is given by

$$\overline{X} \pm 1.96\sigma_{\overline{X}} = 182.00 \pm 1.96\,(3.18)$$
$$= 182.00 \pm 6.23$$

Thus, the 95% confidence interval ranges from €175.77 to €188.23. The probability of finding the true population mean to be within €175.77 and €188.23 is 95%.

Sample size determination: means

The approach used here to construct a confidence interval can be adapted to determine the sample size that will result in a desired confidence interval.[3] Suppose that the researcher wants to estimate the monthly household savings investment more precisely so that the estimate will be within ±€5.00 of the true population value. What should be the size of the sample? The following steps, summarised in Table 15.2, will lead to an answer.

1 Specify the level of precision. This is the maximum permissible difference (D) between the sample mean and the population mean. In our example, $D = \pm$€5.00.
2 Specify the level of confidence. Suppose that a 95% confidence level is desired.
3 Determine the z value associated with the confidence level using Table 2 in the Appendix of statistical tables. For a 95% confidence level, the probability that the population mean will fall outside one end of the interval is 0.025 (0.05/2). The associated z value is 1.96.
4 Determine the standard deviation of the population. This may be known from secondary sources. If not, it might be estimated by conducting a pilot study. Alternatively, it might be estimated on the basis of the researcher's judgement. For example, the range of a normally distributed variable is approximately equal to ±3 standard deviations, and one can thus estimate the standard deviation by dividing the range by 6. The researcher can often estimate the range based on knowledge of the phenomenon.

Table 15.2 Summary of sample size determination for means and proportions

Steps	Means	Proportions
1 Specify the level of precision.	$D = \pm€5.00$	$D = p - \pi = \pm0.05$
2 Specify the confidence level (CL).	CL = 95%	CL = 95%
3 Determine the z value associated with the CL.	z value is 1.96	z value is 1.96
4 Determine the standard deviation of the population.	Estimate σ: $\sigma = 55$	Estimate π: $\pi = 0.64$
5 Determine the sample size using the formula for the standard error.	$n = \dfrac{\sigma^2 z^2}{D^2}$ $n = \dfrac{55^2 (1.96)^2}{5^2}$ $= 465$	$n = \dfrac{\pi(1 - \pi) z^2}{D^2}$ $n = \dfrac{0.64 (1 - 0.64) (1.96)^2}{(0.05)^2}$ $= 355$
6 If the sample size represents 10% of the population, apply the finite factor popular correction (fpc)	$n_c = \dfrac{nN}{N + n - 1}$ $= X + zs_{\bar{x}}$	$n_c = \dfrac{nN}{N + n - 1}$ $p \pm zs_p$
7 If necessary, re-estimate the confidence interval by employing s to estimate σ.	$D = R\mu$	$D = R\pi$
8 If precision is specified in relative rather than absolute terms, determine the sample size by substituting for D.	$n = \dfrac{C^2 z^2}{R^2}$	$n = \dfrac{z^2 (1 - \pi)}{R^2 \pi}$

5 Determine the sample size using the formula for the standard error of the mean:

$$z = \frac{\bar{X} - \mu}{\sigma_{\bar{X}}}$$

$$= \frac{D}{\sigma_{\bar{X}}}$$

or

$$\sigma_{\bar{X}} = \frac{D}{z}$$

or

$$\frac{\sigma}{\sqrt{n}} = \frac{D}{z}$$

or

$$n = \frac{\sigma^2 z^2}{D^2}$$

In our example,

$$n = \frac{55^2 (1.96)^2}{5^2}$$

$$= 464.83$$
$$= 465 \text{ (rounded to the next highest integer)}$$

It can be seen from the formula for sample size that sample size increases with an increase in the population variability, the degree of confidence and the precision level required of the estimate. Because the sample size is directly proportional to σ^2, the larger the population variability, the larger the sample size. Likewise, a higher degree of confidence implies a larger value of z, and thus a larger sample size. Both σ^2 and z appear in the numerator. Greater precision means a smaller value of D, and thus a larger sample size because D appears in the denominator.

6 If the resulting sample size represents 10% or more of the population, the finite population correction (fpc) should be applied.[4] The required sample size should then be calculated from the formula

$$n_c = \frac{nN}{(N+n-1)}$$

where n = sample size without fpc

n_c = sample size with fpc

7 If the population standard deviation, σ, is unknown and an estimate is used, it should be re-estimated once the sample has been drawn. The sample standard deviation, s, is used as an estimate of σ. A revised confidence interval should then be calculated to determine the precision level actually obtained.

Suppose that the value of 55.00 used for σ was an estimate because the true value was unknown. A sample of n = 465 is drawn, and these observations generate a mean $\overline{X}$ of 180.00 and a sample standard deviation s of 50.00. The revised confidence interval is then

$$\overline{X} \pm z_{\overline{X}} = 180.00 \pm 1.96 \times \left(\frac{50.0}{\sqrt{465}} \right)$$

$$= 180.00 \pm 4.55$$

or $175.45 \leqslant \mu \geqslant 184.55$. Note that the confidence interval obtained is narrower than planned, because the population standard deviation was overestimated, as judged by the sample standard deviation.

8 In some cases, precision is specified in relative rather than absolute terms. In other words, it may be specified that the estimate be within plus or minus R percentage points of the mean. Symbolically,

$$D = R\mu$$

In these cases, the sample size may be determined by

$$n = \frac{\sigma^2 z^2}{D^2}$$

$$= \frac{C^2 z^2}{R^2}$$

where the coefficient of variation $C = \sigma/\mu$ would have to be estimated.

The population size, N, does not directly affect the size of the sample, except when the fpc factor has to be applied. Although this may be counter-intuitive, upon reflection it makes sense. For example, if all the population elements are identical on the characteristics of interest, then a sample size of one will be sufficient to estimate the mean perfectly. This is true whether there are 50, 500, 5,000 or 50,000 elements in the population. What directly affects the sample size is the variability of the characteristic in the population. This variability enters into the sample size calculation by way of population variance σ^2 or sample variance s^2.

Sample size determination: proportions

If the statistic of interest is a proportion rather than a mean, the approach to sample size determination is similar. Suppose that the researcher is interested in estimating the proportion of households that own a dog as a pet. The following steps should be followed:[5]

1 Specify the level of precision. Suppose that the desired precision is such that the allowable interval is set as $D = p - \pi = \pm0.05$.
2 Specify the level of confidence. Suppose that a 95% confidence level is desired.
3 Determine the z value associated with the confidence level. As explained in the case of estimating the mean, this will be $z = 1.96$.
4 Estimate the population proportion π. As explained earlier, the population proportion may be estimated from secondary sources, or from a pilot study, or may be based on the judgement of the researcher. Suppose that based on secondary data the researcher estimates that 64% of the households in the target population own a dog. Hence, $\pi = 0.64$.
5 Determine the sample size using the formula for the standard error of the proportion:

$$\sigma_p = \frac{p - \pi}{z}$$

$$= \frac{D}{z}$$

$$= \sqrt{\frac{\pi(1 - \pi)}{n}}$$

or

$$n = \frac{\pi(1 - \pi)z^2}{D^2}$$

In our example,

$$n = \frac{0.64\,(1 - 0.64)\,(1.96)^2}{(0.05)^2}$$

$$= 354.04$$

$$= 355 \text{ (rounded to the next highest interger)}$$

6 If the resulting sample size represents 10% or more of the population, the fpc should be applied. The required sample size should then be calculated from the formula

$$n_c = \frac{nN}{(N + n - 1)}$$

where n = sample size without fpc
n_c = sample size with fpc

7 If the estimate of π turns out to be poor, the confidence interval will be more or less precise than desired. Suppose that after the sample has been taken, the proportion p is calculated to have a value of 0.55. The confidence interval is then re-estimated by employing s_p to estimate the unknown σ_p as

$$p \pm zs_p$$

where

$$S_p = \sqrt{\frac{p(1 - p)}{n}}$$

In our example

$$S_p = \sqrt{\frac{0.55\,(1-0.55)}{355}}$$

$$= 0.0264$$

The confidence interval, then, is

$$0.55 \pm 1.96\,(0.0264) = 0.55 \pm 0.052$$

which is wider than that specified. This is because the sample standard deviation based on $p = 0.55$ was larger than the estimate of the population standard deviation based on $\pi = 0.64$.

If a wider interval than specified is unacceptable, the sample size can be determined to reflect the maximum possible variation in the population. This occurs when the product $\pi(1-\pi)$ is the greatest, which happens when π is set at 0.5. This result can also be seen intuitively. Since one half of the population has one value of the characteristic and the other half the other value, more evidence would be required to obtain a valid inference than if the situation was more clear cut and the majority had one particular value. In our example, this leads to a sample size of

$$n = \frac{0.05\,(0.5)\,(1.96)^2}{(0.05)^2}$$

$$= 384.16$$

$$= 385 \text{ (rounded to the next higher integer)}$$

8 Sometimes, precision is specified in relative rather than absolute terms. In other words, it may be specified that the estimate be within plus or minus R percentage points of the population proportion. Symbolically,

$$D = R\pi$$

In such a case, the sample size may be determined by

$$n = \frac{z^2\,(1-\pi)}{R^2\pi}$$

Example | Statistical sampling: not always an emergency[6]

The city of Los Angeles wished to evaluate demand for non-emergency city services and service usage patterns. The aim was to implement a new system that would alleviate some of the strain on the city's 911 emergency phone system. A telephone survey of 1,800 randomly selected city residents was conducted.

The survey was stratified into two groups of 900 each: residents who had requested a service in the past six months and a group of other residents. The sample size was determined by using a 95% confidence interval and a margin of error of 3.5%. At this confidence level, one would expect that if all the residents of Los Angeles were asked the same survey, the responses to the survey would change by no more than ±3.5%.

To confirm that the sample size of 900 was adequate, calculations for sample size determination by proportions were made as follows, using the maximum population variation ($\pi = 0.05$). The precision of D in this study is 0.035 for a 95% confidence level.

$$n = \pi(1-\pi)z^2/D^2$$
$$n = [(0.05)(1-0.05)(1.96^2)]/(0.035)^2 = 784$$

Therefore, the 900 sample size was more than sufficient.

Multiple characteristics and parameters

In the preceding examples, we focused on the estimation of a single parameter. In most marketing research projects, several characteristics, not just one, are of interest. The researcher is required to estimate several parameters, not just one. The calculation of sample size in these cases should be based on a consideration of all the parameters that must be estimated.

For example, suppose that in addition to the mean household spend at a supermarket, it was decided to estimate the mean household spend on clothes and on gifts. The sample sizes needed to estimate each of the three mean monthly expenses are given in Table 15.3 and are 465 for supermarket shopping, 246 for clothes and 217 for gifts. If all three variables were equally important, the most conservative approach would be to select the largest value of $n = 465$ to determine the sample size. This will lead to each variable being estimated at least as precisely as specified. If the researcher was most concerned with the mean household monthly expense on clothes, however, a sample size of $n = 246$ could be selected.

Table 15.3 Sample size for estimating multiple parameters

	Variable Monthly household spend on:		
	Supermarket	Clothes	Gifts
Confidence level	95%	95%	95%
z value	1.96	1.96	1.96
Precision level (D)	€5	€5	€4
Standard deviation of the population (σ)	€55	€40	€30
Required sample size (n)	465	246	217

Other probability sampling techniques

So far, the discussion of sample size determination has been based on the methods of traditional statistical inference and has assumed simple random sampling. Next, we discuss the determination of sample size when other sampling techniques are used. The determination of sample size for other probability sampling techniques is based on the same underlying principles. The researcher must specify the level of precision and the degree of confidence and estimate the sampling distribution of the test statistic.

In simple random sampling, cost does not enter directly into the calculation of sample size. In the case of stratified or cluster sampling, however, cost has an important influence. The cost per observation varies by strata or cluster, and the researcher needs some initial estimates of these costs.[7] In addition, the researcher must take into account within-strata variability or within- and between-cluster variability. Once the overall sample size is determined, the sample is apportioned among strata or clusters. This increases the complexity of the sample size formulae. The interested reader is referred to standard works on sampling theory for more information.[8] In general, to provide the same reliability as simple random sampling, sample sizes are the same for systematic sampling, smaller for stratified sampling and larger for cluster sampling.

Adjusting the statistically determined sample size

Sample size determined statistically represents the final sample size that must be achieved to ensure that the parameters are estimated with the desired degree of precision and set level of confidence. In surveys, this represents the number of completed interviews or questionnaires. To achieve this final sample size, a much greater number of potential respondents have to be contacted. In other words, the initial sample size has to be much larger because typically the incidence rates and completion rates are less than 100%.[9]

Incidence rate refers to the rate of occurrence or the percentage of persons eligible to participate in the study. Incidence rate determines how many contacts need to be screened for a given sample size requirement.[10] For example, suppose that a study of pet ownership targets a sample of households. Of the households that might be approached to see if they qualify, approximately 75% own a pet. This means that, on average, 1.33 households would be approached to obtain one qualified respondent. Additional criteria for qualifying respondents (e.g. product usage behaviour) will further increase the number of contacts. Suppose that an added eligibility requirement is that the household should have bought a toy for their pet during the last two months. It is estimated that 60% of the households contacted would meet this criterion. Then the incidence rate is $0.75 \times 0.6 = 0.45$. Thus the final sample size will have to be increased by a factor of $(1/0.45)$ or 2.22.

Incidence rate
The rate of occurrence of persons eligible to participate in the study expressed as a percentage.

Similarly, the determination of sample size must take into account anticipated refusals by people who qualify. The **completion rate** denotes the percentage of qualified respondents who complete the interview. If, for example, the researcher expects an interview completion rate of 80% of eligible respondents, the number of contacts should be increased by a factor of 1.25. The incidence rate and the completion rate together imply that the number of potential respondents contacted – that is, the initial sample size – should be 2.22×1.25 or 2.78 times the sample size required. In general, if there are c qualifying factors with an incidence of $Q_1 \times Q_2 \times Q_3 \ldots \times Q_c$ each expressed as a proportion, the following are true:

Completion rate
The percentage of qualified respondents who complete the interview. It enables researchers to take into account anticipated refusals by people who qualify.

$$\text{Incidence rate} = Q_1 \times Q_2 \times Q_3 \times \ldots \times Q_c$$

$$\text{Initial sample size} = \frac{\text{final sample size}}{\text{incidence rate} \times \text{completion rate}}$$

The number of units that will have to be sampled will be determined by the initial sample size. Often a number of variables are used for qualifying potential respondents, thereby decreasing the incidence rate. Completion rates are affected by non-response issues. These issues deserve particular attention and are detailed in the next section.

Non-response issues in sampling

The two major non-response issues in sampling are improving response rates and adjusting for non-response. Non-response error arises when some of the potential respondents included in the sample do not respond (see Chapter 3). This is one of the most significant problems in survey research. Non-respondents may differ from respondents in terms of demographic, psychographic, personality, attitudinal, motivational and behavioural variables.[11] Evaluating these differences was detailed in Chapter 14 in the process of sample validation. For a given study, if the non-respondents differ from the respondents on the characteristics of interest, the sample estimates can be seriously biased. Higher response rates, in general, imply lower rates of non-response bias, yet response rate may not be an adequate indicator of non-response bias. Response rates themselves do not indicate whether

Source: © Getty Images

the respondents are representative of the original sample.[12] Increasing the response rate may not reduce non-response bias if the additional respondents are no different from those who have already responded but do differ from those who still do not respond. As low response rates increase the probability of non-response bias, an attempt should be made to improve the response rate.[13] This is not an issue that should be considered after a survey approach has been decided and a questionnaire designed. Factors that improve response rates are integral to survey and questionnaire design. As detailed in Chapter 13, the marketing researchers should build up an awareness of what motivates their target respondents to participate in a research study. The researchers should ask themselves what their target respondents get in return for spending time and effort, answering set questions in a full and honest manner. The following sub-section details the techniques involved in improving response rates and adjusting for non-response.

Improving the response rates

The primary causes of low response rates are refusals and not-at-homes, as shown in Figure 15.2.

Refusals. Refusals, which result from the unwillingness or inability of people included in the sample to participate, result in lower response rates and increased potential for non-response bias. The following examples illustrate some of the factors that drive refusals, terminations and completed interviews.

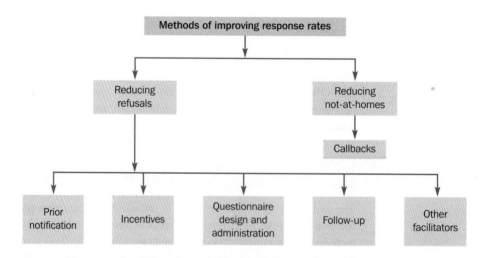

Figure 15.2 Improving response rates

Example ### Reasons for refusal[14]

In a study investigating the refusal problem in telephone surveys, telephone interviews were conducted with responders and non-responders to a previous survey, using quotas of 100 for each subsample. The results are presented in the following table:

Refusals, terminations and completed interviews

Property	Total sample	Responders	Non-responders
Number of refusals (1)	224	31	193
Number of terminations (2)	100	33	67
Number of completed interviews (3)	203	102	101
Total number of contacts $(1 + 2 + 3)^*$	527	166	361
Refusal rate $[1/(1 + 2 + 3)]$	42.5%	18.7%	53.5%
Termination rate $[2/(1 + 2 + 3)]$	19.0%	19.9%	18.5%
Completion rate $[3/(1 + 2 + 3)]$ [†]	38.5%	61.4%	28.0%

* A total of 1,388 attempts was required to make these contacts: the 166 responder contacts required 406 attempts (with one call-back per respondent), and the 361 non-responder contacts required 982 attempts (with two call-backs per respondent). The sampling frame contained 965 phone numbers – 313 respondents and 652 non-responders.
[†] Responder/non-responder differences were significant at $\alpha = 0.05$ (two-tail test).

The study found that people who are likely to participate in a telephone survey (responders) differ from those who are likely to refuse (non-responders) in the following ways:

1 Confidence in survey research
2 Confidence in the research organisation
3 Demographic characteristics
4 Beliefs and attitudes about telephone surveys.

A 2002 study by the Council for Marketing and Opinion Research (CMOR) in the USA showed that 18% of respondents say that the Internet is their first choice when doing a survey, up from 10% in 1999. On respondent cooperation, only 7% of respondents called were willing to answer questions. The situation in the USA reflects conditions in other developed markets such as Europe and Japan. Although average response rates in Japan are significantly higher than in the USA and Europe, they show a continuous downward trend, mainly by the rise of refusals.

Example 'No time' main reason for refusal[15]

Research conducted by Paul Iavrakas, Vice President of Nielsen Media Research (**www.nielsenmedia.com**), showed that there were four basic 'causes' for non-cooperation. These are 'no time or interest', 'privacy and confidentiality concerns', 'not enjoying the survey experience' and 'not believing one's opinions are important'. Paul says it is known that mentioning the survey's topic can significantly affect response rates:

Response rates for surveys on topics that are of higher interest to respondents can be up to 40% higher. Health issue surveys for instance, usually get high response rates. But is it acceptable to mention the topic in the introduction to a survey? One professor at the Ohio State University Survey Center insisted that we not mention the survey topic because of the risk of non-response due to only people being interested in the survey being willing to be interviewed. Balancing effective measures to improve response rates and concerns about non-response errors will always be a very difficult trade off.

Given the potential differences between respondents and non-respondents, researchers should attempt to lower refusal rates. This can be done by prior notification, incentives, good questionnaire design and administration, follow-up and other facilitators:

● *Prior notification.* In prior notification, potential respondents are telephoned, sent a letter or email notifying them of the imminent mail, telephone personal or Internet survey. Prior notification increases response rates, as the respondent's attention is drawn to the purpose of a study and the potential benefits, without the apparent 'chore' of the questionnaire. With the potential respondent's attention focused upon the purpose and benefits, the chances increase for a greater reception when approached actually to complete a survey.[16] A key element of notifying potential respondents lies in how surveys are introduced as illustrated in the following example.

Example | **Only incentives increase response rates?[17]**

In a study organised by a New Zealand marketing research agency that conducted omnibus surveys using CATI, a measure of the effectiveness of 'introductions' upon response rates was made. Four introduction elements were tested: an incentive (prize draw for a weekend holiday); an assurance that the survey was not a sales pitch; an assurance of confidentiality; and a short versus longer description of the survey topic. Overall, only the incentive significantly increased the response rate. In combination, the best result and the only one to achieve a significantly higher response rate was the use of the incentive coupled with a 'no-sales' assurance. The use of the incentive did not appear to encourage people to lie about their eligibility as respondents.

● *Incentives.* Response rates can be increased by offering monetary as well as non-monetary incentives to potential respondents. Monetary incentives can be prepaid or promised. The prepaid incentive is included with the survey or questionnaire. The promised incentive is sent to only those respondents who complete the survey. The most commonly used non-monetary incentives are premiums and rewards, such as pens, pencils, books and offers of survey results.[18] Prepaid incentives have been shown to increase response rates to a greater extent than promised incentives. The amount of incentive can vary from trivial amounts to tens of euros. The amount of incentive has a positive relationship with response rate, but the cost of large monetary incentives may outweigh the value and quality of additional information obtained.

● *Questionnaire design and administration.* A well-designed questionnaire can decrease the overall refusal rate as well as refusals to specific questions (see Chapter 13). If the questionnaire and experience of answering the questions are interesting for the respondent, using words and logic that are meaningful to them, the response rate can improve. Likewise, the skill used to administer the questionnaire in telephone and personal interviews can increase the response rate. Trained interviewers are skilled in refusal conversion or persuasion. They do not accept a no response without an additional plea. The additional plea might emphasise the brevity of the questionnaire or importance of the respondent's opinion. Interviewing procedures are discussed in more detail in Chapter 16.

● *Follow-up.* Follow-up, or contacting the non-respondents periodically after the initial contact, is particularly effective in decreasing refusals in mail and Internet surveys. The researcher might send a reminder to non-respondents to complete and return the questionnaire. Two or three mailings may be needed in addition to the original one. With proper follow-up, the response rate in mail surveys can be increased to 80% or more.[19] Follow-ups can be done by postcard, letter, telephone, email or personal contacts.

● *Other facilitators.* Personalisation, or sending letters addressed to specific individuals, is effective in increasing response rates, especially when practised in conjunction with prior notification.[20] The only downside of such an approach is actually obtaining the names and contact details of those to whom a questionnaire should be sent. The following example illustrates the two approaches to increasing response rates. The first is a procedure used by *Bicycling* magazine specific to its postal survey, the second, used by the research agency Arbitron, is designed to encompass all of its survey work.

Example

Bicycling **magazine's procedure for increasing response to traditional mail surveys[21]**

Bicycling magazine (**www.bicycling.com**) conducts a semi-annual survey of individual bicycle dealers. The following procedure is used to increase the response to the survey:

1 An 'alert' letter is sent to advise the respondent that a questionnaire is coming.
2 A questionnaire package is posted five days after the 'alert' letter. The package contains a cover letter, a five-page questionnaire, a new $1 bill, and a stamped addressed envelope.
3 A second package containing a reminder letter, a questionnaire and a stamped return envelope is posted five days after the first package.
4 A follow-up postcard is sent a week after the second package.
5 A second follow-up postcard is sent a week after the first.

Example

Arbitron's response to low response rates[22]

Arbitron (**www.arbitron.com**), a major marketing research agency, set about trying to improve response rates in order to improve the quality of its surveys. It created a cross-functional team of employees to evaluate the problem and to make recommendations. Their method was named the 'breakthrough method' and resulted in a complete change in the Arbitron approach to surveys. The team recommended six major strategies to improve response rates:

1 Maximise the effectiveness of placement/follow-up calls.
2 Make materials more appealing and easier to complete.
3 Increase Abritron name awareness.
4 Improve survey participant rewards.
5 Optimise the arrival of respondent materials.
6 Increase usability of returned diaries.

Eighty initiatives were launched to implement these six strategies. As a result, response rates improved significantly. However, in spite of encouring results, marketing researchers at Arbitron remain cautious. They appreciate that there is a daily challenge to maintain high response rates that encompasses everything they do in designing and implementing surveys.

Not-at-homes. The second major cause of low response rates is not-at-homes. In telephone and in-home personal interviews, low response rates can result if the potential respondents are not at home when contact is attempted. A study analysing 182 commercial telephone surveys involving a total sample of over 1 million consumers revealed that a large percentage of potential respondents were never contacted. The median non-contact rate was 40%. In nearly 40% of the surveys, only a single attempt was made to contact potential respondents. The results of 259,088 first-call attempts using a sophisticated random-digit dialling system show that less than 10% of the calls resulted in completed interviews, and 14.3% of those contacted refused to participate.[23]

The likelihood that potential respondents will not be at home varies with several factors. People with small children are more likely to be at home. Consumers are more likely to be at home at weekends than on weekdays and in the evening as opposed to during the afternoon. Pre-notification and appointments increase the likelihood that the respondent will be at home when contact is attempted.

The percentage of not-at-homes can be substantially reduced by employing a series of call-backs, or periodic follow-up attempts to contact non-respondents. The decision about the number of call-backs should weigh the benefits of reducing non-response bias against the additional costs. As call-backs are completed, the call-back respondents should be compared with those who have already responded to determine the usefulness of making further call-backs. In most consumer surveys, three or four call-backs may be desirable. Although the first call yields the most responses, the second and third calls have a higher response per call. It is important that call-backs be made and controlled according to a prescribed plan.

Adjusting for non-response

Low response rates increase the probability that non-response bias will be substantial. Response rates should always be reported, and, whenever possible, the effects of non-response should be estimated. This can be done by linking the non-response rate to estimated differences between respondents and non-respondents. Information on differences between the two groups may be obtained from the sample itself. For example, differences found through call-backs could be extrapolated, or a concentrated follow-up could be conducted on a subsample of the non-respondents. Alternatively, it may be possible to estimate these differences from other sources.[24] To illustrate, in a survey of owners of vacuum cleaners, demographic and other information may be obtained for respondents and non-respondents from their guarantee cards. For a mail panel, a wide variety of information is available for both groups from syndicate organisations. If the sample is supposed to be representative of the general population, then comparisons can be made with census figures. Even if it is not feasible to estimate the effects of non-response, some adjustments can still be made during data analysis and interpretation.[25] The strategies available to adjust for non-response error include subsampling of non-respondents, replacement, substitution, subjective estimates, trend analysis, simple weighting and imputation.

Subsampling of non-respondents. Subsampling of non-respondents, particularly in the case of mail surveys, can be effective in adjusting for non-response bias. In this technique, the researcher contacts a subsample of the non-respondents, usually by means of telephone or personal interviews. This often results in a high response rate within that subsample. The values obtained for the subsample are then projected to all the non-respondents, and the survey results are adjusted to account for non-response. This method can estimate the effect of non-response on the characteristic of interest.

Replacement. In replacement, the non-respondents in the current survey are replaced with non-respondents from an earlier, similar survey. The researcher attempts to contact these non-respondents from the earlier survey and administer the current survey questionnaire to them, possibly by offering a suitable incentive. It is important that the nature of non-response in the current survey be similar to that of the earlier survey. The two surveys should use similar kinds of respondents, and the time interval between them should be short. As an example, as the Formula One Racetrack Project is repeated each year, the non-respondents in the present survey may be replaced by the non-respondents in the original survey.

Substitution
A procedure that substitutes for non-respondents other elements from the sampling frame who are expected to respond.

Substitution. In substitution, the researcher substitutes for non-respondents other elements from the sampling frame who are expected to respond. The sampling frame is divided into subgroups that are internally homogeneous in terms of respondent characteristics but heterogeneous in terms of response rates. These subgroups are then used to identify substitutes who are similar to particular non-respondents but dissimilar to respondents already in the sample. Note that this approach would not reduce non-response bias if the substitutes are similar to respondents already in the sample.

Subjective estimates. When it is no longer feasible to increase the response rate by subsampling, replacement or substitution, it may be possible to arrive at subjective estimates of the nature and effect of non-response bias. This involves evaluating the likely effects of non-response based on experience and available information. For example, married adults with young children are more likely to be at home than single or divorced adults or than married adults with no children. This information provides a basis for evaluating the effects of non-response due to not-at-homes in personal or telephone surveys.

Trend analysis
A method of adjusting for non-response in which the researcher tries to discern a trend between early and late respondents. This trend is projected to non-respondents to estimate their characteristic of interest.

Trend analysis. Trend analysis is an attempt to discern a trend between early and late respondents. This trend is projected to non-respondents to estimate where they stand on the characteristic of interest. For example, Table 15.4 presents the results of several waves of a mail survey. The characteristic of interest is money spent on shopping in supermarkets during the last two months. The known value of the characteristic for the total sample is given at the bottom of the table. The value for each successive wave of respondents becomes closer to the value for non-respondents. For example, those responding to the second mailing spent 79% of the amount spent by those who responded to the first mailing. Those responding to the third mailing spent 85% of the amount spent by those who responded to the second mailing. Continuing this trend, one might estimate that those who did not respond spent 91% [85 + (85 − 79)] of the amount spent by those who responded to the third mailing. This results in an estimate of €252 (277 × 0.91) spent by non-respondents and an estimate of €288 [(0.12 × 412) + (0.18 × 325) + (0.13 × 277) + (0.57 × 252)] for the average amount spent in shopping at supermarkets during the last two months for the overall sample. Note that the actual amount spent by the respondents was €230 rather than €252, and that the actual sample average was €275 rather than the €288 estimated by trend analysis. Although the trend estimates are wrong, the error is smaller than the error that would have resulted from ignoring the non-respondents. Had the non-respondents been ignored, the average amount spent would have been estimated at €335 [(0.12 × 412) + (0.18 × 325) + (0.13 × 277)]/(0.12 + 0.18 + 0.13) for the sample.

Table 15.4 Use of trend analysis in adjusting for non-response

	Percentage response	Average euro expenditure	Percentage of previous wave's response
First mailing	12	412	–
Second mailing	18	325	79
Third mailing	13	277	85
Non-response	(57)	(230)	91
Total	100	275	

Weighting
A statistical procedure that attempts to account for non-response by assigning differential weights to the data depending on the response rates.

Weighting. Weighting attempts to account for non-response by assigning differential weights to the data depending on the response rates.[26] For example, in a survey on PC, the sample was stratified according to income. The response rates were 85%, 70% and 40%, respectively, for the high-, medium- and low-income groups. In analysing the data, these subgroups are assigned weights inversely proportional to their response rates. That is, the weights assigned would be 100/85, 100/70 and 100/40, respectively, for the high-, medium- and low-income groups. Although weighting can correct for the differential effects of non-response, it destroys the self-weighting nature of the sampling design and can introduce complications. Weighting is further discussed in Chapter 17 on data preparation.

Imputation
A method to adjust for non-response by assigning the characteristic of interest to the non-respondents based on the similarity of the variables available for both non-respondents and respondents.

Imputation. Imputation involves imputing, or assigning, the characteristic of interest to the non-respondents based on the similarity of the variables available for both non-respondents and respondents.[27] For example, a respondent who does not report brand usage may be imputed based on the usage of a respondent with similar demographic characteristics. Often there is a high correlation between the characteristic of interest and some other variables. In such cases, this correlation can be used to predict the value of the characteristic for the non-respondents (see Chapter 14).

International marketing research

When conducting marketing research in international environments, statistical estimation of sample size may be difficult because estimates of the population variance in particular countries may be unavailable. Hence, the sample size is often determined by qualitative considerations, as discussed in Chapter 14: (1) the importance of the decision, (2) the nature of the research, (3) the number of variables, (4) the nature of the analysis, (5) sample sizes used in similar studies, (6) incidence rates, (7) completion rates, and (8) resource constraints. If statistical estimation of sample size is at all attempted, it should be realised that the estimates of the population variance may vary from country to country. For example, in measuring consumer preferences, a greater degree of heterogeneity may be encountered in countries where consumer preferences are not well developed. Thus, it may be a mistake to assume that the population variance is the same or to use the same sample size in different countries as illustrated in the following example.

Example

The Chinese take to the sky[28]

The airline industry seems to have a strong and promising market potential in China. The airline market in China is growing rapidly. With the equivalent of billions of euros spent, China is trying to satisfy surging demand and to catch up with the rest of the world. The domestic airline traffic is growing at a rate of up to 30% a year. Strong economic growth, surging foreign trade, heavy investment in new airports, and a desire to travel overseas after many years of restriction, have helped to fuel the boom. China is making rapid progress in increasing its fleet and training pilots. For millions of Chinese, air travel is a relatively new experience and many more millions have never flown. Hence, Chinese preferences for air travel are likely to exhibit much more variability compared with Europeans. In a survey to compare attitudes towards air travel in China and European countries, the sample size of the Chinese survey would have to be larger than the European survey in order for the two survey estimates to have comparable precision.

It is important to realise that survey response rates can vary widely across countries. In a 2000 business mail survey conducted in 22 countries, the response rates varied from a low of 7.1% in Hong Kong to a high of 42.1% in Denmark with the overall response rate being 20%. The study also analysed factors to help explain the differences in response rates. Factors included the cultural and geographical distance from the Netherlands (where the survey was mailed), the level of foreign sales, number of employees and size of corporation.[29]

Ethics in marketing research

As discussed in this chapter, statistical methods can be used to determine the sample size and, therefore, have an impact on the cost of the project. While this is usually an objective way of determining the sample size, it is, nonetheless, susceptible to fraud. The sample size is heavily dependent on the standard deviation of the variable and there is no way of knowing the standard deviation until the data have been collected. To resolve this paradox, the computation of the sample size must be performed using an estimate of the standard deviation. This estimate is derived based on secondary data, judgement or a small pilot study. By inflating the standard deviation, it is possible to increase the sample size and thus the project revenue. Using the sample size formula, it can be seen that increasing the standard deviation by 20%, for example, will increase the sample size by 44%. But this is clearly unethical.

Ethical dilemmas can arise even when the standard deviation is estimated honestly. It is possible, indeed common, that the standard deviation in the actual study is different from that estimated initially. When the standard deviation is larger than initially estimated, the confidence interval will also be larger than desired. When such a situation arises, the researcher has the responsibility to disclose this to the client and jointly decide on a course of action. The ethical ramifications of mis-communicating the confidence intervals of survey estimates based on statistical samples are underscored in political polling.

| Example | ### Surveys serve up elections[30] |

The dissemination of some survey results has been strongly criticised as manipulative and unethical. In particular, the ethics of releasing political poll results before and during the election have been questioned. Opponents of such surveys claim that voters are misled by these results. First, before the election, voters are influenced by whom the polls predict will win. If they see that the candidate they favour is trailing, they may decide not to vote; they assume that there is no way their candidate can win. The attempt to predict the election results while the election is in progress has come under even harsher criticism. Opponents of this practice feel that this predisposes voters to vote for the projected winner or that it may even discourage voters from voting, even though the polls have not closed, because the media projects that there is already a winner. Furthermore, not only are the effects of these projections questionable, but frequently the accuracy of the projections is questionable as well. Although voters may be told a candidate has a certain percentage of the votes within 1 per cent, the confidence interval may be much larger, depending on the sample size.

Researchers also have the ethical responsibility to investigate the possibility of non-response bias, and make a reasonable effort to adjust for non-response. The methodology adopted and the extent of non-response bias found should be clearly communicated.

Internet and computer applications

The main use of the Internet in sample size calculations is to track down potential sampling frames that could be used to define and classify a population. With different sampling frames collected and 'cleaned' in a database package, the ultimate population size can be determined. If there is a finite size to a population, the Internet can play a vital role in tracking down all elements of that population.

Using database packages to record the identity of survey respondents, the researcher can keep track of non-respondents. The database can help to determine whether there are particular geographic locations or types of non-respondent that are problematic. The rapid identification of non-respondents enables researchers to develop tactics to encourage a response.

The use of the Internet itself is thought to increase response rates for certain types of respondent. Primarily this is because of the ease of the survey process. Because the length of a survey on the Internet is hidden from respondents, they are less likely not to respond due to survey length. The inclusion of electronic skip patterns in the questionnaire design also helps to promote higher response rates by making it easier for the respondent to manoeuvre through the survey. Internet surveys can also use attractive design and plug-ins such as music and video to make the process more interesting.

For electronic mail surveys, prior emails sent by the sponsor to announce the survey are strongly suggested by many of the Internet marketing research firms. These firms also send reminder emails to non-respondents a few days after the initial survey has been sent. Another way to motivate respondents to complete surveys is to tell them whether and the extent to which a service will be enhanced. Another motivator is to provide incentives for completion of surveys. A Research Information Chat Board request on how to recruit respondents for web-based interviewing drew a note that a respondent had participated in a survey because he would be entered into a 'cash-draw' for participating. Another technique cited was to give points redeemable for merchandise or discounts to survey respondents.

There are a number of websites on the Internet that offer free use of sample size and confidence interval calculators. A simple web search will reveal a great array of sources from software designers such as **www.surveysystem.com** (in Research Aids) to statistics faculties in universities. You will be expected to specify a desired precision level, confidence level and population variance. By incorporating the cost of each sampling unit, the sample size can be adjusted based upon budget considerations.

Summary

The statistical approaches to determining sample size are based on confidence intervals. These approaches may involve the estimation of the mean or proportion. When estimating the mean, determination of sample size using the confidence interval approach requires the specification of precision level, confidence level and population standard deviation. In the case of proportion, the precision level, confidence level and an estimate of the population proportion must be specified. The sample size determined statistically represents the final or net sample size that must be achieved. To achieve this final sample size, a much greater number of potential respondents have to be contacted to account for reduction in response due to incidence rates and completion rates.

Non-response error arises when some of the potential respondents included in the sample do not respond. The primary causes of low response rates are refusals and not-at-homes. Refusal rates may be reduced by prior notification, incentives, excellent questionnaire design and administration, and follow-up. The percentage of not-at-homes can be substantially reduced by call-backs. Adjustments for non-response can be made by subsampling non-respondents, replacement, substitution, subjective estimates, trend analysis, simple weighting and imputation.

The statistical estimation of sample size is even more complicated in international marketing research because the population variance may differ from one country to the next. The preliminary estimation of population variance for the purpose of determining the sample size also has ethical ramifications.

Questions

1 Define:
  a the sampling distribution
  b finite population correction
  c confidence intervals.

2 What is the standard error of the mean?

3 What is the procedure for constructing a confidence interval around a mean?

4 Describe the difference between absolute precision and relative precision when estimating a population mean.

5 How do the degree of confidence and the degree of precision differ?

6 Describe the procedure for determining the sample size necessary to estimate a population mean, given the degree of precision and confidence and a known population variance. After the sample is selected, how is the confidence interval generated?

7 Describe the procedure for determining the sample size necessary to estimate a population mean, given the degree of precision and confidence but where the population variance is unknown. After the sample is selected, how is the confidence interval generated?

8 How is the sample size affected when the absolute precision with which a population mean is estimated is doubled?

9 How is the sample size affected when the degree of confidence with which a population mean is estimated is increased from 95% to 99%?

10 Define what is meant by absolute precision and relative precision when estimating a population proportion.

11 Describe the procedure for determining the sample size necessary to estimate a population proportion given the degree of precision and confidence. After the sample is selected, how is the confidence interval generated?

12 How can the researcher ensure that the generated confidence interval will be no larger than the desired interval when estimating a population proportion?

13 When several parameters are being estimated, what is the procedure for determining the sample size?

14 Define incidence rate and completion rate. How do these rates affect the determination of the final sample size?

15 What strategies are available for adjusting for non-response?

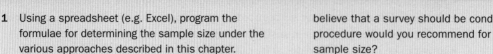

Exercises

1 Using a spreadsheet (e.g. Excel), program the formulae for determining the sample size under the various approaches described in this chapter.

2 Using the website of a major newspaper in your country, search for reports of three recent major surveys. Write a report on the sample sizes used and the extent to which details of precision, confidence levels and any other factors affecting the sample were reported. Note any reporting that sensationalises statistical changes over time that are within the margin of error tolerances.

3 A major electric utility company would like to determine the average amount spent per household for air-conditioning during summer months. From its own records it knows how much electricity is consumed per household but not how much is spent on particular appliances and the attitudes towards the use of those appliances. Thus management

believe that a survey should be conducted. What procedure would you recommend for determining the sample size?

4 You work as the marketing research manager for a chain of theme restaurants. A new menu has been developed based upon organic and fair-trade produce. Before the new menu is introduced, management are concerned about how existing and potential customers will react. How would you approach the sample size calculations for this task? Present your plan to a group of students representing the board of the chain.

5 In a small group discuss the following issues: 'Statistical considerations are more important than administrative considerations in determining sample size' and 'The real determinant of sample size is what managers feel confident with; it has little to do with statistical confidence.'

Video Case Exercise: Subaru

Evaluate the reasons for the high response rates to Subaru surveys. What lessons of Subaru's success can be generalised to other survey designs.

video case

download from
www.pearsoned.co.uk/
malhotra_euro

Appendix: The normal distribution

In this appendix, we provide a brief overview of the normal distribution and the use of the normal distribution table. The normal distribution is used in calculating the sample size, and it serves as the basis for classical statistical inference. Many continuous phenomena follow the normal distribution or can be approximated by it. The normal distribution can, likewise, be used to approximate many discrete probability distributions.[31]

The normal distribution has some important theoretical properties. It is bell shaped and symmetrical in appearance. Its measures of central tendency (mean, median and mode) are all identical. Its associated random variable has an infinite range $(-\infty < x < +\infty)$.

The normal distribution is defined by the population mean μ and population standard deviation σ. Since an infinite number of combinations of μ and σ exist, an infinite number of normal distributions exist and an infinite number of tables would be required. By standardising the data, however, we need only one table, such as Table 2 in the Appendix of statistical tables. Any normal random variable X can be converted to a standardised normal random variable z by the formula

$$z = \frac{X - \mu}{}$$

Note that the random variable z is always normally distributed with a mean of 0 and a standard deviation of 1. The normal probability tables are generally used for two purposes: (1) finding probabilities corresponding to known values of X or z, and (2) finding values of X or z corresponding to known probabilities. Each of these uses is discussed.

Finding probabilities corresponding to known values

Suppose that Figure 15A.1 represents the distribution of the number of engineering contracts received per year by an engineering firm. Because the data span the entire history of the firm, Figure 15A.1 represents the population. Therefore, the probabilities or proportion of area under the curve must add up to 1.0. The marketing director wishes to determine the probability that the number of contracts received next year will be between 50 and 55. The answer can be determined by using Table 2 of the Appendix of statistical tables.

Table 2 gives the probability or area under the standardised normal curve from the mean (zero) to the standardised value of interest, z. Only positive entries of z are listed in the table. For a symmetrical distribution with zero mean, the area from the mean to $+z$ (i.e. z standard deviations above the mean) is identical to the area from the mean to $-z$ (z standard deviations below the mean).

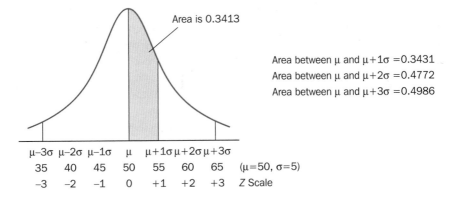

Figure 15A.1
Finding probability corresponding to a known value

Note that the difference between 50 and 55 corresponds to a z value of 1.00. Note that, to use Table 2, all z values must be recorded to two decimal places. To read the probability or area under the curve from the mean to $z = +1.00$, scan down the z column of Table 2 until the z value of interest (in tenths) is located. In this case, stop in the row $z = 1.00$. Then read across this row until you intersect the column containing the hundredths place of the z value. Thus, in Table 2, the tabulated probability for $z = 1.00$ corresponds to the intersection of the row $z = 1.0$ with the column $z = 0.00$. This probability is 0.3413. As shown in Figure 15A.1, the probability is 0.3413 that the number of contracts received by the firm next year will be between 50 and 55. It can also be concluded that the probability is 0.6826 (2×0.3413) that the number of contracts received next year will be between 45 and 55.

This result could be generalised to show that for any normal distribution the probability is 0.6826 that a randomly selected item will fall within 1 standard deviation above or below the mean. Also, it can be verified from Table 2 that there is a 0.9544 probability that any randomly selected, normally distributed observation will fall within ±2 standard deviations above or below the mean, and a 0.9973 probability that the observation will fall within ±3 standard deviations above or below the mean.

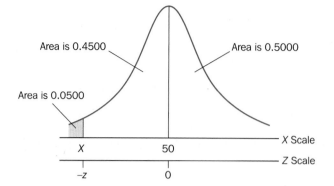

Figure 15A.2
Finding values
corresponding to
known probabilities

Finding values corresponding to known properties values

Suppose that the marketing director wishes to determine how many contracts must come in so that 5% of the contracts for the year have come in. If 5% of the contracts have come in, 95% of the contracts have yet to come. As shown in Figure 15A.2, this 95% can be broken down into two parts: contracts above the mean (i.e. 50%) and contracts between the mean and the desired z value (i.e. 45%). The desired z value can be determined from Table 2, since the area under the normal curve from the standardised mean, 0, to this z must be 0.4500. From Table 2, we search for the area or probability 0.4500. The closest value is 0.4495 or 0.4505. For 0.4495, we see that the z value corresponding to the particular z row (1.6) and z column (0.04) is 1.64. The z value, however, must be recorded as negative (i.e. $z = -1.64$), since it is below the standardised mean of 0. Similarly, the z value corresponding to the area of 0.4505 is -1.65. Since 0.4500 is midway between 0.4495 and 0.4505, the appropriate z value could be midway between the two z values and estimated as -1.645. The corresponding X value can then be calculated from the standardisation formula, as follows:

$$X = \mu + z\sigma$$
$$= 50 + (-1.645)5$$
$$= 41.775$$

Suppose that the marketing director wanted to determine the interval in which 95% of the contracts for the next year are expected to lie. As can be seen from Figure 15A.3, the corresponding z values are ± 1.96. This corresponds to X values of $50 \pm (1.96)5$, or 40.2 and 59.8. this range respresents the 95% confidence interval.

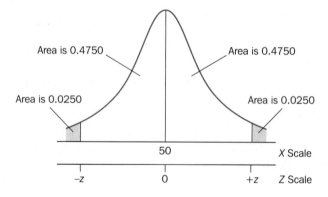

Figure 15A.3
Finding values
corresponding to
known probabilities:
confidence interval

Notes

1 A discussion of the sampling distribution may be found in any basic statistics textbook. For example, see Berenson, M.L., Levine, D.M. and Krehbiel, T., *Basic Business Statistics: Concepts and Applications*, 8th edn (Englewood Cliffs, NJ: Prentice Hall, 2002).

2 Other statistical approaches are also available. A discussion of these is beyond the scope of this book, however. The interested reader is referred to Reynolds, M.R. Jr., 'EWMA control charts with variable sample sizes and variable sampling intervals', *IEE Transactions* 33 (6) (June 2001), 511–530; Sampath, S., *Sampling theory and methods* (Boca Raton, FL: CRC Press, 2000); Yeh, L. and Van, L.C., 'Bayesian double-sampling plans with normal distributions', *Statistician* 46 (2) (1997), 193–207; Blyth, W.G. and Marchant, L.J., 'A self-weighting random sampling technique', *Journal of the Market Research Society* 38 (4) (October 1996), 473–479; Nowell, C. and Stanley, L.R., 'Length-biased sampling in mall intercept surveys', *Journal of Marketing Research* 28 (November 1991), 475–479; Gillett, R., 'Confidence interval construction by Stein's method: a practical and economical approach to sample size determination', *Journal of Marketing Research* 26 (May 1989), 237.

3 Thompson, S.K., *Sampling* (New York: Wiley, 2002); Wall, M.M., 'An effective confidence interval for the mean with samples of size one and two', *American Statistician* (May 2001), 102–105; Chow, S.L., *Statistical Significance* (Thousand Oaks, CA: Sage, 1996).

4 Valliant, R.L., Dorfinan, A.H. and Royall, R.M., *Finite Population Sampling and Inference: A Prediction Approach* (New York: Wiley, 2000).

5 Joseph, L. and Wolfson, D.B., 'Interval based versus decision-theoretic criteria for the choice of a sample size', *Statistician* 46 (2) (1997), 145–149; Frankel, M., 'Sampling theory', in Rossi, P.H., Wright, J.D. and Anderson, A.B. (eds), *Handbook of Survey Research* (New York: Academic Press, 1983), 21–67.

6 'City of Los Angeles Internet Services Project: Market Analysis and Best Practices Report', *e-Government Services Project Reports* (29 October 1999).

7 For a discussion of estimating sample costs, see Kish, L., *Survey Sampling* (New York: Wiley, 1965); Sudman, S., *Applied Sampling* (New York: Academic Press, 1976).

8 See, for example, Sampath, S., *Sampling theory and methods* (Boca Raton, FL: CRC Press, 2000); Bradley, N., 'Sampling for Internet surveys: an examination of respondent selection for internet research', *Journal of the Market Research Society* 41 (4) (October 1999), 387–395; Adcock, C.J., 'Sample size determination a review', *Statistician* 46 (2) (1997), 261–283; Sudman, S., 'Applied sampling', in Rossi, P.H., Wright, J.D. and Anderson, A.B. (eds), *Handbook of Survey Research* (New York: Academic Press, 1983), 145–194.

9 Adjusting for incidence and completion rates is discussed in Rao, P.S., *Sampling Methodologies with Applications* (Boca Raton, FL: CRC Press, 2001); Bickart, B., 'The distribution of survey contact and participation in the United States: constructing a survey based estimate', *Journal of Marketing Research* 36 (2) (May 1999), 286–294; Dillman, D.A., Singer, E., Clark, J.R. and Treat, J.B., 'Effects of benefits appeals, mandatory appeals, and variations in statements of confidentiality on completion rates for census questionnaires', *Public Opinion Quarterly* 60 (3) (Fall 1996), 376–389; Pol,

L.G. and Pak, S., 'The use of two stage survey design in collecting data from those who have attended periodic or special events', *Journal of the Market Research Society* 36 (October 1994), 315–326.

10 Lee, K.G., 'Incidence is a key element', *Marketing News* (13 September 1985), 50.

11 Van Kenhove, P., 'The influence of topic involvement on mail-survey response behaviour', *Psychology & Marketing* 19 (3) (March 2002), 293; Fisher, M.R., 'Estimating the effect of nonresponse bias on angler surveys', *Transactions of the American Fisheries Society* 125 (1) (January 1996), 118–126; Martin, C., 'The impact of topic interest on mail survey response behaviour', *Journal of the Market Research Society* 36 (October 1994), 327–338.

12 Cummings, S.M., 'Reported response rates to mailed physician questionnaires', *Health Services Research* 35 (6) (February 2001), 1347–1355; Hill, A., Roberts, J., Ewings, P. and Gunnell, D., 'Nonresponse bias in a lifestyle survey', *Journal of Public Health Medicine* 19 (2) (June 1997), 203–207; McDaniel, S.W., Madden, C.S. and Verille, P., 'Do topic differences affect survey non-response?', *Journal of the Market Research Society* (January 1987), 55–66.

13 For minimising the incidence of non-response and adjusting for its effects, see Columbo, R., 'A model for diagnosing and reducing non-response bias', *Journal of Advertising Research* 40 (1/2) (January/April 2000), 85–93; Chen, H.C., 'Direction, magnitude, and implications of nonresponse bias in mail surveys', *Journal of the Market Research Society* 38 (3) (July 1996), 267–276; Brown, M., 'What price response?', *Journal of the Market Research Society* 36 (July 1994), 227–244.

14 Jarvis, S., 'CMOR finds survey refusal rate still rising', *Marketing News* 36 (3) (4 February 2002), 4; Baldauf, A., 'Examining motivations to refuse in industrial mail surveys', *Journal of the Market Research Society* 41 (3) (July 1999), 345–353; Baker, R., 'Nobody's talking', *Marketing Research: A magazine of management and applications* 8 (1) (Spring 1996), 22–24; Struebbe, J.M., Kernan, J.B. and Grogan, T.J. 'The refusal problem in telephone surveys', *Journal of Advertising Research* (June/July 1986), 29–38.

15 Havermans, J., 'Strict rules for telemarketers may help research', *Research World* (June 2004), 14.

16 Van Kenhove, P., 'The influence of topic involvement on mail-survey response behaviour', *Psychology & Marketing* 19 (3) (March 2002), 293; Groves, R.M., 'Leverage-saliency theory of survey participation: description and an illustration', *Public Opinion Quarterly* 64 (3) (Fall 2000), 299–308; Everett, S.A., Price, J.H., Bedell, A.W. and Telljohann, S.K., 'The effect of a monetary incentive in increasing the return rate of a survey of family physicians', *Evaluation and the Health Professions* 20 (2) (June 1997), 207–214; Armstrong, J.S. and Lusk, E.J., 'Return postage in mail surveys: a meta-analysis', *Public Opinion Quarterly* (Summer 1987), 233–248; Yu, J. and Cooper, H., 'A quantitative review of research design effects on response rates to questionnaires', *Journal of Marketing Research* 20 (February 1983), 36–44.

17 Brennan, M., Benson, S. and Kearns, Z., 'The effect of introductions on telephone survey participation rates', *International Journal of Market Research* 47 (1) (January 2005) 65–74.

18 Shaw, M.J., 'The use of monetary incentives in a community survey: impact on response rates, data, quality and cost', *Health Services Research* 35 (6) (February 2001), 1339–1346; Wayman, S., 'The buck stops here when it comes to dollar incentives', *Marketing News* 31 (1) (6 January 1997), 9; Biner, P.M. and Kidd, H.J., 'The interactive effects of monetary incentive justification and questionnaire length on mail survey response rates', *Psychology and Marketing* 11 (5) (September/October 1994), 483–492.

19 Zafer Erdogan, B., 'Increasing mail survey response rates from an industrial population: a cost effectiveness analysis of four follow-up techniques', *Industrial Marketing Management* 31 (1) (January 2002), 65.

20 Byrom, J., 'The effect of personalization on mailed questionnaire response rates', *International Journal of Market Research* (Summer 2000), 357–359; Dillman, D.A., Singer, E., Clark, J.R. and Treat, J. LB., 'Effects of benefits appeals, mandatory appeals, and variations in statements of confidentiality on completion rates for census questionnaires', *Public Opinion Quarterly* 60 (3) (Fall 1996), 376–389; Gendall, P., Hoek, J. and Esslemont, D., 'The effect of appeal, complexity and tone in a mail survey covering letter', *Journal of the Market Research Society* 37 (3) (July 1995), 251–268; Greer, T.V. and Lohtia, R., 'Effects of source and paper color on response rates in mail surveys', *Industrial Marketing Management* 23 (February 1994), 47–54.

21 *Bicycling Magazine's 1997 Semi-annual Study of US Retail Bicycle Stores* (September 1997).

22 Smith, J, 'How to boost DM response rates quickly', *Marketing News* 35 (9) (23 April 2001), 5; Peacock, J.D., 'Yes, you can raise response rates', *Journal of Advertising Research* 36 (1) (January 1996), RC7–RC10.

23 Keeter, S., 'Consequences of reducing non-response in a national telephone survey', *Public Opinion Quarterly,* 64 (2) (Summer 2000), 125–148; Bowen, G.L., 'Estimating the reduction in nonresponse bias from using a mail survey as a backup for nonrespondents to a telephone interview survey', *Research on Social Work Practice* 4 (1) (January 1994), 115–128; Kerin, R.A. and Peterson, R.A., 'Scheduling telephone interviews', *Journal of Advertising Research* (May 1983), 44.

24 Columbo, R., 'A model for diagnosing and reducing nonresponse bias,' *Journal of Advertising Research,* (January/April 2000), 85–93; Rowland, M.L. and Forthofer, R.N., 'Adjusting for nonresponse bias in a health examination survey', *Public Health Reports* 108 (3) (May–June 1993), 380–386.

25 Larsen, M.D., 'The psychology of survey response,' *Journal of the American Statistical Association* 97 (457) (March 2002), 358–359; Dey, E.L., 'Working with low survey response rates the efficacy of weighting adjustments', *Research in Higher Education* 38 (2) (April 1997), 215–227.

26 Qin, J., 'Estimation with survey data under non-ignorable non-response or informative sampling', *Journal of the American Statistical Association* 97 (457) (March 2002), 193–200; Kessler, R.C., Little, R.J. and Grover, R.M., 'Advances in strategies for minimising and adjusting for survey nonresponse', *Epidemiologic Reviews* 17 (1) (1995), 192–204; Ward, J.C., Russick, B. and Rudelius, W., 'A test of reducing call-backs and not-at-home bias in personal interviews by weighting at-home respondents', *Journal of Marketing Research* 2 (February 1985), 66–73.

27 Brewer, K., *Design and estimation in survey sampling* (London; Edward Arnold, 2001); Sao, J., 'Variance estimation for survey data with composite imputation and non-negligible sampling fractions', *Journal of American Statistical Association* (March, 1999), 254–265; Drane, J.W., Richter, D. and Stoskopf, C., 'Improved imputation of nonresponse to mailback questionnaires', *Statistics in Medicine* 12 (34) (February 1993), 283–288.

28 Dolven, B., 'The best little airline in China', *Far Eastern Economic Review* 165 (2) (17 January 2002), 32–35; Tse, A., 'Estimating the design factor for surveys in Hong Kong', *Marketing Intelligence and Planning* 13 (9) (1995), 28–29.

29 Harzing, A.-W., 'Cross-national industrial mail surveys: why do response rates differ between countries?', *Industrial Marketing Management* 29 (3) (May 2000), 243–254.

30 Taylor, H., 'Using Internet polling to forecast the 2000 elections', *Marketing Research* 13 (1) (Spring 2001), 26–30; Morwitz, V.G. and Pluzinski, C., 'Do polls reflect opinions or do opinions reflect polls? The impact of political polling on voters' expectations, preferences and behaviour', *Journal of Consumer Research* 23 (1) (June 1996), 53–67.

31 This material is drawn from Berenson, M.L., Levine, D.M. and Krehbiel, T., *Basic Business Statistics: Concepts and Applications* 8th edn (Upper Saddle River, NJ: Prentice Hall, 2002).

Visit the *Marketing Research* Companion Website at www.pearsoned.co.uk/malhotra_euro for additional learning resources including annotated weblinks, an online glossary and a suite of downloadable video cases.

Source: © Getty Images

16

Survey fieldwork

> *No matter how well the research process is designed, the individuals working in the field hold the key to quality data.*

Objectives

After reading this chapter, you should be able to:

1 describe the survey fieldwork process and explain the selecting, training and supervising of fieldworkers, validating fieldwork and evaluating fieldworkers;

2 discuss the training of fieldworkers in making the initial contact, asking the questions, probing, recording the answers and terminating the interview;

3 discuss supervising fieldworkers in terms of quality control and editing, sampling control, control of cheating and central office control;

4 describe evaluating fieldworkers in areas of cost and time, response rates, quality of interviewing and the quality of data;

5 explain the issues related to fieldwork when conducting international marketing research;

6 discuss ethical aspects of survey fieldwork.

STAGE 1
Problem definition

STAGE 2
Research approach developed

STAGE 3
Research design developed

STAGE 4
Fieldwork or data collection

STAGE 5
Data preparation and analysis

STAGE 6
Report preparation and presentation

Overview

Survey fieldwork is a vital process, helping to generate sound marketing research data. During this phase, fieldworkers make contact with potential respondents, administer the questionnaires or observation forms, record the data, and turn in the completed forms for processing. A personal interviewer administering questionnaires door to door, an interviewer intercepting shoppers in the street, a telephone interviewer calling from a central location, a worker mailing questionnaires from an office, an observer counting customers in a particular section of a store, a mystery shopper experiencing the service of a retail outlet, and others involved in data collection and supervision of the process are all quantitative fleldworkers.

The marketing researcher faces two major problems when managing fieldwork operations. First of all, fieldwork should be carried out in a consistent manner so that regardless of who administers a questionnaire, the same process is adhered to. This is vital to allow comparisons between all completed questionnaires. Second, fleldworkers to some extent have to approach and motivate potential respondents in a manner that sets the correct purpose for a study and motivates the respondent to spend time answering the questions properly. This cannot be done in a 'robotic' manner; it requires good communication skills and an amount of empathy with respondents, but could be interpreted as a means to bias responses. These two problems may be seen as conflicting, but for the marketing researcher, fieldwork management means resolving these conflicts for each individual data gathering process. This makes survey fieldwork an essential task in the generation of sound research data.

This chapter describes the nature of survey fieldwork and the general survey fieldwork/data collection process. This process involves selecting, training and supervising fieldworkers, validating fieldwork, and evaluating fieldworkers. We briefly discuss survey fieldwork in the context of international marketing research and identify the relevant ethical issues. To begin, we illustrate the rigours of survey fieldwork: imagine trying to conduct interviews in a professional and consistent manner at one of the biggest street parties in Europe.

Example — Event of the century[1]

Edinburgh's Hogmanay (www.edinburghshogmanay.org) is branded as the biggest street party in Europe, attracting around 250,000 people into the Scottish capital city, to welcome in the New Year along with national and international coverage. Over the past 10 years, the celebration, which is actually a programme of events held in the city over five days, has generated around £55 million (€80 million) in economic benefit to the city. All the city centre hotels are fully booked and around half of the visitors are from outside Scotland. The major research challenge is to conduct face-to-face interviews with a representative sample of visitors attending the event over the five days, but especially with those in the city centre on New Year's Eve itself. The party mood and enhanced interviewer rates mean that they are never short of interviewers eager to work on this survey! The questionnaire is designed carefully to produce considerable detail on the patterns of expenditure by visitors to the event but also to establish the extent to which the event attracted visitors from outside the city.

The nature of survey fieldwork

Marketing research data are rarely collected by the persons who design the research. Researchers have two major options for collecting their data: they can develop their own organisations or they can contract with a fieldwork agency. In either case, data collection involves the use of some kind of field force. The field force may operate either in the field (personal inhome or in office, street interview, CAPI and observation) or from an office (telephone, mail and Internet surveys). The fieldworkers who collect the data typically may have little formal marketing research or marketing training. Their training primarily focuses upon the essential tasks of selecting the correct respondents, motivating them to take part in the research, eliciting the correct answers from them, accurately recording the answers and conveying those answers for analysis. An appreciation of why these tasks fit into the overall context of conducting marketing research is important, but it is not necessary for the survey fieldworker to be trained in the whole array of marketing research skills.

Survey fieldwork and the data collection process

All survey fieldwork involves selecting, training and supervising persons who collect data.[2] The validation of fieldwork and the evaluation of fieldworkers are also parts of the process. Figure 16.1 represents a general framework for the survey fieldwork and data collection process. Even though we describe a general process, it should be recognised that the nature of survey fieldwork varies with the mode of data collection and that the relative emphasis on the different steps will be different for telephone, personal, mail and Internet surveys.

Selecting survey fieldworkers

The first step in the survey fieldwork process is the selection of fieldworkers. The researcher should (1) develop job specifications for the project, taking into account the mode of data collection; (2) decide what characteristics the fieldworkers should have; and (3) recruit appropriate individuals.[3] Interviewers' background characteristics, opinions, perceptions, expectations and attitudes can affect the responses they elicit.[4]

For example, the social acceptability of a fieldworker to the respondent may affect the quality of data obtained, especially in personal interviewing. Researchers generally agree that the more characteristics the interviewer and the respondent have in common, the greater the probability of a successful interview, as illustrated in the following example.

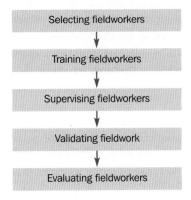

Figure 16.1
Survey fieldwork/data selection process

Example Searching for common ground[5]

In a study dealing with emotional well being and mental health, older interviewers got better cooperation from older respondents than younger interviewers, and this performance appeared to be independent of years of experience. When the interviewer and the respondent were of the same race the cooperation rate was higher than when there was a mismatch on race. The more the interviewer and the respondent had in common, the greater the cooperation and the better the quality of the data.

Thus, to the extent possible, interviewers should be selected to match respondents' characteristics. The job requirements will also vary with the nature of the problem and the type of data collection method. But there are some general qualifications of survey fieldworkers:

- *Healthy.* Fieldwork can be strenuous, and workers must have the stamina required to do the job.
- *Outgoing.* Interviewers should be able to establish rapport with respondents. They should be able to relate quickly to strangers.
- *Communicative.* Effective speaking, observation and listening skills are a great asset.
- *'Pleasant' appearance.* If a fieldworker's physical appearance is unusual (from the respondents' perspective), it may be difficult to get respondents to cooperate.
- *Educated.* Interviewers must have good reading and writing skills and communicating with respondents of varying levels of intellect requires a sound education.
- *Experienced.* Experienced interviewers are likely to do a better job in following instructions, obtaining respondent cooperation and conducting the interview, as illustrated in the following example.

Example Your experience counts[6]

Research has found the following effects of interviewer experience on the interviewing process:

- Inexperienced interviewers are more likely to commit coding errors, to mis-record responses, and to fail to probe.
- Inexperienced interviewers have a particularly difficult time filling quotas of respondents.
- Inexperienced interviewers have larger refusal rates. They also accept more 'don't know' responses and refusals to answer individual questions.

Training survey fieldworkers

Training survey fieldworkers is critical to the quality of data collected. Training may be conducted in person at a central location or, if the interviewers are geographically dispersed, by mail. Training ensures that all interviewers administer the questionnaire in the same manner so that the data can be collected uniformly. Training should cover making the initial contact, asking the questions, probing, recording the answers and terminating the interview.[7]

Making the initial contact

The initial contact can result in cooperation or the loss of potential respondents.[8] It also sets the potential respondent in a 'frame of mind' to answer subsequent questions. Thus interviewers should be trained to make opening remarks that will convince potential respondents that their participation is important. They should also motivate potential respondents to reflect properly upon the questions posed to them and to answer honestly.

Asking the questions

Even a slight change in the wording, sequence or manner in which a question is asked can distort its meaning and bias the response. Training in asking questions can yield high dividends in eliminating potential sources of bias. Changing the phrasing or order of questions during the interview can make significant differences in the response obtained.

> *While we could be faulted for not writing as perfect a questionnaire as we possibly could, still it must be asked in the exact way it is written. It's a challenge for us to try to get the interviewers more conversational, but despite this, the field force absolutely must ask questions as they are written!*[9]

It was argued in Chapter 13 that questionnaire design is a craft. The researcher has to understand and step into the shoes of the respondents they hope to elicit information from. Researchers impose their language and logic onto respondents as they lead them through a questionnaire. If the interviewer is to behave as stated in the above quotation, researchers must appreciate what interviewers go through as they pose questions, probe and motivate respondents. This is because asking questions is an art. The subtle smiles, body language, tone of voice all get the most out of the vast array of personalities, intellects and contexts in which the interviewer must work. The art of interviewing develops with experience, allowing questions to be posed in a consistent manner.

The following are guidelines for interviewers in becoming consistent in asking questions:[10]

1 Be thoroughly familiar with the purpose of the questionnaire.
2 Be thoroughly familiar with the structure of the questionnaire.
3 Ask the questions in the order in which they appear in the questionnaire.
4 Use the exact wording given in the questionnaire.
5 Read each question slowly.
6 Repeat questions that are not understood.
7 Ask every applicable question.
8 Follow instructions, working through any filter questions, and probe carefully.

Probing

Probing
A motivational technique used when asking questions to induce the participants to enlarge on, clarify or explain their answers.

Probing is intended to motivate respondents to enlarge on, clarify or explain their answers. Probing also helps respondents focus on the specific content of the interview and provide only relevant information. Probing should not introduce any bias. An example of the effect of interviewer bias comes from a survey in which one of the authors helped in data analysis (but not in the management of the whole research process!). The survey related to bread and cake buying habits with one particular question focusing upon 'large cakes' that respondents had bought over the previous 12 months. In analysing the data a percentage had replied 'Christmas cake'. When analysed further, all the respondents who said 'Christmas cake' had been interviewed by the same interviewer. The conclusion from this analysis was that the interviewer in question had used his or her own probe to make the interview process work. None of the other interviewers had used this probe, which meant there was an inconsistent approach in eliciting answers from respondents. The paradox faced by the survey designers in this example was that the 'rogue' interviewer *may* have used a probe that elicited a true representation of large cake purchasing, the other interviewers consistently failing to draw out a 'true' response.

To help in the process of probing, the following list details some commonly used techniques:[11]

1 *Repeating the question.* Repeating the question in the same words can be effective in eliciting a response.

2 *Repeating the respondent's reply.* Respondents can be stimulated to provide further comments by repeating their replies verbatim. This can be done as the interviewer records the replies.

3 *Using a pause or silent probe.* A silent probe, or an expectant pause or look, can cue the respondent to provide a more complete response. The silence should not become embarrassing, however.

4 *Boosting or reassuring the respondent.* If the respondent hesitates, the interviewer should reassure the respondent with comments such as 'There are no right or wrong answers. We are just trying to get your opinions.' If the respondent needs an explanation of a word or phrase, the interviewer should not offer an interpretation, unless written instructions to do so have been provided. Rather, the responsibility for the interpretation should be returned to the respondent. This can be done with a comment such as 'Just whatever it means to you.'

5 *Eliciting clarification.* The respondent's motivation to cooperate with the interviewer and provide complete answers can be aroused with a question: 'I don't quite understand what you mean by that. Could you please tell me a little more?'

6 *Using objective or neutral questions or comments.* Table 16.1 provides several examples of the common questions or comments used as probes.[12] Corresponding abbreviations are also provided. The interviewer should record the abbreviations on the questionnaire in parentheses next to the question asked.

Table 16.1 Commonly used probes and abbreviations

Standard interviewer's probe	Abbreviation
Any other reason?	(AO?)
Any others?	(Other?)
Anything else?	(AE or Else?)
Could you tell me more about your thinking on that?	(Tell more)
How do you mean?	(How mean?)
Repeat question	(RQ)
What do you mean?	(What mean?)
Which would be closer to the way you feel?	(Which closer?)
Why do you feet this way?	(Why?)
Would you tell me what you have in mind?	(What in mind?)

The above list seems there are hidden dangers. For example, probing '*why*' respondents behave in a particular manner or feel about a particular issue takes the interview into the realms of the qualitative interview. Compare the context of the street interview with a short structured questionnaire with the context of the qualitative interview with a questioning approach structured to the respondent and where a greater amount of rapport may be developed. The latter scenario is much more conducive to eliciting '*why*' respondents behave or feel as they do. The question '*why*' is an example of a seemingly simple question that can create many problems of consistency in fieldwork. In the greater majority of circumstances, '*why*' should be treated as a qualitative issue.

Recording the answers

Source: © Getty Images

Although recording respondent answers seems simple, several mistakes are common.[13] All interviewers should use the same format and conventions to record the interviews and edit completed interviews. Although the rules for recording answers to structured questions vary with each specific questionnaire, the general rule is to check the box that reflects the respondent's answer. The general rule for recording answers to unstructured questions is to record the responses verbatim. The following guidelines help to record answers to unstructured questions.

1 Record responses during the interview.
2 Use the respondent's own words.
3 Do not summarise or paraphrase the respondent's answers.
4 Include everything that pertains to the question objectives.
5 Include all probes and comments.
6 Repeat the response as it is written down.

Terminating the interview

The interview should not be closed before all the information is obtained. Any spontaneous comments the respondent offers after all the formal questions have been asked should be recorded. The interviewer should answer the respondent's questions about the project. The respondent should be left with a positive feeling about the interview. It is important to thank the respondent and express appreciation.

The Association of Market Survey Organisations (**www.amso.co.uk**) publishes a 'Thank You' pamphlet that can be handed out to respondents who have taken part in an interview. As well as thanking respondents for their cooperation, it serves the purpose of educating respondents about the nature and purpose of marketing research, distinguishing marketing research from 'sugging' and 'frugging' as explained in the ethics section of Chapter 10.

The pamphlet explains why the respondent was chosen, the manner in which the interview was conducted and the purpose of marketing research interviewing. The following example presents extracts from the AMSO pamphlet.

Example **Your time has been of great value, thank you!**

Thank you, for taking the time to give this interview; we hope you enjoyed it. Your interviewer is professionally trained by the company for which he/she works, a company which belongs to the Association of Market Survey Organisations. The Association exists to ensure that its members maintain the highest professional standards of market research. Your interviewer carries an identity card which guarantees they are a genuine market researcher.
AND
The way in which you were interviewed. In order to make sure that a representative sample was interviewed you may have been asked certain questions about your age, occupation, income and other descriptive details. These questions will be used in the research analysis to check the sample against other statistical information.

The questionnaire which the interviewer used will have been carefully constructed and tested by experienced researchers. The interviewer will have been instructed to read out the questions exactly as they are printed, and is not allowed to change the wording or give a personal opinion. These precautions are taken to ensure that your answers are not influenced in any way by the interviewer.

Summary of training issues

To encapsulate the process of interviewer training, the following list summarises the nature and scope of areas in which a marketing research interviewer should be trained:

1 The marketing research process: how a study is developed, implemented and reported.
2 The importance of the interviewer to this process; the need for honesty, objectivity, organisational skills and professionalism.
3 Confidentiality of the respondent and the client.
4 Familiarity with marketing research terminology.
5 The importance of following the exact wording and recording responses verbatim.
6 The purpose and use of probing and clarifying techniques.
7 The reason for and use of classification and respondent information questions.
8 A review of samples of instructions and questionnaires.
9 The importance of the respondent's positive feelings about survey research.

Conversely, marketing researchers should be trained in the 'experience' of gathering data in the field with a practical knowledge of what works in terms of:

- Motivating potential respondents to take part in a survey.
- Questions that will elicit the required data.
- Probes that can be consistently applied.
- An interview process that does not confuse or cause boredom in the respondent.

The marketing researcher needs to appreciate what the respondent and the interviewer go through in the interview process. Without such an understanding, the questionnaires and interview procedures, which seem fine on paper, can lead to very poor-quality data. The following example illustrates the experiences of a 'typical' respondent and researcher. Whilst the feelings expressed cannot be generalised to all interview situations, the lesson from this is that the marketing researcher should aim to understand how the target respondents and interviewers feel about the process. These feelings must form an integral part of any research design that generates sound and accurate data.

Example	How was it for you?[14]

A respondent and an interviewer describe what their interview experiences were like for them.

The respondent

'I felt sorry for the interviewer, she was going around all these houses and nobody was in, so I agreed to take part in the survey. The interview did not take that long, only about 10 to 15 minutes, slightly less time than the interviewer said it would. The interviewer was smartly dressed, professional and helpful. She prompted me but did not actually push me. The experience was enjoyable, it was fun, and not a bad way to spend 10 to 15 minutes, although I think that is long enough. I like taking part in a survey if the subject matter is relevant to your life and you feel that your views are being taken into account. I think a lot of women prefer other females (or gay men) to interview them as there is an empathy there, and they might not feel they can be as honest or chatty with men. The age of the interviewer should relate to the subject matter. For example, if you are asking about children, then you should have an interviewer in a mother's age group. I think it is important to actually be in the same position as someone being surveyed. In an interview, you should be honest, do not tell them what you think they want to hear, relax, be friendly and go with the flow. A lot depends on the respondent as well as the interviewer. There has to be a bit of banter between the two of you.

The interviewer

'I do not have a typical day. If I am doing quota sampling I will do around 10 interviews a day. If it is preselected, then I will do 3 to 4 indepth interviews. But if it's exit interviewing, I can do as many as 20 in a shift. There are pressures to the job sometimes. Getting your quota is like looking for a needle in a haystack. People are much more suspicious, and fewer will open the doors these days. I have interviewed through wrought iron gates, letter boxes, front room windows, and with the chain on the door. For your own safety, you must be aware of where you are and what's around you. Technology has not made my job easier. I hate CAM and I do not use it now. It's slower, heavy to carry around, it sometimes crashes and I feel that interviewing using pen and paper flows better.

My job could be made easier by keeping questionnaires short, and using proper screening questions. The essence is to keep it interesting. The worst thing in the world is when you have got a survey that repeats itself and is boring; huge lists are our worst enemy. All I ask of a respondent is that they are honest, they do not have to be articulate or have strong opinions. There are two keys to successful interviewing, smile and be polite at all times, so that it is very hard for people to be rude to you, and be firm and in control of the interview.'

Supervising survey fieldworkers

Supervising survey fieldworkers means making sure that they are following the procedures and techniques in which they were trained. Supervision involves quality control and editing, sampling control, control of cheating and central office control.

Quality control and editing

Quality control of fieldworkers requires checking to see whether the field procedures are being properly implemented.[15] If any problems are detected, the supervisor should discuss them with the fieldworkers and provide additional training if necessary. To understand the interviewers' problems related to a specific study, the supervisors should also do some interviewing. Supervisors should collect questionnaires and other observation forms and check them daily. They should examine the questionnaires to make sure all appropriate questions have been completed, that unsatisfactory or incomplete answers have not been accepted, and that the writing is legible.

Supervisors should also keep a record of hours worked and expenses. This will allow a determination of the cost per completed interview, whether the job is moving on schedule, and whether any interviewers are having problems.

Sampling control

Sampling control
An aspect of supervising that ensures that the interviewers strictly follow the sampling plan rather than select sampling units based on convenience or accessibility.

An important aspect of supervision is **sampling control**, which attempts to ensure that the interviewers are strictly following the sampling plan rather than selecting sampling units based on convenience or accessibility.[16] Interviewers tend to avoid homes, offices and people (sampling units) that they perceive as difficult or undesirable. If the sampling unit is not at home, for example, interviewers may be tempted to substitute the next available unit rather than call back. Interviewers sometimes stretch the requirements of quota samples. For example, a 58-year-old person may be placed in the 46–55 category and interviewed to fulfil quota requirements.

To control these problems, supervisors should keep daily records of the number of calls made, the number of not-at-homes, the number of refusals, the number of completed interviews for each interviewer, and the total for all interviewers under their control.

Control of cheating

Cheating involves falsifying part of a questionnaire or the entire questionnaire.

Central office control

Supervisors provide quality and cost-control information to the central office so that a total progress report can be maintained. In addition to the controls initiated in the field, other controls may be added at the central office to identify potential problems. Central office control includes tabulation of quota variables, important demographic characteristics and answers to key variables.

Validating survey fieldwork

An interviewer may falsify part of an answer to make it acceptable or may fake answers. The most blatant form of cheating occurs when the interviewer falsifies the entire questionnaire, merely filling in fake answers, either on his or her own or through the use of friends or family members. Cheating can be minimised through proper training, supervision and by rewarding interviewers properly. Most importantly their work should be validated, which includes recording the names and contact details of respondents.[17] Supervisors usually call 10–25% of the respondents to enquire whether the fieldworkers actually conducted the interviews. The supervisors ask about the length and quality of the interview, reaction to the interviewer and basic demographic data. The demographic information is cross-checked against the information reported by the interviewers on the questionnaires. The major drawback of this approach is that respondents may not trust interviewers with a name and telephone number, perhaps believing that it is to be used to generate a sale, i.e. it can be confused with a 'sugging' or 'frugging' approach.

Evaluating survey fieldworkers

It is important to evaluate survey fieldworkers to provide them with feedback on their performance as well as to identify the better fieldworkers and build a better, high-quality field force. The evaluation criteria should be clearly communicated to the fieldworkers during their training. The evaluation of fieldworkers should be based on the criteria of cost and time, response rates, quality of interviewing and quality of data.[18]

Cost and time

Interviewers can be compared in terms of the total cost (salary and expenses) per completed interview. If the costs differ by city size, comparisons should be made only among fieldworkers working in comparable cities. Fieldworkers should also be evaluated on how they spend their time. Time should be broken down into categories such as actual interviewing, travel and administration.

Response rates

It is important to monitor response rates on a timely basis so that corrective action can be taken if these rates are too low.[19] Supervisors can help interviewers with an inordinate number of refusals by listening to the introductions they use and providing immediate feedback. When all the interviews are over, different fieldworkers' percentage of refusals can be compared to identify the more able interviewers.

Quality of interviewing

To evaluate interviewers on the quality of interviewing, the supervisor must directly observe the interviewing process. The supervisor can do this in person or the fieldworker can record the interview on tape. The quality of interviewing should be evaluated in terms of (1) the appropriateness of the introduction, (2) the precision with which the fieldworker asks questions, (3) the ability to probe in an unbiased manner, (4) the ability to ask sensitive questions, (5) interpersonal skills displayed during the interview, and (6) the manner in which the interview is terminated.

Quality of data

The completed questionnaires of each interviewer should be evaluated for the quality of data. Some indicators of quality data are that (1) the recorded data are legible; (2) all instructions, including skip patterns, are followed; (3) the answers to unstructured questions are recorded verbatim; (4) the answers to unstructured questions are meaningful and complete enough to be coded; and (5) item non-response occurs infrequently.

International marketing research

The selection, training, supervision and evaluation of survey fleldworkers are critical in international marketing research. Local fieldwork agencies are unavailable in many countries. Therefore, it may be necessary to recruit and train local fieldworkers or import trained foreign workers. The use of local fieldworkers is desirable, because they are familiar with the local language and culture. They can create an appropriate climate for the interview and sensitivity to the concerns of the respondents. Even with these advantages, extensive training may be required and close supervision in order to ensure that the questions are presented as intended. As observed in many countries, local interviewers tend to help the respondent with the answers and select household or sampling units based on personal considerations rather than the sampling plan. This means that the validation of fieldwork is critical. Proper application of fieldwork procedures can greatly reduce these difficulties and result in consistent and useful findings, as the following example illustrates.

Example   Americanism unites Europeans[20]

An image study conducted by Research International (**www.researchint.com**), a British market research company, showed that European consumers still tend to favour certain American products. The survey was conducted in the UK, France, Germany, Italy and the Netherlands. In each country, local interviewers and supervisors were used because it was felt they would be able to identify better with the respondents. The fleidworkers, however, were trained extensively and supervised closely to ensure quality results and to minimise the variability in country-to-country results due to differences in interviewing procedures.

A total of 6,724 personal interviews were conducted. Some of the findings were that Europeans gave American products high marks for being innovative and some countries also regarded them as fashionable and of high quality. Interestingly, France, usually considered anti-American, also emerged as pro-American. Among the 1,034 French consumers surveyed, 40% considered American products fashionable and 38% believed that they were innovative, whereas 15% said American products were of high quality. In addition, when asked what nationality they preferred for a new company in their area, an American company was the first choice. These findings were comparable and consistent across the four countries. A key to the discovery of these findings was the use of local fieldworkers and extensive training and supervision which resulted in high-quality data.

Ethics in marketing research

Marketing researchers and survey fieldworkers should make respondents feel comfortable when participating in research activities. This is vital in order to elicit the correct responses for a specific project but also more broadly for the health of the marketing research industry. A respondent who feels that his or her trust has been abused, who found an interview to be cumbersome and boring, or who fails to see the purpose of a particular study, is less likely to participate in further marketing research efforts. Collectively, the marketing research industry has the responsibility to look after its most precious assets – willing and honest respondents.

Many marketing researchers do not meet respondents face to face, or if they have done it may have occurred many years ago. Not being in the field, marketing researchers can lose an awareness of what it is like actually to collect data in the field. Without this awareness, research designs that on paper seem feasible are difficult to administer in the field in a consistent manner. If there are problems in collecting data in the field, these may not always be attributable to the training and quality of fieldworkers; the blame may lie with the research designer. The marketing researcher, therefore, has an ethical responsibility to the fieldworker and the respondent. The researcher's responsibility lies in an awareness of the process that the fieldworker and respondent go through in the field for each individual piece of research they design. Poor design can leave fieldworkers facing very disgruntled respondents and can cause great damage.

Good marketing researchers have an awareness of their responsibilities to fieldworkers and respondents. The marketing researcher may take great care in understanding the difficulties of collecting data in the field and go to great pains to ensure that the data gathering process works well for the fieldworker and respondent alike. The fieldworker may have been told about the purpose of the study, the purpose of particular questions, the means to select and approach respondents and the means to elicit responses correctly from respondents. However, fieldworkers may behave in an unethical manner. They may cut corners in terms of selecting the correct respondents, posing questions and probes, and recording responses. In such circumstances the fieldworker can cause much damage to an individual study and to the long-term relationship with potential respondents. Thus it becomes a vital part of fieldworker training to demonstrate the ethical responsibilities fieldworkers have in collecting data.

The use of codes of conduct and guidelines can help fieldworkers to be aware of their responsibilities (see the esomar code on **www.esomar.nl**). It is good to have a specific set of guidelines to help with fieldwork, but applying them is another matter. Marketing researchers who train, develop and reward their survey fieldworkers well create an atmosphere where these guidelines work in practice.

Internet and computer applications

Regardless of which method is used for interviewing (telephone, personal, mail or electronic), the Internet can play a valuable role in all the phases of survey fieldwork: selection, training, supervision, validation and evaluation of fieldworkers. As far as selection is concerned, interviewers can be located, interviewed and hired by using the Internet. This process can be initiated, for example, by posting job vacancies notices for interviewers on the company website, bulletin boards and at other suitable locations. While this would confine the search to only Internet-savvy interviewers, this may well be a qualification to look for in the current marketing research environment.

Similarly, the Internet with its multimedia capabilities can be a good supplementary tool for training the fieldworkers in all aspects of interviewing. Training in this manner can complement personal training programmes and add value to the process. Supervision is enhanced by facilitating communication between the supervisors and the interviewers via email and secured chat rooms. Central office control can be strengthened by posting progress reports, quality and cost control information at a secured location on a website, so that it is easily available to all the relevant parties.

Validation of fieldwork, especially for personal and telephone interviews, can be easily accomplished for those respondents who have an email address or access to the Internet. These respondents can be sent a short verification survey by email or asked to visit a website where the survey is posted. Finally, the evaluation criteria can be communicated to the fieldworkers during the training stage by using the Internet, and performance feedback can also be provided to them by using this medium.

Call disposition
Call disposition records the outcome of an interview call.

Computers can be used in fieldwork for respondent selection, interviewer planning, supervision and control. They can also be used to manage mailing lists. For example, mailing lists can be sorted according to postal codes, geographical regions (which may include drive times from the centre of a city or from a shopping centre) or other prespecified respondent characteristics. Computers can generate accurate and timely reports for supervision and control purposes. These include quota reports, **call disposition** reports, incidence reports, topline reports of respondent data and interviewer productivity reports. Automatic reporting enhances supervision and control and increases the overall quality of data collection. Because less time is spent compiling reports, more time can be spent on data interpretation and on supervision.

Summary

Researchers have two major options in the generation of sound research data: developing their own organisations or contracting with fieldwork agencies. In either case, data collection involves the use of a field force. Fieldworkers should be healthy, outgoing, communicative, pleasant, educated and experienced. They should be trained in important aspects of fieldwork, including making the initial contact, asking the questions, probing, recording the answers and terminating the interview. Supervising fieldworkers involves quality control and editing, sampling control, control of cheating and central office control. Validating fieldwork can be accomplished by calling 10–25% of those who have been identified as interviewees and enquiring whether the interviews took place. Fieldworkers should be evaluated on the basis of cost and time, response rates, quality of interviewing and quality of data collection.

Fieldwork should be carried out in a consistent manner so that, regardless of who administers a questionnaire, the same process is adhered to. This is vital to allow comparisons between collected data. Fieldworkers to some extent have to approach and motivate potential respondents in a manner that sets the correct purpose for a study and motivates the respondent to spend time answering the questions properly. This cannot be done in a 'robotic' manner; it requires good communication skills and an amount of empathy with respondents. This makes the issue of managing fieldwork an essential task in the generation of sound research data.

Selecting, training, supervising and evaluating fieldworkers is even more critical in international marketing research because local fieldwork agencies are not available in many countries. Ethical issues include making the respondents feel comfortable in the data collection process so that their experience is positive.

Questions

1 Why do marketing researchers need to use survey fieldworkers?

2 Describe the survey fieldwork/data collection process.

3 What qualifications should survey fieldworkers possess?

4 What are the guidelines for asking questions?

5 Describe and illustrate the differences between probing in a survey and in an in-depth interview.

6 Evaluate what may be done to help interviewers probe correctly and consistently.

7 Outline the advantages and disadvantages of the interviewer developing a rapport with respondents.

8 How should the answers to unstructured questions be recorded?

9 How should the survey fieldworker terminate the interview?

10 What aspects are involved in the supervision of survey fieldworkers?

11 How can respondent selection problems be controlled?

12 What is validation of survey fieldwork? How is this done?

13 Describe the criteria that should be used for evaluating survey fieldworkers.

14 Describe the major sources of error related to survey fieldwork.

15 Comment on the following field situations, making recommendations for corrective action:
   a One of the interviewers has an excessive rate of refusals in in-home personal interviewing.
   b In a CATI situation, many phone numbers are giving a busy signal during the first dialling attempt.
   c An interviewer reports that at the end of the interviews many respondents asked if they had answered the questions correctly.
   d While validating the fieldwork, a respondent reports that she cannot remember being interviewed over the telephone, but the interviewer insists that the interview was conducted.

Exercises

1 Visit the websites of three major marketing research agencies. Evaluate how they present their quality management of fieldwork. Write a report that details what you feel to be the best elements of their respective practices. Note also what additional practices they should be highlighting to reassure potential marketing research buyers and users.

2 You are a field supervisor. Ask a fellow student to assume the role of an interviewer and another student the role of a respondent. Train the interviewer to conduct an in-home interview by giving a live demonstration.

3 In teams of four, design a questionnaire to be used in a street interview. One of the team then takes on the role of the interviewer, the other three to act as respondents. Conduct three interviews and video the process. Replay the video and write a report that focuses upon:

   a The questionnaire design
   b Stopping and motivating respondents
   c Interviewer instructions
   d The consistency of the process
   e Ethical issues involved in the process.

4 Contact a marketing research agency (so that everyone is aware and agreeable about the process) and arrange a field trip to a shopping centre where street interviews are being conducted. Working in pairs, observe the interviewing process of a number of interviewers over a time span of four hours. Write a report on what you feel worked well or not in the exchanges.

5 In a small group discuss the following issues: 'What makes street interviewing an art?' and 'Why do interviewers cheat?'

Notes

1 Costley, T., 'Event of the century', *Research* (June 1999), 44–45.

2 Gubrium, J.F. and Holstein, J.A., *Handbook of Survey Research: Context and Method* (Thousand Oaks, CA: Sage, 2000); Frey, J.H. and Oishi, SM., *How to Conduct Interviews by Telephone and In Person* (Thousand Oaks, CA: Sage, 1995).

3 Muller, G.D. and Miller, J., 'Interviewers make the difference', *Marketing Research: A Magazine of Management and Applications* 8 (1) (Spring 1996), 8–9; Morton Williams, J., *Interviewer Approaches* (Brookfield: Ashgate, 1993); Groves, R.M. and Magilavy, L.J., 'Measuring and explaining interviewer effects in centralized telephone surveys', *Public Opinion Quarterly* 50 (Summer 1986), 251–266.

4 McCombie, S.C., 'The influences of sex of interviewer on the results of an AIDS survey in Ghana', *Human Organization* 61 (1) (Spring 2002), 51–55; Catina, LA., Binson, D., Canchola, J., Pollack, L.M. *et al.*, 'Effects of interviewer gender, interviewer choice, and item wording on responses to questions concerning sexual behaviour', *Public Opinion Quarterly* 60 (3) (Fall 1996), 345–375; Coulter, P.B., 'Race of interviewer effects on telephone interviews', *Public Opinion Quarterly* 46 (Summer 1982), 278–284; Singer, E., Frankel, M.R. and Glassman, M.B., 'The effect of interviewer characteristics and expectations on response', *Public Opinion Quarterly* 41 (Spring 1983), 68–83.

5 Newman, J.C., 'The differential effects of face-to-face and computer interview models', *American Journal of Public Health* 92 (2) (February 2002), 294–297; Davis, D.W., 'Nonrandom measurement error and race of interviewer effects among African Americans', *Public Opinion Quarterly* 61 (1) (Spring 1997), 183–207; Barker, R.E., 'A demographic profile of marketing research interviewers', *Journal of the Market Research Society* 29 (July 1987), 279–292.

6 Anon., 'Dextra hands out vital interview advice', *Management Services* 46 (2) (February 2002); 6; Kacmar, M.K. and Hochwater, W.A., 'The interview as a communication event: a field examination of demographic effects on interview outcomes', *Journal of Business Communication*, 32 (3) (July 1995), 207–232; Collins, M. and Butcher, B., 'Interviewer and clustering effects in an attitude survey', *Journal of the Market Research Society* 25 (January 1983), 39–58.

7 Anon., 'renewing your interviewing skills', *Healthcare Executive* 17 (1) (January/February 2002), 29; Kiecker, P. and Nelson, J.E., 'Do interviewers follow telephone survey instructions?', *Journal of the Market Research Society* 38 (2) (April 1996), 161–176; Guenzel, P.1., Berkmans, T.R. and Cannell, C.F., *General Interviewing Techniques* (Ann Arbor, MI: Institute for Social Research, 1983).

8 Robertson, B., 'The effect of an introductory letter on participation rates using telephone recruitment', *Australian & New Zealand Journal of Public Health*, 24 (5) (October 2000) 552; Feld, K., 'Good introductions save time, money', *Marketing News* 34 (5) (28 February 2000); 19–20; Couper, M.P., 'Survey introductions and data quality', *Public Opinion Quarterly* (Summer 1997), 317–338.

9 Bordeaux, D.B., 'Interviewing Part II: Getting the most out of interview questions', *Motor Age* 121 (2) (February 2002), 38–40; Anon., 'Market research industry sets up interviewing quality standards', *Management Auckland* 44 (2) (March 1997), 12.

10 This section follows closely the material in *Interviewer's Manual*, rev. edn (Ann Arbor, MI: Survey Research Center, Institute for Social Research, University of Michigan, 1976); Guenzel, P.J., Berkmans, T.R. and Cannell, C.E., *General Interviewing Techniques* (Ann Arbor, MI: Institute for Social Research, 1983).

11 For an extensive treatment of probing, see Gubrium, J.F. and Holstein, J.A., *Handbook of interview research: Context and method* (Thousand Oaks, CA: Sage, 2001) 15–19.

12 Institute for Social Research, University of Michigan, *Interviewer's Manual*, rev. edn (Ann Arbor, MI: Survey Research Center, 1976) 16.

13 Trembly, A.C., 'Poor data quality: a $600 billion issue', *National Underwriter*, 106 (11) (18 March 2002), 48; Anon., 'Market research industry sets up interviewing quality standards', *Management-Auckland* 44 (2) (March 1997), 12; Morton-Williams, J. and Sykes, W., 'The use of interaction coding and follow-up interviews to investigate comprehension of survey questions', *Journal of the Market Research Society* 26 (April 1984), 109–127.

14 Park, C., 'How was it for you?', *Research*, Fieldwork Supplement (July 2000), 8–9.

15 Pallister, J., 'Navigating the righteous course: a quality issue', *Journal of the Market Research Society*, 41 (3) (July 1999), 327–343; Hurley, R.F. and Laitamaki, J.M., 'Total quality research: integrating markets and the organization', *California Management Review* 38 (1) (Fall 1995), 59–78; Collins, M. and Butcher, B., 'Interviewer and clustering effects in an attitude survey', *Journal of the Market Research Society* 25 (January 1983), 39–58.

16 Czaja, R., Blair, J. and Sebestik, J.P., 'Respondent selection in telephone survey: a comparison of three techniques', *Journal of Marketing Research* (August 1982), 381–385.

17 Fielding, N.G., *Interviewing: Four volume set* (Thousand Oaks, CA: Sage, 2003); Greengard, S., '50% of your employees are lying, cheating & stealing', *Workforce* 76 (10) (October 1997), 44–53; Tull, D.S. and Richards, L.E., 'What can be done about interviewer bias'? in Sheth, J. (ed.), *Research in Marketing* (Greenwich, CT: SAT Press, 1980), 143–162.

18 Johnson, C., 'Making sure employees measure up', *HRMagazine* 46 (3) (March 2001), 36–41; Pulakos, E.D., Schmitt, N., Whitney, D. and Smith, M., 'Individual differences in interviewer ratings: the impact of standardization, consensus discussion and sampling error on the validity of a structured interview', *Personnel Psychology* 49 (1) (Spring 1996), 85–102.

19 Smith, J., 'How to boost DM response rates quickly', *Marketing News* 35 (9) (23 April 2001) 5; Turley, S.K., 'A case of response rate success', *Journal of the Market Research Society* 41 (3) (July 1999), 301–309; Edmonston, S., 'Why response rates are declining', *Advertising Age's Business Marketing* 82 (8) (September 1997), 12.

20 Dougherty, C., 'European Union asks US to follow rules, end exports spat', *Knight Union Tribune Business News* (26 January 2002), 1; Semon, T.T., 'Select local talent when conducting research abroad', *Marketing News* 31 (19) (15 September 1997), 28; Wentz, L., 'Poll: Europe favors US products', *Advertising Age* (23 September 1991).

Source: © Getty Images

17

Data preparation

Perhaps the most neglected series of activities in the marketing research process. Handled with care, data preparation can substantially enhance the quality of statistical results.

Objectives

After reading this chapter, you should be able to:

1 discuss the nature and scope of data preparation and the data preparation process;

2 explain questionnaire checking and editing and the treatment of unsatisfactory responses by returning to the field, assigning missing values and discarding unsatisfactory responses;

3 describe the guidelines for coding questionnaires, including the coding of structured and unstructured questions;

4 discuss the data cleaning process and the methods used to treat missing responses: substitution of a neutral value, imputed response, casewise deletion and pairwise deletion;

5 state the reasons for and methods of statistically adjusting data: weighting, variable respecification and scale transformation;

6 describe the procedure for selecting a data analysis strategy and the factors influencing the process;

7 classify statistical techniques and give a detailed classification of univariate techniques as well as a classification of multivariate techniques;

8 understand the intra-cultural, pan-cultural and cross-cultural approaches to data analysis in international marketing research;

9 identify the ethical issues related to data processing, particularly the discarding of unsatisfactory responses, violation of the assumptions underlying the data analysis techniques, and evaluation and interpretation of results and paired samples.

STAGE 1
Problem definition

STAGE 2
Research approach developed

STAGE 3
Research design developed

STAGE 4
Fieldwork or data collection

STAGE 5
Data preparation and analysis

STAGE 6
Report preparation and presentation

Overview

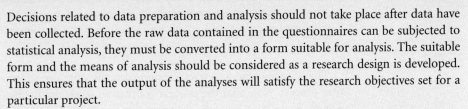

Decisions related to data preparation and analysis should not take place after data have been collected. Before the raw data contained in the questionnaires can be subjected to statistical analysis, they must be converted into a form suitable for analysis. The suitable form and the means of analysis should be considered as a research design is developed. This ensures that the output of the analyses will satisfy the research objectives set for a particular project.

The care exercised in the data preparation phase has a direct effect upon the quality of statistical results and ultimately the support offered to marketing decision-makers. Paying inadequate attention to data preparation can seriously compromise statistical results, leading to biased findings and incorrect interpretation.

This chapter describes the data collection process, which begins with checking the questionnaires for completeness. Then we discuss the editing of data and provide guidelines for handling illegible, incomplete, inconsistent, ambiguous or otherwise unsatisfactory responses. We also describe coding, transcribing and data cleaning, emphasising the treatment of missing responses and statistical adjustment of data. We discuss the selection of a data analysis strategy and classify statistical techniques. The intra-cultural, pan-cultural and cross-cultural approaches to data analysis in international marketing research are explained. Finally, the ethical issues related to data processing are identified with emphasis on discarding unsatisfactory responses, violation of the assumptions underlying the data analysis techniques, and evaluation and interpretation of results.

We begin with an illustration of the data preparation process set in the context of Formula One Racetrack Project.

 Focus on ## Sports Marketing Surveys

Data preparation

In the Formula One Racetrack Project, the data were obtained by face-to-face and telephone interviews. As the questionnaire was developed and finalised a preliminary plan was drawn up of how the findings could be analysed. The questionnaires were edited by a supervisor as they were being returned from Australia, Brazil, France, Germany, Italy, Japan, Spain and the UK. The questionnaires were checked for incomplete, inconsistent and ambiguous responses. Questionnaires with problematic responses were queried with supervisors in each of the eight countries. In some circumstances, the supervisors were asked to recontact the respondents to clarify certain issues. Thirty-five questionnaires were discarded because the proportion of unsatisfactory responses rendered them too poor to use. This resulted in a final sample size of 2,050.

A codebook was developed for coding the questionnaires; this was done automatically as the questionnaire was designed using the SNAP software (fully integrated survey software with on-screen questionnaire design, data collection and analysis for all types of surveys, **www.snapsurveys.com**). The data were transcribed by being directly keyed in as telephone interviews were conducted and onto personal digital assistants (PDAs) as face-to-face interviews were conducted. The SNAP software has a built-in error check that identifies out-of-range responses. About 10% of the data were verified for other data entry errors. The data were cleaned by identifying logically inconsistent responses. Most of the rating information was obtained using five-point scales, so responses of 0, 6 and 7 were considered

→

out of range and a code of 9 was assigned to missing responses. If an out-of-range response was keyed in, the SNAP software package did not allow any continuation of data entry; an audible warning was made. New variables that were composites of original variables were created. Finally, a data analysis strategy was developed.

The Formula One Racetrack example describes the various phases of the data preparation process. Note that the process is initiated while the fieldwork is still in progress. A systematic description of the data preparation process follows.

The data preparation process

Editing
A review of the questionnaires with the objective of increasing accuracy and precision.

Coding
Assigning a code to represent a specific response to a specific question along with the data record and column position that the code will occupy.

The data preparation process is shown in Figure 17.1. The entire process is guided by the preliminary plan of data analysis that was formulated in the research design phase. The first step is to check for acceptable questionnaires. This is followed by **editing**, **coding** and transcribing the data. The data are cleaned and a treatment for missing responses is prescribed. Often, after the stage of sample validation, statistical adjustment of the data may be necessary to make them representative of the population of interest. The researcher should then select an appropriate data analysis strategy. The final data analysis strategy differs from the preliminary plan of data analysis due to the information and insights gained since the preliminary plan was formulated. Data preparation should begin as soon as the first batch of questionnaires is received from the field, while the fieldwork is still going on. Thus, if any problems are detected, the fieldwork can be modified to incorporate corrective action.

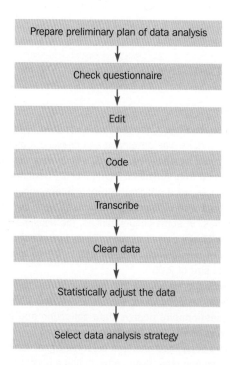

Figure 17.1
Data preparation process

Checking the questionnaire

The initial step in questionnaire checking involves reviewing all questionnaires for completeness and interviewing or completion quality as illustrated in the following example.

Example **Custom cleaning**[1]

According to Johan Harristhal of Gfk Custom Research (**www.cresearch.com**), completed questionnaires from the field often have many small errors because of the inconsistent quality of interviewing. For example, qualifying responses are not circled, or skip patterns are not followed accurately. These small errors can be costly. When responses from such questionnaires are put into a computer, Custom Research runs a cleaning program that checks for completedness and logic. Discrepancies are identified on a computer printout, which is checked by the tabulation supervisors. Once the errors are identified, appropriate corrective action is taken before data analysis is carried out. Custom research has found that this procedure substantially increases the quality of statistical results.

Researchers do not just depend upon error checks at the data entry stage; checks should be made whilst fieldwork is still under way. If the fieldwork was contracted to a data collection agency, the researcher should make an independent check after it is over. A questionnaire returned from the field may be unacceptable for several reasons:

1 Parts of the questionnaire may be incomplete.
2 The pattern of responses may indicate that the respondent did not understand or follow the instructions. For example, filter questions may not have been followed.
3 The responses show little variance. For example, a respondent has ticked only 4s on a series of seven-point rating scales.
4 The returned questionnaire is physically incomplete: one or more pages is missing.
5 The questionnaire is received after the pre-established cut-off date.
6 The questionnaire is answered by someone who does not qualify for participation.

If quotas or cell group sizes have been imposed, the acceptable questionnaires should be classified and counted accordingly. Any problems in meeting the sampling requirements should be identified, and corrective action, such as conducting additional interviews in the under-represented cells, should be taken where this is possible, before the data are edited.

Editing

Editing is the review of the questionnaires with the objective of increasing accuracy and precision. It consists of screening questionnaires to identify illegible, incomplete, inconsistent or ambiguous responses. Responses may be illegible if they have been poorly recorded. This is particularly common in questionnaires with a large number of unstructured questions. The data must be legible if they are to be properly coded. Likewise, questionnaires may be incomplete to varying degrees. A few or many questions may be unanswered.

At this stage, the researcher makes a preliminary check for consistency. Certain obvious inconsistencies can be easily detected. For example, respondents may have answered a whole series of questions relating to their perceptions of a particular bank, yet in other questions may have indicated that they have not used that particular bank or even heard of it.

Responses to unstructured questions may be ambiguous and difficult to interpret clearly. The answer may be abbreviated, or some ambiguous words may have been used. For structured questions, more than one response may be marked for a question designed to elicit a single response. Suppose that a respondent circles 2 and 3 on a five-point rating scale. Does this mean that 2.5 was intended? To complicate matters further, the coding procedure may allow for only a single-digit response.

Treatment of unsatisfactory responses

Unsatisfactory responses are commonly handled by returning to the field to get better data, assigning missing values, and discarding unsatisfactory respondents.

Returning to the field. Questionnaires with unsatisfactory responses may be returned to the field, where the interviewers recontact the respondents. This approach is particularly attractive for business and industrial marketing surveys, where the sample sizes are small and the respondents are easily identifiable. The data obtained the second time, however, may be different from those obtained during the original survey. These differences may be attributed to changes over time or differences in the mode of questionnaire administration (e.g. telephone versus in-person interview).

Assigning missing values. If returning the questionnaires to the field is not feasible, the editor may assign missing values to unsatisfactory responses. This approach may be desirable if (1) the number of respondents with unsatisfactory responses is small; (2) the proportion of unsatisfactory responses for each of these respondents is small; or (3) the variables with unsatisfactory responses are not the key variables.

Discarding unsatisfactory respondents. In another approach, the respondents with unsatisfactory responses are simply discarded. This approach may have merit when (1) the proportion of unsatisfactory respondents is small (less than 10%); (2) the sample size is large; (3) the unsatisfactory respondents do not differ from satisfactory respondents in obvious ways (e.g. demographics, product usage characteristics); (4) the proportion of unsatisfactory responses for each of these respondents is large; or (5) responses on key variables are missing. Unsatisfactory respondents may differ from satisfactory respondents in systematic ways, however, and the decision to designate a respondent as unsatisfactory may be subjective. Both these factors bias the results. If the researcher decides to discard unsatisfactory respondents, the procedure adopted to identify these respondents and their number should be reported, as in the following example.

Example Declaring 'discards'[2]

In a cross-cultural survey of marketing managers from English-speaking African countries, questionnaires were posted to 565 firms. A total of 192 completed questionnaires were returned, of which four were discarded because respondents suggested that they were not in charge of overall marketing decisions. The decision to discard the four questionnaires was based on the consideration that the sample size was sufficiently large and the proportion of unsatisfactory respondents was small.

Coding

Many questionnaire design and data entry software packages code data automatically. Examples of the options available will be presented in the Internet and computer applications section and on the Companion Website. Learning how to use such packages or even using spreadsheet packages means that the process of coding is now a much simpler task for the marketing researcher. Many of the principles of coding are based on the days of data processing using 'punched cards' or even, much more recently, DOS files. Whilst there may be many data analysts who could present coherent cases for the use of original forms of data entry, the greater majority of researchers enjoy the benefits of a simpler, speedier and less error-prone form of data entry, using proprietary software packages such as SNAP (**www.snapsurveys.com**) or Keypoint2 (**www.camsp.com**). The nature and importance of coding for qualitative data was introduced in Chapters 6 and 9. For quantitative data, which can include coping with open-ended responses or responses to 'Other – Please State…', it is still important to understand the principles of coding, as reference to the process is made by so many in the marketing research industry. The examples of coding presented are based on the Formula One Racetrack Project.

Coding means assigning a code, usually a number, to each possible answer to each question. For example, a question on the gender of respondents may be assigned a code of 1 for females and 2 for males. For every individual question in a questionnaire, the researcher decides which codes should be assigned to all its possible answers.

If the question posed has only two possible answers, the codes assigned of 1 or 2 take up one digit space. If the question posed had 25 possible answers such as *'Apart from Formula One, what other sports do you follow on TV or through any other media?'*, the possible answers and assigned codes of 1 to 25 would take up two digit spaces. The reason for focusing upon the digit spaces required for any particular question relates to the convention in marketing research to record the answers from individual questionnaire respondents in 'flat ASCII files'. Such files were typically 80 columns wide. The columns would be set out into 'fields', i.e. assigned columns that relate to specific questions. Thus the task for the researcher after assigning codes to individual question responses was to set out a consecutive series of fields or columns. These fields would represent where the answers to particular questions would be positioned in the ASCII file. In each row of a computer file would be the coded responses from individual questionnaire respondents. Each row is termed a 'record', i.e. all the fields that make up the response from one respondent. All the attitudinal, behavioural, demographic and other classification characteristics of a respondent may be contained in a single record.

Table 17.1 shows an extract from the Formula One Racetrack questionnaire and Table 17.2 illustrates the answers to these questions from a selection of respondents as set out in codes, fields and records. The classification questions set out on Table 17.1 were placed at the start of the questionnaire, forming the 'Screening' part of the questionnaire. It is followed by the first question in the section on 'Attitudes and Opinions towards F1'.

Question 2 has two possible answers, coded 1 to 2, that take up one digit space (there could be a space for 'Refused' to cope with the very rare occasions where the respondents refuse to state their gender and the interviewer cannot discern their gender. It is usually more prevalent in postal questionnaires. Question 3 has eight possible answers, coded 1 to 8, that take up one digit space. Question 4 has seven possible answers, coded 1 to 7, that take up one digit space. Note that if the actual number of Grands Prix viewed were entered (rather than a category) two digit spaces would be needed. Question 5 has 12 possible answers which are coded 01 to 12, taking up two digit spaces. Note that at the end of each question is a small number in parentheses. These numbers represent the first field positions of each question as illustrated in Table 17.2.

Table 17.1 Classification questions from the Formula One Racetrack survey

Question 1 – Have you watched at least one hour of a Formula One race on television in the 2003 season? (5)		
1	☐	Yes
2	☐	No (terminate interview)

Question 2 – Please enter gender (6)		
1	☐	Male
2	☐	Female
3	☐	Refused

Question 3 – Please could you tell me how old you are? (7)		
1	☐	18–24
2	☐	25–29
3	☐	30–34
4	☐	35–39
5	☐	40–44
6	☐	45–49
7	☐	50–55
8	☐	Refused

Question 4 – Out of 16 Formula One Grands Prix held in the 2003 season, how many have you watched on television? (8)		
1	☐	1–2
2	☐	3–4
3	☐	5–6
4	☐	7–9
5	☐	10–12
6	☐	13–15
7	☐	16

Question 5 – Which one Formula One team do you support? (DO NOT READ OUT AND TICK ONLY ONE.)   (9–10)

01	☐	Don't have a favourite team
02	☐	Don't know
03	☐	BAR (Honda)
04	☐	Ferrari
05	☐	Jaguar (Cosworth)
06	☐	Jordan (Ford)
07	☐	McLaren (Mercedes)
08	☐	European Minardi
09	☐	Renault
10	☐	Sauber
11	☐	Toyota
12	☐	Williams (BMW)

Table 17.2 Illustrative computer file held on a flat ASCII file

Records	Fields					
	1–4	5	6	7	8	9–10
Record #1	0001	1	1	2	2	01
Record #11	0011	1	1	3	1	03
Record #21	0021	1	2	7	6	04
Record #2050	2050	1	1	5	4	11

In Table 17.2, the columns represent the fields and the rows represent the records of each respondent. The field space 1–4 is used to record an assigned number to each respondent. Table 17.3 illustrates how the same data may be entered using a spreadsheet. Each row represents an individual respondent and each column represents the fields required to hold the response to an individual question. Note that there is a column that identifies a specific number attached to each record. Many survey analysis packages record a unique ID for each record so that, as the answers to an individual questionnaire are entered, the ID is automatically updated. However, if a unique ID is attached to each questionnaire before it is sent out (e.g. in a postal survey), the ID may be entered as a distinct field (see column A).

Table 17.3 Example of computer file held on a spreadsheet program

Records in rows	Individual fields in columns					
	A	B	C	D	E	F
	ID	Question 1	Question 2	Question 3	Question 4	Question 5
2	1	1	1	2	2	01
12	11	1	1	3	1	03
22	21	1	2	7	6	04
2051	2050	1	1	5	4	11

Coding is still required to identify the individual responses to individual questions. Spreadsheets are normally wide enough to allow an individual record to be recorded on one line, and they can be set up so that whoever is entering the data can clearly keep track of which questions relate to which columns. Spreadsheets can be used as a format to analyse data in a wide variety of data analysis packages and so are very versatile. They do, however, have shortcomings. The next paragraph will go on to illustrate these.

In many surveys, multiple-choice questions are widely used. An example of a multiple-choice question is shown in Table 17.4, a question from the Formula One Racetrack survey which examines respondents' perceptions of Formula One.

Table 17.4 Multiple-choice question from the Formula One Racetrack survey

Question 8 – Please tell me which of the following words you think best describe Formula One. (READ OUT AND TICK ALL THAT APPLY.)		
01		Boring
02	✓	Competitive
03		Dangerous
04		Dynamic
05	✓	Elitist
06	✓	Exciting
07		Expensive
08		Extravagant
09	✓	Innovative
10		Inspirational
11		Prestigious
12		Safe
13		Sexy
14		Too technical

In essence, each of the options presented in question 8 is an individual 'yes' or 'no' question. In the example shown, the respondent has replied 'yes' to the second, fifth, sixth and ninth variables. Using a spreadsheet, this question would be coded as shown in Table 17.5 where the response in Table 17.4 is represented as 'Record 1'. The 'ticks' above have been coded as a '1' to represent 'yes' and '0' as 'no'.

Table 17.5 Formula One Racetrack, question 8 spreadsheet presentation

Records	Individual fields in columns								
	Question 8								
	AJ Q8(1)	AK Q8(2)	AL Q8(3)	AM Q8(4)	AN Q8(5)	AO Q8(6)	AP Q8(7)	AQ Q8(8)	AU Q8(9)
1	1	0	0	0	1	1	0	0	1
2	1	1	0	0	0	1	1	0	0
3	0	0	1	1	1	0	0	0	0
4	1	1	0	0	1	0	1	1	1
... n	0	1	1	0	0	1	1	0	0

Entering data for multiple-choice questions is a simple task on a spreadsheet, provided that there are not so many of these question types in a survey. In the Formula One Racetrack questionnaire there was one question related to which cars 'belonged' (owned, leased or a company car) to particular households. Had the open-ended question been closed into a multiple-choice question of 38 different car manufacturers, this would have meant a spreadsheet of 38 columns. Had the question gone beyond the manufacturer, e.g. Renault, to the type of Renault, e.g. Clio, the number of columns could have run to thousands. If respondents had indicated that they had a Renault, this would mean finding the precise column to enter a '1' and then 37 '0s'. This is a lengthy and potentially error-prone task. This is where proprietary questionnaire design and survey packages really hold many advantages, i.e. they make the data entry task very simple for multiple-choice questions of any length and check for errors. Again, the use of proprietary packages will be outlined at the end of this chapter.

Codebook

Whether, the researcher uses DOS-based systems or a spreadsheet, a summary of the whole questionnaire, showing the position of the fields and the key to all the codes, should be produced. With proprietary software packages, this summary is created automatically as the questionnaire is designed. Such a summary is called a codebook. Table 17.6 shows an extract from the Formula One Racetrack codebook. The codebook shown is based upon using a spreadsheet to enter the data. Depending upon which type of data entry is used, the codebook style will change, but in essence the type of information recorded is the same.

Codebook
A book containing coding instructions and the necessary information about the questions and potential answers in a survey.

A **codebook** contains instructions and the necessary information about the questions and potential answers in a survey. A codebook guides the 'coders' in their work and helps the researcher identify and locate the questions properly. Even if the questionnaire has been pre-coded, it is helpful to prepare a formal codebook. As illustrated in Table 17.6, a codebook generally contains the following information: (1) column identifier, (2) question name, (3) question number, and (4) coding instructions.

Table 17.6 Extract from the Formula One Racetrack survey codebook

Column identifier	Question name	Question number	Coding instructions
A	Respondent ID		Enter handwritten number from top right-hand corner of the questionnaire
B	Watched Formula One	1	Yes = '1' No = '2'
C	Gender	2	Male = '1' Female = '2'
D	Age band	3	Enter number as seen alongside ticked box: 18–24 = '1' 25–29 = '2' 30–34 = '3' 35–39 = '4' 40–44 = '5' 45–49 = '6' 50–55 = '7' Refused = '8'
E	Viewing frequency	4	Enter number as seen alongside ticked box: 1–2 = '1' 3–4 = '2' 5–6 = '3' 7–9 = '4' 10–12 = '5' 13–15 = '6' 16 = '7'

Coding open-ended questions

The coding of structured questions, be they single or multiple choice, is relatively simple because the response options are predetermined. The researcher assigns a code for each response to each question and specifies the appropriate field or column in which it will appear; this is termed 'pre-coding'.[3] The coding of unstructured or open-ended questions is more complex; this is termed 'post-coding'. Respondents' verbatim responses are recorded on the questionnaire. One option the researcher has is to go through all the completed questionnaires, list the verbatim responses and then develop and assign codes to these responses. Another option that is allowed on some data entry packages is to enter the verbatim responses directly onto the computer, allowing a print-off of the collective responses and codes to be assigned before all of the questionnaires have been entered. The coding process here is similar to the process of assigning codes in the analysis of qualitative data as described in Chapter 9. The verbatim responses to 1,000 questionnaires may generate 1,000 different answers. The words may be different but the essence of the response may mean that 20 issues have been addressed. The researcher decides what those 20 issues are, names the issues and assigns codes from 1–20, and then goes through all the 1,000 questionnaires to enter the code alongside the verbatim response.

The following guidelines are suggested for coding unstructured questions and questionnaires in general.[4] Category codes should be mutually exclusive and collectively exhaustive. Categories are mutually exclusive if each response fits into one and only one category code. Categories should not overlap. Categories are collectively exhaustive if every response fits into one of the assigned category codes. This can be achieved by adding an additional category code of 'other' or 'none of the above'. An absolute maximum of 10% of responses should fall into the 'other' category; the researcher should strive to assign all responses into meaningful categories.

Category codes should be assigned for critical issues even if no one has mentioned them. It may be important to know that no one has mentioned a particular response. For example, a car manufacturer may be concerned about its new web page design. In a question 'How did you learn about the new Renault Clio?', the Web should be included as a distinct category, even if no respondents gave this as an answer.

Transcribing

Transcribing data involves keying the coded data from the collected questionnaires into computers. If the data have been collected via the Internet, CATI or CAPI, this step is unnecessary because the data are entered directly into the computer as they are collected. Besides the direct keying of data, they can be transferred by using mark sense forms, optical scanning or computerised sensory analysis (see Figure 17.2). Mark sense forms require responses to be recorded in a pre-designated area coded for that response, and the data can then be read by a machine. Optical scanning involves direct machine reading of the codes and simultaneous transcription. A familiar example of optical scanning is the transcription of universal product code (UPC) data, scanned at supermarket checkout counters. Technological advances have resulted in computerised sensory analysis systems, which automate the data collection process. The questions appear on a computerised gridpad, and responses are recorded directly into the computer using a sensing device.

Except for CATI and CAPI, an original record exists which can be compared with what was either automatically read or keyed. Errors can occur in an automatic read or as data are keyed and it is necessary to verify the dataset, or at least a portion of it, for these errors.

A second operator re-punches the data from the coded questionnaires. The transcribed data from the two operators are compared record by record. Any discrepancy between the

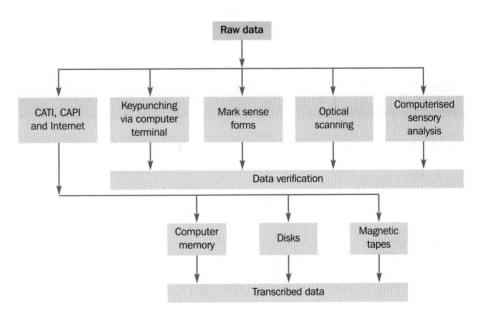

Figure 17.2
Data transcription

two sets of transcribed data is investigated to identify and correct for data keyed in error. Verification of the entire dataset will double the time and cost of data transcription. Given the time and cost constraints, and that experienced operators who key data are quite accurate, it is sufficient to verify 10–25% of the data. With automatically read data, the completed dataset that has been read can be compared with original records. Again, a percentage may be selected and checks made to see what may have caused differences between the original record and the read data (e.g. respondents entering two ticks when only one was requested).

When CATI, CAPI or the Internet are employed, data are verified as they are collected. In the case of inadmissible responses, the computer will prompt the interviewer or respondent. In the case of admissible responses, the interviewer or the respondent can see the recorded response on the screen and verify it before proceeding.

The selection of a data transcription method is guided by the type of interviewing method used and the availability of equipment. If CATI, CAPI or the Internet are used, the data are entered directly into the computer. Keypunching via a computer terminal is most frequently used for ordinary telephone, in-home and street interviewing and traditional mail interviews. The use of computerised sensory analysis systems in personal interviews is increasing with the growing use of handheld computers. Optical scanning can be used in structured and repetitive surveys, and mark sense forms are used in special cases.[5] The following example illustrates the use of scanned data, and, in this circumstance, the advantage it has over keypunching.

Example	Scanning the seas[6]

Princess Cruises (**www.princess.com**) operates large cruise ships around the world. It is the third largest cruise line, carrying around 700,000 passengers annually with 27 ships. Princess wished to know what passengers thought of the cruise experience, but wanted to determine this information in a cost-effective way. A scannable questionnaire was developed that allowed the cruise line to transcribe the data quickly from thousands of responses, thus expediting data preparation and analysis. This questionnaire is distributed to measure customer satisfaction on all voyages. In addition to saving time as compared with keypunching, scanning has also increased the accuracy of survey results. The Senior Marketing Researcher for Princess Cruises, Jamie Goldfarb, commented, 'When we compared the data files from the two methods, we found that although the scanned system occasionally missed marks because they had not been filled in properly, the scanned data was still more accurate than the keypunched file.'

Cleaning the data

Data cleaning
Thorough and extensive checks for consistency and treatment of missing responses.

Data cleaning includes consistency checks and treatment of missing responses. Even though preliminary consistency checks have been made during editing, the checks at this stage are more thorough and extensive, because they are made by computer.

Consistency checks

Consistency checks
A part of the data cleaning process that identifies data that are out of range, logically inconsistent or have extreme values. Data with values not defined by the coding scheme are inadmissible.

Consistency checks identify data that are out of range or logically inconsistent or have extreme values. Out-of-range data values are inadmissible and must be corrected. For example, respondents were asked to express their degree of agreement with a series of lifestyle statements on a 1–5 scale. Assuming that 9 has been designated for missing values, data values of 0, 6, 7 and 8 would be out of range. Computer packages can be programmed to identify out-of-range values for each variable and will not progress to another variable within a record until a value in the set range is entered. Other packages can be programmed to print out the respondent code, variable code, variable name, record number, column number and out-of-range value.[7] This makes it easy to check each variable systematically for out-of-range values. The correct responses can be determined by going back to the edited and coded questionnaire.

Responses can be logically inconsistent in various ways. For example, respondents may indicate that they charge long-distance calls to a calling card from a credit card company, although they do not have such a credit card. Or respondents report both unfamiliarity with and frequent usage of the same product. The necessary information (respondent code, variable code, variable name, record number, column number and inconsistent values) can be printed to locate these responses and to take corrective action.

Finally, extreme values should be closely examined. Not all extreme values result from errors, but they may point to problems with the data. For example, in the Formula One Racetrack survey, respondents were asked to name the manufacturer of the cars that 'belonged' to their households. Certain respondents recorded 10 or more cars. In these circumstances the extreme values can be identified and the actual figure validated in many cases by recontacting the respondent.

Treatment of missing responses

Missing responses
Values of a variable that are unknown because the respondents concerned provided ambiguous answers to the question or because their answers were not properly recorded.

Missing responses represent values of a variable that are unknown either because respondents provided ambiguous answers or because their answers were not properly recorded. Treatment of missing responses poses problems, particularly if the proportion of missing responses is more than 10%. The following options are available for the treatment of missing responses.[8]

Substitute a neutral value. A neutral value, typically the mean response to the variable, is substituted for the missing responses. Thus, the mean of the variable remains unchanged, and other statistics such as correlations are not affected much. Although this approach has some merit, the logic of substituting a mean value (say 4) for respondents who, if they had answered, might have used either high ratings (6 or 7) or low ratings (1 or 2) is questionable.[9]

Substitute an imputed response. The respondents' pattern of responses to other questions is used to impute or calculate a suitable response to the missing questions. The researcher attempts to infer from the available data the responses the individuals would have given if they had answered the questions. This can be done statistically by determining the relationship of the variable in question to other variables based on the available data. For example, product usage could be related to household size for respondents who have provided data on both variables. Given that respondent's household size, the missing product usage response for a respondent could then be calculated. This approach, however, requires considerable effort and can introduce serious bias. Sophisticated statistical procedures have been developed to calculate imputed values for missing responses.[10]

Casewise deletion
A method for handling missing responses in which cases or respondents with any missing responses are discarded from the analysis.

Casewise deletion. In **casewise deletion**, cases or respondents with any missing responses are discarded from the analysis. Because many respondents may have some missing responses, this approach could result in a small sample. Throwing away large amounts of data is undesirable because it is costly and time consuming to collect data. Furthermore, respondents with missing responses could differ from respondents with complete responses in systematic ways. If so, casewise deletion could seriously bias the results.

Pairwise deletion
A method for handling missing responses in which all cases or respondents with any missing responses are not automatically discarded; rather, for each calculation, only the cases or respondents with complete responses are considered.

Pairwise deletion. In **pairwise deletion**, instead of discarding all cases with any missing responses, the researcher uses only the cases or respondents with complete responses for each calculation. As a result, different calculations in an analysis may be based on different sample sizes. This procedure may be appropriate when (1) the sample size is large, (2) there are few missing responses, and (3) the variables are not highly related. However, this procedure can produce unappealing or even infeasible results.

The different procedures for the treatment of missing responses may yield different results, particularly when the responses are not missing at random and the variables are related. Hence, missing responses should be kept to a minimum. The researcher should carefully consider the implications of the various procedures before selecting a particular method for the treatment of non-response.

Statistically adjusting the data

Procedures for statistically adjusting the data consist of weighting, variable respecification and scale transformation. These adjustments are not always necessary but can enhance the quality of data analysis.

Weighting

Weighting
A statistical procedure that attempts to account for non-response by assigning differential weights to the data depending on the response rates.

In **weighting**, each case or respondent in the database is assigned a weight to reflect its importance relative to other cases or respondents. The value 1.0 represents the unweighted case. The effect of weighting is to increase or decrease the number of cases in the sample that possess certain characteristics. (See Chapter 15, which discussed the use of weighting to adjust for non-response bias.)

Weighting is most widely used to make the sample data more representative of a target population on specific characteristics. For example, it may be used to give greater importance to cases or respondents with higher quality data. Yet another use of weighting is to adjust the sample so that greater importance is attached to respondents with certain characteristics. If a study is conducted to determine what modifications should be made to an existing product, the researcher might want to attach greater weight to the opinions of heavy users of the product. This could be accomplished by assigning weights of 3.0 to heavy users, 2.0 to medium users and 1.0 to light users and non-users. Because it destroys the self-weighting nature of the sample design, weighting should be applied with caution. If used, the weighting procedure should be documented and made a part of the project report.[11]

Example **Determining the weight of community centre users**

A mail survey was conducted in the Scottish city of Edinburgh to determine the patronage of a community centre. The resulting sample composition differed in age structure from the area population distribution as compiled from recent census data. Therefore, the sample was weighted to make it representative in terms of age structure. The weights applied were determined by dividing the population percentage by the corresponding sample percentage. The distribution of age structure for the sample and population, as well as the weights applied, are given in the following table.

Source: © Alamy

Age group percentage	Sample percentage	Population	Weight
13–18	4.32	6.13	1.42
19–24	5.89	7.45	1.26
25–34	12.23	13.98	1.14
35–44	17.54	17.68	1.01
45–54	14.66	15.59	1.06
55–64	13.88	13.65	0.98
65–74	15.67	13.65	0.87
75 plus	15.81	11.87	0.75
Totals	100.00	100.00	

Age groups under-represented in the sample received higher weights, whereas over-represented age groups received lower weights. Thus, the data for a respondent aged 13–18 would be overweighted by multiplying by 1.42, whereas the data for a respondent aged 75 plus would be underweighted by multiplying by 0.75.

Variable respecification

Variable respecification
The transformation of data to create new variables or the modification of existing variables so that they are more consistent with the objectives of the study.

Variable respecification involves the transformation of data to create new variables or to modify existing variables. The purpose of respecification is to create variables that are consistent with the objectives of the study. For example, suppose that the original variable was product usage, with 10 response categories. These might be collapsed into four categories: heavy, medium, light and non-user. Or the researcher may create new variables that are composites of several other variables. For example, the researcher may create an Index of Information Search (ISS), which is the sum of information new car customers seek from dealers, promotional sources, the Internet and other independent sources. Likewise, one may take the ratio of variables. If the amount of purchases at a clothes shop (X_1) and the amount of purchases where a credit card was used (X_2) have been measured, the proportion of purchases charged to a credit card can be a new variable, created by taking the ratio of the two (X_2/X_1). Other respecifications of variables include square root and log transformations, which are often applied to improve the fit of the model being estimated.

Dummy variables
A respecification procedure using variables that take on only two values, usually 0 or 1.

An important respecification procedure involves the use of **dummy variables** for respecifying categorical variables. Dummy variables are also called binary, dichotomous, instrumental or qualitative variables. They are variables that may take on only two values, such as 0 or 1. The general rule is that to respecify a categorical variable with K categories, $K - 1$ dummy variables are needed. The reason for having $K - 1$, rather than K, dummy variables is that only $K - 1$ categories are independent. Given the sample data, information about the Kth category can be derived from information about the other $K - 1$ categories. Consider gender, a variable having two categories. Only one dummy variable is needed. Information on the number or percentage of males in the sample can be readily derived from the number or percentage of females. The following example further illustrates the concept of dummy variables.

Example

'Frozen' consumers treated as dummies

In a survey of consumer preferences for frozen foods, the respondents were classified as heavy users, medium users, light users and non-users, and they were originally assigned codes of 4, 3, 2 and 1, respectively. This coding was not meaningful for several statistical analyses. To conduct these analyses, product usage was represented by three dummy variables, X_1, X_2 and X_3, as shown.

Product usage category	Original variable code	Dummy variable code		
		X_1	X_2	X_3
Non-users	1	1	0	0
Light users	2	0	1	0
Medium users	3	0	0	1
Heavy users	4	0	0	0

Note that $X_1 = 1$ for non-users and 0 for all others. Likewise, $X_2 = 1$ for light users and 0 for all others, and $X_3 = 1$ for medium users and 0 for all others. In analysing the data, X_1, X_2, and X_3 are used to represent all user/non-user groups.

Scale transformation

Scale transformation
A manipulation of scale values to ensure compatibility with other scales or otherwise to make the data suitable for analysis.

Scale transformation involves a manipulation of scale values to ensure comparability with other scales or otherwise to make the data suitable for analysis. Frequently, different scales are employed for measuring different variables. For example, image variables may be measured on a seven-point semantic differential scale, attitude variables on a continuous rating scale, and lifestyle variables on a five-point Likert scale. Therefore, it would not be meaningful to make comparisons across the measurement scales for any respondent. To compare attitudinal scores with lifestyle or image scores, it would be necessary to transform the various scales. Even if the same scale is employed for all the variables, different respondents may use the scale differently. For example, some respondents consistently use the upper end of a rating scale whereas others consistently use the lower end. These differences can be corrected by appropriately transforming the data.

Example

Health care services: transforming consumers[12]

In a study examining preference segmentation of health care services, respondents were asked to rate the importance of 18 factors affecting preferences for hospitals on a three-point scale (very, somewhat, or not important). Before analysing the data, each individual's ratings were transformed. For each individual, preference responses were averaged across all 18 items. Then this mean $\bar{X}$ was subtracted from each item rating X_i, and a constant C was added to the difference. Thus, the transformed data, X_t, were obtained by

$$X_t = X_i - \bar{X} + C$$

Subtraction of the mean value corrected for any uneven use of the importance scale. The constant C was added to make all the transformed values positive, since negative importance ratings are not meaningful conceptually. This transformation was desirable because some respondents, especially those with low incomes, had rated almost all the preference items as very important. Others, high-income respondents in particular, had assigned the very important rating to only a few preference items. Thus, subtraction of the mean value provided a more accurate idea of the relative importance of the factors.

Standardisation
The process of correcting data to reduce them to the same scale by subtracting the sample mean and dividing by the standard deviation.

In this example, the scale transformation is corrected only for the mean response. A more common transformation procedure is **standardisation**. To standardise a scale X_i, we first subtract the mean, $\bar{X}$, from each score and then divide by the standard deviation, s_x. Thus, the standardised scale will have a mean of 0 and a standard deviation of 1. This is essentially the same as the calculation of z scores (see Chapter 15). Standardisation allows the researcher to compare variables that have been measured using different types of scales.[13] Mathematically, standardised scores, z_i, may be obtained as

$$z_i = \frac{(X_i - \bar{X})}{s_x}$$

Selecting a data analysis strategy

The process of selecting a data analysis strategy is described in Figure 17.3. The selection of a data analysis strategy should be based on the earlier steps of the marketing research process, known characteristics of the data, properties of statistical techniques and the background and philosophy of the researcher.

Data analysis is not an end in itself. Its purpose is to produce information that will help address the problem at hand. The selection of a data analysis strategy must begin with a consideration of the earlier steps in the process: problem definition (step 1), development of an approach (step 2) and research design (step 3). The preliminary plan of data analysis prepared as part of the research design should be used as a springboard. Changes may be necessary in the light of additional information generated in subsequent stages of the research process.

The next step is to consider the known characteristics of the data. The measurement scales used exert a strong influence on the choice of statistical techniques (see Chapter 12). In addition, the research design may favour certain techniques. For example, analysis of variance (see Chapter 19) is suited for analysing experimental data from causal designs. The insights into the data obtained during data preparation can be valuable for selecting a strategy for analysis.

It is also important to take into account the properties of the statistical techniques, particularly their purpose and underlying assumptions. Some statistical techniques are appropriate for examining differences in variables, others for assessing the magnitudes of the relationships between variables, and still others for making predictions. The techniques also involve different assumptions, and some techniques can withstand violations of the underlying assumptions better than others. A classification of statistical techniques is presented below.

Finally, the researcher's background and philosophy affect the choice of a data analysis strategy. The experienced, statistically trained researcher will employ a range of techniques, including advanced statistical methods. Researchers differ in their willingness to make

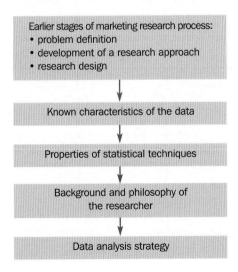

Figure 17.3
Selecting a data analysis strategy

assumptions about the variables and their underlying populations. Researchers who are conservative about making assumptions will limit their choice of techniques to distribution-free methods. In general, several techniques may be appropriate for analysing the data from a given project. We use the Formula One Racetrack Project to illustrate how a data analysis strategy can be developed.

Formula One Racetrack Project

Data analysis strategy[14]

As part of the analysis conducted in the Formula One Racetrack Project, Formula One Image was modelled in terms of the most important issues that shaped perceptions of the sport. The sample was split into halves. The respondents in each half were clustered on the basis of their perceptions. Statistical tests for clusters were conducted, and eight segments were identified. Formula One image was modelled in terms of the evaluations of the race teams. The model was estimated separately for each segment. Differences between segment preference functions were statistically tested. Finally, model verification and cross-validation were conducted for each segment. The data analysis strategy adopted is depicted in this figure:

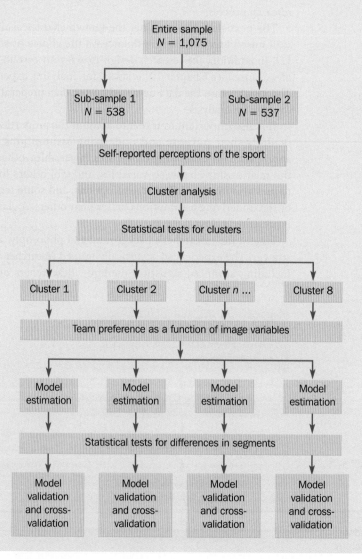

A classification of statistical techniques

Univariate techniques
Statistical techniques appropriate for analysing data when there is a single measurement of each element in the sample, or, if there are several measurements on each element, when each variable is analysed in isolation.

Multivariate techniques
Statistical techniques suitable for analysing data when there are two or more measurements on each element and the variables are analysed simultaneously. Multivariate techniques are concerned with the simultaneous relationships among two or more phenomena.

Metric data
Data that are interval or ratio in nature.

Non-metric data
Data derived from a nominal or ordinal scale.

Independent samples
The samples are independent if they are drawn randomly from different populations.

Paired samples
The samples are paired when the data for the two samples relate to the same group of respondents.

Dependence techniques
Multivariate techniques appropriate when one or more of the variables can be identified as dependent variables and the remaining ones as independent variables.

Interdependence techniques
Multivariate statistical techniques that attempt to group data based on underlying similarity and thus allow for interpretation of the data structures. No distinction is made as to which variables are dependent and which are independent.

Statistical techniques can be classified as univariate or multivariate. **Univariate techniques** are appropriate when there is a single measurement of each element in the sample or when there are several measurements of each element but each variable is analysed in isolation. **Multivariate techniques**, on the other hand, are suitable for analysing data when there are two or more measurements of each element and the variables are analysed simultaneously. Multivariate techniques are concerned with the simultaneous relationships among two or more phenomena. Multivariate techniques differ from univariate techniques in that they shift the focus away from the levels (averages) and distributions (variances) of the phenomena, concentrating instead on the degree of relationships (correlations or covariances) among these phenomena.[15] The univariate and multivariate techniques are described in detail in Chapters 18–24, but here we show how the various techniques relate to each other in an overall scheme of classification.

Univariate techniques can be further classified based on whether the data are metric or non-metric (as introduced in Chapter 12). **Metric data** are measured on an interval or ratio scale, whereas **non-metric data** are measured on a nominal or ordinal scale. These techniques can be further classified based on whether one, two or more samples are involved. It should be noted that the number of samples is determined based on how the data are treated for the purpose of analysis, not based on how the data were collected. For example, the data for males and females may well have been collected as a single sample, but if the analysis involves an examination of gender differences, two samples will be used. The samples are **independent** if they are drawn randomly from different populations. For the purpose of analysis, data pertaining to different groups of respondents, e.g. males and females, are generally treated as independent samples. On the other hand, the samples are **paired** when the data for the two samples relate to the same group of respondents.

For metric data, when there is only one sample, the *z* test and the *t* test can be used. When there are two or more independent samples, the *z* test and *t* test can be used for two samples, and one-way analysis of variance (one-way ANOVA) can be used for more than two samples. In the case of two or more related samples, the paired *t* test can be used. For non-metric data involving a single sample, frequency distribution, chi-square, Kolmogorov–Smirnov (K–S), runs and binomial tests can be used. For two independent samples with non-metric data, the chi-square, Mann–Whitney, median, K–S and Kruskal–Wallis one-way analysis of variance (K–W ANOVA) can be used. In contrast, when there are two or more related samples, the sign, Wilcoxon, McNemar and chi-square tests should be used (see Figure 17.4).

Multivariate statistical techniques can be classified as dependence techniques or interdependence techniques (see Figure 17.5). **Dependence techniques** are appropriate when one or more variables can be identified as dependent variables and the remaining ones as independent variables. When there is only one dependent variable, cross-tabulation, analysis of variance and covariance, multiple regression, two-group discriminant analysis and conjoint analysis can be used. If there is more than one dependent variable, however, the appropriate techniques are multivariate analysis of variance and covariance, canonical correlation and multiple discriminant analysis. In **interdependence techniques**, the variables are not classified as dependent or independent; rather, the whole set of interdependent relationships is examined. These techniques focus on either variable interdependence or interobject similarity. The major technique for examining variable interdependence is factor analysis. Analysis of inter-object similarity can be conducted by cluster analysis and multidimensional scaling.[16]

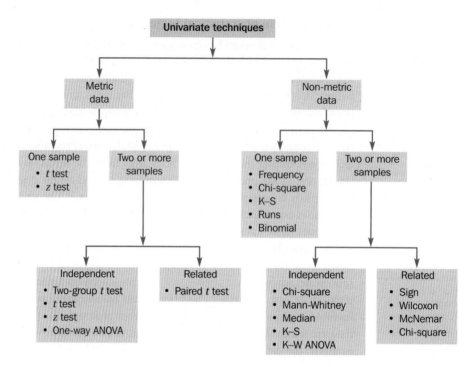

Figure 17.4
A classification of
univariate techniques

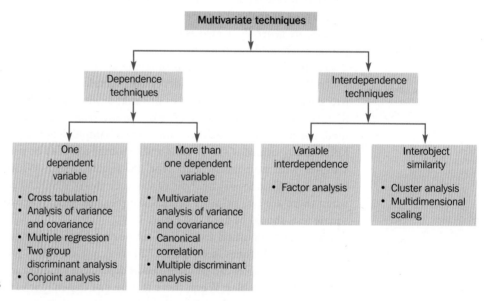

Figure 17.5
A classification of
multivariate techniques

International marketing research

Before analysing the data, the researcher should ensure that the units of measurement are comparable across countries or cultural units. For example, the data may have to be adjusted to establish currency equivalents or metric equivalents. Furthermore, standardisation or normalisation of the data may be necessary to make meaningful comparisons and achieve consistent results.

Example A worldwide scream for ice cream[17]

Over half the sales of Häagen-Dazs (**www.haagen-dazs.com**), the US ice cream manufacturer, come from markets outside the USA. Its sales in Asia, the UK, France and Germany are increasing at a phenomenal rate. In December 2001, General Mills, Inc. sold its 50% stake in Häagen-Dazs to the Swiss company Nestlé for $641 million (£500 million). How has Häagen-Dazs achieved this situation? Marketing research conducted in several European countries (e.g. the UK, France and Germany) and several Asian countries (e.g. Japan, Singapore and Taiwan) revealed that consumers were hungry for a high-quality ice cream with a high-quality image and were willing to pay a premium price for it. These consistent findings emerged after the price of ice cream in each country was standardised to have a mean of zero and a standard deviation of unity. Standardisation was desirable because the prices were specified in different local currencies and a common basis was needed for comparison across countries. Also, in each country, the premium price had to be defined in relation to the prices of competing brands. Standardisation accomplished both of these objectives.

Based on these findings, Häagen-Dazs first introduced the brand at a few high-end retailers; it then built company-owned stores in high-traffic areas; and finally it rolled into convenience stores and supermarkets. It maintained the premium quality brand name by starting first with a few high-end retailers. It also supplied free freezers to retailers. Hungry for quality products, consumers in the new markets paid double or triple the price of home brands. In the USA, Häagen-Dazs remains popular, although faced with intense competition and a health-conscious market. This added to the impetus to enter international markets.

Data analysis could be conducted at three levels: (1) individual, (2) within country or cultural unit, and (3) across countries or cultural units. Individual-level analysis requires that the data from each respondent be analysed separately. For example, one might compute a correlation coefficient or run a regression analysis for each respondent. This means that enough data must be obtained from each individual to allow analysis at the individual level, which is often not feasible. Yet it has been argued that, in international marketing or cross-cultural research, the researcher should possess a sound knowledge of the consumer in each culture. This can best be accomplished by individual-level analysis.[18]

Intra-cultural analysis
Within-country analysis of international data.

In within-country or cultural unit analysis, the data are analysed separately for each country or cultural unit. This is also referred to as **intra-cultural analysis**. This level of analysis is quite similar to that conducted in domestic marketing research. The objective is to gain an understanding of the relationships and patterns existing in each country or cultural unit.

Pan-cultural analysis
Across-countries analysis in which the data for all respondents from all the countries are pooled and analysed.

Cross-cultural analysis
A type of across-countries analysis in which the data could be aggregated for each country and these aggregate statistics analysed.

In across-countries analysis, the data from all the countries are analysed simultaneously. Two approaches to this method are possible. The data for all respondents from all the countries can be pooled and analysed. This is referred to as **pan-cultural analysis**. Alternatively, the data can be aggregated for each country, and then these aggregate statistics can be analysed. For example, one could compute means of variables for each country, and then compute correlations on these means. This is referred to as **cross-cultural analysis**. The objective of this level of analysis is to assess the comparability of findings from one country to another. The similarities as well as the differences between countries should be investigated. When examining differences, not only differences in means but also differences in variance and distribution should be assessed.

All the statistical techniques that have been discussed in this book can be applied to within-country or across-country analysis and, subject to the amount of data available, to individual-level analysis as well.[19]

Ethics in marketing research

Ethical issues that arise during the data preparation and analysis step of the marketing research process pertain mainly to the researcher. While checking, editing, coding, transcribing and cleaning, researchers should try to get some idea about the quality of the data. An attempt should be made to identify respondents who have provided data of questionable quality. Consider, for example, a respondent who ticks the '7' response to all the 20 items measuring attitude to spectator sports on a 1–7 Likert scale. Apparently, this respondent did not realise that some of the statements were negative whereas others were positive. Thus, this respondent indicates an extremely favourable attitude towards spectator sports on all the positive statements and an extremely negative attitude on the statements that were reversed. Decisions on whether such respondents should be discarded, i.e. not included in the analysis, can raise ethical concerns. A good rule of thumb is to make such decisions during the data preparation phase before conducting any analysis.

In contrast, suppose that the researcher conducted the analysis without first attempting to identify unsatisfactory responses. The analysis, however, does not reveal the expected relationship; the analysis does not show that attitude towards spectator sports influences attendance at spectator sports. The researcher then decides to examine the quality of data obtained. In checking the questionnaires, a few respondents with unsatisfactory data are identified. In addition to the type of unsatisfactory responses mentioned earlier, there were responses as '4', the 'neither agree nor disagree' response, to all the 20 items measuring attitude towards spectator sports. When these respondents are eliminated and the reduced dataset is analysed, the expected results are obtained showing a positive influence of attitude on attendance of spectator sports. Discarding respondents after analysing the data raises ethical concerns, particularly if the report does not state that the initial analysis was inconclusive. Moreover, the procedure used to identify unsatisfactory respondents and the number of respondents discarded should be clearly disclosed, as in the following example.

Example   Elimination of decision-makers unwilling to be ethical[20]

In a study of MBA graduates' responses to marketing ethics dilemmas, respondents were required to respond to 14 questions regarding ethically ambiguous scenarios by writing a simple sentence on what action they would take if they were the manager. The responses were then analysed to determine whether the respondent's answer was indicative of ethical behaviour. However, in the data preparation phase, six respondents out of the 561 total respondents were eliminated from further analysis because their responses indicated that they did not follow the directions which told them to state clearly their choice of action. This is an example of ethical editing of the data. The criterion for unsatisfactory responses is clearly stated, the unsatisfactory respondents are identified before the analysis, and the number of respondents eliminated is disclosed.

While analysing the data, the researcher may also have to deal with ethical issues. The assumptions underlying the statistical techniques used to analyse the data must be satisfied to obtain meaningful results. Any departure from these assumptions should be critically examined to determine the appropriateness of the technique for analysing the data at hand. The researcher has the responsibility of justifying the statistical techniques used for analysis. When this is not done, ethical questions can be raised. Moreover, there should be no intentional or deliberate misrepresentation of research methods or results.

Similarly, ethical issues can arise in interpreting the results, drawing conclusions, making recommendations, and in implementation. For example, the error terms in bivariate regression must be normally distributed about zero, with a constant variance, and be uncorrelated (Chapter 20). The researcher has the responsibility to test these assumptions and take appropriate corrective actions if necessary. Although interpretations, conclusions, recommendations and implementations necessarily involve subjective judgement, this judgement must be exercised honestly, free from personal biases or agendas of the researcher or the client.

Internet and computer applications

In evaluating software that can help the marketing researcher with data preparation tasks, a distinction should be made between survey design and analysis packages such as SNAP (**www.snapsurveys.com**), Keypoint2 (**www.camsp.com**) and Sphinxsurvey (**www.scolari. co.uk**), and statistical packages such as SPSS (**www.spss.com**), SAS (**www.sas.com**) and Minitab (**www.minitab.com**), and office products such as Microsoft Excel (**www. microsoft.com**). It is advised that these websites are visited to view the demonstration versions of the packages to gain a feel for their capabilities and applications.

Survey design and analysis packages such as SNAP, Keypoint2 and Sphinx perform a much broader range of tasks to help with the array of data preparation tasks than either the statistical packages or the more generic office products. Primarily, they allow the physical format of a questionnaire to be designed. The designed questionnaire can be printed out and used for traditional mail surveys, formatted for interviewer-led surveys using CATI or CAPI, or formatted for self-completion Internet surveys. As the questionnaire is designed on screen, the underlying structure of the questionnaire is automatically created. This results in the coding of question replies and the associated field positions automatically being worked out. It also means that any alterations in the design of the questionnaire automatically maintain the structure and integrity of the data being collected, ensuring accuracy in the later analysis stages.

Data can be entered directly by respondents as an Internet survey progresses, or entered by an interviewer on a CATI or CAPI survey. Alternatively, the data can be keyed directly from a paper questionnaire onto the computer. The packages have built-in checks for 'out-of-range' responses which halt the progress of data entry; for example, if a five-point Likert scale is used and a '7' is entered, there is an audible warning and the data entry halts until the error is corrected.

Multiple-choice questions typically appear as tick boxes and can be set as either a single response or a multiple response, and it is a simple task to highlight one or more of the boxes. Alternatively, numbers, dates or verbatim responses can be entered. The verbatim data can be transferred to qualitative data analysis packages if needed, or can be post-coded (coded later) and a new variable established for subsequent analysis.

Data preparation effort is considerably reduced when replies are entered directly onto the computer as each question is asked. For paper-based surveys this is not practical and optical scanning can be a cost-effective solution, particularly when there are a large proportion of multiple-response questions. The pages of the questionnaire are scanned and the systems search for marks within boxes, and even allow for situations where a reply has been altered or removed. The following example illustrates conditions where scanning is beneficial and an example of SPSS software to support the process.

$\rightarrow$

How Walcheren Hospital perked up its patients[21]

In 1996, the Netherlands passed the Quality Act for health care institutions. This placed a requirement on all health care organisations in the country to evaluate the quality of their services based on patient feedback. The hospital of Walcheren admits 120,000 patients each year, which creates a huge amount of data to analyse. Walcheren chose the SPSS suite of market research tools called Dimensions. Using the software helped the hospital to design a survey that could be scanned to capture the data, but eliminated the need for it to go through the time-consuming process of actually setting up the questionnaire for scanning. The survey has significantly contributed to patient well-being and satisfaction. Many patients noted that they did not receive enough details about their illnesses and treatment. These complaints led to hospital staff making changes to their communication processes.

Scanning becomes less cost effective when the proportion of open questions increases, as there is often a high level of manual intervention to clean and code the responses. Scanning systems currently recognise and interpret numbers and hand-printed text, but are not yet capable of accurately recognising handwritten text. Some systems can be 'trained' to recognise an individual style of handwriting, but such a task is inappropriate for normal marketing research surveys, particularly if they are self-completion. For certain types of surveys, scanning is a great time saver. For others, the scanning, coding and cleaning are no faster than manually entering the data onto the computer.

Verification is the process of manually re-entering a proportion of the questionnaires to check the accuracy of data entry, and this facility is regularly used for paper-based surveys. Options are available to set a percentage level (perhaps 5–10%) and the programs then randomly select questionnaires to be re-entered. The programs also allow for validation checks between questions to be set up, completing a comprehensive error avoidance and checking ability, which in total means that the full array of data cleaning tasks can be performed.

Once the dataset has been created, checked and cleaned, SNAP and Keypoint2 allow statistical adjustment of the data through the creation of weights, scale transformation and the ability to create new variables or modify existing ones. Univariate and basic multivariate statistical analyses can be performed and presented in an array of styles of tables and graphs. Before questionnaires are sent out, the forms of analysis and the resulting tables and graphs as dummy tables can be designed and the instructions for these forms stored. This means that, as questionnaire responses start to build up in any survey format, a full set of tables and graphs as an interim analysis can be performed at any time by the researcher.

In essence, these packages perform the complete array of tasks faced by the marketing researcher, from designing a questionnaire and ensuring a sound dataset is built up to analysing the data and presenting the findings. There are limitations to the extent and array of multivariate statistical analyses that can be performed by these packages. However, they do allow for links to statistical analysis packages. For example, SNAP has the option to transform the files that describe the question and answer structure, and the raw data of a survey, into a fully labelled and coded SPSS SAV file, ready to perform any of the multivariate analysis tasks as detailed in Chapters 18–24. Alternatively, SNAP can both export and import triple s files (**www.triple-s.org**), a standard used by over 50 survey-related software companies worldwide to represent both the definitions of the survey and the associated data.

Summary

Data preparation begins with a preliminary check of all questionnaires for completeness and interviewing quality. Then more thorough editing takes place. Editing consists of screening questionnaires to identify illegible, incomplete, inconsistent or ambiguous responses. Such responses may be handled by returning questionnaires to the field, assigning missing values or discarding unsatisfactory respondents.

The next step is coding. A numeric or alphanumeric code is assigned to represent a specific response to a specific question along with the column position or field that code will occupy. It is often helpful to prepare a codebook containing the coding instructions and the necessary information about the variables in the dataset. The coded data are transcribed onto discs or magnetic tapes or entered directly into a data analysis package. Mark sense forms, optical scanning or computerised sensory analysis may also be used. Good survey desgin software packages completely automate the coding process.

Cleaning the data requires consistency checks and treatment of missing responses. Options available for treating missing responses include substitution of a neutral value such as a mean, substitution of an imputed response, casewise deletion and pairwise deletion. Statistical adjustments such as weighting, variable respecification and scale transformations often enhance the quality of data analysis. The selection of a data analysis strategy should be based on the earlier steps of the marketing research process, known characteristics of the data, properties of statistical techniques, and the background and philosophy of the researcher. Statistical techniques may be classified as univariate or multivariate.

Before analysing the data in international marketing research, the researcher should ensure that the units of measurement are comparable across countries or cultural units. The data analysis could be conducted at three levels: (1) individual, (2) within-country or cultural unit (intra-cultural analysis), and (3) across countries or cultural units (pancultural or cross-cultural analysis). Several ethical issues are related to data processing, particularly the discarding of unsatisfactory responses, violation of the assumptions underlying the data analysis techniques, and evaluation and interpretation of results.

Questions

1 Describe the data preparation process. Why is this process needed?

2 What activities are involved in the preliminary checking of questionnaires that have been returned from the field?

3 What is meant by editing a questionnaire?

4 How are unsatisfactory responses that are discovered in editing treated?

5 What is the difference between pre-coding and post-coding?

6 Describe the guidelines for the coding of unstructured questions.

7 What does transcribing the data involve?

8 What kinds of consistency checks are made in cleaning the data?

9 What options are available for the treatment of missing data?

10 What kinds of statistical adjustments are sometimes made to the data?

11 Describe the weighting process. What are the reasons for weighting?

12 What are dummy variables? Why are such variables created?

13 Explain why scale transformations are made.

14 Which scale transformation procedure is most commonly used? Briefly describe this procedure.

15 What considerations are involved in selecting a data analysis strategy?

Exercises

1 Using the SNAP software package that accompanies this text (you are able to design nine questions of your survey and administer these to up to 25 respondents), design a short questionnaire on any topic and write out five potential sets of responses to the questions you have set. Enter these responses using SNAP's full range of data entry methods. Write a report on the pros and cons of the different data entry methods and the error checks that are built into the software.

2 To a sample of five male and five female fellow students, pose the question 'Which of the following sports have you participated in over the last 12 months?' Create a list of what you think may be the top 10 sports that fellow students may have participated in, with space for 'Others – please specify'. After conducting the 10 interviews, how would you cope with the coding of the 'Others'? How would you rewrite this question and potential list of sports if you were to repeat the exercise?

3 You are the Marketing Research manager for AGA (**www.AGA.com**). AGA has developed a luxury refrigerator and matching freezer at €4,000 each. A European survey was conducted to determine consumer response to the proposed models. The data were obtained by conducting interviews at shopping malls in 10 European capital cites. Although the resulting sample of 2,500 is fairly representative on all other demographic variables, it under-represents the upper income households. The marketing research analyst who reports to you feels that weighting is not necessary. Discuss this question with the analyst (a student in your class).

4 You are the project manager for a data analysis firm. You are supervising the data preparation process for a large survey on personal hygiene issues. The data were collected via a postal survey and 1,823 questionnaires have been returned. The response rate was excellent, partially due to an excellent prize draw that accompanied the survey. However, you are suspicious about the quality of many responses and 290 questionnaires have missing responses. The data analyst preparing the data has not seen such a level of missing data and does not know how to cope with this survey. Explain to the data analyst how the missing responses and checks on the quality of data to be analysed should be performed.

5 In a small group discuss the following issues: 'Data processing is tedious, time consuming and costly; it should be circumvented whenever possible' and 'Conducting robust sampling is tedious, time consuming and costly; any structural problems in a sample can be simply resolved through weighting.'

Notes

1 Trembly, A.C., 'Poor data quality: A $600 billion issue', *National Underwriter* 106 (11) (18 March 18 2002), 48; Higgins, K.T., 'Never ending journey', *Marketing Management* 6 (1) (Spring 1997), 4–7; Harristhal, J., 'Interviewer tips', *Applied Marketing Research* 28 (Fall 1988), 42–45.

2 Keillor, B., Owens, D. and Pettijohn, C., 'A cross-cultural/cross-national study of influencing factors and socially desirable response biases', *International Jornal of Market Research* 43 (1) (First Quarter 2001), 63–84; Dadzie, K.Q., 'Demarketing strategy in shortage marketing environment', *Journal of the Academy of Marketing Science* (Spring 1989), 157–165. See also Nishisato, S., *Measurement and multivariate analysis* (New York: Springer-Verlag, 2002).

3 Jenkins, S., 'Automating questionnaire design and construction', *Journal of the Market Research Society* 42 (1) (Winter 1999–2000), 79–85; Fink, A., *How to analyze survey data* (Thousand Oaks, CA: Sage, 1995); Alreck, P.L. and Settle, R.B., *The Survey Research Handbook* (Homewood, IL: Irwin, 1985), 254–286; Sidel, P.S., 'Coding', in Ferber, R. (ed.), *Handbook of Marketing Research* (New York: McGraw-Hill, 1974), 2-178–2–199.

4 Kearney, I., 'Measuring consumer brand confusion to comply with legal guidelines', *International Journal of Market Research* 43 (1) (First Quarter 2001), 85–91; Luyens, S., 'Coding verbatims by computer', *Marketing Research: A Magazine of Management and Applications* 7(2) (Spring 1995), 20–25.

5 Studt, T., 'Exclusive survey reveals move to high-tech solutions', *Research & Development* 43 (3) (March 2001), 37–38; Frendberg, N., 'Scanning questionnaires efficiently', *Marketing Research: A Magazine of Management and Applications* 5 (2) (Spring 1993), 38–42.

6 Rydholm, J., 'Scanning the seas', *Marketing Research Review* (May 1993), www.princes.com (23 May 2002).

7 Cronk, B.C., *How to use SPSS: A step by step guide to analysis and interpretation* (Los Angeles, CA: Pyrczak, 2002); Aster, R., *Professional SAS programming shortcuts: Over 1000 ways to improve your SAS programs* (Phoenixville, PA: Breakfast Communications, 2002); Sincich, T., Levine, D.M., Stephan, D. and Berenson, M., *Practical statistics by example using Microsoft Excel and Minitab* (Paramus, NJ: Prentice Hall, 2002); Middleton, M.R., *Data analysis using Microsoft Excel: Updated for Office XP* (Pacific Grove, CA: Duxbury, 2002).

8 Allison, P.D., *Missing data* (Thousand Oaks, CA: Sage, 2001); Lee, B.-J., 'Sample selection bias correction for missing response observations', *Oxford Bulletin of Economics and Statistics* 62 (2) (May 2000), 305; Freedman, V.A. and Wolf, D.A., 'A case study on the use of multiple imputation', *Demography* 32 (3) (August 1995), 459–470; Malhotra, N.K., 'Analysing marketing research data with incomplete information on the dependent variable', *Journal of Marketing Research* 24 (February 1987), 74–84.

9 A meaningful and practical value should be imputed. The value imputed should be a legitimate response code. For example, a mean of 3.86 may not be practical if only single-digit response codes have been developed. In such cases, the mean should be rounded to the nearest integer.

10 Murphy, K.M., 'Estimation and inference in two-step econometric models', *Journal of Business & Economic Statistics* 20 (1) (January 2002), 88–97; Kara, A., Nielsen, C., Sahay, S. and Sivasubramaniam, N., 'Latent information in the pattern of missing observations in global mail surveys', *Journal of Global Marketing* 7 (4) (1994), 103–126.

11 Some weighting procedures require adjustments in subsequent data analysis techniques. See Batholomew, D.J., *The analysis and interpretation of multivariate data for social scientists* (Boca Raton, FL: CRC Press, 2002); Yaniv, L., 'Weighting and trimming: heuristics for aggregating judgments under uncertainty', *Organizational Behaviour & Human Decision Processes* 69 (3) (March 1997), 237–249; Taylor, H., 'The very different methods used to conduct telephone surveys of the public', *Journal of the Market Research Society* 39 (3) (July 1997), 421–432.

12 Bradford, M., 'Health care access services for expats gain in popularity', *Business Insurance* 36 (1) (7 January 2002), 19–20; Woodside, A.G., Nielsen, R.L., Walters, F. and Muller, G.D., 'Preference segmentation of health care services: the old-fashioneds, value conscious, affluents, and professional want-it-alls', *Journal of Health Care Marketing* (June 1988), 14–24. See also Jayanti, R., 'Affective responses toward service providers: implications for service encounters', *Health Marketing Quarterly* 14 (1) (1996), 49–65.

13 See Johnson, R.A. and Wichern, D.W., *Applied Multivariate Statistical Analysis* (Paramus, NJ: Prentice Hall, 2001); Swift, B., 'Preparing numerical data', in Sapsford, R. and Jupp, V. (eds), *Data Collection and Analysis* (Thousand Oaks, CA: Sage, 1996); Frank, R.E., 'Use of transformations', *Journal of Marketing Research* 3 (August 1966), 247–253, for specific transformations frequently used in marketing research.

14 Vesset, D., 'Trends in the market for analytic applications', *KM World* 11 (4) (April 2002), 14. For a similar data analysis strategy, see Malhotra, N.K., 'Modelling store choice based on censored preference data', *Journal of Retailing* (Summer 1986), 128–144; Birks, D.F. and Birts, A.N., 'Service quality in domestic banks', in Birks, D.F. (ed.), *Global Cash Management in Europe* (Basingstoke: Macmillan, 1998), 175–205.

15 Bivariate techniques have been included here with multivariate techniques. Although bivariate techniques are concerned with pairwise relationships, multivariate techniques examine more complex simultaneous relationships among phenomena. See Tacq, J., *Multivariate Analysis Techniques in Social Science Research Analysis* (Thousand Oaks, CA: Sage ,1996).

16 DeSarbo, W.S., 'The joint spatial representation of multiple variable batteries collected in marketing research', *Journal of Marketing Research* 38 (2) (May 2001), 244–253; Carroll, J.D. and Green, P.E., 'Psychometric methods in marketing research: Part ii: Multidimensional scaling', *Journal of Marketing Research* 34 (2) (May 1997), 193–204.

17 Anon., 'For a scoop of their own', *Businessline* (17 January 2002), 1; Kilburn, D., 'Häagen-Dazs is flavor of month', *Marketing Week* 20 (23) (4 September 1997), 30; Maremont, M., 'They're all screaming for Häagen-Dazs', *Business Week* (14 October 1991).

18 McDonald, G., 'Cross-cultural methodological issues in ethical research', *Journal of Business Ethics* 27 (1/2) (September 2000), 89–104; Alasuutari, P., *Researching Culture* (Thousand Oaks, CA: Sage, 1995); Tan, C.T., McCullough, J. and Teoh, J., 'An individual analysis approach to cross-cultural research', in Wallendorf, M. and Anderson, P. (eds), *Advances in Consumer Research* 14 (Provo, UT: Association for Consumer Research, 1987), 394–397.

19 See, for example, Tian, R.G., 'Cross-cultural issues in Internet marketing', *Journal of American Academy of Business* 1 (2) (March 2002) 217–224; Spiller, L.D. and Campbell, A.J., 'The use of international direct marketing by small businesses in Canada, Mexico, and the United States: a comparative analysis', *Journal of Direct Marketing* 8 (Winter 1994), 7–16; Nyaw, M.K. and Ng, I., 'A comparative analysis of ethical beliefs: a four country study', *Journal of Business Ethics* 13 (July 1994), 543–556.

20 Newman, D.L. and Brown, R.D., *Applied Ethics for Program Evaluation Analysis* (Thousand Oaks, CA: Sage, 1996); Zinkhan, G.M., Bisesi, M. and Saxton, M.J., 'MBAs' changing attitudes toward marketing dilemmas: 1981–1987', *Journal of Business Ethics* 8 (1989), 963–974.

21 Anon, 'How Walcheren hospital perked up their patients', *Research in Business* (March 2004), 15.

Source: © Getty Images

18

Frequency distribution, cross-tabulation and hypothesis testing

> *Frequency distribution, cross-tabulation and hypothesis testing are the fundamental building blocks of quantitative data analysis. They provide insights into the data, guide subsequent analyses and aid the interpretation of results.*

Objectives

After reading this chapter, you should be able to:

1 describe the significance of preliminary data analysis and the insights that can be obtained from such an analysis;

2 discuss data analysis associated with frequencies, including measures of location, measures of variability and measures of shape;

3 explain data analysis associated with cross-tabulations and the associated statistics: chi-square, phi coefficient, contingency coefficient, Cramer's *V* and lambda coefficient;

4 describe data analysis associated with parametric hypothesis testing for one sample, two independent samples and paired samples;

5 understand data analysis associated with non-parametric hypothesis testing for one sample, two independent samples and paired samples.

STAGE 1
Problem definition

STAGE 2
Research approach developed

STAGE 3
Research design developed

STAGE 4
Fieldwork or data collection

STAGE 5
Data preparation and analysis

STAGE 6
Report preparation and presentation

Overview

Once the data have been prepared for analysis (Chapter 17), the researcher should conduct basic analyses. This chapter describes basic data analyses, including frequency distribution, cross-tabulation and hypothesis testing. First, we describe the frequency distribution and explain how it provides both an indication of the number of out-of-range, missing or extreme values as well as insights into the central tendency, variability and shape of the underlying distribution. Next, we introduce hypothesis testing by describing the general procedure. Hypothesis testing procedures are classified as tests of associations or tests of differences. We consider the use of cross-tabulation for understanding the associations between variables taken two or three at a time. Although the nature of the association can be observed from tables, statistics are available for examining the significance and strength of the association. Finally, we present tests for examining hypotheses related to differences based on one or two samples.

Many marketing research projects do not go beyond basic data analysis. These findings are often displayed using tables and graphs, as discussed further in Chapter 25. Although the findings of basic analysis are valuable in their own right, they also provide guidance for conducting multivariate analysis. The insights gained from the basic analysis are also invaluable in interpreting the results obtained from more sophisticated statistical techniques. The following examples provide a 'flavour' of basic data analysis techniques. We illustrate the use of cross-tabulation, chi-square analysis and hypothesis testing.

 Focus on

Sports Marketing Surveys

Basic data analyses

In the Formula One Racetrack Project, basic data analysis formed the foundation for conducting subsequent multivariate analysis. Data analysis began by obtaining a frequency distribution and descriptive statistics for each variable or question asked in the survey. In addition to identifying possible problems with the data, this information provided a good idea of the data and insights into how specific variables should be treated in subsequent analyses. For example, should the interval scaled variable 'number of Grand Prix races watched on television' be treated as categorical? If so, how many categories should there be? (See the following example.) Several two- and three-variable cross-tabulations were also conducted to identify associations in the data. The effects of variables with two categories on the metric-dependent variables of interest were examined by means of t tests and other hypothesis testing procedures.

Focus on

Sports Marketing surveys

Formula One viewing habits

Formula One fans watched an average of 6.2 races during the 2003 season, a slight increase on 2002 (5.8). This was seen as good news after the impact of Michael Schumacher's runaway victory in 2002. The following table focuses upon the viewing habits of male and female respondents. The first question tackled was 'Out of the 16 Formula One Grands Prix held in the 2003 season, how many have you watched on television?' Sports Marketing Surveys used the question to create three different viewing groups:

- **Occasional** = watched 4 or less Grands Prix
- **Regular** = watched between 5 and 9 Grands Prix
- **Avid** = watched 10 or more Grand Prixs.

The responses to this question were broken down into male and female respondents. Cross-tabulation and chi-square analysis provided the following:

Formula One races watched on TV	Respondent gender (%)	
	Male	Female
Occasional	59	74
Regular	6	7
Avid	35	19
	$\chi^2 = 6.51$	$p \leqslant 0.05$

These results indicate that there is little difference in male and female viewers in terms of regular viewing of Formula One races. However, there is a much higher proportion of men that are avid viewers.

Example Catalogues are risky business[1]

Twelve product categories were examined to compare shopping by catalogue with store shopping. The hypothesis that there is no significant difference in the overall amount of risk perceived when buying products by catalogue compared with buying the same products in a retail store was rejected. The hypothesis was tested by computing 12 paired observation *t* tests, one for each product. Mean scores for overall perceived risk for some of the products in both buying situations are presented in the following table, with higher scores indicating greater risk.

Product	Overall perceived risk	
	Catalogue	Store
Shoes	58.60	50.80*
Pocket calculator	49.62	42.00*
Hi-fi	48.89	41.98*
Portable television	48.53	40.91*
Digital camera	48.13	39.52*
Athletic socks	35.22	30.22*
Perfume	34.85	29.79*
CDs	32.65	28.74*

* Significant at 0.01 level

As can be seen, a significantly ($p < 0.01$) higher overall amount of perceived risk was attached to products purchased by catalogue as compared with those purchased from a retail store.

The first Sports Marketing Surveys example illustrates the role of basic data analysis used in conjunction with multivariate procedures, whereas the other two examples show how such analysis can be useful in its own right. The cross-tabulation and chi-square analysis in the Formula One Racetrack example and the paired *t* tests in the catalogue shopping example enabled us to draw specific conclusions from the data. These and other concepts discussed in this chapter are illustrated in the context of explaining Internet usage for personal (non-professional) reasons. Table 18.1 contains data for 30 respondents giving the gender (1 = male, 2 = female), familiarity with the Internet (1 = very unfamiliar, 7 = very familiar), Internet usage in hours per week, attitude towards the Internet and towards technology, both measured on a seven-point scale (1 = very unfavourable, 7 = very favourable), and whether the respondents have done shopping or banking on the Internet (1 = yes, 2 = no). As a first step in the analysis, it is useful to examine the frequency distributions of the relevant variables.

Table 18.1 Internet usage data

Respondent No.	Gender	Familiarity	Internet usage	Attitude towards Internet	Attitude towards technology	Usage of Internet shopping	Usage of Internet banking
1	1	7	14	7	6	1	1
2	2	2	2	3	3	2	2
3	2	3	3	4	3	1	2
4	2	3	3	7	5	1	2
5	1	7	13	7	7	1	1
6	2	4	6	5	4	1	2
7	2	2	2	4	5	2	2
8	2	3	6	5	4	2	2
9	2	3	6	6	4	1	2
10	1	9	15	7	6	1	2
11	2	4	3	4	3	2	2
12	2	5	4	6	4	2	2
13	1	6	9	6	5	2	1
14	1	6	8	3	2	2	2
15	1	6	5	5	4	1	2
16	2	4	3	4	3	2	2
17	1	6	9	5	3	1	1
18	1	4	4	5	4	1	2
19	1	7	14	6	6	1	1
20	2	6	6	6	4	2	2
21	1	6	9	4	2	2	2
22	1	5	5	5	4	2	1
23	2	3	2	4	2	2	2
24	1	7	15	6	6	1	1
25	2	6	6	5	3	1	2
26	1	6	13	6	6	1	1
27	2	5	4	5	5	1	1
28	2	4	2	3	2	2	2
29	1	4	4	5	3	1	2
30	1	3	3	7	5	1	2

Frequency distribution

Marketing researchers often need to answer questions about a single variable. For example:

- How many users of the brand may be characterised as brand loyal?
- What percentage of the market consists of heavy users, medium users, light users and non-users?
- How many customers are very familiar with a new product offering? How many are familiar, somewhat familiar, or unfamiliar with the brand? What is the mean familiarity rating? Is there much variance in the extent to which customers are familiar with the new product?
- What is the income distribution of brand users? Is this distribution skewed towards low-income brackets?

Frequency distribution
A mathematical distribution whose objective is to obtain a count of the number of responses associated with different values of one variable and to express these counts in percentage terms.

The answers to these kinds of questions can be determined by examining **frequency distributions**. In a frequency distribution, one variable is considered at a time.

The objective is to obtain a count of the number of responses associated with different values of the variable. The relative occurrence, or frequency, of different values of the variable is expressed in percentages. A frequency distribution for a variable produces a table of frequency counts, percentages and cumulative percentages for all the values associated with that variable.

Table 18.2 gives the frequency distribution of familiarity with the Internet. In the table, the first column contains the labels assigned to the different categories of the variable and the second column indicates the codes assigned to each value. Note that a code of 9 has been assigned to missing values. The third column gives the number of respondents ticking each value. For example, three respondents ticked value 5, indicating that they were somewhat familiar with the Internet. The fourth column displays the percentage of respondents ticking each value.

The fifth column shows percentages calculated by excluding the cases with missing values. If there are no missing values, the fourth and fifth columns are identical. The last column represents cumulative percentages after adjusting for missing values. As can be seen, of the 30 respondents who participated in the survey, 10% entered a figure of '5'. If the one respondent with a missing value is excluded, this changes to 10.3%. The cumulative percentage corresponding to the value of 5 is 58.6. In other words, 58.6% of the respondents with valid responses indicated a familiarity value of 5 or less.

Table 18.2 Frequency distribution of 'Familiarity with the Internet'

Value label	Value	Frequency (N)	Percentage	Valid percentage	Cumulative percentage
Very unfamiliar	1	0	0.0	0.0	0.0
	2	2	6.7	6.9	6.9
	3	6	20.0	20.7	27.6
	4	6	20.0	20.7	48.3
	5	3	10.0	10.3	58.6
	6	8	26.7	27.6	86.2
Very familiar	7	4	13.3	13.8	100.0
Missing	9	1	3.3		
Total		30	100.0	100.0	

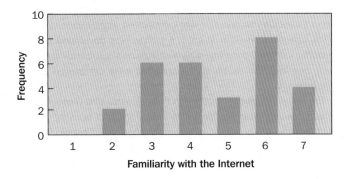

Figure 18.1
Frequency histogram

A frequency distribution helps determine the extent of item non-response (1 respondent out of 30 in Table 18.1). It also indicates the extent of illegitimate responses. Values of 0 and 8 would be illegitimate responses, or errors. The cases with these values could be identified and corrective action could be taken. The presence of outliers or cases with extreme values can also be detected. For example, in the case of a frequency distribution of household size, a few isolated families with household sizes of nine or more might be considered outliers. A frequency distribution also indicates the shape of the empirical distribution of the variable. The frequency data may be used to construct a histogram, or a vertical bar chart in which the values of the variable are portrayed along the x axis and the absolute or relative frequencies of the values are placed along the y axis.

Figure 18.1 is a histogram of the frequency data in Table 18.1. From the histogram, one could examine whether the observed distribution is consistent with an expected or assumed distribution.

Example

Basic analysis yields Olympic results[2]

For the 1996 Olympic Games in Atlanta, more than 2 million unique visitors came to the games and more than 11 million tickets were sold. Researchers at the University of

Motivational factors that influenced the decision to attend the Olympic Games

Motivational factor	Frequency	Percentage
Once-in-a-lifetime opportunity	95	29.7
Availability of housing	36	11.2
Availability of tickets	27	8.4
Distance away from home	24	7.5
Business/employment	17	5.3
Availability of money – overall expenses	17	5.3
Availability of time	12	3.8
Personal relationship with participant or official	8	2.5
Other motivational factor	8	2.5
Visit Atlanta	4	1.3
Security	3	0.9
Did not respond	69	21.6
Total	320	100.0

Colorado decided to discover what motivated international and domestic travellers to come to the Olympic Games in Atlanta. A survey was developed and administered to visitors via personal interviews during a nine-day period surrounding the completion of the games. Three hundred and twenty questionnaires were completed correctly and were used in the data analysis.

The results showed that the top three factors that motivated people to attend the games were: 'once-in-a-lifetime opportunity', 'availability of housing' and 'availability of tickets'. The results of this study helped planners for the 2000 Olympic Games in Sydney find what specific characteristics the city needed to improve. For instance, Sydney put funds into projects that added hotel rooms to the city. Sydney also constructed state-of-the-art transportation (a new elevated rail system) and unique venues (Olympic Park) so that visitors truly felt they were getting a once-in-a-lifetime experience. As this survey evolved over the years the findings have a cumulative effect in supporting future host cities.

Note that the numbers and percentages in the preceding example indicate the extent of the various motivational factors that attract individuals to the Olympic Games. Because numbers are involved, a frequency distribution can be used to calculate descriptive or cumulative statistics.

Statistics associated with frequency distribution

As illustrated in the previous section, a frequency distribution is a convenient way of looking at different values of a variable. A frequency table is easy to read and provides basic information, but sometimes this information may be too detailed and the researcher must summarise it by the use of descriptive statistics.[3] The most commonly used statistics associated with frequencies are measures of location (mean, mode and median), measures of variability (range, interquartile range, variance, standard deviation and coefficient of variation) and measures of shape (skewness and kurtosis).[4]

Measures of location

Measure of location
A statistic that describes a location within a dataset. Measures of central tendency describe the centre of the distribution.

The **measures of location** that we discuss are measures of central tendency because they tend to describe the centre of the distribution. If the entire sample is changed by adding a fixed constant to each observation, then the mean, mode and median change by the same fixed amount.

Mean
The average; that value obtained by summing all elements in a set and dividing by the number of elements.

Mean. The **mean**, or average value, is the most commonly used measure of central tendency. The measure is used to estimate the mean when the data have been collected using an interval or ratio scale. The data should display some central tendency, with most of the responses distributed around the mean.

The mean, $\bar{X}$, is given by

$$\bar{X} = \frac{\sum_{i=1}^{n} X^i}{n}$$

where

X_i = observed values of the variable X
n = number of observations (sample size).

Generally, the mean is a robust measure and does not change markedly as data values are added or deleted. For the frequencies given in Table 18.1, the mean value is calculated as follows:

$$\bar{X} = (2 \times 2) + (6 \times 3) + (6 \times 4) + (3 \times 5) + (8 \times 6) + (4 \times 7)/29$$
$$= (4 + 18 + 24 + 15 + 48 + 28)/29$$
$$= 137/29$$
$$= 4.724$$

Mode
A measure of central tendency given as the value that occurs with the most frequency in a sample distribution.

Median
A measure of central tendency given as the value above which half of the values fall and below which half of the values fall.

Mode. The **mode** is the value that occurs most frequently. It represents the highest peak of the distribution. The mode is a good measure of location when the variable is inherently categorical or has otherwise been grouped into categories. The mode in Table 18.2 is 6.

Median. The **median** of a sample is the middle value when the data are arranged in ascending or descending order. If the number of data points is even, the median is usually estimated as the midpoint between the two middle values by adding the two middle values and dividing their sum by 2. The median is the 50th percentile. The median is an appropriate measure of central tendency for ordinal data. In Table 18.2, the middle value is 5, so the median is 5.

As can be seen from Table 18.1, the three measures of central tendency for this distribution are different (mean = 4.724, mode = 6, median = 5). This is not surprising, since each measure defines central tendency in a different way. So which measure should be used? If the variable is measured on a nominal scale, the mode should be used. If the variable is measured on an ordinal scale, the median is appropriate. If the variable is measured on an interval or ratio scale, the mode is a poor measure of central tendency. This can be seen from Table 18.2. Although the modal value of 6 has the highest frequency, it represents only 27.6% of the sample. In general, for interval or ratio data, the median is a better measure of central tendency, although it too ignores available information about the variable. The actual values of the variable above and below the median are ignored. The mean is the most appropriate measure of central tendency for interval or ratio data. The mean makes use of all the information available since all of the values are used in computing it. However, it is sensitive to extremely small or extremely large values (outliers). When there are outliers in the data, the mean is not a good measure of central tendency, and it is useful to consider both the mean and the median.

Measures of variability

Measure of variability
A statistic that indicates the distribution's dispersion.

Range
The difference between the smallest and largest values of a distribution.

The **measures of variability**, which are calculated on interval or ratio data, include the range, interquartile range, variance or standard deviation and coefficient of variation.

Range. The **range** measures the spread of the data. It is simply the difference between the largest and smallest values in the sample:

$$range = X_{largest} - X_{smallest}$$

As such, the range is directly affected by outliers. If all the values in the data are multiplied by a constant, the range is multiplied by the same constant. The range in Table 18.2 is $7 - 2 = 5$.

Interquartile range
The range of a distribution encompassing the middle 50% of the observations.

Interquartile range. The **interquartile range** is the difference between the 75th and 25th percentiles. For a set of data points arranged in order of magnitude, the pth percentile is the value that has $p\%$ of the data points below it and $(100 - p)\%$ above it. If all the data points are multiplied by a constant, the interquartile range is multiplied by the same constant. The interquartile range in Table 18.2 is $6 - 3 = 3$.

Variance
The mean squared deviation of all the values of the mean.

Variance. The difference between the mean and an observed value is called the deviation from the mean. The **variance** is the mean squared deviation from the mean. The variance can never be negative. When the data points are clustered around the mean, the variance

509

is small. When the data points are scattered, the variance is large. If all the data values are multiplied by a constant, the variance is multiplied by the square of the constant.

Standard deviation
The square root of the variance.

Standard deviation. The **standard deviation** is the square root of the variance. Thus, the standard deviation is expressed in the same units as the data, rather than in squared units. The standard deviation of a sample, s is calculated as

$$s = \sqrt{\sum_{i=1}^{n} \frac{(X_i - \bar{X})^2}{n-1}}$$

We divide by $n - 1$ instead of n because the sample is drawn from a population and we are trying to determine how much the responses vary from the mean of the entire population. The population mean is unknown, however; therefore, the sample mean is used instead. The use of the sample mean makes the sample seem less variable than it really is. By dividing by $n - 1$ instead of by n, we compensate for the smaller variability observed in the sample. For the data given in Table 18.1, the variance is calculated as follows:

$$
\begin{aligned}
S^2 &= [2 \times (2 - 4.724)^2 + 6 \times (3 - 4.724)^2 + 6 \times (4 - 4.724)^2 + 3 \times (5 - 4.724)^2 \\
&\quad + 8 \times (6 - 4.724)^2 + 4 \times (7 - 4.724)^2]/ 28 \\
&= [14.840 + 17.833 + 3.145 + 0.229 + 13.025 + 20.721]/28 \\
&= 69.793/28 \\
&= 2.493
\end{aligned}
$$

The standard deviation, therefore, is calculated as

$$
\begin{aligned}
S &= \sqrt{2.493} \\
&= 1.579
\end{aligned}
$$

Coefficient of variation
A useful expression in sampling theory for the standard deviation as a percentage of the mean.

Coefficient of variation. The **coefficient of variation** is the ratio of the standard deviation to the mean expressed as a percentage, and it is a unitless measure of relative variability. The coefficient of variation, CV, is expressed as

$$CV = \frac{S}{\bar{X}}$$

The coefficient of variation is meaningful only if the variable is measured on a ratio scale. It remains unchanged if all the data values are multiplied by a constant. Because familiarity with the Internet is not measured on a ratio scale, it is not meaningful to calculate the coefficient of variation for the data in Table 18.2.

Measures of shape

In addition to measures of variability, measures of shape are also useful in understanding the nature of the distribution. The shape of a distribution is assessed by examining skewness and kurtosis.

Skewness
A characteristic of a distribution that assesses its symmetry about the mean.

Skewness. Distributions can be either symmetric or skewed. In a symmetric distribution, the values on either side of the centre of the distribution are the same, and the mean, mode and median are equal. The positive and corresponding negative deviations from the mean are also equal. In a skewed distribution, the positive and negative deviations from the mean are unequal. **Skewness** is the tendency of the deviations from the mean to be larger in one direction than in the other. It can be thought of as the tendency for one tail of the distribution to be heavier than the other (see Figure 18.2). The skewness value for the data of Table 18.1 is −0.094, indicating a slight negative skew.

Kurtosis. **Kurtosis** is a measure of the relative peakedness or flatness of the curve defined by the frequency distribution. The kurtosis of a normal distribution is zero. If the kurtosis is positive, then the distribution is more peaked than a normal distribution. A negative value means that the distribution is flatter than a normal distribution. The value of this statistic for Table 18.2 is −1.261, indicating that the distribution is flatter than a normal distribution.

A general procedure for hypothesis testing

Basic analysis invariably involves some hypothesis testing. Examples of hypotheses generated in marketing research abound:

- A cinema is being patronised by more than 10% of the households in a city.
- The heavy and light users of a brand differ in terms of psychographic characteristics.
- One hotel has a more 'luxurious' image than its close competitor.
- Familiarity with a restaurant results in greater preference for that restaurant.

Chapter 15 covered the concepts of the sampling distribution, standard error of the mean or the proportion, and the confidence interval.[5] All these concepts are relevant to hypothesis testing and should be reviewed. We now describe a general procedure for hypothesis testing that can be applied to test hypotheses about a wide range of parameters. The following steps are involved in hypothesis testing (Figure 18.3).

1 Formulate the null hypothesis H_0 and the alternative hypothesis H_1.
2 Select an appropriate statistical technique and the corresponding test statistic.
3 Choose the level of significance, α.
4 Determine the sample size and collect the data. Calculate the value of the test statistic.
5 Determine the probability associated with the test statistic under the null hypothesis, using the sampling distribution of the test statistic. Alternatively, determine the critical values associated with the test statistic that divide the rejection and non-rejection region.
6 Compare the probability associated with the test statistic with the level of significance specified. Alternatively, determine whether the test statistic has fallen into the rejection or the non-rejection region.
7 Make the statistical decision to reject or not reject the null hypothesis.
8 Express the statistical decision in terms of the marketing research problem.

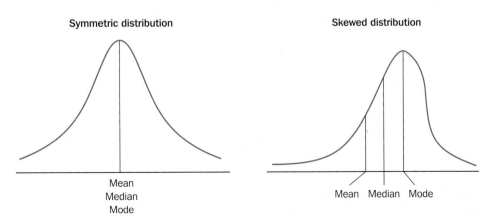

Figure 18.2
Skewness of a distribution

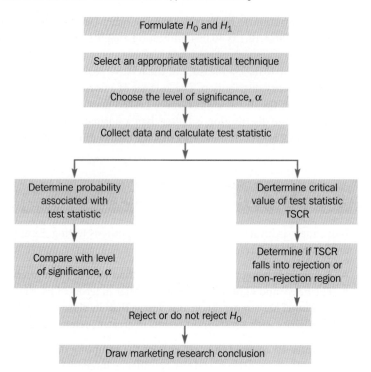

Figure 18.3
A general procedure
for hypothesis testing

Step 1: Formulate the hypothesis

Null hypothesis
A statement in which no difference or effect is expected. If the null hypothesis is not rejected, no changes will be made.

Alternative hypothesis
A statement that some difference or effect is expected. Accepting the alternative hypothesis will lead to changes in opinions or actions.

The first step is to formulate the null and alternative hypotheses. A **null hypothesis** is a statement of the status quo, one of no difference or no effect. If the null hypothesis is not rejected, no changes will be made. An **alternative hypothesis** is one in which some difference or effect is expected. Accepting the alternative hypothesis will lead to changes in opinions or actions. Thus, the alternative hypothesis is the opposite of the null hypothesis.

The null hypothesis is always the hypothesis that is tested. The null hypothesis refers to a specified value of the population parameter (e.g. μ, σ, π), not a sample statistic (e.g. $\bar{X}$). A null hypothesis may be rejected, but it can never be accepted based on a single test. A statistical test can have one of two outcomes: that the null hypothesis is rejected and the alternative hypothesis accepted, or that the null hypothesis is not rejected based on the evidence. It would be incorrect, however, to conclude that since the null hypothesis is not rejected, it can be accepted as valid. In classical hypothesis testing, there is no way to determine whether the null hypothesis is true.

In marketing research, the null hypothesis is formulated in such a way that its rejection leads to the acceptance of the desired conclusion. The alternative hypothesis represents the conclusion for which evidence is sought. For example, a Formula One sponsor is considering introducing an Internet shopping service. Given the investment in systems and personnel to make this plan work, it will only be introduced if more than 40% of Internet users shop via the Internet. The appropriate way to formulate the hypotheses is

$$H_0:\ \pi \leq 0.40$$
$$H_1:\ \pi > 0.40$$

One-tailed test
A test of the null hypothesis where the alternative hypothesis is expressed directionally.

If the null hypothesis H_0 is rejected, then the alternative hypothesis H_1 will be accepted and the new Internet shopping service introduced. On the other hand, if H_0 is not rejected, then the new Internet shopping service should not be introduced unless additional evidence is obtained. The test of the null hypothesis is a **one-tailed test** because the alternative hypothesis is expressed directionally: the proportion of customers who express a preference is greater than 0.40.

On the other hand, suppose that the researcher wanted to determine whether the proportion of Internet users who shop via the Internet is different than 40%. Then a **two-tailed test** would be required, and the hypotheses would be expressed as

$$H_0: \pi = 0.40$$

$$H_1: \pi \neq 0.40$$

In commercial marketing research, the one-tailed test is used more often than a two-tailed test. Typically, there is some preferred direction for the conclusion for which evidence is sought. For example, the higher the profits, sales and product quality, the better. The one-tailed test is more powerful than the two-tailed test. The power of a statistical test is discussed further in step 3.

Step 2: Select an appropriate statistical technique

To test the null hypothesis, it is necessary to select an appropriate statistical technique. The researcher should take into consideration how the **test statistic** is computed and the sampling distribution that the sample statistic (e.g. the mean) follows. The test statistic measures how close the sample has come to the null hypothesis. The test statistic often follows a well-known distribution, such as the normal, t, or chi-square distribution. Guidelines for selecting an appropriate test or statistical technique are discussed later in this chapter. In our example, the z statistic, which follows the standard normal distribution, would be appropriate. This statistic would be computed as follows:

$$z = \frac{p - \pi}{\sigma_p} \text{ where } \sigma_p = \sqrt{\frac{\pi(1 - \pi)}{n}}$$

Step 3: Choose the level of significance

Whenever we draw inferences about a population, there is a risk that an incorrect conclusion will be reached. Two types of error can occur.

Type I error occurs when the sample results lead to the rejection of the null hypothesis when it is in fact true. In our example, a Type I error would occur if we concluded, based on sample data, that the proportion of customers preferring the new service plan was greater than 0.40, when in fact it was less than or equal to 0.40. The probability of Type I error (α) is also called the **level of significance**. The Type I error is controlled by establishing the tolerable level of risk of rejecting a true null hypothesis. The selection of a particular risk level should depend on the cost of making a Type I error.

Type II error occurs when, based on the sample results, the null hypothesis is not rejected when it is in fact false. In our example, the Type II error would occur if we concluded, based on sample data, that the proportion of customers preferring the new service plan was less than or equal to 0.40 when in fact it was greater than 0.40. The probability of Type II error is denoted by β. Unlike α, which is specified by the researcher, the magnitude of β depends on the actual value of the population parameter (proportion). The probability of Type I error (α) and the probability of Type II error (β) are shown in Figure 18.4.

The complement $(1 - \beta)$ of the probability of a Type II error is called the **power of a statistical test**. The power of a test is the probability $(1 - \beta)$ of rejecting the null hypothesis when it is false and should be rejected. Although β is unknown, it is related to α. An extremely low value of α (e.g. 0.001) will result in intolerably high β errors. So it is necessary to balance the two types of errors. As a compromise, α is often set at 0.05; sometimes it is 0.01; other values of α are rare. The level of along with the sample size will determine the level of for a particular research design. The risk of both α and β can be controlled by increasing the sample size. For a given level of α, increasing the sample size will decrease β, thereby increasing the power of the test.

Two-tailed test
A test of the null hypothesis where the alternative hypothesis is not expressed directionally.

Test statistic
A measure of how close the sample has come to the null hypothesis. It often follows a well-known distribution, such as the normal, t, or chi-square distribution.

Type I error
An error that occurs when the sample results lead to the rejection of a null hypothesis that is in fact true. Also called alpha error (α)

Level of significance
The probability of making a Type I error.

Type II error
An error that occurs when the sample results lead to acceptance of a null hypothesis that is in fact false. Also called beta error (β).

Power of a statistical test
The probability of rejecting the null hypothesis when it is in fact false and should be rejected.

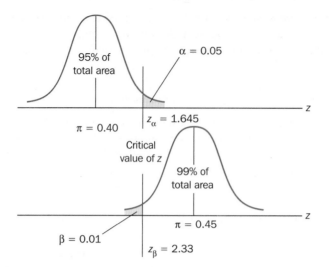

Figure 18.4
Type I error (α) and
Type II error (β)

Step 4: Collect the data and calculate the test statistic

Sample size is determined after taking into account the desired a and β errors and other qualitative considerations, such as budget constraints. Then the required data are collected and the value of the test statistic is computed. In our example, 30 users were surveyed and 17 indicated that they used the Internet for shopping. Thus the value of the sample proportion is $p = 17/30 = 0.567$. The value of σ_p can be determined as follows:

$$\sigma_p = \sqrt{\pi(1-\pi)/n}$$
$$= \sqrt{0.4 \times 0.6/30}$$
$$= 0.089$$

The test statistic z can be calculated as follows:

$$z = p - \pi/\sigma_p$$
$$= 0.567 - 0.40/0.089$$
$$= 1.88$$

Step 5: Determine the probability or the critical value

Using standard normal tables (Table 2 of the Appendix of statistical tables), the probability of obtaining a z value of 1.88 can be calculated (see Figure 18.5). The shaded area between $-\infty$ and 1.88 is 0.96. Therefore, the area to the right of $z = 1.88$ is $1.0000 - 0.9699 = 0.03$.

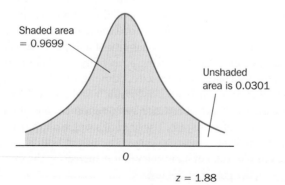

Figure 18.5
Probability of z with a
one-tailed test

Alternatively, the critical value of z, which will give an area to the right side of the critical value of 0.05, is between 1.64 and 1.65 and equals 1.645. Note that, in determining the critical value of the test statistic, the area to the right of the critical value is either α or $\alpha/2$. It is α for a one-tailed test and $\alpha/2$ for a two-tailed test.

Steps 6 and 7: Compare the probability or critical values and make the decision

The probability associated with the calculated or observed value of the test statistic is 0.0301. This is the probability of getting a p value of 0.567 when $\pi = 0.40$. This is less than the level of significance of 0.05. Hence, the null hypothesis is rejected. Alternatively, the calculated value of the test statistic $z = 1.88$ lies in the rejection region, beyond the value of 1.645. Again, the same conclusion to reject the null hypothesis is reached. Note that the two ways of testing the null hypothesis are equivalent but mathematically opposite in the direction of comparison. If the probability associated with the calculated or observed value of the test statistic (TS_{CAL}) is less than the level of significance (α), the null hypothesis is rejected. If the calculated value of the test statistic is greater than the critical value of the test statistic (TS_{CR}), however, the null hypothesis is rejected. The reason for this sign shift is that the larger the value of TS_{CAL}, the smaller the probability of obtaining a more extreme value of the test statistic under the null hypothesis. This sign shift can be easily seen:

$$\text{if probability of } \text{TS}_{\text{CAL}} < \text{significance level } (\alpha), \text{ then reject } H_0$$

but

$$\text{if } \text{TS}_{\text{CAL}} > \text{TS}_{\text{CR}}, \text{ then reject } H_0$$

Step 8: Draw the marketing research conclusion

The conclusion reached by hypothesis testing must be expressed in terms of the marketing research problem. In our example, we conclude that there is evidence that the proportion of Internet users who shop via the Internet is significantly greater than 0.40. Hence, the recommendation would be to introduce the new Internet shopping service.

As can be seen from Figure 18.6, hypothesis testing can be related to either an examination of associations or an examination of differences. In tests of associations the null hypothesis is that there is no association between the variables (H_0: ... is *not* related to ...). In tests of differences the null hypothesis is that there is no difference (H_0: ... is *not* different than ...). Tests of differences could relate to distributions, means, proportions, or medians or rankings. First, we discuss hypotheses related to associations in the context of cross-tabulations.

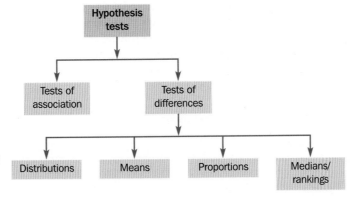

Figure 18.6
A broad classification of hypothesis testing procedures

Cross-tabulations

Although answers to questions related to a single variable are interesting, they often raise additional questions about how to link that variable to other variables. To introduce the frequency distribution, we posed several representative marketing research questions. For each of these, a researcher might pose additional questions to relate these variables to other variables. For example:

- How many brand-loyal users are males?
- Is product use (measured in terms of heavy users, medium users, light users and non-users) related to interest in outdoor leisure activities (high, medium and low)?
- Is familiarity with a new product related to age and income levels?
- Is product ownership related to income (high, medium and low)?

Cross-tabulation
A statistical technique that describes two or more variables simultaneously and results in tables that reflect the joint distribution of two or more variables that have a limited number of categories or distinct values.

The answers to such questions can be determined by examining **cross-tabulations**. A frequency distribution describes one variable at a time, but a cross-tabulation describes two or more variables simultaneously. Cross-tabulation results in tables that reflect the joint distribution of two or more variables with a limited number of categories or distinct values. The categories of one variable are cross-classified with the categories of one or more other variables. Thus, the frequency distribution of one variable is subdivided according to the values or categories of the other variables.

Suppose we are interested in determining whether Internet usage is related to gender. For the purpose of cross-tabulation, respondents are classified as 'light' or 'heavy' users. Those reporting five hours or less usage were classified as 'light' users, and the remaining were 'heavy' users. The cross-tabulation is shown in Table 18.3. A cross-tabulation includes a cell for every combination of the categories of the two variables. The number in each cell shows how many respondents gave that combination of responses. In Table 18.3, 10 respondents were females who reported light Internet usage. The marginal totals in this table indicate that of the 30 respondents with valid responses on both variables, 15 reported light usage and 15 were heavy users. In terms of gender, 15 respondents were females and 15 were males. Note that this information could have been obtained from a separate frequency distribution for each variable. In general, the margins of a cross-tabulation show the same information as the frequency tables for each of the variables.

Contingency table
A cross-tabulation table. It contains a cell for every combination of categories of the two variables.

Cross-tabulation tables are also called **contingency tables**. The data are considered to be qualitative or categorical data, because each variable is assumed to have only a nominal scale.[6] Cross-tabulation is widely used in commercial marketing research because (1) cross-tabulation analysis and results can be easily interpreted and understood by managers who are not statistically oriented; (2) the clarity of interpretation provides a stronger link between research results and managerial action; (3) a series of cross-tabulations may provide greater insights into a complex phenomenon than a single multivariate analysis; (4) cross-tabulation may alleviate the problem of sparse cells, which could be serious in discrete multivariate analysis; and (5) cross-tabulation analysis is simple to conduct and appealing to both qualitative and quantitative researchers.[7] We will discuss cross-tabulation for two and three variables.

Table 18.3 Gender and Internet usage

Internet usage	Gender		Row total
	Male	Female	
Light (1)	5	10	15
Heavy (2)	10	5	15
Column total	15	15	

Two variables

Cross-tabulation with two variables is also known as bivariate cross-tabulation. Consider again the cross-classification of Internet usage with gender given in Table 18.3. Is usage related to gender? It appears to be from Table 18.3. We see that disproportionately more of the respondents who are male are heavy Internet users as compared with females. Computation of percentages can provide more insight.

Because two variables have been cross-classified, percentages could be computed either column-wise, based on column totals (Table 18.4), or row-wise, based on row totals (Table 18.5). Which table is more useful?

Table 18.4 Gender and Internet usage – column totals

Internet usage	Gender	
	Male	Female
Light (1)	33.3%	66.7%
Heavy (2)	66.7%	33.3%
Column total	100%	100%

Table 18.5 Gender and Internet usage – row totals

Internet usage	Gender		Row total
	Male	Female	
Light (1)	33.3%	66.7%	100%
Heavy (2)	66.7%	33.3%	100%

The answer depends on which variable will be considered as the independent variable and which as the dependent variable.[8] The general rule is to compute the percentages in the direction of the independent variable, across the dependent variable. In our analysis, gender may be considered as the independent variable and Internet usage as the dependent variable, and the correct way of calculating percentages is shown in Table 18.4. Note that whereas 66.7% of the males are heavy users, only 33.3% of females fall into this category. This seems to indicate that males are more likely to be heavy users of the Internet as compared with females.

Note that computing percentages in the direction of the dependent variable across the independent variable, as shown in Table 18.5, is not meaningful in this case. Table 18.5 implies that heavy Internet usage causes people to be males. This latter finding is implausible. It is possible, however, that the association between Internet usage and gender is mediated by a third variable, such as age or income. This kind of possibility points to the need to examine the effect of a third variable.

Three variables

Often the introduction of a third variable clarifies the initial association (or lack of it) observed between two variables. As shown in Figure 18.7, the introduction of a third variable can result in four possibilities:

1 It can refine the association observed between the two original variables.
2 It can indicate no association between the two original variables, although an association was initially observed. In other words, the third variable indicates that the initial association between the two variables was spurious.

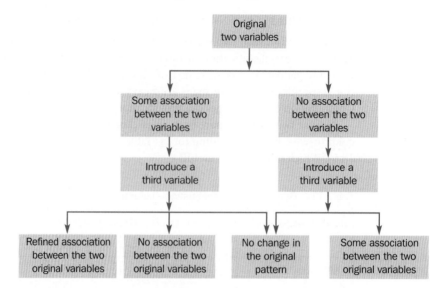

Figure 18.7
The introduction of a third variable in cross-tabulation

3 It can reveal some association between the two original variables, although no association was initially observed. In this case, the third variable reveals a suppressed association between the first two variables.

4 It can indicate no change in the initial association. [9]

These cases are explained with examples based on a sample of 1,000 respondents. Although these examples are contrived to illustrate specific cases, such cases are not uncommon in commercial marketing research.

Refine an initial relationship. An examination of the relationship between the purchase of 'designer' clothing and marital status resulted in the data reported in Table 18.6. The respondents were classified into either high or low categories based on their purchase of 'designer' clothing. Marital status was also measured in terms of two categories: currently married or unmarried. As can be seen from Table 18.6, 52% of unmarried respondents fell in the high-purchase category as opposed to 31% of the married respondents. Before concluding that unmarried respondents purchase more 'designer' clothing than those who are married, a third variable, the buyer's gender, was introduced into the analysis.

Table 18.6 Purchase of 'designer' clothing by marital status

Purchase of 'designer' clothing	Marital status	
	Married	Unmarried
High	31%	52%
Low	69%	48%
Column	100%	100%
Number of respondents	700	300

The buyer's gender was selected as the third variable based on past research. The relationship between purchase of 'designer' clothing and marital status was re-examined in light of the third variable, as shown in Table 18.7. In the case of females, 60% of the unmarried respondents fall in the high-purchase category compared with 25% of those who are married. On the other hand, the percentages are much closer for males, with 40%

Table 18.7 Purchase of 'designer' clothing by marital status and gender

Purchase of 'designer' clothing	Gender			
	Male marital status		Female marital status	
	Married	Unmarried	Married	Unmarried
High	35%	40%	25%	60%
Low	65%	60%	75%	40%
Column	100%	100%	100%	100%
Number of respondents	400	120	300	180

of the unmarried respondents and 35% of the married respondents falling in the high-purchase category. Hence, the introduction of gender (third variable) has refined the relationship between marital status and purchase of 'designer' clothing (original variables). Unmarried respondents are more likely to fall into the high-purchase category than married ones, and this effect is much more pronounced for females than for males.

Initial relationship was spurious. A researcher working for an advertising agency promoting a car brand costing more than €70,000 was attempting to explain the ownership of expensive cars (see Table 18.8). The table shows that 32% of those with university degrees own an expensive (more than €70,000) car compared with 21% of those without university degrees. The researcher was tempted to conclude that education influenced ownership of expensive cars. Realising that income may also be a factor, the researcher decided to re-examine the relationship between education and ownership of expensive cars in the light of income level. This resulted in Table 18.9. Note that the percentages of those with and without university degrees who own expensive cars are the same for each income group. When the data for the high-income and low-income groups are examined separately, the association between education and ownership of expensive cars disappears, indicating that the initial relationship observed between these two variables was spurious.

Source: © Alamy

Table 18.8 Ownership of expensive cars by education level

Own expensive car	Education	
	Degree	No degree
Yes	32%	21%
No	68%	79%
Column	100%	100%
Number of respondents	250	750

Table 18.9 Ownership of expensive cars by education and income levels

Own expensive car	Income			
	Low-income education		High-income education	
	Degree	No degree	Degree	No degree
Yes	20%	20%	40%	40%
No	80%	80%	60%	60%
Column totals	100%	100%	100%	100%
Number of respondents	100	700	150	50

Reveal suppressed association. A researcher suspected that desire to travel abroad may be influenced by age. A cross-tabulation of the two variables produced the results in Table 18.10, indicating no association. When gender was introduced as the third variable, Table 18.11 was obtained. Among men, 60% of those under 45 indicated a desire to travel abroad compared with 40% of those 45 or older. The pattern was reversed for women, where 35% of those under 45 indicated a desire to travel abroad as opposed to 65% of those 45 or older. Since the association between desire to travel abroad and age runs in the opposite direction for males and females, the relationship between these two variables is masked when the data are aggregated across gender as in Table 18.10. But when the effect of gender is controlled, as in Table 18.11, the suppressed association between preference and age is revealed for the separate categories of males and females.

Table 18.10 Desire to travel abroad by age

Desire to travel abroad	Age	
	Under 45	45 or older
Yes	50%	50%
No	50%	50%
Column totals	100%	100%
Number of respondents	500	500

Table 18.11 Desire to travel abroad by age and gender

Desire to travel abroad	Gender			
	Male age		Female age	
	Under 45	45 or older	Under 45	45 or older
Yes	60%	40%	35%	65%
No	40%	60%	65%	35%
Column totals	100%	100%	100%	100%
Number of respondents	300	300	200	200

No change in initial relationship. In some cases, the introduction of the third variable does not change the initial relationship observed, regardless of whether the original variables were associated. This suggests that the third variable does not influence the relationship between the first two. Consider the cross-tabulation of family size and the tendency to eat in fast-food restaurants frequently, as shown in Table 18.12. The respondents' families were classified into small- and large-size categories based on a median split of the distribution, with 500 respondents in each category. No association is observed. The

Table 18.12 Eating frequently in fast-food restaurants by family size

Eat frequently in fast-food restaurants	Family size	
	Small	Large
Yes	65%	65%
No	35%	35%
Column totals	100%	100%
Number of respondents	500	500

respondents were further classified into high- or low-income groups based on a median split. When income was introduced as a third variable in the analysis, Table 18.13 was obtained. Again, no association was observed.

Table 18.13 Eating frequently in fast-food restaurants by family size and income

Eat frequently in fast-food restaurants	Income			
	Low-income family size		High-income family size	
	Small	Large	Small	Large
Yes	65%	65%	65%	65%
No	35%	35%	35%	35%
Column total	100%	100%	100%	100%
Number of respondents	250	250	250	250

General comments on cross-tabulation

More than three variables can be cross-tabulated; the interpretation is quite complex. Also, because the number of cells increases multiplicatively, maintaining an adequate number of respondents or cases in each cell can be problematic. As a general rule, there should be at least five expected observations in each cell for the computed statistics to be reliable. Thus, cross-tabulation is an inefficient way of examining relationships when there are more than a few variables. Note that cross-tabulation examines association between variables, not causation. To examine causation, the causal research design framework should be adopted (see Chapter 11).

Statistics associated with cross-tabulation

We now discuss the statistics commonly used for assessing the statistical significance and strength of association of cross-tabulated variables. The statistical significance of the observed association is commonly measured by the chi-square statistic. The strength of association, or degree of association, is important from a practical or substantive perspective. Generally, the strength of association is of interest only if the association is statistically significant. The strength of the association can be measured by the phi correlation coefficient, the contingency coefficient, Cramer's V and the lambda coefficient. These statistics are described in detail.

Chi-square statistic
The statistic used to test the statistical significance of the observed association in a cross-tabulation. It assists us in determining whether a systematic association exists between the two variables.

Chi-square

The **chi-square statistic** (χ^2) is used to test the statistical significance of the observed association in a cross-tabulation. It assists us in determining whether a systematic association exists between the two variables. The null hypothesis, H_0, is that there is no association between the variables. The test is conducted by computing the cell frequencies that would be expected if no association were present between the variables, given the existing row and column totals. These expected cell frequencies, denoted f_e, are then compared with the actual observed frequencies, f_0, found in the cross-tabulation to calculate the chi-square statistic. The greater the discrepancies between the expected and observed frequencies, the larger the value of the statistic. Assume that a cross-tabulation has r rows and c columns and a random sample of n observations. Then the expected frequency for each cell can be calculated by using a simple formula:

$$f_e = \frac{n_r n_c}{n}$$

where n_r = total number in the row
n_c = total number in the column
n = total sample size

For the data in Table 18.3, the expected frequencies for the cells, going from left to right and from top to bottom, are

$$15 \times 15/30 = 7.50 \quad 15 \times 15/30 = 7.50 \quad 15 \times 15/30 = 7.50 \quad 15 \times 15/30 = 7.50$$

Then the value of χ^2 is calculated as follows:

$$\chi^2 = \sum_{all\ cells} \frac{(f_0 - f_e)^2}{f_e}$$

For the data in Table 18.2, the value of χ^2 is calculated as

$$\chi^2 = (5 - 7.5)^2/7.5 + (10 - 7.5)^2/7.5 + (10 - 7.5)^2/7.5 + (5 - 7.5)^2/7.5$$
$$= 0.833 + 0.833 + 0.833 + 0.833$$
$$= 3.333$$

To determine whether a systematic association exists, the probability of obtaining a value of chi-square as large as or larger than the one calculated from the cross-tabulation is estimated. An important characteristic of the chi-square statistic is the number of degrees of freedom (df) associated with it. In general, the number of degrees of freedom is equal to the number of observations less the number of constraints needed to calculate a statistical term. In the case of a chi-square statistic associated with a cross-tabulation, the number of degrees of freedom is equal to the product of number of rows (r) less one and the number of columns (c) less one. That is, $df = (r - 1) \times (c - 1)$.[10] The null hypothesis (H_0) of no association between the two variables will be rejected only when the calculated value of the test statistic is greater than the critical value of the chi-square distribution with the appropriate degrees of freedom, as shown in Figure 18.8.

Chi-square distribution
A skewed distribution whose shape depends solely on the number of degrees of freedom. As the number of degrees of freedom increases, the chi-square distribution becomes more symmetrical.

The **chi-square distribution** is a skewed distribution whose shape depends solely on the number of degrees of freedom.[11] As the number of degrees of freedom increases, the chi-square distribution becomes more symmetrical. Table 3 in the Appendix of statistical tables contains upper tail areas of the chi-square distribution for different degrees of freedom. In this table, the value at the top of each column indicates the area in the upper portion (the right side, as shown in Figure 18.8) of the chi-square distribution. To illustrate, for 1 degree of freedom, the value for an upper tail area of 0.05 is 3.841. This indicates that for 1 degree of freedom the probability of exceeding a chi-square value of 3.841 is 0.05. In other words, at the 0.05 level of significance with 1 degree of freedom, the critical value of the chi-square statistic is 3.841.

For the cross-tabulation given in Table 18.3, there are $(2 - 1) \times (2 - 1) = 1$ degree of freedom. The calculated chi-square statistic had a value of 3.333. Because this is less than the critical value of 3.841, the null hypothesis of no association cannot be rejected, indicating that the association is not statistically significant at the 0.05 level.

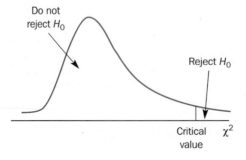

Figure 18.8
Chi-square test of association

The chi-square statistic can also be used in goodness-of-fit tests to determine whether certain models fit the observed data. These tests are conducted by calculating the significance of sample deviations from assumed theoretical (expected) distributions and can be performed on cross-tabulations as well as on frequencies (one-way tabulations). The calculation of the chi-square statistic and the determination of its significance are the same as illustrated above.

The chi-square statistic should be estimated only on counts of data. When the data are in percentage form, they should first be converted to absolute counts or numbers. In addition, an underlying assumption of the chi-square test is that the observations are drawn independently. As a general rule, chi-square analysis should not be conducted when the expected or theoretical frequency in any of the cells is less than five. If the number of observations in any cell is less than 10, or if the table has two rows and two columns (a 2 × 2 table), a correction factor should be applied.[12] With the correction factor, the value is 2.133, which is not significant at the 0.05 level. In the case of a 2 × 2 table, the chi-square is related to the phi coefficient.

Phi coefficient

Phi coefficient (ϕ)
A measure of the strength of association in the special case of a table with two rows and two columns (a 2 × 2 table).

The **phi coefficient** (ϕ) is used as a measure of the strength of association in the special case of a table with two rows and two columns (a 2 × 2 table). The phi coefficient is proportional to the square root of the chi-square statistic. For a sample of size n, this statistic is calculated as

$$\phi = \sqrt{\frac{\chi^2}{n}}$$

It takes the value of 0 when there is no association, which would be indicated by a chi-square value of 0 as well. When the variables are perfectly associated, phi assumes the value of 1 and all the observations fall just on the main or minor diagonal. (In some computer programs, phi assumes a value of –1 rather than +1 when there is perfect negative association.) In our case, because the association was not significant at the 0.05 level, we would not normally compute the phi value. However, for the purpose of illustration, we show how the values of phi and other measures of the strength of association would be computed. The value of phi is

$$\phi = \sqrt{3.333/30} = 0.333$$

Thus, the association is not very strong. In the more general case involving a table of any size, the strength of association can be assessed by using the contingency coefficient.

Contingency coefficient

Contingency coefficient
A measure of the strength of association in a table of any size.

Although the phi coefficient is specific to a 2 × 2 table, the **contingency coefficient** (C) can be used to assess the strength of association in a table of any size. This index is also related to chi-square, as follows:

$$C = \sqrt{\frac{\chi^2}{\chi^2 + n}}$$

The contingency coefficient varies between 0 and 1. The value of 0 occurs in the case of no association (i.e. the variables are statistically independent), but the maximum value of 1 is never achieved. Rather, the maximum value of the contingency coefficient depends on the size of the table (number of rows and number of columns). For this reason, it should be used only to compare tables of the same size. The value of the contingency coefficient for Table 18.3 is

$$C = \sqrt{3.333/(3.333 + 30)} = 0.316$$

This value of C indicates that the association is not very strong. Another statistic that can be calculated for any table is Cramer's V.

Cramer's V

Cramer's V is a modified version of the phi correlation coefficient, ϕ, and is used in tables larger than 2×2. When phi is calculated for a table larger than 2×2, it has no upper limit. Cramer's V is obtained by adjusting phi for either the number of rows or the number of columns in the table based on which of the two is smaller. The adjustment is such that V will range from 0 to 1. A large value of V merely indicates a high degree of association. It does not indicate how the variables are associated. For a table with r rows and c columns, the relationship between Cramer's V and the phi correlation coefficient is expressed as

$$V = \sqrt{\frac{\phi^2}{\min(r-1),(c-1)}}$$

or

$$V = \sqrt{\frac{\chi^2/n}{\min(r-1),(c-1)}}$$

The value of Cramer's V for Table 18.3 is

$$V = \sqrt{(3.333/30)/1} = 0.333$$

Thus, the association is not very strong. As can be seen, in this case $V = \phi$. This is always the case for a 2×2 table. Another statistic commonly estimated is the lambda coefficient.

Lambda coefficient

The lambda coefficient assumes that the variables are measured on a nominal scale. **Asymmetric lambda** measures the percentage improvement in predicting the value of the dependent variable, given the value of the independent variable. The lambda coefficient also varies between 0 and 1. A value of 0 means no improvement in prediction. A value of 1 indicates that the prediction can be made without error. This happens when each independent variable category is associated with a single category of the dependent variable.

Asymmetric lambda is computed for each of the variables (treating it as the dependent variable). The two asymmetric lambdas are likely to be different, since the marginal distributions are not usually the same. A **symmetric lambda**, a kind of average of the two asymmetric values, is also computed. The symmetric lambda does not make an assumption about which variable is dependent. It measures the overall improvement when prediction is done in both directions.[13] The value of asymmetric lambda in Table 18.3, with usage as the dependent variable, is 0.333. This indicates that knowledge of gender increases our predictive ability by the proportion of 0.333, i.e. a 33% improvement. The symmetric lambda is also 0.333.

Other statistics

Note that in the calculation of the chi-square statistic the variables are treated as being measured only on a nominal scale. Other statistics such as **tau b**, **tau c** and **gamma** are available to measure association between two ordinal-level variables. All these statistics use information about the ordering of categories of variables by considering every possible pair of cases in the table. Each pair is examined to determine whether its relative ordering on the first variable is the same as its relative ordering on the second variable (concordant), the ordering is reversed (discordant), or the pair is tied. The manner in which the ties are treated is the basic difference between these statistics. Both tau b and tau c adjust for ties. Tau b is the most appropriate with square tables in which the number of rows and the number of columns are equal. Its value varies between +1 and −1. For a rectangular table in which the number of rows is different from the number of columns, tau c should be used. Gamma does not make an adjustment for either ties or table size. Gamma also varies between +1 and −1 and generally has a higher numerical value than tau b or tau c. For the data in Table 18.3, as gender is a nominal variable, it is not appropriate to calculate ordinal statistics. All these statistics can be estimated by using the appropriate computer software that incorporates cross-tabulation. Other statistics for measuring the strength of association, namely product moment correlation and non-metric correlation, are discussed in Chapter 20.

Cross-tabulation in practice

While conducting cross-tabulation analysis in practice, it is useful to proceed through the following steps:

1 Test the null hypothesis that there is no association between the variables using the chi-square statistic. If you fail to reject the null hypothesis, then there is no relationship.
2 If H_0 is rejected, then determine the strength of the association using an appropriate statistic (phi coefficient, contingency coefficient, Cramer's V, lambda coefficient, or other statistics).
3 If H_0 is rejected, interpret the pattern of the relationship by computing the percentages in the direction of the independent variable, across the dependent variable.
4 If the variables are treated as ordinal rather than nominal, use tau b, tau c or gamma as the test statistic. If H_0 is rejected, then determine the strength of the association using the magnitude, and the direction of the relationship using the sign of the test statistic.

Hypothesis testing related to differences

The previous section considered hypothesis testing related to associations. We now focus on hypothesis testing related to differences. A classification of hypothesis testing procedures for examining differences is presented in Figure 18.9. Note that this figure is consistent with the classification of univariate techniques presented in Figure 17.4. The major difference is that Figure 17.4 also accommodates more than two samples and thus deals with techniques such as one-way ANOVA and K–W ANOVA (Chapter 17), whereas Figure 18.9 is limited to no more than two samples. Also, one-sample techniques such as frequencies, which do not involve statistical testing, are not covered in Figure 18.9.

Hypothesis testing procedures can be broadly classified as parametric or non-parametric, based on the measurement scale of the variables involved. **Parametric tests** assume that the variables of interest are measured on at least an interval scale. **Non-parametric tests** assume that the variables are measured on a nominal or ordinal scale. These tests can be further classified based on whether one or two or more samples are involved. As explained in Chapter 17, the number of samples is determined based on how the data are treated for the purpose of analysis, not based on how the data were collected. The samples are independent if they are drawn randomly from different populations. For the purpose of analysis, data pertaining to different groups of respondents, e.g. males and females, are generally treated as independent samples. On the other hand, the samples are paired when the data for the two samples relate to the same group of respondents.

The most popular parametric test is the t test conducted for examining hypotheses about means. The t test could be conducted on the mean of one sample or two samples of observations. In the case of two samples, the samples could be independent or paired.

Parametric tests
Hypothesis testing procedures that assume that the variables of interest are measured on at least an interval scale.

Non-parametric tests
Hypothesis testing procedures that assume that the variables are measured on a nominal or ordinal scale.

Non-parametric tests based on observations drawn from one sample include the chi-square test, the Kolmogorov–Smirnov test, the runs test and the binomial test. In the case of two independent samples, the chi-square test, the Mann–Whitney U test, the median test and the Kolmogorov–Smirnov two-sample test are used for examining hypotheses about location. These tests are non-parametric counterparts of the two-group t test. For paired samples, non-parametric tests include the Wilcoxon matched-pairs signed-ranks test and the sign test. These tests are the counterparts of the paired t test. Parametric as well as non-parametric tests are also available for evaluating hypotheses relating to more than two samples. These tests are considered in later chapters.

Parametric tests

Parametric tests provide inferences for making statements about the means of parent populations. A t test is commonly used for this purpose. This test is based on Student's t statistic. The **t statistic** assumes that the variable is normally distributed and the mean is known (or assumed to be known) and the population variance is estimated from the sample. Assume that the random variable X is normally distributed, with mean μ and unknown population variance σ^2, which is estimated by the sample variance s^2. Recall that the standard deviation of the sample mean, $\overline{X}$, is estimated as $s_{\overline{x}} = s/\sqrt{n}$. Then $t = (\overline{X} - \mu)/s_{\overline{x}}$ is t distributed with $n-1$ degrees of freedom.

The **t distribution** is similar to the normal distribution in appearance. Both distributions are bell shaped and symmetric. Compared with the normal distribution, however, the t distribution has more area in the tails and less in the centre. This is because the population variance σ^2 is unknown and is estimated by the sample variance s^2. Given the uncertainty in the value of s^2, the observed values of t are more variable than those of z. Thus, we must go out a larger number of standard deviations from zero to encompass a certain percentage of values from the t distribution than is the case with the normal distribution. Yet, as the number of degrees of freedom increases, the t distribution approaches

t test
A univariate hypothesis test using the t distribution, which is used when the standard deviation is unknown and the sample size is small.

t statistic
A statistic that assumes that the variable has a symmetric bell-shaped distribution, that the mean is known (or assumed to be known), and that the population variance is estimated from the sample.

t distribution
A symmetrical bell-shaped distribution that is useful for sample testing ($n < 30$). It is similar to the normal distribution in appearance.

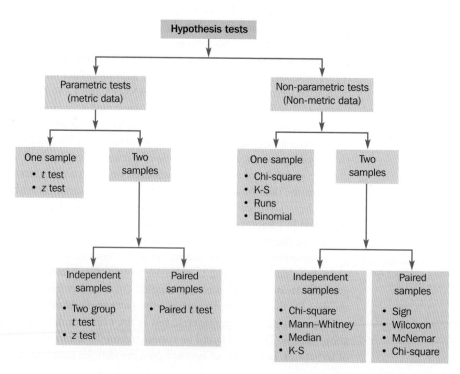

Figure 18.9
Hypothesis testing procedures

the normal distribution. In fact, for large samples of 120 or more, the t distribution and the normal distribution are virtually indistinguishable. Table 4 in the Appendix of statistical tables shows selected percentiles of the t distribution. Although normality is assumed, the t test is quite robust to departures from normality.

The procedure for hypothesis testing, for the special case when the t statistic is used, is as follows:

1 Formulate the null (H_0) and the alternative (H_1) hypotheses.
2 Select the appropriate formula for the t statistic.
3 Select a significance level, a, for testing H_0. Typically, the 0.05 level is selected.[14]
4 Take one or two samples and compute the mean and standard deviation for each sample.
5 Calculate the t statistic assuming that H_0 is true.
6 Calculate the degrees of freedom and estimate the probability of getting a more extreme value of the statistic from Table 4 in the Appendix. (Alternatively, calculate the critical value of the t statistic.)
7 If the probability computed in step 6 is smaller than the significance level selected in step 3, reject H_0. If the probability is larger, do not reject H_0. (Alternatively, if the value of the calculated t statistic in step 5 is larger than the critical value determined in step 6, reject H_0. If the calculated value is smaller than the critical value, do not reject H_0.) Failure to reject H_0 does not necessarily imply that H_0 is true. It only means that the true state is not significantly different from that assumed by H_0.[15]
8 Express the conclusion reached by the t test in terms of the marketing research problem.

We illustrate the general procedure for conducting t tests in the following sections, beginning with the one-sample case.

One sample

In marketing research, the researcher is often interested in making statements about a single variable against a known or given standard. Examples of such statements are that the market share for a new product will exceed 15%, at least 65% of customers will like a new package design, and 80% of retailers will prefer a new pricing policy. These statements can be translated to null hypotheses that can be tested using a one-sample test, such as the t test or the z test. In the case of a t test for a single mean, the researcher is interested in testing whether the population mean conforms to a given hypothesis (H_0). For the data in Table 18.2, suppose we wanted to test the hypothesis that the mean familiarity rating exceeds 4.0, the neutral value on a seven-point scale. A significance level of $a = 0.05$ is selected. The hypothesis may be formulated as

$$H_0: \mu \leqslant 4.0$$
$$H_1: \mu > 4.0$$
$$t = (\bar{X} - \mu)/s_{\bar{x}}$$
$$s_{\bar{x}} = s/\sqrt{n}$$
$$s_{\bar{x}} = 1.579/\sqrt{29} = 1.579/5.385 = 0.293$$
$$t = (4.724 - 4.0)/0.293 = 0.724/0.293 = 2.471$$

The degrees of freedom for the t statistic to test the hypothesis about one mean are $n - 1$. In this case, $n - 1 = 29 - 1$, or 28. From Table 4 in the Appendix, the probability of getting a more extreme value than 2.471 is less than 0.05. (Alternatively, the critical t value for 28 degrees of freedom and a significance level of 0.05 is 1.7011, which is less than the calculated value.) Hence, the null hypothesis is rejected. The familiarity level does not exceed 4.0.

Note that if the population standard deviation was assumed to be known as 1.5, rather than estimated from the sample, a *z* test would be appropriate. In this case, the value of the *z* statistic would be

$$z = \frac{\overline{X} - \mu}{\sigma_{\overline{x}}}$$

where

$$\sigma_{\overline{x}} = 1.5/\sqrt{29} = 1.5/5.385 = 0.279$$

and

$$z = (4.724 - 4.0)/0.279 = 0.724/0.279 = 2.595$$

From Table 2 in the Appendix of statistical tables, the probability of getting a more extreme value of *z* than 2.595 is less than 0.05. (Alternatively, the critical *z* value for a one-tailed test and a significance level of 0.05 is 1.645, which is less than the calculated value.) Therefore, the null hypothesis is rejected, reaching the same conclusion arrived at earlier by the *t* test.

The procedure for testing a null hypothesis with respect to a proportion was illustrated earlier in this chapter when we introduced hypothesis testing.

Two independent samples

Several hypotheses in marketing relate to parameters from two different populations: for example, the users and non-users of a brand differ in terms of their perceptions of the brand, high-income consumers spend more on leisure activities than low-income consumers, or the proportion of brand-loyal users in segment I is more than the proportion in segment II. Samples drawn randomly from different populations are termed **independent samples**. As in the case for one sample, the hypotheses could relate to means or proportions.

Means. In the case of means for two independent samples, the hypotheses take the following form:

$$H_0:\ \mu_1 = \mu_2$$
$$H_1:\ \mu_1 \neq \mu_2$$

The two populations are sampled and the means and variances are computed based on samples of sizes n_1 and n_2. If both populations are found to have the same variance, a pooled variance estimate is computed from the two sample variances as follows:

$$s^2 = \frac{\sum_{i=1}^{n_1} (X_{i_1} - \overline{X}_1)^2 + \sum_{i=1}^{n_2} (X_{i_2} - \overline{X}_2)^2}{n_1 + n_2 - 2} \qquad s^2 = \frac{(n_1 - 1)s_1^2 + (n^2 - 1)\, s_2^2}{n_1 + n_2 - 2}$$

The standard deviation of the test statistic can be estimated as

$$s_{\overline{X}_1 - \overline{X}_2} = \sqrt{s^2\left(\frac{1}{n_1} + \frac{1}{n_2}\right)}$$

The appropriate value of *t* can be calculated as

$$t = \frac{(\overline{X}_1 - \overline{X}_2) - (\mu_1 - \mu_2)}{s_{\overline{X}_1 - \overline{X}_2}}$$

The degrees of freedom in this case are $(n_1 + n_2 - 2)$.

If the two populations have unequal variances, an exact t cannot be computed for the difference in sample means. Instead, an approximation to t is computed. The number of degrees of freedom in this case is usually not an integer, but a reasonably accurate probability can be obtained by rounding to the nearest integer.[16]

An **F test** of sample variance may be performed if it is not known whether the two populations have equal variance. In this case the hypotheses are

$$H_0: \ \sigma_1^2 = \sigma_2^2$$
$$H_1: \ \sigma_1^2/\sigma_2^2$$

The **F statistic** is computed from the sample variances as follows:

$$F_{(n_1 - 1),(n_2 - 1)} = \frac{s_1^2}{s_2^2}$$

where n_1 = size of sample 1

n_2 = size of sample 2

$n_1 - 1$ = degrees of freedom for sample 1

$n_2 - 1$ = degrees of freedom for sample 2

s_1^2 = sample variance for sample 1

s_2^2 = sample variance for sample 2.

As can be seen, the critical value of the **F distribution** depends on two sets of degrees of freedom: those in the numerator and those in the denominator. The critical values of F for various degrees of freedom for the numerator and denominator are given in Table 5 of the Appendix of statistical tables. If the probability of F is greater than the significance level a, H_0 is not rejected and t based on the pooled variance estimate can be used. On the other hand, if the probability of F is less than or equal to a, H_0 is rejected and t based on a separate variance estimate is used.

Using the data in Table 18.1, suppose we wanted to determine whether Internet usage was different for males as compared with females. A two-independent-samples t test can be conducted. The results of this test are presented in Table 18.14. Note that the F test of sample variances has a probability that is less than 0.05. Accordingly H_0 is rejected and the t test based on the 'equal variances not assumed' should be used. The t value is –4.492

F test
A statistical test of the equality of the variances of two populations.

F statistic
The ratio of two sample variances.

F distribution
A frequency distribution that depends upon two sets of degrees of freedom: the degrees of freedom in the numerator and the degrees of freedom in the denominator.

Table 18.14 Two independent samples t test

Summary statistics			
	Number of cases	Mean	Standard error mean
Male	15	9.333	1.137
Female	15	3.867	0.435
F test for equality of variances			
F value		Two-tail probability	
15.507		0.000	
t test			
Equal variances assumed			Equal variances not assumed		

t value	Degrees of freedom	Two-tail probability	t value	Degrees of freedom	Two-tail probability
–4.492	28	0.000	–4.492	18.014	0.000

and with 18.014 degrees of freedom, this gives a probability of 0.000, which is less than the significance level of 0.05. Therefore, the null hypothesis of equal means is rejected. Because the mean usage for males (gender = 1) is 9.333 and that for females (gender = 2) is 3.867, males use the Internet to a significantly greater extent than females. We also show the t test assuming equal variances because most software packages automatically conduct the t test both ways.

For another application of the t test, consider the following example.

Example

Shops seek to suit elderly to a 't'[17]

A study based on a sample of 789 respondents who were 65 or older attempted to determine the effect of lack of mobility on shop patronage. A major research question related to the differences in the physical requirements of dependent and self-reliant elderly persons. That is, did the two groups require different things to get to the shop or after they arrived at the shop? A more detailed analysis of the physical requirements conducted by the t tests of two independent samples (shown in the table) indicated that dependent elderly persons are more likely to look for shops that offer home delivery and phone orders and for shops to which they have accessible transportation. They are also more likely to look for a variety of shops located close together.

Differences in physical requirements between dependent and self-reliant elderly

Physical requirement items	Mean*		
	Self-reliant	Dependent	t test probability
Delivery to home	1.787	2.000	0.023
Phone in order	2.030	2.335	0.003
Transportation to store	2.188	3.098	0.000
Convenient parking	4.001	4.095	0.305
Location close to home	3.177	3.325	0.137
Variety of shops close together	3.456	3.681	0.023

* Measured on a five-point scale from not important (1) to very important (5).

In this example, we tested the difference between means. A similar test is available for testing the difference between proportions for two independent samples.

Proportions. A case involving proportions for two independent samples is also illustrated using the data from Table 18.1, which gives the number of males and females who use the Internet for shopping. Is the proportion of respondents using the Internet for shopping the same for males and females? The null and alternative hypotheses are

$$H_0: \pi_1 = \pi_2$$
$$H_1: \pi_1 \neq \pi_2$$

A z test is used as in testing the proportion for one sample. In this case, however, the test statistic is given by

$$z = \frac{P_1 - P_2}{S_{\bar{P}_1 - \bar{P}_2}}$$

In the test statistic, the numerator is the difference between the proportions in the two samples, P_1 and P_2. The denominator is the standard error of the difference in the two proportions and is given by

$$s_{P_1 - P_2} = \sqrt{P(1-P)\left(\frac{1}{n_1} + \frac{1}{n_2}\right)}$$

where

$$P = \frac{n_1 P_1 + n_2 P_2}{n_1 + n_2}$$

A significance level of $a = 0.05$ is selected. Given the data in Table 18.1, the test statistic can be calculated as

$$P_1 - P_2 = (11/15) - (6/15)$$
$$= 0.733 - 0.400 = 0.333$$
$$P = (15 \times 0.733 + 15 \times 0.4)/(15 + 15) = 0.567$$
$$s_{P_1 - P_2} = \sqrt{0.567 \times 0.433 \,(1/15 + 1/15)} = 0.181$$
$$z = 0.333/0.181 = 1.84$$

Given a two-tail test, the area to the right of the critical value is $a/2$, or 0.025. Hence, the critical value of the test statistic is 1.96. Because the calculated value is less than the critical value, the null hypothesis cannot be rejected. Thus, the proportion of users (0.733) for males and (0.400) for females is not significantly different for the two samples. Note that although the difference is substantial, it is not statistically significant due to the small sample sizes (15 in each group).

Paired samples

Paired samples
The samples are paired when the data for the two samples relate to the same group of respondents.

Paired samples t test
A test for differences in the means of paired samples.

In many marketing research applications, the observations for the two groups are not selected from independent samples. Rather, the observations relate to **paired samples** in that the two sets of observations relate to the same respondents. A sample of respondents may rate competing brands, may indicate the relative importance of two attributes of a product, or may evaluate a brand at two different times. The differences in these cases are examined by a **paired samples t test**. To compute t for paired samples, the paired difference variable, denoted by D, is formed and its mean and variance calculated. Then the t statistic is computed. The degrees of freedom are $n - 1$, where n is the number of pairs. The relevant formulae are

$$H_0: \mu_D = 0$$
$$H_1: \mu_D \neq 0$$

$$t_{n-1} = \frac{\bar{D} - \mu_D}{\dfrac{s_D}{\sqrt{n}}}$$

where

$$\bar{D} = \frac{\displaystyle\sum_{i=1}^{n} D_i}{n}$$

$$S_{\bar{D}} = \sqrt{\frac{\displaystyle\sum_{i=1}^{n}(D_i - \bar{D})^2}{n-1}}$$

$$S_{\bar{D}} = S_D/\sqrt{n}$$

In the Internet usage example (Table 18.1), a paired *t* test could be used to determine if the respondents differed in their attitude towards the Internet and attitude towards technology. The resulting output is shown in Table 18.15. The mean attitude towards the Internet is 5.167 and that towards technology is 4.10. The mean difference between the variables is 1.067, with a standard deviation of 0.828 and a standard error of 0.1511. This results in a *t* value of (1.067/0.1511) = 7.06, with 30 – 1 = 29 degrees of freedom and a probability of less than 0.001. Therefore the respondents have a more favourable attitude towards the Internet as compared with technology in general. Another application is provided in the context of determining the relative effectiveness of 15-second versus 30-second TV commercials.

Table 18.15 Paired samples *t* test

Variable	Number of cases	Mean	Standard deviation	Standard error
Internet attitude	30	5.167	1.234	0.225
Technology attitude	30	4.100	1.398	0.255

Difference mean	Standard deviation	Standard error	Correlation	Two-tail probability	t value	Degrees of freedom	Two-tail probability
1.067	0.828	0.1511	0.809	0.000	7.059	29	0.000

Example

Seconds count[18]

A survey of 83 media directors of the largest Canadian advertising agencies was conducted to determine the relative effectiveness of 15-second versus 30-second commercial advertisements. By use of a five-point rating scale (1 being excellent and 5 being poor), 15- and 30-second commercials were rated by each respondent for brand awareness, main idea recall, persuasion, and ability to tell an emotional story. The table indicates that 30-second commercials were rated more favourably on all the dimensions. Paired *t* tests indicated that these differences were significant, and the 15-second commercials were evaluated as less effective.

Mean rating 15- and 30-second commercials on four communication variables

Brand awareness		Main idea recall		Persuasion		Ability to tell an emotional story	
15	30	15	30	15	30	15	30
2.5	1.9	2.7	2.0	3.7	2.1	4.3	1.9

The difference in proportions for paired samples can be tested by using the McNemar test or the chi-square test, as explained in the following section on non-parametric tests.

Non-parametric tests

Non-parametric tests are used when the variables are non-metric. Like parametric tests, non-parametric tests are available for testing variables from one sample two independent samples or two related samples.

One sample

Sometimes the researcher wants to test whether the observations for a particular variable could reasonably have come from a particular distribution, such as the normal, uniform or Poisson distribution. Knowledge of the distribution is necessary for finding probabilities corresponding to known values of the variable, or variable values corresponding to known probabilities (see the Appendix at the end of Chapter 15). The **Kolmogorov–Smirnov (K–S) one-sample test** is one such goodness-of-fit test. The K–S test compares the cumulative distribution function for a variable with a specified distribution. A_i denotes the cumulative relative frequency for each category of the theoretical (assumed) distribution, and O_i denotes the comparable value of the sample frequency. The K–S test is based on the maximum value of the absolute difference between A_i and O_i. The test statistic is

$$K = \max | A_i - O_i |$$

The decision to reject the null hypothesis is based on the value of K. The larger K is, the more confidence we have that H_0 is false. Note that this is a one-tailed test, since the value of K is always positive, and we reject H_0 for large values of K. For $a = 0.05$, the critical value of K for large samples (over 35) is given by $1.36/\sqrt{n}$.[19] Alternatively, K can be transformed into a normally distributed z statistic and its associated probability determined.

Table 18.16 K–S one-sample test for normality for Internet usage

Test distribution, normal				
Mean			6.600	
Standard deviation			4.296	
Cases			30	
Most extreme differences				
Absolute	Positive	Negative	K–S z	Two-tailed p
0.222	0.222	–0.142	1.217	0.103

In the context of the Internet usage example, suppose we wanted to test whether the distribution of Internet usage was normal. A K–S one-sample test is conducted, yielding the data shown in Table 18.16. The largest absolute difference between the observed and normal distribution was $K = 0.222$. Although our sample size is only 30 (less than 35), we can use the approximate formula and the critical value of K is $1.36/\sqrt{30} = 0.248$. Because the calculated value of K is smaller than the critical value, the null hypothesis cannot be rejected. Alternatively, Table 18.16 indicates that the probability of observing a K value of 0.222, as determined by the normalized z statistics, is 0.103. Because this is more than the significance level of 0.05, the null hypothesis cannot be rejected, leading to he same conclusion. Hence the distribution of Internet usage does not deviate significantly from the normal distribution.

As mentioned earlier, the chi-square test can also be performed on a single variable from one sample. In this context, the chi-square serves as a goodness-of-fit test. It tests whether a significant difference exists between the observed number of cases in each category and the expected number.

Other one-sample non-parametric tests include the **runs test** and the **binomial test**. The runs test is a test of randomness for the dichotomous variables. This test is conducted by determining whether the order or sequence in which observations are obtained is

Kolmogorov–Smirnov (K–S) one-sample test
A one-sample non-parametric goodness-of-fit test that compares the cumulative distribution function for a variable with a specified distribution.

Runs test
A test of randomness for a dichotomous variable.

Binominal test
A goodness-of-fit statistical test for dichotomous variables. It tests the goodness of fit of the observed number of observations in each category to the number expected under a specified binominal distribution.

random. The binomial test is also a goodness-of-fit test for dichotomous variables. It tests the goodness of fit of the observed number of observations in each category to the number expected under a specified binomial distribution. For more information on these tests, refer to the standard statistical literature.[20]

Two independent samples

Mann-Whitney U test
A statistical test for a variable measured on an ordinal scale, comparing the differences in the location of two populations based on observations from two independent samples.

When the difference in the location of two populations is to be compared based on observations from two independent samples and the variable is measured on an ordinal scale, the **Mann–Whitney U test** can be used.[21] This test corresponds to the two-independent-samples t test, for interval scale variables, when the variances of the two populations are assumed equal.

In the Mann-Whitney U test, the two samples are combined and the cases are ranked in order of increasing size. The test statistic, U, is computed as the number of times a score from sample or group 1 precedes a score from group 2. If the samples are from the same population, the distribution of scores from the two groups in the rank list should be random. An extreme value of U would indicate a non-random pattern pointing to the inequality of the two groups. For samples of less than 30, the exact significance level for U is computed. For larger samples, U is transformed into a normally distributed z statistic. This z can be corrected for ties within ranks.

We examine again the difference in the Internet usage of males and females. This time, though, the Mann–Whitney test is used. The results are given in Table 18.17. Again, a significant difference is found between the two groups, corroborating the results of the two-independent-samples t test reported earlier. Because the ranks are assigned from the smallest observation to the largest, the higher mean rank of males (20.93) indicates that they use the Internet to a greater extent than females (mean rank = 10.07).

Table 18.17 Mann–Whitney U–Wilcoxon rank sum W test: Internet usage by gender

Gender	Mean rank	Cases	
Male	20.93	15	
Female	10.07	15	
Total		30	
U	W	z	Corrected for ties, two-tailed p
31.000	151.000	–3.406	0.001

Note: U = Mann–Whitney test statistics, W = Wilcoxon W statistic, z = U transformed into normally distributed z statistics.

Two-sample median test
Non-parametric test statistic that determines whether two groups are drawn from populations with the same median. This is not as powerful as the Mann–Whitney U test.

Kolmogorov–Smirnov (K–S) two-sample test
Non-parametric test statistic that determines whether two distributions are the same. It takes into account any differences in the two distributions, including median, dispersion and skewness.

Researchers often wish to test for a significant difference in proportions obtained from two independent samples. In this case, as an alternative to the parametric z test considered earlier, one could also use the cross-tabulation procedure to conduct a chi-square test.[22] In this case, we will have a 2×2 table. One variable will be used to denote the sample and will assume a value of 1 for sample 1 and a value of 2 for sample 2. The other variable will be the binary variable of interest.

Two other independent-samples non-parametric tests are the median test and K–S test. The **two-sample median test** determines whether the two groups are drawn from populations with the same median. It is not as powerful as the Mann–Whitney U test because it merely uses the location of each observation relative to the median, and not the rank, of each observation. The **K–S two-sample test** examines whether the two distributions are the same. It takes into account any differences between the two distributions, including the median, dispersion and skewness, as illustrated by the following example.

Example	**Directors change direction[23]**

How do marketing research directors and users in Fortune 500 manufacturing firms perceive the role of marketing research in initiating changes in marketing strategy formulation? It was found that the marketing research directors were more strongly in favour of initiating changes in strategy and less in favour of holding back than were users of marketing research. Using the K–S test, these differences of role definition were statistically significant at the 0.05 level, as shown below

The role of marketing research in strategy formulation

Sample	n	Responses (%)				
		Absolutely must	Preferably should	May or may not	Preferably should not	Absolutely must not
D	77	7	26	43	19	5
U	68	2	15	32	35	16

K–S significance = 0.05.
D = directors, U = users.

In this example, the marketing research directors and users comprised two independent samples. The samples, however, are not always independent. In the case of paired samples, a different set of tests should be used.

Paired samples

Wilcoxon matched-pairs signed-ranks test
A non-parametric test that analyses the differences between the paired observations, taking into account the magnitude of the differences.

An important non-parametric test for examining differences in the location of two populations based on paired observations is the **Wilcoxon matched-pairs signed-ranks test**. This test analyses the differences between the paired observations, taking into account the magnitude of the differences. It computes the differences between the pairs of variables and ranks the absolute differences. The next step is to sum the positive and negative ranks. The test statistic, z, is computed from the positive and negative rank sums. Under the null hypothesis of no difference, z is a standard normal variate with mean 0 and variance 1 for large samples. This test corresponds to the paired t test considered earlier.[24]

The example considered for the paired t test, whether the respondents differed in terms of attitude towards the Internet and attitude towards technology, is considered again. Suppose we assume that both these variables are measured on ordinal rather than interval scales. Accordingly, we use the Wilcoxon test. The results are shown in Table 18.18. Again, a significant difference is found in the variables, and the results are in accordance with the conclusion reached by the paired t test. There are 23 negative differences (attitude towards technology is less favourable than attitude towards the Internet). The mean rank of these negative differences is 12.72. On the other hand, there is only one positive difference (attitude towards technology is more favourable than attitude towards the Internet). The mean rank of the difference is 7.50. The are six ties, or observations with the same value for both variables. These numbers indicate that the attitude towards the Internet is more favourable than that towards technology. Furthermore, the probability associated with the z statistic is less than 0.05, indicating that the difference is indeed significant.

Table 18.18 Wilcoxon matched-pairs signed-ranks test

Internet with technology		
(Technology–Internet)	*Cases*	*Mean rank*
– Ranks	23	12.72
+ Ranks	1	7.50
Ties	6	
Total	30	
$z = -4.207$		Two-tailed $p = 0.000$

Sign test
A non-parametric test for examining differences in the location of two populations, based on paired populations, that compares only the signs of the differences between pairs of variables without taking into account the magnitude of the differences.

Another paired sample non-parametric test is the **sign test**.[25] This test is not as powerful as the Wilcoxon matched-pairs signed-ranks test because it only compares the signs of the differences between pairs of variables without taking into account the magnitude of the differences. In the special case of a binary variable where the researcher wishes to test differences in proportions, the McNemar test can be used. Alternatively, the chi-square test can also be used for binary variables.

The various parametric and non-parametric tests are summarised in Table 18.19. The tests in Table 18.19 can be easily related to those in Figure 18.9. Table 18.19 classifies the tests in more detail, as parametric tests (based on metric data) are classified separately for

Table 18.19 A summary of hypothesis testing

Sample	*Application*	*Level of scaling*	*Test/comments*
One sample			
One sample	Distributions	Non-metric	K–S and chi-square for goodness of fit Runs test for randomness Binomial test for goodness of fit for dichotomous variables
One sample	Means	Metric	t test, if variance is unknown z test, if variance is known
One sample	Proportions	Metric	z test
Two independent samples			
Two independent samples	Distributions	Non-metric	K–S two-sample test for examining equivalence of two distributions
Two independent samples	Means	Metric	Two-group t test F test for equality of variances
Two independent samples	Proportions	Metric Non-metric	z test Chi-square test
Two independent samples	Rankings/medians	Non-metric	Mann–Whitney U test more powerful than median test
Paired samples			
Paired samples	Means	Metric	Paired t test
Paired samples	Proportions	Non-metric	McNemar test for binary variables Chi-square test
Paired samples	Rankings/medians	Non-metric	Wilcoxon matched-pairs ranked-signs test more powerful than sign test

means and proportions. Likewise, non-parametric tests (based on non-metric data) are classified separately for distributions and rankings/medians. The final example illustrates the use of hypothesis testing in international branding strategy.

Example   ### International brand equity – the name of the game[26]

In an era of global marketing, how can marketers develop theirs brands overseas in diverse social, cultural and historical envirnoments? A study showed that, in general, a firm's international brand structure includes firm-based characteristics, product market characteristics, and market dynamics. More specifically, according to Bob Kroll, the former President of Del Monte International, uniform packaging may be an asset to marketing internationally, but catering to the culinary taste preferences of individual countries is more important. One survey on international product marketing makes this clear. Respondents included 100 brand and product managers and marketing executives from some of the world's largest food, pharmaceutical and personal product companies. For overseas markets, 39% said it was not a good idea to use uniform packaging and 38% said it was a good idea. Those who said it was not a good idea mentioned, however, the desirability of maintaining as much brand equity and package consistency from market to market. But they also believed it was necessary to tailor the package to fit the linguistic and regulatory needs of different markets.

Based on this finding, a suitable research question can be: 'Do consumers in different countries prefer to buy global name brands with different packaging customised to suit their local needs?' Based on this research question, one can frame a hypothesis that, other things being constant, standardised branding with customised packaging for a well-established brand name will result in a greater market share. The hypotheses may be formulated as follows:

H_0: Standardised branding with customised packaging for a well-established brand name will not lead to greater market share in an international market.
H_1: Other factors remaining equal, standardised branding with customised packaging for a well-established brand name will lead to greater market share in the international market.

To test the null hypothesis, a well-established brand such as Colgate toothpaste, which has followed a mixed strategy, can be selected. The market share in countries with standardised branding and standardised packaging can be compared with market share in countries with standardised branding and customised packaging, after controlling for the effect of other factors. A two-independent-samples t test can be used.

Internet and computer applications

SPSS (www.spss.com)

The main program in SPSS is FREQUENCIES. It produces a table of frequency counts, percentages and cumulative percentages for the values of each variable. It gives all of the associated statistics except for the coefficient of variation. If the data are interval scaled and only the summary statistics are desired, the DESCRIPTIVES procedure can be used. All of the statistics computed by DESCRIPTIVES are available in FREQUENCIES. However, DESCRIPTIVES is more efficient because it does not sort values into a frequency table. An additional program, MEANS, computes means and standard deviations for a dependent variable over subgroups of cases defined by independent variables.

CROSSTABS displays cross-classification tables and provides cell counts, row and column percentages, the chi-square test for significance, and all the measures of the strength of the association that have been discussed. The major program for conducting t tests is T-TEST. This program can be used to conduct t tests on independent as well as paired samples. All the non-parametric tests that we have discussed can be conducted by using the NPAR TESTS program.

SAS (www.sas.com)

The main program is UNIVARIATE. In addition to providing a frequency table, this program provides all the associated statistics. Another procedure available is FREQ. For one-way frequency distribution, FREQ does not provide any associated statistics. If only summary statistics are desired, procedures such as MEANS, SUMMARY and TABULATE can be used.

FREQ displays cross-classification tables and provides cell counts, row and column percentages, the chi-square test for significance, and all the measures of the strength of the association that have been discussed. TABULATE can be used for obtaining cell counts and row and column percentages, although it does not provide any of the associated statistics. The program T-TEST can be used. The non-parametric tests may be conducted by using NPAR1WAY. This program will conduct the two-independent-samples test (Mann–Whitney, median and K–S) as well as the Wilcoxon test for paired samples.

Minitab (www.minitab.com)

The main function is stats>descriptive statistics. The output values include the mean, median, mode, standard deviation, minimum, maximum and quartiles. A histogram in a bar chart or graph can be produced from the Graph>Histogram selection. Cross-tabulations (crosstabs) and chi-square are under the Stats>Tables function. Parametric tests available in Minitab in descriptive stat function are z test for means, t test for mean, and two-sample t test. The non-parametric tests can be accessed under the Stat>Time series function. The output includes the one-sample sign, one-sample Wilcoxon, Mann–Whitney, Kruskal–Wallis, median test, Friedman, runs test and pairwise differences.

Excel (www.microsoft.com)

In Excel the output produces the mean, standard error, median, mode, standard deviation, variance, kurtosis, skewness, range, minimum, maximum, sum, count and confidence level. Frequencies can be selected under the histogram function. A histogram can be produced in bar format. The Data>Pivot Table performs crosstabs in Excel. To do additional analysis or customise data, select a different summary function such as max, min, average or standard deviation. In addition, a custom calculation can be selected to calculate based on other cells in the data plane. The chi-square test can be accessed under the Insert>Function>Statistical>Chitest function. The available parametric tests include the t test: paired samples for means; t test: two independent samples assuming equal variances; t test: two independent samples assuming unequal variances; z test: two samples for means; and F test for variances of two samples.

SNAP (www.snapsurveys.com)

In SNAP, Descriptive Statistics produces the count, mean, mode, quartiles, median, sum, minimum, maximum, range, standard error, standard deviation, variance, skewness and kurtosis. In either Tables or Charts, the following can be produced displaying absolute values, percentages or means:

- A single question or several questions together.
- Comparing one question against another, or several questions against one or more other questions (cross-tabulation).
- Grids of a body of scaled items, e.g. a body of Likert scales.
- Holecount tables, i.e. a summary of all or any chosen responses to the questionnaire.
- Summary results in counts or percentages in the format of the original questionnaire. Chi-square and t tests can be calculated using the Charts option.

Summary

Basic data analysis provides valuable insights and guides the rest of the data analysis as well as the interpretation of the results. A frequency distribution should be obtained for each variable in the data. This analysis produces a table of frequency counts, percentages and cumulative percentages for all the values associated with that variable. It indicates the extent of out-of-range, missing or extreme values. The mean, mode and median of a frequency distribution are measures of central tendency. The variability of the distribution is described by the range, the variance or standard deviation, coefficient of variation and interquartile range. Skewness and kurtosis provide an idea of the shape of the distribution.

Cross-tabulations are tables that reflect the joint distribution of two or more variables. In cross-tabulation, the percentages can be computed either by column, based on column totals, or by row, based on row totals. The general rule is to compute the percentages in the direction of the independent variable, across the dependent variable. Often the introduction of a third variable can provide additional insights. The chi-square statistic provides a test of the statistical significance of the observed association in a cross-tabulation. The phi coefficient, contingency coefficient, Cramer's V and lambda coefficient provide measures of the strength of association between the variables.

Parametric and non-parametric tests are available for testing hypotheses related to differences. In the parametric case, the t test is used to examine hypotheses related to the population mean. Different forms of the t test are suitable for testing hypotheses based on one sample, two independent samples or paired samples. In the non-parametric case, popular one-sample tests include the chi-square, Kolmogorov–Smirnov and binomial tests. For two independent non-parametric samples, the chi-square, Mann–Whitney U, median and Kolmogorov–Smirnov tests can be used. For paired samples, the sign, Wilcoxon matched-pairs signed-ranks, McNemar and chi-square tests are useful for examining hypotheses related to measures of location.

Questions

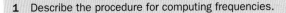

1   Describe the procedure for computing frequencies.

2   What measures of location are commonly computed?

3   What measures of variability are commonly computed?

4   How is the relative flatness or peakedness of a distribution measured?

5   What is a skewed distribution? What does it mean?

6   What is the major difference between cross-tabulation and frequency distribution?

7   What is the general rule for computing percentages in cross-tabulation?

8   Define a spurious correlation.

9   What is meant by a suppressed association? How is it revealed?

10   Discuss the reasons for the frequent use of cross-tabulations. What are some of the limitations?

11   Present a classification of hypothesis testing procedures.

12   Describe the general procedure for conducting a t test.

13   What is the major difference between parametric and non-parametric tests?

14   Which non-parametric tests are the counterparts of the two-independent-samples t test for parametric data?

15   Which non-parametric tests are the counterparts of the paired samples t test for parametric data?

Exercises

1 in each of the following situations, indicate the statistical analysis you would conduct and the appropriate test or test statistic that should be used.

  a Consumer preferences for Body Shop shampoo were obtained on an 11-point Likert scale. The same consumers were then shown a commercial about the Body Shop. After the commercial, preferences for the Body Shop were again measured. Has the commercial been successful in inducing a change in preferences?

  b Does the preference for Body Shop shampoo follow a normal distribution?

  c Respondents in a survey of 1,000 households were classified as heavy, medium, light and non-users of ice cream. They were also classified as being in high-, medium- or low-income categories. Is the consumption of ice cream related to income level?

  d In a survey of 2,000 households, respondents were asked to rank 10 supermarkets, including Lidl, in order of preference. The sample was divided into small and large households based on a median split of the household size. Does preference for shopping in Lidl vary by household size?

2 The current advertising campaign for Red Bull would be changed if less than 30% of consumers like it.

  a Formulate the null and alternative hypotheses.

  b Discuss the Type I and Type II errors that could occur in hypothesis testing.

  c Which statistical test would you use? Why?

  d A random sample of 300 consumers was surveyed and 84 respondents indicated that they liked the campaign. Should the campaign be changed? Why?

3 An electrical goods chain is having a New Year sale of refrigerators. The number of refrigerators sold during this sale at a sample of 10 stores was:

  80   110   0   40   70   80   100   50   80   30

  a Is there evidence that an average of more than 50 refrigerators per store were sold during this sale? Use $a = 0.05$.

  b What assumption is necessary to perform this test?

4 In a survey pretest, data were obtained from 45 respondents on Benetton clothes. These data are given in the table opposite, which gives the usage, gender, awareness, attitude, preference, intention and loyalty towards Benetton of a sample of Benetton users. Usage was coded as 1, 2, or 3, representing light, medium or heavy users. Gender was coded as 1 for females and 2 for males. Awareness, attitude, preference, intention and loyalty were measured on a 7-point Likert type scale (1 = very unfavourable, 7 = very favourable). Note that 5 respondents have missing values that are denoted by 9.

Analyse the Benetton data to answer the following questions. In each case, formulate the null and alternative hypotheses and conduct the appropriate statistical test(s).

  a Obtain a frequency distribution for each of the following variables and calculate the relevant statistics: awareness, attitude, preference, intention and loyalty towards Benetton.

  b Conduct a cross-tabulation of the usage with gender. Interpret the results.

  c Does the awareness for Benetton exceed 3.0?

  d Do males and females differ in their awareness for Benetton? Their attitude towards Benetton? Their loyalty for Benetton?

  e Do the respondents in the pretest have a higher level of awareness than loyalty?

  f Does awareness of Benetton follow a normal distribution?

  g Is the distribution of preference for Benetton normal?

  h Assume that awareness towards Benetton was measured on an ordinal scale rather than an interval scale. Do males and females differ in their loyalty towards Benetton?

  i Assume that loyalty towards Benetton was measured on an ordinal scale rather than an interval scale. Do males and females differ in their loyalty towards Benetton?

  j Assume that attitude and loyalty towards Benetton was measured on an ordinal scale rather than an interval scale. Do the respondents have a greater awareness of Benetton than loyalty for Benetton?

Number	Usage	Gender	Awareness	Attitude	Preference	Intention	Loyalty
1	3	2	7	6	5	5	6
2	1	1	2	2	4	6	5
3	1	1	3	3	6	7	6
4	3	2	6	5	5	3	2
5	3	2	5	4	7	4	3
6	2	2	4	3	5	2	3
7	2	1	5	4	4	3	2
8	1	1	2	1	3	4	5
9	2	2	4	4	3	6	5
10	1	1	3	1	2	4	5
11	3	2	6	7	6	4	5
12	3	2	6	5	6	4	4
13	1	1	4	3	3	1	1
14	3	2	6	4	5	3	2
15	1	2	4	3	4	5	6
16	1	2	3	4	2	4	2
17	3	1	7	6	4	5	3
18	2	1	6	5	4	3	2
19	1	1	1	1	3	4	5
20	3	1	5	7	4	1	2
21	3	2	6	6	7	7	5
22	2	2	2	3	1	4	2
23	1	1	1	1	3	2	2
24	3	1	6	7	6	7	6
25	1	2	3	2	2	1	1
26	2	2	5	3	4	4	5
27	3	2	7	6	6	5	7
28	2	1	6	4	2	5	6
29	1	1	9	2	3	1	3
30	2	2	5	9	4	6	5
31	1	2	1	2	9	3	2
32	1	2	4	6	5	9	3
33	2	1	3	4	3	2	9
34	2	1	4	6	5	7	6
35	3	1	5	7	7	3	3
36	3	1	6	5	7	3	4
37	3	2	6	7	5	3	4
38	3	2	5	6	4	3	2
39	3	2	7	7	6	3	4
40	1	1	4	3	4	6	5
41	1	1	2	3	4	5	6
42	1	1	1	3	2	3	4
43	1	1	2	4	3	6	7
44	1	1	3	3	4	6	5
45	1	1	1	1	4	5	3

5   In a small group discuss the following issues: 'Why waste time doing basic forms of data analysis? Why not just go straight to performing multivariate analyses – whose outputs from most software packages will include basic analyses?' and 'Why do managers find cross-tabulations so appealing? What would it take to make managers more appreciative of statistical analyses that go beyond the cross-tabulation?'

Notes

1 Mathwick, C., Malhotra, N.K. and Rigdon, E., 'The effect of dynamic retail experience on experiential perceptions of value: an Internet and catalog comparison', *Journal of Retailing* 78 (2002), 51–60; Festervand, T.A., Snyder, DR. and Tsalikis, J.D., 'Influence of catalog vs. store shopping and prior satisfaction on perceived risk', *Journal of the Academy of Marketing Science* (Winter 1986), 28–36.

2 Neirtti, L.D., Bosetti, HA, and Teed, K.C., 'Motivation to attend the 1996 Summer Olympic Games,' *Journal of Travel Research* 39 (3) (February 2001), 327–331.

3 For an application of frequencies and descriptive statistics, see Bitner, M.J., Booms, B.H. and Mohr, L.A., 'Critical service encounters: the employee's viewpoint', *Journal of Marketing* 58 (October 1994), 95–106.

4 See any introductory statistics book for a more detailed description of these statistics; for example, see Berenson, M.L., Levine, D.M. and Krehbiel, T.C., *Basic Business Statistics: Concepts and Applications*, 8th edn (Englewood Cliffs, NJ: Prentice Hall, 2002).

5 For our purposes, no distinction will be made between formal hypothesis testing and statistical inference by means of confidence intervals.

6 Excellent discussions of ways to analyse cross-tabulations can be found in Denham, B.E., 'Advanced categorical statistics: issues and applications in communication research', *Journal of Communication* 52 (1) (March 2002), 162; Hellevik, 0., *Introduction to Causal Analysis: Exploring Survey Data by Crosstabulation* (Beverly Hills, CA: Sage, 1984).

7 Kivetz, R., Simonson, I., 'Earning the right to indulge: effort as a determinant of customer preferences toward frequency program rewards', *Journal of Marketing Research* 39 (2) (May 2002), 155–170; Feick, L.F., 'Analyzing marketing research data with association models', *Journal of Marketing Research* 21 (November 1984), 376–386. For an application, see Kamakura, W.A. and Wedel, M., 'Statistical data fusion for cross tabulation', *Journal of Marketing Research* 34 (4) (November 1997), 485-498.

8 Lenell, W. and Boissoneau, it, 'Using causal-comparative and correlational designs in conducting market research', *Journal of Professional Services Marketing* 13 (2) (1996), 59–69. See also the classic book by Zeisel, H., *Say It with Figures*, 5th edn (New York: Harper & Row, 1968).

9 Wright, D.B., *First steps in statistics* (Thousand Oaks, CA: Sage, 2002); Sirkin, R.M., *Statistics for the Social Sciences* (Thousand Oaks, CA: Sage, 1994).

10 Higgins, J.J., *Introduction to modern nonparametric statistics*, (Pacific Grove, CA: Duxbury, 2002); Pet, M.A., *Nonparametric Statistics for Health Care Research* (Thousand Oaks, CA: Sage, 1997). For a more extensive treatment see Lancaster, HO., *The Chi Squared Distribution* (New York: Wiley, 1969).

11 Berenson, M.L., Levine) D.M. and Krehbiel, T.C., *Basic Business Statistics: Concepts and Applications*, 8th edn (Englewood Cliffs, NJ: Prentice Hall, 2002).

12 Some statisticians, however, disagree. They feel that a correction should not be applied. See, for example, Overall, J.E., 'Power of chi-square tests for 2 × 2 contingency tables with small expected frequencies', *Psychological Bulletin* (January 1980), 132–135.

13 Significance tests and confidence intervals are also available for either lambda asymmetric or lambda symmetric. See Goodman, L.A. and Kruskal, W.H., 'Measures of association for cross classification: appropriate sampling theory', *Journal of the American Statistical Association* 88 (June 1963), 310–364.

14 Hoenig, J.M., 'The abuse of power: the pervasive fallacy of power calculation for data analysis', *American Statistician* 55 (1) (February 2001), 19–24; Cowles, M. and Davis, C., 'On the origins of the .05 level of statistical significance', *American Psychologist* (May 1982), 553–558. See also Kotabe, M., Duhan, D.E., Smith, D.K. Jr and Wilson, RID., 'The perceived veracity of PIMS strategy principles in Japan: an empirical inquiry', *Journal of Marketing* 55 (January 1991), 26–41.

15 Technically, a null hypothesis cannot be accepted. It can be either rejected or not rejected. This distinction, however, is inconsequential in marketing research.

16 The condition when the variances cannot be assumed to be equal is known as the Behrens–Fisher problem. There is some controversy over the best procedure in this case. For an example, see Heilman, C.M., Nakamoto, K. and Rao, A.G., 'Pleasant surprises: consumer response to unexpected in-store coupons', *Journal of Marketing Research* 39 (2) (May 2002), 242–252.

17 Chandler, S., 'Some retailers begin to cater to growing group of aging shoppers', *Knight Ridder Tribune Business News* (17 March 2001), 1; Lumpkin, J.R. and Hunt, J.B., 'Mobility as an influence on retail patronage behavior of the elderly: testing conventional wisdom', *Journal of the Academy of Marketing Science* (Winter 1989), 1–12.

18 Hainon, A., 'Skip the ads TV has Madison Ave. upset', *New York Times* (23 May 2002), Al; Dunst, L., 'Is it possible to get creative in 15 seconds?', *Advertising Age* 64 (50) (29 November 1993), 18; Rosenblatt, J.A. and Mainprize, J., 'The history and future of 15-second commercials: an empirical investigation of the perception of ad agency media directors ', in Lazer, W., Shaw, E. and Wee, C.H. (eds), *World Marketing Congress*, International Conference Series, Vol. 4 (Boca Raton, FL: Academy of Marketing Science, 1989), 169–177.

19 Kanji, G.K., *100 Statistical Tests* (Thousand Oaks, CA: Sage, 1999); Harnett, D.L., *Statistical Methods*, 3rd edn (Reading, MA: Addison-Wesley, 1982).

20 Higgins, J.J., *Introduction to modern nonparametric statistics* (Pacific Grove, CA: Duxbury, 2002); Pen, M.A., *Nonparametric Statistics for Health Care Research* (Thousand Oaks, CA: Sage, 1997).

21 There is some controversy over whether non-parametric statistical techniques should be used to make inferences about population parameters. See also Cheung, Y.K. and Klotz, J.H, 'The Mann–Whitney–Wilcoxon distribution using linked lists', *Statistica Sinica* 7 (3) (July 1997), 805–813.

22 The *t* test in this case is equivalent to a chi-square test for independence in a 2 × 2 contingency table. The relationship is

$$\chi^2.95(1) = t^2.0005(n_1 + n_2 - 2)$$

For large samples, the *t* distribution approaches the normal distribution and so the *t* test and the *z* test are equivalent.

23 Swaddling, D., 'Good data still worth the investment', *Marketing News* 35 (2) (15 January 2001), 20–21; Krum, J.R.,

Rau, P.A. and Keiser, S.K., 'The marketing research process: role perceptions of researchers and users', *Journal of Advertising Research* (December-January 1988), 9–21. See also Miller, C., 'Gallup Brothers analyze the research industry', *Marketing News* 31 (1) (6 January 1997), 2.

24 Bergmann, R., 'Different outcomes of the Wilcoxon–Mann–Whitney test from different statistics packages', *American Statistician* 54 (1) (February 2000), 72–77; and for an example of Wilcoxon matched-pairs signed-ranks test, see Kalwani, M.U. and Narayandas, N., 'Long-term manufacturer-supplier relationships: do they pay off for supplier firms?', *Journal of Marketing* 59 (January 1995), 1–16.

25 Pett, M.A., *Nonparametric Statistics for Health Care Research* (Thousand Oaks, CA: Sage, 1997); Field, J.G., 'The world's simplest test of significance', *Journal of the Market Research Society* (July 1971), 170–172.

26 Miles, L., 'Finding a balance in global research', *Marketing* (29 November 2001), 33; de Chernatony, L., Halliburton, C. and Bernath, R., 'International branding: demand or supply driven?', *International Marketing Review* 12 (2) (1995), 9–21.

Visit the *Marketing Research* Companion Website at www.pearsoned.co.uk/malhotra_euro for additional learning resources including annotated weblinks, an online glossary and a suite of downloadable video cases.

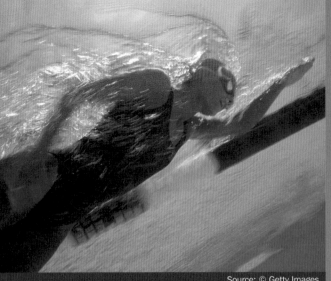

Source: © Getty Images

19

Analysis of variance and covariance

> *Analysis of variance is a straightforward way to examine the differences between groups of responses that are measured on interval or ratio scales.*

Objectives

After reading this chapter, you should be able to:

1 discuss the scope of the analysis of variance (ANOVA) technique and its relationship to the t test, and regression;

2 describe one-way analysis of variance, including decomposition of the total variation, measurement of effects significance testing and interpretation of results;

3 describe n-way analysis of variance and the testing of the significance of the overall effect, the interaction effect and the main effect of each factor;

4 describe analysis of covariance and show how it accounts for the influence of uncontrolled independent variables;

5 explain key factors pertaining to the interpretation of results with emphasis on interactions, relative importance of factors and multiple comparisons;

6 discuss specialised ANOVA techniques applicable to marketing, such as repeated measures ANOVA, non-metric ANOVA, and multivariate analysis of variance (MANOVA).

STAGE 1
Problem
definition

STAGE 2
Research approach
developed

STAGE 3
Research design
developed

STAGE 4
Fieldwork or data
collection

STAGE 5
Data preparation
and analysis

STAGE 6
Report preparation
and presentation

Overview

In Chapter 18, we examined tests of differences between two means or two medians. In this chapter, we discuss procedures for examining differences between more than two means or medians. These procedures are called analysis of variance and analysis of covariance. These procedures have traditionally been used for analysing experimental data, but they are also used for analysing survey or observational data.

We describe analysis of variance and covariance procedures and discuss their relationship to other techniques. Then we describe one-way analysis of variance, the simplest of these procedures, followed by *n*-way analysis of variance and analysis of covariance. Special attention is given to issues in interpretation of results as they relate to interactions, relative importance of factors and multiple comparisons. Some specialised topics such as repeated measures analysis of variance, non-metric analysis of variance and multivariate analysis of variance are briefly discussed. We begin with an example illustrating the application of analysis of variance.

Example Analysis of tourism destinations[1]

A survey conducted by EgeBank in Istanbul, Turkey, focused upon the importance of tour operators and travel agents' perceptions of selected Mediterranean tourist destinations (Egypt, Greece, Italy and Turkey). Operators/travel agents were mailed questionnaires

Image variations of destinations promoted to tour operators and travel agencies

Image items	Turkey (n=36)	Egypt (n=29)	Greece (n=37)	Italy (n=34)	Sig.
Affective (scale 1–7)					
Unpleasant–pleasant	6.14	5.62	6.43	6.50	0.047*
Sleepy–arousing	6.24	5.61	6.14	6.56	0.053
Distressing–relaxing	5.60	4.86	6.05	6.09	0.003*
Gloomy–exciting	6.20	5.83	6.32	6.71	0.061
Perceptual (scale 1–5)					
Good value for money	4.62	4.32	3.89	3.27	0.000*
Beautiful scenery and natural attractions	4.50	4.04	4.53	4.70	0.011*
Good climate	4.29	4.00	4.41	4.35	0.133
Interesting cultural attractions	4.76	4.79	4.67	4.79	0.781
Suitable accommodations	4.17	4.28	4.35	4.62	0.125
Appealing local food (cuisine)	4.44	3.57	4.19	4.85	0.000*
Great beaches and water sports	3.91	3.18	4.27	3.65	0.001*
Quality of infrastructure	3.49	2.97	3.68	4.09	0.000*
Personal safety	3.83	3.28	4.19	4.15	0.000*
Interesting historical attractions	4.71	4.86	4.81	4.82	0.650
Unpolluted and unspoiled environment	3.54	3.34	3.43	3.59	0.784
Good nightlife and entertainment	3.44	3.15	4.06	4.27	0.000*
Standard hygiene and cleanliness	3.29	2.79	3.76	4.29	0.000*
Interesting and friendly people	4.34	4.24	4.35	4.32	0.956

*Significant at 0.05 level.

based on the location of tours, broken down as follows: Egypt (53), Greece (130), Italy (150) and Turkey (65). The survey consisted of questions on affective and cognitive evaluations of the 4 destinations. The 4 affective questions were asked on a seven-point semantic differential scale, whereas the 14 cognitive evaluations were measured on a five-point Likert scale (1 = offers very little, 2 = offers somewhat little, 3 = offers neither little nor much, 4 = offers somewhat much, and 5 = offers very much). The differences in the evaluations of the four locations were examined using one-way analysis of variance (ANOVA) as seen in the table on the previous page.

The ANOVA table shows that 'unpleasant–pleasant' and 'distressing–relaxing' affective factors have significant differences among the four destinations. For instance, Greece and Italy were perceived as being significantly more relaxing than Egypt. As for the perceptual factors, 8 of the 14 factors were significant. Turkey was perceived as significantly better value for money than Greece and Italy. Turkey's main strength appears to be 'good value', and the country's tourist agencies should promote this in their marketing strategies. On the other hand, Turkey needs to improve the perception of its infrastructure, cleanliness and entertainment to attract more tour operators and travel agencies.

In this example, *t* tests were not appropriate to examine the overall difference in the four category means, so analysis of variance was used instead.

Relationship among techniques

Analysis of variance and analysis of covariance are used for examining the differences in the mean values of the dependent variable associated with the effect of the controlled independent variables, after taking into account the influence of the uncontrolled independent variables. Essentially, **analysis of variance (ANOVA)** is used as a test of means for two or more populations. The null hypothesis, typically, is that all means are equal. For example, suppose that the researcher was interested in examining whether heavy users, medium users, light users and non-users of yogurt differed in their preference for Müller yogurt, measured on a nine-point Likert scale. The null hypothesis that the four groups were not different in preference for Müller could be tested using ANOVA.

In its simplest form, ANOVA must have a dependent variable (preference for Müller yogurt) that is metric (measured using an interval or ratio scale). There must also be one or more independent variables (product use: heavy, medium, light and non-users). The independent variables must be all categorical (non-metric). Categorical independent variables are also called factors. A particular combination of **factor** levels, or categories, is called a **treatment**. **One-way analysis of variance** involves only one categorical variable, or a single factor. The differences in preference of heavy users, medium users, light users and non-users would be examined by one-way ANOVA. In this, a treatment is the same as a factor level (medium users constitute a treatment). If two or more factors are involved, the analysis is termed *n*-way analysis of variance. If, in addition to product use, the researcher also wanted to examine the preference for Müller yogurt of customers who are loyal and those who are not, an *n*-way ANOVA would be conducted.

If the set of independent variables consists of both categorical and metric variables, the technique is called **analysis of covariance (ANCOVA)**. For example, analysis of covariance would be required if the researcher wanted to examine the preference of product use groups and loyalty groups, taking into account the respondents' attitudes towards nutrition and the importance they attached to dairy products. The latter two variables would be measured on nine-point Likert scales. In this case, the categorical independent variables (product use and brand loyalty) are still referred to as factors, whereas the

Analysis of variance (ANOVA)
A statistical technique for examining the differences among means for two or more populations.

Factors
Categorical independent variables in ANOVA. The independent variables must all be categorical (non-metric) to use ANOVA.

Treatment
In ANOVA, a particular combination of factor levels or categories.

One-way analysis of variance
An ANOVA technique in which there is only one factor.

n-way analysis of variance
An ANOVA model where two or more factors are involved.

Analysis of covariance (ANCOVA)
An advanced ANOVA procedure in which the effects of one or more metric-scaled extraneous variables are removed from the dependent variable before conducting the ANOVA.

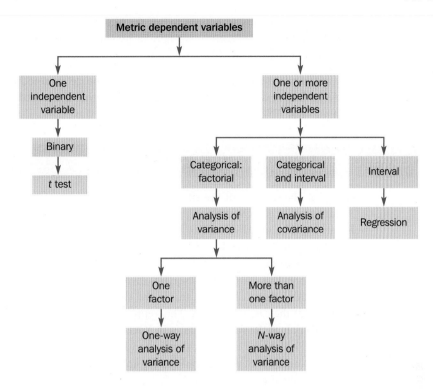

Figure 19.1
Relationship between
_t_ test, analysis of
variance, analysis of
covariance and
regression

Covariate
A metric-independent variable
used in ANCOVA.

metric-independent variables (attitude towards nutrition and importance attached to dairy products) are referred to as **covariates**.

The relationship of ANOVA to _t_ tests and other techniques, such as regression (see Chapter 20), is shown in Figure 19.1. These techniques all involve a metric-dependent variable. ANOVA and ANCOVA can include more than one independent variable (product use, brand loyalty, attitude, importance, etc.). Furthermore, at least one of the independent variables must be categorical, and the categorical variables may have more than two categories (in our example, product use has four categories). A _t_ test, on the other hand, involves a single, binary independent variable. For example, the difference in the preferences of loyal and non-loyal respondents could be tested by conducting a _t_ test. Regression analysis, like ANOVA and ANCOVA, can also involve more than one independent variable. All the independent variables, however, are generally interval scaled, although binary or categorical variables can be accommodated using dummy variables. For example, the relationship between preference for Müller yogurt, attitude towards nutrition, and importance attached to dairy products could be examined via regression analysis, with preference for Müller serving as the dependent variable and attitude and importance as independent variables.

One-way ANOVA

Marketing researchers are often interested in examining the differences in the mean values of the dependent variable for several categories of a single independent variable or factor. For example:

- Do various market segments differ in terms of their volume of product consumption?
- Do brand evaluations of groups exposed to different commercials vary?
- Do retailers, wholesalers and agents differ in their attitudes towards the firm's distribution policies?

- How do consumers' intentions to buy the brand vary with different price levels?
- What is the effect of consumers' familiarity with a car manufacturer (measured as high, medium and low) on preference for the car?

The answer to these and similar questions can be determined by conducting one-way ANOVA. Before describing the procedure, we define the important statistics associated with one-way ANOVA.[2]

Statistics associated with one-way ANOVA

eta^2 (η^2). The strength of the effects of X (independent variable or factor) on Y (dependent variable) is measured by eta^2 (η^2). The value of η^2 varies between 0 and 1.

F statistic. The null hypothesis that the category means are equal in the population is tested by an *F statistic* based on the ratio of mean square related to X and mean square related to error.

Mean square. This is the sum of squares divided by the appropriate degrees of freedom.

$SS_{between}$. Also denoted as SS_x, this is the variation in Y related to the variation in the means of the categories of X. This represents variation between the categories of X or the portion of the sum of squares in Y related to X.

SS_{within}. Also denoted as SS_{error}, this is the variation in Y due to the variation within each of the categories of X. This variation is not accounted for by X.

SS_y. This is the total variation in Y.

Conducting one-way ANOVA

The procedure for conducting one-way ANOVA is described in Figure 19.2. It involves identifying the dependent and independent variables, decomposing the total variation, measuring the effects, testing significance and interpreting the results. We consider these steps in detail and illustrate them with some applications.

Identifying the dependent and independent variables

The dependent variable is denoted by Y and the independent variable by X, and X is a categorical variable having c categories. There are n observations on Y for each category of X, as shown in Table 19.1. As can be seen, the sample size in each category of X is n, and the total sample size $N = n \times c$. Although the sample sizes in the categories of X (the group sizes) are assumed to be equal for the sake of simplicity, this is not a requirement.

Decomposing the total variation

Decomposition of the total variation
In one-way ANOVA, separation of the variation observed in the dependent variable into the variation due to the independent variables plus the variation due to error.

In examining the differences among means, one-way ANOVA involves the **decomposition of the total variation** observed in the dependent variable. This variation is measured by the sums of squares corrected for the mean (SS). ANOVA is so named because it examines the variability or variation in the sample (dependent variable) and, based on the variability, determines whether there is reason to believe that the population means differ.

The total variation in Y, denoted by SS_y, can be decomposed into two components:

$$SS_y = SS_{between} + SS_{within}$$

where the subscripts *between* and *within* refer to the categories of X. $SS_{between}$ is the variation in Y related to the variation in the means of the categories of X. It represents variation between the categories of X. In other words, $SS_{between}$ is the portion of the sum of squares in Y related to the independent variable or factor X. For this reason, $SS_{between}$ is

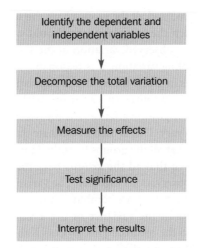

**Figure 19.2
Conducting one-way
ANOVA**

Table 19.1 Decomposition of the total variation: one-way ANOVA

Independent variable			X
Categories			*Total sample*
X_1	X_2	X_3 ... X_c	
Y_1	Y_1	Y_1 ... Y_1	Y_1
Y_2	Y_2	Y_2 ... Y_2	Y_2
⋮			⋮
Y_n	Y_n	Y_n ... Y_n	Y_n
$\bar{Y}_1$	$\bar{Y}_2$	$\bar{Y}_3$ ... $\bar{Y}_c$	

Within-category variation = SS_{within}

Category mean

Total variation = SS_y

Between-category variation = $SS_{between}$

also denoted as SS_x. SS_{within} is the variation in Y related to the variation within each category of X. SS_{within} is not accounted for by X. Therefore, it is referred to as SS_{error}. The total variation in Y may be decomposed as

$$SS_y = SS_x + SS_{error}$$

where $SS_y = \sum_{i=1}^{N} (Y_i - \bar{Y})^2$

$$SS_x = \sum_{j=1}^{c} n(\bar{Y}_j - \bar{Y})^2$$

$$SS_{error} = \sum_{j}^{c}\sum_{i}^{n} (\bar{Y}_{ij} - \bar{Y}_j)^2$$

and Y_i = indivdual observation

$\bar{Y}_j$ = mean for category j

$\bar{Y}$ = mean over the whole sample or grand mean

Y_{ij} = ith observation in the jth category

The logic of decomposing the total variation in Y, SS_y into $SS_{between}$ and SS_{within} to examine differences in group means can be intuitively understood. Recall from Chapter 18 that, if the variation of the variable in the population was known or estimated, one could estimate how much the sample mean should vary because of random variation alone. In ANOVA, there are several different groups (e.g. heavy, medium and light users and non-users). If the null hypothesis is true and all the groups have the same mean in the population, one can estimate how much the sample means should vary because of sampling (random) variations alone. If the observed variation in the sample means is more than what would be expected by sampling variation, it is reasonable to conclude that this extra variability is related to differences in group means in the population.

In ANOVA, we estimate two measures of variation: within groups (SS_{within}) and between groups ($SS_{between}$). Within-group variation is a measure of how much the observations, Y values, within a group vary. This is used to estimate the variance within a group in the population. It is assumed that all the groups have the same variation in the population. But because it is not known that all the groups have the same mean, we cannot calculate the variance of all the observations together. The variance for each of the groups must be calculated individually, and these are combined into an 'average' or 'overall' variance. Likewise, another estimate of the variance of the Y values may be obtained by examining the variation between the means. (This process is the reverse of determining the variation in the means, given the population variances.) If the population mean is the same in all the groups, then the variation in the sample means and the sizes of the sample groups can be used to estimate the variance of Y. The reasonableness of this estimate of the Y variance depends on whether the null hypothesis is true. If the null hypothesis is true and the population means are equal, the variance estimate based on between-group variation is correct. On the other hand, if the groups have different means in the population, the variance estimate based on between-group variation will be too large. Thus, by comparing the Y variance estimates based on between-group and within-group variation, we can test the null hypothesis. Decomposition of the total variation in this manner also enables us to measure the effects of X on Y.

Measuring the effects

The effects of X on Y are measured by SS_x. Because SS_x is related to the variation in the means of the categories of X, the relative magnitude of SS_x increases as the differences among the means of Y in the categories of X increase. The relative magnitude of SS_x also increases as the variations in Y within the categories of X decrease. The strength of the effects of X on Y is measured as follows:

$$\eta^2 = \frac{SS_x}{SS_y} = \frac{SS_y - SS_{error}}{SS_y}$$

The value of η^2 varies between 0 and 1. It assumes a value of 0 when all the category means are equal, indicating that X has no effect on Y. The value of η^2 will be 1 when there is no variability within each category of X but there is some variability between categories. Thus, η^2 is a measure of the variation in Y that is explained by the independent variable X. Not only can we measure the effects of X on Y, but we can also test for their significance.

Testing the significance

In one-way ANOVA, the interest lies in testing the null hypothesis that the category means are equal in the population.[3] In other words,

$$H_0: \mu_1 = \mu_2 = \mu_3 = \ldots = \mu_c$$

Under the null hypothesis, SS_x and SS_{error} come from the same source of variation. In such a case, the estimate of the population variance of Y can be based on either between-category variation or within-category variation. In other words, the estimate of the population variance of Y,

$$S_y^2 = \frac{SS_x}{c-1}$$
$$= \text{mean square due to } X$$
$$= MS_x$$

or

$$S_y^2 = \frac{SS_{error}}{N-c}$$
$$= \text{mean square due to error}$$
$$= MS_{error}$$

The null hypothesis may be tested by the F statistic based on the ratio between these two estimates:

$$F = \frac{SS_x/(c-1)}{SS_{error}/(N-c)} = \frac{MS_x}{MS_{error}}$$

This statistic follows the F distribution, with $(c-1)$ and $(N-c)$ degrees of freedom (df). A table of the F distribution is given as Table 5 in the Appendix of statistical tables at the end of the book. As mentioned in Chapter 18, the F distribution is a probability distribution of the ratios of sample variances. It is characterised by degrees of freedom for the numerator and degrees of freedom for the denominator.[4]

Interpreting results

If the null hypothesis of equal category means is not rejected, then the independent variable does not have a significant effect on the dependent variable. On the other hand, if the null hypothesis is rejected, then the effect of the independent variable is significant. In other words, the mean value of the dependent variable will be different for different categories of the independent variable. A comparison of the category mean values will indicate the nature of the effect of the independent variable. Other salient issues in the interpretation of results, such as examination of differences among specific means, are discussed later.

Illustrative applications of one-way ANOVA

We illustrate the concepts discussed in this section using the data presented in Table 19.2. These data were generated by an experiment in which Renault wanted to examine the effect of direct mail offers and dealership promotions upon the level of sales of new cars. Dealership promotion was varied at three levels: high (1), medium (2) and low (3). Direct mail efforts were manipulated at two levels. Either an exclusive boxed set of DVDs covering the history of Formula One Racing was offered to customers who bought a new car (denoted by 1) or it was not (denoted by 2 in Table 19.2). Dealership promotion and direct mail offer were crossed, resulting in a 3×2 design with six cells. Thirty Renault dealerships were randomly selected, and five dealerships were randomly assigned to each treatment condition. The experiment ran for two months. The sales level of new cars were measured, normalised to account for extraneous factors (e.g. dealership size, competitive dealerships in town) and converted to a 1 to 10 scale (10 representing the highest level of sales). In addition, a qualitative assessment was made of the relative affluence of the clientele of each dealership, again using a 1 to 10 scale (10 representing the most affluent client base).

Table 19.2 Direct mail offer, dealership promotion, sales of new cars and clientele rating

Dealership number	Direct mail offer	Dealership promotion	Sales	Clientele rating
1	1	1	10	9
2	1	1	9	10
3	1	1	10	8
4	1	1	8	4
5	1	1	9	6
6	1	2	8	8
7	1	2	8	4
8	1	2	7	10
9	1	2	9	6
10	1	2	6	9
11	1	3	5	8
12	1	3	7	9
13	1	3	6	6
14	1	3	4	10
15	1	3	5	4
16	2	1	8	10
17	2	1	9	6
18	2	1	7	8
19	2	1	7	4
20	2	1	6	9
21	2	2	4	6
22	2	2	5	8
23	2	2	5	10
24	2	2	6	4
25	2	2	4	9
26	2	3	2	4
27	2	3	3	6
28	2	3	2	10
29	2	3	1	9
30	2	3	2	8

To illustrate the concepts of ANOVA, we begin with an example showing calculations done by hand and then by computer. Suppose that only one factor, namely dealership promotion, was manipulated; that is, let us ignore the direct mail efforts for the purpose of this illustration. Renault is attempting to determine the effect of dealership promotion (X) on the sales of new cars (Y). For the purpose of illustrating hand calculations, the data of Table 19.2 are transformed in Table 19.3 to show the dealership (Y_{ij}) for each level of promotion.

The null hypothesis is that the category means are equal:

$$H_0: \ \mu_1 = \mu_2 = \mu_3$$

To test the null hypothesis, the various sums of squares are computed as follows:

$$
\begin{aligned}
SS_y = {} & (10-6.067)^2 + (9-6.067)^2 + (10-6.067)^2 + (8-6.067)^2 + (9-6.067)^2 + (8-6.067)^2 \\
& + (8-6.067)^2 + (7-6.067)^2 + (9-6.067)^2 + (6-6.067)^2 + (5-6.067)^2 + (7-6.067)^2 \\
& + (6-6.067)^2 + (4-6.067)^2 + (5-6.067)^2 + (8-6.067)^2 + (9-6.067)^2 + (7-6.067)^2 \\
& + (7-6.067)^2 + (6-6.067)^2 + (4-6.067)^2 + (5-6.067)^2 + (5-6.067)^2 + (6-6.067)^2 \\
& + (4-6.067)^2 + (2-6.067)^2 + (3-6.067)^2 + (2-6.067)^2 + (1-6.067)^2 + (2-6.067)^2 \\
= {} & 185.867
\end{aligned}
$$

$$SS_x = 10(8.3 - 6.067)^2 + 10(6.2 - 6.067)^2 + 10(3.7 - 6.067)^2$$
$$= 106.067$$

$$SS_{error} = (10 - 8.3)^2 + (9 - 8.3)^2 + (10 - 8.3)^2 + (8 - 8.3)^2 + (9 - 8.3)^2 + (8 - 8.3)^2 + (9 - 8.3)^2$$
$$+ (7 - 8.3)^2 + (7 - 8.3)^2 + (6 - 8.3)^2 + (8 - 8.3)^2 + (8 - 6.2)^2 + (7 - 6.2)^2 + (9 - 6.2)^2$$
$$+ (6 - 6.2)^2 + (4 - 6.2)^2 + (5 - 6.2)^2 + (5 - 6.2)^2 + (6 - 6.2)^2 + (4 - 6.2)^2 + (5 - 3.7)^2$$
$$+ (7 - 3.7)^2 + (6 - 3.7)^2 + (4 - 3.7)^2 + (5 - 3.7)^2 + (2 - 3.7)^2 + (3 - 3.7)^2 + (2 - 3.7)^2$$
$$+ (1 - 3.7)^2 + (2 - 3.7)^2$$
$$= 79.8$$

Table 19.3 Effect of dealership promotion on sales of new cars

Dealership number	Level of dealership promotion		
	High	Medium	Low
	Normalised sales		
1	10	8	5
2	9	8	7
3	10	7	6
4	8	9	4
5	9	6	5
6	8	4	2
7	9	5	3
8	7	5	2
9	7	6	1
10	6	4	2
Column totals	83	62	37
Category means: $\bar{Y}_j$	$\dfrac{83}{10} = 8.3$	$\dfrac{62}{10} = 6.2$	$\dfrac{37}{10} = 3.7$
Grand means: $\bar{Y} = \dfrac{83 + 62 + 37}{30} = 6.067$			

It can be verified that

$$SS_y = SS_x + SS_{error}$$

as follows:

$$185.867 = 106.067 + 79.80$$

The strength of the effects of X on Y are measured as follows:

$$\eta^2 = \frac{SS_x}{SS_y}$$

$$= \frac{106.067}{185.897}$$

$$= 0.571$$

In other words, 57.1% of the variation in sales (Y) is accounted for by dealership promotion (X), indicating a modest effect. The null hypothesis may now be tested:

$$F = \frac{SS_x/(c-1)}{SS_{error}/(N-c)} = \frac{MS_x}{MS_{error}}$$

$$= \frac{106.067/(3-1)}{79.8/(30-3)}$$

$$= 17.944$$

From Table 5 in the Appendix of statistical tables we see that, for 2 and 27 degrees of freedom, the critical value of F is 3.35 for $a = 0.05$. Because the calculated value of F is greater than the critical value, we reject the null hypothesis. We conclude that the population means for the three levels of dealership promotion are indeed different. The relative magnitudes of the means for the three categories indicate that a high level of dealership promotion leads to significantly higher sales of new car sales.

We now illustrate the ANOVA procedure using a computer program. The results of conducting the same analysis by computer are presented in Table 19.4.

Table 19.4 One-way ANOVA: effect of dealership promotion on the sale of new cars

Source of variation	Sum of squares	df	Mean square	F ratio	F probability
Between groups (dealership promotion)	106.067	2	53.033	17.944	0.000
Within groups (error)	79.800	27	2.956		
Total	185.867	29	6.409		

Cell means		
Level of dealership promotion	Count	Mean
High (1)	10	8.300
Medium (2)	10	6.200
Low (3)	10	3.700
Total	30	6.067

The value of SS_x denoted by main effects is 106.067 with 2 df; that of SS_{error} (within-group sums of squares) is 79.80 with 27 df. Therefore, $MS_x = 106.067/2 = 53.033$ and $MS_{error} = 79.80/27 = 2.956$. The value of $F = 53.033/2.956 = 17.944$ with 2 and 27 df, resulting in a probability of 0.000. Since the associated probability is less than the significance level of 0.05, the null hypothesis of equal population means is rejected. Alternatively, it can be seen from Table 5 in the Appendix that the critical value of F for 2 and 27 df is 3.35. Since the calculated value of F (17.944) is larger than the critical value, the null hypothesis is rejected. As can be seen from Table 19.4, the sample means with values of 8.3, 6.2 and 3.7 are quite different. Dealerships with a high level of promotions have the highest average sales (8.3) and dealerships with a low level of promotions have the lowest average sales (3.7). Dealerships with a medium level of promotions have an intermediate level of sales (6.2). These findings seem plausible.

Assumptions in ANOVA

The procedure for conducting one-way ANOVA and the illustrative applications help us understand the assumptions involved. The salient assumptions in ANOVA can be summarised as follows:

1 Ordinarily, the categories of the independent variable are assumed to be fixed. Inferences are made only to the specific categories considered. This is referred to as the *fixed-effects model*. Other models are also available. In the *random-effects model*, the categories or treatments are considered to be random samples from a universe of treatments. Inferences are made to other categories not examined in the analysis. A *mixed-effects model* results if some treatments are considered fixed and others random.[5]

2 The error term is normally distributed, with a zero mean and a constant variance. The error is not related to any of the categories of *X*. Modest departures from these assumptions do not seriously affect the validity of the analysis. Furthermore, the data can be transformed to satisfy the assumption of normality or equal variances.

3 The error terms are uncorrelated. If the error terms are correlated (i.e. the observations are not independent), the *F* ratio can be seriously distorted.

In many data analysis situations, these assumptions are reasonably met. ANOVA is therefore a common procedure.

N-way ANOVA

In marketing research, one is often concerned with the effect of more than one factor simultaneously.[6] For example:

- How do consumers' intentions to buy a brand vary with different levels of price and different levels of distribution?
- How do advertising levels (high, medium and low) interact with price levels (high, medium and low) to influence a brand's sale?
- Do income levels (high, medium and low) and age (younger than 35, 35–55, older than 55) affect consumption of a brand?
- What is the effect of consumers' familiarity with a bank (high, medium and low) and bank image (positive, neutral and negative) on preference for taking a loan out with that bank?

In determining such effects, *n*-way ANOVA can be used as illustrated in the following example. This example involves a comparison of means where there were two factors (independent variables), each of which was varied at two levels.

Example   ### Electronic shopping risks[7]

Analysis of variance was used to test differences in preferences for electronic shopping for products with different economic and social risks. In a 2 × 2 design, economic risk and social risk were varied at two levels each (high, low). Preference for electronic shopping served as the dependent variable. The results indicted a significant interaction of social risk with economic risk. Electronic shopping was not favoured for high-social-risk products, regardless of the level of economic product risk. It was preferred for low-economic-risk products over high-economic-risk products when the level of social risk was low. Despite the results of this study, year on year, the number of online shoppers has increased significantly. The increase in shoppers can be attributed to bargain-seeking consumers, convenience of using the Internet and, surprisingly, an added sense of safety associated with purchasing online. Improved websites, streamlined order taking and delivery, and assurances of more secure payment systems have increased the flow of new shoppers to the Internet while decreasing the traditional risk associated with online transactions.

Interaction
When assessing the relationship between two variables, an interaction occurs if the effect of X_1 depends on the level of X_2, and vice versa.

A major advantage of *n*-way ANOVA is that it enables the researcher to examine **interactions** between the factors. Interactions occur when the effects of one factor on the dependent variable depend on the level (category) of the other factors. The procedure for conducting n-way ANOVA is similar to that for one-way ANOVA. The statistics associated with n-way ANOVA are also defined similarly. Consider the simple case of two factors X_1 and X_2 having categories c_1 and c_2. The total variation in this case is partitioned as follows:

$$SS_{total} = SS \text{ due to } X_1 + SS \text{ due to } X_2 + SS \text{ due to interraction of } X_1 \text{ and } X_2 + SS_{within}$$

or

$$SS_y = SS_{x_1} + SS_{x_2} + SS_{x_1 x_2} + SS_{error}$$

A larger effect of X_1 will be reflected in a greater mean difference in the levels of X_1 and a larger SS_{x_1}. The same is true for the effect of X_2. The larger the interaction between X_1 and X_2, the larger $SS_{x_1 x_2}$ will be. On the other hand, if X_1 and X_2 are independent, the value of $SS_{x_1 x_2}$ will be close to zero.[8]

Multiple η^2
The strength of the joint effect of two (or more) factors, or the overall effect.

The strength of the joint effect of two factors, called the overall effect, or **multiple η^2**, is measured as follows:

$$\text{multiple } \eta^2 = (SS_{x_1} + SS_{x_2} + SS_{x_1 x_2})/SS_y$$

Significance of the overall effect
A test that some differences exist between some of the treatment groups.

The **significance of the overall effect** may be tested by an F test, as follows:

$$F = \frac{(SS_{x_1} + SS_{x_2} + SS_{x_1 x_2})/df_n}{SS_{error}/df_d}$$

$$= \frac{SS_{x_1,x_2,x_1 x_2}/df_n}{SS_{error}/df_d}$$

$$= \frac{MS_{x_1,x_2,x_1 x_2}}{MS_{error}}$$

where df_n = degrees of freedom for the numerator
$\qquad = (c_1 - 1) + (c_2 - 1) + (c_1 - 1)(c_2 - 1)$
$\qquad = c_1 c_2 - 1$
$\qquad df_d$ = degrees of freedom for the denominator
$\qquad\quad = N - c_1 c_2$
$\qquad MS$ = mean square

Significance of the interaction effect
A test of the significance of the interaction between two or more independent variables.

If the overall effect is significant, the next step is to examine the **significance of the interaction effect**.[9] Under the null hypothesis of no interaction, the appropriate F test is:

$$F = \frac{SS_{x_1 x_2}/df_n}{SS_{error}/df_d}$$

$$= \frac{MS_{x_1 x_2}}{MS_{error}}$$

where $df_n = (c_1 - 1)(c_2 - 1)$
$\qquad df_d = N - c_1 c_2$

Significance of the main effect of each factor
A test of the significance of the main effect for each individual factor.

If the interaction effect is found to be significant, then the effect of X_1 depends on the level of X_2, and vice versa. Since the effect of one factor is not uniform but varies with the level of the other factor, it is not generally meaningful to test the **significance of the main effect of each factor**. It is meaningful to test the significance of each main effect of each factor, if the interaction effect is not significant.[10]

The significance of the main effect of each factor may be tested as follows for X_1:

$$F = \frac{SS_{x_1}/df_n}{SS_{error}/df_d}$$

$$= \frac{MS_{x_1}}{MS_{error}}$$

where $df_n = c_1 - 1$
$df_d = N - c_1 c_2$

The foregoing analysis assumes that the design was orthogonal, or balanced (the number of cases in each cell was the same). If the cell size varies, the analysis becomes more complex.

Returning to the data in Table 19.2, let us now examine the effect of the level of dealership promotion and direct mail efforts on the sales of new cars. The results of running a 3×2 ANOVA on the computer are presented in Table 19.5.

Table 19.5 Two-way ANOVA

Source of variation	Sum of squares	df	Mean square	F	Sig. of F	ω^2
Main effects						
Dealer promotions	106.067	2	53.033	54.862	0.000	0.557
Direct mail	53.333	1	53.333	55.172	0.000	0.280
Combined	159.400	3	53.133	54.966	0.000	
Two-way interaction	3.267	2	1.633	1.690	0.206	
Model	162.667	5	32.533	33.655	0.000	
Residual (error)	23.200	24	0.967			
Total	185.867	29	6.409			
Cell means						
Dealership promotions	Direct mail		Count		Mean	
High	Yes		5		9.200	
High	No		5		7.400	
Medium	Yes		5		7.600	
Medium	No		5		4.800	
Low	Yes		5		5.400	
Low	No		5		2.000	
Factor-level means						
Dealership promotions	Direct mail		Count		Mean	
High			10		8.300	
Medium			10		6.200	
Low			10		3.700	
	Yes		15		7.400	
	No		15		4.733	
Grand mean			30		6.067	

For the main effect of level of promotion, the sum of squares SS_{xp}, degrees of freedom and mean square MS_{xp} are the same as earlier determined in Table 19.4. The sum of squares for direct mail $SS_{xd} = 53.333$ with 1 df, resulting in an identical value for the mean square MS_{xd}. The combined main effect is determined by adding the sum of squares due to the two main effects ($SS_{xp} + SS_{xd} = 106.067 + 53.333 = 159.400$) as well as adding the degrees of freedom $(2 + 1 = 3)$. For the promotions and direct mail interaction effect, the sum of squares $SS_{xpxd} = 3.267$ with $(3 - 1) \times (2 - 1) = 2$ df, resulting in $MS_{xpxd} = 3.267/2 = 1.633$. For the overall (model) effect, the sum of squares is the sum of squares for promotions main effect, direct mail main effect and interaction effect $= 106.067 + 53.333 + 3.267 = 162.667$ with $2 + 1 + 2 = 5$ df, resulting in a mean square of $162.667/5 = 32.533$. Note, however, that the error statistics are now different from those in Table 19.4. This is due to the fact that we now have two factors instead of one, $SS_{error} = 23.2$ with $[30 - (3 \times 2)]$ or 24 df resulting in $MS_{error} = 23.2/24 = 0.967$.

The test statistic for the significance of the overall effect is

$$F = \frac{32.533}{0.967}$$
$$= 33.643$$

with 5 and 24 df, which is significant at the 0.05 level.

The test statistic for the significance of the interaction effect is

$$F = \frac{1.633}{0.967}$$
$$= 1.69$$

with 2 and 24 df, which is not significant at the 0.05 level.

As the interaction effect is not significant, the significance of the main effects can be evaluated. The test statistic for the significance of the main effect of promotion is

$$F = \frac{53.033}{0.967}$$
$$= 54.843$$

with 2 and 24 df, which is significant at the 0.05 level.

The test statistic for the significance of the main effect of direct mail is

$$F = \frac{53.333}{0.967}$$
$$= 55.153$$

with 1 and 24 df, which is significant at the 0.05 level. Thus, higher levels of promotions result in higher sales. The use of a direct mail campaign results in higher sales. The effect of each is independent of the other.

The following example illustrates the use of n-way analysis.

Example

Country affects TV reception[11]

A study examined the impact of country affiliation on the credibility of product-attribute claims for TVs. The dependent variables were the following product-attribute claims: good sound, reliability, crisp-clear picture and stylish design. The independent variables which were manipulated consisted of price, country affiliation and store distribution. A 2 × 2 × 2 between-subjects design was used. Two levels of price, 'low' and 'high', two levels of country affiliation, South Korea and Germany, and two levels of store distribution, Kaufhof and without Kaufhof, were specified.

Source: © Getty Images

Data were collected from two shopping centres in a large German city. Thirty respondents were randomly assigned to each of the eight treatment cells for a total of 240 subjects. Table 1 presents the results for manipulations that had significant effects on each of the dependent variables.

The directions of country-by-distribution interaction effects for the three dependent variables are shown in Table 2. Although the credibility ratings for the crisp-clear picture, reliability and stylish design claims are improved by distributing the Korean-made TV set through Kaufhof rather than some other distributor, the same is not true of a German-made set. Similarly, the directions of country-by-price interaction effects for the two dependent variables are shown in Table 3. At the 'high' price level, the credibility ratings for the 'good sound' and 'reliability' claims are higher for the German-made TV set than for its Korean counterpart, but there is little difference related to country affiliation when the product is at the 'low' price.

Table 1 Analyses for significant manipulations

Effect	Univariate			
	Dependent variable	F	df	p
Country × price	Good sound	7.57	1.232	0.006
Country × price	Reliability	6.57	1.232	0.011
Country × distribution	Crisp-clear picture	6.17	1.232	0.014
Country × distribution	Reliability	6.57	1.232	0.011
Country × distribution	Stylish design	10.31	1.232	0.002

Table 2 Country-by-distribution interaction means

Country × distribution	Crisp-clear picture	Reliability	Stylish design
South Korea			
Kaufhof	3.67	3.42	3.82
Without Kaufhof	3.18	2.88	3.15
Germany			
Kaufhof	3.60	3.47	3.53
Without Kaufhof	3.77	3.65	3.75

Table 3 **Country-by-price interaction means**

Country × price	Good sound	Reliability
Low price		
Kaufhof	3.75	3.40
Without Kaufhof	3.53	3.45
High price		
Kaufhof	3.15	2.90
Without Kaufhof	3.73	3.67

This study demonstrates that credibility of attribute claims, for products traditionally exported to Germany by a company in a newly industrialised country, can be significantly improved if the same company distributes the product through a prestigious German retailer and considers making manufacturing investments in Europe. Specifically, three product-attribute claims (crisp-clear picture, reliability and stylish design) are perceived as more credible when the TVs are made in South Korea if they are also distributed through a prestigious German retailer. Also, the 'good sound' and 'reliability' claims for TVs are perceived to be more credible for a German-made set sold at a higher price, possibly offsetting the potential disadvantage of higher manufacturing costs in Europe.

Analysis of covariance (ANCOVA)

When examining the differences in the mean values of the dependent variable related to the effect of the controlled independent variables, it is often necessary to take into account the influence of uncontrolled independent variables. For example:

- In determining how consumers' intentions to buy a brand vary with different levels of price, attitude towards the brand may have to be taken into consideration.
- In determining how different groups exposed to different commercials evaluate a brand, it may be necessary to control for prior knowledge.
- In determining how different price levels will affect a household's breakfast cereal consumption, it may be essential to take household size into account.

In such cases, ANCOVA should be used. ANCOVA includes at least one categorical independent variable and at least one interval or metric-independent variable. The categorical independent variable is called a *factor*, whereas the metric-independent variable is called a *covariate*. The most common use of the covariate is to remove extraneous variation from the dependent variable, because the effects of the factors are of major concern. The variation in the dependent variable due to the covariates is removed by an adjustment of the dependent variable's mean value within each treatment condition.

An ANOVA is then performed on the adjusted scores.[12] The significance of the combined effect of the covariates, as well as the effect of each covariate, is tested by using the appropriate F tests. The coefficients for the covariates provide insights into the effect that the covariates exert on the dependent variable. ANCOVA is most useful when the covariate is linearly related to the dependent variable and is not related to the factors.[13]

Illustrative application of covariance

We again use the data of Table 19.2 to illustrate ANCOVA. Suppose that we wanted to determine the effect of dealership promotion and direct mail on sales while controlling for the affluence of clientele. It is felt that the affluence of the clientele may also have an effect on the sales of new cars. The dependent variable consists of new car sales. As before, promotion has three levels and direct mail has two. Clientele affluence is measured on an interval scale and serves as the covariate. The results are shown in Table 19.6.

Table 19.6 ANCOVA

Source of variation	Sum of squares	df	Mean square	F	Sig. of F
Covariates					
Clientele	0.838	1	0.838	0.862	0.363
Main effects					
Promotions	106.067	2	53.033	54.546	0.000
Direct mail	53.333	1	53.333	54.855	0.000
Combined	159.400	3	53.133	54.649	0.000
Two-way interaction					
Promotions*Direct mail	3.267	2	1.633	1.680	0.208
Model	163.505	6	27.251	28.028	0.000
Residual (error)	22.362	23	0.972		
Total	185.867	29	6.409		
Covariate	Raw coefficient				
Clientele	−0.078				

As can be seen, the sum of squares attributable to the covariate is very small (0.838) with 1 *df* resulting in an identical value for the mean square. The associated *F* value is 0.838/0.972 = 0.862, with 1 and 23 *df*, which is not significant at the 0.05 level. Thus, the conclusion is that the affluence of the clientele does not have an effect on the sales of new Renault cars. If the effect of the covariate is significant, the sign of the raw coefficient can be used to interpret the direction of the effect on the dependent variable.

Issues in interpretation

Important issues involved in the interpretation of ANOVA results include interactions, relative importance of factors, and multiple comparisons.

Interactions

The different interactions that can arise when conducting ANOVA on two or more factors are shown in Figure 19.3.

One outcome is that ANOVA may indicate that there are no interactions (the interaction effects are not found to be significant). The other possibility is that the interaction is significant. An interaction effect occurs when the effect of an independent variable on a dependent variable is different for different categories or levels of another independent

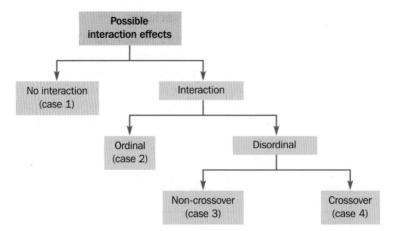

Figure 19.3
A classification of interaction effects

Ordinal interaction
An interaction where the rank order of the effects attributable to one factor does not change across the levels of the second factor.

Disordinal interaction
The change in the rank order of the effects of one factor across the levels of another.

variable. The interaction may be ordinal or disordinal. In **ordinal interaction**, the rank order of the effects related to one factor does not change across the levels of the second factor. **Disordinal interaction**, on the other hand, involves a change in the rank order of the effects of one factor across the levels of another. If the interaction is disordinal, it could be of a non-crossover or crossover type.[14] These interaction cases are displayed in Figure 19.4, which assumes that there are two factors, X_1 with three levels (X_{11}, X_{12} and X_{13}) and X_2 with two levels (X_{21} and X_{22}). Case 1 depicts no interaction.

The effects of X_1 on Y are parallel over the two levels of X_2. Although there is some departure from parallelism, this is not beyond what might be expected from chance. Parallelism implies that the net effect of X_{22} over X_{21} is the same across the three levels of X_1. In the absence of interaction, the joint effect of X_1 and X_2 is simply the sum of their individual main effects.

Case 2 depicts an ordinal interaction. The line segments depicting the effects of X_1 and X_2 are not parallel. The difference between X_{22} and X_{21} increases as we move from X_{11} to X_{12} and from X_{12} to X_{13}, but the rank order of the effects of X_1 is the same over the two levels of X_2. This rank order, in ascending order, is X_{11}, X_{12}, X_{13}, and it remains the same for X_{21} and X_{22}.

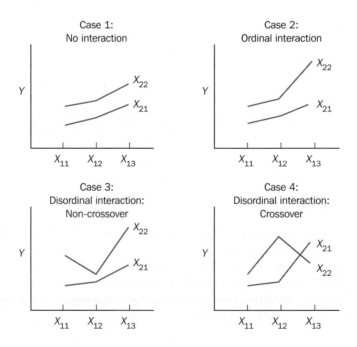

Figure 19.4
Patterns of interaction

Disordinal interaction of a non-crossover type is displayed by case 3. The lowest effect of X_1 at level X_{21} occurs at X_{11}, and the rank order of effects is X_{11}, X_{12}, X_{13}. At level X_{22}, however, the lowest effect of X_1 occurs at X_{12}, and the rank order is changed to X_{12}, X_{11}, X_{13}. Because it involves a change in rank order, disordinal interaction is stronger than ordinal interaction.

In disordinal interactions of a crossover type, the line segments cross each other, as shown by case 4 in Figure 19.4. In this case, the relative effect of the levels of one factor changes with the levels of the other. Note that X_{22} has a greater effect than X_{21} when the levels of X_1 are X_{11} and X_{12}. When the level of X_1 is X_{13}, the situation is reversed, and X_{21} has a greater effect than X_{22}. (Note that in cases 1, 2 and 3, X_{22} had a greater impact than X_{21} across all three levels of X_1.) Hence, disordinal interactions of a crossover type represent the strongest interactions.[15]

Relative importance of factors

Experimental designs are usually balanced in that each cell contains the same number of respondents. This results in an orthogonal design in which the factors are uncorrelated. Hence, it is possible to determine unambiguously the relative importance of each factor in explaining the variation in the dependent variable.[16] The most commonly used measure in ANOVA is **omega squared** (ω^2). This measure indicates what proportion of the variation in the dependent variable is related to a particular independent variable or factor. The relative contribution of a factor X is calculated as follows:[17]

$$\omega_x^2 = \frac{SS_x - (df_x \times MS_{error})}{SS_{total} + MS_{error}}$$

Omega squared (ω^2)
A measure indicating the proportion of the variation in the dependent variable that is related to a particular independent variable or factor.

Note that the estimated value of ω^2 can be negative, in which case the estimated value of ω^2 is set equal to zero. Normally, ω^2 is interpreted only for statistically significant effects.[18] In Table 19.4, ω^2 associated with level of dealership promotions is calculated as follows:

$$\omega_p^2 = \frac{106.067 - (2 \times 0.967)}{185.867 + 0.967}$$

$$= \frac{104.133}{186.834}$$

$$= 0.557$$

In Table 19.5 note that

$$SS_{total} = 106.067 + 53.333 + 3.267 + 23.2$$
$$= 185.867$$

Likewise, the ω^2 associated with direct mail is

$$\omega^2 = \frac{53.333 - (1 \times 0.967)}{185.867 + 0.967}$$

$$= \frac{52.366}{186.834}$$

$$= 0.280$$

As a guide to interpreting ω^2, a large experimental effect produces an ω^2 of 0.15 or greater, a medium effect produces an index of around 0.06, and a small effect produces an index of 0.01.[19] In Table 19.5, while the effects of promotions and direct mail are both large, the effect of promotions is much larger. Therefore, dealership promotions will be more effective in increasing sales than direct mail.

Multiple comparisons

The ANOVA *F* test examines only the overall difference in means. If the null hypothesis of equal means is rejected, we can only conclude that not all the group means are equal. Only some of the means may be statistically different, however, and we may wish to examine differences among specific means. This can be done by specifying appropriate **contrasts**, or comparisons used to determine which of the means are statistically different. Contrasts may be a priori or a posteriori. **A priori contrasts** are determined before conducting the analysis, based on the researcher's theoretical framework. Generally, a priori contrasts are used in lieu of the ANOVA *F* test. The contrasts selected are orthogonal (they are independent in a statistical sense).

A posteriori contrasts are made after the analysis. These are generally **multiple comparison tests**. They enable the researcher to construct generalised confidence intervals that can be used to make pairwise comparisons of all treatment means. These tests, listed in order of decreasing power, include least significant difference, Duncan's multiple range test, Student–Newman–Keuls, Tukey's alternate procedure, honestly significant difference, modified least significant difference and Scheffé's tests. Of these tests, least significant difference is the most powerful and Scheffé's the most conservative. For further discussion on a priori and a posteriori contrasts, refer to the literature.[20]

Our discussion so far has assumed that each subject is exposed to only one treatment or experimental condition. Sometimes subjects are exposed to more than one experimental condition, in which case repeated measures ANOVA should be used.

Contrasts
In ANOVA, a method of examining differences among two or more means of the treatment groups.

A priori contrasts
Contrasts determined before conducting the analysis, based on the researcher's theoretical framework.

A posteriori contrasts
Contrasts made after conducting the analysis. These are generally multiple comparison tests.

Multiple comparison tests
A posteriori contrasts that enable the researcher to construct generalised confidence intervals that can be used to make pairwise comparisons of all treatment means.

Repeated measures ANOVA

In marketing research, there are often large differences in the background and individual characteristics of respondents. If this source of variability can be separated from treatment effects (effects of the independent variable) and experimental error, then the sensitivity of the experiment can be enhanced. One way of controlling the differences between subjects is by observing each subject under each experimental condition (see Table 19.7).

In this sense, each subject serves as its own control. For example, in a survey attempting to determine differences in evaluations of various airlines, each respondent evaluates all the major competing airlines. In a study examining the differences among heavy users, medium users, light users and non-users of a brand, each respondent provides ratings on the relative importance of each attribute. Because repeated measurements are obtained from each respondent, this design is referred to as within-subjects design or **repeated measures ANOVA**. This differs from the assumption we made in our earlier discussion that each respondent is exposed to only one treatment condition, also referred to as between-subjects design.[21] Repeated measures ANOVA may be thought of as an extension of the paired samples *t* test to the case of more than two related samples.

In the case of a single factor with repeated measures, the total variation, with $n(c-1)$ degrees of freedom, may be split into between-people variation and within-people variation:

Repeated measures ANOVA
An ANOVA technique used when respondents are exposed to more than one treatment condition and repeated measurements are obtained.

$$SS_{total} = SS_{between\ people} + SS_{within\ people}$$

The between-people variation, which is related to the differences between the means of people, has $n-1$ degrees of freedom. The within-people variation has $n(c-1)$ degrees of freedom. The within-people variation may, in turn, be divided into two different sources of variation. One source is related to the differences between treatment means, and the second consists of residual or error variation. The degrees of freedom corresponding to the treatment variation are $c-1$ and those corresponding to residual variation are $(c-1)(n-1)$. Thus,

Table 19.7 Decomposition of the total variation: repeated measures ANOVA

Independent variable X

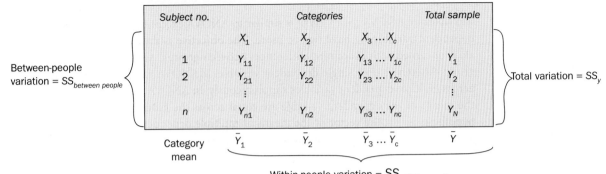

$$SS_{within\ people} = SS_x + SS_{error}$$

A test of the null hypothesis of equal means may now be constructed in the usual way:

$$F = \frac{SS_x/(c-1)}{SS_{error}/(n-1)(c-1)}$$

$$= \frac{MS_x}{MS_{error}}$$

So far we have assumed that the dependent variable is measured on an interval or ratio scale. If the dependent variable is non-metric, however, a different procedure should be used.

Non-metric ANOVA

Non-metric ANOVA
An ANOVA technique for examining the difference in the central tendencies of more than two groups when the dependent variable is measured on an ordinal scale.

k-sample median test
A non-parametric test used to examine differences among more than two groups when the dependent variable is measured on an ordinal scale.

Kruskal–Wallis one-way ANOVA
A non-metric ANOVA test that uses the rank value of each case, not merely its location relative to the median.

Non-metric ANOVA examines the difference in the central tendencies of more than two groups when the dependent variable is measured on an ordinal scale. One such procedure is the *k-sample median test*. As its name implies, this is an extension of the median test for two groups, which was considered in Chapter 18. The null hypothesis is that the medians of the k populations are equal. The test involves the computation of a common median over the k samples. Then, a $2 \times k$ table of cell counts based on cases above or below the common median is generated. A chi-square statistic is computed. The significance of the chi-square implies a rejection of the null hypothesis.

A more powerful test is the **Kruskal–Wallis one-way ANOVA**. This is an extension of the Mann–Whitney test (Chapter 18). This test also examines the difference in medians. The null hypothesis is the same as in the *k-sample median test*, but the testing procedure is different. All cases from the k groups are ordered in a single ranking. If the k populations are the same, the groups should be similar in terms of ranks within each group. The rank sum is calculated for each group. From these, the Kruskal–Wallis H statistic, which has a chi-square distribution, is computed.

The Kruskal–Wallis test is more powerful than the *k-sample median test* because it uses the rank value of each case, not merely its location relative to the median. If there are a large number of tied rankings in the data, however, the *k-sample median test* may be a better choice.

Non-metric ANOVA is not popular in marketing research. Another procedure that is also only rarely used is multivariate ANOVA.

Multivariate ANOVA

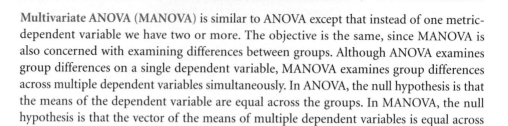

Multivariate ANOVA (MANOVA)
An ANOVA technique using two or more metric dependent variables.

Multivariate ANOVA (MANOVA) is similar to ANOVA except that instead of one metric-dependent variable we have two or more. The objective is the same, since MANOVA is also concerned with examining differences between groups. Although ANOVA examines group differences on a single dependent variable, MANOVA examines group differences across multiple dependent variables simultaneously. In ANOVA, the null hypothesis is that the means of the dependent variable are equal across the groups. In MANOVA, the null hypothesis is that the vector of the means of multiple dependent variables is equal across groups. MANOVA is appropriate when there are two or more dependent variables that are correlated. If there are multiple dependent variables that are uncorrelated or orthogonal, ANOVA on each of the dependent variables is more appropriate than MANOVA.[22]

As an example, suppose that four groups, each consisting of 100 randomly selected individuals, were exposed to four different commercials about the 'Series 1' BMW. After seeing the commercial, each individual provided ratings on preference for the 'Series 1', preference for BMW, and preference for the commercial itself. Because these three preference variables are correlated, MANOVA should be conducted to determine which commercial is the most effective (produced the highest preference across the three preference variables). The following example illustrates the application of ANOVA and MANOVA in international marketing research.

Example   ### The commonality of unethical research practices worldwide[23]

A study examined marketing professionals' perceptions of how common unethical practices in marketing research were across different countries, i.e. 'the commonality of unethical marketing research practices'. A sample of marketing professionals was drawn from Australia, the UK, Canada and the USA.

Respondents' evaluations were analysed using MANOVA and ANOVA techniques. The predictor variable was the 'country of respondent' and 15 evaluations of 'commonality' served as the criterion variables. The F values from the ANOVA analyses indicated that only 2 of the 15 commonality evaluations achieved significance ($p < 0.05$ or better). Further, the MANOVA F value was not statistically significant, implying the lack of overall differences in commonality evaluations across respondents of the four countries. It was concluded that marketing professionals in the four countries demonstrate similar perceptions of the commonality of unethical research practices. This finding is not surprising, given other research evidence that organisations in the four countries reflect similar corporate cultures. ■

Internet and computer applications

The computer packages SPSS and SAS have programs for conducting ANOVA and ANCOVA. In addition to the basic analysis that we have considered, these programs can also perform more complex analysis. Minitab and Excel also offer some programs. Given the importance of ANOVA and ANCOVA, several programs are available in each package.

SPSS

One-way ANOVA can be efficiently performed using the program ONEWAY. This program also allows the user to test a priori and a posteriori contrasts. For performing *n*-way ANOVA, the program ANOVA can be used. Although covariates can be specified, the program ANOVA does not perform a full ANCOVA. For comprehensive ANOVA or ANCOVA, including repeated measures and multiple dependent measures, the MANOVA procedure is recommended. For non-metric ANOVA, including the *k*-sample median test and Kruskal–Wallis one-way ANOVA, the program NPAR TESTS should be used.

SAS

The main program for performing ANOVA in the case of a balanced design is the program ANOVA. This program can handle data from a wide variety of experimental designs, including MANOVA and repeated measures. Both a priori and a posteriori contrasts can be tested. For unbalanced designs, the more general GLM procedure can be used. This program performs ANOVA, ANCOVA, repeated measures ANOVA and MANOVA. It also allows the testing of a priori and a posteriori contrasts. Whereas GLM can also be used for analysing balanced designs, it is not as efficient as ANOVA for such models. The VARCOMP procedure computes variance components. For non-metric ANOVA, the NPAR1WAY procedure can be used. For constructing designs and randomised plans, the PLAN procedure can be used.

Minitab

ANOVA and ANCOVA can be accessed from the Stats>ANOVA function. This function performs one-way ANOVA, one-way unstacked ANOVA, two-way ANOVA, analysis of means, balanced ANOVA, ANCOVA, general linear model, main-effects plot, interactions plot and residual plots. In order to compute the mean and standard deviation, the CROSSTAB function must be used. To obtain *F* and *p* values, use the balanced ANOVA.

Excel

Both a one-way ANOVA and two-way ANOVA can be performed under the Tools>DATA ANALYSIS function. The two-way ANOVA has the features of a two-factor with replication and a two-factor without replication. The two-factor with replication includes more than one sample for each group of data, while the two-factor without replication does not include more than one sampling per group.

Summary

In ANOVA and ANCOVA, the dependent variable is metric and the independent variables are all categorical and metric variables. One-way ANOVA involves a single independent categorical variable. Interest lies in testing the null hypothesis that the category means are equal in the population. The total variation in the dependent variable may be decomposed into two components: variation related to the independent variable and variation related to error. The variation is measured in terms of the sum of squares corrected for the mean (*SS*). The mean square is obtained by dividing the *SS* by the corresponding degrees of freedom (*df*). The null hypothesis of equal means is tested by an *F* statistic, which is the ratio of the mean square related to the independent variable to the mean square related to error.

N-way ANOVA involves the simultaneous examination of two or more categorical independent variables. A major advantage is that the interactions between the independent variables can be examined. The significance of the overall effect, interaction terms and the main effects of individual factors are examined by appropriate *F* tests. It is meaningful to the significance of main effects only if the corresponding interaction terms are not significant.

ANCOVA includes at least one categorical independent variable and at least one interval or metric-independent variable. The metric-independent variable, or covariate, is commonly used to remove extraneous variation from the dependent variable.

When ANOVA is conducted on two or more factors, interactions can arise. An interaction occurs when the effect of an independent variable on a dependent variable is different for different categories or levels of another independent variable. If the interaction is significant, it may be ordinal or disordinal. Disordinal interaction may be of a non-crossover or crossover type. In balanced designs, the relative importance of factors in explaining the variation in the dependent variable is measured by omega squared (ω^2). Multiple comparisons in the form of a priori or a posteriori contrasts can be used for examining differences among specific means.

In repeated measures ANOVA, observations on each subject are obtained under each treatment condition. This design is useful for controlling for the differences in subjects that exist prior to the experiment. Non-metric ANOVA involves examining the differences in the central tendencies of two or more groups when the dependent variable is measured on an ordinal scale. MANOVA involves two or more metric-dependent variables.

Questions

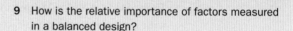

1 Discuss the similarities and differences between analysis of variance and analysis of covariance.

2 What is the relationship between analysis of variance and the *t* test?

3 What is total variation? How is it decomposed in a one-way analysis of variance?

4 What is the null hypothesis in one-way ANOVA? What basic statistic is used to test the null hypothesis in one-way ANOVA? How is this statistic computed?

5 How does *n*-way analysis of variance differ from the one-way procedure?

6 How is the total variation decomposed in *n*-way analysis of variance?

7 What is the most common use of the covariate in ANCOVA?

8 What is the difference between ordinal and disordinal interaction?

9 How is the relative importance of factors measured in a balanced design?

10 What is an a priori contrast?

11 What is the most powerful test for making a posteriori contrasts? Which test is the most conservative?

12 What is meant by repeated measures ANOVA? Describe the decomposition of variation in repeated measures ANOVA.

13 What are the differences between metric and non-metric analyses of variance?

14 Describe two tests used for examining differences in central tendencies in non-metric ANOVA.

15 What is multivariate analysis of variance? When is it appropriate?

Exercises

1 A marketing researcher wants to test the hypothesis that there is no difference in the importance attached to shopping by consumers living in Belgium, France, Germany and the Netherlands. A study is conducted and analysis of variance is used to analyse the data. The results obtained are presented in the following table:

Source	df	Sum of squares	Mean squares	F ratio	F probability
Between groups	3	70.212	23.404	1.12	0.3
Within groups	996	20812.416	20.896		

   a   Is there sufficient evidence to reject the null hypothesis?
   b   What conclusion can be drawn from the table?
   c   If the average importance was computed for each group, would you expect the sample means to be similar or different?
   d   What was the total sample size in this study?

2 In a pilot study examining the effectiveness of three commercials (A, B, and C), 10 consumers were assigned to view each commercial and rate it on a nine-point Likert scale. The data obtained from the 30 respondents are shown in the following table:

Commercial A	Commercial B	Commercial C
4	7	8
5	4	7
3	6	7
4	5	6
3	4	8
4	6	7
4	5	8
3	5	8
5	4	5
5	4	6

   a   Calculate the category means and the grand mean.
   b   Calculate SS_y into SS_x and SS_{error}.
   c   Calculate η^2.
   d   Calculate the value of F.
   e   Are the three commercials equally effective?

3 An experiment tested the effects of package design and shelf display on the likelihood of buying a breakfast cereal. Package design and shelf display were varied at two levels each, resulting in a 2×2 design. Purchase likelihood was measured on a seven-point scale. The results are partially described in the following table:

Source of variation	Sum of squares	df	Mean square	F	Sig. of F	ω^2
Package design	68.76	1				
Shelf display	320.19	1				
Two-way interaction	55.05	1				
Residual error	176.00	40				

   a   Complete the table by calculating the mean square, F, significance of F, and ω^2 values.
   b   How should the main effects be interpreted?

4 In an experiment designed to measure the effect of gender and frequency of travel on preference for long-haul holidays, a 2 (gender) × 3 (frequency of travel) between-subjects design was adopted. Five respondents were assigned to each cell for a total sample size of 30. Preference for long-haul holidays was measured on a nine-point scale (1 = no preference, 9= strong preference). Gender was coded as male = 1 and female = 2. Frequency of travel was coded as light = 1, medium = 2, and heavy = 3. The data obtained are shown in the table.

Number	Gender	Travel group	Preference
1	1	1	2
2	1	1	3
3	1	1	4
4	1	1	4
5	1	1	2
6	1	2	4
7	1	2	5
8	1	2	5
9	1	2	3
10	1	2	3
11	1	3	8
12	1	3	9
13	1	3	8
14	1	3	7
15	1	3	7
16	2	1	6
17	2	1	7
18	2	1	6
19	2	1	5
20	2	1	7
21	2	2	3
22	2	2	4
23	2	2	5
24	2	2	4
25	2	2	5
26	2	3	6
27	2	3	6
28	2	3	6
29	2	3	7
30	2	3	8

Using software of your choice, perform the following analysis.

a Do males and females differ in their preference for long-haul travel?
b Do the light, medium and heavy travellers differ in their preference for long-haul travel?
c Conduct a 2 × 3 analysis of variance with preference for long-haul travel as the dependent variable and gender and travel frequency as the independent variables or factors. Interpret the results.

5 In a small group discuss the following issues: 'Which procedure is more useful in marketing research – analysis of variance or analysis of covariance?' and 'There are few marketing research applications where t tests are used; the complexity of marketing phenomena mean that analysis of variance or analysis of covariance are much more commonplace.'

Notes

1   Mangaloglu, S.B.M., 'Tourism destination images of Turkey, Egypt, Greece and Italy as perceived by US based tour operators and travel agents', *Tourism Management* 22 (1) (February 2001), 1–9.

2   For applications of ANOVA, see Sengupta, J., and Gorn, G.J., 'Absence makes the mind grow sharper: effects of element omission on subsequent recall', *Journal of Marketing Research* 39 (2) (May 2002), 186–201; Varki, S. and Rust, R.T., 'Satisfaction is relative', *Marketing Research: A Magazine of Management and Applications* 9 (2) (Summer 1997), 14–19; Deshpande, R. and Stayman, D.M., 'A tale of two cities: distinctiveness theory and advertising effectiveness', *Journal of Marketing Research* 31 (February 1994), 57–64.

3   Janky, D.G., 'Sometimes pooling for analysis of variance hypothesis tests: a review and study of a split level model', *American Statistician* 54 (4) (November 2000), 269–279; Driscoll, W.C., 'Robustness of the ANOVA and Tukey-Kramer statistical tests', *Computers and Industrial Engineering* 31 (1,2) (October 1996), 265–268; Burdick, R.K., 'Statement of hypotheses in the analysis of variance', *Journal of Marketing Research* (August 1983), 320–324.

4   The *F* test is a generalised form of the *t* test. If a random variable is *t* distributed with *N* degrees of freedom, then t^2 is *F* distributed with 1 and *N* degrees of freedom. Where there are two factor levels or treatments, ANOVA is equivalent to the two-sided *t* test.

5   Although computations for the fixed-effects and random-effects models are similar, interpretations of results differ. A comparison of these approaches is found in Turner, J.R. and Thayer, J., *Introduction to Analysis of Variance: Design, Analysis and Interpretation*, (Thousand Oaks, CA: Sage, 2001); Erez, A., Bloom, M.C. and Wells, M.T., 'Using random rather than fixed effects models in meta-analysis: implications for situational specificity and validity generalization', *Personnel Psychology* 49 (2) (Summer 1996), 275–306; Neter, J.W., *Applied Linear Statistical Models*, 4th edn (Burr Ridge, IL: Irwin, 1996).

6   We consider only the full factorial designs, which incorporate all possible combinations of factor levels. For example, see Menon, G., 'Are the parts better than the whole? The effects of decompositional questions on judgments of frequent behaviors', *Journal of Marketing Research* 34 (August 1997), 335–346.

7   Miyazaki, A.D., 'Consumer perceptions of privacy and security risks for online shopping', *Journal of Consumer Affairs* 35 (1) (Summer 2001), 27; Burnett, R., 'As internet sales rise, so do shoppers' complaints', *Knight Ridder Tribune Business News* (20 December 2001), 1.

8   Sengupta, J., and Gorn, G. 'Absence makes the mind grow sharper: effects of element omission on subsequent recall', *Journal of Marketing Research* 39 (2) (May 2002), 186–201; Jaccard, J., *Interaction Effects in Factorial Analysis of Variance* (Thousand Oaks, CA: Sage, 1997); Mayers, J.L., *Fundamentals of Experimental Design*, 3rd edn (Boston, MA: Allyn & Bacon, 1979).

9   Tacq, J., *Multivariate Analysis Techniques in Social Science Research* (Thousand Oaks, CA: Sage, 1997); Daniel, W.W. and Terrell, LC., *Business Statistics*, 7th edn (Boston, MA: Houghton Muffin, 1995).

10 Nishisato, S., *Measurement and Multivariate Analysis* (New York: Springer-Verlag, New York, 2002).

11 Desai, K.K., 'The effects of ingredient branding strategies on host brand extendibility', *Journal of Marketing* 66 (1) (January 2002), 73–93; Peterson, R.A. and Jolibert, A.J.P., 'A meta-analysis of country-of-origin effects', *Journal of International Business Studies* 26 (4) (Fourth Quarter 1995), 883–900; Chao, P., 'The impact of country affiliation on the credibility of product attribute claims', *Journal of Advertising Research* (April–May 1989), 35–41.

12 Although this is the most common way in which analysis of covariance is performed, other situations are also possible. For example, covariate and factor effects may be of equal interest, or the set of covariates may be of major concern. For applications, see Pham, M.T. and Muthukrishnan, A.V., 'Search and alignment in judgment revision: implications for brand positioning', *Journal of Marketing Research* 39 (1) (February 2002), 18–30; Lane Keller, K. and Aaker, D.A., 'The effects of sequential introduction of brand extensions', *Journal of Marketing Research* 29 (February 1992), 35–50.

13 For more detailed discussions, see Turner, J.R. and Thayer, J., *Introduction to Analysis of Variance: Design, Analysis and Interpretation*, (Thousand Oaks, CA: Sage, 2001); Glantz, S.A. and Slinker, B.K., *Primer of Applied Regression and Analysis of Variance* (Blacklick, OH: McGraw-Hill, 2000); Neter, J.W., *Applied Linear Statistical Models*, 4th edn (Burr Ridge, IL: Irwin, 1996); Wildt, A.R. and Ahtola, O.T., *Analysis of Covariance* (Beverly Hills, CA: Sage, 1978).

14 See Zhang, S. and Schmitt, B.H., 'Creating local brands in multilingual international markets', *Journal of Marketing Research* 38 (3) (August 2001), 313–325; Umesh, U.N., Peterson, R.A., McCann-Nelson, M. and Vaidyanathan, R., 'Type IV error in marketing research: the investigation of ANOVA interactions', *Journal of the Academy of Marketing Science* 24 (1) (Winter 1966), 17–26; Ross W.T. Jr., and Creyer, E.H., 'Interpreting interactions: raw means or residual means', *Journal of Consumer Research* 20 (2) (September 1993), 330–338; Leigh, J.H. and Kinnear, T.C., 'On interaction classification', *Educational and Psychological Measurement* 40 (Winter 1980), 841–843.

15 For an examination of interactions using an ANOVA framework, see Jaccard, J., *Interaction Effects in Factorial Analysis of Variance* (Thousand Oaks, CA: Sage, 1997); Wansink, B., 'Advertising's impact on category substitution', *Journal of Marketing Research* 31 (November 1994), 505–515; Peracchio, L.A. and Meyers-Levy, J., 'How ambiguous cropped objects in ad photos can affect product evaluations', *Journal of Consumer Research* 21 (June 1994), 190–204.

16 Verma, R. and Goodale, J.C., 'Statistical power in operations management', *Journal of Operations Management* 13 (2) (August 1995), 139–152; Wyner, G.A., 'The significance of marketing research', *Marketing Research: A Magazine of Management and Applications* 5 (1) (Winter 1993), 43–45; Sawyer, A. and Peter, J.P., 'The significance of statistical significance tests in marketing research', *Journal of Marketing Research* 20 (May 1983), 125; Beltramini, R.F., 'A meta-analysis of effect sizes in consumer behavior experiments', *Journal of Consumer Research* 12 (June 1985), 97–103.

17 This formula does not hold if repeat measurements are made on the dependent variable. See Fern, E.F. and Monroe, K.B., 'Effect size estimates: Issues and problems in interpretation', *Journal of Consumer Research* 23 (2) (September 1996), 89–105; Dodd, D.H. and Schultz, Jr., R.F., 'Computational

procedures for estimating magnitude of effect for some analysis of variance designs', *Psychological Bulletin* (June 1973), 391–395.

18 The ω^2 formula is attributed to Hays. See Hays, W.L., *Statistics for Psychologists* (New York: Holt, Rinehart & Winston, 1963). For an application, see Ratneshwar, S. and Chaiken, S., 'Comprehension's role in persuasion: the case of its moderating effect on the persuasive impact of source cues', *Journal of Consumer Research* 18 (June 1991), 52–62. For an alternative approach, see also Finn, A. and Kayande, U., 'Reliability assessment and optimisation of marketing measurement', *Journal of Marketing Research* 34 (February 1997), 262–275.

19 Johnson, R.A. and Wichern, D.W., *Applied Multivariate Statistical Analysis* (Paramus, NJ: Prentice Hall, 2001); Fern, E.F. and Monroe, K.B., 'Effect-size estimates: issues and problems in interpretation', *Journal of Consumer Research* 23 (2) (September 1996), 89–105; Cohen, J., *Statistical Power Analysis for the Behavioral Sciences* (New York: Academic Press, 1969).

20 Turner, J.R. and Thayer, J., *Introduction to Analysis of Variance: Design, Analysis and Interpretation* (Thousand Oaks, CA: Sage, 2001); Neter, J.W., *Applied Linear Statistical Models*, 4th edn (Burr Ridge, IL: Irwin, 1996); Winer, B.J., Brown, D.R. and Michels, K.M., *Statistical Principles in Experimental Design*, 3rd edn (New York: McGraw-Hill, 1991).

21 It is possible to combine between-subjects and within-subjects factors in a single design. See, for example, Ahluwalia, R., Unnava, H.R. and Burnkrant, R.E., 'The moderating role of commitment on the spillover effect of marketing communi-
cations', *Journal of Marketing Research* 38 (4) (November 2001), 458–470; Mount, M.K., Sytsma, M.A., Hazucha, J.F. and Holt, K.E., 'Rater-ratee effects in developmental performance ratings of managers', *Personnel Psychology* 50 (1) (Spring 1997), 51–69; Broniarczyk, S.M. and Alba, J.W., 'The importance of the brand in brand extension', *Journal of Marketing Research* 31 (May 1994), 214–228; Krishna, A., 'The effect of deal knowledge on consumer purchase behavior', *Journal of Marketing Research* 31 (February 1994), 76–91.

22 See Roehm, M.L. Pullins, E.B. and Roehm, H.A., Jr. 'Designing loyalty-building programs for packaged goods brands', *Journal of Marketing* 39 (2) (May 2002), 202–213; Bray, J.H. and Maxwell, S.E., Multivariate Analysis of Variance (Beverly Hills, CA: Sage, 1985). For an application of MANOVA, see Piercy, N.F., 'Sales manager behaviour control strategy and its consequences: the impact of gender differences', *Journal of Personal Selling & Sales Management* 21(1) (Winter 2001), 39–49.

23 Kimmel, A.J. and Smith, N.C., 'Deception in marketing research: ethical, methodological and disciplinary implications', *Psychology and Marketing* 18 (7) (July 2001), 663–689; Abramson, N.R., Keating, R.J. and Lane, H.W., 'Cross-national cognitive process differences: a comparison of Canadian, American and Japanese managers', *Management International Review* 36 (2) (Second Quarter 1996), 123–147; Akaah, 1.P., 'A cross-national analysis of the perceived commonality of unethical practices in marketing research', in Lazer, L., Shaw, E. and Wee, C.-H. (eds), *World Marketing Congress*, International Conference Series, Vol. 4 (Boca Raton, FL: Academy of Marketing Science, 1989), 2–9.

Source: © Cadmium

20

Identifying relationships

> *Correlation is the simplest way to understand the association between two metric variables. When extended to multiple regression, the relationship between one variable and several others becomes more clear.*

Objectives

After reading this chapter, you should be able to:

1 discuss the concepts of product moment correlation, partial correlation and part correlation, and show how they provide a foundation for regression analysis;

2 explain the nature and methods of bivariate regression analysis and describe the general model, estimation of parameters, standardised regression coefficient, significance testing, prediction accuracy, residual analysis and model cross-validation;

3 explain the nature and methods of multiple regression analysis and the meaning of partial regression coefficients;

4 describe specialised techniques used in multiple regression analysis, particularly stepwise regression, regression with dummy variables, and analysis of variance and covariance with regression;

5 discuss non-metric correlation and measures such as Spearman's rho and Kendall's tau;

6 discuss the nature of structural equation modelling and its applications in marketing research.

STAGE 1
Problem definition

STAGE 2
Research approach developed

STAGE 3
Research design developed

STAGE 4
Fieldwork or data collection

STAGE 5
Data preparation and analysis

STAGE 6
Report preparation and presentation

Overview

Chapter 19 examined the relationship among the *t* test, analysis of variance and covariance, and regression. This chapter describes regression analysis, which is widely used for explaining variation in market share, sales, brand preference and other marketing results. This is done in terms of marketing management variables such as advertising, price, distribution and product quality. Before discussing regression, however, we describe the concepts of product moment correlation and partial correlation coefficient, which lay the conceptual foundation for regression analysis.

In introducing regression analysis, we discuss the simple bivariate case first. We describe estimation, standardisation of the regression coefficients, and testing and examination of the strength and significance of association between variables, prediction accuracy, and the assumptions underlying the regression model. Next, we discuss the multiple regression model, emphasising the interpretation of parameters, strength of association, significance tests and examination of residuals.

We then cover topics of special interest in regression analysis, such as stepwise regression, multicollinearity, relative importance of predictor variables, and cross-validation. We describe regression with dummy variables and the use of this procedure to conduct analysis of variance and covariance. Finally, we describe and present an application of structural equation modelling in marketing. We begin with an example that illustrates an application of regression analysis.

Example Retailing revolution[1]

Many retailing experts suggest that electronic shopping will be the next revolution in shopping. Although e-tailing continues to make up a very small portion of the overall retail sales, the prospects look very promising for the future. A research project investigating this trend looked for correlates of consumers' preferences for electronic shopping services via home videotex (computerised in-home shopping services). The sample was made up of respondents who were familiar with the concept of computerised shopping from home. The explanation of consumers' preferences was sought in psychographic, demographic and communications variables suggested in the literature.

Multiple regression was used to analyse the data. The overall multiple regression model was significant at a 0.05 level. Univariate *t* tests indicated that the following variables in the model were significant at a 0.05 level or better: price orientation, gender, age, occupation, ethnicity and education. None of the three communication variables (mass media word of mouth and publicity) was significantly related to consumer preference, the dependent variable. The results suggested that electronic shopping was preferred by white females who were older, better educated, working in supervisory or higher level occupations, and price orientated.

This example illustrates the use of regression analysis in determining which independent variables explain a significant variation in the dependent variable of interest, the structure and form of the relationship, the strength of the relationship, and predicted values of the dependent variable. Fundamental to regression analysis is an understanding of the product moment correlation.

Product moment correlation

In marketing research, we are often interested in summarising the strength of association between two metric variables, as in the following situations:

- How strongly are sales related to advertising expenditures?
- Is there an association between market share and size of the sales force?
- Are consumers' perceptions of quality related to their perceptions of prices?

Product moment correlation (r)
A statistic summarising the strength of association between two metric variables.

In situations like these, the **product moment correlation** (*r*) is the most widely used statistic, summarising the strength of association between two metric (interval or ratio scaled) variables, say *X* and *Y*. It is an index used to determine whether a linear or straight line relationship exists between *X* and *Y*. It indicates the degree to which the variation in one variable, *X*, is related to the variation in another variable, *Y*. Because it was originally proposed by Karl Pearson, it is also known as the *Pearson correlation coefficient* and also referred to as *simple correlation, bivariate correlation* or merely the *correlation coefficient*. From a sample of *n* observations, *X* and *Y*, the product moment correlation, *r*, can be calculated as

$$r = \frac{\sum_{i=1}^{n}(X_i - \bar{X})(Y_i - \bar{Y})}{\sqrt{\sum_{i=1}^{n}(X_i - \bar{X})^2 \sum_{i=1}^{n}(Y_i - \bar{Y})^2}}$$

Division of the numerator and denominator by *n* – 1 gives

$$r = \frac{\sum_{i=1}^{n}\dfrac{(X_i - \bar{X})(Y_i - \bar{Y})}{n-1}}{\sqrt{\sum_{i=1}^{n}\dfrac{(X_i - \bar{X})^2}{n-1} \sum_{i=1}^{n}\dfrac{(Y_i - \bar{Y})^2}{n-1}}}$$

$$= \frac{COV_{xy}}{S_x S_y}$$

Covariance
A systematic relationship between two variables in which a change in one implies a corresponding change in the other (COV_{xy}).

In these equations, $\bar{X}$ and $\bar{Y}$ denote the sample means, and S_x and S_y the standard deviations. COV_{xy}, the **covariance** between *X* and *Y*, measures the extent to which *X* and *Y* are related. The covariance may be either positive or negative. Division by $S_x S_y$ achieves standardisation so that *r* varies between –1.0 and +1.0. Note that the correlation coefficient is an absolute number and is not expressed in any unit of measurement. The correlation coefficient between two variables will be the same regardless of their underlying units of measurement.

As an example, suppose that a researcher wants to explain attitudes towards a respondent's city of residence in terms of duration of residence in the city. The attitude is measured on an 11-point scale (1 = do not like the city, 11 = very much like the city), and the duration of residence is measured in terms of the number of years the respondent has lived in the city. In a pretest of 12 respondents, the data shown in Table 20.1 are obtained.

Table 20.1 Explaining attitude towards the city of residence

Respondent number	Attitude towards the city	Duration of residence	Importance attached to weather
1	6	10	3
2	9	12	11
3	8	12	4
4	3	4	1
5	10	12	11
6	4	6	1
7	5	8	7
8	2	2	4
9	11	18	8
10	9	9	10
11	10	17	8
12	2	2	5

The correlation coefficient may be calculated as follows:

$$\bar{X} = (10 + 12 + 12 + 4 + 12 + 6 + 8 + 2 + 18 + 9 + 17 + 2)/12$$
$$= 9.333$$
$$\bar{Y} = (6 + 9 + 8 + 3 + 10 + 4 + 5 + 2 + 11 + 9 + 10 + 2)/12$$
$$= 6.583$$

$$\sum_{i=1}^{n}(X_i - \bar{X})(Y_i - \bar{Y}) = (10 - 9.33)(6 - 6.58)$$
$$+ (12 - 9.33)(9 - 6.58)$$
$$+ (12 - 9.33)(8 - 6.58) + (4 - 9.33)(3 - 6.58)$$
$$+ (12 - 9.33)(10 - 6.58) + (6 - 9.33)(4 - 6.58)$$
$$+ (8 - 9.33)(5 - 6.58) + (2 - 9.33)(2 - 6.58)$$
$$+ (18 - 9.33)(11 - 6.58) + (9 - 9.33)(9 - 6.58)$$
$$+ (17 - 9.33)(10 - 6.58) + (2 - 9.33)(2 - 6.58)$$
$$= -0.3886 + 6.4614 + 3.7914 + 19.0814 + 9.1314 + 8.5914$$
$$+ 2.1014 + 33.5714 + 38.3214 - 0.7986 + 26.2314 + 33.5714$$
$$= 179.6668$$

$$\sum_{i=1}^{n}(X_i - \bar{X})^2 = (10 - 9.33)^2 + (12 - 9.33)^2 + (12 - 9.33)^2 + (4 - 9.33)^2$$
$$+ (12 - 9.33)^2 \ (6 - 9.33)^2 + (8 - 9.33)^2 + (2 - 9.33)^2 + (18 - 9.33)^2$$
$$+ (9 - 9.33)^2 + (17 - 9.33)^2 + (2 - 9.33)^2$$
$$= 0.4489 + 7.1289 + 7.1289 + 28.4089 + 7.1289 + 11.0889 + 1.7689$$
$$+ 53.7289 + 75.1689 + 0.1089 + 58.8289 + 53.7289$$
$$= 304.6668$$

$$\sum_{i=1}^{n}(Y_i - \bar{Y})^2 = (6 - 6.58)^2 + (9 - 6.58)^2 + (8 - 6.58)^2 + (3 - 6.58)^2 + (3 - 6.58)^2$$
$$+ (10 - 6.58)^2 + (4 - 6.58)^2 + (5 - 6.58)^2 + (2 - 6.58)^2 + (11 - 6.58)^2$$
$$+ (9 - 6.58)^2 + (10 - 6.58)^2 + (2 - 6.58)^2$$
$$= 0.3364 + 5.8564 + 2.0164 + 12.8164 + 11.6964 + 6.6564 + 2.4964$$
$$+ 20.9764 + 19.5364 + 5.8564 + 11.6964 + 20.9764$$
$$= 120.9168$$

Thus,

$$r = \frac{179.6668}{\sqrt{(304.6668)(120.9168)}}$$

$$= 0.9361$$

In this example, $r = 0.9361$, a value close to 1.0. This means that respondents' duration of residence in the city is strongly associated with their attitude towards the city. Furthermore, the positive sign of r implies a positive relationship; the longer the duration of residence, the more favourable the attitude and vice versa.

Since r indicates the degree to which variation in one variable is related to variation in another, it can also be expressed in terms of the decomposition of the total variation (see Chapter 19). In other words,

$$r^2 = \frac{\text{explained variation}}{\text{total variation}}$$

$$= \frac{SS_x}{SS_y}$$

$$= \frac{\text{total variation} - \text{error variation}}{\text{total variation}}$$

$$= \frac{SS_y - SS_{error}}{SS_y}$$

Hence, r^2 measures the proportion of variation in one variable that is explained by the other. Both r and r^2 are symmetric measures of association. In other words, the correlation of X with Y is the same as the correlation of Y with X. It does not matter which variable is considered to be the dependent variable and which the independent. The product moment coefficient measures the strength of the linear relationship and is not designed to measure non-linear relationships. Thus $r = 0$ merely indicates that there is no linear relationship between X and Y. It does not mean that X and Y are unrelated. There could well be a non-linear relationship between them, which would not be captured by r (see Figure 20.1).

When computed for a population rather than a sample, the product moment correlation is denoted by the Greek letter rho, ρ. The coefficient r is an estimator of ρ. Note that the calculation of r assumes that X and Y are metric variables whose distributions have the same shape. If these assumptions are not met, r is deflated and underestimates ρ. In marketing research, data obtained by using rating scales with a small number of categories may not be strictly interval. This tends to deflate r, resulting in an underestimation of ρ.[2]

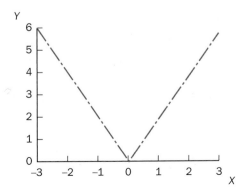

Figure 20.1
A non-linear relationship for which $r = 0$

The statistical significance of the relationship between two variables measured by using r can be conveniently tested. The hypotheses are

$$H_0: \rho = 0$$
$$H_1: \rho \neq 0$$

The test statistic is

$$t = r \left[\frac{n-2}{1-r^2} \right]^{\frac{1}{2}}$$

which has a t distribution with $n - 2$ degrees of freedom.[3] For the correlation coefficient calculated based on the data given in Table 20.1,

$$t = 0.9361 \left[\frac{12-2}{1-(0.36)^2} \right]^{\frac{1}{2}}$$
$$= 8.414$$

and $df = 12 - 2 = 10$. From the t distribution table (Table 4 in the Appendix of statistical tables), the critical value of t for a two-tailed test and $a = 0.05$ is 2.228. Hence, the null hypothesis of no relationship between X and Y is rejected. This, along with the positive sign of r, indicates that attitude towards the city is positively related to the duration of residence in the city. Moreover, the high value of r indicates that this relationship is strong.

In conducting multivariate data analysis, it is often useful to examine the simple correlation between each pair of variables. These results are presented in the form of a correlation matrix, which indicates the coefficient of correlation between each pair of variables. Usually, only the lower triangular portion of the matrix is considered. The diagonal elements all equal 1.00, since a variable correlates perfectly with itself. The upper triangular portion of the matrix is a mirror image of the lower triangular portion, since r is a symmetric measure of association. The form of a correlation matrix for five variables, V_1 to V_5 is as follows:

	V_1	V_2	V_3	V_4	V_5
V_1					
V_2	0.5				
V_3	0.3	0.4			
V_4	0.1	0.3	0.6		
V_5	0.2	0.5	0.3	0.7	

Although a matrix of simple correlations provides insights into pairwise associations, sometimes researchers want to examine the association between two variables after controlling for one or more other variables. In the latter case, partial correlation should be estimated.

Partial correlation

Partial correlation coefficient
A measure of the association between two variables after controlling or adjusting for the effects of one or more additional variables.

Whereas the product moment or simple correlation is a measure of association describing the linear association between two variables, a **partial correlation coefficient** measures the association between two variables after controlling for or adjusting for the effects of one or more additional variables. This statistic is used to answer the following questions:

● How strongly are sales related to advertising expenditures when the effect of price is controlled?

- Is there an association between market share and size of the sales force after adjusting for the effect of sales promotion?
- Are consumers' perceptions of quality related to their perceptions of prices when the effect of brand image is controlled?

As in these situations, suppose that a researcher wanted to calculate the association between X and Y after controlling for a third variable, Z. Conceptually, one would first remove the effect of Z from X. To do this, one would predict the values of X based on knowledge of Z by using the product moment correlation between X and Z, r_{xz}. The predicted value of X is then subtracted from the actual value of X to construct an adjusted value of X. In a similar manner, the values of Y are adjusted to remove the effects of Z. The product moment correlation between the adjusted values of X and the adjusted values of Y is the partial correlation coefficient between X and Y, after controlling for the effect of Z, and is denoted by $r_{xy \cdot z}$. Statistically, since the simple correlation between two variables completely describes the linear relationship between them, the partial correlation coefficient can be calculated by knowledge of the simple correlations alone, without using individual observations:

$$r_{xy \cdot z} = \frac{r_{xy} - (r_{xz})(r_{yz})}{\sqrt{1 - r_{xz}^2}\ \sqrt{1 - r_{yz}^2}}$$

To continue our example, suppose that the researcher wanted to calculate the association between attitude towards the city, Y, and duration of residence, X_1, after controlling for a third variable, importance attached to weather, X_2. These data are presented in Table 20.1.

The simple correlations between the variables are

$$r_{xy_1} = 0.9361\ r_{yx_2} = 0.7334\ r_{x_1 x_2} = 0.5495$$

The required partial correlation may be calculated as follows:

$$r_{xy_1 \cdot x_2} = \frac{0.9361 - (0.5495)(0.7334)}{\sqrt{1 - (0.5495)^2}\ \sqrt{1 - (0.7334)^2}}$$

$$= 0.9386$$

As can be seen, controlling for the effect of importance attached to weather has little effect on the association between attitude towards the city and duration of residence.

Partial correlations have an *order* associated with them that indicates how many variables are being adjusted or controlled for. The simple correlation coefficient, r, has a zero order, because it does not control for any additional variables while measuring the association between two variables. The coefficient $r_{xy \cdot z}$ is a first-order partial correlation coefficient, because it controls for the effect of one additional variable, Z. A second-order partial correlation coefficient controls for the effects of two variables, a third-order for the effects of three variables, and so on. The higher order partial correlations are calculated similarly. The $(n + 1)$th-order partial coefficient may be calculated by replacing the simple correlation coefficients on the right side of the preceding equation with the nth order partial coefficients.

Partial correlations can be helpful for detecting spurious relationships (see Chapter 18). The relationship between X and Y is spurious if it is solely because X is associated with Z, which is indeed the true predictor of Y. In this case, the correlation between X and Y disappears when the effect of Z is controlled. Consider a case in which consumption of a breakfast cereal brand (C) is positively associated with income (I), with $r_{ci} = 0.28$. Because this brand was popularly priced, income was not expected to be a significant factor. Therefore, the researcher suspected that this relationship was spurious. The sample results also indicated that income is positively associated with household size (H), $r_{hi} = 0.48$, and that household size is associated with breakfast cereal consumption, $r_{ch} = 0.56$. These figures seem to indicate that the real predictor of breakfast cereal consumption is not income but household size. To test this assertion, the first-order partial correlation between cereal consumption and income is calculated, controlling for the effect of household size. The reader can verify that this partial correlation, $r_{ci·h}$, is 0.02, and the initial correlation between cereal consumption and income vanishes when the household size is controlled. Therefore, the correlation between income and cereal consumption is spurious. The special case when a partial correlation is larger than its respective zero-order correlation involves a suppressor effect (see Chapter 18).[4]

Another correlation coefficient of interest is the **part correlation coefficient**. This coefficient represents the correlation between Y and X when the linear effects of the other independent variables have been removed from X but not from Y. The part correlation coefficient, $r_{y(x·z)}$, is calculated as follows:

Part correlation coefficient
A measure of the correlation between Y and X when the linear effects of the other independent variables have been removed from X (but not from Y).

$$r_{y(x·z)} = \frac{r_{xy} - r_{yz}r_{xz}}{\sqrt{1 - r_{xz}^2}}$$

The part correlation between attitude towards the city and the duration of residence, when the linear effects of the importance attached to weather have been removed from the duration of residence, can be calculated as

$$r_{y(x_1·x_2)} = \frac{0.9361 - (0.5495)(0.7334)}{\sqrt{1 - (0.5495)^2}}$$

$$= 0.63806$$

The partial correlation coefficient is generally viewed as more important than the part correlation coefficient. The product moment correlation, partial correlation and part correlation coefficient all assume that the data are interval or ratio scaled. If the data do not meet these requirements, the researcher should consider the use of non-metric correlation.

Example   Selling ads to home shoppers[5]

Advertisements play a very important role in forming attitudes and preferences for brands. Source credibility in advertisements may emerge from 'celebrity endorsement' or 'corporate credibility', either or both of which can influence consumer reactions to advertisements and shape brand attitudes. In general, it has been found that for low-involvement products, attitude towards the advertisement mediates brand cognition (beliefs about the brand) and attitude towards the brand.

What would happen to the effect of this mediating variable when products are purchased through a home shopping network? Home Shopping Budapest in Hungary conducted research to assess the impact of advertisements towards purchase. A survey was conducted in which several measures were taken, such as attitude towards the product, attitude towards the brand, attitude towards the ad characteristics and brand cognitions. It was hypothesised that in a home shopping network, advertisements largely determined attitude towards the brand. To find the degree of association of attitude towards the ad with both attitude towards the brand and brand cognition, a partial correlation coefficient could be computed. The partial correlation would be calculated between attitude towards the brand and brand cognitions after controlling for the effects of attitude towards the ad on the two variables. If attitude towards the ad is significantly high, then the partial correlation coefficient should be significantly less than the product moment correlation between brand cognition and attitude towards the brand. Research was conducted which supported this hypothesis. Then Saatchi & Saatchi (**www.saatchi.com**) designed the ads aired on Home Shopping Budapest to generate positive attitude towards the advertising. This turned out to be a major competitive weapon for the network.

Non-metric correlation

Non-metric correlation
A correlation measure for two non-metric variables that relies on rankings to compute the correlation.

At times the researcher may have to compute the correlation coefficient between two variables that are non-metric. It may be recalled that non-metric variables do not have interval or ratio scale properties and do not assume a normal distribution. If the non-metric variables are ordinal and numeric, Spearman's rho, ρ_s, and Kendall's tau, τ, are two measures of **non-metric correlation** which can be used to examine the correlation between them. Both these measures use rankings rather than the absolute values of the variables, and the basic concepts underlying them are quite similar. Both vary from -1.0 to $+1.0$. (See Chapter 18.)

In the absence of ties, Spearman's ρ_s yields a closer approximation to the Pearson product moment correlation coefficient, ρ, than does Kendall's τ. In these cases, the absolute magnitude of τ tends to be smaller than Pearson's ρ. On the other hand, when the data contain a large number of tied ranks, Kendall's τ seems more appropriate. As a rule of thumb, Kendall's τ is to be preferred when a large number of cases fall into a relatively small number of categories (thereby leading to a large number of ties). Conversely, the use of Spearman's ρ_s is preferable when we have a relatively larger number of categories (thereby having fewer ties).[6]

The product moment as well as the partial and part correlation coefficients provide a conceptual foundation for bivariate as well as multiple regression analysis.

Regression analysis

Regression analysis
A statistical procedure for analysing associative relationships between a metric-dependent variable and one or more independent variables.

Regression analysis is a powerful and flexible procedure for analysing associative relationships between a metric-dependent variable and one or more independent variables. It can be used in the following ways:

1 To determine whether the independent variables explain a significant variation in the dependent variable: whether a relationship exists.
2 To determine how much of the variation in the dependent variable can be explained by the independent variables: strength of the relationship.
3 To determine the structure or form of the relationship: the mathematical equation relating the independent and dependent variables.
4 To predict the values of the dependent variable.
5 To control for other independent variables when evaluating the contributions of a specific variable or set of variables.

Although the independent variables may explain the variation in the dependent variable, this does not necessarily imply causation. The use of the terms 'dependent or criterion variables' and 'independent or predictor variables' in regression analysis arises from the mathematical relationship between the variables. These terms do not imply that the criterion variable is dependent on the independent variables in a causal sense. Regression analysis is concerned with the nature and degree of association between variables and does not imply or assume any causality. Bivariate regression is discussed first, followed by multiple regression.

Bivariate regression

Bivariate regression
A procedure for deriving a mathematical relationship, in the form of an equation, between a single metric-dependent variable and a single metric-independent variable.

Bivariate regression is a procedure for deriving a mathematical relationship, in the form of an equation, between a single metric-dependent or criterion variable and a single metric-independent or predictor variable. The analysis is similar in many ways to determining the simple correlation between two variables. Since an equation has to be derived, however, one variable must be identified as the dependent variable and the other as the independent variable. The examples given earlier in the context of simple correlation can be translated into the regression context:

- Can variation in sales be explained in terms of variation in advertising expenditures? What is the structure and form of this relationship, and can it be modelled mathematically by an equation describing a straight line?
- Can the variation in market share be accounted for by the size of the sales force?
- Are consumers' perceptions of quality determined by their perceptions of price?

Before discussing the procedure for conducting bivariate regression, we define some important statistics associated with bivariate regression analysis.

Statistics associated with bivariate regression analysis

The following statistics and statistical terms are associated with bivariate regression analysis.

Bivariate regression model. The basic regression equation is $Y_i = \beta_0 + \beta_1 X_i + e_i$, where $Y =$ dependent or criterion variable, $X =$ independent or predictor variable, $\beta_0 =$ intercept of the line, $\beta_1 =$ slope of the line, and e_i is the error term associated with the ith observation.

Coefficient of determination. The strength of association is measured by the coefficient of determination, r^2. It varies between 0 and 1 and signifies the proportion of the total variation in Y that is accounted for by the variation in X.

Estimated or predicted value. The estimated or predicted value of Y_i is $\hat{Y}i = a + bx$, where $\hat{Y}_i$ is the predicted value of Y_i, and a and b are estimators of β_0 and β_1, respectively.

Regression coefficient. The estimated parameter b is usually referred to as the non-standardised regression coefficient.

Scattergram. A scatter diagram, or scattergram, is a plot of the values of two variables for all the cases or observations.

Standard error of estimate. This statistic, the *SEE*, is the standard deviation of the actual Y values from the predicted $\hat{Y}$ values.

Standard error. The standard deviation of b, SE_b, is called the standard error.

Standardised regression coefficient. Also termed the beta coefficient or beta weight, this is the slope obtained by the regression of Y on X when the data are standardised.

Sum of squared errors. The distances of all the points from the regression line are squared and added together to arrive at the sum of squared errors, which is a measure of total error, $\sum e_j^2$.

t statistic. A t statistic with $n - 2$ degrees of freedom can be used to test the null hypothesis that no linear relationship exists between X and Y, or $H_0 : \beta_1 = 0$, where

$$t = \frac{b}{SE_b}$$

Conducting bivariate regression analysis

The steps involved in conducting bivariate regression analysis are described in Figure 20.2.

Plot the scatter diagram

Suppose that the researcher wants to explain attitudes towards the city of residence in terms of the duration of residence (see Table 20.2). In deriving such relationships, it is often useful first to examine a scatter diagram. A scatter diagram, or scattergram, is a plot

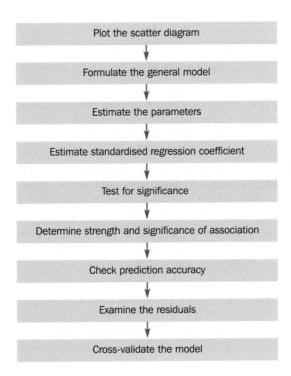

Figure 20.2
Conducting bivariate regression analysis

Plot the scatter diagram
↓
Formulate the general model
↓
Estimate the parameters
↓
Estimate standardised regression coefficient
↓
Test for significance
↓
Determine strength and significance of association
↓
Check prediction accuracy
↓
Examine the residuals
↓
Cross-validate the model

Table 20.2 Bivariate regression

Multiple R	0.93608			
R^2	0.87624			
Adjusted R^2	0.86387			
Standard error	1.22329			
Analysis of variance				
	df	Sum of squares	Mean square	
Regression	1	105.95222	105.95222	
Residual	10	14.96444	1.49644	
$F = 70.80266$	Significance of $F = 0.0000$			
Variables in the equation				
Variable	b	SE_b	Beta (β)	T	Sig. of T
Duration	0.58972	0.07008	0.93608	8.414	0.0000
(Constant)	1.07932	0.74335		1.452	0.1772

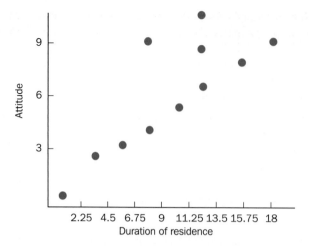

Figure 20.3
Plot of attitude with duration

of the values of two variables for all the cases or observations. It is customary to plot the dependent variable on the vertical axis and the independent variable on the horizontal axis. A scatter diagram is useful for determining the form of the relationship between the variables. A plot can alert the researcher to patterns in the data or to possible problems. Any unusual combinations of the two variables can be easily identified. A plot of Y (attitude towards the city) against X (duration of residence) is given in Figure 20.3. The points seem to be arranged in a band running from the bottom left to the top right. One can see the pattern: as one variable increases, so does the other. It appears from this scattergram that the relationship between X and Y is linear and could be well described by a straight line. How should the straight line be fitted to best describe the data?

The most commonly used technique for fitting a straight line to a scattergram is the **least squares procedure**. This technique determines the best-fitting line by minimising the vertical distances of all the points from the line. The best-fitting line is called the regression line. Any point that does not fall on the regression line is not fully accounted for. The vertical distance from the point to the line is the error, e_j (see Figure 20.4). The distances of all the points from the line are squared and added together to arrive at the sum of squared errors, which is a measure of total error, $\sum e_j^2$. In fitting the line, the least squares procedure minimises the sum of squared errors. If Y is plotted on the vertical axis

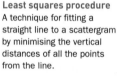

Least squares procedure
A technique for fitting a straight line to a scattergram by minimising the vertical distances of all the points from the line.

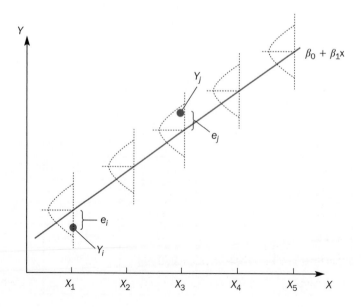

Figure 20.4
Bivariate regression

and X on the horizontal axis, as in Figure 20.4, the best-fitting line is called the regression of Y on X, since the vertical distances are minimised. The scatter diagram indicates whether the relationship between Y and X can be modelled as a straight line and, consequently, whether the bivariate regression model is appropriate.

Formulate the general model

In the bivariate regression model, the general form of a straight line is

$$Y = \beta_0 + \beta_1 X$$

where Y = dependent or criterion variable
X = independent or predictor variable
β_0 = intercept of the line
β_1 = slope of the line

This model implies a deterministic relationship in that Y is completely determined by X. The value of Y can be perfectly predicted if β_0 and β_1 are known. In marketing research, however, very few relationships are deterministic. Thus, the regression procedure adds an error term to account for the probabilistic or stochastic nature of the relationship. The basic regression equation becomes

$$Y_i = \beta_0 + \beta_1 X_i + e_i$$

where e_i is the error term associated with the ith observation.[7] Estimation of the regression parameters, β_0 and β_1, is relatively simple.

Estimate the parameters

In most cases, β_0 and β_1 are unknown and are estimated from the sample observations using the equation

$$\hat{Y}_i = a + bx_i$$

Estimated or predicted value
The value $Y_i = a + b_x$, where a and b are, respectively, estimators of β_0 and β_1, the corresponding population parameters.

where $\hat{Y}_i$ is the **estimated or predicted value** of Y_i, and a and b are estimators of β_0 and β_1 respectively. The constant b is usually referred to as the non-standardised regression coefficient. It is the slope of the regression line, and it indicates the expected change in Y when X is changed by one unit. The formulae for calculating a and b are simple.[8] The slope, b, may be computed in terms of the covariance between X and Y (COV_{xy}) and the variance of X as

$$b = \frac{COV_{xy}}{S_x^2}$$

$$= \frac{\sum_{i=1}^{n}(X_i - \bar{X})(Y_i - \bar{Y})}{\sum_{i=1}^{n}(X_i - \bar{X})^2}$$

$$= \frac{\sum_{i=1}^{n}X_iY_i - n\bar{X}\bar{Y}}{\sum_{i=1}^{n}X_i^2 - n\bar{X}^2}$$

The intercept, a, may then be calculated using

$$a = \bar{Y} - b\bar{X}$$

For the data in Table 20.2, the estimation of parameters may be illustrated as follows:

$$\sum_{i=1}^{12} X_i Y_i = (10)(6) + (12)(9) + (12)(8) + (4)(3) + (12)(10) + (6)(4) + (8)(5) + (2)(2)$$
$$+ (18)(11) + (9)(9) + (17)(10) + (2)(2)$$
$$= 917$$

$$\sum_{i=1}^{12} X_i^2 = 10^2 + 12^2 + 12^2 + 4^2 + 12^2 + 6^2 + 8^2 + 2^2 + 18^2 + 9^2 + 17^2 + 2^2$$
$$= 1350$$

It may be recalled from earlier calculations of the simple correlation that

$$\overline{X} = 9.333$$
$$\overline{Y} = 6.583$$

Given $n = 12$, b can be calculated as

$$b = \frac{917 - (12)(9.333)(6.583)}{1350 - (12)(9.333)^2}$$
$$= 0.5897$$
$$a = \overline{Y} - b\overline{X}$$
$$= 6.583 - (0.5897)(9.333)$$
$$= 1.0793$$

Note that these coefficients have been estimated on the raw (untransformed) data. Should standardisation of the data be considered desirable, the calculation of the standardised coefficients is also straightforward.

Estimate the standardised regression coefficient

Standardisation is the process by which the raw data are transformed into new variables that have a mean of 0 and a variance of 1 (Chapter 17). When the data are standardised, the intercept assumes a value of 0. The term *beta coefficient* or *beta weight* is used to denote the standardised regression coefficient. In this case, the slope obtained by the regression of Y on X, B_{yx}, is the same as the slope obtained by the regression of X on Y, B_{xy}. Moreover, each of these regression coefficients is equal to the simple correlation between X and Y:

$$B_{yx} = B_{xy} = r_{xy}$$

There is a simple relationship between the standardised and non-standardised regression coefficients:

$$B_{yx} = b_{yx}\left(\frac{S_x}{S_y}\right)$$

Note that this is also the value of r calculated earlier in this chapter.

Once the parameters have been estimated, they can be tested for significance.

Test for significance

The statistical significance of the linear relationship between X and Y may be tested by examining the hypotheses

$$H_0: \beta_1 = 0$$
$$H_1: \beta_1 \neq 0$$

The null hypothesis implies that there is no linear relationship between X and Y. The alternative hypothesis is that there is a relationship, positive or negative, between X and Y. Typically, a two-tailed test is done. A t statistic with $n - 2$ degrees of freedom can be used, where

$$t = \frac{b}{SE_b}$$

and SE_b denotes the standard deviation of b, called the *standard error*.[9] The t distribution was discussed in Chapter 18.

Using a software package, the regression of attitude on duration of residence, using the data shown in Table 20.1, yielded the results shown in Table 20.2. The intercept, a, equals 1.0793, and the slope, b, equals 0.5897. Therefore, the estimated equation is

$$\text{attitude } (\hat{Y}) = 1.0793 + 0.5897(\text{duration of residence})$$

The standard error or standard deviation of b is estimated as 0.07008, and the value of the t statistic, $t = 0.5897/0.0701 = 8.414$, with $n - 2 = 10$ df. From Table 4 in the Appendix of statistical tables, we see that the critical value of t with 10 df and $a = 0.05$ is 2.228 for a two-tailed test. Since the calculated value of t is larger than the critical value, the null hypothesis is rejected. Hence, there is a significant linear relationship between attitude towards the city and duration of residence in the city. The positive sign of the slope coefficient indicates that this relationship is positive. In other words, those who have lived in the city for a longer time have more positive attitudes towards it.

For the regression results given in Table 20.2, the value of the beta coefficient is estimated as 0.9361.

Determine strength and significance of association

A related inference involves determining the strength and significance of the association between Y and X. The strength of association is measured by the coefficient of determination, r^2. In bivariate regression, r^2 is the square of the simple correlation coefficient obtained by correlating the two variables. The coefficient r^2 varies between 0 and 1. It signifies the proportion of the total variation in Y that is accounted for by the variation in X. The decomposition of the total variation in Y is similar to that for analysis of variance (Chapter 19). As shown in Figure 20.5, the total variation SS_y may be decomposed into the variation accounted for by the regression line, SS_{reg}, and the error or residual variation, SS_{error} or SS_{res}, as follows:

$$SS_y = SS_{reg} + SS_{res}$$

$$SS_y = \sum_{i=1}^{n} (Y_i - \bar{Y})^2$$

$$SS_{reg} = \sum_{i=1}^{n} (\hat{Y}_i - \bar{Y})^2$$

$$SS_{res} = \sum_{i=1}^{n} (Y_i - \hat{Y}_i)^2$$

The strength of the association may then be calculated as follows:

$$r^2 = \frac{SS_{reg}}{SS_y}$$

$$= \frac{SS_y - SS_{res}}{SS_y}$$

To illustrate the calculations of r^2, let us consider again the effect of attitude towards the city on the duration of residence. It may be recalled from earlier calculations of the simple correlation coefficient that

$$SS_y = \sum_{i=1}^{n} (Y_i - \bar{Y})^2$$

$$= 120.9168$$

The predicted values ($\hat{Y}$) can be calculated using the regression equation

$$\text{attitude } (\hat{Y}) = 1.0793 + 0.5897(\text{duration of residence})$$

For the first observation in Table 20.1, this value is

$$(\hat{Y}) = 1.0793 + (0.5897 \times 10) = 6.9763$$

For each successive observation, the predicted values are, in order, 8.1557, 8.1557, 3.4381, 8.1557, 4.6175, 5.7969, 2.2587, 11.6939, 6.3866, 11.1042, 2.2587. Therefore,

$$SS_{reg} = \sum_{i=1}^{n} (\hat{Y}_i - \bar{Y})^2$$

$$= (6.9763 - 6.5833)^2 + (8.1557 - 6.5833)^2 + (8.1557 - 6.5833)^2$$
$$+ (3.4381 - 6.5833)^2 + (8.1557 - 6.5833)^2 + (4.6175 - 6.5833)^2$$
$$+ (5.7969 - 6.5833)^2 + (2.2587 - 6.5833)^2 + (11.6939 - 6.5833)^2$$
$$+ (6.3866 - 6.5833)^2 + (11.1042 - 6.5833)^2 + (2.2587 - 6.5833)^2$$
$$= 0.1544 + 2.42724 + 2.4724 + 9.8922 + 2.4724 + 3.8643 + 0.6184$$
$$+ 18.7021 + 26.1182 + 0.0387 + 20.4385 + 18.7021$$
$$= 105.9466$$

$$SS_{res} = \sum_{i=1}^{n} (Y_i - \hat{Y}_i)^2$$

$$= (6 - 6.69763)^2 + (9 - 8.1557)^2 + (8 - 8.1557)^2 + (3 - 3.4381)^2$$
$$+ (10 - 8.1557)^2 + (4 - 4.6175)^2 + (5 - 5.7969)^2 + (2 - 2.2587)^2$$
$$+ (11 - 11.6939)^2 + (9 - 6.3866)^2 + (10 - 11.1042)^2 + (2 - 2.2587)^2$$
$$= 14.9644$$

It can be seen that $SS_y = SS_{reg} + SS_{res}$. Furthermore,

$$r^2 = \frac{SS_{reg}}{SS_y}$$

$$= \frac{105.9466}{120.9168}$$

$$= 0.8762$$

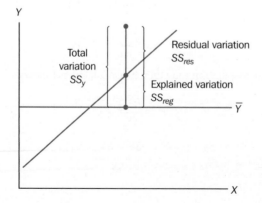

Figure 20.5
Decomposition of the total variation in bivariate regression

Another equivalent test for examining the significance of the linear relationship between X and Y (significance of b) is the test for the significance of the coefficient of determination. The hypotheses in this case are

$$H_0: R^2_{pop} = 0$$

$$H_1: R^2_{pop} > 0$$

The appropriate test statistic is the F statistic

$$F = \frac{SS_{reg}}{SS_{res}/(n-2)}$$

which has an F distribution with 1 and $(n-2)$ df. The F test is a generalised form of the t test (see Chapter 18). If a random variable is t distributed with n degrees of freedom, then t^2 is F distributed with 1 and n df. Hence, the F test for testing the significance of the coefficient of determination is equivalent to testing the following hypotheses:

$$H_0: \beta_1 = 0$$
$$H_1: \beta_1 \neq 0$$

or

$$H_0: \rho = 0$$
$$H_1: \rho \neq 0$$

From Table 20.2, it can be seen that

$$r^2 = \frac{105.9522}{105.9522 + 14.9644}$$

$$= 0.8762$$

which is the same as the value calculated earlier. The value of the F statistic is

$$F = \frac{105.9522}{14.9644/10}$$

$$= 70.8028$$

with 1 and 10 df. The calculated F statistic exceeds the critical value of 4.96 determined from Table 5 in the Appendix. Therefore, the relationship is significant at $a = 0.05$, corroborating the results of the t test. If the relationship between X and Y is significant, it is meaningful to predict the values of Y based on the values of X and to estimate prediction accuracy.

Check prediction accuracy

To estimate the accuracy of predicted values, $\hat{Y}$, it is useful to calculate the standard error of estimate, SEE. This statistic is the standard deviation of the actual $\hat{Y}$ values from the predicted $\hat{Y}$ values:

$$SEE = \sqrt{\frac{\sum_{i=1}^{n}(Y_i - \hat{Y})^2}{n-2}}$$

or

$$SEE = \sqrt{\frac{SS_{res}}{n-2}}$$

or, more generally, if there are k independent variables

$$SEE = \sqrt{\frac{SS_{res}}{n - k - 1}}$$

SEE may be interpreted as a kind of average residual or average error in predicting Y from the regression equation.[10]

Two cases of prediction may arise. The researcher may want to predict the mean value of Y for all the cases with a given value of X, say X_0, or predict the value of Y for a single case. In both situations, the predicted value is the same and is given by $\hat{Y}$, where

$$\hat{Y} = a + bX_0$$

But the standard error is different in the two situations, although in both situations it is a function of SEE. For large samples, the standard error for predicting the mean value of Y is $SEE/\sqrt{n}$ and for predicting individual Y values it is SEE. Hence, the construction of confidence intervals (see Chapter 15) for the predicted value varies, depending upon whether the mean value or the value for a single observation is being predicted. For the data given in Table 20.2, SEE is estimated as follows:

$$SEE = \sqrt{\frac{14.9644}{12 - 2}}$$

$$= 1.22329$$

The final two steps in conducting bivariate regression, namely examination of residuals and model cross-validation, are considered later, and we now turn to the assumptions underlying the regression model.

Assumptions

The regression model makes a number of assumptions in estimating the parameters and in significance testing, as shown in Figure 20.4:

1 The error term is normally distributed. For each fixed value of X, the distribution of Y is normal.[11]
2 The means of all these normal distributions of Y, given X, lie on a straight line with slope b.
3 The mean of the error term is 0.
4 The variance of the error term is constant. This variance does not depend on the values assumed by X.
5 The error terms are uncorrelated. In other words, the observations have been drawn independently.

Insights into the extent to which these assumptions have been met can be gained by an examination of residuals, which is covered in the next section on multiple regression.[12]

Multiple regression

Multiple regression
A statistical technique that simultaneously develops a mathematical relationship between two or more independent variables and an interval-scaled dependent variable.

Multiple regression involves a single dependent variable and two or more independent variables. The questions raised in the context of bivariate regression can also be answered via multiple regression by considering additional independent variables:

● Can variation in sales be explained in terms of variation in advertising expenditures, prices and level of distribution?
● Can variation in market shares be accounted for by the size of the sales force, advertising expenditures and sales promotion budgets?

- Are consumers' perceptions of quality determined by their perceptions of prices, brand image and brand attributes?

Additional questions can also be answered by multiple regression:

- How much of the variation in sales can be explained by advertising expenditures, prices and level of distribution?
- What is the contribution of advertising expenditures in explaining the variation in sales when the levels of prices and distribution are controlled?
- What levels of sales may be expected given the levels of advertising expenditures, prices and level of distribution?

Example | **Global brands, local ads[13]**

Europeans welcome brands from other countries, but when it comes to advertising, they seem to prefer brands from their own country. A survey conducted by Yankelovich and Partners (www.yankelovich.com) and its affiliates found that most European consumers' favourite commercials were for local brands even though they were more than likely to buy foreign brands. Respondents in the UK, France and Germany named Coca-Cola as the most often purchased soft drink. The French, however, selected the famous award-winning spot for France's Perrier bottled water as their favourite commercial. Similarly, in Germany, the favourite advertising was for a German brand of non-alcoholic beer, Clausthaler. In the UK, though, Coca-Cola was the favourite soft drink and also the favourite advertising. In the light of such findings, the important question was: does advertising help? Does it help increase the purchase probability of the brand or does it merely maintain the brand recognition rate high? One way of finding out was by running a regression where the dependent variable was the likelihood of brand purchase and the independent variables were brand attribute evaluations and advertising evaluations. Separate models with and without advertising could be run to assess any significant difference in the contribution. Individual t tests could also be examined to find out the significant contribution of both the brand attributes and advertising. The results could indicate the degree to which advertising plays an important part in brand purchase decisions.

Multiple regression model
An equation used to explain the results of multiple regression analysis.

The general form of the **multiple regression model** is as follows:

$$Y = \beta_0 + \beta_1 X_1 + \beta_2 X_2 + \beta_3 X_3 + \ldots + \beta_k X_k + e$$

which is estimated by the following equation:

$$\hat{Y} = a + b_1 X_1 + b_2 X_2 + b_3 X_3 + \ldots + b_k X_k$$

As before, the coefficient a represents the intercept, but the bs are now the partial regression coefficients. The least squares criterion estimates the parameters in such a way as to minimise the total error, SS_{res}. This process also maximises the correlation between the actual values of Y and the predicted values of $\hat{Y}$. All the assumptions made in bivariate regression also apply in multiple regression. We define some associated statistics and then describe the procedure for multiple regression analysis.[14]

Statistics associated with multiple regression

Most of the statistics and statistical terms described under bivariate regression also apply to multiple regression. In addition, the following statistics are used:

Adjusted R^2. R^2, the coefficient of multiple determination, is adjusted for the number of independent variables and the sample size to account for the diminishing returns. After the first few variables, the additional independent variables do not make much contribution.

Coefficient of multiple determination. The strength of association in multiple regression is measured by the square of the multiple correlation coefficient, R^2, which is also called the *coefficient of multiple determination.*

F test. The F test is used to test the null hypothesis that the coefficient of multiple determination in the population, R^2_{pop}, is zero. This is equivalent to testing the null hypothesis $H_0: \beta_1 = \beta_2 = \beta_3 = \dots \beta_k = 0$. The test statistic has an F distribution with k and $(n - k - 1)$ *df*.

Partial F test. The significance of a partial regression coefficient, β_i, of X_i may be tested using an incremental F statistic. The incremental F statistic is based on the increment in the explained sum of squares resulting from the addition of the independent variable X_i to the regression equation after all the other independent variables have been included.

Partial regression coefficient. The partial regression coefficient, b_1, denotes the change in the predicted value, $\hat{Y}$, per unit change in X_1 when the other independent variables, X_2 to X_k, are held constant.

Conducting multiple regression analysis

The steps involved in conducting multiple regression analysis are similar to those for bivariate regression analysis. The discussion focuses on partial regression coefficients, strength of association, significance testing and examination of residuals.

Estimating the partial regression coefficients

To understand the meaning of a partial regression coefficient, let us consider a case in which there are two independent variables, so that

$$\hat{Y} = a + b_1 X_1 + b_2 X_2$$

First, note that the relative magnitude of the partial regression coefficient of an independent variable is, in general, different from that of its bivariate regression coefficient. In other words, the partial regression coefficient, b_1, will be different from the regression coefficient, b, obtained by regressing Y on only X_1. This happens because X_1 and X_2 are usually correlated. In bivariate regression, X_2 was not considered, and any variation in Y that was shared by X_1 and X_2 was attributed to X_1. In the case of multiple independent variables, however, this is no longer true.

The interpretation of the partial regression coefficient, b_1, is that it represents the expected change in Y when X_1 is changed by one unit but X_2 is held constant or otherwise controlled. Likewise, b_2 represents the expected change in Y for a unit change in X_2 when X_1 is held constant. Thus, calling b_1 and b_2 partial regression coefficients is appropriate. It can also be seen that the combined effects of X_1 and X_2 on Y are additive. In other words, if X_1 and X_2 are each changed by one unit, the expected change in Y would be $(b_1 + b_2)$.

Conceptually, the relationship between the bivariate regression coefficient and the partial regression coefficient can be illustrated as follows. Suppose that one were to remove the effect of X_2 from X_1. This could be done by running a regression of X_1 on X_2. In other words, one would estimate the equation $X_1 = a + bX_2$ and calculate the residual $X_r = (X_1 - \hat{X}_1)$. The partial regression coefficient, b_1, is then equal to the bivariate regression coefficient, b, obtained from the equation $\hat{Y} = a + bX_r$. In other words, the partial regression coefficient, b_2, is equal to the regression coefficient, b_r, between Y and the residuals of X_1 from which the effect of X_2 has been removed. The partial coefficient, b_2, can also be interpreted along similar lines.

Extension to the case of k variables is straightforward. The partial regression coefficient, b_1, represents the expected change in Y when X_1 is changed by one unit and X_2 to X_k are held constant. It can also be interpreted as the bivariate regression coefficient, b, for the regression of Y on the residuals of X_1, when the effect of X_2 to X_k has been removed from X_1.

The beta coefficients are the partial regression coefficients obtained when all the variables $(Y, X_1, X_2, ..., X_k)$ have been standardised to a mean of 0 and a variance of 1 before estimating the regression equation. The relationship of the standardised to the non-standardised coefficients remains the same as before:

$$B_1 = b_1 \left(\frac{S_{x_1}}{S_y} \right)$$

$$\vdots$$

$$B_k = b_k \left(\frac{S_{xk}}{S_y} \right)$$

The intercept and the partial regression coefficients are estimated by solving a system of simultaneous equations derived by differentiating and equating the partial derivatives to zero. Since these coefficients are automatically estimated by various computer programs, we will not present the details. Yet it is worth noting that the equations cannot be solved if (1) the sample size, n, is smaller than or equal to the number of independent variables, k, or (2) one independent variable is perfectly correlated with another.

Suppose that in explaining the attitude towards the city we now introduce a second variable, importance attached to the weather. The data for the 12 pretest respondents on attitude towards the city, duration of residence and importance attached to the weather are given in Table 20.1. The results of multiple regression analysis are depicted in Table 20.3. The partial regression coefficient for duration (X_1) is now 0.4811, different from what it was in the bivariate case. The corresponding beta coefficient is 0.7636.

Table 20.3 Multiple regression

Multiple R	0.97210		
R^2	0.94498		
Adjusted R^2	0.93276		
Standard error	0.85974		
Analysis of variance			
	df	Sum of squares	Mean square
Regression	2	114.26425	57.13213
Residual	9	6.65241	0.73916
$F = 77.29364$	Significance of $F = 0.0000$		
Variables in the equation			
Variable	b	SE_b	Beta (β)	T	Sig. of T
Importance	0.28865	0.08608	0.31382	3.353	0.0085
Duration	0.48108	0.05895	0.76363	8.160	0.0000
(Constant)	0.33732	0.56736		0.595	0.5668

The partial regression coefficient for importance attached to weather (X_2) is 0.2887, with a beta coefficient of 0.3138. The estimated regression equation is

$$(\hat{Y}) = 0.33732 + 0.48108X_1 + 0.28865X_2$$

or

$$\text{attitude} = 0.33732 + 0.48108(\text{duration}) + 0.28865(\text{importance})$$

This equation can be used for a variety of purposes, including predicting attitudes towards the city, given a knowledge of the respondents' duration of residence in the city and the importance they attach to weather. Note that Duration and Importance are significant and useful in the prediciton.

Strength of association

The strength of the relationship stipulated by the regression equation can be determined by using appropriate measures of association. The total variation is decomposed as in the bivariate case:

$$SS_y = SS_{reg} + SS_{res}$$

where
$$SS_y = \sum_{i=1}^{n} (Y_i - \bar{Y})^2$$

$$SS_{reg} = \sum_{i=1}^{n} (\hat{Y}_i - \bar{Y})^2$$

$$SS_{res} = \sum_{i=1}^{n} (Y_i - \hat{Y})^2$$

The strength of association is measured by the square of the multiple correlation coefficient, R^2, which is also called the coefficient of multiple determination:

$$R^2 = \frac{SS_{reg}}{SS_y}$$

The multiple correlation coefficient, R, can also be viewed as the simple correlation coefficient, r, between Y and $\hat{Y}$. Several points about the characteristics of R^2 are worth noting. The coefficient of multiple determination, R^2, cannot be less than the highest bivariate, r^2, of any individual independent variable with the dependent variable. R^2 will be larger when the correlations between the independent variables are low. If the independent variables are statistically independent (uncorrelated), then R^2 will be the sum of bivariate r^2 of each independent variable with the dependent variable. R^2 cannot decrease as more independent variables are added to the regression equation. Yet diminishing returns set in, so that after the first few variables, the additional independent variables do not make much of a contribution.[15] For this reason, R^2 is adjusted for the number of independent variables and the sample size by using the following formula:

$$\text{adjusted } R^2 = R^2 - \frac{k(1 - R^2)}{n - k - 1}$$

For the regression results given in Table 20.3, the value of R^2 is

$$R^2 = \frac{114.2643}{114.2643 + 6.6524}$$

$$= 0.9450$$

This is higher than the r^2 value of 0.8762 obtained in the bivariate case. The r^2 in the bivariate case is the square of the simple (product moment) correlation between attitude towards the city and duration of residence. The R^2 obtained in multiple regression is also higher than the square of the simple correlation between attitude and importance attached to weather (which can be estimated as 0.5379). The adjusted R^2 is estimated as

$$\text{adjusted } R^2 = 0.9450 - \frac{2(1.0 - 0.9450)}{12 - 2 - 1}$$

$$= 0.9328$$

Note that the value of adjusted R^2 is close to R^2 and both are higher than r^2 for the bivariate case. This suggests that the addition of the second independent variable, importance attached to weather, makes a contribution in explaining the variation in attitude towards the city.

Test for significance

Significance testing involves testing the significance of the overall regression equation as well as specific partial regression coefficients. The null hypothesis for the overall test is that the coefficient of multiple determination in the population, R^2_{pop}, is zero:

$$H_0: R^2_{pop} = 0$$

This is equivalent to the following null hypothesis:

$$H_0: \beta_1 = \beta_2 = \beta_3 = \ldots = \beta_k = 0$$

The overall test can be conducted by using an F statistic

$$F = \frac{SS_{reg}/k}{SS_{reg}/(n-k-1)}$$

$$= \frac{R^2/k}{(1 - R^2)/(n-k-1)}$$

which has an F distribution with k and $(n-k-1)$ df.[16] For the multiple regression results given in Table 20.3,

$$F = \frac{114.2642/2}{6.6524/9} = 77.2937$$

which is significant at $a = 0.05$.

If the overall null hypothesis is rejected, one or more population partial regression coefficients have a value different from 0. To determine which specific coefficients (the β_is) are non-zero, additional tests are necessary. Testing for the significance of the β_is can be done in a manner similar to that in the bivariate case by using t tests. The significance of the partial coefficient for importance attached to weather may be tested by the following equation:

$$t = \frac{b}{SE_b}$$

$$= \frac{0.2887}{0.08608} = 3.354$$

which has a t distribution with $(n-k-1)$ df. This coefficient is significant at $\alpha = 0.05$. The significance of the coefficient for duration of residence is tested in a similar way and found to be significant. Therefore, both the duration of residence and importance attached to weather are important in explaining attitude towards the city.

Some computer programs provide an equivalent F test, often called the partial F test, which involves a decomposition of the total regression sum of squares, SS_{reg}, into components related to each independent variable. In the standard approach, this is done by assuming that each independent variable has been added to the regression equation after all the other independent variables have been included. The increment in the explained sum of squares, resulting from the addition of an independent variable, X_i, is the component of the variation attributed to that variable and is denoted by SS_{xi}.[17] The significance of the partial regression coefficient for this variable, b_i, is tested using an incremental F statistic

$$F = \frac{SS_{xi}/1}{SS_{res}/(n-k-1)}$$

which has an F distribution with 1 and $(n-k-1)$ df.

Although high R^2 and significant partial regression coefficients are comforting, the efficacy of the regression model should be evaluated further by an examination of the residuals.

Examine the residuals

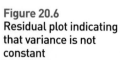

Residual
The difference between the observed value of Y_i and the value predicted by the regression equation $\hat{Y}_i$.

A **residual** is the difference between the observed value of Y_i and the value predicted by the regression equation $\hat{Y}_i$. Residuals are used in the calculation of several statistics associated with regression. In addition, scattergrams of the residuals – in which the residuals are plotted against the predicted values, $\hat{Y}_i$, time, or predictor variables – provide useful insights in examining the appropriateness of the underlying assumptions and regression model fitted.[18]

The assumption of a normally distributed error term can be examined by constructing a histogram of the residuals. A visual check reveals whether the distribution is normal. Additional evidence can be obtained by determining the percentages of residuals falling within ± 1 SE or ± 2 SE. These percentages can be compared with what would be expected under the normal distribution (68% and 95%, respectively). More formal assessment can be made by running the K–S one-sample test.

The assumption of constant variance of the error term can be examined by plotting the residuals against the predicted values of the dependent variable, $\hat{Y}_i$. If the pattern is not random, the variance of the error term is not constant. Figure 20.6 shows a pattern whose variance is dependent on the $\hat{Y}_i$ values.

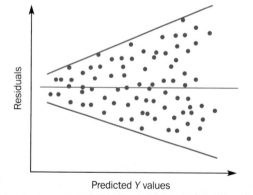

Figure 20.6
Residual plot indicating that variance is not constant

A plot of residuals against time, or the sequence of observations, will throw some light on the assumption that the error terms are uncorrelated. A random pattern should be seen if this assumption is true. A plot like the one in Figure 20.7 indicates a linear relationship between residuals and time. A more formal procedure for examining the correlations between the error terms is the Durbin–Watson test.[19]

Plotting the residuals against the independent variables provides evidence of the appropriateness or inappropriateness of using a linear model. Again, the plot should result in a random pattern. The residuals should fall randomly, with relatively equal distribution dispersion about zero. They should not display any tendency to be either positive or negative.

To examine whether any additional variables should be included in the regression equation, one could run a regression of the residuals on the proposed variables. If any variable explains a significant proportion of the residual variation, it should be considered for inclusion. Inclusion of variables in the regression equation should be strongly guided by the researcher's theory. Thus, an examination of the residuals provides valuable insights into the appropriateness of the underlying assumptions and the model that is fitted. Figure 20.8 shows a plot that indicates that the underlying assumptions are met and that the linear model is appropriate. If an examination of the residuals indicates that the assumptions underlying linear regression are not met, the researcher can transform the variables in an attempt to satisfy the assumptions. Transformations, such as taking logs, square roots or reciprocals, can stabilise the variance, make the distribution normal or make the relationship linear. We further illustrate the application of multiple regression with an example.

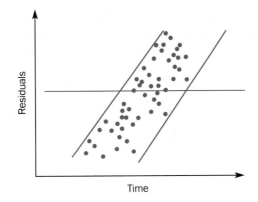

Figure 20.7
Plot indicating a linear relationship between residuals and time

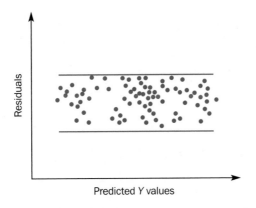

Figure 20.8
Plot of residuals indicating that a fitted model is appropriate

Example

At no 'Ad'ditional cost[20]

It is widely believed that consumer magazines' prices are subsidised by the advertising carried within the magazines. A study examined the contribution of advertising to the price per copy of magazines.

Multiple regression analysis was used to examine the relationships among price per copy and editorial pages, circulation, percentage of news-stand circulation, promotional expenditures, percentage of colour pages, and per copy advertising revenues. The form of the analysis was

Source: © Getty Images

$$PPC = b_0 + b_1(\text{ed. pages}) + b_2(\text{circ.}) + b_3(\% \text{ news circ.}) + b_4(\text{PE}) + b_5(\% \text{ colour}) + b_6(\text{ad revs.})$$

where

PPC	= price per copy (in €)
ed. pages	= editorial pages per average issue
circ.	= the log of average paid circulation (in thousands)
% news circ.	= percentage news-stand circulation
PE	= promotional expenditures (in €)
% colour	= percentage of pages printed in colour
ad revs.	= per copy advertising revenues (in €)

Table 1 shows the zero-order Pearson product moment correlations among the variables. The correlations provide directional support for the predicted relationships and show that collinearity among the independent variables is sufficiently low so as not to affect the stability of the regression analysis. The highest correlation among the independent variables was between promotional expenditures and circulation ($r = 0.42$).

Table 1 Zero-order correlation matrix of variables in analyses

	Price per copy	Price per editorial page	Circulation	Editorial pages	Pro- motional expendi- tures	% colour pages	% news- stand circ.
Price per editorial page	0.60*						
Circulation	−0.21*	−0.42*					
Editorial pages	0.52*	−0.30*	0.29*				
Promotional expenditures	−0.22*	−0.06	0.42*	−0.19			
% colour pages	0.01	−0.15	0.33*	0.19	−0.15		
% news-stand circ.	0.46*	0.17	0.09	0.31*	0.26*	0.02	
Ad revenues per copy	0.29*	−0.04	−0.25*	0.30*	−0.14	0.15	0.08

*$p < 0.05$.

The results of the regression analysis using price per copy as the dependent variable are given in Table 2. Of the six independent variables, three were significant ($p < 0.05$): the number of editorial pages, average circulation and percentage news-stand circulation. The three variables accounted for virtually all of the explained variance ($R^2 = 0.51$; adjusted $R^2 = 0.48$). The direction of the coefficients was consistent with prior expectations: the number of editorial pages was positive, circulation was negative, and percentage news-stand circulation was positive. This was expected, given the structure of the magazine publishing industry, and it confirmed the hypothesised relationship.

Table 2 Regression analysis using price per copy as dependent variable

	b	SE	F
Dependent variable: price per copy **Independent variables:**			
Editorial pages	0.0084	0.0017	23.04[a]
Circulation	−0.4180	0.1372	9.29[a]
Percentage news-stand circulation	0.0067	0.0016	18.46[a]
Promotional expenditures	0.13 − 0.04[b]	0.0000	0.59
Percentage colour pages	0.0227	0.0092	0.01
Per copy ad revenues	0.1070	0.0412	0.07
Overall R^2 = 0.51		$df = 6, 93$ Overall $F = 16.19$[a]	

[a] $p < 0.05$.
[b] Decimal moved by four zeros.

Promotional expenditures, use of colour and per copy advertising revenues were found to have no relationship with price per copy, after the effects of circulation, percentage news-stand circulation and editorial pages were controlled in the regression analysis.

Because the effect of per copy advertising revenue was not significant, no support was found for the contention that advertising decreases the price per copy of consumer magazines. It was concluded that advertising in magazines is provided free to consumers, but does not subsidise prices.

In this example, promotional expenditures, percentage of colour pages and per copy advertising revenues were not found to be significantly related to the price per copy of magazines. Some of the independent variables considered in a study often turn out to be non-significant. When there are a large number of independent variables and the researcher suspects that not all of them are significant, stepwise regression should be used.

Stepwise regression

Stepwise regression
A regression procedure in which the predictor variables enter or leave the regression equation one at a time.

The purpose of **stepwise regression** is to select, from a large number of predictor variables, a small subset of variables that account for most of the variation in the dependent or criterion variable. In this procedure, the predictor variables enter or are removed from the regression equation one at a time.[21] There are several approaches to stepwise regression:

1 *Forward inclusion.* Initially, there are no predictor variables in the regression equation. Predictor variables are entered one at a time, only if they meet certain criteria specified in terms of F ratio. The order in which the variables are included is based on the contribution to the explained variance.
2 *Backward elimination.* Initially, all the predictor variables are included in the regression equation. Predictors are then removed one at a time based on the F ratio.
3 *Stepwise solution.* Forward inclusion is combined with the removal of predictors that no longer meet the specified criterion at each step.

Stepwise procedures do not result in regression equations which are optimal, in the sense of producing the largest R^2, for a given number of predictors.[22] Because of the correlations between predictors, an important variable may never be included or less important variables may enter the equation. To identify an optimal regression equation, one would have to compute combinatorial solutions in which all possible combinations are examined. Nevertheless, stepwise regression can be useful when the sample size is large in relation to the number of predictors, as shown in the following example.

Example

Browsers step out[23]

Many commentators consider store-based retailers to have an advantage over web-based retailers when it comes to browsing, because store-based retailers are larger in size and product offerings. Although the Web can appeal to younger shoppers, the shopping mall can remain a dominant force with so many entertainment factors being built into shopping malls. A profile of browsers in regional shopping centres was constructed using three sets of independent variables: demographics, shopping behaviour, and psychological and attitudinal variables. The dependent variable consisted of a browsing index. In a stepwise regression including all three sets of variables, demographics were found to be the most powerful predictors of browsing behaviour. The final regression equation, which contained

Regression of browsing index on descriptive and attitudinal variables by order of entry into stepwise regression

Variable description	Coefficient	SE	Significance
Gender (0 = male, 1 = female)	−0.485	0.164	0.001
Employment status (0 = employed)	0.391	0.182	0.003
Self-confidence	−0.152	0.128	0.234
Education	0.079	0.072	0.271
Brand intention	−0.063	0.028	0.024
Watch daytime TV? (0 = yes)	0.232	0.144	0.107
Tension	−0.182	0.069	0.008
Income	0.089	0.061	0.144
Frequency of shopping centre visits	−0.130	0.059	0.028
Fewer friends than most	0.162	0.084	0.054
Good shopper	−0.122	0.090	0.174
Others' opinions important	−0.147	0.065	0.024
Control over life	−0.069	0.069	0.317
Family size	−0.086	0.062	0.165
Enthusiastic person	−0.143	0.099	0.150
Age	0.036	0.069	0.603
Number of purchases made	−0.068	0.043	0.150
Purchases per store	0.209	0.152	0.167
Shop on tight budget	−0.055	0.067	0.412
Excellent judge of quality	−0.070	0.089	0.435
Constant	3.250		
Overall R^2 = 0.477			

20 of the possible 36 variables, included all the demographics. The table presents the regression coefficients, standard errors of the coefficients, and their significance levels.

In interpreting the coefficients, it should be recalled that the smaller the browsing index (the dependent variable), the greater the tendency to exhibit behaviours associated with browsing. The two predictors with the largest coefficients were gender and employment status. Browsers were more likely to be employed females. They also tend to be somewhat 'downscale', compared with other shopping centre patrons, exhibiting lower levels of education and income, after accounting for the effects of gender and employment status. Although browsers tend to be somewhat younger than non-browsers, they are not necessarily single; those who reported larger family sizes tended to be associated with smaller values of the browsing index.

The 'downscale' profile of browsers relative to other patrons indicates that speciality stores in shopping centres should emphasise moderately priced products. This may explain the historically low rate of failure in shopping centres among such stores and the tendency of high-priced speciality shops to be located in only the prestigious shopping centres or 'upscale' non-enclosed shopping centres.

Multicollinearity

Multicollinearity
A state of high intercorrelations among independent variables.

Stepwise regression and multiple regression are complicated by the presence of **multicollinearity**. Virtually all multiple regression analyses done in marketing research involve predictors or independent variables that are related. Multicollinearity, however, arises when intercorrelations amongst the predictors are very high.[24] Multicollinearity can result in several problems, including the following:

1 The partial regression coefficients may not be estimated precisely. The standard errors are likely to be high.
2 The magnitudes as well as the signs of the partial regression coefficients may change from sample to sample.
3 It becomes difficult to assess the relative importance of the independent variables in explaining the variation in the dependent variable.
4 Predictor variables may be incorrectly included or removed in stepwise regression.

What constitutes serious multicollinearity is not always clear, although several rules of thumb and procedures have been suggested in the literature. Procedures of varying complexity have also been suggested to cope with multicollinearity.[25] A simple procedure consists of using only one of the variables in a highly correlated set of variables.

Alternatively, the set of independent variables can be transformed into a new set of predictors that are mutually independent by using techniques such as principal components analysis (see Chapter 22). More specialised techniques, such as ridge regression and latent root regression, can also be used.[26]

Relative importance of predictors

When multicollinearity is present, special care is required in assessing the relative importance of independent variables. In marketing research, it is valuable to determine the *relative importance of the predictors*. In other words, how important are the independent variables in accounting for the variation in the criterion or dependent variable?[27] Unfortunately, because the predictors are correlated, there is no unambiguous measure of relative importance of the predictors in regression analysis.[28] Several approaches, however, are commonly used to assess the relative importance of predictor variables:

1 *Statistical significance.* If the partial regression coefficient of a variable is not significant, as determined by an incremental F test, that variable is judged to be unimportant. An exception to this rule is made if there are strong theoretical reasons for believing that the variable is important.

2 *Square of the simple correlation coefficient.* This measure, r^2, represents the proportion of the variation in the dependent variable explained by the independent variable in a bivariate relationship.

3 *Square of the partial correlation coefficient.* This measure, $R^2_{yx_i.x_jx_k}$, is the coefficient of determination between the dependent variable and the independent variable, controlling for the effects of the other independent variables.

4 *Square of the part correlation coefficient.* This coefficient represents an increase in R^2 when a variable is entered into a regression equation that already contains the other independent variables.

5 *Measures based on standardised coefficients or beta weights.* The most commonly used measures are the absolute values of the beta weights, $|\beta_i|$, or the squared values, β_i^2. Because they are partial coefficients, beta weights take into account the effect of the other independent variables. These measures become increasingly unreliable as the correlations among the predictor variables increase (multicollinearity increases).

6 *Stepwise regression.* The order in which the predictors enter or are removed from the regression equation is used to infer their relative importance.

Given that the predictors are correlated, at least to some extent, in virtually all regression situations, none of these measures is satisfactory. It is also possible that the different measures may indicate a different order of importance of the predictors.[29] Yet if all the measures are examined collectively, useful insights may be obtained into the relative importance of the predictors.

Cross-validation

Cross-validation
A test of validity that examines whether a model holds on comparable data not used in the original estimation.

Before assessing the relative importance of the predictors or drawing any other inferences, it is necessary to cross-validate the regression model. Regression and other multivariate procedures tend to capitalise on chance variations in the data. This could result in a regression model or equation that is unduly sensitive to the specific data used to estimate the model. One approach for evaluating the model for this and other problems associated with regression is cross-validation. **Cross-validation** examines whether the regression model continues to hold on comparable data not used in the estimation. The typical cross-validation procedure used in marketing research is as follows.

1 The regression model is estimated using the entire dataset.

2 The available data are split into two parts, the *estimation sample* and the *validation sample*. The estimation sample generally contains 50–90% of the total sample.

3 The regression model is estimated using the data from the estimation sample only. This model is compared with the model estimated on the entire sample to determine the agreement in terms of the signs and magnitudes of the partial regression coefficients.

4 The estimated model is applied to the data in the validation sample to predict the values of the dependent variable, $\hat{Y}_i$, for the observations in the validation sample.

Double cross-validation
A special form of validation in which the sample is split into halves. One half serves as the estimation sample and the other as a validation sample. The roles of the estimation and validation halves are then reversed and the cross-validation process is repeated.

5 The observed values, Y_i, and the predicted values, $\hat{}$, in the validation sample are correlated to determine the simple r^2. This measure, r^2, is compared with R^2 for the total sample and with R^2 for the estimation sample to assess the degree of shrinkage.

A special form of validation is called **double cross-validation**. In double cross-validation the sample is split into halves. One half serves as the estimation sample, and the other is used as a validation sample in conducting cross-validation. The roles of the estimation and validation halves are then reversed, and the cross-validation is repeated.[30]

Regression with dummy variables

Cross-validation is a general procedure that can be applied even in some special applications of regression, such as regression with dummy variables. Nominal or categorical variables may be used as predictors or independent variables by coding them as dummy variables. The concept of dummy variables was introduced in Chapter 17. In that chapter, we explained how a categorical variable with four categories (heavy users, medium users, light users and non-users) can be coded in terms of three dummy variables, D_1, D_2 and D_3, as shown.

Suppose that the researcher was interested in running a regression analysis of the effect of attitude towards the brand on product use. The dummy variables D_1, D_2 and D_3 would be used as predictors. Regression with dummy variables would be modelled as

$$\hat{Y}_i = a + b_1 D_1 + b_2 D_2 + b_3 D_3$$

Product usage category	Original variable code	Dummy variable code		
		D_1	D_2	D_3
Non-users	1	1	0	0
Light users	2	0	1	0
Medium users	3	0	0	1
Heavy users	4	0	0	0

In this case, 'heavy users' have been selected as a reference category and have not been directly included in the regression equation. Note that for heavy users, D_1, D_2 and D_3 assume a value of 0, and the regression equation becomes

$$\hat{Y}_i = a$$

For non-users, $D_1 = 1$ and $D_2 = D_3 = 0$, and the regression equation becomes

$$\hat{Y}_i = a + b_1$$

Thus, the coefficient b_1 is the difference in predicted $\hat{Y}_i$ for non-users, as compared with heavy users. The coefficients b_2 and b_3 have similar interpretations. Although heavy users was selected as a reference category, any of the other three categories could have been selected for this purpose.[31]

Analysis of variance and covariance with regression

Regression with dummy variables provides a framework for understanding the analysis of variance and covariance. Although multiple regression with dummy variables provides a general procedure for the analysis of variance and covariance, we show only the equivalence of regression with dummy variables to one-way analysis of variance. In regression with dummy variables, the predicted $\hat{Y}$ for each category is the mean of Y for each category. To illustrate using the dummy variable coding of product use we just considered, the predicted $\hat{Y}$ and mean values for each category are as follows:

Product usage category	Predicted value $\hat{Y}$	Mean value $\bar{Y}$
Non-users	$a + b_1$	$a + b_1$
Light users	$a + b_2$	$a + b_2$
Medium users	$a + b_3$	$a + b_3$
Heavy users	a	a

Given this equivalence, it is easy to see further relationships between dummy variable regression and one-way ANOVA.[32]

Thus, we see that regression in which the single independent variable with c categories has been recoded into $c - 1$ dummy variables is equivalent to one-way ANOVA. Using similar correspondences, one can also illustrate how n-way ANOVA and analysis of covariance can be performed using regression with dummy variables:

Dummy variable regression	One-way ANOVA
$SS_{res} = \displaystyle\sum_{i=1}^{n} (Y_i - \hat{Y}_i)^2$	$= SS_{within} = SS_{error}$
$SS_{reg} = \displaystyle\sum_{i=1}^{n} (\hat{Y}_i - \bar{Y})^2$	$= SS_{between} = SS_x$
R^2	$= \eta^2$
Overall F test	$= F$ test

Structural equation modelling

Structural equation modelling (SEM)
Collection of statistical techniques including factor analysis and multiple regression. It allows the researcher to examine relationships between several continuous or discrete independent variables and several continuous or discrete dependent variables. The independent and dependent variables can be latent or measured variables.

Structural equation modelling (SEM) estimates the unknown coefficients in a set of linear structural equations. Variables in the equation system are usually directly observed variables plus unmeasured latent variables that are not observed but relate to the observed variables. SEM assumes there is a causal structure among a set of latent variables, and that the observed variables are indicators of the latent variables. The latent variables may appear as linear combinations of observed variables, or they may be intervening variables in a causal chain.

The following example,[33] will help to illustrate the application of this technique. Consider Omote-sando, one of Tokyo's chic fashion districts. Here in Omote-sando we observe a young woman – let us call her Yumi – emerging from one of the trendy and very expensive boutiques which abound in this area. Elegantly and expensively dressed and coiffured, it is apparent to us that Yumi pays a great deal of attention to her appearance. In marketing jargon, we might say she appears to be 'fashion conscious'.

Though we often use terms like 'fashion conscious' casually, it is important to recognise that fashion consciousness is in reality a theoretical construct; we cannot actually see it but can only infer its presence from what we can observe. In other words, it is a latent or unobserved variable. We can observe Yumi's dress and manner and the Omote-sando boutique at which she's been shopping and make the inference that she is fashion-conscious. However, other people may think differently and conclude instead that Yumi is simply materialistic. Materialism is another example of a latent or unobserved variable. Still others may think she is both fashion conscious and materialistic. In this case we would, in effect, be saying that these two latent variables are correlated.

Measurable and unmeasurable variables

In marketing research we would not normally venture into Omote-sando, observe young women like Yumi and speculate about latent variables. We often do, however, administer questionnaires to consumers which probe for concepts such as 'fashion consciousness' or 'materialism'. By asking them to make self-assessments on items such as 'I usually have one or more outfits that are of the very latest style', we are attempting to measure the extent of their fashion consciousness, though we recognise that we cannot do so perfectly. (That is, we can measure but only with error.) The statement 'I usually have one or more outfits that are of the very latest style' is an example of a measurable variable and, similarly, 'fashion-consciousness' is an example of an unmeasurable, latent variable. To relate this to our earlier discussion, by asking Yumi to make self-assessments such as this, we are attempting to measure indirectly a latent variable that is, in fact, a theoretical construct that cannot be measured directly.

Latent variables

Thus, unobserved or unmeasured, latent variables are those that represent abstract concepts or theoretical constructs that cannot be measured directly. Such variables are often referred to as 'factors' or 'common factors'. That is, they are presumed to underlie what can be observed, in the sense that the latent variables directly influence the outcome or values taken by the observed variables. In pictorial form, latent variables can be represented as ellipses (Figure 20.9). Latent variables can be correlated with each other, as represented by the double-headed arrow in Figure 20.10. Latent variables can also influence other latent variables directly, via a regression-type relationship, as represented by the single-headed arrows in Figure 20.11.

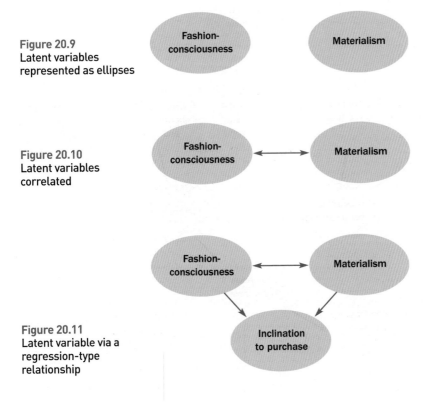

Figure 20.9
Latent variables represented as ellipses

Figure 20.10
Latent variables correlated

Figure 20.11
Latent variable via a regression-type relationship

Observed variables

Because latent variables are, by definition, unobservable, their measurement must be obtained indirectly. This is done by linking one or more observed variables to each unobserved variable. With SEM, the linking of observed (or indicator) variables with latent (or unobserved) variables is the first step in a formal statistically valid procedure. In pictorial form, observed or indicator variables can be represented as rectangles (Figure 20.12). In this diagram, the single-headed arrows connecting the latent and observed variables indicate that the latent variables directly influence the outcome or values taken by the observed variables, again through a regression-type relationship. We can go still further, in terms of identifying observed variables, for the completely endogenous latent variable labelled as 'inclination to purchase', as illustrated in Figure 20.13.

Still more variables

Apart from latent and observed variables, there are residual and error terms associated with each of these which also form a key part of the overall model. For simplicity, however, we omit these from the discussion and refer the interested reader to more specialised

Figure 20.12
Linking observed (or indicator) variables with latent (or unobserved) variables

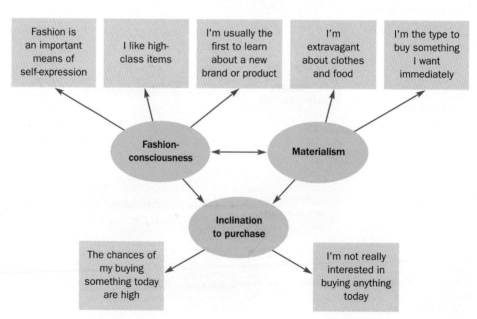

Figure 20.13
Identifying observed variables for the completely endogenous latent variable, labelled as 'inclination to purchase'

texts on this topic.[34] Suffice it to say that a fully specified structural equation model is potentially a complex interplay between a large number of observed and unobserved variables, and residual and error terms.

Example | **Japanese single women**

To illustrate the concepts of observed/measured and unmeasured/latent variables we introduced a fictitious young woman called Yumi. Fashion-consciousness and materialism were used as examples of unmeasured/latent variables, and we hypothesised that these two latent variables might be intercorrelated. We now proceed beyond allegory and discuss the results of an actual study conducted among consumers who, in many aspects, are very much like Yumi. Recently, SRG Japan conducted a study on overseas travel among young Japanese single women – OLs in the local vernacular. The term OL is an abbreviation of 'Office Lady' and is widely used in Japan to refer to single women working in non-management and non-technical occupations, most often clerical work. Although their earned incomes are typically not high, OLs are one of the most important consumer groups in Japan because they often live with their parents, rent-free, and tend to have significant disposable incomes – incomes which they frequently spend quite freely. Another distinction of OLs that is important to the travel industry is that they often have more freedom to travel during any time of the year than other consumer groups. A key objective of this research was to explore personality factors underlying OLs' preferences for overseas destinations and travel arrangements. Consequently, during the interviews, respondents rated themselves on a battery of psychographic items which had been developed through preliminary qualitative research. The qualitative phase of the research had suggested five principal psychographic factors of relevance to overseas travel experience and tastes:

- Fashion-consciouness
- Materialism
- Assertiveness
- Conservatism
- Hedonism.

Each of these latent constructs was measured by three or four measured variables (items). These are shown in Table 1 overleaf.

Based on the qualitative research and exploratory factor analysis (EFA) of the quantitative results, a number of structural equation models were developed and tested, each of which hypothesised different interrelationships among the five latent constructs listed in the table. The path diagram, representing the model that was considered most meaningful in light of the overall findings of the research, is shown in Figure 20.14. In this path diagram, latent constructs (unmeasured variables) are shown in ellipses and the questionnaire items used to measure these latent constructs (i.e. measured variables) are shown in rectangles. Arrows pointing from the circles to the rectangles are equivalent to factor loadings in factor analysis. With two exceptions, all loadings were above 0.50. Arrows between the unobserved variables represent correlations among these factors (since correlations are two-way associations, all arrows between the unobserved variables are two-headed). The overall results may seem surprisingly intuitive: fashion-consciousness and materialism were found to be highly associated and in a positive direction. In fact, this correlation (0.84) was strong enough to suggest that these two factors may actually be functions of a second-order factor, although confirmation of this would need further research. Materialism and assertiveness were also found to be positively related, but more weakly. The correlation between assertiveness and fashion-consciousness was weakly positive (0.26) but, nonetheless, statistically significant. Looking to the right side of the diagram in Figure 20.14, we see that conservatism and hedonism are negatively associated. This relationship is also weak but significant. Note also that fashion-consciousness, materialism and assertiveness are all moderately positively associated with hedonism. And, as had been anticipated, materialism

Table 1 Measured variables

Fashion-consciousness	
V13	Fashion is an important means of self-expression
V20	I like high-class items
V21	I'm usually the first among my friends to learn about a new brand or product

Materialism	
V31	I'm extravagant about my clothes and food
V34	I'm the type to buy something I want immediately even if I have to borrow money
V37	I'm the type that doesn't hesitate to buy necessary things even if they are somewhat expensive

Assertiveness	
V14	I make friends quickly even with people I've just met
V17	I challenge anything without fear of failure
V33	I socialise with many different types of people
V39	I'm the type to clearly state my opinions to others

Conservatism (or 'Deliberateness')	
V3	I tend to achieve my goals one step at a time
V6	I'm the type to deliberate things
V7	I gather various information and study well when deciding to buy a specific item

Hedonism	
V1	I want to enjoy the present rather than think about the future
V9	I like to go out to night-time entertainment spots
V12	I want to lead a life with lots of ups and downs

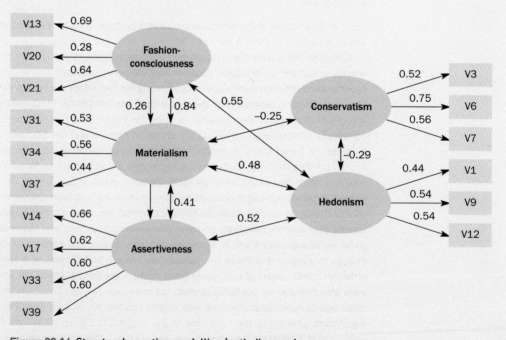

Figure 20.14 Structural equation modelling 'path diagram'

and conservatism were negatively related in this research, although this relationship is not strong. In an earlier preliminary model, fashion-consciousness and assertiveness were not found to be associated with conservatism, and these paths were deleted before testing the present model. To recapitulate, fashion-conscious OLs are inclined to be on the spendthrift side and to have a hedonistic streak, although they are not necessarily exceptionally assertive or extroverted. Given these patterns, we might expect that, when vacationing abroad, they would tend to look for an abundance of places to shop, especially for high-priced/fashion goods. Choice restaurants and perhaps nightspots would probably also be considerations for many of them when choosing a travel destination and/or travel package. More conservative or methodical types, on the other hand, would be expected to be less extravagant, fashion conscious and assertive and also less hedonistic. Other results for this survey suggested that these young women might, instead, be more inclined to enjoy the local flavour of their destination, or simply relax.

Calibration and hypothesis testing

So far, we have a model that makes a certain amount of sense in terms of describing the key relationships in a model of market behaviour. In fact, what we have is more than that. First, the diagram in Figure 20.14 indicates that there is a hypothesised relationship between a number of latent variables which forms the underpinning causal structure of behaviour in this market. This is the so-called *structural model*. Second, the diagram indicates that there are several variables that we can observe directly, with statistical relationships between them that we may be able to use to calibrate the underlying structural model. This set of statistical relationships is the so-called *measurement model*. (Recall that the latent variables are linked to each other via regression-type relationships, so that calibration in this context simply means estimating values for the relevant regression coefficients.) The central ideas behind SEM are then:

- To determine the statistical relationship between the observed variables and estimates of the regression coefficients that link the unobserved, latent variables.
- To determine the adequacy, or goodness of fit, of the hypothesised structural model.

Internet and computer applications

The computer packages contain several programs to perform correlation analysis and regression analysis, calculating the associated statistics, performing tests for significance and plotting the residuals.

SPSS

The CORRELATIONS can be used for computing Pearson product moment correlations with significance levels. Univariate statistics, covariance and cross-product deviations may also be requested. PARTIAL CORR computes partial correlations. The effects of one or more confounding variables can be controlled when describing the relationship between two variables. Significance levels are included in this output.

REGRESSION calculates bivariate and multiple regression equations, associated statistics and plots. It allows for easy examination of residuals. Stepwise regression can also be conducted. Regression statistics can be requested with PLOT, which produces simple scattergrams and some other types of plots.

Within the SPSS suite of products, Amos provides powerful and easy-to-use structural equation modelling (SEM) software. This allows the creation of more realistic models than standard multivariate statistics or multiple regression models alone. With Amos, a model is specified, estimated, assessed and presented in an intuitive path diagram to show hypothesised relationships amongst variables. This enables the rapid testing and confirmation of claims such as 'value drives loyalty'.

SAS

CORR produces metric and non-metric correlations between variables, including Pearson's product moment correlation. It also computes partial correlations.

REG is a general-purpose regression procedure that fits bivariate and multiple regression models using the least squares procedure. All the associated statistics are computed, and residuals can be plotted. Stepwise methods can be implemented. RSREG is a more specialised procedure that fits a quadratic response surface model using least squares regression. It is useful for determining factor levels that optimise a response. The ORTHOREG procedure is recommended for regression when the data are ill-conditioned. GLM uses the method of least squares to fit general linear models and can also be used for regression analysis. NLIN computes the parameters of a non-linear model using least squares or weighted least squares procedures.

Minitab

Correlation can be computed using the STAT>BASIC STATISTICS>CORRELATION function. It calculates Pearson's product moment. Spearman's procedure ranks the columns first and then performs the correlation on the ranked columns. To compute partial correlation, use the menu commands STAT>BASIC STATISTICS>CORRELATION and STAT>REGRESSION>REGRESSION. Partial correlations can also be calculated using session commands.

Regression analysis, under the STATS>REGRESSION function, can perform simple, polynomial and multiple analysis. The output includes a linear regression equation, table of coefficients, R^2, R^2 adjusted, analysis of variance table, and a table of fits and residuals that provide unusual observations. Other available features include stepwise, best subsets, fitted line plot and residual plots.

Excel

Correlations can be determined in Excel by using the TOOLS>DATA ANALYSIS>CORRELATION function. Utilise the Correlation Worksheet function when a correlation coefficient for two cell ranges is needed. There is no separate function for partial correlations.

Regression can be accessed from the TOOLS>DATA ANALYSIS menu. Depending on the features selected, the output can consist of a summary output table, including an ANOVA table, a standard error of Y estimate, coefficients, standard error of coefficients, R^2 values and the number of observations. In addition, the function computes a residual output table, a residual plot, a line fit plot, a normal probability plot and a two-column probability data output table.

Summary

The product moment correlation coefficient, r, measures the linear association between two metric (interval or ratio scaled) variables. Its square, r^2, measures the proportion of variation in one variable explained by the other. The partial correlation coefficient measures the association between two variables after controlling, or adjusting for, the effects of one or more additional variables. The order of a partial correlation indicates how many variables are being adjusted or controlled. Partial correlations can be very helpful for detecting spurious relationships.

Bivariate regression derives a mathematical equation between a single metric criterion variable and a single metric predictor variable. The equation is derived in the form of a straight line by using the least squares procedure. When the regression is run on standardised data, the intercept assumes a value of zero, and the regression coefficients are called beta weights. The strength of association is measured by the coefficient of determination, r^2, which is obtained by computing a ratio of SS_{reg} to SS_y. The standard error of estimate is used to assess the accuracy of prediction and may be interpreted as a kind of average error made in predicting Y from the regression equation.

Multiple regression involves a single dependent variable and two or more independent variables. The partial regression coefficient, b_1, represents the expected change in Y when X_1 is changed by one unit and X_2 to X_k are held constant. The strength of association is measured by the coefficient of multiple determination, R^2. The significance of the overall regression equation may be tested by the overall F test. Individual partial regression coefficients may be tested for significance using the incremental F test. Scattergrams of the residuals, in which the residuals are plotted against the predicted values, $\hat{Y}_i$, time, or predictor variables, are useful for examining the appropriateness of the underlying assumptions and the regression model fitted.

In stepwise regression, the predictor variables are entered or removed from the regression equation one at a time for the purpose of selecting a smaller subset of predictors that account for most of the variation in the criterion variable. Multicollinearity, or very high intercorrelations among the predictor variables, can result in several problems. Because the predictors are correlated, regression analysis provides no unambiguous measure of relative importance of the predictors. Cross-validation examines whether the regression model continues to hold true for comparable data not used in estimation. It is a useful procedure for evaluating the regression model.

Nominal or categorical variables may be used as predictors by coding them as dummy variables. Multiple regression with dummy variables provides a general procedure for the analysis of variance and covariance. Structural equation modelling (SEM) estimates the unknown coefficients in a set of linear structural equations. Variables in such an equation system are usually directly observed variables plus unmeasured latent variables that are not observed but relate to the observed variables.

Questions

1 What is the product moment correlation coefficient? Does a product moment correlation of zero between two variables imply that the variables are not related to each other?

2 What are the main uses of regression analysis?

3 What is the least squares procedure?

4 Explain the meaning of standardised regression coefficients.

5 How is the strength of association measured in bivariate regression? In multiple regression?

6 What is meant by prediction accuracy? What is the standard error of the estimate?

7 What is multiple regression? How is it different from bivariate regression?

8 Explain the meaning of a partial regression coefficient. Why is it called that?

9 State the null hypothesis in testing the significance of the overall multiple regression equation. How is this null hypothesis tested?

10 What is gained by an examination of residuals?

11 Explain the stepwise regression approach. What is its purpose?

12 What is multicollinearity? What problems can arise because of multicollinearity?

13 Describe the cross-validation procedure. Describe double cross-validation.

14 Demonstrate the equivalence of regression with dummy variables to one-way ANOVA.

15 Explain what structural equation modelling attempts to achieve. How can SEM be applied in marketing research?

Exercises

1 A supermarket chain wants to determine the effect of promotion on relative competitiveness. Data were obtained from 15 cities on the promotional expenses relative to a major competitor (competitor expenses = 100) and on sales relative to this competitor (competitor sales = 100).

City number	Relative promotional expense	Relative sales
1	95	98
2	92	94
3	103	110
4	115	125
5	77	82
6	79	84
7	105	112
8	94	99
9	85	93
10	101	107
11	106	114
12	120	132
13	118	129
14	75	79
15	99	105

You are assigned the task of telling the manager whether there is any relationship between relative promotional expense and relative sales.

a Plot the relative sales (*Y* axis) against the relative promotional expense (*X* axis), and interpret the diagram.
b Which measure would you use to determine whether there is a relationship between the two variables? Why?
c Run a bivariate regression analysis of relative sales on relative promotional expense.
d Interpret the regression coefficients.
e Is the regression relationship significant?
f If the company matched the competitor in terms of promotional expense (if the relative expense was 100), what would the company's relative sales be?
g Interpret the resulting r^2.

2 To understand the role of quality and price in influencing the patronage of shoe shops, 14 major shoe shops in a large city were rated in terms of preference to shop, quality of shoes sold and price fairness. All the ratings were obtained on an 11-point scale, with higher numbers indicating more positive ratings.

Shoe shop number	Preference	Quality	Price
1	6	5	3
2	9	6	11
3	8	6	4
4	3	2	1
5	10	6	11
6	4	3	1
7	5	4	7
8	2	1	4
9	11	9	8
10	9	5	10
11	10	8	8
12	2	1	5
13	9	8	5
14	5	3	2

a Run a multiple regression analysis explaining shoe shop preference in terms of shoe quality and price fairness.
b Interpret the partial regression coefficients.
c Determine the significance of the overall regression.
d Determine the significance of the partial regression coefficients.
e Do you think that multicollinearity is a problem in this case? Why or why not?

3 You come across a magazine article reporting the following relationship between annual expenditure on prepared dinners (*PD*) and annual income (*INC*):

$$PD = 23.4 + 0.003INC$$

The coefficient of the *INC* variable is reported as significant.

a Does this relationship seem plausible? Is it possible to have a coefficient that is small in magnitude and yet significant?
b From the information given, can you tell how good the estimated model is?
c What are the expected expenditures on prepared dinners of a family earning €30,000?
d If a family earning €40,000 spent €130 annually on prepared dinners, what is the residual?
e What is the meaning of the negative residual?

4   In a survey pretest, data were obtained from 20 respondents on preference for boots on a seven-point scale
    (1 = not preferred, 7= greatly preferred) (V_1). The respondents also provided their evaluations of the boots on
    comfort (V_2), style (V_3) and durability (V_4), also on seven-point scales (1 = poor, 7 = excellent). The resulting data
    are given in the following table:

Number	(V_1)	(V_2)	(V_3)	(V_4)
1	6	6	3	5
2	2	3	2	4
3	7	5	6	7
4	4	6	4	5
5	1	3	2	2
6	6	5	6	7
7	5	6	7	5
8	7	3	5	4
9	2	4	6	3
10	3	5	3	6
11	1	3	2	3
12	5	4	5	4
13	2	2	1	5
14	4	5	4	6
15	6	5	4	7
16	3	3	4	2
17	4	4	3	2
18	3	4	3	2
19	4	4	3	2
20	2	3	2	4

a   Calculate the simple correlations between V_1 and V_4 and interpret the results.
b   Run a bivariate regression with preference for boots (V_1) as the dependent variable and evaluation on comfort
    (V_2) as the independent variable. Interpret the results.
c   Run a bivariate regression with preference for boots (V_1) as the dependent variable and evaluation on style (V_3)
    as the independent variable. Interpret the results.
d   Run a bivariate regression with preference for boots (V_1) as the dependent variable and evaluation on durability
    (V_4) as the independent variable. Interpret the results.
e   Run a multiple regression with preference for boots (V_1) as the dependent variable and V_2 to V_4 as the
    independent variables. Interpret the results. Compare the coefficients for V_2, V_3 and V_4 obtained in the bivariate
    and the multiple regressions.

5   In a small group discuss the following issues: 'Regression is such a basic technique that it should always be used
    in analysing data' and 'What is the relationship between bivariate correlation, bivariate regression, multiple
    regression and analysis of variance?'

1 Brown, J., Green, H. and Zeilner, W., 'Shoppers are beating apath to the web', *Business Week*, (3763) (24 December 2001), 41; Korgaonkar, P.K. and Smith, A.E., 'Shopping orientation, demographic and media preference correlates of electronic shopping', in Balm, K.D. (ed.), *Developments in Marketing Science*, Vol. 11 (Blacksburg, VA: Academy of Marketing Science, 1988), 52–55.

2 Chen, P.Y. and Popovich, P.M., *Correlation: Parametric and nonparametric measures*, (Thousand Oaks, CA: Sage, 2002); Bobko, P., Roth, P.L. and Bobko, C., 'Correcting the effect size of *d* for range restriction and unreliability', *Organizational Research Methods* 4 (1) (January 2001), 46–61; Draper, N.R. and Smith, H., *Applied Regression Analysis*, 3rd edn (New York: Wiley, 1998); Doherty, M.E. and Sullivan, J.A., 'rho = *p*', *Organizational Behaviour and Human Decision Processes* 43 (1) (February 1989),136–144; Martin, W.S., 'Effects of scaling on the correlation coefficient: additional considerations', *Journal of Marketing Research* 15 (May 1978), 304–308; Bollen, K.A. and Barb, RH., 'Pearson's *R* and coarsely categorized measures', *American Sociological Review* 46 (1981), 232–239.

3 Cox, T. and Branco, J., *Introduction to multivariate analysis* (New York: Oxford University Press, 2002); Tacq, J., *Multivariate Analysis Techniques in Social Science Research* (Thousand Oaks, CA: Sage, 1997); Neter, J., Wasserman, W. and Kutner, M.J., *Applied Linear Statistical Models*, 3rd edn (Burr Ridge, IL: Irwin, 1990).

4 Although the topic is not discussed here, partial correlations can also be helpful in locating intervening variables and making certain types of causal inferences.

5 Harvey, J.E., 'Home shopping "NET" work', *Business First* 18 (30) (22 February 2002), 27; Goldsmith, RE., 'The impact of corporate credibility and celebrity credibility on consumer reaction to advertisements and brands'. *Journal of Advertising* 29 (3) (Fall 2000), 43–54; 'Bates Saatchi & Saatchi, Budapest: accounting for change', *Accountancy* 116 (224) (August 1995), 31; Kasriel, K., 'Hungary's million-dollar slap', *Advertising Age* (8 June 1992).

6 Another advantage to τ is that it can be generalised to a partial correlation coefficient. Higgins, J.J., *Introduction to modern nonparametric statistics* (Pacific Grove, CA: Duxbury, 2002); Pett, M.A., *Nonparametric Statistics for Health Care Research* (Thousand Oaks, CA: Sage, 1997); Siegel, S. and Castellan, N.J., *Nonparametric Statistics*, 2nd edn (New York: McGraw-Hill, 1988).

7 In a strict sense, the regression model requires that errors of measurement be associated only with the criterion variable and that the predictor variables be measured without error. For serially correlated errors, see Canjels, E. and Watson, M.W., 'Estimating deterministic trends in the presence of serially correlated errors', *Review of Economics and Statistics* 79 (2) (May 1997), 184–200. See also Bobko, P., *Correlation and Regression: Applications for Industrial/Organizational Psychology and Management*, 2nd edn (Thousand Oaks, CA: Sage, 2001).

8 See any text on regression, such as Goldberg, M.A., *Introduction to Regression Analysis* (Southhampton: WIT Press, 2002); Kahane, L.H., *Regression Basics* (Thousand Oaks, CA: Sage, 2001); Draper, N.R. and Smith, H., *Applied Regression Analysis*, 3rd edn (New York: Wiley, 1998); Neter, J., Wasserman, W. and Kutner, M.J., *Applied Linear Statistical Models*, 3rd edn (Burr Ridge, IL: Irwin, 1990).

9 Technically, the numerator is $b - \beta$. Since it has been hypothesised that $\beta = 0.0$, however, it can be omitted from the formula.

10 The larger the *SEE*, the poorer the fit of the regression.

11 The assumption of fixed levels of predictors applies to the 'classical' regression model. It is possible, if certain conditions are met, for the predictors to be random variables. Their distribution is not allowed to depend on the parameters of the regression equation. See Miles, J. and Shevlin, M., *Applying regression and correlation: A guide for students and researchers* (Thousand Oaks, CA: Sage, 2001); Draper, N.R. and Smith, H., *Applied Regression Analysis*, 3rd edn (New York: Wiley, 1998).

12 For an approach to handling the violations of these assumptions, see Zellner, A., 'Further results on Bayesian method of moments analysis of the multiple regression model', *International Economic Review* 42 (1) (February 2001), 121–140; Dispensa, G.S., 'Use logistic regression with customer satisfaction data', *Marketing News* 31 (1) (6 January 1997), 13; Reddy, S.K., Holak, S.L. and Bhat, S., 'To extend or not to extend: success determinants of line extensions', *Journal of Marketing Research* 31 (May 1994), 243–262.

13 Fan, Y., 'The national image of global brands', *Journal of Brand Management* 9 (3) (January 2002), 180–192; Donthu, N., Lee, S. and Yoo, B., 'An examination of selected marketing mix elements and brand equity', *Academy of Marketing Science* 28 (2) (Spring 2000), 195–211; Giges, N., 'Europeans buy outside goods, but like local ads', *Advertising Age International* (27 April 1992).

14 For other applications of multiple regression see Wertenbroch, K. and Skiera, B., 'Measuring consumers' willingness to pay at the point of purchase', *Journal of Marketing Research* 39 (2) (May 2002), 228–241; Irwin, JR., 'Misleading heuristics and moderated multiple regression models', *Journal of Marketing Research* 38 (1) (February 2001), 100–109; Griffin, A., 'The effect of project and process characteristics on product development cycle time', *Journal of Marketing Research* 34 (February 1997), 24–35; Gatignon, H. and Xuereb, J.M., 'Strategic orientation of the firm and new product performance', *Journal of Marketing Research* 34 (February 1997), 77–90.

15 Yet another reason for adjusting R^2 is that as a result of the optimising properties of the least squares approach, it is a maximum. Thus, to some extent, R^2 always overestimates the magnitude of a relationship. For applications of adjusted R^2 see Smith, N.C. and Cooper-Martin, E., 'Ethics and target marketing: the role of product harm and consumer vulnerability', *Journal of Marketing* 61 (3) (January 1997), 1–20; Cohen, M.A. and Ho, T.H., 'An anatomy of a decision support system for developing and launching line extensions', *Journal of Marketing Research* 34 (February 1997), 117–129.

16 If R^2_{pop} is zero, then the sample R^2 reflects only sampling error, and the *F* ratio will tend to be equal to unity.

17 Another approach is the hierarchical method, in which the variables are added to the regression equation in an order specified by the researcher. For an application of multiple regression, see Corfinan, K.P., 'Perceptions of relative influence: formation and measurement', *Journal of Marketing Research* 28 (May 1991), 125–136.

18 Irwin, J.R. and McClelland, G.H., 'Misleading heuristics and moderated multiple regression models', *Journal of Marketing Research*, 38 (1) (February 2001), 100–109; Atkinson, A.C., Koopman, S.J. and Shephard, N., 'Detecting shocks: outliers and breaks in time series', *Journal of Econometrics* 80 (2) (October 1997), 387–422; Wang, G.C.S. and Akabay, C.K., 'Autocorrelation: problems and solutions in regression modeling', *Journal of Business Forecasting Methods and Systems* 13

(4) (Winter 1994/95), 18–26; Belsley, D., Kub, E. and Walsh, R.E., *Regression Diagnostics* (New York: Wiley, 1980).

19 The Durbin–Watson test is discussed in virtually all regression textbooks. See also Marmol, F., 'Near observational equivalence and fractionally integrated processes', *Oxford Bulletin of Economics and Statistics* 61 (2) (May 1999), 283; Hisamatsu, H. and Maekawa, K., 'The distribution of the Durbin–Watson statistic in integrated and near-integrated models', *Journal of Econometrics* 61 (2) (April 1994), 367–382; Draper, N.R. and Smith, H., *Applied Regression Analysis*, 3rd edn (New York: Wiley, 1998).

20 Koschat, M.A. and Putsis, W.P., Jr 'Audience characteristics and bundling: a hedonic analysis of magazine advertising rates', *Journal of Marketing Research* 39 (2) (May 2002), 262–273; Berman, H., 'Selling the advertising/trade show partnership', *Folio: The Magazine for Magazine Management* (Special Sourcebook Issue for 1997 Supplement) 25 (18) (1997), 214–215; Soley. L. and Krishnan, R., 'Does advertising subsidise consumer magazine prices?', *Journal of Advertising* 16 (Spring 1987), 4–9.

21 Schmitt, N., 'Estimates for cross-validity for stepwise regression and with predictor selection', *Journal of Applied Psychology* 84 (1) (February 1999), 50; Fox, J., *Applied Regression Analysis, Linear models and Related Methods* (Thousand Oaks, CA: Sage, 1997); McIntyre, S.H., Montgomery, D.B., Srinivasan, V. and Weitz, B.A., 'Evaluating the statistical significance of models developed by stepwise regression', *Journal of Marketing Research* 20 (February 1983), 1–11.

22 For applications of stepwise regression, see Ittner, D. and Larcker, D.F., 'Product development cycle time and organisational performance', *Journal of Marketing Research* 34 (February 1997), 13–23: Laroche, M. and Sadokierski, R., 'Role of confidence in a multi-brand model of intentions for a high-involvement service', *Journal of Business Research* 29 (January 1994), 1–12.

23 Forseter, M. and Mahler, D.Q., 'The Roper Starch Report', *Drug Store News* (2000), 46–63; Jarboe, G.R. and McDaniel, C.D., 'A profile of browsers in regional shopping malls', *Journal of the Academy of Marketing Science* (Spring 1987), 46–53.

24 Greenberg, E. and Parks, R.P., 'A predictive approach to model selection and multicollinearity', *Journal of Applied Econometrics* 12 (1) (January/February 1997), 67–75; Ofir, C. and Khuri, A., 'Multicollinearity in marketing models: diagnostics and remedial measures', *International Journal of Research in Marketing* 3 (1986), 181–205.

25 Possible procedures are given in Sethi, R., Smith, D.C. and Whan Park, C., 'Cross-functional product development teams, creativity and the innovations of new consumer products', *Journal of Marketing Research* 38 (1) (February 2001), 73–85; Grapentine, T., 'Path analysis vs. structural equation modeling', *Journal of Business Forecasting Methods and Systems* 15 (1) (Spring 1996), 23–27; Wang, G.C.S., 'How to handle multicollinearity in regression modelling', *Journal of Business Forecasting Methods and Systems* 15 (1) (Spring 1996), 23–27; Mason, C.H. and Perreault, W.D., Jr 'Collinearity, power, and interpretation of multiple regression analysis', *Journal of Marketing Research* 28 (August 1991), 268–280; Hocking, R.R., 'Developments in linear regression methodology: 1959–1982', *Technometrics* 25 (August 1983), 219–230; Snee, R.D., 'Discussion', *Technometrics* 25 (August 1983), 230–237.

26 Billor, N., 'An application of the local influence approach to ridge regression', *Journal of Applied Statistics* 26 (2) (February 1999), 177–183; Holzworth, J.R., 'Policy capturing with ridge

regression', *Organizational Behavior and Human Decision Processes* 68 (2) (November 1996), 171–179; Wildt, A.R., 'Equity estimation and assessing market response', *Journal of Marketing Research* 31 (February 1994), 437–451; Shanna, S. and James, W.L., 'Latent root regression: an alternative procedure for estimating parameters in the presence of multicollinearity', *Journal of Marketing Research* 18 (May 1981), 154–161.

27 Only relative importance can be determined, since the importance of an independent variable depends upon all the independent variables in the regression model.

28 McClendon, M.J., *Multiple Regression and Causal Analysis* (Prospect Heights, IL: Waveland Press, 2002); Rugimbana, R., 'Predicting automated teller machine usage: the relative importance of perceptual and demographic factors', *International Journal of Bank Marketing* 13 (4) (1995), 26–32; Green, P.E., Carroll, S.D. and DeSarbo, W.S., 'A new measure of predictor variable importance in multiple regression', *Journal of Marketing Research* 15 (August 1978), 356–360; Jackson, B.B., 'Comment on "A new measure of predictor variable importance in multiple regression"', *Journal of Marketing Research* 17 (February 1980), 116–118.

29 In the rare situation in which all the predictors are uncorrelated, simple correlations = partial correlations = part correlations = betas. Hence, the squares of these measures will yield the same rank order of the relative importance of the variables.

30 For more on cross-validation, see Schmitt, N., 'Estimates for cross-validity for stepwise regression and predictor selection', *Journal of Applied Psychology* 84 (1) (February 1999), 50; Litwin, M.S., *How to Measure Survey Reliability and Validity* (Thousand Oaks, CA: Sage, 1997); Song, X.M. and Perry, M.E., 'The determinants of Japanese new product success', *Journal of Marketing Research* 34 (February 1997), 64–76; Cooil, B., Winer, R.S. and Rados, D.L., 'Cross-validation for prediction', *Journal of Marketing Research* 24 (August 1987), 271–279.

31 For further discussion and applications of dummy variable regression, see Glantz, S.A. and Slinker, B.K., *Primer of applied regression and analysis of variance* (Blacklick, OH: McGraw-Hill, 2000); Yavas, U., 'Demand forecasting in a service setting', *Journal of International Marketing and Marketing Research* 21 (1) (February 1996), 3–11. For further discussion on dummy variable coding, see Cohen, J. and Cohen, P., *Applied Multiple Regression Correlation Analysis for the Behavioural Sciences*, 2nd edn (Hillsdale, NJ: Lawrence Eribaum, 1983), 191–222.

32 Glantz, S.A. and Slinker, B.K., *Primer of applied regression and analysis of variance* (Blacklick, OH: McGraw-Hill, 2000); Fox, J., *Applied Regression Analysis, Linear Models and Related Methods* (Thousand Oaks, CA: Sage, 1997). For an application of regression analysis to conduct analysis of covariance, see Grier, S.A. and Deshpande, R., 'Social dimensions of consumer distinctiveness: the influence of social status on group identity and advertising persuasion', *Journal of Marketing Research* 38 (2) (May 2001), 216–224; Dancin, P.A. and Smith, D.C., 'The effect of brand portfolio characteristics on consumer evaluations of brand extensions', *Journal of Marketing Research* 31 (May 1994), 229–242.

33 MacLean, S. and Gray, K., 'Structural equation modeling in market research', *Australasian Journal of Market Research* 6 (1) (January 1998).

34 For further discussion see Byrne, A., *Structural Equation Modelling with AMOS* (Hillsdale NJ: Lawrence Erlbaum, 2001).

Source: © Getty Images

21

Discriminant analysis

Objectives

After reading this chapter, you should be able to:

1 describe the concept of discriminant analysis, its objectives and its applications in marketing research;

2 outline the procedures for conducting discriminant analysis, including the formulation of the problem, estimation of the discriminant function coefficients, determination of significance, interpretation and validation;

3 discuss multiple discriminant analysis and the distinction between two-group and multiple discriminant analysis;

4 explain stepwise discriminant analysis and describe the Mahalanobis procedure.

| STAGE 1 Problem definition | STAGE 2 Research approach developed | STAGE 3 Research design developed | STAGE 4 Fieldwork or data collection | STAGE 5 Data preparation and analysis | STAGE 6 Report preparation and presentation |

Overview

This chapter discusses the technique of discriminant analysis. We begin by examining the relationship of this procedure to regression analysis (Chapter 20) and analysis of variance (Chapter 19). We present a model and describe the general procedure for conducting discriminant analysis, with an emphasis on formulation, estimation, determination of significance, interpretation, and validation of the results. The procedure is illustrated with an example of two-group discriminant analysis, followed by an example of multiple (three-group) discriminant analysis. The stepwise discriminant analysis procedure is also covered.

We begin with an example that illustrates an application of multiple discriminant analysis.

Example   An eye for a bargain[1]

A study of 294 consumers was undertaken to determine the correlates of 'rebate proneness': in other words, the characteristics of consumers who respond favourably to direct mail promotions that offer a discount on the normal purchase price. The predictor variables were four factors related to household shopping attitudes and behaviour and selected demographic characteristics (gender, age and income). The dependent variable was the extent to which respondents were predisposed to take up the offer of a rebate, of which three levels were identified. Respondents who reported no purchases triggered by a rebate during the past 12 months were classified as *non-users*, those who reported one or two such purchases as *light users*, and those with more than two purchases as *frequent users* of discounts. Multiple discriminant analysis was used to analyse the data.

Two primary findings emerged. First, consumers' perception of the effort/value relationship was the most effective variable in discriminating among frequent users, light users and non-users of rebate offers. Clearly, 'rebate-prone' consumers associate less effort with fulfilling the requirements of the rebated purchase, and are willing to accept a relatively smaller refund than other customers. Second, consumers who were aware of the regular prices of products, so that they recognise bargains, are more likely than others to respond to rebate offers.

These findings were used by DIRECTV (**www.directtv.com**) when it added the National Geographic Channel to its programming. As a way to promote its service, DIRECTV offered three levels of rebates for new customers. The company felt that this would encourage the rebate-sensitive new customers to choose DIRECTV, which it did.

In this example, significant intergroup differences were found using multiple predictor variables. An examination of differences across groups lies at the heart of the basic concept of discriminant analysis.

Basic concept

Discriminant analysis
A technique for analysing marketing research data when the criterion or dependent variable is categorical and the predictor or independent variables are interval in nature.

Discriminant analysis is a technique for analysing data when the criterion or dependent variable is categorical and the predictor or independent variables are interval in nature.[2] For example, the dependent variable may be the choice of the make of a new car (A, B or C) and the independent variables may be ratings of attributes of PCs on a seven-point Likert scale. The objectives of discriminant analysis are as follows:

1 Development of discriminant functions, or linear combinations of the predictor or independent variables, that best discriminate between the categories of the criterion or dependent variable (groups).
2 Examination of whether significant differences exist among the groups, in terms of the predictor variables.
3 Determination of which predictor variables contribute to most of the intergroup differences.
4 Classification of cases to one of the groups based on the values of the predictor variables.
5 Evaluation of the accuracy of classification.

Discriminant analysis techniques are described by the number of categories possessed by the criterion variable. When the criterion variable has two categories, the technique is known as **two-group discriminant analysis**. When three or more categories are involved, the technique is referred to as **multiple discriminant analysis**. The main distinction is that in the two-group case it is possible to derive only one **discriminant function**, but in multiple discriminant analysis more than one function may be computed.[3]

Examples of discriminant analysis abound in marketing research. This technique can be used to answer questions such as the following:[4]

- In terms of demographic characteristics, how do customers who exhibit loyalty to a particular car manufacturer differ from those who do not?
- Do heavy users, medium users and light users of soft drinks differ in terms of their consumption of frozen foods?
- What psychographic characteristics help differentiate between price-sensitive and non-price-sensitive buyers of groceries?
- Do market segments differ in their media consumption habits?
- What are the distinguishing characteristics of consumers who respond to direct mail offers?

Two-group discriminant analysis
Discriminant analysis technique where the criterion variable has two categories.

Multiple discriminant analysis
Discriminant analysis technique where the criterion variable involves three or more categories.

Discriminant function
The linear combination of independent variables developed by discriminant analysis that will best discriminate between the categories of the dependent variable.

Relationship to regression and ANOVA

The relationships between discriminant analysis, analysis of variance (ANOVA) and regression analysis are shown in Table 21.1.

We explain these relationships with an example in which the researcher is attempting to explain the amount of life insurance purchased in terms of age and income. All three procedures involve a single criterion or dependent variable and multiple predictor or independent variables. The nature of these variables differs, however. In ANOVA and regression analysis, the dependent variable is metric or interval scaled (amount of life

Table 21.1 Similarities and differences among ANOVA, regression and discriminant analysis

	ANOVA	*Regression*	*Discriminant analysis*
Similarities			
Number of dependent variables	One	One	One
Number of independent variables	Multiple	Multiple	Multiple
Differences			
Nature of the dependent variable	Metric	Metric	Categorical Binary
Nature of the independent variable	Categorical	Metric	Metric

insurance purchased in euros), whereas in discriminant analysis, it is categorical (amount of life insurance purchased classified as high, medium or low). The independent variables are categorical in the case of ANOVA (age and income are each classified as high, medium or low) but metric in the case of regression and discriminant analysis (age in years and income in euros, i.e. both measured on a ratio scale).

Two-group discriminant analysis, in which the dependent variable has only two categories, is closely related to multiple regression analysis. In this case, multiple regression, in which the dependent variable is coded as a 0 or 1 dummy variable, results in partial regression coefficients that are proportional to discriminant function coefficients (see the following section on the discriminant analysis model).

Discriminant analysis model

Discriminant analysis model
The statistical model on which discriminant analysis is based.

The **discriminant analysis model** involves linear combinations of the following form:

$$D = b_0 + b_1 X_1 + b_2 X_2 + b_3 X_3 + ... + b_k X_k$$

where D = discriminant score
b's = discriminant coefficients or weights
X = predictor or independent variable

The coefficients or weights (b) are estimated so that the groups differ as much as possible on the values of the discriminant function. This occurs when the ratio of between-group sum of squares to within-group sum of squares for the discriminant scores is at a maximum. Any other linear combination of the predictors will result in a smaller ratio. The technical details of estimation are described in the appendix to this chapter.

Statistics associated with discriminant analysis

The important statistics associated with discriminant analysis include the following:

Canonical correlation. Canonical correlation measures the extent of association between the discriminant scores and the groups. It is a measure of association between the single discriminant function and the set of dummy variables that define the group membership.

Centroid. The centroid is the mean values for the discriminant scores for a particular group. There are as many centroids as there are groups, as there is one for each group. The means for a group on all the functions are the *group centroids*.

Classification matrix. Sometimes also called confusion or prediction matrix, the classification matrix contains the number of correctly classified and misclassified cases. The correctly classified cases appear on the diagonal, because the predicted and actual groups are the same. The off-diagonal elements represent cases that have been incorrectly classified. The sum of the diagonal elements divided by the total number of cases represents the *hit ratio*.

Discriminant function coefficients. The discriminant function coefficients (unstandardised) are the multipliers of variables, when the variables are in the original units of measurement.

Discriminant scores. The unstandardised coefficients are multiplied by the values of the variables. These products are summed and added to the constant term to obtain the discriminant scores.

Eigenvalue. For each discriminant function, the eigenvalue is the ratio of between-group to within-group sums of squares. Large eigenvalues imply superior functions.

F **values and their significance.** *F* values are calculated from a one-way ANOVA, with the grouping variable serving as the categorical independent variable. Each predictor, in turn, serves as the metric-dependent variable in the ANOVA.

Group means and group standard deviations. Group means and group standard deviations are computed for each predictor for each group.

Pooled within-group correlation matrix. The pooled within-group correlation matrix is computed by averaging the separate covariance matrices for all the groups.

Standardised discriminant function coefficients. The standardised discriminant function coefficients are the discriminant function coefficients that are used as the multipliers when the variables have been standardised to a mean of 0 and a variance of 1.

Structure correlations. Also referred to as discriminant loadings, the structure correlations represent the simple correlations between the predictors and the discriminant function.

Total correlation matrix. If the cases are treated as if they were from a single sample and the correlations are computed, a total correlation matrix is obtained.

Wilks' λ. Sometimes also called the *U* statistic, Wilks' λ for each predictor is the ratio of the within-group sum of squares to the total sum of squares. Its value varies between 0 and 1. Large values of λ (near 1) indicate that group means do not seem to be different. Small values of λ (near 0) indicate that the group means seem to be different.

The assumptions in discriminant analysis are that each of the groups is a sample from a multivariate normal population and that all the populations have the same covariance matrix. The role of these assumptions and the statistics just described can be better understood by examining the procedure for conducting discriminant analysis.

Conducting discriminant analysis

The steps involved in conducting discriminant analysis consist of formulation, estimation, determination of significance, interpretation and validation (see Figure 21.1). These steps are discussed and illustrated within the context of two-group discriminant analysis. Discriminant analysis with more than two groups is discussed later in this chapter.

Formulate the problem

The first step in discriminant analysis is to formulate the problem by identifying the objectives, the criterion variable and the independent variables. The criterion variable

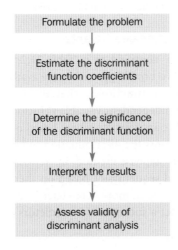

Figure 21.1
Conducting
discriminant analysis

must consist of two or more mutually exclusive and collectively exhaustive categories. When the dependent variable is interval or ratio scaled, it must first be converted into categories. For example, attitude towards the brand, measured on a seven-point scale, could be categorised as unfavourable (1, 2, 3), neutral (4) or favourable (5, 6, 7). Alternatively, one could plot the distribution of the dependent variable and form groups of equal size by determining the appropriate cut-off points for each category. The predictor variables should be selected based on a theoretical model or previous research, or in the case of exploratory research, the experience of the researcher should guide their selection.

The next step is to divide the sample into two parts. One part of the sample, called the *estimation* or **analysis sample**, is used for estimation of the discriminant function. The other part, called the *holdout* or **validation sample**, is reserved for validating the discriminant function. When the sample is large enough, it can be split in half. One half serves as the analysis sample, and the other is used for validation. The roles of the halves are then interchanged and the analysis is repeated. This is called double cross-validation and is similar to the procedure discussed in regression analysis (Chapter 20).

Often, the distribution of the number of cases in the analysis and validation samples follows the distribution in the total sample. For instance, if the total sample contained 50% loyal and 50% non-loyal consumers, then the analysis and validation samples would each contain 50% loyal and 50% non-loyal consumers. On the other hand, if the sample contained 25% loyal and 75% non-loyal consumers, the analysis and validation samples would be selected to reflect the same distribution (25% vs. 75%).

Finally, it has been suggested that the validation of the discriminant function should be conducted repeatedly. Each time, the sample should be split into different analysis and validation parts. The discriminant function should be estimated and the validation analysis carried out. Thus, the validation assessment is based on a number of trials. More rigorous methods have also been suggested.[5]

To illustrate two-group discriminant analysis better, let us look at an example. Suppose that we want to determine the salient characteristics of families that have visited a skiing resort during the last two years. Data were obtained from a pretest sample of 42 households. Of these, 30 households, shown in Table 21.2, were included in the analysis sample and the remaining 12, shown in Table 21.3, were part of the validation sample. The households that visited a resort during the last two years were coded as 1; those that did not, as 2 (VISIT). Both the analysis and validation samples were balanced in terms of VISIT. As can be seen, the analysis sample contains 15 households in each category, whereas the validation sample had 6 in each category. Data were also obtained on annual family income (INCOME), attitude towards travel (TRAVEL, measured on a nine-point scale), importance attached to a family skiing holiday (HOLIDAY, measured on a nine-point scale), household size (HSIZE) and age of the head of the household (AGE).

Estimate the discriminant function coefficients

Once the analysis sample has been identified, as in Table 21.2, we can estimate the discriminant function coefficients. Two broad approaches are available. The **direct method** involves estimating the discriminant function so that all the predictors are included simultaneously. In this case, each independent variable is included, regardless of its discriminating power. This method is appropriate when, based on previous research or a theoretical model, the researcher wants the discrimination to be based on all the predictors. An alternative approach is the stepwise method. In **stepwise discriminant analysis**, the predictor variables are entered sequentially, based on their ability to discriminate among groups. This method, described in more detail later in this chapter, is appropriate when the researcher wants to select a subset of the predictors for inclusion in the discriminant function.

Analysis sample
Part of the total sample used to check the results of the discriminant function.

Validation sample
That part of the total sample used to check the results of the estimation sample.

Direct method
An approach to discriminant analysis that involves estimating the discriminant function so that all the predictors are included simultaneously.

Stepwise discriminant analysis
Discriminant analysis in which the predictors are entered sequentially based on their ability to discriminate between the groups.

The results of running two-group discriminant analysis on the data of Table 21.2 using a popular statistical analysis package are presented in Table 21.4. Some intuitive feel for the results may be obtained by examining the group means and standard deviations. It appears that the two groups are more widely separated in terms of income than other

Table 21.2 Information on resort visits: analysis sample

Number	Resort visit	Annual family income (e000)	Attitude towards travel	Importance attached to family skiing holiday	Household size	Age of head of household	Amount spent spent on family skiing holiday
1	1	50.2	5	8	3	43	M (2)
2	1	70.3	6	7	4	61	H (3)
3	1	62.9	7	5	6	52	H (3)
4	1	48.5	7	5	5	36	L (1)
5	1	52.7	6	6	4	55	H (3)
6	1	75.0	8	7	5	68	H (3)
7	1	46.2	5	3	3	62	M (2)
8	1	57.0	2	4	6	51	M (2)
9	1	64.1	7	5	4	57	H (3)
10	1	68.1	7	6	5	45	H (3)
11	1	73.4	6	7	5	44	H (3)
12	1	71.9	5	8	4	64	H (3)
13	1	56.2	1	8	6	54	M (2)
14	1	49.3	4	2	3	56	H (3)
15	1	62.0	5	6	2	58	H (3)
16	2	32.1	5	4	3	58	L (1)
17	2	36.2	4	3	2	55	L (1)
18	2	43.2	2	5	2	57	M (2)
19	2	50.4	5	2	4	37	M (2)
20	2	44.1	6	6	3	42	M (2)
21	2	38.3	6	6	2	45	L (1)
22	2	55.0	1	2	2	57	M (2)
23	2	46.1	3	5	3	51	L (1)
24	2	35.0	6	4	5	64	L (1)
25	2	37.3	2	7	4	54	L (1)
26	2	41.8	5	1	3	56	M (2)
27	2	57.0	8	3	2	36	M (2)
28	2	33.4	6	8	2	50	L (1)
29	2	37.5	3	2	3	48	L (1)
30	2	41.3	3	3	2	42	L (1)

variables, and there appears to be more of a separation on the importance attached to the family skiing holiday than on attitude towards travel. The difference between the two groups on age of the head of the household is small, and the standard deviation of this variable is large.

Table 21.3 Information on resort visits: validation sample

Number	Resort visit	Annual family income (e000)	Attitude towards travel	Importance attached to family skiing holiday	Household size	Age of head of household	Amount spent on family skiing holiday
1	1	50.8	4	7	3	45	M (2)
2	1	63.6	7	4	7	55	H (3)
3	1	54.0	6	7	4	58	M (2)
4	1	45.0	5	4	3	60	M (2)
5	1	68.0	6	6	6	46	H (3)
6	1	62.1	5	6	3	56	H (3)
7	2	35.0	4	3	4	54	L (1)
8	2	49.6	5	3	5	39	L (1)
9	2	39.4	6	5	3	44	H (3)
10	2	37.0	2	6	5	51	L (1)
11	2	54.5	7	3	3	37	M (2)
12	2	38.2	2	2	3	49	L (1)

Table 21.4 Results of two-group discriminant analysis

Group means

Visit	INCOME	TRAVEL	HOLIDAY	HSIZE	AGE
1	60.52000	5.40000	5.80000	4.33333	53.73333
2	41.91333	4.33333	4.06667	2.80000	50.13333
Total	51.21667	4.86667	4.93333	3.56667	51.93333

Group standard deviations

1	9.83065	1.91982	1.82052	1.23443	8.77062
2	7.55115	1.95180	2.05171	0.94112	8.27101
Total	12.79523	1.97804	2.09981	1.33089	8.57395

Pooled within-groups correlation matrix

INCOME	1.00000				
TRAVEL	0.19745	1.00000			
HOLIDAY	0.09148	0.08434	1.00000		
HSIZE	0.08887	−0.01681	0.07046	1.00000	
AGE	−0.01431	−0.19709	0.01742	−0.04301	1.00000

Table 21.4 Continued

Wilks' λ (U statistic) and univariate F ratio with 1 and 28 degrees of freedom

Variable	Wilks' λ	F	Significance
INCOME	0.45310	33.800	0.0000
TRAVEL	0.92479	2.277	0.1425
HOLIDAY	0.82377	5.990	0.0209
HSIZE	0.65672	14.640	0.0007
AGE	0.95441	1.338	0.2572

Canonical discriminant functions

Function	Eigenvalue	Per cent of variance	Cumulative percentage	Canonical correlation	After function	Wilks' λ	Chi-square	df	Sig.
1*	1.7862	100.00	100.00	0.8007	0	0.3589	26.13	5	0.0001

*Marks the one canonical discriminant function remaining in the analysis.

Standard canonical discriminant function coefficients

	Func 1
INCOME	0.74301
TRAVEL	0.09611
HOLIDAY	0.23329
HSIZE	0.46911
AGE	0.20922

Structure matrix: pooled within-groups correlations between discriminating variables and canonical discriminant functions (variables ordered by size of correlation within function)

	Func 1
INCOME	0.82202
HSIZE	0.54096
HOLIDAY	0.34607
TRAVEL	0.21337
AGE	0.16354

Unstandardised canonical discriminant function coefficients

	Func 1
INCOME	0.8476710E-01
TRAVEL	0.4964455E-01
HOLIDAY	0.1202813
HSIZE	0.4273893
AGE	0.2454380E-01
(Constant)	−7.975476

Table 21.4 Continued

Canonical discriminant functions evaluated at group means (group centroids)	
Group	Func 1
1	1.29118
2	−1.29118

Classification results

			Predicted group membership		Total
		Visit	1	2	
Original	Count	1	12	3	15
		2	0	15	15
	%	1	80.0	20.0	100.0
		2	0.0	100.0	100.0
Cross-validated	Count	1	11	4	15
		2	2	13	15
	%	1	73.3	26.7	100.0
		2	13.3	86.7	100.0

[a] Cross-validation is done only for those cases in the analysis. In cross-validation, each case is classified by the functions derived from all cases other than that case.
[b] 90.0% of original grouped cases correctly classified.
[c] 80.0% of cross-validated grouped cases correctly classified.

Classification results for cases not selected for use in analysis (holdout sample)

	Actual group	No. of cases	Predicted group membership	
			1	2
Group	1	6	4	2
			66.7%	33.3%
Group	2	6	0	6
			0.0%	100%

Percentage of grouped cases correctly classified: 83.33%

The pooled within-groups correlation matrix indicates low correlations between the predictors. Multicollinearity is unlikely to be a problem. The significance of the univariate F ratios indicates that, when the predictors are considered individually, only income, importance of holiday and household size significantly differentiate between those who visited a resort and those who did not.

Because there are two groups, only one discriminant function is estimated. The eigenvalue associated with this function is 1.7862, and it accounts for 100% of the explained variance. The canonical correlation associated with this function is 0.8007. The square of this correlation, $(0.8007)^2 = 0.64$, indicates that 64% of the variance in the dependent variable (VISIT) is explained or accounted for by this model. The next step is determination of significance.

Determine the significance of the discriminant function

It would not be meaningful to interpret the analysis if the discriminant functions estimated were not statistically significant. The null hypothesis that, in the population, the means of all discriminant functions in all groups are equal can be statistically tested. In SPSS, this test is based on Wilks' λ. If several functions are tested simultaneously (as in the case of multiple discriminant analysis), the Wilks' λ statistic is the product of the univariate λ for each function. The significance level is estimated based on a chi-square transformation of the statistic. In testing for significance in the holiday resort example (see Table 21.4), it may be noted that the Wilks' λ associated with the function is 0.3589, which transforms to a chi-square of 26.13 with 5 degrees of freedom. This is significant beyond the 0.05 level. In SAS, an approximate F statistic, based on an approximation to the distribution of the likelihood ratio, is calculated. If the null hypothesis is rejected, indicating significant discrimination, one can proceed to interpret the results.[6]

Interpret the results

The interpretation of the discriminant weights, or coefficients, is similar to that in multiple regression analysis. The value of the coefficient for a particular predictor depends on the other predictors included in the discriminant function. The signs of the coefficients are arbitrary, but they indicate which variable values result in large and small function values and associate them with particular groups.

Given the multicollinearity in the predictor variables, there is no unambiguous measure of the relative importance of the predictors in discriminating between the groups.[7] With this caveat in mind, we can obtain some idea of the relative importance of the variables by examining the absolute magnitude of the standardised discriminant function coefficients. Generally, predictors with relatively large standardised coefficients contribute more to the discriminating power of the function, as compared with predictors with smaller coefficients, and are therefore more important.

Some idea of the relative importance of the predictors can also be obtained by examining the structure correlations, also called *canonical loadings* or *discriminant loadings*. These simple correlations between each predictor and the discriminant function represent the variance that the predictor shares with the function. Like the standardised coefficients, these correlations must also be interpreted with caution.

An examination of the standardised discriminant function coefficients for the holiday resort example is instructive. Given the low intercorrelations between the predictors, one might cautiously use the magnitudes of the standardised coefficients to suggest that income is the most important predictor in discriminating between the groups, followed by household size and importance attached to the family skiing holiday. The same observation is obtained from examination of the structure correlations. These simple correlations between the predictors and the discriminant function are listed in order of magnitude.

The unstandardised discriminant function coefficients are also given. These can be applied to the raw values of the variables in the holdout set for classification purposes. The group centroids, giving the value of the discriminant function evaluated at the group means, are also shown. Group 1, those who have visited a resort, has a positive value, whereas Group 2 has an equal negative value. The signs of the coefficients associated with all the predictors are positive, which suggests that higher family income, household size, importance attached to family skiing holiday, attitude towards travel and age are more likely to result in the family visiting the resort. It would be reasonable to develop a profile of the two groups in terms of the three predictors that seem to be the most important: income, household size and importance of holiday. The values of these three variables for the two groups are given at the beginning of Table 21.4.

The determination of relative importance of the predictors is further illustrated by the following example.

Example

Satisfied salespeople stay[8]

A survey asked business people about the climate of hiring and maintaining employees in harsh economic conditions. It was reported that 85% of respondents were concerned about recruiting employees and 81% said they were concerned about retaining employees. When the economy is down, turnover is rapid. Generally speaking, if an organisation wants to retain its employees, it must learn why people leave their jobs and why others stay and are satisfied with their jobs. Discriminant analysis was used to determine what factors explained the differences between salespeople who left a large computer manufacturing company and those who stayed. The independent variables were company rating, job security, seven job satisfaction dimensions, four role-conflict dimensions four role-ambiguity dimensions and nine measures of sales performance. The dependent variable was the dichotomy between those who stayed and those who left. The canonical correlation, an

Discriminant analysis results

Variable		Coefficients	Standardised coefficients	Structure correlations
1	Work[a]	0.0903	0.3910	0.5446
2	Promotion[a]	0.0288	0.1515	0.5044
3	Job security	0.1567	0.1384	0.4958
4	Customer relations[b]	0.0086	0.1751	0.4906
5	Company rating	0.4059	0.3240	0.4824
6	Working with others[b]	0.0018	0.0365	0.4651
7	Overall performance[b]	−0.0148	−0.3252	0.4518
8	Time-territory management[b]	0.0126	0.2899	0.4496
9	Sales produced[b]	0.0059	0.1404	0.4484
10	Presentation skill[b]	0.0118	0.2526	0.4387
11	Technical information[b]	0.0003	0.0065	0.4173
12	Pay benefits[a]	0.0600	0.1843	0.3788
13	Quota achieved[b]	0.0035	0.2915	0.3780
14	Management[a]	0.0014	0.0138	0.3571
15	Information collection[b]	−0.0146	−0.3327	0.3326
16	Family[c]	−0.0684	−0.3408	−0.3221
17	Sales manager[a]	−0.0121	−0.1102	0.2909
18	Coworker[a]	0.0225	0.0893	0.2671
19	Customer[c]	−0.0625	−0.2797	−0.2602
20	Family[d]	0.0473	0.1970	0.2180
21	Job[d]	0.1378	0.5312	0.2119
22	Job[c]	0.0410	0.5475	−0.1029
23	Customer[d]	−0.0060	−0.0255	0.1004
24	Sales manager[c]	−0.0365	−0.2406	−0.0499
25	Sales manager[d]	−0.0606	−0.3333	0.0467
26	Customer[a]	−0.0338	−0.1488	0.0192

Note: Rank order of importance is based on the magnitude of the canonical loadings:
[a] Satisfaction
[b] Performance
[c] Ambiguity
[d] Conflict.

index of discrimination (R = 0.4572), was significant (Wilks' λ = 0.7909, $F(26,173)$ = 1.7588, p = 0.0180). This result indicated that the variables discriminated between those who left and those who stayed.

The results from simultaneously entering all variables in discriminant analysis are presented in the table opposite. The rank order of importance, as determined by the relative magnitude of the canonical loadings, is presented in the first column. Satisfaction with the job and promotional opportunities were the two most important discriminators, followed by job security. Those who stayed in the company found the job to be more exciting, satisfying, challenging and interesting than those who left.

In this example, promotion was identified as the second most important variable based on the canonical loadings. However, it is not the second most important variable based on the absolute magnitude of the standardised discriminant function coefficients. This anomaly results from multicollinearity.

Characteristic profile
An aid to interpreting discriminant analysis results by describing each group in terms of the group means for the predictor variables.

Another aid to interpreting discriminant analysis results is to develop a **characteristic profile** for each group by describing each group in terms of the group means for the predictor variables. If the important predictors have been identified, then a comparison of the group means on these variables can assist in understanding the intergroup differences. Before any findings can be interpreted with confidence, however, it is necessary to validate the results.

Assess the validity of discriminant analysis

Many computer programs, such as SPSS, offer a leave-one-out cross-validation option. In this option, the discriminant model is re-estimated as many times as there are respondents in the sample. Each re-estimated model leaves out one respondent and the model is used to predict for that respondent. When a large holdout sample is not possible, this gives a sense of the robustness of the estimate using each respondent in turn, as a holdout.

As explained earlier, the data are randomly divided into two subsamples. One, the analysis sample, is used for estimating the discriminant function, and the validation sample is used for developing the classification matrix. The discriminant weights, estimated by using the analysis sample, are multiplied by the values of the predictor variables in the holdout sample to generate discriminant scores for the cases in the holdout sample. The cases are then assigned to groups based on their discriminant scores and an appropriate decision rule. For example, in two-group discriminant analysis, a case will be assigned to the group whose centroid is the closest. The **hit ratio**, or the percentage of cases correctly classified, can then be determined by summing the diagonal elements and dividing by the total number of cases.[9]

Hit ratio
The percentage of cases correctly classified by discriminant analysis.

It is helpful to compare the percentage of cases correctly classified by discriminant analysis with the percentage that would be obtained by chance. When the groups are equal in size, the percentage of chance classification is one divided by the number of groups. How much improvement should be expected over chance? No general guidelines are available, although some authors have suggested that classification accuracy achieved by discriminant analysis should be at least 25% greater than that obtained by chance.[10]

Most discriminant analysis programs also estimate a classification matrix based on the analysis sample. Because they capitalise on chance variation in the data, such results are invariably better than the classification obtained on the holdout sample.[11]

Table 21.4, for the holiday resort example, also shows the classification results based on the analysis sample. The hit ratio, or the percentage of cases correctly classified, is (12 + 15)/30 = 0.90, or 90%. One might suspect that this hit ratio is artificially inflated, as the data used for estimation were also used for validation. Leave-one-out cross-validation correctly classifies only (11 + 13)/30 = 0.80 or 80% of the cases. Conducting classification analysis on an independent holdout set of data results in the classification matrix with a slightly lower hit ratio of $(4 + 6)/12 = 0.833$, or 83.3% (see Table 21.4). Given two groups of equal size, by chance one would expect a hit ratio of $1/2 = 0.50$, or 50%. Hence, the improvement over chance is more than 25%, and the validity of the discriminant analysis is judged as satisfactory.

Another application of two-group discriminant analysis is provided by the following example.

Example   Home bodies and couch potatoes[12]

Two-group discriminant analysis was used to assess the strength of each of five dimensions used in classifying individuals as TV users or non-users. The discriminant analysis procedure was appropriate for this use because of the nature of the predefined categorical groups (users and non-users) and the interval scales used to generate individual factor scores.

Source: © Getty Images

Two equal groups of 185 elderly consumers, users and non-users (total $n = 370$), were created. The discriminant equation for the analysis was estimated by using a subsample of 142 respondents from the sample of 370. Of the remaining respondents, 198 were used as a validation subsample in a cross-validation of the equation. Thirty respondents were excluded from the analysis because of missing discriminant values.

The canonical correlation for the discriminant function was 0.4291, significant at the $p < 0.0001$ level. The eigenvalue was 0.2257. The table opposite summarises the standardised canonical discriminant coefficients. A substantial portion of the variance is explained by the discriminant function. In addition, as the table shows, the home-orientation dimension made a fairly strong contribution to classifying individuals as users or non-users of TV. Morale, security and health, and respect also contributed significantly. The social factor appeared to make little contribution.

The cross-validation procedure using the discriminant function from the analysis sample gave support to the contention that the dimensions aided researchers in discriminating between users and non-users of TV. As the table shows, the discriminant function was successful in classifying 75.76% of the cases. This suggests that consideration of the identified dimensions will help marketers understand the elderly market.

Summary of discriminant analysis

Standard canonical discriminant function coefficients

Morale	0.27798
Security and health	0.39850
Home orientation	0.77496
Respect	0.32069
Social	−0.01996

Classification results for cases selected for use in the analysis

		Predicted group membership	
Actual group	*No. of cases*	*Non-users*	*Users*
TV non-users	77	56	21
		72.7%	27.3%
TV users	65	24	41
		36.9%	63.1%

Per cent of grouped cases correctly classified: 68.31%

Classification results for cases selected for cross-validation

		Predicted group membership	
Actual group	*No. of cases*	*Non-users*	*Users*
TV non-users	108	85	23
		78.7%	21.3%
TV users	90	25	65
		27.8%	72.2%

Per cent of grouped cases correctly classified: 75.76%

The extension from two-group discriminant analysis to multiple discriminant analysis involves similar steps and is illustrated with an application.

Conducting multiple discriminant analysis

Formulate the problem

The data presented in Tables 21.2 and 21.3 can also be used to illustrate three-group discriminant analysis. In the last column of these tables, the households are classified into three categories, based on the amount spent on their family skiing holiday (high, medium or low). Ten households fall in each category. The question of interest is whether the households that spend high, medium or low amounts on their holidays (AMOUNT) can be differentiated in terms of annual family income (INCOME), attitude towards travel (TRAVEL), importance attached to family skiing holiday (HOLIDAY), household size (HSIZE) and age of the head of household (AGE).[13]

Estimate the discriminant function coefficients

Table 21.5 presents the results of estimating three-group discriminant analysis. An examination of group means indicates that income appears to separate the groups more widely than any other variable. There is some separation on travel and holiday. Groups 1 and 2 are very close in terms of household size and age. Age has a large standard deviation relative to the separation between the groups. The pooled within-groups correlation matrix indicates some correlation of holiday and household size with income. Age has some negative correlation with travel. Yet these correlations are on the lower side, indicating that, although multicollinearity may be of some concern, it is not likely to be a serious problem. The significance attached to the univariate F ratios indicates that, when the predictors are considered individually, only income and travel are significant in differentiating between the two groups.

In multiple discriminant analysis, if there are G groups, $G-1$ discriminant functions can be estimated if the number of predictors is larger than this quantity. In general, with G groups and k predictors, it is possible to estimate up to the smaller of $G-1$, or k, discriminant functions. The first function has the highest ratio of between-groups to within-groups sum of squares. The second function, uncorrelated with the first, has the second highest ratio, and so on. Not all the functions may be statistically significant, however.

Because there are three groups, a maximum of two functions can be extracted. The eigenvalue associated with the first function is 3.8190, and this function accounts for 93.93% of variance in the data. The eigenvalue is large, so the first function is likely to be superior. The second function has a small eigenvalue of 0.2469 and accounts for only 6.07% of the variance.

Table 21.5 Results of three-group discriminant analysis

Group means					
Visit	INCOME	TRAVEL	HOLIDAY	HSIZE	AGE
1	38.57000	4.50000	4.70000	3.10000	50.30000
2	50.1100	4.00000	4.20000	3.40000	49.50000
3	64.97000	6.10000	5.90000	4.20000	56.00000
Total	51.21667	4.86667	4.93333	3.56667	51.93333
Group standard deviations					
1	5.29718	1.71594	1.88856	1.19722	8.09732
2	6.00231	2.35702	2.48551	1.50555	9.25263
3	8.61434	1.19722	1.66333	1.13529	7.60117
Total	12.79523	1.97804	2.09981	1.33089	8.57395
Pooled within-groups correlation matrix					
INCOME	1.00000				
TRAVEL	0.05120	1.00000			
HOLIDAY	0.30681	0.03588	1.00000		
HSIZE	0.38050	0.00474	0.22080	1.00000	
AGE	–0.20939	–0.34022	–0.01326	–0.02512	1.00000

Table 21.5 Continued

Wilks' λ (*U* statistic) and univariate *F* ratio with 2 and 27 degrees of freedom

Variable	Wilks' λ	F	Significance
INCOME	0.26215	38.000	0.0000
TRAVEL	0.78790	3.634	0.0400
HOLIDAY	0.88060	1.830	0.1797
HSIZE	0.87411	1.944	0.1626
AGE	0.88214	1.804	0.1840

Canonical discriminant functions

Function	Eigenvalue	Per cent of variance	Cumulative percentage	Canonical correlation	After function	Wilks' λ	Chi-square	df	Sig.
					0	0.1664	44.831	10	0.00
1*	3.8190	93.93	93.93	0.8902	1	0.8020	5.517	4	0.24
2*	0.2469	6.07	100.00	0.4450					

* Marks the two canonical discriminant functions remaining in the analysis.

Standardised canonical discriminant function coefficients

	Func 1	Func 2
INCOME	1.04740	−0.42076
TRAVEL	0.33991	0.76851
HOLIDAY	−0.14198	0.53354
HSIZE	−0.16317	0.12932
AGE	0.49474	0.52447

Structure matrix: pooled within-groups correlations between discriminating variables and canonical discriminant functions (variables ordered by size of correlation within function)

	Func 1	Func 2
INCOME	0.85556*	−0.27833
HSIZE	0.19319*	0.07749
HOLIDAY	0.21935	0.58829*
TRAVEL	0.14899	0.45362*
AGE	0.16576	0.34079*

Unstandardised canonical discriminant function coefficients

	Func 1	Func 2
INCOME	0.1542658	−0.6197148E-01
TRAVEL	0.1867977	0.4223430
HOLIDAY	−0.6952264E-01	0.2612652
HSIZE	−0.1265334	0.1002796
AGE	0.5928055E-01	0.6284206E-01
(Constant)	−11.09442	−3.791600

Table 21.5 Continued

Canonical discriminant functions evaluated at group means (group centroids)

Group	Func 1	Func 2
1	–2.04100	0.41847
2	–0.40479	–0.65867
3	2.44578	0.24020

Classification results

			Predicted group membership			
		Amount	1	2	3	Total
Original	Count	1	9	1	0	10
		2	1	9	0	10
		3	0	2	8	10
	%	1	90.0	10.0	0.0	100.0
		2	10.0	90.0	0.0	100.0
		3	0.0	20.0	80.0	100.0
Cross-validated	Count	1	7	3	0	10
		2	4	5	1	10
		3	0	2	8	10
	%	1	70.0	30.0	0.0	100.0
		2	40.0	50.0	10.0	100.0
		3	0.0	20.0	80.0	100.0

[a] Cross-validation is done only for those cases in the analysis. In cross-validation, each case is classified by the functions derived from all cases other than that case.

[b] 86.7% of original grouped cases correctly classified.

[c] 66.7% of cross-validated grouped cases correctly classified.

Classification results for cases not selected for use in analysis

	Actual group	No. of cases	Predicted group membership		
			1	2	3
Group	1	4	3	1	0
			75.0%	25.0%	0.0%
Group	2	4	0	3	1
			0.0%	75.0%	25.0%
Group	3	4	1	0	3
			25.0%	0.0%	75.0%
Percentage of grouped cases correctly classified: 75.00%					

Determine the significance of the discriminant function

To test the null hypothesis of equal group centroids, both the functions must be considered simultaneously. It is possible to test the means of the functions successively by first testing all means simultaneously. Then one function is excluded at a time, and the means of the remaining functions are tested at each step. In Table 21.5, the 0 below the 'After function' heading indicates that no functions have been removed. The value of Wilks' λ is 0.1644. This transforms to a chi-square of 44.831, with 10 degrees of freedom, which is significant beyond the 0.05 level. Thus, the two functions together significantly discriminate among the three groups. When the first function is removed, however, the Wilks' λ associated with the second function is 0.8020, which is not significant at the 0.05 level. Therefore, the second function does not contribute significantly to group differences.

Interpret the results

The interpretation of the results is aided by an examination of the standardised discriminant function coefficients, the structure correlations and certain plots. The standardised coefficients indicate a large coefficient for income on function 1, whereas function 2 has relatively larger coefficients for travel, holiday and age. A similar conclusion is reached by an examination of the structure matrix (see Table 21.5). To help interpret the functions, variables with large coefficients for a particular function are grouped together. These groupings are shown with asterisks. Thus income and household size have asterisks for function 1 because these variables have coefficients which are larger for function 1 than for function 2. These variables are associated primarily with function 1. On the other hand, travel, holiday and age are predominantly associated with function 2, as indicated by the asterisks.

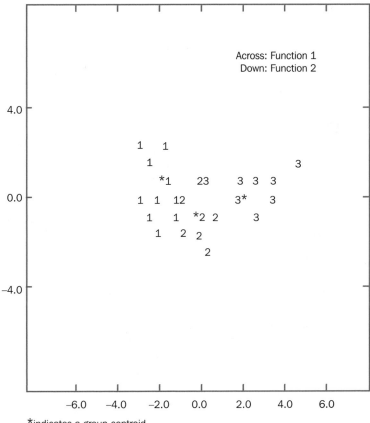

Figure 21.2
All-groups scattergram
*indicates a group centroid

Figure 21.2 is a scattergram plot of all the groups on function 1 and function 2. It can be seen that group 3 has the highest value on function 1, and group 1 the lowest. Because function 1 is primarily associated with income and household size, one would expect the three groups to be ordered on these two variables. Those with higher incomes and higher household size are likely to spend large amounts of money on holidays. Conversely, those with low incomes and smaller household size are likely to spend small amounts on holidays. This interpretation is further strengthened by an examination of group means on income and household size.

Figure 21.2 further indicates that function 2 tends to separate group 1 (highest value) and group 2 (lowest value). This function is primarily associated with travel, holiday and age. Given the positive correlations of these variables with function 2 in the structure matrix, we expect to find group 1 to be higher than group 2 in terms of travel, holiday and age. This is indeed true for travel and holiday, as indicated by the group means of these variables. If families in group 1 have more favourable attitudes towards travel and attach more importance to a family skiing holiday than group 2, why do they spend less? Perhaps they would like to spend more on holidays but cannot afford it because they have low incomes.

Territorial map
A tool for assessing discriminant analysis results by plotting the group membership of each case on a graph.

A similar interpretation is obtained by examining a **territorial map**, as shown in Figure 21.3. In a territorial map, each group centroid is indicated by an asterisk. The group boundaries are shown by numbers corresponding to the groups. Thus, group 1 centroid is bounded by 1s, group 2 centroid by 2s and group 3 centroid by 3s.

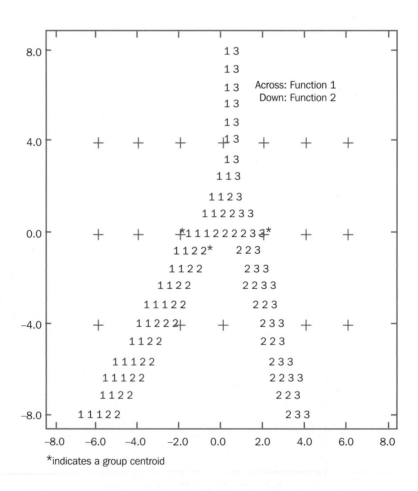

Figure 21.3
Territorial map

*indicates a group centroid

Assess the validity of discriminant analysis

The classification results based on the analysis sample indicate that (9 + 9 + 8)/30 = 86.67% of the cases are correctly classified. Leave-one-out cross-validation correctly classifies only (7 + 5 + 8)/30 = 0.667 or 66.7% of the cases. When the classification analysis is conducted on the independent holdout sample of Table 21.3, a hit ratio of (3 + 3 + 3)/12 = 75% is obtained. Given three groups of equal size, by chance alone one would expect a hit ratio of 1/3 = 0.333 or 33.3%. The improvement over chance is more than 25%, indicating at least satisfactory validity.[14]

Further illustration of multiple group discriminant analysis is provided by the following example.

Example | ### The home is where the patient's heart is[15]

In the majority of developed nations, the largest sector in the economy is the health care industry. Over the next decade, it is expected that spending on health care services will grow significantly faster than their economies. Contributing to this growth are demographic forces, with shrinking birth rates, ageing populations, longer life expectancies and with rapidly growing numbers of elderly patients seeking health support of some kind.

Consumers were surveyed to determine their attitudes towards four systems of health care delivery (home health care, hospitals, nursing homes and outpatient clinics) along 10 attributes. A total of 102 responses were obtained, and the results were analysed using multiple discriminant analysis (Table 1). Three discriminant functions were identified. Chi-square tests performed on the results indicated that all three discriminant functions were significant at the 0.01 level. The first function accounted for 63% of the total discriminative power, and the remaining two functions contributed 29.4% and 7.6%, respectively.

Table 1 gives the standardised discriminant function coefficients of the 10 variables in the discriminant equations. Coefficients ranged in value from –1 to +1. In determining the ability of each attribute to classify the delivery system, absolute values were used. In the first discriminant function, the two variables with the largest coefficients were comfort (0.53) and privacy (0.40). Because both related to personal attention and care, the first dimension was labelled 'personalised care'. In the second function, the two variables with the largest coefficients were quality of medical care (0.67) and likelihood of faster recovery (0.32). Hence, this dimension was labelled 'quality of medical care'. In the third discriminant function, the most significant attributes were sanitation (–0.70) and expense (0.52). Because these two attributes represent value and price, the third discriminant function was labelled 'value'.

The four group centroids are shown in Table 2. This table shows that home health care was evaluated most favourably along the dimension of personalised care, and hospitals were evaluated least favourably. Along the dimension of quality of medical care, there was a substantial separation between nursing homes and the other three systems. Also, home health care received higher evaluations on the quality of medical care than did outpatient clinics. Outpatient clinics, on the other hand, were judged to offer the best value.

Classification analysis of the 102 responses, reported in Table 3, showed correct classifications ranging from 86% for hospitals to 68% for outpatient clinics. The misclassifications for hospitals were 6% each to nursing homes and outpatient clinics and 2% to home health care. Nursing homes showed misclassifications of 9% to hospitals, 10% to outpatient clinics and 3% to home health care. For outpatient clinics, 9% misclassifications were made to hospitals, 13% to nursing homes and 10% to home health care. For home health care, the misclassifications were 5% to hospitals, 4% to nursing homes and 13% to outpatient clinics. The results demonstrated that the discriminant functions were fairly accurate in predicting group membership.

Table 1 Standardised discriminant function coefficients

Variable system	Discriminant function		
	1	2	3
Safe	−0.20	−0.04	0.15
Convenient	0.08	0.08	0.07
Chance of medical complications[a]	−0.27	0.10	0.16
Expensive[a]	0.30	−0.28	0.52
Comfortable	0.53	0.27	−0.19
Sanitary	−0.27	−0.14	−0.70
Best medical care	−0.25	0.67	−0.10
Privacy	0.40	0.08	0.49
Faster recovery	0.30	0.32	−0.15
Staffed with best medical personnel	−0.17	−0.03	0.18
Percentage of variance explained	63.0	29.4	7.6
Chi-square	663.3[b]	289.2[b]	70.1[b]

[a] These two items were worded negatively on the questionnaire. They were reverse coded for purposes of data analysis.

[b] $p < 0.01$.

Table 2 Centroids of health care systems in discriminant space

System	Discriminant function		
	1	2	3
Hospital	−1.66	0.97	−0.08
Nursing home	−0.60	−1.36	−0.27
Outpatient clinic	0.54	−0.13	0.77
Home health care	1.77	0.50	−0.39

Table 3 Classification table

System	Classification (%)			
	Hospital	Nursing home	Outpatient clinic	Home health care
Hospital	86	6	6	2
Nursing home	9	78	10	3
Outpatient clinic	9	13	68	10
Home health care	5	4	13	78

Stepwise discriminant analysis

Stepwise discriminant analysis is analogous to stepwise multiple regression (see Chapter 20) in that the predictors are entered sequentially based on their ability to discriminate between the groups. An F ratio is calculated for each predictor by conducting a univariate ANOVA in which the groups are treated as the categorical variable and the predictor as the criterion variable. The predictor with the highest F ratio is the first to be selected for inclusion in the discriminant function, if it meets certain significance and tolerance criteria. A second predictor is added based on the highest adjusted or partial F ratio, taking into account the predictor already selected.

Each predictor selected is tested for retention based on its association with other predictors selected. The process of selection and retention is continued until all predictors meeting the significance criteria for inclusion and retention have been entered in the discriminant function. Several statistics are computed at each stage. In addition, at the conclusion, a summary of the predictors entered or removed is provided. The standard output associated with the direct method is also available from the stepwise procedure.

The selection of the stepwise procedure is based on the optimising criterion adopted. The **Mahalanobis procedure** is based on maximising a generalised measure of the distance between the two closest groups. This procedure allows marketing researchers to make maximal use of the available information.[16]

Mahalanobis procedure
A stepwise procedure used in discriminant analysis to maximise a generalised measure of the distance between the two closest group.

The Mahalanobis method was used to conduct a two-group stepwise discriminant analysis on the data pertaining to the visit variable in Tables 21.2 and 21.3. The first predictor variable to be selected was income, followed by household size and then holiday. The order in which the variables were selected also indicates their importance in discriminating between the groups. This was further corroborated by an examination of the standardised discriminant function coefficients and the structure correlation coefficients. Note that the findings of the stepwise analysis agree with the conclusions reported earlier by the direct method.

The next example illustrates an application of discriminant analysis in marketing research.

Example **Satisfactory results of satisfaction programmes in Europe[17]**

In their marketing strategies, computer companies are emphasising the quality of their customer service programmes rather than focusing upon computer features and capabilities. Hewlett-Packard learned this lesson in Europe. Research conducted in the European market revealed that there was a difference in emphasis on service requirements across age segments. Focus groups revealed that customers above 40 years of age had a hard time with the technical aspects of the computer and greatly required the customer service programmes. On the other hand, younger customers appreciated the technical aspects of the product that added to their satisfaction. To uncover the factors leading to differences in the two segments, further research in the form of a large single cross-sectional survey was done. A two-group discriminant analysis was conducted with satisfied and dissatisfied customers as the two groups, with several independent variables such as technical information, ease of operation, variety and scope of customer service programmes, etc. Results confirmed the fact that the variety and scope of customer satisfaction programmes was indeed a strong differentiating factor. This was a crucial finding because Hewlett-Packard could better handle dissatisfied customers by focusing more on customer services than on technical details. Consequently, Hewlett-Packard successfully started three programmes on customer satisfaction: customer feedback, customer satisfaction surveys and total quality control. This effort resulted in increased customer satisfaction.

After seeing the successful results of this approach in Europe, HP Malaysia decide to launch a customer service programme called HP Cares!. This programme was developed in Malaysia as part of HP's Total Customer Experience (TCE) initiative to be rolled out worldwide. HP Malaysia's marketing and sales manager belives this programme will allow HP to build brand value and to differentiate the company from its competitors. HP realises that no matter how great its products may be, brand loyalty can be achieved only through continuous improvements in customer service.

Internet and computer applications

SPSS

The DISCRIMINANT procedure is used for conducting discriminant analysis. This is a general program that can be used for two-group or multiple discriminant analysis. Furthermore, the direct or the stepwise method can be adopted.

SAS

The DISCRIM procedure can be used for performing two-group or multiple discriminant analysis. If the assumption of a multivariate normal distribution cannot be met, the NEIGHBOR procedure can be used. In this procedure, a non-parametric nearest neighbour rule is used for classifying the observations. CANDISC performs canonical discriminant analysis and is related to principal components analysis and canonical correlation. The STEPDISC procedure can be used for performing stepwise discriminant analysis.

Minitab

Discriminant analysis can be conducted using the STATS>MULTIVARIATE>DISCRIMINANT ANALYSIS function. It computes both linear and quadratic discriminant analysis in the classification of observations into two or more groups.

Excel

At the time of writing, discriminant analysis was not available.

Summary

Discriminant analysis is useful for analysing data when the criterion or dependent variable is categorical and the predictor or independent variables are interval scaled. When the criterion variable has two categories, the technique is known as two-group discriminant analysis. Multiple discriminant analysis refers to the case when three or more categories are involved.

Conducting discriminant analysis is a five-step procedure. First, formulating the discriminant problem requires identification of the objectives and the criterion and predictor variables. The sample is divided into two parts. One part, the analysis sample, is used to estimate the discriminant function. The other part, the holdout sample, is reserved for validation. Estimation, the second step, involves developing a linear combination of the predictors, called discriminant functions, so that the groups differ as much as possible on the predictor values.

Determination of statistical significance is the third step. It involves testing the null hypothesis that, in the population, the means of all discriminant functions in all groups are equal. If the null hypothesis is rejected, it is meaningful to interpret the results.

The fourth step, the interpretation of discriminant weights or coefficients, is similar to that in multiple regression analysis. Given the multicollinearity in the predictor variables, there is no unambiguous measure of the relative importance of the predictors in discriminating between the groups. Some idea of the relative importance of the variables, however, may be obtained by examining the absolute magnitude of the standardised discriminant function coefficients and by examining the structure correlations or discriminant loadings. These simple correlations between each predictor and the discriminant function represent the variance that the predictor shares with the function. Another aid to interpreting discriminant analysis results is to develop a characteristic profile for each group, based on the group means for the predictor variables.

Validation, the fifth step, involves developing the classification matrix. The discriminant weights estimated by using the analysis sample are multiplied by the values of the predictor variables in the holdout sample to generate discriminant scores for the cases in the holdout sample. The cases are then assigned to groups based on their discriminant scores and an appropriate decision rule. The percentage of cases correctly classified is determined and compared with the rate that would be expected by chance classification.

Two broad approaches are available for estimating the coefficients. The direct method involves estimating the discriminant function so that all the predictors are included simultaneously. An alternative is the stepwise method in which the predictor variables are entered sequentially, based on their ability to discriminate among groups.

In multiple discriminant analysis, if there are G groups and k predictors, it is possible to estimate up to the smaller of $G - 1$, or k, discriminant functions. The first function has the highest ratio of between-group to within-group sums of squares; the second function, uncorrelated with the first, has the second highest ratio; and so on.

Questions

1 What are the objectives of discriminant analysis?

2 Describe four examples of the application of discriminant analysis.

3 What is the main distinction between two-group and multiple discriminant analysis?

4 Describe the relationship of discriminant analysis to regression and ANOVA.

5 What are the steps involved in conducting discriminant analysis?

6 How should the total sample be split for estimation and validation purposes?

7 What is Wilks' λ? For what purpose is it used?

8 Define discriminant scores.

9 Explain what is meant by an eigenvalue.

10 What is a classification matrix?

11 Explain the concept of structure correlations.

12 How is the statistical significance of discriminant analysis determined?

13 Describe a common procedure for determining the validity of discriminant analysis.

14 When the groups are of equal size, how is the accuracy of chance classification determined?

15 How does the stepwise discriminant procedure differ from the direct method?

Exercises

1 In investigating the differences between heavy and light or non-users of frozen foods, it was found that the two largest standardised discriminant function coefficients were 0.97 for convenience orientation and 0.61 for income. Is it correct to conclude that convenience orientation is more important than income when each variable is considered by itself?

2 Given the following information, calculate the discriminant score for each respondent. The value of the constant is 2.04.

Unstandardised discriminant function coefficients				
Age	0.38			
Income	0.44			
Risk taking	–0.39			
Optimistic	1.26			

Respondent ID	Age	Income	Risk taking	Optimistic
0246	36	43.7	21	65
1337	44	62.5	28	56
2375	57	33.5	25	40
2454	63	38.7	16	36

3 Analyse the Benetton data (taken from Exercise 4, Chapter 18). Do the three usage groups differ in terms of awareness, attitude, preference, intention and loyalty towards Benetton when these variables are considered simultaneously?

4 Conduct a two-group discriminant analysis on the data given in Tables 21.2 and 21.3 using different statistical analysis packages, e.g. SPSS, SAS and Minitab. Compare the output from all the packages. Discuss the similarities and differences.

5 In a small group discuss the following issue: 'Is it meaningful to determine the relative importance of predictors in discriminating between the groups? Why or why not?'

Appendix: Estimation of discriminant function coefficients

Suppose that there are G groups, $i = 1, 2, 3, \ldots, G$, each containing n_i observations on K independent variables, $X_1, X_2, \ldots, X_k$. The following notations are used:

$$N = \text{total sample size} = \sum_{i=1}^{G} n_i$$

W_i = matrix of mean corrected sum of squares and cross-products for the ith group

W = matrix of pooled within-groups mean corrected sum of squares and cross-products

B = matrix of between-groups mean corrected sum of squares and cross-products

T = matrix of total mean corrected sum of squares and cross-products for all the N observations = $W + B$

$\overline{X}_i$ = vector of means of observations in the ith group

$\overline{X}$ = vector of grand means for all the N observations

λ = ratio of between-groups to within-group sums of squares

b = vector of discriminant coefficients or weights

Then,

$$T = \sum_{i=1}^{G} \sum_{j=1}^{n_i} (X_{ij} - \overline{X})(X_{ij} - \overline{X})'$$

$$W_i = \sum_{j=1}^{n_i} (X_{ij} - \overline{X}_i)(X_{ij} - \overline{X}_i)'$$

$$W = W_1 + W_2 + W_3 + \ldots + W_G$$

$$B = T - W$$

Define the linear composite $D = b_1'X$. Then, with reference to D, the between-groups and within-groups sums of squares are $b_1'Bb$ and $b_1'Wb$, respectively. To discriminate the groups maximally, the discriminant functions are estimated to maximise the between-group variability. The coefficients b are calculated to maximise λ, by solving

$$\text{Max } \lambda = \frac{b'Bb}{b'Wb}$$

Taking the partial derivative with respect to λ and setting it equal to zero, with some simplification, yields

$$(B - \lambda W)b = 0$$

To solve for b, it is more convenient to premultiply by W^{-1} and solve the following characteristic equation:

$$(W^{-1}B - \lambda I)b = 0$$

The maximum value of λ is the largest eigenvalue of the matrix $W^{-1}B$, and b is the associated eigenvector. The elements of b are the discriminant coefficients, or weights, associated with the first discriminant function. In general, it is possible to estimate up to the smaller of $G - 1$ or k discriminant functions, each with its associated eigenvalue. The discriminant functions are estimated sequentially. In other words, the first discriminant function exhausts most of the between-group variability, the second function maximises the between-group variation that was not explained by the first one, and so on.

Notes

1 Anon., 'DirecTv adds National Geographic Channel', *Satellite News* (15 January 2001), 1; Lichtenstein, D.R., Burton, S. and Netemeyer, R.G., 'An examination of deal proneness across sales promotion types: a consumer segmentation perspective', *Journal of Retailing* 73 (2) (Summer 1997), 283–297; Jolson, M.A., Wiener, J.L. and Rosecky, R.B., 'Correlates of rebate proneness', *Journal of Advertising Research* (February–March 1987), 33–43.

2 A detailed discussion of discriminant analysis may be found in Kemsley, E.K., *Discriminant Analysis and Class Modeling of Spectroscopic Data* (New York: Wiley, 1998); Tacq, J., *Multivariate Analysis Techniques in Social Science Research* (Thousand Oaks, CA: Sage, 1996); Lachenbruch, P.A., *Discriminant Analysis* (New York: Hafner Press, 1975). For an application, see Deal, K., 'Determining success criteria for financial products: a comparative analysis of CART, logit and factor/discriminant analysis', *Service Industries Journal* 17 (3) (July 1997), 489–506.

3 See Johnson, R.A. and Wichern, D.W., *Applied Multivariate Statistical Analysis*, 5th edn (Paramus, NJ: Prentice Hall, 2001); Klecka, W.A., *Discriminant Analysis* (Beverly Hills, CA: Sage, 1980). See also Sinclair, S.A. and Stalling, E.C., 'How to identify differences between market segments with attribute analysis', *Industrial Marketing Management* 19 (February 1990), 31–40.

4 For an application, see Khan, Z., Chawla, S.K. and Cianciolo, T.A., 'Multiple discriminant analysis: tool for effective marketing of computer information systems to small business clients', *Journal of Professional Systems Marketing* 12 (2) (1995), 153–162; Sager, J.K. and Menon, A., 'The role of behavioural intentions in turnover of salespeople', *Journal of Business Research* 29 (March 1994), 179–188; Kijewski, V., Yoon, E. and Young, G., 'How exhibitors select trade shows', *Industrial Marketing Management* 22 (November 1993), 287–298.

5 Franses, P.H., 'A test for the hit rate in binary response models', *International Journal of Market Research* 42 (2) (Spring 2000), 239–245; Mitchell, V.-W., 'How to identify psychographic segments: Part 2', *Marketing Intelligence and Planning* 12 (7) (1994), 11–16; Crask, M.R. and Perrault, W.D. Jr, 'Validation of discriminant analysis in marketing research', *Journal of Marketing Research* 14 (February 1977), 60–68.

6 Strictly speaking, before testing for the equality of group means, the equality of group covariance matrices should be tested. Box's M test can be used for this purpose. If the equality of group covariance means is rejected, the results of discriminant analysis should be interpreted with caution. In this case, the power of the test for the equality of group means decreases.

7 See Hanna, N., 'Brain dominance and the interpretation of advertising messages', *International Journal of Commerce & Management* 9 (3/4) (1999), 19–32; Fok, L., Angelidis, J.P., Ibrahim, N.A. and Fok, W.M., 'The utilization and interpretation of multivariate statistical techniques in strategic management', *International Journal of Management* 12 (4) (December 1995), 468–481; Morrison, D.G., 'On the interpretation of discriminant analysis', *Journal of Marketing Research* 6 (May 1969), 156–163. For the use of other techniques in conjunction with discriminant analysis to aid interpretation, see Dant, R.P., Lumpkin, J.R. and Bush, R.P., 'Private physicians or walk-in clinics: do the patients differ?', *Journal of Health Care Marketing* 10 (June 1990), 23–35.

8 Sahl, R.J., 'Retention reigns as economy suffers drought', *Workspan* 44 (11) (November 2001), 6–8; Hawes, J.M., Rao, C.P. and Baker, T.L., 'Retail salesperson attributes and the role of dependability in the selection of durable goods', *Journal of Personal Selling and Sales Management* 13 (4) (Fall 1993), 61–71; Fern, E.E., Avila, R.A. and Grewal, D., 'Salesforce turnover: those who left and those who stayed', *Industrial Marketing Management* (1989), 1–9.

9 For the validation of discriminant analysis, see Reinartz, W.J. and Kumar, V., 'On the profitability of long life customers in a non-contractual setting: an empirical investigation and implications for marketing', *Journal of Marketing* 64 (4) (October 2000), 17–35.

10 Hair, J.E. Jr, Anderson, R.E., Tatham, R.L. and Black, W.C., *Multivariate Data Analysis with Readings*, 5th edn (Upper Saddle River, NJ: Prentice Hall, 1999). See also Glen, J.J., 'Classification accuracy in discriminant analysis: a mixed integer programming approach', *Journal of the Operational Research Society* 52 (3) (March 2001), 328.

11 Mitchell, V.W., 'How to identify psychographic segments: Part 2', *Marketing Intelligence and Planning* 12 (7) (1994), 11–16; Albaum, G. and Baker, K., 'The sampling problem in validation of multiple discriminant analysis', *Journal of the Market Research Society* 18 (July 1976).

12 Anon., 'Interactive TV growth to erupt over the next five years', *Satellite News* 24 (2) (8 January, 2001), 1; Rahtz, D.R., Sirgy, M.J. and Kosenko, R., 'Using demographics and psychographic dimensions to discriminate between mature heavy and light television users: an exploratory analysis', in Bahn, K.D. (ed.), *Developments in Marketing Science*, Vol. 11 (Blacksburg, VA: Academy of Marketing Science, 1988), 2–7.

13 For advanced discussion of multiple discriminant analysis, see Johnson, R.A. and Wichern, D.W., *Applied Multivariate Statistical Analysis*, 5th edn (Upper Saddle River, NJ: Prentice Hall, 2002). For an application, see Reinartz, W.J. and Kumar, V., 'On the profitability of long life customers in a non-contractual setting: an empirical investigation and implications for marketing', *Journal of Marketing* 64 (4) (October 2000), 17–35.

14 Loucopoulos, C. and Pavur, R.M., 'Computational characteristics of a new mathematical programming model for the three-group discriminant problem', *Computers and Operations Research* 24 (2) (February 1997), 179–191. For an application of multiple discriminant analysis, see O'Connor, S.J., Shewchuk, R.M. and Camey, L.W., 'The great gap', *Journal of Health Care Marketing* 14 (Summer 1994), 32–39.

15 Tudor, J., 'Valuation of the health services industry', *Weekly Corporate Growth Report* (1133) (26 March, 2001), 11237–11238; Dansky, K.H. and Brannon, D., 'Discriminant analysis: a technique for adding value to patient satisfaction surveys', *Hospital and Health Services Administration* 41 (4) (Winter 1996), 503–513; Lim, J.S. and Zallocco, R., 'Determinant attributes in formulation of attitudes toward four health care systems', *Journal of Health Care Marketing* 8 (June 1988), 25–30.

16 Johnson, R.A. and Wichern, D.A., *Applied Multivariate Statistical Analysis*, 5th edn (Upper Saddle River, NJ: Prentice Hall, 2002); Hair, J.E. Jr, Anderson, R.E., Tatham, R.L. and Black, W.C., *Multivariate Data Analysis with Readings*, 5th edn (Englewood Cliffs, NJ: Prentice Hall, 1999), 178–255.

17 Raman, P., 'Taking customer service a step ahead', *Computimes* (22 October 2001), 1; Whitelock, J., Roberts, C. and Blakeley, J., 'The reality of the eurobrand: an empirical analysis', *Journal of International Marketing* 3 (3) (1995), 77–95.

Visit the *Marketing Research* Companion Website at www.pearsoned.co.uk/malhotra_euro for additional learning resources including annotated weblinks, an online glossary and a suite of downloadable video cases.

Source: © EMPICS

22

Factor analysis

> *Factor analysis allows an examination of the potential interrelationships among a number of variables and the evaluation of the underlying reasons for these relationships.*

Objectives

After reading this chapter, you should be able to:

1 describe the concept of factor analysis and explain how it is different from analysis of variance, multiple regression and discriminant analysis;

2 discuss the procedure for conducting factor analysis, including problem formulation, construction of the correlation matrix, selection of an appropriate method, determination of the number of factors, rotation and interpretation of factors;

3 understand the distinction between principal component factor analysis and common factor analysis methods;

4 explain the selection of surrogate variables and their application with emphasis on their use in subsequent analysis;

5 describe the procedure for determining the fit of a factor analysis model using the observed and the reproduced correlations.

STAGE 1
Problem definition

STAGE 2
Research approach developed

STAGE 3
Research design developed

STAGE 4
Fieldwork or data collection

STAGE 5
Data preparation and analysis

STAGE 6
Report preparation and presentation

Overview

In analysis of variance (Chapter 19), regression (Chapter 20) and discriminant analysis (Chapter 21), one of the variables is clearly identified as the dependent variable. We now turn to a procedure, factor analysis, in which variables are not classified as independent or dependent. Instead, the whole set of interdependent relationships among variables is examined. This chapter discusses the basic concept of factor analysis and gives an exposition of the factor model. We describe the steps in factor analysis and illustrate them in the context of principal components analysis. Next, we present an application of common factor analysis. To begin, we provide an example to illustrate the usefulness of factor analysis.

Example

Personal alarms[1]

In a study of personal alarms, women were asked to rate eight personal alarms using the following 15 statements:

1 Feels comfortable in the hand.
2 Could be easily kept in the pocket.
3 Would fit easily into a handbag.
4 Could be easily worn on the person.
5 Could be carried to be very handy when needed.
6 Could be set off almost as a reflex action.
7 Would be difficult for an attacker to take it off me.
8 Could keep a very firm grip on it if attacked.
9 An attacker might be frightened that I might attack him with it
10 Would be difficult for an attacker to switch off.
11 Solidly built.
12 Would be difficult to break.
13 Looks as if it would give off a very loud noise.
14 An attacker might have second thoughts about attacking me if he saw me with it.
15 I would be embarrassed to carry it around with me.

The question was 'Could these 15 variables be reduced to a smaller number of derived variables, known as factors, in such a way that too much information was not lost?' Factor analysis enabled these 15 variables to be reduced to four underlying dimensions or factors that women used to evaluate the alarms. Factor 1 seemed to measure a dimension of *size*, on a continuum of small to large. Factor 2 tapped into aspects of the *appearance* of a personal alarm. Factor 3 revealed *robustness* characteristics, with factor 4 related to *hand feel*.

Basic concept

Factor analysis
A class of procedures primarily used for data reduction and summarisation.

Factor
An underlying dimension that explains the correlations among a set of variables.

Factor analysis is a general name denoting a class of procedures primarily used for data reduction and summarisation. In marketing research, there may be a large number of variables, most of which are correlated and which must be reduced to a manageable level. Relationships among sets of many interrelated variables are examined and represented in terms of a few underlying factors. For example, car manufacturer image may be measured by asking respondents to evaluate car(s) on a series of items on a semantic differential scale or a Likert scale. These item evaluations may then be analysed to determine the **factors** underlying car manufacturer image.

In analysis of variance, multiple regression and discriminant analysis, one variable is considered the dependent or criterion variable, and the others are considered independent or predictor variables. But no such distinction is made in factor analysis. Rather, factor analysis is an interdependence technique in that an entire set of **interdependent relationships** is examined.[2]

Factor analysis is used in the following circumstances:

1 To identify underlying dimensions, or factors, that explain the correlations among a set of variables. For example, a set of lifestyle statements may be used to measure the psychographic profiles of consumers. These statements may then be factor analysed to identify the underlying psychographic factors.[3]

2 To identify a new, smaller, set of uncorrelated variables to replace the original set of correlated variables in subsequent multivariate analysis (regression or discriminant analysis). For example, the psychographic factors identified may be used as independent variables in explaining the differences between loyal and non-loyal consumers.

3 To identify a smaller set of salient variables from a larger set for use in subsequent multivariate analysis. For example, a few of the original lifestyle statements that correlate highly with the identified factors may be used as independent variables to explain the differences between the loyal and non-loyal users.

Factor analysis has numerous applications in marketing research. For example:

- Factor analysis can be used in market segmentation for identifying the underlying variables on which to group the customers. New car buyers might be grouped based on the relative emphasis they place on economy, convenience, performance, comfort and luxury.
- This might result in five segments: economy seekers, convenience seekers, performance seekers, comfort seekers and luxury seekers.
- In product research, factor analysis can be employed to determine the brand attributes that influence consumer choice. Toothpaste brands might be evaluated in terms of protection against cavities, whiteness of teeth, taste, fresh breath and price.
- In advertising studies, factor analysis can be used to understand the media consumption habits of the target market. The users of frozen foods may be heavy viewers of satellite TV, see a lot of videos, and listen to country music.
- In pricing studies, factor analysis can be used to identify the characteristics of price-sensitive consumers. For example, these consumers might be methodical, economy minded and home centred.

Interdependence technique
A multivariate statistical technique in which the whole set of interdependent relationships is examined.

Factor analysis model

Mathematically, factor analysis is somewhat similar to multiple regression analysis in that each variable is expressed as a linear combination of underlying factors. The amount of variance a variable shares with all other variables included in the analysis is referred to as *communality*. The covariation among the variables is described in terms of a small number of common factors plus a unique factor for each variable. These factors are not overtly observed. If the variables are standardised, the factor model may be represented as

$$X_i = A_{i1}F_i + A_{i2}F_2 + A_{i3}F_3 + ... + A_{im}F_m + V_iU_i$$

where X_i = ith standardised variable
A_{ij} = standardised multiple regression coefficient of variable i on common factor j
F = common factor
V_i = standardised regression coefficient of variable i on unique factor i
U_i = the unique factor for variable i
m = number of common factors

The unique factors are correlated with each other and with the common factors.[4] The common factors themselves can be expressed as linear combinations of the observed variables

$$F_i = W_{i1}X_1 + W_{i2}X_2 + W_{i3}X_3 + \ldots + W_{ik}X_k$$

where F_i = estimate of ith factor
W_i = weight or factor score coefficient
k = number of variables

It is possible to select weights or factor score coefficients so that the first factor explains the largest portion of the total variance. Then a second set of weights can be selected so that the second factor accounts for most of the residual variance, subject to being uncorrelated with the first factor. This same principle could be applied to selecting additional weights for the additional factors. Thus, the factors can be estimated so that their factor scores, unlike the values of the original variables, are not correlated. Furthermore, the first factor accounts for the highest variance in the data, the second factor the second highest, and so on. A technical treatment of the factor analysis model is presented in the appendix to this chapter.

Statistics associated with factor analysis

The key statistics associated with factor analysis are as follows:

Bartlett's test of sphericity. Bartlett's test of sphericity is a test statistic used to examine the hypothesis that the variables are uncorrelated in the population. In other words, the population correlation matrix is an identity matrix; each variable correlates perfectly with itself ($r = 1$) but has no correlation with the other variables ($r = 0$).

Communality. Communality is the amount of variance a variable shares with all the other variables being considered. This is also the proportion of variance explained by the common factors.

Correlation matrix. A correlation matrix is a lower triangular matrix showing the simple correlations, r, between all possible pairs of variables included in the analysis. The diagonal elements, which are all one, are usually omitted.

Eigenvalue. The eigenvalue represents the total variance explained by each factor.

Factor loadings. Factor loadings are simple correlations between the variables and the factors.

Factor loading plot. A factor loading plot is a plot of the original variables using the factor loadings as coordinates.

Factor matrix. A factor matrix contains the factor loadings of all the variables on all the factors extracted.

Factor scores. Factor scores are composite scores estimated for each respondent on the derived factors.

Kaiser–Meyer–Olkin (KMO) measure of sampling adequacy. The Kaiser–Meyer–Olkin (KMO) measure of sampling adequacy is an index used to examine the appropriateness of factor analysis. High values (between 0.5 and 1.0) indicate that factor analysis is appropriate. Values below 0.5 imply that factor analysis may not be appropriate.

Percentage of variance. The percentage of the total variance attributed to each factor.

Residuals. Residuals are the differences between the observed correlations, as given in the input correlation matrix, and the reproduced correlations, as estimated from the factor matrix.

Scree plot. A scree plot is a plot of the eigenvalues against the number of factors in order of extraction.

We describe the uses of these statistics in the next section, in the context of the procedure for conducting factor analysis.

Conducting factor analysis

The steps involved in conducting factor analysis are illustrated in Figure 22.1. The first step is to define the factor analysis problem and identify the variables to be factor analysed. Then a correlation matrix of these variables is constructed and a method of factor analysis is selected. The researcher decides on the number of factors to be extracted and the method of rotation. Next, the rotated factors should be interpreted. Depending on the objectives, the factor scores may be calculated, or surrogate variables selected, to represent the factors in subsequent multivariate analysis. Finally, the fit of the factor analysis model is determined. We discuss these steps in more detail in the following subsections.[5]

Formulate the problem

Formulating the problem includes several tasks. First, the objectives of factor analysis should be identified. The variables to be included in the factor analysis should be specified based on past research (quantitative or qualitative), theory and judgement of the researcher. It is important that the variables be appropriately measured on an interval or ratio scale. An appropriate sample size should be used. As a rough guide, there should be at least four or five times as many observations (sample size) as there are variables.[6] In many marketing research situations, the sample size is small, and this ratio is considerably lower. In these cases, the results should be interpreted cautiously.

To illustrate factor analysis, suppose that the researcher wants to determine the underlying benefits consumers seek from the purchase of a toothpaste. A sample of 30 respondents was interviewed using street interviewing. The respondents were asked to indicate their degree of agreement with the following statements using a seven-point scale (1 = strongly disagree, 7 = strongly agree):

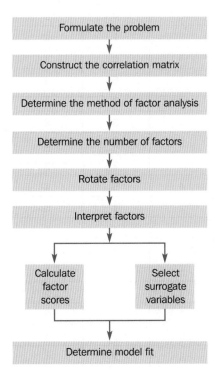

Figure 22.1
Conducting factor analysis

V_1 It is important to buy a toothpaste that prevents cavities.

V_2 I like a toothpaste that gives shiny teeth.

V_3 A toothpaste should strengthen your gums.

V_4 I prefer a toothpaste that freshens breath.

V_5 Prevention of tooth decay should be an important benefit offered by a toothpaste.

V_6 The most important consideration in buying a toothpaste is attractive teeth.

The data obtained are given in Table 22.1. A correlation matrix was constructed based on these ratings data.

Table 22.1 Toothpaste attribute ratings

Respondent number	V_1	V_2	V_3	V_4	V_5	V_6
1	7	3	6	4	2	4
2	1	3	2	4	5	4
3	6	2	7	4	1	3
4	4	5	4	6	2	5
5	1	2	2	3	6	2
6	6	3	6	4	2	4
7	5	3	6	3	4	3
8	6	4	7	4	1	4
9	3	4	2	3	6	3
10	2	6	2	6	7	6
11	6	4	7	3	2	3
12	2	3	1	4	5	4
13	7	2	6	4	1	3
14	4	6	4	5	3	6
15	1	3	2	2	6	4
16	6	4	6	3	3	4
17	5	3	6	3	3	4
18	7	3	7	4	1	4
19	2	4	3	3	6	3
20	3	5	3	6	4	6
21	1	3	2	3	5	3
22	5	4	5	4	2	4
23	2	2	1	5	4	4
24	4	6	4	6	4	7
25	6	5	4	2	1	4
26	3	5	4	6	4	7
27	4	4	7	2	2	5
28	3	7	2	6	4	3
29	4	6	3	7	2	7
30	2	3	2	4	7	2

Construct the correlation matrix

The analytical process is based on a matrix of correlations between the variables. Valuable insights can be gained from an examination of this matrix. For factor analysis to be meaningful, the variables should be correlated. In practice, this is usually the case. If the correlations between all the variables are small, factor analysis may not be appropriate. We would also expect that variables that are highly correlated with each other would also highly correlate with the same factor or factors.

Formal statistics are available for testing the appropriateness of the factor model. Bartlett's test of sphericity can be used to test the null hypothesis that the variables are uncorrelated in the population; in other words, the population correlation matrix is an identity matrix. In an identity matrix, all the diagonal terms are one, and all off-diagonal terms are zero. The test statistic for sphericity is based on a chi-square transformation of the determinant of the correlation matrix. A large value of the test statistic will favour the rejection of the null hypothesis. If this hypothesis cannot be rejected, then the appropriateness of factor analysis should be questioned. Another useful statistic is the Kaiser–Meyer–Olkin (KMO) measure of sampling adequacy. This index compares the magnitudes of the observed correlation coefficients with the magnitudes of the partial correlation coefficients. Small values of the KMO statistic indicate that the correlations between pairs of variables cannot be explained by other variables and that factor analysis may not be appropriate. Generally, a value greater than 0.5 is desirable.

The correlation matrix, constructed from the data obtained to understand toothpaste benefits, is shown in Table 22.2. There are relatively high correlations among V_1 (prevention of cavities), V_3 (strong gums) and V_5 (prevention of tooth decay). We would expect these variables to correlate with the same set of factors. Likewise, there are relatively high correlations among V_2 (shiny teeth), V_4 (fresh breath) and V_6 (attractive teeth). These variables may also be expected to correlate with the same factors.[7]

Table 22.2 Correlation matrix

Respondent	V_1	V_2	V_3	V_4	V_5	V_6
V_1	1.00					
V_2	–0.053	1.00				
V_3	0.873	–0.155	1.00			
V_4	–0.086	0.572	–0.248	1.00		
V_5	–0.858	0.020	–0.778	–0.007	1.00	
V_6	0.004	0.640	–0.018	0.640	–0.136	1.00

The results of factor analysis are given in Table 22.3. The null hypothesis, that the population correlation matrix is an identity matrix, is rejected by Bartlett's test of sphericity. The approximate chi-square statistic is 111.314 with 15 degrees of freedom, which is significant at the 0.05 level. The value of the KMO statistic (0.660) is also large (>0.5). Thus factor analysis may be considered an appropriate technique for analysing the correlation matrix of Table 22.2.

Determine the method of factor analysis

Once it has been determined that factor analysis is an appropriate technique for analysing the data, an appropriate method must be selected. The approach used to derive the weights or factor score coefficients differentiates the various methods of factor analysis.

The two basic approaches are principal components analysis and common factor analysis. In principal components analysis, the total variance in the data is considered. The diagonal of the correlation matrix consists of unities, and full variance is brought into the factor matrix. **Principal components analysis** is recommended when the primary concern is to determine the minimum number of factors that will account for maximum variance in the data for use in subsequent multivariate analysis. The factors are called *principal components*.

In **common factor analysis**, the factors are estimated based only on the common variance. Communalities are inserted in the diagonal of the correlation matrix. This method is appropriate when the primary concern is to identify the underlying dimensions and the common variance is of interest. This method is also known as *principal axis factoring*.

Other approaches for estimating the common factors are also available. These include the methods of unweighted least squares, generalised least squares, maximum likelihood, alpha method and image factoring. These methods are complex and are not recommended for inexperienced users.[8]

Table 22.3 shows the application of principal components analysis to the toothpaste example.

Principal components analysis
An approach to factor analysis that considers the total variance in the data.

Common factor analysis
An approach to factor analysis that estimates the factors based only on the common variance. Also called principal axis factoring.

Table 22.3 Results of principal components analysis

Bartlett test of sphericity
Approximate chi-square = 111.314, *df* = 15, significance = 0.00000
Kaiser–Meyer–Olkin measure of sampling adequacy = 0.660

Communalities

Variable	Initial	Extraction
V_1	1.000	0.926
V_2	1.000	0.723
V_3	1.000	0.894
V_4	1.000	0.739
V_5	1.000	0.878
V_6	1.000	0.790

Initial eigenvalues

Factor	Eigenvalue variance	Percentage of percentage	Cumulative
1	2.731	45.520	45.520
2	2.218	36.969	82.488
3	0.442	7.360	89.848
4	0.341	5.688	95.536
5	0.183	3.044	98.580
6	0.085	1.420	100.000

Extraction sums of squared loadings

Factor	Eigenvalue	Percentage of variance	Cumulative percentage
1	2.731	45.520	45.520
2	2.218	36.969	82.488

Table 22.3 Continued

Factor matrix

	Factor 1	Factor 2
V_1	0.928	0.253
V_2	−0.301	0.795
V_3	0.936	0.131
V_4	−0.342	0.789
V_5	−0.869	−0.351
V_6	−0.177	0.871

Rotation sums of squared loadings

Factor	Eigenvalue	Percentage of variance	Cumulative percentage
1	2.688	44.802	44.802
2	2.261	37.687	82.488

Rotated factor matrix

	Factor 1	Factor 2
V_1	0.962	−0.027
V_2	−0.057	0.848
V_3	0.934	−0.146
V_4	−0.098	0.854
V_5	−0.933	−0.084
V_6	0.083	0.885

Factor score coefficient matrix

	Factor 1	Factor 2
V_1	0.358	0.011
V_2	−0.001	0.375
V_3	0.345	−0.043
V_4	−0.017	0.377
V_5	−0.350	−0.059
V_6	0.052	0.395

Reproduced correlation matrix

Variables	V_1	V_2	V_3	V_4	V_5	V_6
V_1	0.926*	0.024	−0.029	0.031	0.038	−0.053
V_2	−0.078	0.723*	0.022	−0.158	0.038	−0.105
V_3	0.902	−0.177	0.894*	−0.031	0.081	0.033
V_4	−0.117	0.730	−0.217	0.739*	−0.027	−0.107
V_5	−0.895	−0.018	0.859	0.020	0.878*	0.016
V_6	0.057	−0.746	−0.051	0.748	−0.152	0.790

*The lower left triangle contains the reproduced correlation matrix; the diagonal, the communalities; and the upper right triangle, the residuals between the observed correlations and the reproduced correlations.

Under 'Communalities', 'Initial' column, it can be seen that the communality for each variable, V_1 to V_6, is 1.0 as unities were inserted in the diagonal of the correlation matrix. The table labelled 'Initial eigenvalues' gives the eigenvalues. The eigenvalues for the factors are, as expected, in decreasing order of magnitude as we go from factor 1 to factor 6. The eigenvalue for a factor indicates the total variance attributed to that factor. The total variance accounted for by all the six factors is 6.00, which is equal to the number of variables. Factor 1 accounts for a variance of 2.731, which is (2.731/6) or 45.52% of the total variance. Likewise, the second factor accounts for (2.218/6) or 36.97% of the total variance, and the first two factors combined account for 82.49% of the total variance. Several considerations are involved in determining the number of factors that should be used in the analysis.

Determine the number of factors

It is possible to compute as many principal components as there are variables, but in doing so, no parsimony is gained, i.e. we would not have summarised the information nor revealed any underlying structure. To summarise the information contained in the original variables, a smaller number of factors should be extracted. The question is: how many? Several procedures have been suggested for determining the number of factors. These included a priori determination and approaches based on eigenvalues, scree plot, percentage of variance accounted for, split-half reliability and significance tests:

A priori determination. Sometimes, because of prior knowledge, the researcher knows how many factors to expect and thus can specify the number of factors to be extracted beforehand. The extraction of factors ceases when the desired number of factors has been extracted. Most computer programs allow the user to specify the number of factors, allowing for an easy implementation of this approach.

Determination based on eigenvalues. In this approach, only factors with eigenvalues greater than 1.0 are retained; the other factors are not included in the model. An eigenvalue represents the amount of variance associated with the factor. Hence, only factors with a variance greater than 1.0 are included. Factors with a variance less than 1.0 are no better than a single variable because, due to standardisation, each variable has a variance of 1.0. If the number of variables is less than 20, this approach will result in a conservative number of factors.

Determination based on scree plot. A scree plot is a plot of the eigenvalues against the number of factors in order of extraction. The shape of the plot is used to determine the number of factors. Typically, the plot has a distinct break between the steep slope of factors, with large eigenvalues and a gradual trailing off associated with the rest of the factors. This gradual trailing off is referred to as the scree. Experimental evidence indicates that the point at which the scree begins denotes the true number of factors. Generally, the number of factors determined by a scree plot will be one or a few more than that determined by the eigenvalue criterion.

Determination based on percentage of variance. In this approach, the number of factors extracted is determined so that the cumulative percentage of variance extracted by the factors reaches a satisfactory level. What level of variance is satisfactory depends upon the problem. It is recommended that the factors extracted should account for at least 60% of the variance.

Determination based on split-half reliability. The sample is split in half, and factor analysis is performed on each half. Only factors with high correspondence of factor loadings across the two subsamples are retained.

Determination based on significance tests. It is possible to determine the statistical significance of the separate eigenvalues and retain only those factors that are statistically significant. A drawback is that with large samples (size greater than 200) many factors are likely to be statistically significant, although from a practical viewpoint many of these account for only a small proportion of the total variance.

In Table 22.3, we see that the eigenvalue greater than 1.0 (default option) results in two factors being extracted. Our a priori knowledge tells us that toothpaste is bought for two major reasons. The scree plot associated with this analysis is given in Figure 22.2. From the scree plot, a distinct break occurs at three factors. Finally, from the cumulative percentage of variance accounted for, we see that the first two factors account for 82.49% of the variance and that the gain achieved in going to three factors is marginal. Furthermore, split-half reliability also indicates that two factors are appropriate. Thus, two factors appear to be reasonable in this situation.

The second column under the 'Communalities' heading in Table 22.3 gives relevant information after the desired number of factors has been extracted. The communalities for the variances under 'Extraction' are different from those under 'Initial' because all of the variances associated with the variables are not explained unless all the factors are retained. The 'Extraction sums of squared loadings' table gives the variances associated with the factors that are retained. Note that these are the same as those under 'Initial eigenvalues'. This is always the case in principal components analysis. The percentage variance accounted for by a factor is determined by dividing the associated eigenvalue by the total number of factors (or variables) and multiplying by 100. Thus, the first factor accounts for $(2.731/6) \times 100$ or 45.52% of the variance of the six variables. Likewise, the second factor accounts for $(2.218/6) \times 100$ or 36.967% of the variance. Interpretation of the solution is often enhanced by a rotation of the factors.

Rotate factors

An important output from factor analysis is the factor matrix, also called the *factor pattern matrix*. The factor matrix contains the coefficients used to express the standardised variables in terms of the factors. These coefficients, the factor loadings, represent the correlations between the factors and the variables. A coefficient with a large absolute value indicates that the factor and the variable are closely related. The coefficients of the factor matrix can be used to interpret the factors.

Although the initial or unrotated factor matrix indicates the relationship between the factors and individual variables, it seldom results in factors that can be interpreted, because the factors are correlated with many variables. For example, in Table 22.3, factor 1 is at least somewhat correlated with five of the six variables (absolute value of factor loading greater than 0.3). How should this factor be interpreted? In such a complex matrix, it

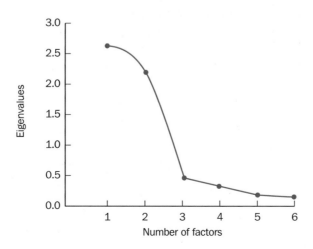

Figure 22.2
Scree plot

is difficult to interpret the factors. Therefore, through rotation, the factor matrix is transformed into a simpler one that is easier to interpret.

In rotating the factors, we would like each factor to have non-zero, or significant, loadings or coefficients for only some of the variables. Likewise, we would like each variable to have non-zero or significant loadings with only a few factors, and if possible with only one. If several factors have high loadings with the same variable, it is difficult to interpret them. Rotation does not affect the communalities and the percentage of total variance explained. The percentage of variance accounted for by each factor does change, however. This is seen in Table 22.3. The variance explained by the individual factors is redistributed by rotation. Hence, different methods of rotation may result in the identification of different factors.

The rotation is called **orthogonal rotation** if the axes are maintained at right angles. The most commonly used method for rotation is the **varimax procedure**. This is an orthogonal method of rotation that minimises the number of variables with high loadings on a factor, thereby enhancing the interpretability of the factors.[9] Orthogonal rotation results in factors that are uncorrelated. The rotation is called **oblique rotation** when the axes are not maintained at right angles, and the factors are correlated. Sometimes, allowing for correlations among factors can simplify the factor pattern matrix. Oblique rotation should be used when factors in the population are likely to be strongly correlated.

In Table 22.3, by comparing the varimax rotated factor matrix with the unrotated matrix (entitled factor matrix), we can see how rotation achieves simplicity and enhances interpretability. Whereas five variables correlated with factor 1 in the unrotated matrix, only variables V_1, V_3 and V_5 correlate highly with factor 1 after rotation. The remaining variables, V_2, V_4 and V_6, correlate highly with factor 2. Furthermore, no variable correlates highly with both the factors. The rotated factor matrix forms the basis for interpretation of the factors.

Orthogonal rotation
Rotation of factors in which the axes are maintained at right angles.

Varimax procedure
An orthogonal method of factor rotation that minimises the number of variables with high loadings on a factor, thereby enhancing the interpretability of the factors.

Oblique rotation
Rotation of factors when the axes are not maintained at right angles.

Interpret factors

Interpretation is facilitated by identifying the variables that have large loadings on the same factor. That factor can then be interpreted in terms of the variables that load high on it. Another useful aid in interpretation is to plot the variables, using the factor loadings as coordinates. Variables at the end of an axis are those that have high loadings on only that factor and hence describe the factor. Variables near the origin have small loadings on both the factors. Variables that are not near any of the axes are related to both the factors. If a factor cannot be clearly defined in terms of the original variables, it should be labelled as an undefined or a general factor.

In the rotated factor matrix of Table 22.3, factor 1 has high coefficients for variables V_1 (prevention of cavities) and V_3 (strong gums), and a negative coefficient for V_5 (prevention of tooth decay is not important). Therefore, this factor may be labelled a health benefit factor. Note that a negative coefficient for a negative variable (V_5) leads to a positive interpretation that prevention of tooth decay is important. Factor 2 is highly related with variables V_2 (shiny teeth), V_4 (fresh breath) and V_6 (attractive teeth). Thus factor 2 may be labelled a social benefit factor. A plot of the factor loadings, given in Figure 22.3, confirms this interpretation. Variables V_1, V_3 and V_5 (denoted 1, 3 and 5, respectively) are at the end of the horizontal axis (factor 1), with V_5 at the end opposite to V_1 and V_3, whereas variables V_2, V_4 and V_6 (denoted 2, 4 and 6) are at the end of the vertical axis (factor 2). One could summarise the data by stating that consumers appear to seek two major kinds of benefits from toothpaste: health benefits and social benefits.

Calculate factor scores

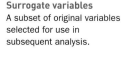

Factor scores
Composite scores estimated for each respondent on the derived factors.

Following interpretation, **factor scores** can be calculated, if necessary. Factor analysis has its own stand-alone value. If the goal of factor analysis is to reduce the original set of variables to a smaller set of composite variables (factors) for use in subsequent multivariate analysis, however, it is useful to compute factor scores for each respondent. A factor is simply a linear combination of the original variables. The factor scores for the ith factor may be estimated as follows:

$$F_i = W_{i1}X_1 + W_{i2}X_2 + W_{i3}X_3 + \ldots + W_{ik}W_k$$

where the symbols are as defined earlier in the chapter.

The weights or factor score coefficients used to combine the standardised variables are obtained from the factor score coefficient matrix. Most computer programs allow you to request factor scores. Only in the case of principal components analysis is it possible to compute exact factor scores. Moreover, in principal components analysis, these scores are uncorrelated. In common factor analysis, estimates of these scores are obtained, and there is no guarantee that the factors will be uncorrelated with each other. Factor scores can be used instead of the original variables in subsequent multivariate analysis. For example, using the factor score coefficient matrix in Table 22.3, one could compute two factor scores for each respondent. The standardised variable values would be multiplied by the corresponding factor score coefficients to obtain the factor scores.

Select surrogate variables

Surrogate variables
A subset of original variables selected for use in subsequent analysis.

Sometimes, instead of computing factor scores, the researcher wishes to select surrogate variables. Selection of substitute or **surrogate variables** involves singling out some of the original variables for use in subsequent analysis. This allows the researcher to conduct subsequent analysis and to interpret the results in terms of original variables rather than factor scores. By examining the factor matrix, one could select for each factor the variable with the highest loading on that factor. That variable could then be used as a surrogate variable for the associated factor. This process works well if one factor loading for a variable is clearly higher than all other factor loadings. The choice is not as easy, however, if two or more variables have similarly high loadings. In such a case, the choice between these variables should be based on theoretical and measurement considerations. For example, theory may suggest that a variable with a slightly lower loading is more important than one with a slightly higher loading. Likewise, if a variable has a slightly lower loading but has been measured more precisely, it should be selected as the

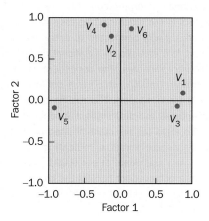

Figure 22.3
Factor loading plot

surrogate variable. In Table 22.3, the variables V_1, V_3 and V_5 all have high loadings on factor 1, and all are fairly close in magnitude, although V_1 has relatively the highest loading and would therefore be a likely candidate. However, if prior knowledge suggests that prevention of tooth decay is a very important benefit, V_5 would be selected as the surrogate for factor 1. Also, the choice of a surrogate for factor 2 is not straightforward. Variables V_2, V_4 and V_6 all have comparable high loadings on this factor. If prior knowledge suggests that attractive teeth are the most important social benefit sought from a toothpaste, the researcher would select V_6.

Determine the model fit

The final step in factor analysis involves the determination of model fit. A basic assumption underlying factor analysis is that the observed correlation between variables can be attributed to common factors. Hence, the correlations between the variables can be deduced or reproduced from the estimated correlations between the variables and the factors. The differences between the observed correlations (as given in the input correlation matrix) and the reproduced correlations (as estimated from the factor matrix) can be examined to determine model fit. These differences are called residuals. If there are many large residuals, the factor model does not provide a good fit to the data and the model should be reconsidered. In Table 22.3, we see that only five residuals are larger than 0.05, indicating an acceptable model fit.

The following example further illustrates principal components factoring in the context of trade promotion.

Example · **Manufacturing promotion components[10]**

The objective of this study was to develop a comprehensive inventory of manufacturer-controlled trade promotion variables and to demonstrate that an association exists between these variables and the retailer's promotion support decision. Retailer or trade support was defined operationally as the trade buyer's attitude towards the promotion.

Factor analysis was performed on the explanatory variables with the primary goal of data reduction. The principal components method, using varimax rotation, reduced the 30 explanatory variables to eight factors having eigenvalues greater than 1.0. For the purpose of interpretation, each factor was composed of variables that loaded 0.40 or higher on that factor. In two instances, where variables loaded 0.40 or above on two factors, each variable was assigned to the factor where it had the highest loading. Only one variable, ease of handling/stocking at retail, did not load at least 0.40 on any factor. In all, the eight factors explained 62% of the total variance. Interpretation of the factor loading matrix was straightforward. Table 1 lists the factors in the order in which they were extracted.

Stepwise discriminant analysis was conducted to determine which, if any, of the eight factors predicted trade support to a statistically significant degree. The factor scores for the eight factors were the explanatory variables. The dependent variable consisted of the retail buyer's overall rating of the deal (rating), which was collapsed into a three-group (low, medium and high) measure of trade support. The results of the discriminant analyses are shown in Table 2. All eight entered the discriminant functions. Goodness-of-fit measures indicated that, as a group, the eight factors discriminated between high, medium and low levels of trade support. Multivariate F ratios, indicating the degree of discrimination between each pair of groups, were significant at $p < 0.001$. Correct classification into high, medium and low categories was achieved for 65% of the cases. The order of entry into discriminant analysis was used to determine the relative importance of factors as trade support influencers, as shown in Table 3.

Table 1 Factors influencing trade promotional support

Factor	Factor interpretation (% variance explained)	Loading	Variables included in the factor
F1	Item importance (16.3%)	0.77	Item is significant enough to warrant promotion
		0.75	Category responds well to promotion
		0.66	Closest trade competitor is likely to promote item
		0.64	Importance of promoted product category
		0.59	Item regular (non-deal) sales volume
		0.57	Deal meshes with trade promotional requirements
			Buyer's estimate of sales increase on the basis of:
F2	Promotion elasticity (9.3%)	0.86	Price reduction and display
		0.82	Display only
		0.80	Price reduction only
		0.70	Price reduction, display and advertising
			Manufacturer's brand support in the form of:
F3	Manufacturer brand support (8.2%)	0.85	Coupons
		0.81	Radio and television advertising
		0.80	Newspaper advertising
		0.75	Point of purchase promotion (e.g. display)
F4	Manufacturer reputation (7.3%)	0.72	Manufacturer's overall reputation
		0.72	Manufacturer's cooperation in meeting trade's promotional needs
		0.64	Manufacturer's cooperation on emergency orders
		0.55	Quality of sales presentation
		0.51	Manufacturer's overall product quality
F5	Promotion wearout (6.4%)	0.93	Product category is overpromoted
		0.93	Item is overpromoted
F6	Sales velocity (5.4%)	−0.81	Brand market share rank*
		0.69	Item regular sales volume*
		0.46	Item regular sales volume
F7	Item profitability (4.5%)	0.79	Item regular gross margin
		0.72	Item regular gross margin*
		0.49	Reasonableness of deal performance requirements
F8	Incentive amount (4.2%)	0.83	Absolute amount of deal allowances
		0.81	Deal allowances as per cent of regular trade cost*
		0.49	Absolute amount of deal allowances*

* Denotes objectives (archival) measure.

Table 2 Discriminant analysis results: analysis of rating ($n = 564$)

Factor		Standardised Discrimination Coefficients	Analysis of Rating
		Function 1	Function 2
F1	Item importance	0.861	−0.253
F2	Promotion elasticity	0.081	0.398
F3	Manufacturer brand support	0.127	−0.036
F4	Manufacturer reputation	0.394	0.014
F5	Promotion wearout	−0.207	0.380
F6	Sales velocity	0.033	−0.665
F7	Item profitability	0.614	0.357
F8	Incentive amount	0.461	0.254
Wilks' λ (for each factor)		All significant at $p < 0.001$	
Multivariate F ratios		All significant at $p < 0.001$	
Percentage of cases correctly classified		65% correct ($t = 14.4$, $p < 0.001$)	

Table 3 Relative importance of trade support influencers (as indicated by order of entry into the discriminant analysis)

Analysis of rating	
Order of entry	Factor name
1	Item importance
2	Item profitability
3	Incentive amount
4	Manufacturer reputation
5	Promotion wearout
6	Sales velocity
7	Promotion elasticity
8	Manufacturer brand support

Applications of common factor analysis

The data of Table 22.1 were analysed using the common factor analysis model. Instead of using unities in the diagonal, the communalities were inserted. The output, shown in Table 22.4, is similar to the output from principal components analysis presented in Table 22.3. Beneath the 'Communalities' heading, below the 'Initial' column, the communalities for the variables are no longer 1.0. Based on the eigenvalue criterion, again two factors are extracted. The variances, after extracting the factors, are different from the initial eigenvalues. The first factor accounts for 42.84% of the variance, whereas the second accounts for 31.13%, in each case a little less than what was observed in principal components analysis.

Table 22.4 Results of common factor analysis

Bartlett test of sphericity
Approximate chi-square = 111.314, *df* = 15, significance = 0.00000
Kaiser–Meyer–Olkin measure of sampling adequacy = 0.660

Communalities

Variable	Initial	Extraction
V_1	0.859	0.928
V_2	0.480	0.562
V_3	0.814	0.836
V_4	0.543	0.600
V_5	0.763	0.789
V_6	0.587	0.723

Initial eigenvalues

Factor	Eigenvalue	Percentage of variance	Cumulative percentage
1	2.731	45.520	45.520
2	2.218	36.969	82.488
3	0.442	7.360	89.848
4	0.341	5.688	95.536
5	0.183	3.044	98.580
6	0.085	1.420	100.000

Extraction sums of squared loadings

Factor	Eigenvalue	Percentage of variance	Cumulative percentage
1	2.570	42.837	42.837
2	1.868	31.126	73.964

Factor matrix

	Factor 1	Factor 2
V_1	**0.949**	**0.168**
V_2	**−0.206**	**0.720**
V_3	**0.914**	**0.038**
V_4	**−0.246**	**0.734**
V_5	**−0.850**	**−0.259**
V_6	−0.101	0.844

Rotation sums of squared loadings

Factor	Eigenvalue	Percentage of variance	Cumulative percentage
1	2.541	42.343	42.343
2	1.897	31.621	73.964

Table 22.4 Continued

Rotated factor matrix

	Factor 1	Factor 2
V_1	0.963	−0.030
V_2	−0.054	0.747
V_3	0.902	−0.150
V_4	−0.090	0.769
V_5	−0.885	−0.079
V_6	0.075	0.847

Factor score coefficient matrix

	Factor 1	Factor 2
V_1	0.628	0.101
V_2	−0.024	0.253
V_3	0.217	−0.169
V_4	−0.023	0.271
V_5	−0.166	−0.059
V_6	0.083	0.500

Reproduced correlation matrix

Variables	V_1	V_2	V_3	V_4	V_5	V_6
V_1	0.928*	0.022	−0.000	0.024	−0.008	−0.042
V_2	−0.075	0.562*	0.006	−0.008	0.031	0.012
V_3	0.873	−0.161	0.836*	−0.051	0.008	0.042
V_4	−0.110	0.580	−0.197	0.600*	−0.025	−0.004
V_5	−0.850	−0.012	0.786	0.019	0.789*	−0.003
V_6	0.046	0.629	−0.060	0.645	−0.133	0.723*

* The lower left triangle contains the reproduced correlation matrix; the diagonal, the communalities; and the upper right triangle, the residuals between the observed correlations and the reproduced correlations.

The values in the unrotated factor pattern matrix of Table 22.4 are a little different from those in Table 22.3, although the pattern of the coefficients is similar. Sometimes, however, the pattern of loadings for common factor analysis is different from that for principal components analysis, with some variables loading on different factors. The rotated factor matrix has the same pattern as that in Table 22.3, leading to a similar interpretation of the factors.

We end with another application of common factor analysis, in the context of consumer perception of rebates.

Example   **'Common' rebate perceptions[11]**

Rebates are effective in obtaining new users, brand switching and repeat purchases among current users. Microsoft deployed a rebate programme as a means to draw new users to its MSN Internet service. Microsoft's intent behind this rebate plan was to acquire new users from rivals such as AOL. Under the rebate plan, Microsoft offered a cash-back option for new users who committed to two years of MSN service. The question faced by marketers at Microsoft was 'What makes rebates effective?'

A study was undertaken to determine the factors underlying consumer perception of rebates. A set of 24 items measuring consumer perceptions of rebates was constructed. Respondents were asked to express their degree of agreement with these items on five-point Likert scales. The data were collected by telephone survey, with a total of 303 usable questionnaires.

The 24 items measuring perceptions of rebates were analysed using common factor analysis. The initial factor solution did not reveal a simple structure of underlying rebate perceptions. Therefore, items that had low loadings were deleted from the scale, and the factor analysis was performed on the remaining items. This second solution yielded three interpretable factors. The factor loadings and the reliability coefficients are presented in the table. The three factors contained four, four and three items, respectively. Factor 1 seemed to capture the consumers' perceptions of the efforts and difficulties associated with rebate redemption (**Efforts**). Factor 2 was defined as a representation of consumers' faith in the rebate system (**Faith**). Factor 3 represented consumers' perceptions of the manufacturers' motives for offering rebates (**Motives**). The loadings of items on their respective factors ranged from 0.527 to 0.744. Significant loadings are in bold.

Therefore, companies such as Microsoft that employ rebates should ensure that the effort and difficulties of consumers in taking advantage of the rebates are minimised. They should also try to build consumers' faith in the rebate system and portray honest motives for offering rebates.

Factor analysis of perceptions of rebates

Scale items[a]	Factor loading		
	Factor 1	Factor 2	Factor 3
Manufacturers make the rebate process too complicated	0.194	**0.671**	−0.127
Postal rebates are not worth the trouble involved	−0.031	**0.612**	0.352
It takes too long to receive the rebate cheque from the manufacturer	0.013	**0.718**	0.051
Manufacturers could do more to make rebates easier to use	0.205	**0.616**	0.173
Manufacturers offer rebates because consumers want them[b]	**0.660**	0.172	0.101
Today's manufacturers take real interest in consumer welfare[b]	**0.569**	0.203	0.334
Consumer benefit is usually the primary consideration in rebate offers[b]	**0.660**	0.002	0.318
In general, manufacturers are sincere in their rebate offers to consumers[b]	**0.716**	0.047	−0.033
Manufacturers offer rebates to get consumers to buy something they do not really need	0.099	0.156	**0.744**
Manufacturers use rebate offers to induce consumers to buy slow-moving items	0.090	0.027	**0.702**
Rebate offers require you to buy more of a product than you need	0.230	0.066	0.527
Eigenvalues	2.030	1.344	1.062

[a] The response categories for all items were strongly agree (I), agree (2), neither agree nor disagree (3), disagree (4), strongly disagree (5) and don't know (6). 'Don't know' responses were excluded from data analysis.
[b] The scores of these items were reversed.

In this example, when the initial factor solution was not interpretable, items which had low loadings were deleted and the factor analysis was performed on the remaining items. If the number of variables is large (greater than 15), principal components analysis and common factor analysis result in similar solutions. Principal components analysis is less prone to misinterpretation, however, and is recommended for the non-expert user.

Internet and computer applications

SPSS

The program FACTOR may be used for principal components analysis as well as for common factor analysis. Some other methods of factor analysis are also available and factor scores are available.

SAS

The program PRINCOMP performs principal components analysis and calculates principal components scores. To perform common factor analysis, the program FACTOR can be used. The FACTOR program also performs principal components analysis.

SNAP

Multiple factor analyses can be run within any survey, and each will be stored separately and listed within the multivariate statistics window. The factors that are produced are effectively DERIVED QUANTITY variables and can be used within tables and charts in the same way as other QUANTITY variables.

Minitab

Factor analysis can be accessed using MULTIVARIATE>FACTOR ANALYSIS. Principal components or maximum likelihood can be used to determine the initial factor extraction. If maximum likelihood is used, specify the number of factors to extract. If a number is not specified with a principal component extraction, the program will set it equal to a number of variables in the dataset.

Summary

Factor analysis is a class of procedures used for reducing and summarising data. Each variable is expressed as a linear combination of the underlying factors. Likewise, the factors themselves can be expressed as linear combinations of the observed variables. The factors are extracted in such a way that the first factor accounts for the highest variance in the data, the second the next highest, and so on. Additionally, it is possible to extract the factors so that the factors are uncorrelated, as in principal components analysis.

In formulating the factor analysis problem, the variables to be included in the analysis should be specified based on past research, theory and the judgement of the researcher. These variables should be measured on an interval or ratio scale. Factor analysis is based on a matrix of correlation between the variables. The appropriateness of the correlation matrix for factor analysis can be statistically tested.

The two basic approaches to factor analysis are principal components analysis and common factor analysis. In principal components analysis, the total variance in the data is considered. Principal components analysis is recommended when the researcher's primary concern is to determine the minimum number of factors that will account for maximum variance in the data for use in subsequent multivariate analysis. In common factor analysis, the factors are estimated based only on the common variance. This method is appropriate when the primary concern is to identify the underlying dimensions and when the common variance is of interest. This method is also known as principal axis factoring.

The number of factors that should be extracted can be determined a priori or based on eigenvalues, scree plots, percentage of variance, split-half reliability or significance tests. Although the initial or unrotated factor matrix indicates the relationships between the factors and individual variables, it seldom results in factors that can be interpreted, because the factors are correlated with many variables. Therefore, rotation is used to transform the factor matrix into a simpler one that is easier to interpret. The most commonly used method of rotation is the varimax procedure, which results in orthogonal factors. If the factors are highly correlated in the population, oblique rotation can be used. The rotated factor matrix forms the basis for interpreting the factors.

Factor scores can be computed for each respondent. Alternatively, surrogate variables may be selected by examining the factor matrix and selecting a variable with the highest or near highest loading for each factor. The differences between the observed correlations and the reproduced correlations, as estimated from the factor matrix, can be examined to determine model fit.

Questions

1. How is factor analysis different from multiple regression and discriminant analysis?

2. What are the major uses of factor analysis?

3. Describe the factor analysis model.

4. What hypothesis is examined by Bartlett's test of sphericity? For what purpose is this test used?

5. What is meant by the term 'communality of a variable'?

6. Briefly define the following: eigenvalue, factor loadings, factor matrix and factor scores.

7. For what purpose is the Kaiser–Meyer–Olkin measure of sampling adequacy used?

8. What is the major difference between principal components analysis and common factor analysis?

9. Explain how eigenvalues are used to determine the number of factors.

10. What is a scree plot? For what purpose is it used?

11. Why is it useful to rotate the factors? Which is the most common method of rotation?

12. What guidelines are available for interpreting the factors?

13. When is it useful to calculate factor scores?

14. What are surrogate variables? How are they determined?

15. How is the fit of the factor analysis model examined?

Exercises

1 Complete the following portion of an output from principal components analysis:

Variable	Communality	Factor	Eigenvalue	% of variance
V_1	1.0	1	3.25	
V_2	1.0	2	1.78	
V_3	1.0	3	1.23	
V_4	1.0	4	0.78	
V_5	1.0	5	0.35	
V_6	1.0	6	0.30	
V_7	1.0	7	0.19	
V_8	1.0	8	0.12	

   a Draw a scree plot based on these data.
   b How many factors should be extracted? Explain your reasoning.

2 In a study of the relationship between household behaviour and shopping behaviour, data on the following lifestyle statements were obtained on a seven-point scale (1 = disagree, 7 = agree):

V_1 I would rather spend a quiet evening at home than go out to a party.
V_2 I always check prices, even on small items.
V_3 Magazines are more interesting than movies.
V_4 I would not buy products advertised on billboards.
V_5 I am a homebody.
V_6 I save and cash coupons.
V_7 Companies waste a lot of money advertising.

The data obtained from a pretest sample of 25 respondents are given below:

No.	V_1	V_2	V_3	V_4	V_5	V_6	V_7
1	6	2	7	6	5	3	5
2	5	7	5	6	6	6	4
3	5	3	4	5	6	6	7
4	3	2	2	5	1	3	2
5	4	2	3	2	2	1	3
6	2	6	2	4	3	7	5
7	1	3	3	6	2	5	7
8	3	5	1	4	2	5	6
9	7	3	6	3	5	2	4
10	6	3	3	4	4	6	5
11	6	6	2	6	4	4	7
12	3	2	2	7	6	1	6
13	5	7	6	2	2	6	1
14	6	3	5	5	7	2	3
15	3	2	4	3	2	6	5
16	2	7	5	1	4	5	2
17	3	2	2	7	2	4	6
18	6	4	5	4	7	3	3
19	7	2	6	2	5	2	1
20	5	6	6	3	4	5	3
21	2	3	3	2	1	2	6
22	3	4	2	1	4	3	6
23	2	6	3	2	1	5	3
24	6	5	7	4	5	7	2
25	7	6	5	4	6	5	3

a Analyse these data using principal components analysis, using the varimax rotation procedure.
b Interpret the factors extracted.
c Calculate factor scores for each respondent.
d If surrogate variables were to be selected, which ones would you select?
e Examine the model fit.
f Analyse the data using common factor analysis, and answer parts **b** to **e**.

3 Analyse the Benetton data (taken from Exercise 4, Chapter 18). Consider only the following variables: awareness, attitude, preference, intention and loyalty towards Benetton.

a Analyse these data using principal components analysis, using the varimax rotation procedure.
b Interpret the factors extracted.
c Calculate factor scores for each respondent.
d If surrogate variables were to be selected, which ones would you select?
e Examine the model fit.
f Analyse the data using common factor analysis, and answer parts **b** to **e**.

4 You are a marketing research analyst for a manufacturer of fashion clothing targeted at teenage boys. You have been asked to develop a set of 10 statements for measuring psychographic characteristics and lifestyles that you feel would relate to their fashion personas. The respondents would be asked to indicate their degree of agreement with the statements using a seven-point scale (1 = completely disagree, 7 = completely agree). Question 40 students on campus using these scale items. Factor analyse the data to identify the underlying psychographic factors.

5 In a small group identify the uses of factor analysis in each of the following major decision areas in marketing:

a Market segmentation
b Product decisions
c Promotions decisions
d Pricing decisions
e Distribution decisions
f Service delivery decisions.

Appendix: Fundamental equations of factor analysis[12]

In the factor analysis model, hypothetical components are derived that account for the linear relationship between observed variables. The factor analysis model requires that the relationships between observed variables be linear and that the variables have non-zero correlations between them. The derived hypothetical components have the following properties:

1 They form a linearly independent set of variables. No hypothetical component is derivable from the other hypothetical components as a linear combination of them.

2 The hypothetical components' variables can be divided into two basic kinds of components: common factors and unique factors. These two components can be distinguished in terms of the patterns of weights in the linear equations that derive the observed variables from the hypothetical components' variables. A common factor has more than one variable with a non-zero weight or factor loading associated with the factor. A unique factor has only one variable with a non-zero weight associated with the factor. Hence, only one variable depends on a unique factor.

3 Common factors are always assumed to be uncorrelated with the unique factors. Unique factors are also usually assumed to be mutually uncorrelated, but common factors may or may not be correlated with each other.

4 Generally, it is assumed that there are fewer common factors than observed variables. The number of unique factors is usually assumed to be equal to the number of observed variables, however.

The following notations are used:

$$X = \text{an } n \times 1 \text{ random vector of observed random variables } X_1, X_2, X_3, \ldots X_n$$

It is assumed that

$$E(X) = 0$$
$$E(XX') = R_{xx}, \text{ a correlation matrix with unities in the main diagonal}$$
$$F = \text{an } m \times 1 \text{ vector of } m \text{ common factors } F_1, F_2, \ldots, F_m$$

It is also assumed that

$$E(F) = 0$$
$$E(FF') = R_{ff}, \text{ a correlation matrix}$$
$$U = \text{an } n \times 1 \text{ random vector of the } n \text{ unique factor variables, } U_1, U_2, \ldots, U_n$$

and

$$E(U) = \mathbf{0}$$
$$E(UU') = I$$

The unique factors are normalised to have unit variances and are mutually uncorrelated:

$$A = \text{an } n \times m \text{ matrix of coefficients called the factor pattern mix}$$
$$V = \text{an } n \times n \text{ diagonal matrix of coeffieicients for the unique factors}$$

The observed variables, which are the coordinates of X, are weighted combinations of the common factors and the unique factors. The fundamental equation of factor analysis can then be written as

$$X = AF + VU$$

The correlations between variables in terms of the factors may be derived as follows:

$$\begin{aligned}
R_{xx} &= E(XX') \\
&= E[(AF + VU)(AF + VU'] \\
&= E[(AF + VU)(F'A' + U'V')] \\
&= E(AFF'A' + AFU'V'] + VUF'A' + VUU'V') \\
&= AR_{ff}A' + AR_{fu}V' + VR_{uf}A' + V^2
\end{aligned}$$

Given that the common factors are uncorrelated with the unique factors, we have

$$R_{fu} = R'_{uf} = 0$$

Hence,

$$R_{xx} = AR_{ff}A' + V^2$$

Suppose that we subtract the matrix of unique factor variance, V^2, from both sides. We then obtain

$$R_{xx} - V^2 = AR_{ff}A'$$

R_{xx} is dependent only on the common factor variables, and the correlations among the variables are related only to the common factors. Let $R_c = R_{xx} - V^2$ be the reduced correlation matrix.

We have already defined the factor pattern matrix A. The coefficients of the factor pattern matrix are weights assigned to the common factors when the observed variables are expressed as linear combinations of the common and unique factors. We now define the factor structure matrix. The coefficients of the factor structure matrix are the covariances between the observed variables and the factors. The factor structure matrix is helpful in the interpretation of factors as it shows which variables are similar to a common factor variable. The factor structure matrix, A_s, is defined as

$$A_s = E(XF')$$
$$= E[(AF + VU)F']$$
$$= AR_{ff} + VR_{uf}$$
$$= AR_{ff}$$

Thus, the factor structure matrix is equivalent to the factor pattern matrix A multiplied by the matrix of covariances among the factors R_{ff}. Substituting A_s for AR_{ff}, the reduced correlation matrix becomes the product of the factor structure and the factor pattern matrix:

$$R_c = AR_{ff}A'$$

Notes

1 Alt, M., *Exploring Hyperspace* (New York: McGraw-Hill, 1990), 74.

2 For a detailed discussion of factor analysis, see Tacq, J., *Multivariate Analysis Techniques in Social Science Research* (Thousand Oaks, CA: Sage, 1996); Dunteman, G.H., *Principal Components Analysis* (Newbury Park, CA: Sage, 1989). For applications, see Aaker, J.L., 'Dimensions of brand personality', *Journal of Marketing Research* 34 (August 1997), 347–356; Birks, D.F. and Birts, A.N., 'Service quality in domestic cash management banks', in Birks, D.F. (ed.), *Global Cash Management in Europe* (Basingstoke: Macmillan, 1998), 175–205. See also Mels, G., Boshof, C. and Nel, D., 'The dimensions of service quality: the original European perspective revisited', *Service Industries Journal* 17 (January 1997), 173–189.

3 See, for example, Bo Edvardsson, S., Larsson, G. and Setterlind, S., 'Internal service quality and the psychosocial work environment: an empirical analysis of conceptual interrelatedness', *Service Industries Journal* 17 (2) (April 1997), 252–263; Taylor, S., 'Waiting for service: the relationship between delays and evaluations of service', *Journal of Marketing* 58 (April 1994), 56–69.

4 See Ding, A.A., 'Prediction intervals, factor analysis models and high-dimensional empirical linear prediction,' *Journal of the American Statistical Association*, 94 (446) (June 1999), 446–455; Gaur, S., 'Adelman and Morris factor analysis of developing countries', *Journal of Policy Modeling* 19 (4) (August 1997), 407–415; Lastovicka, J.L. and Thamodaran, K., 'Common factor score estimates in multiple regression problems', *Journal of Marketing Research* 28 (February 1991), 105–112; Dillon, W.R. and Goldstein, M., *Multivariate Analysis: Methods and Applications* (New York: Wiley, 1984), 23–99.

5 For applications of factor analysis, see Johns, N., Gyimothy, S., 'Market segmentation and the prediction of tourist behaviour: the case of Bornholm, Denmark', *Journal of Travel Research* 40 (3) (February 2002), 316–327.

6 Bartholomew, D.J. and Knott, M., *Latent variable models and factor analysis* (London Edward Arnold, 1999); Hair J.E. Jr,

Anderson, R.E., Tatham, R.L. and Black, W.C., *Multivariate Data Analysis with Readings*, 5th edn (Englewood Cliffs, NJ: Prentice Hall, 1999), 364–419; Basilevsky, A., *Statistical Factor Analysis and Related Methods: Theory and Applications* (New York: Wiley, 1994).

7 Factor analysis is influenced by the relative size of the correlations rather than the absolute size.

8 See Kamakura, W.A. and Wedel, M, 'Factor analysis and missing data', *Journal of Marketing Research* 37 (4) (November 2000), 49–498; Roberts, J.A. and Beacon, D.R., 'Exploring the subtle relationships between environmental concern and ecologically conscious behavior', *Journal of Business Research* 40 (1) (September 1997), 79–89; Chatterjee, S., Jamieson, L. and Wiseman, F., 'Identifying most influential observations in factor analysis', *Marketing Science* (Spring 1991), 145–160; Acito, F. and Anderson, R.D., 'A Monte Carlo comparison of factor analytic methods', *Journal of Marketing Research* 17 (May 1980), 228–236.

9 Other methods of orthogonal rotation are also available. The quartimax method minimises the number of factors needed to explain a variable. The equimax method is a combination of varimax and quartimax.

10 Silva-Risso, J.M., Bucklin, R.E. and Morrison, D.G., 'A decision support system for planning manufacturers' sales promotion calendars', *Marketing Science* 18 (3) (1999), 274; Curhan, R.C. and Kopp, R.J., 'Obtaining retailer support for trade deals: key success factors', *Journal of Advertising Research* (December 1987–January 1988), 51–60.

11 Anon., 'Microsoft to discontinue MSN rebate promotion', *The Los Angeles Times* (3 February, 2001) C1; Lichtenstein, D.R., Ridgway, N.M. and Netemeyer, R.G., 'Price perceptions and consumer shopping behaviour: a field study', *Journal of Marketing* Research 30 (2) (May 1993), 234–45; Tat, P., Cunningham, W.A. III and Babakus, E., 'Consumer perceptions of rebates', *Journal of Advertising Research* (August–September 1988), 45–50.

12 The material in this appendix has been drawn from Stanley A. Muliak, *The Foundations of Factor Analysis* (New York: McGraw-Hill, 1972).

Source: © Getty Images

23

Cluster analysis

> *Cluster analysis aims to identify and classify similar entities, based upon the characteristics they possess. It helps the researcher to understand patterns of similarity and difference that reveal naturally occurring groups.*

Objectives

After reading this chapter, you should be able to:

1 describe the basic concept and scope of cluster analysis and its importance in marketing research;

2 discuss the statistics associated with cluster analysis;

3 explain the procedure for conducting cluster analysis, including formulating the problem, selecting a distance measure, selecting a clustering procedure, deciding on the number of clusters, interpreting clusters and profiling clusters;

4 describe the purpose and methods for evaluating the quality of clustering results and assessing reliability and validity;

5 discuss the applications of non-hierarchical clustering and clustering of variables.

STAGE 1
Problem definition

STAGE 2
Research approach developed

STAGE 3
Research design developed

STAGE 4
Fieldwork or data collection

STAGE 5
Data preparation and analysis

STAGE 6
Report preparation and presentation

Overview

Like factor analysis (Chapter 22), cluster analysis examines an entire set of interdependent relationships. Cluster analysis makes no distinction between dependent and independent variables. Rather, interdependent relationships between the whole set of variables are examined. The primary objective of cluster analysis is to classify objects into relatively homogeneous groups based on the set of variables considered. Objects in a group are relatively similar in terms of these variables and different from objects in other groups. When used in this manner, cluster analysis is the obverse of factor analysis in that it reduces the number of objects, not the number of variables, by grouping them into a much smaller number of clusters.

This chapter describes the basic concept of cluster analysis. The steps involved in conducting cluster analysis are discussed and illustrated in the context of hierarchical clustering by using a popular computer program. Then an application of non-hierarchical clustering is presented, followed by a discussion of clustering of variables. We begin with an example that illustrates the use of clustering to aid the process of defining target markets.

Example Ice cream 'hot spots'[1]

In order to achieve an expanded customer base, Häagen-Dazs (**www.haagen-dazs.com**) identified potential consumer segments that could generate additional sales. It used geodemographic techniques (as discussed in Chapter 5), which are based upon clustering consumers, using geographic, demographic and lifestyle data. Additional primary data were collected to develop an understanding of the demographic, lifestyle and behavioural characteristics of Häagen-Dazs Café users, which included frequency of purchase, time of day to visit café, day of the week and a range of other product variables. The postcodes or zip codes of respondents were also obtained. With a postcode or zip code, respondents can be assigned to one of the arrays of established geodemographic classifications. Häagen-Dazs compared its profile of customers with the profile of geodemographic classifications to develop a clearer picture of the types of consumer it was attracting. From this it decided which profiles of consumer or target markets it believed to hold the most potential for additional sales.

Basic concept

Cluster analysis is a class of techniques used to classify objects or cases into relatively homogeneous groups called clusters. Objects in each cluster tend to be similar to each other and dissimilar to objects in the other clusters. Cluster analysis is also called classification analysis or numerical taxonomy.[2] We are concerned with clustering procedures that assign each object to one and only one cluster.[3] Figure 23.1 shows an ideal clustering situation in which the clusters are distinctly separated on two variables: quality consciousness (variable 1) and price sensitivity (variable 2). Note that each consumer falls into one cluster and there are no overlapping areas. Figure 23.2, on the other hand, presents a clustering situation more likely to be encountered in practice. In Figure 23.2, the boundaries for some of the clusters are not clear cut, and the classification of some consumers is not obvious, because many of them could be grouped into one cluster or another.

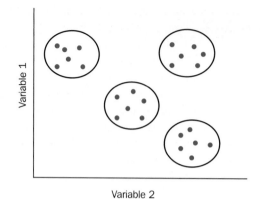

Figure 23.1
An ideal clustering solution

Figure 23.2
A practical clustering solution

Both cluster analysis and discriminant analysis are concerned with classification. Discriminant analysis, however, requires prior knowledge of the cluster or group membership for each object or case included, to develop the classification rule. In contrast, in cluster analysis there is no a priori information about the group or cluster membership for any of the objects. Groups or clusters are suggested by the data, not defined a priori.[4] Cluster analysis has been used in marketing for a variety of purposes, including the following:[5]

- *Segmenting the market.* For example, consumers may be clustered on the basis of benefits sought from the purchase of a product. Each cluster would consist of consumers who are relatively homogeneous in terms of the benefits they seek.[6] This approach is called *benefit segmentation* as illustrated in the following example.

Example   **Thailand escapists[7]**

A study assessed examined 510 tourists' image of Thailand as an international travel destination. It examined the impact of the destination's image on the likelihood of the traveller returning to Thailand. The sample was made up of international travellers who visited Thailand and were departing from Bangkok International Airport. The study involved the use of a three-stage sampling approach that included proportionate stratified, cluster and systematic random sampling. Cluster sampling was used to randomly select departure flights from Bangkok International Airport. The results of the study revealed that Thailand has a negative image of environmental and social problems. At the same time, it has a positive image as a safe travel destination, associated with the benefits of: scenic natural beauty, culture, cuisine and hotels, and good shopping. Overall, most tourists, but especially a group classified as 'escapists', indicated that they would return to Thailand for a vacation. Thus Thailand should make a special effort to reach the 'escapists' segment, as the country would appeal the most to these tourists.

- *Understanding buyer behaviours.* Cluster analysis can be used to identify homogeneous groups of buyers. Then the buying behaviour of each group may be examined separately, as can happen for example with different types of car buyers. Cluster analysis has been used to identify the kinds of strategies car buyers use to obtain information to support their buying decisions.
- *Identifying new product opportunities.* By clustering brands and products, competitive sets within the market can be determined. Brands in the same cluster compete more fiercely with each other than with brands in other clusters. A firm can examine its current offerings compared with those of its competitors to identify potential new product opportunities.
- *Selecting test markets.* By grouping cities into homogeneous clusters, it is possible to select comparable cities to test various marketing strategies.
- *Reducing data.* Cluster analysis can be used as a general data reduction tool to develop clusters or subgroups of data that are more manageable than individual observations. Subsequent multivariate analysis is conducted on the clusters rather than on the individual observations. For example, to describe differences in consumers' product usage behaviour, the consumers may first be clustered into groups. The differences among the groups may then be examined using multiple discriminant analysis.

Statistics associated with cluster analysis

Before discussing the statistics associated with cluster analysis, it should be mentioned that most clustering methods are relatively simple procedures that are not supported by an extensive body of statistical reasoning. Rather, most clustering methods are heuristics, which are based on algorithms. Thus, cluster analysis contrasts sharply with analysis of variance, regression, discriminant analysis and factor analysis, which are based upon an extensive body of statistical reasoning. Although many clustering methods have important statistical properties, the fundamental simplicity of these methods needs to be recognised.[8] The following statistics and concepts are associated with cluster analysis.

Agglomeration schedule. An agglomeration schedule gives information on the objects or cases being combined at each stage of a hierarchical clustering process.

Cluster centroid. The cluster centroid is the mean values of the variables for all the cases or objects in a particular cluster.

Cluster centres. The cluster centres are the initial starting points in non-hierarchical clustering. Clusters are built around these centres or seeds.

Cluster membership. Cluster membership indicates the cluster to which each object or case belongs.

Dendrogram. A dendrogram, or tree graph, is a graphical device for displaying clustering results. Vertical lines represent clusters that are joined together. The position of the line on the scale indicates the distances at which clusters were joined. The dendrogram is read from left to right. Figure 23.8 later in this chapter is a dendrogram.

Distances between cluster centres. These distances indicate how separated the individual pairs of clusters are. Clusters that are widely separated are distinct and therefore desirable.

Icicle diagram. An icicle diagram is a graphical display of clustering results, so called because it resembles a row of icicles hanging from the eaves of a house. The columns correspond to the objects being clustered, and the rows correspond to the number of clusters. An icicle diagram is read from bottom to top. Figure 23.7 later in this chapter is an icicle diagram.

Similarity/distance coefficient matrix. A similarity/distance coefficient matrix is a lower triangular matrix containing pairwise distances between objects or cases.

Conducting cluster analysis

The steps involved in conducting cluster analysis are listed in Figure 23.3. The first step is to formulate the clustering problem by defining the variables on which the clustering will be based. Then, an appropriate distance measure must be selected. The distance measure determines how similar or dissimilar the objects being clustered are. Several clustering procedures have been developed, and the researcher should select one that is appropriate for the problem at hand. Deciding on the number of clusters requires judgement on the part of the researcher. The derived clusters should be interpreted in terms of the variables used to cluster them and profiled in terms of additional salient variables. Finally, the researcher must assess the validity of the clustering process.

Formulate the problem

Perhaps the most important part of formulating the clustering problem is selecting the variables on which the clustering is based. Inclusion of even one or two irrelevant variables may distort an otherwise useful clustering solution. Basically, the set of variables selected should describe the similarity between objects in terms that are relevant to the marketing research problem. The variables should be selected based on past research, theory or a consideration of the hypotheses being developed or tested. If cluster analysis is used as an exploratory approach, the researcher naturally exercises his or her judgement and intuition.

To illustrate, we consider a clustering of consumers based on attitudes towards shopping. Based on past research, six attitudinal variables were identified as being the most relevant to the marketing research problem. Consumers were asked to express their degree of agreement with the following statements on a seven-point scale (1 = disagree, 7 = agree):

V_1 Shopping is fun.
V_2 Shopping is bad for your budget.
V_3 I combine shopping with eating out.
V_4 I try to get the best buys while shopping.
V_5 I don't care about shopping.
V_6 You can save a lot of money by comparing prices.

Data obtained from a pretest sample of 20 respondents are shown in Table 23.1. Note that, in practice, clustering is done on much larger samples of 100 or more. A small sample size has been used to illustrate the clustering process.

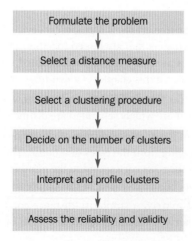

Figure 23.3
Conducting cluster analysis

Table 23.1 Attitudinal data for clustering

Case number	V_1	V_2	V_3	V_4	V_5	V_6
1	6	4	7	3	2	3
2	2	3	1	4	5	4
3	7	2	6	4	1	3
4	4	6	4	5	3	6
5	1	3	2	2	6	4
6	6	4	6	3	3	4
7	5	3	6	3	3	4
8	7	3	7	4	1	4
9	2	4	3	3	6	3
10	3	5	3	6	4	6
11	1	3	2	3	5	3
12	5	4	5	4	2	4
13	2	2	1	5	4	4
14	4	6	4	6	4	7
15	6	5	4	2	1	4
16	3	5	4	6	4	7
17	4	4	7	2	2	5
18	3	7	2	6	4	3
19	4	6	3	7	2	7
20	2	3	2	4	7	2

Select a distance measure

Because the objective of clustering is to group similar objects together, some measure is needed to assess how similar or different the objects are. The most common approach is to measure similarity in terms of distance between pairs of objects. Objects with smaller distances between them are more similar to each other than are those at larger distances. There are several ways to compute the distance between two objects.[9]

Euclidean distance
The square root of the sum of the squared differences in values for each variable.

The most commonly used measure of similarity is the Euclidean distance or its square.[10] The Euclidean distance is the square root of the sum of the squared differences in values for each variable. Other distance measures are also available. The city-block or Manhattan distance between two objects is the sum of the absolute differences in values for each variable. The Chebychev distance between two objects is the maximum absolute difference in values for any variable. For our example, we use the squared Euclidean distance.

If the variables are measured in vastly different units, the clustering solution will be influenced by the units of measurement. In a supermarket shopping study, attitudinal variables may be measured on a nine-point Likert-type scale; patronage, in terms of frequency of visits per month and the amount spent; and brand loyalty, in terms of percentage of grocery shopping expenditure allocated to the favourite supermarket. In these cases, before clustering respondents, we must standardise the data by rescaling each variable to have a mean of 0 and a standard deviation of 1. Although standardisation can remove the influence of the unit of measurement, it can also reduce the differences between groups on variables that may best discriminate groups or clusters. It is also desirable to eliminate outliers (cases with atypical values).[11]

Use of different distance measures may lead to different clustering results. Hence, it is advisable to use different measures and to compare the results. Having selected a distance or similarity measure, we can next select a clustering procedure.

Select a clustering procedure

Figure 23.4 is a classification of clustering procedures.

Clustering procedures can be hierarchical or non-hierarchical. **Hierarchical clustering** is characterised by the development of a hierarchy or treelike structure. Hierarchical methods can be agglomerative or divisive. **Agglomerative clustering** starts with each object in a separate cluster. Clusters are formed by grouping objects into bigger and bigger clusters. This process is continued until all objects are members of a single cluster. **Divisive clustering** starts with all the objects grouped in a single cluster. Clusters are divided or split until each object is in a separate cluster.

Agglomerative methods are commonly used in marketing research. They consist of linkage methods, error sums of squares or variance methods, and centroid methods. **Linkage methods** include single linkage, complete linkage and average linkage. The **single linkage** method is based on minimum distance or the nearest neighbour rule. The first two objects clustered are those that have the smallest distance between them. The next shortest distance is identified, and either the third object is clustered with the first two or a new two-object cluster is formed. At every stage, the distance between two clusters is the distance between their two closest points (see Figure 23.5). Two clusters are merged at any stage by the single shortest link between them. This process is continued until all objects are in one cluster. The single linkage method does not work well when the clusters are poorly defined. The **complete linkage** method is similar to single linkage, except that it is based on the maximum distance or the farthest neighbour approach. In complete linkage, the distance between two clusters is calculated as the distance between their two farthest points (see Figure 23.5). The **average linkage** method works similarly. In this method, however, the distance between two clusters is defined as the average of the distances

Hierarchical clustering
A clustering procedure characterised by the development of a hierarchy or treelike structure.

Agglomerative clustering
A hierarchical clustering procedure where each object starts out in a separate cluster. Clusters are formed by grouping objects into bigger and bigger clusters.

Divisive clustering
A hierarchical clustering procedure where all objects start out in one giant cluster. Clusters are formed by dividing this cluster into smaller and smaller clusters.

Linkage methods
Agglomerative methods of hierarchical clustering that cluster objects based on a computation of the distance between them.

Single linkage
A linkage method based on minimum distance or the nearest neighbour rule.

Complete linkage
A linkage method that is based on maximum distance or the farthest neighbour approach.

Average linkage
A linkage method based on the average distance between all pairs of objects, where one member of the pair is from each of the clusters.

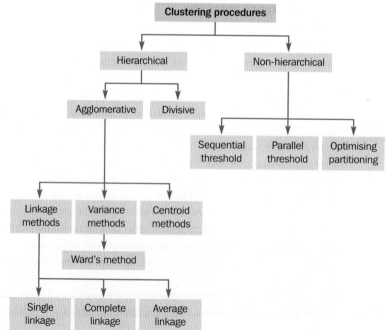

Figure 23.4
A classification of clustering procedures

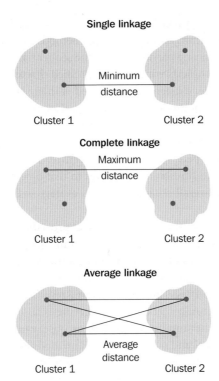

Single linkage

Minimum distance

Cluster 1   Cluster 2

Complete linkage

Maximum distance

Cluster 1   Cluster 2

Average linkage

Average distance

Cluster 1   Cluster 2

Figure 23.5
Linkage methods of clustering

between all pairs of objects, where one member of the pair is from each of the clusters (Figure 23.5). As can be seen, the average linkage method uses information on all pairs of distances, not merely the minimum or maximum distances. For this reason, it is usually preferred to the single and complete linkage methods.

The **variance methods** attempt to generate clusters to minimise the within-cluster variance. A commonly used variance method is **Ward's procedure**. For each cluster, the means for all the variables are computed. Then, for each object, the squared Euclidean distance to the cluster means is calculated (Figure 23.6), and these distances are summed for all the objects. At each stage, the two clusters with the smallest increase in the overall sum of squares within cluster distances are combined. In the **centroid method**, the distance between two clusters is the distance between their centroids (means for all the variables), as shown in Figure 23.6. Every time objects are grouped, a new centroid is computed. Of the hierarchical methods, the average linkage method and Ward's procedure have been shown to perform better than the other procedures.[12]

Variance method
An agglomerative method of hierarchical clustering in which clusters are generated to minimise the within-cluster variance.

Ward's procedure
A variance method in which the squared Euclidean distance to the cluster means is minimised.

Centroid method
A variance method of hierarchical clustering in which the distance between two clusters is the distance between their centroids (means for all the variables).

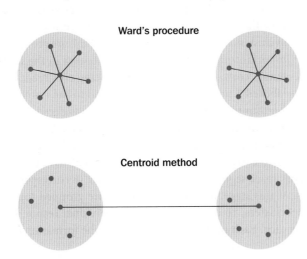

Ward's procedure

Centroid method

Figure 23.6
Other agglomerative clustering methods

Non-hierarchical clustering
A procedure that first assigns or determines a cluster centre and then groups all objects within a pre-specified threshold value from the centre.

Parallel threshold method
A non-hierarchical clustering method that specifies several cluster centres at once. All objects that are within a pre-specified threshold value from the centre are grouped together.

Optimising partitioning method
A non-hierarchical clustering method that allows for later reassignment of objects to clusters to optimise an overall criterion.

The second type of clustering procedures, the **non-hierarchical clustering** methods, are frequently referred to as k-means clustering. These methods include sequential threshold, parallel threshold and optimising partitioning. In the sequential threshold method, a cluster centre is selected and all objects within a pre-specified threshold value from the centre are grouped together. A new cluster centre or seed is then selected, and the process is repeated for the unclustered points. Once an object is clustered with a seed, it is no longer considered for clustering with subsequent seeds. The **parallel threshold method** operates similarly except that several cluster centres are selected simultaneously and objects within the threshold level are grouped with the nearest centre. The **optimising partitioning method** differs from the two threshold procedures in that objects can later be reassigned to clusters to optimise an overall criterion, such as average within-cluster distance for a given number of clusters.

Two major disadvantages of the non-hierarchical procedures are that the number of clusters must be pre-specified and that the selection of cluster centres is arbitrary. Furthermore, the clustering results may depend on how the centres are selected. Many non-hierarchical programs select the first k cases (k = number of clusters) without missing values as initial cluster centres. Thus, the clustering results may depend on the order of observations in the data. Yet non-hierarchical clustering is faster than hierarchical methods and has merit when the number of objects or observations is large. It has been suggested that the hierarchical and non-hierarchical methods be used in tandem. First, an initial clustering solution is obtained using a hierarchical procedure, such as average linkage or Ward's. The number of clusters and cluster centroids so obtained are used as inputs to the optimising partitioning method.[13]

The choice of a clustering method and the choice of a distance measure are interrelated. For example, squared Euclidean distances should be used with Ward's and the centroid methods. Several non-hierarchical procedures also use squared Euclidean distances.

We will use Ward's procedure to illustrate hierarchical clustering. The output obtained by clustering the data of Table 23.1 is given in Table 23.2. Useful information is contained in the agglomeration schedule, which shows the number of cases or clusters being combined at each stage. The first line represents stage 1, with 19 clusters. Respondents 14 and 16 are combined at this stage, as shown in the columns labelled 'Clusters combined'. The squared Euclidean distance between these two respondents is given under the column labelled 'Coefficients'. The column entitled 'Stage cluster first appears' indicates the stage at which a cluster is first formed. To illustrate, an entry of 1 at stage 6 indicates that respondent 14 was first grouped at stage 1. The last column, 'Next stage', indicates the stage at which another case (respondent) or cluster is combined with this one. Because the number in the first line of the last column is 6, we see that, at stage 6, respondent 10 is combined with 14 and 16 to form a single cluster. Similarly, the second line represents stage 2 with 18 clusters. In stage 2, respondents 6 and 7 are grouped together.

Another important part of the output is contained in the icicle plot given in Figure 23.7. The columns correspond to the objects being clustered; in this case, they are the respondents labelled 1 to 20. The rows correspond to the number of clusters. This figure is read from bottom to top. At first, all cases are considered as individual clusters. Since there are 20 respondents, there are 20 initial clusters. At the first step, the two closest objects are combined, resulting in 19 clusters. The last line of Figure 23.7 shows these 19 clusters. The two cases, respondents 14 and 16, that have been combined at this stage have no blank space separating them. Row number 18 corresponds to the next stage, with 18 clusters. At this stage, respondents 6 and 7 are grouped together. Thus, at this stage there are 18 clusters; 16 of them consist of individual respondents, and 2 contain two respondents each. Each subsequent step leads to the formation of a new cluster in one of

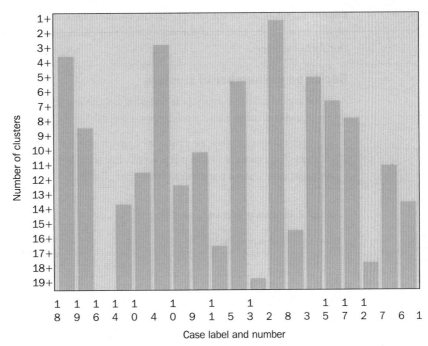

Figure 23.7
Vertical icicle plot using Ward's procedure

three ways: (1) two individual cases are grouped together, (2) a case is joined to an already existing cluster, or (3) two clusters are grouped together.

Another graphic device that is useful in displaying clustering results is the dendrogram (see Figure 23.8). The dendrogram is read from left to right. Vertical lines represent clusters that are joined together. The position of the line on the scale indicates the distances at which clusters were joined. Because many distances in the early stages are of similar magnitude, it is difficult to tell the sequence in which some of the early clusters are formed. It is clear, however, that in the last two stages, the distances at which the clusters are being combined are large. This information is useful in deciding on the number of clusters.

It is also possible to obtain information on cluster membership of cases if the number of clusters is specified. Although this information can be discerned from the icicle plot, a tabular display is helpful. Table 23.2 contains the cluster membership for the cases,

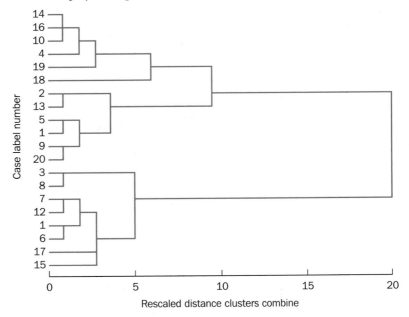

Figure 23.8
Dendrogram using Ward's procedure

depending on whether the final solution contains two, three or four clusters. Information of this type can be obtained for any number of clusters and is useful for deciding on the number of clusters.

Decide on the number of clusters

A major issue in cluster analysis is deciding on the number of clusters. Although there are no hard and fast rules, some guidelines are available.

1 Theoretical, conceptual or practical considerations may suggest a certain number of clusters. For example, if the purpose of clustering is to identify market segments, management may want a particular number of clusters.

Table 23.2 Results of hierarchical clustering

Case processing summary[a,b]

Cases					
Valid		Missing		Total	
N	%	N	%	N	%
20	100.0	0	0.0	20	100.0

[a] Squared Euclidean distance used. [b] Ward linkage.

Ward linkage: agglomeration schedule

	Clusters combined			Stage cluster first appears		
Stage	Cluster 1	Cluster 2	Coefficients	Cluster 1	Cluster 2	Next stage
1	14	16	1.000	0	0	6
2	6	7	2.000	0	0	7
3	2	13	3.500	0	0	15
4	5	11	5.000	0	0	11
5	3	8	6.500	0	0	16
6	10	14	8.167	0	1	9
7	6	12	10.500	2	0	10
8	9	20	13.000	0	0	11
9	4	10	15.583	0	6	12
10	1	6	18.500	0	7	13
11	5	9	23.000	4	8	15
12	4	19	27.750	9	0	17
13	1	17	33.100	10	0	14
14	1	15	41.333	13	0	16
15	2	5	51.833	3	11	18
16	1	3	64.500	14	5	19
17	4	18	79.667	12	0	18
18	2	4	172.667	15	17	19
19	1	2	328.600	16	18	0

Table 23.2 Continued

Cluster membership			
Case	Number of clusters		
	Four clusters	Three clusters	Two clusters
1	1	1	1
2	2	2	2
3	1	1	1
4	3	3	2
5	2	2	2
6	1	1	1
7	1	1	1
8	1	1	1
9	2	2	2
10	3	3	2
11	2	2	2
12	1	1	1
13	2	2	2
14	3	3	2
15	1	1	1
16	3	3	2
17	1	1	1
18	4	3	2
19	3	3	2
20	2	2	2

2 In hierarchical clustering, the distances at which clusters are combined can be used as criteria. This information can be obtained from the agglomeration schedule or from the dendrogram. In our case, we see from the agglomeration schedule in Table 23.2 that the value in the 'Coefficients' column suddenly more than doubles between stages 17 (three clusters) and 18 (two clusters). Likewise, at the last two stages of the dendrogram in Figure 23.8, the clusters are being combined at large distances. Therefore, it appears that a three-cluster solution is appropriate.

3 In non-hierarchical clustering, the ratio of total within-group variance to between-group variance can be plotted against the number of clusters. The point at which an elbow or a sharp bend occurs indicates an appropriate number of clusters. Increasing the number of clusters beyond this point is usually not worthwhile.

4 The relative sizes of the clusters should be meaningful. In Table 23.2, by making a simple frequency count of cluster membership, we see that a three-cluster solution results in clusters with eight, six and six elements. If we go to a four-cluster solution, however, the sizes of the clusters are eight, six, five and one. It is not meaningful to have a cluster with only one case, so a three-cluster solution is preferable in this situation.

Interpret and profile clusters

Interpreting and profiling clusters involves examining the cluster centroids. The centroids represent the mean values of the objects contained in the cluster on each of the variables. The centroids enable us to describe each cluster by assigning it a name or label. If the clustering program does not print this information, it may be obtained through discriminant analysis. Table 23.3 gives the centroids or mean values for each cluster in our example. Cluster 1 has relatively high values on variables V_1 (Shopping is fun) and V_3 (I combine shopping with eating out). It also has a low value on V_5 (I don't care about shopping). Hence cluster 1 could be labelled 'fun-loving and concerned shoppers'. This cluster consists of cases 1, 3, 6, 7, 8, 12, 15 and 17. Cluster 2 is just the opposite, with low values on V_1 and V_3 and a high value on V_5; this cluster could be labelled 'apathetic shoppers'. Members of cluster 2 are cases 2, 5, 9, 11, 13 and 20. Cluster 3 has high values on V_2 (Shopping is bad for your budget), V_4 (I try to get the best buys while shopping) and V_6 (You can save a lot of money by comparing prices). Thus, this cluster could be labelled 'economical shoppers'. Cluster 3 is composed of cases 4, 10, 14, 16, 18 and 19.

Table 23.3 Cluster centroids

Cluster number	Means of variables					
	V_1	V_2	V_3	V_4	V_5	V_6
1	5.750	3.625	6.000	3.125	1.750	3.875
2	1.667	3.000	1.833	3.500	5.500	3.333
3	3.500	5.833	3.333	6.000	3.500	6.000

It is often helpful to profile the clusters in terms of variables that were not used for clustering, such as demographic, psychographic, product usage, media usage or other variables. For example, the clusters may have been derived based on benefits sought. Further profiling may be done in terms of demographic and psychographic variables to target marketing efforts for each cluster. The variables that significantly differentiate between clusters can be identified via discriminant analysis and one-way analysis of variance.

Assess the reliability and validity

Given the several judgements entailed in cluster analysis, no clustering solution should be accepted without some assessment of its reliability and validity. Formal procedures for assessing the reliability and validity of clustering solutions are complex and not fully defensible.[14] Hence, we omit them here. The following procedures, however, provide adequate checks on the quality of clustering results. These are vital if managers are to appreciate what constitutes robust clustering solutions.[15]

1 Perform cluster analysis on the same data using different distance measures. Compare the results across measures to determine the stability of the solutions.
2 Use different methods of clustering and compare the results.
3 Split the data randomly into halves. Perform clustering separately on each half. Compare cluster centroids across the two subsamples.
4 Delete variables randomly. Perform clustering based on the reduced set of variables. Compare the results with those obtained by clustering based on the entire set of variables.
5 In non-hierarchical clustering, the solution may depend on the order of cases in the dataset. Make multiple runs using different order of cases until the solution stabilises.

We further illustrate hierarchical clustering with a study of differences in marketing strategy among British, Japanese and American firms.

Example   It is a small world[16]

Data for a study of British, Japanese and American competitors were obtained from detailed personal interviews with chief executives and top marketing decision-makers for defined product groups in 90 companies. To control for market differences, the methodology was based upon matching 30 British companies with their major Japanese and American competitors in the British market. The study involved 30 triads of companies, each composed of a British, American and Japanese business that competed directly with one another.

Most of the data on the characteristics of the companies' performance, strategy and organisation were collected on five-point semantic differential scales. The first stage of the analysis involved factor analysis of variables describing the firms' strategies and marketing activities. The factor scores were used to identify groups of similar companies using Ward's hierarchical clustering routine. A six-cluster solution was developed.

Strategic clusters

Cluster	I	II	III	IV	V	VI
Name	Innovators	Quality marketers	Price promoters	Product marketers	Mature marketers	Aggressive pushers
Size	22	11	14	13	13	17
Successful (%)	55	100	36	38	77	41
Nationality (%)						
British	23	18	64	38	31	29
Japanese	59	46	22	31	15	18
American	18	36	14	31	54	53

Source: © Getty Images

Membership in the six clusters was then interpreted against the original performance, strategy and organisational variables. All the clusters contained some successful companies, although some contained significantly more than others. The clusters lent support to the hypothesis that successful companies were similar irrespective of nationality, since British, Japanese and American companies were found in all the clusters. There was, however, a preponderance of Japanese companies in the more successful clusters and a predominance of British companies in the two least successful clusters. Apparently, Japanese companies do not deploy strategies that are unique to them; rather, more of them pursue strategies that work effectively in the British market.

The findings indicate that there are generic strategies that describe successful companies irrespective of their industry. Three successful strategies can be identified. The first is the quality marketing strategy. These companies have strengths in marketing and research and development. They concentrate their technical developments on achieving high-quality rather than pure innovation. These companies are characterised by entrepreneurial organisations, long-range planning and a well-communicated sense of mission. The second generic strategy is that of the Innovators who are weaker on advanced research and development but are entrepreneurial and driven by a quest for innovation. The last successful group are the mature marketers, who are highly profit oriented and have in-depth marketing skills. All three appear to consist of highly marketing-oriented businesses.

Applications of non-hierarchical clustering

We illustrate the non-hierarchical procedure using the data in Table 23.1 and an optimising partitioning method. Based on the results of hierarchical clustering, a three-cluster solution was pre-specified. The results are presented in Table 23.4.

Table 23.4 Results of non-hierarchical clustering

Initial cluster centres

Cluster	V_1	V_2	V_3	V_4	V_5	V_6
1	4	6	3	7	2	7
2	2	3	2	4	7	2
3	7	2	6	4	1	3

Iteration history*

Change in cluster centres

Iteration	1	2	3
1	2.154	2.102	2.550
2	0.000	0.000	0.000

*Convergence achieved due to no or small distance change. The maximum distance by which any centre has changed is 0.000. The current iteration is 2. The minimum distance between initial centres is 7.746.

Cluster membership

Case number	Cluster	Distance
1	3	1.414
2	2	1.323
3	3	2.550
4	1	1.404
5	2	1.848
6	3	1.225
7	3	1.500
8	3	2.121
9	2	1.756
10	1	1.143
11	2	1.041

Table 23.4 Continued

Case number	Cluster	Distance
12	3	1.581
13	2	2.598
14	1	1.404
15	3	2.828
16	1	1.624
17	3	2.598
18	1	3.555
19	1	2.154
20	2	2.102

Final cluster centres

Cluster	V_1	V_2	V_3	V_4	V_5	V_6
1	4	6	3	6	4	6
2	2	3	2	4	6	3
3	6	4	6	3	2	4

Distances between final cluster centres

Cluster	1	2	3
1	0.000		
2	5.568	0.000	
3	5.698	6.928	0.000

Analysis of variance

Variable	Cluster MS	df	Error MS	df	F	p
V_1	29.108	2	0.608	17	47.888	0.000
V_2	13.546	2	0.630	17	21.505	0.000
V_3	31.392	2	0.833	17	37.670	0.000
V_4	15.713	2	0.728	17	21.585	0.000
V_5	22.537	2	0.816	17	27.614	0.000
V_6	12.171	2	1.071	17	11.363	0.001

The F tests should be used only for descriptive purposes because the clusters have been chosen to maximise the differences among cases in different clusters. The observed significance levels are not corrected for this and thus cannot be interpreted as tests of the hypothesis that the cluster means are equal.

Number of cases in each cluster

Cluster	
1	6
2	6
3	8
Missing	0
Total	20

The initial cluster centres are the values of the first three cases. The classification cluster centres are interim centres used for the assignment of cases. Each case is assigned to the nearest classification cluster centre. The classification centres are updated until the stopping criteria are reached. The final cluster centres represent the variable means for the cases in the final clusters.

Table 23.4 also displays cluster membership and the distance between each case and its classification centre. Note that the cluster memberships given in Table 23.2 (hierarchical clustering) and Table 23.4 (non-hierarchical clustering) are identical. (Cluster 1 of Table 23.2 is labelled cluster 3 in Table 23.4, and cluster 3 of Table 23.2 is labelled cluster 1 in Table 23.4.) The distances between the final cluster centres indicate that the pairs of clusters are well separated. The univariate F test for each clustering variable is presented. These F tests are only descriptive. Because the cases or objects are systematically assigned to clusters to maximise differences on the clustering variables, the resulting probabilities should not be interpreted as testing the null hypothesis of no differences among clusters.

The following example of hospital choice further illustrates non-hierarchical clustering.

Example   ## Segmentation with surgical precision[17]

Cluster analysis was used to classify and segment respondents, based upon their preferences for hospitals that provide inpatient care. The clustering was based on the reasons respondents gave for preferring a particular hospital. The demographic profiles of the grouped respondents were compared to learn whether the segments could be identified more efficiently.

Quick Cluster (SPSS), a minimum variance clustering method, was used for grouping the respondents based on their answers to the hospital preference items. The squared Euclidean distances between all clustering variables were minimised. Because different individuals perceive scales of importance differently, each individual's ratings were normalised before clustering. The results indicated that the respondents could be best classified into four clusters. The cross-validation procedure for cluster analysis was run twice, on halves of the total sample.

As expected, the four groups differed substantially by their distributions and average responses to the reasons for their hospital preferences. The names assigned to the four groups reflected the demographic characteristics and reasons for hospital preferences: *old-fashioned*, *affluent*, *value conscious* and *professional want-it-alls*.

Clustering variables

Sometimes cluster analysis is also used for clustering variables to identify homogeneous groups. In this instance, the units used for analysis are the variables, and the distance measures are computed for all pairs of variables. For example, the correlation coefficient, either the absolute value or with the sign, can be used as a measure of similarity (the opposite of distance) between variables.

Hierarchical clustering of variables can aid in the identification of unique variables, or variables that make a unique contribution to the data. Clustering can also be used to reduce the number of variables. Associated with each cluster is a linear combination of the variables in the cluster, called the cluster component. A large set of variables can often be replaced by the set of cluster components with little loss of information. A given number of cluster components does not generally explain as much variance as the same number of principal components, however. Why, then, should the clustering of variables be used?

Cluster components are usually easier to interpret than the principal components, even if the latter are rotated.[18] We illustrate the clustering of variables with an example from advertising research.

Example

Feelings – nothing more than feelings[19]

Polaroid has been faced with increasing competition from digital cameras, so marketing executives decided to focus on the emotional potential of its core camera line. A €15 million campaign rolled out the tagline 'click, instantly' with the implication that the Polaroid camera could change a feeling 'right there and then'. An advertising campaign was designed to evoke emotional feelings in consumers when viewing the new Polaroid commercials.

Polaroid based this campaign on a study conducted to identify feelings that were intuitively evoked. A total of 655 feelings were reduced to a set of 180 that were judged by respondents to be most likely to be stimulated by advertising. This group was clustered on the basis of judgements of similarity between feelings resulting in 31 'feelings' clusters. These were divided into 16 positive and 15 negative clusters, as shown in the table

	Positive feelings		Negative feelings
1	Playful/childish	1	Fear
2	Friendly	2	Bad/sick
3	Humorous	3	Confused
4	Delighted	4	Indifferent
5	Interested	5	Bored
6	Strong/confident	6	Sad
7	Warm/tender	7	Anxious
8	Relaxed	8	Helpless/timid
9	Energetic/impulsive	9	Ugly/stupid
10	Eager/excited	10	Pity/deceived
11	Contemplative	11	Mad
12	Pride	12	Disagreeable
13	Persuaded/expectant	13	Disgusted
14	Vigorous/challenged	14	Irritated
15	Amazed	15	Moody/frustrated
16	Set/informed		

Thus, 655 feelings responses to advertising were reduced to a core set of 31 feelings. In this way, advertisers now have a manageable set of feelings for understanding and measuring responses to advertising. When measured, these feelings can provide information on a commercial's ability to persuade target consumers, as in the case of Polaroid cameras.

Internet and computer applications

SPSS

The main program for hierarchical clustering of objects or cases is CLUSTER. Different distance measures can be computed, and all the hierarchical clustering procedures discussed here are available. For non-hierarchical clustering, the QUICK CLUSTER program can be used. This program is particularly helpful for clustering a large number of cases. All the default options will result in a k-means clustering. To cluster variables, the distance measures should be computed across variables using the PROXIMITIES program. This proximity matrix can be read into CLUSTER to obtain a grouping of the variables.

SAS

The CLUSTER program can be used for the hierarchical clustering of cases or objects. All the clustering procedures discussed here are available, as well as some additional ones. Non-hierarchical clustering of cases or objects can be accomplished using FAST-CLUS. For clustering of variables, the VARCLUS program can be used. Dendrograms are not automatically computed but can be obtained using the TREE program.

SNAP

Uses k-Means Clustering, the model most commonly used for survey data. It allows multiple cluster analyses to be run and saved, creating a new Single Response variable for each saved cluster analysis. The variable appears in the variables window, now available for use in further analysis including standard tables and charts.

Minitab

Cluster analysis can be accessed in the Multivariate>Cluster observation function. Also available are Clustering of Variables and Cluster *K*-Means.

Summary

Cluster analysis is used for classifying objects or cases, and sometimes variables, into relatively homogeneous groups. The groups or clusters are suggested by the data and are not defined a priori.

The variables on which the clustering is based should be selected based on past research, theory, the hypotheses being tested, or the judgement of the researcher. An appropriate measure of distance or similarity should be selected. The most commonly used measure is the Euclidean distance or its square.

Clustering procedures may be hierarchical or non-hierarchical. Hierarchical clustering is characterised by the development of a hierarchy or treelike structure. Hierarchical methods can be agglomerative or divisive. Agglomerative methods consist of linkage methods, variance methods and centroid methods. Linkage methods are composed of single linkage, complete linkage and average linkage. A commonly used variance method is Ward's procedure. The non-hierarchical methods are frequently referred to as *k*-means clustering. These methods can be classified as sequential threshold, parallel threshold and optimising partitioning. Hierarchical and non-hierarchical methods can be used in tandem. The choice of a clustering procedure and the choice of a distance measure are interrelated.

The number of clusters may be based on theoretical, conceptual or practical considerations. In hierarchical clustering, the distance at which the clusters are being combined is an important criterion. The relative sizes of the clusters should be meaningful. The clusters should be interpreted in terms of cluster centroids. It is often helpful to profile the clusters in terms of variables that were not used for clustering. The reliability and validity of the clustering solutions may be assessed in different ways.

Questions

1 Discuss the similarity and difference between cluster analysis and discriminant analysis.

2 What is a 'cluster'?

3 What are some of the uses of cluster analysis in marketing?

4 Briefly define the following terms: dendrogram, icicle plot, agglomeration schedule and cluster membership.

5 What is the most commonly used measure of similarity in cluster analysis?

6 Present a classification of clustering procedures.

7 Upon what basis may a researcher decide which variables should be selected to formulate a clustering problem?

8 Why is the average linkage method usually preferred to single linkage and complete linkage?

9 What are the two major disadvantages of non-hierarchical clustering procedures?

10 What guidelines are available for deciding the number of clusters?

11 What is involved in the interpretation of clusters?

12 What role may qualitative methods play in the interpretation of clusters?

13 What are some of the additional variables used for profiling the clusters?

14 Describe some procedures available for assessing the quality of clustering solutions.

15 How is cluster analysis used to group variables?

Exercises

1 Analyse the data in Table 23.1 using the following hierarchical methods:

  a Single linkage (nearest neighbour).
  b Complete linkage (furthest neighbour).
  c Method of centroid.

  Use SPSS, SAS or Minitab. Compare your results with those given in Table 20.2.

2 Conduct the following analysis on the boots data (taken from Exercise 4, Chapter 20). Consider only the following variables: evaluations of the boots on comfort (V_2), style (V_3) and durability (V_4).

  a Cluster the respondents based on the identified variables using hierarchical clustering. Use Ward's method and squared Euclidean distances. How many clusters do you recommend and why?
  b Cluster the respondents based on the identified variables using k-means clustering and the number of clusters identified in part a. Compare the results to those obtained in part a.

3 Analyse the Benetton data (taken from Exercise 4, Chapter 18). Consider only the following variables: awareness, attitude, preference, intention and loyalty towards Benetton.

  a Cluster the respondents based on the identified variables using hierarchical clustering. Use Ward's method and squared Euclidean distances. How many clusters do you recommend and why?
  b Cluster the respondents based on the identified variables using k-means clustering and the number of clusters identified in part a. Compare the results to those obtained in part a.

4 You are a marketing research analyst for a major airline. You have been set the task of determining consumers' attitudes towards budget airlines. Construct a 15-item scale for this purpose. In a group of 5 students, obtain data on this scale and standard demographic characteristics from 25 male and 25 females in your community. These data should then be used to cluster respondents and to cluster the 15 variables measuring consumer attitudes to budget airlines.

5 In a small group discuss the following issues: 'The consequences of inappropriate validation of cluster analysis solutions can be disastrous' and 'user-friendly statistical packages can create cluster solutions in situations where naturally occurring clusters do not exist'.

Notes

1 Reynolds, E., 'Is Häagen-Dazs shrewd to drop its sexy image?', *Marketing* (6 September, 2001), 17; Stuart, L., 'Häagen-Dazs aims to scoop a larger share', *Marketing Week* 19 (46/2) (21 February 1997), 26.

2 For applications of cluster analysis, see Moe, W.W. and Fader, P.S., 'Modeling hedonic portfolio products: a joint segmentation analysis of music compact disc sales', *Journal of Marketing Research* 38 (3) (August 2001), 376–388; Arimond, G., 'A clustering method for categorical data in tourism market segmentation research', *Journal of Travel Research* 39 (4) (May 2001), 391–397; Birks, D.F. and Birts, A.N., 'Cash management market segmentation', in Birks, D.F. (ed.), *Global Cash Management in Europe* (Basingstoke: Macmillan, 1998), 83–109.

3 Overlapping clustering methods that permit an object to be grouped into more than one cluster are also available. See Chaturvedi, A., Carroll, J.D., Green, P.E. and Rotondo, J.A., 'A feature based approach to market segmentation via overlapping k-centroids clustering', *Journal of Marketing Research* 34 (August 1997), 370–377.

4 Excellent discussions on the various aspects of cluster analysis may be found in Everitt, B.S., Landau, S. and Leese, M., *Cluster Analysis* 4th edn. (Oxford: Oxford University Press, 2001); Romsburg, H.C., *Cluster Analysis for Researchers* (Melbourne: Krieger, 1990).

5 Ali, J., 'Micro-market segmentation using a neural network model approach', *Journal of International Consumer Marketing*, (2001), 7; Douglas, V., 'Questionnaires too long? Try variable clustering', *Marketing News* 29 (5) (27 February 1995), 38; Punj, G. and Stewart, D., 'Cluster analysis in marketing research: review and suggestions for application', *Journal of Marketing Research* 20 (May 1983), 134–148.

6 For use of cluster analysis for segmentation, see Stewart-Hunter, M. and Bergenthal, M., 'The art and science of consumer segmentation', *Admap*, (October 2004), 65–68; Arimond, G., 'A clustering method for categorical data in tourism market segmentation research', *Journal of Travel Research* 39 (4) (May 2001), 391–397; Neal, W.D., 'Advances in market segmentation', *Marketing Research* (Spring 2001), 14–18; Peterson, M. and Malhotra, N.K., 'A global view of quality of life: segmentation analysis of 165 countries', *International Marketing Review* 17 (1) (2000), 56–73.

7 Brown, T. J., Qu, H. and Rittichainuwat, B.N., 'Thailand's international travel image: mostly favourable', *Cornell Hotel and Restaurant Administration Quarterly*, 42 (2) (April 2001), 85–95.

8 Sambandam, R., 'Cluster analysis gets complicated', *Marketing Research*, (Spring 2003), 16–21; Everitt, B.S., Landau, S. and Leese, M., *Cluster Analysis*, 4th edn. (Oxford: Oxford University Press, 2001).

9 For a detailed discussion on the different measures of similarity, and formulaes for computing them, see Bradlow, E.T., 'Subscale distance and item clustering effects in self-administered surveys: a new metric', *Journal of Marketing Research* (May 2001) 254–261; Chepoi, V. and Dragan, F., 'Computing a median point of a simple rectilinear polygon', *Information Processing Letters* 49 (6) (22 March 1994), 281–285; Romsburg, H.C., *Cluster Analysis for Researchers* (Belmont, CA: Lifetime Learning, 1984).

10 Hirata, T., 'A unified linear-time algorithm for computing distance maps', *Information Processing Letters* 58 (3) (13 May 1996), 129–133; Hair, J.E., Jnr Anderson, R.E., Tatham, R.L. and Black, W.C., *Multivariate Data Analysis with Readings*, 4th edn (Englewood Cliffs, NJ: Prentice Hall, 1995), 420–483.

11 For further discussion of the issues involved in standardisation, see Romsburg, H.C., *Cluster Analysis for Researchers* (Melbourne: Krieger, 1990).

12 Everitt, B.S., Landau, S. and Leese, M., *Cluster Analysis*, 4th edn (Oxford: Oxford University Press, 2001); Johnson, R.A. and Wichern, D.W., *Applied Multivariate Statistical Analysis*, 5th edn (Paramus, NJ: Prentice Hall, 2001); Milligan, G., 'An examination of the effect of six types of error perturbation on fifteen clustering algorithms', *Psychometrika* 45 (September 1980), 325–342.

13 Everitt, B.S., Landau, S. and Leese, M., *Cluster Analysis*, 4th edn (Oxford: Oxford University Press, 2001); Punj, G. and Stewart, D., 'Cluster analysis in marketing research: reviews and suggestions for application', *Journal of Marketing Research* 20 (May 1983), 134–148.

14 For a formal discussion of reliability, validity and significance testing in cluster analysis, see Brusco, M.J., Cradit, J.D. and Stahl, S., 'A simulated annealing heuristic for a bicriterion partitioning problem in market segmentation', *Journal of Marketing Research* 39 (1) (February 2002), 99–109; Chen, H.-M., 'Using clustering techniques to detect usage patterns in a web-based information system', *Journal of the American Society for Information Science and Technology*, 52 (11) (September 2001), 888; Dibbs, S. and Stern, P., 'Questioning the reliability of market segmentation techniques', *Omega* 23 (6) (December 1995), 625–36; Funkhouser, G.R., 'A note on the reliability of certain clustering algorithms', *Journal of Marketing Research* 30 (February 1983), 99–102; Klastorin, T.D., 'Assessing cluster analysis results', *Journal of Marketing Research* 20 (February 1983), 92–98; Arnold, S.J., 'A test for clusters', *Journal of Marketing Research* 16 (November 1979), 545–551.

15 Bottomley, P. and Nairn, A., 'Blinded by science: the managerial consequences of inadequately validated cluster analysis solutions,' *International Journal of Market Research* 46 (2) (2004), 171–187.

16 Saunders, J., Wong, V. and Doyle, P., 'The congruence of successful international competitors: a study of successful international competitors: a study of the marketing strategies and organisations of Japanese and US competitors in the UK', *Journal of Global Marketing* 7 (3) (1994), 41–59; Doyle, P., Saunders, J. and Wong, V., 'International marketing strategies and organisations: a study of U.S., Japanese, and British competitors', in Bloom, P., Winer, R., Kassarjian, H.H., Scammon, D.L., Weitz, B., Spekman, R.E., Mahajan, V. and Levy, M. (eds), *Enhancing Knowledge Development in Marketing*, Series No. 55 (Chicago: American Marketing Association, 1989), 100–104.

17 Lin, A., Lenert, L.A., Hlatky, M.A. and McDonald, K.M., 'Clustering and the design of preference-assessment surveys in healthcare,' *Health Services Research* 34 (5) (December 1999), 1033–1045; Holohean, E.J. Jr, Banks, S.M. and Maddy, B.A., 'System impact and methodological issues in the development of an empirical typology of psychiatric hospital

residents', *Journal of Mental Health Administration* 22 (2) (Spring 1995), 177–188.

18 Everitt, B.S., Landau, S. and Leese, M., *Cluster Analysis*, 4th edn (Oxford: Oxford University Press, 2001); Douglas, V., 'Questionnaire too long? Try variable clustering', *Marketing News* 29 (5) (27 February 1995), 38.

19 Baar, A., 'Polaroid asd play up emotion', *Adweek* 42 (15) (9 April, 2001); Helgesen, T., 'The power of advertising – myths and realities', *Marketing and Research Today* 24 (2) (May 1996), 63–71; Aaker, D.A., Stayman, D.M. and Vezina, R., 'Identifying feelings elicited by advertising', *Psychology and Marketing* (Spring 1988), 1–16.

Visit the *Marketing Research* Companion Website at www.pearsoned.co.uk/malhotra_euro for additional learning resources including annotated weblinks, an online glossary and a suite of downloadable video cases.

Source: © Getty Images

24

Multidimensional scaling and conjoint analysis

Multidimensional scaling allows the perceptions and preferences of consumers to be clearly represented in a spatial map. Conjoint analysis helps to determine the relative importance of attributes that consumers use in choosing products.

Objectives

After reading this chapter, you should be able to:

1 discuss the basic concept and scope of multidimensional scaling (MDS) in marketing research and describe its various applications;

2 describe the steps involved in MDS of perception data, including formulating the problem, obtaining input data, selecting an MDS procedure, deciding on the number of dimensions, labelling the dimensions and interpreting the configuration, and assessing reliability and validity;

3 explain the MDS scaling of preference data and distinguish between internal and external analysis of preferences;

4 explain correspondence analysis and discuss its advantages and disadvantages;

5 understand the relationship between MDS discriminant analysis and factor analysis;

6 discuss the basic concepts of conjoint analysis, contrast it with MDS and discuss its various applications;

7 describe the procedure for conducting conjoint analysis, including formulating the problem, constructing the stimuli, deciding the form of input data, selecting a conjoint analysis procedure, interpreting the results, and assessing reliability and validity;

8 define the concept of hybrid conjoint analysis and explain how it simplifies the data collection task.

STAGE 1
Problem definition

STAGE 2
Research approach developed

STAGE 3
Research design developed

STAGE 4
Fieldwork or data collection

STAGE 5
Data preparation and analysis

STAGE 6
Report preparation and presentation

Overview

This final chapter on quantitative data analysis presents two related techniques for analysing consumer perceptions and preferences: multidimensional scaling (MDS) and conjoint analysis. We outline and illustrate the steps involved in conducting MDS and discuss the relationships among MDS, factor analysis and discriminant analysis. Then we describe conjoint analysis and present a step-by-step procedure for conducting it. We also provide brief coverage of hybrid conjoint models.

We begin with examples illustrating MDS and conjoint analysis.

Example **Colas collide[1]**

In a survey, respondents were asked to rank-order all the possible pairs of nine brands of soft drinks in terms of their similarity. These data were analysed via MDS and resulted in the following spatial representation of soft drinks.

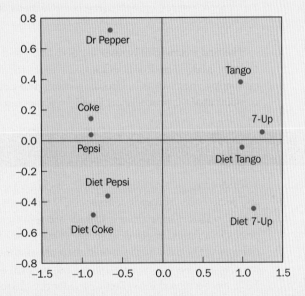

From other information obtained in the questionnaire, the horizontal axis was labelled 'cola flavour'. Diet Coke was perceived to be the most cola flavoured and 7-Up the least cola flavoured. The vertical axis was labelled 'dietness', with Diet Coke being perceived to be the most dietetic and Dr Pepper the least dietetic. Note that Coke and Pepsi were perceived to be very similar as indicated by their closeness in the perceptual map. Close similarity was also perceived between 7-Up and Tango, Diet 7-Up and Diet Tango, and Diet Coke and Diet Pepsi. Notice that Dr Pepper is perceived to be relatively dissimilar to the other brands. Such MDS maps are very useful in understanding the competitive structure of the soft drink market.

Example **The conjoint path over the cultural divide[2]**

Boots the Chemist was considering whether to open new stores in the Netherlands, Japan and Thailand. Research was conducted to help decide whether to enter these markets and also to decide which element of Boots' product and service offering to prioritise.

The key research objectives were to:

- Understand the key drivers of store choice.
- Assess the performance of main competitors already in the market.
- Estimate the proportion of shoppers likely to visit new Boots stores.

Conjoint analysis was used to understand the key drivers of store choice, the impact of features such as range, price, quality, service and convenience, and the trade-offs made in prioritising these features.

To understand the strengths and weaknesses of existing retailers, respondents stated for each of the attributes under review what the named competitors offered. To enable take-up of the new stores to be forecast, respondents were first shown a video of the Boots concept store. The concept store was then assessed on the same series of attributes used for the existing competitors. Over 1,000 interviews were conducted in each country. The research results found:

- The characteristics of the target market in terms of age, sex, income and lifestage, frequency of and attitudes to shopping.
- The key success factors in each product area, which influenced store design, merchandising, staff training and marketing decisions.
- Which existing players posed the greatest threat, in terms of being differentiated from current competitors and having possible areas of leverage against Boots.

The first example illustrates the derivation and use of perceptual maps, which lie at the heart of MDS. The Boots example involves the trade-offs that respondents make while evaluating alternatives in choosing stores and desirable features within those stores. The conjoint analysis procedure is based on these trade-offs.

Basic concepts in MDS

Multidimensional scaling (MDS)
A class of procedures for representing perceptions and preferences of respondents spatially by means of a visual display.

Multidimensional scaling (MDS) is a class of procedures for representing perceptions and preferences of respondents spatially by means of a visual display. Perceived or psychological relationships among stimuli are represented as geometric relationships among points in a multidimensional space. These geometric representations are often called spatial maps. The axes of the spatial map are assumed to denote the psychological bases or underlying dimensions respondents use to form perceptions and preferences for stimuli.[3] MDS has been used in marketing to identify the following:

1 The number and nature of dimensions consumers use to perceive different brands.
2 The positioning of brands on these dimensions.
3 The positioning of consumers' ideal brand on these dimensions.

Information provided by MDS has been used for a variety of marketing applications, including:

- *Image measurement.* Comparing the customers' and non-customers' perceptions of the firm with the firm's perceptions of itself and thus identifying perceptual gaps.
- *Market segmentation.* Positioning brands and consumers in the same space and then identifying groups of consumers with relatively homogeneous perceptions.
- *New product development.* To look for gaps in a spatial map, which indicate potential opportunities for positioning new products. Also to evaluate new product concepts and existing brands on a test basis to determine how consumers perceive the new concepts. The proportion of preferences for each new product is one indicator of its success.
- *Assessing advertising effectiveness.* Spatial maps can be used to determine whether advertising has been successful in achieving the desired brand positioning.

- *Pricing analysis.* Spatial maps developed with and without pricing information can be compared to determine the impact of pricing.
- *Channel decisions.* Judgements on compatibility of brands with different retail outlets could lead to spatial maps useful for making channel decisions.
- *Attitude-scale construction.* MDS techniques can be used to develop the appropriate dimensionality and configuration of the attitude space.

Statistics and terms associated with MDS

The important statistics and terms associated with MDS include the following:

Similarity judgements. Similarity judgements are ratings on all possible pairs of brands or other stimuli in terms of their similarity using a Likert-type scale.

Preference rankings. Preference rankings are rank orderings of the brands or other stimuli from the most preferred to the least preferred. They are normally obtained from respondents.

Stress. Stress is a lack-of-fit measure; higher values of stress indicate poorer fits.

R-square. *R*-square is a squared correlation index that indicates the proportion of variance of the optimally scaled data that can be accounted for by the MDS procedure. This is a goodness-of-fit measure.

Spatial map. Perceived relationships among brands or other stimuli are represented as geometric relationships among points in a multidimensional space.

Coordinates. Coordinates indicate the positioning of a brand or a stimulus in a spatial map.

Unfolding. The representation of both brands and respondents as points in the same space.

Conducting MDS

Figure 24.1 shows the steps in MDS. The researcher must formulate the MDS problem carefully because a variety of data may be used as input into MDS. The researcher must also determine an appropriate form in which data should be obtained and select an MDS procedure for analysing the data. An important aspect of the solution involves determining the number of dimensions for the spatial map. Also, the axes of the map should be labelled and the derived configuration interpreted. Finally, the researcher must assess the quality of the results obtained.[4] We describe each of these steps, beginning with problem formulation.

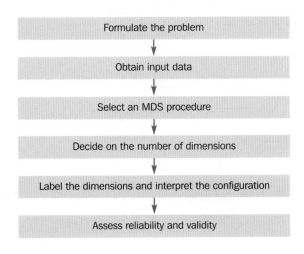

Figure 24.1
Conducting MDS

Formulate the problem

Formulating the problem requires that the researcher specify the purpose for which the MDS results would be used and select the brands or other stimuli to be included in the analysis. The number of brands or stimuli selected and the specific brands included determine the nature of the resulting dimensions and configurations. At a minimum, eight brands or stimuli should be included to obtain a well-defined spatial map. Including more than 25 brands is likely to be cumbersome and may result in respondent fatigue.[5]

The decision regarding which specific brands or stimuli to include should be made carefully. Suppose that a researcher is interested in obtaining consumer perceptions of cars. If luxury cars are not included in the stimulus set, this dimension may not emerge in the results. The choice of the number and specific brands or stimuli to be included should be based on the statement of the marketing research problem, theory and the judgement of the researcher.

MDS will be illustrated in the context of obtaining a spatial map for 10 brands of beer. These brands are Becks, Budvar, Budweiser, Carlsberg, Corona, Grolsch, Harp, Holsten, San Miguel and Stella Artois. Given the list of brands, the next question is: how should we obtain data on these 10 brands?

Obtain input data

As shown in Figure 24.2, input data obtained from the respondents may be related to perceptions or preferences. Perception data, which may be direct or derived, is discussed first.

Perception data: direct approaches In direct approaches to gathering perception data, respondents are asked to judge how similar or dissimilar various brands or stimuli are, using their own criteria. Respondents are often required to rate all possible pairs of brands or stimuli in terms of similarity on a Likert scale. These data are referred to as similarity judgements. For example, similarity judgements on all the possible pairs of bottled beer brands may be obtained in the following manner:

	Very dissimilar						Very similar
Becks versus Budweiser	1	2	3	4	5	6	7
Budweiser versus Carlsberg	1	2	3	4	5	6	7
Carlsberg versus Corona	1	2	3	4	5	6	7
⋮	⋮	⋮	⋮	⋮	⋮	⋮	⋮
Becks versus Stella Artois	1	2	3	4	5	6	7

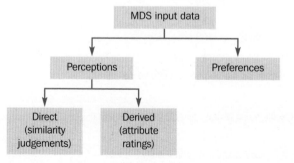

Figure 24.2
Input data for MDS

The number of pairs to be evaluated is $n(n-1)/2$, where n is the number of stimuli. Other procedures are also available. Respondents could be asked to rank order all the possible pairs from the most similar to the least similar. In another method, the respondent rank orders the brands in terms of their similarity to an anchor brand. Each brand, in turn, serves as the anchor. In our example, the direct approach was adopted. Subjects were asked to provide similarity judgements for all 45 $(10 \times 9/2)$ pairs of bottled beer brands, using a seven-point scale. The data obtained from one respondent are given in Table 24.1.[6]

Source: © Alamy

Derived approaches
In MDS, attribute-based approaches to collecting perception data requiring respondents to rate the stimuli on the identified attributes using semantic differential or Likert scales.

Perception data: derived approaches Derived approaches to collecting perception data are attribute-based approaches requiring the respondents to rate the brands or stimuli on the identified attributes using semantic differential or Likert scales. For example, the different brands of bottled beer may be rated on attributes like these:

Best drunk with food ——————————— Best drunk on its own

Bottle feels good to hold ——————————— Bottle does not feel good to hold

Has a strong smell of hops ——————————— No smell of hops

Sometimes an ideal brand is also included in the stimulus set. The respondents are asked to evaluate their hypothetical ideal brand on the same set of attributes. If attribute ratings are obtained, a similarity measure (such as Euclidean distance) is derived for each pair of brands.

Direct vs. derived approaches. Direct approaches have the advantage that the researcher does not have to identify a set of salient attributes. Respondents make similarity judgements using their own criteria, as they would under normal circumstances. The disadvantages are that the criteria are influenced by the brands or stimuli being evaluated. If the various

Table 24.1 Similarity ratings of bottled beer brands

	Becks	Budvar	Budweiser	Carlsberg	Corona	Grolsch	Harp	Holsten	San Miguel	Stella Artois
Becks										
Budvar	5									
Budweiser	6	7								
Carlsberg	4	6	6							
Corona	2	3	4	5						
Grolsch	3	3	4	4	5					
Harp	2	2	2	3	5	5				
Holsten	2	2	2	2	6	5	6			
San Miguel	2	2	2	2	6	6	7	6		
Stella Artois	1	2	4	2	4	3	3	4	3	

brands of cars being evaluated are in the same price range, then price will not emerge as an important factor. It may be difficult to determine before analysis if and how the individual respondent's judgements should be combined. Furthermore, it may be difficult to label the dimensions of the spatial map.

The advantage of the attribute-based approach is that it is easy to identify respondents with homogeneous perceptions. The respondents can be clustered based on the attribute ratings. It is also easier to label the dimensions. A disadvantage is that the researcher must identify all the salient attributes, a difficult task. The spatial map obtained depends on the attributes identified.

The direct approaches are more frequently used than the attribute-based approaches. It may, however, be best to use both these approaches in a complementary way. Direct similarity judgements may be used for obtaining the spatial map, and attribute ratings may be used as an aid to interpreting the dimensions of the perceptual map. Similar procedures are used for preference data.

Preference data Preference data order the brands or stimuli in terms of respondents' preference for some property. A common way in which such data are obtained is preference rankings. Respondents are required to rank the brands from the most preferred to the least preferred. Alternatively, respondents may be required to make paired comparisons and indicate which brand in a pair they prefer. Another method is to obtain preference ratings for the various brands. (The rank order, paired comparison and rating scales were discussed in Chapter 12 on scaling techniques.) When spatial maps are based on preference data, distance implies differences in preference. The configuration derived from preference data may differ greatly from that obtained from similarity data. Two brands may be perceived as different in a similarity map yet similar in a preference map, and vice versa. For example, Becks and Harp may be perceived by a group of respondents as very different brands and thus appear far apart on a perception map. But these two brands may be about equally preferred and may appear close together on a preference map.

We continue using the perception data obtained in the bottled beer example to illustrate the MDS procedure and then consider the scaling of preference data.

Select an MDS procedure

Non-metric MDS
A type of MDS which assumes that the input data are ordinal.

Metric MDS
An MDS method that assumes that input data are metric.

Selecting a specific MDS procedure depends on whether perception or preference data are being scaled or whether the analysis requires both kinds of data. The nature of the input data is also a determining factor. Non-metric MDS procedures assume that the input data are ordinal, but they result in metric output. The distances in the resulting spatial map may be assumed to be interval scaled. These procedures find, in a given dimensionality, a spatial map whose rank orders of estimated distances between brands or stimuli best preserve or reproduce the input rank orders. In contrast, metric MDS methods assume that input data are metric. Since the output is also metric, a stronger relationship between the output and input data is maintained, and the metric (interval or ratio) qualities of the input data are preserved. The metric and non-metric methods produce similar results.[7]

Another factor influencing the selection of a procedure is whether the MDS analysis will be conducted at the individual respondent level or at an aggregate level. In individual-level analysis, the data are analysed separately for each respondent, resulting in a spatial map for each respondent. Although individual-level analysis is useful from a research perspective, it is not appealing from a managerial standpoint. Marketing strategies are typically formulated at the segment or aggregate level, rather than at the individual level. If aggregate-level analysis is conducted, some assumptions must be made in aggregating individual data. Typically, it is assumed that all respondents use the same dimensions to evaluate the brands or stimuli, but that different respondents weight these common dimensions differentially.

The data of Table 24.1 were treated as rank ordered and scaled using a non-metric procedure. Because these data were provided by one respondent, an individual-level analysis was conducted. Spatial maps were obtained in one to four dimensions, and then a decision on an appropriate number of dimensions was made. This decision is central to all MDS analyses; therefore, it is explored in greater detail in the following section.

Decide on the number of dimensions

The objective in MDS is to obtain a spatial map that best fits the input data in the smallest number of dimensions. However, spatial maps are computed in such a way that the fit improves as the number of dimensions increases, which means that a compromise has to be made. The fit of an MDS solution is commonly assessed by the stress measure. Stress is a lack-of-fit measure; higher values of stress indicate poorer fits. The following guidelines are suggested for determining the number of dimensions:

1 *A priori knowledge.* Theory or past research may suggest a particular number of dimensions.
2 *Interpretability of the spatial map.* Generally, it is difficult to interpret configurations or maps derived in more than three dimensions.
3 *Elbow criterion.* A plot of stress versus dimensionality should be examined. The points in this plot usually form a convex pattern, as shown in Figure 24.3. The point at which an elbow or a sharp bend occurs indicates an appropriate number of dimensions. Increasing the number of dimensions beyond this point is usually not worth the improvement in fit. This criterion for determining the number of dimensions is called the elbow criterion.
4 *Ease of use.* It is generally easier to work with two-dimensional maps or configurations than with those involving more dimensions.
5 *Statistical approaches.* For the sophisticated user, statistical approaches are also available for determining the dimensionality.[8]

Elbow criterion
A plot of stress versus dimensionality used in MDS. The point at which an elbow or a sharp bend occurs indicates an appropriate dimensionality.

Based on the plot of stress versus dimensionality (Figure 24.3), interpretability of the spatial map and ease-of-use criteria, it was decided to retain a two-dimensional solution. This is shown in Figure 24.4.

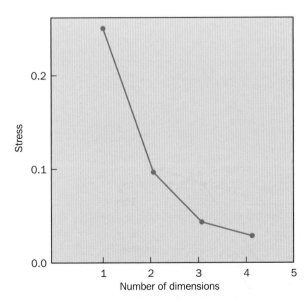

Figure 24.3
Plot of stress versus dimensionality

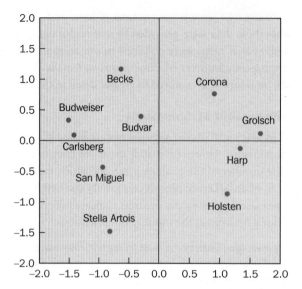

Figure 24.4
A spatial map of
beer brands

Label the dimensions and interpret the configuration

Once a spatial map is developed, the dimensions must be labelled and the configuration interpreted. Labelling the dimensions requires subjective judgement on the part of the researcher. The following guidelines can assist in this task:

1 Even if direct similarity judgements are obtained, ratings of the brands on researcher-supplied attributes may still be collected. Using statistical methods such as regression these attribute vectors may be fitted in the spatial map (see Figure 24.5). The axes may then be labelled for the attributes with which they are most closely aligned.

2 After providing direct similarity or preference data, the respondents may be asked to indicate the criteria they used in making their evaluations. These criteria may then be subjectively related to the spatial map to label the dimensions.

3 If possible, the respondents can be shown their spatial maps and asked to label the dimensions by inspecting the configurations.

4 If objective characteristics of the brands are available (e.g. horsepower or kilometres per litre for cars), these could be used as an aid in interpreting the subjective dimensions of the spatial maps.

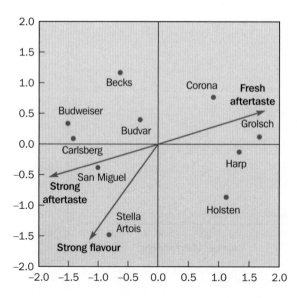

Figure 24.5
Using attribute vectors
to label dimensions

Often, the dimensions represent more than one attribute. The configuration or the spatial map may be interpreted by examining the coordinates and relative positions of the brands. For example, brands located near each other compete more fiercely than brands far apart. An isolated brand has a unique image. Brands that are farther along in the direction of a descriptor are stronger on that characteristic than others. Thus, the strengths and weaknesses of each product can be understood. Gaps in the spatial map may indicate potential opportunities for introducing new products.

In Figure 24.5, the vertical axis may be labelled as 'strength', representing the power of particular flavours and smells when the beer is first tasted. Brands with high positive values on this axis include Grolsch, Harp, Holsten and Corona. The horizontal axis may be labelled as 'aftertaste', representing the flavour of the beer that lingers on the palate after the beer has been drunk. Brands with large negative values on this dimension include Stella Artois, Holsten and San Miguel. Note that negative scores on the map do not necessarily represent negative characteristics for certain consumers. Thus, the strength of flavour from initial smell and taste through to a strong aftertaste in a brand such as Stella Artois may be seen as desirable characteristics for many beer drinkers.

The gaps in the spatial map indicate potential opportunities for new brands: for example, one that has a strong initial taste but does not have a strong lingering aftertaste.

Assess reliability and validity

The input data, and consequently the MDS solutions, are invariably subject to substantial random variability. Hence, it is necessary that some assessment be made of the reliability and validity of MDS solutions. The following guidelines are suggested:

1 The index of fit, or R-square, should be examined. This is a squared correlation index that indicates the proportion of variance of the optimally scaled data that can be accounted for by the MDS procedure. Thus, it indicates how well the MDS model fits the input data. Although higher values of R-square are desirable, values of 0.60 or better are considered acceptable.

2 Stress values are also indicative of the quality of MDS solutions. Whereas R-square is a measure of goodness of fit, stress measures badness of fit, or the proportion of variance of the optimally scaled data that is not accounted for by the MDS model. Stress values vary with the type of MDS procedure and the data being analysed. For Kruskal's stress formula 1, the recommendations for evaluating stress values are as follows:[9]

Stress (%)	Goodness of fit
20	Poor
10	Fair
5	Good
2.5	Excellent
0	Perfect

3 If an aggregate-level analysis has been done, the original data should be split into two or more parts. MDS analysis should be conducted separately on each part and the results compared.

4 Stimuli can be selectively eliminated from the input data and the solutions determined for the remaining stimuli.

5 A random error term could be added to the input data. The resulting data are subjected to MDS analysis and the solutions compared.

6 The input data could be collected at two different points in time and the test–retest reliability determined.

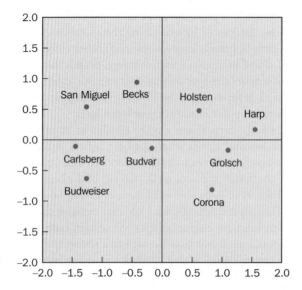

Figure 24.6
Assessment of stability by deleting one brand

Formal procedures are available for assessing the validity of MDS.[10] In the case of our illustrative example, the stress value of 0.095 indicates a fair fit. One brand, namely Stella Artois, is different from the others. Would the elimination of Stella Artois from the stimulus set appreciably alter the relative configuration of the other brands? The spatial map obtained by deleting Stella Artois is shown in Figure 24.6. There is some change in the relative positions of the brands, particularly Corona and Holsten, yet the changes are modest, indicating fair stability.[11]

Assumptions and limitations of MDS

It is worthwhile to point out some assumptions and limitations of MDS. It is assumed that the similarity of stimulus A to B is the same as the similarity of stimulus B to A. There are some instances where this assumption may be violated. For example, New Zealand is perceived as more similar to Australia than Australia is to New Zealand.

MDS assumes that the distance (similarity) between two stimuli is some function of their partial similarities on each of several perceptual dimensions. Not much research has been done to test this assumption. When a spatial map is obtained, it is assumed that inter-point distances are ratio scaled and that the axes of the map are multidimensional interval scaled. A limitation of MDS is that dimension interpretation relating physical changes in brands or stimuli to changes in the perceptual map is difficult at best. These limitations also apply to the scaling of preference data.

Scaling preference data

Internal analysis of preferences
A method of configuring a spatial map such that the spatial map represents both brands or stimuli and respondent points or vectors and is derived solely from the preference data.

Analysis of preference data can be internal or external. In **internal analysis of preferences**, a spatial map representing both brands or stimuli and respondent points or vectors is derived solely from the preference data. Thus, by collecting preference data, both brands and respondents can be represented in the same spatial map. In **external analysis of preferences**, the ideal points or vectors based on preference data are fitted in a spatial map derived from perception (e.g. similarities) data. To perform external analysis, both preference and perception data must be obtained. The representation of both brands and respondents as points in the same space, by using internal or external analysis, is referred to as *unfolding*.

External analysis of preferences
A method of configuring a spatial map such that the ideal points or vectors based on preference data are fitted in a spatial map derived from the perception data.

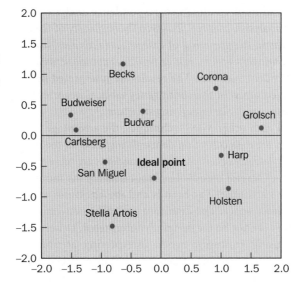

Figure 24.7
External analysis of preference data

External analysis is preferred in most situations.[12] In internal analysis, the differences in perceptions are confounded with differences in preferences. It is possible that the nature and relative importance of dimensions may vary between the perceptual space and the preference space. Two brands may be perceived to be similar (located closely to each other in the perceptual space), yet one brand may be distinctly preferred over the other (i.e. the brands may be located apart in the preference space). These situations cannot be accounted for in internal analysis. In addition, internal analysis procedures are beset with computational difficulties.[13]

We illustrate external analysis by scaling the preferences of our respondent into his spatial map. The respondent ranked the brands in the following order of preference (most preferred first): Stella Artois, Holsten, Harp, San Miguel, Carlsberg, Grolsch, Budvar, Budweiser, Corona and Becks. These preference rankings, along with the coordinates of the spatial map (Figure 24.5), were used as input into a preference scaling program to derive Figure 24.7. Notice the location of the ideal point. It is close to Stella Artois, Holsten, Carlsberg and San Miguel, the four most preferred brands, and far from Corona and Becks, the two least preferred brands. If a new brand were to be located in this space, its distance from the ideal point, relative to the distances of other brands from the ideal point, would determine the degree of preference for this brand.

Although we have considered only quantitative data so far, qualitative data can also be mapped using procedures such as correspondence analysis.

Correspondence analysis

Correspondence analysis
An MDS technique for scaling qualitative data that scales the rows and columns of the input contingency table in corresponding units so that each can be displayed in the same low-dimensional space.

Correspondence analysis is an MDS technique for scaling qualitative data in marketing research. The input data are in the form of a contingency table indicating a qualitative association between the rows and columns. Correspondence analysis scales the rows and columns in corresponding units so that each can be displayed graphically in the same low-dimensional space. These spatial maps provide insights into:

1 Similarities and differences within the rows with respect to a given column category.
2 Similarities and differences within the column categories with respect to a given row category.
3 Relationships among the rows and columns.[14]

The interpretation of results in correspondence analysis is similar to that in principal components analysis (Chapter 22), given the similarity of the algorithms. Correspondence analysis results in the grouping of categories (activities, brands or other stimuli) found within the contingency table, just as principal components analysis involves the grouping of the independent variables. The results are interpreted in terms of proximities among the rows and columns of the contingency table. Categories that are closer together than others are more similar in underlying structure.[15]

Compared with other MDS techniques, the advantage of correspondence analysis is that it reduces the data collection demands imposed on the respondents, since only binary or categorical data are obtained. The respondents are merely asked to tick which attributes apply to each of several brands. The input data are the number of 'yes' responses for each brand on each attribute. The brands and the attributes are then displayed in the same multidimensional space. The disadvantage is that between-set (i.e. between column and row) distances cannot be meaningfully interpreted. Other users have criticised the technique as causing confusion when interpreting attribute–brand relationships and complications in the tracking of perceptual changes.[16] Ultimately, it must be remembered that correspondence analysis is an exploratory data analysis technique that is not suitable for hypothesis testing.[17]

Relationship between MDS, factor analysis and discriminant analysis

MDS, including correspondence analysis, is not the only procedure available for obtaining perceptual maps. Two other techniques that we have discussed before, discriminant analysis (Chapter 21) and factor analysis (Chapter 22), can also be used for this purpose.

If the attribute-based approaches are used to obtain input data, spatial maps can also be obtained by using factor or discriminant analysis. In this approach, each respondent rates n brands on m attributes. By factor analysing the data, one could derive for each respondent n factor scores for each factor, one for each brand. By plotting brand scores on the factors, a spatial map could be obtained for each respondent. If an aggregate map is desired, the factor score for each brand for each factor can be averaged across respondents. The dimensions would be labelled by examining the factor loadings, which are estimates of the correlations between attribute ratings and underlying factors.[18]

The goal of discriminant analysis is to select the linear combinations of attributes that best discriminate between the brands or stimuli. To develop spatial maps by means of discriminant analysis, the dependent variable is the brand rated and the independent or predictor variables are the attribute ratings. A spatial map can be obtained by plotting the discriminant scores for the brands. The discriminant scores are the ratings on the perceptual dimensions, based on the attributes which best distinguish the brands. The dimensions can be labelled by examining the discriminant weights, or the weightings of attributes that make up a discriminant function or dimension.[19]

Basic concepts in conjoint analysis

Conjoint analysis
A technique that attempts to determine the relative importance consumers attach to salient attributes and the utilities they attach to the levels of attributes.

Conjoint analysis attempts to determine the relative importance consumers attach to salient attributes and the utilities they attach to the levels of attributes. This information is derived from consumers' evaluations of brands or from brand profiles composed of these attributes and their levels. The respondents are presented with stimuli that consist of combinations of attribute levels. They are asked to evaluate these stimuli in terms of their desirability. Conjoint procedures attempt to assign values to the levels of each attribute so that the resulting values or utilities attached to the stimuli match, as closely as possible, the input evaluations provided by the respondents. The underlying assumption is that any set of stimuli – such as products, brands or banks – are evaluated as a bundle of attributes.[20]

Like MDS, conjoint analysis relies on respondents' subjective evaluations. In MDS, however, the stimuli are products or brands. In conjoint analysis, the stimuli are combinations of attribute levels determined by the researcher. The goal in MDS is to develop a spatial map depicting the stimuli in a multidimensional perceptual or preference space. Conjoint analysis, on the other hand, seeks to develop the part-worth or utility functions describing the utility consumers attach to the levels of each attribute. The two techniques are complementary.

Conjoint analysis has been used in marketing for a variety of purposes, including the following:

- *Determining the relative importance of attributes in the consumer choice process.* A standard output from conjoint analysis consists of derived relative importance weights for all the attributes used to construct the stimuli presented in an evaluation task. The relative importance weights indicate which attributes are important in influencing consumer choice.
- *Estimating market share of brands that differ in attribute levels.* The utilities derived from conjoint analysis can be used as input into a choice simulator to determine the share of choices, and hence the market share, of different brands.
- *Determining the composition of the most preferred brand.* Brand features can be varied in terms of attribute levels and the corresponding utilities determined. The brand features that yield the highest utility indicate the composition of the most preferred brand.
- *Segmenting the market based on similarity of preferences for attribute levels.* The part-worth functions derived for the attributes may be used as a basis for clustering respondents to arrive at homogeneous preference segments.[21]

Applications of conjoint analysis have been made in consumer goods, industrial goods and financial and other services. Moreover, these applications have spanned all areas of marketing. A survey of conjoint analysis reported applications in the areas of new product and concept identification, competitive analysis, pricing, market segmentation, advertising and distribution.[22]

Statistics and terms associated with conjoint analysis

The important statistics and terms associated with conjoint analysis include the following:

Part-worth functions. The part-worth or *utility functions* describe the utility consumers attach to the levels of each attribute.

Relative importance weights. The relative importance weights are estimated and indicate which attributes are important in influencing consumer choice.

Attribute levels. Denote the values assumed by the attributes.

Full profiles. Full profiles or complete profiles of brands are constructed in terms of all the attributes by using the attribute levels specified by the design.

Pairwise tables. Respondents evaluate two attributes at a time until all the required pairs of attributes have been evaluated.

Cyclical designs. Designs employed to reduce the number of paired comparisons.

Fractional factorial designs. Designs employed to reduce the number of stimulus profiles to be evaluated in the full-profile approach.

Orthogonal arrays. A special class of fractional designs that enable the efficient estimation of all main effects.

Internal validity. This involves correlations of the predicted evaluations for the holdout or validation stimuli with those obtained from the respondents.

Conducting conjoint analysis

Figure 24.8 lists the steps in conjoint analysis. Formulating the problem involves identifying the salient attributes and their levels. These attributes and levels are used for constructing the stimuli to be used in a conjoint evaluation task. The respondents rate or rank the stimuli using a suitable scale, and the data obtained are analysed. The results are interpreted and their reliability and validity assessed. We now describe each of the steps of conjoint analysis in detail.

Formulate the problem

In formulating the conjoint analysis problem, the researcher must identify the attributes and attribute levels to be used in constructing the stimuli. Attribute levels denote the values assumed by the attributes. From a theoretical standpoint, the attributes selected should be salient in influencing consumer preference and choice. For example, in the choice of a car, price, fuel efficiency, interior space and so forth should be included. From a managerial perspective, the attributes and their levels should be characteristics that management can change and take action upon. To tell a manager that consumers prefer a sporty car to one that is conservative looking is not helpful, unless sportiness and conservativeness are defined in terms of attributes over which a manager has control. The attributes can be identified through discussions with management and industry experts, analysis of secondary data, qualitative research and pilot surveys. A typical conjoint analysis study may involve six or seven attributes.

Once the salient attributes have been identified, their appropriate levels should be selected. The number of attribute levels determines the number of parameters that will be estimated and also influences the number of stimuli that will be evaluated by the respondents. To minimise the respondent evaluation task and yet estimate the parameters with reasonable accuracy, it is desirable to restrict the number of attribute levels. The utility or part-worth function for the levels of an attribute may be non-linear. For example, a consumer may prefer a medium-sized car to either a small or a large one. Likewise, the utility for price may be non-linear. The loss of utility in going from a low price to a medium

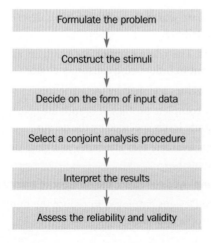

Figure 24.8
Conducting conjoint analysis

price may be much smaller than the loss in utility in going from a medium price to a high price. In these cases, at least three levels should be used. Some attributes, though, may naturally occur in binary form (two levels): a car does or does not have a sunroof.

The attribute levels selected will affect the consumer evaluations. If the price of a car brand is varied at €14,000, €16,000 and €18,000, price will be relatively unimportant. On the other hand, if the price is varied at €20,000, €30,000 and €40,000, it will be an important factor. Hence, the researcher should take into account the attribute levels prevalent in the marketplace and the objectives of the study. Using attribute levels that are beyond the range reflected in the marketplace will decrease the believability of the evaluation task, but it will increase the accuracy with which the parameters are estimated. The general guideline is to select attribute levels so that the ranges are somewhat greater than those prevalent in the marketplace but not so large as to impact the believability of the evaluation task adversely.

We illustrate the conjoint methodology by considering the problem of how students evaluate boots, e.g. brands such as Dr Martens, Timberland, Bally and Caterpillar. Qualitative research identified three attributes as salient: the material used for the upper, the country or region in which the boots were designed and manufactured and the price. Each was defined in terms of three levels, as shown in Table 24.2. These attributes and their levels were used for constructing the conjoint analysis stimuli. Note that, to keep the illustration simple, we are using only a limited number of attributes, i.e. only three. It has been argued that pictorial stimuli should be used when consumers' marketplace choices are strongly guided by the product's styling, such that the choices are heavily based on an inspection of actual products or pictures of products.[23]

Table 24.2 Boot attributes and levels

Attribute	Level	
	Number	*Description*
Uppers	3	Leather
	2	Suede
	1	Imitation leather
Country	3	Italy
	2	USA
	1	Far East
Price	3	€50
	2	€125
	1	€200

Construct the stimuli

Two broad approaches are available for constructing conjoint analysis stimuli: the pairwise approach and the full-profile procedure. In the pairwise approach, also called two-factor evaluations, respondents evaluate two attributes at a time until all the possible pairs of attributes have been evaluated. This approach is illustrated in the context of the boots example in Figure 24.9. For each pair, respondents evaluate all the combinations of levels of both the attributes, which are presented in a matrix.

You will be presented with information on boots in terms of pairs of features described in the form of a matrix. For each matrix, please rank the nine feature combinations in terms of your preference. A rank of 1 should be assigned to the most preferred combination and 9 to least preferred.

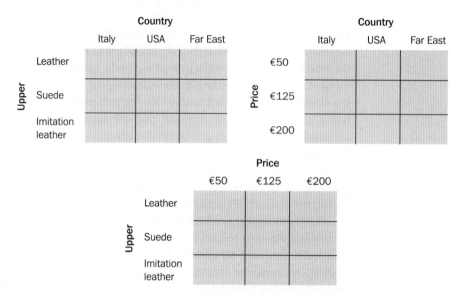

Figure 24.9
Pairwise approach to collecting conjoint data

In the full-profile approach, also called multiple-factor evaluations, full or complete profiles of brands are constructed for all the attributes. Typically, each profile is described on a separate index card. This approach is illustrated in the context of the boots example in Table 24.3.

Table 24.3 Full-profile approach to collecting conjoint data

Example of boot product profile	
Upper	Made of leather
Country	Designed and made in Italy
Price	Costing €200

It is not necessary to evaluate all the possible combinations, nor is it feasible in all cases.[24] In the pairwise approach, it is possible to reduce the number of paired comparisons by using cyclical designs. Likewise, in the full-profile approach, the number of stimulus profiles can be greatly reduced by means of fractional factorial designs. A special class of fractional designs, orthogonal arrays, allows for the efficient estimation of all main effects. Orthogonal arrays permit the measurement of all main effects of interest on an uncorrelated basis. These designs assume that all interactions are negligible. Orthogonal arrays are constructed from basic full factorial designs by substituting a new factor for selected interaction effects that are presumed to be negligible.[25] Generally, two sets of data are obtained. One, the *estimation set*, is used to calculate the part-worth functions for the attribute levels. The other, the *holdout set*, is used to assess reliability and validity.

The advantage of the pairwise approach is that it is easier for the respondents to provide these judgements. Its relative disadvantage, however, is that it requires more evaluations than the full-profile approach. Also, the evaluation task may be unrealistic when only two attributes are being evaluated simultaneously. Studies comparing the two approaches indicate that both methods yield comparable utilities, yet the full-profile approach is more commonly used.

The boots example follows the full-profile approach. Given three attributes, defined at three levels each, a total of $3 \times 3 \times 3 = 27$ profiles can be constructed. To reduce the respondent evaluation task, a fractional factorial design was employed and a set of nine profiles was constructed to constitute the estimation stimuli set (see Table 24.4). Another set of nine stimuli was constructed for validation purposes. Input data were obtained for both the estimation and validation stimuli. Before the data could be obtained, however, it was necessary to decide on the form of the input data.[26]

Decide on the form of input data

As in the case of MDS, conjoint analysis input data can be either non-metric or metric. For non-metric data, respondents are typically required to provide rank order evaluations. For the pairwise approach, respondents rank all the cells of each matrix in terms of their desirability. For the full-profile approach, they rank all the stimulus profiles. Rankings involve relative evaluations of the attribute levels. Proponents of ranking data believe that such data accurately reflect the behaviour of consumers in the marketplace.

In the metric form, respondents provide ratings, rather than rankings. In this case, the judgements are typically made independently. Advocates of rating data believe they are more convenient for the respondents and easier to analyse than rankings. In recent years, the use of ratings has become increasingly common.

In conjoint analysis, the dependent variable is usually preference or intention to buy. In other words, respondents provide ratings or rankings in terms of their preference or intentions to buy. The conjoint methodology, however, is flexible and can accommodate a range of other dependent variables, including actual purchase or choice.

In evaluating boot profiles, respondents were required to provide preference ratings for the boots described by the nine profiles in the estimation set. These ratings were obtained using a nine-point Likert scale (1 = not preferred, 9 = greatly preferred). Ratings obtained from one respondent are shown in Table 24.4.

Table 24.4 Boot profiles and their ratings

Profile number	Attribute levels*			
	Upper	Country	Price	Preference rating
1	1	1	1	9
2	1	2	2	7
3	1	3	3	5
4	2	1	2	6
5	2	2	3	5
6	2	3	1	6
7	3	1	3	5
8	3	2	1	7
9	3	3	2	6

*The attribute levels correspond to those in Table 24.2.

Select a conjoint analysis procedure

Conjoint analysis model
The mathematical model expressing the fundamental relationship between attributes and utility in conjoint analysis.

The basic **conjoint analysis model** may be represented by the following formula:[27]

$$U(X) = \sum_{i=1}^{m} \sum_{j=1}^{k_i} a_{ij} x_{ij}$$

where $U(X)$ = overall utility of an alternative

a_{ij} = the part-worth contribution or utility associated with the jth level
$(j, j = 1, 2, \ldots, k_i)$ of the ith attribute $(i, i = 1, 2, \ldots, m)$
k_i = number of levels of attribute i
m = number of attributes
x_{ij} = 1 if the jth level of the ith attribute is present
= 0 otherwise

The importance of an attribute, I_i, is defined in terms of the range of the part-worths, a_{ij}, across the levels of that attribute:

$$I_i = \{\max(a_{ij}) - \min(a_{ij})\} \text{ for each } i$$

The attribute's importance is normalised to ascertain its importance relative to other attributes, W_i:

$$W_i = \frac{I_i}{\sum_{i=1}^{m} I_i}$$

so that

$$\sum_{i=1}^{m} W_i = 1$$

Several different procedures are available for estimating the basic model. The simplest, and one which is gaining in popularity, is dummy variable regression (see Chapter 20). In this case, the predictor variables consist of dummy variables for the attribute levels. If an attribute has k_i levels, it is coded in terms of $k_i - 1$ dummy variables. If metric data are obtained, the ratings, assumed to be interval scaled, form the dependent variable. If the data are non-metric, the rankings may be converted to 0 or 1 by making paired comparisons between brands. In this case, the predictor variables represent the differences in the attribute levels of the brands being compared. Other procedures that are appropriate for non-metric data include LINMAP, MONANOVA and the LOGIT model.[28]

The researcher must also decide whether the data will be analysed at the individual respondent or the aggregate level. At the individual level, the data of each respondent are analysed separately. If an aggregate-level analysis is to be conducted, some procedure for grouping the respondents must be devised. One common approach is to estimate individual-level part-worth or utility functions first. Respondents are then clustered on the basis of the similarity of their part-worth functions. Aggregate analysis is then conducted for each cluster.[29] An appropriate model for estimating the parameters should be specified.[30]

The data reported in Table 24.4 were analysed using ordinary least squares (OLS) regression with dummy variables. The dependent variable was the preference ratings. The independent variables or predictors were six dummy variables, two for each variable. The transformed data are shown in Table 24.5. Since the data pertain to a single respondent, an individual-level analysis was conducted. The part-worth or utility functions estimated for each attribute, as well as the relative importance of the attributes, are given in Table 24.6.[31]

Table 24.5 Boot data coded for dummy variable regression

Preference ratings	Attributes					
	Upper		Country		Price	
Y	X_1	X_2	X_3	X_4	X_5	X_6
9	1	0	1	0	1	0
7	1	0	0	1	0	1
5	1	0	0	0	0	0
6	0	1	1	0	0	1
5	0	1	0	1	0	0
6	0	1	0	0	1	0
5	0	0	1	0	0	0
7	0	0	0	1	1	0
6	0	0	0	0	0	1

Table 24.6 Boot attributes and levels

Attribute	Level			
	Number	Description	Utility	Importance
Uppers	3	Leather	0.778	
	2	Suede	−0.556	
	1	Imitation leather	−0.222	0.268
Country	3	Italy	0.445	
	2	USA	0.111	
	1	Far East	−0.556	0.214
Price	3	€50	1.111	
	2	€125	0.111	
	1	€200	−1.222	0.500

The model estimated may be represented as

$$U = b_0 + b_1 X_1 + b_2 X_2 + b_3 X_3 + b_4 X_4 + b_5 X_5 + b_6 X_6$$

where X_1, X_2 = dummy variables representing uppers
X_3, X_4 = dummy variables representing country
X_5, X_6 = dummy variables representing price

For uppers, the attribute levels were coded as follows:

	X_1	X_2
Level 1	1	0
Level 2	0	1
Level 3	0	0

The levels of the other attributes were coded similarly. The parameters were estimated as follows:

$$
\begin{aligned}
b_0 &= 4.222 \\
b_1 &= 1.000 \\
b_2 &= -0.333 \\
b_3 &= 1.000 \\
b_4 &= 0.667 \\
b_5 &= 2.333 \\
b_6 &= 1.333
\end{aligned}
$$

Given the dummy variable coding, in which level 3 is the base level, the coefficients may be related to the part-worths. As explained in Chapter 20, each dummy variable coefficient represents the difference in the part-worth for that level minus the part-worth for the base level. For upper, we have the following:

$$
\begin{aligned}
a_{11} - a_{13} &= b_1 \\
a_{12} - a_{13} &= b_2
\end{aligned}
$$

To solve for the part-worths, an additional constraint is necessary. The part-worths are estimated on an interval scale, so the origin is arbitrary. Therefore, the additional constraint imposed is of the form

$$
a_{11} + a_{12} + a_{13} = 0
$$

These equations for the first attribute, uppers, are

$$
\begin{aligned}
a_{11} - a_{13} &= 1.000 \\
a_{12} - a_{13} &= -0.333 \\
a_{11} + a_{12} + a_{13} &= 0
\end{aligned}
$$

Solving these equations, we get

$$
\begin{aligned}
a_{11} &= 0.778 \\
a_{12} &= -0.556 \\
a_{13} &= -0.222
\end{aligned}
$$

The part-worths for other attributes reported in Table 24.6 can be estimated similarly. For country, we have

$$
\begin{aligned}
a_{21} - a_{23} &= b_3 \\
a_{22} - a_{23} &= b_4 \\
a_{21} + a_{22} + a_{23} &= 0
\end{aligned}
$$

For the third attribute, price, we have

$$
\begin{aligned}
a_{31} - a_{33} &= b_5 \\
a_{32} - a_{33} &= b_6 \\
a_{31} + a_{32} + a_{33} &= 0
\end{aligned}
$$

The relative importance weights were calculated based on ranges of part-worths, as follows:

$$
\begin{aligned}
\text{Sum of ranges of part-worths} &= [0.778 \ (-0.556)] + [0.445 - (-0.556)] \\
&\quad + [1.111 - (-1.222)] \\
&= 4.668
\end{aligned}
$$

$$
\text{Relative importance of uppers} = \frac{1.334}{4.668} = 0.286
$$

$$\text{Relative importance of country} = \frac{1.001}{4.668} = 0.214$$

$$\text{Relative importance of price} = \frac{2.333}{4.668} = 0.500$$

The estimation of the part-worths and the relative importance weights provides the basis for interpreting the results.

Interpret the results

For interpreting the results, it is helpful to plot the part-worth functions. The part-worth function values for each attribute given in Table 24.6 are graphed in Figure 24.10. As can be seen from Table 24.6 and Figure 24.10, this respondent has the greatest preference for leather uppers when evaluating boots. Second preference is for imitation leather uppers, and suede uppers are least preferred. An Italian boot is most preferred, followed by American boots and boots from the Far East. As may be expected, a price of €50.00 has the highest utility and a price of €200.00 the lowest. The utility values reported in Table 24.6 have only interval scale properties, and their origin is arbitrary. In terms of relative importance of the attributes, we see that price is number one. Second most important is uppers, followed closely by country. Because price is by far the most important attribute for this respondent, this person could be labelled as price sensitive.

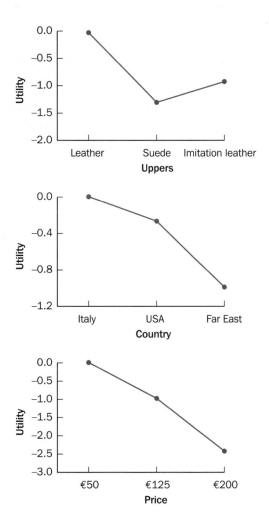

Figure 24.10
Part-worth functions

Assess the reliability and validity

Several procedures are available for assessing the reliability and validity of conjoint analysis results:[32]

1 The goodness of fit of the estimated model should be evaluated. For example, if dummy variable regression is used, the value of R^2 will indicate the extent to which the model fits the data. Models with poor fit are suspect.

2 Test–retest reliability can be assessed by obtaining a few replicated judgements later in data collection. In other words, at a later stage in the interview, the respondents are asked to evaluate certain selected stimuli again. The two values of these stimuli are then correlated to assess test–retest reliability.

3 The evaluations for the holdout or validation stimuli can be predicted by the estimated part-worth functions. The predicted evaluations can then be correlated with those obtained from the respondents to determine internal validity.

4 If an aggregate-level analysis has been conducted, the estimation sample can be split in several ways and conjoint analysis conducted on each subsample. The results can be compared across subsamples to assess the stability of conjoint analysis solutions.

In running a regression analysis on the data of Table 24.5, an R^2 of 0.934 was obtained, indicating a good fit. The preference ratings for the nine validation profiles were predicted from the utilities reported in Table 24.6. These were correlated with the input ratings for these profiles obtained from the respondent. The correlation coefficient was 0.95, indicating a good predictive ability. This correlation coefficient is significant at $\alpha = 0.05$.

Assumptions and limitations of conjoint analysis

Although conjoint analysis is a popular technique, like MDS it carries a number of assumptions and limitations. Conjoint analysis assumes that the important attributes of a product can be identified. Furthermore, it assumes that consumers evaluate the choice alternatives in terms of these attributes and make trade-offs. In situations where image or brand name is important, however, consumers may not evaluate the brands or alternatives in terms of attributes. Even if consumers consider product attributes, the trade-off model may not be a good representation of the choice process. Another limitation is that data collection may be complex, particularly if a large number of attributes are involved and the model must be estimated at the individual level. This problem has been mitigated to some extent by procedures such as interactive or adaptive conjoint analysis and hybrid conjoint analysis. It should also be noted that the part-worth functions are not unique.

Hybrid conjoint analysis

Hybrid conjoint analysis
A form of conjoint analysis that can simplify the data collection task and estimate selected interactions as well as all main effects.

Hybrid conjoint analysis is an attempt to simplify the burdensome data collection task required in traditional conjoint analysis. Each respondent evaluates a large number of profiles, yet usually only simple part-worth functions, without any interaction effects, are estimated. In the simple part-worths or main-effects model, the value of a combination is simply the sum of the separate main-effects (simple part-worths). In actual practice, two attributes may interact in the sense that the respondent may value the combination more than the average contribution of the separate parts. Hybrid models have been developed to serve two main purposes: (1) to simplify the data collection task by imposing less of a burden on each respondent, and (2) to permit the estimation of selected interactions (at the subgroup level) as well as all main (or simple) effects (at the individual level).

In the hybrid approach, the respondents evaluate a limited number, generally no more than nine, of conjoint stimuli, such as full profiles. These profiles are drawn from a large master design and different respondents evaluate different sets of profiles so that, over a group of respondents, all the profiles of interest are evaluated. In addition, respondents directly evaluate the relative importance of each attribute and desirability of the levels of each attribute. By combining the direct evaluations with those derived from the evaluations of the conjoint stimuli, it is possible to estimate a model at the aggregate level and still retain some individual differences.[33]

MDS and conjoint analysis are complementary techniques and may be used in combination, as the following examples show.

Example — Herit-age or merit-age in Europe?[34]

European car manufacturers are increasingly focusing on an attribute that competitors will not be able to buy or build, namely heritage. For BMW, it is superior engineering. Volvo has a reputation for safe cars. Alfa Romeo rides on the laurels of engines that have won numerous races. Renault has *savoir-faire*. On the other hand, Japanese cars are advanced technologically but they lack an amount of 'class' or heritage. Philip Gamba, Vice President of Marketing at Renault, believes Japanese brands lack the 'French touch' encapsulated in Renault's design and credibility. These days, Renault builds cars with increasing focus on safety, BMW is trying to emphasise not the prestige of owning a luxury car but the 'inner value' of its cars. To communicate value in cars is of growing importance, and BMW certainly has an edge with its German heritage.

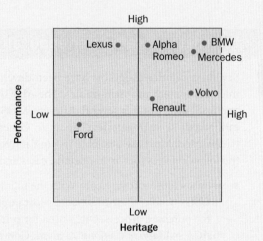

Because performance and heritage are important attributes or dimensions in car preferences of Europeans, the positioning of different European cars on these two dimensions is shown. Note that BMW has attained the best positioning on both these dimensions. Typical of most American and Japanese cars in the 2000s has been the emphasis on quality, reliability and efficiency. However, to compete in the European market, American, Japanese and car manufacturers from developing nations worldwide are faced with the challenge of an added dimension – heritage.

Example — Weeding out the competition[35]

ICI Agricultural Products did not know whether it should lower the price of Fusilade, its herbicide. It knew that it had developed a potent herbicide, but it was not sure that the weedkiller would survive in a price-conscious market. So a survey was designed to assess the relative importance of different attributes in selecting herbicides and to measure and map perceptions of major herbicides on the same attributes. Personal interviews were conducted with 601 soybean and cotton farmers who had at least 120 hectares dedicated to growing these crops and who had used herbicides during the past growing season. First, conjoint analysis was used to determine the relative importance of attributes farmers use when selecting herbicides. Then MDS was used to map farmers' perceptions of herbicides. The study showed that price greatly influenced herbicide selections, and respondents were particularly sensitive when costs were more than €10 per hectare. But price was not the only determinant. Farmers also considered how much weed control the herbicide provided. They were willing to pay higher prices to keep weeds off their land. The study showed that herbicides that failed to control even one of the four most common weeds would have to be very inexpensive to attain a reasonable market share. Fusilade promised good weed control. Furthermore, MDS indicated that one of Fusilade's competitors was considered to be expensive. Hence, ICI kept its original pricing plan and did not lower the price of Fusilade.

As of 2003, however, the agriculture industry has changed. One factor that has changed the industry is a shift in technology, especially biotechnology. Roundup Ready soybeans had a huge effect on the herbicide market, by making farmers switch from using traditional soybean herbicides to a new combined technology of Roundup and transgenic seed. The new technology cut the cost of per-acre herbicides in half, and, as a result, competing chemical companies were forced to meet the price of the new technology. It is very important for companies to research consumer acceptance of technological innovations using techniques such as MDS and conjoint analysis.

Internet and computer applications

Several computer programs have been developed for conducting MDS analysis using microcomputers and mainframes. The ALSCAL program, available in versions of SPSS and SAS, incorporates several different MDS models and can be used for conducting individual- or aggregate-level analysis. Other MDS programs are easily available and widely used. Most are available in both microcomputer and mainframe versions. Visit the following sites for further details, cases and demos:

- **www.sawtoothsoftware.com** With the following variations:
  CBC – Choice-Based Conjoint. Most popular conjoint method. The choices mimic the purchase process. Often used for pricing research.
  ACA – Adaptive Conjoint Analysis. Computer interview customises the experience for respondent. Especially useful with many attributes.
  CVA – Conjoint Value Analysis. Traditional full-profile conjoint method. For few attributes and single-version design plans.
  ASM – Advanced Simulation Module. Add-on to the market simulator for automated product optimisation searches.
  CCS – Client Conjoint Simulator. Client version of the market simulator.
- **www.newmdsx.com** A resource base for MDS.
- **www.statpac.com** Click on 'Advanced Statistical Analysis' to see an array of multivariate data analysis programs, including correspondence analysis.

Summary

Multidimensional scaling (MDS) is used for obtaining spatial representations of respondents' perceptions and preferences. Perceived or psychological relationships among stimuli are represented as geometric relationships among points in a multi-dimensional space. Formulating the MDS problem requires a specification of the brands or stimuli to be included. The number and nature of brands selected influence the resulting solution. Input data obtained from the respondents can be related to perceptions or preferences. Perception data can be direct or derived. The direct approaches are more common in marketing research.

The selection of an MDS procedure depends on the nature (metric or non-metric) of the input data and whether perceptions or preferences are being scaled. Another determining factor is whether the analysis will be conducted at the individual or aggregate level. The decision about the number of dimensions in which to obtain a solution should be based on theory, interpretability, elbow criterion and ease-of-use considerations. Labelling of the dimensions is a difficult task that requires subjective judgement. Several guidelines are available for assessing the reliability and validity of MDS solutions. Preference data can be subjected to either internal or external analysis. If the input data are of a qualitative nature, they can be analysed via correspondence analysis. If the attribute-based approaches are used to obtain input data, spatial maps can also be obtained by means of factor or discriminant analysis.

Conjoint analysis is based on the notion that the relative importance that consumers attach to salient attributes, and the utilities they attach to the levels of attributes, can be determined when consumers evaluate brand profiles that are constructed using these attributes and their levels. Formulating the problem requires an identification of the salient attributes and their levels. The pairwise and the full-profile approaches are commonly employed for constructing the stimuli. Statistical designs are available for reducing the number of stimuli in the evaluation task. The input data can be either non-metric (rankings) or metric (ratings). Typically, the dependent variable is preference or intention to buy.

Although other procedures are available for analysing conjoint analysis data, regression using dummy variables is becoming increasingly important. Interpreting the results requires an examination of the part-worth functions and relative importance weights. Several procedures are available for assessing the reliability and validity of conjoint analysis results.

Questions

1 For what purposes are MDS procedures used?

2 Identify two marketing research problems where MDS could be applied. Explain how you would apply MDS in these situations.

3 What is meant by a spatial map?

4 Describe the steps involved in conducting MDS.

5 Describe the direct and derived approaches to obtaining MDS input data.

6 What factors influence the choice of an MDS procedure?

7 What guidelines are used for deciding on the number of dimensions in which to obtain an MDS solution?

8 Describe the ways in which the reliability and validity of MDS solutions can be assessed.

9 What is the difference between internal and external analysis of preference data?

10 What is involved in formulating a conjoint analysis problem?

11 Describe the full-profile approach to constructing stimuli in conjoint analysis.

12 Describe the pairwise approach to constructing stimuli in conjoint analysis.

13 How can regression analysis be used for analysing conjoint data?

14 Graphically illustrate what is meant by part-worth functions.

15 What procedures are available for assessing the reliability and validity of conjoint analysis results?

Exercises

1 Identify two marketing research problems where MDS could be applied and two where conjoint analysis could be applied. Explain how you would use these techniques in these situations.

2 A respondent's ratings of nine luxury car brands on four dimensions are shown. Each brand was evaluated on each dimension (prestige, performance, luxury and value) on a seven-point scale with 1 = poor and 7 = excellent. Develop an MDS plot in two dimensions. Explain the plot.

Brand	Prestige	Performance	Luxury	Value
Ferrari	5	7	5	7
Jaguar	5	6	5	7
BMW	5	7	6	5
Mercedes	6	6	6	6
Audi	5	5	6	5
Lexus	6	6	5	5
Porsche	5	6	5	4
Bentley	7	4	7	3
Rolls	7	4	7	1

3 Consider 12 brands of bath soap (you can use the following – or other brands that you are more familiar with): Dove, Zest, Dial, Imperial Leather, Body Shop, Camay, Ivory, Palmolive, Irish Spring, Lux, Safeguard, Fairy. Form all the possible 66 pairs of these brands. Rate these pairs of brands in terms of similarity using a seven-point scale. Write a report on what you would see as the respondent experience in completing the task of comparing these brands.

4 Construct the nine boot profiles given in Table 24.4. Rate these nine profiles in terms of your preference, using a nine-point rating scale.

5 In a small group discuss the similarities and differences between MDS, factor analysis and discriminant analysis, and 'simplifying MDS solutions to two-dimensional graphics works well in conveying a solution, but they can only rarely convey the complexity of how consumers differentiate between brands'.

Notes

1 Anon., 'Soft drink product tops survey', *Businessworld* (14 August 2001), 1; Green, P.E., Carmone, F.J. Jr and Smith, S.M., *Multidimensional Scaling: Concepts and Applications* (Boston, MA: Allyn & Bacon, 1989), 16–17.

2 Kara, A., Kaynak, E. and Kucukemiroglu, O., 'Credit card development strategies for the youth market: the use of conjoint analysis', *International Journal of Bank Marketing* 12 (6) (1994), 30–36; Barrett, P., Burr, P. and Dolman, N., 'The conjoint path over the cultural divide', *Marketing Week* (14 October 1997).

3 For a review of MDS studies in marketing, see Bijmolt, T.H.A. and Wedel, M., 'A comparison of multidimensional scaling methods for perceptual mapping', *Journal of Marketing Research* 36 (2) (May 1999), 277–285; Carroll, J.D. and Green, P.E., 'Psychometric methods in marketing research: Part II. Multidimensional scaling', *Journal of Marketing Research* 34 (February 1997), 193–204; Cooper, L.G., 'A review of multidimensional scaling in marketing research', *Applied Psychological Measurement* 7 (Fall 1983), 427–450.

4 An excellent discussion of the various aspects of MDS may be found in Bijmolt, T.H.A. and Wedel, M., 'A comparison of multidimensional scaling methods for perceptual mapping', *Journal of Marketing Research* 36 (2) (May 1999), 277–285; Davison, M.L., *Multidimensional Scaling* (Melbourne: Krieger, 1992).

5 Lines, R. and Denstadli, J.M., 'Information overload in conjoint experiments', *International Journal of Market Research* 46 (3) (2004) 297–310.

6 The data are commonly treated as symmetric. For an asymmetric approach, see Desarbo, W.S. and Manrai, A.K., 'A new multidimensional scaling methodology for the analysis of asymmetric proximity data in marketing research', *Marketing Science* 11 (1) (Winter 1992), 1–20. For other approaches to MDS data, see Juvoung, K., 'Incorporating context effects in the multidimensional scaling of "Pick Any/N" choice data', *International Journal of Research in Marketing* 16 (1) (February 1999), 35–55; Bijmolt, T.H.A. and Wedel, M., 'The effects of alternative methods of collecting similarity data for multidimensional scaling', *International Journal of Research in Marketing* 12 (4) (November 1995), 363–371.

7 See Cox, T.F. and Cox, M.A., *Multidimensional scaling*, 2nd edn (New York: Chapman & Hall, 2000); Steenkamp, J.-B.E.M. and Van Trijp, H.C.M., 'Task experience and validity in perceptual mapping: a comparison of two consumer-adaptive techniques', *International Journal of Research in Marketing* 13 (3) (July 1996), 265–276; Malhotra, N.K., Jain, A.K. and Pinson, C., 'The robustness of MDS configurations in the case of incomplete data', *Journal of Marketing Research* 25 (February 1988), 95–102.

8 See Cox, T.F. and Cox, M.A., *Multidimensional scaling*, 2nd edn (New York: Chapman & Hall, 2000).

9 Kruskal's stress is probably the most commonly used measure for lack of fit. See Borg, I. and Groenen, P.J., *Modern Multidimensional Scaling Theory and Applications* (New York: Springer-Verlag, 1996). For the original article, see Kruskal, J.B., 'Multidimensional scaling by optimising goodness of fit to a nonmetric hypothesis', *Psychometrika* 29 (March 1964), 1–27.

10 Carroll, J.D. and Green, P.E., 'Psychometric methods in marketing research: Part II. Multidimensional scaling', *Journal of Marketing Research* 34 (February 1997), 193–204; Malhotra, N.K., 'Validity and structural reliability of multidimensional scaling', *Journal of Marketing Research* 24 (May 1987), 164–173.

11 For an examination of the reliability and validity of MDS solutions, see DeSarbo, W.S., 'The joint spatial representation of multiple variable batteries collected in marketing research', *Journal of Marketing Research* 38 (2) (May 2001), 244–253.

12 Hair, J.E., Jr Anderson, R.E., Tatham, R.L. and Black, W.C., *Multivariate Data Analysis with Readings*, 5th edn (Englewood Cliffs, NJ: Prentice Hall, 1999), 484–555.

13 See, for example, Lee, J.K.H., Sudhir, K. and Steckel, J.H., 'A multiple ideal point model: capturing multiple preference effects from within an ideal point framework', *Journal of Marketing Research* 39 (1) (February 2002), 73–86; DeSarbo, W.S., Hoffman, D. and Rangaswamy, A., 'A parametric multidimensional unfolding procedure for incomplete nonmetric preference/choice set data marketing research', *Journal of Marketing Research* 34 (4) (November 1997), 499–516; Mackay, D.B., Easley, R.F. and Zinnes, J.L., 'A single ideal point model for market structure analysis', *Journal of Marketing Research* 32 (4) (November 1995), 433–443.

14 For an application of correspondence analysis, see Malhotra, N.K. and Charles, B., 'Overcoming the attribute prespecification bias in international marketing research by using nonattribute based correspondence analysis', *International Marketing Review* 19 (1) (2002), 65–79; Reed, K., 'The use of correspondence analysis to develop a scale to measure workplace morale from multi-level data', *Social Indicators Research* 57 (3) (March 2002), 339.

15 Kara, A., Kaynak, E. and Kucukemiroglu, O., 'Positioning of fast food outlets in two regions of north America: a comparative study using correspondence analysis', *Journal of Professional Services Marketing* 14 (2) (1996), 99–119; O'Brien, T.V., 'Correspondence analysis', *Marketing Research: A Magazine of Management and Applications* 5 (4) (Fall 1993), 54–56; Green, P.E., Carmone, F.J. Jr and Smith, S.M., *Multidimensional Scaling: Concepts and Applications* (Boston, MA: Allyn & Bacon, 1989), 16–17.

16 Whitlark, D.B. and Smith, S.M., 'Using correspondence analysis to map relationships', *Marketing Research: A Magazine of Management and Applications* 13 (4) (Fall 2001), 22–27.

17 See Blasius, J. and Greenacre, M.J., *Visualization of Categorical Data* (New York: Academic Press, 1998); Greenacre, M.J., *Correspondence Analysis in Practice* (New York: Academic Press, 1993); Greenacre, M.J., 'The Carroll–Green–Schaffer scaling in correspondence analysis: a theoretical and empirical appraisal', *Journal of Marketing Research* 26 (August 1989), 358–365; Greenacre, M.J., *Theory and Applications of Correspondence Analyses* (New York: Academic Press, 1984); Hoffman, D.L. and Franke, G.R., 'Correspondence analysis: graphical representation of categorical data in marketing research', *Journal of Marketing Research* 23 (August 1986), 213–227.

18 For the use of factor analysis in constructing spatial maps, see Hasson, L., 'Monitoring social change', *Journal of the Market Research Society* 37 (January 1995), 69–80.

19 Bijmolt, T.H.A. and Wedel, M., 'A comparison of multidimensional scaling methods for perceptual mapping', *Journal of Marketing Research* 36 (2) (May 1999), 277–285; Hauser, J.R. and Koppelman, F.S., 'Alternative perceptual mapping techniques: relative accuracy and usefulness', *Journal of Marketing Research* 16 (November 1979), 495–506. Hauser and Koppelman conclude that factor analysis is superior to discriminant analysis. See also Borg, I. and Groenen, P.J., *Modern Multidimensional Scaling Theory and Applications* (New York: Springer-Verlag, 1996).

20 For applications and issues in conjoint analysis, see Andrews, R.L., Ansari, A. and Currim, I.S., 'Hierarchical Bayes versus finite mixture conjoint analysis models: a comparison of fit, prediction and partworth recovery', *Journal of Marketing Research* 39 (1) (February 2002), 87–98; Srinivasan, V. and Park, C.S., 'Surprising robustness of the self-explicated approach to customer preference structure measurement', *Journal of Marketing Research* 34 (May 1997), 286–291; Naude, P. and Buttle, F., 'Assessing relationship quality', *Industrial Marketing Management* 29 (2000), 351–361; Carroll, J.D. and Green, P.E., 'Psychometric methods in marketing research: Part I. Conjoint analysis', *Journal of Marketing Research* 32 (November 1995), 385–391; Green, P.E. and Krieger, A.M., 'Segmenting markets with conjoint analysis', *Journal of Marketing* 55 (October 1991), 20–31.

21 Vriens, M., 'Linking attributes, benefits, and consumer values', *Marketing Research* 12 (3) (Fall 2000), 4–10; Thomas-Miller, J., Ogden, J.R. and Latshaw, C.A., 'Using trade-off analysis to determine value–price sensitivity of custom calling features', *American Business Review* 16 (1) (January 1998), 8–13.

22 Sandor, Z. and Wedel, M., 'Designing conjoint choice experiments using managers' prior beliefs', *Journal of Marketing Research* 38 (4) (November 2001), 430–444; Srinivasan, V., 'Predictive validation of multiattribute choice models', *Marketing Research* 11 (4) (Winter 1999/Spring 2000), 29–34; Wittink, D.R., Vriens, M. and Burhenne, W., 'Commercial uses of conjoint analysis in Europe: results and critical reflections', *International Journal of Research in Marketing* 11 (1) (January 1994), 41–52; Wittink, D.R. and Cattin, P., 'Commercial use of conjoint analysis: an update', *Journal of Marketing* 53 (July 1989), 91–97. For using conjoint analysis to measure price sensitivity, see 'Multi-stage conjoint methods to measure price sensitivity', *Sawtooth News* 10 (Winter 1994–1995), 5–6.

23 Wetzels, M., 'Measuring service quality trade-offs in Asian distribution channels: a multilayer perspective', *Total Quality Management* 11 (3) (May 2000), 307–318; Loosschilder, G.H., Rosbergen, E., Vriens, M. and Wittink, D.R., 'Pictorial stimuli in conjoint analysis – to support product styling decisions', *Journal of the Market Research Society* 37 (January 1995), 17–34.

24 McCullough, D., 'A users guide to conjoint analysis', *Marketing Research* (Summer 2002), 19–23.

25 See Green, P.A., Krieger, A.M. and Wind, Y., 'Thirty years of conjoint analysis: reflections and prospects', *Interfaces* 31 (3) (May/June 2001), S56; Carroll, J.D. and Green, P.E., 'Psychometric methods in marketing research: Part I. Conjoint analysis', *Journal of Marketing Research* 32 (November 1995), 385–391; Kuhfeld, W.F., Tobias, R.D. and Garratt, M., 'Efficient experimental designs with marketing applications', *Journal of Marketing Research* 31 (November 1994), 545–557; Addleman, S., 'Orthogonal main-effect plans for asymmetrical factorial experiments', *Technometrics* 4 (February 1962), 21–36; Green, P.E., 'On the design of choice experiments involving multifactor alternatives', *Journal of Consumer Research* 1 (September 1974), 61–68.

26 More complex conjoint designs are also possible. See Oppewal, H., Louviere, J.J. and Timmermans, H.J.P., 'Modeling hierarchical conjoint processes with integrated choice experiments', *Journal of Marketing Research* 31 (February 1994), 15–27.

27 Haaijer, R., Kamakura, W. and Wedel, M., 'Response latencies in the analysis of conjoint choice experiments', *Journal of Marketing Research* 37 (3) (August 2000), 376–382; Carroll, J.D. and Green, P.E., 'Psychometric methods in marketing research: Part I. Conjoint analysis', *Journal of Marketing Research* 32 (November 1995), 385–391.

28 Sandor, Z. and Wedel, M., 'Designing conjoint choice experiments using managers' prior beliefs', *Journal of Marketing Research* 38 (4) (November 2001), 430–444; Oppewal, H., Timmermans, H.J. and Louviere, J.J., 'Modeling the effect of shopping center size and store variety in consumer choice behaviour', *Environment and Planning* 29 (6) (June 1997), 1073–1090.

29 Arora, N. and Allenby, G.M., 'Measuring the influence of individual preference structures in group decision making', *Journal of Marketing Research* 36 (4) (November 1999), 476–487; Brice, R., 'Conjoint analysis: a review of conjoint paradigms and discussion of the outstanding design issues', *Marketing and Research Today* 25 (4) (November 1997), 260–266; Carroll, J.D. and Green, P.E., 'Psychometric methods in marketing research: Part I. Conjoint analysis', *Journal of Marketing Research* 32 (November 1995), 385–391; Carmone, E.J. and Green, P.E., 'Model mis-specification in multiattribute parameter estimation', *Journal of Marketing Research* 18 (February 1981), 87–93.

30 For an application of conjoint analysis using OLS regression see Haaijer, R., Kamakura, W. and Wedel, M., 'The "No–Choice" alternative to conjoint choice experiments', *International Journal of Market Research* 43 (1) (First Quarter 2001), 93–106; Ostrom, A. and Iacobucci, D., 'Consumer trade-offs and the evaluation of services', *Journal of Marketing* 59 (January 1995), 17–28; Danaher, P.J., 'Using conjoint analysis to determine the relative importance of service attributes measured in customer satisfaction surveys', *Journal of Retailing* 73 (2) (Summer 1997), 235–260.

31 Ibid.

32 Andrews, R.L., 'Hierarchical Bayes versus finite mixture conjoint analysis: a comparison of fit, prediction and partworth recovery', *Journal of Marketing Research* 39 (1) (February 2002), 87–98; Carroll, J.D. and Green, P.E., 'Psychometric methods in marketing research: Part I. Conjoint analysis', *Journal of Marketing Research* 32 (November 1995), 385–391; Malhotra, N.K., 'Structural reliability and stability of nonmetric conjoint analysis', *Journal of Marketing Research* 19 (May 1982), 199–207; Leigh, T.W., MacKay, D.B. and Summers, J.O., 'Reliability and validity of conjoint analysis and self-explicated weights: a comparison', *Journal of Marketing Research* 21 (November 1984), 456–462; Segal, M.N., 'Reliability of conjoint analysis: contrasting data collection procedures', *Journal of Marketing Research* 19 (February 1982), 139–143.

33 Hofstede, F.T., Kim, Y. and Wedel, M., 'Bayesian prediction in hybrid conjoint analysis', *Journal of Marketing Research* 39 (2) (May 2002), 253–261; Vavra, T.G., Green, P.E. and Krieger, A.M., 'Evaluating EZPass', *Marketing Research* 11 (2) (Summer 1999), 4–14; Hu, C. and Hiemstra, S.J., 'Hybrid conjoint analysis as a research technique to measure meeting planners' preferences in hotel selection', *Journal of Travel Research* 35 (2) (Fall 1996), 62–69; Green, P.E. and Krieger, A.M., 'Individualized hybrid models for conjoint analysis', *Management Science* 42 (6) (June 1996), 850–867; Green, P.E., 'Hybrid models for conjoint analysis: an expository review', *Journal of Marketing Research* 21 (May 1984), 155–169.

34 McSheehy, W., 'Think globally, act locally', *Corporate Location* (July/August 2001), 12; McCarthy, M., 'Marketers reduce national ad spending', *USA Today* (17 April 2001), B3; Anon., 'Luxury car makers assemble world view', *Corporate Location* (January/February 1997), 4.

35 Boyle, K.J., 'A comparison of conjoint analysis response formats', *American Journal of Agricultural Economics* 83 (2) (May 2001), 441–454; McDonald, D., 'Industry giants', *Farm Industry News* 34 (3) (February 2001), 6; Schneidman, D., 'Research method designed to determine price for new products, line extensions', *Marketing News* (23 October 1987), 11.

Visit the *Marketing Research* Companion Website at www.pearsoned.co.uk/malhotra_euro for additional learning resources including annotated weblinks, an online glossary and a suite of downloadable video cases.

Source: © Cadmium

25

Report preparation and presentation

Managers should find reports easy to understand, be confident in the findings, and be clear about the action they should take, based on the researcher's approach, insight and integrity.

Objectives

After reading this chapter, you should be able to:

1 discuss the basic requirements of report preparation, including report format, report writing, graphs and tables;

2 discuss the nature and scope of the oral presentation;

3 describe the approach to the marketing research report from the client's perspective;

4 explain the reason for follow-up with the client and describe the assistance that should be given to the client and the evaluation of the research project;

5 understand the report preparation and presentation process in international marketing research;

6 identify the ethical issues related to the interpretation and reporting of the research process and findings to the client and the use of these results by the client.

STAGE 1
Problem definition

STAGE 2
Research approach developed

STAGE 3
Research design developed

STAGE 4
Fieldwork or data collection

STAGE 5
Data preparation and analysis

STAGE 6
Report preparation and presentation

Overview

This chapter describes the importance of report preparation and presentation and outlines the process of producing written and oral presentations. We provide guidelines for report preparation, including report writing and preparing tables and graphs, and we discuss oral presentation of the report. Research follow-up, including assisting the client and evaluating the research process, is described. The special considerations for report preparation and presentation in international marketing research are discussed, and relevant ethical issues are identified. We begin with an example of a report based upon an ongoing customer satisfaction survey that is fed to different levels of an organisation, helping it to maintain its customer orientation. This is followed with an example of a very creative means to present findings to a study that is primarily presenting qualitative findings. Both examples illustrate the different styles and means to present marketing research reports.

Example   Reporting the friendly skies[1]

United Airlines conducts an ongoing in-flight customer satisfaction tracking survey. Each month, 192,000 passengers on 900 flights are selected and surveyed using a four-page scannable form. The survey covers the satisfaction of passengers on both 'on-the-ground' services (flight reservation, airport service) and 'in-the-air' services (flight attendants, meals, aircraft). Each month a report is produced, summarising customer satisfaction. The report is also posted on the Internet and available online to managers all over the world. Because of the large size of the sample, the data are very reliable and all departments of the company use the report, such as:

- *Marketing department* uses it for strategic planning, product positioning and target marketing decisions.
- *Finance department* uses it to measure the success of its product investments.
- *Airport* uses it to evaluate ground services, including speed and efficiency of check-in.
- *Executive board* evaluate the corporate performance of United, both internally in achieving its goals and externally compared with the competition.

The result of this report is that it enables a coordinated and integrated approach to United's customer orientation. This helps United to differentiate itself in an environment where all companies have the same schedules, the same service and the same prices.

Example   Meet Matthias, Stephanie, Seb, Justine and Stan[2]

Allied Domecq Spirits and Wines (ADSW) commissioned an innovative study to understand the factors of brand adoption of young emergent adult drinkers. The innovative approach to gathering data continued into communicating the findings. ADSW managers were invited to spend a day of 'discovery'. The day started by holding breakout sessions to gauge current assumptions about young drinkers. They then 'met' a set of fictional characters that represented the adult emergent drinker generation that had been the focus of the study. The idea behind this was to allow ADSW managers to be able to visualise their consumers when developing new products or communications strategies. Personalities were created and brought to life using actors. In France, for example, the clients were able to meet Matthias, Stephanie, Seb, Justine and Stan. These five characters symbolised the richness and the diversity of the generation. Each of the characters engaged with the manager audience via dialogue, discussing for example their lifestyle, behaviours, what's 'in' or 'out', values, concerns and expectations for the future, as well as their current attitudes towards alcohol. In addition, the audience were presented with workshop 'souvenirs' and notebooks with pictures and biographies of the character types where they could take notes during the presentation. The effect was immediate; with a bar as a cue, managers were able to step into a new world and easily meet and interact with their consumers. Moreover, their 'consumers' were eager to explain what was and wasn't important to them. This multimedia/multi-layered presentation of findings allowed information to be assimilated visually, audibly and kinesthetically.

Importance of the report and presentation

For the following reasons, the report and its presentation are important parts of the marketing research project:

1 They are the tangible products of the research effort. After the project is complete and management have made the decision, there is little documentary evidence of the project other than the written report. The report serves as a historical record of the project.
2 Management decisions are guided by the report and the presentation. If the first five steps in the project are carefully conducted but inadequate attention is paid to the sixth step, the value of the project to management will be greatly diminished.
3 The involvement of many marketing managers in the project is limited to the written report and the oral presentation. These managers evaluate the quality of the entire project on the quality of the report and presentation.
4 Management's decision to undertake marketing research in the future or to use the particular research supplier again will be influenced by the perceived usefulness of the report and the presentation.

Preparation and presentation process

Figure 25.1 illustrates report preparation and presentation.

The process begins by interpreting the results of data analysis in the light of the marketing research problem, approach, research design and fieldwork. Instead of merely summarising the quantitative and/or qualitative analyses, the researcher should present the findings in such a way that they can be used directly as input into decision making. Wherever appropriate, conclusions should be drawn and recommendations made. The researcher should aim to make the recommendations actionable. Before writing the report, the researcher should discuss the major findings, conclusions and recommendations with the key decision-makers. These discussions play a major role in ensuring that the report meets the client's needs and is ultimately accepted. These discussions should confirm specific dates for the delivery of the written report and other data.

The entire marketing research project should be summarised in a single written report or in several reports addressed to different readers. Generally, an oral presentation supplements the written documents. The client should be given an opportunity to read the report. After that, the researcher should take the necessary follow-up actions. The researcher should assist the client in understanding the report, help in interpretations of the findings that can affect their implementation, offer to undertake further research and reflect upon the research process to evaluate its overall worth.

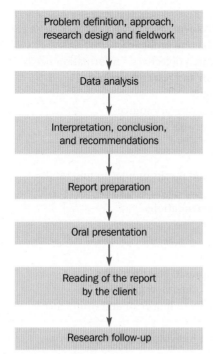

Figure 25.1
The report preparation and presentation process

Report preparation

Researchers differ in the way they prepare a research report. The personality, background, expertise and responsibility of the researcher, along with the marketing decision-maker to whom the report is addressed, interact to give each report a unique character. Yet there are guidelines for formatting and writing reports and designing tables and graphs.[3]

Report format

Report formats are likely to vary with the researcher or the marketing research firm conducting the project, the client for whom the project is being conducted, and the nature of the project itself. Hence, the following is intended as a guide from which the researcher can develop a format for the research project at hand. Most research reports include the following elements:

1 **Submission letter**
2 **Title page**
3 **Table of contents**
   a Main sections
   b List of tables
   c List of graphs
   d List of appendices
   e List of exhibits
4 Executive summary
   a Summary of prime objectives
   b Major findings
   c Conclusions and recommendations

    5 **Problem definition**
- a Background to the problem
- b Statement of the marketing problem
- c Statement of the research objectives – information needs

    6 **Approach to the problem and research design**
- a Type of research design
- b Data collection from secondary sources
- c Data collection from primary sources

    7 **Data analysis**
- a Research design
- b Plan of data analysis and means of interpreting results

    8 **Results**

    9 **Conclusions and recommendations**

  10 **Limitations and caveats**

  11 **Appendices**
- a Letter of authorisation
- b Questionnaire development and pretesting
- c Questionnaires, forms, interview guides
- d Sampling techniques, including error and confidence levels
- e Fieldwork
- f Lists including contact individuals and organisations.

This format closely follows the earlier steps of the marketing research process. The results may be presented in several chapters of the report. For example, in a national survey, data analysis may be conducted for the overall sample and then the data for each geographical region may be analysed separately. If so, the results from each analysis may be presented in a separate chapter.

Submission letter. A formal report generally contains a letter of submission that delivers the report to the client and summarises the researcher's overall experience with the project, without mentioning the findings. The letter should also identify the need for further action on the part of the client, such as implementation of the findings or further research that should be undertaken.

Title page. The title page should include the title of the report, information (name, address and telephone number) about the researcher or organisation conducting the research, the name of the client for whom the report was prepared, and the date of release. The title should encapsulate the nature of the project with a tone that is meaningful to the target managers, not one of technical 'research-speak'.

Table of contents. The table of contents should list the topics covered and the appropriate page numbers. In most reports, only the major headings and subheadings are included. The table of contents is followed by a list of tables, a list of graphs, a list of appendices and a list of exhibits.

Executive summary. The executive summary is an extremely important part of the report, because this is often the only portion of the report that executives read. The summary should concisely describe the problem, approach and research design that were adopted. A summary section should be devoted to the major results, conclusions and recommendations. The executive summary should be written after the rest of the report has been written.

Problem definition. The problem definition section of the report gives the background to the problem. This part summarises elements of the marketing and research problem diagnosis. Key elements of any discussions with decision-makers, industry experts and initial secondary data analyses are presented. Having set this context for the whole project, a clear statement of the marketing decision problem(s) and the marketing research problem(s) should be presented.

Approach to the problem and research design. The approach to the problem section should discuss the broad approach that was adopted in addressing the problem. This section should summarise the theoretical foundations that guided the research, any analytical models formulated, research questions, hypotheses and the factors that influenced the research design. The research design should specify the details of how the research was conducted, preferably with a graphical presentation of the stages undertaken, showing the relationships between stages. This should detail the methods undertaken in the data collection from secondary and primary sources. These topics should be presented in a non-technical, easy-to-understand manner. The technical details should be included in an appendix. This section of the report should justify the specific methods selected.

Data analysis. The section on data analysis, be it quantitative or qualitative, should describe the plan of data analysis and justify the data analysis strategy and techniques used. The techniques used for analysis should be described in simple, non-technical terms, with examples to guide the reader through the interpretations.

Results. The results section is normally the longest part of the report and may entail several chapters. It may be presented in any of the following ways:

1 *Forms of analysis.* For example, in a health care marketing survey of hospitals, the results were presented in four chapters. One chapter presented the overall results, another examined the differences between geographical regions, a third presented the differences between for-profit and non-profit hospitals, and a fourth presented the differences according to bed capacity. Often, results are presented not only at the aggregate level but also at the subgroup (market segment, geographical area, etc.) level.
2 *Forms of data collection.* For example, a study may contain significant elements of secondary data collection and analyses, a series of focus group interviews and a survey. The results in such circumstances may be best presented by drawing conclusions from one method before moving on to another method. The conclusions derived from focus groups, for example, may need to be established to show the link to a sample design and questions used in a survey.
3 *Objectives.* There may be a series of research objectives whose fulfilment may incorporate a variety of data collection methods and levels of analysis. In these circumstances the results combine methods and levels of analyses to show connections and to develop and illustrate emerging issues.

The results should be organised in a coherent and logical way. Choosing whether to present by *forms of analysis, forms of data collection,* or *objectives* helps to build that coherence and logic. The presentation of the results should be geared directly to the components of the marketing research problem and the information needs that were diagnosed in the initial research brief and proposal. The nature of the information needs and characteristics of the recipients of the report ultimately determine the best way to present results.

Conclusions and recommendations. Presenting a mere summary of the quantitative or qualitative findings is not enough for most marketing research users. The researcher should interpret the results in light of the problem being addressed to arrive at major conclusions. Based on the results and conclusions, the researcher may make recommendations to the decision-makers. Sometimes, marketing researchers are not asked to make recommendations because they research only one area and do not understand the bigger picture at the client firm. The researcher may not have been fully involved in the diagnosis of the marketing and research problems, in which case the researcher's interpretations may not fit into the context that the marketer understands.

In any research project there are many approaches that can be taken to analyse the data. This can result in a potential overabundance of data (quantitative and/or qualitative), and distilling the 'meaning' from the data and presenting this in a clear report can result in much of the original meaning or richness being lost.[4] To maintain the meaning or richness, the researcher should strive to understand the nature of the decision-making process that is being supported. Only then can sound interpretations of the collected data be made. This is illustrated in the following example, where the main factor in selecting a research agency to work with is an understanding of the decision-making process that is being supported.

> ### *Example* | French marketing research looks abroad[5]
>
> Mark Whiting, Research Director at Hennessy, is quite content with the support he gets from French marketing research agencies. He points out that 99% of the cognac brand's business is conducted outside France, and he therefore cannot expect to find everything he needs amongst French agencies. What drives his desire to work with a particular agency?
>
> *Above all, I'm looking to work with agencies who understand the business issues which concern us and who can make recommendations as to how to solve those issues, based on the research data that they have collected. This means searching near and far, so sometimes I find what I'm looking for in France, and sometimes I use agencies in the UK, the US and Asia.*

Limitations and caveats. All marketing research projects have limitations caused by time, budget and other organisational constraints. Furthermore, the research design adopted may be limited in terms of the various types of errors, and some of these may be serious enough to warrant discussion. This section should be written with great care and a balanced perspective. On the one hand, the researcher must make sure that management do not rely too heavily on the results or use them for unintended purposes, such as projecting them to unintended populations. On the other hand, this section should not erode management's confidence in the research or unduly minimise its importance.

Appendices. At the end of the report, documents can be compiled that may be used by different readers to help them to understand characteristics of the research project in more detail. These should include the letter of authorisation to conduct the research; this authorisation could include the agreed research proposal. Details that relate to individual techniques should be included relating to questionnaires, interview guides, sampling and fieldwork activities. The final part of the appendix should include lists of contacts, references used and further sources of reference.

Report writing

Readers. A report should be written for a specific reader or readers: namely, the marketing decision-makers who will use the results. The report should take into account the readers' technical sophistication and interest in the project as well as the circumstances under which they will read the report and how they will use it.[6]

Technical jargon should be avoided. As expressed by one expert, 'The readers of your reports are busy people; and very few of them can balance a research report, a cup of coffee, and a dictionary at one time.'[7] Instead of technical terms such as maximum likelihood, heteroscedasticity and non-parametric, use descriptive explanations. If some technical terms cannot be avoided, briefly define them in an appendix. When it comes to marketing research, decision-makers would rather live with a problem they cannot solve than accept a solution they cannot understand.

Often the researcher must cater to the needs of several audiences with different levels of technical sophistication and interest in the project. Such conflicting needs may be met by including different sections in the report for different readers or separate reports entirely.

Easy to follow. The report should be easy to follow.[8] It should be structured logically and written clearly. The material, particularly the body of the report, should be structured in a logical manner so that the reader can easily see the inherent connections and linkages. Headings should be used for different topics and subheadings for subtopics.

A logical organisation also leads to a coherent report. Clarity can be enhanced by using well-constructed sentences that are short and to the point. The words used should express precisely what the researcher wants to communicate. Difficult words, slang and clichés should be avoided. An excellent check on the clarity of a report is to have two or three people who are unfamiliar with the project read it and offer critical comments. Several revisions of the report may be needed before the final document emerges.

Presentable and professional appearance. The look of a report is important. The report should be professionally reproduced with quality paper, typing and binding. The typography should be varied. Variation in type size and skilful use of white space can greatly contribute to the appearance and readability of the report. However, a balance should be sought with styles of variation. Too much variation can lead to confusion; variation is only useful if it aids understanding.

Objective. Objectivity is a virtue that should guide report writing. Researchers can become so fascinated with their project that they overlook their 'objective' role. The report should accurately present the research design, results and conclusions of the project, without slanting the findings to conform to the expectations of management. Decision-makers are unlikely to receive with enthusiasm a report that reflects unfavourably on their judgement or actions. Yet the researcher must have the courage to present and defend the results objectively.

Reinforce text with tables and graphs. It is important to reinforce key information in the text with tables, graphs, pictures, maps and other visual devices. Visual aids can greatly facilitate communication and add to the clarity and impact of the report. Guidelines for tabular and graphical presentation are discussed later.

Reinforce tables and graphs with text. Conversely it is important to illustrate tables and graphs with verbatim quotes from questionnaires and interviews. Quotes can bring to life the meaning in tables and graphs and, used carefully, can make the reading of the report far more interesting than a solid body of statistics.

Terse. A report should be terse and concise. Anything unnecessary should be omitted. If too much information is included, important points may be lost. Avoid lengthy discussions of common procedures. Yet brevity should not be achieved at the expense of completeness.

Guidelines for tables

Statistical tables are a vital part of the report and deserve special attention. We illustrate the guidelines for tables using data from the Racetrack study. Table 25.1 presents the findings from three questions. The rows in Table 25.1 show groupings of Formula One viewing habits. The columns in Table 25.1 present gender and age groupings of the respondents.

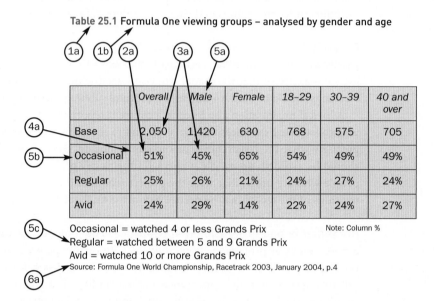

Table 25.1 Formula One viewing groups – analysed by gender and age

	Overall	Male	Female	18–29	30–39	40 and over
Base	2,050	1,420	630	768	575	705
Occasional	51%	45%	65%	54%	49%	49%
Regular	25%	26%	21%	24%	27%	24%
Avid	24%	29%	14%	22%	24%	27%

Note: Column %

Occasional = watched 4 or less Grands Prix
Regular = watched between 5 and 9 Grands Prix
Avid = watched 10 or more Grands Prix
Source: Formula One World Championship, Racetrack 2003, January 2004, p.4

The numbers in parentheses in the following paragraphs refer to the numbered sections of the table.

Title and number. Every table should have a number (1a) and title (1b). The title should be brief yet clearly descriptive of the information provided. Arabic numbers are used to identify tables so that they can be referenced in the text.[9]

Arrangement of data items. The arrangement of data items in a table should emphasise the most significant aspect of the data. For example, when the data pertain to time, the items should be arranged by appropriate time period. When order of magnitude is most important, the data items should be arranged in that order (2a). If ease of locating items is critical, an alphabetical arrangement is most appropriate.

Basis of measurement. The basis or unit of measurement should be clearly stated (3a). In Table 25.1, the total sample size is shown and the subsample sizes of the different ways of classifying respondents. The main body of data is shown in percentages. The % signs would normally be removed, with a note to tell the reader that the main body is based upon column percentages or row percentages, or percentages related to the total sample size.

Leaders, rulings and spaces. The reader's eye should be guided to be able to read across the table clearly. This can be achieved with ruled lines (4a), alternate shaded rows, or white spaces with dotted lines leading from the row headings to the data.

Explanations and comments: headings, stubs and footnotes. Explanations and comments clarifying the table can be provided in the form of captions, stubs and footnotes.

Designations placed over the vertical columns are called headings (5a). Designations placed in the left-hand column are called stubs (5b). Information that cannot be incorporated in the table should be explained by footnotes (5c). Letters or symbols should be used for footnotes rather than numbers. The footnotes that are part of the original source should come after the main table, but before the source note.

Sources of the data. If the data contained in the table are secondary, the source of data should be cited (6a).

Guidelines for graphs

As a general rule, graphical aids should be employed whenever practical. Graphical display of information can effectively complement the text and tables to enhance clarity of communication and impact.[10] As the saying goes, a picture is worth a thousand words. The guidelines for preparing graphs are similar to those for tables. Therefore, this section focuses on the different types of graphical aids.[11] We illustrate several of these using the Racetrack data from Table 25.1.

Geographic and other maps. Geographic and other maps, such as product positioning maps, can communicate relative location and other comparative information. Geographic maps form the bases of presentations in geodemographic analyses as discussed in Chapter 5. The maps used in geodemographic analyses can portray customer locations and types, potential consumers, location of competitors, road networks to show consumer flows, and other facilities that may attract consumers to certain locations.

Pie chart
A round chart divided into sections.

Round or pie charts. In a pie chart, the area of each section, as a percentage of the total area of a circle, reflects the percentage associated with the value of a specific variable. Pie charts are very useful in presenting simple relative frequencies in numbers or percentages. A pie chart is not useful for displaying relationships over time or relationships among several variables. As a general guide, a pie chart should not require more than seven sections.[12] Figure 25.2 shows the percentages of Formula One viewing groups. Great care must be taken with 3D pie charts as the relative sizes of the pie segments become distorted.

Line chart
A chart that connects a series of data points using continuous lines.

Line charts. A line chart connects a series of data points using continuous lines. This is an attractive way of illustrating trends and changes over time. Several series can be compared on the same chart, and forecasts, interpolations and extrapolations can be shown. If several series are displayed simultaneously, each line should have a distinctive colour or form (see Figure 25.3).[13]

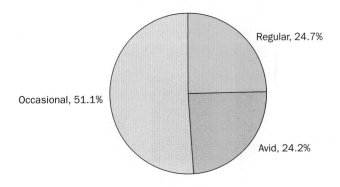

Figure 25.2
Pie chart that shows the percentage of Formula One viewing groups

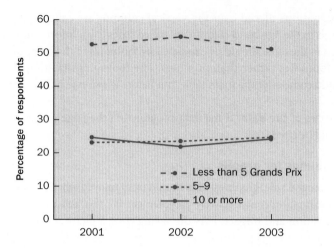

Figure 25.3
Line chart of the number of Formula One races watched in a season

Bar chart
A chart that displays data in bars positioned horizontally or vertically.

Histogram
A vertical bar chart in which the height of the bar represents the relative or cumulative frequency of occurrence.

Histograms and bar charts. A **bar chart** displays data in various bars that may be positioned horizontally or vertically. Bar charts can be used to present absolute and relative magnitudes, differences and change. A **histogram** is a vertical bar chart in which the height of the bar represents the relative or cumulative frequency of occurrence of a specific variable (see Figure 25.4). Other variations on the basic bar chart include the stacked bar chart (Figure 25.5) and the cluster bar chart (Figure 25.6). Stacked and cluster bar charts can work well with a few data items presented, to represent differences qualitatively between groups. As noted with pie charts, 3D charts should be used with great caution as they can distort the message and confuse an audience. Most graphics packages have a great array of 3D options; however, there are few circumstances where they can be used to present data in a clear and unbiased manner.

Schematic figures and flow charts. Schematic figures and flow charts take on a number of different forms. They can be used to display the steps or components of a process, as in Figure 25.1. They can also be of great value in presenting qualitative data analyses by representing the nature and interconnection of ideas that have been uncovered (see Chapter 9). Another useful form of these charts is classification diagrams. Examples of classification charts for classifying secondary data were provided in Chapter 4 (Figures 4.1 to 4.4). An example of a flow chart for questionnaire design was given in Chapter 13 (Figure 13.3).[14]

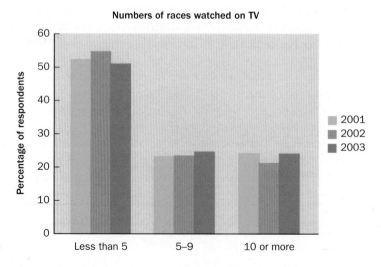

Figure 25.4
Bar chart of the number of Grand Prix races watched on TV in the 2001–2003 seasons

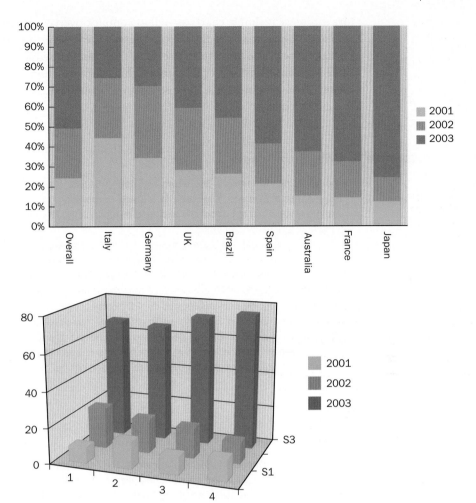

Figure 25.5
Stacked bar chart of the viewing frequency by country

Figure 25.6
The 3D cluster bar chart of Japanese respondents' viewing frequency, 1999–2003

Oral presentation

The entire marketing research project should be presented to the management of the client firm. This presentation will help management understand and accept the written report. Any preliminary questions that management may have can be addressed in the presentation. Because many executives form their first and lasting impressions about the project based on the oral presentation, its importance cannot be overemphasised.[15]

The key to an effective presentation is preparation. A written script or detailed outline should be prepared following the format of the written report. The presentation must be geared to the audience. For this purpose, the researcher should determine the backgrounds, interests and involvement of those in the project, as well as the extent to which they are likely to be affected by it. The presentation should be rehearsed several times before it is made to management.

Visual aids such as tables and graphs should be displayed with a variety of media. Flip charts of large pads of blank paper mounted on an easel enable the researcher to manipulate numbers. They are particularly useful in communicating answers to technical questions. Visual aids can also be drawn on the pages in advance, and the speaker flips through the pages during the presentation. Although not as flexible, magnetic boards and felt boards allow for rapid presentation of previously prepared material. Overhead projectors can present simple charts as well as complex overlays produced by the successive additions of new images to the screen. The use of computer packages such as Microsoft's PowerPoint can also be of immense help. They can be used for making computer-controlled presentations or for presenting technical information such as analytical models. However, the presenter must not lose sight of the message, as illustrated in the following two examples.

Example

Bridging the gap[16]

The following summarises the views of Cristina Stuart, Managing Director of SpeakEasy Training, and Khalid Aziz, Chairman of the Aziz Corporation. In essence they argue that the oral presentation is not about the slick use of technology – the presenter should add something to the visual presentation.

Actors understand that there is a gap between the speaker and the audience and that you have to do a certain amount of work to bridge that gap. Actors spend their lives at interviews and are constantly having to present themselves to new people. Like actors, some speakers use props to enhance their performance, but these need to be handled with care. It is the person that must be persuasive, not the PC. People often hide behind their visuals, but if that is all that you are presenting, you might as well have sent them in the post. Technology may be used where it is appropriate, but too often people overdo the visuals to the detriment of the message. Even at Microsoft, where with its PowerPoint software the medium is the message, the presenter presides over the technology, not the other way around.

Example

Screen saviours[17]

Phillip Redding, Deputy Managing Director of The Presentation Company, emphasises that technology is only part of the presentation picture. For him, it is just as important to get the content and structure of the argument right, and to create designs that put them over in a powerful way:

If the content and structure are not clear, the presentation is not going to stand a chance. People think that by adding 3D animation the audience will be impressed. They will, but they still won't think the argument is very good.

Video recorders (VCRs) and large-screen projectors are particularly effective in presenting focus groups and other aspects of fieldwork that are dynamic in nature. It is important to maintain eye contact and to interact with the audience during the presentation. Sufficient opportunity should be provided for questions, both during and after the presentation. The presentation should be made interesting and convincing with the use of appropriate stories, examples, experiences and quotations. Filler words like 'uh', 'y'know' and 'all right' should not be used.

Body language should be employed. Descriptive gestures are used to clarify or enhance verbal communication. Emphatic gestures are used to emphasise what is being said. Suggestive gestures are symbols of ideas and emotions. Prompting gestures are used to elicit a desired response from the audience. The speaker should vary the volume, pitch, voice quality, articulation and rate while speaking. The presentation should terminate with a strong closing. To stress its importance, the presentation should be sponsored by a top-level manager in the client's organisation.

After the presentation, key executives in the client firm should be given time to read the report in detail.

The researcher's task does not end with the oral presentation. Two other tasks remain. The researcher should help the client understand and implement the findings and take follow-up action. Second, while it is still fresh in the researcher's mind, the entire marketing research project should be evaluated.

Assisting the client

After the client has read the report in detail, several questions may arise. Parts of the report, particularly those dealing with technical matters, may not be understood and the researcher should provide the help needed. Sometimes the researcher helps implement the findings. Often, the client retains the researcher to help with the selection of a new product or advertising agency, development of a pricing policy, market segmentation or other marketing actions. An important reason for client follow-up is to discuss further research projects. For example, the researcher and management may agree to repeat the study after two years. Where possible, the researcher should also aim to make links between the findings of a project and other studies. By reviewing 'historical' findings in the context of current issues, project findings can be seen as more valid and decision-makers may increase their trust in the process.[18] Finally, the researcher should help the client firm make the information generated in the marketing research project a part of the firm's marketing or management information system. Ad hoc marketing research should be seen as a significant component of an ongoing link and understanding of target consumers. A key element of researchers being able to assist marketing decision-makers is the level of trust that exists between the two parties. The nature of personal interaction between managers and researchers is very important in creating trust in the researcher and consequently in the results of the research. The quality of personal interaction affects managers' perceptions of the overall quality of the report itself.[19] Trust between the decision-maker and the researcher has been found to influence the perceived quality of user–researcher interactions, the level of researcher involvement, the level of user commitment to the relationship and the level of market research utilisation.[20]

Evaluation of the research project

Although marketing research is scientific, which may seem to imply a rigid, systematic process, it clearly involves creativity, intuition and personal judgement. Hence, every marketing research project provides an opportunity for learning, and the researcher should critically evaluate the entire project to obtain new insights and knowledge. The key question to ask is: 'Could this project have been conducted more effectively or efficiently?' This question, of course, raises several more specific questions. Could the problem have been defined differently so as to enhance the value of the project to the client or reduce the costs? Could a different approach have yielded better results? Was the research design that was used the best? How about the method of data collection? Should street interviews have been used instead of telephone interviews? Was the sampling plan employed the most appropriate? Were the sources of possible design error correctly anticipated and kept under control, at least in a qualitative sense? If not, what changes could have been made? How could the selection, training and supervision of fieldworkers be altered to improve data collection? Was the data analysis strategy effective in yielding information useful for decision making? Were the conclusions and recommendations appropriate and useful to the client? Was the report adequately written and presented? Was the project completed within the time and budget allocated? If not, what went wrong? The insights gained from such an evaluation will benefit the researcher and the subsequent projects conducted.

International marketing research

The guidelines presented earlier in this chapter apply to international marketing research as well, although report preparation may be complicated by the need to prepare reports for management in different countries and in different languages. In such a case, the researcher should prepare different versions of the report, each geared to specific readers. The different reports should be comparable, although the formats may differ. The guidelines for oral presentation are also similar to those given earlier, with the added proviso that the presenter should be sensitive to cultural norms. For example, making jokes, which is frequently done in many countries, is not appropriate in all cultures (which may also include particular organisational cultures). The potential impact of cultural variations in humour is illustrated in the following example.

Example Camry chicken fries Ford[21]

The advertising campaign designed for the Toyota Camry in Australia was very different from the one used in Japan. 'Why did the chicken cross the road?' Toyota asked in a continuing series of TV commercials in Australia. The answer: 'To sell more Toyota Camry's of course.' The adverts, showing an animated chicken trying to cross the road and getting its feathers blown off by a passing Camry, were created by Saatchi & Saatchi Advertising. When Bob Miller, Toyota's General Manager, tried to explain the advertisement to colleagues in Japan, they thought he was insane. The humour was offensive to the Japanese but it clearly worked well with the Australians. As a continuing series, the next advertisement sees a chicken sitting on a pile of eggs in the middle of the road and hatching chicks as the Camry speeds past. The advertisements helped Toyota topple Ford's dominance in Australia.

Most marketing decisions are made from facts and figures arising out of marketing research. But these figures and how they have been arrived at have to be credible to decision-makers. The subjective experience and gut feeling of managers could vary widely across countries, necessitating that different recommendations be made for implementing the research findings in different countries. This is particularly important when making innovative or creative recommendations such as in advertising campaigns.

Ethics in marketing research

Many issues pertaining to research integrity arise during report preparation and presentation. A survey of 254 marketing researchers found that 33% believed that the most difficult ethical problems they face pertain to issues of research integrity. These issues included ignoring pertinent data, compromising the research design, deliberately misusing statistics, falsifying figures, altering research results, misinterpreting the results with the objective of supporting a personal or corporate point of view, and withholding information.[22] It is important that researchers deal with these issues in a satisfactory manner and prepare a report which accurately and fully discloses the details of all the procedures and findings.

Objectivity should be maintained throughout the research process. For example, when data are analysed and no meaningful results are found, researchers are tempted to see findings which are not supported by the analysis. One example is meaningfully interpreting a regression equation when all the independent variables turn out to be non-significant (Chapter 20). Ethical dilemmas can arise in these instances. The researchers are being paid for their expert interpretation of data, and can nothing meaningful be said?

> *To arrive at some rational, logical, and convincing conclusion is so much more satisfying intellectually than to admit that the findings are inconsistent and inconclusive. No wonder we find ourselves mentally selecting and shaping what might otherwise be shapeless into a coherent, well-defined story.*[23]

Such temptations must be resisted to avoid unethical conduct.

Like researchers, clients also have the responsibility for full and accurate disclosure of the research findings and are obligated to employ these findings honourably. For example, the public can be negatively affected by a client who distorts the research findings to develop a more favourable TV advertising campaign. Ethical issues also arise when client firms, such as tobacco companies, use marketing research findings to formulate questionable marketing programmes.

Internet and computer applications

Marketing research reports are being published or posted directly on the Internet or on intranets. Reports on the Internet are not located in publicly accessible areas but in locations protected by passwords or corporate intranets. The various word-processing, spreadsheet and presentation packages have the capability to produce material in a format that can be posted directly on the Web, thus facilitating the process.

There are a number of advantages to publishing marketing research reports on the Web. These reports can incorporate all kinds of multimedia presentations, including graphs, pictures, animation, audio and full-motion video. The dissemination is immediate and the reports can be accessed by authorised persons online on a worldwide basis. These reports can be electronically searched to identify materials of specific interest. For example, a manager in Kuala Lumpur can electronically locate the portions of a report that pertain to Malaysia or South East Asia. Storage or future retrieval is efficient and effortless. It is easy to integrate these reports to become part of a decision support system. The main disadvantage is that the readers may not have permanent access to the reports, as websites may change periodically.

Given the ability to search electronically and tailor reports on the Internet, information published on websites is now becoming more 'pull' oriented, as opposed to the 'push' orientation of a printed report. The standard analysis that the researcher generates can continue to be written, but can now be accessed as a result of a search, instigation of a link, or even just rolling the mouse pointer over an icon. In addition, using database-driven technology it is possible to have a completely interactive website that allows data interrogation through the specification of questions, filters, cross-tabulations and even applied weighting.

The basic structure of a website, and the ease with which it is possible to navigate around a large amount of information, ensures that managers can quickly find exactly what they want. It is also possible to have index areas constantly visible on the screen to ensure that areas of information contained within a single report, or indeed multiple reports, can be accessed quickly.

Examples of how marketing research reports on the Internet are making decision-makers' lives easier are as follows:[24]

- Reporting and interrogating real-time data (not just from web interviews but from CATI and CAPI data).
- Linking different research projects' reports together to create a more detailed overview.
- Building charts and tables by adding different elements (such as confidence limits and explanation of chart movements).
- Applying rules to the reporting to ensure the robustness of the presented results.
- Applying complex modelling calculations and processes to data as they are made available.

Though these benefits are clear, the use of the Web to publish marketing research findings is still primarily 'locked' into static presentations, and there is some way to go to realise these benefits as illustrated in the following example.

Example ### The missing off-ramp[25]

Before embarking upon an online marketing research project, a vital issue to bear in mind is how the results are presented. Research buyers are looking for their results to be delivered online virtually instantaneously, through individual stakeholder-centric reporting portals. These need to allow a hierarchy of managers to log in and see their own cut of the data, compared with norms or aggregate totals for other divisions, and all presented as easy-to-follow charts and with exceptions highlighted. Some would even like to be able to drill down from the high-level data to the underlying results and even perform some extra calculations. There is little doubt that the e-delivery of marketing research findings can transform the relationship between research user and research findings. In most web survey packages, this is still extremely difficult to achieve without a dedicated team of technicians and web programmers. A few packages provide integrated tools to allow the building of integrative reports, but most are still tricky to use.

Viewing marketing research reports using the Internet is effectively the same as conducting a search for secondary data as detailed in Chapter 4. In order to get a feel for the different styles of report presentation, based upon the types of research technique used, the country in which it was conducted and the industry supported, visit the websites of leading marketing research agencies. Click on **www.tnsofres.com**, the web address of Taylor Nelson Sofres, and **www.gfk.de**, the web address of the German marketing research company GfK. On both sites (which cover the many countries they operate in, with different languages) you will see case studies, descriptions of special studies related to specific industry sectors and examples of reports that they produce.

Summary

Report preparation and presentation is the final step in the marketing research project. This process begins with interpretation of data analysis results and leads to conclusions and recommendations. Next, the formal report is written and an oral presentation made. After management have read the report, the researcher should conduct a follow-up, assisting management and undertaking a thorough evaluation of the marketing research project.

In international marketing research, report preparation may be complicated by the need to prepare reports for management in different countries and in different languages. Several ethical issues are pertinent, particularly those related to the interpretation and reporting of the research process and findings to the client and the use of these results by the client.

The final example presents a metaphor of the use of the guitar in supporting presentations. It is a final reminder that the power of computing software can never replace the creative skills of conveying the story and impact of a piece of research upon a decision-making situation.

Example ## My paradigm is the guitar[26]

Developments in modern technology have had a profound impact on the art of business presentation, most notably through PC-driven presentations. There is no doubt that the standard of visualisation in presentations has improved immeasurably, but has the presentation itself? Technically good presentations are becoming commonplace, perhaps even predictable. Predictability precedes boredom.

Source: © Jim Craigmyle/CORBIS

Presenters spend too much time at the PC creating a slide show and not enough on their performance. Presenters have forgotten to plan their personal involvement and the involvement of their audience.

My paradigm is the guitar. The guitar represents a tool that supports presentation, rather like a PC, but that can never do the performance for you. From my own experience as a guitarist, presentations and gigs have many parallels. You have to prepare diligently, and have a good plan for the progress of the performance. You should know your material. You must be able to excite the audience and get them involved. You must be able to improvise and respond to requests. You should have a good guitar, but the good guitar on its own won't carry the day. You will.

Questions

1 Describe the process of report preparation.

2 Why is the quality of report presentation vital to the success of a marketing research project?

3 Describe a commonly used format for writing marketing research reports.

4 Describe the following parts of a report: title page, table of contents, executive summary, problem definition, research design, data analysis, conclusions and recommendations.

5 Why is the 'limitations and caveats' section included in the report?

6 Discuss the importance of objectivity in writing a marketing research report.

7 Describe the guidelines for report writing.

8 How should the data items be arranged in a table?

9 What is a pie chart? For what type of information is it suitable? For what type of information is it not suitable?

10 Describe a line chart. What kind of information is commonly displayed using such charts?

11 What are the advantages and disadvantages of presenting data using 3D charts?

12 What is the purpose of an oral presentation? What guidelines should be followed in an oral presentation?

13 To what extent should marketing researchers interpret the information they present in a report?

14 Describe the evaluation of a marketing research project in retrospect.

15 Graphically represent the consumer decision-making process described in the following paragraph:

The consumer first becomes aware of the need. Then the consumer simultaneously searches for information from several sources: retailers, advertising, word of mouth, and independent publications. After that a criterion is developed for evaluating the available brands in the marketplace. Based on this evaluation, the most preferred brand is selected.

Exercises

1 Obtain a copy of an old marketing research report (many marketing research agencies or companies that have commissioned research will provide copies of old reports for educational purposes). Evaluate the ways in which you could improve the structure and style of presentation in this report.

2 Prepare an oral presentation of the report above, to be targeted at senior marketing managers. Deliver your presentation to a group of fellow students (role playing the managers) and ask them to critique the presentation.

3 Visit **www.gallup.com** to identify a recent report prepared by this company. How does the format of this report compare to the one in this book?

4 You are a researcher preparing a report for a high-tech firm on 'The demand potential for digital cameras in Europe'. Develop a format for your report. How is that format different from the one given in this book? Discuss the format and purposes of each section with your boss (role played by a student in your class).

5 In a small group discuss the following issues: 'Writing reports is an art. Presenting reports is an art. Reading reports is an art. It is all a matter of art.' and 'Writing a report that is concise and yet complete is virtually impossible as these two objectives are conflicting'.

Video Case Exercise: Burke Inc.

Burke describe how they communicate marketing research findings to their clients. What factors of success do you see in their approach to reporting? Are there any other factors not mentioned that you feel could create more successful reporting?

video case

download from
www.pearsoned.co.uk/
malhotra_euro

Notes

1 Tatum, C., 'United Airlines banks on new network, customer data to fill more seats', *Knight Ridder Tribune Business News* (1 April 2002); Rydholm, J., 'Surveying the friendly skies', *Marketing Research* (May 1996).

2 Acreman, S. and Pegram, B., 'Getting to know you', *Research* (November 1999), 36–41.

3 Anon. 'Research Reports', *Barron's* 82 (14) (8 April 2002), 30; Tufte, E.R., *Visual Explanations: Images and Quantities, Evidence and Narrative* (Cheshire, CT: Graphic, 1997); Fink, A., *How to Report on Surveys* (Thousand Oaks, CA: Sage, 1995).

4 Birks, D.F., 'Market research', in Baker, M.J. (ed.), *The Marketing Book*, 3rd edn (Oxford: Butterworth–Heinemann, 1994), 262.

5 Heeg, R., 'We have some catching up to do', *Research World* (November 2004), 6–7.

6 Keys, T., Jr 'Report writing', *Internal Auditor* 53 (4) (August 1996), 65–66.

7 Wolcott, H.F., *Writing up qualitative research*, 2nd edn (Thousand Oaks, CA: Sage, 2001); Britt, S.H., 'The writing of readable research reports', *Journal of Marketing Research* (May 1971), 265. See also Mort, S., *Professional Report Writing* (Brookfield, IL: Ashgate, 1995); Shair, D.I., 'Report writing', *HR Focus* 71 (2) (February 1994), 20.

8 Low, G.S., 'Factors affecting the use of information in the evaluation of marketing communications productivity', *Academy of Marketing Science Journal* 29 (1) (Winter 2001), 70–88; Boland, A., 'Got report-o-phobia? Follow these simple steps to get those ideas onto paper', *Chemical Engineering* 103 (3) (March 1996), 131–132.

9 Tanase, G., 'Real-life data mart processing', *Intelligent Enterprise* 5 (5) (8 March 2002), 22–24; Wilson, L.D., 'Are appraisal reports logical fallacies?', *Appraisal Journal* 64 (2) (April 1996), 129–133; Leach, J., 'Seven steps to better writing', *Planning* 59 (6) (June 1993), 26–27; Ehrenberg, A.S.C., 'The problem of numeracy', *American Statistician* 35 (May 1981), 67–71.

10 Wallgren, A., Wallgren, B., Persson, R., Jorner, U. and Haaland, J.A., *Graphing Statistics and Data* (Thousand Oaks, CA: Sage, 1996); Tufte, E.R., *Visual Display of Quantitative Information* (Cheshire, CT: Graphic, 1992).

11 Dean, J., 'High-powered charts and graphs', *Government Executive* 34 (1) (January 2002), 58; Kauder, N.B., 'Pictures worth a thousand words', *American Demographics* (Tools Supplement) (November/December 1996), 64–68.

12 Gutsche, A.M., 'Visuals make the case', *Marketing News* 35 (20) (24 September 2001), 21–22; Hinkin, S., 'Charting your course to effective information graphics', *Presentations* 9 (11) (November 1995), 28–32.

13 Lee, M., 'Its all in the charts', *Malaysian Business* (1 February 2002), 46; Chen, M.T., 'An innovative project report', *Cost Engineering* 38 (4) (April 1996), 41–45; Zelazny, G., *Say It with Charts*, 3rd edn (Homewood, IL: Business One Irwin, 1996).

14 Anon., 'Flow chart', *B-to-B* 87 (4) (8 April 2002), 16; Johnson, S. and Regan, M., 'A new use for an old tool', *Quality Progress* 29 (11) (November 1996), 144; Parr, G.L., 'Pretty-darned-quick flowchart creation', *Quality* (August 1996), 62–63.

15 Desiderio, L., 'At the sales presentation: ask and listen', *ID* 38 (4) (April 2002), 55; McConnell, C.R., 'Speak up: the manager's guide to oral presentations', *Health Care Manager* 18 (3) (March 2000), 70–77; Verluyten, S.P., 'Business communication and intercultural communication in Europe: the state of the art', *Business Communication Quarterly* 60 (2) (June 1997), 135–143.

16 Miller, R., 'In the spotlight', *Marketing* (19 March 1997), 35.

17 Condon, R., 'Screen saviours', *Marketing* (8 January 1998), 24.

18 Eshpeter, B., 'Communicating research findings: eight common pitfalls', *Imprints* (January 2004), 8–9.

19 Deshpande, R. and Zaltman, G., 'Factors affecting the use of market research information: a path analysis', *Journal of Marketing Research* 19 (February 1982), 25.

20 Moorman, C., Deshpande, R. and Zaltman, G., 'Factors affecting trust in market research relationships', *Journal of Marketing* 57 (January 1993), 81–101.

21 Anon., 'Toyota Camry', *Consumer Reports* 67 (4) (April 2002), 67; Garnaut, R., 'Australian cars in a global economy', *Australian Economic Review* 30 (4) (December 1997), 359–373; Martin, G.L., 'Aussies chicken fries Ford', *Advertising Age* (18 January 1993).

22 Liebman, M., 'Beyond ethics: companies deal with legal attacks on marketing practices', *Medical Marketing and Media* 37 (2) (February 2002), 74–77; Giacobbe, R.W., 'A comparative analysis of ethical perceptions in marketing research: USA vs Canada', *Journal of Business Ethics* 27 (3) (October 2000), 229–245; Milton-Smith, J., 'Business ethics in Australia and New Zealand', *Journal of Business Ethics* 16 (14) (October 1997), 1485–1497; Chonko, L.B., *Ethical Decision Making in Marketing* (Thousand Oaks, CA: Sage, 1995).

23 Day, R.L., 'A comment on "Ethics in marketing research"', *Journal of Marketing Research* 11 (1974), 232–233.

24 Hummerston, A., 'Net reporting comes of age', *Research* (May 2000), 36.

25 Macer, T., 'On your marks, get set...', *Research in Business* (May 2006), 7–8: Macer, T., 'PowerPoint slammed as research results delivery device', *Research* (May 2006), 14.

26 Willetts N.J., 'Going live', *Marketing Week* (13 November 1997), 47–48.

Source: © EMPICS

26

International marketing research

> " *Marketing across national boundaries remains one of the most difficult activities for many manufacturers in many product and service areas. Likewise, the research problems involved in multi-country coordination can be formidable.*[1] "

Objectives

After reading this chapter, you should be able to:

1 develop a framework for conducting international marketing research;

2 explain in detail the marketing, governmental, legal, economic, structural, informational and technological, and socio-cultural environmental factors and how they have an impact on international marketing research;

3 describe characteristics of the use of secondary data, qualitative techniques, telephone, personal and mail survey methods in different countries;

4 discuss how to establish the equivalence of scales and measures, including construct, operational, scalar and linguistic equivalence;

5 describe the processes of back translation and parallel translation in translating a questionnaire into a different language;

6 discuss the ethical considerations in international marketing research.

STAGE 1
Problem definition

STAGE 2
Research approach developed

STAGE 3
Research design developed

STAGE 4
Fieldwork or data collection

STAGE 5
Data preparation and analysis

STAGE 6
Report preparation and presentation

Overview

This chapter starts by evaluating the need for international marketing research. It then discusses the environment in which international marketing research is conducted, focusing on the marketing, governmental, legal, economic, structural, informational and technological, and socio-cultural environment.[2] Although illustrations of how the six steps of the marketing research process should be implemented in an international setting have been presented in earlier chapters, here we present additional details on secondary data, qualitative techniques, survey methods, scaling techniques and questionnaire translation. Relevant ethical issues in international marketing research are identified. We begin with some examples illustrating the role of marketing research in international marketing. The first example illustrates the use of ethnographic techniques, as introduced in Chapter 6. It also illustrates the point that research techniques may have to be adapted and developed to suit the nature of consumers in different cultures. The second example illustrates the great potential in international markets and some of the cultural challenges that must be overcome to conduct good-quality marketing research.

Example

Tasty wisdom[3]

'The most accurate research is done for pet food companies because it is not possible to ask pets what they think, only observe what they do.' Such an approach is just as feasible with humans! Economies of scale may be driving some research companies to harmonise their methodologies when conducting international marketing research, but Nestlé decided it needed more than just traditional focus groups to understand why its products were not thriving in Russia. It needed an ethnographic study of culinary habits to help develop a unified marketing approach. Incorporating video observation into a study of cooking habits by Russian housewives enabled Nestlé to sift out how people see themselves versus how they really are. Nestlé's study, using a range of different techniques, unmasked the myth of the creative cook interested in exotic recipes. The food giant reviewed its product portfolio accordingly.

Example

In India, familiarity breeds better content[4]

Hewlett-Packard is using Linux as a standard operating system (OS) in India after extensive marketing research. Through focus groups and survey research, the company found that many people in India felt that Linux was the fastest growing OS, with about 10,000 users already. This was mainly due to the cost of the OS, which was free. Hewlett-Packard publicly agreed to support Linux on its computers, hoping to grab market share in the international market's newest technology consumer powerhouse. In India, differences in culture and infrastructure had to be noted and respected when Hewlett-Packard conducted their research. The focus groups used were designed with homogeneity in mind because of traditions held with regard to class, gender and age. They were conducting in hotels to make the respondents they were targeting feel comfortable. The findings helped Hewlett-Packard identify the preferred Indian OS so that it could position its product in line with respondents' preferences.

What is international marketing research?

The term 'international marketing research' can be used very broadly. It denotes research for true international products (international research), research carried out in a country other than the country of the research-commissioning organisation (foreign research), research conducted in all important countries where the company is represented (multi-national research), and research conducted in and across different cultures (cross-cultural research). The last category of cross-cultural research does not have to cross national boundaries. Many European countries have a vast array of ethnic groups, giving the marketing researcher many challenges in understanding consumers in these groups within their home country. The following example is a brief illustration of the array of problems faced by researchers working in a London local authority.

> **Example** **Qualitative research among ethnic minority communities in the UK[5]**
>
> Although the language barrier remains a problem among non-English-speaking minorities in the UK, communicating or conducting research with them can still be done provided their traditional patterns of behaviour are observed. Two examples of the issues faced in studies of ethnic minorities in the London Borough of Newham include:
>
> ● Is there a difference between the Punjabi spoken by Pakistanis and Indians in the UK? This will depend on the exact area from which the people come: the written forms are entirely different, and the more formal spoken forms may differ too, but there can be no hard and fast rules. Punjabi is the language spoken in the Punjab region of India and Pakistan. Indian Punjabis usually speak Hindi (the national language of India) as well, while Pakistani Punjabis usually speak Urdu (the national language of Pakistan) as well.
> ● Should one use Bengali or Sylheti for written stimulus directed at the Bangladeshi population? Sylheti is not a written language, so if people from the Sylhet region are literate in their mother tongue, they will read Bengali.

The example above supports the contention that, methodologically, there is no difference between domestic and international marketing research. In other words, marketing researchers have to adapt their techniques to their target respondents, and the subtle cultural differences within a country offer the same challenges as the much more apparent differences over thousands of kilometres. The following example does not present an actual case but the opinions of the respected international marketing researcher Mary Goodyear. Her views support the contention that there is no difference between domestic and international research but then show why international marketing research should be examined as a distinct subject area.

> **Example** **The world over, a group is a group is a group[6]**
>
> It has become the convention to talk about international research as if it were a discrete sector of the industry. Methodologically, in qualitative research at least, it is not really very different from what is done at home. A group is a group is a group. However, it is important to realise that international research is different: firstly, in terms of analysing the social and cultural dynamics of the society, how the foreign society is structured, how power is gained and expressed, the roles allotted to men and women, the interactions between different sectors of society and so on; and secondly, in the practical problems involved in organising the research.

The first point established in the above example is that many of the cultural and societal assumptions that we take for granted have to be examined. This we discussed when considering how researchers 'see' in Chapter 9. Without such an examination we have the potential to be naive in the questions we pose, who we pose those questions to, and the manner in which we interpret the answers we generate. The second point reminds us of the features of the infrastructure that supports the research process, features that we may get used to and take for granted. For example, without the benefits of accurate sampling frames, accurate and up-to-date secondary data and reliable and widespread use of telephones, our research plans may be weak. Our whole approach to organising and conducting research in international markets has to reflect these physical conditions. The following example builds upon Mary Goodyear's notion that, the world over, a group is a group is a group. It illustrates that even if methodologically the focus group can be conducted in the same manner anywhere in the world, the cultural and societal assumptions and the infrastructure for conducting research have to be appraised.

Example   ### Managing research among Saudi women[7]

What you find behind the veil is what you would find anywhere: outgoing women, shy women, women with a sense of humour, serious women – the entire spectrum of characters and temperaments is present among Saudi women.

In a qualitative project (for a financial institution interested in managing the assets of Saudi women), some women stressed that their husbands should never know that they had a bank account or even that they had money or other assets. Hana Balaa, Director of TNS's Saudi Female Research Centre, found it fascinating to learn about this confident determination to maintain a level of independence, and to think about the marketing communication implications.

Focus group participants are selected through referrals and will be driven to the focus group by their driver, husband or son, as women are not allowed to drive in Saudi Arabia. Five years ago it would have been impossible to conduct this type of focus group in Jeddah, Riyadh or the Kingdom's other major cities. But Saudi society is opening up, slowly, but steadily.

Overseas expansion has become more important for European companies due to increasing economic integration, the lowering of trade barriers and in some instances intensive competition in domestic markets. International markets such as the vast developing economies of China, India and Russia offer huge prospective returns. As attractive as these markets may be, companies must realise that setting up operations in these countries does not guarantee success. Understanding the nature and scope of these markets is vital to realising the opportunities and presents a major challenge to marketing researchers. This challenge also lies in overcoming the 'red tape' in countries that may well have laws and policies designed to protect their own businesses. Realising the opportunities and overcoming the challenges may mean, at one extreme, that marketing researchers work with decision-makers in their own domestic markets, trying to coordinate research in distant lands. It may mean that companies have operations in overseas markets which extend to indigenous marketing research operations; an example of this is the Indian subsidiary of Unilever.

Unilever's Indian subsidiary has a marketing research department that the global group considers to be a laboratory for research in developing markets. The marketing research team is manned by 65 people, including 25 highly respected senior managers, a field force of over 1,600 and an annual budget equivalent to over €7 million. The team operates in a wide range of areas, from basic product and advertising testing, to trend forecasting and media research. The urban consumer panel it runs, of 50,000 households in 43 towns, must be one of the largest in the world. The following example illustrates how the team's rich local knowledge helped to create a successful research programme and financially successful marketing decisions.

Example   **Mud and lemons[8]**

Hindustan Lever Limited (HLL), Unilever's Indian subsidiary, is big in India but has regularly faced competition from small, local entrepreneurs who have competed on price. This was the situation that HLL faced in 1997, when sales of the Vim soap bar for dishwashing had stagnated, being undercut by the Odopic bar which was selling at half the price of Vim. HLL panicked, but its marketing research department began a general study of consumer behaviour in this category, which found that Vim bar's basic position seemed strong if one looked only at dishwashing bars, but compared with all other products, it was not.

Competition came from low-cost detergents, ash, lemons and even mud, which were essentially scourers. They got dishes fairly clean and they were cheap – free, in fact, in the case of ash taken from the residue of cooking. Taking these products into account, Vim's share of the market dropped from 52% to just 8%. Clearly the real issue for HLL was not Odopic, but how to grow the category by encouraging conversions from these dishwashing rivals. To determine consumer attitudes, HLL Marketing Research set up in-depth research projects, which concluded that no one particularly liked the alternatives to Vim, but their low prices made them hard to resist.

HLL decided to avoid the price game, where the smaller players always had an advantage. Instead it would create a significantly better product for only a small increase in the price, one that would have to be better in quantifiable terms, like the ability to remove grease, and in terms of consumer perceptions. HLL Marketing Research used a sequential recycling technique where product development went hand in hand with continuous research with the same group of consumers. HLL and its consumer panel reached a product and price they were satisfied with. The end result was that Vim brand sales rose nearly threefold in the year 2000.

It could well be argued that the above example does not represent international marketing research, as it is domestic research conducted by an Indian company. This adds further support to the contention that, methodologically, there is no difference between domestic and international marketing research. For companies with such a global reach as Unilever, whose economies of scale allow it to operate in this manner, their international research does ultimately become a domestic issue. However, for companies without the financial muscle of Unilever that wish to realise the opportunities in international markets, decisions have to be made about how they plan and implement research from their domestic base.

A framework for international marketing research

Conducting international marketing research can be much more complex than conducting domestic marketing research. Although the basic six-step framework for domestic marketing research is applicable, the environment prevailing in the countries, cultural units or international markets that are being researched influences the way the six steps of the marketing research process should be performed. Figure 26.1 presents a framework for conducting international marketing research.

The differences in the environments of countries, cultural units or foreign markets should be considered when conducting international marketing research. These differences may arise in the marketing, governmental, legal, economic, structural, informational and technological, and socio-cultural environments, as shown in Figure 26.1.

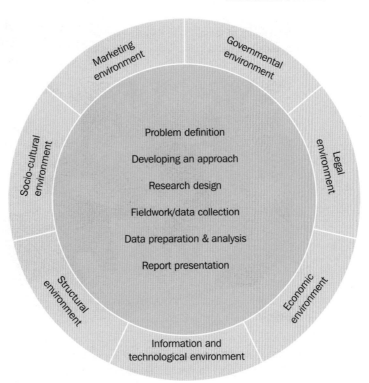

Figure 26.1
A framework for international marketing research

The figure shows concentric circles. The inner core lists: Problem definition, Developing an approach, Research design, Fieldwork/data collection, Data preparation & analysis, Report presentation. The outer ring is labelled with environments: Marketing environment, Governmental environment, Legal environment, Economic environment, Information and technological environment, Structural environment, Socio-cultural environment.

Marketing environment

The role of marketing in economic development varies in different countries. For example, many developing countries are frequently oriented towards production rather than marketing. Demand typically exceeds supply, and there is little concern about customer satisfaction, especially because the level of competition is low. In assessing the marketing environment, the researcher should consider the variety and assortment of products available, pricing policies, government control of media and the public's attitude towards advertising, the efficiency of the distribution system, the level of marketing effort undertaken, and the unsatisfied needs and behaviour of consumers. For example, surveys conducted in Europe usually involve questions on the variety and selection of merchandise. These questions would be inappropriate in many African countries, which are characterised by shortage economies. Likewise, questions about pricing may have to incorporate bargaining as an integral part of the exchange process. Questions about promotion should be modified as well. TV advertising, an extremely important promotion vehicle in Europe, is restricted or prohibited in many countries where TV stations are owned and operated by the government. Certain themes, words and illustrations used in Europe are taboo in some countries. This is illustrated in the following example which describes characteristics of research in the Middle East.

Example **Warming responses from the Levant to the Gulf[9]**

Marketing research is no longer a novelty for people in the Middle East and is relatively well developed in most countries. Local Arab females' mobility is generally restricted and all interviews have to be conducted at the recruiter's or respondent's home. However, this means that the chances of finding women at home and obtaining an interview from them are much higher than in Europe. Using visuals in research can be problematic if they are not carefully selected before they are sent and presented to local custom. It is particularly essential to control the amount of female skin visually exposed. One should never forget that sexual connotations, verbal as well as visual, are unacceptable in most Middle Eastern countries.

One of the main difficulties encountered in interviewing Arabs (and females in particular) is their natural tendency to want to please others, including researchers. Careful formulation of questions is essential to a fruitful interview or discussion, together with a non-complacent interviewer or moderator. Indeed, true feelings, opinions or preferences are often disguised, if felt to be socially unacceptable: ratings are generally higher, especially when related to product attributes or purchase propensity.

Governmental environment

An additional relevant factor is the governmental environment. The type of government has a bearing on the emphasis on public policy, regulatory agencies, government incentives and penalties, and investment in government enterprises. Some governments, particularly in developing countries, do not encourage foreign competition. High tariff barriers create disincentives to the efficient use of marketing research approaches. Also, the role of government in setting market controls, developing infrastructure and acting as an entrepreneur should be carefully assessed. The role of government is also crucial in many developed countries, where government has traditionally worked with industry towards a common national industrial policy. At the tactical level, the government determines tax structures, tariffs and product safety rules and regulations, often imposing special rules and regulations on foreign multinationals and their marketing practices. In many countries, the government may be an important member of the distribution channel. The government purchases essential products on a large scale and then sells them to consumers, perhaps on a rationed basis.

Legal environment

The legal environment encompasses common law, foreign law, international law, transaction law, antitrust, bribery and taxes. From the standpoint of international marketing research, particularly salient are laws related to the elements of the marketing mix. Product laws include those dealing with product quality, packaging, warranty and after-sales service, patents, trademarks and copyright. Laws on pricing deal with price fixing, price discrimination, variable pricing, price controls and retail price maintenance. Distribution laws relate to exclusive territory arrangements, type of channels, and cancellation of distributor or whole-saler agreements. Likewise, laws govern the type of promotional methods that can be employed. Although all countries have laws regulating marketing activities, some countries have only a few laws that are loosely enforced and others have many complicated laws that are strictly enforced. In many countries the legal channels are clogged and the settlement of court cases is prolonged. In addition, home-country laws may also apply while conducting business or marketing research in foreign countries.

Economic environment

Economic environmental characteristics include economic size (gross domestic product, or GDP); level, source and distribution of income; growth trends; and sectoral trends. A country's stage of economic development determines the size, the degree of modernisa-tion and the standardisation of its markets. Consumer, industrial and commercial markets become more standardised and consumers' work, leisure and lifestyles become more homogenised by economic development and advances in technology. The following example illustrates the problems inherent in understanding the characteristics of a coun-try's stage of economic development and in forecasting the potential that exists there.

Example	**The East gets out of the red and into the black**[10]

Dr Rudolf Bretschneider of the GfK Group (**www.gfk.de**) is credited for making the first bold steps into Eastern Europe: GfK credits itself with being the first Western agency to spot mar-keting research potential in the region. Bretschneider cautions against relying too greatly on official economic indicators which, given the substantial size of the black and grey markets, can never give more than an illusory and fragmentary picture. GfK discovered that it had over-estimated its knowledge of the region. GfK's experience highlights the pace of change and the meteoric swings that are commonplace, requiring extra vigilance from all observers.

Marketing research markets in the former Eastern Bloc now show very healthy growth fig-ures, boosted by large EU projects and growing at twice the rate of the original EU15 states. For example, Romania's marketing research industry grew at a real rate of 30.5% in 2003–2004.

Informational and technological environment

Elements of the informational and technological environment include information and communication systems, computerisation, use of electronic equipment, energy, production technology, science and invention. For example, in India, South Korea and many Latin American countries, advances in science and technology have not had a proportionate impact on the lifestyle of the majority of citizens. Computers and electronic information transfer have still to make an impact at grassroots level. Information handling and record keeping are performed in the traditional way. Again, this has an impact on the type of information that can be solicited from consumers, businesses and other enterprises.

Structural environment

Structural factors relate to transportation, communication, utilities and infrastructure. For example, telephone usage in many parts of the Far East, where many households do without telephones, is much lower than in Europe. The mail service may be inefficient in many developing countries resulting in reports of up to 99% of research done on a face-to-face basis, door to door in many parts of Africa.[11] Even so, personal contact with respondents is difficult because city people work during the day and rural residents are inaccessible. Block statistics and maps are not available or can be obtained only with great difficulty. Many households and homes are unidentified.

Based on geography alone, national samples in China and Indonesia are almost unthinkable. China is predominantly rural and Indonesia consists of several thousand islands. In Thailand, only 21% of the population live in urban areas and two-thirds of the total urban population live in a single city, Bangkok. In these three countries, interviewing by telephone is, for the most part, not a consideration.[12]

Socio-cultural environment

Socio-cultural factors include values, literacy, language, religion, communication patterns, and family and social institutions. Relevant values and attitudes towards time, achievement, work, authority, wealth, scientific method, risk, innovation, change, and the Western world should be considered. The marketing research process should be modified so that it does not conflict with the cultural values. In many developing countries, 60% or more of the population is illiterate. In tradition-directed, less developed societies, the ability of respondents to formulate opinions of their own seems to be all but absent; consequently, it is difficult to solicit information from these respondents. As a result, the sophisticated rating scales employed in Europe are not useful. There may also be several distinct spoken languages and dialects in a given nation or region.

In India, for example, there are 19 major languages and more than 200 dialects. India is divided into linguistic states. The country can be described as a mini-Europe, each state like a separate country within Europe, with its own language and cultural peculiarities. A survey which even approaches national representation in scope will generally be printed in at least 12 languages.[13]

A country with a homogeneous family structure is likely to be more culturally homogeneous than a country with multiple family structures. For example, Japan is culturally more homogeneous than many European or African countries, which have many different kinds of family structures.

Finally, what is meant by terms such as 'the youth market'? Many marketers believe that youth markets on a global basis are becoming more alike in their attitudes, lifestyles and aspirations. The following two examples urge caution in such assumptions, presenting small sketches of the forces shaping 'youth markets' in Asia and Europe.

Example · 'I want my MTV, but in Mandarin, please'[14]

Many magazines would have you believe that Asian teens, in appearance, attitude and posture, increasingly resemble American and European teens. However, this convergence view of global teen lifestyle overlooks the reality of Asian cultural diversity. The paradox is that, as Asian teens have become more globally aware, they have also grown increasingly confident in their local identity. This conflict between global and local is becoming more important, being reflected in food, music, language and brands. To appreciate this conflict, it is important to understand what 'Asianness' means to Asian teens. What makes Asianness a valid concept is its communities' resistance to deep cultural change, despite rapid technological and economic progress. Asia's open and purposeful resistance to change in general is rooted in fear of failure and its resultant loss of 'face'. In risk-averse Asia, the status quo is not such a bad place and any change is incremental. The salience of race, community and the family unit, downsizing notwithstanding, is unchallenged. The obvious signs of these include the enduring popularity of traditional costumes and aesthetics; the continued strength of extended families, family associations and networks; the continued power of religion; and a Confucian respect for elders. Even more interesting is how these values have over time been institutionalised into formal political or business practice.

Example   **Euro-youth: myth or reality?[15]**

A major area of difference in European youth stems from the role of the family and attitudes to parenting. As expectations regarding living standards rise, and parental working hours extend to compensate, we are increasingly seeing a 'hands-off' style of parenting. Consequently, family-related need-states become more difficult to satisfy, as parents are increasingly absent. This is especially true in Northern Europe, and nowhere more so than in the UK (which has the highest teen pregnancy and alcohol/drug abuse rates). Southern and certain Eastern European Catholic countries tend to have more united family units, with extended support networks firmly in place. A distinct approach to personal space means that family members are likely to be resident close by and very much involved in young people's lives. Offspring remain living within the family home until much later (as late as 30 in Italy, for example) and parenting is much more 'hands-on'. This makes for a slower transition to emotional and financial independence. Tighter families provide an all-important sense of belonging to Southern/Eastern European teenagers. This is often denied to those from the north (with its more fragmented families), who are forced to make up for this deficit by turning to communal activities such as sports and clubbing to feel they are part of something.

Each country's environment is unique, so international marketing research must take into consideration the environmental characteristics of the countries or foreign markets involved. For companies that wish to expand into a large geographical region, this can cause problems. Should they invest in research into every country or even regions within countries, or will these be prohibitive in time and cost terms? If they cannot manage to research individual countries in a region, which countries should they focus upon? Questioning the resource issues of this dilemma, Martin Stollan, Associate Director of the research company IPSOS-Insight, offers the following argument.[16]

Americans often tend to treat Europe as a single market, so that they feel that doing one country is enough, often choosing Britain because of the language, and that can be very misleading. An improvement is to choose one country in northern Europe and another in southern Europe. But ideally, you need to research each local market. Think of Britain and the differences between England, Wales and Scotland and you can understand the dangers of assuming that Portuguese consumers have the same attitudes as Spanish consumers (and by Spanish consumers do we mean Catalan and Basque as well as Castilian?).

Researching from the security of a key market may miss subtleties that local researchers would be quick to pick up on. Another benefit of local researchers is that desk research and their knowledge can help to fill in many gaps. The ideal is to have a multi-country project, coordinated from one location with local suppliers carrying out individual country 'legs' within a common framework. The research approach should ensure quality control and consistency, and it should lead to actionable and global strategic recommendations, with all local markets represented. Such a maxim is fine, provided that international marketing researchers can demonstrate the potential returns from such an investment, which is inherently very difficult to achieve.

The extent to which companies may invest in research targeted at individual countries may be evaluated in terms of not only the potential returns and idiosyncrasies of that country, but also the complexities of implementing research techniques that will work well. To help understand the problems of implementing international marketing research, we provide additional details for implementing secondary data, qualitative techniques, survey methods, measurement and scaling techniques and questionnaire translation.[17]

Secondary data

The topic of secondary data was covered in detail in Chapters 4 and 5. It is worth recalling where secondary data can support the research process, especially given some of the difficulties of conducting primary research in international markets. Secondary data can help to:

1 Diagnose the research problem.
2 Develop an approach to the problem.
3 Develop a sampling plan.
4 Formulate an appropriate research design (e.g. by identifying the key variables to measure or understand).
5 Answer certain research questions and test some hypotheses.
6 Interpret primary data with more insight.
7 Validate qualitative research findings.

Obtaining secondary data on international markets to gain support for the above is much simpler with the advent of the Internet. The Internet may allow access to international markets which in the past may have required travel to the country and a great amount of time-consuming searching. Judicious use of the Internet does not mean that the international researcher will automatically gain support in the above areas. There may still be little or no secondary data that relate to the issues we wish to research in an international market. For what data we can obtain, the principles of evaluating secondary data, as set out in Table 4.2, still apply. Conducting an evaluation of the nature, specifications, accuracy, currency and dependability may be far more difficult in international markets. The process and specifications of research conducted in international markets may not be explicit; one may need a deep understanding of conducting primary research in a country to understand why data have been collected in a particular manner. Language is also a major issue, not only in reading and interpreting data, but in the definitions used in measurements. Finally, secondary research from a target country may have been heavily influenced by political forces. The researcher may need to be aware of such influences in order to interpret and make use of the findings.

Another major development in the use of secondary data is in the development of geographic information systems. In the use of geodemographic classifications of consumers, systems already exist in many countries across the globe. The systems work well in defining consumers within each country and, as described in Chapter 5, can be used as a foundation to add transactional and survey data generated within an organisation operating within each country. The international research problem emerges from the means of comparing classifications across the different countries. This problem emerges from the different data sources that are used to build the classifications in each country. There are different types of data that may be accessible, different standards and definitions used in data collection and different laws allowing the use, or not, of certain types of data. As discussed in Chapter 5, Experian (**www.experian.com**) have produced 'Mosaic Global' as an attempt to produce a consistent segmentation system that covers over 284 million of the world's households. Using local data from 16 countries and clustering methods, Experian has identified 10 distinct types of residential neighbourhood, each with a distinctive set of values, motivations and consumer preferences, which can be found in each of the countries. Mosaic Global uses the data from the national Mosaic classification systems for the following countries: Australia, China (Beijing, Guangzhou, Shanghai), Denmark, Finland, France, Germany, Greece, Hong Kong, Ireland, the Netherlands, New Zealand, Norway, Spain, Sweden, the UK and the USA.

Geodemographic databases can give an excellent introduction to a particular country and can form a foundation upon which other data sources can be built. At present, comparing consumer types across borders is problematic.

Qualitative techniques

Chapter 6 discussed the differences between European and American researchers in their approach to focus groups. In essence, an American approach is far more structured and tends to be a foundation for subsequent surveys, while the European approach tends to be more evolutionary and exploratory. The question of the perspective from which one plans and conducts qualitative research is not really important until other researchers or moderators from international markets become involved in the process. The approach adopted may not match the expectations of the decision-maker who will be supported by the research. These circumstances are outlined and illustrated in the following example.

Example | When East meets West, quite what does 'qualitative' mean?[18]

International marketers have always been aware that qualitative research as it developed in the USA and in Europe had quite different practices, stemming from different premises and yielding different results. American-style qualitative research started from the same evaluative premise as quantitative research but on a smaller scale. European-style qualitative research started from the opposite premise: it was developmental, exploratory and creative rather than evaluative.

The rest of the world tended to adopt one or the other style of qualitative research depending upon the history and trading partners of the country. For example, India adopted the European model, whereas Japan largely followed the American model. The difficulty for the Asia–Pacific region is that the influences of both schools are found there concurrently. The founders of commercial research in the region came from the UK, Australia, New Zealand and North America, bringing with them varying approaches. From a marketer's point of view, the problem is that both styles of qualitative research are currently on offer under the same description. Marketers may not be sure what they are getting; even worse, some research agencies seem unclear about what they are offering, serving up a confused mixture of both styles of qualitative research, falling short of achieving the objectives of either approach.

Decision-makers often require global answers to develop global marketing campaigns, yet data are often single-market related and cannot be easily interpreted across various countries. Researchers are wary of using varying methods across different countries and cultures and are especially wary of qualitative approaches. Using surveys, where far more control of the design and implementation can be afforded, many forms of bias can emerge when working across cultures. The problems of cross-cultural comparisons grow when qualitative techniques are used. Some researchers argue that international marketing researchers would be better off using direct observational approaches, rather than being misled by findings based upon the 'dubious' application of qualitative research techniques.[19] The following example presents the advice of an experienced international qualitative marketing researcher, addressing cross-cultural research problems. It illustrates the challenges faced by researchers in their attempts to be consistent in qualitative research designs and techniques.

Example | The world at your feet[20]

Kate Anderson is Director of Qualitative Research at RS Consulting (**www.rsconsulting.com**). With many years' experience of conducting qualitative research all over the world, she offers a few 'trade secrets' to help cope with tailoring research design within target markets:

- **Design**. Focus groups may well be suitable for a European or American audience but, when researching Asia (and particularly Japan) or the Middle East, it may be necessary to conduct one-to-one interviews, paired depth interviews, mini or friendship groups, all to avoid the effects of social deference on group dynamics. It may be taboo to mix male and female consumers in the same focus group in many Middle Eastern markets. The same is also true of mixed age groups in Asia where in some markets it can be impolite to challenge the opinions of an elder.
- **Scheduling**. Late work hours in South Korea and Japan mean that it is unlikely that you will be able to schedule two groups per night with business audiences. Consider weekend groups to save time.
- **Moderators**. Ensure a moderator who can communicate with you in a common language. Beware management middlemen who prevent you from dealing directly with the moderator – insist that you are allowed direct access or key points will be lost in translation. Groups in Asia need longer to warm up, so do not be nervous if the moderator spends more time on this part of the discussion.
- **Interpreters**. If an observer is present, an interpreter will need to be briefed to ensure they know which questions and wordings are of key interest. Not knowing what respondents are talking about makes observers uneasy and concerned that they are missing something. The interpreter may also have to work with the moderator. They have to control the group so that comments can be heard, summarising key points of the discussion which may have been lost in the hubbub.
- **Viewing**. Do not assume that it will be possible for clients to view focus groups. In the Middle East, videotaping female respondents can be a problem. Where real-time viewing is available, do not assume that this will be via a mirror wall. In some markets this is considered too distracting and viewing may be via video links.

Direct observational approaches are not feasible or even desirable for all international marketing researchers. Conducting qualitative research in a number of countries may mean approaching a local research company which is aware of local customs, language issues and administrative requirements. Nearly all international marketing researchers choose an in-country marketing research firm to complete the actual fieldwork, whether for focus group moderating or for interviews.[21] However, for some multi-country projects that are qualitative in nature, it may be impossible to find researchers with the cultural, linguistic and administrative experience that can allow some degree of consistency and means to compare findings. The following example illustrates how bilingual researchers working in teams tackle this problem.

Example | In-depth research? A bit controversial[22]

Consumer markets such as soft drinks or processed foods are important enough to be regularly researched across many countries. Wherever you go there are professional qualitative researchers who really understand them. The same cannot be said for most business-to-business markets. Just sending a topic guide and recruitment questionnaire to local agencies is not enough.

Some research agencies have responded by recruiting bilingual researchers, so that the same research team that does the 'home' interviews can, with as much ease, do interviews in target foreign countries. They feel that this is the only way to guarantee consistency in how the research is carried out. More fundamentally, it is the only way to keep the approach flexible. Why is flexibility so important? True qualitative research entails wording questions to suit respondents: if necessary, to keep rewording the question until the answer makes sense. It means the freedom to adapt the interview to suit the interviewer's developing understanding of the subject.

This example also illustrates the essence of qualitative research in terms of exploring through rewording, of adapting an interview until sense is made. In international marketing research this calls for linguistic skills matching the native speaker in any target country. This may not be a solution that is feasible for all international research projects. Depending upon the array of countries to be researched, recruiting researchers with the relevant linguistic skills may not be possible, but it is the best alternative should local research companies not exist or be considered to be of poor quality. Good-quality local researchers should be sought out, because, even if researchers with the relevant linguistic abilities are available, there are other cultural nuances that can affect the trust, rapport and comfort of qualitative research respondents. Often participants are unfamiliar with the process or simply do not trust the researcher. In many Asian cultures, respondents are unwilling to offer an individual opinion that may differ from that of the group. For instance, the need for politeness can thwart the researcher's desire to get at respondents' real feelings in a typical Japanese focus group.

In general, patience and sensitivity are required to overcome cultural problems in conducting qualitative research in international markets.[23] An excellent working relationship with a local research company can be absolutely vital to success and in many cultures can only be achieved by developing a personal relationship. Listening to the advice of local research companies will also enhance sensitivity to respondents. Patience is expressed by a preparedness to lengthen the research schedule, extra care in translation, pretests of wording and tact, and respect for respondents and local researchers. Great care should be taken to be more selective in recruiting and grouping respondents for focus groups.

Whether shaped by European or American paradigms, good qualitative research should be open and a learning process. This openness and learning should be shared among decision-makers, the researchers coordinating research activities and local researchers working in individual countries. All parties should clearly understand the premises for exploring particular issues, probing certain individuals and the bases for interpreting data. In qualitative international marketing research, where there may be confusion about the premises for the whole approach, there is a much greater need for openness between all parties involved.

Survey methods

The following sections discuss the major interviewing methods in light of the challenges of conducting research in foreign countries.[24]

Telephone interviewing and CATI

In the USA and Canada, the telephone has achieved almost total penetration of households. In North America, telephone interviewing is the dominant mode of questionnaire administration. Throughout Europe there are also many countries, regions and cities that have almost total telephone penetration. Even with high penetration rates, in recent years, telephone interviewing techniques in Europe have started to decline. Many Europeans are reluctant to divulge personal details over the telephone. European countries with the highest use of telephone surveys include Denmark (41%) and Italy (39%). Low usage of telephone surveys in Europe includes the UK (19%) and Belgium (20%) with Japan at a level of (4%).[25]

The successful use of the telephone in international research depends upon three factors. The first is the level of telephone penetration (see Chapter 10 for a discussion of the issues related to the selection of probability samples in telephone interviewing). The second is the completeness and accuracy of telephone directories (the growth of the use of mobile phones and of 'ex-directory' numbers has compounded this factor). The third is the cultural acceptance of using the telephone to divulge personal details.

In Hong Kong, for example, 96% of households (other than those on outlying islands and on boats) can be contacted by telephone. With some persistence, evening telephone interviewing can successfully achieve interviews with 70–75% of selected respondents. Residents are uninhibited about using telephones and relaxed about telephone interviews. Even in these circumstances, this is not the most important mode of data collection.

In most developing countries, telephone penetration is low. There may be relatively high concentrations of telephone usage in particular cities and with particular types of consumer (especially in professional classes). Telephone interviews are most useful with respondents in these countries who are accustomed to business transactions by phone.

With the decline of costs for international telephone calls, multi-country studies can be conducted from a single location. This greatly reduces the time and costs associated with the organisation and control of the research project in each country. Furthermore, international calls can obtain a high response rate, and the results have been found to be stable (i.e. the same results are obtained from the first 100 interviews as from the next 200 or 500). It is necessary to find interviewers fluent in the relevant languages, but in most major European cities this is not a problem.

In-home and in-office personal interviews

In many European countries such as Greece, Portugal and Spain, home interviewing is the dominant means to conduct surveys.[26] Given that in-home interviews require a large pool of qualified interviewers and are time consuming and costly, this may seem odd. However, when one considers the quality of rapport that can be built up between the interviewer and respondent, the amount of probing and the quality of audio-visual stimuli that can be used, there are clear benefits that outweigh the costs. In many areas of industrial marketing research, the only means to contact certain managers may be through the personal interview, held in their office. The following example further illustrates a cultural problem faced with in-office interviews.

Example	### Russian roulette: exciting once you learn the new rules[27]

Executives find it odd, and sometimes sinister, that people should just come to ask questions which often seem irrelevant. One respondent, a high official in a major city, kept interrupting the interview with offers to sell the product under discussion and asked our agency to supply some other products. He considered it fatuous that he should face a stream of questions without seeing any concrete result at the end. It is usually assumed that the researcher belongs to the company commissioning the research, even when the relationship is made clear. Guarantees that the respondents' identity will remain confidential can be treated with disbelief.

Street interviews

In many countries, with low telephone penetration and comparatively low literacy rates, the street interview offers an excellent means to survey. This is illustrated in the following example, showing Chinese respondents enjoying the marketing research task.

Example   **Foreign policy[28]**

Interviewing is not usually an obstacle in mainland China, says Richard Necchi, Taylor Nelson Audits of Great Britain Group Director for Greater China. The problem is ensuring that you have a representative sample to work from. Census data are simply not up to Western standards, he says, and researchers try to rely on government statistics as little as possible. The huge migrant population of about 100 million also means that the actual population of certain cities is much greater than official figures suggest, and this problem is likely to grow. 'In China we have to do face-to-face every time, as there are so few telephones. But people love answering questions.'

Provided that the environment of the street allows an interview to be conducted, the street interview is an excellent means to identify and interview individuals where there are poor or non-existent sampling frames. Given the congestion in many major international cities, the locations where interviews will be conducted have to be carefully selected. However, this does not differ from planning and conducting street interviews in 'home' markets. As with in-home and in-office interviews, the differences lie in the culture of approaching someone in the street and their willingness to divulge information to a stranger.

Mail surveys

Because of their low cost, mail interviews continue to be used in most developed countries where literacy is high and the postal system is well developed. At 7%, mail surveys globally constitute the lowest form of quantitative data collection. Japan (14%), Denmark (12%) and Sweden (10%) constitute the highest levels of mail surveys worldwide. In many parts of Africa, Asia and South America, the use of mail surveys and mail panels is low because of illiteracy and the large proportion of population living in rural areas. Examples in these regions of the use of mail surveys versus face-to-face methods include Kenya (1% vs. 60%), Bangladesh (0.5% vs. 85%) and Peru (0.5% vs. 64%). Mail surveys are, typically, more effective in b2b international marketing research (see Chapter 27), although it can be a major challenge to identify the appropriate respondent within each firm and to personalise the address.

Electronic surveys

Globally, the use of email and the Internet has grown enormously. As such, the use of these methods for conducting surveys is growing not only with business and institutional respondents, but also within households. Both these methods have become viable for conducting surveys, mail panels and access panels. The highest incidences of the use of online survey work include Australia (20%), the Netherlands (18%) and the UK (17%). In Japan, online research (12%) now exceeds the incidence of telephone surveying (4%). Given the global nature of the Internet, for certain topics (such as home shopping using the Internet) this may be the cheapest and quickest means to conduct an international survey. However, given the sampling problems associated with Internet usage, great care must be taken in validating samples from such surveys. As the penetration of Internet usage increases globally, the technique has great potential for both survey work and qualitative techniques; it is ideally suited to reaching out across national boundaries. The sampling problems of email and Internet surveys mean that they are not viable in many developing countries. However, as penetration levels to the Internet are developing so quickly, these techniques are enabling researchers to reach out to important target groups in developing countries, as illustrated in the following example.

Example India braced for online panel explosion[29]

Research agencies are looking to capitalise on booming Internet uptake in India's major urban centres with plans to launch access panels in the country. Global agency TNS is planning to extend its multi-country 6th Dimension online access panel to India. Approximately 40 million people have online access, with the majority of web users based in major markets such New Dehli, Mumbai, Calcutta and Chennai. Pulse Group has already recruited 245,000 members for its new access panel. Mark Walton, TNS Regional Director of Asia–Pacific Access Panels, believes speed and cost are not the only reasons why online panels will be useful in India. 'In emerging markets, web research can be the best way to target groups such as the rich urban classes as they are more likely to provide feedback on products online compared to face-to-face interviews.'

The criteria for the selection of survey methods were discussed in Chapter 10. As discussed and illustrated in that chapter, an important consideration in selecting the methods of administering questionnaires is to ensure equivalence and comparability across countries. This is illustrated in the following example, where comparability between countries is of paramount importance. The example leads on to issues of equivalence in measurement and scaling.

Example The strengths and flaws[30]

For big multinational firms, almost any marketing research is international and, as a consequence, their focus is upon standardisation and a consistency of quality standards. For example, the electronics multinational Philips is very specific in what it wants from research agencies in international projects: speed and comparability. Among other things, Philips has developed a questionnaire for tracking brand positioning, expecting the agencies it works with to use a set list of questions. 'Many agencies are taken aback at first,' Marjolein van Nieuwkasteele, Chief of Global Marketing Management at Philips Electronics, says:

Some disagree with the scales or they suggest adjustments in other areas. However, for us standardisation is very important. We want to be able to compare the results of surveys, for instance on brand awareness, across the different divisions of our company. We agreed internally to develop standard questionnaires. We now expect agencies to use them and not re-invent the wheel over and over again. Standardisation speeds up the research process.

Measurement and scaling

In international marketing research, it is critical to establish the equivalence of scales and measures used to obtain data from different countries. As illustrated in Figure 26.2, this requires an examination of construct equivalence, operational equivalence, scalar equivalence and linguistic equivalence.[31]

Construct equivalence
A type of equivalence that deals with the question of whether the marketing constructs have the same meaning and significance in different countries.

Construct equivalence deals with the question of whether the marketing constructs (e.g. opinion leadership, variety seeking and brand loyalty) have the same meaning and significance in different countries. In many countries, the number of brands available in a given product category is limited. In some countries, the dominant brands have become generic labels symbolising the entire product category. Consequently, a different perspective on brand loyalty may have to be adopted in these countries.

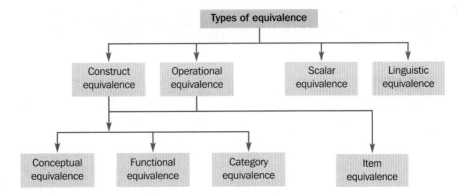

Figure 26.2 Scaling and measurement equivalence in international research

Conceptual equivalence
A construct equivalence issue that deals with whether the interpretation of brands, products, consumer behaviour and the marketing effort are the same in different countries.

Functional equivalence
A construct equivalence issue that deals specifically with whether a given concept or behaviour serves the same role or function in different countries.

Category equivalence
A construct equivalence issue that deals specifically with whether the categories in which brands, products and behaviour are grouped are the same in different countries.

Operational equivalence
A type of equivalence that measures how theoretical constructs are operationalised in different countries to measure marketing variables.

Item equivalence
Use of the same instrument in different countries.

Scalar equivalence
The demonstration that two individuals from different countries with the same value on some variable will score at the same level on the same test. Also called metric equivalence.

Linguistic equivalence
The equivalence of both spoken and written language forms used in scales and questionnaires.

Construct equivalence comprises conceptual equivalence, functional equivalence and category equivalence. **Conceptual equivalence** deals with the interpretation of brands, products, consumer behaviour and marketing effort. For example, sales promotion techniques are an integral component of marketing effort throughout Europe. On the other hand, in countries with shortage economies, where the market is dominated by the sellers, consumers view sales with suspicion because they believe that the product being promoted is of poor quality. **Functional equivalence** examines whether a given concept or behaviour serves the same role or function in different countries. For example, in many developing countries, bicycles are predominantly a means of transportation rather than of recreation. Marketing research related to the use of bicycles in these countries must examine different motives, attitudes, behaviours and even different competing products than such research would in Europe. **Category equivalence** refers to the category in which stimuli such as products, brands and behaviours are grouped. In Europe, the category of the principal shopper may be defined as either the male or female head of household. This category may be inappropriate in countries where routine daily shopping is done by a domestic servant. Furthermore, the category 'household' itself varies across countries.

Operational equivalence concerns how theoretical constructs are operationalised to make measurements. In Europe, leisure may be operationalised as playing golf, tennis or other sports, watching TV, or basking in the sun for example. This operationalisation may not be relevant in countries where people do not play these sports or do not have round-the-clock TV transmission. Lying in the sun is generally not normal behaviour in countries with hot climates. **Item equivalence**, which is closely connected to operational equivalence, presupposes both construct and operational equivalence. To establish item equivalence, the construct should be measured by the same instrument in different countries.

Scalar equivalence, also called metric equivalence, is established if the other types of equivalence have been attained. This involves demonstrating that two individuals from different countries with the same value on some variable, such as brand loyalty, will score at the same level on the same test. Scalar equivalence has two aspects. The specific scale or scoring procedure used to establish the measure should be equivalent. The equivalence of response to a given measure in different countries should be considered. For example, do scores from the top box or from the top two boxes on a purchase–intent scale reflect similar likelihood of purchase in different countries? Finally, **linguistic equivalence** refers to both the spoken and the written language forms used in scales, questionnaires and interviewing. The scales and other verbal stimuli should be translated so that they are readily understood by respondents in different countries and have equivalent meaning.[32]

Questionnaire translation

Focus on | **Sports Marketing Surveys**

Translation into eight languages[33]

Robert Kirby, who was the Telephone Research Director at Research Services Ltd and has many years' experience of pan-European telephone surveys, offers the following advice in coping with translation:

> Translations require the most rigorous checking. In my experience it is not advisable to use someone from a home country who can speak the language fluently, because frequently a current idiomatic knowledge is required. A translation agency with no expertise could have the idiom but not the interviewing skills.

His advice mirrors the practice in the Formula One Racetrack Project that has been illustrated in many chapters. The Racetrack questionnaire was translated from English into French, German, Italian, Japanese, Portuguese and Spanish. In the 2005 version a Chinese translation was added. The translation for the Racetrack Project was undertaken by its local agents (beyond the UK it has offices in Australia, Belgium, Brazil, France, Greece, Italy, Japan, Korea, Spain, Singapore, Turkey, the USA) in the target countries of the survey. These agents understood the idiom and the elicitation task required to connect with Formula One fans in their particular country.

Example | **Taking the people's temperature – right across Europe[34]**

Eurobarometer measures public opinion across Europe on behalf of the European Commission. First published in 1974, it runs twice a year, in spring and autumn, and now interviews some 25,000 respondents in each wave. The objectives set by the EC for the Eurobarometer are threefold. First, to evaluate the activities of the European Commission and indicate how the public might welcome a particular proposition, e.g. nuclear energy. Second, to measure how European public opinion has changed over a period of time. Third, to observe and anticipate public attitudes towards important events directly or indirectly linked to the development of the EU.

One of the most challenging steps of the Eurobarometer is to ensure that question meaning is the same across all countries surveyed, taking into account specific national and cultural differences. For example, in France, the phrase 'mobile phone' is translated as 'téléphone mobile'. In French-speaking Belgium, that would mean 'wireless handset'. To address such issues, TNS always starts with a bilingual (English/French) version of the initial questionnaire. From this point, a meeting takes place to review the quality of the bilingual version to check if the meaning of each question is clear for all countries. A final bilingual version of the questionnaire is then made available so that each country can carry out its translation into the local language(s). The translations are carried out, working from the final questionnaire by two different translators. After this, all questionnaires are back translated into English or French by external experts. Any differences between the back-translated version and the original are immediately identified and reviewed.

As in the above examples, questions may have to be translated for administration in different cultures. Direct translation, in which a bilingual translator translates the questionnaire directly from a base language to the respondent's language, is frequently used. If the trans-

Back translation
A translation technique that translates a questionnaire from the base language by a translator whose native language is the one into which the questionnaire is being translated. This version is then retranslated back into the original language by someone whose native language is the base language. Translation errors can then be identified.

Parallel translation
A translation method in which a committee of translators, each of whom is fluent in at least two languages, discuss alternative versions of a questionnaire and make modifications until consensus is reached.

lator is not fluent in both languages and is not familiar with both cultures, however, direct translation of certain words and phrases may be erroneous. Procedures like back translation and parallel translation have been suggested to avoid these errors. In **back translation**, the questionnaire is translated from the base language by a bilingual speaker whose native language is the language into which the questionnaire is being translated. This version is then retranslated back into the original language by a bilingual whose native language is the initial or base language. Translation errors can then be identified. Several repeat translations and back translations may be necessary to develop equivalent questionnaires, and this process can be cumbersome and time consuming.[35]

An alternative procedure is **parallel translation**. A committee of translators, each of whom is fluent in at least two of the languages in which the questionnaire will be administered, discuss alternative versions of the questionnaire and make modifications until consensus is reached. In countries where several languages are spoken, the questionnaire should be translated into the language of each respondent subgroup. It is important that any non-verbal stimuli (pictures and advertisements) also be translated using similar procedures. The following example underscores the importance of translation that does not impose the structure of a 'home country' from which the research is commissioned, in this case the UK.

Example   **The search for focus – brand values across Europe[36]**

Land Rover wished to understand the values associated with its brand in Belgium, the UK, France, Germany, Italy, the Netherlands, Portugal and Spain. The project involved the use of CAPI and required the development of a questionnaire that could allow comparisons between the countries. The issue of questionnaire translation was a sensitive and pertinent one. What was crucial was that the translation was meaningful in all languages rather than forcing the English-language requirements into the local language. The translation was a difficult process and required an understanding of both the research process and the cultural context of the individual markets. It was the case that certain concepts that are expressive in English could not easily be translated into other languages. For instance, the word 'aspirational' does not easily translate into French, Spanish or Italian with the same meaning as in English. Consequently, in order to ensure comparability the translation process involved a series of iterative steps changing the master questionnaire to fit what was achievable overall in each market.

Ethics in marketing research

Ethical responsibilities for marketing research conducted abroad are very similar to those for research conducted domestically. In conducting marketing research across Europe (and indeed globally), ESOMAR produced a code of conduct that guides professional practice that protects the interests of all research stakeholders. In general, for each of the six stages of the marketing research design process, the same four stakeholders (client, researcher, respondent and public) should act honourably and respect their responsibilities to one another. For individual countries, a key development in honourable practice lies in the development of professional associations. These can guide researchers through the development of specific codes of practice that may reflect their culture and industrial heritage. For example, in the Czech Republic, Hungary, Poland and Russia, major market research suppliers are forming associations and introducing or discussing quality standard systems for fieldwork. Research was not unknown in the region prior to the collapse of communism and most countries have had a tradition of government-sponsored research spanning 40–50 years. Most major suppliers are investing in their future by training their staff in Western Europe and North America.[37]

For all the similarities that may exist in conducting research in international markets, some ethical issues become more difficult to solve. Consider the dilemma presented by David Mendoza, Director of Gobi International, an Anglo-Russian industrial research company:

> *Some people will, Soviet style, still refuse to answer any questions of any kind. Others, often the same type of former Soviet apparatchik, but totally disillusioned, will promise to tell you whatever you need in return for dollars. Frankly, this is highly unsatisfactory and something we try to avoid, although often there is no choice.[38]*

Internet and computer applications

The Internet and computers can be extensively used in all phases of the international marketing research process. These uses parallel those discussed in earlier chapters and hence will not be repeated here. The fact that the Internet can be used to communicate with respondents and marketing decision-makers anywhere in the world has given a new dimension to international marketing research. For example, the online survey overcomes geographic boundaries and differences in postal systems to solicit responses from around the world. The online survey also takes advantage of one interviewer (the computer) that can present the same survey in several different translations. As well as the benefits of speed and cost reductions, the Internet can also enhance the quality of data supplied to respondents, generating more meaningful and relevant responses, as illustrated in the following example.

Example

How online research helped to track reaction to a campaign designed to boost tourism[39]

Tourism Australia (**www.australia.com**) has tracked the effectiveness of the 'Uniquely Australian Invitation' campaign (which incorporates the line 'So where the bloody hell are you?'). TNS (**www.tns-global.com**) is conducting the research globally through 14 key markets in Asia–Pacific, Europe and the USA. Tracking within 11 of these markets is now conducted online with only China, India and Malaysia using CATI or face-to-face methods. Five of the eight Asia–Pacific markets are now run online, disproving the myth that Asia–Pacific is not yet ready for online research. In addition to the benefits of cost and speed, online access panels also provide a more sensitive evaluation of advertising, Senior Researcher David Holderness of Tourism Australia explains:

> As with many advertising campaigns, the soundtrack plays a vital role in or campaign, complementing the visuals and helping reinforce key messages, not least the 'So where the bloody hell are you?' line. Online interviewing enables us to play the soundtrack to respondents to achieve accurate recognition and gain a more detailed understanding of advertising response. By using TNS access panels, we also have the opportunity to recontact respondents for future research with a specific focus. This would be valuable for us if we want some 'deep dives' into the data and understand the nuances of a particular subsample.

The environmental characteristics of international markets detailed in this chapter present a formidable research task, especially when first learning about a country. The Internet is the ideal means to access quickly material that helps to shape an understanding of the environmental context of a particular country. This is particularly relevant in tracking down secondary data sources that may not be available in the home country of a researcher.

The Internet has also been extremely beneficial in conducting qualitative interviews. One of the most difficult administrative tasks in conducting focus groups is getting participants together at an agreed location. Because of the travel problems for certain respondents, many focus groups may have to be conducted to cover a wide geographical area. The Internet can help to overcome these problems, first of all by the convenience it offers the participants – not having to leave their homes – and second by the breaking down of geographical boundaries.

Summary

With the globalisation of markets, international marketing research is burgeoning rapidly. As well as the technical requirements of conducting successful marketing research as outlined in this text, the researcher has to cope with new cultures and languages in targeted international markets. Given the array of ethnic groups within most European countries, the challenges of understanding new cultures and languages can exist within a 'home' country.

The environment prevailing in the international markets being researched influences all six steps of the marketing research process. Important aspects of this environment include the marketing, governmental, legal, economic, structural, informational and technological, and socio-cultural environment.

In collecting data from different countries, it is desirable to use techniques with equivalent levels of reliability rather than the same method. Repeating identical techniques across borders may result in subtle cultural and linguistic differences being ignored, which may have a great effect upon the nature and quality of data that are generated. It is critical to establish the equivalence of scales and measures in terms of construct equivalence, operational equivalence, scalar equivalence and linguistic equivalence. Questionnaires used should be adapted to the specific cultural environment and should not be biased in favour of any one culture or language. Back translation and parallel translation are helpful in detecting translation errors.

The ethical concerns facing international marketing researchers are similar in many ways to the issues confronting domestic researchers. Working in countries where professional marketing research associations exist should allow access to codes of conduct that reflect the culture and industrial heritage of the particular country. However, the international researcher being exposed to an array of cultures and economic scenarios should always expect to find new situations and ethical dilemmas.

Questions

1 Evaluate the meaning of 'international' from the perspective of the marketing researcher.

2 What characteristics distinguish international marketing research from domestic marketing research?

3 Describe the aspects of the environment of each country that should be taken into account in international marketing research.

4 Describe the importance of considering the marketing environment in conducting international marketing research.

5 What is meant by the structural environment? How do the variables comprising the structural environment influence international marketing research?

6 What is meant by the informational and technological environment? How do the variables comprising the informational and technological environment influence international marketing research?

7 What is meant by the socio-cultural environment? How do the variables comprising the socio-cultural environment influence international marketing research?

8 How should the researcher evaluate secondary data obtained from foreign countries?

9 Describe the factors that may influence the approach to qualitative techniques in different countries.

10 Select a country, using environmental characteristics to illustrate why CATI works particularly well as a survey technique.

11 Select a country, using environmental characteristics to illustrate why in-home interviewing does not work particularly well as a survey technique.

12 Select a country, using environmental characteristics to illustrate why Internet surveys work particularly well as a survey technique.

13 How should the equivalence of scales and measures be established when the data are to be obtained from different countries or cultural units?

14 What problems are involved in the direct translation of a questionnaire into another language?

15 Briefly describe the procedures that may be adopted to ensure translation is correctly conducted in the development of a questionnaire.

Exercises

1 Obtain a copy of an old marketing research report that has been conducted in the country where you are studying (many marketing research agencies or companies that have commissioned research will provide copies of old reports for educational purposes). Evaluate how the research would have been conducted if the same project were conducted in Malaysia.

2 Compile data on the GDP, level of literacy and percentage of households with telephones for 20 different countries. Using a proprietary statistics package, run a regression analysis with GDP as the dependent variable and the other two variables as the independent variables. Interpret your results.

3 Visit the website of Kodak at **www.kodak.com**. What can you learn about the company's international marketing efforts? Write a report on what you see as its main international marketing research challenges.

4 You are the Marketing Research Director of Unilever (**www.unilever.com**). What challenges do you see in researching markets for household products in the Far East? Prepare a report for the Unilever Board in Europe making the case for a higher investment in marketing research in this region.

5 In a small group discuss the following issues: 'Some marketing strategists have argued that a standardised marketing strategy should be adopted for all foreign markets. Does this imply that the research design and techniques should be standardised no matter where the research is being conducted?' and 'Given the huge cultural diversity that exists in many parts of Europe, should marketing researchers have a mindset of "home" and "foreign" markets'?

Video Case Exercise: Nike

Given Nikes desire to operate globally, what internal marketing research challenges do they face in:
a) developing sponsorship partnerships?
b) understanding the culture of soccer?

video case

download from
www.pearsoned.co.uk/
malhotra_euro

Notes

1 Goodyear, M., Guest editorial – 'International Research and Marketing', *Journal of the Market Research Society* 38 (1) (January 1996), 1.

2 See Malhotra, N.K., 'Cross-cultural marketing research in the twenty-first century', *International Marketing Review* 18 (3) (2001), 230–234; Douglas, S.P., 'Exploring new worlds: the challenge of global marketing', *Journal of Marketing* 65 (1) (January 2001), 103–107; Malhotra, N.K., Agarwal, J. and Peterson, M., 'Cross-cultural marketing research: methodological issues and guidelines', *International Marketing Review* 13 (5) (1996), 7–43; Malhotra, N.K., 'Administration of questionnaires for collecting quantitative data in international marketing research', *Journal of Global Marketing* 4 (2) (1991), 63–92; Malhotra, N.K., 'Designing an international marketing research course: framework and content', *Journal of Teaching in International Business* 3 (1992), 1–27.

3 Petrin, K., 'Tasty wisdom for ESOMAR delegates', *Research* (1 December 2001), 9.

4 LeHardy, M., 'In India, familiarity breeds better content', *Marketing News* 35 (9) (23 April 2001), 40.

5 Sills, A. and Desai, P., 'Qualitative research amongst ethnic minorities in Britain', *Journal of the Market Research Society* 38 (3) (July 1996), 247.

6 Goodyear, M., 'The world over, a group is a group is a group', *ResearchPlus* (November 1992), 5.

7 Havermans, J., 'Connecting with Saudi women', *Research World* (August 2005), 16.

8 Doctor, V., 'Levering the market', *Research* (1 August 2001), 14.

9 Dunlop, C., 'Warming responses from the Levant to the Gulf', *Research* (November 1995), 24.

10 Savage, M., 'The East gets out of the red and into the black', *Research* (October 1997), 22; ESOMAR – *Industry study on 2004*, p. 5.

11 Havermans, J., 'Connecting with Saudi women', *Research World* (August 2005), 17.

12 Hutton, G., 'If you board the Asian bus, better mind your language', *ResearchPlus* (February 1996), 9.

13 Ibid.

14 Lau, S., 'I want my MTV, but in Mandarin, please', *Admap* (March 2001), 34–36.

15 Pasco, M., 'Euro-youth: myth or reality?', *Admap* (June 2001), 14–15.

16 Miles, L., 'Finding a balance in global research', *Marketing* (29 November 2001), 33.

17 See Dawar, N. and Parker, P., 'Marketing universals: consumers' use of brand name, price, physical appearance, and retailer reputation as signals of product quality', *Journal of Marketing* 58 (April 1994), 81–95.

18 Broadbent, K., 'When East meets West, quite what does "qualitative" mean?', *ResearchPlus* (March 1997), 15.

19 Choudry, Y.A., 'Pitfalls in international marketing research: are you speaking French like a Spanish cow?', *Akron Business and Economic Review* 17 (4) (Winter 1986), 18–28.

20 Anderson, K., 'The world at your feet', *Research*, Special Report – Qualitative Research (August, 2004), 30–31.

21 Zimmerman, A.S. and Szenberg, M., 'International primary market research techniques: availability, effectiveness and relative costs', *Proceedings of the International Trade and Finance Association*, Vol. III (San Jose, Costa Rica, May 1995), 773–806.

22 Bloom, N., 'In-depth research? A bit controversial!', *ResearchPlus* (June 1993), 13.

23 Zimmerman, A.S. and Szenberg, M., 'Implementing international qualitative research: techniques and obstacles', *Qualitative Market Research: An International Journal* 3 (3) (2000), 158–164.

24 The work on survey methods is drawn from Malhotra, N.K., 'Cross-cultural marketing research in the twenty-first century', *International Marketing Review* 18 (3) (2001), 230–234; Douglas, S.P., 'Exploring new worlds: the challenge of global marketing', *Journal of Marketing* 65 (1) (January 2001), 103–107; Malhotra, N.K., Agarwal, J. and Peterson, M., 'Cross-cultural marketing research: methodological issues and guidelines', *International Marketing Review* 13 (5) (1996), 7–43.

25 ESOMAR – *Industry study on 2004*, p. 26.

26 Ibid.

27 Ibid.

28 Gander, P., 'Foreign policy', *Marketing Week* (30 April 1998), 46.

29 Secker, M., 'India braced for online panel explosion as Internet uptake rockets in urban centres', *Research* (May 2006), 8.

30 Havermans, J., 'The strengths and flaws', *ResearchWorld* (April 2005), 12–13.

31 Myers, M.B., 'Academic insights: an application of multiple-group causal models in assessing cross cultural measurement equivalence', *Journal of International Marketing* 8 (4) (2000), 108–121; and guidelines', Malhotra, N.K., Agarwal, J. and Peterson, M., 'Cross-cultural marketing research: methodological issues and guidelines', *International Marketing Review* 13 (5) (1996), 7–43.

32 Thorne, L., 'The sociocultural embeddedness of individuals' ethical reasoning in organisations (cross cultural ethics)', *Journal of Business Ethics* 35 (1) (January 2002), 1–13; McDonald, G., 'Cross-cultural methodological issues in ethical research', *Journal of Business Ethics* 27 (1/2) (September 2000), 89–104.

33 Kirby, R., 'A pan-European view of the executive at lunch', *ResearchPlus* (October 1992), 7.

34 De Voogd, L. and Carballo, M., 'Taking the temperature', *Research* (January 2006), 38–39.

35 Behling, O. and Law, K.S., *Translating Questionnaires and other research instruments: problems and solutions* (Thousand Oaks, CA: Sage, 2000); Malhotra, N. K. and McCort, D., 'A cross-cultural comparison of behavioural intention models: theoretical consideration and an empirical investigation', *International Marketing Review* 18 (3) (2001), 235–269.

36 Bull, N. and Oxley, M., 'The search for focus – brand values across Europe', *Marketing and Research Today* (November 1996), 243.

37 Bartonova, M., 'The markets are emerging – and research is hard on their heels', *ResearchPlus* (January 1996), 4.

38 Mendoza, D., 'Russian roulette: exciting once you learn the new rules', *Research* (January 1995), 21.

39 Anon., 'How online research helped to track reaction to a campaign to boost tourism', *Research in Business – Case Studies* (May 2006), 14.

Source: © Mark Dadwell/Getty Images

27

Business-to-business (b2b) marketing research

> *The management of customer relationships is the core task of the b2b marketer. The marketing researcher must help to unlock the nature and dynamism of these relationships.*

Objectives

After reading this chapter, you should be able to:

1 explain what b2b marketing is;

2 understand the differences between b2b and consumer marketing;

3 explain the marketing research challenges that emerge from the differences between b2b and consumer marketing decision making;

4 understand how the concepts of networks and relationships underpin the distinctive challenges faced by b2b decision-makers;

5 understand what competitor intelligence is and how it may supplement or even take the place of marketing research for some businesses;

6 discuss the cultural challenges faced in conducting b2b marketing research in an international setting;

7 discuss the ethical considerations in b2b marketing research by comparing the challenges set in competitor intelligence with conventional marketing research.

| STAGE 1 Problem definition | STAGE 2 Research approach developed | STAGE 3 Research design developed | STAGE 4 Fieldwork or data collection | STAGE 5 Data preparation and analysis | STAGE 6 Report preparation and presentation |

Overview

This chapter starts by defining the nature of b2b marketing, presenting a definition that introduces the concept of 'relationships'. This is followed by a short introduction to the differences between b2b and consumer marketing. The evaluation of differences is crucial if one is to consider whether these have any impact upon the practice of b2b marketing research. The chapter then sets out the bases in which to evaluate the key challenges faced by b2b marketing decision-makers. These bases describe the importance of nurturing and developing relationships and the use of networks. From these bases, the key differences between b2b and consumer marketing are explained in more detail. There are five key areas of difference that are explored, followed in each case by the marketing research challenges these differences present. The 'threat' to conventional marketing research is then explored with a review of the nature and use of competitor intelligence. The challenges faced by b2b marketing researchers in an international setting are then evaluated, discussing how language and cultural differences impact upon gaining access to businesses. This is followed by a discussion of the ethical issues raised in implementing competitive intelligence compared with conventional marketing research. The chapter finally evaluates the implications of using the Internet in b2b research, especially the benefits of briefing and supporting fieldworkers when they have been given the task of interviewing respondents about technical questions.

We begin with two examples illustrating how marketing research may be used in b2b marketing. The first example demonstrates the use of quantitative and qualitative techniques in an international setting. The case could well refer to any consumer marketing organisation, investing in the use of exhibitions and wishing to evaluate the worth of that investment. It basically illustrates that all the techniques that have been presented and discussed in this text can be used in a b2b context. It could also be used to support the argument that there is no difference between marketing research in b2b contexts compared with consumer marketing, as the case clearly shows that all techniques can be utilised. What it does not reveal are the many challenges facing b2b marketing researchers when generating information in which b2b decision-makers will have confidence.

Example   Fair's fair for Ericsson[1]

As the world's largest supplier of mobile systems and a leading player in fixed-line networks, Ericsson operates in more than 140 countries. It provides total solutions from systems and applications to services and core technology for mobile handsets. Its customers are network operators from around the world; indeed, the top 10 largest mobile operators are all customers of Ericsson. Telecoms companies like Ericsson recognise that trade shows play a crucial role in building the brand as well as providing showcases to demonstrate new products and technologies. They also provide the means to nurture and develop relationships by meeting and entertaining customers and other parties.

Ericsson has a clearly defined strategy for participation at trade shows and typically takes part in the 3GSM World Congress (France), CTIA (USA), CeBIT (Germany), CommunicAsia (Singapore) and ITU Telecom Asia (Hong Kong). Given the high levels of expenditure to participate and the importance of this communication channel, Ericsson determined that it needed to ensure that:

- the return on investment in a show could be measured;
- best practice guidelines were developed;
- the Ericsson brand was being communicated consistently.

In order to support the decisions involved in these areas, Ericsson used marketing research to provide feedback in five key areas:

- the 'quality' of visitors;
- their performance at an individual show;
- the impact on customer/employee relationships;
- the impact on the brand;
- the value of participation relative to other communication tools.

Working with the research company BPRI, Ericsson used an array of research techniques. Depending upon the nature of the target audience, CAPI, ethnography, telephone, web and self-completion surveys were used. The CAPI approach was used daily and enabled the company to capture findings from the previous day and to make changes to the visitor experience. For example, at the beginning of the 3GSM World Congress, some concern was expressed about the processes used for directing visitors to key Ericsson staff, as well as about the need for a more tailored approach. The daily briefings by the BPRI team highlighted these areas of concern and alternative solutions to these issues were implemented on the same day. Marked improvement was subsequently reflected in much higher scores for these aspects of performance.

The second example comes from the many technical challenges in a study of cash-management banking.

Example — Supporting b2b decision making

GlobalCash[2] was a study designed to support b2b decision-makers in major pan-European banks. Examples from GlobalCash will be used to illustrate a number of techniques and challenges throughout this chapter.

The array of techniques used in GlobalCash included:

- a traditional postal survey to the largest companies in Europe;
- a telephone survey to these companies prior to the launch of the euro;
- an Internet survey regarding company responses to the introduction of the euro (€);
- qualitative in-depth interviews with key decision-makers;
- a feedback workshop in Brussels where survey findings were presented to respondents, followed by qualitative workshops based on group discussions.

These techniques were targeted at chief executives, finance directors and cash managers. The decision-makers in major banks from the UK, France, Germany, Ireland, Spain and the USA that required decision support included: customer relationship managers, systems designers, brand managers, marketing managers and strategists.

The main challenge in this study lay in gaining access to such prominent and busy executives. Over the 10 years that the study unfolded, different research techniques were tried and developed to draw out the most meaningful, valid and reliable information from the target executives. The researchers involved in the study were fortunate to be able to repeat the study every two years and to learn very valuable lessons in implementing the next study. The majority of b2b marketing researchers do not have this luxury, having to do their best in a one-off situation, learning from their experiences and the case material of b2b research practices in many specific contexts.

There are many marketing researchers who believe that b2b marketing research is quite distinctive from consumer marketing research. There is a professional group, the Business Intelligence Group (BIG) (**www.b2bresearch.org**), that was launched in 2001 to support the interests of individuals involved in b2b marketing research. We will progress by evaluating whether there are distinctive characteristics of b2b marketing decision making that may require a different approach to marketing research. To begin such an evaluation we continue by evaluating the nature of b2b marketing and what are contended to be the similarities and distinctions when compared with consumer marketing.

What is b2b marketing?

The term 'b2b marketing' is a relatively new one used to describe business marketing, industrial marketing or even organisational marketing. It is a simple acronym that was initially used to distinguish online business transactions, but is now used as the generic term for business marketing. In very simple terms b2b means businesses that sell products or services to other businesses, such as Intel selling processors to Dell or other computer manufacturers.

Such a simple term masks the challenges faced by b2b marketers. In the following definition, Dibb et al.[3] highlight the activities involved in the process of exchange between two parties. This definition presents little distinction between b2b marketing and the generic process of marketing, as discussed in Chapter 1:

> Industrial [b2b] marketing concerns activities directed towards facilitating and expediting exchanges between industrial markets and industrial producers.

In the second definition, Ford et al.[4] present a view of b2b marketing that goes beyond the more traditional marketing notions of exchange as presented above:

> Business [b2b] marketing is the task of selecting, developing and managing customer relationships for the advantage of both customer and supplier, with regard to their respective skills, resources, technologies, strategies and objectives.

In this definition the key element to emphasise is the task of managing customer relationships. This can be seen as a process that goes beyond the facilitating and expediting exchanges of goods, although it could be argued that the facilitation of exchanges could include the management of relationships. Nonetheless, Ford et al.'s emphasis upon the management of relationships forming the essence of b2b marketing could lead to the case that there are more differences than similarities between b2b marketing and consumer marketing.

Introducing the distinction between b2b and consumer marketing

There are many products and services which may be clearly identified as b2b transactions, such as electrical components used in the manufacture of earthmoving equipment. Other products and services, which at first glance may appear to be b2b transactions, may also be sold to consumer markets. For example, electrical components used in car manufacturing may be sold direct to consumers who wish to service, repair or even transform their own cars. Other more obvious examples of products and services which may be bought by both businesses and consumers include: cars, private health insurance, meals in restaurants, laptop computers and stationery equipment – the list could go on! Littler[5] contends that the key factor that distinguishes b2b and consumer transactions is *the purpose for which they are sold*. In b2b transactions, he argues that products are bought for resale or for the production of other goods, and services are bought to facilitate the resale and production of goods. In consumer transactions, products and services are generally bought for oneself, the household or as gifts. This distinction clearly does not rule out consumers reselling products, as any glance at the classified columns of newspapers for 'unwanted Christmas presents' or a search on eBay (**www.ebay.com**) would quickly reveal!

If there are different purposes for which goods and services are sold in the two sectors, the approaches to marketing them could differ quite significantly, the nature of target markets may be fundamentally different, and the marketing techniques that communicate and generate sales could differ. However, the underlying reason for such a difference may be simply that business consumers tend to be seen as rational buyers, whilst consumers tend to be seen as more intuitive and emotive. In examining the differences between business and consumer purchases, Wilson[6] argues that it is difficult to dispel the persistent images of professional committees deciding proactively on organisational purchases, and wilful or manipulated individual consumers engaging in semi-rational or impulsive buying behaviour. Such images can be defended if one is circumspect in choosing examples to illustrate the argument, from either perspective. For example, if one were to contrast the buying decision for a train manufacturer selecting the supplier of braking mechanisms compared with a consumer buying chocolates, there would very different time frames and stages to the decision-making process. If one were to compare the differences between the two sectors in the decision to buy a Christmas hamper as a gift, the time frame and stages to the decision-making process may be very similar. The purposes behind the decision to buy a Christmas hamper may also be very similar. There are also many examples of consumer purchasing that may be very 'professional' in terms of knowledge of prices, quality, source reliability, product availability and product applications, but which can make the difference between competitive survival or failure – in the sense of sustaining accustomed standards of organisational (i.e. family) performance.[7] There are clearly many grey areas between a notion of business purchasing = professional and consumer purchasing = emotive and impulsive. The task of setting out clear differences is difficult given the breadth of products and services that are purchased by businesses and consumers and the great overlap in the nature and intention of the purchase. One of the foremost industrial marketing writers, Frederick Webster,[8] recognised that many of the differences may be only by degree, but that there are substantial differences:

> If we are to understand and intelligently attack industrial marketing problems, a number of substantial differences between industrial and consumer marketing must be recognized. While it may be true that these are often differences of degree rather than kind, the degrees of difference are substantial.

In examining the similarities and differences between b2b and consumer marketing, the strength of the argument lies in the examples chosen to make the case for the difference to be 'substantial'. These differences may not be absolutes; there may always be specialised b2b and consumer markets that can be used to counter-argue a point. The emphasis may be upon the propensity or tendency for b2b and consumer marketing problems to be different. The 'tendencies' for b2b purchases to develop distinctive characteristics do have implications for the b2b marketing researcher. Before examining these implications, two factors at the heart of the defence for the distinction of b2b marketing need addressing, namely *relationships* and *networks*. These factors are founded in Ford *et al.*'s definition of business marketing and are the basis for the contention that there are fundamental differences between b2b and consumer marketing, and thus differences in the approaches and challenges faced by b2b and consumer marketing researchers.

Bases for the distinction of b2b marketing research

Relationships

Ford *et al.* use the term 'relationship' to describe 'the pattern of interactions and mutual conditioning of behaviours over time, between a company and a customer, a supplier or other organisation'.[9] The time dimension of a relationship requires decision-makers to shift their emphasis away from each single discrete transaction, towards tracking how things unfold in the relationship over time and changing them when appropriate. Relationships with business customers are likely to be complex. A business's relationships with its suppliers, development partners and financial institutions that constitute its network all depend upon its relationships with its customers and on solving their problems in those relationships. Ford *et al.* make the clear distinction between the growth of customer relationship management (CRM) systems and the stream of books and articles dealing with 'relationship marketing'. They contend that the idea that underpins most relationship marketing literature is that relationships are the creation of the marketing company. Such views do not help b2b marketers who have to cope with:

- The history of their relationship and the impact of those events upon how different individuals in separate businesses react to each other.
- Relationships that are not necessarily positive and coping with differences in aims and understanding that may result in conflict as well as cooperation.
- Both businesses interacting with each other, both attempting to manage the relationship in a way that they think appropriate.

The b2b relationship is not a relationship that is managed in a unilateral manner, i.e. a relationship that the marketer can 'drive'. CRM systems that hold the details relating to every customer, that are typically used to ensure all interactions with the customer are consistent and knowledge driven, are typically 'unilateral'. Though CRM systems may measure and model characteristics of transactions that develop over time, they are electronic observations of measurable characteristics of those transactions. CRM systems are not a means to acquire a realistic understanding of the rich and qualitative complexities of continually developing b2b relationships.

In the context of understanding networks and relationships, the prime objective of marketing researchers in business markets therefore is to establish and support an understanding of how successful relationships evolve and how networks operate. There is a need to understand how networks develop and how businesses and individuals in them relate to each other. By being able to recognise patterns of behaviour in the network, businesses should gain some guidance on how they should act and react. To develop such an understanding of patterns requires more than analysis in the traditional sense of gathering and interpreting the available data on patterns of sales and market shares. It means capitalising on the tacit knowledge inside the business and in other networked businesses. Tacit knowledge in this sense could mean, for example, understanding the psychological barriers that may exist in managers when presented to new offerings that evidently offer better monetary value than they get from their present suppliers. They may have worked with their present suppliers for many years and developed economically and socially together; what price would they pay to sever that relationship?

The network

Ford *et al.*[10] argue that the transactions between a business supplier and its customers are not isolated events that are unrelated to each other. Instead, each of the transactions takes place in a relationship and each is related to the previous experience of the companies and what they plan for the future. Business marketers have relationships with their suppliers and these relationships are vital if the marketer aims to build strong relationships with their customers. Each of their suppliers will have relationships with other suppliers and with their customers. All of these relationships are affected by the other ones and are intertwined in a network, and it is in this network that the b2b market operates. The distinctive element of seeing b2b marketing as a series of relationships in a network is that, if marketing researchers wish to understand the behaviour of an individual company, then they have to understand its relationships with other companies. Businesses are not seen as free agents, able to develop and implement their strategy in isolation; each is dependent upon the other in order to act and react to the strategies of others. In other words, the basic assumption of network thinking is that 'no business is an island'.[11] Figure 27.1 illustrates a distribution network from the perspective of a large supplying company: IBM. The figure demonstrates the different ways that computers can reach customers in Italy.

In order to understand a network, a focal relationship is usually chosen. By choosing a particular relationship the network can be examined from that perspective. As soon as the focal relationship changes, a new set of relationships emerges. By examining a network carefully, b2b marketers can achieve a realistic and balanced understanding of their own position in the minds of customers and suppliers. It is very important to evaluate the network from different focal points because drawing the network from the perspective of just one business can lead it to believe that it is more important to others than it actually is. The existence of a network should not cloud the fact that the key task of b2b marketing is to manage each single relationship. It is through its relationships that a business learns and adapts to its surrounding network; that a business exploits and develops its own abilities and gains access to others; and it is also through relationships that a business can influence different businesses elsewhere in the network.

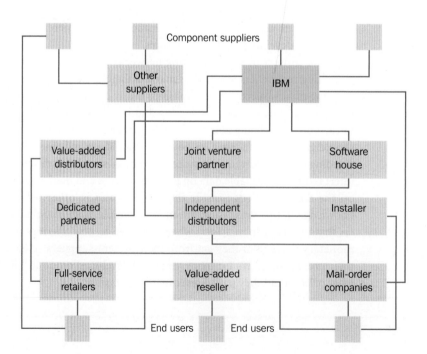

Figure 27.1
IBM's distribution network

Faced with such a challenge in understanding networks and relationships, b2b marketing researchers have all the techniques as detailed and illustrated in this text at their disposal. Having the techniques available is one thing, implementing them is another. The challenge for b2b marketing researchers is to adapt creatively and develop the techniques to overcome the obstacles in the b2b environment. In order to understand the challenge set for these researchers we now examine the implications they face from the differences between business and consumer purchases.

Implications of the differences between business and consumer purchases for marketing researchers

The differences between b2b and consumer purchases have implications for the approach, research design and individual data gathering and analysis techniques that may be employed by marketing researchers. We now examine the nature of the differences between business and consumer marketing and the challenges faced in applying marketing research techniques using the framework of arguments as presented by Ford et al.[12] As we work through the individual challenges you will also see how these challenges become interrelated. The five key differences are summarised in Figure 27.2 and then individually evaluated.

The number of people who may be involved in a b2b purchasing decision

The concept of the 'buying centre' is well established in business purchasing. Collective decisions are more typical of complex, expensive or controversial purchasing decisions in larger businesses, whereas routine decisions and/or decisions made by smaller organisations are typically made by individuals rather than by groups.[13] However, even in cases of decisions apparently made by an individual, there could still be many other roles of influence involved in the phases of the purchasing process before and after the actual decision itself.

Webster and Wind[14] famously identified five buying 'roles' within the context of 'buying centres'. We can illustrate these roles by using an example of a b2b scenario involving an FMCG business buying marketing research services!

1 *Users*. This may be a brand manager seeking marketing research support for the decisions faced in the launch of a new product.
2 *Influencers*. This may be a human resources director who has used a range of research organisations for staff surveys over the past two years.
3 *Buyers*. This may be a purchaser who is responsible for drawing up a research brief, contacting research organisations, gathering research proposals and managing the negotiation process.

Figure 27.2
Summary of differences between b2b and consumer marketing

Key differences between b2b and consumer marketing	b2b marketing tends towards	Consumer marketing tends towards
1 Number of people involved in purchasing decision	High	Low
2 Professionalism of those involved in the purchasing decision	More rational	More emotive
3 Time taken to negotiate from decision to buy to actual purchase	Lengthy	Short
4 Importance of individual consumer to supplier	High	Low
5 Relationship development	Joint negotiation	Unilateral

4 *Deciders.* This may be the marketing director if the budget for the project exceeds a set amount.

5 *Gatekeeper.* This may be another brand manager who may be supportive or downright secretive and may help or hinder in feeding information and the interpretation of that information.

Further categories have been suggested such as those of:

6 *Initiator.*[15] This may be a more senior manager to the brand manager who recognises the decision problems faced by the brand manager/user and encourages that manager to purchase marketing research support or even champions the case for marketing research support.

7 *Analyst.*[16] This may be an individual who has the technical ability to critically evaluate the offerings and associated costs as presented in the proposals from competing research agencies.

8 *Spectator.* This may be the brand manager of a competing brand who may react in the way the brand manager/user desires. A feeling of 'sheer panic' may be introduced by the thought that the competition is employing a major ethnographic study to support the development of a new integrated communications strategy.

This example shows eight people involved in the decision. In some organisations, these roles may be performed by one person, in others there may be numerous influencers and gatekeepers, sometimes working in different managerial functions, hierarchical levels and geographic locations. The people in the 'buying centre' will have different needs because of their different responsibilities, so a buyer is likely to be more interested in price and contractual details than a user is. Behind these roles there are individuals who will have their own perceptions, expectations and objectives based on their personalities and backgrounds.[17] The marketing researcher needs to help decision-makers measure and understand these individuals and their interrelationships.

Marketing research challenges. The main challenge of the number of people involved in a business purchase is one of sampling. In a team such as that illustrated above, who would be the target *element* when putting together a sampling plan? Even if there were sampling frames that listed the managerial roles of individuals in an organisation, it is highly improbable that they will be listed by their roles in a 'buying centre'. The views of the marketing researcher Ruth McNeil illustrate this point.

Example | **Open for business?**[18]

Sampling is becoming ever more demanding. Clients are requiring specialist samples, targeting particular people with particular job titles or skill sets. Such detailed specifications require the fieldwork company to know both where to find and how to access good lists. The absence of good, globally relevant sampling frames is still an issue. Given that SIC codes are rapidly becoming out of date, the increasingly specific demands for respondent type mean that a b2b researcher's skill now lies as much in finding the right respondent as in conducting and analysing a good interview.

The above example illustrates something of the 'detective' skills in tracking down the right respondent for a survey or interview. Even when we have tracked down the right individual, the challenge of getting him or her to respond in the way we would like is a great challenge. This challenge is developed in the next difference between b2b and consumer purchases discussed below.

The people involved in a b2b purchase are professional

The concept of the professional buyer is well established in business purchasing. Businesses use professional buyers to make economically sound purchases that support their strategic and operational decisions. Such professionals establish auditable systems of purchasing to cope with relatively cheap and routine goods through to expensive, complex and risky one-off products and services such as the purchase of a new accounting information system in a multinational company. Purchasing professionals in essence aim to manage b2b transactions in a rational and economic manner. The following example briefly describes the nature and mission of the professional body that represents purchasing professionals.

Example ### The professional buyer – a Chartered Purchaser

The Chartered Institute of Purchasing and Supply (CIPS) is an international education and qualification body representing purchasing and supply chain professionals. CIPS exists to promote and develop high standards of professional skill, ability and integrity among all those engaged in purchasing and supply chain management. It is the largest organisation of its kind in Europe and a central reference point worldwide on matters relating to purchasing and supply chain management. Its Professional Code of Ethics is the model for the international code and the domestic codes of many countries. CIPS acts as a centre of excellence for the whole profession of purchasing and supply chain management.

A body of professionals with rational, economic and ethical practices and who are auditable in a business should make the research challenge of measuring their practices relatively easy when compared with emotive and fickle consumers. However, even assuming that it is the professional buyers who make the purchasing decision, one has to consider why they should divulge or share their practices with marketing researchers.

Marketing research challenges. The first major challenge for marketing researchers targeting professionals is *access*. Access can be described as working at two levels:

1 *Initial contact* – getting to meet target respondents in the first instance so that they understand the nature, purpose and benefits of taking part in an interview or completing a questionnaire.
2 *True feelings* – assuming that a researcher has managed to persuade target respondents to participate, are they able to access what they really feel or think about the research subject? How guarded or sensitive may the respondents be in responding to the set questions and probes? Will they be responsive to research techniques that seek to uncover issues that are difficult to conceive and/or express?

The example on page 782 illustrated how increasingly difficult it is to gain access to chief executive officers, especially in a b2b context. It illustrates the despair faced by marketing researchers when they are briefed to interview managers who the researchers know have been targeted in many other studies, and they realise the difficulty or impossibility of gaining access to them, at both levels of access described above. The views of the marketing researcher Richard Field further illustrate this point.

Example ### Is nothing straightforward in b2b research?[19]

Organisational changes are making it increasingly difficult to complete business research. It is, for example, harder to contact business executives. Routes to them are less likely to be through a secretary or even a switchboard. Phone numbers are more likely to be direct, unlisted or routed through a central department or an automatic exchange that is immune to the persuasive interviewer. On a wider level, researchers have also had to contend with both the seemingly inexorable conglomeration of the business world and policy changes on compliance. Increasingly, corporate policy forbids interviews – even in corporations that need, and commission, research themselves. In areas where there is a restricted pool of potential respondents, one cannot afford low strike rates. It doesn't just take longer to complete the quotas; one just runs out of contacts.

The second level of access ('true feelings') also presents major challenges for the b2b marketing researcher. The issue raised by professional purchasers at this level is whether they actually behave in a rational and economic manner and whether they understand or are willing to discuss any emotive or subjective reasons for their purchasing behaviour. The following quote illustrates that, although business purchasers may be professional and strive to be rational in economic terms, the reality is somewhat different:[20]

> No organisation has the resources (in terms of time, energy, money and brain capacity) to look at all the possibly relevant information about all the competitive alternatives available.

At some point in the evaluation of potential alternatives, professional purchasers will determine that they have considered enough information to be able to make a decision. Professional purchasers may strive for and project an image of rationality. The marketing researcher Neil McPhee[21] does not see it this way:

> There is a strand of business teaching that has put forward a model that decision-making in corporates is logical and unemotional. This has never been true and is not true now. Research respondents remain human, even when they are at work, and human emotions have a habit of clouding rationalism.

The following example illustrates the techniques used by Insight Research Group to clarify the issues that may cloud rationalism in b2b purchases.

Example **A spoonful of research helps the medicine go down[22]**

The only difference between doctors and other consumers is that this is a classic b2b market, in which customers are not in themselves the end consumers. However, they still have a set of beliefs about the value of a brand for themselves and their patients. It is imperative therefore that researchers get beyond doctors' rational and logical outer shell. They need to find a robust way to underpin functional data with the kind of emotionally driven information that could be used to feed into differentiated pharmaceutical products. Having long known that doctors were adept at assuming and maintaining a professional, logical 'distance' in research, the Insight Research Group began looking at how this behaviour might affect the depth of the overall findings. The often thoughtful, cogent, technical and articulate responses from doctors were in themselves something of a barrier to getting at the more fundamental drivers and triggers for prescribing which were required to make really compelling campaigns. This led to the development of a research approach which placed a greater emphasis on non-direct questioning, increased observation and interpretation of materials, generated from purpose-designed exercises. In small workshops, doctors participated in group and individual work that helped to dismantle the 'doctor' behaviour and facilitate access to their deeper 'sensing' levels. At the analysis stage, the specific sorts of communication, imagery, language and even tone that would help the brand to trigger response at both rational and emotional levels became the focus.

It could be quite easily argued that such research approaches are commonplace in consumer marketing research; there is nothing distinctive in such an approach for b2b marketing researchers. What makes it distinctive is the juxtaposition of the access issues discussed above, i.e. getting to interview professional purchasers in the first instance and, if access is gained, getting them to cooperate – with the implementation of qualitative techniques. The following example illustrates the difficulties and expense involved in making such approaches work.

Example   Engineering the group discussion – the GlobalCash solution

Trying to bring together finance directors and cash managers from the largest companies in Europe to participate in focus groups could be viewed as an impossible task. The logistics of bringing together such senior managers, the rewards they may demand for attending such an event and the question of how much they would reveal to other managers and researchers in such a forum make the whole technique questionable. The solution demanded many months of planning, great expense to create an event that would draw managers together and the careful setting of a context that made managers relaxed enough to be open with their responses.

Part of the incentive to complete the GlobalCash questionnaire was an invitation to take part in a 'closed forum for respondents'. This meant that a date was set to present findings from the survey exclusively to respondents. The date and meeting place of The Management Centre in Brussels (a forum for 'serious' discussion of high quality) were established well in advance to allow managers the chance to put the date in their diaries. The day started with an initial session of presenting statistical findings to the whole group of managers who had responded to the questionnaire. As questions were fielded in this forum, particular topics of interest were identified and focus groups (never named as focus groups but as 'workshops') were built around these topics. By mid-morning, groups of around 10–12 managers were together tackling a theme of importance to them. With a loose set of topics to develop into questions and probes, the format for a focus group was

---

The second major challenge of the people involved in a business purchase being professional is one of *interviewer credibility*. The subject of an interview may be technical in nature given the complexity of the product or service. This was discussed in Chapter 8 in the context of qualitative depth interviewing. The interviewer with credibility in the eyes of the respondent would appreciate the significance of particular revelations, understand the language (even technical language and jargon in certain areas) and ultimately get the respondent to open up, i.e. gain a greater level of access.

The nature of networks or relationships within an industry may have a level of complexity that could prove to be difficult for an interviewer to comprehend. These complexities may not present problems when a structured interview is being conducted. However, if there are open-ended questions or areas where probing is required, as would be necessary in any qualitative interview, the 'technical competence' of the interviewer will be revealed. If the interviewer has technical knowledge, probing can be much more meaningful to the respondent, the process of building a rapport can be much stronger, and a richer and more revealing response may be obtained. In the GlobalCash study, the very precise technical nature of the subject and the seniority of the respondents meant that interviewer credibility had to be tackled when the series of in-depth interviews was planned. The supporting researchers from business schools in individual European countries helped in gaining access to key respondents, and a local professor would be at hand to help with any language and cultural issues. The nature of the questions and probes were handled by a consultant with an international reputation in the field of cash management, who the respondents respected, wanted to talk to and could relate to at their technical level. The consultant had knowledge of the banking techniques, and, just as important, the nature of networks and relationships that operated in a highly competitive industry.

A b2b purchase may take a long time from the moment when the issue is first raised until final delivery

Given the complexity of a business customer's requirements, the importance or value of its purchase, the number of individuals involved in the purchase and the level of their knowledge and the help and advice that negotiating suppliers can give, a business purchase can be a very lengthy process. The following example illustrates the time taken for what may seem to be a simple decision, i.e. to choose to work with a new bank.

Example	**Interfering parents**

Hitachi Europe operates from offices in the UK and Germany. It manages transactions with wholesalers and retailers throughout Europe involving the euro and other currencies, e.g. Swiss francs and British pounds. It manages these transactions and the relationships with the parent company in Japan through a number of domestic and international banks.

One of the key challenges that Hitachi Europe faced was trying to simplify the process of managing transactions and cutting down on the expense incurred in its thousands of transactions. The first route that it took was to purchase and implement a new accounting system, which in itself took three years from the moment of recognising the nature of the problem through to evaluating possible solutions, negotiations with alternative suppliers and on to buying and implementing the system through to changes in practices and training the staff. The second route was to concentrate the banking business by cutting down on the number of banks Hitachi Europe had accounts with and to develop a new business relationship with a bank that had the international expertise, compatible information systems and service support of the quality level it sought.

For an organisation like Hitachi, choosing a new bank and setting up a new account is not like a consumer going into a bank branch or to a website and selecting a product from a range of standard products. The main obstacle to change faced by Hitachi Europe was the parent company's insistence that the European offices worked with certain Japanese banks. It is left to your imagination to appreciate the nature and intricacy of the networks and relationships between individuals working in Hitachi headquarters, regional offices, country offices, wholesalers, retailers and the banks that support their operations. Developing a new relationship between Hitachi Europe and a new bank, which would involve the demise of many established relationships, would involve much negotiation within Hitatchi and between existing banks and the new bank. For Hitatchi Europe, the process started at the time of choosing a new accounting system. Working with the new bank took another two years to complete, five years in all.

In this example, the compounding factors of the time taken from the moment when an issue is first raised, to final delivery, emerge from the numbers of individuals who may be involved in the negotiations and the fact that they are professionals expected to present clear cost/benefit analyses. Assuming then that marketing researchers can identify who to talk to and gain access to them, what new challenges emerge given lengthy decision-making processes?

Telescoping
A psychological phenomenon that takes place when an individual telescopes or compresses time by remembering an event as occurring more recently than it actually occurred.

Marketing research challenges. The main challenge of the time taken to make a business purchase is one of *respondent error*.

In Chapter 13 we discussed the errors caused when administering questionnaires through the inability of respondents to remember events. Telescoping takes place when an individual telescopes or compresses time by remembering an event as occurring more recently than it actually occurred.[23] The ability to remember an event is influenced by (1) the event itself, (2) the time elapsed since the event, and (3) the presence or absence of things that would aid memory. We tend to remember events that are important or unusual or that occur frequently. Decision-makers that are part of a 'buying centre' are more likely to remember the negotiations, events and individuals associated with their most recent decisions. In the Hitachi example, the time taken to conduct negotiations developed over five years. During that time, negotiations may unfold in different geographic locations, involving different business functions and types of decision-maker. The personnel involved may even change as decision-makers move on to other projects or other organisations. For the marketing researcher this presents challenges in terms of accessing potential respondents who were present through the process of negotiations. If such decision-makers can be accessed, the next challenge is to get them to remember key events and individuals. Questions that do not provide the respondent with cues to the event, and that rely on unaided recall, can underestimate the actual occurrence and nature of an event.

In Chapter 3 we discussed the non-sampling errors termed 'response errors'. It was noted that a non-sampling error is likely to be more problematic than a sampling error. Its problematic nature emerges from the difficulties involved in identifying the error, measuring it and making changes in estimates. Response errors can be broken down into 'respondent inability' and 'respondent unwillingness':

- *Inability error* results from the respondent's inability to provide accurate answers. Respondents may provide inaccurate answers because language and logic used in a survey or questionnaire bear no relevance to their experiences, or the question format and content may be taking them into issues that are meaningless in their work context. Such an experience may result in respondents suffering from fatigue, boredom and a general lack of engagement with the process of questioning. For example, in the GlobalCash example, imagine a respondent being asked to respond to a series of Likert-scale items about the service quality of online technical support. Though the organisation may use such support, a professional buyer responding to the scales may see the overall issue of online technical support as being of very low priority in the context of all the issues involved in negotiating with a new bank. Could the marketing researcher trust that the respondent has thought through the measured issues carefully and is being honest?
- *Unwillingness error* arises from the respondent's unwillingness to provide accurate information. Respondents may intentionally misreport their answers because of a desire to provide socially acceptable answers, to avoid embarrassment or to please the interviewer. More especially in the b2b scenario, their answer has great commercial sensitivity and responding truthfully would reveal their commercial intellectual property. For example, to impress the interviewer respondents may intentionally say that their business works with The Cooperative Bank in order to portray themselves as having relationships with organisations that profess a socially responsible agenda. They may not have any business with this bank, but would the interviewer be able to validate this response? As another example, the interviewer may pose questions about weaknesses in the services offered by a particular bank. The respondents may consider this sensitive as the weaknesses may reveal flaws and, by implication, the individuals involved in these flaws in their own organisation. The respondents may also question what may happen to their responses. If given directly to other banks in an unaggregated form, it would present all the elements required for another bank to make a sales pitch that may upset an established relationship.

Overcoming telescoping and respondent errors raises fundamental questions about the techniques used to elicit information and the benefits and rewards given to respondents. These types of error cannot be simply managed by larger samples as we will explore in the next subsection.

In many cases each business customer is individually important to a supplier and responsible for a significant proportion of its total sales

An example to illustrate this difference between b2b and consumer marketing is the extreme situation of dependence which can occur in commercial aviation, where there are only two main suppliers of airliners and only a few dozen major customers. Of course, not all b2b marketers have so few target customers. A manufacturer selling photocopier paper could have potentially huge numbers of businesses to sell its wares to, from major multi-nationals through to home businesses. In consumer marketing, a manufacturer of bespoke tailor-made shoes, selling at €2,000 a pair, may have relatively small numbers of target consumers that are responsible for a significant proportion of its total sales.

In b2b and consumer marketing, examples can be found of businesses that have a few high-value customers and those that have huge numbers of customers with low-value transactions. In general, however, b2b marketers have a higher propensity to deal with fewer customers of high value when compared with consumer marketers. The comparison between the two is illustrated in Figure 27.3.

To illustrate further the comparison between b2b and consumer marketing, an example based upon the relationship of Renault and its banks is presented below.

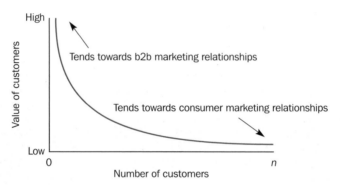

**Figure 27.3
Customer
number/value trade-off**

> ***Example***   **Size matters**
>
> One would imagine that in commercial banking the number of target businesses is huge: every business requires banking services of some sort. 'Some sort' of services covers a vast array of services that banks can deliver. When these services are individually analysed, the individual number of consumers is not so big. We will examine such an analysis in the case of cash-management banking.
>
> Imagine yourself going on holiday and wanting to exchange your local currency for Australian dollars. All banks can help you make currency exchanges. The transaction is paid for through an exchange rate that is constantly changing and a commission fee. If you were a small business conducting transactions that involved a few currency exchanges per year, then you may have to pay the 'going rates' at your local bank or shop around for the best rates. However, for a company like Renault, imagine the variation in its profits depending upon the relative value of the euro to the US dollar and how much it costs for each currency transfer. Think of the currencies that Renault may have to deal in and the number of trans-actions and flows of funds. To Renault, the fluctuations in currency values and timing of cash transfers are crucial factors that can make the difference between sound profits and a loss. Given the volume of its business and the size of its transactions, Renault would not pay the 'going rate' to a bank that yourself or a small business would. Renault would expect a cash-management banking service tailored specifically to its operations that may be radi-cally different from the operations and expectations of BMW.

> The target markets in cash-management banking sought by major banks are those companies that operate internationally or even globally, dealing in huge sums and a variety of currencies. There may be millions of individual transactions to manage, huge networks of transactions across many countries or very high values to the transactions. When examining the nature of businesses that fulfil these requirements, there are relatively few compared with the total number of businesses, which is why the GlobalCash study, conducted on behalf of 15 of the largest pan-European banks, targeted just the largest 5,000 companies in Europe, a very small fraction of the total number of European businesses.

This example illustrates how the essence of relatively few consumers may be of high value – through careful target marketing. Some businesses may have a mass marketing strategy that aims to target a great breadth of business types; others may have to tailor their offerings specifically to suit the specific needs of quite distinctive businesses. From the following example you are encouraged to track down the Kelly's directory (see the web link references below) for a British and global illustration of how businesses may be classified and the extent to which b2b marketers may finely tune the nature of their offerings to generate business with a few high-value businesses.

Example Kelly's – a 205-year-old success story[24]

Kelly's, a subsidiary of the publishers Reed Elselvier, is the UK's premier brand for industrial purchasing and supplies. Its print directory, popularly known as 'the Big Red Book' for industrial product and part manufacturers, comes out yearly, and has done since 1799. Its current directory aggregates more than 150,000 companies in 110,000 categories. Kelly's added a CD-ROM version of the directory in 1989 so that users could more easily search the listings. In 2001 a dynamic search-based site was established enabling customers to look for anything from abrasives to water pumps. Since then, the number of searches on **www.kellysearch.com** has risen from 10,000 to 12.5 million a month. The number of companies it represents has also ballooned from 150,000 to 1.3 million and each business receives quarterly figures tracking the responses the site has generated.

Marketing research challenges. The main challenge of each business customer being individually important to a supplier and responsible for a significant proportion of its total sales, is one of coping with relatively few target consumers. As most quantitative marketing research techniques tend to assume large numbers of potential target consumers and survey respondents, the challenge faced by b2b marketing researchers is one of *sampling methods* and the subsequent *analyses that may be performed given sample selection*.

We have already presented the challenges of 'element' definition in a sampling plan, gaining access to respondents (and the effect upon response rates) and response error. If we add on the challenge of conducting surveys when there are relatively few target respondents, it is clear to see that the whole sampling process becomes very challenging.

In choosing a sampling method for a small target population, probability methods such as random and systematic sampling can be utilised. With simple random sampling it is often difficult to construct a sampling frame that will permit a simple random sample to be drawn. Simple random sampling may or may not result in a representative sample; this is the paradox faced when drawing a random sample – one does not know if it will be representative of a target population, only the probability that it will be, within margins of error. Although samples drawn will represent the population well on average, a given simple random sample may grossly misrepresent the target population. This is more likely if the size of the sample is small, as faced in many b2b surveys.

With systematic sampling, when the ordering of the sample elements is related to the characteristic of interest the technique increases the representativeness of the sample. If businesses within an industry are arranged in increasing order of annual sales, a systematic sample will include some small and some large firms. A simple random sample may be unrepresentative because it may contain, for example, only small firms or a disproportionate number of small firms. Choosing the right characteristics by which to order sample elements is crucial. With the wrong criteria, systematic sampling may decrease the representativeness of the sample. Thus, the power of systematic sampling lies in the accuracy of the sampling frame and the criteria used to order or arrange the sample elements.

With the time and cost factors of sourcing and building up-to-date and accurate sampling frames, with details of sample elements, many b2b marketing researchers will favour administrative, i.e. timing and cost, criteria in preference to statistical criteria, and ultimately be forced to use non-probability sampling techniques. **Non-probability sampling** relies on the personal judgement of the researcher rather than on chance to select sample elements. The b2b marketing researcher would aim to build the elements to include in a sample, rather than starting from a point of having an up-to-date and accurate sampling frame that resembles the target population. Building up the sample in this manner leads the b2b researcher commonly to use judgemental sampling and snowball sampling techniques (as discussed in Chapter 14). Samples created using these techniques may yield good estimates of the population characteristics, but they do not allow for objective evaluation of the precision of the sample results. Because there is no way of determining the probability of selecting any particular element for inclusion in the sample, the estimates obtained are not statistically projectable to the population.

The following example illustrates the challenges faced in the IT industry in sourcing accurate sampling frames and how researchers spend time building their own.

Non-probability sampling
Sampling techniques that do not use chance selection procedures but rather rely on the personal judgement of the researcher.

Example **Traditional market-share research is dead in the water**[25]

Data concerning IT market share have been one of the most visible aspects of b2b research, with IT trade magazines headlining leading IT companies' latest research findings. Traditionally, these data have been collected from large panels of retailers and resellers and often audited against shipment data provided by many of the manufacturers. Major changes in the IT market now mean that such panels provide only a partial view. Many key IT vendors are working to reposition themselves with their customers, targeting after-sales revenue which may spread over many years. For example, IBM is evolving from a manufacturer of hardware and associated software to a provider of IT services. As a result, for many key IT products, market size bears only an indirect relationship to the most recent purchase data. Measuring the data therefore requires complex calculations based on combining the installed base of the product with the after-sales revenue flow it generates. In most cases, the raw data can only be collected by researching customers directly.

Contacting customers directly means that researchers have to collect data about a product which could be purchased by multiple decision-makers at dozens of different locations – and at site, department, or an individual level. These factors present quite formidable sampling challenges. Incompatibility between business sampling frames and official statistics regarding the number of businesses, where the latter exist at all, is common. Many research agencies are forced to build their own sampling frames, often from telephone directories. The result can be sampling frames that miss whole sections of the business population, such as sub-branches or government offices and perhaps the most 'invisible' group, the home-office sector.

Summary of sampling challenges. Whilst the theory of sampling is the same for all types of markets whatever their nature, there are key differences between sampling in b2b and consumer markets. These may be summarised as:[26]

1 *Unit definition.* Is it the site (establishment), organisation, legal entity or some other business unit? Each definition offers different benefits and drawbacks, depending upon the research objectives. In consumer research only the individual or household has to be considered.

2 *Element definition.* In b2b research, an individual is interviewed as a representative of the business. We have to be sure to interview the right individual in each business, and be consistent across businesses. This can be complex as business titles and responsibilities vary widely across businesses of different sizes and sectors.

3 *Heterogeneity.* There is a lack of homogeneity in the business universe. There is much more variance between a small business and a large organisation than between any two consumers. There is also great variation between different types of small business.

4 *Sampling frames.* The available sampling frames of businesses and the nature of their detail that could allow stratification vary considerably in accuracy and coverage.

5 *Public sector.* The public sector generally counts as business, though the usage and buying patterns are frequently very different from the private sector.

A b2b purchase or sale is not an isolated event

Salespeople, purchasing professionals and indeed anyone making decisions in a 'buying centre' do not just meet, negotiate a deal and move on to other things. Imagine a cement manufacturer wishing to buy a furnace that is expected to be part of its cement production process for over 20 years. There would be many meetings with staff from the cement company, the various competing furnace manufacturers and many potential suppliers of key components for the furnace. Even when the decision to buy from one particular supplier has been made, the interactions between technical, financial, production and legal staff could take place over many months or even years. The purchase could be the forerunner to servicing and repair contracts and the installation of similar equipment in other cement-making plants.

In the above example of buying a new furnace, there could be a time when modifications need to be made. There are locations where local authorities allow cement manufacturers to burn old car tyres in their furnaces. Adding old tyres to a gas-fired furnace may require modifications to allow the tyres to be fed in, changes to the chimneys to get rid of different fumes and the lining of the furnace. All of these developments may again unfold over time, involving purchasing, technical, production, logistics, marketing and legal personnel. There may be components that need to be replaced frequently given the immense temperatures in the furnace. The delivery of these components may involve a repeat order which may need a simple telephone call or even be generated by computer.

In all of these cases, the customer and supplier interact on the basis of their experiences of previous purchases between them, and given the nature of their expectations for future purchases. The interaction between a customer and supplier is a single episode in the relationship between them. Each episode is affected by the relationship of which it forms part and each interaction in turn affects the relationship itself.[27] Each interaction and each purchase or sale can only be understood in the context of that relationship, and ultimately within the network or businesses that enable the relationships to work.

Cross-sectional design
A type of research design involving the collection of information from any given sample of population elements only once.

Marketing research challenges. The main challenge of a b2b purchase or sale not being an isolated event is finding a research design that is appropriate to understanding complex networks and relationships. The cross-sectional study is the most frequently used descriptive design in marketing research. **Cross-sectional designs** involve the collection of

Single cross-sectional design
A cross-sectional design in which one sample of respondents is drawn from the target population and information is obtained from this sample once.

Multiple cross-sectional design
A cross-sectional design in which there are two or more samples of respondents, and information from each sample is obtained only once.

Longitudinal design
A type of research design involving a fixed sample of population elements measured repeatedly. The sample remains the same over time, thus providing a series of pictures that, when viewed together, vividly illustrate the situation and the changes that are taking place.

information from any given sample of population elements only once. They may be either single cross-sectional or multiple cross-sectional designs. In **single cross-sectional designs**, only one sample of respondents is drawn from the target population, and information is obtained from this sample only once. These designs are also called sample survey research designs. In **multiple cross-sectional designs**, there are two or more samples of respondents, and information from each sample is obtained only once. In either variation of the design, much of the richness of the context of individual relationships and the network of relationships is lost. A more appropriate though more expensive and resource-intensive design is the longitudinal design. In **longitudinal designs**, a fixed sample (or samples) of population elements is measured repeatedly. A longitudinal design differs from a cross-sectional design in that the sample or samples remain the same over time. In other words, the same people are studied over time. In contrast to the typical cross-sectional design, which gives a snapshot of the variables of interest at a single point in time, a longitudinal study provides a series of 'pictures'. These 'pictures' give an in-depth view of the situation and the changes that take place over time.

A key feature of creating such 'pictures' of relationships and networks is the building of contextual material from sources such as sales data, customer data, secondary data statistics, intelligence through press and trade commentary that focuses upon particular markets or industries, and a vast resource of intelligence held within the employees of a business that may be seeking research support.[28] In the following example, the SevenHR company was built around secondary data and intelligence sources, plus in-depth interviews within SevenHR.

Example   **A new approach to FMCG and retail recruitment – SevenHR[29]**

Frustrated by current practices in the recruitment industry, a group of FMCG and retail professionals decided to form a new recruitment consultancy. SevenHR considered that a researched understanding of its markets and target customers should be at the core of its business. It commissioned the research agency Propaganda to develop a launch strategy. Propaganda was briefed to evaluate the perceptions of key industry decision-makers and to explore the opportunities of developing a differentiated recruitment brand. Propaganda used a two-stage strategy. First it conducted desk research using secondary data and intelligence to audit the competitors of SevenHR, with focus on how they portrayed themselves and what reputations they had earned among industry influencers. Second, internal research was conducted which included in-depth interviews with each of the founding members of the company. The findings of the research project enabled Propaganda to establish a cultural mission statement for SevenHR, and formed the basis of its communications tactics. Having launched in October 2002, within six months the business was already 75% ahead of forecast. Significantly, almost every client had placed repeat business, some returning up to five times.

There may be a lack of resources devoted to allowing b2b marketing researchers to use longitudinal studies and uncover the wider contextual issues that would allow detailed knowledge of relationships and networks. There could be a limitation on the way that b2b researchers view the value of contextual material. It has been argued that many b2b marketing researchers demonstrate a 'tunnel vision', which fails to recognise the wider business context of business findings.[30] Many researchers work comfortably within the standard research process of: a brief, proposal, research setup, fieldwork, presentation and report. They continue to argue that 'desk research is a dying art and that the multitude of excellent Internet resources are sadly neglected'; many b2b researchers are consistently failing to put their research into a wider market or business context. Such a failing can affect the briefing/proposal stage as well as the analysis/reporting stage. This means that research findings are often set in a 'vacuum' without reference to the challenges faced by b2b marketers. The danger of this is that b2b marketing research is seen by decision-makers as a 'nice-to-know' or luxury item rather than a key part of the planning and decision-making process. Adding value by drawing on the various sources of market intelligence available reduces the risk of marketing research appearing irrelevant to decision-makers. It can also improve the research process so that decision-makers value the information provided.

The weaknesses of cross-sectional research designs, the resources required to perform longitudinal designs and the limitations of some b2b researchers to appreciate the wider context of their investigations may result in b2b decision-makers looking to other sources for decision support. Over recent years there has been a growth in the use and practice of competitor intelligence. Many organisations have developed competitor intelligence systems that allow them to have a relatively low-cost 'picture' of their environment, competitors and sometimes even their customers. Competitive intelligence uses many marketing research techniques and by using multiple sources aims to set a broad context to allow the b2b decision-makers to understand the networks in which they operate. The next section briefly explores the nature of competitor intelligence and its 'threat' to the nature and standards of conventional marketing research.

The growth of competitive intelligence

The research designs and techniques employed in competitive intelligence may in some respects differ from the structured methods of marketing research; in other respects there are many similarities. Over the past 15 years or so, those who professionally gather competitive intelligence have continued to refine research techniques and to distinguish their approach from industrial espionage. In general, the research design employed for competitive intelligence is exploratory, using primarily secondary data, intelligence sources and qualitative primary data.[31] Competitive intelligence has been defined as a systematic process by which a firm gathers, analyses and disseminates information about its rivals[32] or as a process of researching a competitor's organisation, products, prices, financial performance, technology and strategy.[33]

From these definitions we can see in 'systematic' and 'process' the continuous development of an understanding or knowledge of competitors. In the first definition we see the

elements of managing data that replicate the marketing research process in terms of gathering, analysing and disseminating data. In the second definition we see the focus of data gathering in terms of products, prices, financial performance, technology and strategy. These are areas of measurement and understanding that go beyond the remit of conventional marketing researchers.

While the nature of competitive intelligence has evolved there has been much confusion over what competitive intelligence is and what it is not. Competitive intelligence is not corporate espionage, stealing competitive documents or accessing competitors' computer files.

Source: © Laureen March/CORBIS

Rather, the discipline is a structured approach to a different type of research which has evolved as an outgrowth of strategic planning and market research. The Society of Competitive Professionals (SCIP) was formed in 1986 to develop behavioural standards and a code of ethics.[34]

The most commonly used techniques in competitive intelligence are:

1 *Review of public records* – monitoring secondary sources of information such as government records, commercial databases, media reports and news clippings, and company-produced literature, for potential threats and opportunities.

2 *Observational techniques* – directly observing competitors' activities or facilities through overt surveillance as another way to acquire competitive data, though such practices may be viewed with suspicion. Likewise, learning about a competitor's capabilities, strengths and weaknesses through physical inspection of its products or actual use of its services is seen to be within the bounds of acceptable practice. Observers contribute to the gathering of 'informal' information concerning the market and business at different levels. Observers are not formal researchers but members of business departments, marketing specialists, technicians in engineering departments or plant-building departments. Employees in every department, including sales, purchasing and research and development, hear industry news well before it appears in a trade journal or in databases.[35] These observers and their contacts form key components of b2b relationships set in the context of networks.

3 *Personal interviews* – conversing with informed sources is beneficial when hard-to-find information about a competitor's strategies and intentions is used to fill critical gaps in secondary data and provide a more complete understanding of the competition.[36]

In the gathering and interpretation of 'public records', conducting personal interviews and overt observations, competitive intelligence targets individuals from the following types of organisation:[37]

- Competitor companies
- Customers
- Suppliers
- Distributors
- Government organisations
- Trade associations
- Financial institutions.

Given the array of data sources, data gathering techniques, institutions and individuals that may be targeted (including consumers in some instances), and the array of employees that may be used to 'observe', competitor intelligence is clearly a 'broad-brush' approach. Competitor intelligence can offer the broad context and in many instances detail specific areas to b2b decision-makers that may be missing in conventional marketing research. Marketing research techniques may be more error free, less subjective and carried out with much stronger and more well-established codes of conduct when compared with competitor intelligence. However, for the b2b decision-makers needing to understand the long-term development of relationships and the dynamics of the network in which those relationships work, conventional views of marketing research may not offer the support they seek. They may forego an amount of error, interpret subjective and biased views and even push the boundaries of ethical practice to gain support that is more attuned to the decisions they face. In the following example we see how Texas Instruments, as long ago as 1995, moved this way by utilising its marketing research practices and findings as a foundation for its competitor intelligence system.

Example

The evolution of marketing research archives to a comprehensive competitive intelligence system[38]

When Alicia Helton was Director of Corporate Market Research at Texas Instruments, she championed the placing of semiconductor marketing research archives on the corporate intranet. The market research team began with current research reports and gradually added two years of earlier reports. At the time the team used Microsoft PowerPoint for all research presentations, so it was easy to convert to HTML. The team required all research suppliers to follow the same standards with a policy that the entire research presentation was available on the intranet within one week of the original presentation. The whole site used a portion of the semiconductor marketing site and, as this was already established, it proved to be the ideal foundation for the company's competitive intelligence system. From this point, Texas Instruments began to improve its acquisition, analysis and dissemination of competitive intelligence. The strategic leadership team worked with consultants The Futures Group to integrate fully competitive intelligence into strategic decision making. Marketing research was seen as but one component of competitive intelligence. However, because the competitor intelligence system was built around marketing research archives, the company found that the use and influence of marketing research grew.

This example illustrates that competitor intelligence need not replace marketing research. In this case, the well-thought-out use of competitor intelligence increased the use and influence of marketing research. This relationship happened because competitor intelligence helped to provide the broader context needed to get the most out of interpreting marketing research findings. There still remain ethical issues to consider with competitor intelligence, which will be tackled later in the chapter.

International marketing research

It is clear from many examples throughout the book that b2b marketing research is practised in international settings. The challenges involved in conducting international research detailed in Chapter 26, i.e. adapting research techniques based upon different cultures and languages, simply add to the challenges of b2b marketing research detailed in this chapter. The following example illustrates a few of the challenges faced by international b2b marketing researchers with possible solutions where budgets may be limited.

Example

Balancing act[39]

In an increasingly global market, and with research budgets having to cover more and more countries, it can be difficult to find cost-effective solutions to researching niche b2b markets across multiple borders. Suppose a marketing manager wished to understand the niche market of large format printers. From a 'purist' perspective, the approach would be to measure the markets with large samples producing statistically significant findings. However, this is often not practical, and even if it were, it can be prohibitively expensive. Therefore 'traditional' marketing research techniques and standards have to be adapted for these 'difficult' markets to produce usable and actionable insights at an affordable price. For example, by speaking to industry experts, be they journalists, analysts or industry bodies, one can gain different estimates of market sizes and, as more conversations take place, these estimates become more and more refined. The skill is in knowing who to talk to and being able to gauge good information from bad. In addition, secondary data collection and analysis can be used to identify key competitors. This may be very easy in the case of major software suppliers across the globe, but can be much more difficult for something such as compatible inkjet and toner cartridges in South America. Indeed, in Asia–Pacific countries, South America and Africa, it can require extensive research just to find out who the competitors are. Assuming one can establish who the competitors are, the challenge is to conduct interviews in multiple countries with multiple offices without breaking the budget.

However, the b2b marketing researcher Stephen Connell of the Research Agency MOR-PACE International argues that in his experience international b2b research is getting easier for a number of reasons.[40] He contends that globalisation in b2b as well as consumer industries is making marketing research interviews more familiar and acceptable. The Web allows survey and focus group respondents to be accessed in almost any country of the world. Technology allows for more centralisation of data collection and field operations alongside the more traditional options of using local subcontractors or partners.

The following two examples summarise recent projects completed by Connell.[41] In both examples he highlights how small the potential sample may be and how that can help in managing the project from a central location.

Example — Customer satisfaction survey in global telecoms

A survey was undertaken of 95 telephone companies from around the world, from Argentina to Inner Mongolia, in which up to six face-to-face interviews were carried out per company. The interviews, a total of 420 individuals in 200 organisations, combined scoring and rating questions with a considerable amount of open-ended discussion of business and technical issues. Appointments were set up by telephone and email, and interviewers travelled from the UK or, in one or two cases, from the USA. A total of nine languages, including Mandarin, Russian and Polish, were used to make appointments and to conduct the interviews.

The process worked well with response rates of over 85%; the no-show rate when the interviewer arrived was below 5%. The small team of interviewers achieved a very high standard of probing and issues analysis. The travel budget was only 15% of the total cost.

Example — Revenue loss in telecoms

A survey was carried out of how telecom operators saw the problem of 'revenue loss' caused by billing problems, resulting in a failure to charge for calls, or by deliberate fraud. This was of major concern in the industry and the survey was designed to assess: the extent to which the problem was recognised; quality perceptions of the amount of revenue lost in this way; and approaches to detecting and minimising loss. A total of 50 telephone in-depth interviews were carried out, in more than 30 countries, using a list of fixed and mobile operators assembled by a leading consultancy.

In this last example, note that a specialist consultancy was used to develop a sampling frame. A further difficulty faced even when the name and telephone number were listed in the sampling frame was identifying the sample elements. Identifying the relevant decision-maker in each business was difficult as the persons responsible for limiting revenue loss had a wide variety of titles, e.g. Manager Network Operation, Vice President – Finance, Controller, Risk Management Manager, etc. Once these were tracked down, the next challenge was persuading them that the survey was bona fide and worth responding to. In the end the survey was a success given that a wide range of companies participated despite the clearly sensitive nature of the subject matter.

Connell also presents some generalised observations of cultural differences in applying b2b marketing research which are worth debating:

- Telephone and web interviews with b2b respondents can be very difficult to achieve in China. Managers are often unwilling to discuss important issues without the reassurance of face-to-face contact. On the other hand, personal interviews, once started, can yield as much information and ideas as anywhere in the world, though it can be difficult to tie down respondents to precise appointments in advance.
- b2b respondents in other countries, including some Southern European countries where marketing research is less familiar, require more reassurance about confidentiality and security. Faxes explaining the research agency, the sponsoring client and the project credentials are more likely to be required after initial contact by telephone (for a telephone or face-to-face survey). Once the interview is granted, excellent information can be provided.
- Telephone and self-completion questionnaires sometimes elicit less detailed and informative responses from Nordic (Denmark, Finland, Iceland, Norway, Sweden) respondents than elsewhere. In this region b2b respondents were more cautious, using formal ways to respond to unstructured questions, although this behaviour can be modified in the context of a face-to-face interview.

This last observation was certainly the same experience as in the GlobalCash studies. the Nordic/Scandinavian respondents were most cautious in responding to the more sensitive questions, with the Danes having the highest non-response levels to questions that referred to their experiences of specific banks.

With the spread of globalisation and increase of international trade, international marketing research has similarly grown. The marketing research industry has had to respond to the challenges set, with major agencies developing account or relationship teams that serve the worldwide operations of their customers.

Ethics in marketing research

In Chapter 1, we highlighted how ESOMAR distinguishes marketing research from other competitive forms of data gathering, primarily through the issue of the anonymity of respondents. It stresses that in marketing research the identity of the provider of information is not disclosed. In b2b marketing research, the nature of the relationship between clients, researchers and respondents has been undergoing a transformation in recent years. The change has been most evident in customer satisfaction research, where the research interview is tending now to be treated as an active component of customer relationship management. Rather than using aggregated research findings to guide process changes in customer-facing operations, clients are seeking to use the survey process as a tool for maintaining dialogue with individual customers. In response to this, customers are increasingly keen to lose their anonymity and have their responses passed on in an attributable form to appropriate people such as account management teams. Their motivation is that their responses will be used in a way that will improve the service or product they receive. Survey anonymity has to remain a fundamental right of any respondent for both ethical and data validity reasons. However, the trend in b2b customer research is clearly towards respondents choosing to forego this.[42]

Another major ethical challenge facing b2b marketing researchers lies in the growth of competitive intelligence. One of the major differences in competitive intelligence and traditional market research is the knowledge of the purpose of the study. Ethical marketing research should reveal the purpose of the study to the respondent, and, sometimes, how the information will be used, especially when explaining why particularly sensitive questions are being asked. Competitive intelligence studies in contrast generally do not reveal the purpose of the study and how the information will be used. Essentially, the competitive intelligence interviewers must develop a 'story' as to why they are calling the respondents, e.g. they are interested in their products, they are conducting a general industry study, they are conducting a study as part of their degree or they are looking at specific issues within the industry (e.g. legislation or product safety). This may generate a response and some respondents may be happy to cooperate. However, this would clearly be considered as unethical by traditional marketing research organisations.[43] Being duplicitous in gaining access to respondents could potentially damage the reputation of legitimate marketing researchers and ultimately damage response rates, making access continually more difficult.

For bona fide b2b marketing researchers, it is usual to disclose the identity of their clients, i.e. who commissioned the research, either up-front or in the course of an interview. This means that marketing research has to play an ambassadorial role. Marketing researchers are not speaking for their clients, but are representing them in asking respondents for their views. As a result the behaviour of researchers must be highly professional and care must be taken of client and respondent reputation. The size of respondent populations is often so small that treating respondents with care is becoming evermore important and sometimes b2b marketing researchers need to dissuade their clients from trying to cram more into ever longer interviews. Although it is tempting to ask as much as possible in the one 'hit', this rebounds on researchers and their clients in the long run.[44] Look back to Chapter 15, where non-response issues were discussed, and re-examine the proposed means to improve response rates. Now consider how feasible it is to increase response rates with a small pool of respondents who may be very irritated by the number of requests for interviews and the length of those interviews.

Internet and computer applications

For business respondents, the Web is a useful additional access and information exchange tool beyond the more traditional methods of gathering data. As a means to gain access to b2b respondents, it does not always offer the potential that many commentators believed it would: b2b respondents are busy and, although they may be delighted to talk if asked questions, they often do not have the time to complete Web-based questionnaires, however good their intentions. In the GlobalCash surveys, the Web-based survey, whilst much shorter than the postal survey, did not achieve anything like the same success in terms of response rate. This is only one example and does not dismiss the hugely important role of the Web in b2b interviewing. It can be used to send respondents stimulus or advertising material to look at, to confirm appointments, thank the respondents, and deliver incentives or summary reports; and to publish research results so that respondents, equipped with access passwords can look at such data and even manipulate data relevant to them. A whole spectrum of management-tiered tailored results and interactivity has opened up through the Web.

The Web can also be used for interviewer briefing. One chemical company for instance commonly used to bring sheets of polythene and other materials used for insulation to interviewer briefing sessions. Now, however, it can point the interviewers to the websites, which is a great advantage to all those managing the field force and the interviewers working in the field. Interviewers can develop a clear understanding of esoteric topics such as insulation, aviation fuel, cabling or the solvents industry. The Web, together with the collection of accurate email addresses, is becoming increasingly important, but in limited, facilitating areas rather than as the overall vehicle for data collection.[45]

Summary

This chapter was founded upon the key question of whether there are substantial differences between b2b and consumer marketing and thus differences in the approaches and challenges faced by b2b and consumer marketing researchers. The two main bases of b2b marketing are the concepts of relationships and networks. In the context of understanding relationships and networks, the prime objective of marketing researchers in business markets therefore is to support an understanding of how successful relationships evolve and how the network operates. The nature of relationships and networks underpins five key differences between b2b marketing and consumer marketing. These can be summarised as differences in the: number of people who may be involved in a b2b purchasing decision; people involved in a b2b purchase being professionals; nature of b2b purchases taking a long time from the moment when an issue is first raised until final delivery; many cases where each business customer is individually important to a supplier and responsible for a significant proportion of its total sales; b2b purchases or sales not being isolated events. These differences are the reason that there are distinctive differences in the approaches adopted and challenges faced by b2b and consumer marketing researchers. The key challenges they face are in:

- Administering effective sampling plans with the associated problems of finding appropriate sampling techniques and the limitations of inference from the statistics that they may generate.
- Gaining access to key respondents, in terms of getting to interview respondents in the first instance and getting them to be open and honest. A key element of this access lies in how credible interviewers are perceived by business respondents.
- Business respondents actually remembering what has happened and why they or their organisation behaved as they did. The events may have taken a long time to unfold, involved numerous individuals and taken a great deal of time.
- Creating research designs that can measure or help to create an understanding of the dynamics of relationships and networks.

The b2b marketing researchers face further challenges from practitioners in competitor intelligence who have to work with decision-makers who may forgo an amount of error, interpret subjective and biased views and even push the boundaries of ethical practice to gain support that is more attuned to the decisions they face. Competitor intelligence need not be a direct replacement for conventional marketing research; it can be a strong supplement that allows research findings to be understood in a more dynamic and broader context. Even though many of the techniques adopted in competitor research match those in marketing research and may be quite removed from notions of industrial espionage, there still remain clear ethical issues about such approaches.

b2b marketing researchers tackle the challenges summarised above mostly in very creative ways, as illustrated in the examples throughout this chapter and indeed throughout the text – so well in fact that b2b researchers sometimes see themselves as superior to consumer researchers![46] With the spread of globalisation and increase of international trade, international b2b marketing research has similarly grown. The marketing research industry has had to respond to the challenges set, with major agencies developing account or relationship teams that serve the worldwide operations of their customers. The use of the Web has enabled the management and control of international b2b marketing research to become far more cost effective. The Web has also enabled the briefing and training of field interviewers to become much more effective in terms of enabling them to understand the technical issues of the questions they are posing. This in turn can increase their credibility with business respondents and improve the quality of their responses.

Questions

1 Why is it important to ask the question 'Is b2b marketing research significantly different from consumer marketing research?'

2 What characteristics distinguish b2b marketing from consumer marketing?

3 From what focal point should a business network be analysed?

4 What challenges do b2b marketers face in managing relationships?

5 How do the concepts of business networks and relationships relate to each other?

6 What are the five major differences between b2b and consumer marketing?

7 Describe the sampling challenges that the b2b marketing researcher faces.

8 What does 'access' mean in the context of b2b marketing research?

9 Evaluate the reasons why gaining access to key respondents may be so difficult. Why may gaining access grow more difficult over time?

10 What is meant by 'interviewer credibility'? What may interviewers do to be seen as more credible in the eyes of target respondents?

11 Describe the potential respondent errors that may occur in b2b marketing research. What may be done to reduce these potential errors?

12 What is competitor intelligence? How does this definition differ from notions of 'conventional marketing research'?

13 What sampling frame challenges exist in international b2b marketing research?

14 To what extent do you think that competitor analysts have benefits to offer to potential respondents in any interviews they conduct?

15 Describe the means by which the Web may improve the process of conducting b2b marketing research.

Exercises

1 Visit the website of Business Intelligence Group (BIG) (www.b2bresearch.org). Evaluate why it came into existence and present a case for why b2b marketing researchers need a distinctive professional body to represent their interests.

2 You are the marketing research manager of a bank. Management have asked you to assess the demand potential for 'high-growth start-up businesses'. What sources of secondary data and intelligence would you consult? What kinds of information would you expect to obtain from each source? Ask a group of fellow students to play the role of management and explain to them the role of secondary data in this project.

3 You are a marketing manager for a company that manufactures adhesives for the construction industry. You wish to invest in an Internet focus group study of construction engineers and architects. Explain how you would identify and recruit such respondents from across the globe. What incentive(s) would you offer potential participants?

4 A manufacturer would like to survey users to determine the demand potential for a new power press. The new press has a capacity of 500 tonnes and costs €400,000. It is used for forming products from lightweight and heavyweight steel and can be used by automobile, construction equipment and household appliance manufacturers.

a Identify the population and sampling frame that could be used for this study.

b Describe how simple random sampling could be used with your identified sampling frame.

c Could a stratified sample be used? If so, how?

d Could a cluster sample be used? If so, how?

e Which sampling technique (it need not be random, stratified or cluster) would you recommend? Why?

5 In a small group discuss the following issues: 'What is the ideal educational background for someone seeking a career in competitive intelligence?' and 'There can never be any convergence in values between the professional bodies representing marketing research and competitive intelligence.'

Video Case Exercise: Eaton

video case

download from www.pearsoned.co.uk/malhotra_euro

1 What 'relationship' challenges does Eaton have to manage? How can marketing research help them to understand the nature and dynamics of relationships?

2 What 'network' challenges does Eaton have to manage? How can marketing research help them to understand the nature and dynamics of networks.

3 What would you see as being the main challenges faced by marketing researchers working for Eaton?

Notes

1 Chilvers, V., 'Fair's fair at trade shows', *Research* (November 2003), 63.

2 GlobalCash was a study conducted between 1996 and 2002 on behalf of 15 leading pan-European banks. It was conducted across 20 European countries using different survey methods and qualitative techniques.

3 Dibb, S., Simkin, L., Pride, W.M. and Ferrell, O.C., *Marketing: Concepts and Strategies*, 4th edn (Boston: Houghton-Mifflin, 2000), 158.

4 David Ford conducts his work with a team of researchers in the IMP (International Marketing and Purchasing) Group. This group was founded in 1976 by researchers from five European countries. The group's 'interaction approach' is based on the importance for both researchers and managers of understanding the *interaction* between *active* buyers and sellers in continuing business *relationships*. Ford, D., *The Business Marketing Course: Managing in Complex Networks* (Chichester: Wiley, 2002), 6. See www.impgroup.org.

5 Littler, D., 'Organizational marketing', in Baker, M.J. (ed.), *The Marketing Book*, 3rd edn (Oxford: Butterworth–Heinneman, 1994), 610.

6 Wilson, D.F., 'Why divide consumer and organizational buyer behaviour?', *European Journal of Marketing* 34 (7) (2000), 780–796.

7 Ibid., p. 789.

8 Webster, F.E. Jr, 'Management science in industrial marketing', *Journal of Marketing* 42 (January 1978), 22.

9 Ford, D., Gadde, L.E., Hakansson, H. and Snehota, I., *Managing Business Relationships*, 2nd edn (Chichester: Wiley, 2003), 38.

10 Ford, D., *The Business Marketing Course: Managing in Complex Networks* (Chichester: Wiley, 2002), 29.

11 Hakansson, H. and Snehota, I., 'No business is an island: the network concept of business strategy', *Scandinavian Journal of Management* 14 (3) (1990), 177–200.

12 Ford, D., *The Business Marketing Course: Managing in Complex Networks* (Chichester: Wiley, 2002), 3–6.

13 Spekman, R.E. and Stern, L.W., 'Environmental uncertainty and buying group structure: an empirical investigation', *Journal of Marketing* 43 (1979), 54–64.

14 Webster, F.E. Jr and Wind, Y., 'A general model of organizational buying behaviour', *Journal of Marketing* 36 (2) (1972), 12–19.

15 Bonoma, T.V., 'Major sales: who really does the buying?', *Harvard Business Review* 60 (3) (1982), 111–119.

16 Wilson, D.F., *Organizational Marketing* (London: Routledge, 1998).

17 Ford, D., *The Business Marketing Course: Managing in Complex Networks* (Chichester: Wiley, 2002), 79.

18 McNeil, R., 'Open for business', *Research* (May 2003), 3.

19 Field, R., 'Open for business', *Research* (May 2003), 6.

20 Minett, S., *B2B Marketing* (Harlow: Financial Times Prentice Hall, 2002), 63.

21 McPhee, N., 'Gaining insight on business and organisational behaviour: the Qualitative Dimension', *International Journal of Marketing Research*, 44 (1) (January 2002).

22 Hamilton-Stent, S., 'A spoonful of research helps the medicine go down', *Research* (November 2003), 63.

23 Menon, G., Raghubir, P and Schwarz, N., 'Behavioural frequency judgments: an accessibility–diagnosticity framework', *Journal of Consumer Research*, 22 (2) (September 1995), 212–228; Cook, W.A., 'Telescoping and memory's other tricks', *Journal of Advertising Research* (February–March 1987), 5–8; Sudman, S., Finn, A. and Lannom, L., 'The use of bounded recall procedures in single interviews', *Public Opinion Quarterly* (Summer 1984), 520–524.

24 Hemsley, S., 'Book, online and tinker', *Marketing Week* (17 June), 39–41.

25 Stubington, P., 'Traditional market share research is dead in the water', *Research* (November 2004), 63.

26 Macfarlane, P., 'Structuring and measuring the size of business markets', *International Journal of Market Research* 44 (1) (2002).

27 Ford, D., Gadde, L.E., Hakansson, H. and Snehota, I., *Managing Business Relationships*, 2nd edn (Chichester: Wiley, 2003), 4.

28 Cummings, S., 'Secondary research: an essential part of the b2b toolkit', *Imprints* (May 2003), 30–31.

29 Anon., 'Special supplement on Marketing Research Awards – Business and Professional', *Marketing* (7 July 2004).

30 Bairfelt, S. and Wilkinson, T., 'Future proof', *Research* (May 2003), 13.

31 Stanat, R., 'The relationship between market research and competitive intelligence', *ESOMAR Journal* (1998).

32 Kahaner, L., *Competitive Intelligence: From Black Ops to Boardrooms. How Businesses Gather, Analyze, and Use Information to Succeed in a Global Marketplace* (New York: Simon and Schuster, 1996).

33 Stanat, R., 'The relationship between market research and competitive intelligence', *Proceedings of the ESOMAR Congress Berlin* (1998).

34 van Hamersveld, M., 'What are we talking about?', *ESOMAR Journal* (1999), **www.warc.com/fulltext/ESOMAR/13800. htm** (12 February 2005).

35 Jakobiak, F., *ESOMAR Journal* (1999), **www.warc.com/ fulltext/ESOMAR/13801.htm** (18 February 2005).

36 Lithwick, D., 'How to conduct a competitive intelligence phone interview', *Imprints* (December 2004), 15–16; Kassler, H.S., 'Mining the Internet for competitive intelligence', *Online* (September/October 1997), 34–45.

37 Stanat, R., 'The relationship between market research and competitive intelligence', *ESOMAR Journal* (1998).

38 Helton, A.S., 'Data, data everywhere, but no competitive intelligence in sight', *ESOMAR Journal* (1999), **www.warc.com/ print/13808p.asp** (12 February 2005).

39 Hannay, S., 'Balancing act', *Research* (July 2005), 46–47.

40 Connell, S., 'Travel broadens the mind – the case for international research', *International Journal of Market Research* 44 (1) (2002), 7.

41 Ibid., pp. 3–4.

42 Joseph, M., 'Loud and clear', *Research* (February 2005), 26–27.

43 Stanat, R., 'The relationship between market research and competitive intelligence', *ESOMAR Journal* (1998).

44 McNeil, R., 'Open for business', *Research* (May 2003), 3.

45 Ibid.

46 Britton, T. 'Superiority "devalues" b2b research', *Research* (21 May 2003), **www.research-live.com/index.aspx?pageid =30&newsid=259** (21 February 2005).

Visit the *Marketing Research* Companion Website at www.pearsoned.co.uk/malhotra_euro for additional learning resources including annotated weblinks, an online glossary and a suite of downloadable video cases.

Appendix: Statistical tables

Table 1 Simple random numbers

Line/col.	(1)	(2)	(3)	(4)	(5)	(6)	(7)	(8)	(9)	(10)	(11)	(12)	(13)	(14)
1	10480	15011	01536	02011	81647	91646	69179	14194	62590	36207	20969	99570	91291	90700
2	22368	46573	25595	85393	30995	89198	27982	53402	93965	34095	52666	19174	39615	99505
3	24130	48390	22527	97265	76393	64809	15179	24830	49340	32081	30680	19655	63348	58629
4	42167	93093	06243	61680	07856	16376	39440	53537	71341	57004	00849	74917	97758	16379
5	37570	39975	81837	16656	06121	91782	60468	81305	49684	60072	14110	06927	01263	54613
6	77921	06907	11008	42751	27756	53498	18602	70659	90655	15053	21916	81825	44394	42880
7	99562	72905	56420	69994	98872	31016	71194	18738	44013	48840	63213	21069	10634	12952
8	96301	91977	05463	07972	18876	20922	94595	56869	69014	60045	18425	84903	42508	32307
9	89579	14342	63661	10281	17453	18103	57740	84378	25331	12568	58678	44947	05585	56941
10	85475	36857	53342	53988	53060	59533	38867	62300	08158	17983	16439	11458	18593	64952
11	28918	69578	88231	33276	70997	79936	56865	05859	90106	31595	01547	85590	91610	78188
12	63553	40961	48235	03427	49626	69445	18663	72695	52180	20847	12234	90511	33703	90322
13	09429	93969	52636	92737	88974	33488	36320	17617	30015	08272	84115	27156	30613	74952
14	10365	61129	87529	85689	48237	52267	67689	93394	01511	26358	85104	20285	29975	89868
15	07119	97336	71048	08178	77233	13916	47564	81056	97735	85977	29372	74461	28551	90707
16	51085	12765	51821	51259	77452	16308	60756	92144	49442	53900	70960	63990	75601	40719
17	02368	21382	52404	60268	89368	19885	55322	44819	01188	65255	64835	44919	05944	55157
18	01011	54092	33362	94904	31273	04146	18594	29852	71685	85030	51132	01915	92747	64951
19	52162	53916	46369	58586	23216	14513	83149	98736	23495	64350	94738	17752	35156	35749
20	07056	97628	33787	09998	42698	06691	76988	13602	51851	46104	88916	19509	25625	58104
21	48663	91245	85828	14346	09172	30163	90229	04734	59193	22178	30421	61666	99904	32812
22	54164	58492	22421	74103	47070	25306	76468	26384	58151	06646	21524	15227	96909	44592
23	32639	32363	05597	24200	13363	38005	94342	28728	35806	06912	17012	64161	18296	22851
24	29334	27001	87637	87308	58731	00256	45834	15398	46557	41135	10307	07684	36188	18510
25	02488	33062	28834	07351	19731	92420	60952	61280	50001	67658	32586	86679	50720	94953
26	81525	72295	04839	96423	24878	82651	66566	14778	76797	14780	13300	87074	79666	95725
27	29676	20591	68086	26432	46901	20849	89768	81536	86645	12659	92259	57102	80428	25280
28	00742	57392	39064	66432	84673	40027	32832	61362	98947	96067	64760	64584	96096	98253
29	05366	04213	25669	26422	44407	44048	37937	63904	45766	66134	75470	66520	34693	90449
30	91921	26418	64117	94305	26766	25940	39972	22209	71500	64568	91402	42416	07844	69618
31	00582	04711	87917	77341	42206	35126	74087	99547	81817	42607	43808	76655	62028	76630
32	00725	69884	62797	56170	86324	88072	76222	36086	84637	93161	76038	65855	77919	88006
33	69011	65795	95876	55293	18988	27354	26575	08625	40801	59920	29841	80150	12777	48501
34	25976	57948	29888	88604	67917	48708	18912	82271	65424	69774	33611	54262	85963	03547
35	09763	83473	73577	12908	30883	18317	28290	35797	05998	41688	34952	37888	38917	88050
36	91567	42595	27959	30134	04024	86385	29880	99730	55536	84855	29088	09250	79656	73211
37	17955	56349	90999	49127	20044	59931	06115	20542	18059	02008	73708	83517	36103	42791
38	46503	18584	18845	49618	02304	51038	20655	58727	28168	15475	56942	53389	20562	87338
39	92157	89634	94824	78171	84610	82834	09922	25417	44137	48413	25555	21246	35509	20468
40	14577	62765	35605	81263	39667	47358	56873	56307	61607	49518	89656	20103	77490	18062
41	98427	07523	33362	64270	01638	92477	66969	98420	04880	45585	46565	04102	46880	45709
42	34914	63976	88720	82765	34476	17032	87589	40836	32427	70002	70663	88863	77775	69348
43	70060	28277	39475	46473	23219	53416	94970	25832	69975	94884	19661	72828	00102	66794
44	53976	54914	06990	67245	68350	82948	11398	42878	80287	88267	47363	46634	06541	97809
45	76072	29515	40980	07391	58745	25774	22987	80059	39911	96189	41151	14222	60697	59583

(continued)

Table 1 (continued)

Line/col.	(1)	(2)	(3)	(4)	(5)	(6)	(7)	(8)	(9)	(10)	(11)	(12)	(13)	(14)
46	90725	52210	83974	29992	65831	38857	50490	83765	55657	14361	31720	57375	56228	41546
47	64364	67412	33339	31926	14883	24413	59744	92351	97473	89286	35931	04110	23726	51900
48	08962	00358	31662	25388	61642	34072	81249	35648	56891	69352	48373	45578	78547	81788
49	95012	68379	93526	70765	10592	04542	76463	54328	02349	17247	28865	14777	62730	92277
50	15664	10493	20492	38301	91132	21999	59516	81652	27195	48223	46751	22923	32261	85653
51	16408	81899	04153	53381	79401	21438	83035	92350	36693	31238	59649	91754	72772	02338
52	18629	81953	05520	91962	04739	13092	97662	24822	94730	06496	35090	04822	86774	98289
53	73115	35101	47498	87637	99016	71060	88824	71013	18735	20286	23153	72924	35165	43040
54	57491	16703	23167	49323	45021	33132	12544	41035	80780	45393	44812	12515	98931	91202
55	30405	83946	23792	14422	15059	45799	22716	19792	09983	74353	68668	30429	70735	25499
56	16631	35006	85900	98275	32388	52390	16815	69293	82732	38480	73817	32523	41961	44437
57	96773	20206	42559	78985	05300	22164	24369	54224	35083	19687	11052	91491	60383	19746
58	38935	64202	14349	82674	66523	44133	00697	35552	35970	19124	63318	29686	03387	59846
59	31624	76384	17403	53363	44167	64486	64758	75366	76554	31601	12614	33072	60332	92325
60	78919	19474	23632	27889	47914	02584	37680	20801	72152	39339	34806	08930	85001	87820
61	03931	33309	57047	74211	63445	17361	62825	39908	05607	91284	68833	25570	38818	46920
62	74426	33278	43972	10119	89917	15665	52872	73823	73144	88662	88970	74492	51805	99378
63	09066	00903	20795	95452	92648	45454	69552	88815	16553	51125	79375	97596	16296	66092
64	42238	12426	87025	14267	20979	04508	64535	31355	86064	29472	47689	05974	52468	16834
65	16153	08002	26504	41744	81959	65642	74240	56302	00033	67107	77510	70625	28725	34191
66	21457	40742	29820	96783	29400	21840	15035	34537	33310	06116	95240	15957	16572	06004
67	21581	57802	02050	89728	17937	37621	47075	42080	97403	48626	68995	43805	33386	21597
68	55612	78095	83197	33732	05810	24813	86902	60397	16489	03264	88525	42786	05269	92532
69	44657	66999	99324	51281	84463	60563	79312	93454	68876	25471	93911	25650	12682	73572
70	91340	84979	46949	81973	37949	61023	43997	15263	80644	43942	89203	71795	99533	50501
71	91227	21199	31935	27022	84067	05462	35216	14486	29891	68607	41867	14951	91696	85065
72	50001	38140	66321	19924	72163	09538	12151	06878	91903	18749	34405	56087	82790	70925
73	65390	05224	72958	28609	81406	39147	25549	48542	42627	45233	57202	94617	23772	07896
74	27504	96131	83944	41575	10573	03619	64482	73923	36152	05184	94142	25299	94387	34925
75	37169	94851	39117	89632	00959	16487	65536	49071	39782	17095	02330	74301	00275	48280
76	11508	70225	51111	38351	19444	66499	71945	05422	13442	78675	84031	66938	93654	59894
77	37449	30362	06694	54690	04052	53115	62757	95348	78662	11163	81651	50245	34971	52974
78	46515	70331	85922	38329	57015	15765	97161	17869	45349	61796	66345	81073	49106	79860
79	30986	81223	42416	58353	21532	30502	32305	86482	05174	07901	54339	58861	74818	46942
80	63798	64995	46583	09785	44160	78128	83991	42865	92520	83531	80377	35909	81250	54238
81	82486	84846	99254	67632	43218	50076	21361	64816	51202	88124	41870	52689	51275	83556
82	21885	32906	92431	09060	64297	51674	64126	62570	26123	05155	59194	52799	28225	85762
83	60336	98782	07408	53458	13564	59089	26445	29789	85205	41001	12535	12133	14645	23541
84	43937	46891	24010	25560	86355	33941	25786	54990	71899	15475	95434	98227	21824	19535
85	97656	63175	89303	16275	07100	92063	21942	18611	47348	20203	18534	03862	78095	50136
86	03299	01221	05418	38982	55758	92237	26759	86367	21216	98442	08303	56613	91511	75928
87	79626	06486	03574	17668	07785	76020	79924	25651	83325	88428	85076	72811	22717	50585
88	85636	68335	47539	03129	65651	11977	02510	26113	99447	68645	34327	15152	55230	93448
89	18039	14367	61337	06177	12143	46609	32989	74014	64708	00533	35398	58408	13261	47908
90	08362	15656	60627	36478	65648	16764	53412	09013	07832	41574	17639	82163	60859	75567
91	79556	29068	04142	16268	15387	12856	66227	38358	22478	73373	88732	09443	82558	05250
92	92608	82674	27072	32534	17075	27698	98204	63863	11951	34648	88022	56148	34925	57031
93	23982	25835	40055	67006	12293	02753	14827	23235	35071	99704	37543	11601	35503	85171
94	09915	96306	05908	97901	28395	14186	00821	80703	70426	75647	76310	88717	37890	40129
95	59037	33300	26695	62247	69927	76123	50842	43834	86654	70959	79725	93872	28117	19233
96	42488	78077	69882	61657	34136	79180	97526	43092	04098	73571	80799	76536	71255	64239
97	46764	86273	63003	93017	31204	36692	40202	35275	57306	55543	53203	18098	47625	88684
98	03237	45430	55417	63282	90816	17349	88298	90183	36600	78406	06216	95787	42579	90730
99	86591	81482	52667	61582	14972	90053	89534	76036	49199	43716	97548	04379	46370	28672
100	38534	01715	94964	87288	65680	43772	39560	12918	80537	62738	19636	51132	25739	56947

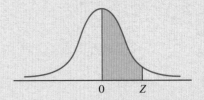

Table 2 Area under the normal curve

Z	.00	.01	.02	.03	.04	.05	.06	.07	.08	.09
0.0	.0000	.0040	.0080	.0120	.0160	.0199	.0239	.0279	.0319	.0359
0.1	.0398	.0438	.0478	.0517	.0557	.0596	.0636	.0675	.0714	.0753
0.2	.0793	.0832	.0871	.0910	.0948	.0987	.1026	.1064	.1103	.1141
0.3	.1179	.1217	.1255	.1293	.1331	.1368	.1406	.1443	.1480	.1517
0.4	.1554	.1591	.1628	.1664	.1700	.1736	.1772	.1808	.1844	.1879
0.5	.1915	.1950	.1985	.2019	.2054	.2088	.2123	.2157	.2190	.2224
0.6	.2257	.2291	.2324	.2357	.2389	.2422	.2454	.2486	.2518	.2549
0.7	.2580	.2612	.2642	.2673	.2704	.2734	.2764	.2794	.2823	.2852
0.8	.2881	.2910	.2939	.2967	.2995	.3023	.3051	.3078	.3106	.3133
0.9	.3159	.3186	.3212	.3238	.3264	.3289	.3315	.3340	.3365	.3389
1.0	.3413	.3438	.3461	.3485	.3508	.3531	.3554	.3577	.3599	.3621
1.1	.3643	.3665	.3686	.3708	.3729	.3749	.3770	.3790	.3810	.3830
1.2	.3849	.3869	.3888	.3907	.3925	.3944	.3962	.3980	.3997	.4015
1.3	.4032	.4049	.4066	.4082	.4099	.4115	.4131	.4147	.4162	.4177
1.4	.4192	.4207	.4222	.4236	.4251	.4265	.4279	.4292	.4306	.4319
1.5	.4332	.4345	.4357	.4370	.4382	.4394	.4406	.4418	.4429	.4441
1.6	.4452	.4463	.4474	.4484	.4495	.4505	.4515	.4525	.4535	.4545
1.7	.4554	.4564	.4573	.4582	.4591	.4599	.4608	.4616	.4625	.4633
1.8	.4641	.4649	.4656	.4664	.4671	.4678	.4686	.4693	.4699	.4706
1.9	.4713	.4719	.4726	.4732	.4738	.4744	.4750	.4756	.4761	.4767
2.0	.4772	.4778	.4783	.4788	.4793	.4798	.4803	.4808	.4812	.4817
2.1	.4821	.4826	.4830	.4834	.4838	.4842	.4846	.4850	.4854	.4857
2.2	.4861	.4864	.4868	.4871	.4875	.4878	.4881	.4884	.4887	.4890
2.3	.4893	.4896	.4898	.4901	.4904	.4906	.4909	.4911	.4913	.4916
2.4	.4918	.4920	.4922	.4925	.4927	.4929	.4931	.4932	.4934	.4936
2.5	.4938	.4940	.4941	.4943	.4945	.4946	.4948	.4949	.4951	.4952
2.6	.4953	.4955	.4956	.4957	.4959	.4960	.4961	.4962	.4963	.4964
2.7	.4965	.4966	.4967	.4968	.4969	.4970	.4971	.4972	.4973	.4974
2.8	.4974	.4975	.4976	.4977	.4977	.4978	.4979	.4979	.4980	.4981
2.9	.4981	.4982	.4982	.4983	.4984	.4984	.4985	.4985	.4986	.4986
3.0	.49865	.49869	.49874	.49878	.49882	.49886	.49889	.49893	.49897	.49900
3.1	.49903	.49906	.49910	.49913	.49916	.49918	.49921	.49924	.49926	.49929
3.2	.49931	.49934	.49936	.49938	.49940	.49942	.49944	.49946	.49948	.49950
3.3	.49952	.49953	.49955	.49957	.49958	.49960	.49961	.49962	.49964	.49965
3.4	.49966	.49968	.49969	.49970	.49971	.49972	.49973	.49974	.49975	.49976
3.5	.49977	.49978	.49978	.49979	.49980	.49981	.49981	.49982	.49983	.49983
3.6	.49984	.49985	.49985	.49986	.49986	.49987	.49987	.49988	.49988	.49989
3.7	.49989	.49990	.49990	.49990	.49991	.49991	.49992	.49992	.49992	.49992
3.8	.49993	.49993	.49993	.49994	.49994	.49994	.49994	.49995	.49995	.49995
3.9	.49995	.49995	.49996	.49996	.49996	.49996	.49996	.49996	.49997	.49997

Each entry represents the area under the standard normal distribution from the mean to Z.

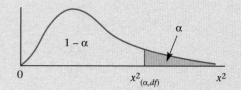

Table 3 Chi-square distribution

Degrees of freedom	Upper tail area (a)											
	.995	.99	.975	.95	.90	.75	.25	.10	.05	.025	.01	.005
1			0.001	0.004	0.016	0.102	1.323	2.706	3.841	5.024	6.635	7.879
2	0.010	0.020	0.051	0.103	0.211	0.575	2.773	4.605	5.991	7.378	9.210	10.597
3	0.072	0.115	0.216	0.352	0.584	1.213	4.108	6.251	7.815	9.348	11.345	12.838
4	0.207	0.297	0.484	0.711	1.064	1.923	5.385	7.779	9.488	11.143	13.277	14.860
5	0.412	0.554	0.831	1.145	1.610	2.675	6.626	9.236	11.071	12.833	15.086	16.750
6	0.676	0.872	1.237	1.635	2.204	3.455	7.841	10.645	12.592	14.449	16.812	18.548
7	0.989	1.239	1.690	2.167	2.833	4.255	9.037	12.017	14.067	16.013	18.475	20.278
8	1.344	1.646	2.180	2.733	3.490	5.071	10.219	13.362	15.507	17.535	20.090	21.955
9	1.735	2.088	2.700	3.325	4.168	5.899	11.389	14.684	16.919	19.023	21.666	23.589
10	2.156	2.558	3.247	3.940	4.865	6.737	12.549	15.987	18.307	20.483	23.209	25.188
11	2.603	3.053	3.816	4.575	5.578	7.584	13.701	17.275	19.675	21.920	24.725	26.757
12	3.074	3.571	4.404	5.226	6.304	8.438	14.845	18.549	21.026	23.337	26.217	28.299
13	3.565	4.107	5.009	5.892	7.042	9.299	15.984	19.812	22.362	24.736	27.688	29.819
14	4.075	4.660	5.629	6.571	7.790	10.165	17.117	21.064	23.685	26.119	29.141	31.319
15	4.601	5.229	6.262	7.261	8.547	11.037	18.245	22.307	24.996	27.488	30.578	32.801
16	5.142	5.812	6.908	7.962	9.312	11.912	19.369	23.542	26.296	28.845	32.000	34.267
17	5.697	6.408	7.564	8.672	10.085	12.792	20.489	24.769	27.587	30.191	33.409	35.718
18	6.265	7.015	8.231	9.390	10.865	13.675	21.605	25.989	28.869	31.526	34.805	37.156
19	6.844	7.633	8.907	10.117	11.651	14.562	22.718	27.204	30.144	32.852	36.191	38.582
20	7.434	8.260	9.591	10.851	12.443	15.452	23.828	28.412	31.410	34.170	37.566	39.997
21	8.034	8.897	10.283	11.591	13.240	16.344	24.935	29.615	32.671	35.479	38.932	41.401
22	8.643	9.542	10.982	12.338	14.042	17.240	26.039	30.813	33.924	36.781	40.289	42.796
23	9.260	10.196	11.689	13.091	14.848	18.137	27.141	32.007	35.172	38.076	41.638	44.181
24	9.886	10.856	12.401	13.848	15.659	19.037	28.241	33.196	36.415	39.364	42.980	45.559
25	10.520	11.524	13.120	14.611	16.473	19.939	29.339	34.382	37.652	40.646	44.314	46.928
26	11.160	12.198	13.844	15.379	17.292	20.843	30.435	35.563	38.885	41.923	45.642	48.290
27	11.808	12.879	14.573	16.151	18.114	21.749	31.528	36.741	40.113	43.194	46.963	49.645
28	12.461	13.565	15.308	16.928	18.939	22.657	32.620	37.916	41.337	44.461	48.278	50.993
29	13.121	14.257	16.047	17.708	19.768	23.567	33.711	39.087	42.557	45.722	49.588	52.336
30	13.787	14.954	16.791	18.493	20.599	24.478	34.800	40.256	43.773	46.979	50.892	53.672
31	14.458	15.655	17.539	19.281	21.434	25.390	35.887	41.422	44.985	48.232	52.191	55.003
32	15.134	16.362	18.291	20.072	22.271	26.304	36.973	42.585	46.194	49.480	53.486	56.328
33	15.815	17.074	19.047	20.867	23.110	27.219	38.058	43.745	47.400	50.725	54.776	57.648
34	16.501	17.789	19.806	21.664	23.952	28.136	39.141	44.903	48.602	51.966	56.061	58.964
35	17.192	18.509	20.569	22.465	24.797	29.054	40.223	46.059	49.802	53.203	57.342	60.275
36	17.887	19.233	21.336	23.269	25.643	29.973	41.304	47.212	50.998	54.437	58.619	61.581
37	18.586	19.960	22.106	24.075	26.492	30.893	42.383	48.363	52.192	55.668	59.892	62.883
38	19.289	20.691	22.878	24.884	27.343	31.815	43.462	49.513	53.384	56.896	61.162	64.181
39	19.996	21.426	23.654	25.695	28.196	32.737	44.539	50.660	54.572	58.120	62.428	65.476
40	20.707	22.164	24.433	26.509	29.051	33.660	45.616	51.805	55.758	59.342	63.691	66.766
41	21.421	22.906	25.215	27.326	29.907	34.585	46.692	52.949	56.942	60.561	64.950	68.053
42	22.138	23.650	25.999	28.144	30.765	35.510	47.766	54.090	58.124	61.777	66.206	69.336

(*continued*)

Table 3 *(continued)*

Degrees of freedom	Upper tail areas (α)											
	.995	.99	.975	.95	.90	.75	.25	.10	.05	.025	.01	.005
43	22.859	24.398	26.785	28.965	31.625	36.436	48.840	55.230	59.304	62.990	67.459	70.616
44	23.584	25.148	27.575	29.787	32.487	37.363	49.913	56.369	60.481	64.201	68.710	71.893
45	24.311	25.901	28.366	30.612	33.350	38.291	50.985	57.505	61.656	65.410	69.957	73.166
46	25.041	26.657	29.160	31.439	34.215	39.220	52.056	58.641	62.830	66.617	71.201	74.437
47	25.775	27.416	29.956	32.268	35.081	40.149	53.127	59.774	64.001	67.821	72.443	75.704
48	26.511	28.177	30.755	33.098	35.949	41.079	54.196	60.907	65.171	69.023	73.683	76.969
49	27.249	28.941	31.555	33.930	36.818	42.010	55.265	62.038	66.339	70.222	74.919	78.231
50	27.991	29.707	32.357	34.764	37.689	42.942	56.334	63.167	67.505	71.420	76.154	79.490
51	28.735	30.475	33.162	35.600	38.560	43.874	57.401	64.295	68.669	72.616	77.386	80.747
52	29.481	31.246	33.968	36.437	39.433	44.808	58.468	65.422	69.832	73.810	78.616	82.001
53	30.230	32.018	34.776	37.276	40.308	45.741	59.534	66.548	70.993	75.002	79.843	83.253
54	30.981	32.793	35.586	38.116	41.183	46.676	60.600	67.673	72.153	76.192	81.069	84.502
55	31.735	33.570	36.398	38.958	42.060	47.610	61.665	68.796	73.311	77.380	82.292	85.749
56	32.490	34.350	37.212	39.801	42.937	48.546	62.729	69.919	74.468	78.567	83.513	86.994
57	33.248	35.131	38.027	40.646	43.816	49.482	63.793	71.040	75.624	79.752	84.733	88.236
58	34.008	35.913	38.844	41.492	44.696	50.419	64.857	72.160	76.778	80.936	85.950	89.477
59	34.770	36.698	39.662	42.339	45.577	51.356	65.919	73.279	77.931	82.117	87.166	90.715
60	35.534	37.485	40.482	43.188	46.459	52.294	66.981	74.397	79.082	83.298	88.379	91.952

For a particular number of degrees of freedom, each entry represents the critical value of χ^2 corresponding to a specified upper tail area, α.

For larger values of degrees of freedom (df), the expression $z = \sqrt{2\chi^2} - \sqrt{2(df) - 1}$ may be used and the resulting upper tail area can be obtained from the table of the standardised normal distribution.

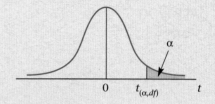

Table 4 *t* distribution

Degrees of freedom	Upper tail area					
	.25	.10	.05	.025	.01	.005
1	1.0000	3.0777	6.3138	12.7062	31.8207	63.6574
2	0.8165	1.8856	2.9200	4.3027	6.9646	9.9248
3	0.7649	1.6377	2.3534	3.1824	4.5407	5.8409
4	0.7407	1.5332	2.1318	2.7764	3.7469	4.6041
5	0.7267	1.4759	2.0150	2.5706	3.3649	4.0322
6	0.7176	1.4398	1.9432	2.4469	3.1427	3.7074
7	0.7111	1.4149	1.8946	2.3646	2.9980	3.4995
8	0.7064	1.3968	1.8595	2.3060	2.8965	3.3554
9	0.7027	1.3830	1.8331	2.2622	2.8214	3.2498
10	0.6998	1.3722	1.8125	2.2281	2.7638	3.1693
11	0.6974	1.3634	1.7959	2.2010	2.7181	3.1058
12	0.6955	1.3562	1.7823	2.1788	2.6810	3.0545
13	0.6938	1.3502	1.7709	2.1604	2.6503	3.0123
14	0.6924	1.3450	1.7613	2,1448	2.6245	2.9768
15	0.6912	1.3406	1.7531	2.1315	2.6025	2.9467
16	0.6901	1.3368	1.7459	2.1199	2.5835	2.9208
17	0.6892	1.3334	1.7396	2.1098	2.5669	2.8982
18	0.6884	1.3304	1.7341	2.1009	2.5524	2.8784
19	0.6876	1.3277	1.7291	2.0930	2.5395	2.8609
20	0.6870	1.3253	1.7247	2.0860	2.5280	2.8453
21	0.6864	1.3232	1.7207	2.0796	2.5177	2.8314
22	0.6858	1.3212	1.7171	2.0739	2.5083	2.8188
23	0.6853	1.3195	1.7139	2.0687	2.4999	2.8073
24	0.6848	1.3178	1.7109	2.0639	2.4922	2.7969
25	0.6844	1.3163	1.7081	2.0595	2.4851	2.7874
26	0.6840	1.3150	1.7056	2.0555	2.4786	2.7787
27	0.6837	1.3137	1.7033	2.0518	2.4727	2.7707
28	0.6834	1.3125	1.7011	2.0484	2.4671	2.7633
29	0.6830	1.3114	1.6991	2.0452	2.4620	2.7564
30	0.6828	1.3104	1.6973	2.0423	2.4573	2.7500
31	0.6825	1.3095	1.6955	2.0395	2.4528	2.7440
32	0.6822	1.3086	1.6939	2.0369	2.4487	2.7385
33	0.6820	1.3077	1.6924	2.0345	2.4448	2.7333
34	0.6818	1.3070	1.6909	2.0322	2.4411	2.7284
35	0.6816	1.3062	1.6896	2.0301	2.4377	2.7238
36	0.6814	1.3055	1.6883	2.0281	2.4345	2.7195
37	0.6812	1.3049	1.6871	2.0262	2.4314	2.7154
38	0.6810	1.3042	1.6860	2.0244	2.4286	2.7116
39	0.6808	1.3036	1.6849	2.0227	2.4258	2.7079
40	0.6807	1.3031	1.6839	2.0211	2.4233	2.7045
41	0.6805	1.3025	1.6829	2.0195	2.4208	2.7012
42	0.6804	1.3020	1.6820	2.0181	2.4185	2.6981
43	0.6802	1.3016	1.681 1	2.0167	2.4163	2.6951

(continued)

Table 4 *(continued)*

Degrees of freedom	.25	.10	.05	.025	.01	.005
				Upper tail area		
44	0.6801	1.3011	1.6802	2.0154	2.4141	2.6923
45	0.6800	1.3006	1.6794	2.0141	2.4121	2.6896
46	0.6799	1.3002	1.6787	2.0129	2.4102	2.6870
47	0.6797	1.2998	1.6779	2.0117	2.4083	2.6846
48	0.6796	1.2994	1.6772	2.0106	2.4066	2.6822
49	0.6795	1.2991	1.6766	2.0096	2.4049	2.6800
50	0.6794	1.2987	1.6759	2.0086	2.4033	2.6778
51	0.6793	1.2984	1.6753	2.0076	2.4017	2.6757
52	0.6792	1.2980	1.6747	2.0066	2.4002	2.6737
53	0.6791	1.2977	1.6741	2.0057	2.3988	2.6718
54	0.6791	1.2974	1.6736	2.0049	2.3974	2.6700
55	0.6790	1.2971	1.6730	2.0040	2.3961	2.6682
56	0.6789	1.2969	1.6725	2.0032	2.3948	2.6665
57	0.6788	1.2966	1.6720	2.0025	2.3936	2.6649
58	0.6787	1.2963	1.6716	2.0017	2.3924	2.6633
59	0.6787	1.2961	1.6711	2.0010	2.3912	2.6618
60	0.6786	1.2958	1.6706	2.0003	2.3901	2.6603
61	0.6785	1.2956	1.6702	1.9996	2.3890	2.6589
62	0.6785	1.2954	1.6698	1.9990	2.3880	2.6575
63	0.6784	1.2951	1.6694	1.9983	2.3870	2.6561
64	0.6783	1.2949	1.6690	1.9977	2.3860	2.6549
65	0.6783	1.2947	1.6686	1.9971	2.3851	2.6536
66	0.6782	1.2945	1.6683	1.9966	2.3842	2.6524
67	0.6782	1.2943	1.6679	1.9960	2.3833	2.6512
68	0.6781	1.2941	1.6676	1.9955	2.3824	2.6501
69	0.6781	1.2939	1.6672	1.9949	2.3816	2.6490
70	0.6780	1.2938	1.6669	1.9944	2.3808	2.6479
71	0.6780	1.2936	1.6666	1.9939	2.3800	2.6469
72	0.6779	1.2934	1.6663	1.9935	2.3793	2.6459
73	0.6779	1.2933	1.6660	1.9930	2.3785	2.6449
74	0.6778	1.2931	1.6657	1.9925	2.3778	2.6439
75	0.6778	1.2929	1.6654	1.9921	2.3771	2.6430
76	0.6777	1.2928	1.6652	1.9917	2.3764	2.6421
77	0.6777	1.2926	1.6649	1.9913	2.3758	2.6412
78	0.6776	1.2925	1.6646	1.9908	2.3751	2.6403
79	0.6776	1.2924	1.6644	1.9905	2.3745	2.6395
80	0.6776	1.2922	1.6641	1.9901	2.3739	2.6387
81	0.6775	1.2921	1.6639	1.9897	2.3733	2.6379
82	0.6775	1.2920	1.6636	1.9893	2.3727	2.6371
83	0.6775	1.2918	1.6634	1.9890	2.3721	2.6364
84	0.6774	1.2917	1.6632	1.9886	2.3716	2.6356
85	0.6774	1.2916	1.6630	1.9883	2.3710	2.6349
86	0.6774	1.2915	1.6628	1.9879	2.3705	2.6342
87	0.6773	1.2914	1.6626	1.9876	2.3700	2.6335
88	0.6773	1.2912	1.6624	1.9873	2.3695	2.6329
89	0.6773	1.2911	1.6622	1.9870	2.3690	2.6322
90	0.6772	1.2910	1.6620	1.9867	2.3685	2.6316
91	0.6772	1.2909	1.6618	1.9864	2.3680	2.6309
92	0.6772	1.2908	1.6616	1.9861	2.3676	2.6303
93	0.6771	1.2907	1.6614	1.9858	2.3671	2.6297
94	0.6771	1.2906	1.6612	1.9855	2.3667	2.6291
95	0.6771	1.2905	1.6611	1.9853	2.3662	2.6286

(continued)

Table 4 *(continued)*

Degrees of freedom	Upper tail area					
	.25	.10	.05	.025	.01	.005
96	0.6771	1.2904	1.6609	1.9850	2.3658	2.6280
97	0.6770	1.2903	1.6607	1.9847	2.3654	2.6275
98	0.6770	1.2902	1.6606	1.9845	2.3650	2.6269
99	0.6770	1.2902	1.6604	1.9842	2.3646	2.6264
100	0.6770	1.2901	1.6602	1.9840	2.3642	2.6259
110	0.6767	1.2893	1.6588	1.9818	2.3607	2.6213
120	0.6765	1.2886	1.6577	1.9799	2.3578	2.6174
130	0.6764	1.2881	1.6567	1.9784	2.3554	2.6142
140	0.6762	1.2876	1.6558	1.9771	2.3533	2.6114
150	0.6761	1.2872	1.6551	1.9759	2.3515	2.6090
∞	0.6745	1.2816	1.6449	1.9600	2.3263	2.5758

For a particular number of degrees of freedom, each entry represents the critical value of t corresponding to a specified upper tail area α.

Table 5 F distribution

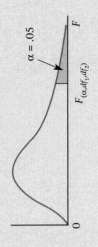

$\alpha = .05$

$F_{(\alpha, df_1, df_2)}$

Numerator df_1

Denominator df_2	1	2	3	4	5	6	7	8	9	10	12	15	20	24	30	40	60	120	∞
1	161.4	199.5	215.7	224.6	230.2	234.0	236.8	238.9	240.5	241.9	243.9	245.9	248.0	249.1	250.1	251.1	252.2	253.3	254.3
2	18.51	19.00	19.16	19.25	19.30	19.33	19.35	19.37	19.38	19.40	19.41	19.43	19.45	19.45	19.46	19.47	19.48	19.49	19.50
3	10.13	9.55	9.28	9.12	9.01	8.94	8.89	8.85	8.81	8.79	8.74	8.70	8.66	8.64	8.62	8.59	8.57	8.55	8.53
4	7.71	6.94	6.59	6.39	6.26	6.16	6.09	6.04	6.00	5.96	5.91	5.86	5.80	5.77	5.75	5.72	5.69	5.66	5.63
5	6.61	5.79	5.41	5.19	5.05	4.95	4.88	4.82	4.77	4.74	4.68	4.62	4.56	4.53	4.50	4.46	4.43	4.40	4.36
6	5.99	5.14	4.76	4.53	4.39	4.28	4.21	4.15	4.10	4.06	4.00	3.94	3.87	3.84	3.81	3.77	3.74	3.70	3.67
7	5.59	4.74	4.35	4.12	3.97	3.87	3.79	3.73	3.68	3.64	3.57	3.51	3.44	3.41	3.38	3.34	3.30	3.27	3.23
8	5.32	4.46	4.07	3.84	3.69	3.58	3.50	3.44	3.39	3.35	3.28	3.22	3.15	3.12	3.08	3.04	3.01	2.97	2.93
9	5.12	4.26	3.86	3.63	3.48	3.37	3.29	3.23	3.18	3.14	3.07	3.01	2.94	2.90	2.86	2.83	2.79	2.75	2.71
10	4.96	4.10	3.71	3.48	3.33	3.22	3.14	3.07	3.02	2.98	2.91	2.85	2.77	2.74	2.70	2.66	2.62	2.58	2.54
11	4.84	3.98	3.59	3.36	3.20	3.09	3.01	2.95	2.90	2.85	2.79	2.72	2.65	2.61	2.57	2.53	2.49	2.45	2.40
12	4.75	3.89	3.49	3.26	3.11	3.00	2.91	2.85	2.80	2.75	2.69	2.62	2.54	2.51	2.47	2.43	2.38	2.34	2.30
13	4.67	3.81	3.41	3.18	3.03	2.92	2.83	2.77	2.71	2.67	2.60	2.53	2.46	2.42	2.38	2.34	2.30	2.25	2.21
14	4.60	3.74	3.34	3.11	2.96	2.85	2.76	2.70	2.65	2.60	2.53	2.46	2.39	2.35	2.31	2.27	2.22	2.18	2.13
15	4.54	3.68	3.29	3.06	2.90	2.79	2.71	2.64	2.59	2.54	2.48	2.40	2.33	2.29	2.25	2.20	2.16	2.11	2.07
16	4.49	3.63	3.24	3.01	2.85	2.74	2.66	2.59	2.54	2.49	2.42	2.35	2.28	2.24	2.19	2.15	2.11	2.06	2.01
17	4.45	3.59	3.20	2.96	2.81	2.70	2.61	2.55	2.49	2.45	2.38	2.31	2.23	2.19	2.15	2.10	2.06	2.01	1.96
18	4.41	3.55	3.16	2.93	2.77	2.66	2.58	2.51	2.46	2.41	2.34	2.27	2.19	2.15	2.11	2.06	2.02	1.97	1.92
19	4.38	3.52	3.13	2.90	2.74	2.63	2.54	2.48	2.42	2.38	2.31	2.23	2.16	2.11	2.07	2.03	1.98	1.93	1.88
20	4.35	3.49	3.10	2.87	2.71	2.60	2.51	2.45	2.39	2.35	2.28	2.20	2.12	2.08	2.04	1.99	1.95	1.90	1.84
21	4.32	3.47	3.07	2.84	2.68	2.57	2.49	2.42	2.37	2.32	2.25	2.18	2.10	2.05	2.01	1.96	1.92	1.87	1.81
22	4.30	3.44	3.05	2.82	2.66	2.55	2.46	2.40	2.34	2.30	2.23	2.15	2.07	2.03	1.98	1.94	1.89	1.84	1.78
23	4.28	3.42	3.03	2.80	2.64	2.53	2.44	2.37	2.32	2.27	2.20	2.13	2.05	2.01	1.96	1.91	1.86	1.81	1.76
24	4.26	3.40	3.01	2.78	2.62	2.51	2.42	2.36	2.30	2.25	2.18	2.11	2.03	1.98	1.94	1.89	1.84	1.79	1.73
25	4.24	3.39	2.99	2.76	2.60	2.49	2.40	2.34	2.28	2.24	2.16	2.09	2.01	1.96	1.92	1.87	1.82	1.77	1.71
26	4.23	3.37	2.98	2.74	2.59	2.47	2.39	2.32	2.27	2.22	2.15	2.07	1.99	1.95	1.90	1.85	1.80	1.75	1.69
27	4.21	3.35	2.96	2.73	2.57	2.46	2.37	2.31	2.25	2.20	2.13	2.06	1.97	1.93	1.88	1.84	1.79	1.73	1.67
28	4.20	3.34	2.95	2.71	2.56	2.45	2.36	2.29	2.24	2.19	2.12	2.04	1.96	1.91	1.87	1.82	1.77	1.71	1.65
29	4.18	3.33	2.93	2.70	2.55	2.43	2.35	2.28	2.22	2.18	2.10	2.03	1.94	1.90	1.85	1.81	1.75	1.70	1.64
30	4.17	3.32	2.92	2.69	2.53	2.42	2.33	2.27	2.21	2.16	2.09	2.01	1.93	1.89	1.84	1.79	1.74	1.68	1.62
40	4.08	3.23	2.84	2.61	2.45	2.34	2.25	2.18	2.12	2.08	2.00	1.92	1.84	1.79	1.74	1.69	1.64	1.58	1.51
60	4.00	3.15	2.76	2.53	2.37	2.25	2.17	2.10	2.04	1.99	1.92	1.84	1.75	1.70	1.65	1.59	1.53	1.47	1.39
120	3.92	3.07	2.68	2.45	2.29	2.17	2.09	2.02	1.96	1.91	1.83	1.75	1,66	1.61	1.55	1.50	1.43	1.35	1.25
∞	3.84	3.00	2.60	2.37	2.21	2.10	2.01	1.94	1.88	1.83	1.75	1.67	1.57	1.52	1.46	1.39	1.32	1.22	1.00

(continued)

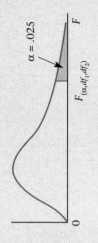

$\alpha = .025$

Table 5 (continued)

Numerator df_1

Denominator df_2	1	2	3	4	5	6	7	8	9	10	12	15	20	24	30	40	60	120	∞
1	647.8	799.5	864.2	899.6	921.8	937.1	948.2	956.7	963.3	968.6	976.7	984.9	993.1	997.2	1001	1006	1010	1014	1018
2	38.51	39.00	39.17	39.25	39.30	39.33	39.36	39.37	39.39	39.40	39.41	39.43	39.45	39.46	39.46	39.47	39.48	39.49	39.50
3	17.44	16.04	15.44	15.10	14.88	14.73	14.62	14.54	14.47	14.42	14.34	14.25	14.17	14.12	14.08	14.04	13.99	13.95	13.90
4	12.22	10.65	9.98	9.60	9.36	9.20	9.07	8.98	8.90	8.84	8.75	8.66	8.56	8.51	8.46	8.41	8.36	8.31	8.26
5	10.01	8.43	7.76	7.39	7.15	6.98	6.85	6.76	6.68	6.62	6.52	6.43	6.33	6.28	6.23	6.18	6.12	6.07	6.02
6	8.81	7.26	6.60	6.23	5.99	5.82	5.70	5.60	5.52	5.46	5.37	5.27	5.17	5.12	5.07	5.01	4.96	4.90	4.85
7	8.07	6.54	5.89	5.52	5.29	5.12	4.99	4.90	4.82	4.76	4.67	4.57	4.47	4.42	4.36	4.31	4.25	4.20	4.14
8	7.57	6.06	5.42	5.05	4.82	4.65	4.53	4.43	4.36	4.30	4.20	4.10	4.00	3.95	3.89	3.84	3.78	3.73	3.67
9	7.21	5.71	5.08	4.72	4.48	4.32	4.20	4.10	4.03	3.96	3.87	3.77	3.67	3.61	3.56	3.51	3.45	3.39	3.33
10	6.94	5.46	4.83	4.47	4.24	4.07	3.95	3.85	3.78	3.72	3.62	3.52	3.42	3.37	3.31	3.26	3.20	3.14	3.08
11	6.72	5.26	4.63	4.28	4.04	3.88	3.76	3.66	3.59	3.53	3.43	3.33	3.23	3.17	3.12	3.06	3.00	2.94	2.88
12	6.55	5.10	4.47	4.12	3.89	3.73	3.61	3.51	3.44	3.37	3.28	3.18	3.07	3.02	2.96	2.91	2.85	2.79	2.72
13	6.41	4.97	4.35	4.00	3.77	3.60	3.48	3.39	3.31	3.25	3.15	3.05	2.95	2.89	2.84	2.78	2.72	2.66	2.60
14	6.30	4.86	4.24	3.89	3.66	3.50	3.38	3.29	3.21	3.15	3.05	2.95	2.84	2.79	2.73	2.67	2.61	2.55	2.49
15	6.20	4.77	4.15	3.80	3.58	3.41	3.29	3.20	3.12	3.06	2.96	2.86	2.76	2.70	2.64	2.59	2.52	2.46	2.40
16	6.12	4.69	4.08	3.73	3.50	3.34	3.22	3.12	3.05	2.99	2.89	2.79	2.68	2.63	2.57	2.51	2.45	2.38	2.32
17	6.04	4.62	4.01	3.66	3.44	3.28	3.16	3.06	2.98	2.92	2.82	2.72	2.62	2.56	2.50	2.44	2.38	2.32	2.25
18	5.98	4.56	3.95	3.61	3.38	3.22	3.10	3.01	2.93	2.87	2.77	2.67	2.56	2.50	2.44	2.38	2.32	2.26	2.19
19	5.92	4.51	3.90	3.56	3.33	3.17	3.05	2.96	2.88	2.82	2.72	2.62	2.51	2.45	2.39	2.33	2.27	2.20	2.13
20	5.87	4.46	3.86	3.51	3.29	3.13	3.01	2.91	2.84	2.77	2.68	2.57	2.46	2.41	2.35	2.29	2.22	2.16	2.09
21	5.83	4.42	3.82	3.48	3.25	3.09	2.97	2.87	2.80	2.73	2.64	2.53	2.42	2.37	2.31	2.25	2.18	2.11	2.04
22	5.79	4.38	3.78	3.44	3.22	3.05	2.93	2.84	2.76	2.70	2.60	2.50	2.39	2.33	2.27	2.21	2.14	2.08	2.00
23	5.75	4.35	3.75	3.41	3.18	3.02	2.90	2.81	2.73	2.67	2.57	2.47	2.36	2.30	2.24	2.18	2.11	2.04	1.97
24	5.72	4.32	3.72	3.38	3.15	2.99	2.87	2.78	2.70	2.64	2.54	2.44	2.33	2.27	2.21	2.15	2.08	2.01	1.94
25	5.69	4.29	3.69	3.35	3.13	2.97	2.85	2.75	2.68	2.61	2.51	2.41	2.30	2.24	2.18	2.12	2.05	1.98	1.91
26	5.66	4.27	3.67	3.33	3.10	2.94	2.82	2.73	2.65	2.59	2.49	2.39	2.28	2.22	2.16	2.09	2.03	1.95	1.88
27	5.63	4.24	3.65	3.31	3.08	2.92	2.80	2.71	2.63	2.57	2.47	2.36	2.25	2.19	2.13	2.07	2.00	1.93	1.85
28	5.61	4.22	3.63	3.29	3.06	2.90	2.78	2.69	2.61	2.55	2.45	2.34	2.23	2.17	2.11	2.05	1.98	1.91	1.83
29	5.59	4.20	3.61	3.27	3.04	2.88	2.76	2.67	2.59	2.53	2.43	2.32	2.21	2.15	2.09	2.03	1.96	1.89	1.81
30	5.57	4.18	3.59	3.25	3.03	2.87	2.75	2.65	2.57	2.51	2.41	2.31	2.20	2.14	2.07	2.01	1.94	1.87	1.79
40	5.42	4.05	3.46	3.13	2.90	2.74	2.62	2.53	2.45	2.39	2.29	2.18	2.07	2.01	1.94	1.88	1.80	1.72	1.64
60	5.29	3.93	3.34	3.01	2.79	2.63	2.51	2.41	2.33	2.27	2.17	2.06	1.94	1.88	1.82	1.74	1.67	1.58	1.48
120	5.15	3.80	3.23	2.89	2.67	2.52	2.39	2.30	2.22	2.16	2.05	1.94	1.82	1.76	1.69	1.61	1.53	1.43	1.31
∞	5.02	3.69	3.12	2.79	2.57	2.41	2.29	2.19	2.11	2.05	1.94	1.83	1.71	1.64	1.57	1.48	1.39	1.27	1.00

(continued)

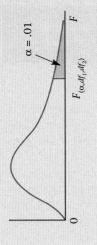

Table 5 *(continued)*

Denominator df_2	Numerator df_1																		
	1	2	3	4	5	6	7	8	9	10	12	15	20	24	30	40	60	120	∞
1	4052	4999.5	5403	5625	5764	5859	5928	5982	6022	6056	6106	6157	6209	6235	6261	6287	6313	6339	6366
2	98.50	99.00	99.17	99.25	99.30	99.33	99.36	99.37	99.39	99.40	99.42	99.43	99.45	99.46	99.47	99.47	99.48	99.49	99.50
3	34.12	30.82	29.46	28.71	28.24	27.91	27.67	27.49	27.35	27.23	27.05	26.87	26.69	26.60	26.50	26.41	26.32	26.22	26.13
4	21.20	18.00	16.69	15.98	15.52	15.21	14.98	14.80	14.66	14.55	14.37	14.20	14.02	13.93	13.84	13.75	13.65	13.56	13.46
5	16.26	13.27	12.06	11.39	10.97	10.67	10.46	10.29	10.16	10.05	9.89	9.72	9.55	9.47	9.38	9.29	9.20	9.11	9.02
6	13.75	10.92	9.78	9.15	8.75	8.47	8.26	8.10	7.98	7.87	7.72	7.56	7.40	7.31	7.23	7.14	7.06	6.97	6.88
7	12.25	9.55	8.45	7.85	7.46	7.19	6.99	6.84	6.72	6.62	6.47	6.31	6.16	6.07	5.99	5.91	5.82	5.74	5.65
8	11.26	8.65	7.59	7.01	6.63	6.37	6.18	6.03	5.91	5.81	5.67	5.52	5.36	5.28	5.20	5.12	5.03	4.95	4.86
9	10.56	8.02	6.99	6.42	6.06	5.80	5.61	5.47	5.35	5.26	5.11	4.96	4.81	4.73	4.65	4.57	4.48	4.40	4.31
10	10.04	7.56	6.55	5.99	5.64	5.39	5.20	5.06	4.94	485	4.71	4.56	4.41	4.33	4.25	4.17	4.08	4.00	3.91
11	9.65	7.21	6.22	5.67	5.32	5.07	4.89	4.74	4.63	4.54	4.40	4.25	4.10	4.02	3.94	3.86	3.78	3.69	3.60
12	9.33	6.93	5.95	5.41	5.06	4.82	4.64	4.50	4.39	4.30	4.16	4.01	3.86	3.78	3.70	3.62	3.54	3.45	3.36
13	9.07	6.70	5.74	5.21	4.86	4.62	4.44	4.30	4.19	4.10	3.96	3.82	3.66	3.59	3.51	3.43	3.34	3.25	3.17
14	8.86	6.51	5.56	5.04	4.69	4.46	4.28	4.14	4.03	3.94	3.80	3.66	3.51	3.43	3.35	3.27	3.18	3.09	3.00
15	8.68	6.36	5.42	4.89	4.56	4.32	4.14	4.00	3.89	3.80	3.67	3.52	3.37	3.29	3.21	3.13	3.05	2.96	2.87
16	8.53	6.23	5.29	4.77	4.44	4.20	4.03	3.89	3.78	3.69	3.55	3.41	3.26	3.18	3.10	3.02	2.93	2.84	2.75
17	8.40	6.11	5.18	4.67	4.34	4.10	3.93	3.79	3.68	3.59	3.46	3.31	3.16	3.08	3.00	2.92	2.83	2.75	2.65
18	8.29	6.01	5.09	4.58	4.25	4.01	3.84	3.71	3.60	3.51	3.37	3.23	3.08	3.00	2.92	2.84	2.75	2.66	2.57
19	8.18	5.93	5.01	4.50	4.17	3.94	3.77	3.63	3.52	3.43	3.30	3.15	3.00	2.92	2.84	2.76	2.67	2.58	2.49
20	8.10	5.85	4.94	4.43	4.10	3.87	3.70	3.56	3.46	3.37	3.23	3.09	2.94	2.86	2.78	2.69	2.61	2.52	2.42
21	8.02	5.78	4.87	4.37	4.04	3.81	3.64	3.51	3.40	3.31	3.17	3.03	2.88	2.80	2.72	2.64	2.55	2.46	2.36
22	7.95	5.72	4.82	4.31	3.99	3.76	3.59	3.45	3.35	3.26	3.12	2.98	2.83	2.75	2.67	2.58	2.50	2.40	2.31
23	7.88	5.66	4.76	4.26	3.94	3.71	3.54	3.41	3.30	3.21	3.07	2.93	2.78	2.70	2.62	2.54	2.45	2.35	2.26
24	7.82	5.61	4.72	4.22	3.90	3.67	3.50	3.36	3.26	3.17	3.03	2.89	2.74	2.66	2.58	2.49	2.40	2.31	2.21
25	7.77	5.57	4.68	4.18	3.85	3.63	3.46	3.32	3.22	3.13	2.99	2.85	2.70	2.62	2.54	2.45	2.36	2.27	2.17
26	7.72	5.53	4.64	4.14	3.82	3.59	3.42	3.29	3.18	3.09	2.96	2.81	2.66	2.58	2.50	2.42	2.33	2.23	2.13
27	7.68	5.49	4.60	4.11	3.78	3.56	3.39	3.26	3.15	3.06	2.93	2.78	2.63	2.55	2.47	2.38	2.29	2.20	2.10
28	7.64	5.45	4.57	4.07	3.75	3.53	3.36	3.23	3.12	3.03	2.90	2.75	2.60	2.52	2.44	2.35	2.26	2.17	2.06
29	7.60	5.42	4.54	4.04	3.73	3.50	3.33	3.20	3.09	3.00	2.87	2.73	2.57	2.49	2.41	2.33	2.23	2.14	2.03
30	7.56	5.39	4.51	4.02	3.70	3.47	3.30	3.17	3.07	2.98	2.84	2.70	2.55	2.47	2.39	2.30	2.21	2.11	2.01
40	7.31	5.18	4.31	3.83	3.51	3.29	3.12	2.99	2.89	2.80	2.66	2.52	2.37	2.29	2.20	2.11	2.02	1.92	1.80
60	7.08	4.98	4.13	3.65	3.34	3.12	2.95	2.82	2.72	2.63	2.50	2.35	2.20	2.12	2.03	1.94	1.84	1.73	1.60
120	6.85	4.79	3.95	3.48	3.17	2.96	2.79	2.66	2.56	2.47	2.34	2.19	2.03	1.95	1.86	1.76	1.66	1.53	1.38
∞	6.63	4.61	3.78	3.32	3.02	2.80	2.64	2.51	2.41	2.32	2.18	2.04	1.88	1.79	1.70	1.59	1.47	1.32	1.00

For a particular combination of numerator and denominator degrees of freedom, each entry represents the critical value of F corresponding to a specified upper tail area a.

Glossary

A posteriori contrasts Contrasts made after conducting the analysis. These are generally multiple comparison tests.

A priori contrasts Contrasts determined before conducting the analysis, based on the researcher's theoretical framework.

Access panel A general 'pool' of individuals or households who have agreed to be available for surveys of widely varying types and topics.

Action research A team research process, facilitated by a professional researcher(s), linking with decision-makers and other stakeholders who together wish to improve particular situations.

Agglomerative clustering A hierarchical clustering procedure where each object starts out in a separate cluster. Clusters are formed by grouping objects into bigger and bigger clusters.

Alpha error (a) See Type I error.

Alternative hypothesis A statement that some difference or effect is expected. Accepting the alternative hypothesis will lead to changes in opinions or actions.

Alternative-forms reliability An approach for assessing reliability that requires two equivalent forms of the scale to be constructed and then the same respondents to be measured at two different times.

Analysis of covariance (ANCOVA) An advanced ANOVA procedure in which the effects of one or more metric-scaled extraneous variables are removed from the dependent variable before conducting the ANOVA.

Analysis of variance (ANOVA) A statistical technique for examining the differences among means for two or more populations.

Analysis sample Part of the total sample used to check the results of the discriminant function.

Analytical model An explicit specification of a set of variables and their interrelationships designed to represent some real system or process in whole or in part.

Analytical services Companies that provide guidance in the development of research design.

Area sampling A common form of cluster sampling in which the clusters consist of geographical areas such as counties, housing tracts, blocks or other area descriptions.

Association techniques A type of projective technique in which participants are presented with a stimulus and are asked to respond with the first thing that comes to mind.

Asymmetric lambda A measure of the percentage improvement in predicting the value of the dependent variable given the value of the independent variable in contingency table analysis. Lambda also varies between 0 and 1.

Audit A data collection process derived from physical records or performing inventory analysis. Data are collected personally by the researcher, or by representatives of the researcher, and are based on counts usually of physical objects rather than people.

Average linkage A linkage method based on the average distance between all pairs of objects, where one member of the pair is from each of the clusters.

Back translation A translation technique that translates a questionnaire from the base language by a translator whose native language is the one into which the questionnaire is being translated. This version is then retranslated back into the original language by someone whose native language is the base language. Translation errors can then be identified.

Balanced scale A scale with an equal number of favourable and unfavourable categories.

Bar chart A chart that displays data in bars positioned horizontally or vertically.

Bayesian approach A selection method where the elements are selected sequentially. The Bayesian approach explicitly incorporates prior information about population parameters as well as the costs and probabilities associated with making wrong decisions.

Beta error (β) See Type II error.

Bibliographic databases Databases composed of citations to articles in journals, magazines, newspapers, marketing research studies, technical reports, government documents, and the like. They often provide summaries or abstracts of the material cited.

Binominal test A goodness-of-fit statistical test for dichotomous variables. It tests the goodness of fit of the observed number of observations in each category to the number expected under a specified binominal distribution.

Bivariate regression A procedure for deriving a mathematical relationship, in the form of an equation, between a single metric-dependent variable and a single metric-independent variable.

Branching question A question used to guide an interviewer (or respondent) through a survey by directing the interviewer (or respondent) to different spots on the questionnaire depending on the answers given.

Branded market research products Specialised data collection and analysis procedures developed to address specific types of marketing research problems.

Broad statement of the problem The initial statement of the marketing research problem that provides an appropriate perspective on the problem.

Call disposition Call disposition records the outcome of an interview call.

Carryover effects Where the evaluation of a particular scaled item significantly affects the respondent's judgement of subsequent scaled items.

Cartoon tests Cartoon characters are shown in a specific situation related to the problem. Participants are asked to indicate the dialogue that one cartoon character might make in response to the comment(s) of another character.

Case study A detailed study based upon the observation of the intrinsic details of individuals, groups of individuals and organisations.

Casewise deletion A method for handling missing responses in which cases or respondents with any missing responses are discarded from the analysis.

Category equivalence A construct equivalence issue that deals specifically with whether the categories in which brands, products and behaviour are grouped are the same in different countries.

Causal research A type of conclusive research where the major objective is to obtain evidence regarding cause-and-effect (causal) relationships.

Causality Causality applies when the occurrence of X increases the probability of the occurrence of Y.

Census A complete enumeration of the elements of a population or study objects.

Centroid method A variance method of hierarchical clustering in which the distance between two clusters is the distance between their centroids (means for all the variables).

Characteristic profile An aid to interpreting discriminant analysis results by describing each group in terms of the group means for the predictor variables.

Chi-square distribution A skewed distribution whose shape depends solely on the number of degrees of freedom. As the number of degrees of freedom increases, the chi-square distribution becomes more symmetrical.

Chi-square statistic The statistic used to test the statistical significance of the observed association in a cross-tabulation. It assists us in determining whether a systematic association exists between the two variables.

Classification information Socio-economic and demographic characteristics used to classify respondents.

Cluster sampling A two-step probability sampling technique where the target population is first divided into mutually exclusive and collectively exhaustive subpopulations called clusters, and then a random sample of clusters is selected based on a probability sampling technique such as SRS. For each selected cluster, either all the elements are included in the sample, or a sample of elements is drawn probabilistically.

Codebook A book containing coding instructions and the necessary information about the questions and potential answers in a survey.

Coding Assigning a code to represent a specific response to a specific question along with the data record and column position that the code will occupy.

Coding and data entry services Companies whose primary service offering is their expertise in converting completed surveys or interviews into a usable database for conducting statistical analysis.

Coding data Breaking down qualitative data into discrete chunks and attaching a reference to those chunks of data.

Coding data in grounded theory A form of shorthand that distills events and meanings without losing their essential properties.

Coefficient alpha A measure of internal consistency reliability that is the average of all possible split-half coefficients resulting from different splittings of the scale items.

Coefficient of variation A useful expression in sampling theory for the standard deviation as a percentage of the mean.

Cohort analysis A multiple cross-sectional design consisting of surveys conducted at appropriate time intervals. The cohort refers to the group of respondents who experience the same event within the same interval.

Common factor analysis An approach to factor analysis that estimates the factors based only on the common variance. Also called principal axis factoring.

Comparative scales One of two types of scaling technique in which there is direct comparison of stimulus objects with one another.

Complete linkage A linkage method that is based on maximum distance of the farthest neighbour approach.

Completion rate The percentage of qualified respondents who complete the interview. It enables researchers to take into account anticipated refusals by people who qualify.

Completion technique A projective technique that requires particpants to complete an incomplete stimulus situation.

Conceptual equivalence A construct equivalence issue that deals with whether the interpretation of brands, products, consumer behaviour and the marketing effort are the same in different countries.

Conclusive research A research design characterised by the measurement of clearly defined marketing phenomena.

Concomitant variation A condition for inferring causality that requires that the extent to which a cause, X, and an effect, Y, occur together or vary together is predicted by the hypothesis under consideration.

Concurrent validity A type of validity that is assessed when the data on the scale being evaluated and on the criterion variables are collected at the same time.

Confidence intervals The range into which the true population parameter will fall, assuming a given level of confidence.

Confounding variables Variables used to illustrate that extraneous variables can confound the results by influencing the dependent variable; synonymous with extraneous variables.

Conjoint analysis A technique that attempts to determine the relative importance consumers attach to salient attributes and the utilities they attach to the levels of attributes.

Conjoint analysis model The mathematical model expressing the fundamental relationship between attributes and utility in conjoint analysis.

Consistency checks A part of the data cleaning process that identifies data that are out of range, logically inconsistent or have extreme values. Data with values not defined by the coding scheme are inadmissible.

Constant sum scaling A comparative scaling technique in which respondents are required to allocate a constant sum of units such as points, euros, chits, stickers or chips among a set of stimulus objects with respect to some criterion.

Construct equivalence A type of equivalence that deals with the question of whether the marketing constructs have the same meaning and significance in different countries.

Construct validity A type of validity that addresses the question of what construct or characteristic the scale is measuring. An attempt is made to answer theoretical questions of why a scale works and what deductions can be made concerning the theory underlying the scale.

Construction technique A projective technique in which participants are required to construct a response in the form of a story, dialogue or description.

Content analysis The objective, systematic and quantitative description of the manifest content of a communication.

Content validity A type of validity, sometimes called face validity, that consists of a subjective but systematic evaluation of the representativeness of the content of a scale for the measuring task at hand.

Contingency coefficient A measure of the strength of association in a table of any size.

Contingency table A cross-tabulation table. It contains a cell for every combination of categories of the two variables.

Continuous rating scale A measurement scale that has respondents rate the objects by placing a mark at the appropriate position on a line that runs from one extreme of the criterion variable to the other. The form may vary considerably. Also called graphic rating scale.

Contrasts In ANOVA, a method of examining differences among two or more means of the treatment groups.

Contrived observation Observing behaviour in an artificial environment.

Controlled test market A test-marketing programme conducted by an outside research company in field experimentation. The research company guarantees distribution of the product in retail outlets that represent a predetermined percentage of the market.

Convenience sampling A non-probability sampling technique that attempts to obtain a sample of convenient elements. The selection of sampling units is left primarily to the interviewer.

Convergent validity A measure of construct validity that measures the extent to which the scale correlates positively with other measures of the same construct.

Cookie technology A group of letters and numbers stored in a web surfer's browser that identify the browser's computer.

Correspondence analysis An MDS technique for scaling qualitative data that scales the rows and columns of the input contingency table in corresponding units so that each can be displayed in the same low-dimensional space.

Covariance A systematic relationship between two variables in which a change in one implies a corresponding change in the other (COV_{xy}).

Covariate A metric-independent variable used in ANCOVA.

Cramer's V A measure of the strength of association used in tables larger than 2×2.

Criterion validity A type of validity that examines whether the measurement scale performs as expected in relation to other selected variables as meaningful criteria.

Critical request The target behaviour being researched.

Cross-cultural analysis A type of across-countries analysis in which the data could be aggregated for each country and these aggregate statistics analysed.

Cross-sectional design A type of research design involving the collection of information from any given sample of population elements only once.

Cross-tabulation A statistical technique that describes two or more variables simultaneously and results in tables that reflect the joint distribution of two or more variables that have a limited number of categories or distinct values.

Cross-validation A test of validity that examines whether a model holds on comparable data not used in the original estimation.

Customer database A database that details characteristics of customers and prospects that can include names and addresses, geographic, demographic and buying behaviour data.

Customised services Companies that tailor research procedures to best meet the needs of each client.

Data analysis services Firms whose primary service is to conduct statistical analysis of quantative data.

Data assembly The gathering of data from a variety of disparate sources.

Data cleaning Thorough and extensive checks for consistency and treatment of missing responses.

Data display Involves summarising and presenting the structure that is seen in collected qualitative data.

Data mining The process of discovering meaningful correlations, patterns and trends by sifting through large amounts of data stored in repositories, using pattern recognition as well as statistical and mathematical techniques.

Data reduction The organising and structuring of qualitative data.

Data verification Involves seeking alternative explanations of the interpretations of qualitative data, through other data sources.

Datawarehouse This may be seen as a 'super-database', but more specifically it may be defined as a process of gathering disparate data from database and survey sources, and converting the data into a consistent format that can aid business decision making.

Debriefing After a disguised experiment, informing test subjects what the experiment was about and how the experimental manipulations were performed.

Decision support system (DSS) An information system that enables decision-makers to interact directly with both databases and analysis models. The important components of a DSS include hardware and a communication network, database, model base, software base and the DSS user (decision-maker).

Decomposition of the total variation In one-way ANOVA, separation of the variation observed in the dependent variable into the variation due to the independent variables plus the variation due to error.

Deduction A form of reasoning in which a conclusion is validly inferred from some premises, and must be true if those premises are true.

Demand artefacts Responses given because the respondents attempt to guess the purpose of the experiment and respond accordingly.

Dependence techniques Multivariate techniques appropriate when one or more of the variables can be identified as dependent variables and the remaining ones as independent variables.

Dependent variables Variables that measure the effect of the independent variables on the test units.

Depth interview An unstructured, direct, personal interview in which a single respondent is probed by an experienced interviewer to uncover underlying motivations, beliefs, attitudes and feelings on a topic.

Derived approaches In MDS, attribute-based approaches to collecting perception data requiring respondents to rate the stimuli on the identified attributes using semantic differential or Likert scales.

Descriptive research A type of conclusive research that has as its major objective the description of something, usually market characteristics or functions.

Design control A method of controlling extraneous variables that involves using specific experimental designs.

Determinism A doctrine espousing that everything that happens is determined by a necessary chain of causation.

Diary media panels A data gathering technique composed of samples of respondents whose television viewing behaviour is automatically recorded by electronic devices, supplementing the purchase information recorded in a diary.

Diary purchase panels A data gathering technique in which respondents record their purchases in a diary.

Dichotomous question A structured question with only two response alternatives, such as yes and no.

Direct approach A type of qualitative research in which the purposes of the project are disclosed to the participant or are obvious given the nature of the interview.

Direct method An approach to discriminant analysis that involves estimating the discriminant function so that all the predictors are included simultaneously.

Directory databases Databases that provide information on individuals, organisations and services.

Discriminant analysis A technique for analysing marketing research data when the criterion or dependent variable is categorical and the predictor or independent variables are interval in nature.

Discriminant analysis model The statistical model on which discriminant analysis is based.

Discriminant function The linear combination of independent variables developed by discriminant analysis that will best discriminate between the categories of the dependent variable.

Discriminant validity A type of construct validity that assesses the extent to which a measure does not correlate with other constructs from which it is supposed to differ.

Disordinal interaction The change in the rank order of the effects of one factor across the levels of another.

Divisive clustering A hierarchical clustering procedure where all objects start out in one giant cluster. Clusters are formed by dividing this cluster into smaller and smaller clusters.

Double-barrelled question A single question that attempts to cover two issues. Such questions can be confusing to respondents and result in ambiguous responses.

Double cross-validation A special form of validation in which the sample is split into halves. One half serves as the estimation sample and the other as a validation sample. The roles of the estimation and validation halves are then reversed and the cross-validation process is repeated.

Double sampling A sampling technique in which certain population elements are sampled twice.

Dummy variables A respecification procedure using variables that take on only two values, usually 0 or 1.

Editing A review of the questionnaires with the objective of increasing accuracy and precision.

Elbow criterion A plot of stress versus dimensionality used in MDS. The point at which an elbow or a sharp bend occurs indicates an appropriate dimensionality.

Electronic observation An observational research strategy in which electronic devices, rather than human observers, record the phenomenon being observed.

Element An object that possesses the information sought by the researcher and about which inferences are to be made.

Empiricism A theory of knowledge. A broad category of the philosophy of science that locates the source of all knowledge in experience.

Estimated or predicted value The value $Y_i = a + b_x$, where a and b are, respectively, estimators of β_0 and β_1, the corresponding population parameters.

Ethnography A research approach based upon the observation of the customs, habits and differences between people in everyday situations.

Euclidean distance The square root of the sum of the squared differences in values for each variable.

Evolving research design A research design where particular research techniques are chosen as the researcher develops an understanding of the issues and respondents.

Experiment The process of manipulating one or more independent variables and measuring their effect on one or more dependent variables, while controlling for the extraneous variables.

Experimental design The set of experimental procedures specifying (1) the test units and sampling procedures, (2) the independent variables, (3) the dependent variables, and (4) how to control the extraneous variables.

Experimental group An initial focus group run to test the setting of the interview, the opening question, the topic guide and the mix of participants that make up the group.

Exploratory research A research design characterised by a flexible and evolving approach to understand marketing phenomena that are inherently difficult to measure.

Expressive technique A projective technique in which participants are presented with a verbal or visual situation and are asked to relate the feelings and attitudes of other people to the situation.

External analysis of preferences A method of configuring a spatial map such that the ideal points or vectors based on preference data are fitted in a spatial map derived from the perception data.

External data Data that originate outside the organisation.

External suppliers Outside marketing research companies hired to supply marketing research services.

External validity A determination of whether the cause-and-effect relationships found in the experiment can be generalised.

Extraneous variables Variables, other than dependent and independent variables, which may influence the results of an experiment.

Eye tracking equipment Instruments that record the gaze movements of the eye.

F distribution A frequency distribution that depends upon two sets of degrees of freedom: the degrees of freedom in the numerator and the degrees of freedom in the denominator.

F statistic The ratio of two sample variances.

F test A statistical test of the equality of the variances of two populations.

Factor An underlying dimension that explains the correlations among a set of variables.

Factor analysis A class of procedures primarily used for data reduction and summarisation.

Factor scores Composite scores estimated for each respondent on the derived factors.

Factorial design A statistical experimental design used to measure the effects of two or more independent variables at various levels and to allow for interactions between variables.

Factors Categorical independent variables in ANOVA. The independent variables must all be categorical (non-metric) to use ANOVA.

Field environment An experimental location set in actual market conditions.

Field force Both the actual interviewers and the supervisors involved in data collection.

Field notes A log or diary of observations, events and reflections made by a researcher as a study is planned, implemented and analysed.

Field services Companies whose primary service is offering their expertise in collecting data for research projects.

Filter question An initial question in a questionnaire that screens potential respondents to ensure they meet the requirements of the sample.

Fixed-response alternative questions Questions that require respondents to choose from a set of predetermined answers.

Focus group A discussion conducted by a trained moderator among a small group of participants in an unstructured and natural manner.

Forced rating scale A rating scale that forces respondents to express an opinion because a 'no opinion' or 'no knowledge' option is not provided.

Frequency distribution A mathematical distribution whose objective is to obtain a count of the number of responses associated with different values of one variable and to express these counts in percentage terms.

Friendship pair A technique used to interview children as two friends or classmates together.

Frugging The use of marketing research to deliberately disguise fundraising activities.

Full-service suppliers Companies that offer a full range of marketing research activities.

Full-text databases Databases that contain the complete text of secondary source documents comprising the database.

Functional equivalence A construct equivalence issue that deals specifically with whether a given concept or behaviour serves the same role or function in different countries.

Funnel approach A strategy for ordering questions in a questionnaire in which the sequence starts with the general questions, which are followed by progressively specific questions, to prevent specific questions from biasing general questions.

Galvanic skin response Changes in the electrical resistance of the skin that relate to a respondent's affective state.

Gamma A test statistic that measures the association between two ordinal-level variables. It does not make an adjustment for ties.

Generalisability The degree to which a study based on a sample applies to the population as a whole.

Geodemographic classification This groups consumers together based on the types of neighbourhood in which they live. If a set of neighbourhoods are similar across a wide range of demographic measures, they may also offer similar potential across most products, brands, services and media.

Geodemographic information system (GIS) At a base level, a GIS matches geographic information with demographic information. This match allows subsequent data analyses to be presented on maps.

Graphic rating scale See Continuous rating scale.

Graphical models Analytical models that provide a visual picture of the relationships between variables.

Grounded theory Theory derived from data, systematically gathered and analysed. Or, a qualitative approach to generating theory through the systematic and simultaneous process of data collection and analysis.

Hierarchical clustering A clustering procedure characterised by the development of a hierarchy or treelike structure.

Histogram A vertical bar chart in which the height of the bar represents the relative or cumulative frequency of occurrence.

History Specific events that are external to the experiment but that occur at the same time as the experiment.

Hit ratio The percentage of cases correctly classified by discriminant analysis.

Hybrid conjoint analysis A form of conjoint analysis that can simplify the data collection task and estimate selected interactions as well as all main effects.

Hypertext markup language (HTML) The language of the Web.

Hypothesis An unproven statement or proposition about a factor or phenomenon that is of interest to a researcher.

Identification information A type of information obtained in a questionnaire that includes name, address and phone number.

Implicit alternative An alternative that is not explicitly expressed.

Implicit assumptions An assumption that is not explicitly stated in a question.

Imputation A method to adjust for non-response by assigning the characteristic of interest to the non-respondents based on the similarity of the variables available for both non-respondents and respondents.

Incidence rate The rate of occurrence of persons eligible to participate in the study expressed as a percentage.

Independent samples The samples are independent if they are drawn randomly from different populations.

Independent variables Variables that are manipulated by the researcher and whose effects are measured and compared.

In-depth interview An unstructured, direct, personal interview in which a single participant is probed by an experienced interviewer to uncover underlying motivations, beliefs, attitudes and feelings on a topic.

Indirect approach A type of qualitative research in which the purposes of the project are disguised from the participants.

Induction A form of reasoning that usually involves the inference that an instance or repeated combination of events may be universally generalised.

Instrumentation An extraneous variable involving changes in the measuring instrument, in the observers, or in the scores themselves.

Integrating analysis Creating an order and connectivity that is seen to be emerging from memos.

Interaction When assessing the relationship between two variables, an interaction occurs if the effect of X_1 depends on the level of X_2, and vice versa.

Interactive testing effect An effect in which a prior measurement affects the test unit's response to the independent variable.

Interdependence technique A multivariate statistical technique in which the whole set of inter-dependent relationships is examined.

Interdependence techniques Multivariate statistical techniques that attempt to group data based on underlying similarity and thus allow for interpretation of the data structures. No distinction is made as to which variables are dependent and which are independent.

Internal analysis of preferences A method of configuring a spatial map such that the spatial map represents both brands or stimuli and respondent points or vectors and is derived solely from the preference data.

Internal consistency reliability An approach for assessing the internal consistency of a set of items, where several items are summated in order to form a total score for the scale.

Internal data Data available within the organisation for whom the research is being conducted.

Internal supplier Marketing research department located within a firm.

Internal validity A measure of accuracy of an experiment. It measures whether the manipulation of the independent variables, or treatments, actually caused the effects on the dependent variable(s).

Internet databases Databases that can be accessed, searched and analysed on the Internet. It is also possible to download data from the Internet and store it on the computer or an auxiliary device.

Internet services Companies which specialise in the use of the Internet to collect, analyse and distribute marketing research information.

Interquartile range The range of a distribution encompassing the middle 50% of the observations.

Interval scale A scale in which the numbers are used to rank objects such that numerically equal distances on the scale represent equal distances in the characteristic being measured.

Intra-cultural analysis Within-country analysis of international data.

Item equivalence Use of the same instrument in different countries.

Itemised rating scale A measurement scale having numbers or brief descriptions associated with each category. The categories are ordered in terms of scale position.

Judgemental sampling A form of convenience sampling in which the population elements are purposely selected based on the judgement of the researcher.

_k_-sample median test A non-parametric test used to examine differences among more than two groups when the dependent variable is measured on an ordinal scale.

Kolmogorov–Smirnov (K–S) one-sample test A one-sample non-parametric goodness-of-fit test that compares the cumulative distribution function for a variable with a specified distribution.

Kolmogorov–Smirnov (K–S) two-sample test Non-parametric test statistic that determines whether two distributions are the same. It takes into account any differences in the two distributions, including median, dispersion and skewness.

Kruskal–Wallis one-way ANOVA A non-metric ANOVA test that uses the rank value of each case, not merely its location relative to the median.

Kurtosis A measure of the relative peakedness of the curve defined by the frequency distribution.

Laboratory environment An artificial setting for experimentation in which the researcher constructs the desired conditions.

Laddering A technique for conducting depth interviews in which a line of questioning proceeds from product characteristics to user characteristics.

Latin square design A statistical design that allows for the statistical control of two non-interacting external variables in addition to the manipulation of the independent variable.

Leading question A question that gives the respondent a clue as to what the answer should be.

Least squares procedure A technique for fitting a straight line into a scattergram by minimising the vertical distances of all the points from the line.

Level of significance The probability of making a Type I error.

Lifestyles Distinctive patterns of living described by the activities people engage in, the interests they have, and the opinions they hold of themselves and the world around them.

Likert scale A measurement scale with five response categories ranging from 'strongly disagree' to 'strongly agree' that requires respondents to indicate a degree of agreement or disagreement with each of a series of statements related to the stimulus objects.

Limited-service suppliers Companies that specialise in one or a few phases of a marketing research project.

Line chart A chart that connects a series of data points using continuous lines.

Linguistic equivalence The equivalence of both spoken and written language forms used in scales and questionnaires.

Linkage methods Agglomerative methods of hierarchical clustering that cluster objects based on a computation of the distance between them.

Longitudinal design A type of research design involving a fixed sample of population elements measured repeatedly. The sample remains the same over time, thus providing a series of pictures that, when viewed together, vividly illustrate the situation and the changes that are taking place.

Loyalty card At face value, a sales promotion device used by supermarkets, pharmacists, department stores, petrol stations and even whole shopping centres and towns to encourage repeat purchases. For the marketing researcher, the loyalty card is a device that can link customer characteristics to actual product purchases.

Mahalanobis procedure A stepwise procedure used in discriminant analysis to maximise a generalised measure of the distance between the two closest groups.

Mail panel A large and nationally representative sample of households that have agreed to participate in periodic mail questionnaires and product tests.

Main testing effect An effect of testing occurring when a prior observation affects a later observation.

Mann–Whitney *U* test A statistical test for a variable measured on an ordinal scale, comparing the differences in the location of two populations based on observations from two independent samples.

Marketing decision problem The problem confronting the marketing decision-maker, which asks what the decision-maker has to do.

Marketing information systems (MkIS) A formalised set of procedures for generating, analysing, sorting and distributing pertinent information to marketing decision-makers on an ongoing basis.

Marketing intelligence Qualified observations of events and developments in the marketing environment.

Marketing research A key element within the total field of marketing information. It links the consumer, customer and public to the marketer through information which is used to identify and define marketing opportunities and problems; to generate, refine and evaluate marketing actions; and to improve understanding of marketing as a process and of the ways in which specific marketing activities can be made more effective.

Marketing research problem A problem that entails determining what information is needed and how it can be obtained in the most feasible way.

Marketing research process A set of six steps which define the tasks to be accomplished in conducting a marketing research study. These include problem definition, developing an approach to the problem, research design formulation, fieldwork, data preparation and analysis, and report generation and presentation.

Matching A method of controlling extraneous variables that involves matching test units on a set of key background variables before assigning them to the treatment conditions.

Mathematical models Analytical models that explicitly describe the relationship between variables, usually in equation form.

Maturation An extraneous variable attributable to changes in the test units themselves that occur with the passage of time.

Mean The average; that value obtained by summing all elements in a set and dividing by the number of elements.

Measure of location A statistic that describes a location within a dataset. Measures of central tendency describe the centre of the distribution.

Measure of variability A statistic that indicates the distribution's dispersion.

Measurement The assignment of numbers or other symbols to characteristics of objects according to certain pre-specified rules.

Measurement error The variation in the information sought by the researcher and the information generated by the measurement process employed.

Media panels A data gathering technique composed of samples of respondents whose TV viewing behaviour is automatically recorded by electronic devices, supplementing the purchase information recorded in a diary.

Median A measure of central tendency given as the value above which half of the values fall and below which half of the values fall.

Memo writing Loosely written notes through to fully formed analytical arguments which are added to the original data and interpretations.

Metric data Data that are interval or ratio in nature.

Metric equivalence See Scalar equivalence.

Metric MDS An MDS scaling method that assumes the input data are metric.

Metric scale A scale that is either interval or ratio in nature.

Missing responses Values of a variable that are unknown because the respondents concerned provided ambiguous answers to the question or because their answers were not properly recorded.

Mode A measure of central tendency given as the value that occurs with the most frequency in a sample distribution.

Moderator An individual who conducts a focus group interview, by setting the purpose of the interview, questioning, probing and handling the process of discussion.

Monadic scale See Non-comparative scale.

Mood board A collage created in a focus group setting. Focus group participants are asked to snip words and pictures from magazines that they see as representing the values a particular brand is perceived to have. In some circumstances, collages can also be made up from audio- and videotapes.

Mortality An extraneous variable attributable to the loss of test units while the experiment is in progress.

Multicollinearity A state of high intercorrelations among independent variables.

Multidimensional scaling (MDS) A class of procedures for representing perceptions and preferences of respondents spatially by means of a visual display.

Multiple comparison tests A posteriori contrasts that enable the researcher to construct generalised confidence intervals that can be used to make pairwise comparisons of all treatment means.

Multiple cross-sectional design A cross-sectional design in which there are two or more samples of respondents, and information from each sample is obtained only once.

Multiple discriminant analysis Discriminant analysis technique where the criterion variable involves three or more categories.

Multiple regression A statistical technique that simultaneously develops a mathematical relationship between two or more independent variables and an interval-scaled dependent variable.

Multiple regression model An equation used to explain the results of multiple regression analysis.

Multiple time series design A time series design that includes another group of test units to serve as a control group.

Multiple η^2 The strength of the joint effect of two (or more) factors, or the overall effect.

Multivariate ANOVA (MANOVA) An ANOVA technique using two or more metric dependent variables.

Multivariate techniques Statistical techniques suitable for analysing data when there are two or more measurements on each element and the variables are analysed simultaneously. Multivariate techniques are concerned with the simultaneous relationships among two or more phenomena.

Mystery shopper An observer visiting providers of goods and services as if he or she was really a customer, and recording characteristics of the service delivery.

n-way analysis of variance An ANOVA model where two or more factors are involved.

Natural observation Observing behaviour as it takes place in the environment.

Neuromarketing The application of neuroscience in marketing, primarily to measure emotions through brain imaging.

Nominal scale A scale whose numbers serve only as labels or tags for identifying and classifying objects with a strict one-to-one correspondence between the numbers and the objects.

Nomological validity A type of validity that assesses the relationship between theoretical constructs. It seeks to confirm significant correlations between the constructs as predicted by a theory.

Non-comparative scale One of two types of scaling techniques in which each stimulus object is scaled independently of the other objects in the stimulus set. Also called monadic scale.

Non-hierarchical clustering A procedure that first assigns or determines a cluster centre and then groups all objects within a pre-specified threshold value from the centre.

Non-metric ANOVA An ANOVA technique for examining the difference in the central tendencies of more than two groups when the dependent variable is measured on an ordinal scale.

Non-metric correlation A correlation measure for two non-metric variables that relies on rankings to compute the correlation.

Non-metric data Data derived from a nominal or ordinal scale.

Non-metric MDS A type of MDS which assumes that the input data are ordinal.

Non-metric scale A scale that is either nominal or ordinal in nature.

Non-parametric tests Hypothesis testing procedures that assume that the variables are measured on a nominal or ordinal scale.

Non-probability sampling Sampling techniques that do not use chance selection procedures but rather rely on the personal judgement of the researcher.

Non-response bias Bias caused when actual respondents differ from those who refuse to participate.

Non-response error A type of non-sampling error that occurs when some of the respondents included in the sample do not respond. This error may be defined as the variation between the true mean value of the variable in the original sample and the true mean value in the net sample.

Non-sampling error An error that can be attributed to sources other than sampling and that can be random or non-random.

Null hypothesis A statement in which no difference or effect is expected. If the null hypothesis is not rejected, no changes will be made.

Numeric databases Databases containing numerical and statistical information that may be important sources of secondary data.

Objective evidence Perceived to be unbiased evidence, supported by empirical findings.

Oblique rotation Rotation of factors when the axes are not maintained at right angles.

Offline databases Databases that are available on diskette or CD-ROM.

Omega squared (ω^2) A measure indicating the proportion of the variation in the dependent variable that is related to a particular independent variable or factor.

Omnibus survey A distinctive form of survey that serves the needs of a syndicated group. The omnibus survey targets particular types of respondents such as those in specific geographic locations, e.g. Luxembourg residents, or consumers of particular types of products, e.g. business air travellers. With that target group of respondents, a core set of questions can be asked, with other questions added as syndicate members wish.

One-group pretest–posttest design A pre-experimental design in which a group of test units is measured twice.

One-shot case study A pre-experimental design in which a single group of test units is exposed to a treatment **X**, and then a single measurement of the dependent variable is taken.

One-tailed test A test of the null hypothesis where the alternative hypothesis is expressed directionally.

One-way analysis of variance An ANOVA technique in which there is only one factor.

Online databases Databases, stored in computers, that require a telecommunications network to access.

Operational data Data generated about an organisation's customers, through day-to-day transactions.

Operational equivalence A type of equivalence that measures how theoretical constructs are operationalised in different countries to measure marketing variables.

Operationalised The derivation of measurable characteristics to encapsulate marketing phenomena, e.g. the concept of 'customer loyalty' can be operationalised through measurements such as frequency of repeat purchases or the number of years that a business relationship has existed.

Optimising partitioning method A non-hierarchical clustering method that allows for later reassignment of objects to clusters to optimise an overall criterion.

Order bias (position bias) A respondent's tendency to choose an alternative merely because it occupies a certain position or is listed in a certain order.

Ordinal interaction An interaction where the rank order of the effects attributable to one factor does not change across the levels of the second factor.

Ordinal scale A ranking scale in which numbers are assigned to objects to indicate the relative extent to which some characteristic is possessed. Thus, it is possible to determine whether an object has more or less of a characteristic than some other object.

Orthogonal rotation Rotation of factors in which the axes are maintained at right angles.

Paired comparison scaling A comparative scaling technique in which a respondent is presented with two objects at a time and asked to select one object in the pair according to some criterion. The data obtained are ordinal in nature.

Paired samples The samples are paired when the data for the two samples relate to the same group of respondents.

Paired samples *t* test A test for differences in the means of paired samples.

Pairwise deletion A method for handling missing responses in which all cases or respondents with any missing responses are not automatically discarded; rather, for each calculation, only the cases or respondents with complete responses are considered.

Pan-cultural analysis Across-countries analysis in which the data for all respondents from all the countries are pooled and analysed.

Panel A sample of respondents who have agreed to provide information at specified intervals over an extended period.

Pantry audit A type of audit where the researcher inventories the brands, quantities and package sizes of products in a consumer's home.

Paradigm A set of assumptions consisting of agreed-upon knowledge, criteria of judgement, problem fields and ways to consider them.

Parallel threshold method A non-hierarchical clustering method that specifies several cluster centres at once. All objects that are within a pre-specified threshold value from the centre are grouped together.

Parallel translation A translation method in which a committee of translators, each of whom is fluent in at least two languages, discuss alternative versions of a questionnaire and make modifications until consensus is reached

Parametric tests Hypothesis testing procedures that assume that the variables of interest are measured on at least an interval scale.

Part correlation coefficient A measure of the correlation between Y and X when the linear effects of the other independent variables have been removed from X (but not from Y).

Partial correlation coefficient A measure of the association between two variables after controlling or adjusting for the effects of one or more additional variables.

Perceived respondent anonymity The respondents' perceptions that their identities will not be discerned by the interviewer or researcher.

Personal observation An observational research strategy in which human observers record the phenomenon being observed as it occurs.

Personification technique Participants are asked to imagine that the brand is a person and then describe characteristics of that person.

Phi coefficient (ϕ) A measure of the strength of association in the special case of a table with two rows and two columns (a 2×2 table).

Picture response technique A projective technique in which participants are shown a picture and are asked to tell a story describing it.

Pie chart A round chart divided into sections.

Pilot-testing Testing the questionnaire on a small sample of particpants for the purpose of improving the questionnaire by identifying and eliminating potential problems.

Population The aggregate of all the elements, sharing some common set of characteristics, that comprise the universe for the purpose of the marketing research problem.

Position bias See Order bias.

Positivism A philosophy of language and logic consistent with an empiricist philosophy of science.

Posttest-only control group design Experimental design in which the experimental group is exposed to the treatment but the control group is not and no pretest measure is taken.

Power of a statistical test The probability of rejecting the null hypothesis when it is in fact false and should be rejected.

Pre-coding In questionnaire design, assigning a code to every conceivable response before data collection.

Predictive validity A type of validity that is concerned with how well a scale can forecast a future criterion.

Pre-experimental designs Designs that do not control for extraneous factors by randomisation.

Pretest–posttest control group design An experimental design in which the experimental group is exposed to the treatment but the control group is not. Pretest and posttest measures are taken on both groups.

Primary data Data originated by the researcher specifically to address the research problem.

Principal axis factoring See Common factor analysis.

Principal components analysis An approach to factor analysis that considers the total variance in the data.

Probability proportionate to size (PPS) A selection method where the probability of selecting a sampling unit in a selected cluster varies inversely with the size of the cluster. Therefore, the size of all the resulting clusters is approximately equal.

Probability sampling A sampling procedure in which each element of the population has a fixed probabilistic chance of being selected for the sample.

Probing A motivational technique used when asking questions to induce the participants to enlarge on, clarify or explain their answers.

Problem audit A comparative examination of a marketing problem to understand its origin and nature.

Problem definition A broad statement of the general problem and identification of the specific components of the marketing research problem.

Problem identification research Research undertaken to help identify problems that are not necessarily apparent on the surface, yet exist or are likely to arise in the future.

Problem-solving research Research undertaken to help solve marketing problems.

Product moment correlation (r) A statistic summarising the strength of association between two metric variables.

Projective technique An unstructured and indirect form of questioning that encourages participants to project their underlying motivations, beliefs, attitudes or feelings regarding the issues of concern.

Psycho-galvanometer An instrument that measures a respondent's galvanic skin response.

Psychographics Quantified profiles of individuals based upon lifestyle characteristics.

Pupilometer An instrument that measures changes in the eye pupil diameter.

Purchase panels A data gathering technique in which respondents record their purchases in a diary.

Q-sort scaling A comparative scaling technique that uses a rank order procedure to sort objects based on similarity with respect to some criterion.

Qualitative research An unstructured, primarily exploratory design based on small samples, intended to provide insight and understanding.

Quantitative observation The recording and counting of behavioural patterns of people, objects and events in a systematic manner to obtain information about the phenomenon of interest.

Quantitative research Research techniques that seek to quantify data and, typically, apply some form of statistical analysis.

Quasi-experimental designs Designs that apply part of the procedures of true experimentation yet lack full experimental control.

Questionnaire A structured technique for data collection consisting of a series of questions, written or verbal, that a respondent answers.

Quota sampling A non-probability sampling technique that is two-stage restricted judgemental sampling. The first stage consists of developing control categories or quotas of population elements. In the second stage, sample elements are selected based on convenience or judgement.

Random error An error that arises from random changes or differences in respondents or measurement situations.

Random sampling error The error because the particular sample selected is an imperfect repesentation of the population of interest. It may be defined as the variation between the true mean value for the sample and the true mean value of the population.

Randomisation A method of controlling extraneous variables that involves randomly assigning test units to experimental groups by using random numbers. Treatment conditions are also randomly assigned to experimental groups.

Randomised block design A statistical design in which the test units are blocked on the basis of an external variable to ensure that the various experimental and control groups are matched closely on that variable.

Range The difference between the smallest and largest values of a distribution.

Rank order scaling A comparative scaling technique in which respondents are presented with several objects simultaneously and asked to order or rank them according to some criterion.

Ratio scale The highest scale. This scale allows the researcher to identify or classify objects, rank order the objects, and compare intervals or differences. It is also meaningful to compute ratios of scale values.

Regression analysis A statistical procedure for analysing associative relationships between a metric-dependent variable and one or more independent variables.

Reliability The extent to which a scale produces consistent results if repeated measurements are made on the characteristic.

Repeated measures ANOVA An ANOVA technique used when respondents are exposed to more than one treatment condition and repeated measurements are obtained.

Research brief A document produced by the users of research findings or the buyers of a piece of marketing research. The brief is used to communicate the perceived requirements of a marketing research project.

Research design A framework or blueprint for conducting the marketing research project. It specifies the details of the procedures necessary for obtaining the information needed to structure or solve marketing research problems.

Research proposal The official layout of the planned marketing research activity.

Research questions Refined statements of the specific components of the problem.

Residual The difference between the observed value of Y_i and the value predicted by the regression equation $\hat{Y}_i$.

Response error A type of non-sampling error arising from respondents who do respond but who give inaccurate answers or whose answers are mis-recorded or mis-analysed. It may be defined as a variation between the true mean value of the variable in the net sample and the observed mean value obtained in the market research project.

Response latency The amount of time it takes to respond to a question.

Response rate The percentage of the total attempted interviews that are completed.

Role playing Participants are asked to assume the behaviour of someone else.

Runs test A test of randomness for a dichotomous variable.

Sample A subgroup of the elements of the population selected for participation in the study.

Sample control The ability of the survey mode to reach the units specified in the sample effectively and efficiently.

Sample size The number of elements to be included in a study.

Sampling control An aspect of supervising that ensures that the interviewers strictly follow the sampling plan rather than select sampling units based on convenience or accessibility.

Sampling distribution The distribution of the values of a sample statistic computed for each possible sample that could be drawn from the target population under a specified sampling plan.

Sampling frame A representation of the elements of the target population that consists of a list or set of directions for identifying the target population.

Sampling unit An element, or a unit containing the element, that is available for selection at some stage of the sampling process.

Sampling with replacement A sampling technique in which an element can be included in the sample more than once.

Sampling without replacement A sampling technique in which an element cannot be included in the sample more than once.

Scalar equivalence The demonstration that two individuals from different countries with the same value on some variable will score at the same level on the same test. Also called metric equivalence

Scale transformation A manipulation of scale values to ensure compatibility with other scales or otherwise to make the data suitable for analysis.

Scaling The generation of a continuum upon which measured objects are located.

Scanner data Data obtained by passing merchandise over a laser scanner that reads the UPC from the packages.

Scanner diary panels Scanner data where panel members are identified by an ID card, allowing information about each panel member's purchases to be stored with respect to the the individual shopper.

Scanner diary panels with cable TV The combination of a scanner diary panel with manipulations of the advertising that is being broadcast by cable TV companies.

Scanning device Technology that reads the UPC from merchandise by passing it over a laser scanner.

Secondary data Data collected for some purpose other than the problem at hand.

Selection bias An extraneous variable attributable to the improper assignment of test units to treatment conditions.

Semantic differential A seven-point rating scale with end points associated with bipolar labels.

Semiotics The study of signs in the context of consumer experience.

Sentence completion A projective technique in which participants are presented with a number of incomplete sentences and are asked to complete them.

Sequential sampling A probability sampling technique in which the population elements are sampled sequentially, data collection and analysis are done at each stage, and a decision is made as to whether additional population elements should be sampled.

Shadow team A small cross-functional boundary spanning group that learns everything about a competitive unit.

Sign test A non-parametric test for examining differences in the location of two populations, based on paired populations, that compares only the signs of the differences between pairs of variables without taking into account the magnitude of the differences.

Significance of the interaction effect A test of the significance of the interaction between two or more independent variables.

Significance of the main effect of each factor A test of the significance of the main effect for each individual factor.

Significance of the overall effect A test that some differences exist between some of the treatment groups.

Simple random sampling (SRS) A probability sampling technique in which each element has a known and equal probability of selection. Every element is selected independently of every other element, and the sample is drawn by a random procedure from a sampling frame.

Simulated test market A quasi-test market in which respondents are preselected; they are then interviewed and observed on their purchases and attitudes towards the product.

Single cross-sectional design A cross-sectional design in which one sample of respondents is drawn from the target population and information is obtained from this sample once.

Single linkage A linkage method based on minimum distance or the nearest neighbour rule.

Skewness A characteristic of a distribution that assesses its symmetry about the mean.

Snowball sampling A non-probability sampling technique in which an initial group of respondents is selected randomly. Subsequent respondents are selected based on the referrals or information provided by the initial respondents. By obtaining referrals from referrals, this process may be carried out in waves.

Social desirability The tendency of respondents to give answers that may not be accurate but may be desirable from a social standpoint.

Solomon four-group design An experimental design that explicitly controls for interactive testing effects, in addition to controlling for all the other extraneous variables.

Special-purpose databases Databases that contain information of a specific nature, e.g. data on a specialised industry.

Specific components of the problem The second part of the marketing research problem definition that focuses on the key aspects of the problem and provides clear guidelines on how to proceed further.

Split-half reliability A form of internal consistency reliability in which the items constituting the scale are divided into two halves and the resulting half scores are correlated.

Standard deviation The square root of the variance.

Standard error The standard deviation of the sampling distribution of the mean or proportion.

Standard test market A test market in which the product is sold through regular distribution channels. For example, no special considerations are given to products simply because they are being test marketed.

Standardisation The process of correcting data to reduce them to the same scale by subtracting the sample mean and dividing by the standard deviation.

Standardised services Companies that use standardised procedures to provide marketing research to various clients.

Stapel scale A scale for measuring attitudes that consists of a single adjective in the middle of an even-numbered range of values.

Static group A pre-experimental design in which there are two groups: the experimental group (EG), which is exposed to the treatment, and the control group (CG). Measurements on both groups are made only after the treatment, and test units are not assigned at random.

Statistical control A method of controlling extraneous variables by measuring the extraneous variables and adjusting for their effects through statistical methods.

Statistical designs Designs that allow for the statistical control and analysis of external variables.

Statistical inference The process of generalising the sample results to a target population.

Statistical regression An extraneous variable that occurs when test units with extreme scores move closer to the average score during the course of the experiment.

Stepwise discriminant analysis Discriminant analysis in which the predictors are entered sequentially based on their ability to discriminate between the groups.

Stepwise regression A regression procedure in which the predictor variables enter or leave the regression equation one at a time.

Story completion A projective technique in which participants are provided with part of a story and are required to give the conclusion in their own words.

Stratified sampling A probability sampling technique that uses a two-step process to partition the population into subsequent subpopulations, or strata. Elements are selected from each stratum by a random procedure.

Structural equation modelling (SEM) Collection of statistical techniques including factor analysis and multiple regression. It allows the researcher to examine relationships between several continuous or discrete independent variables and several continuous or discrete dependant variables. The independent and dependent variables can be latent or measured variables.

Structured data collection Use of a formal questionnaire that presents questions in a prearranged order.

Structured observation Observation where the researcher clearly defines the behaviours to be observed and the techniques by which they will be measured.

Structured questions Questions that pre-specify the set of response alternatives and the response format. A structured question could be multiple-choice, dichotomous or a scale.

Substitution A procedure that substitutes for non-respondents other elements from the sampling frame who are expected to respond.

Sugging The use of marketing research to deliberately disguise a sales effort.

Surrogate variables A subset of original variables selected for use in subsequent analysis.

Survey techniques Technniques based upon the use of structured questionnaires given to a sample of a population.

Surveys Interviews with a large number of people using a questionnaire.

Symmetric lambda The symmetric lambda does not make an assumption about which variable is dependent. It measures the overall improvement when prediction is done in both directions.

Syndicated services Companies that collect and sell common pools of data designed to serve information needs shared by a number of clients.

Syndicated sources (services) Information services offered by marketing research organisations that provide information from a common database to different firms that subscribe to their services.

Systematic error An error that affects the measurement in a constant way and represents stable factors that affect the observed score in the same way each time the measurement is made.

Systematic sampling A probability sampling technique in which the sample is chosen by selecting a random starting point and then picking every ith element in succession from the sampling frame.

t distribution A symmetrical bell-shaped distribution that is useful for sample testing ($n < 30$). It is similar to the normal distribution in appearance.

t statistic A statistic that assumes that the variable has a symmetric bell-shaped distribution, that the mean is known (or assumed to be known), and that the population variance is estimated from the sample.

t test A univariate hypothesis test using the t distribution, which is used when the standard deviation is unknown and the sample size is small.

Target population The collection of elements or objects that possess the information sought by the researcher and about which inferences are to be made.

tau b A test statistic that measures the association between two ordinal-level variables. It makes an adjustment for ties and is the most appropriate when the table of variables is square.

tau c A test statistic that measures the association between two ordinal-level variables. It makes an adjustment for ties and is most appropriate when the table of variables is not square but a rectangle.

Telescoping A psychological phenomenon that takes place when an individual telescopes or compresses time by remembering an event as occurring more recently than it actually occurred.

Territorial map A tool for assessing discriminant analysis results by plotting the group membership of each case on a graph.

Test market A carefully selected part of the marketplace particularly suitable for test marketing.

Test marketing An application of a controlled experiment done in limited, but carefully selected, test markets. It involves a replication of the planned national marketing programme for a product in test markets.

Test statistic A measure of how close the sample has come to the null hypothesis. It often follows a well-known distribution, such as the normal, t, or chi-square distribution.

Test units Individuals, organisations or other entities whose response to independent variables or treatments is being studied.

Testing effects Effects caused by the process of experimentation.

Test–retest reliability An approach for assessing reliability, in which respondents are administered identical sets of scale items at two different times, under as nearly equivalent conditions as possible.

Thematic maps Maps that solve marketing problems. They combine geography with demographic information and a company's sales data or other proprietary information and are generated by a computer.

Theoretical sampling Data gathering driven by concepts derived from evolving theory and based on the concept of 'making comparisons'.

Theory A conceptual scheme based on foundational statements, or axioms, that are assumed to be true.

Third-person technique A projective technique in which participants are presented with a verbal or visual situation and are asked to relate the beliefs and attitudes of a third person in that situation.

Time series design A quasi-experimental design that involves periodic measurements of the dependent variable for a group of test units. Then the treatment is administered by the researcher or occurs naturally. After the treatment, periodic measurements are continued to determine the treatment effect.

Topic guide A list of topics, questions and probes that are used by a moderator to help manage a focus group discussion.

Total error The variation between the true mean value in the population of the variable of interest and the observed mean value obtained in the marketing research project

Trace analysis An approach in which data collection is based on physical traces, or evidence, of past behaviour.

Transcripts 'Hard copies' of the questions and probes and the corresponding answers and responses in focus group or in-depth interviews.

Transitivity of preference An assumption made to convert paired comparison data with rank order data. It implies that if Brand A is preferred to Brand B, and Brand B is preferred to Brand C, then Brand A is preferred to Brand C.

Treatment In ANOVA, a particular combination of factor levels or categories.

Trend analysis A method of adjusting for non-response in which the researcher tries to discern a trend between early and late respondents. This trend is projected to non-respondents to estimate their characteristic of interest.

True experimental designs Experimental designs distinguished by the fact that the researcher can randomly assign test units to experimental groups and also randomly assign treatments to experimental groups.

True score model A mathematical model that provides a framework for understanding the accuracy of measurement.

Two-group discriminant analysis Discriminant analysis technique where the criterion variable has two categories.

Two-sample median test Non-parametric test statistic that determines whether two groups are drawn from populations with the same median. This test is not as powerful as the Mann–Whitney *U* test.

Two-tailed test A test of the null hypothesis where the alternative hypothesis is not expressed directionally.

Type I error An error that occurs when the sample results lead to the rejection of a null hypothesis that is in fact true. Also known as alpha error (α).

Type II error An error that occurs when the sample results lead to acceptance of a null hypothesis that is in fact false. Also known as beta error (β).

Univariate techniques Statistical techniques appropriate for analysing data when there is a single measurement of each element in the sample, or, if there are several measurements on each element, when each variable is analysed in isolation.

Unstructured observation Observation that involves a researcher monitoring all relevant phenomena, without specifying the details in advance.

Unstructured questions Open-ended questions that respondents answer in their own words.

Validation sample That part of the total sample used to check the results of the estimation sample.

Validity The extent to which a measurement represents characteristics that exist in the phenomenon under investigation.

Variable respecification The transformation of data to create new variables or the modification of existing

variables so that they are more consistent with the objectives of the study.

Variance The mean squared deviation of all the values of the mean.

Variance method An agglomerative method of hierarchical clustering in which clusters are generated to minimise the within-cluster variance.

Varimax procedure An orthogonal method of factor rotation that minimises the number of variables with high loadings on a factor, thereby enhancing the interpretability of the factors.

Verbal models Analytical models that provide a written representation of the relationships between variables.

Verbal protocol A technique used to understand respondents' cognitive responses or thought processes by having them think aloud while completing a task or making a decision.

Viewing laboratory A room where a focus group may be conducted and simultaneously observed, usually by using a two-way mirror.

Voice pitch analysis Measurement of emotional reactions through changes in the respondent's voice.

Volume tracking data Scanner data that provide information on purchases by brand, size, price and flavour or formulation.

Ward's procedure A variance method in which the squared Euclidean distance to the cluster means is minimised.

Weighting A statistical procedure that attempts to account for non-response by assigning differential weights to the data depending on the response rates.

Wilcoxon matched-pairs signed-ranks test A non-parametric test that analyses the differences between the paired observations, taking into account the magnitude of the differences.

Word association A projective technique in which participants are presented with a list of words, one at a time. After each word, they are asked to give the first word that comes to mind.

***z* test** A univariate hypothesis test using the standard normal distribution.

***z* value** The number of standard errors a point is away from the mean.

abbreviations used in interviewing 464
ABC Global Kids Study 33
academic approach to marketing
    research 50
access to business leaders 775–7, 791
access panels 76
accuracy
    of measurement 356
    of secondary data 97–8
action-oriented problems 46
action research 149, 169–72, 176, 254
    applications of 171
    essential elements of 169
    stages in 171
A-C-V chain (attributes>
        consequences>values) 212–13
added value 39
administration of research projects 38
advertising 108–11, 154, 180, 226, 235,
        239, 253–4, 270, 302, 326, 532,
        580–1, 591, 598–9, 694, 736
after-only designs 313
agglomerative clustering 673, 676–7,
        688
agreed-upon knowledge 49
aided recall 379
airline services 93–4, 99, 450, 723
algorithms, use of 673
Alliance for Research 26
alpha coefficient 358
alternative-forms reliability 357
alternative hypotheses 512
American products, attitudes to 469
American style of research 156–7,
        198–9, 202, 753
analysis of covariance (ANCOVA) 311,
        545–7, 560–1, 566, 568
    interpretation of 561
    with regression 603
analysis of variance (ANOVA) 491, 493,
        545–7, 566
    assumptions involved in 554–5
    multivariate 566
    n-way 546, 555–60, 567–8
    non-metric 565, 568
    one-way 546–55, 567
    repeated-measures type 564–5, 568
    with regression 603–4
analysis samples in discriminant
        analysis 622, 640
analytical models 51–2
animatics 109

anonymity of research respondents 27,
        142–5, 172–3, 176, 225, 227, 280,
        292, 297, 390, 425, 789
anthropology 157
appendices of research reports 728
Apple Mac computers 397
a priori and a posteriori contrasts 564,
        568
Arab societies 747–7
area sampling 419
articulation of responses 379
ASCII files 479, 481
asking of questions, training in 463
association
    strength and significance of 587, 594,
        611
    suppressed 520
Association of Market Survey
        Organisations 465
association techniques 217
assumptions, implicit 386–7
asymmetric lamda 524
Atlanta Olympics 507–8
attitude-scale construction 695
attitudinal data 99, 128, 145, 197
attribute-based approach to perception
        data 696–8, 705, 717
audience figures 110–11, 288
audimeters 286
audit 107, 114, 287–9
Audit Bureau of Circulations 98
Australia 132, 279, 702, 736, 757, 762
average linkage method of clustering
        676
axioms 49

back translation 761, 763
background information for research
        36–9, 43–5
balanced and unbalanced scales 352
Bangladesh 757
banking services 136–9, 143, 223–4,
        271, 373–4, 778–81
bar charts 732–3
bar codes 113, 126, 286
barriers to entry into marketing
        research 28
Bartlett's test of sphericity 648, 651
Bayesian sampling 408
beer market 12, 696–703
BEHAVIOSCAN 113–14
behavioural data 128

behavioural patterns and processes 165,
        283, 290
Belgium 756
Bengali language 744
beta coefficients (or beta weights) 582,
        586, 593, 602, 611
bias 6, 78, 97, 159, 259, 279–82, 289–90,
        297, 381–2, 385–6, 414, 419,
        443–4, 449, 460
    cultural 361–2, 395
    deliberate 396
bibliographic databases 105
Bicycling magazine 447
bilingual researchers 754–5
binomial test 526, 533–4, 539
body language in presentations 734
boots, attributes of 707–13
brainstorming 150, 195
branching questions 389, 391
branded marketing research products
        17
brands and brand development 12–13,
        45, 109, 220–1, 238, 253–4, 281,
        325, 343, 537, 580, 591, 705
Brazil 55, 335–6
breakfast cereals 12
bricolage 51
broad-based patterns of consumer
        behaviour 214
Bulgaria 28
Business Intelligence Group 768–9
business research 196, 209, 271, 281,
        425
    distinctive characteristics of 769–73
business-to-business (b2b) marketing
        766–92
    connectedness of different purchases
        and sales 783–5
    importance of individual customers
        780–3
    number of people involved in
        purchasing decisions 773–8
    time taken over purchases 778–9
buyer behaviours 673–5
buying centres and buying roles 773–4,
        783

cable television 107, 113
calibration 609
call-backs to non-responders 448
call disposition 471
Canada 290–1, 755

Professional Marketing Research
Society 396
canonical correlation 620
canonical loadings 627
carryover effects 341
cars, attributes and ownership of 519,
715
cartoon tests 220
case studies 159, 313
casewise deletion 487
catalogue shopping 504
categorical variables 546, 560
category codes 484–5
category equivalence 759
causal research 79, 89, 155, 159, 302–5,
323–4, 329–30
causality
concept of 302–3
conditions for 303–4
caveats in research reports 728
census data 96, 98, 103, 116, 278, 757,
405–6
centiles 340
Central and Eastern European Business
Directory 102
Central Statistics Office of Ireland 104
central tendency, measures of 508–9
centroid values 620; see also cluster
centroids
channel decisions 695
characteristic profiles 629
Chartered Institute of Purchasing and
Supply 775
charts in research reports 731
cheating error 85, 468
Chebychev distance 675
checkout scanners 113
children
as consumers 108
interviewing of 210, 227
Chile 28
China 28, 86, 116, 450, 745, 756–7, 789
chi-square (x^2) statistic, distribution
and test 493, 521–3, 526, 532–3,
538–9, 798–9
choice-based conjoint (CBC) analysis
50
cities, attitudes towards 575–8
civil liberties 143
clarification of responses 464
classification information 388
classification matrices 620
cleaning of data 486–8, 499
Clementine tool 139–40
click-stream intercepts 426
client assistance 735
client-specific information 58
cluster analysis 131, 215, 493, 671–88

applications of 684–6
basic concept of 671–3
clustering of variables 686–7
interpretation and profiling of
clusters 682
number of clusters 680–1
reliability and validity of 682–3
statistics associated wirh 673
steps in conduct of 674–84
cluster-bar charts 733
cluster centres 673
cluster centroids 673, 677, 682
cluster membership 673
cluster sampling 418–19, 423, 442
codebooks 483–4, 499
codes of conduct 26–7, 142, 259, 470,
763, 775, 786
coding of data 17, 236, 240–4, 247, 251,
256–7, 381, 476, 479–85, 499
in grounded theory 249
from open-ended questions 484–5
coefficient of determination 582, 587,
611
coefficient of multiple determination
592–5, 611
coefficient of variation 510
cognitive structures 212
cohort analysis 75
cold-calling 269
collaborative filtering 138
colour coding 391
combination of data sources 135–6,
140, 283, 297
combination of research techniques
80–2
commercial sensitivity 154, 281
common factor analysis 652, 665
applications of 660–4
common ground between interviewers
and respondents 462
communalities 648, 655
communication, non-verbal forms of
226–7, 239
comparative and *non-comparative*
scaling techniques 335, 341–2,
363–4
competitive advantage 76
competitive intelligence 785–7, 790–1
competitor companies 683–4
complete linkage method of clustering
676
completion rates 443, 452
completion techniques 218–19, 227
computer-assisted personal interviewing
(CAPI) 271, 275–82, 291–4, 297,
375, 378, 486
computer-assisted qualitative data
analysis 257–8

computer-assisted telephone
interviewing (CATI) 265–7,
275–82, 292, 297, 375, 378, 486
computer literacy 174
computer-mediated communication
(CMC) 173, 176
computer technology and applications
27–8, 88, 143, 226, 254–5, 291,
295, 426, 471
computerised databases 118
classification of 104–6
conceptual equivalence 759
conceptual thinking 23
conclusions of research reports 727–8
conclusive research 69–72, 88–9, 152,
285, 409, 421
concomitant variation 303–5
concurrent validity 359
confidence intervals 411, 434–41,
451–2, 564, 590
confidence levels 434
confidentiality 225, 292
confounding variables 310
conjoint analysis 50, 344, 694, 704–17
applications of 705
assumptions and limitations of 714
basic concepts of 704–5
form of input data 709
hybrid 714–16
interpretation of results 713
model for 710
in relation to MDS 715
reliability and validity of 714
selection of procedure in 710–13
statistics associated with 705–6
steps in conduct of 706–14
Conservative Party 280
consistency checks 478, 486–7
constant-sum scaling 345–6
constraints on research 37
construct elicitation 214
construct equivalence 758–9
construct validity 359
construction techniques 219–20, 227
constructs 355
consumer choice process 705
consumer classification 126
consumer relationships 63; see also
customer relationship
management
consumer theory 254
consumption patterns 130
content analysis 244, 251–3, 260
limitations of 251–2
content validity 358
contents tables of research reports 726
context 162, 165, 207, 228, 257–8, 278,
379–80, 784–5

cultural 252
of questioning 223
contingency coefficient 523–4, 539
contingency tables 516
continuous rating scales 348, 362–3
Continuous Tracking Survey 410
contrasts in ANOVA 564
control characteristics 413–14
control groups 314, 329
controlled experiments 305
controlled test markets 326
convenience foods 56
convenience sampling 411–12, 425–6
convergent validity 359
cookie technology 288
coordinates in spatial maps 695
corporate territorialism 100
correlation coefficient 352, 575
   multiple 594
   partial 578–81, 602, 611
correlation matrices 578, 621, 648, 651
correspondence analysis 703–4, 717
cost of sampling 442
Council for Marketing and Opinion
      Research (CMOR) 26, 268, 445
Council of American Survey Research
      Organisations (CASRO) 26
covariance 575
covariates 547, 560
Cramer's *V* 524, 539
creation error 378
creativity 20, 22, 24, 41, 50, 72, 139–40,
      150, 188–9, 244
credibility of interviewers 777
criterion validity 358–9
criterion variables 581
critical path charts 40
critical requests 280
Cronbach's alpha 358
cross-cultural analysis 495
cross-sectional research designs 74–7,
      89, 783–5
cross-selling 143
cross-tabulation 503, 516–25, 539
   bivariate 517
   definition of 516
   in practice 525
   qualitative 246
   statistics associated with 521–5
   with three variables 517–18
cross-validation 602–3, 611
   double 522, 602
cruise business 130–1, 486
cultural influences and differences 224,
      232–3, 236, 252–4, 258–60, 789
currency of data 98
customer databases 123–5, 128–9, 132,
      135, 142–3, 197

customer needs 4–5
customer relationship management
      (CRM) 125, 144, 771
customer satisfaction 134, 271, 788
customer service research 284, 639
customised services 16
cyclical designs 705
Cyprus 103

data
   accuracy and dependability of
         97–100
   nature and content of 99
   overview of 257
   retrieval, organisation and
         interpretation of 242
   statistical adjustment of 488–91,
         498–8
data analysis 10, 17, 40
   coverage in research reports 727
   for focus groups 193
   in grounded theory 249–50
   strategy for 476, 491–4, 499
data analysis error 84
data assembly 237
data collection 9, 40
   environment for 278
   flexibility of 275
   in grounded theory 167
   purpose of 99
   structured 265–6
data display 244–8
data entry services 17
data mining 72, 128, 137–40, 144–5,
      152–3
data preparation 10, 475–99
data protection legislation 143
data reduction 239–40
data richness 182, 202
database analyses 27
database marketing 27, 142
database packages 426
database technology 123
databases 145
   computerised 104–6, 118
   geodemographic 753
   and marketing research 139–40
   see also customer databases
datawarehousing 136–9, 145
debriefing 328, 392
deception of research respondents 328
decision-makers and marketing research
      2–3, 6, 17–23, 28–9, 34–8, 41–2,
      43–4, 58–9, 64–5, 138–9, 235
decomposition of total variation
      548–50, 567, 577, 588, 596
deduction 160
deep understanding 207

degrees of freedom 522, 526–9
deletion, *casewise* and *pairwise* 487–8
demand effects 323
demo disc 255
demographic characteristics 394–5
dendrograms 673, 681
Denmark 21, 103, 267, 450, 755, 757
dependability of data 99–100
dependence techniques 493
dependent and *independent* variables 50,
      306, 548, 581, 584
depth psychology 153
descriptive research 73–9, 89, 265,
      323–4
design control of experiments 311
determinism 159
developing countries, research in 86,
      142, 424, 747, 756
diary-keeping by researchers 168
diary panels 107, 110–14
dichotomous questions 382–3
dichotomous variables 533–4
difficult questions 388
directories
   of business information 102
   of email and Internet addresses 296
   see also telephone directories
directory databases 105
Directory of Research Organisations 102
discarding of unsatisfactory
      respondents 478, 496
discriminant analysis 618–41
   model for 620
   multiple 619, 631–41
   in relation to factor analysis and MDS
         704
   in relation to regression and ANOVA
         619–20
   statistics associated with 620–1
   steps in conduct of 621–31, 640
   stepwise 622, 638–9
   two-group type 619–20, 640
   validity of 629–31, 637
discriminant function 619–20, 640–1
   coefficients of 620–6, 632–4
   significance of 627, 635
discriminant loadings 627
discriminant scores 620
discriminant validity 359
discussion groups 88
disordinal interaction 562–3, 568
distance measures 675–6
distribution research 13
divisive clustering 676
double-barrelled questions 377
double cross-validation 602, 622
double sampling 421
dummy tables 374, 392

dummy variables 489–90, 547, 603–4, 611, 717
Duncan's multiple range test 564
Durbin-Watson test 597

eating out 520–1
economic environment 749
Edinburgh 460, 488–9
editing of data 476–8, 499
effort required of survey respondents 379
eigenvalues 620, 648, 654–5
elbow criterion 699
Electron debit card 45
electronic interviews 267, 273–5
electronic observation 286–9
electronic scanner services 112
electronic shopping 555, 574
electronic surveillance of behaviour (ESOB) 164
electronic surveys 757–8
element selection and element comparisons 214
elements about which information is wanted 406–7
email as a research resource 58, 226–7, 273–82, 425, 452, 757
embarrassment of research participants 200, 281, 380
emergent knowledge 166–7
emotions, assessment of 287
empathy with respondents 460
empiricism 155
employee recruitment 628–9
English language, use of 41
environmental context 8, 43, 55–6, 59, 86, 747–50
epilepsy 413
equivalence concepts in international studies 758–9, 763
errors
  in measurement 356–7
  in regression 584
  in research designs 83–5
  in secondary data 97–8
ESOMAR *see* European Society for Opinion and Marketing Research
estimated values (in regression) 582, 585
estimates asked of respondents 387
eta-squared (η^2) statistic 548, 550, 556
ethical issues 25–9, 57–8, 292–7, 362, 364, 396–7
  for b2b research 789–91
  for causal research 327–8
  for data preparation and analysis 496–9
  for fieldwork 470–1

for focus groups 200, 202
for international marketing research 761, 763
for qualitative research 172–3, 182, 224–5, 259–60
for report preparation and presentation 736–7, 739
for research design 87, 89
for sampling 425, 451, 453
for secondary data 116–17, 119, 142–3, 145
ethnic minorities 744
ethnographic research 161–6, 197, 222, 239, 249, 284
  aims of 162
  criticisms of 166, 176
Euclidian distance 675, 688
euro currency 25
Eurobarometer surveys 760
EUROPA portal website 106
European Commission 106, 410, 760
European Society for Opinion and Marketing Research (ESOMAR) 6, 11, 26–7, 87, 102, 142, 259, 294, 296, 761, 789
  2005 Price Study 28
  Global Market Research Industry Study 13
European Toiletries and Cosmetics Database 27
European Union (EU) 26
Eurostat publications 104
evaluation apprehension 195
evaluation of research projects 735
everyday events, deep understanding of 207
evolving analysis 193
evolving research design 1 60
Excel software package 416, 426, 538, 566–7, 610, 640
executive summaries 38, 726
expenditure on marketing research 14–15, 28, 57, 153, 183, 266, 269, 272–3
experimental designs 306–19, 330
  classification 312–13, 330
  compared with non-experimental designs 323–4
  potential sources of invalidity 318
experimental groups 314
experimentation
  field and *laboratory* environments for 322–3
  time, cost and administration needed for 324
  validity in 307–8, 327, 330
expert information 44–5, 58–9, 71
exploratory research 69–72, 79–80, 88,

152–3, 381, 412, 421
expressive techniques 220–1
extended text 244
external secondary data 100, 117–18
  published sources of 101–4
external suppliers 16–17, 28
external validity 307, 327, 330
externally-generated data 81
extraneous variables 159, 306–10, 327
  control of 310–12
extreme values 486–7
eye-tracking equipment 286–7

F distributioin, table of 803–5
F statistic 529–30, 538, 548, 551, 556, 560, 564, 567–8, 589, 592, 595, 621
F test, partial 592, 596
face-to-face contacts 27–8, 82, 227, 275, 280, 293, 470
factor analysis 215, 493, 646–65
  applications of 647
  fundamental equations of 667–9
  model for 647–8
  in relation to discriminant analysis and MDS 704
  statistics associated with 648–9
  steps in conduct of 649–60
factor loadings 648, 657–8
factor matrices 648
factor pattern matrix 655
factor scores 648, 657, 665
factorial designs 321–2
factors
  in factor analysis 646, 656
  in ANCOVA 546, 560, 563
'fair samples' 161
fake answers to questionnaires 468
fast-moving consumer goods (FMCG) 112
feedback to fieldworkers 468
feelings of respondents and interviewers about research 466–7
field environment 322–3
field experiments 326–7
field notes 236–8, 247, 260
fieldwork 9, 16–17, 40, 460–71
  management of operations 278, 282–3, 460, 471
  nature of 461
  researchers' independent checks on 477
  validatioin of 468–71
fieldworkers
  evaluation of 468–71
  local or 'imported' 469
  selection of 461–2, 471
  supervision of 467–8, 471

training of 462–4, 471
unethical behaviour by 470
FIFA (International Federation of
Football Associations) 335
filter questions 378
filtering 267
financial services sector 48
Financial Times Index 102
fingerprints 288
finite population correction (fpc) 433
fixed-effects model of ANOVA 555
fixed-response alternative questions
266
flat ASCII files 479, 481
flow charts
for display of data 246–7
for navigating through questionnaires
389–90
in research reports 732
focus groups 10, 50, 56, 67–8, 82, 86,
173, 176, 180–203, 211, 221–2,
234, 237–40, 245, 256, 415, 745,
754–5, 763, 777
advantages and disadvantages of
187–8
American and European styles in
198–9, 202
characteristics of 183–4
cognitive and *conative* types 156–7,
198
data analysis for 193
ethical issues for 200, 202
experimental 191, 200, 202
length of discussion periods 184–6
misconceptions about 196–8
moderators of 180–3, 186–8, 193–9,
202
number of discussion periods 191–2
online 180, 188, 201–2
participants in 183–4, 189–91, 201
planning of 188–91
rewards for attendance 190
running of 191–3
serving of alcoholic drink at 200, 203
variants of 194
follow-up
of non-response 446
on research results 735
football rankings 335–6
forced and *non-forced* choices on rating
scales 353
Formula One racing 53–4, 217–18, 336,
339–40, 344, 350, 375–8, 388,
407, 448, 475–6, 479–84, 487,
492, 503–5, 551–2, 760
fractional factorial designs 705
fragmentation of data 251
France 14, 25, 103, 116, 424, 591

fraud 451, 788
free newspapers 268
frequency distributions 503, 506–10
friendship pairs 211
'frugging' 293, 465, 468
full profiles in conjoint analysis 705,
707–9, 717
full-service suppliers 16, 28–9
full-text databases 105
functional equivalence 759
functional Magnetic Resonance Imaging
(fMRI) 287
'funnel' approach to questioning 389
'fusing' of data from different sources
128, 135–6, 139

galvanic skin response (GSR) 286
gamma statistic 524–5
generalisability and generalisability
studies 360, 412
generalisations in questions 387
geodemographic information systems
(GISs) 129–36, 141–5, 426, 752
Germany 21, 25, 103, 110, 279, 424,
558–60, 591
Global Village study 154
GlobalCash study 768, 777–81, 789–90
globalisation 95
goodness-of-fit tests 523, 533–4, 714
goodwill towards marketing research
294, 296
government sources of information
103–4, 118
governmental environment 748
graphical models 51–2, 59
graphs in research reports 729, 731
Greece 269
grounded theory 51, 155, 166–8, 176,
192, 234, 248–50, 260
limitations of 250
group means and group standard
deviations in discriminant
analysis 621
'guerilla ethnography' 172
guidelines for marketing research 26,
87, 294, 296, 470
guides to sources of business
information 101

handheld computers 486
health care services 167, 637–8
Henley Centre 163
heterogeneous populations 422
heuristics 673
'hidden' responses 225
hierarchical and non-hierarchical
clustering 676–8, 688
high-intensity situations 165

histograms 507, 732
'history' of events simultaneous with
experiments 308
hit ratio 629
holdouts 622, 640
holistic thinking 23, 154–5, 235
'honestly significant difference' 564
Hong Kong 450, 756
humour in the research process 238
hypermarkets 191–2
Hypertext Markup Language (HTML)
273
hypothesis testing 54–5, 59, 161, 503
classification of procedures for 515
procedure for 511–15, 527
related to difference 525–6
summary of 536

ice cream sales 495, 671
icicle diagrams 673, 678–9
identification information 388
illiteracy 291
image
corporate 143
of marketing research industry 293
image measurement 694
implicit alternatives and implicit
assumptions 386–7
imputed responses 450, 487
inability error 85
incentives for respondents 446
incidence rate 443, 452
independent samples 528
in-depth interviews 68, 173, 176, 181,
206–17, 221–8, 240
advantages and disadvantages of 211
applications of 216
procedure for 208–10
see also 'laddering' technique;
repertory grid technique
indexes of business information 102
India 424, 743, 745, 758
induction 161
industrial espionage 791
industrial firms
databanks on 107
discussions between 195
syndicated data on 115
information technology (IT) services
782
informational environment 749
information-oriented problems 46
in-home interviews 269–70, 276–82,
396, 756
initial relationships
refinement of 518–19
spurious 519
innovative products 19

in-office interviews 271, 276–82, 756
insight 168
instant analysis 199
instrumentation effects in experiments 309–10
insurance industry 143–4
integrating analysis 250
interaction effects in statistical analysis 555–63, 558–9
interactions between customers and suppliers 783
interactive testing effects (ITs) 309
interconnectivity, models of 243
interdependence techniques 493, 647
interest groups 174
internal consistency reliability 358
internal secondary data 100, 117–18, 124–5
   ethical issues for 142–3, 145
   international 141–2
internal validity 307, 327, 330
   in conjoint analysis 706
International Business Locator 115
international marketing research 24–5, 29, 55–6, 59, 223, 258–9, 361, 364, 494–5, 499, 743–63
   business-to-business 787–9
   causal 326–7
   definition and nature of 744–6
   fieldwork for 469, 471
   focus groups in 198
   framework for 746–51
   interviewing techniques for 290–2
   measurement and scaling in 758–9
   questionnaires for 394–5, 760–1
   reports on 736, 739
   research design for 86
   sampling in 424, 450, 453
   secondary data for 115–16, 119, 141–2, 752–3, 763
   survey techniques for 292, 755–8
International Olympic Committee 412
Internet resources 16, 27–9, 48, 58, 88, 95, 104–5, 110–11, 117–18, 125, 143, 173–6, 227–8, 240, 273–82, 295–7, 329, 362–3, 398, 425, 452, 470–1, 486, 737–8, 791
   advantages and disadvantages of 173–4, 296
   consumers' familiarity with 506
   for focus groups 180, 188, 201–2
   for international marketing research 752, 757, 762–3
   usage of 516–17, 533–4
   see also World Wide Web
interobject similarity 493
interpretation
   logic of 254

of research results 497
interpretation bias 221
interpreters, use of 754
interpretevism 157–61, 168, 175, 213
interquartile range 509
interval scales 340, 363
interviewer error 85
interviews 10, 28, 469
   with children 210, 227
   with industry experts 44–5, 58–9, 71
   locations for 223–4, 228
   protocols for conduct of 223–4, 228
   responses to 66
   termination of 465
   see also computer-assisted personal interviewing; computer-assisted telephone interviewing; electronic interviews; in-depth interviews; personal interviews; semi-structured interviews; street interviews; virtual interviews
intra-cultural analysis 495
intranets 117, 425, 737
inventory-sales ratio 112
investigative reporters 161–2
isomorphic assignment 336
issues, definition of 384
Italy 273, 755
item equivalence 759
item non-response 384
itemised rating scales 348–54, 363

Japan 56, 267, 272, 395, 607, 736, 756–7
journals see diary-keeping
judgemental sampling 411–12

k-means clustering 688
k-sample median test 565
Kaiser-Meyer-Olkin (KMO) statistic 648, 651
Kdnuggets resource 144
Kelly's Directory 781
Kendall's tau (τ) 581
Kenya 757
key questions 189
Keypoint 2 software package 479, 497–8
Kitchen Stories (film) 163
Kolmogorov-Smirnov (K-S) test 493, 526, 533–5, 539
Korea see South Korea
Kruskal–Wallis one-way analysis of variance (K-W ANOVA) 493, 565
kurtosis 511

laboratory environment 322–3

Labour Party 280
'laddering' technique 206, 212–13, 227
lamda coefficient 524, 539
language
   of researchers 159, 224, 266
   rules of 258–9
   of teenagers 154, 241–2
language divisions 395, 424, 744, 752, 755
latent root regression 601
latent variables 604–5, 609–11
Latin square design 320–1
laughter, meaning of 238
leading questions 386, 396
least-squares procedure 584
legal environment 748–9
legitimacy of research 380
library facilities 106
lifestyles 108, 129–30, 134
Likert scales 348–52
limited-service suppliers 16, 29
line charts 731–2
linguistic equivalence 759
'Link' tests 109
linkage methods in cluster analysis 676–7, 688
linking different kinds of data 134–5
Linux operating system 73
listening 168
listservers 88
literature, enjoyment of 233–4
literature reviews 49
local advice and assistance, need for 755
location, measures of 508–9
logical inconsistencies 486–7
logical order of questions 389
London Marathon 24, 73, 270
longitudinal studies 76–7, 87, 89, 111, 272–3, 784–5
Los Angeles 441
Los Medios Mercados de Latinoamerica (LMML) 116
loyalty card schemes 126–9, 145, 286

McNemar test 493, 532, 536, 539
magazines
   popularity of 288
   prices of 598–9
magnetic resonance imaging 287
magnitude estimation technique 346
Mahalanobis procedure 639
mail panels 107, 272–3, 277–82, 291–2
mail surveys 267, 272–3, 276–82, 291–2, 375, 390, 757
mailing lists 272, 277–8, 471
main testing effects (MTs) 309
Malaysia 395
management decision problem 8

managers, discussions between 196
manifest content 251
Mann-Whitney test 493, 526, 534, 539
maps in research reports 731
Market Research Abstracts 102
Market Research Society 102, 172, 259, 280
market share 705
market testing 324
market tracking studies 422
marketing decision problem 46–7, 59, 80
marketing environment in different countries 747
marketing intelligence 94–6, 123
marketing research
    classiification of 11–13
    definition of 6–7, 11
    future prospects for 21–4
    limitations of 17–21
    long-term benefits of 19
    misconceptions about 19
    purpose of 11, 28
    role of 4–5
marketing research industry 13–17, 23
marketing research problem 8, 46–9, 54–9
marketing research process 6–11, 18–19, 28, 59
Marketing Surveys Index 102
marketing understanding 235
matching of test units 311
mathematical models 52–3, 59
mathematically-derived scales 360–1
maturation effects in test units 309
mean square statistic 548
means 508–9
    differences between 528–30, 546
means-end-chain (MEC) 212
measurable and *unmeasurable* variables 605
measurement
    concept of 335–6
    primary scales of 336–41
measurement error 84, 356–7
measurement models 609
mechanistic data analysis 257, 260
media exposure analysis 109
Media Monitor 110
media panels 110–11
Media Watch 111
median test 526, 534, 539, 565
medians 509
memory, limitations of 165, 237, 378–9
memo-writing 249–50
mental maps 212
Metaphoria software 216
metaphors, use of 215–16

metric and *non-metric* data 493
metric and *non-metric* scales 341–2
metric and *non-metric* variables 546–7, 567
Metro newspapers 268
Mexico 55, 291, 424
Minitab software package 329, 497, 538, 566–7, 610, 640, 664, 688
missing responses 487, 499
missing values, assignment of 478
mixed-effects model of ANOVA 555
mixed-mode research 265, 283
mobile phone technology 111, 174, 294
mode of a distribution 509
model-building 51–3
modified least significant difference test 564
monadic scales 342
Le Monde Index 102
Money magazine 93–5, 99
monotonic positive transformations 338
mood boards 192–3, 240
mortality of test units 310
Mosaic Global 131–4, 141, 752
motivation for consumption 212
multicollinearity 601, 611
multidimensional scaling (MDS) 493, 694–704, 716–17
    applications of 694–5
    assumptions and limitations of 702
    basic concepts of 694–5
    labelling of dimensions 700–1, 717
    non-metric 698
    number of dimensions 699–70
    of preference data 702–3
    in relation to conjoint analysis 715
    in relation to factor analysis and discriminant analysis 704
    reliability and validity of 701–2, 717
    statistics associated with 695
    steps in conduct of 695–702
multi-disciplinary working 23–4
multi-item scales 355–8, 364
multimode data collection 295
multiple-choice questions 381–2, 482–3, 497
multiple comparison tests 564
multiple time-series designs 317–19
multivariate statistical techniques 10, 493, 498, 566, 578
mystery shoppers 283–5, 293–4

narrative, use of 234–5
national research cultures 24
'natural experiments' 169
negative statements 387
Nestea project 24, 39–40

Netherlands, the 86, 103, 110, 498, 757
network relationships 772–3, 784, 791
neuromarketing 287
neutral responses to rating scales 352
neutral values, subtitution of 487
new products
    development of 19, 183, 214–15, 694
    experimental research on 311–12
    opportunities for 673
    testing of 76, 162
New Year celebrations 460
New Zealand 702
Newham, London Borough of 744
newspapers
    readership figures 98, 268
    sports coverage 109
'next birthday' method of respondent selection 408
'nice-to-know' information 785
The Nikkei Weekly 102
nomimal scales 336–41, 363
nomological validity 359
normal distribution 432, 526–7
    table of areas under 797
not-at-homes 447–8, 453
note-taking by researchers 236–40, 249–50, 260
NUD*IST 256
null hypotheses 512, 515, 527, 551
numbering of questions and questionnaires 390
numeric databases 105
NVIVO 256

O symbol in marketing research 307
objectives of research 36–9
objectivity in research 6, 49, 167, 729, 736
oblique rotation 656, 665
observation techniques of research 173, 182, 200, 202, 754, 786
    advantages and disadvantages of 290
    comparative evaluation of 288–90
    disguised and *undisguised* 284–5, 297
    by mode of administration 285–8
    natural and *contrived* 285, 297
    structured and *unstructured* 283–4, 297
    see also electronic observation
observed and *unobserved* variables 611
Office for National Statistics 103
offline databases 104–5, 118
Olympic Games 412, 507–8
omega-squared (ω^2) measure 563, 568
omnibus surveys 108, 270, 395–6
    international 291
one-group pretest-posttest designs 313–14

one-shot case studies 313
one-tailed tests 512–14
online databases 105, 118
online focus groups 180, 188, 201–2
online panels 76, 78, 118, 273
online research methods 27–8, 173–4,
    266, 295, 426, 757–8, 762
open-ended questions 381–2, 395–8,
    498
  coding of 484–5
opening questions 388
operational equivalence 759
operational data 124
operationalisation 155
opinion polls 268, 280, 432–3, 451
optical scanning 485–6, 497
optimising partitioning method of
    clustering 678
oral presentations 11, 733–4
order bias 382
ordinal interaction 562, 568
ordinal scales 338–41, 363
orthogonal arrays 706
orthogonal rotation 656
Orthopedics Global Industry Guide
    101–2
outliers 507
out-of-range data values 486–7
over-sampling 413

paired comparative scaling techniques
    342–3
paired samples 493, 531–2, 535, 538
pairwise analysis 705–8, 717
pairwise deletion 488
pan-cultural analysis 495
panels 76–8, 107, 110–14, 118, 272–3,
    276–82, 291–2
pan-European research, dos and don'ts
    of 41
pantry audits 287
paradigms 4, 11, 49, 156
parallel threshold method of clustering
    678
parallel translation 761, 763
parameters 433, 585
parametric and non-parametric tests
    525–39
part correlation coefficient 580, 602
participant observation 161, 175, 248
participant validation 247
participants in research 149, 170
  investigators as 159
  potential harm to 173
  see also focus groups: participants in
partitioning of a population 417
part-worth functions 705, 713
passwords 425, 790

pattern recognition 138
pauses, use of 464
people meters 286
Peperami 220–1
perception data, gathering of 696–8
personal alarms 646
personal construct psychology 213
personal digital assistants (PDAs)
    294–5
personal interviews 269–71, 275–82,
    377, 786
personal observation 286–9
personal people meters (PPMs) 110
personalisation of letters to respondents
    446
personification technique 220
perspiration 286–7
Peru 757
phi (ϕ) coefficient 523, 539
philosophy of qualitative research
    155–61
photographs, use of 239
physiological reactions of customers
    287
picture response technique 219–20
piggybacking 396
pilot-testing 391–2, 395, 412
principal axis factoring 665
pocket PCs 294
point-of-purchase data 164
point-of-purchase buying decisions
    302, 305
point-of-sale systems 134
political pressures 19
pooled within-group correlation matrix
    621
population definition error 84
populations 405–7
Portugal 45, 272
position bias 382
positive statements 387
positivism 155–61, 175, 192, 213
postcodes 133, 143
Pot Noodle 252–3
power of statistical tests 513
PowerPoint software 734, 787
precision 415–18, 433
pre-coding of responses 381, 390, 484
predicted values (in regression) 582,
    585, 589
predictive analysis and predictive
    models 128, 137–40, 144
predictive validity 359
predictor variables 611
predictors, relative importance of
    601–2
pre-experimental designs 312–14
preference, transitivity of 343

preference data 695, 698, 717
  internal and external analysis of
    702–3
  scaling of 702–3
presentations of research findings 11,
    733–4
pretest-posttest control groups designs
    313–16, 412
pre-testing of questionnaires 412
pricing research 13, 695
primary data 45, 86, 266
  definition of 94
  in qualitative and in quantitative
    research 152–3
primary research 9
primary scales of measurement 336–41
principal components analysis 601,
    652–4, 664–5, 704
prior notification to respondents 446
privacy, invasion of 173, 293, 396
probability sampling 408–11, 414–22,
    425
probing 186–8, 209, 212, 225, 237,
    281–2, 463–4
problem audits 43–4, 55, 59
problem components 48
problem definition 8, 11–13, 28, 33–5,
    39, 42–8, 55–9, 726–7
problem-solving research 11–13, 28
product moment correlation
    co-efficient (r) 574–7, 611
product research 13
production blocking 195
professinal buyers 775–6
professional appearance of research
    reports 729
profile analysis 350
profiles of customers and markets 127,
    132–6, 139, 145
profits of marketing research agencies
    38
projective techniques 182, 184, 186,
    200, 202, 206, 217–28, 238
  advantages and disadvantages of
    221–2
  applications of 221–2
  definition of 217
promotions research 13
proof-checking 397
proportionate and disproportionate
    sampling 418
proportions, differences between 530
protocol analysis 392
protocols, verbal 346–7, 364
psycho-galvanometers 286–9
psychographics 108, 134
psychological characteristics of
    customers 134–5, 139

public records, review of 786
Pulse 252–3
Punjabi language 744
pupilometers 286–7
purchase panels 111

Q-sort scaling 346, 362
qualitative data analysis 232, 256–60
  computer-assisted 257–8
  process of 236–48, 260
  stages in 232, 236–7
qualitative learning by researchers
    235–6
qualitative research 9–10, 50, 56, 65,
    71–2, 109, 149–76, 226, 228, 744
  American and European styles of
      156–7, 753
  comparison between techniques
      222–4
  definition of 152
  direct and indirect approaches to
      181–2, 202
  ethical issues for 172–3, 182, 224–5
  on international markets 753–5
  nature of 153
  philosophy of 155–61
  rationale for use of 153–5
  using the Internet 173–4
  see also ethnographic research; focus
      groups; in-depth interviews;
      projective techniques
qualitative researchers 233–6
quality control in fieldwork 467
'quality individuals' 227
quality of interviewing and data 469
quantitative research 9–10, 65, 175, 232,
    251, 259
  definition of 152
  observation techniques as 265, 283
QuarkXpress software 397
quasi-experimental designs 312, 317–19
'question purposes' 373
questioning, context of 223
questioning error 85
questionnaires 10, 279, 370–99
  as exchanges of values between
      researchers and respondents
      371–2
  checking of 477
  content of questions 377–8
  definition of 371–2
  design process for 372–4, 392–4,
      398–9
  diversity of questions in 276–7
  electronic 275
  excessive length of 396
  form and layout of 390
  modes of administration 267

objectives of 371, 398
ordering of questions in 387–90
physical production of 390–1
pilot-testing of 391–2
respondents' inability or
    unwillingness to answer 378–81
returned to the field 478
specification of information needed
    374–5
specification of interviewing method
    375–7
structured 265–6
trade-offs involved in 372–4
translation of 760–1
verification of 498
wording of questions 384–5
questions, structured and unstructured
    381–3, 395, 478, 484
'quirks' website 118
Quo Vadis project 26
quota sampling 411–14, 424, 426
quotas 278

R symbol in marketing research 307
R-squared (R^2) in MDS 695
Racetrack project 24, 53–4, 217–19,
    339–40, 375–8, 388, 407, 436,
    448, 475–6, 479–84, 487, 492,
    503–5, 760
radio
  advertising on 163
  audiences for 288
  sports coverage on 109
random-effects model of ANOVA 555
random error 357
random numbers, table of 795–6
random sampling 83, 85, 88, 225, 406,
    415–19, 423, 426, 781–2
randomisation 311, 319–20, 380–1
range of data 509
rank-order scaling 344–5
rapport, building of 282, 756
rating scales 350–4
  continuous 348, 362–3
  development and evaluation of
      355–60
  itemised 348–54, 363
  multi-item 355–6
  physical form of 354
ratio scales 341, 363
'real time' communication 202
reality, contrasting views of 158–9
rebates 618, 662–3
recall, aided 379
recommendations in research reports
    727–8
recording error 85
recording of respondents' answers

465–7
reduction of data 673
referrals 414, 424
reflexivity 10, 67, 207, 225–6
refusals to participate 444–6
regression analysis 310, 547, 574, 581,
    603
  assumptions involved in 590
  bivariate 582–90, 611
  multiple 590–601, 611
  in relation to discriminant analysis
      and ANOVA 619–20
  stepwise 599–602, 611
regression coefficients 582
  partial 592–3, 611
  standardised 582, 586
regression lines 584
relative importance weights 705
relevance of research findings 65
reliability
  of data 97
  of measurement 159
  of scales 357–9, 364
repeated-measures ANOVA 564–5, 568
repertory grid technique 206, 213–15,
    227
repetition of questions or replies 464
replacement of non-respondents 448
reporting bias 297
reports on research 10–11, 40, 723–33
  importance of 724
  oral presentation of 11, 733–4
  preparation of 724–33
  writing of 728–9
representativeness 296, 412–17, 781–2
Reputation Excellence survey 4
research briefs 34–9, 42–3, 59
research design 9, 39–42, 64–89, 97, 727
  classification of 69–73
  components of 64
  from the decision-makers' perspective
      65–6
  definition of 64
  ethical issues in 87, 89
  evolution of 160
  flexibility in 162–3
  for international studies 86
  from the respondents' perspective
      66–9
  selection of 79
  sources of error in 83–5
  and theory 159–60
research proposals 34, 38–42, 59
  ownership of 58
research questions 53–5, 59
Research World (magazine) 13
researcher-participants 159
residuals,

in factor analysis 648
plotting of 596–7, 611
respecification of variables 489–90
respondent inability and respondent
unwillingness 779
respondent selection error 85
response bias 385
response error 84, 85, 89, 384
response latency 287
response rates 83, 89, 265, 268–9,
279–80, 283, 293, 295
achieved by different fieldworkers
468
improvement of 44–8
results presented in research reports
727
retail audits 114–15
ridge regression 601
rigour in data analysis 257
role-playing 220–1
rotation of factors in factor analysis
655–6, 665
Royal Statistical Society 280
rugby league, study of 151, 184–5, 243
runs test 533–4
Russia 269, 326–7, 361, 743, 745

sample size 85, 408–9, 418, 432, 514
adjustment for incidence rate and
completion rate 443, 452
apportionment of overall total 442
for estimation of a mean 437–9, 452
for estimation of a proportion 440–1,
452
for estimation of several parameters
442
statistical approaches to
determination of 436
sampling 257, 405–27
adjustment for non-response 448
in business research 781–3
classification of techniques 410–11
design process 404–10, 424
execution of process 409
non-probability techniques 408–15,
421–2, 782
non-response 443–50
probability techniques 408–11,
414–22, 425, 437–42
proportionate and disproportionate
418–19
relative strengths and weaknesses of
techniques 422–3
selection of techniques 408
sequential 420–1
stratified 417–19, 423, 442
systematic 416–17, 423, 442, 782
two-phase 421

validation of 410
with and without replacement 408
sampling control 277–8, 467
sampling distributions 434
sampling efficiency 415
sampling error 83, 85, 88–9, 409, 415,
417, 425
compared with non-sampling error
406
of a percentage 432
sampling frame error 84
sampling frames 275, 277, 407–11, 415,
420, 424, 426, 452, 774, 782–3
sampling intervals 416
sampling theory 225
sampling units 406
São Paulo 55
SAS software package 329, 497, 538,
566–7, 610, 640, 664, 688, 716
Saudi Arabia 86, 424, 745
Save the Children 180
scalar equivalence 759
scale categories, number of 351–2
scale transformation 490–1
scaling, concept of 335–6
scaling techniques
choice of 360, 364
comparative 335, 342–7
comparision of 341–2
constant-sum 345–6
magnitude estimation 346
mathematically-derived 360–1
non-comparative 335, 347–8
paired comparative 342–3
Q-sort 346
rank order 344–5
validity of 358–9, 364
see also rating scales
scanned data 107, 112–15, 125–6, 145,
288, 485–6, 497–8
scanning of blood flows to the brain
287
scatter diagrams (scattergrams) 582–5,
611
Scheffé's test 564
schematic figures in research reports
732
scientific approaches to research 51, 155
Scottish Epilepsy Association 413
scree plots 648, 654–5
screening
of respondents 407–10, 426
of responses to questionnaires 477
search engines 58, 117
secondary data 42, 45–6, 49, 58–9,
81–119, 123
secondary data
advantages and uses of 96

classification of 100
criteria for evaluation of 97–100
definition of 94
disadvantages of 96
ethical issues for 116–17, 119
internal 124–5
on international markets 115–17,
118–19, 752–3, 763
sources of 9–10, 101–7
segmentation 13, 123, 126, 134, 139–41,
686, 752
of markets 672, 694, 705
selection bias 310
semantic differential scales 350, 361
semiotics 232, 252–4, 260
limitations of 254
semi-structured interviews 82, 173, 176,
212, 227
sensitive information 154, 167–8, 174,
197, 227, 266, 281, 80, 396
sentence completion 218–19
sequential sampling 420–1
serendipity 187
shadow teams 95
shame on the part of respondents 165
shapes of distributions 510–11
shopping centres 600–1
sign test 526, 536
significance levels 513–14
significance testing 550–1, 556–7, 578,
586–9, 595, 602
similarity/distance coefficient matrix
673
similarity judgements 695
simple random sampling (SRS) 415–19,
423, 426, 442, 781–2
limitations of 416
simulations 426
simultaneous use of different research
techniques 80–1
Singapore 395
single linkage method of clustering 676
skewness 510–11
skip patterns 389, 398, 452
Small Area Statistics (SAS) 103
'smiling face' rating scales 354
SNAP software package 397, 479,
497–8, 538, 664, 688
snowball sampling 187, 411, 414–15,
424
soaps and detergents 56, 206, 218, 226
Social Trends 103
socially-acceptable responses 280, 288
Society of Competitive Professionals
786
socio-cultural environment 750–1
sociology 157
soft drinks market 693

software packages 247, 255–60, 295–6
  for data analysis 497–8
  for questionnaire design 483
Solomon four-group design 316
'sophisticated singles' 132
South Korea 395, 558–60
Spain 25, 45
spatial maps 695, 699–705
Spearman's rho (ρ) 581
special-purpose databases 105
spectator studies 40
Sphinxsurvey software 497
split-half reliability 358, 654–5
'sponsorship impact' 52
spontaneity of responses 187, 198
sports car owners 190
Sports Council 420
sports goods 86
spreadsheets 244–5, 482–3
SPSS software package 128, 139, 144,
    258, 329, 497–8, 537, 566–7,
    609–10, 627, 629, 640, 664,
    687–8, 716
spurious relationships 519, 579–80, 611
SS$_{between}$, SS$_{within}$, SS$_x$ and SS$_y$ statistics
    548, 550
SS$_{reg}$ statistic 596
stacked bar charts 733
standard deviation 510
  dishonest estimation of 451
  of a mean 409
standard errors 416, 434–6, 582,
    589–90, 611
standard test markets 325–6
standardisation
  of coefficients 602, 621
  of data 586
  of scales 490–1
  of variables 593
standardised services 16
Stapel scales 350–1
statements, positive and negative 387
static group designs 314
statistical adjustment of data 488–91,
    498–9
statistical analysis packages 497
statistical control of experiments 311
statistical data, published 102–4
statistical designs 312, 319–22
statistical inference 434
Statistical Office of the European
    Communities (SOEC) 104
statistical techniques
  classification of 493
  properties of 491
  selection of 513
statistics of samples 433
stepwise discriminant analysis 622,

638–9
stepwise regression 599–602, 611
stimuli 235, 277, 286–7, 398
  in conjoint analysis 706–8, 714
story completion 218–19
strategic marketing 127, 129
stratification variables 417
stratified sampling 417–19, 423, 442
street interviews 172, 271, 277–82, 292,
    412, 414, 464, 756–7
stress for survey respondents 293
stress measure 695, 699
structural environment 749–50
structural equation modelling (SEM)
    604–11
structural models 609
structure correlations 621
structured and *unstructured* questions
    381–3, 395, 478, 484
structured data collection 265–6
structured observation 283
Student–Newman–Keuls test 564
Student's *t* 526; *see also t* statistic and
    test
subconscious feelings 154, 221
subjective estimates of non-response
    bias 449
subjectivity in research 167
submission letters with research reports
    726
subpopulations 418
subsampling of non-respondents 448
substitution for non-respondents
    448–9
subtext 253
'sugging' 293, 465, 468
sums of squares 567, 582; *see also under*
    SS
The Sun 226
supermarkets 10, 55
supervision of fieldwork 467–8, 471
suppressed association 520
Surf 56, 226
surrogate information error 84
surrogate variables 657–8, 665
survey techniques 265–6, 274, 296–7
  comparative evaluation of 275–83
  selection of 292
  unethical use of 292–4
  see also mail surveys; web surveys
surveys, use of 10, 64, 82, 107–10, 133,
    136, 224–5
Sweden 14, 25, 102, 132, 269, 291, 757
Switzerland 110, 324
Sydney Olympics 412
Sylheti language 744
symbols, definition of 307
symbols for population and sample

variables 433–4
symmetric distributions 511
symmetric lamda 524
syndicated data 16, 106–15, 118–19
  about industrial firms 115
  from households 108–14
  from institutions 114–15
synergy 187
systematic error 357
systematic sampling 416–17, 423, 442,
    782

t distribution, table of 800–2
t statistic and test 493, 525–7, 538–9,
    546–7, 578, 582
tables in research reports 729–31
taboos 747, 754
tacit knowledge 771
tape-recording 392
target groups for research 37
target markets 5–6, 40, 56, 127, 134,
    235–6
target populations 159, 406–11, 414,
    420, 424–5
target respondents 374, 384, 444
tau *b* and tau *c* statistics 524
teamwork in data analysis 257
technological environment 749
telemarketing 26, 293
telephone directories 277, 756, 782
telephone research 27, 35, 195, 269,
    280–2, 290–2
  international 755–6
  see also computer-assisted telephone
    interviewing
telescoping 378, 778–9
television
  advertising on 108, 180, 326
  audience research 99, 110–11
  reception of 558–9
  sports coverage on 109
  users and non-users of 630–1
  see also cable television
tender documents 35–6
Tennis magazine 48–9, 417
Terminator 2 235
terse language in research reports 729
test markets and test marketing 324–6,
    673
test-retest reliability 357, 714
test statistics 513–14
testing effects 309
Thailand 395, 672
'thank you' pamphlets 465
thematic apperception test (TAT) 219
thematic maps 129
theoretical sampling 160, 250, 257, 260
theory

application of 50–3
challenges to 249
definitions of 49, 155, 166
development and evolution of 155, 249–50
incompleteness of 51
need for 355
and research design 8–9, 159–60, 234
'thermometer' scales 354
third-person technique 220
time, orientation to 56
time intervals between tests 357
time order of occurrence of variables 304–5
time-series designs 317–19
The Times 98
title pages of research reports 726
tomato ketchup 55
topic guides 188, 208, 245
total correlation matrix 621
'total field of information' 6
tourism 545–6, 762
trace analysis 288–9
trade promotions 658–60
training of fieldworkers 462–6, 471
transaction data 100, 125, 128, 135
transcription of data 485–6
transcripts 193, 240, 259–60
transformation of data 597
transition questions 189
transitivity of preference 343
translation 395
    back translation and parallel translation 761, 763
    of questionnaires 760–1
    of transcripts 259–60
travel 520, 607; see also tourism
treatments in ANOVA 546
trend analysis to adjust for non-response 449
triangulation 247
true experimental designs 312, 315–17
true score model 356
Tukey's alternate procedure 564
two-tailed tests 513
two-way mirrors 186, 198–200

Type I error and Type II error 513

U statistic 621; see also Wilks' λ
unconscious mind 233–4
under-sampling 413
unfolding in MDS 695
United Nations 102–3
United States 14, 26, 28, 156, 279, 290–3, 424, 755; see also American products; American style of research
units of measurement 99
univariate statistical techniques 493
universal product code (UPC) data 485
university libraries 106
unsatisfactory responses to questionnaires 478, 496
unwillingness error 85
user-friendliness of computer software 258

vacuum cleaners 19
validation
    of fieldwork 468–71
    of samples 410
    see also cross-validation; participant validation
validation samples in discriminant analysis 622
validity
    of data 97
    in experimentation 307–8. 327, 330
    of measurement 159
    of scales 358–9, 364
values 159, 233, 236, 259–60
variability, measures of 509–10
variable respecification 489–90
variables
    measurable and unmeasurable 605
    observed and unobserved 606–7, 611
variance 509–10
variance methods of clustering 677
variation within and between groups 548, 550
varimax procedure 656, 665
verbal description of scales, nature and

degree of 353–4, 364
verbal models 51–2, 59
verbal protocols 346–7, 364
verbatim reporting 381, 425, 484, 497
verification
    of data 10, 247–8, 486, 498
    of survey respondents 296
video camera analysis 10
video games 20–1
video recording 186, 200, 221, 225
viewing laboratories 198–9
virtual communities 173, 176
virtual interviews 226
'vision' of markets 5
visual aids 733
visual data 239
voice pitch analysis 287
volume-tracking data 113

Walcheren hospital 498
Ward's procedure 677–81, 688
web publishng of research findings 737–8
web surveys 265, 273, 788–92
webcams 226
websites 48, 329, 452
weighting 408, 410, 449–50, 488–9
wholesale audits 114–15
'why' questions 464
Wilcoxon test 493, 526, 535–6, 539
Wilks' λ 621, 627
word association 217–18, 221–2
word-processing packages 397
wording of questions 384–5
workshops 196
World Wide Web 117; see also under websites

X symbol in marketing research 307
Xsight software 232, 255–6

z statistic and test 435, 493, 514–15, 528, 530, 538
Zaltman metaphor elicitation technique 215–16, 227
zero points on scales 340–1, 363

Allison, John 265
Anderson, Kate 754
Armes, Tim 98
Attfield, John 279
Authers, Alex 193

Balaa, Hana 745
Beattie, Trevor 20
Berelson, B. 251–2
Bevolo, Marco 150
Birks, David 18
Birks, James 18
Brandes, Dieter 168
Brenner, Marc 37
Bretschneider, Rudolf 749
Brown, Colin 294

Connell, Stephen 788–9
Cooper, Peter 157

Derrida, J. 254
Dibb, S. 769
Dyson, James 19

Emery, Anita 108
Evans, Malcolm 258–9

Fawcus, Jem 20
Featherstone, Shirley 294
Field, Richard 775
Ford, David 769–73
Forrest, Chris 238
Forsyth, John 23
Friedman, Larry 109

Gamba, Philip 715
Glaser, B. 166, 248
Goffman, E. 239
Goldfarb, Jamie 486
Goodyear, Mary 744–5

Gordon, Wendy 18
Grant, Andrew 25
Guttman, J. 212

Hackbarth, Knut 324
Harristhal, Johan 477
Hashemi, Sahar 17
Helton, Alicia 787
Henchoz, Richard 22–3
Holderness, David 762
Holsheimer, Marcel 144
Hourston, Neil 20–1

Iavrakas, Paul 445

James, Meril 25
Jowell, Roger 293–4

Kelly, George
Kirby, Robert 760
Kirkby, Robin 95
Kohl, Helmut 76
Kroll, Bob 537

Lewin, Kurt 169
Likert, Rensis 348
Liljeberg, Eric 21
Littler, D. 769
Lynch, David 20–1

McGown, Stuart 274
McNeill, Ruth 774
McPhee, Neil 776
Manoussakis, Dimitris 268–9
March, Wendy 151
Mendoza, David 762
Metcalf, Peter 162
Miller, Bob 736
Miln, David 37
Murray, Anne 150

Necchi, Richard 757

O'Konis, Chris 265

Pearson, Karl 575
Penn, David 50
Price, Kevin 164

Quartz, Steve 287

Redding, Phillip 734
Roddick, Anita 18
Rowland, Greg 252

Schumacher, Michael 53–4, 503
Spichiger-Carlsson, Peter 324
Stapel, Jan 350
Stollan, Martin 751
Strauss, A. 166, 248
Stuart, Christina 734

Terhanian, George 426

Valentine, Virginia 258–9
van der Herberg, Bert L.J. 3
van Nieuwkasteele, Marjolein 758

Walton, Mark 758
Walton, Paul 193
Ward, Greg 139
Webster, Frederick 770, 773
Whiting, Mark 728
Wilson, D.F. 770
Wilson, Simon 22
Wimmer, Frank 21–2
Wind, Y. 773
Wübbenhorst, Klaus 25

Zaltman, Jerry 215

Company index

ABN AMRO 132
A.C. Nielsen 3, 111, 114, 118, 191–2, 286
Aldi 168
Alfa Romeo 715
Allied Domecq 63, 723–4
Amazon 138
Anheuser-Busch 302
Arbitron 447
Ariba 266
Asda 126
AT&T 215
Audi 404

BASES 319, 326
Bass 325
Blue Trail 175
BMW 404, 715
The Body Shop 18
Boots the Chemist 693–4
Bose Corporation 284–5

Canon 274
CAPIBUS Europe 291
Capital Radio 163
Cheeseborough Ponds 326
CIGNA Retirement and Investment Services 418
Citrosuco Paulista 55
Clausthaler 591
Coca-Cola 95, 117, 168, 342, 377, 591
Coffee Republic 17
Colgate 537
Continental Research 71
Cooperative Bank 779
Credit Suisse 138–9
CustomerSat.com 266

Dalgety Animal Feeds 415
Datamonitor 101
Dell 769
DIRECTV 618
Domino's Pizza 363
Dunn & Bradstreet 115
Dyson 19

Ebay 207
Eckerd 302
EgeBank 545
Electrolux 162
Ericsson 162, 767–8
Euromonitor 102, 118

EVO Research and Consulting 186
Experian 131–2

Ferrari 53, 339, 341
Firefish 20
Flora 24
Ford 736
Fred Olsen 130–1
Future Publishing 71

Gallup 75, 268
General Electric 95
GfK Group 113, 326, 329, 738, 749

Häagen Dazs 495
Harris Interactive 404
Heinz 55
Hewlett-Packard 95, 743
Hindustani Lever Limited (HLL) 746
Hitachi 778–9
Homebase 123–4
Hotwired 288

IBM 95, 772, 782
ICI 715–16
ID Magasin 10
Insight Research Group 776
Intel 95, 151, 769
Interpolis 144
IPSOS 291

Kaufhof 559
Kellogg's 12–13

Land Rover 761
Lange Uhren 327
Lidl 221

MacLaren 339
MARE 149
Markedsconsult 4
Mars 326–7
Mercedes 404
Mercury Asset Management 125
Microsoft 95
Millward Brown 109
Mintel 118
MORI 75, 255–6, 133
Motorola 95

National Opinion Polls (NOP) 133
Nestlé 743

New Solutions 193
News International 226
Nike 328
Nordea Bank 3–4

Ocean Spray 344
L'Oréal 150

Parfümerie Douglas 133
Pegram Walters International 63, 154
Pepsi Cola 154, 302
Perrier 591
Pfizer 302
Philips 3–4, 150, 758
Phillip Morris 22
Pillsbury 74–5
PlayStation 20–1, 213
Point of Purchasing International 302
Polaroid 687
Premier Automotive Group 22
Princess Cruises 486
Procter & Gamble 95, 215, 218, 302, 326–7

QSR International 255–6
Quæstor 210–11
QualiQuant 226

Ralston-Purina 302
Red Bull 175
Reed Elselvier 781
Renault 54, 144, 312–16, 320–2, 339, 348–9, 377–8, 483, 551–4, 715, 780
Research International 268, 469
Research Services Limited 291
Roper Audits and Surveys Worldwide 116
Royal Ahold 2–5, 9

Saatchi & Saatchi 581, 736
Sainsbury's 126
Sauber 340–1
SevenHR 784
Sports Marketing Surveys 2, 24, 39–41, 52–4, 73–8, 109, 150–1, 184–5, 217–19, 243, 269–70, 313–16, 320–1, 339–41, 375–7, 407, 475–6, 503–5, 760
Staropramen 325

Taylor Nelson 27, 108, 118, 133, 139, 738

TBWA 20
Techneos 294
Tesco 126
Texas Instruments 786–7
TFG 95
TNS 78, 109, 268, 271, 758
Toyota 736
TrustMark CFI 140

Unilever 56, 745–6
United Airlines 723

The Value Engineers 193
Visa 45
Volvo 715

Williams 340

Xerox 361

Yankelovich and Partners 591